FIFTEENTH EDITION

HUMAN RESOURCE MANAGEMENT

Robert L. Mathis
*University of
Nebraska at Omaha*

John H. Jackson
*University of
Wyoming*

Sean R. Valentine
*University of
North Dakota*

Patricia A. Meglich
*University of
Nebraska at Omaha*

CENGAGE
Learning®

Australia • Brazil • Mexico • Singapore • United Kingdom • United States

Human Resource Management, Fifteenth Edition
Robert L. Mathis, John H. Jackson
Sean R. Valentine, Patricia A. Meglich

Vice President, General Manager, Social Science & Qualitative Business: Erin Joyner

Product Director: Jason Fremder

Senior Product Manager: Scott Person

Content Developer: Jamie Mack

Product Assistant: Brian Pierce

Marketing Director: Kristen Hurd

Marketing Manager: Emily Horowitz

Marketing Coordinator: Chris Walz

Art and Cover Direction, Production Management, and Composition: Lumina Datamatics, Inc

Intellectual Property

Analyst: Diane Garrity

Project Manager: Betsy Hathaway

Manufacturing Planner: Ron Montgomery

Cover and Internal Image: aleisha/ Shutterstock.com

For product information and technology assistance, contact us at
Cengage Learning Customer & Sales Support, 1-800-354-9706

For permission to use material from this text or product, submit all requests online at **www.cengage.com/permissions**
Further permissions questions can be emailed to
permissionrequest@cengage.com

Library of Congress Control Number: 2015949189

Student Edition:
ISBN: 978-1-305-50070-9

Loose-leaf Edition:
ISBN: 978-1-305-50075-4

Cengage Learning
20 Channel Center Street
Boston, MA 02210
USA

Cengage Learning is a leading provider of customized learning solutions with employees residing in nearly 40 different countries and sales in more than 125 countries around the world. Find your local representative at **www.cengage.com**.

Cengage Learning products are represented in Canada by Nelson Education, Ltd.

To learn more about Cengage Learning Solutions, visit **www.cengage.com**

Purchase any of our products at your local college store or at our preferred online store **www.cengagebrain.com**

Unless otherwise noted all items © Cengage Learning.

Printed in the United States of America
Print Number: 01   Print Year: 2015

DEDICATIONS

TO

Jo Ann Mathis,
for managing efforts on this book, and
Julie Foster and Lee Skoda as key supporters.

R.D. and M.M. Jackson,
who were successful managers of people for many years.

Page and Will,
for their love and support, as well as my parents, family,
and friends who have helped through the years.

Thank you to my parents,
Robert and Margaret Meglich, and to family, friends, and colleagues
who have encouraged me along life's journey.

BRIEF CONTENTS

TABLE OF CONTENTS

SECTION 2

Jobs and Labor 121

CHAPTER 10
Performance Management and Appraisal 362

SECTION 4

Compensation 399

In comparing the fifteenth edition of *Human Resource Management* with the first edition, the evolution that has occurred in the HR field is very apparent. Because we have carefully researched and recorded the changes in this book, we are told it has become the leader in both the academic and professional segments of the market. The book is a longtime standard in HR classes, and the authors are very gratified that their efforts are appreciated by so many.

While developing this text, we paid close attention to presenting information at an appropriate reading level and length, using many practical examples, and offering other learning devices to make the book more "student friendly." It is also worth noting that the authors have all won teaching and/or research awards, which illustrates knowledge of what it takes to effectively communicate the latest HR information both orally and in written form.

Casual comments from colleagues reveal a lack of clarity about how one successfully revises a textbook in a field that changes as rapidly as Human Resources. There are many hundreds of articles in the academic and professional literatures that have appeared in the three years since our last book was researched. When business examples from *The Wall Street Journal, Business Week, HR Magazine*, and other trade publications are added, the number is staggering. These articles, as well as the themes that appear in them, represent the changing nature of the subject matter in HR and must be added to the overall knowledge of the field. Consequently, this information must be added to a university text that effectively summarizes the field. This book has provided a comprehensive overview of the HR profession for many editions, and it has successfully done that again in this current edition. You can be confident it contains the most current content that reflects current HR practices in the field.

The field of HR management is different from some other areas of business. There is a definite academic/research side that explores new theories and knowledge, but HR has a more professional/applied side too. Just ask leaders who deal with HR issues on a daily basis. This book focuses on both sides of the HR field, which has resulted in it being used by many individuals to prepare for certification in the HR profession. Our approach has always been that both perspectives are very important in understanding the field, and this strategy is continued in the fifteenth edition.

With this edition, we welcome a new author. Patricia Meglich is an accomplished scholar who has a special interest and expertise in the applied areas of HR given her extensive professional background. You will note more consideration of the practical implications of many HR issues in this current edition of the text. She is a strong addition to the author team.

The Fifteenth Edition

HR takes place in an environment that changes rapidly and impacts the field, resulting in necessary changes to the book being recognized between editions. The fifteenth edition identifies these changes and how they are being dealt with in the field. A few of the most significant characteristics of the fifteenth edition are detailed next. This new edition also contains many other positive content attributes, and you will find them throughout the text.

"What's Trending" Chapter Sections

Human resource management is a complex field, and highlighting all the current trends is difficult. However, there are a number of issues that are currently affecting organizations, particularly with regard to how they manage people at work. Employees are expected to have the proper knowledge, skills, and abilities to perform in a workplace that has many challenges and new expectations, which requires organizations to implement practices that help employees get better at what they do and perform well. Each chapter provides an overview of the current trends pertaining to the particular topics explored.

Measuring HR Effectiveness

The trend toward holding HR groups accountable for corporate performance has expanded, giving HR professionals a "seat at the strategic table." The days when an HR manager could be successful because "she just loves working with people" are long gone. Benchmarking, metrics, and now analytics are a part of the analysis of how well HR is doing its job. The fifteenth edition uses a metrics icon to indicate where material on measuring HR is covered throughout the book. Such measurement is welcome, as it documents how HR contributes to organizational goals in a tangible way.

Global Human Resource Management

Business is now global in scope, a reality that has dramatically changed the HR profession. Offshoring, global mergers and acquisitions, and cultural differences continue to challenge HR departments. The fifteenth edition covers global issues throughout the chapters to ensure proper coverage of global issues throughout the textbook. Globally related material is indicated with a global icon.

HR Ethics

The study of ethics is emphasized in the academic business community, and HR is a fertile area for the practical application of ethics material. The potential for unethical dealings in compensation, staffing, Equal Employment Opportunity (EEO), and other areas is significant and problematic. At a minimum, investigation of these issues can provide a basis for discussion of HR ethics in the classroom, hopefully leading to greater consideration of ethical challenges in the HR profession. There is an HR ethics icon where HR ethics issues are covered.

Organization of the book

- Each chapter opens with an "HR Headline" designed to introduce chapter material with a real company dilemma or problem. Learning objectives are provided at the beginning of each chapter.
- The latest trends and cutting-edge practices are highlighted in each chapter in a new feature called "What's Trending."
- Chapters contain a mix of three boxed features designed to do different things: *HR Perspective* sections provide real examples of how companies deal with the issue covered. *HR Competencies & Applications* provide a "how to do it" view of the material based on key competencies identified in many professional models of HR. Finally, *HR Ethics* features highlight some of the ethical issues encountered in the profession.

- Each chapter ends with a point-by-point "Summary."
- The "Critical Thinking Challenges" at the end of each chapter provide questions and exercises that allow readers to apply what has been learned in each chapter.
- New in-depth end of chapter cases showcase HR innovations in current organizations and present readers with a chance to critically assess the effectiveness of innovative people practices.

Material is organized around five sections:

- The Environment of Human Resource Management
- Workforce, Jobs, and Staffing
- Training, Development, and Performance
- Compensation
- Employee Relations

The fifteenth edition presents both the continuity and changes occurring within human resource management. The chapters in each section will be highlighted next, along with some of the topics explored in each chapter.

Section One: The Environment of Human Resource Management

Section One contains chapters emphasizing the changing environment in which HR operates, as well as how HR can effectively adapt. *Chapter 1* explains why HR is needed and how employees can function as key assets for an organization. Basic HR functions and current HR challenges are covered. Ethics and HR as a career field are discussed. Different HR competencies that are important in the profession are also explored in this edition. *Chapter 2* discusses two primary ways of dealing with the changing environment—strategy and HR planning. The strategic planning process and HR's role in it are covered. A process for conducting HR planning is identified, including environmental analysis, assessing internal and external labor markets, and managing imbalances. The chapter also covers HR metrics and analytics and presents benchmarking and balanced scorecard processes. Good and bad strategy distinctions, HR analytics, and the HR audit are among topics investigated. *Chapter 3* deals with the EEO environment, including legal requirements and concepts. This comprehensive chapter also investigates the challenges presented by EEO issues. Gender inequity in compensation, discrimination based on sexual orientation, and religious discrimination/accommodation are discussed.

Section Two: Workforce, Jobs, and Staffing

Section Two looks at people, the jobs they do, and how to bring these two factors together for the purposes of accomplishing work requirements. *Chapter 4* profiles the United States' workforce participation rates and skills gaps, before turning to the nature of jobs, including job design and redesign, flexibility, telework, and work–life balance. The chapter then presents the most comprehensive coverage of job analysis available in a basic HR text. Treatment of the workforce is also covered, as is presentation of jobs, and flexible work opportunities. *Chapter 5* investigates the individual–organizational relationship and retention. Individual performance factors, including a very brief summary of the leading work motivation ideas and the psychological contract, are identified. Absenteeism and turnover, including measurement issues, are covered. The discussion then turns to retaining employees and the available management options for improving retention. The focus on individual performance factors is emphasized, as is employee engagement, loyalty, and drivers of retention for high-performing employees. *Chapter 6* considers labor markets and recruiting. Online recruiting and the other common recruiting methods are examined, and this information is followed by a comprehensive look at measuring the success of recruiting. Recruiting and employer ethics and the use of technology and social media in recruiting are expanded. *Chapter 7* looks at placement, selection testing, interviewing, and background investigations, among other topics. An assessment of person–environment fit as part of the attraction-selection-attrition framework is also presented.

Section Three: Training, Development, and Performance

Section Three considers bringing people along in their careers in organizations through training, talent management, and career and performance management. *Chapter 8* explores different potential strategies for training in the organization. A comprehensive model of the training process leads ultimately to training delivery and evaluation. Issues associated with sales training, the expansion of e-learning (online training) and m-learning (using mobile devices) based on new research, and the increased use of simulation and games in training are also covered. *Chapter 9* looks at talent management, leadership development, succession planning, and career issues, topics that have been very much in the literature since the last edition. This is reflected through the entire chapter, with special emphasis on integrating talent management into the organization's strategy and ideas for keeping high performers invested in their jobs. *Chapter 10* considers identifying and measuring employee performance. Performance appraisal with all its pros and cons is covered, as well as hints for the appraisal interview. In this edition, ethical issues surrounding performance appraisal are reviewed, and the voluminous new literature in performance has been reviewed and integrated.

Section Four: Compensation

Section Four summarizes compensation, incentives, and benefits. *Chapter 11* introduces basic compensation, total rewards, and the development of a pay system. This edition covers strategic compensation decisions, linkage of pay to motivation theories, and current compensation challenges, including the use of two-tier wage systems. *Chapter 12* considers variable pay (incentives), sales compensation, and executive pay. Individual, group, and organizational incentive systems are reviewed, and the controversial topic of executive compensation is presented. Clawbacks, commissions, "say-on-pay," and exit package changes are also discussed. *Chapter 13* explains the different types of benefits that organizations offer, as well as how to effectively administer and manage these benefits so that employees are satisfied. New or expanded content includes international benefits, the Patient Protection and Affordable Care Act, outsourcing benefit administration, and technology-driven, self-service benefits administration.

Section Five: Employee Relations

Section Five covers risk and safety, employee rights and responsibilities, and unions. *Chapter 14* looks at threats to the well-being of both organizations and employees.

OSHA, legal requirements for well-being, safety management, and security concerns are specified. Expanded discussions of medical marijuana, counterproductive employee behaviors, and drug testing are provided. *Chapter 15* looks at rights existing in the employment agreement, including privacy rights, workplace monitoring, investigations, and discipline. This edition are covers alternative dispute-resolution techniques and material on employee rights and ethical issues. *Chapter 16* evaluates the union–management relationship through labor laws, history, collective bargaining, and grievance management. New since the last edition is material on politics and unionization, changes in union membership, and union tactics.

Appendices

To keep the chapters sized appropriately, yet provide additional specific information, the book contains seven appendices. These provide details on the bodies of knowledge/ competence for HR certification, HR literature, EEO laws, Uniform Guidelines, illegal preemployment inquires, EEO enforcement, and HR job descriptions.

Supplements

Instructor's Resource Website

The Instructor's Resource website puts all of the core resources in one place. The website contains the Instructor's Manual, Test Bank, and PowerPoint presentation slides.

- *Instructor's Manual:* The Instructor's Manual represents one of the most exciting and useful aids available. Comprehensive teaching materials are provided for each chapter—including overviews; outlines; instructor's notes; suggested answers to end-of-chapter Review and Applications Questions; suggested questions for the "HR Headline," "HR Perspective," "HR Ethics," and "HR Competencies & Applications" features; suggested answers to the end-of-chapter case questions; and suggested questions and comments on the supplemental cases for each chapter.
- *Cognero Test Bank:* The test bank contains more than 1,800 questions, including multiple-choice, true/false, and essay questions. Questions are additionally identified by type—definition, application, and analytical—and also include AACSB tags for general (NATIONAL) and topic-specific (LOCAL) designations.
- *PowerPoint Slide Presentation:* The PowerPoint presentation contains approximately 400 slides to aid in class lectures.

Print on Demand Student Study Guide

Designed from a student's perspective, this useful guide provides aids that students can use to maximize results in the classroom and on exams, and, ultimately, in the practice of human resources. Chapter objectives and chapter outlines aid students in reviewing for exams. Study questions include matching, true/false, idea completion, multiple-choice, and essay questions. Answer keys are provided for immediate feedback to reinforce learning.

MindTap

MindTap is the digital learning solution that helps instructors engage students and relate HR management concepts to their lives. Through interactive assignments, students connect HR management concepts to real-world organizations and say how managers should perform in given situations. Finally, all activities are designed to teach students to problem-solve and think like management leaders. Through these activities, real-time course analytics, and an accessible reader, MindTap helps you turn cookie cutter into cutting edge, apathy into engagement, and memorizers into higher-level thinkers.

Acknowledgments

The success of each edition of *Human Resource Management* can largely be attributed to our reviewers, who have generously offered both suggestions for improvements and new ideas for the text. We sincerely thank the following reviewers:

Deloris Oliver	*LeMoyne-Owen College*
David F. Orf	*Webster University*
Vallari Chandna	*University of North Texas*
Clare A Francis	*University of North Dakota*
Kathleen Jones	*University of North Dakota*
Dr. Sheri Bias	*Saint Leo University*
Dr. Dave Calland	*Liberty University*
LCDR Thomas R. Kelley, USN, Ret.	*Averett University*
Robert W.Sopo, PhD	*Carnegie Mellon University*
A. Eads	*Texas A&M University–Central Texas*

The authors also wish to thank the publishing team at Cengage Learning: Jason Fremder, Product Director; Scott Person, Senior Product Manager; Sarah Ginn, Content Developer; Jamie Mack, Associate Content Developer; Jennifer Ziegler, Senior Content Project Manager; and Joseph Malcolm, Project Manager (at Lumina Datamatics).

As the authors, we are confident the fifteenth edition of *Human Resource Management* will continue to set the standard for the Human Resource field. As the users of the text, we certainly hope you agree.

Robert L. Mathis, SPHR
John H. Jackson
Sean R. Valentine
Patricia A. Meglich, SPHR, SHRM-SCP

Robert L. Mathis Dr. Robert L. Mathis is professor emeritus of management at the University of Nebraska at Omaha (UNO). Born and raised in Texas, he received his BBA and MBA from Texas Tech University and a PhD in Management and Organization from the University of Colorado. At UNO, he has received the Excellence in Teaching award. Dr. Mathis has co-authored several books and published numerous articles covering a variety of topics. He also has held national offices in the Society for Human Resource Management (SHRM) and served as president of the Human Resource Certification Institute (HRCI). In addition, he is certified as a Senior Professional in Human Resources (SPHR) by HRCI. Dr. Mathis has extensive specialized consulting experience in establishing or revising compensation plans for small and medium-sized firms.

John H. Jackson Dr. John H. Jackson is professor emeritus of management at the University of Wyoming. Born in Alaska, he received his BBA and MBA from Texas Tech University. He worked in the telecommunications industry in human resources management for several years before completing his PhD in Management and Organization at the University of Colorado. During his academic career, Dr. Jackson authored six other college texts and more than 50 articles and papers, including those appearing in *Academy of Management Review, Journal of Management, Human Resource Management*, and *Human Resources Planning*. He has consulted with a variety of organizations on HR and management development matters and has served as an expert witness in a number of HR-related cases. At the University of Wyoming, he served four terms as department head in the Department of Management and Marketing. Dr. Jackson received the university's highest teaching award and has been recognized for his work with two-way interactive television for MBA students. Two Wyoming governors have appointed him to the Wyoming Business Council and the Workforce Development Council. Dr. Jackson serves as president of Silverwood Ranches, Inc.

Sean R. Valentine Dr. Sean R. Valentine is the University of North Dakota alumni leadership and ethics professor and professor of management. Originally from Texas, he received a BS in Management/Human Resources from Park University, a BS in Hotel, Restaurant, and Tourism Management from New Mexico State University, an MBA in Business Administration from Texas State University, and a DBA in Management from Louisiana Tech University. He was employed in the hospitality industry for many years and was an officer in the Army National Guard. During his academic career, Dr. Valentine published more than 75 articles in journals such as *Human Resource Management, Human Relations, Human Resource Development Quarterly, Employee Responsibilities and Rights Journal, Journal of Business Research, Journal of Business Ethics, Journal of Personal Selling & Sales Management, Contemporary Accounting Research*, and *Behavioral Research in Accounting*. His primary research and teaching interests include human resource management, business ethics, and organizational behavior, and he has received numerous awards and other recognition for his work. He also has consulted with a variety of organizations on different business matters.

Patricia A. Meglich Dr. Patricia A. Meglich is associate professor of management at the University of Nebraska at Omaha. Born and raised in Ohio, she earned her BSBA from Bowling Green State University, MBA from Cleveland State University, and PhD from Kent State University. Prior to entering academia, she spent 20 years as the human resources director for an automotive supplier, where she designed and implemented talent management programs and participated in numerous acquisitions and business process reengineering initiatives. Dr. Meglich was active in professional activities with SHRM and was awarded the national SHRM Award for Professional Excellence. She is certified SPHR and SHRM-SCP. She has published numerous articles in scholarly journals such as *Employee Rights and Responsibilities, Journal of Leadership and Organizational Studies*, and the *Journal of Applied Business and Economics*. She has developed several learning modules and course materials for SHRM and has received a number of teaching awards at UNO. She serves as a visiting professor at the University of Ljubljana (Slovenia) and the Osnabruck University of Applied Sciences (Germany). She is committed to bridging research to the practice of HR and ensuring that HR professionals have the timely, relevant information that is needed to successfully lead their organizations to success

SECTION 1

The Environment of Human Resource Management

CHAPTER

1

Human Resource Management in Organizations

Learning Objectives

After you have read this chapter, you should be able to:

LO1 Understand human resource management and define human capital.

LO2 Identify how human resource management and employees can be core competencies for organizations.

LO3 Name the seven categories of HR functions.

LO4 Provide an overview of four challenges facing HR today.

LO5 Explain how ethical issues in organizations affect HR management.

LO6 Explain the key competencies needed by HR professionals and why certification is important.

WHAT'S TRENDING IN HUMAN RESOURCE MANAGEMENT

There are a number of current HR trends that affect how companies manage people at work. Employees are expected to have the proper knowledge, skills, and abilities (KSAs) to perform in an environment that presents constant changes and new expectations. This requires HR professionals to be at the top of their game when it comes to developing policies that help people get better at what they do. Here are some issues that are currently trending in HR:

1. The rapidly changing workplace focuses HR efforts on the development of human capital factors that address organizational needs (e.g., customer service, quality, productivity). Once employees are developed, they need to be placed in the proper jobs with positive work cultures that enable them to effectively use their talents.
2. Globalization and workforce diversity present a number of ways for individual differences to help companies. However, challenges associated with the proper placement of employees and the development of positive HR policies in diverse environments are common.
3. Technology is viewed as a key means to an end when it comes to managing human resources. Increased social media, online interactions, and the use of software to manage traditional HR functions can enhance how individuals are supervised at work.
4. The ability of companies to develop ethics policies, social responsibility, and sustainable practices is viewed as a source of competitive advantage. Developing an ethical culture, offering ethics training, and encouraging employees to give back are all ways that HR leaders can help improve business ethics.

Entrepreneurial HR Culture at MGM Resorts International

any companies are creating an entrepreneurial culture for employees so that they can be innovative. Part of this process includes making them business partners and giving them good jobs. Another aspect includes allowing them to voice their opinions, make suggestions about how work gets done, and follow up with positive action. Some HR functions are also changed to offer a worksite that encourages individuals to take chances with new approaches and participate in decision making, and resources that help people develop new ideas can be provided. The HR department is in a unique position to develop these opportunities.

MGM Resorts International, a Las Vegas–based gaming organization, relies on this entrepreneurial approach. Since many of the firm's employees earn their income from tips, the

HEADLINE

Entrepreneurial
HR Culture at
MGM Resorts
International 3

PERSPECTIVE

Transforming
HR at Popeyes
Louisiana
Kitchen 7

COMPETENCIES & APPLICATIONS

Building Healthy
Organizations 14

ETHICS

HR Links
Employee
Volunteering
to Social
Responsibility 30

Andrew Zarivny/Shutterstock.com

3

company encourages them to ask questions and develop ideas that help improve service delivery and workforce management. Innovation is also emphasized in the company's Leadership Institute for executives, where people attend a seminar on innovation, participate in brainstorming sessions, and create new processes that enable the company to cut expenses. One idea, which involved developing a consistent brand of water bottles in the different properties, saved MGM about $400,000 a year.

MGM relied on a number of other strategic HR ideas to create a culture of innovation. Some of these included:

- Using focus groups to obtain feedback from line employees as part of a broader communication strategy at each of the properties
- Developing a directory called Workday, which contained the contact information for all employees and executives, as a way of sharing information
- Encouraging employees to develop ideas that improved responsiveness to customers' needs

Michelle DiTondo, Senior Vice President of HR, believes that the resulting culture established a workplace where employees feel valued and empowered, leading to greater decision making and participation.[1]

Employees are the necessary resources that organizations use to satisfy important business objectives. Having talented individuals employed in a company is the cornerstone of developing a competitive advantage. If an organization is to compete on whatever distinctive core competencies are considered important in its industry (e.g., customer service, quality, strategic planning), having qualified and motivated employees is critical.

By earning the reputation as good employers, companies can attract and retain productive, creative, and reliable people who possess competitive advantages that reach strategic goals. Finding knowledgeable and motivated employees, training them to perform critical jobs, paying them appropriately, giving them important work responsibilities, and providing them opportunities to succeed and gain recognition are but a few of the issues that an organization must address. But how does an employer create these policies and earn such a positive reputation? Most often, it is an HR department that develops and coordinates practices that enable people to make important contributions at work.

Developing sound HR activities can enhance an organization's reputation as a desirable place to work. A company must also look ahead and address emerging challenges and opportunities so that employees are satisfied and perform their jobs at high levels. In particular, there is a need to understand the current trends that are occurring in the field of human resource management.

LO1 Understand
human resource
management and
define human capital.

1-1 What Is Human Resource Management?

What is now called human resource management has evolved a great deal since its beginnings around the year 1900. What began as a primarily clerical operation in larger companies concerned with payroll and employee records began to face changes with the social legislation of the 1960s and 1970s. "Personnel departments," as they came to be called, became concerned with the legal implications of policies and procedures affecting employees. In the 1990s, globalization and competition required human resource departments to become more concerned with costs, planning, and the implications of various HR strategies for both organizations and their employees. More recently, human resource operations in some companies have been involved with mergers and acquisitions, outsourcing, and managing vendors of certain traditional HR activities such as payroll and executive search. HR may also advise the CEO or chairman of the board as he or she works to fill vacancies among executives and directors.[2] Rising concerns over corporate scandals and unethical behavior are also encouraging HR professionals to get more involved in programs that increase ethics, compliance, and social responsibility.

**Human resource
management**
Designing formal systems
in an organization to
manage human talent for
accomplishing organiza-
tional goals

Human resource management is designing formal systems in an organization to manage human talent for accomplishing organizational goals. Whether you work in a big company with 10,000 employees or a small nonprofit organization with 10 employees, employees must be recruited, selected, trained, managed, and retained. Employees must also be paid, which means an appropriate and legal compensation system is needed. Each of these activities requires thought and understanding about what works well given current employee concerns and company conditions. Research into these issues and the knowledge gained from successful approaches form the basis of effective HR management.

1-1a Why Organizations Need HR Management

Not every organization has an HR department. In a company with an owner and 10 employees, for example, the owner usually addresses HR issues. However, despite the obvious differences between large and small organizations, the same HR issues must be dealt with in every firm. Luckily, *every* leader in an organization is an HR manager, so there are usually many people who can help address HR issues. Sales managers, head nurses, drafting supervisors, food and beverage directors, college deans, and accounting department supervisors all engage in managing human resources, and their effectiveness depends in part on their ability to understand the principles of HR management.

It is unrealistic, however, to expect these individuals to understand all the details of equal employment regulations, how to design a complex compensation system, or when to conduct a job analysis. Therefore, the presence of an HR department and leaders who understand important HR issues can be helpful. For that reason, larger organizations frequently have people who specialize in these activities, and these professionals are organized into an HR function or department. Yet some firms have never employed HR professionals or have eliminated their HR departments. But their experiences suggest that companies without HR support must deal with a variety of personnel challenges.[3] Companies such as Zappos are even trying a "holacracy" approach where departments are dismantled, job titles are dropped, and management structures are flattened so that self-managed groups are given flexibility to perform tasks that fit their abilities.[4]

Despite these trends, there are many benefits associated with having a dedicated HR department. However, HR professionals must respond appropriately to current business challenges and opportunities if they want to be helpful. A recent survey indicates that worker engagement and performance, leadership development, and employee retention are key issues in companies today, so HR leaders need to effectively address these concerns.[5] Another survey shows that management of health care issues, loss of senior talent, retirement concerns, and hiring skilled and educated individuals are key challenges that should be addressed.[6] Other trends include a globalized workforce, greater age diversity, a focus on sustainability, and an emphasis on social media. HR leaders can address these issues by adopting an interdisciplinary business approach (e.g., working with marketing, operations, and finance talent), connecting with outside constituencies, identifying critical organizational challenges, and facilitating organizational change.[7] HR professional might also adapt HR processes to fit workplace changes, work more closely with IT personnel to manage technology, hire more high performers who have the right skills, and be innovation leaders.[8] Finally, sharing employee knowledge and expertise has become a big issue, so HR staff can modify work that limits collaboration.[9] The following "HR Perspective: Transforming HR at Popeyes Louisiana Kitchen" feature highlights some of these emerging trends, as well as others.

Greater cooperation between operating managers and the HR department is also needed for HR efforts to succeed. In many cases, the HR department designs processes and systems that operating managers must help implement. The exact division of labor between the two varies from firm to firm. Throughout this book there will be examples of how HR responsibilities in various areas are divided in organizations that have HR departments.

How Human Resource Management Is Sometimes Seen in Organizations

HR departments have been viewed in different ways, both positively and negatively. HR management is necessary, especially when dealing with the many government regulations enacted over the past several decades. However, the need to protect corporate assets against the many legal issues often makes the HR function play a different role, which may be seen as negative, restrictive, and not focused on getting work done.

The legal compliance role can cause other people to have negative views of HR staff. The negative perception that some employees, managers, and executives have is that HR departments are too bureaucratic, detail oriented, and costly, and that they are comprised of naysayers. Some managers also believe that HR departments reduce innovation and negatively impact the ability to complete work because of poorly executed programs. The availability of software that automates different functions and farms out various HR functions also fuels the belief that HR support is not really needed.[10] Critics think HR groups don't make important contributions. Despite such concerns, the HR function can benefit the workplace if it is managed well.

Human Resources in Smaller Organizations

In the United States and worldwide, small businesses employ more than half of all private-sector employees and generate many new jobs each year. In surveys over several years by the U.S. Small Business Administration (SBA), the issues identified as significant concerns in small organizations were consistent: not having enough qualified workers, the rapidly increasing costs of employee benefits, payroll taxes, and compliance with government regulations. Notice that all these concerns have an HR focus, especially when compliance with wage/hour, safety, equal employment, and other regulations are considered. This is why some degree of HR support and expertise is always needed in smaller organizations. However, a recent study shows that smaller firms tend to offer much more work flexibility to their employees in the form of working from home, flextime, and personal time,[11] which suggests that small businesses are quite progressive in their approach to HR management.

When new employees are hired in a small business, line managers usually do the recruiting, selecting, and orienting. These HR activities, however, reduce the amount of time managers have available to focus on their regular jobs. As a result, when such activities occur frequently, hiring someone to do them allows managers to spend more time on their primary duties. With about 80 to 100 employees,

PERSPECTIVE

Transforming HR at Popeyes Louisiana Kitchen

Evidence shows that HR departments have grown, with more money being dedicated to corporate HR efforts. However, changing work environments are challenging HR professionals to do more, even though their numbers and support have steadily risen. People employed in HR have much more responsibility in today's workplace, something that likely won't change as expectations have increased.

This is the case at the Atlanta-based fast-food firm Popeyes Louisiana Kitchen. While the organization's HR group grew from seven to 10 individuals over several years, the work also increased, according to Lynne Zappone, the company's Chief Talent Officer. The group manages as many as three times the number of issues it did in the past. Some of these include creating leadership development opportunities, enhancing customer service, and building food outlets. Popeyes focuses on *servant leadership*, which requires leaders to believe that the needs of the company and employees outweigh their own concerns. Further, Zappone and her colleagues evaluate how HR can address issues through a strategic lens. All of these responsibilities take time and energy.

Zappone also claims that many HR functions are being altered as the workplace changes. Besides being more focused on strategy, HR staff at Popeyes work on cross-functional project teams, and the HR function is structured so that each business area has a dedicated HR professional who operates as an advisor on various personnel issues. This enables staff to be more strategic because they work directly with the business units. Zappone also looks to redesign how different HR activities are performed so that more might be done with fewer people.[12]

Despite the growing need for HR personnel, the ability to manage the increasing number of HR responsibilities with current staff is a challenge. Expectations are higher, regardless of how many HR professionals are present. Consider the following questions:

1. Given the issues at Popeyes, how would you redesign an HR department in any organization to better tackle a company's needs?

2. What needs do you think deserve the most attention given the current trends in HR?

smaller organizations often find that they would benefit from designating some-one to specialize in HR practices. Other specialist HR positions are added (e.g., in compensation, training, or recruiting) as the company grows larger. The need for HR increases as an organization grows until it evolves into a distinct function with specialists assigned to specific duties. However, for HR to be most useful, it must remain firmly attached to the operating management of the organization. Without that attachment, HR functions cannot reach their potential.

LO2 Identify how human resource management and employees can be core competencies for organizations.

1-2 Managing Human Resources in Organizations

Human resources (or more simply, people) who work in organizations may have valuable contributions they can make to a firm's mission based on their human capital. But this will occur only if people are developed and have a reasonable opportunity to contribute. Employees must be placed into the right job, be trained, and be given feedback if they are to perform at high levels. As noted earlier, it is not just the HR department that takes care of these issues—it is often a joint effort between the organization's managers and HR staff members. Managing people ulti-mately has to do with the decisions these leaders make from among the wide range of possible choices on the formal policies, practices, and methods for managing employees.[13] Examples of such systems and policies are pay system design, perfor-mance measurement, vacation policy, and hiring processes.

1-2a Human Resource Management as a Core Competency

Core competency
A unique capability that creates high value for a company

The development and implementation of specific strategies must be based on an organization's areas of strength. Referred to as *core competencies*, those strengths are the foundation for creating the organization's competitive advantage. A core competency is a unique capability that creates high value for a company.

Certainly, many organizations have identified that their HR practices differenti-ate them from their competitors and that HR is a key determinant of competitive advantage. Recognizing this, organizations as diverse as FedEx, Nordstrom, and Dow Corning have focused on people as having special strategic value for the organization.

The same can be true with small companies as well. For example, small com-munity banks have gained numerous small- and medium-sized commercial loan cus-tomers because the banks emphasize that their customers can deal with the same employees directly every time they need help rather than having to call an auto-mated service center in another state as is sometimes the case with larger nation-wide banks. The focus here is on using people (in this example, loan officers) to help build core competencies in companies.

1-2b Employees as a Core Competency

How might employees become a core competency for an organization? One of the main issues that must be addressed is developing human capital in employees. Build-ing positive human capital brings together all assets of an organization so that work gets done and the company functions well.

FIGURE 1-1   Four Types of Organizational Assets

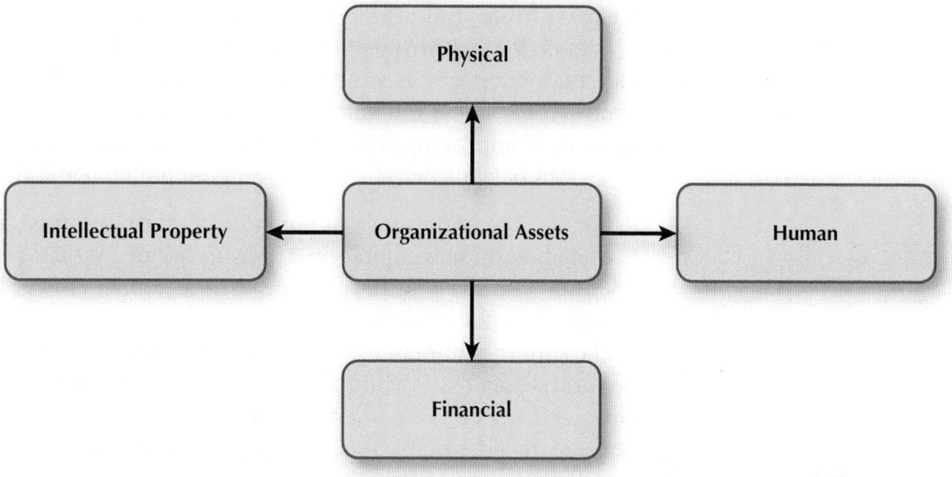

Human Capital Organizations must manage four types of assets to be successful (see Figure 1-1):

- *Physical assets*: Buildings, land, furniture, computers, vehicles, equipment, and so on
- *Financial assets*: Cash, financial resources, stocks, bonds or debt, and so on
- *Intellectual property assets*: Specialized research capabilities, patents, information systems, designs, operating processes, copyrights, and so on
- *Human assets*: Individuals with their talents, capabilities, experience, professional expertise, relationships, and so on

All of these assets are important to varying degrees in different firms. But the human assets are the "glue" that holds all the other parts together to achieve results. Certainly, the waiters, bartenders, hosts, and cooks at a Red Lobster restaurant or the stockpersons, cashiers, courtesy clerks, and customer service attendants working for a Kroger grocery store enable all the other assets of their organizations to be used to provide products and services to customers. Effective use of the firm's human capital can often explain a big part of the differences in company success.

Human capital is not just the people in organizations—it also involves what individuals contribute to organizational achievements. Broadly defined, human capital is the collective value of the capabilities, knowledge, skills, life experiences, and motivation of an organization's workforce.

Sometimes human capital is called *intellectual capital* to reflect the thinking, knowledge, creativity, and decision making that people in organizations contribute. For example, firms with high intellectual capital may have highly educated and trained managers who develop new ways of supervising employees, new business processes that improve quality, or new software for specialized uses. All of these contributions illustrate the potential value of human capital to companies.

A fundamental question involves how organizations and HR groups should most effectively manage human capital. A recent poll suggests that focusing on

Human capital
The collective value of the capabilities, knowledge, skills, life experiences, and motivation of an organization's workforce

valued rewards is one approach that helps with the management of human capital; other approaches include increasing levels of feedback to employees about their work expectations and taking steps to enhance their job satisfaction.[14] Focusing on a "personal value proposition," similar to marketing used to sell a company's product and/or services, is another strategy that enables employees to identify how their knowledge, skills, and abilities can help their organization perform better, with an eye toward improving these characteristics as new needs arise.[15] The following principles can be considered when developing human capital:[16]

- Recognize the importance of human capital to business success.
- Closely link human capital programs to organizational performance.
- Focus on your current business needs rather than always benchmarking the best practices of other firms.
- Make sure that human capital plans match the best practices that are selected.
- Be future-oriented in your planning to anticipate new human capital needs.
- Give managers a voice in and allow them to lead human capital programs.
- Be ready to alter plans as situations unfold; be flexible.
- Prioritize human capital planning and don't invest in too many initiatives.
- Be sure to track the value of human capital investments and monitor how they affect customers.

There are many other possible areas in which employees can be core competencies for organizations. As shown in Figure 1-2, productivity, customer service and quality, and organizational culture represent several of these areas.

MEASURE

Productivity Employee productivity can be a competitive advantage because when the costs to produce goods and services are lowered through increased

FIGURE 1-2   Areas in Which Employees Can Be Core Competencies

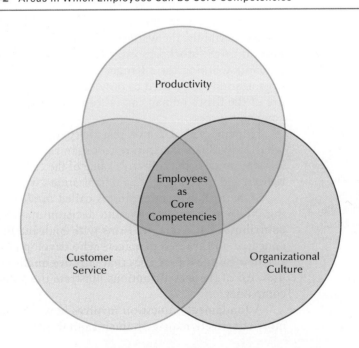

individual production, lower prices can be charged to consumers. The result is often incremental increases in sales. However, increased productivity does not necessarily mean greater output. Perhaps fewer people (or less money and/or time) are used to produce the same amount. In its most basic sense, productivity is a measure of the quantity and quality of work done, considering the cost of the resources used.

A useful way to measure the productivity of human resources is to consider unit labor cost, which is computed by dividing the average cost of workers by their average levels of output. Using unit labor costs, one can see that relatively high wages will not affect competitiveness if high productivity levels are achieved. Low unit labor costs can be a basis for a strategy focusing on human resource competency. Productivity and unit labor costs can be evaluated at the global, country, organizational, departmental, or individual level.

Improving Productivity Organizational-level productivity ultimately affects profitability and competitiveness in a for-profit organization and total costs in a not-for-profit organization. Perhaps of all the resources used in organizations, the ones most closely scrutinized are human resources. It is estimated that the average employee completes work requirements on time and according to standard at a rate of around 30% to 60%, which suggests that managing productivity is a key challenge.[17] The use of poor business approaches such as bureaucratic policies, poorly managed meetings, and low teamwork and collaboration can cause much of this decreased productivity (something called *coordination waste*), but giving employees autonomy and regular performance feedback can decrease many of these problems.[18] In the retail industry, HR can further invest in human capital to enhance productivity and customer service, such as providing better compensation, using cross-training to help customer service, and relying on empowerment.[19]

Additional HR management efforts are designed to enhance productivity as Figure 1-3 indicates. Among the major ways to increase employee productivity are

- *organizational restructuring*, which involves eliminating layers of management and changing reporting relationships as well as cutting staff through downsizing, layoffs, and early retirement buyout programs;
- *redesigning work*, which often involves making changes to the way work gets done by focusing on the characteristics of jobs and altering how tasks are structured and coordinated;
- *aligning HR activities*, which means ensuring that HR efforts and practices are consistent with organizational efforts to improve productivity and satisfy strategic goals; and
- *outsourcing analyses*, which require the HR department to conduct cost–benefit assessments that indicate the overall positive or negative impact of outsourcing—HR then manages outsourcing efforts if they occur.

Customer Service and Quality In addition to productivity, both customer service and quality efforts can significantly affect organizational effectiveness, making them key areas that HR can emphasize when developing employees as core competencies. Having managers and employees focus on customers' needs contributes significantly to achieving organizational goals and maintaining a competitive advantage.

Unfortunately, customer satisfaction is still a challenge in the United States and other countries, and it must be managed. One example illustrates the importance

Productivity
Measure of the quantity and quality of work done, considering the cost of the resources used

Unit labor cost
Computed by dividing the average cost of workers by their average levels of output

FIGURE 1-3 HR Approaches to Improving Productivity

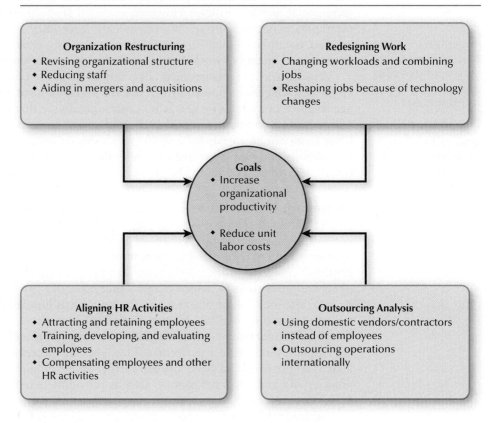

of service excellence. Within the first six months after being hired, a new CEO of a large retail company directed that labor costs and staffing in the company stores be reduced. As a result, many customers complained about not being able to find employees to help them, having to wait a long time to check out, and encountering shortages of merchandise on shelves. At the same time, a major competitor expanded its staff and advertised its customer service. The result was that the competitor's sales and profitability grew significantly, while the new CEO's cost-cutting approach created customer problems and hurt the firm's performance. After several years, the CEO resigned, and the retail company took steps to repair its customer service image.

Delivering quality services and/or products can also impact organizational effectiveness. Whether producing automobiles, as General Motors and Toyota do, or providing cellular phone service, as Verizon and AT&T do, a firm must consider how well its products and services meet customer needs. Therefore, many organizations have emphasized efforts to enhance quality. These programs seek to get tasks done correctly and efficiently so that employees deliver high quality. The problems with quality that some U.S. auto manufacturers have had compared with other firms such as Honda and Nissan illustrate the important effect of quality on sales, revenue, costs, and ultimately organizational effectiveness. Attempts to improve quality have worked better for some organizations than for others, but they usually can be impacted by HR efforts.

Organizational Culture Another important element of the workplace that drives the ability to use human resources as core competencies to meet strategic objectives is organizational culture. Organizational culture consists of the shared values and beliefs that give members of an organization meaning and provide them with rules for behavior. These values are deeply embedded in organizations and affect how their members view themselves, define opportunities, and plan strategies. In this sense, such a culture establishes the personality of a company in a similar way that personality shapes an individual, shaping its members' responses and defining what an organization can or is willing to do. The culture of an organization is therefore witnessed by employees in the norms, values, philosophies, rituals, and symbols adopted by the firm. Culture is particularly important because it tells individuals how to behave (or not to behave) in the workplace.

Culture often requires considerable time to develop, but once it is established, it is relatively constant and enduring over time. Newcomers learn the culture from senior employees, and the rules of behavior are therefore perpetuated. These rules are ideally beneficial, so culture can facilitate high employee job performance when it contains positive characteristics. But culture can also be negative, which means changes need to be made to improve the workplace.

Before focusing on the development and implementation of HR policies, managers should develop a positive culture within the organization. When they do so, excellent ideas can be enhanced by a culture that is compatible with the needs of the business. This is how culture can be used to create a competitive advantage.

Organizational culture is often viewed by employees, managers, customers, and others as the social environment that exists within a firm and that affects how a firm gets work done. This culture affects service and quality, organizational productivity, and financial results. From a critical perspective, it is the culture of a company that affects the attraction and retention of competent employees. Aligning the culture with what management is trying to accomplish also determines the health of an organization by creating an environment that capitalizes on human capital strengths. The following "HR Competencies & Applications: Building Healthy Organizations" feature discusses how culture can be enhanced by focusing on organizational health.

Organizational culture Consists of the shared values and beliefs that give members of an organization meaning and provide them with rules for behavior

LO3 Name the seven categories of HR functions.

1-3 HR Management Functions

HR management involves designing the *formal systems* that are used to manage people in an organization. Usually, both HR managers and line managers provide input into the policies, regulations, and rules that guide HR matters. For example, consider the question of how many days of vacation an employee receives after three years. There is no "right" answer for a given organization that is trying to devise a vacation policy, but the vacation policy that is finally designed is one of the formal systems used to manage people in the organization. Such systems need to be

Building Healthy Organizations

Companies like Southwest Airlines, Zappos .com, and Nordstrom have been successful because they rely on sound technology and business strategy. However, "organizational health" often drives employee motivation and customer loyalty. Organizational health is much broader than corporate culture because it establishes the workplace in which other business functions can operate well. In other words, healthy organizations create a positive workplace that keeps employees satisfied and committed. Low political behavior and turnover, high cohesion and morale, and a more unified sense of purpose are often characteristics of this environment.

A firm's HR department and top managers are key to making companies healthier. HR professionals function as leaders by developing good policies that make the workplace more positive. This often includes management development, performance feedback, and fair rewards. They also act as advisors to top leaders and provide a sounding board for the CEO. The CEO often pushes the idea that organizational health is an important issue. The following approaches should help managers lead efforts to create healthy cultures:

- *Developing a positive leadership unit*: Put together a group of leaders who trust each

other and who can develop a positive way of interacting.
- *Creating alignment around a common purpose*: The leadership team should identify and agree on the company's mission, vision, and goals for success.
- *Communicating the company's approach*: Once a purpose is established, it needs to be discussed frequently with employees to unify them and build a common understanding of the workplace.
- *Using HR practices to support the workplace*: All of the traditional HR functions should be utilized to create alignment around the purpose.[20]

The ability to develop healthy organizations and business cultures is a key leadership competency within the HR profession. If you were given the responsibility of improving your firm's health:

1. How would you encourage the CEO and other top leaders to focus their efforts on creating a healthy organization culture? What issues do you think deserve the most attention?

2. In addition to the points already mentioned, what steps would you take to develop a healthy organization?

KEY COMPETENCIES: Leadership & Navigation (Behavioral Competency) and Organization (Technical Competency)

formal, that is, agreed upon, written down, and shared with employees. Try to picture the chaos that would result if every supervisor in a very large company could set his or her own vacation policy!

Grouping the areas for which HR typically creates formal systems yields seven interlocking functions, as shown in Figure 1-4. In each organization, these functions are carried out in that firm's unique format that is influenced by external forces that

FIGURE 1-4 HR Management Functions

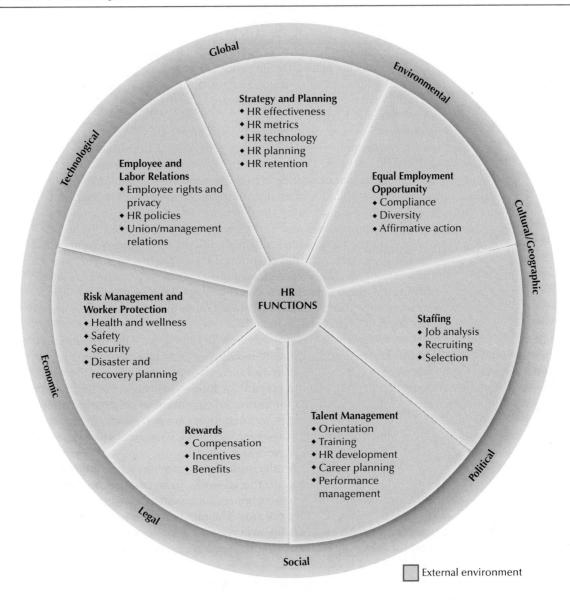

are global, environmental, cultural/geographic, political, social, legal, economic, and technological in nature. The seven HR functions can be visualized as follows:

- Strategy and planning
- Equal employment opportunity
- Staffing
- Talent management
- Rewards
- Risk management and worker protection
- Employee and labor relations

Each of these functions consists of several areas (which are covered in the forthcoming chapters of this book) as follows:

- *HR strategy and planning*: As part of achieving organizational competitiveness, *strategic planning* for the organization and HR's role in those strategic plans are good starting places. Dealing with workforce surpluses and shortages and predicting human capital needs and availabilities are challenges here. How well HR does what it plans to do is measured by HR metrics and analytics, which are covered in Chapter 2.
- *Equal employment opportunity*: *Compliance* with federal, state, and even local equal employment opportunity (EEO) laws and regulations affects all other HR activities. The nature of these laws is discussed in Chapter 3.
- *Staffing*: The aim of staffing is to provide a sufficient supply of qualified individuals to fill jobs in an organization. The nature of the workforce, job design, and job analysis lay the foundation for staffing by identifying what people do in their jobs and how they are affected by these job characteristics Relationships between individuals and the employing organization affect employee performance and retention. Turnover helps determine how many new employees will be needed, an important piece of information when the firm is recruiting applicants for job openings. The selection process is focused on choosing qualified individuals to fill those jobs. These staffing activities are discussed in Chapters 4, 5, 6, and 7.
- *Talent management and development*: Beginning with the *orientation* of new employees, talent management and development includes different types of *training*. *HR development* and *succession planning* for employees and managers are necessary to prepare for future challenges. *Career planning* identifies paths and activities for individual employees as they move within the organization. Assessing how well employees are performing their jobs is the focus of *performance management*. Activities associated with talent management are examined in Chapters 8, 9, and 10.
- *Rewards*: *Compensation* in the form of *pay*, *incentives*, and *benefits* rewards people for performing organizational work. To be competitive, employers develop and refine their basic *compensation* systems and may use *variable pay programs* as incentive rewards. The rapid increase in the cost of *benefits*, especially health care benefits, will continue to be a major issue for most employers. Compensation, variable pay, and benefits activities are discussed in Chapters 11, 12, and 13.
- *Risk management and worker protection*: Employers must address various workplace risks to ensure workers are protected, meet legal requirements, and respond to concerns for workplace *health* and *safety*. Also, workplace *security* has grown in importance along with *disaster and recovery planning*. HR's roles in activities are examined in Chapter 14.
- *Employee and labor relations*: The relationship between managers and their employees must be handled legally and effectively. *Employer and employee rights* must be addressed. It is important to develop, communicate, and update *HR policies and procedures* so that managers and employees alike know what is expected. In some organizations, *union–management relations* must be addressed as well. Activities associated with employee rights and labor–management relations are discussed in Chapters 15 and 16.

These various HR management functions are translated into the daily activities of the HR department if such a group exists in an organization. Operating managers typically perform these activities if a company does not have an HR department.

1-4 Roles for Human Resource Departments

If an organization has a formal HR department or group, there are typically three different roles these individuals might play in the organization. Which role dominates, or whether all three roles are performed, depends on what management wants HR to do and what competencies the HR staff members possess. The potential mix of roles is shown in Figure 1-5, as is how the emphasis on the different roles is likely to change. The following list describes these roles in more depth:

- *Administrative*: Focusing on clerical administration and recordkeeping, including essential legal paperwork and policy implementation
- *Operational and employee advocate*: Managing HR activities based on the strategies and operations that have been identified by management and serving as "champion" for employee issues and concerns
- *Strategic*: Helping define and implement the business strategy relative to human capital and its contribution to the organization's results

While the administrative role has traditionally been the dominant one for HR, the operational and employee advocate roles are increasingly being emphasized in many organizations. The strategic role requires the ability and focus to contribute to strategic decisions and to be recognized by upper management for these efforts. This practice is likely to grow as firms expect HR groups to be involved in the strategic planning process and to prepare employees to be more strategic. HR staff should understand the business so that their strategies match its needs.

FIGURE 1-5 Mix of Roles for HR Departments

PAST

FUTURE

Strategic

Operational/ Employee Advocate

Administrative

1-4a Administrative Role for Human Resources

The administrative role of HR management involves processing information and recordkeeping. This role has given HR management in some organizations the reputation of being staffed by people who primarily tell managers and employees what *cannot* be done, usually because of some policy or problem from the past. If limited to the administrative role, HR staff members are often clerical and lower-level administrative aides to the organization. Two major shifts driving the transformation of the administrative role are greater use of technology and outsourcing.

Technology and the Administrative Role   More HR functions are being performed electronically or done using web-based technology. Technology has changed most HR activities, from employment applications and employee benefits enrollment to e-learning. There will always be a recordkeeping responsibility within HR departments but it can now be done electronically or outsourced. Having employees manage their own records also increases the accuracy of the records.

Outsourcing the Administrative Role   Some HR administrative functions can be outsourced to vendors. This outsourcing of HR administrative activities has grown dramatically in HR areas such as employee assistance (counseling), retirement planning, benefits administration, payroll services, and outplacement services. The primary reasons HR functions are outsourced are to save money on HR staffing and to take advantage of specialized vendor expertise and technology. These activities are being outsourced to firms both in the United States and around the world. A growing trend among companies that outsource HR functions is to evaluate the quality and effectiveness of the services provided and base the amounts paid to vendors on these assessments.[21]

1-4b Operational and Employee Advocate Role for Human Resources

HR personnel are often viewed as employee advocates because they must effectively balance the needs of employees with the needs of organizations. As the voice for employee concerns, HR professionals may serve as "company morale officers," but they spend considerable time on HR "crisis management" when dealing with employee problems that are related to work. Employee advocacy helps ensure fair and equitable treatment for employees regardless of personal background or circumstances. Despite these benefits, the HR advocate role sometimes creates conflict with operating managers because there may be differences of opinion about how to manage employees. However, without the HR advocate role, employers could face lawsuits, regulatory complaints, and employees with poor work attitudes.

The operational role requires the HR function to cooperate with various managers and identify and implement needed programs and policies in the organization. Operational activities are tactical in nature because they affect how work gets done. Compliance with equal employment opportunity and other laws is ensured, employment applications are processed, current openings are filled through interviews, supervisors are trained, safety problems are resolved, and wage and benefit questions are answered. HR staff must make certain that these efforts support the strategies of the organization.

1-4c Strategic Role for Human Resources

The strategic role for HR involves addressing business realities, focusing on future business requirements, and understanding how the management of human capital fits into the organization's plans. The HR department may or may not assist directly in the formulation of business strategies, but it often helps carry them out. However, HR managers are increasingly being seen as strategic contributors to the success of organizations. The role of HR as a *strategic business partner* is often described as "having a seat at the table" and contributing to the strategic direction and success of the organization. That means HR is involved in *devising* and *implementing* strategy.

The opportunity for the HR department to adopt a strategic role exists in many firms. In for-profit companies, the HR group can develop policies that place the right people in the right jobs at the right times to ensure that goals are being met. In not-for-profit organizations such as governmental and social service entities, HR leaders can manage employees in a business-like manner to accomplish other functional goals. Overall, instead of just understanding HR issues and concerns, HR staff should have a broad business focus to help companies reach their strategic goals.

HR can make strategic contributions in a number of areas. For instance, HR should identify the kinds of employees needed and where to find them. Building worker engagement, retaining good employees, and creating development opportunities for leaders are other key issues that enable HR staff to participate in strategic planning.[22] HR should also know what the true costs of human capital are for an employer. For example, in some situations, it costs twice the annual salaries to replace employees who leave. Turnover is something HR can help control, and successful retention and talent management strategies that the department develops and that save a company money represent important contributions to the bottom line.

Some other examples of areas where HR can make strategic contributions are

- Evaluating mergers and acquisitions for organizational compatibility, potential structural changes, and future staffing needs;
- conducting workforce planning to anticipate the retirement of employees at all levels and identify workforce expansion in organizational strategic plans;
- leading site selection efforts for new facilities or transferring operations to international locations on the basis of workforce needs;
- instituting HR management systems to reduce administrative time, equipment, and staff costs with technology;
- working with executives to develop a revised sales compensation and incentives plan as new products or services are rolled out to customers; and
- identifying organizational training opportunities that will more than pay back the costs.

LO4 Provide an overview of four challenges facing HR today.

1-5 Human Resources Management Challenges

As the field of HR management evolves, a challenging employment environment applies pressure for even more and faster change. These issues are often driven by competitive factors that exist in an industry and that require the HR group to respond with positive practices to enable the organization to remain competitive. Challenges are also embedded in economic forces that lead to cost pressures and job changes, globalization, changes in the workforce, and technology advancement.

Global competitors, technology changes, and cost concerns are also reflected in changing jobs. As work must be done differently, jobs must sometimes be changed or downsized. Jobs are seldom static; rather, they change and evolve as the organization changes. The following sections discuss these various challenges.

1-5a Competition, Cost Pressures, and Restructuring

Competition keeps pressure on business organizations to keep costs down so that prices will not become excessive, which can result in lost customers. An overriding theme facing managers and organizations is the need to operate in a "cost-less" mode, which means continually looking for ways to reduce costs of all types, including financial, operational, equipment, and labor expenses. Pressure from global competitors has forced many U.S. firms to close facilities, use international outsourcing, change management practices, increase productivity, and decrease labor costs to become more competitive. These shifts have caused some organizations to reduce the number of employees while at the same time scrambling to attract and retain employees with different capabilities than were previously needed.

The human costs associated with downsizing have resulted in increased workloads, some loss of employee loyalty, and turnover among remaining employees. Shifts in the United States and global economy in the past years have changed the number and types of jobs found in the United States. The last recession affected many types of companies, including automotive and financial firms. In general, organizations in the United States have continued to offer private- and public-sector jobs that fall within the service economy, and many of the jobs to be filled in the next several years will be in the service industry rather than in the manufacturing sector.

Job Shifts The growth in some jobs and decline in others illustrate that shifts are indeed occurring. Figure 1-6 lists occupations that are expected to experience the greatest growth in percentage and numbers by 2022. Many of the fastest-growing occupations percentage-wise are related to health care. However, when the growth in the number of jobs is compared to percentage growth, an interesting factor becomes apparent. The highest growth of jobs by percentage is in occupations that generally require more education and training. However, much of the growth in absolute numbers of jobs is expected to be in areas requiring less education and jobs that are generally considered to be lower-skilled occupations.

Overall, many people feel that the job market is improving, with more companies looking to hire workers. For instance, there is increased demand for skilled employees due to job growth in the United States and the corresponding improving economy, with enhanced consumer spending being reported for auto purchases, tourism, property rentals, and home sales.[23] There is also a growing need for freelance professionals (those who perform work on a contract basis) because of their unique training, experiences, and backgrounds.[24] Another example of the shifting economy involves the types of jobs that are expected to disappear in the near future, including social media expert, taxi dispatcher, toll booth operator, word processor/typist, and retail cashier. However, the number of culture officers is expected to

FIGURE 1-6 Some of the Fastest Growing Occupations by 2022

Occupation	Change, 2012–2022	
	Number	Percentage
Industrial-organizational psychologists	900.0	53.4
Personal care aides	580,800.0	48.8
Home health aides	424,200.0	48.5
Insulation workers, mechanical	13,500.0	46.7
Interpreters and translators	29,300.0	46.1
Diagnostic medical sonographers	27,000.0	46.0
Helpers—brick masons, block masons, stonemasons, and tile and marble setters	10,500.0	43.0
Occupational therapy assistants	12,900.0	42.6
Genetic counselors	900.0	41.2
Physical therapist assistants	29,300.0	41.0
Physical therapist aides	20,100.0	40.1
Skincare specialists	17,700.0	39.8
Physician assistants	33,300.0	38.4
Segmental pavers	700.0	38.1
Helpers—electricians	22,400.0	36.9
Information security analysts	27,400.0	36.5
Occupational therapy aides	3,000.0	36.2
Health specialties teachers, postsecondary	68,600.0	36.1
Medical secretaries	189,200.0	36.0
Physical therapists	73,500.0	36.0
Orthotists and prosthetists	3,000.0	35.5
Brick masons and block masons	25,200.0	35.5
Nursing instructors and teachers, postsecondary	24,000.0	35.4
Nurse practitioners	37,100.0	33.7
Audiologists	4,300.0	33.6
Dental hygienists	64,200.0	33.3
Meeting, convention, and event planners	31,300.0	33.2
Therapists, all other	9,100.0	31.7
Market research analysts and marketing specialists	131,500.0	31.6
Substance abuse and behavioral disorder counselors	28,200.0	31.4

Source: Employment Projections Program, U.S. Department of Labor, U.S. Bureau of Labor Statistics, www.bls.gov.

grow because these individuals help develop and strengthen an organization's climate and overall well-being.[25] Other occupations that are expected to grow in the future include accountants, civil engineers, electricians, forest firefighters, massage therapists, radiologists, and wind energy operations managers.[26]

Skills Shortages Various regions of the United States and different industries face significant workforce shortages because of an inadequate supply of workers with the skills needed to perform emerging jobs. It may not be that there are too few people—only that there are too few with many of the required skills. For instance, some of the most difficult jobs to fill include engineers, nurses, technicians, sales representatives, and certain teachers. Positions that require high skills and experience in a trade have been particularly difficult to fill in some cities, for example, Philadelphia, Dallas, Cleveland, and New York. Many of these shortages are leading to increased compensation to attract good employees.[27] It has become more critical for employees to maintain up-to-date skills if they want to remain marketable and obtain work where opportunities are available.[28]

Even though many Americans today graduate from high school and college, employers are concerned about new graduates' job readiness and specific job-related skills. Test results show that students in the United States perform respectably overall in math and science, but well below students in some other competitive nations. Also, college graduates with degrees in computer science, engineering, and the health sciences remain in short supply relative to the demand for them. Unless major improvements are made to the U.S. educational systems, U.S. employers will be unable to find enough qualified workers for the growing number of skilled jobs.

GLOBAL

1-5b Globalization

The globalization of business has shifted from trade and investment to the integration of global operations, management, and strategic alliances, which has significantly affected how human resources are managed. Many U.S. firms, both large and small, generate a substantial portion of their sales and profits from other countries; firms such as Coca-Cola, Exxon/Mobil, Microsoft, and General Electric derive a significant portion of total sales and profits from outside the United States. Research suggests that about 400 midsized cities in emerging markets will generate 40% of global growth in the next 15 years; many of these cities are relatively unknown in the West.[29] However, many foreign organizations have taken advantage of growth opportunities in the United States. For example, Toyota, based in Japan, has grown its market share and increased its number of jobs in the United States and elsewhere in North America. Also, Toyota, Honda, Nissan, and other Japanese automobile manufacturers, electronics firms, and suppliers have maintained operations in the United States.

Companies often send individuals to foreign worksites to ensure that business operations are consistent with home office expectations. An expatriate is a citizen of one country who is working in a second country and employed by an organization headquartered in the first country. Experienced expatriates can provide a pool of talent that can be tapped as the organization expands its operations more broadly into even more countries. There is growing interest in providing expatriates with appropriate housing options that convey the importance of overseas job assignments to them and outsiders. Housing decisions can be facilitated by working with destination consultants who know about potential living areas. Helping expatriates

Expatriate
A citizen of one country who is working in a second country and employed by an organization headquartered in the first country

move into their new homes, preparing them for cultural differences via appropriate educational material and/or counseling, and monitoring the value of the properties on an ongoing basis can help improve expatriate experiences.[30] However, some HR leaders are starting to question the use of expatriates, with some firms considering shorter assignments and relying on technology to help build overseas business relationships.[31]

Attracting and placing the proper talent in global organizations can be difficult. A recent survey of Latin American organizations indicated that talent acquisition and poor succession planning were key challenges in overseas locations, particularly when dealing with mergers and acquisitions.[32] A number of Canadian organizations are dealing with a lack a qualified tradespersons to staff mining, engineering, construction, and energy jobs in Alberta, and some of these employers are looking to the United States for potential workers.[33] Global staffing has also created political issues. For instance, U.S. employers are having a difficult time hiring enough engineers and educated technology workers because federal legislation restricts the number of high-skilled workers that can be admitted from other countries.

Wage Comparisons across Countries Many economic factors are linked to different political, legal, cultural, and economic systems. For example, in many developed countries, especially in Europe, employment restrictions and wage levels are high. When manufacturing labor costs in the United States are compared with those in Germany and in the Philippines, the differences are significant, as Figure 1-7 shows. Thus, many U.S. and European firms are moving jobs to lower-wage countries.

Critics of globalization cite the extremely low wage rates paid by some international firms and the substandard working conditions that exist in some underdeveloped countries, for example, those found in Apple computer factories in China.[34] Various advocacy groups have accused global firms of being "sweatshop" employers. As a result, some global employers have made efforts to ensure that foreign factories adhere to higher HR standards, but others have not. Global employers

FIGURE 1-7 Hourly Compensation for Manufacturing Workers (2012)

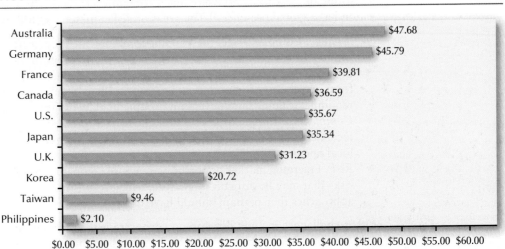

Australia	$47.68
Germany	$45.79
France	$39.81
Canada	$36.59
U.S.	$35.67
Japan	$35.34
U.K.	$31.23
Korea	$20.72
Taiwan	$9.46
Philippines	$2.10

$0.00 $5.00 $10.00 $15.00 $20.00 $25.00 $30.00 $35.00 $40.00 $45.00 $50.00 $55.00 $60.00

Source: U.S. Bureau of Labor Statistics, www.bls.gov.

counter that even though some countries in which they operate have low wage rates, employees at their firms often receive the highest wages and experience the best overall working conditions compared to others in the country. They also argue that their presence enables more people to have jobs in the host countries, which allows employees to improve their living standards.

Legal and Political Factors   Firms in the United States, Europe, and elsewhere are accustomed to relatively stable political and legal systems. However, many nations function under turbulent and varied legal and political systems. Grupo Clarin, a large media organization located in Buenos Aires, Argentina, faces a number of HR issues related to blending the different cultures in its various businesses, but the company also deals with high inflation and a government that is trying break up the firm over claims that it is a monopoly.[35] International firms in many industries have dramatically increased security measures for both operations and employees. Terrorist threats and incidents have significantly affected airlines, travel companies, construction firms, and even retailers such as McDonald's. HR management gets involved in such concerns as part of its transnational operations and risk-management efforts.

Compliance with laws and company actions on wages, benefits, union relations, worker privacy, workplace safety, and other issues illustrate the importance of HR management when operating in other countries. As a result, HR leaders should conduct comprehensive reviews of the political environment and employment laws before beginning operations in a country. The role and nature of labor unions should be a part of that review to avoid potential problems. For example, two managers at a Goodyear Tire plant in France were detained in an office as part of a protest by union members after being accused by another leader in the company of not working hard enough. Goodyear had almost fully shut down operations in the plant and was trying to close or sell it but had to keep paying workers because of strict French labor laws.[36]

Common Challenges for Global Human Resources   Although individual companies do not respond to all HR challenges exactly the same way, research suggests that all must face and overcome a common set of difficulties when an organization has a global presence.[37] The areas of difficulties are as follows:

- *Strategy*: Companies feel they do not communicate their strategy clearly, finding it difficult to be flexible as they expand to other markets.
- *People*: Executives feel their companies are not good at transferring lessons from one country to another and are not sufficiently effective at recruiting, retaining, training, and developing people in all geographic locations.
- *Complexity*: Complexity arises as standardization of processes clashes with local needs and sharing the cost of distant centers increases the expense of local operations.
- *Risk*: Emerging market opportunities expose companies to unfamiliar risks that may be difficult to analyze, which results in sometimes rejecting approaches they perhaps should have taken.

Other challenges include developing corporate leaders, retaining employee talent, and building needed skills in HR groups.[38] Opportunities to address some of these challenges involve changing the structures of HR groups and using more self-service technology that executives can take advantage of to manage HR services.[39]

1-5c A Changing Workforce

Chapter 4 will present a more comprehensive profile of the workforce, but the following text will introduce some workforce changes that present challenges for human resources. The U.S. workforce today is more racially and ethnically diverse, more women are employed than ever before, and the average age of its members is increasing. As a result of these demographic shifts, HR management in organizations has had to adapt to a more varied labor force both externally and internally.

Racial and Ethnic Diversity Racial and ethnic minorities such as Hispanics and African Americans account for a growing percentage of the overall labor force. Immigrants will continue to expand that growth. An increasing number of individuals characterize themselves as *multiracial*, suggesting that the American "melting pot" is blurring racial and ethnic identities.

Racial and ethnic differences have also created greater cultural diversity because of the accompanying differences in traditions, languages, and so on. For example, global events have increased employers' attention to individuals who have diverse religious beliefs, and more awareness of and accommodation for various religious practices have become common issues in organizations.

Gender in the Workforce Women constitute about 50% of the U.S. workforce, but they may be a majority in certain occupations. For instance, the membership of HR professionals in the Society for Human Resource Management (SHRM) is more than 75% female. Additionally, numerous female workers are single, separated, divorced, or widowed and are primary income earners in a household unit. A growing number of U.S. households also include domestic partners, who are committed to each other though not married, and who may be of the same or the opposite sex.

For many workers in the United States, balancing the demands of family and work is a significant challenge. Although that balancing has always been a concern, the increase in the number of working women and dual-career couples has resulted in greater tension for many workers, both male and female. Employers have had to respond to work–family concerns to retain employees. Responses have included greater use of job sharing, the establishment of child care services, increased flexibility in hours worked, and work-life programs. A panel of successful female HR managers noted that work-life balance is a key area of success for women in leadership roles, along with getting good mentors and being confident and unique on the job.[40]

Age Considerations in the Workforce In many areas of the world, the population is aging, resulting in an older workforce. In the United States, a significant number of experienced employees will be retiring in the near future, changing to part-time work, or otherwise shifting their employment. Replacing the experience and talents of longer-service workers is a challenge facing employers in all industries. Loss of these individuals is frequently referred to as a brain drain because of their capabilities and experience. Employers often focus on programs that help retain them, possibly having them mentor and transfer knowledge to younger employees or finding ways for them to continue contributing to the workplace in a more limited capacity (e.g., part-time work).

Millennials (also called Generation Y) are an emerging group of workers in organizations today, and their numbers are expected to represent 75% of the workforce by the year 2025. These individuals value flexibility in work characteristics, transparency in decision making, and a culture of community.[41] Members of Generation Y are often negatively stereotyped as entitled and wanting everything now, but Millennials are often energetic, committed, and industrious.[42] Reverse mentoring is becoming popular in firms such as General Electric, Johnson & Johnson, and Cisco, which encourage Millennials to mentor seasoned managers on how to use technology.[43]

1-5d Human Resources and Technology

In the 1980s, most large companies used a mainframe computer to run a Human Resource Information System (HRIS). These systems processed payroll, tracked employees and their benefits, and produced reports for HR managers. All of this was run by Information Technology (IT) staff/professionals. In 1989, a software package called PeopleSoft became wildly popular—it allowed HR to run its own reports and make changes without help from IT. Today, Software as a Service (or SaaS) functions in a vendor's data center or in the cloud, and the self-service it allows has probably done more to change the work of HR than anything else.[44] SaaS agreements enable firms to rent software packages from vendors instead of buying licenses, but there are concerns. Data security and privacy are concerns because even though a company owns its own data, information is still stored with a vendor. HR professionals need to be aware of contract details to understand how these issues (as well as others) will be addressed by vendors.[45] Many organizations are also replacing some of their aging HR software, particularly programs that focus on the management of human capital, with new technology that allows firms to bring together different types of information, conduct more robust analyses, and identify important relationships and trends.[46]

Benefits and Challenges of Technology The increased use of technologies in the workplace is greatly impacting the way HR activities and other managerial functions are performed in organizations. In particular, the rapid expansion of HR technology serves a number of important purposes. Administrative and operational efficiency and effectiveness can be enhanced when technology is appropriately incorporated into the workplace. For instance, technology can improve the efficiency with which data on employees and HR activities are compiled. The most basic example is the automation of payroll and benefits activities. Numerous firms also provide web-based employee self-service programs that enable employees to go online and access and change their personal data, enroll in or change benefits programs, and prepare for performance reviews.

Another common use of technology is tracking EEO/affirmative action activities. HR technology can also facilitate strategic HR planning. Having accessible data enables HR planning and managerial decision making to be based to a greater degree on information rather than on managerial perceptions and intuition, thus making organizational management more effective. Using technology to support HR activities increases the efficiency of the administrative HR functions and reduces costs. Managers benefit from the availability of relevant information about employees. Properly designed systems provide historical information on performance, pay, training, career progress, and disciplinary actions. On the basis of this information, managers can make better HR-related decisions. To maximize the value of technology, systems should be integrated into the overall IT plan and enterprise software of the organization.[47]

Technology is used extensively by many organizations to help hire the best employees. Automation tools enable hiring managers to quickly work through large numbers of resumes with keyword assessments and to more effectively evaluate candidates' human capital factors.[48] Technology can also be used to improve employee training and development. For example, PersonifyLive is a videoconferencing application that allows trainers to provide enhanced interactive sessions that link real-time presentations with background content on the screen.[49]

Despite these benefits, the use of technology in organizations has some inherent challenges. An overreliance on technology could negatively impact individual learning.[50] The use of the small computerized device known as Google Glass, which individuals wear like eyeglasses to access the Internet with voice commands, take photos, and record videos, prompts many concerns about privacy and security.[51] Companies' HR information systems can also be targeted by harmful cyberattacks that access sensitive employee information.[52]

Mobile Devices One emerging trend is the use of mobile devices to manage various HR and business functions. For instance, ADP offers a popular mobile app called ADP Mobile that allows individuals to view employee information and perform other HR functions. A recent study by the company showed that payroll data was viewed more frequently with mobile devices than it was with traditional computers.[53] Some organizations are encouraging employees to bring their personal devices into the workplace so that they can be used to complete work. This is called a bring you own device (or BYOD) policy.[54] The cloud technology firm Rackspace Hosting has such a policy and encourages employees to perform more of their HR functions and activities—everything from payroll administration to knowledge transfer—on mobile devices.[55]

There are several issues that should be considered to successfully manage mobile technology. One consideration is that HR leaders should encourage the use of mobile devices with BYOD policies. The HR department should also work closely with IT professionals to establish practices that will be the most beneficial. There should be a close working relationship between the Chief Information Officer and Chief Human Resource Officer. Another concern is that to avoid complexity, companies need to be selective about what types of information are available on mobile devices. HR people also need to figure out how to use mobile technology to help them at work. They should select apps that make information easily accessible and can be used with multiple devices.[56]

Social Media The growth of the Internet has resulted in many employees and managers using wikis, blogs, tweets, text messaging, and other techniques. In a wiki, which is a widely available website where individuals can make comments, employees can communicate both positive and negative messages on many topics. Employers have used wikis to increase the exchange of ideas and information among a wide range of individuals. Social media can even be used to increase communication during crisis situations and emergencies.[57]

Blogs are web logs kept by individuals or groups to post and exchange information on a variety of topics. People create and use more than 1 million blogs daily. The subjects of blogs vary. An example of company use would be CEOs or HR executives immediately exchanging information with employees about operational issues or other important events.

Another technology tool is Twitter, which is a microblog that allows people to send and receive tweets, quick messages of less than 140 characters each; through these messages, individuals quickly send information to others. Some firms use tweets to send out policy changes and many other organizational messages. However, individuals in an organization can also use tweets inappropriately, sending critical, obscene, or even harassing details to other employees.

ETHICS

The Risk of Social Media The risk of social media is becoming apparent to employers, and some fear that its use will lead to disclosure of trade secrets such as customer lists and many other problems. Some managers also worry that negative comments made by employees will harm a firm's reputation. While companies may want to establish policies that regulate how technology can and should be used, recent developments suggest that such an approach might not be positive. The general counsel of the National Labor Relations Board has advanced a number of complaints about corporate social networking policies on the grounds that they violate workers' right to engage in conversations about the workplace as part of the provisions outlined in the National Labor Relations Act.[58] Another concern relates to how social media might be used to screen job candidates. Many states, including New Mexico, Arkansas, California, and Utah, now have laws that prevent hiring companies from requesting passwords to obtain access to job applicants' social media accounts.[59]

LO5 Explain how ethical issues in organizations affect HR management.

1-6 Organizational Ethics and Human Resource Management

Closely linked with the strategic role of HR is the way managers and HR staff influence the ethics of employees, as well as the ethical practices of organizations as a whole. These various levels of ethics should be managed in a manner that affects individuals and the workplace in a positive manner, thus aiding in the development of better work outcomes. As Figure 1-8 indicates, violating HR protocols can lead to negative organizational and individual consequences, while institutionalizing ethical practices can prompt many positive outcomes.[60]

Attention to ethics has been growing for many years, driven in part by the corporate scandals at numerous firms in the United States and globally. These scandals show that ethical lapses are common, and they can erode corporate culture so that employers, employees, and other stakeholders are negatively impacted. Research also suggests that the presence of "moral disengagement," a tendency for individuals to make unethical decisions without feeling any regret or remorse, might also be driving unethical conduct in the workplace.[61] This means that firms must develop a culture of ethics so that employees are less likely to witness unethical acts and feel more encouraged to do the right thing on the job.

FIGURE 1-8 HR and Organizational Ethics

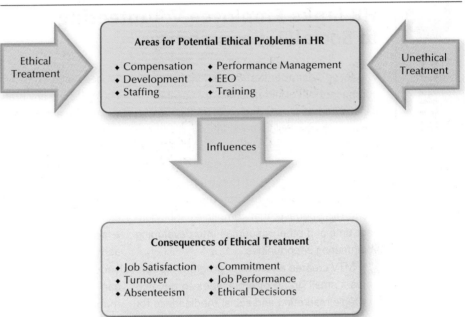

1-6a Ethical Culture and Practices

Writers on business ethics consistently stress that one of the primary determinants of ethical behavior is a positive organizational culture, which, as mentioned earlier, involves the shared values and beliefs that are embedded within an organization. Every organization has a culture, whether it is newly created or well developed, and that culture influences how executives, managers, and employees make organizational decisions. For example, if meeting objectives and financial targets is stressed as a cultural characteristic, then executives and managers may feel encouraged to falsify numbers or doctor cost records. However, when an ethical culture exists in an organization, employees are often more motivated to behave according to appropriate ethical standards. If trustworthiness is emphasized as a cultural value and is upheld by ethical managers, then a company can develop an enhanced image, and its employees can feel more engaged in the workplace.[62]

Companies often rely on a number of programs to increase employees' awareness of ethical issues. For instance, when the following programs exist, an ethical culture often develops, and ethical behavior is encouraged:

- A written code of ethics and standards of conduct
- Training on ethical behavior for all executives, managers, and employees
- Advice to employees on ethical situations they face, often given by HR
- Systems for confidential reporting of ethical misconduct or questionable behavior

Companies can also develop programs related to corporate social responsibility that focus on the enhancement of stakeholder interests and the advancement of social good. There is growing awareness that socially responsible business practices are artifacts of cultural values and can prompt positive employee outcomes.[63] Firms

ETHICS

HR Links Employee Volunteering to Social Responsibility

Employee volunteerism is often viewed as a component of social responsibility because individuals agree to work on projects outside the organization that help stakeholders and address different social issues. Millennials are especially interested in volunteering their time, with some evidence indicating that these projects can improve their work commitment and engagement. This suggests that companies should invest time and other resources into developing volunteering opportunities.

MTV created a volunteer program that enables a small group of employees to develop strategic marketing and social media ideas for the Center for Employment Opportunities, a nonprofit firm based in New York City that provides job search assistance to former inmates. According to Senior Vice President of Public Affairs Jason Rzepka, the program was a success, with a majority of the 15 participants giving it high praise. This shows that volunteering can be a key consideration when managing recruitment and retention. Companies can support these activities by (1) making sure that there is a good match between a program and the participants, (2) enlisting the help of an intermediary organization to help manage the

process, and (3) being aware that surprises do occur despite any preparations made.

There are some risks associated with volunteering programs, so organizations should plan ahead. For instance, employees with high job skills might be hard to replace while they are volunteering, and selecting the right participants can be difficult without arousing claims of favoritism. Other concerns include a lack of clear guidelines and/or expectations, as well as confusion over whether employees should be paid for their time. The HR group can enhance volunteer projects by building management support, structuring the process, properly tracking compensation of volunteer time, and increasing communication about the program.[64]

Based on current interest in employee volunteerism, consider the following questions:

1. If you were working as an HR professional, how would you develop an employee volunteer program that would lead to great worker engagement?

2. What kinds of activities would you include in an engaging employee volunteer program?

---

that are interested in sustainable practices that help the environment and society can also incorporate as "benefit corporations," which makes companies show how they are operating in a responsible way. This designation can enhance HR activities such as hiring good employees.[65]

ETHICS

1-6b Ethics and Global Differences

Variations in legal, political, and cultural values and practices in different countries often raise ethical issues for global employers that must comply with both their home-country laws and the laws of other countries. These differences can also lead to ethical and legal conflicts for global managers. Some firms have established guidelines and policies, for example, to reduce the payments of bribes, but even these efforts do not provide guidance for all situations that can arise. Companies can develop ethics codes and training so that employees understand the problems they might face in global environments. These guidelines could be wrapped into regular cultural and/or expatriation training that prepares individuals for working in a diverse global workplace. They might also concentrate on issues such as sustainability and social responsibility. Telefonica, the prominent Spanish telecommunications company, focuses on developing programs that emphasize corporate social responsibility, including employee work-life balance and flexible work scheduling.[66]

GLOBAL

1-6c Role of Human Resources in Organizational Ethics

People in organizations face many different ethical decisions, and they are often guided by their own values and personal behavior codes, as well as by various organizational, professional, and societal principles. Employees may ask the following questions when dealing with ethical dilemmas:

- Does the behavior or result meet all applicable *laws*, *regulations*, and *government codes*?
- Does the behavior or result meet both *organizational standards* and *professional standards* of ethical behavior?

Organizations that are known to be ethical have better long-term success because they develop policies that guide individual ethics. In this sense, HR management plays a key role as the keeper and voice of organizational ethics. HR departments can help develop corporate compliance efforts and an ethical culture by coordinating ethics training and creating policies that encourage employees to report misconduct.[67] They can also evaluate the current state of ethical culture by surveying employees, monitoring corporate values, and being alert for conditions that encourage unethical behavior.[68] There are many different views about the importance of HR in ensuring that ethical practices, justice, and fairness are embedded in HR practices. Figure 1-9 identifies some of the most frequent areas of ethical misconduct that involve HR activities.

Ethical issues pose fundamental questions about fairness, justice, truthfulness, and social responsibility. Just complying with a wider range of requirements, laws, and regulations cannot cover every ethical situation that executives, managers, HR professionals, and employees will face. Yet having all the elements of an ethics program may not prevent individual managers or executives from engaging in or failing to report unethical behavior. Even HR staff members may be reluctant to report ethics concerns, primarily because of fears that doing so may affect their current and future employment.[69] However, when HR develops programs that encourage ethics, employees should be more motivated to behave ethically. The preceding "HR Ethics: HR Links Employee Volunteering to Social Responsibility" feature provides an example of how employee volunteering can be used to support social responsibility by building positive ties with different communities.

Another critical approach for guiding employees' ethical decisions and behavior is ethics training, with research showing that many more companies are using such instruction to enhance an ethical culture.[70] Firms such as Best Buy, Caterpillar, and others have ethics training for all employees via the Internet or in person.

FIGURE 1-9 Examples of HR-Related Ethical Misconduct

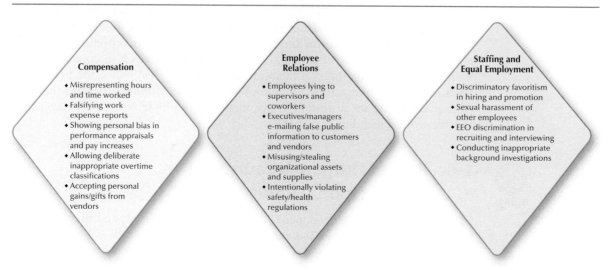

How to address difficult and conflicting situations is part of effective HR management training efforts. To help HR staff members deal with ethical issues, the Society for Human Resource Management has developed a code of ethics for its members and provides information on handling ethical issues and policies.[71]

HR Ethics and Sarbanes-Oxley The Sarbanes-Oxley (SOX) Act was passed in 2002 by Congress to make certain that publicly traded companies follow accounting controls that could reduce the likelihood of illegal and unethical behaviors. Many HR issues must be managed in line with SOX. The biggest concerns are linked to executive compensation and benefits, but SOX sections 404, 406, 802, and 806 require companies to establish ethics codes, develop employee complaint systems, and have antiretaliation policies for employees who act as whistle-blowers to identify wrongful actions. HR has been involved in routing people through the massive compliance verification effort that has occurred.

LO6 Explain the key competencies needed by HR professionals and why certification is important.

1-7 Human Resources Management Competencies and Careers

The intent of this book is not to train all who read it to be HR managers. Most will take this knowledge and work at another job in the organization but understand the duties HR must accomplish, which they must often share. Given that, it is useful to understand the necessary competencies and certifications for HR professionals.

1-7a Human Resources Competencies

There has been much discussion in the HR profession about the competencies HR leaders should possess. The transformation of HR into a more strategic and professional field has implications for the kinds of competencies that individuals should develop.[72] HR professionals at all levels certainly need to have a basic

FIGURE 1-10 SHRM HR Competency Model

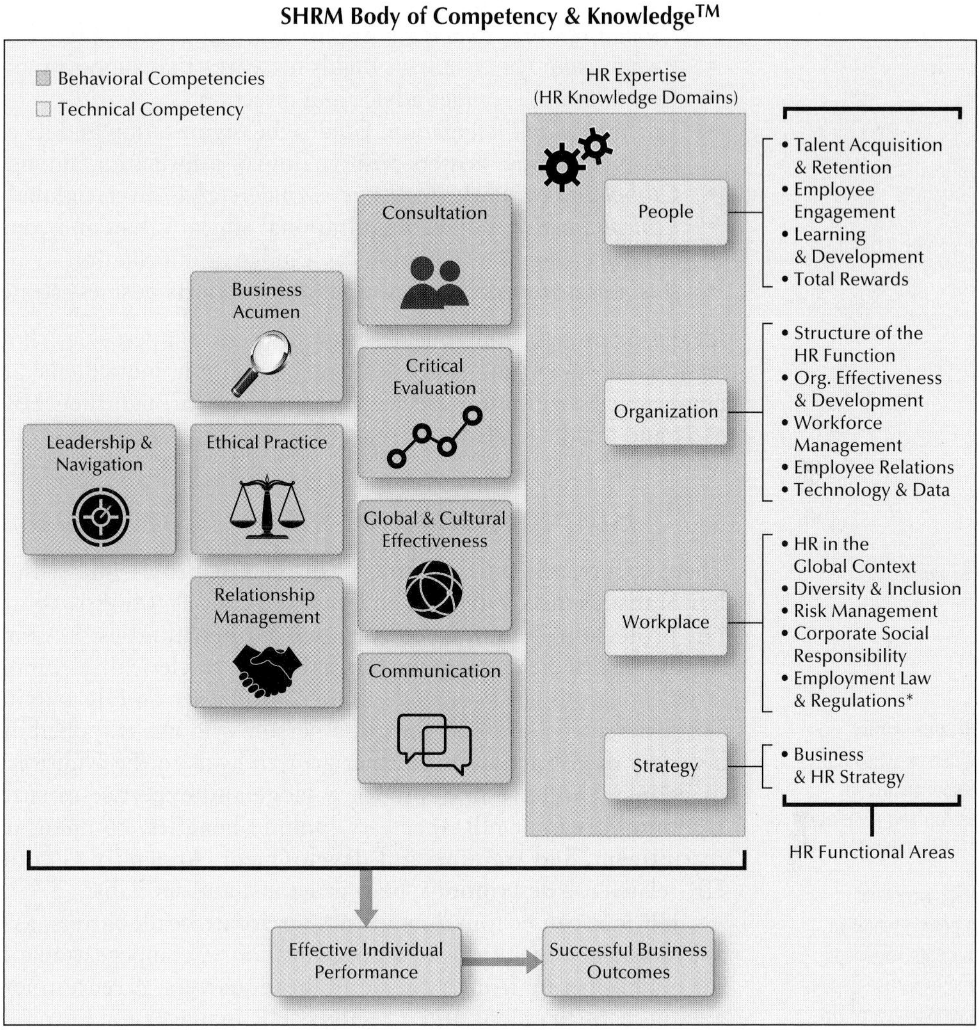

SHRM Body of Competency & Knowledge™

☐ Behavioral Competencies
☐ Technical Competency

HR Expertise
(HR Knowledge Domains)

Consultation

Business Acumen

Critical Evaluation

Leadership & Navigation

Ethical Practice

Global & Cultural Effectiveness

Relationship Management

Communication

People
- Talent Acquisition & Retention
- Employee Engagement
- Learning & Development
- Total Rewards

Organization
- Structure of the HR Function
- Org. Effectiveness & Development
- Workforce Management
- Employee Relations
- Technology & Data

Workplace
- HR in the Global Context
- Diversity & Inclusion
- Risk Management
- Corporate Social Responsibility
- Employment Law & Regulations*

Strategy
- Business & HR Strategy

HR Functional Areas

Effective Individual Performance → Successful Business Outcomes

*Applicable only to examinees testing within the United States
Source: www.shrm.org.

understanding of strategic management; legal, administrative, and operational issues; and how technology is applied. A recent study identified other competency-based factors that a typical HR professional should develop, including being a strategic positioner, a credible activist, a capacity builder, a change champion, an innovator and integrator, and a technology proponent.[73]

The Society of Human Resource Management (SHRM), the leading professional association for HR, recently developed a list of competencies that are arranged in a new model. Figure 1-10 provides a summary of the SHRM competency framework. The model was developed based on advice given by more than 1,200 practitioners who participated in focus groups; survey responses provided by more than 32,000 other professionals; and analysis of multiple performance outcomes that were linked back to the competencies. The nine competencies highlighted include:

- *Human resource expertise*: Applies knowledge of HR functions
- *Relationship management*: Builds networks that support the firm
- *Consultation*: Provides advice and direction
- *Leadership and navigation*: Guides the organization and its employees
- *Communication*: Fosters positive flow of information among different parties
- *Global and cultural effectiveness*: Understands diverse global issues
- *Ethical practice*: Builds organizational ethical values and compliance
- *Critical evaluation*: Functions as a judge of information
- *Business acumen*: Provides input that supports business strategy

Ideally, awareness and consideration of these competencies should guide the professional development of HR leaders. In addition, individuals' application of these competencies will often vary as they progress through their HR careers, from the early and middle levels to the senior and executive levels.[74]

1-7b Human Resource Management as a Career Field

There is currently much optimism in the HR profession, with the Bureau of Labor Statistics indicating that there is tremendous job growth in the field and few HR professionals looking for new work opportunities.[75] A variety of jobs exist within the HR field, ranging from executive to clerical. As an organization grows large enough to need someone to focus primarily on HR activities, the role of the HR generalist is needed—that is, a person who has responsibility for performing a variety of HR activities. Further growth leads to the addition of HR specialists, or people who have in-depth knowledge and expertise in specific areas of HR. Common areas of HR specialty include benefits, compensation, staffing and recruitment, and training and development. Appendix G contains examples of HR-related job descriptions, both generalist and specialist.

HR jobs can be found in a firm's corporate headquarters, as well as in the field and subsidiary operations of an organization. A compensation analyst or HR director might operate from a corporate headquarters. A recruitment coordinator for a manufacturing plant and a regional HR manager for European operations in a global food company are examples of field and subsidiary HR professionals. These types of jobs have different career appeals and challenges based on their varying responsibilities. Another job within the HR profession that is gaining momentum is Chief Human Resource Officer. These individuals are expected to have a broad understanding of the different complex areas of HR management, and their presence is linked to higher organizational performance and profitability.[76]

1-7c Human Resource Professionalism and Certification

Depending on the job, HR professionals may need considerable knowledge about employment regulations, finance, tax law, statistics, and information systems.[77] In most cases, they also need extensive knowledge about specific HR activities. The broad range of issues faced by HR professionals has made involvement in professional associations and organizations important. For HR generalists, the largest

HR generalist
A person who has responsibility for performing a variety of HR activities

HR specialist
A person who has in-depth knowledge and expertise in a specific area of HR

organization is SHRM. Public-sector HR professionals tend to be concentrated in the International Personnel Management Association (IPMA). Two other prominent specialized HR organizations are the WorldatWork Association and the Association for Talent Development (ATD).

One characteristic of a professional field is having a means to certify that members have the knowledge and competencies needed in the profession. The CPA for accountants and the CLU for life insurance underwriters are examples. Certification can be valuable to individuals and useful to employers as they select and promote certified individuals. Earning certification is an important step in establishing proficiency and credibility in the profession. Equally important is the continuing education and recertification process that ensures that individuals maintain up-to-date skills and knowledge so that they can effectively manage HR programs and practices.

HRCI Certification The most widely known HR certifications are the Professional in Human Resources (PHR), the Senior Professional in Human Resources (SPHR), and the Global Professional in Human Resources (GPHR), all sponsored by the Human Resource Certification Institute (HRCI). More than 100,000 professionals have at least one of these designations, and thousands of individuals take the certification exams annually. Eligibility requirements for PHR, SPHR, and GPHR are shown in Appendix A.

Eligible individuals must pass the appropriate exam. Appendix A identifies test specifications and knowledge areas covered by the PHR and SPHR exams. Readers of this book will be introduced to specific competencies that they should understand in order to earn a PHR or SPHR designation. Certification from HRCI also exists for global HR professionals in the GPHR. Global certification recognizes the growth in HR responsibilities in international organizations and covers appropriate global HR subject areas.

SHRM Exams and Certifications The growth of the HR profession has fueled interest in the development of many university-based HR programs. Given these trends, SHRM developed the Assurance of Learning Assessment in 2011. This exam evaluates a student's ability to apply the knowledge learned in college, and by successfully completing the exam, a person shows he or she is ready for entry-level positions within the HR profession.[78]

In 2015, SHRM began offering a certification based on its competency model for HR professionals. The certification focuses on the application of HR knowledge to increase organizational performance. Certification of competency can be earned at two levels, one that focuses on executive competencies and another that focuses on entry, middle, and senior competencies. Once certified, a professional's credentials will last for three years, and then he or she will need to be recertified.[79]

SHRM recently partnered with the Associacion Mexicana en Direccion de Recuros Humanos, the largest HR group in Mexico, to develop an eight-month certification course to be completed by HR professionals in that country. Individuals have to successfully complete an interview and have no fewer than five years of HR experience and a college degree to enroll; having seven or more years of experience waives the college degree requirement. Participants learn information about strategic HR, staffing, compensation, employee development, and other areas, and they must complete a project at the end of the course to demonstrate mastery of the course content.[80]

WorldatWork Certifications The WorldatWork Association has four certifications emphasizing compensation and benefits:

- Certified Compensation Professional (CCP)
- Certified Benefits Professional (CBP)
- Certified Work-Life Professional (CWLP)
- Certified Global Remuneration (CGR)

Other Human Resource Certifications Increasingly, employers hiring or promoting HR professionals are requesting certifications as a "plus." HR certifications give HR professionals more credibility with corporate peers and senior managers. Additional certification programs for HR specialists and generalists are sponsored by various organizations, and the number of certifications is being expanded. For specialists, some well-known programs include the following:

- Certified Recognition Professional (CRP) sponsored by the Recognition Professionals International
- Certified Employee Benefits Specialist Program sponsored by the International Foundation of Employee Benefits Plans
- Certified Professional in Learning and Performance sponsored by the Association for Talent Development
- Certified Safety Professional (CSP) and Occupational Health and Safety Technologist (OHST) sponsored by the American Society of Safety Engineers
- Certified Graphics Communications Manager (CGCM) and Certified Mail Manager (CMM) sponsored by the International Personnel Management Association

Most individuals who want to succeed in the field update their knowledge continually. One way of staying current in HR is to review current information that appears in the HR literature or that is provided by relevant associations, as listed in Appendix B of this book. Overall, certifying knowledge and competency is a trend in many professions, and HR illustrates the importance of certification by making many types available. Given that some people enter HR jobs with limited formal HR training, certifications help both individuals and their employers ensure that appropriate HR practices are implemented to improve the performance of their organizations.

SUMMARY

- HR management should ensure that human talent is used effectively and efficiently to accomplish organizational goals.
- All organizations need HR management, but larger ones are more likely to have a specialized HR function.
- Organizations need HR because HR functions must be done by *someone* in all organizations.
- Human capital is the collective value of the capabilities, knowledge, skills, life experiences, and motivation of an organization's workforce.
- HR management activities can be grouped as follows: strategic HR management; equal

employment opportunity; staffing; talent management; compensation and benefits; health, safety, and security; and employee and labor relations.
- HR departments can take administrative, operations, and/or strategic roles in the organization.
- As an organization core competency, HR has a unique capability to create high value that differentiates an organization from competitors in areas such as productivity, quality and service, and organizational climate.

- Numerous HR challenges currently exist, including organizational cost pressures, globalization, a changing workforce, and technology.
- Ethical behavior is crucial in HR management, and HR professionals regularly face many ethical issues and consequences both domestically and globally.
- All levels of HR professionals need competencies in strategic knowledge and impacts; legal, administrative, and operational areas; and technology. Senior HR leaders need these competencies plus others to be effective.
- Current knowledge about HR management is required for professionals in the field of HR and professional certification has grown in importance for HR generalists and specialists.

CRITICAL THINKING CHALLENGES

1. Discuss several areas in which HR can affect organizational culture positively or negatively.

2. Give some examples of ethical issues that you have experienced in jobs and explain how HR did or did not help resolve them.

3. Why is it important for HR management to transform from being primarily administrative and operational to a more strategic contributor?

4. Assume you are an HR Director with a staff of seven people. A departmental objective is for all staff members to become professionally certified within a year. Using the Internet resources of HR associations, such as www.shrm.org and www.WorldatWork.org, develop a table that identifies four to six certifications that could be obtained by your staff members and show the important details for each certification.

5. Your company, a growing firm in the financial services industry, is extremely sensitive to the issues surrounding business ethics.

The company wants to be proactive in developing a business ethics training program for all employees, both to ensure the company's reputation as an ethical organization in the community and to help maintain the industry's high standards. As the HR Director and someone who values the importance of having all employees trained in the area of business ethics, you are in charge of developing the ethics training program. It needs to be a basic program that can be presented to all employees in the company. Resources for business ethics information can be found at www.business-ethics.org/.

A. What legislative act prompted many U.S. companies to develop internal ethical policies and procedures?

B. What are key concepts related to business ethics that should be considered in the development of the ethics training program?

CASE   Water Quality Association: Building Competencies with Technology

The Water Quality Association (WQA) is a trade association that focuses on the delivery of drinking water to residents and businesses. This organization has developed a learning environment for its employees based on the development of important competencies and skills that are needed for work. Experiential and informal learning is emphasized, which represents approximately 90% of training that is often overlooked in favor of more formal instruction. What makes approaches such as these unique is the reliance on technologies such as mobile devices, customized software, analytical assessments of data, and computer-based awards that enhance learning.

The basis for using experiential and informal learning, in conjunction with extensive technology support, is apprenticeships. Apprenticeships are traditionally used to build critical skills for individuals working in trade occupations. But they can also be used to develop important cognitive competencies when they are supported by technology (a process referred to as Apprenticeship 3.0). The following guidelines can be considered when developing cognitive apprenticeships:

- Ask job experts to develop a list of all the critical circumstances that surround a job and then identify the knowledge, skills, and abilities needed to effectively work under these circumstances.
- Create a list of performance objectives and link them to competencies; training topics should be identified and should ultimately focus on job situations.
- The learning experiences should progressively become more challenging over time, while focusing on providing learners with more responsibility.
- Time should be provided for individual reflection and coaching from others (some of which can be technology based).
- To enhance motivation and satisfaction, recognize employees as they progress through the training.

- Continuous learning should be emphasized so that employees constantly develop important competencies that help them be more effective.

WQA has immersed itself in Apprenticeship 3.0 to better prepare its employees for workplace challenges and opportunities. The organization is using mobile technology to deliver a series of learning modules to individuals, and their progress is tracked in the system. Badges are also awarded to employees as they successfully complete various activities.

WQA developed the process by empowering job experts to develop a list of important competencies for different jobs in the firm, and the badges reflect the mastery of these areas. WQA also specified various learning opportunities such as work experience with mobile evaluations and feedback, online study and tutoring, and active coaching. These experiences help individuals earn the badges.[81]

QUESTIONS

1. How did the Water Quality Association's use of technology help enhance how employees acquired important work competencies? Can you think of any other mobile technology applications that might be used to enhance WQA's learning activities?

2. What is your opinion of Apprenticeship 3.0? Is it an approach that you would consider using as an HR manager, or does it need further development?

SUPPLEMENTAL CASES

Rio Tinto: Redesigning HR

This case describes a company that must reduce its workforce due to the 2008 global recession. The approach used was global in nature, and downsizing efforts were highly coordinated and consistent across all areas of the business. (For the case, go to www.cengage.com/management/mathis.)

Phillips Furniture

This case describes a small company that has grown large enough to need a full-time HR person. You have been selected to be the HR manager, and you have to decide what HR activities are needed as well as the role HR is to play. (For the case, go to www.cengage.com/management/mathis.)

Sysco

Large food services and distribution firm Sysco had to revise its HR management. Review this case and identify how the changes at Sysco modified HR's importance. (For the case, go to www.cengage.com/management/mathis.)

HR, Culture, and Success at Google, Scripps, and UPS

This case describes HR's role in the culture of three different companies. HR's contribution to organizational success in each case can be identified and further researched. (For the case go to www.cengage.com/management/mathis.)

END NOTES

1. Based on Carol Patton, "Leap of Faith," *Human Resource Executive,* May 2014, pp. 14–16.
2. Peter Cappelli, "The Restructuring of the Top HR Job," *Human Resource Executive Online,* May 21, 2012, pp. 1–2.
3. Lauren Weber and Rachel Feintzeig, "Is It a Dream or a Drag? Companies without HR," *Wall Street Journal,* April 9, 2014, p. B1.
4. "Holacracy," *T+D,* March 2014, p. 17.
5. Mark McGraw, "What's Keeping HR up at Night," *Human Resource Executive,* 2013, pp. 32–36.
6. Jennifer Schramm, "HR Professionals Forecast the Future," *HR Magazine,* May 2013, p. 96.
7. John Boudreau, Carrie Gibson, and Ian Ziskin, "What Is the Future of HR?" *Workforce,* January 5, 2014, http://www.workforce.com/articles/20179-what-is-the-future-of-hr.
8. Stowe Boyd, "A New Charter for HR," *Gigaom Research,* February 6, 2014, pp. 1–16.
9. Donna M. Owens, "Is Management Obsolete?" *HR Magazine,* May 2012, p. 28.
10. Lauren Weber and Rachel Feintzeig, "Is It a Dream or a Drag? Companies without HR," *Wall Street Journal,* April 9, 2014, p. B1.
11. Kenneth Matos and Ellen Galinsky, *2014 National Study of Employers,* sponsored by Families and Work Institute, Society for Human Resource Management, and *When Work Works,* pp. 1–63.
12. Adapted from Eric Krell, "Is HR Doing More with Less?" *HR Magazine,* September 2013, pp. 63–66.
13. Bruce E. Kaufman and Benjamin I. Miller, "The Firm's Choice of HRM Practices: Economics Meets Strategic Human Resource Management," *Industrial and Labor Relations Review* 64 (2011) 526–557.
14. Sara Hill, "The Challenges Facing HR in Human Capital Management," *Human Resource Executive,* November 2013, p. 25.
15. Annabelle Reitman and Caitlin Williams, "Distinguish Yourself and Excel in the Profession," *T+D,* September 2013, pp. 42–46.
16. Tim Weyland, "10 Principles for Building an Effective Human Capital Plan," TriNet White Paper, March 2010, pp. 1–10.
17. Chris Majer, "Silent Killers' Measureable Cost," *Talent Management,* July 29, 2014, http://talentmgt.com/articles/print/6658-silent-killers-measureable-cost.
18. Chris Majer, "Productivity and Inactivity," *Talent Management,* July 29, 2014, http://talentmgt.com/articles/print/6659-productivity-and-inactivity.
19. Peter Cappelli, "Rethinking the Retail Model," *Human Resource Executive Online,* January 28, 2014, http://www.hreonline.com/HRE/print.jhtml?id=534356654.
20. Adapted from Patrick Lencioni, "The Age of HR Has Finally Arrived," *Human Resource Executive,* 2013, pp. 38–41.
21. Eric Krell, "Results-Oriented Outsourcing," *HR Magazine,* July 2014, pp. 47–49.
22. Jeff Wangler, "HR Helps Set the Course for the Future," *Human Resource Executive,* November 13, 2012, p. 36.
23. Sarah Portlock, "Demand for Skilled Workers Perking Up, Fed Survey Says," *Wall Street Journal,* June 5, 2014, p. A2.
24. Lauren Weber, "Elance Taps Growing Demand for Freelancers," *Wall Street Journal,* February 5, 2014.
25. "Five Jobs That Won't Exist in 10 Years...," *HR Magazine,* February 2014, p. 16; Kathy Gurchiek, "Social Media Expert an Obsolete Job in 10 Years," *SHRM Online,* December 12, 2013, http://www.shrm.org/Publications/HRNews/Pages/Job-Trends-Social-Media-Expert.aspx.
26. "Bright Outlook Occupations," *O*NET Online,* http://www.onetonline.org/help/bright/.
27. Sarah Portlock, "Demand for Skilled Workers Perking Up, Fed Survey Says," *Wall Street Journal,* June 5, 2014, p. A2.
28. Lauren Weber, "Elance Taps Growing Demand for Freelancers," *Wall Street Journal,* February 5, 2014.
29. Markin Dewhurst et al., "The Global Company's Challenge," *McKinsey Quarterly,* June 2012, pp. 1–5.
30. Sheryl Nance-Nash, "Discerning Digs," *Human Resource Executive,* January-February 2014, pp. 20–24.
31. Eric Krell, "Easy Come, Easy Go," *HR Magazine,* March 2013, pp. 59–61.
32. Roy Maurer, "Latin American Multinationals Challenged by HR Issues," *SHRM Online,* November 11, 2013, http://www.shrm.org/hrdisciplines/global/articles/pages/latin-american-multinationals-hr-challenges.aspx.
33. Catherine Skrzypinski, "Study: U.S. Workers Head North to Bridge Skills Gap," *SHRM Online,* November 18, 2013, http://www.shrm.org/

hrdisciplines/global/articles/pages/us-canada-skills-gap.aspx.

34. Rex Nutting, "Apple's Chinese Labor Problem," *Denver Post*, February 19, 2012, p. 4K.

35. Robert J. Grossman, "Delivering HR in a Media Giant," *HR Magazine*, February 2014, pp. 28–29.

36. Gabrielle Parussini, "Goodyear Managers Held Hostage," *Wall Street Journal*, January 7, 2014, p. B3.

37. Markin Dewhurst et al., "The Global Company's Challenge," *McKinsey Quarterly*, June 2012, pp. 2–5.

38. Dori Meinert, " 'Re-skilling' HR among Top Challenges Facing Companies," *HR Magazine*, May 2014, p. 18.

39. Roy Maurer, "Global HR Service-Delivery Processes, Technologies in Flux," *SHRM Online*, November 19, 2013, http://www.shrm.org/hrdisciplines/global/articles/pages/global-hr-service-delivery-processes-technology.aspx.

40. Pamela Babcock, "Female HR Leaders Share Lessons They've Learned," *SHRM Online*, March, 28, 2013, http://www.shrm.org/hrdisciplines/diversity/articles/pages/female-hr-leaders-lessons.aspx.

41. Kathryn Tyler, "New Kids on the Block," *HR Magazine*, October 2013, pp. 35–40.

42. Rick Bell, "The Last Word: You Talk about Annoying," *Workforce*, December 11, 2013, http://www.workforce.com/articles/20133-the-last-word-you-talk-about-annoying; Ladan Nikravan, "Gen Y Isn't Entitled: Here's Why," *Chief Learning Officer*, January 17, 2014, http://www.clomedia.com/articles/gen-y-isn-t-entitled-here-s-why.

43. Ryann K. Ellis, "Revise Mentoring: Letting Millennials Lead the Way," *T+D*, September 2013, p. 13.

44. Bill Kutik, "Lifetimes of Tech Change," *Human Resource Executive Online*, April 3, 2012, pp. 1–2.

45. Bill Roberts, "Contract Competence," *HR Magazine*, June 2014, pp. 101–104.

46. Stephanie Castellano, "New Software Helps HR Drive Business Decisions," *T+D*, September 2013, p. 18.

47. Clinton Wingrove, "Why Automating Bad HR Processes Isn't a Solution," *Workspan*, February 2012, pp. 47–50.

48. Drew Robb, "Better Hiring through Technology," *HR Magazine*, June 2013, pp. 46–52.

49. "Getting inside Your Digital Content," *T+D*, September 2013, p. 19.

50. Pat Galagan, "Technology and the Interrupted Brain," *T+D*, September 2013, pp. 2–25.

51. Max Mihelich, "Forward to the Future: How Workforce Tech Promises to Change the Way We Do Business," *Workforce*, December 12, 2013, http://www.workforce.com/articles/20129-forward-to-the-future-how-workforce-tech-promises-to-change-the-way-we-do-business.

52. Drew Robb, "Could HR Be the Next Target?" *HR Magazine*, July 2014, pp. 50–52.

53. Aliah D. Wright, "Study: More Using HR Apps on Mobile Devices," *SHRM Online*, March 6, 2014, http://www.shrm.org/hrdisciplines/technology/articles/pages/study-more-using-hr-apps-on-mobile-devices.aspx.

54. Aliah D. Wright, "BYOD Policy, Security Highlighted as Apple, IBM Join Forces," *SHRM Online*, July 25, 2014, http://www.shrm.org/hrdisciplines/technology/articles/pages/why-byod-policy-is-important.aspx.

55. Dave Zielinski, "The Mobilization of HR Tech," *HR Magazine*, February 2014, pp. 30–36.

56. Sarah Fister Gale, "Mobile HR Technology Is on the Move," *Workforce*, March 18, 2014, http://www.workforce.com/articles/20332-mobile-hr-technology-is-on-the-move; Drew Robb, "Partnering with CIOs," *HR Magazine*, March 2014, pp. 51–53.

57. Dave Zielinski, "Emergency Channels," *HR Magazine*, September 2013, pp. 69–72.

58. David S. Rubin, "Get Antisocial," *HR Magazine*, February 2013, pp. 69–70.

59. Joanne Deschenaux, "Seven States Protect Social Media Privacy," *HR Magazine*, June 2013, p. 16; Dana Wilkie and Aliah Wright, "Balance Risks of Screening Social Media Activity," *HR Magazine*, May 2014, p. 14.

60. David M. Mayer et al, "Who Displays Ethical Leadership and Why Does It Matter?" *Academic of Management Journal* 55 (February 2012), 151–171.

61. Celia Moore, James R. Detert, Linda Klebe Trevino, Vicki L. Baker, and David M. Mayer, "Why Employees Do Bad Things: Moral Disengagement and Unethical Organizational Behavior," *Personnel Psychology* 65 (2012), 1–48.

62. Matthew Brodsky, "A Matter of Trust," *Human Resource Executive Online*, July 15, 2014, http://www.hreonline.com/HRE/print.jhtml?id=534357297.

63. Frederick P. Morgeson, Herman Aguinis, David A. Waldman, and Donald S. Siegel, "Extending Corporate Social Responsibility Research to the Human Resource Management and Organizational Behavior Domains: A Look to the Future," *Personnel Psychology* 66 (2013), 805–824.

64. Based on Pamela Babcock, "MTV Engages Millennials with 'Pro-Social' Programs," October 21, 2013, www.shrm.org; Lin Grensing-Pophal, "Pitfalls of Employee Volunteerism and How to Avoid Them," September 13, 2013, www.shrm.org.

65. Pamela Babcock, "Businesses Commit to Greater Good," *SHRM Online*, December 21, 2012, http://www.shrm.org/hrdisciplines/ethics/articles/pages/businesses-commit-greater-good.aspx.

66. Daniel Palacios-Marques and Carlos A. Devece-Caranana, "Policies to Support Corporate Social Responsibility: The Case of Telefonica," *Human Resource Management* 52 (2013), 145–152.

67. Pamela Babcock, "HR: Play to Your Strengths to Boost Compliance," *SHRM Online*, November 27, 2012, http://www.shrm.org/hrdisciplines/ethics/articles/pages/hr-strengths-boost-compliance.aspx.

68. Pamela Babcock, "Roadblocks to Creating a Culture of Ethics," *SHRM Online*, May 13, 2013, http://www.shrm.org/hrdisciplines/ethics/articles/pages/culture-of-ethics.aspx.

69. Susan R. Meisinger, "Examining Organizational Ethics," *Human Resource Executive Online*, June 11, 2012, pp. 1–2.

70. Dori Meinert, "Creating an Ethical Workplace," *SHRM Online*, April 1, 2014, http://www.shrm.org/publications/hrmagazine/

editorialcontent/2014/0414/
pages/0414-ethical-workplace-
culture.aspx.

71. To view the code of ethics and its
development, go to www.shrm.org.

72. Marja-Liisa Payne, "A Comparative
Study of HR Manager's
Competencies in Strategic Roles,"
International Management Review 6
(2010), 5–12.

73. Dave Ulrich, Jon Younger, Wayne
Brockbank, and Michael D. Ulrich,
"The State of the HR Profession,"
Human Resource Management 52
(2013), 457–471.

74. *SHRM HR Competency Model*,
http://www.shrm.org/hrcompetencies/
pages/default.aspx; http://www.shrm
.org/HRCompetencies/Documents/
SHRM_CompetencyModel.
pdf; http://www.shrm.org/
HRCompetencies/Documents/

Competency%20Model%2011%
202_10%201%202014.pdf.

75. Jennifer Schramm, "The Pulse of
the HR Profession," *HR Magazine*,
February 2014, p. 64.

76. Dinah Wisenberg Brin, "Want to
Turn a Profit? Hire a CHRO,"
SHRM Online, November 22,
2013, http://www.shrm.org/
hrdisciplines/businessleadership/
articles/pages/want-to-turn-a-profit-
hire-a-chro.aspx; Aliah D. Wright,
"Each One, Reach One, Says
CHROs," *SHRM Online*, October
7, 2013, http://www.shrm.org/
publications/hrnews/pages/career-
advancement-chro-panel-strategy-
conference.aspx.

77. Kristen B. Frasch, "The Changing
Face of HR," *Human Resource
Executive Online*, June 2, 2010,
pp. 1–4. Peter Cappelli, "The Last

25 Years Point to the Future,"
Human Resource Executive Online,
March 26, 2012, pp. 1–2.

78. Jennifer Schramm, "Teaching Human
Resources," *HR Magazine*, July 2013,
p. 72.

79. Kathy Gurchiek, "SHRM Announces
Details of New Certification,"
SHRM Online. May 15, 2014,
http://www.shrm.org/publications/
hrnews/pages/new-shrm-
certification.aspx.

80. Kathy Gurchiek, "SHRM, Mexico
HR Group Create Certificate
Program," *SHRM Online*, May
7, 2014, http://www.shrm.org/
hrdisciplines/global/articles/pages/
shrm-mexico-hr-certificate-
program.aspx.

81. Adapted from Marty Rosenheck,
"Harnessing the 90%," *T+D*,
September 2013, pp. 54–59.

CHAPTER

2

Human Resource Strategy and Planning

Learning Objectives

After you have read this chapter, you should be able to:

LO1 Summarize the organization's strategic planning process.

LO2 Explain the key differences between effective and ineffective strategies and suggest ways to implement strategic asset reallocation.

LO3 Outline how HR's strategies are merged with organizational strategies and give two examples.

LO4 Discuss how to forecast the supply and demand of Human Resources.

LO5 List options for handling a shortage and a surplus of employees.

LO6 Identify how organizations can measure and analyze the effectiveness of HR management practices.

WHAT'S TRENDING IN
HR STRATEGY AND PLANNING

Over the past several decades, the strategic role of HR has been emphasized because firms realize that high-quality employees are needed to help them reach strategic objectives. The strategic landscape is expected to continually change as new issues challenge companies to more effectively use their employees. There are also opportunities that companies can seize to be more successful, which all require support and guidance from HR leaders. These realities require HR departments to develop people strategies that make sense given current business conditions. Here's what's currently trending in HR strategy and planning:

1. Human resource management is expected to play a more important strategic role in organizations in the future. There is much discussion and speculation about how HR groups can fulfill such expectations.
2. A number of strategic issues are emerging in businesses today. These include an emphasis on sustainability (or giving back), a focus on work–life balance, and the creation of policies that enhance talent.
3. Globalization has created challenges for HR professionals because strategies often need to be revised to address issues in different areas of the world. HR needs to evaluate how employees are compensated, determine if they have a broad understanding of global business, and assess whether specific strategies work in foreign worksites.
4. HR planning can be found in the driver's seat of strategic planning. Consequently, HR leaders should be aware of the latest approaches to help companies find and retain the right talent.
5. The number of mergers and acquisitions is expected to increase over the next several years. To make these changes work, HR professionals should understand important best practices.

HR Planning and the North Dakota Oil Boom

North Dakota is now the second-largest oil producing state in the United States. An exciting part of the state's recent oil boom is that many jobs are available for individuals living around the town of Williston, the fastest-growing small city in the nation. Many people are moving there hoping that they can land high-paying work with the region's oil extraction companies and service firms.

However, there have been a number of challenges associated with this growth. There is increased competition for talented workers, so getting and keeping employees can be difficult. Walmart starts workers at $17 an hour so that it can attract individuals, and some fast-food chains use signing bonuses to court potential employees. Other companies highlight good working conditions and employment stability to help with hiring. Yet oil companies are paying anywhere from $25 to $35 an hour, which makes recruiting difficult for other companies, particularly when people are so focused on earning money. Turnover is also high in this region's organizations. Employees often leave their jobs to make a few extra dollars an hour someplace else, which challenges companies to think about how they can more effectively retain good workers. Finally, public services in Williston have been heavily burdened by the increased numbers of people living there.

One of the biggest challenges has involved living arrangements, with some firms offering housing and other allowances. Acme Tools built several apartments above its store and bought a house to provide temporary housing for its workers. Walmart has provided employees per diem and placed them in hotel rooms. The oilfield services company JMAC Resources provides housing to many of its workers such as

Tom Reichner/Shutterstock.com

townhomes, mobile homes, and crew camps. Many oil companies in the region also rely on crew camps to house employees.

There are a number of planning issues that should be considered by HR professionals when facing conditions such as these. Some of them include:

- Plan ahead of time for HR challenges but be adaptable.
- Do some research about the area where operations will be established.
- Establish good relationships with regional partners; companies may elect to use liaisons to help coordinate and communicate with constituencies.
- Invest in the local community and plan for long-term sustainable operations.

When companies practice sound HR planning, positive relationships can be established with stakeholders.[1]

Strategy
A plan an organization follows for how to compete successfully, survive, and grow

The strategy an organization follows is its plan for how to compete successfully, survive, and grow. Many organizations have a relatively formal process for developing a written strategy encompassing a certain period of time, with objectives and goals identified for each business unit. Strategic planning in these companies is often performed by top managers. Other firms are more informal in their approach to developing a strategy and sometimes involve employees and staff in the creation of business goals.

Organizations want to achieve and maintain a competitive advantage by delivering high-quality products and services to their customers in a way that competitors cannot duplicate. Strategies to do so might include revising existing products, acquiring new businesses, or developing new products or services using existing capabilities. Other strategic approaches might be to maintain a secure position with stable products or to emphasize a constant stream of new products that customers want to buy. Whatever strategies are chosen will determine the number and capabilities of people needed in the organization. This is why the management of people in companies is an inherently strategic process—strategic plans cannot be met unless talent is used effectively.

Different companies in the same industry may have different strategies to succeed, and firms in different industries that are located in the same geographic area may have to use similar strategies to be effective. It all depends on the current business situation. Successful strategic management requires companies to accurately analyze their situations, decide what their goals will be, and implement the right actions to achieve those goals. At the end of the day, strategy is about the actions to be taken[2] as well as the proper HR planning that is completed to support the business strategy, which is illustrated by Walmart and other firms in the chapter opener about the North Dakota oil boom.

Strategic planning
The process of defining organizational strategy, or direction, and allocating resources toward its achievement

LO1 Summarize the organization's strategic planning process.

2-1 Organizational Strategic Planning

Strategic planning is the process of defining organizational strategy, or direction, and allocating resources (capital and people) toward its achievement. Successful organizations engage in this core business process on an ongoing basis.

FIGURE 2-1 Strategic Planning Process for the Organization

The strategic plan serves as the road map that gives the organization direction and aligns resources. The strategic planning process involves several sequential steps that focus on the future of the firm; Figure 2-1 shows these steps.

2-1a Strategy Formulation

The strategic planning cycle typically covers a three- to five-year time frame, although some firms conduct long-term planning that can cover 10 years or more. When formulating the strategic plan, management often considers both internal and external forces that affect a company, including the conditions that exist in the industry overall. The guiding force behind the strategic planning process is the organizational mission, which is the core reason for the existence of the organization and what makes it unique. The mission statement is usually determined by the organizational founders or leaders and sets the general direction of the firm.

The planning process begins with an assessment of the current state of the business and the environmental forces that may be important during the strategic planning cycle. Analysis of strengths, weaknesses, opportunities, and threats (SWOT) is a common starting point because it allows managers to consider both internal and external conditions that the business faces. The SWOT analysis helps managers formulate a strategic plan that considers the organization's ability to deal with the situation at hand based on its own strengths and weaknesses, as well as the external opportunities and threats that exist in the firm's external environment. The planning process requires continuous monitoring and responding to environmental changes and competitive conditions, which means that strategic planning is an ongoing process that is never fully complete and must be constantly revisited.

Managers then determine the objectives for the planning cycle and formulate organization-level strategies to accomplish those objectives. Each function within the organization (such as the HR department) then formulates strategies that link to and support the organization-level strategies. The strategic plan is reevaluated periodically because conditions may change and managers must react to a fluid business environment.

Organizational mission
The core reason for the existence of the organization and what makes it unique

2-1b Good versus Bad Strategy

LO2 Explain the key differences between effective and ineffective strategies and suggest ways to implement strategic asset reallocation.

Many companies generate strategies that by their own admission are substandard. In one survey, McKinsey consultants asked 2,000 executives to rate their company's strategies on a set of 10 strategic measures and found that only 35% of the executives felt their company passed more than three of the tests.[3] They concluded that top management teams need to focus as much time on strategy as they do on operating issues on an ongoing basis if they are to have a useful strategy.

Suppose Company A allocates money consistently each year, making only small changes to the allocation of talent, capital, and research dollars. Company B, on the other hand, evaluates each division's market opportunities and performance, and adjusts allocations on the basis of that analysis. Which company should perform better? Company B does almost 40% better, although most companies function the way Company A does. Managers in Company A can shift resources to achieve their goals or run the risk that the market will do it for them.[4] The following "HR Perspective: Encouraging the Evaluation and Reallocation of Strategic Assets" feature shows one way to do this analysis and reallocation.

ETHICS

Effective strategy often relies on managers who are willing to closely assess current conditions and develop a game plan that enables the firm to overcome obstacles and sustain success. At Walgreens, the company's communication strategy relies on social media, blogs, and surveys to provide important information to employees on an ongoing basis.[5] However, such a focus on communication does not preclude generating strategy ideas by opening up the process to stakeholders who

PERSPECTIVE

Encouraging the Evaluation and Reallocation of Strategic Assets

A company may elect to classify its various units into different categories on the basis of their market opportunity and performance. For instance, a unit might be labeled "grow," "maintain," or "dispose" to indicate its likely degrees of success. In addition, each category has guidelines that show how resources will be assigned. This approach allows managers to determine whether the different areas of the company will be successful. It also removes many of the politics from the process and focuses attention on how each unit is contributing to important strategic goals.

When Lee Raymond was CEO of Exxon Mobil, he required that 3% to 5% of the company's assets be designated for disposal each year. The burden to prove that an asset should be kept was on a particular division. A division could keep an asset *only* if it could present a compelling plan that a unit was improving. The net effect was healthy turnover and upgraded units despite the natural desire on the part of executives to keep all of the units, even the

ones that were not performing well.[6] Such a process encourages the evaluation and reallocation of assets within a company and causes people to rethink how the firm can best achieve its strategic goals. This approach also makes managers constantly assess the overall health of their business units so that changes can be made if necessary.

Companies should be proactive about assessing their strategic assets so that critical decisions can be made about which assets are eliminated and which are retained. Consider the following questions that explore these issues:

1. If you were given the task of evaluating and reallocating the strategic assets of your employer, how would you approach these duties?

2. How should HR professionals assess human resources as strategic assets? Should they be treated any differently in the assessment process than other assets of an organization?

might have been previously frozen out of strategic direction setting. For example, 3M, Rite-Solutions, Red Hat, and Wikimedia have all used or experimented with improving their strategy development through *crowdsourcing*, or opening up the strategic planning process to more people.[7] Such an approach enables a company to improve employee engagement and be seen as a participative and responsible employer. A variation of this theme is *crowdfunding*, which involves aligning social responsibility efforts with the decision making that takes place in a company. Campaigns related to worthy causes that are important to external stakeholders and employees alike can be developed, and employees are given the opportunity to support these campaigns by donating money. Such efforts can be key strategic initiatives for companies that want to be more ethical.[8]

2-2 Human Resources and Strategy

LO3 Outline how HR's strategies are merged with organizational strategies and give two examples.

Regardless of which specific strategies are adopted for guiding an organization, having the right people is necessary to make the strategies work. If a strategy requires specific skills that are currently not available in the company, it will take time to either recruit people who have those skills or train current employees to adapt to the new strategy. Strategic HR management (HRM) provides input for strategic planning and develops specific HR initiatives to help achieve organizational goals. Getting HR involved is the key, with one study finding that the participation of HR in strategic processes is enhanced as HR's service quality and the expectations of the contributions of HR increase.[9] This means that the HR department must demonstrate that its support is helpful to the company. But even though considering HR in a company's strategy seems obvious, estimates are that only 30% of HR professionals are full strategic partners. Their primary role remains one of providing input to top management.[10] Part of this could be driven by HR's inability to justify how it helps the bottom line or the kinds of issues on which it focuses. For instance, one of the criticisms of strategic HR research is that it pays too much attention to basic managerial issues rather than exploring how HR strategy benefits companies economically.[11]

Some businesses are also less dependent on human capital for a competitive advantage than others, a situation that lowers the strategic impact of HR in some firms. For example, the productivity of a steel mill depends more on the efficiency of furnaces and quality of raw materials than on human resources. However, the argument can be made that every business strategy must be carried out by people, so human capital always has some impact on business success. An important concept covered later in this chapter is measuring and determining the value of human capital and HR in a given organization.

Although administrative and legally mandated tasks are important, HR's strategic contribution should add value to the organization by improving the performance of the business. Strategic HR management refers to the appropriate use of HR management practices to gain or keep a competitive advantage. There are different areas that HR professionals can improve to help firms be more competitive, including hiring good employees, placing them in the right jobs, and rewarding them fairly. For example, JetBlue developed a corporate culture that established a clear sense of purpose and supported positive values and then hired individuals who matched this culture, which helped the company succeed.[12]

Strategic HR management
The appropriate use of HR management practices to gain or keep a competitive advantage

FIGURE 2-2 Positioning HR to Be a Strategic Partner

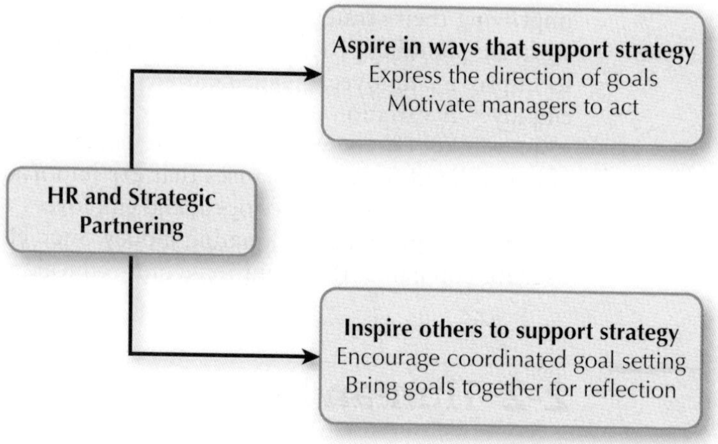

Source: Adapted from Torben Juul Anderson and Dana Minbaeva, "The Role of Human Resource Management in Strategy Making," *Human Resource Management* 52 (2013), 809–827.

An important element of strategic HRM is creating processes in a company that help connect employee performance with strategic objectives. For instance, some contend that HR should be a strategic partner by providing aspirations to a company and functioning as an inspiration for strategic planning.[13] Figure 2-2 shows how these partnerships can be developed. These partnerships can be strengthened when HR professionals know what the organization does and when they make good decisions about building human capital, being willing to change, communicating the intent of HR policies, and following through on their plans.[14]

Individual workers also need to understand relevant HR priorities so that they can better contribute by applying their skills to advance the strategic goals, so partnerships should also be fostered with employees. Employees who understand the big picture can do their jobs in ways that help the firm reach its objectives. Effective HR practices include talent development and reward systems that direct employee efforts toward the bottom line. Employees must also be prepared for strategic HR initiatives with proper training, good communication from managers, and appropriate performance standards and rewards.[15] For instance, W.W. Grainger, the maintenance, repair, and operating products distributor located in Illinois, instituted a brand-based strategy, which required HR professionals in the firm to be engaged with planning so that employees were kept informed about change efforts.[16]

2-2a Human Resource Contributions to Strategy

The strategies developed by HR managers depend heavily on the plans and objectives created within an organization; HR departments need to be involved in strategic planning so that HR executives are aware of the overall strategic direction of a firm. Some common areas where HR can develop and implement appropriate strategies are creating HR policies at the top, middle, and lower levels of the firm that best match organizational strategies, as well as developing metrics that help determine how well strategies at the different levels are being met. To contribute in the strategic planning process, HR leaders can provide their perspectives and expertise to operating managers by doing the following:

- *Having a seat at the strategic table*: Companies must include HR professionals in discussions about strategy and encourage them to provide input.
- *Being knowledgeable about business operations*: Understanding how the business works and knowing the need for certain strategies are important components.
- *Focusing on the future*: Strategic planning requires leaders to think about the future based on past experiences.
- *Prioritizing business goals*: Efforts that have the greatest impact on the business and its objectives are emphasized first.
- *Understanding what to measure*: Metrics are a vital part of assessing success, which means identifying the right metrics that are linked to business goals.

One way HR professionals can contribute to strategy is by introducing high-performance approaches into the workplace that lead to increased performance. These HR practices often focus on enhancing participation, teamwork, and work attitudes so that employees are more engaged in their jobs.[17] Using information collected from top HR professionals working for financial and manufacturing organizations in Jordan, a recent study found that high-performance HR practices influenced the positive relationship between the strategic role of HR and corporate financial performance.[18] Another study found that certain strategies were linked either positively or negatively to the adoption of high-performance work systems and that adoption of these practices was related to the use of work–life balance programs.[19] Overall, these studies show that high-performance HR practices are beneficial to companies.

ETHICS

There is also growing awareness that HR professionals can assist in developing strategies for organizational sustainability. Figure 2-3 highlights a model summarizing HR professionals' interests in sustainability management. An HR department can provide expertise that is needed to prepare employees to focus on sustainability, including talent acquisition, training and development, and performance management. HR professionals also focus on social concerns, so they are well suited to prepare employees to help external stakeholders. Even more important is the central leadership role the HR department plays in the creation of a positive workplace, making the HR group keenly positioned to help lead sustainability efforts.[20]

GLOBAL

2-2b Human Resources Strategies for Global Competitiveness

The globalization of business means that more organizations now operate across borders and have ties to foreign operations along with international suppliers, vendors, employees, and other business partners. A global presence can range from importing and exporting to operating as a multinational corporation (MNC). An MNC, sometimes called a transnational corporation, is an organization that has facilities and other assets in at least one country other than its home country.

Even organizations that operate primarily in the domestic market face pressure from foreign competitors. The supply chain is often internationally dispersed, and foreign business practices influence operations in the United States. Technological advancements have eliminated many barriers that previously limited operating on a global scale.

Multinational corporation (MNC)
An organization that has facilities and other assets in at least one country other than its home country

FIGURE 2-3   The HR Department's Contribution to Organizational Sustainability

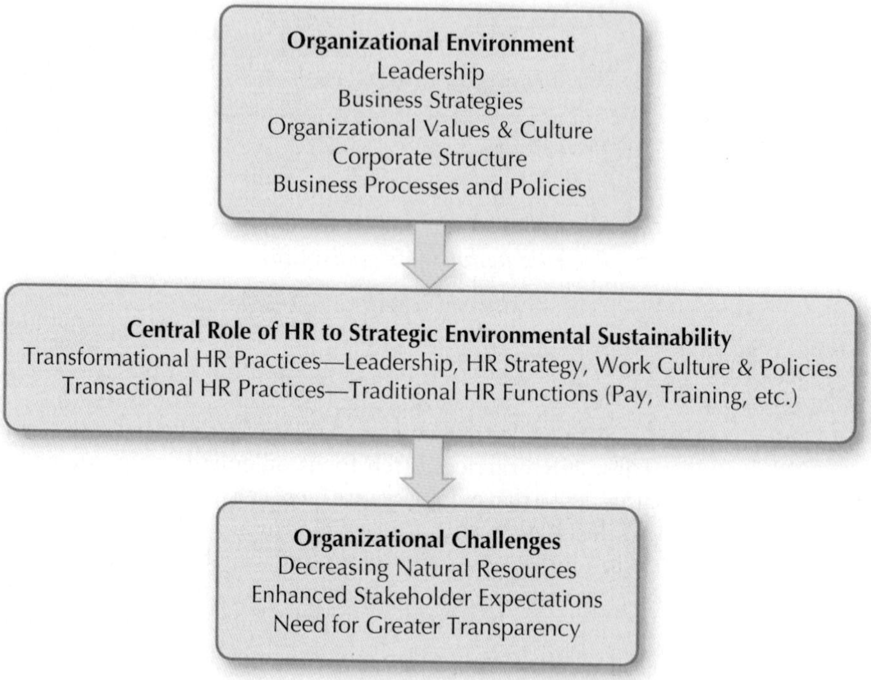

Source: Adapted from Cathy L. Z. Dubois and David A. Dubois, "Strategic HRM as Social Design for Environmental Sustainability in Organization," *Human Resource Management* 51 (2012), 799–826.

For HR to complement the organization's strategy, it has to consider how to merge HR strategies with those of the company. To effectively compete on an international scale, the organization needs expertise to administer HR activities in a wide range of nations. For example, the firm may decide to standardize talent development and succession planning but permit local managers to establish compensation and labor relations policies. An ideal international strategy strikes a balance between home-country and host-country policies, and it utilizes the best practices available in each. Companies must also prepare employees to have a *global mindset*, which is based on their ability to understand diverse cultural values and global business operations. A recent study found that a global mindset can be increased with greater global job experiences, psychological capital (or a positive outlook), and varied experiences in different countries.[21]

Consider two international topics that are frequently the basis for HR strategies that are developed to support organizational strategy—*offshoring* and global staffing. Both actions require leaders to merge organizational and HR strategies.

Offshoring Strategies Competitive pressure to lower costs has resulted in many jobs being moved overseas in recent years. Offshoring occurs when a company relocates a business process or operation from one country to another. Firms can offshore the production of goods as well as the delivery of services to lower-wage countries. Call centers in India are an example of business service offshoring to countries with well-educated English-speaking workers. The movement of product and software development projects to other countries because the United States

Offshoring
A company's relocation of a business process or operation from one country to another

lacks the right talent is another example. Due to its advantages, offshoring is likely to increase for the foreseeable future.

Other factors might be considered when offshoring business operations, such as whether practices in other countries match those employed in the United States. For instance, a recent study found that some companies in China might be utilizing high-performance work systems to increase organizational performance.[22] Another study determined that firms located in Germany are adopting positive HR practices used in other European nations and the United States.[23] These finding show that global HR approaches can be important considerations when making offshoring decisions.

GLOBAL

Global Staffing Strategies A wide variety of alternatives can be considered when planning for staffing global operations. The optimal solution is to combine the expertise of local employees with organization-specific knowledge of employees from the home country (headquarters). Some countries require that the organization employ a certain percentage of workers from the host country. Figure 2-4 shows four strategic HR approaches to international staffing. Each organization will use a staffing model that best fits its culture and strategic goals.

As discussed in the previous chapter, an expatriate is a citizen of one country who is working in a second country and employed by an organization headquartered in the first country. To make the experience a success, moving an employee to an overseas assignment must be planned effectively. The return of an expatriate (a process called repatriation) must also be executed well for the organization to capitalize on the benefits of the overseas assignment when the employee gets back to the home country.

Leadership development is critical in global organizations because more top management jobs require greater understanding of international management. Leading in different cultures requires greatly varied skills, and organizations can

FIGURE 2-4 Strategic HR Approaches to International Staffing

Ethnocentric Policy	• Managers from headquarters staff key positions • Ensures control over subsidiary location operations • Eases transfer of policies from headquarters to subsidiary
Polycentric Policy	• Host-country nationals staff key positions • Reduces cultural mishaps and misunderstanding • Coordination with headquarters may be problematic
Regiocentric Policy	• Key positions are filled by individuals in the region of the subsidiary (e.g., European Union countries) • Capitalizes on cultural and language similarities within the region
Geocentric Policy	• An international cadre of skilled managers are assigned to global subsidiaries regardless of nationality • Leverages technical and managerial expertise

provide formal training and job assignments that develop leaders. Effective compensation and selection processes are also needed to ensure that the right individuals are attracted to and chosen for these international assignments. For instance, global firms can attract more outstanding employees with performance-based pay and generous total reward packages.[24] Companies might also need to develop more customized HR programs that fit the preferences of the local talent in different countries,

COMPETENCIES & APPLICATIONS

Latin American Firms Face Staffing Problems

A recent survey of large global Latin American firms headquartered in countries such as Brazil, Mexico, and Argentina showed that many have expanded into international markets through mergers and acquisitions. On average, each of these organizations managed worksites in 13 different nations, with operations frequently located in North America and western Europe. There is also high interest for continued expansion into current and new markets. Despite these exciting trends, the survey results suggested that the firms faced a number of staffing challenges that potentially hurt their ability to grow in new regions.

The survey found that mergers and acquisitions were one of the most troubling issues, and determining how to function in different cultures was identified as one of the key difficulties. However, Latin American firms may be better able to deal with these issues given that they have experience with challenging political, legal, and economic conditions. Getting good workers and figuring out how to manage the flow of talent were also key problems that these companies faced. HR professionals in these organizations will need to determine how to most effectively manage recruiting efforts and succession plans so that people are hired and placed into the right jobs at the proper time; promotions and other placement issues will also have to be planned well to ensure that mergers and acquisitions are successful. The following

considerations can help firms plan HR staffing in the global environment:

- *Pay attention to the firm's HR strategies.* Understand where and how a company plans to expand so that the right HR strategies are considered.
- *Develop consistent expansion plans.* An organization's global expansion plans should be similar across the board to ensure consistency.
- *Think about succession plans.* Have an idea about how exiting employees will be replaced with current staff so that vacancies can be filled quickly.
- *Partner with HR to lower risks.* The HR department needs to have a seat at the risk management table so that staffing and other workplace issues can be explored strategically.[25]

The ability to manage international expansion is certainly an important global competency within the HR profession. If you were given the responsibility of managing mergers and acquisitions in a global firm:

1. How would you focus HR leaders on the development of positive strategies for expansion? What HR issues do you think deserve the most attention?

2. What other steps would you take to help a global company expand into new markets?

KEY COMPETENCIES: Global & Cultural Effectiveness (Behavioral Competency) and Organization (Technical Competency) particularly because there are growing numbers of highly educated professionals in developing markets abroad.[26]

Another issue in HR is planning, which is frequently a direct consequence of implementing strategies to move the organization forward. HR planning deals with determining how many people will be needed to execute an organization's specific functions, a key concern in both global and domestic firms. The preceding "HR Competencies & Applications: Latin American Firms Face Staffing Problems" feature discusses how companies in Latin America face challenges related to HR planning.

2-3 Human Resource Planning

Human Resource planning

The process of analyzing and identifying the need for and availability of people so that the organization can meet its strategic objectives

Human Resource planning is the process of analyzing and identifying the need for and availability of people so that the organization can meet its strategic objectives. The focus of HR planning is ensuring that the organization has the *right number of people* with the *right capabilities* at the *right times* and in the *right places*. In HR planning, an organization must consider the availability and allocation of people to jobs over longer periods of time, not just for the next month or even the next year.[27] For example, leaders at Prudential Financial are asked to determine what jobs are emerging in the company so that work areas can be properly staffed in the future.[28]

HR plans can include several approaches. Actions may include shifting employees to other jobs in the organization, laying off employees or otherwise cutting back the number of employees, retraining current employees, and/or increasing the number of employees in certain areas. Factors to consider include the current employees' knowledge, skills, abilities (KSAs), and career aspirations as well as vacancies expected as the result of retirements, promotions, transfers, and discharges. To do this, HR professionals work with executives and managers.[29] Human capital solutions are also available that enable HR managers to identify how to develop talent to allow the organization to reach its strategic goals.[30]

2-3a Human Resources Planning Process

The steps in the HR planning process are shown in Figure 2-5. Notice that the process begins with considering the organizational plans and the environmental analysis that went into developing strategies. The process includes an environmental analysis to identify the context in which HR is operating. Strengths, weaknesses,

FIGURE 2-5 HR Planning Process

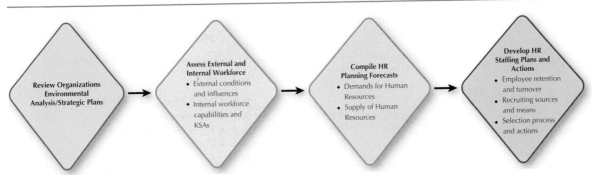

opportunities, and threats are considered. Then the possible *available workforce* is evaluated by identifying both the internal and the external workforce.

Once those assessments are complete, forecasts must be developed to determine both the demand for and supply of human resources. Management then formulates HR staffing plans and actions needed to address imbalances, in both the short and the long term. Particular strategies may be developed to fill vacancies or deal with surplus employees. For example, a strategy might be to fill 50% of expected vacancies by training employees in lower-level jobs and promoting them.

Finally, HR plans are developed to provide specific direction for the management of HR activities related to recruiting, selecting, and retaining employees. The most telling evidence of successful HR planning is consistent alignment of the availabilities and capabilities of human resources with the needs of the organization over a considerable period of time.[31]

2-3b Environmental Analysis

Environmental scanning
The assessment of external and internal environmental conditions that affect the organization

Before managers in a company begin strategic planning, they study and assess the dynamics of the environment to better understand how these conditions might affect their plans. The process of environmental scanning involves the assessment of external and internal environmental conditions that affect the organization. The HR department should be involved in this process to make sure that the employee perspective is considered.

The external environment includes many economic, political, and competitive forces that shape the future. From an HR perspective, the internal environment includes the quality and quantity of talent, the organizational culture, and the talent pipeline and leadership bench strength. Figure 2-6 shows the HR elements of a SWOT analysis that are included in the environmental analysis.

Opportunities and threats emerge from the external environment and can impact an organization's outcomes. Many of these forces are not within the company's control but must be considered in the scanning process because they can affect the viability of the business. Being able to deal with uncertainty in the external environment is an important skill for planners. The external environmental scan includes an assessment of economic conditions, legislative and political influences, demographic changes, and geographic and competitive issues.

FIGURE 2-6 HR Factors in the SWOT Analysis

Strengths
- Intellectual capital
- Loyal, committed employees
- Innovative, adaptive employees
- High-performance practices

Weaknesses
- Lack of skilled employees
- Lack of leadership pipeline
- Outdated talent management practices

Opportunities
- Market position
- Unexplored markets
- Global expansion
- Technology advances

Threats
- Legal mandates and restrictions
- Competitor power
- Economic uncertainty
- Talent shortage

Population shifts and demographic changes can affect an organization's strategy. For example, by 2042, non-Hispanic whites will no longer comprise the majority of the U.S. population.[32] Such workforce demographics will affect the labor available to organizations. It also means that diversity management will remain an important HR issue.

Where an organization locates its operations plays a role in how well it will perform. But more importantly, an understanding of geographic advantages and disadvantages can help managers develop appropriate plans. The strengths and weaknesses of the organization also represent internal factors that either create or destroy value. When assessing the internal environment, managers should evaluate the quantity and quality of employees, HR practices, and the organizational culture.

The strength of the talent pipeline is a particularly important internal consideration as the organization plans its HR future. Fulfilling strategic objectives is difficult without employees who can provide sufficient skills and talent. Leadership development and succession planning programs ensure that high-quality talent will be available to carry out business strategies. For instance, effective development programs can reduce the high failure rate of people in leadership positions. Selecting individuals with the right talents and teaching them leadership skills can also improve the quality of leaders and promote strategic success. Succession planning is the process of identifying a plan for the orderly replacement of key employees. The discussion will now turn to how these and other concerns are incorporated into HR planning.

Succession planning
The process of identifying a plan for the orderly replacement of key employees

2-4 Planning for External Workforce Availability

If a network technology company plans to double its number of client accounts from 100 to 200 in a three-year period, the firm must also identify how many and what types of new employees will be needed to staff the expanded services, locations, and facilities. These new employees will probably be obtained from outside the current pool of employees, which means that the company and its HR department will need to be aware of the forces that impact external labor markets. Several specific factors that affect the external pool of potential employees are highlighted next.

2-4a Economic and Governmental Factors

Like the issues discussed in this chapter's "HR Headline" feature, the general economic cycles of recession and boom affect HR planning. Factors such as interest rates, inflation, and economic decline or growth affect the availability of workers and should be considered when organizational and HR plans and objectives are formulated. There is a considerable difference between finding qualified applicants in a 4% unemployment market compared to a 9% unemployment market. As the unemployment rate rises, the number of qualified people looking for work increases, which often makes it easier for companies to fill some jobs. However, the people who are hired may receive lower pay and benefits because companies have more hiring options and leverage. As the unemployment rate decreases, there are fewer potential employees who are available, meaning that companies must provide more attractive compensation to recruit qualified employees.

A broad array of government regulations affects the labor supply and therefore HR planning. As a result, HR planning must be done by individuals who understand the legal requirements of various government regulations. In the United States and other countries, tax legislation at local, state, and federal levels affects HR planning. Pension provisions and Social Security legislation may change retirement patterns and funding options. Elimination or expansion of tax benefits for job-training expenses might alter some job-training activities associated with workforce expansions. In summary, an organization must consider a variety of economics factors and government policies, regulations, and laws during the HR planning process, focusing on those that specifically affect the company.

2-4b Geographic and Competitive Evaluations

When making HR plans, employers must consider a number of geographic and competitive concerns. The *net migration* into a particular region is important. For example, in the past decade, the populations of some U.S. cities in the South, Southwest, and West have grown rapidly and provide sources of labor. However, areas in the Northeast and Midwest have experienced declining populations or net outmigration, which affects the number of people available to be hired.

Direct competitors are another important external force to consider in HR planning. Failure to consider the competitive labor market and to offer pay scales and benefits comparable with those of organizations in the same general industry and geographic location may cost a company dearly in the long run. Finally, the impact of *international competition* must be considered as part of environmental scanning. Global competition for labor intensifies as global competitors shift jobs and workers around the world, something that is seen when jobs from the United States are outsourced to countries with cheaper labor.

2-4c Changing Workforce Considerations

Significant changes in the workforce, both in the United States and globally, must be considered when examining the outside workforce during HR planning. Shifts in the composition of the workforce, combined with the use of different work patterns, have created workplaces and organizations that are notably different from those of the past. For instance, many employers provide flexible workplaces that enable employees to balance their work and personal responsibilities, but recent evidence suggests that some firms are scaling back these opportunities because their businesses have become leaner due to the recent recession.[33] When scanning the potential and future workforce, it is important to consider a number of variables, including:

- Aging of the workforce
- Growing diversity of workers
- Female workers and work–life balance concerns
- Availability of contingent workers
- Outsourcing possibilities

When assessing these factors, it is important to analyze how they affect the current and future availability of workers with specific capabilities and experience. For instance, in a number of industries, the median age of highly specialized professionals is more than 50 years, and the supply of potential replacements with adequate education and experience is not sufficient to replace such employees as they retire. Many firms have planned for workforce shortages because of the brain drain created by the retirement of existing older workers.

2-5 Planning for Internal Workforce Availability

Analyzing the jobs that will need to be done and the capabilities of people who are currently available in the organization to do them is the next step in HR planning. The needs of the organization must be compared to the existing labor supply, as well as the potential labor supply available outside the firm.

2-5a Current and Future Jobs Audit

The starting point for evaluating internal workforce strengths and weaknesses is an audit of the jobs that are expected in the planning period. A comprehensive analysis of all current jobs provides a basis for forecasting what jobs will need to be done in the future. Much of the data required for the audit should be available from existing staffing and organizational databases. The following are key questions addressed during the internal jobs assessment:

- What jobs exist now, and how essential is each job?
- How many individuals are performing each job?
- What are the reporting relationships of jobs?
- What are the vital KSAs (knowledge, skills, and abilities) needed in the jobs?
- What jobs will be needed to implement future organizational strategies?
- What are the characteristics of those anticipated jobs?

2-5b Employee and Organizational Capabilities Inventory

As HR planners gain an understanding of the current and future jobs that will be necessary to carry out organizational plans, they can conduct a detailed audit of current employees and their capabilities. The basic data on employees should be available in the organization's HR records.

An inventory of organizational skills and capabilities may consider a number of elements. The following are especially important:

- Individual employee demographics (age, length of service in the organization, time in present job)
- Individual career progression (jobs held, time in each job, education and training levels, promotions or other job changes, pay rates)
- Individual performance data (work accomplishments, growth in skills, working relationships)

Detailed information about each individual employee's skills are stored in an HRIS database. Since this data may affect employees' careers, its use must meet the same standards of job-relatedness and nondiscrimination as those met when the employee was initially hired. Security measures must ensure that sensitive information is available only to those who have a specific appropriate use for it.

Managers and HR staff members can gather data on individual employees and aggregate details into a profile of the organization's current workforce. This profile may reveal many of the current strengths and deficiencies of people in the organization. For instance, a skills mismatch may be identified in which some workers are either overqualified or underqualified for their jobs. The profile may also highlight potential future problems. For example, if many workers lack some specialized expertise, such as advanced technical skills, the organization may find it difficult to take advantage of changing technological opportunities. Or if a large number of experienced employees are in the same age bracket, their eventual retirements that will likely occur about the same time might lead to future gaps in the organization.

LO4 Discuss how to forecast the supply and demand of Human Resources.

Forecasting
Using information from the past and present to predict future conditions

2-6 Forecasting HR Supply and Demand

Forecasting uses information from the past and present to predict future conditions. When forecasting future HR conditions, the information comes from workforce availability and requirements. Projections for the future are, of course, subject to error. Fortunately, experienced people usually are able to forecast with enough accuracy to positively affect long-range organizational planning.

2-6a Forecasting Methods and Periods

Forecasting methods may be either judgmental or mathematical, as Figure 2-7 shows. Methods for forecasting human resources range from a manager's best guess to rigorous and complex computer simulation. Despite the availability of sophisticated judgmental and mathematical models and techniques, forecasting is still a combination of quantitative methods and subjective judgment. The facts must be evaluated and weighed by knowledgeable individuals, who use the mathematical models as tools and make judgments to arrive at decisions.[34]

HR forecasting should be done over three planning periods: short range, intermediate range, and long range. The most commonly used planning period of six months to one year focuses on *short-range* forecasts for the immediate HR needs of an organization. Intermediate- and long-range forecasting are much more difficult processes. *Intermediate-range* plans usually project one to three years into the future, and *long-range* plans extend beyond three years.

2-6b Forecasting the Demand (Need) for Human Resources

The demand for employees can be calculated for an entire organization and/or for individual units in the organization. For example, a forecast might indicate that a firm needs 125 new employees next year or that it needs 25 new people in sales and customer service, 45 in production, 20 in accounting and information systems, 2 in HR, and 33 in the warehouse. The unit breakdown obviously allows HR planners to better pinpoint the specific skills needed than does the aggregate method.

Demand for human resources can be forecast by considering specific openings that are likely to occur. The openings (or demands) are made when new jobs are created or current jobs are changed. Additionally, forecasts must consider when employees leave positions because of promotion, transfer, turnover, and termination.

An analysis is used to develop decision rules (or fill rates) for each job or level. For example, a decision rule for a financial institution might state that 50% of branch supervisor openings will be filled through promotions from customer service tellers, 25% through promotions from personal bankers, and 25% from new hires. Forecasters must be aware of multiple effects throughout the organization because as people are promoted from within, their previous positions become available. Continuing

FIGURE 2-7 HR Forecasting Methods

Judgmental Methods

- *Estimates* can be either top-down or bottom-up, but essentially people who are in a position to know are asked, "How many people will you need next year?"
- The *rule of thumb* method relies on general guidelines applied to a specific situation within the organization. For example, a guideline of "one operations manager per five reporting supervisors" aids in forecasting the number of supervisors needed in a division. However, it is important to adapt the guideline to recognize widely varying departmental needs.
- The *Delphi technique* uses input from a group of experts whose opinions of forecasted situations are sought. These expert opinions are then combined and returned to the experts for a second anonymous opinion. The process continues through several rounds until the experts essentially agree on a judgment. For example, this approach is used to forecast effects of technology on HR management and staffing needs.
- *Nominal groups*, unlike the Delphi method, require experts to meet face to face. Their ideas maybe cited independently at first, discussed as a group, and then compiled as a report.

Mathematical Methods

- *Statistical regression analysis* makes a statistical comparison of past relationships among various factors. For example, a statistical relationship between gross sales and number of employees in a retail chain may be useful in forecasting the number of employees that will be needed if the retailer's sales increase 15% or decrease 10%.
- *Simulation models* are representations of real situations in abstract form. For example, an econometric model of the growth in software usage would lead to forecasts of the need for software developers. Numerous simulation methods and techniques are available.
- *Productivity ratios* calculate the average number of units produced per employee. These averages can be applied to sales forecasts to determine the number of employees needed. For example, a firm could forecast the number of needed sales representatives using these ratios.
- *Staffing ratios* can be used to estimate indirect labor. For example, if the company usually uses one clerical person for every 25 production employees, that ratio can be used to estimate the need for clerical employees.

the example, forecasts for the need for customer service tellers and personal bankers would also have to be developed. The overall purpose of the forecast is to identify needs for Human Resources by number and type for the forecasting period.

2-6c Forecasting the Supply (Availability) of Human Resources

Once HR needs have been forecast, the availability of qualified individuals must be determined. Forecasting availability considers both *external* and *internal* supplies.

Although the internal supply may be somewhat easier to calculate, it is important to calculate the external supply as accurately as possible.

External Supply The external supply of potential employees available to the organization can be identified. Government estimates of labor force populations, trends in the industry, and many more complex and interrelated factors must be considered. Such information is often available from state or regional economic development offices. The following items may be included:

- Net migration into and out of the area
- Individuals entering and leaving the workforce
- Individuals graduating from colleges and other schools
- Changing workforce composition and patterns
- Economic forecasts for the next few years
- Technological developments and shifts
- Actions of competing employers
- Government regulations and pressures
- Circumstances affecting persons entering and leaving the workforce

Internal Supply Figure 2-8 shows in general terms how internal supply can be calculated for a specific employer. Estimating internal supply considers the number of external hires and the employees who move from their current jobs into others through promotions, lateral moves, and demotions. It also considers that the

FIGURE 2-8 Estimating Internal Labor Supply for a Given Unit

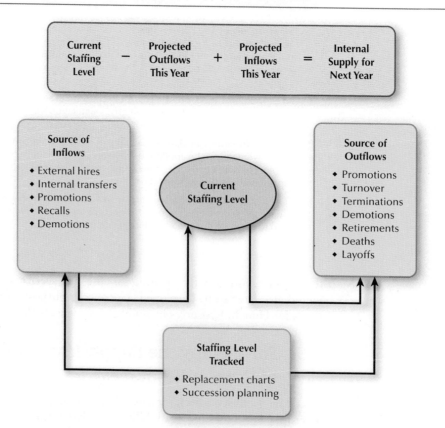

internal supply is influenced by transfer and promotion policies, and retirement policies, among other factors. In forecasting internal supply, data from replacement charts and succession planning efforts are used to project potential personnel changes, identify possible backup candidates, and keep track of attrition (resignations, retirements, etc.) for each department in an organization.

Positive HR planning can be a source of competitive advantage for organizations. This is true because planning helps companies identify their future needs and how to get the right employees to satisfy these needs, thus making the hiring process more efficient. The "HR Competencies & Applications: Using Workforce Planning

COMPETENCIES & APPLICATIONS

Using Workforce Planning to Improve Hiring

HR professionals do their best to make the hiring process more efficient by identifying the right talent to fill needs in companies. Results of a recent SHRM survey showed that open positions take an average of 34 days to fill; jobs that require more knowledge and positions in larger firms take more time. The goal should be to hire quality people more quickly, thus generating lower than average fill rates.

This can be done by looking for bottlenecks in the hiring process and making appropriate changes to HR policy. Companies used to be negatively affected by the vast number of applications they received for positions, but technology has accelerated candidate screening, made communication much easier, and provided unique ways to identify good talent. However, there are other potential problems that companies face. For instance, according to Chrissy A. Cacioppo, a benefits specialist, hiring at the Omaha-based Centris Federal Credit Union is often slowed down by candidate background checks. Other delays can occur when managers can't coordinate interviews with candidates or when managers can't agree about which individuals to hire. Another problem involves unrealistic and/or unclear job descriptions that cloud the hiring process, says Kevin Wheeler, president of the

California-based consulting company Global Learning Resources.

The bottom line is that companies must conduct solid HR planning to decrease these concerns. In other words, the future staffing needs of a company should be identified ahead of time. The following planning approaches can help firms with their hiring processes:

- *Make good workplace projections.* Constantly project what jobs need to be filled and when they will be needed.
- *Identify an appropriate pool of talent.* Have a group of possible job candidates ready to fill positions as they become available.
- *Work with outside parties who can help.* Develop good relationships with universities and other groups that have access to potential employees.
- *Educate leaders about the importance of hiring.* Make sure that managers understand the costs associated with unfilled positions.[35]

Based on these issues, consider the following questions:

1. What other challenges do you think companies face when trying to manage HR planning?

2. In what other ways could workforce planning be used to improve the hiring process?

KEY COMPETENCIES: Critical Evaluation (Behavioral Competency) and Strategy (Technical Competency) to Improve Hiring" feature discusses how organizations can enhance the efficiency of their hiring efforts with solid HR planning.

LO5 List options for handling a shortage and a surplus of employees.

2-7 Workforce Supply ≠ Demand

Since the objective of strategic planning is to anticipate and react to future events and conditions, managers should evaluate and revise the strategic plan on a periodic basis. Some have called into question the value of strategic planning in light of economic volatility. However, organizations would fare much worse with no plan in place. Surprises are not good when hiring a workforce, and planning helps reduce surprises.

Attracting and retaining the right talent is an ongoing challenge as the needs of the business change over time. The United States has continued to move from a manufacturing economy to a service economy. This shifting economic base leads to structural mismatches between workers and jobs. Workers with the wrong skills are unable to fill the technical and health service jobs employers need. Ongoing retraining can help overcome some of these problems if strategic planning has identified them. Organizations need to plan for both the quantity and the quality of the workforce over the planning horizon. Having sufficient workers with the right qualifications is essential if the strategic plan is to be achieved. If the firm employs too many people for its needs, a talent surplus exists, and if too few, a talent shortage. Because of rapidly changing conditions, the organization may face a surplus in some parts of the business and a shortage in others. Figure 2-9 shows the tactics organizations might use to deal with workforce supply imbalances.

FIGURE 2-9 Managing Talent Supply Imbalances

Managing a Talent Surplus	Managing a Talent Shortage
Reduce employee work hours or compensation	Increase employee work hours through overtime
Attrition	Outsource to a third party
Hiring freezes	Implement alternative work arrangements
Voluntary separation programs	Use contingent workers (temporaries, independent contractors)
Workforce downsizing/reduction in force (RIF)	Reduce employee turnover

2-7a Managing a Talent Surplus

A talent surplus can be managed within a strategic HR plan in a number of ways. The reasons for the surplus will guide the ultimate steps taken by the organization. If the workforce has the right qualifications but sales revenue has fallen, the primary strategies would involve retaining the best workers and cutting costs. However, if the workforce is not appropriately trained for the jobs needed, the organization may lay off those employees who cannot perform the work. Managers may use various strategies in a progressive fashion to defer workforce reductions until absolutely necessary.

Reduction in Work Hours or Compensation To retain qualified employees, managers may temporarily institute reduced work hours. Selected groups of employees may have their workweek reduced, or all employees could be asked to take a day or week off without pay. For example, a small family-owned company asked its 15 full-time workers to take a day off without pay each week to keep all of them on the payroll and avoid layoffs. When the economy improved, these skilled employees were available to handle the increased workload.

Across-the-board pay cuts can reduce labor costs while retaining some skilled employees. It is important that pay cuts start at the very top of the organization so that employees do not bear all of the hardship. Uniform pay cuts can be seen as a shared sacrifice for the survival of the firm. Organizations may also reduce employee benefits, such as eliminating matching 401(k) contributions or raising employee health insurance premiums. To maintain employee loyalty and a sense of fairness, HR personnel should closely monitor the situation and reinstate pay and benefit levels when the economic outlook improves.

Attrition and Hiring Freezes Attrition occurs when individuals quit, die, or retire and are not replaced. Using attrition with no additional hiring means that no one loses a job, but those who remain must handle the same workload with fewer people. Unless turnover is high, attrition will eliminate only a relatively small number of employees in the short run, but it can be a viable alternative over a longer period of time. Therefore, for greater impact, employers may combine attrition with a freeze on hiring. Employees usually accept this approach more readily than they do other downsizing methods.

Voluntary Separation Programs If employees volunteer to leave, organizations can reduce the workforce while also minimizing legal risks. Firms often entice employees to volunteer by offering additional severance, training, and benefit payments. Early retirement buyouts are widely used to encourage more senior workers to leave organizations early. As an incentive, employers may offer expanded health coverage and additional buyout payments so that the employees will not be penalized economically until their pensions and Social Security benefits take effect. These programs are viewed as a way to accomplish workforce reductions without resorting to layoffs.

Voluntary separation programs appeal to employers because they can significantly reduce payroll costs over time. Although the organization faces some up-front costs, it does not incur as many continuing payroll costs. Using such programs is also viewed as a more humane way to reduce staff than terminating long-serving, loyal employees. In addition, as long as buyouts are truly voluntary, an organization offering them is less exposed to age discrimination suits. One drawback is that some employees the company would like to retain might take advantage of a buyout.

Workforce Downsizing This workforce process has been given many names, including downsizing, rightsizing, and reduction in force (RIF), but it almost always means cutting employees. Layoffs on a broad scale have occurred with frightening regularity in recent years. Trimming underperforming units or employees as part of a plan that is based on sound organizational strategies may make sense. After a decade of many examples and studies, it is clear that downsizing has worked for some firms.[36] However, it does not increase revenues; it is a short-term cost-cutting measure that can result in a long-term lack of talent. When companies cannibalize the human resources needed to change, restructure, or innovate, disruption follows for some time.[37] Also, downsizing can hurt productivity by leaving "surviving" employees overburdened and demoralized.

Many HR professionals believe that their organizations have mishandled layoffs in the past by getting rid of too many employees, not getting rid of enough, or letting the wrong ones go. Groupthink (a herd mentality), framing effects (thinking about decisions only in certain ways), focusing on inappropriate criteria, and making decisions too quickly can lead to some of these poor decisions.[38] Best practices for companies to successfully carry out layoffs include the following:

- Identify the work that is core to sustaining a profitable business.
- Identify the knowledge, skills, and competencies needed to execute the business strategy.
- Protect the bottom line and the corporate brand.
- Constantly communicate with employees.
- Pay attention to the survivors.

A common myth is that individuals who are still employed after downsizing are so grateful to have a job that they won't cause any problems in the workplace. However, some observers draw an analogy between those who survive downsizing and those who survive wartime battles. Bitterness, anger, disbelief, and shock all are common reactions. For those who survive workforce cuts, the culture and image of the firm as a "lifetime" employer often are gone forever.

Companies may offer severance benefits, outplacement services, and employee assistance programs to cushion the shock of layoffs and protect the company from litigation. Severance benefits are temporary payments made to laid-off employees to ease the financial burden of unemployment. One common strategy is to offer laid-off employees severance benefits that require the employees to release the organization from legal claims. Severance benefits are typically based on length of service with the company, often one or two weeks' pay per year of service. Outplacement services and employee assistance programs are provided to give displaced employees support and assistance. This support often includes personal career counseling, résumé-preparation services, interviewing workshops, and referral assistance. Such services can be provided by outside firms that specialize in outplacement assistance and whose fees usually are paid by the employer, or they can be provided by the HR staff. Helping laid-off workers gain new employment can ease the financial burden on employees and preserve the company's image.[39]

Severance benefits
Temporary payments made to laid-off employees to ease the financial burden of unemployment

2-7b Legal Considerations for Workforce Reductions

HR must be involved during workforce adjustments to ensure that the organization does not violate any of the nondiscrimination or other laws governing workforce reductions. Selection criteria for determining which employees will be laid off must comply with Title VII of the Civil Rights Act as well as the Age Discrimination in

Employment Act and the Americans with Disabilities Act. A careful analysis and disparate impact review should be conducted before final decisions are made.

There is no legal requirement to provide severance benefits, and loss of medical benefits is a major problem for laid-off employees. However, under the federal Consolidated Omnibus Budget Reconciliation Act (COBRA), displaced workers can retain their group medical coverage for up to 18 months for themselves and for up to 36 months for their dependents, if they pay the premiums themselves.

Employers must also comply with the Older Workers Benefit Protection Act (OWBPA) when implementing RIFs. The OWBPA requires employers to disclose the ages of both terminated and retained employees in layoff situations, and a waiver of rights to sue for age discrimination must meet certain requirements. The worker must be given something of value ("consideration"), typically severance benefits, in exchange for waiving the right to sue. When a group of employees is laid off, workers over age 40 in this group must be granted 45 days in which to consider accepting severance benefits and waiving their right to sue.

To ensure employees have adequate notice of plant closings or mass layoffs, a federal law was passed—the Worker Adjustment and Retraining Notification (WARN) Act. This law requires private and commercial organizations that employ 100 or more full-time workers who have worked more than six months in the previous year to give a 60-day notice before implementing a layoff or facility closing that involves more than 50 people. However, workers who have been employed less than six months in the prior year, as well as part-time staff members working fewer than 20 hours per week, are not counted toward the total of 50 employees. Despite not being formally counted to determine implementation of the law, these individuals should still be given some form of notice. The WARN Act imposes heavy fines on employers who do not follow the required process and fail to give proper notice.

2-7c Managing a Talent Shortage

Managing a shortage of employees seems simple enough—just hire more people. However, as mentioned earlier, there can be mismatches between the qualifications needed by employers and the skills possessed by available workers. The list of the 10 hardest jobs to fill in the United States includes engineers, nurses, certain teachers, IT staff, and skilled trades. For these jobs, there may not always be sufficient qualified workers to hire. Companies can use a number of alternative tactics to manage a talent shortage, as Figure 2-10 shows.

FIGURE 2-10 Ways to Manage a Talent Shortage

The following are in a common order of usage:

First	—	Use overtime
Second	—	Outsource work
Third	—	Try alternative work arrangements
Fourth	—	Bring back recent retirees
Fifth	—	Increase contingent workers
Sixth	—	Reduce turnover

One tactic is having existing employees work overtime. This strategy can work on a short-term basis but is not a solution for a longer-term talent shortage. Workers may appreciate the extra hours and pay for a while, but eventually fatigue sets in, productivity and quality may drop, and injuries and absenteeism may increase.

Outsourcing involves transferring the management and performance of a business function to an external service provider. Organizations in the United States outsource a wide variety of noncore functions to reduce costs or to obtain skills and expertise not available in the organization.

Alternate work arrangements are nontraditional schedules that provide flexibility to employees and include job sharing and telecommuting. These are creative solutions to attract and retain skilled employees who want flexibility. Employees can be given more freedom in determining when and how they will perform their jobs. Overall, these arrangements have become popular and widely used in many organizations, but certain programs such as job sharing and sabbaticals are used less frequently today than in the past.[40] Retirees may be rehired on a part-time or temporary basis to fill talent gaps. The advantage is that these individuals are already trained and can be productive immediately. Care must be taken not to interfere with pension payments or other benefits tied to retirement.

Contingent employees, that is, noncore employees working for a company on a temporary or as-needed basis, can provide short-term help. Professional employer organizations can lease employees to the firm, which is often a good solution for technical talent. Independent contractors can be hired when needed to fill talent shortages. The use of independent contractors must be managed closely to ensure compliance with wage and hour, safety, and employee benefit statutes. When using contingent workers, special efforts are needed to assimilate them into the workforce and avoid an "us-and-them" mentality. Contingent workers fill an important need, and managers can maximize their contributions through good employee relations practices.

Reducing turnover of qualified employees should be part of an ongoing effort to maintain a talented workforce. Special attention may be required in times of talent shortages to retain skilled employees. Providing these individuals desirable compensation and a desirable workplace can improve retention of qualified workers.

2-8 Human Resources Planning in Mergers and Acquisitions

The purpose of a merger or acquisition is to generate growth by combining two existing companies and creating a more competitive company. Recent evidence suggests that companies frequently use mergers and acquisitions (M&As), and more efforts more planned for the future. Thus, HR professionals should be involved in managing these business ventures.[41]

HR departments can contribute to the strategic success of M&As through sound HR planning. Unfortunately, many mergers and acquisitions don't live up to their full potential. Due diligence is even more complex when the M&A involves companies in different countries. For instance, cultural differences in global operations, poor leadership, and inappropriate workplace practices can cause problems during M&As.[42] A significant number of failed ventures can also trace their roots to HR issues that were not properly addressed such as loss of key staff, culture clashes, and poor communication. To ensure successful integration, HR should be involved

FIGURE 2-11 HR Activities during M&A

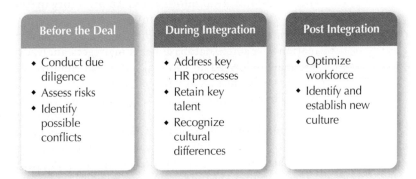

Before the Deal	During Integration	Post Integration
• Conduct due diligence • Assess risks • Identify possible conflicts	• Address key HR processes • Retain key talent • Recognize cultural differences	• Optimize workforce • Identify and establish new culture

before, during, and after the deal is completed. Figure 2-11 shows HR activities and focus during each stage of the merger process.

2-8a Before the Deal

Due diligence
A comprehensive assessment of all aspects of the business being acquired

To determine whether the two organizations should combine, a rigorous process of due diligence is conducted. Due diligence is a comprehensive assessment of all aspects of the business being acquired. Financial, sales and marketing, operations, and human resource staffs can all be involved before the final decision is made to merge with or acquire the company. Each function determines the assets and liabilities of the target company to ascertain whether there are serious risks to the buyer. HR professionals can review broad issues related to legal compliance and labor contract obligations. HR should also assess what HR policies have been used in a firm, the available talent, and the organizational culture.[43]

A process can be developed for due diligence that can be used over and over again for greater consistency. In addition, a document can be created that summarizes the details of the M&A process, including assessments of compensation, the associated expenses, and overall HR findings.[44] These efforts can help companies identify potential problems early on and enable managers to plan for an orderly transition. A thorough, objective analysis of HR-related issues is therefore critical to making good business decisions. Organizations should also invite HR professionals and other key stakeholders to help with M&A efforts early on in the process, and the implications for employees should be reviewed constantly.[45]

2-8b During Integration

After the deal is closed, the focus of HR activity switches to the orderly transition of basic HR processes such as payroll and benefits migration. During the first 60 days after the acquisition, HR must deliver high-quality administrative and operational support to employees and managers. Immediate concerns often focus on basic services needed to run the operations. Frequent communication, employee hotlines, and guidance for managers all contribute to employee retention and loyalty during the chaotic early days of the transition. Managers focus on identifying key talent and establishing initiatives to retain needed employees. Attractive compensation and job assignments can be offered to retain employees during integration.

Integrating HR information systems is important to provide managers with information about employee capabilities, performance, and potential. The acquiring organization cannot make optimum human resource assessments without access to employees' historical information. An inventory of knowledge, skills, and expertise along with performance information provide the data needed to make suitable assignments for employees from both organizations. Gathering all relevant HR information in a single database helps managers analyze and compare employee skills and make informed decisions about which employees should be retained.

As the businesses are merged, culture-based conflicts can emerge. For example, when HP and Compaq merged, cultural differences were recognized and addressed. HP had a culture that fostered innovation by giving employees autonomy and opportunities for professional development. Compaq, on the other hand, was a fast-paced company that made decisions quickly. The merger was successful because the best parts of the culture in each company were blended. Changing the organizational culture depends on changing behavior in the organization. Four important factors in changing culture include:

- *Define the desired behaviors.* Provide behavioral examples of how people are expected to act and tie these behaviors to the performance management system.
- *Deploy role models.* Select leaders who exemplify the desired behaviors and make them visible throughout the organization.
- *Provide meaningful incentives.* Reward the role models with recognition to reinforce their behavior and to signal to the rest of the organization.
- *Provide clear and consistent messages.* Align what you say with what you do and reward.

2-8c Post-Integration

To realize the expected benefits of a merger, the months following the initial integration are important. Cultural changes started in the early days must be maintained. Practical issues regarding talent management and development along with combined compensation systems will solidify the new united organization. Failure to effectively blend the workforces and move beyond competing interests can harm the merger. Continued change efforts are needed to bring all employees to a *one organization* mentality. Breaking down the barriers between the previous practices used in each company and implementing the best from both firms will give employees a sense of value and importance. Ultimately, the outcomes of the deal depend on how HR issues are addressed.

M&As can be challenging strategic moves for companies. They can be particularly tough for employees because they often must deal with new cultural values. The following "HR Perspective: A Tale of Two Cultures: Vocon and Conant Architects" feature illustrates how M&As can be performed in a way that helps employees adjust.

Effectiveness
The ability of a program, project, or task to produce a specific desired effect or result that can be measured

Efficiency
The degree to which operations are carried out in an economical manner

MEASURE

LO6 Identify how organizations can measure and analyze the effectiveness of HR management practices.

2-9 Measuring the Effectiveness of Human Resources and Human Capital

Effectiveness for organizations is a measure of the ability of a program, project, or task to produce a specific desired effect or result that can be measured. Efficiency is the degree to which operations are carried out in an economical manner. Efficiency can also be thought of as a short-term measure that compares inputs and costs directly against outputs and benefits.

PERSPECTIVE

A Tale of Two Cultures: Vocon and Conant Architects

Organizations use mergers and acquisitions as a way to reduce expenses, break into untapped markets, reach out to new customers, and/or diversify their business plans. In a perfect world, integrating business operations would be an easy and fluid process, but many times the reality is very different. Companies often find it difficult to mesh varying business cultures because employees in the merging companies have grown accustomed to how business is conducted in their different worksites. Consequently, as many as half of all mergers and acquisitions fail, and many more of them don't really help companies improve their overall worth. Merging firms must focus their efforts on creating positive cultural fit.

A good example of how to effectively manage these processes involves the recent merger that took place between the Cleveland-based architectural design company Vocon and New York–based Conant Architects. Vocon acquired Conant to diversify its offerings beyond interior design to include workspace development. Yet, the HR group was concerned about how to make employees feel good about the merger, particularly because the culture in Vocon was considered

to be "fun," while the culture in Conant was thought to be "traditional." So they had to find ways to help reduce employees' fears.

Vocon's Chief Human Resources Officer Susan Austin first looked for any differences in the companies' employee handbooks so that she could describe to workers the changes that would be needed. She also grouped individuals from the two firms together so that they could interview each other in a fun and dynamic way. Finally, the Conant employees were flown to Cleveland for a holiday party at Vocon's headquarters to build morale.[46]

HR professionals need to develop sound strategies for managing mergers and acquisitions. Consider the following questions about cultural fit:

1. What specific cultural challenges do companies face during mergers and acquisitions?

2. What unique strategies could be used to reduce the anxiety experienced by employees during mergers and acquisitions? How could an HR department help with these efforts?

There are many ways of measuring the financial impact of the HR practices, and there are many challenges associated with doing so. Return on investment (ROI) is a common measure used by financial professionals to assess the value of an investment. For example, if a firm invests $20,000 for a supervisory training program, what does it gain in lower worker compensation costs, lower legal costs, higher employee productivity, and lower employee turnover? The benefits of HR practices are not always immediately visible, which is what makes measuring HR's impact such a challenge. However, successful efforts can usually be made to assess HR practices.

A long-standing myth perpetuates the notion that one cannot really measure the value of HR practices. That myth has hurt HR's credibility because it suggests that either HR efforts do not add value or they are too far removed from business results to matter. That notion is, of course, untrue. HR, like all other functions, must be evaluated by considering the results of its actions and the value it adds to the organization. Unfortunately, the perceptions of managers and employees in many organizations are mixed because HR has not historically measured and documented its contributions or communicated those results. Further, accounting practices treat expenditures on human capital and talent development as expenses rather than capital investments. This practice encourages top management to view employees as consumers of capital rather than as a long-term investment.

People-related costs are typically the largest controllable expense in organizations. Effective management of these costs can make a positive difference in the survival of the organization. Collecting and analyzing HR information can pinpoint waste and improper allocation of human resources. It is important that HR managers understand financial and operational measures that drive the business and relate decisions to key performance indicators (KPIs). Metrics, benchmarking, balanced scorecards, and audits can help firms track HR performance and measure the value of different business practices.

2-9a HR Metrics and Analytics

HR metrics
Specific measures of HR practices

HR metrics are specific measures of HR practices. They are performance indicators of various HR issues, like absenteeism and turnover rates. Metrics are typically used to assess HR practices and results within the organization over time. A metric can be developed using cost, quantity, quality, timeliness, and other designated goals. Metrics can be developed to track HR efficiency and effectiveness. A pioneer in developing HR measurements, Jac Fitz-Enz, has identified a wide range of HR metrics. A number of key HR metrics are shown in Figure 2-12.[47]

HR and line managers collect and share the data needed to track performance. Data to track these measures come from several sources within the organization. Financial data are required to determine costs for various HR activities, and performance and turnover data can be found in HR and operations records. The real value in using metrics comes from the interpretation of the data that can lead to improvements in HR practices. Information and historical data are studied to determine the reasons for current performance levels and to learn how to improve these levels in the future.

HR analytics
An evidence-based approach to making HR decisions on the basis of quantitative tools and models

A key challenge that many HR groups face is having enough professionals on staff who know how to properly use HR analytics.[48] Analytics involve using various metrics and complex modeling techniques to answer questions about HR functions. HR analytics can be defined as an evidence-based approach to making HR decisions on the basis of quantitative tools and models.[49]

Unlike financial reporting, there is not yet a standard for the implementation and reporting of HR measures. Managers choose what and how to report to employees, investors, and other interested parties. This lack of consistency in HR reporting makes it difficult to evaluate an organization and to compare HR practices across organizations. Though there have been efforts to develop consistent ways of reporting HR metrics, some of these efforts have been met with opposition.[50] The following should be considered when developing HR metrics and analytics:

- Accurate data can be collected.
- Measures are linked to strategic and operational objectives.

FIGURE 2-12   Key HR Metrics

HR Staff and Expenses	Staffing
• HR-to-employee ratio • Total HR staff • HR expenses per FTE	• Number of positions filled • Time to fill • Cost per hire • Annual turnover rate

Compensation	Training
• Annual wage and salary increases • Payroll as a percentage of operating expenses • Benefit costs as a percentage of payroll	• Hours of training per employee • Total costs for training • Percentage of employees participating in tuition reimbursement program

Retention and Quality	Development
• Average tenure of employees • Percentage of new hires retained for 90 days • Performance quality of employees in first year	• Positions filled internally • Percentage of employees with career plan

- Calculations can be clearly understood.
- Measures provide information valued by executives.
- Results can be compared both externally and internally.
- Measurement data drive HR management efforts.

2-9b Human Resources and Benchmarking

Benchmarking
The process of comparing an organization's business results to industry standards or best practices

Benchmarking is the process of comparing an organization's business results to industry standards or best practices. An organization compares itself to "best-in-class" organizations that demonstrate excellence for a specific process. Benchmarking is focused on external practices that the organization can use to improve its own processes and practices. When implementing benchmarking, managers should be careful to find organizations with similar contexts, cultures, operations, and size so that comparisons are realistic. Practices that would work effectively in an organization of 500 employees might not transfer very well to an organization with 5,000 employees. The organization should also select benchmarks that will have the greatest impact on organizational performance.

Many HR professionals report that their organizations collect benchmark data on a planned, periodic basis, while others collect it on an as-needed basis. Major obstacles to using benchmarks are uncertainty about how to collect the information and what information to collect. Using benchmarking, HR effectiveness is best determined by measures on a year-to-year basis. This way, an organization can track improvements and results by implementing specific HR practices. While benchmarking helps a firm compare its results to those of other organizations, it does not provide the reasons behind the findings. Thus, benchmarking is only a starting point, not the end point, for improving HR practices.

2-9c Human Resources and the Balanced Scorecard

Balanced scorecard
A framework organizations use to report on a diverse set of performance measures

One way companies can effectively measure their strategic performance and HR practices involves using the balanced scorecard. The balanced scorecard is a framework organizations use to report on a diverse set of performance measures. This method balances financial and nonfinancial measures so that managers focus on long-term drivers of performance and organizational sustainability. As shown in Figure 2-13, the balanced scorecard measures performance in four areas:

- *Financial measures*: Traditional financial measures such as profit and loss, operating margins, utilization of capital, return on investment, and return on assets are needed to ensure that the organization manages its bottom line effectively.
- *Internal business processes*: Product and service quality, efficiency and productivity, conformance with standards, and cycle times can be measured to ensure that the operation runs smoothly and efficiently.

FIGURE 2-13 Balanced Scorecard Framework

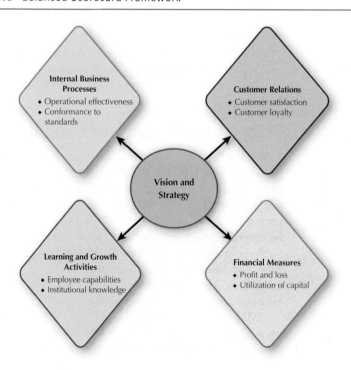

- *Customer relations*: Customer satisfaction, loyalty, and retention are important to ensure that the organization is meeting customer expectations and can depend on repeat business from its customers.
- *Learning and growth activities*: Employee training and development, mentoring programs, succession planning, and knowledge creation and sharing provide the necessary talent and human capital pool to ensure the future of the organization.

Results in each of these four areas determine if the organization is progressing toward its strategic objectives. For example, some firms have noticed that when survey results show a decline in employee satisfaction, several months later there are declines in customer loyalty and repeat customer sales. Further, investing money in employee leadership development training can be linked to lower employee turnover and reduced time to hire managers from outside the organization. Using the balanced scorecard therefore requires considerable time and effort to identify the appropriate HR measures in each of the areas and determine how they tie to strategic organizational success. The balanced scorecard should also be linked to a company's strategic objectives and focus on results that support these goals.

2-9d Human Capital Effectiveness Measures

HR measures outcomes that traditional accounting typically does not explore. Human capital often provides both the biggest value and the biggest cost to organizations; therefore, many metrics reflect people-related *costs*. Measuring the *benefits* of human capital is equally important because it shows how effective HR practices help an organization and its employees. As noted previously, human capital refers to the collective value of the competencies, knowledge, and skills of the employees in the organization. This capital is the renewable source of creativity and innovativeness in the organization but is not reflected in its financial statements.

Revenue per employee is a basic measure of human capital effectiveness. The formula is revenue/head count (full-time employee equivalents). It is a measure of employee productivity and shows the sales revenue generated by each full-time employee. This measure is commonly used in government reporting (see Bureau of Labor Statistics [BLS] on the Internet) as well as by other organizations to track productivity over time. If revenues increase but employee head count remains constant, productivity will increase.

Return on investment (ROI)
Calculation showing the value of investments in human capital

A widely used financial element that can be applied to measure the contribution and cost of HR activities is return on investment (ROI), a calculation showing the value of investments in human capital. It can also be used to show how long it will take for the activities to show results. The following formula can be used to calculate the potential ROI for a new HR practice:

$$ROI = \frac{C}{A + B}$$

where:

A = Operating costs for a new or enhanced system for the time period
B = One-time cost of acquisition and implementation
C = Value of gains from productivity improvements for the time period

ROI is stressed because it is used in many other organizational functions and is the "language" used by financial staff and top management. It allows managers to choose from among various investment opportunities to determine the best use of funds.

Human capital value added (HCVA)
Calculated by subtracting all operating expenses *except* labor expenses from revenue and dividing by the total full-time head count

Human capital value added (HCVA) is an adjusted operating profitability figure calculated by subtracting all operating expenses *except* labor expenses from revenue and dividing by the total full-time head count. It shows the operating profit per full-time employee. Because labor is required to generate revenues, employment costs are added back into operating expenses. The formula for HCVA is:

$$\frac{\text{revenue} - (\text{operating expenses [compensation + benefit costs]})}{\text{full-time head count}}$$

Human capital return on investment (HCROI)
Directly shows the amount of profit derived from investments in labor

Human capital return on investment (HCROI) directly shows the amount of profit derived from investments in labor, which represents the leverage the company has on labor cost. The formula for HCROI uses the same adjusted operating profitability figure as are used for HCVA, but it is divided by the human capital cost:

$$\frac{\text{revenue (operating expenses} - [\text{compensation + benefit costs}])}{(\text{compensation + benefit costs})}$$

Human economic value added (HEVA)
Wealth created per employee

Human economic value added (HEVA) shows the wealth created per employee. It shows how much more valuable the organization has become because of its investment in human capital. Wealth is the net operating profit of a firm after the cost of capital is deducted. The cost of capital is the minimum rate of return demanded by shareholders. When a company is making more than the cost of capital, it is creating wealth for shareholders. An HEVA approach requires that all policies, procedures, measures, and methods use cost of capital as a benchmark against which their return is judged. HR decisions can be subjected to the same analysis. The formula for HEVA is:

$$\frac{\text{net profit after taxes} - \text{cost of capital}}{\text{full-time head count}}$$

A variety of financial measures can be assessed to show the contribution human capital makes to organizational results. Without such measures, it would be difficult to know what is going on in the organization, identify performance gaps, and provide feedback. Managers should require the same level of rigor in measuring HR practices as they do for other functions in the organization. Regardless of the time and effort given to HR measurement and metrics, an important consideration is that HR effectiveness and efficiency is being measured regularly so that managers know how HR practices positively impact the company.

2-9e Human Resources Audit

HR audit
A formal research effort to assess the current state of an organization's HR practices

One means for assessing HR performance is through an HR audit, which is similar to a financial audit. An HR audit is a formal research effort to assess the current state of an organization's HR practices. This audit is used to evaluate how well activities in each of the HR areas (staffing, compensation, health and safety, etc.) have been performing so that management can identify areas for improvement. An HR audit often helps smaller organizations without a formal HR professional identify issues associated with legal compliance, administrative processes and record keeping, employee retention, and other areas.

There are many levels of HR audit, including these common ones:

- *Compliance audit*: Checks record keeping on state and federal documentation requirements
- *Benefit programs audit*: Reviews regulatory compliance, benefits administration, and reporting
- *I-9 audit*: Reviews compliance with immigration regulations and the I-9 form requirement
- *Specific program audit*: Reviews specific HR subareas such as compensation, EEO, or training
- *Full HR audit*: Reviews all of the above plus any and all other HR functions[51]

Audits frequently involve a questionnaire and interviews to collect information about programs, and they may be performed by outside entities for more objective evaluation. They can provide useful assessments about how well HR practices meet established standards and requirements.

SUMMARY

- The strategy an organization follows is its proposition for identifying how to compete successfully and thereby survive and grow.
- HR should be involved in developing and implementing strategic initiatives throughout the organization.
- Strategic planning is a core business process that results in a road map of organizational direction.
- Strategic HR management refers to the use of practices to gain or keep a competitive advantage by aligning individual employee performance with the organization's strategic objectives.
- Environmental scanning helps pinpoint strengths, weaknesses, opportunities, and threats that the organization will face during the planning horizon.
- HR functions may involve merging organizational and HR strategies with offshoring and global staffing strategies.
- HR planning must identify the demand for people and the supply of individuals available.
- Managing a talent surplus may require reducing

work hours, downsizing through use of attrition and hiring freezes, implementing voluntary separation programs, and downsizing the workforce.
- Managing a talent shortage may be addressed through overtime, reducing turnover, using contingent workers, and outsourcing.
- HR plays a crucial role in mergers and acquisitions, particularly in dealing with integration and organizational culture issues.
- HR effectiveness must be measured using HR metrics that consider both strategic and operational effectiveness.
- Benchmarking allows an organization to compare its practices against best practices in different organizations, and HR audits can be used to get a comprehensive overview of HR activities.
- The balanced scorecard can be a useful framework to measure and combine organizational performance measures.
- An HR audit is valuable in providing an overall perspective or a perspective of several specific areas.

CRITICAL THINKING CHALLENGES

1. Discuss how globalization has changed jobs in an organization where you have worked. What are some HR responses to those changes?

2. What steps can HR professionals take to ensure that mergers and acquisitions are successful? How can HR help during the integration process?

3. How can an organization maintain its image while dealing with a talent surplus? If layoffs are necessary, what would you recommend managers do to ensure that survivors remain committed and productive?

4. As the HR manager for a multinational corporation, you want to identify HR competencies that are critical for global companies. Visit the website for the World Federation of People Management Association (www.wfpma.com) to research the topic and to identify differences in the body of knowledge in different parts of the world.

5. As the HR Director of a U.S.-based company that is looking at global opportunities in China, you have been asked by the company president to prepare an outline for an HR strategic plan as part of the company's expansion process. You need to develop an HR strategic plan that will integrate the goals, objectives, and strategies of the HR department with those of the company. The plan also needs to support the objectives of other departments within the company. To get ideas on how to develop an HR strategic plan, go to www.workinfo.com.

   A. What is the process to use for identifying the components of the HR strategic planning process?
   B. What other company strategic objectives must the HR strategic plan integrate and support?

CASE | HR's Performance Consulting at Ingersoll Rand

Many people who work in the HR profession focus their efforts on improving the typical HR activities that are performed in a firm, including staffing, training and development, compensation, and performance appraisal. However, they sometimes overlook the important strategic objectives of their employers. This is why managers in other areas of a company often fail to see the importance of HR staff. There doesn't seem to be any real connection between what the HR function does and what the firm is trying to accomplish strategically. Therefore, HR professionals need to get involved with *performance consulting* in companies, which requires them to be more proactive in their approach to managing HR activities.

This is what Craig Mundy focused on when he was given the opportunity to take over the HR area in Ingersoll Rand's Climate Solutions, a large and valuable business unit within the company that was created by merging Trane and Thermo King under one operational umbrella. The unit employs 25,000 individuals and has locations in over 60 nations. Performance consulting was particularly important to Climate Solutions because the global economic downturn occurred right after the unit was created, which means that costs had to be managed while the organization tried to make global gains.

The HR group worked with managers to create positive talent plans to help the unit reach its strategic goals. In particular, the following issues were addressed by HR:

- The key gaps that stopped individuals from accomplishing their objectives were highlighted.
- Diverse approaches that effectively reduced gaps were identified.
- Solutions tied to talent management were created and utilized.

Another step involved developing a talent solutions framework that enabled leaders to identify the causes of performance problems in the organization and to develop fixes. The framework is based on workforce planning, which involves finding out the firm's talent requirements. Once these needs are known, leaders can determine how and when employees will be hired. Developing individuals once they are hired is the next issue that is addressed in the framework, followed by how to improve employee engagement and retention. Finally, performance needs to be monitored so that successes can be documented. Using this talent solutions framework at Ingersoll Rand enabled the HR group to play a more strategic role in the company.[52]

QUESTIONS

1. Why do HR personnel need to think more strategically in companies? Why might such an approach enable HR to be taken more seriously by other managers?

2. How would you evaluate the talent solutions framework developed for the Climate Solutions unit at Ingersoll Rand? Is the approach something that you could use as a line manager or as an HR professional, or should it be changed or developed further?

SUPPLEMENTAL CASES

Analytics at PricewaterhouseCoopers

This case illustrates how turnover in a company was dealt with by surveying current and former employees to develop better HR strategies. (For the case, go to www.cengage.com/management/mathis.)

Where Do You Find the Bodies?

This case identifies problems associated with HR planning and recruiting in a tight labor market. (For the case, go to www.cengage.com/management/mathis.)

Xerox

This case highlights the challenges of employee retention during stressful and unpredictable times when Xerox was undergoing a significant shift in its strategic focus. (For the case, go to www.cengage.com/management/mathis.)

Pioneers in HR Analytics

HR analytics at four different organizations helped solve several problems, and this case shows how analytics can be used. (For the case, go to www.cengage.com/management/mathis.)

END NOTES

1. Adapted from Dori Meinert, "Hiring Frenzy," *HR Magazine*, June 2013, pp. 31–35.
2. Chris Bradley, "Managing the Strategic Journey," *McKinsey Quarterly*, July 2012, pp. 1–12.
3. Chris Bradley et al., op cit, p. 1.
4. Stephen Hall et al., "How to Put Your Money Where Your Strategy Is," *McKinsey Quarterly*, March 2012, pp. 1–12.
5. Geri Tucker, "HR at the Corner of People and Strategy," *HR Magazine*, May 2014, pp. 42–44.
6. Adapted from Stephen Hall et al., "How to Put Your Money Where Your Strategy Is," *McKinsey Quarterly*, March 2012, p. 9.
7. Arne Gast and Michele Zanini, "The Social Side of Strategy," *McKinsey Quarterly*, May 2012, pp. 1–10.
8. "Crowdfunding," *T+D*, October 2013, p. 17; Tessa MacDougall, "A New Corporate Social Responsibility Strategy: Integrated Corporate Crowdfunding," June 16, 2014, *Crowdfund Insider Online*,

www.crowdfundinsider.com/2014/06/41949-new-corporate-social-responsibility-strategy-integrated-corporate-crowdfunding/.

9. Jin Feng Uen, David Ahlstrom, Shu-Yuan Chen, and Pai-Wei Tseng, "Increasing HR's Strategic Participation: The Effect of HR Service Quality and Contribution Expectations," *Human Resource Management* 51 (2012), 3–24.

10. E. E. Lawler III and J. W. Boudreav, "What Makes HR a Strategic Partner?" CEO (Center for Effective Organizations) Publication G09-01 (555), pp. 1–23. 9.

11. Bruce E. Kaufman, "Strategic Human Resource Management Research in the United States: A Failing Grade after 30 Years," *Academy of Management Perspectives* 26 (May 2012), 12–36.

12. Aliah D. Wright, "JetBlue's Ann Rhoades on Creating a Values-Centric Culture," *SHRM Online*, October 2, 2014, http://www.shrm.org/hrdisciplines/businessleadership/articles/pages/rhoades-emerging-hr-leaders.aspx.

13. Torben Juul Anderson and Dana Minbaeva, "The Role of Human Resource Management in Strategy Making," *Human Resource Management* 52 (2013), 809–827.

14. Aliah D. Wright, "Getting the C-Suite to Take Notice," *SHRM Online*, October 2, 2014, http://www.shrm.org/hrdisciplines/businessleadership/articles/pages/karsh-emerging-leadhr.aspx.

15. "How Do We Help People Adapt to Dynamic Situations," *Workforce Online*, http://www.workforce.com/articles/how-do-we-help-people-adapt-to-dynamic-situations.

16. Pamela Babcock, "Designing for Growth and Success," *SHRM Online*, November 20, 2013, http://www.shrm.org/hrdisciplines/orgempdev/articles/Pages/Designing-for-Growth.aspx.

17. Janet H. Marler, "Strategic Human Resource Management in Context: A Historical and Global Perspective," *Academy of Management Perspectives* 26 (2012), 6–11.

18. Rebecca Mitchell, Shatha Obeidat, and Mark Bray, "The Effect of Stra-tegic Human Resource Management on Organizational Performance: The Mediating Role of High-Performance Human Resource Practices," *Human Resource Management* 52 (2013), 899–921.

19. Jing Wang and Anil Verma, "Explaining Organizational Responsiveness to Work-Life Balance Issues: The Role of Business Strategy and High-Performance Work Systems," *Human Resource Management* 51 (2012), 407–432.

20. Cathy L. Z. Dubois and David A. Dubois, "Strategic HRM as Social Design for Environmental Sustainability in Organization," *Human Resource Management* 51 (2012), 799–826.

21. Joana S. P. Story, John E. Barbuto Jr., Fred Luthans, and James A. Bovaird, "Meeting the Challenges of Effective International HRM: Analysis of the Antecedents of Global Mindset," *Human Resource Management* 53 (2014), 131–155.

22. Xiaoya Liang, Janet H. Marler, and Zhiyu Cui, "Strategic Human Resource Management in China: East Meets West," *Academy of Management Perspectives* 26 (2012), 55–70.

23. Marion Festing, "Strategic Human Resource Management in Germany: Evidence of Convergence to the U.S. Model, the European Model, or a Distinctive National Model?" *Academy of Management Perspectives* 26 (2012), 37–54.

24. Roy Maurer, "Personalize Rewards to Win Global Talent," *SHRM Online*, June 18, 2013, http://www.shrm.org/publications/hrnews/pages/personalize-rewards-to-win-global-talent.aspx.

25. Adapted from Roy Maurer, "Latin American Multinationals Challenged by HR Issues," *SHRM Online*, November 11, 2013, http://www.shrm.org/hrdisciplines/global/articles/pages/latin-american-multinationals-hr-challenges.aspx.

26. Roy Maurer, "Emerging Markets Drive Global Talent Strategy Shift," *SHRM Online*, November 5, 2013, http://www.shrm.org/hrdisciplines/global/articles/pages/emerging-markets-global-talent-strategy.aspx.

27. Steven Balsam et al., "The Impact of Firm Strategy on Performance Measures Used in Executive Compensation," *Journal of Business Research* 64 (2011), 187–193.

28. Frank Kalman, "Firms Plan for Emerging Roles," *Talent Management Online*, May 30, 2014, http://www.talentmgt.com/articles/firms-plan-for-emerging-roles.

29. Harry J. Van Buren III et al., "Strategic HRM and the Decline of Employee Focus," *Human Resource Management Review* 21 (September 2011), 209–219.

30. Ann Pace, "Human Capital Solutions for the 21st Century," *T+D*, May 2013, pp. 64–66.

31. Paul F. Buller and G. M. McEvoy, "Strategy, HRM, and Performance: Sharpening the Line of Sight," *Human Resource Management Review* 22 (March 2012), 43–56.

32. U.S. Census Bureau, Population Division, "U. S. Population Projections," www.census.gov.

33. Lauren Weber, "Employers Are Getting More Flexible, to a Point," *Wall Street Journal*, April 30, 2014, p. B7.

34. Tom Stamer, "A Strategic Workforce Planning Officer?" *Human Resource Executive Online*, June 5, 2012, pp. 1–7.

35. Adapted from Tamara Lytle, "Streamline Hiring," *HR Magazine*, April 2013, pp. 63–65.

36. Robert J. Grossman, "Hidden Costs of Layoffs," *HR Magazine*, February 2012, pp. 24–30.

37. John C. Dencker, "Who Do Firms Lay Off and Why?" *Industrial Relations: A Journal of Economy and Society* 51 (2012), 152–169.

38. Dinah Brin, "Experts: Avoid Costly Layoff Errors," *SHRM Online*, March 28, 2014, http://www.shrm.org/hrdisciplines/businessleadership/articles/pages/avoid-costly-layoff-errors.aspx.

39. Dinah Brin, "Experts: Avoid Costly Layoff Errors," *SHRM Online*, March 28, 2014, http://www.shrm.org/hrdisciplines/businessleadership/articles/pages/avoid-costly-layoff-errors.aspx.

40. Lauren Weber, "Employers Are Getting More Flexible, to a Point," *Wall Street Journal*, April 30, 2014, p. B7.

41. Steve Ostrom, "Mergers and Acquisitions: An HR Guide for Success," *SHRM Online*, October, 23, 2014, http://www.shrm.org/hrdisciplines/businessleadership/articles/pages/

mergers-and-acquisitions-for-hr-professionals.aspx.

42. Carol Gill, "The Role of Leadership in Successful International Mergers and Acquisitions: Why Renault-Nissan Succeeded and DaimlerChrysler-Mitsubishi Failed," *Human Resource Management* 51, May–June 2012, 433–456.

43. Shari Yocum and Niki Lee, "Tackling HR Due Diligence in M&A," *Human Resource Executive Online,* July 21, 2014, http://www.hreonline.com/HRE/view/story.jhtml?id=534357340.

44. Shari Yocum and Niki Lee, "Tackling HR Due Diligence in M&A," *Human Resource Executive*

Online, July 21, 2014, http://www.hreonline.com/HRE/view/story.jhtml?id=534357340.

45. Steve Ostrom, "Mergers and Acquisitions: An HR Guide for Success," *SHRM Online,* October, 23, 2014, http://www.shrm.org/hrdisciplines/businessleadership/articles/pages/mergers-and-acquisitions-for-hr-professionals.aspx.

46. Adapted from Susan Milligan, "Culture Clash!" *HR Magazine,* August 2014, pp. 19–24.

47. "Human Capital Benchmarking Study," *Society for Human Resource Management,* www.shrm.org.

48. Dave Zielinski, "Analyze This!" *SHRM Online,* October 23, 2014, http://www.shrm.org/hrdisciplines/

businessleadership/articles/pages/hr-leaders-shift-focus-to-data-analytics-.aspx.

49. Laurie Bassi, "Raging Debates in HR Analytics," *People and Strategy* 34 (2011), 14–18.

50. Sarah Fister Gale, "Human Capital Metrics Proposal Hits Snag," *Workforce Online,* November 14, 2012, http://www.workforce.com/articles/human-capital-metrics-proposal-hits-snag.

51. Eric Krell, "Auditing Your HR Department," *HR Magazine,* September 2011, pp. 101–103.

52. Adapted from J. Craig Mundy, "Be a Strategic Performance Consultant," *HR Magazine,* March 2013, pp. 44–46.

CHAPTER

3

Equal Employment Opportunity

Learning Objectives

After you have read this chapter, you should be able to:

LO1 Identify the major government agencies that enforce employment discrimination laws.

LO2 Outline key provisions in the Civil Rights Acts of 1964 and 1991 and compare the two theories of unlawful employment discrimination.

LO3 Show how women are affected by pay, job assignments, and career issues.

LO4 Distinguish between the two types of sexual harassment and explain how employers can prevent such misconduct.

LO5 List key elements of disability discrimination laws.

LO6 Discuss the legal protections to prevent bias and discrimination based on age, religion, national origin, and other factors.

WHAT'S TRENDING IN
EQUAL EMPLOYMENT OPPORTUNITY

Equal employment opportunity (EEO) continues to be a critical issue in organizations. In particular, HR professionals must understand the relevant employment laws that govern how organizations are supposed to treat their workers. They must also understand important concepts related to EEO so that they can develop fair and appropriate work policies that protect worker rights. Here's what's currently trending in EEO:

1. Workplace discrimination is an ongoing concern for organizations. HR departments should recognize the different individual characteristics and work processes that can lead to discrimination. They must also take steps to correct these conditions.
2. Sexual harassment is not a new issue in organizations, but it is still an important one. Companies should develop policies that educate employees about sexual misconduct so that they act professionally at work.
3. Providing reasonable accommodations for pregnant employees, workers with disabilities, and individuals with military backgrounds are important EEO issues today. HR professionals should understand the relevant laws and create policies that provide these individuals fair work situations.
4. Diversity enables companies to capitalize on employees' unique attributes. However, it has also created challenges for HR professionals because these differences can cause problems and misunderstandings. HR should create practices that allow employees to capitalize on their diverse characteristics.

HEADLINE

American Airlines Balances Workplace and Faith

Religion is important to many individuals. Almost 70% of people in the United States believe that they are moderately to very religious. Roughly 77% claim to be Christian, 5% believe in a non-Christian faith, and 18% subscribe to no particular religion. Despite these trends, demographic changes will likely alter some of these characteristics as more individuals representing different faiths (e.g., Buddhists, Hindus, and Muslims) immigrate into the country.

Religion in the workplace has been a challenge for HR professionals for some time. While religion helps establish unique identities for many people, it can also create divisions in companies when different beliefs are discussed openly at work. In other words, religion can separate employees on a range of issues that might be better addressed outside of the workplace. Making matters more challenging are federal and state laws that prevent discrimination based on religion affiliation. Recent evidence suggests that many Muslims, atheists, and evangelical Christians believe that they face some prejudice in the workplace, and these perceptions can lead to legal actions. For example, Abercrombie & Fitch was recently involved in a lawsuit involving a conflict between religious attire and the company's dress code.

Despite these challenges, some companies are becoming more faith-friendly to employees by allowing them to openly express their religious beliefs. Such an approach can result in enhanced individual engagement, commitment, and creativity. For example, American Airlines allows workers to express their religious beliefs and has supported several faith-based groups since the 1990s. They are successful because individuals feel more valued. These groups have been excellent resources for the company when it

iStockphoto.com/Justin Sullivan

has had to make workplace accommodations. Managers can make better decisions when using critical information provided by such groups. These faith-based groups also provide seminars for staff so that employees are better prepared to satisfy customers' needs based on their religious beliefs. In addition, American Airlines has increased sales by reaching out to various churches and offering travel discounts.[1]

Basing employment decisions on factors other than worker qualifications is generally illegal in the United States. The costs of litigation, penalties, and harm to the company's reputation can be substantial when violations occur. With the enactment of the Civil Rights Act of 1964 (Title VII), workers of all backgrounds were provided a more level playing field in terms of employment opportunities. Since then, a number of additional laws and executive orders have been implemented to prohibit illegal discrimination in the workplace. While the Civil Rights Act stands as the foundation of equal employment laws, it is by no means the only regulation affecting the employer–employee relationship. There are other laws that regulate how issues such as individual age, disability, and pregnancy are addressed at work.

Employers have paid (and continue to pay) large amounts for violating EEO laws. But companies can find ways to effectively develop workforce diversity to avoid lawsuits and enhance the workplace. This chapter provides an introduction to nondiscrimination requirements and explains some common best practices related to diversity management. To provide context, Appendix C lists the major laws governing workplace nondiscrimination.

LO1 Identify the major government agencies that enforce employment discrimination laws.

3-1 The Nature of Equal Employment Opportunity

Civil rights activists in the United States used nonviolent means to protest unequal treatment during the turbulent 1950s. This led to the passage of important nondiscrimination laws and guaranteed an equal opportunity for employment to all individuals.[2] Equal employment opportunity means that employment decisions must be made on the basis of job requirements and worker qualifications. Unlawful discrimination occurs when those decisions are made based on protected characteristics, which are individual attributes such as race, age, sex, disability, or religion that are protected under EEO laws and regulations. These factors are not work related and should not be considered. Under federal, state, and local laws, employers are prohibited from considering the following factors in making hiring and other employment decisions:

Protected characteristics
Individual attributes that are protected under EEO laws and regulations

- Age
- Color
- Disability
- Genetic information
- Marital status (some states)

- Military status or experience
- National origin
- Pregnancy
- Race
- Religion
- Sexual orientation (some states and cities)

These categories are considered protected characteristics under various employment laws and regulations. All workers are provided equal protection. In other words, the laws do not favor some groups over others. For example, both men and women can file charges on the basis of alleged sex discrimination. Individuals representing all religious backgrounds and faiths (e.g., Christians, Jews, Muslims, atheists) can claim that their religions rights have been violated based on biases that may exist in the workplace.

Equal employment opportunity
Employment that is not affected by illegal discrimination

Status-blind
Employment decisions that are made without regard to individuals' personal characteristics

Equal employment opportunity (EEO) is employment that is not affected by illegal discrimination. It is a broad-reaching concept that essentially requires employers to make status-blind employment decisions. Status-blind decisions are made without regard to individuals' personal characteristics (e.g., age, sex, race). Most employers are required to comply with EEO laws. Alternatively, affirmative action involves taking proactive measures to increase the number of women and minorities in the workplace in an effort to make up for past patterns of discrimination. This approach allows employers to consider various personal characteristics when making employment decisions.

3-1a Sources of Regulation and Enforcement

The employment relationship is governed by a wide variety of regulations, and all three branches of government have played a role in shaping these laws. Federal statutes enacted by Congress form the backbone of the regulatory environment, but state and city governments also enact laws governing activity within their regions. Various state laws add a degree of complexity to the interpretation and prevention of workplace discrimination. Companies should be aware of legislation that may cover employees based on where they actually complete work tasks, where they live, and where the company conducts business.[3] The courts interpret these laws and rule on cases, providing guidance about how companies should comply with EEO regulations. Case law helps employers understand how laws are applied and what they must do to comply. Executive orders are issued by the president of the United States to help government departments, agencies, and contractors manage their operations.

Government agencies responsible for enforcing laws issue guidelines and rules to provide details on how the law will be implemented. Employers then use these guidelines to meet their obligations in complying with the laws. For example, guidelines issued about sexual harassment help companies identify types of misconduct and enable them to more effectively handle work incidents.

The two main enforcement bodies for EEO are the Equal Employment Opportunity Commission (EEOC) and the U.S. Department of Labor (DOL) (in particular, the Office of Federal Contract Compliance Programs [OFCCP]). The EEOC enforces employment laws for employers in both private and public workplaces. For example, the EEOC recently outlined a strategic enforcement plan encouraging companies to develop fair criminal background screening practices, establish equitable pay for both men and women, and take steps to reduce workplace harassment.[4] The DOL has broad enforcement power and oversees compliance with many employment-related laws. The OFCCP enforces employment requirements set out by executive orders for federal contractors and subcontractors. Many states have enforcement agencies to ensure compliance with state employment laws. Compliance can become complex for companies that operate in multiple states.

GLOBAL

Multinational companies face a confusing array of nondiscrimination laws in different countries. For example, many European nations have employment discrimination laws similar to those found in the United States. But nations in Asia and other developing economies can be less restrictive about workplace practices.[5] Leaders often determine the best approach for managing international operations by either electing to use the highest standards in all nations or complying with each nation's specific regulations. The "HR Ethics: Handbooks and Codes Reconcile Global Employment Laws" feature discusses how companies can deal more effectively with the varying labor laws around the world.

ETHICS

Handbooks and Codes Reconcile Global Employment Laws

A significant hurdle that many global companies face is the varying employment laws that exist in different countries. In the United States, employee handbooks are not the basis of an employment contract, but this is not always the case in other nations. In addition, certain U.S. employment laws should be discussed with employees when they work in other parts of the world (for instance, training could be provided). These include rules about bribery (Foreign Corrupt Practices Act), as well as details about what is considered inappropriate workplace behavior (e.g., sexual harassment). Additionally, nations such as Germany, Canada, and Australia require companies to balance their federal legislation with particular laws in their states, provinces, and territories. The wide variety of global and cultural values that firms must reconcile with their corporate culture makes these issues even tougher. Different societies have varying opinions on sexual orientation, women in the workplace, professional conduct, and gift giving. These issues sometimes make the enforcement of U.S. labor law difficult.

Employers should consider creating a team of trained individuals to audit relevant employment laws. This team should partner with the legal department to make sure that all important legislation is identified and understood. The overall purpose of this audit is to identify how various labor laws differ from a company's current employment practices across a wide range of issues such as staffing, appraisals, discipline, and separation. Once these differences are identified, a more appropriate set of employment policies can be developed that will work on a global scale. These policies should be included in a handbook that outlines proper procedures and guidelines for employees. A global code of conduct can also be developed to outline the behaviors that companies expect to see in the global workplace.[6]

HR professionals should understand and manage different international employment laws. If you were given the responsibility of doing this in a global firm:

1. How would you encourage HR leaders to identify differences in relevant employment laws?

2. Once employment law differences are identified, how would you manage around these issues?

FIGURE 3-1   Charges Filed with EEOC, 1997 and 2014

Charge Basis	Claims Filed, 1997 (Number, Percentage)	Claims Filed, 2014 (Number, Percentage)
Age	15,785 19.6%	20,588 23.2%
Color	762 0.9%	2,756 3.15%
Disability	18,108 22.4%	25,369 28.6%
Equal Pay Act	1,134 1.4%	938 1.1%
Genetic information	Not in force	333 0.4%
National origin	6,712 8.3%	9,579 10.8%
Race	29,199 36.2%	31,073 35.0%
Religion	1,709 2.1%	3,549 4.0%
Retaliation	18,198 22.6%	37,955 42.8%
Sex	24,728 30.7%	26,027 29.3%
Total	80,680	93,727

Note: Totals exceed 100% because of multiple charges filed by an individual claimant.

Source: U.S. Equal Employment Opportunity Commission, http://www.eeoc.gov/eeoc/statistics/enforcement/charges.cfm; http://www1.eeoc.gov/eeoc/newsroom/release/2-4-15.cfm.

Discrimination remains a concern as the U.S. workforce becomes more diverse. According to one expert, HR professionals need to be sensitive to trends in the workplace that can precipitate negative legal actions.[7] Charges filed with the EEOC continue to rise, as shown in Figure 3-1. Over the past 17 years, the total number of charges has increased significantly, but the totals have varied from year to year. For instance, the total number of changes for 2014 is higher than the total reported for 1997, but there were fewer charges reported in 2014 compared to the previous three years. While issues related to race and sex have historically represented the highest percentages of complaints, in recent years, charges of retaliation have become much more common and now represent the highest number (and percentage) of complaints. The EEOC investigates charges levied at companies to determine whether employees were treated unlawfully, which can lead to findings of no discrimination, withdrawn changes, settlements, and/or lawsuits. The EEOC has also been held accountable for filing lawsuits against employers without properly investigating charges and has been forced to reimburse employers' attorney costs and expert witness fees, such as with the temporary employment agency Peoplemark.[8]

ETHICS

3-2 Theories of Unlawful Discrimination

Disparate treatment
Occurs when individuals with particular characteristics that are not job related are treated differently from others

Disparate impact
Occurs when an employment practice that does not appear to be discriminatory adversely affects individuals with a particular characteristic so that they are substantially underrepresented as a result of employment decisions that work to their disadvantage

There are two types of unlawful employment discrimination, disparate treatment and disparate impact. The first type, disparate treatment, occurs when individuals with particular characteristics that are not job related are treated differently from others. This type of discrimination is typically overt and intentional, and it often follows a pattern or practice. For example, if female applicants are asked interview questions regarding child care plans while male applicants are not, then disparate treatment may be occurring.

Disparate impact is the second type of illegal discrimination. It occurs when an employment practice that does not appear to be discriminatory adversely affects individuals with a particular characteristic so that they are substantially underrepresented as a result of employment decisions that work to their disadvantage. This type of discrimination is often unintentional because identical criteria are used, but the results can differ for certain groups. For example, using a test for firefighters that requires candidates to carry a 100-pound sack down a ladder could result in more women being eliminated from selection. The same job-related test is used for all candidates, with markedly different results on the basis of sex.

In a landmark case on disparate impact, *Griggs vs. Duke Power* (1971),[9] the U.S. Supreme Court ruled that lack of intent is not sufficient for an employer to prove that a practice is lawful. The Court also stated that the employer has the burden to show that a selection practice is directly job related as a business necessity. Considering the firefighter test that women failed at a higher rate, the test is a true reflection of a job-related duty—carrying a person out of a burning building. Therefore, the test would be lawful even though women would not pass at the same rate as men. A thorough job analysis and a search for alternate selection practices are important steps when disparate impact occurs. The employer must demonstrate that there is no reasonable nondiscriminatory method available to use. Appendix D explains how disparate impact is defined under the federal government's Uniform Guidelines on Employee Selection Procedures.

Unlawful discrimination can occur in any number of employment-related decisions, including recommendations for advancement opportunities, selection for training seminars, allocation of rewards, and layoffs and terminations. Employers should analyze job requirements, keep good records, and review personnel actions to make sure that employment decisions are lawful and prevent claims of disparate treatment and disparate impact. Managers can also be taught to recognize situations that can lead to discrimination. Training can enhance diversity awareness in organizations, efforts that are discussed later in this chapter. Finally, a recent study found that the use of assessment center data compared to top-down appraisals might mitigate adverse impact when many of the raters are white men. The findings also implied that top-down appraisals that were well developed, job specific, and supported by rater training could lead to greater advancement for women and minorities, and they could also reduce legal challenges.[10]

3-2a Equal Employment Opportunity Concepts

Court decisions and administrative rulings have helped define several basic EEO concepts. The four key concepts discussed next (see Figure 3-2) help clarify key EEO ideas that lead to fair treatment and nondiscriminatory employment decisions.

Business Necessity and Job Relatedness A business necessity is a practice necessary for safe and efficient organizational operations, such as restricting employees from wearing garments that might get caught in machinery although the attire may be required by an employee's religion. Business necessity has been the subject of numerous court cases. Educational requirements are often decided on the basis of business necessity. However, an employer that requires a minimum level of education, such as a high school diploma, must be able to defend the requirement as essential to the performance of the job (job related), which may be difficult. For instance, equating a high school diploma with the possession of math or reading abilities is considered questionable.

Employers are expected to use job-related employment practices. For instance, the use of criminal background checks and credit reports in the selection process has come under fire because it can result in disparate impact directed at minority applicants. The EEOC has issued guidelines stating that the nature of the job sought by the applicant is a major determining factor in whether a criminal conviction is job related. Consequently, employers must find a balance between their obligations to provide a safe working environment and their duty to ensure equal employment opportunity. PepsiCo was forced to rescind its rigid policy on criminal background checks because it screened out individuals who had been convicted of minor offenses that were irrelevant to warehouse jobs.[11]

> **Business necessity**
> A practice necessary for safe and efficient organizational operations

FIGURE 3-2 EEO Concepts

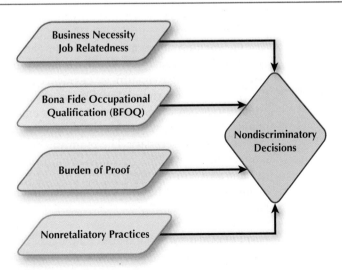

However, the state of Texas recently challenged the EEOC's guidance regarding the hiring of convicted felons. Their position is that it is acceptable for organizations to have policies that ban the employment of criminals. But a recent ruling by the U.S. District Court for the Northern District of Texas rejected the claims made in the lawsuit.[12] On a related issue, even though federal and state laws prevent employers from making inquiries about the arrest records of job candidates, they can investigate current employees' arrests and take appropriate action. While employment decisions cannot be based simply on arrest records, they can be made based on the behaviors that lead to arrests, including conduct that raises concerns about safety and/or security. When disciplining employees who have been arrested, employers should also point out that the conduct is job related and an issue of business necessity.[13]

During the last economic recession, the credit status of many individuals was negatively impacted because of job loss. They were further harmed when employers used credit histories during the hiring process and denied them employment. A number of states enacted laws to prevent the use of negative credit reports in hiring decisions unless the job requires handling money or involves spending authority. There is currently no federal law addressing this issue, but the EEOC has spoken out against the practice, and the U.S. Congress has considered enacting legislation. The crucial outcome is that hiring criteria must be specifically job related and a matter of business necessity.[14]

Bona fide occupational qualification (BFOQ)
Characteristic providing a legitimate reason an employer can exclude persons on otherwise illegal bases of consideration

Bona Fide Occupational Qualification Employers may discriminate on the basis of sex, religion, or national origin if the characteristic can be justified as a bona fide occupational qualification reasonably necessary to the normal operation of the particular business or enterprise. Thus, a bona fide occupational qualification (BFOQ) provides a legitimate reason an employer can use to exclude persons on otherwise illegal bases of consideration. The application of a BFOQ is very narrowly determined and an employer seeking to justify hiring on this basis is advised to obtain prior authorization from the EEOC.

What constitutes a BFOQ has been subject to different interpretations in various courts. Legal uses of BFOQs may occur when gender is used as a BFOQ when hiring women for certain jobs (e.g., a cocktail server at a gentlemen's club) or when religious organizations hire individuals who are members of particular faith.

Burden of proof
What individuals who file suit against employers must prove to establish that illegal discrimination has occurred

Burden of Proof When a legal issue regarding unlawful discrimination is raised, the burden of proof must be satisfied to file suit against an employer and establish that illegal discrimination has occurred. The plaintiff charging discrimination must establish a *prima facie* case of discrimination through either factual or statistical evidence, meaning that sufficient evidence must be provided to the court to support the case and allow the plaintiff to continue with the claim. Once a case has been established, the burden then shifts to the employer, who must provide a legitimate nondiscriminatory reason for the decision, such as focusing on job-related factors and/or business necessity. The plaintiff then must show either that the employer's motivation or rationale was a pretext for discrimination or that there is an alternative employment approach that would not result in discrimination. The plaintiff maintains the final burden of proof that unlawful discrimination underlies an employment decision.

Retaliation
Punitive actions taken by employers against individuals who exercise their legal rights

Nonretaliatory Practices Employers are prohibited from retaliating against individuals who file discrimination charges. Retaliation occurs when employers take punitive actions against individuals who exercise their legal rights. For example, a former police officer filed an EEOC charge alleging sex discrimination when she was transferred to a less prestigious job. She later learned that she was receiving less overtime work than her peers and used the department's copier to copy her coworkers' payroll stubs to substantiate her claim. The city's attorney threatened to criminally prosecute her for making the copies on the department's equipment but offered to drop the charges if she withdrew her EEOC complaint. The plaintiff was awarded over $400,000 in damages and costs.[15] Another case occurred when the EEOC won a judgment against Cognis Corporation for taking retaliatory action against Steven Whitlow, a former employee. The firm implemented a procedure requiring employees

COMPETENCIES & APPLICATIONS

What to Do When the EEOC Comes Knocking

Having to respond to the EEOC when claims of discrimination are levied at a company is a daunting task for HR professionals. Such incidents are becoming more common because there have been steady increases in charges of age, race, and disability discrimination and workplace retaliation. Consequently, HR and other operating managers must be prepared to effectively respond to the EEOC as quickly and succinctly as possible.

But how should they do this? It is important for companies to make a good first impression by taking an allegation seriously. HR professionals and managers should provide the EEOC with any information that is requested and make sure that important files and documents are not discarded. They need to protect confidentiality and ensure that no retaliation occurs. It is important to notify the company's insurer about the incident. An internal investigation should also be conducted, preferably by individuals who have some legal training. Finally, employee interviews should be conducted, and all documentation should be thoroughly reviewed.

A position statement can then be developed that details important points about the company's response to the discrimination claim. The company's position on the charges should be clearly presented, a summary of the business and its policies should be provided, and an overview of the employee's situation in relation to past decisions should be provided. An organization also needs to effectively respond to a request for information (RFI) by providing the EEOC with any materials that are needed. Mediation can sometimes be an option if the claim is deemed eligible and both parties are willing to participate in the process. Settlements can also be formulated between the parties at any point during the process of an investigation. A final consideration is that organizations should do their best to respond quickly to an EEOC investigation.[16]

HR professionals should know how to effectively manage EEOC investigations. If you had to do this in a future job:

1. What kinds of issues would you consider when developing policies related to EEOC investigations? Who would you include in this development process, and what issues do you think are the most important?

2. What other factors do you think companies should consider when dealing with allegations of discrimination?

KEY COMPETENCIES: Consultation (Behavioral Competency) and People (Technical Competency) to sign a "last-chance" agreement in which each employee forfeited the right to ever file discrimination charges for any alleged violations by the company in exchange for continued employment. Whitlow had worked at the company for 19 years, and he refused to comply. Cognis, in turn, fired him in retaliation for not signing the agreement. The court ruled in favor of the EEOC and Whitlow, stating that the company acted unlawfully and violated a fundamental right of employees in the United States to file charges or lawsuits when they believe an employer discriminated against them.[17]

Retaliation claims now constitute many of the charges filed with the EEOC. This is because they can be added to all antidiscrimination charges, and a wide range of workplace decisions might be interpreted as retaliatory. An important aspect of retaliation charges is that the charging party may lose the case on the basis of discrimination but still win if the employer took punitive action against him or her. To prevent charges of retaliation, the following actions are recommended for employers:[18]

- Create and disseminate an antiretaliation policy.
- Train supervisors on what retaliation is and what actions are not appropriate.
- Review all performance evaluation and discipline records to ensure consistency and accuracy.
- Conduct a thorough internal investigation of any claims and document the results.
- Take appropriate action when any retaliation occurs.

Even though HR professionals and operating managers may follow these actions, EEOC investigations sometimes occur when allegations of retaliation and other forms of unlawful discrimination are advanced. These professionals must develop a game plan that enables them to effectively respond to allegations and protect the interests of both the organization and its employees. The previous "HR Competencies & Applications: What to Do When the EEOC Comes Knocking" feature explores important issues that should be considered when the EEOC conducts an investigation.

LO2 Outline key provisions in the Civil Rights Acts of 1964 and 1991 and compare the two theories of unlawful employment discrimination.

3-3 Broad-Based Discrimination Laws

Comprehensive equal employment laws provide broad-based protection for applicants and employees. This section provides an overview of the broad-based discrimination laws, and the various subsections give more specific details about the major laws and compliance requirements.

3-3a Civil Rights Act of 1964, Title VII

Although the very first civil rights act was passed in 1866, it was not until passage of the Civil Rights Act of 1964 that the keystone of antidiscrimination employment legislation was put into place. Title VII, the employment section of the Civil Rights Act of 1964, details the legal protections provided to applicants and employees, and it defines prohibited employment practices. Title VII is the foundation on which all other workplace nondiscrimination legislation is built.

Title VII of the Civil Rights Act states that it is illegal for organizations to discriminate in any way based on a person's sex, race, national origin, color, and/or religion. Coverage includes hiring decisions, terminations, promotions, demotions, compensation, working conditions, and many other personnel actions.

Title VII Coverage Title VII, as amended by the Equal Employment Opportunity Act of 1972, covers most employers in the United States. Any organization meeting one of the following criteria must comply with rules and regulations that specific government agencies have established to enforce the act:

- All private employers of 15 or more employees
- All educational institutions, public and private
- State and local governments
- Public and private employment agencies
- Labor unions with 15 or more members
- Joint labor–management committees for apprenticeships and training

Title VII has been the basis for several extensions of EEO law. For example, in 1980, the EEOC interpreted the law to include sexual harassment. Further, a number of concepts identified in Title VII are the foundation for court decisions, regulations, and other laws discussed elsewhere in this chapter.

3-3b Civil Rights Act of 1991

In response to several U.S. Supreme Court decisions during the 1980s, Congress amended the Civil Rights Act of 1964 to strengthen legal protection for employees, provide for jury trials, and allow for damages payable to successful plaintiffs in employment discrimination cases.[19] A key provision of the 1991 act relates to how U.S. EEO laws are applied globally.

The Civil Rights Act of 1991 requires that employers show that an employment practice is job related for the position and consistent with *business necessity*. The act clarifies that plaintiffs bringing discrimination charges must identify the particular employer practice being challenged and must show only that protected status played *some role in their treatment*. For employers, this means that an individual's race, color, religion, sex, or national origin *must play no role* in employment decisions. The act allows people who have been targets of intentional discrimination based on sex, religion, or national origin to receive both compensatory and punitive damages. The penalties are scaled by the size of employer, as shown in Figure 3-3.

FIGURE 3-3 Penalties under the Civil Rights Act of 1991, by Employer Size

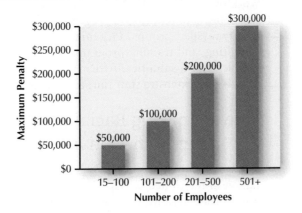

Source: U.S. Equal Employment Opportunity Commission Enforcement Guidance, http://www.eeoc.gov/policy/docs/damages.html.

However, some states have not changed their nondiscriminatory laws to allow for punitive damages, which can limit plaintiffs' ability to receive them in a lawsuit. For example, a recent ruling related to the Iowa Civil Rights Act indicated that three individuals could not receive punitive damages for sex discrimination, sexual harassment, and workplace retaliation because the laws in the state had not been revised.[20]

3-3c Executive Orders 11246, 11375, and 11478

Affirmative action
Proactive employment practices to compensate for historical discrimination against women, minorities, and individuals with disabilities.

Several important executive orders have been issued by the U.S. president that affect the employment practices of federal contractors and subcontractors. The OFCCP in the U.S. Department of Labor is responsible for overseeing federal contractor operations and ensuring that unlawful discrimination does not occur. Executive Orders 11246, 11375, and 11478 require federal contractors to take affirmative action to compensate for historical discrimination against women, minorities, and individuals with disabilities. The concept of affirmative action is not without controversy, and some states have passed laws banning such programs.

Supporters offer many reasons why affirmative action is important, while opponents argue firmly against it. Individuals can consider both sides in the debate and compare them with their personal views of affirmative action. Whether one supports or opposes affirmative action, it is important to understand why its supporters believe that it is needed and why its opponents believe it should be discontinued.

3-3d Managing Affirmative Action Requirements

Affirmative action program (AAP)
A document that outlines proactive steps the organization will take to attract and hire members of underrepresented groups

Federal contractors are required to develop and maintain a written affirmative action program (AAP) that outlines proactive steps the organization will take to attract and hire members of underrepresented groups. This data-driven program includes analysis of the composition of the company's current workforce with a comparison to the availability of workers in the labor market. The overall objective of the AAP is to have the company's workforce demographics reflect as closely as possible the demographics in the labor market from which workers are recruited. The contents of an AAP and the policies flowing from it must be available for review by managers and supervisors within the organization. The AAP is reviewed by the OFCCP and is subject to periodic audits to ensure compliance. In addition to an extensive workforce analysis, the AAP includes goals, timetables, and documentation of good faith efforts to reduce and prevent employment discrimination against historically disadvantaged groups. Organizations implement outreach programs, targeted recruiting, and training programs to recruit and advance women, minorities, and people with disabilities. Affirmative action plans vary in length; some are long and require extensive staff time to prepare.

3-3e Managing Racial and Ethnic Discrimination Issues

The original purpose of the Civil Rights Act of 1964 was to address race discrimination in the United States. This concern continues to be important today. To take appropriate actions, employers should be aware of potential HR issues that are based on race, national origin, and citizenship.

Charges of racial discrimination continue to make up many of the complaints filed with the EEOC. Employment discrimination can occur in numerous ways. This can include refusal to hire someone because of their race or ethnicity and questions found in a selection interview. All employment inquiries and decisions should be based on job-related factors, not personal characteristics. See Appendix E for examples of legal and illegal pre-employment inquiries. The EEOC found that a trucking delivery company failed to hire qualified black applicants for dockworker positions because factors unrelated to job performance were used in their hiring decisions. The company had to pay $120,000 to settle the lawsuit.[21]

Sometimes racial discrimination is very subtle. Some firms have tapped professional and social networking sites to fill open positions. However, networking sites may not be easily accessible to some people, resulting in disparate impact. The use of employee referral programs can lead to a more homogenous workforce because employees may be more likely to refer people who are similar to themselves. One solution is to make sure a hiring organization uses recruitment approaches that secure a diverse applicant pool. This can be done by avoiding procedures that make it difficult for some groups to learn about and apply for open positions. Another possible solution is to use *anonymous application procedures* in which names and other identifying characteristics of applicants are deleted from candidate documents. Decision makers in the hiring process are presented only with credentials and job-relevant information. This procedure, while controversial, may level the playing field and reduce the possibility of selection bias.[22] Under federal law, discriminating against people because of skin color is just as illegal as discriminating because of race. For example, one might be guilty of color discrimination but not racial discrimination if one hired light-skinned African Americans over dark-skinned individuals.

Racial and Ethnic Harassment Racial and ethnic harassment is such a concern that the EEOC has issued guidelines on it. It is recommended that employers adopt policies against harassment of any type, including ethnic jokes, vulgar epithets, racial slurs, and physical actions that could constitute harassment. The consequences of not enforcing these policies are seen in a case involving a major transportation company that subjected African-American employees to a racially hostile working environment and discriminatory employment conditions. The company was fined $11 million in penalties.

Other cases demonstrate the importance of these issues. For instance, an African-American police sergeant was allowed to pursue a discrimination case when he was transferred to a late night shift that reduced his work responsibilities compared to his other colleagues.[23] In another case, a white accountant working for a Korean-owned company claimed that she was not given a promotion to a higher position because she wasn't of Korean heritage. The HR manager stated that Korean leaders in the firm did not want to consider Americans for the promotion, which allowed her to pursue a lawsuit.[24] However, in another case, it was found that an organization did not unlawfully discriminate based on race when it relied on merit-based recruitment procedures to hire a white woman rather than promoting an employee who was black.[25]

LO3 Show how women are affected by pay, job assignments, and career issues.

3-4 Sex and Gender Discrimination Laws and Regulations

The inclusion of sex as a basis for protected status in Title VII of the 1964 Civil Rights Act has led to additional areas of legal protection, and a number of laws and regulations now address discrimination based on sex or gender.

3-4a Pregnancy Discrimination

The Pregnancy Discrimination Act (PDA) of 1978 amended Title VII to require that employers treat maternity leave the same as other personal or medical leaves. Closely related to the PDA is the Family and Medical Leave Act (FMLA) of 1993. The FMLA requires that qualified individuals be given up to 12 weeks of unpaid family leave and also requires that those taking family leave be allowed to return to jobs (see Chapter 13 for details). The FMLA applies to both men and women. The American with Disabilities Act Amendments Act (ADAAA) also expanded the definition of a disability to include less permanent and serious physical and mental issues, which can be interpreted to cover pregnancies.[26] There are also states (Texas, Maryland, Connecticut, and California) that govern the treatment of pregnant employees. For instance, a new law covering individuals working in New York City requires companies to provide bathroom breaks, rest periods, and other reasonable accommodations to pregnant workers.[27]

GLOBAL

Despite these domestic concerns, pregnancy discrimination is a global issue. Women around the world have experienced discrimination because of pregnancy despite legal protections related to childbirth and child rearing. For example, Italian women experience the lowest employment rate in the European Union, Italy ranks below Ghana and Bangladesh in terms of gender equality, and some Italian workers have reported being fired after giving birth.[28]

Discrimination may occur because of employer perceptions of the pregnancy affecting the employee's job performance and attendance. Such discrimination might occur from questions related to pregnancy or child care plans asked during an employment interview. It may also occur because of negative views about pregnancy and/or taking maternity leave. Finally, illegal discrimination can result when a pregnant applicant is not hired or is transferred or terminated.

Courts have generally ruled that the PDA requires employers to treat pregnant employees the same as those who are not pregnant. Employers do have a right to maintain performance standards and expectations of pregnant employees. But they should be cautious to use the same standards for nonpregnant employees and employees with other medical conditions. Finally, managers who are misinformed about issues related to pregnancy discrimination can lead to claims. Companies should provide some training to reduce these concerns.[29]

3-4b Equal Pay and Pay Equity

The Equal Pay Act of 1963 requires employers to pay similar wage rates for similar work without regard to gender. A *common core of tasks* must be similar to justify similar wages. Tasks performed only intermittently or infrequently do not make jobs different enough to justify different wages. Differences in pay between men and women in the same jobs are permitted because of:

1. Differences in seniority
2. Differences in performance
3. Differences in quality and/or quantity of production
4. Factors other than sex, such as skill, effort, and working conditions

In response to a procedural issue in pursuit of a fair pay claim, Congress enacted the Lilly Ledbetter Fair Pay Act in 2009. This law eliminates the statute of limitations for employees who file pay discrimination claims under the Equal Pay

Act. Each paycheck is essentially considered a new act of discrimination. Lawmakers recognized that because pay information is often secret, it might take months or even years for an employee to discover the inequity. The successful plaintiff can recover up to two years of back pay.

Pay equity
The idea that pay for jobs requiring comparable levels of knowledge, skill, and ability should be similar, even if actual duties differ significantly

Pay equity involves the idea that pay for jobs requiring comparable levels of knowledge, skill, and ability should be similar, even if actual duties differ significantly. This theory has also been called *comparable worth* in earlier cases. Some state laws mandate pay equity for public-sector employees. However, U.S. federal courts generally have ruled that the existence of pay differences between the different jobs held by women and men is not sufficient to prove that illegal discrimination has occurred. For instance, a court recently found that a female engineer did not face gender discrimination when she was compensated less than more experienced male colleagues who worked in higher-level engineering jobs.[30]

Ongoing interest in the notion of pay equity is due to the continuing gap between the earnings of women and men. Women have traditionally earned less than men in various occupations and professional fields. However, recent evidence suggests that these differences are slowly eroding, which is good news for gender equity in the workplace.[31] Figure 3-4 shows that the gender pay gap is shrinking, especially for Millennials. In 2012, the income of women who were 25 to 34 years old was 93% of the income earned by men. The income of all working women (ages 16 and older) was 84% of the income earned by men. However, other evidence indicates that pay gaps tend to increase as Millennials are promoted into higher-level positions.[32]

Even though the situation may be improving, gender-based pay inequity is still a concern. Women tend to take more time off during their childbearing years.

FIGURE 3-4 Women's Median Hourly Income as a Percentage of Men's Income

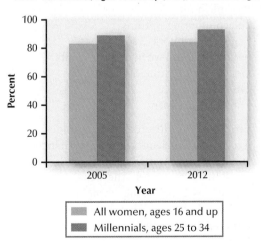

2005—All women, ages 16 and up (83%), Millennials, ages 25 to 34 (89%)
2012—All women, ages 16 and up (84%), Millennials, ages 25 to 34 (93%)

Note: Numbers represent civilian, noninstitutionalized, full-time and part-time employees with positive incomes; they do not include self-employed individuals

Source: Pew Research Survey assessment of Current Population Survey data cited in Dori Meinert, "Young Women Are Narrowing the Gender Pay Gap," *HR Magazine*, February 2014, p. 19.

This makes it difficult to remain on par with their male counterparts, resulting in a pay gap. Persistent, widespread beliefs about how women should act and how they should be treated might also negatively impact women's workplace experiences and pay.[33] One study found that biases might be driving the tendencies of managers to give men higher merit-based raises than women.[34] The following "HR Perspective: Sociometric Solutions Study Reveals Gender Bias" feature discusses that it is likely women still face workplace discrimination based on gender beliefs.

Employers can take steps to reduce pay inequities, including the following:

- For the most accurate overall picture, include all benefits and other items that are part of pay to calculate total compensation.
- Make sure people know how the organization's pay practices work.
- Base pay on the value of jobs and performance.
- Benchmark against local and national markets so that pay structures are competitive.
- Conduct frequent audits to ensure that pay is fair internally and that there are no gender-based inequities.

3-4c Managing Sex and Gender Issues

The influx of women into the workforce has had major social, economic, and organizational consequences. In particular, the growing number of women has led to more sex and gender issues related to jobs and careers. Since women bear children and traditionally play a significant role in raising children, issues of work–life balance can emerge. Respect for employees' lives outside of the workplace can pay off in terms of attracting and retaining high-quality talent. Organizations can offer a range of options to help employees achieve satisfaction in both their work and personal lives. Glassdoor.com reports that organizations on its annual list of the Top 25 Companies for Work–Life Balance have many of the following attributes, characteristics, and/or programs:

- Support from senior leadership for work–life balance programs
- Flexible hours
- Telecommuting options
- Compressed work weeks
- Family-friendly work environments
- Generous paid time off
- On-site cafeteria
- On-site fitness center

Employees at different career stages and with different household structures may seek different elements to help balance work and family obligations. For example, single employees may value flexible work arrangements but not a work–family culture. Parents may value the work–family culture and supervisors' social support. Organizations considering implementing work–family balance programs have a wide range of choices. They benefit most by customizing to their specific cultures and situations rather than adopting a one-size-fits-all approach.[35]

Glass ceiling
Discriminatory practices that have prevented women and minority status employees from advancing to executive-level jobs

Glass Ceiling For years, women's groups have alleged that women in workplaces encounter a glass ceiling, which refers to discriminatory practices that have prevented women and other minority status employees from advancing to executive-level jobs. For instance, women still hold a small percentage of top leadership jobs

PERSPECTIVE

Sociometric Solutions Study Reveals Gender Bias

Women have greatly varied workplace experiences. Some experiences are positive, while others are negative. Sheryl Sandberg, for example, was able to rise above the competitive male-dominated arena of Silicon Valley and become Facebook's chief operating officer. For other women, however, dealing with prevailing gender beliefs, cognitive biases, and work–family conflict issues can be challenging. Women also face gender biases in hiring decisions, preferences for male leadership styles, and differing attitudes about women and child rearing. Current workplace statistics are troubling—women still receive less in earnings than do men in the United States. Only 4.2% of Fortune 500 firms have female CEOs.

A recent study conducted by the data analytics company Sociometric Solutions tried to determine some of the reasons why women face these issues. Information was collected from subjects working for one of three firms in the United States, including a large banking call center, a large maker of office products, and a medium-sized pharmaceutical organization. Sensor ID badges were worn by both men and women for six weeks.

These sensors tracked their discussions with others and movement patterns. Their email, phone, and instant message information was also evaluated.

The researchers found that women outperformed men in the banking call center, but this didn't seem to get them promoted. The data also showed that men and women scored similarly with regard to interactive capabilities. But women filled only 13% of the top leadership positions in the firm (50% of the organization's employees were women). These findings suggest that there is still more that can be done to make the workplace more equitable for both women and men. Employers should focus on key performance measures and objective criteria.[36]

Based on the challenges identified in the Sociometric Solutions study, consider the following questions:

1. What other gender challenges do you think women face in the workplace?

2. What more can companies do to make women's career experiences better? What specific policies could be developed?

in corporations. As recently as 2014, only 54 of the Fortune 1000 companies are led by a female CEO.[37] Women working in other parts of the world also seem to face the glass ceiling. Women employed in Latin American countries such as Brazil, Chile, Argentina, and Mexico are not well represented in upper-level positions.[38]

Another problem is that women have tended to advance to senior management in a limited number of support or staff areas, such as HR and corporate communications. Limits that keep women from progressing only in certain fields have been referred to as glass elevators. Since executive jobs in these areas tend to pay less than jobs in other operational areas, the overall impact can be a reduction in women's career progression and income. A related issue involves the "glass cliff." This situation occurs when women and minorities are promoted into top management positions only when companies are failing, often to be replaced by white men when they don't save the organization.[39]

Breaking the Glass A number of employers have recognized that breaking the glass, whether ceilings, walls, or elevators, is good business for women and racial/ethnic minorities. Some of the most common means used to break the glass are as follows:

- Establish formal mentoring programs for women and members of racial and ethnic minorities.
- For individuals who have shown talent in their current jobs, provide opportunities for career rotation into different work areas.
- Include women and minorities as members of top management and boards of directors.
- Establish clear goals for retention and progression of women and minorities. Also, hold managers accountable for achieving these goals.
- Allow for alternative work arrangements for employees, particularly those who balance work and family responsibilities.

3-4d Sexual Orientation

A small percentage of Americans identify themselves as being lesbian, gay, bisexual, or transgender (LGBT). While there is no federal law prohibiting discrimination on the basis of sexual orientation, 18 states and the District of Columbia have passed laws to protect applicants and employees from such discrimination. In addition, various court decisions prohibit same-sex sexual harassment in the workplace. Sex discrimination based on stereotypical gender attitudes about appropriate and inappropriate mannerisms, appearance, and conduct is also inappropriate.[40]

An issue that some employers have faced is that of individuals who have had or are undergoing gender transition surgery and therapy. Federal court cases and the EEOC have ruled that sex discrimination under Title VII applies to a person's gender at birth. Thus, it does not apply to the new gender of those who have had sex transformation operations. However, managers and employees should be tolerant of such situations and show respect for individuals undergoing these procedures by making the right accommodations when needed.[41]

3-4e Nepotism

Nepotism
Practice of allowing relatives to work for the same employer

Many employers have policies that restrict or prohibit nepotism. This practice involves allowing relatives to work for the same employer. Other firms require only that relatives not work directly for or with each other or not be placed in positions where collusion or conflict could occur. Such policies most frequently cover spouses, siblings, parents, sons, and daughters. Generally, employers' antinepotism policies have been upheld by courts.

3-4f Consensual Relationships and Romance at Work

When work-based friendships lead to romance and off-the-job sexual relationships, managers and employers face a dilemma. Should they "monitor" these relationships to protect the firm from potential legal complaints, thereby "meddling" in employees' private, off-the-job lives? Or do they simply ignore these relationships and the potential problems they present? These concerns are significant given that a company's responses to workplace romances can influence perceptions of fairness and views of the organization as an employer.[42] When workplace romances occur, employees' perceptions of injustice, cognitive dissonance, and negative work norms may lead to poor work attitudes and job performance.[43]

Most executives and HR professionals agree that workplace romances are risky because they can create conflict. Dealing with this as a strategic issue means that leaders consider both the costs and the benefits in addition to the legal factors. Companies should consider developing behavioral guidelines and dating policies to help address romances at work.

LO4 Distinguish between the two types of sexual harassment and explain how employers can prevent such misconduct.

Sexual harassment
Unwelcome verbal, visual, or physical conduct of a sexual nature that is severe and affects working conditions or creates a hostile work environment

3-5 Sexual Harassment

Many women report that they have been harassed at work during their careers. This problem is a form of sex discrimination under Title VII. The Equal Employment Opportunity Commission has issued guidelines designed to curtail sexual harassment. Sexual harassment is unwelcome verbal, visual, or physical conduct of a sexual nature that is severe and affects working conditions or creates a hostile work environment. Sexual harassment can occur between a boss and a subordinate, among coworkers, and when nonemployees have business contact with employees.

Sexual harassers can be either managers or employees. In other words, working in a position of authority is not a prerequisite for such misconduct. Many of the sexual harassment charges filed involve harassment of women by men. However, a small but noteworthy number of sexual harassment claims are filed by men who claim that they were harassed by either men or women. Sexual harassment is therefore not a gender-specific issue. Both men and women can be targeted by perpetrators of either gender. Unfortunately, many claims of harassment go unreported because victims are uncomfortable, embarrassed, and/or concerned about retaliation in the workplace.

3-5a Types of Sexual Harassment

Two basic types of sexual harassment have been defined by EEOC regulations and a number of court cases. Figure 3-5 shows the two types and how they differ. They are defined as follows:

Quid pro quo
Sexual harassment that links employment outcomes to the granting of sexual favors

Hostile environment
Sexual harassment occurs when an individual's work performance or psychological well-being is unreasonably affected by intimidating or offensive working conditions

1. Quid pro quo is sexual harassment that links employment outcomes to the granting of sexual favors.
2. Hostile environment sexual harassment occurs when an individual's work performance or psychological well-being is unreasonably affected by intimidating or offensive working conditions.

In quid pro quo harassment, an employee may be promised a promotion, a special raise, or a desirable work assignment, but only if the employee grants some sexual favors to the supervisor. Since supervisors are agents of the company, the company always bears liability for quid pro quo harassment.

The second type, hostile environment harassment, may include actions such as commenting on appearance or attire, or telling jokes that are suggestive or sexual in nature. It can also include allowing revealing photos and posters to be displayed or making continual requests to get together after work. These actions can lead to the creation of a hostile work environment. If the employer has taken appropriate steps to prevent sexual harassment, it may be possible to offer an affirmative defense and prevail in a lawsuit.

FIGURE 3-5 Sexual Harassment Types

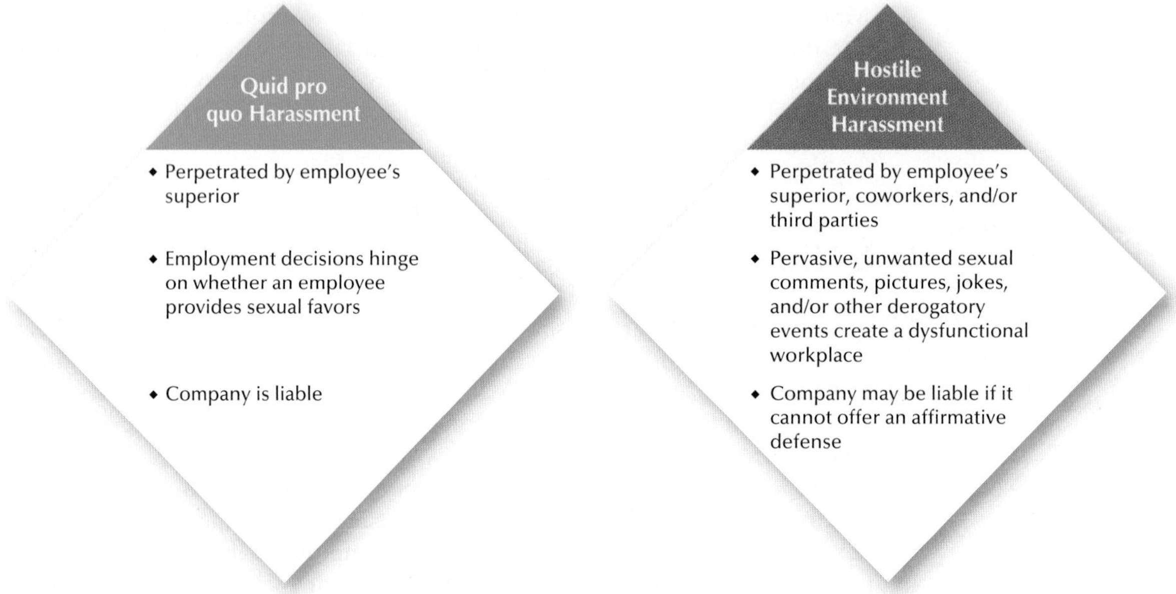

Quid pro quo Harassment

- Perpetrated by employee's superior

- Employment decisions hinge on whether an employee provides sexual favors

- Company is liable

Hostile Environment Harassment

- Perpetrated by employee's superior, coworkers, and/or third parties

- Pervasive, unwanted sexual comments, pictures, jokes, and/or other derogatory events create a dysfunctional workplace

- Company may be liable if it cannot offer an affirmative defense

3-5b Current Sexual Harassment Issues

Gender stereotyping in the workplace is becoming a critical issue related to sexual harassment. In one situation, a male ironworker employed at a construction firm was repeatedly hazed in the workplace by a male supervisor for not acting masculine enough on the job. The mistreatment included name-calling and suggestive gestures and acts. The victim was represented by the EEOC and was eventually awarded punitive and compensatory damages based on the sexual harassment he endured.[44]

GLOBAL

Electronic sexual harassment can also be an issue given the increased use of technology at work. Sexual harassment can occur when employees email each other, when they visit social networking sites, and when they access the Internet. Examples include forwarding sexual jokes through a company's email system and looking at pornographic websites and then sharing the content with coworkers. The seriousness of these issues is compounded in the global business environment because more people with varying beliefs about sexual conduct can be impacted. Companies should consider developing appropriate electronic and Internet use policies that prevent technology-based sexual harassment in international companies. Finally, fundamental differences of opinion regarding the balance of power between men and women and cultures that are more tolerant of sexual harassment lead to very different harassment situations from country to country.

3-5c Preventing Sexual Harassment

A proactive preventive approach is the most effective way to reduce sexual harassment in the workplace. If the workplace culture fosters harassment, and if policies and practices do not inhibit harassment, an employer is wise to reevaluate the workplace and solve the problem before lawsuits occur. This requires managers and HR professionals to take certain steps.

Companies may avoid liability if they take reasonable care to prohibit sexual harassment. This process is tied into what is called the affirmative defense. Important elements of the affirmative defense include the following:

- Establish a sexual harassment policy.
- Communicate the policy regularly.
- Train employees and managers on avoiding sexual harassment.
- Investigate and take action when complaints are voiced.

Companies also need to make sure that sexual harassment policies establish clear standards for appropriate conduct. Employees should also be required to acknowledge in writing that they understand these policies. Effective training to prevent sexual harassment ideally includes information about how to report sexual harassment incidents when they occur. Scenario-based discussions of actual situations can also be beneficial, and companies may want to show videos of real court cases involving sexual harassment.[45]

LO5 List key elements of disability discrimination laws.

3-6 Disability Discrimination

Several federal laws have been enacted to advance the employment of individuals with disabilities and to reduce discrimination based on disability. These laws and regulations affect employment matters as well as public accessibility for individuals with disabilities. Despite these attempts to open the workplace to individuals with disabilities, unemployment among the disabled population has consistently exceeded the overall unemployment rate, particularly during economic downturns.[46]

3-6a Rehabilitation Act

The Rehabilitation Act was passed in 1973 and represents the earliest law regarding individuals with disabilities. The law applies only to federal contractors and requires them to take affirmative action to employ workers with disabilities based on steps outlined in the contractor's AAP. The OFCCP recently established a rule that federal contractors should set a utilization goal of 7% for people who have disabilities. Other recent changes to the law include collecting and accumulating data about the disabilities of job candidates and new workers so that utilization goals can be used to evaluate progress.[47] A standardized form was created by the OFCCP to gather (every five years) disability information from applicants, newly hired employees, and others who have been working for an organization.[48] Also, individuals who claim disability discrimination do not have to "exhaust administrative remedies" (which involves submitting a grievance to a tribunal for evaluation) before pursuing a lawsuit.[49] Overall, the Rehabilitation Act has helped define many of the terms and concepts specified in subsequent laws and provides equal opportunity to applicants and workers with disabilities.

3-6b Americans with Disabilities Act

Two decades after passage of the first law prohibiting discrimination against individuals with disabilities, the Americans with Disabilities Act was enacted in 1990. This act applies to private employers, employment agencies, and labor unions with

15 or more employees; it is enforced by the EEOC. Those employed by state governments are not covered by the Americans with Disabilities Act (ADA). This means that they cannot sue in federal courts for relief and damages. However, they may still bring suits under state laws in state courts. Many of the concepts and definitions included in the ADA were based on the Rehabilitation Act.

3-6c ADA Amendments Act

In 2009, Congress passed amendments to the ADA, overruling several key cases and regulations and reflecting the original intent of the ADA. The effect was to significantly broaden the definition of individuals with disabilities to include anyone with a physical or mental impairment that substantially limits major life functions *without* regard for the helpful effects of medication, prosthetics, hearing aids, and so on. This establishes a very low threshold for establishing whether an individual is "disabled."

Who Is Disabled? A three-pronged test is used to determine whether an individual meets the definition of disabled. A person must meet one of the following three conditions, as stated in the ADA and modified by the Americans with Disabilities Act Amendments Act (ADAAA). A person with a disability is someone who

1. has a mental or physical challenge that greatly reduces the ability to perform important life functions;
2. possesses a record of such a challenge; or
3. is thought to have such a challenge.[50]

Person with a disability
Someone who has a mental or physical challenge that greatly reduces the ability to perform important life functions, who possesses a record of such a challenge, or who is thought to have such a challenge.

A person is considered to have a disability even if any corrective measures are used to reduce the impact of the disability, such as a wheelchair or medication. The only exception is ordinary eyeglasses and contact lenses. Significant life activities and functions include not just visible activities like seeing, breathing, and walking but also internal bodily functions such as those of the neurological, immune, and endocrine systems along with normal cell growth. The definition of disability no longer rests on the individual's inability to *do* something but on his or her medical condition, whether or not it limits functioning. This expanded definition of disability now encompasses a much larger percentage of workers, meaning that employers are likely to encounter situations that require action.

Some impairments such as autism, blindness, bipolar disorder, cancer, diabetes, HIV infection, and major depressive disorder are disabilities covered by the ADA. With regard to substance abuse, the ADA protects individuals who are recovering from addictions. But the law does not protect current users of illegal drugs and substances, so drug policies can still be enforced. For example, employees who suffer relapses after participating in recovery and rehabilitation programs can be terminated when return-to-work agreements have been violated.[51]

Mental Disabilities A growing area of concern to employers under the ADA (as amended) is dealing with mental disabilities. A mental disability is defined by the EEOC as "any mental or psychological disorder, such as an intellectual disability, organic brain syndrome, emotional or mental illness, and specific learning disabilities." Employers may find providing accommodations for workers with mental disabilities is more difficult and that maintaining effective performance standards is a challenge. Mental disabilities may manifest in more unpredictable ways, and medications taken to alleviate these conditions can have negative side effects.[52]

It is advisable to rely on sound medical information and avoid stereotypes regarding individuals with mental impairment or disabilities.

More ADA complaints are being filed by individuals who have or claim to have mental disabilities. Two of the top seven disabilities most frequently cited in EEOC claims for disability discrimination are mental: depression and anxiety disorder. Cases have ranged from individuals with a medical history of paranoid schizophrenia to clinical depression to individuals who claim that job stress has affected their marriage or sex life. Regardless of the type of employees' claims, it is important to treat mental disabilities in the same way as physical disabilities. Obtain medical verification of worker limitations and engage in an interactive process to establish reasonable accommodations.

Employees Who Develop Disabilities For many employers, the impact of the ADA has been the greatest when handling employees who develop disabilities, not when dealing with applicants who already have disabilities. As the workforce ages, it is likely that more employees will develop disabilities. More temporary impairments such as injuries that significantly impair life activities for shorter periods of time can also be covered by the ADA.[53] For instance, a warehouse stocker who suffers a serious leg injury in a motorcycle accident may request reasonable accommodations.

Employers should be prepared to respond to accommodation requests from employees whose contribution to the organization was satisfactory before they became disabled and who now require accommodations to continue working. If situations are handled inappropriately, these individuals can file either ADA complaints with the EEOC or private lawsuits.

Employees can sometimes be shifted to other jobs where their disabilities do not affect them as much. For instance, the warehouse firm might transfer the injured stocker to a sedentary purchasing inventory job so that climbing and lifting are unnecessary. But the problem for employers is what to do with the next worker who develops problems if an alternative job within the organization is not available. Even if the accommodations are just for one employee, the coworkers' reactions must be considered.

3-6d ADA and Job Requirements

Essential job functions
Fundamental job duties

Discrimination is prohibited against individuals with disabilities who can perform the essential job functions—the fundamental job duties—of the employment positions that those individuals hold or desire. These functions do not include marginal functions of the position. For example, an essential function for the job of cosmetologist is to cut and style hair. A marginal function of that job would be answering the telephone to schedule client appointments. An essential job function of a restaurant server is shuttling food from the kitchen to tables on the floor in a prompt manner. A marginal function of the same job is to fold napkins. The EEOC provides guidelines to help employers determine which job functions are essential. To avoid potential lawsuits, it is important that organizations support lists of essential job functions with hard evidence based on the information found in job descriptions and assessments of typical work duties.[54] Figure 3-6 lists the criteria recommended by the EEOC.

Reasonable accommodation
A modification to a job or work environment that gives a qualified individual an equal employment opportunity to perform

For a qualified person with a disability, an employer must make a reasonable accommodation. This involves modifying a job or work environment to give that individual an equal employment opportunity to perform. EEOC guidelines encourage employers and individuals to work together to determine the appropriate reasonable accommodations, rather than employers alone making those judgments.

FIGURE 3-6 Determining if a Job Function Is Essential

A Job Function May Be Considered Essential for Any of Several Reasons, Including but Not Limited to the Following:

1. The function may be essential because the reason the position exists is to perform that function.

2. The function may be essential because there is a limited number of employees available who can perform the job function.

3. The function may be highly specialized so that the job incumbent is hired for that expertise or ability to perform the particular function.

Evidence of whether a Particular Function Is Essential Includes, but Is Not Limited to the Following:

1. The employer's judgment as to which functions are essential.

2. Written job descriptions prepared before advertising or interviewing applicants for the job.

3. The amount of time spent on the job performing the function.

4. The consequences of not requiring the incumbent to perform the function.

5. The terms of a collective bargaining agreement.

6. The work experience of past incumbents in the job.

7. The current work experience of incumbents in similar jobs.

Source: Part 1630 Regulations to Implement the Equal Employment Provisions of the Americans with Disabilities Act.

A recent case demonstrates the need for organizations to provide reasonable accommodations to those with mental or physical impairments. A teacher was granted the right to pursue an ADA lawsuit based on a school district's unwillingness to transfer her to a different job to accommodate a serious back injury, even after she decided to go on disability retirement.[55] The reasonableness of the accommodations provided is also not linked solely to the performance of essential job functions. For instance, an engineer may request better parking from the firm because of a leg injury or affliction. Such a request should be seriously considered, even though it is not related to an essential job function.[56]

Under the ADAAA, the focus has shifted from determining whether an individual has a disability to an emphasis on finding ways to accommodate that individual in the workplace. The process of determining reasonable accommodations is expected to be interactive. The individual with disabilities should be an active participant in the process. Many options may be considered, but the employer has the authority to select the accommodations to be implemented.

Reasonable accommodation is limited to actions that do not place an undue hardship on an employer. An **undue hardship** occurs when making an accommodations for individuals with disabilities imposes a significant difficulty or expense

Undue hardship
Significant difficulty or expense imposed on an employer when making an accommodation for individuals with disabilities

on an employer. The ADA offers only general guidelines for determining when an accommodation becomes unreasonable and will create undue hardship for an employer. The determination of undue hardship is made on a case-by-case basis. Undue hardship might stem from financial requirements to scheduling options or facilities modifications. What might be reasonable for a large multinational company might be an undue hardship for a smaller firm with fewer resources. A recent study found that people who have disabilities are more inclined to ask for accommodations than are individuals who do not have disabilities. But the kinds of requests and associated costs and benefits were similar (an example of such a request could involve asking for an accommodation related to work scheduling). Providing reasonable accommodations also leads to positive work attitudes.[57] Companies are therefore more likely to attract and retain employees if they take steps to ensure a supportive corporate culture. They can do this with managers and supervisors who are trained to deal with the special needs of individuals with disabilities.

The key to making reasonable accommodations is identifying the essential job functions and then determining which accommodations are reasonable so that the individual can perform the core job duties. Common means of reasonable accommodation are shown in Figure 3-7. Architectural barriers should not block individuals with disabilities from accessing work areas or restrooms. Appropriate work tasks must be assigned or modified to allow individuals with disabilities to perform them effectively. This may mean modifying jobs or work area layouts, or providing assistive devices or special equipment. Work hours and break schedules may be adjusted. Fortunately, most necessary accommodations are relatively inexpensive. Free assistance is readily available from the Job Accommodation Network's online resource center.[58]

ADA Restrictions and Medical Information The ADA restricts employers' attempts to obtain and retain medical information related to applicants and

FIGURE 3-7   Common Means of Reasonable Accommodation

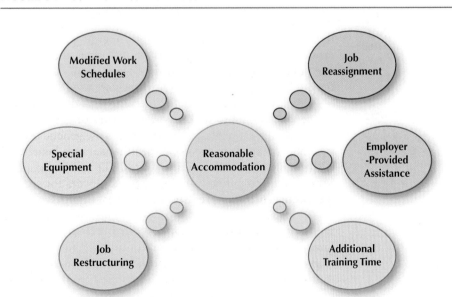

Source: Adapted from Job Accommodation Network, http://askjan.org/index.html.

employees. Restrictions include prohibiting employers from rejecting individuals because of a disability and from asking job applicants any question about current or past medical history until a conditional job offer is made. Also, the ADA prohibits the use of pre-employment medical exams, except for drug tests, until a job has been conditionally offered. An additional ADA requirement is that all medical information be maintained in files separated from general personnel files; they must be stored in a secure location, and access should be granted only on a need-to-know basis.

3-6e Claims of Discrimination

During the decade prior to the enactment of the ADAA, approximately 16,000 disability discrimination claims were filed with the EEOC each year. In 2014, that number skyrocketed to over 25,000 claims, representing a 17% increase in the historical average. Experts attribute this increase to changes made in how the ADAA defines a disability. Prior to the ADAA, employers won 90% of challenges regarding whether an individual actually had a disability. Now that argument is essentially moot. Companies no longer aggressively work to disqualify individuals from that status.

Claims of discrimination are more common at the lower levels of organizations. However, the CEO of a home furnishings retailer filed charges of disability discrimination, claiming that the board of directors perceived her to have a disability—based on a recent diagnosis of breast cancer—and terminated her employment. This case shows that *being regarded* as having a disability qualifies an individual for protection under the law, whether or not the person shows any outward impairment or requests an accommodation. This is an example of the second prong of the definition of *individual with disabilities* and sends a note of caution that treating someone as if they have a disability grants them coverage under the law. In fact, "regarded as" claims represent the highest percentage of claims filed in ADA charges.[59] Figure 3-8 shows the most frequent disabilities identified in ADA charges.

ETHICS

3-6f Genetic Bias Regulations

Related to medical disabilities is the emerging area of workplace genetic bias. As medical research has revealed the human genome, medical tests have been developed that can identify an individual's genetic markers for various diseases. Whether these tests should be used and how they are used can raise ethical issues.

Employers that use genetic screening tests do so for two primary reasons. Some use genetic testing to make workers aware of genetic problems that may exist so that medical treatments can begin. Others use genetic testing to terminate employees who may make extensive use of health insurance benefits, thus raising the employer's benefits costs and utilization rates. The railroad company Burlington Northern Santa Fe had to publicly apologize to employees for secretly testing to determine if they were genetically predisposed to carpal tunnel syndrome.

Genetic Information Nondiscrimination Act Congress passed the Genetic Information Nondiscrimination Act in 2009 to limit health insurance plans' use of genetic information and to prohibit employment discrimination on the basis of this information. Employers are prohibited from collecting genetic information or making employment decisions on the basis of genetic information, which includes information about the employee and/or family members' genetic tests and family medical history.[60]

FIGURE 3-8 Most Frequent ADA Charges Filed in 2013

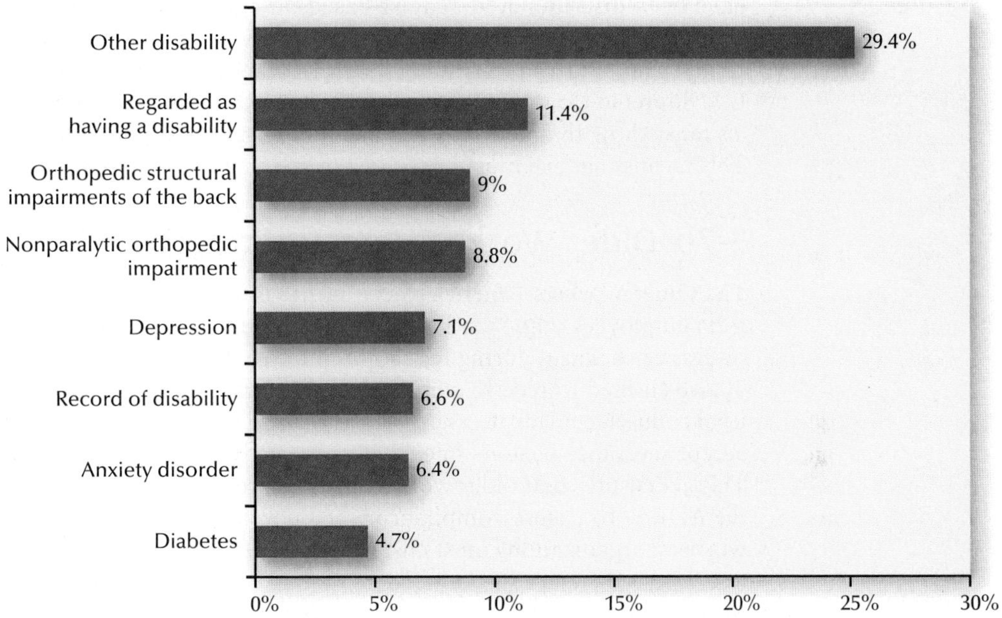

Other disability — 29.4%
Regarded as having a disability — 11.4%
Orthopedic structural impairments of the back — 9%
Nonparalytic orthopedic impairment — 8.8%
Depression — 7.1%
Record of disability — 6.6%
Anxiety disorder — 6.4%
Diabetes — 4.7%

(scale: 0% 5% 10% 15% 20% 25% 30%)

Source: Based on data from the U.S. Equal Employment Opportunity Commission, 2013, http://www.eeoc.gov/eeoc/statistics/enforcement/ada-receipts.cfm

3-7 Age Discrimination Laws

LO6 Discuss the legal protections to prevent bias and discrimination based on age, religion, national origin, and other factors.

The populations of most developed countries, including Australia, Japan, most European countries, and the United States, are aging.[61] These changes mean that as older workers with a lifetime of experiences and skills retire, companies face significant challenges in replacing them with workers with the proper capabilities and work ethic. However, many senior employees decide to continue working beyond what is considered a typical retirement age. This reality can challenge companies to manage various generational differences and preferences in the workplace.

GLOBAL

Many countries have enacted laws prohibiting age discrimination. For example, EU member nations, Australia, India, Argentina, Canada, and Chile focus on preventing age discrimination in recruitment, promotion, training, and retirement-related actions.[62] In the United States, employment discrimination against individuals age 40 and older is prohibited by the Age Discrimination in Employment Act.

3-7a Age Discrimination in Employment Act

The Age Discrimination in Employment Act (ADEA) of 1967, amended in 1978 and 1986, prohibits discrimination in terms, conditions, or privileges of employment against all individuals age 40 or older employed by organizations having 20 or more workers. However, state employees may not sue state government employers in federal courts because the ADEA is a federal law.

As with most equal employment issues, what constitutes age discrimination continues to be defined by the courts and the EEOC. Individuals who believe they have been discriminated against based on age usually must show that they are a member of a protected group based on age, were performing well on the job, were terminated, and were terminated in part based on age.[63] However, based on the U.S. Supreme Court decision in *Gross vs. FBL Financial Services* (2009), individuals must show that age was the "but-for" trigger of a particular personnel decision. This means that age must be the key factor that causes a particular outcome.[64]

3-7b Older Workers Benefit Protection Act

The Older Workers Benefit Protection Act is an amendment to the ADEA and protects employees who sign liability waivers for age discrimination in exchange for severance packages during reductions in force. For example, workers over the age of 40 are entitled to receive complete and accurate information on available benefits, legal counsel from an attorney, and a specified number of weeks to decide whether to accept severance benefits in exchange for waiving their right to sue the employer.[65] This act ensures that older workers are not pressured into waiving their rights under the ADEA. To ensure compliance when developing procedures for laying off older workers, organizations must ensure legal oversight and a strict protocol.

3-7c Managing Age Discrimination

One issue that has led to age discrimination charges is saying older workers are overqualified for certain jobs or promotions. A recent survey found that many older workers find the job search process challenging, and about one-third are called overqualified.[66] In a number of cases, courts have ruled that the term *overqualified* may have been used as a code word for workers being too old, thus causing them not to be considered for employment. Selection and promotion practices must be age neutral. For example, terminating an older salesperson based on inaccurate and undocumented claims of poor performance and hiring younger professionals with no sales experience as replacements are suspicious practices that could lead to a lawsuit.[67] Older workers also face substantial barriers to entry in a number of occupations, especially those requiring significant amounts of training or for which new technology has been recently developed.

In some cases involving older employees, comments made by employers such as "hang up the Superman cape," "shelf life," "let's hire a recent college graduate," or "new blood" were considered to determine if age discrimination existed.[68] Managers and employees need to be careful about making comments that could be viewed as biased or discriminatory.

Stereotypes about older workers abound and are often negative. Many people mistakenly believe that older workers are less productive, resistant to change, more costly to employ and pay, and less trainable. Evidence suggests that many of these stereotypes are unfounded. A recent study found that out of six common stereotypes, only one (older employees are less motivated to attend training and development sessions) was linked to any actual findings.[69] Regardless of their accuracy, these beliefs can adversely impact older workers' ability to make positive contributions to organizations and thus be appropriately rewarded and recognized.

Companies should provide training to managers and employees to educate them about age-related biases and stereotypes. It is also important to encourage them to not make comments that could be seen as biased against older workers.[70] Providing older workers with interesting employment opportunities can also promote diversity in the workplace. A study found that developing inclusive HR policies related to age and creating a climate of age diversity leads to positive employee–employer exchanges, increased organizational performance, and reduced intentions to quit.[71] To counter significant staffing difficulties, some employers recruit older people to return to the workforce through part-time and other attractive scheduling options. During the past decade, the number of older workers holding part-time jobs has increased. It is likely that the number of older workers interested in working part-time will continue to grow.

A strategy employers use to retain the talents of older workers for a period of time is phased retirement, an approach that enables employees to gradually reduce their workloads and pay levels. This option is growing in use as a way to provide greater personal flexibility to older workers with significant knowledge and experience. Organizations also retain them for their valuable capabilities. Some firms rehire their retirees as part-time workers, independent contractors, or consultants, strategies intended to help the company retain its institutional knowledge and history.

Phased retirement
Approach that enables employees to gradually reduce their workloads and pay levels

3-8 Religion and Spirituality in the Workplace

The United States is fairly diverse with regard to religious beliefs, and this wide range of faiths may evolve as immigrant populations bring with them diverse cultural and religious practices. Figure 3-9 shows the percentage of U.S. adults that practice particular faiths. Religious diversity in the United States is also reflected in the workplace, and this increasing diversity requires organizations to put greater emphasis on religious considerations.

FIGURE 3-9   Religious Preferences Found in the United States, 2012

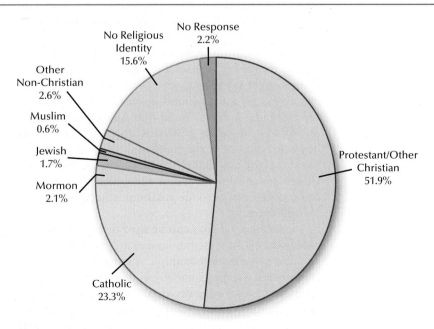

Source: Gallup, January 2–November 30, 2012; cited in Dori Meinert, "Matters of Faith," *HR Magazine*, December 2013, pp. 18–24.

Title VII of the Civil Rights Act prohibits discrimination on the basis of religion. Religious discrimination can take many forms, from hostile remarks to refusal to promote individuals because they have different beliefs. Employees should avoid making comments that could be viewed as offensive to someone's religious beliefs. Employment decisions should not be influenced by workers' religious beliefs.

A related issue concerns religious expression. Employees have sued employers for prohibiting them from expressing their religious beliefs at work. In other situations, employers have taken action because workers complain that their colleagues are aggressively "pushing" their religious views at work, thus creating a hostile environment. For instance, a teacher at an Ohio public school was fired for insubordination because he would not remove religious symbols from his classroom and included specific religious references in his teachings on different subject matters.[72]

Organizations should also be cautious about promoting certain religious practices and faiths. Executives and owners of some firms have strong religious beliefs that are carried over into their companies. Some even display religious symbols, sponsor religious study and prayer sessions, and support other religious efforts. But such actions can alienate those with different beliefs and create a negative work environment. It is generally considered acceptable to display more secularized religious items in the workplace such as Christmas trees or pictures of Santa Claus in a manner that does not offend or attempt to convert others. To achieve consistency, employees of all faiths should be given the opportunity to display religious symbols in similar (and often specified) ways. Also, holiday parties should be more general—rather than specifically religious—in focus, and attendance should be voluntary.[73]

Employers must make reasonable accommodation efforts regarding an employee's religious beliefs unless they create an undue hardship for the employer. Problems can arise because of conflicts between employer policies and employee religious practices such as dress and other aspects of appearance. Some religions have standards about appropriate attire for women and shaving or hair length for men. Generally, employers are encouraged to make exceptions to their dress code policies unless public image is so critical that it represents a business necessity. Deferring to customer preferences in making these determinations is risky and may lead to charges of unlawful discrimination. Employers are also on firmer ground when worker safety is involved and they refuse to modify dress or appearance policies. Employer must be made aware of religious practices so that accommodations can be made. A court found that Abercrombie & Fitch did not commit religious discrimination when a Muslim applicant was denied employment because her headscarf did not fit the company's dress code. She never mentioned the attire was based on faith and that she needed a reasonable accommodation. However, a recent United States Supreme Court ruling overturned this decision, which indicates that companies must provide reasonable accommodations even when not requested by employees.[74]

Sometimes religion can be used directly to make employment decisions. Faith-based schools and institutions can use religion as a BFOQ for employment practices on a limited scale. For example, a university affiliated with a particular religion can lawfully ask questions about job applicants' religious beliefs and evaluate responses when they make hiring decisions when the job involves promoting a particular faith. However, religious organizations must still evaluate jobs on a case by case basis to make sure that they include a faith-based component; otherwise, jobs can be open to all candidates.

3-8a Managing Religious Diversity

Managing religious diversity can be a significant challenge for organizations. The EEOC recommends that employers consider the following reasonable accommodations for employees' religious beliefs and practices:

- Scheduling changes, voluntary substitutes, and shift swaps
- Changing an employee's job tasks or providing a lateral transfer
- Making an exception to dress and grooming rules
- Making accommodations related to paying union dues or agency fees
- Making accommodations related to necessary prayer, proselytizing, and other forms of religious expression

HR staff should also teach employees about diverse religious beliefs and provide managers with proper guidelines about how to make appropriate religious accommodations. They can also instruct workers about their rights and consider all religious holidays before scheduling company activities.[75]

Recent evidence also suggests that religion may not be an overwhelming challenge for organizations. In fact, it may be used to create a competitive advantage. A Workplace Options survey found that 44% of workers discuss religion and politics with their colleagues, but only 9% think that religion is the main cause of workplace conflict. Further, 17% claimed that the main cause of conflict involves disagreements over politics, and 52% pointed to work issues.[76] In an effort to increase understanding and appreciation—as well as to enhance the bottom line—companies such as Tyson Foods and American Airlines are encouraging religious discussions in the workplace. These firms have developed chaplain programs and faith-based educational groups.[77]

3-9 Managing Other Discrimination Issues

A number of other factors such as national origin and immigration, language, military status, and appearance and weight might lead to unlawful discrimination. In addition to Title VII protections, a number of federal laws have been enacted to address these forms of discrimination. Many of these laws were passed in response to improper company decisions that resulted in unfair treatment of applicants or employees.

3-9a Immigration Reform and Control Acts

The United States is home to many millions of foreign-born residents, including people from Latin America, the Middle East, and Asia. The influx of immigrants has led to extensive political, social, and employment-related debates. In particular, growing numbers of children and families have been illegally immigrating to Texas and other border states over the past several years, which has prompted many heated discussions among politicians.[78] Debates (and some associated myths) about immigration have centered on issues such as the payment of taxes, deportation, family unification, and the hiring of needed talent.[79] In addition, some immigration reform proposals have focused on tightening border security, encouraging better enforcement in companies, and verifying individuals' employability.[80] The Immigration Reform and Control Act (IRCA), enacted in 1986, requires that employers verify the employment eligibility status of all employees, while not discriminating because of national origin or ethnic background. Employers may not knowingly hire unauthorized workers for employment in the United States.

Regardless of company size, every employer must comply with the provisions of the act. High-profile Immigration and Customs Enforcement (ICE) raids on employers have led to audits of thousands of employers and the imposition of millions of dollars in penalties.[81] Employers ignore these obligations at their own peril. Within the first three days of employment, each employee must complete an Employment Eligibility Verification (commonly called an I-9) form and provide documents proving that he or she is legally authorized to work in the United States. Figure 3-10 lists the documents accepted in this process. The employer is required to inspect the documents and maintain records for all new hires. The E-verify federal database instantly verifies the employment eligibility of employees. Federal contractors are required to use the system, as are employers in a number of states where it has been mandated. Other employers may use the system to check and verify employees' legal status.[82]

Visa Requirements Various revisions to the IRCA changed some of the restrictions on the entry of immigrants to work in U.S. organizations, particularly organizations with high-technology and other "scarce skill" areas. More immigrants with specific skills have been allowed legal entry, and categories for entry visas were revised. Among the most common visas encountered by employers are the B1 for business visitors, H-1B for professional or specialized workers, and L-1 for intra-company transfers. The O-1A visa designation is reserved for foreigners who have special skill sets that place them at the apex of their professions, for example, successful athletes, scientists, academics, and businesspersons.[83]

To discourage hiring immigrants rather than U.S. workers, an employer must file documents with the Labor Department and pay prevailing U.S. wages to the visa holders. Despite these regulations, a number of unions and other entities view such programs as ways to circumvent the limits on hiring foreign workers. Another issue involves same-sex partners. The U.S. Supreme Court ruling states that same-sex partner applications for citizenship will be treated the same way

FIGURE 3-10   Primary Documents to Certify I-9 Compliance

List A	List B	List C
• U.S. passport	• Driver's license or state-issued ID card	• U.S. social security card
• Certificate of U.S. citizenship	• ID card issued by federal, state, or local government	• Certification of birth abroad
• Certificate of naturalization	• School ID card with photograph	• Original or certified copy of birth certificate
• Unexpired foreign passport	• Voter's registration card	• Native American tribal document
• Permanent residence card	• U.S. military card or draft record	• U.S. citizen ID card

as those submitted by spouses of the opposite sex, which can affect their employment opportunities.[84]

3-9b Language Issues

As the diversity of the workforce increases, more employees have language skills in addition to English. Interestingly, some employers have attempted to restrict the use of foreign languages at work, while other employers have recognized that bilingual employees have valuable skills. There has been much debate on both sides of the issue. EEOC guidelines have not been entirely clear about how companies should address these issues.[85]

Some employers have policies requiring that employees speak only English at work. These employers contend that the policies are necessary for valid business purposes. The EEOC has issued guidelines clearly stating that employers may require workers to speak only English at certain times or in certain situations, but the business necessity of the requirements must be justified.[86] Teaching, customer service, and telemarketing are examples of positions that may require English skills and voice clarity.

Some employers have found it beneficial to have bilingual employees so that foreign-language customers can contact someone who speaks their language. Bilingual employees are especially needed among police officers, airline flight personnel, hospital interpreters, international sales representatives, and travel guides. Employers should also be aware of legal messages that need to be presented in multiple languages, such as posters that discuss the requirements associated with the Family and Medical Leave Act.[87]

3-9c Military Status Protections

The employment rights of military veterans and reservists have been addressed in several laws. The two most important are the Vietnam Era Veterans Readjustment Assistance Act of 1974 and the Uniformed Services Employment and Reemployment Rights Act (USERRA) of 1994. Under the former, federal contractors are supposed to provide employment opportunities for veterans based on percentage benchmarks that are not related to quotas.[88] Under the latter, employees are required to notify their employers of military service obligations. Employers must give employees serving in the military leaves of absence protections under USERRA, as Figure 3-11 highlights.

With the use of reserves and National Guard troops abroad, the provisions of USERRA have had more impact on employers. Requirements regarding benefits, disabilities, and reemployment are covered in the act. For example, USERRA does not require employers to pay employees while they are on military leave, but many firms voluntarily provide additional compensation to bridge the gap between military pay and regular pay. Uniformed military personnel are also provided up to five years of active duty service leave during which the employer must hold their job. Service members who return from duty are to be staffed in the jobs they would have *worked in* or been automatically *promoted into* had they not left the company for military service. These jobs are referred to as "escalator positions."[89] However, federal law may require companies to promote returning service members in situations where there is some certainty that they would have received a discretionary promotion.[90] This does not mean that returning service members have to be retained when they are underperforming. The same is true when the company is conducting employee layoffs.[91]

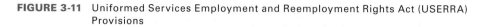

FIGURE 3-11 Uniformed Services Employment and Reemployment Rights Act (USERRA) Provisions

Helping military veterans find work is a key HR issue in organizations today. A number of organizations provide these individuals with employment support. Joining Forces Mentoring Plus is one such group that was started by the Business and Professional Women's Foundation in January 2012 to provide career support for female soldiers, wounded warrior caregivers, and military spouses.[92] Companies can also be awarded the Work Life Legacy Military Award by the Families and Work Institute for outstanding efforts to assist military personnel and their families with available employment opportunities.[93] Some of the top jobs for military personnel based on their professional background include technician, engineer, IT professional, mechanic, and sales representative.[94]

3-9d Appearance and Weight Discrimination

Several EEOC cases have been filed concerning the physical appearance of employees. Court decisions consistently have allowed employers to set dress codes and appearance standards as long as they are applied uniformly. For example, establishing a dress code for women but not for men has been ruled discriminatory. Also, employers should be cautious when enforcing dress standards for female employees whose religions prescribe appropriate and inappropriate dress and appearance standards. Some individuals have brought cases of employment discrimination based on height or weight. Employers must link any weight or height requirements to specific job functions.

Complying with this complex array of regulations requires diligence and careful record keeping. Appendix F provides details on the EEO enforcement process, information about records retention, and the investigation process.

3-10 Diversity Training

Traditional diversity training has a number of goals. A primary goal is to minimize discrimination and harassment lawsuits. Other goals focus on improving acceptance and understanding of people with different backgrounds, experiences, capabilities, and lifestyles. Employees are encouraged to recognize, evaluate, and appreciate differences.

3-10a Components of Traditional Diversity Training

Diversity training programs often have three components. *Legal awareness* is the first and most common component. Here, the training focuses on the legal implications of discrimination. This limited approach to diversity training focuses only on these legal "do's and don'ts."

Through *cultural awareness* training, organizations hope to build greater understanding of the differences among people. Cultural awareness training helps all participants see and accept the differences in people with widely varying cultural backgrounds.

The third component of diversity training—*sensitivity training*—is more difficult. The aim here is to "sensitize" people to the differences among them and how their words and behaviors are seen by others. Some diversity training includes exercises containing examples of harassment and other misbehaviors.

3-10b Mixed Results for Diversity Training

The results of diversity training are viewed as mixed by both organizations and participants. Studies on the effectiveness of diversity training raise some concern that the programs may be interesting or entertaining but may not produce longer-term changes in people's attitudes and behaviors toward others with characteristics different from their own.[95]

Some argue that traditional diversity training more often than not has failed because it has not reduced discrimination and harassment complaints. Rather than reducing conflict, in a number of situations, diversity training has increased hostility and conflict. In some firms, it has produced divisive effects and has not changed behaviors so that employees can work well together in a diverse workplace.

Negative consequences of diversity training may manifest themselves broadly in a backlash against all diversity efforts. Women and members of racial minorities sometimes see diversity programs as inadequate and nothing but "lip service." Thus, by establishing diversity programs, employers may raise expectations but fail to meet them. Some individuals who are in the majority (primarily white males) may also interpret the emphasis on diversity as assigning them blame for societal problems. Finally, diversity programs might be perceived as benefiting only women and racial minorities and taking away opportunities from white men.

3-10c Improving Diversity Training Efforts

Focusing on behavior seems to hold the most promise for making diversity training more effective. For instance, cultural diversity training that teaches sales representatives and managers how to positively communicate with people from diverse backgrounds should produce positive results. Trainers emphasize that the key to avoiding backlash in diversity efforts is to stress that people can believe whatever they wish, but at work, their values are less important than their *behaviors*. Dealing with diversity is not about what people can and cannot *say*. It is about being *respectful* to others.

SUMMARY

- Equal employment is an attempt to level the field of opportunity for all people at work.
- Laws have been enacted to prohibit making employment decisions based on age, color, disability, national origin, race, religion, and other protected characteristics.
- The Equal Employment Opportunity Commission and Office of Federal Contract Compliance programs are the primary enforcement agencies in employment discrimination laws.
- Disparate treatment occurs when individuals are treated differently on the basis of a protected characteristic.
- Disparate impact occurs when employment decisions work to the disadvantage of individuals on the basis of a protected characteristic.
- Employers may be able to use business necessity, job relatedness, and bona fide occupational qualifications (BFOQ) to defend their management practices.
- Title VII of the 1964 Civil Rights Act was the first significant equal employment law. The Civil Rights Act of 1991 altered and expanded the 1964 provisions.
- Retaliation claims now rank as the most common reason individuals file EEO claims.
- Executive orders issued by the president govern the relationship between federal contractors and the U.S. government.
- Affirmative action has been intensely litigated, and the debate continues today.
- Several laws on sex/gender discrimination have addressed issues regarding pregnancy discrimination, unequal pay for similar jobs, and sexual harassment.
- As more women have entered the workforce, sex/gender issues in equal employment have included both discrimination through pay inequity and discrimination in jobs and careers.
- The courts have defined two types of sexual harassment—quid pro quo and hostile environment.
- It is vital that employers train all employees on what constitutes sexual harassment, promptly investigate complaints, and take action when sexual harassment is found to have occurred.
- The Americans with Disabilities Act (ADA) requires that most employers identify the essential functions of jobs and make reasonable accommodations for individuals with disabilities unless doing so would result in undue hardship.
- Employment discrimination against persons older than age 40 is illegal according to the Age Discrimination in Employment Act (ADEA).
- Employers are required to make reasonable accommodations for employees with religious beliefs and practices.
- The Immigration Reform and Control Acts (IRCA) regulate the employment of workers from other countries who work in the United States.
- A number of other employment concerns have been addressed by laws, including discrimination based on religion, military status, and other factors.
- Diversity training has had limited success, possibly because it too often has focused on beliefs rather than behaviors.

CRITICAL THINKING CHALLENGES

1. Discuss some of the protected characteristics covered by equal employment opportunity laws and why they are important in today's employment setting.

2. You recently learned that two of your key female employees will be taking maternity leave around the same time. What procedures or rules do you need to be aware of based on the Pregnancy Discrimination Act (PDA)?

3. Give an example of sexual harassment you may have witnessed or heard about. If you had been the HR manager, how would you have handled the situation?

4. Use the U.S. Department of Labor website (www.usdol.gov) to further research a topic discussed in this chapter. Be sure to understand what the particular law (act) is protecting and what the rules are that companies need to follow to comply with this act.

<table>
<tr><td>CASE</td><td>Conflict over an Employee's Pregnancy at UPS</td></tr>
</table>

There is sometimes pushback in companies when women become pregnant and request changes to their work schedules and responsibilities. In some instances, pregnant women are asked to take unpaid leave or are pressured to quit their positions. The troubling fact is that many of these situations could be more effectively handled with some type of accommodation that is both reasonable and fair. Providing reasonable accommodations to pregnant women, similar to those provided to individuals with physical or mental challenges, is the best strategy for avoiding poor morale and potential lawsuits. Pregnancy discrimination falls under the umbrella of many major employment laws.

A UPS driver, who had been working for the company for seven years at the Landover, Maryland facility, faced some of these issues when she became pregnant. She was sent to the firm's nurse, who told her that she needed to see a doctor to get a more detailed assessment of her needs. The doctor provided her with a note stating that she should not lift packages heavier than 20 pounds. This requirement was not an issue because she mostly dealt with light materials. Upon submitting the note, she was told that the company had a policy stating that lightweight duties could not be given to individuals who had health concerns that were caused outside of the workplace. Her manager indicated that she was a potential liability, and that she should return to her job after her pregnancy was over. Consequently, the individual's pay and benefits came to a halt. The HR department was not contacted because she assumed that the company was following its stated policies.

While on unpaid leave, she pursued a complaint in federal court that UPS violated the requirements of the Pregnancy Discrimination Act (PDA). A district court decided that UPS was not in violation of the PDA. The Fourth U.S. Circuit Court of Appeals supported this decision, stating that UPS's policy did not adversely target the employee based on her pregnancy. It is speculated that the ruling might have been different if the case had occurred after the ADAAA was passed. Maryland also passed a law that provides pregnant employees special accommodations similar to those given to individuals who have short-term physical challenges.[96]

QUESTIONS

1. What can HR professionals do to mitigate concerns about pregnancy discrimination in the workplace? What does the law say companies need to do to avoid violating the rights of pregnant employees?

2. If you were an HR manager at UPS, how would you have handled the situation described in the case? How could the employee's immediate manager have handled the situation differently?

SUPPLEMENTAL CASES

Worker Exploitation at Foxconn/Hon Hai

This case discusses how labor laws in China provide limited protection for workers, raising ethical concerns when U.S. companies do business with firms located there. (For the case, go to http://www.cengage.com/management/mathis.)

Keep on Trucking

This case illustrates the problems that can be associated with the use of employment tests that have not been validated. (For the case, go to http://www.cengage.com/management/mathis.)

Mitsubishi Believes in EEO—Now

This case shows the problems Mitsubishi had with sexual harassment in the United States. (For the case, go to http://www.cengage.com/management/mathis.)

Religious Accommodation?

This case shows how companies must deal with employees from many cultures and religions. (For the case, go to http://www.cengage.com/management/mathis.)

END NOTES

1. Adapted from Dori Meinert, "Matters of Faith," *HR Magazine,* December 2013, pp. 18–24.

2. "Civil Rights Movement," August 2012, http://www.history.com/topics/civil-rights-movement.

3. Debra Steiner Friedman, "State of the States," *HR Magazine,* March 2014, pp. 59–62.

4. Allen Smith, "EEOC to Focus on Hiring, Pay and Harassment," *HR Magazine,* February 2013, p. 11.

5. "Global Employment Law: NLRB Ruling Complicates Employers' Internal Investigations," August 2012, http://www.globalemploymentlaw.com/articles.

6. Adapted from Stephen J. Hirschfeld, "Global Employee Handbooks Must Balance Compliance with Culture," *SHRM Online,* November 18, 2013, http://www.shrm.org/hrdisciplines/global/articles/pages/global-employee-handbooks-compliance.aspx.

7. Dana Wilkie, "Discrimination Trends," *HR Magazine,* December 2013, p. 61.

8. Tara Craft Adams, "EEOC Ordered to Pay Fees for Groundless Pursuit of Criminal Background Check Lawsuit," *SHRM* Online, October 25, 2013, http://www.shrm.org/legalissues/federalresources/pages/eeoc-fees-groundless-lawsuit.aspx.

9. *Griggs v. Duke Power Co.,* 401 U.S. 424, (1971); Mary Birk, "RIFs: Use Statistical Analysis to Avoid Disparate Impact Based on Age," *Legal Report Society for Human Resources Management,* April 2008, pp. 5–8.

10. H. John Bernardin, Robert Konopaske, and Christine M. Hagan, "A Comparison of Adverse Impact Levels Based on Top-Down, Multisource, and Assessment Center Data: Promoting Diversity and Reducing Legal Challenges," *Human Resource Management* 51 (2012), 313–341.

11. David Shadovitz, "Questioning Criminal Backgrounds," *Human Resource Executive,* October 2, 2011, p. 10; Leslie Silverman, "What HR Professionals Need to Know about the EEOC's New Guidance on Criminal Background Checks," www.shrm.org, 2012; Allen Smith, "Pepsi Settles Dispute over Criminal Checks for $3 Million," *HR Magazine,* March 2012, p. 14.

12. Allen Smith, "Texas Challenges EEOC Felon Guidance," *SHRM Online,* November 12, 2013, http://www.shrm.org/legalissues/federalresources/pages/eeoc-felon-guidance.aspx; Allen Smith, "Texas Loses Skirmish with EEOC over Criminal Background Checks," *SHRM Online,* August 26, 2014, http://www.shrm.org/legalissues/federalresources/pages/texas-eeoc-criminal-background-checks.aspx.

13. Naomi Cossack, "Employee Arrests, Part-Timers, Pay Increases," *HR Magazine,* February 2013, p. 20.

14. Sara Murray, "Credit Checks on Job Seekers by Employers Attract Scrutiny," *Wall Street Journal,* October 21, 2010; SHRM White Paper, "Hiring: Background Checks: Can We Run Credit Reports and Use Them as Part of our Employee Selection Process?" April 28, 2012.

15. Amanda Bolliger, "Award of $417,955 Upheld in Retaliation Case," *HR Magazine,* May 2012, p. 65.

16. Adapted from Melanie Pate and Mary Ellen Simonson, "Effective Responses to EEOC Charges," *HR Magazine,* October 2013, pp. 73–75.

17. Based on *EEOC v. Cognis Corp.,* No. 10-CV-2182 C.D. III (2012); http://www1.eeoc.gov//eeoc/newsroom/release/5-29-12.cfm.

18. Jamie Prenkert, "Handle with Care: Avoiding and Managing Retaliation Claims," *Business Horizons,* May 2012, p. 1; Lisa Cooney, "Understanding and Preventing Workplace Retaliation," *Massachusetts Law Review* 88 (2003); http://www.massbar.org/publications/massachusetts-law-review/2003/v88-n1/understanding-and-preventing-workplace-retaliation.

19. "U.S. Equal Employment Opportunity Commission: Title I. Federal Civil Rights Remedies, Damages in Cases of International Discrimination," 2012, http://www.eeoc.gov/laws/statutes/cra-1991.cfm.

20. Susan R. Heylman, "No Punitive Damages Allowed under Iowa's Non-discrimination Law," *HR Magazine,* September 2013, p. 16.

21. "U.S. Equal Employment Opportunity Commission: EEOC Race Discrimination Case against YRC/Yellow Transportation Ends with $11 Million Decree," June 29, 2012, http://www.eeoc.gov/eeoc/newsroom/release/6-29-12a.cfm; "U.S. Equal Employment Opportunity Commission: Caldwell Freight Lines to Pay $120,000 to Settle EEOC Race Discrimination Lawsuit," August 3, 2012, http://www.eeoc.gov/eeoc/newsroom/release/8-3-12.cfm.

22. Olaf Asplundh and Oskar Nordstrom Skans, "Do Anonymous Job Application Procedures Level the Playing Field?" *Industrial and Labor Relations Review* 65 (2012), 82–107.

23. Jennifer Colvin, "Black Police Officer Sergeant Denied Transfer May Pursue Claim," *HR Magazine,* February 2014, p. 49.

24. La Toy M. Palmer, "Was HR Manager's Comment Admissible in Bias Case? *SHRM Online,* October 17, 2013, http://www.shrm.org/legalissues/federalresources/pages/hr-managers-comment-bias-case.aspx.

25. Adam R Gardner, "No Finding of Race Discrimination in Failure-to-Promote Case," *HR Magazine,* April 2013, p. 74.

26. Adrienne Fox, "Great Expectations," *HR Magazine,* February 2014, pp. 22–27.

27. Rita Zeidner, "NYC Employers Must Accommodate Pregnant Employees," *HR Magazine,* March 2014, p. 17.

28. "Italian Women Hoping for Workplace Changes, Protection vs. Discrimination," *Business World,* August 13, 2012.

29. Adrienne Fox, "Great Expectations," *HR Magazine,* February 2014, pp. 22–27.

30. Michael D. Malone, "Female Engineer Lacks Triable Gender-Bias Claim," *HR Magazine,* March 2014, p. 55.

31. Dori Meinert, "Young Women Are Narrowing the Gender Pay Gap," *HR Magazine,* February 2014, p. 19.

32. Dana Wilkie, "Millennials Closing Pay Gap, but Not Cutting Apron Strings, *SHRM Online,* December 4, 2014, http://www.shrm.org/publications/hrmagazine/editorialcontent/2014/1014/pages/1014-execbrief.aspx.

33. Dana Wilkie, "Millennials Closing Pay Gap, but Not Cutting Apron Strings, *SHRM Online,* December 4, 2014, http://www.shrm.org/publications/hrmagazine/

editorialcontent/2014/1014/
pages/1014-execbrief.aspx.

34. Stephen Benard, "Why His Merit
Raise Is Bigger Than Hers," *Harvard
Business Review,* April 2012, p. 26.

35. Jacquelyn Smith, "The Top 25 Com-
panies for Work-Life Balance," *Forbes,*
August 10, 2012; Colette Darcy,
Alma McCarthy, Jimmy Hill, and
Geraldine Grady, "Work-Life Balance:
One Size Fits All? An Exploratory
Analysis of the Differential Effects of
Career Stage," *European Management
Journal,* April 2012, pp. 111–120;
Jing Wang and Anil Verma, "Explain-
ing Organizational Responsiveness
to Work-Life Balance Issues: The
Role of Business Strategy and High-
Performance Work Systems," *Human
Resource Management,* May–June,
2012, pp. 407–432; Lieke ten Brum-
melhuis and Tanja van der Lippe,
"Effective Work-Life Balance Support
for Various Household Structures,"
Human Resource Management,
March–April 2010, pp. 173–193.

36. Adapted from Ben Waber, "Gender Bias
by the Numbers," *Bloomberg Businessweek,* February 3–9, 2014, pp. 8–9.

37. "Catalyst: Women CEOs of the
Fortune 1000," November 7, 2014,
http://www.catalyst.org/knowledge/
women-ceos-fortune-1000.

38. Roy Maurer, "What's Keeping Latin
American Women from the C-Suite?"
SHRM Online, October 23, 2013,
http://www.shrm.org/hrdisciplines/
global/articles/pages/latin-american-
women-c-suite.aspx.

39. Antonio Franquiz, "Watch Out for
the 'Glass Cliff,' " *HR Magazine,*
September 2013, 20.

40. "Sexual Orientation and Gender
Identity," *Public Policy Issue
Statement,* SHRM, June 2014,
http://www.shrm.org/advocacy/
publicpolicystatusreports/federal/
documents/014sexualorientation%20
statement%20final%206-20-14.pdf.

41. Dana Wilkie, "New Name, New
Locker Room," *SHRM Online,*
March 6, 2014, http://www.shrm
.org/hrdisciplines/diversity/articles/
pages/transgender-workplace-
accommodations.aspx.

42. Charles Pierce, Katherine Karl,
and Eric Brey, "Role of Workplace
Romance Policies and Procedures on
Job Pursuit Intentions," *Journal of
Managerial Psychology* 27 (2012),
237–263.

43. G. Stoney Alder and Douglas M.
Quist, "Rethinking Love at the
Office: Antecedents and Conse-
quences of Coworker Evaluations
of Workplace Romances," *Human
Resource Management* 53
(May–June 2014), 329–351.

44. Patricia M. McFall, "Gender-Stere-
otyping Evidence Establishes Same-
Sex Harassment," *SHRM Online,*
November 1, 2013, http://www.
shrm.org/legalissues/federalresources/
pages/gender-stereotyping-evidence-
same-sex-harassment.aspx.

45. Dana Wilkie, "Anti-Harassment
Training Following the Supreme
Court's *Vance* Ruling," *SHRM
Online,* July 16, 2013, http://
www.shrm.org/hrdisciplines/
employeerelations/articles/pages/
anti-harassment-training-following-
supremecourt-vance-ruling.aspx.

46. H. Stephen Kaye, "The Impact of the
2007–09 Recession on Workers with
Disabilities," *Monthly Labor Review,*
October 2010, pp. 19–34.

47. Allen Smith, "OFCCP Rule on Persons
with Disabilities Upheld," *SHR Online,* May 24, 2014, http://www.shrm
.org/LegalIssues/FederalResources/
Pages/OFCCP-rule-upheld.aspx.

48. Allen Smith, "Disability Self-Identifica-
tion Form Approved," *SHRM Online,*
January 1, 2014, http://www.shrm
.org/legalissues/federalresources/pages/
disability-self-identification-form.aspx.

49. Roger S. Achille, "Rehabilitation
Act Does Not Require Exhaus-
tion of Administrative Remedies,"
SHRM Online, November 11, 2013,
http://www.shrm.org/legalissues/
federalresources/pages/rehabilitation-
act-exhaustion-administrative-
remedies.aspx.

50. Laurie A. Petersen and Samantha
J. Wood, "Temporary Impairment
May Be 'Disability' Under ADA," *HR
Magazine,* May 2014, p. 55.

51. Brian D. Pedrow and Mark F.
Kowal, "Firing Alcoholic Employee
for Relapse Not ADA Violation,"
SHRM Online, November 6, 2013,
http://www.shrm.org/legalissues/
federalresources/pages/firing-
alcoholic-employee-relapse-ada.aspx.

52. "ADA Regulations: What Is a
Mental Impairment?" January 5,
2012, http://hr.blr.com/HR-news/
Discrimination/Disabilities-ADA/
znt1-ADA-Regulations-What-is-a-
Mental-Impairment.

53. Laurie A. Petersen and Samantha
J. Wood, "Temporary Impairment
May Be 'Disability' Under ADA," *HR
Magazine,* May 2014, p. 55.

54. Daniel L. Boyer, "Factual Dispute over
Essential Functions of Firefighter Jobs
Revives ADA Claim," *SHRM Online,*
May 27, 2014, http://www.shrm.org/
legalissues/federalresources/pages/esse-
ntial-functions-firefighter-jobs-ada.aspx.

55. Jill Garcia, "School Worker's Disability Retirement Does Not Preclude
ADA Claim," *SHRM Online,* September 26, 2013, http://www.shrm.org/
legalissues/federalresources/pages/
disability-retirement-ada-claim.aspx.

56. Christine M. White and Lindsey M.
Johnson, "Accommodation Request
Need Not Be Tied to Essential Job
Function," *SHRM Online,* October
17, 2013, http://www.shrm.org/
legalissues/federalresources/pages/
accommodation-request-essential-
job-function.aspx.

57. Lisa Schur, Lisa Nishii, Meera Adya,
Douglas Kruse, Susanne M. Bruyere,
and Peter Blanck, "Accommodating
Employees with and without Disabilities," *Human Resource Management*
53 (July–August 2014), 593–621.

58. Job Accommodation Network, http://
askjan.org.

59. Jared Shelly, "Discrimination Deluge,"
Human Resource Executive Online,
April 1, 2011, http://www.hreonline
.com/HRE/view/story.jhtml?id=53333
4825&ss=%22risk+management%22;
Jared Shelly, "Disability Discrimination
Rises," *Human Resource Executive
Online,* February 24, 2011, http://
www.hreonline.com/HRE/view/story
.jhtml?id=533332696; Joann Lublin
and Saabira Chaudhur, "Ex-CEO Says
Cancer Led to Her Ouster," *Wall Street
Journal,* August 4–5, 2012.

60. "The Genetic Information Nondiscrimination Act (GINA) of 2008,"
SHRM Online, http://www.shrm.org/
legalissues/federalresources/federal-
statutesregulationsandguidanc/pages/
thegeneticinformationnondiscrimina-
tionact.aspx.

61. "World Population Ageing, 1950–
2050," UN Department of Economic and Social Affairs-Population
Division, 2002, http://www.un.org/
esa/population/publications/world-
ageing19502050.

62. "Age Discrimination Internationally,"
http://www.agediscrimination.info/
international/Pages/international.aspx.

63. W. Kevin Smith, "Supervisor's Comments Were Evidence of Age Discrimination," *SHRM Online*, September 26, 2013, http://www.shrm.org/legalissues/federalresources/pages/supervisors-comments-evidence-age-discrimination.aspx.

64. Robert E. Bettac, "Possible Nondiscriminatory Motives Do Not Defeat Age-Bias Claims," *SHRM Online*, November 11, 2013, http://www.shrm.org/legalissues/federalresources/pages/possible-nondiscriminatory-motives.aspx.

65. "Age Discrimination in Employment Act of 1967," *SHRM Online*, http://www.shrm.org/legalissues/federalresources/federalstatutesregulationsandguidanc/pages/agediscriminationinemploymentactof1967.aspx.

66. Dana Wilkie, " 'Overqualified': Is It Code for 'Too Old'?" *SHRM Online*, November 19, 2013, http://www.shrm.org/hrdisciplines/diversity/articles/pages/older-workers-discrimination.aspx.

67. Timothy W. Roehrs, "Salesman Entitled to Trial on Age-Bias Claim," *SHRM Online*, November 15, 2013, http://www.shrm.org/legalissues/federalresources/pages/trial-age-bias-claim.aspx.

68. Robert E. Bettac, "Possible Nondiscriminatory Motives Do Not Defeat Age-Bias Claims," *SHRM Online*, November 11, 2013, http://www.shrm.org/legalissues/federalresources/pages/possible-nondiscriminatory-motives.aspx; Craig A. Reutlinger, "HR Comments about Employee's 'Shelf Life' Insufficient to Establish Age Bias," *SHRM Online*, November 22, 2013, http://www.shrm.org/legalissues/federalresources/pages/comments-employees-shelf-life-age-bias.aspx; WW. Kevin Smith, "Supervisor's Comments Were Evidence of Age Discrimination," *SHRM Online*, September 26, 2013, http://www.shrm.org/legalissues/federalresources/pages/supervisors-comments-evidence-age-discrimination.aspx.

69. Thomas W. H. Ng and Daniel C. Feldman, "Evaluating Six Common Stereotypes about Older Workers with Meta-Analytic Data," *Personnel Psychology* 65 (2012), 821–858.

70. Allen Smith, "Five Tips for Avoiding Age Discrimination," *SHRM Online*, October 7, 2014, http://www.shrm.org/publications/managingsmart/pages/avoiding-age-discrimination-.aspx.

71. Stephan A. Boehm, Florian Kunze, and Heike Bruch, "Spotlight on Age-Diversity Climate: The Impact of Age-Inclusive HR Practices on Firm-Level Outcomes," *Personnel Psychology* 67 (2014), 667–704.

72. Susan R. Heylman, "Teacher's Display of Religious Items Justified Firing," *HR Magazine*, February 2014, p. 12.

73. Dana Wilkie, "Deck the Halls … Or Not?" *SHRM Online*, November 12, 2013, http://www.shrm.org/hrdisciplines/employeerelations/articles/pages/office-holiday-religious-accommodations.aspx.

74. Roger S. Achille, "Headscarf Accommodation Not Required for Muslim Applicant," *SHRM Online*, October 25, 2013, http://www.shrm.org/legalissues/federalresources/pages/headscarf-accommodation-muslim-applicant.aspx; Marianne Levine, "Supreme Court Rules Against Abercrombie in Hijab Case," Politico, June 1, 2015, http://www.politico.com/story/2015/06/ambercrombie-fitch-hijab-case-supreme-court-ruling-118492.html.

75. Dori Meinert, "Matters of Faith," *HR Magazine*, December 2013, pp. 18–24.

76. "The Source of Workplace Strife," Fast Fact, *T+D*, November 2013, p. 17.

77. Dori Meinert, "Matters of Faith," *HR Magazine*, December 2013, pp. 18–24.

78. Nathan Koppel, "Child Immigration Is Rising," *Wall Street Journal*, May 8, 2012, p. A3.

79. Darrell M. West, "7 Myths That Have Clouded the Immigration Debate," *USA Today*, September 1, 2010.

80. Roy Maurer, "GOP Immigration Stand Centers on Workplace, Border Security," *HR Magazine*, March 2014, p. 13.

81. Miriam Jordan, "Fresh Raids Target Illegal Hiring," *Wall Street Journal*, May 3, 2012, p. A2; Miriam Jordan, "Chipotle Faces Inquiry on Hiring," *Wall Street Journal*, May 23, 2012, p. B3.

82. "U.S. Citizenship and Immigration Services," ttp://www.uscis.gov/portal/site/uscis.

83. Jessica Cook, "Extraordinary People: Who Are O-1As?" *SHRM Online*, http://www.shrm.org/hrdisciplines/global/articles/pages/extraordinary-outstanding-O1A-.aspx.

84. Allen Smith, "Decision Will Transform Immigration Law," *HR Magazine*, September 2013, p. 12.

85. Dana Wilkie, "English-Only Rules at Work: Discrimination or Business Necessity?" *SHRM Online*, November 14, 2013, http://www.shrm.org/hrdisciplines/diversity/articles/pages/english-only-eeoc.aspx.

86. "English-Only Language Policy," *SHRM Online*, June 30, 2014, http://www.shrm.org/templatestools/samples/policies/pages/cms_013464.aspx.

87. Shari Lau, "Must Employers Provide Labor Law Posters in Languages Other Than English?" *HR Magazine*, Solutions, September 2013, p. 22.

88. David Tobenkin, "Compliance Concerns," *HR Magazine*, December 2013, pp. 46–48.

89. Roger S. Achille, "Termination May Be Valid 'Re-employment Position' under USERRA," *HR Magazine*, March 2013, p. 69; David W. McBride, "Returning Vets Must Be Considered for Promotions," *HR Magazine*, December 2013, p. 56.

90. David W. McBride, "Returning Vets Must Be Considered for Promotions," *HR Magazine*, December 2013, p. 56.

91. Roger S. Achille, "Termination May Be Valid 'Re-employment Position' under USERRA," *HR Magazine*, March 2013, p. 69.

92. Kathy Gurchiek, "BPW Mentoring Program Helps Female Veterans Land Jobs," *SHRM Online*, November 12, 2013, http://www.shrm.org/publications/hrnews/pages/bpw-mentoring-program-female-veterans-jobs.aspx.

93. SHRM Online Staff, "Work Life Agency Award Applications Open," *SHRM Online*, December 13, 2013, http://www.shrm.org/publications/hrnews/pages/fwi-work-life-legacy-award-application-opens.aspx.

94. "Top 10 Jobs for Military Veterans," *T+D*, May 2013, p. 13.

95. Katerina Bezrukova, Karen Jehn, and Chester Spell, "Reviewing Diversity Training: Where We Have Been and Where We Should Go," *Academy of Management Learning & Education*, June 2012, pp. 207–227; Rohini Anand and Mary-Francis Winters, "A Retrospective of Corporate Diversity Training from 1964 to the Present," *Academy of Management Learning and Education*, September 2008, pp. 356–373.

96. Adapted from Adrienne Fox, "Great Expectations," *HR Magazine*, February 2014, pp. 22–27.

Jobs and Labor

CHAPTER

4

Workforce, Jobs, and Job Analysis

Learning Objectives

After you have read this chapter, you should be able to:

LO1 Explain how the workforce is changing in unpredicted ways.

LO2 Identify components of workflow analysis.

LO3 Define job design and identify common approaches to job design.

LO4 Discuss how flexible work arrangements are linked to work–life balancing efforts.

LO5 Describe job analysis and the stages in the process.

LO6 List the components of job descriptions.

WHAT'S TRENDING IN
WORKFORCE, JOBS, AND JOB ANALYSIS

The creation of jobs that motivate employees is a critical issue that companies address. Human resource professionals assist with workforce management, the creation of satisfying work, and the assessment of jobs. In particular, they must understand that jobs play an important role in the effective and efficient use of human resources in companies. Here's what's currently trending in the area of workforce, jobs, and job analysis:

1. The development of important skills in employees is always a concern for human resource professionals and managers. Skills gaps continue to challenge organizations, and proper steps need to be taken to reduce these gaps so that workers are best positioned to make valuable contributions in their jobs.

2. Many employees desire flexible work arrangements so that they can work in ways that accommodate their individual preferences, obligations, and schedules. Companies can offer a wide array of flexible job opportunities to support different preferences and professional goals.

3. Focusing on the right mix between work and home is an important issue that companies address on an ongoing basis. Human resource professionals should create policies that allow workers to establish a healthy balance between their personal and professional lives.

4. Job analysis enables human resource professionals and operating managers to identify the proper tasks, duties, and responsibilities of various organizational jobs. Given its importance, the process of conducting concise and ongoing job analyses is still heavily emphasized in companies. Proper job analysis facilitates the creation of appropriate job descriptions and specifications, which ultimately affect other

important human resource functions such as recruiting, staffing, training and development, appraisals, and compensation.

These trends show that the way the workforce is managed is constantly being altered to accommodate the needs of both companies and employees. The variety of challenges that employers face also suggests that jobs will likely continue to change based on these needs. This chapter explores many of the important workforce issues that affect the jobs employers create and develop, as well as techniques for determining exactly what people do in their jobs and how they should perform.

HEADLINE

Work–Life Balance for All at BDO USA

Creating fair work–life balance policies continues to be an important issue that companies address because work–life balance can keep workers satisfied. Employees must find reasonable ways to take care of increasing demands on their time to fulfill work responsibilities, while at the same time promoting harmony in their personal lives. While work–life balance is often considered a concern for women, recent evidence suggests that men are equally affected by some of the same challenges. A recent survey conducted by the Families and Work Institute (FWI) actually found that work–life balance was a more significant issue for men than it was for women. The findings also showed that men who have children are working more hours compared to women and to men without kids; men are also dedicating more time to child rearing activities and housework.

The public accounting firm BDO USA, which is based in New York, has taken steps to help both men and women manage the potential conflicts that can occur between work and home. The results of a survey revealed that men were actually less satisfied with work–life balance in the company than were women. A task force was developed to address some of these concerns, and adjustments were made to the workplace so that it would be less stressful and more accommodating. As a

Monkey Business Images/Shutterstock.com

result, a vast majority of the firm's employees take advantage of various flexible scheduling opportunities, including adjustable hours that enable employees to plan for personal and family time during the workday. BDO USA has achieved an increase in employee job satisfaction because of these efforts.

BDO USA received an Alfred P. Sloan Award from the Society for Human Resource Management and FWI in 2011 based on its innovative workplace practices. It appears that other companies are paying attention as work–life balance programs are becoming very popular, and many are targeted at men (e.g., paternity leave). Other New York–based organizations such as IBM and Citi have flexible workplaces and maternity leave, with many of male employees taking advantage of such opportunities.[1]

To understand the workforce and the jobs that people perform, it is important to consider the trends driving how the workplace is managed. As discussed in the opening "HR Headline" feature, the use of alternative work arrangements has been driven by employees' preferences for work–life balance and flexible opportunities. This is just one way that changing elements of the workplace affect companies and industries in different ways. For example, it was predicted that the retirement of Baby Boomers (born between 1946 and 1964) would leave a huge talent gap. However, many Boomers have not saved enough money to retire from their jobs, and the rising costs of health care and general living expenses pose a significant issue for many. These realities have pushed these individuals to reconsider retirement; the wave of expected retirements has been delayed because many older employees are choosing to stay in the workforce.

Another prediction is that companies will be challenged by "skills gaps" in certain fields. Skills shortages already exist in a variety of industries; many people do not have the skills needed to fill available jobs. Generational differences in the workforce have also been considered, analyzed, and addressed, and some of these issues were discussed in previous chapters of this text. Will differences between the generations at work really amount to differences in the way jobs get done? How will younger and older workers adapt to changes in the workplace? Human resource professionals must formulate appropriate answers to these questions so that organizations are managed appropriately; policies will likely need to be developed to address these concerns.

Other critical issues must also be considered by human resource professionals and organizational leaders. Historically, part-time positions have not been viewed favorably; people would begrudgingly accept part-time work until they could find a full-time employment opportunity. Yet today, employers want more contingent employees for the flexibility they provide, and more employees now want part-time work, which provides them more flexible work opportunities. These preferences require new approaches to human resource management that recognize the varying needs of employers and employees.

LO1 Explain how the workforce is changing in unpredicted ways.

4-1 The Workforce Profile

Human resource professionals deal with the segment of the population that works in current jobs or that is looking for work. The goal is to develop jobs that are inherently motivating to employees or to create work situations that are desirable enough to attract and hire competent workers. We begin with an overview of the workforce and jobs.

According to the Bureau of Labor Statistics, compared to the labor force of the past, today's workplace is comprised of many diverse individuals, including older adults, female employees, and people representing different racial and ethnic backgrounds.[2] It is expected to grow at a slower rate than in previous decades because population growth in the United States has slowed, and the labor force participation rate has decreased; the labor force participation rate is the percentage of the population working or seeking work. Figure 4-1 shows the racial and gender profile of the U.S. workforce in 1990 and projects today's workforce to 2020.

Labor force participation rate
The percentage of the population working or seeking work

FIGURE 4-1 Thumbnail Profile of U.S. Workforce

Group	Number (in thousands)		Percent Distribution		Annual Growth Rate (in percent)
	1990	2020	1990	2020	2010–2020
Total, 16 years and older	125,840	164,360	100.0	100.0	0.7
Age, years:					
16–24	22,492	18,330	17.9	11.2	–1.3
25–54	88,322	104,619	70.2	63.7	0.2
55+	15,026	41,411	11.9	25.2	3.3
Gender:					
Men	69,011	87,128	54.8	53.0	0.6
Women	56,829	77,232	45.2	47.0	0.7

Source: U.S. Bureau of Labor Statistics.

The Census Bureau projects that the U.S. population in 2020 will be about 341 million, and people aged 55 and older will comprise about 29% of this total. Flows *into* the population include fertility (births) and immigration, while flows out of the population include deaths and outmigration. The fertility (or birth) rate in the United States is roughly at a replacement level of 2.1 children per woman, and population-wide life expectancies continue to increase. Immigration is volatile and difficult to predict because it depends on other countries and economics, but it is estimated that immigration adds 1.4 million people to the population annually.[3]

The labor force participation rate peaked at 67% before 2000 and has since declined to around 65%. Part of the reason for this trend is that older people are still in the population, but they are not as likely to be in the workforce as younger people. Figure 4-2 shows participation rates by age, gender, and race/ethnicity in 2010 (at the last census) and projects them to 2020.

4-1a Important Elements of the Workforce Profile

Participation rates help us understand which segments of the population are more likely to be in the labor market in the future. Several variables—like age, generation status, employee skills (or the lack of in the case of skills gaps), and individual readiness for work—are important factors that illustrate the workforce profile.

Age/Generational Groups Much has been written about the different expectations and participation rates of individuals in various age groups and generations. Some common age/generational groups are labeled as follows:

- Mature (born before 1946)
- Baby Boomers (born 1946 to 1964)
- Generation Xers (born 1965 to 1980)
- Generation Yers (Millennials) (born 1981 to 2000)

Different characteristics have been attributed to these groups. For instance, research indicates that Millennials, who will represent approximately 50% of the workforce by the year 2020, show preferences for high-impact work opportunities that enable them to get ahead in their careers; they are also interested in learning at work so that they can use their knowledge to make valuable contributions. However, Millennials are less loyal to their employers, demonstrated in part by their relatively high job change rates.[4] A recent Ernst and Young survey of business professionals found that Gen Xers received the highest marks for their managerial skills and efforts, while Baby Boomers came in a close second place. Millennials scored the lowest in leadership ability, but they were viewed favorably for their knowledge of technology. A slight majority of survey participants believed that Millennials would be good leaders by the year 2020.[5]

Some of these beliefs might make managing a multigenerational workforce difficult for human resource professionals and line managers. In a workplace that often includes individuals who represent three or more generations, Millennials are increasingly being given the responsibility of supervising Baby Boomers, often because senior individuals are staying employed (instead of retiring), and younger workers are getting promoted rapidly because of their high levels of motivation and talent. In addition, these individuals can have different ideas about appropriate

FIGURE 4-2 Labor Force Participation Rate

Group	Participation Rate (%)		Percentage-Point Change	Group	Participation Rate (%)		Percentage-Point Change	Group	Participation Rate (%)		Percentage-Point Change
	2010	2020	2010–2020		2010	2020	2010–2020		2010	2020	
Total, 16+ years	64.7	62.5	–2.2	Men, 16+ years	71.2	68.2	–3.0	Women, 16+ years	58.6	57.1	–1.5
16–24	55.2	48.2	–7.0	16–24	56.8	50.6	–6.2	16–24	53.6	45.7	–7.9
25–54	82.2	81.3	–0.9	25–54	89.3	88.4	–1.6	25–54	75.2	74.6	0.6
55+	40.2	43.0	2.8	55+	46.4	47.3	0.9	55+	35.1	39.3	4.2
55–64	64.9	68.8	3.9	55–64	70.0	71.1	1.1	55–64	60.2	66.6	6.4
65+	17.4	22.6	5.2	65+	22.1	26.7	4.6	65+	13.8	19.2	5.4
65–74	25.7	31.0	5.3	65–74	30.4	35.1	4.7	65–74	21.6	27.5	5.9
75–79	10.9	15.2	4.3	75–79	14.5	18.2	3.7	75–79	8.2	13.0	4.8
Race:											
White	65.1	62.8	–2.3								
Men	72.0	69.0	–3.0								
Women	58.5	56.9	–1.6								
Black	62.2	60.3	–1.9								
Men	65.0	63.1	–1.9								
Women	59.9	57.9	–2.0								
Asian	64.7	63.1	–1.6								
Men	73.2	71.0	–2.2								
Women	57.0	56.1	–0.9								
Hispanic origin	67.5	66.2	–1.3								
Men	77.8	75.9	–1.9								
Women	56.6	56.1	–0.4								

Source: U.S. Bureau of Labor Statistics.

leadership styles, with younger leaders using technology to communicate and develop working relationships with others and older individuals wanting more close contact with their bosses.[6] Companies can provide training to help reduce the challenges associated with generational differences, and they should also utilize the skills of older workers while building the talents of younger employees.[7]

Skill Gaps Being able to hire people with the skills needed to help a business accomplish its goals is fundamental to sound human resource management. Employees need certain skills to help them make valuable contributions to the workplace. For instance, the skills associated with *mindfulness*, including a focused awareness, a rational mindset, and positive decision making, are all considered to be important in the workplace.[8] Listening skills are also important, particularly when employees are recovering from a traumatic event, and human resource professionals must be a sounding board for a variety of personal issues.[9] The "HR Competencies & Applications: Companies Need Skillful Introverts" feature

COMPETENCIES & APPLICATIONS

Companies Need Skillful Introverts

Organizations are interested in employing diverse individuals who bring with them a host of positive and varied skills. Besides more obvious physical characteristics such as age, ethnicity, and gender, underlying traits such as personality represent some new and emerging characteristics that can benefit companies. In particular, hiring introverted individuals can help firms operate in a more productive manner, despite some of the challenges that are commonly associated with this trait.

Introverts tend to prefer more solitary activities than do extroverts, and they often gain energy by performing work alone. They also value quiet time in the workplace that allows them to reflect and be creative. Alternatively, extroverts like to be more active in stimulating work environments that are characterized by much social interaction. A common misconception is that these characteristics set up extroverts to be creative leaders and introverts to be reserved followers, but this notion is far from the truth. Research shows that introverts are better suited to handle various managerial situations compared to extroverts. For instance, introverts tend to be skillful at communicating with colleagues, and they often possess adept decision-making skills. It is also common for them to be creative in the workplace. Many of these skills are seen in leaders such as Larry Page and Warren Buffet, both of whom are introverts.

Introverts do face some workplace challenges, though. They may be less likely to make quick decisions and connect well with others, which can hurt group synergy. However, organizations can take several steps to capitalize on the positive skills that introverts bring to the table:

- Be sure to provide introverts some time for quiet reflection.
- Reward introverts in ways that match their preferences for solitude.
- Specify areas of the worksite where introverts can go to be alone.
- Give introverts time to develop ideas before they are shared in meetings and other gatherings.[10]

Human resource professionals need to understand how to manage introverts so that their skills are put to good use. If you were given the responsibility of doing this:

1. How would you encourage introverts to make positive contributions to the workplace? What could be done to augment their skills?

2. How could you prepare extroverts to work more effectively with introverts?

KEY COMPETENCIES: Leadership and Navigation (Behavioral Competency) and People (Technical Competency) explores how companies can effectively utilize introverted employees based on their unique skill sets.

There is growing awareness that, unfortunately, individuals don't always have the skills needed to be successful at work. In a recent survey, almost half of managers working for a selection of large companies surveyed in the United States claimed that skills gaps exist in their professions, especially in the areas of information technology, engineering, research/development, and sales.[11] Adding to this challenge is that lower energy costs, rising wages in China and India, and high international shipping costs might make the United States more attractive to manufacturing. Even though there is skepticism about the long-term viability of American manufacturing jobs because of automation, many firms focus on hiring fewer individuals who possess much higher skills.[12] The confluence of these factors means that more jobs requiring science, technology, engineering, and math skills (STEM) should be available. However, there is currently a great shortage of those skills in the U.S. workforce.[13] It is not that there are too few high school and college graduates. Rather, the problems are that students are not studying the proper subjects, and there are concerns about the level and quality of the education received. Figure 4-3 shows educational attainment at the last census.

Other noteworthy skills gaps exist in different industries. Analytical skills are believed to be exceedingly important in business, but a recent survey of business-people found that perceptions of human resource professionals' analytical capabilities and general abilities were low.[14] Skills gaps in trade occupations have been identified in Alberta, Canada, with many organizations there hiring workers from the United States to fill key jobs.[15] Organizations that need high-skilled employees, such as those that operate in the science, medical, technical, and managerial fields, also experience skills gaps, making it difficult to hire the right people. Recent evidence indicates that two-thirds of companies face recruiting challenges because job candidates often lack decision-making, leadership, ethics, math, and communication skills.[16]

Other strategies can be used to manage talent gaps before they become a serious issue. Some companies are moving employees to locations where certain skills are needed the most, particularly for jobs in the oil, gas, and technology fields.[17] Disney is using workforce analytics to identify the talent that is needed for the various films it is developing.[18] The Atlanta-based software company Xpanxion has several offices located in smaller Nebraska towns to tap into the talent that exists in more remote areas, an approach the firm calls rural sourcing.[19]

Improving Readiness for Work Many efforts focus on developing skills to improve employees' readiness for work. For instance, the Workforce Investment Act established a federal program that provides workforce training to individuals, and this legislation is being reviewed for reauthorization.[20] Educational institutions are also developing programs that provide the skills necessary for success in business. Many liberal arts colleges such as Wake Forest University, Wesleyan University, and the University of Chicago are offering learning opportunities that help students develop business and technical skills.[21] Other institutions such as UCLA and the College for America are offering competency-based and online educational programs to senior business professionals to promote skills enhancement.[22] Massive open online courses are also being developed by various start-up businesses and elite universities to address employees' skills gaps.[23]

Organizations, including their human resource departments, can also address skills shortages. A survey of executives working in the United States determined

FIGURE 4-3 Education Profile of Workforce

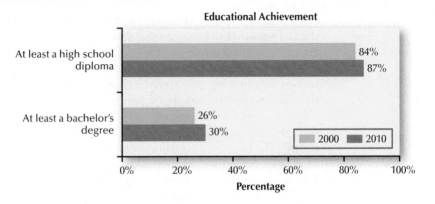

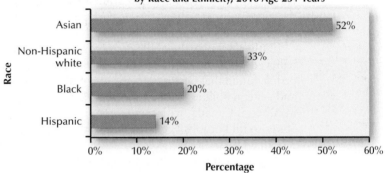

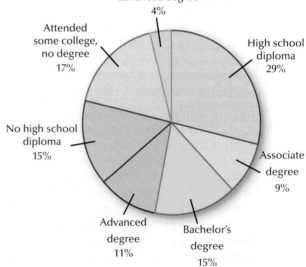

that more than half of organizations planned to dedicate more resources to training their employees. Employees can also shadow their colleagues at work and participate in online discussion boards to develop their skills.[24] The use of online badges that indicate the knowledge and skills obtained by workers is one way to recognize individual development.[25]

LO2 Identify components of workflow analysis.

Work
Effort directed toward accomplishing results

Job
Grouping of tasks, duties, and responsibilities that constitutes the total work assignment for an employee

4-2 The Nature of Work and Jobs

One way to visualize an organization is as an entity that takes inputs from the surrounding environment and then, through some kind of work, turns those inputs into goods or services. Work is effort directed toward accomplishing results, and such effort may be performed by humans, machines, or both. The total amount of work to be performed in an organization must be divided into jobs so that effort can be coordinated in some logical way. A job is a grouping of tasks, duties, and responsibilities that constitutes the total work assignment for an employee; these tasks, duties, and responsibilities may change over time, and therefore, the job may change.

Ideally, when the work processes to be done in all jobs in an organization are combined, the total should equal the amount of work that the organization needs to have done—no more, no less. The degree to which this ideal situation is met drives differences in organizational productivity. In addition, jobs increase in number and/or evolve, and duties change and are combined or eliminated as the needs of the organization change. If this doesn't occur, the organization fails to adapt to the changes in its environment and may become outmoded or noncompetitive. Several approaches are used to deal with common issues related to jobs in any organization.

At Southwest Airlines, jobs involve employees delivering dependable service at low fares while working in an enjoyable organizational culture. Southwest employees have a high degree of flexibility in the jobs they perform, even to the point that customer service agents may help clean planes or unload luggage if the workload demands it. Other airlines, such as American and United, have higher fares, more service amenities, and employees with more narrowly defined jobs, while the cultures are arguably different from the work environment at Southwest Airlines. The ways the work is done and jobs are designed and performed vary significantly under these two approaches, and the differences impact the number of jobs and people needed.

For human resource professionals, the way work flows through the organization and how to make that work more efficient is also important. Formally reviewing jobs through workflow analysis can help identify what is to be accomplished, and changing the way jobs are done through job redesign may make people more satisfied. The following sections explore in more detail these issues related to work and jobs.

Workflow analysis
Study of the way work (inputs, activities, and outputs) moves through an organization

4-2a Workflow Analysis

Workflow analysis is the study of the way work moves through an organization. Such analysis usually begins with an examination of the quantity and quality of the desired and actual *outputs* (goods and services), and then the *activities* (tasks and

FIGURE 4-4   Workflow Analysis

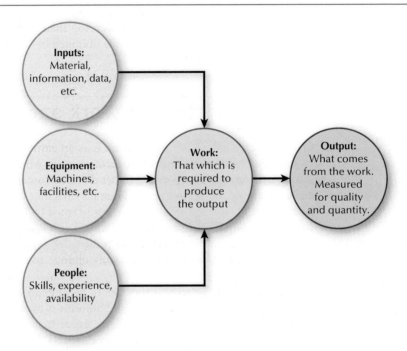

jobs) that lead to the outputs are evaluated to see if they are achieving the desired outputs. Finally, the *inputs* (people, material, information, data, equipment, etc.) must be assessed to determine if they make the outputs and activities more effective and efficient. A workflow analysis framework is shown in Figure 4-4.

An integrated workflow analysis is likely to lead to better employee involvement, greater efficiency, and more customer satisfaction because the organization's work is divided into jobs that can be coordinated. For example, if a customer experiences a service problem in a fine-dining restaurant, a server typically takes the issue to a floor supervisor so that it can be addressed directly at the table. If a floor supervisor is not available, then the server must take the issue to a higher-level manager, assuming one is around. Besides providing certain items free of charge, at better-managed establishments, a supervisor or manager can input the service problem and the customer's name and contact information into a database so that other special offers can be sent later to ensure that the individual will eat at the restaurant again sometime in the future. This action may also be delegated to a line employee such as a host or another customer-contact worker.

A workflow analysis of this process would show that there are too many steps involving too many jobs. So, the restaurant might consider implementing a new customer service system that empowers servers to resolve service problems at the tables immediately as they occur, rather than trying to find managers to discuss these issues. The process necessitates the redefinition of the tasks, duties, and responsibilities of several jobs, particularly the server position. In particular, servers should be trained to understand how they are expected to tackle service problems, including how to remove items from tickets, what types of offers should be given for certain complaints, and how actions should be reported to management later on. The result should be a more responsive workflow for customers, more efficient responses to service problems, and more empowered jobs for servers.

4-2b Job Design/Job Redesign

LO3 Define job design and identify common approaches to job design.

Job design
Organizing tasks, duties, responsibilities, and other elements into a productive unit of work

Job redesign
Changing existing jobs in different ways it to improve them

Job design refers to organizing tasks, duties, responsibilities, and other elements into a productive unit of work. **Job redesign** involves changing existing jobs in different ways to improve them. Identifying the components of a given job so that these factors can ultimately be enhanced is an integral part of the job design process. Job design receives attention for a number of important reasons:

- Job design can influence *performance* in many different jobs, especially those jobs where employee motivation can be influenced substantially by work factors so that performance improves.
- Job design can affect employees' overall *job satisfaction*. Since people are more satisfied with certain job elements and characteristics than others, identifying what makes a "good" job becomes critical. In addition, lower turnover and absenteeism are often associated with effective job design.
- Under many circumstances, job design can impact both *physical* and *mental health*. Problems such as hearing loss, backache, leg pain, stress, high blood pressure, general fatigue, sleeplessness, and heart disease can sometimes be linked directly to job design.

Managers play a significant role in job design because they are commonly the individuals who establish jobs and their design components. Managers must make sure that the expectations, requirements, responsibilities, and accountabilities of work are made clear to all those who work in particular jobs. During job design, managers should consider the nature and characteristics of both jobs and people. As Figure 4-5 indicates, managers can influence or control job characteristics, but they usually cannot easily control the basic characteristics of people.

FIGURE 4-5 Some Characteristics of Jobs and People

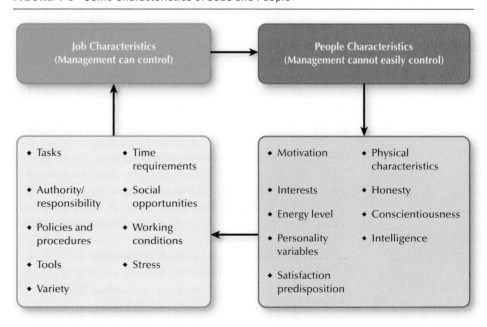

4-2c Using Contingent Workers as Job Design

Organizations employ a wide variety of workers, not just full-time employees. Depending on economic and competitive factors, the types of workers in firms can vary greatly. These may include full-time and part-time employees, independent contractors, and temporary and contingent workers.

The jobs found in organizations can be designed to utilize any of the different types of employees and workers. Although some firms still use the traditional approach of employing full-time and part-time employees, many firms are making significant use of independent, temporary, and contingent workers. These individuals are not considered employees because they generally work at will or on limited contracts, and they may even be working for other employers as well. A contingent worker is not a full-time employee but is a temporary or part-time worker for a specific period of time and type of work.

According to the U.S. Bureau of Labor Statistics, contingent workers are part of a group of "alternative workers" who may be on call, work through an employment agency, or operate as independent contractors. A number of contingent workers have contracts with employers that establish their pay, hours, job requirements, limitations, and time periods. Because of the inherent advantages, more employers are using contingent or temporary workers to staff different positions.

Contingent worker
Someone who is not a full-time employee but is a temporary or part-time worker for a specific period of time and type of work

Person–Job Fit Not everyone would necessarily enjoy being a human resource manager, an engineer, a nurse, or a drill-press operator. However, some people do prefer these specific jobs and do well at them. These issues relate to person–job fit, which involves matching the characteristics of people with the characteristics of jobs.

If a person does not fit a job, he or she can be changed or replaced, or the job can be redesigned to establish greater congruence. However, though an employer can try to make a "round" person fit a "square" job, it is generally difficult to successfully reshape people. If it is possible to redesign a job, the person–job fit may be improved much more easily than it would be if the focus were on developing employees. For example, bank tellers interact with people throughout a typical workday. An individual who prefers not to talk to others at work may perform better in a position that does not require so much interaction because this particular aspect of the bank teller job cannot be changed significantly. Consequently, different people will consider some jobs "good" and others "bad" based on the match between individual characteristics and the unchangeable components of a job. As a result, different people will find that they fit different kinds of work in unique ways.

Person–job fit
Matching the characteristics of people with the characteristics of jobs

4-2d Common Approaches to Job Design

One way to design or redesign jobs is to simplify the job tasks and responsibilities. Job simplification may be appropriate for jobs that are to be staffed with entry-level employees; however, making jobs too simple may result in boring work situations that appeal to few people, causing higher turnover. Several other approaches have also been used as part of job design, including job enlargement, job enrichment, and job rotation.

Job Enlargement and Job Enrichment Attempts to alleviate some of the problems encountered with excessive job simplification fall under the general categories of job enlargement and job enrichment. Job enlargement involves broadening the scope of a job by expanding the number of different tasks that are performed.

Job enlargement
Broadening the scope of a job by expanding the number of different tasks that are performed

Job enrichment
Increasing the depth
of a job by adding
responsibility for
planning, organizing,
controlling, and/or
evaluating the job

Job enrichment involves increasing the depth of a job by adding responsibility for planning, organizing, controlling, and/or evaluating the job. Some examples of job enrichment are:

- Giving employees an entire job to complete rather than just a particular part of the work to be performed
- Providing employees with more flexibility to perform jobs as needed
- Increasing employees' accountability for their work by reducing external control and overly close supervision
- Expanding assignments for employees so that they can perform new tasks and develop special areas of expertise
- Submitting feedback reports to employees rather than only to management so that individuals have more ownership over their development

Job rotation
Process of shifting a
person from job to job

Job Rotation One technique that can break the monotony of an otherwise simple routine job is job rotation, which is the process of shifting a person from job to job. There are advantages to job rotation, including that it develops an employee's capabilities for doing several jobs. For instance, large convention hotels can successfully use job rotation to prepare food and beverage employees to work in different areas of the organization, including banquets, fine dining, and room service. Such varied job experiences also make the workplace more interesting to employees because they get the opportunity to perform in different types of positions. Clear policies that identify the nature of job rotations and provide the appropriate training are more likely to make job rotation a successful strategy.

4-2e Characteristics of Jobs to Consider in Design

A model developed by Hackman and Oldham focuses on five important design characteristics of jobs that managers can target. Figure 4-6 shows that *skill variety*, *task identity*, and *task significance* affect the meaningfulness of work; *autonomy* stimulates responsibility; and *feedback* provides knowledge of results. The more that each component characteristic is present, the better the job situation is for an employee because work is inherently more motivating and satisfying. Using a sample of business professionals employed in a large Taiwanese retail home improvement firm, one study found that positive job characteristics are negatively related to turnover intentions.[26] These findings indicate that appropriate job characteristics can be used as a tool to enhance employee retention. The following sections detail the various job dimensions that can be enhanced to improve the characteristics of work.

Skill variety
Extent to which the work
requires several activities
for successful completion

Task identity
Extent to which the job
includes a recognizable
unit of work that is
carried out from start
to finish and results in
a known consequence

- Skill variety is the extent to which the work requires several activities for successful completion. For example, higher skill variety exists when a production line worker performs many different tasks when assembling products such as adding components, inspecting item quality, and packaging. Skill variety is not to be confused with *multitasking*, which involves doing several tasks at the same time, often with the assistance of computers, telephones, personal organizers, and other means. The impact of multitasking for an employee may be never getting away from the job, which can be an unacceptable outcome for some.
- Task identity is the extent to which the job includes a recognizable unit of work that is carried out from start to finish and results in a known consequence.

FIGURE 4-6 Job Characteristics Model

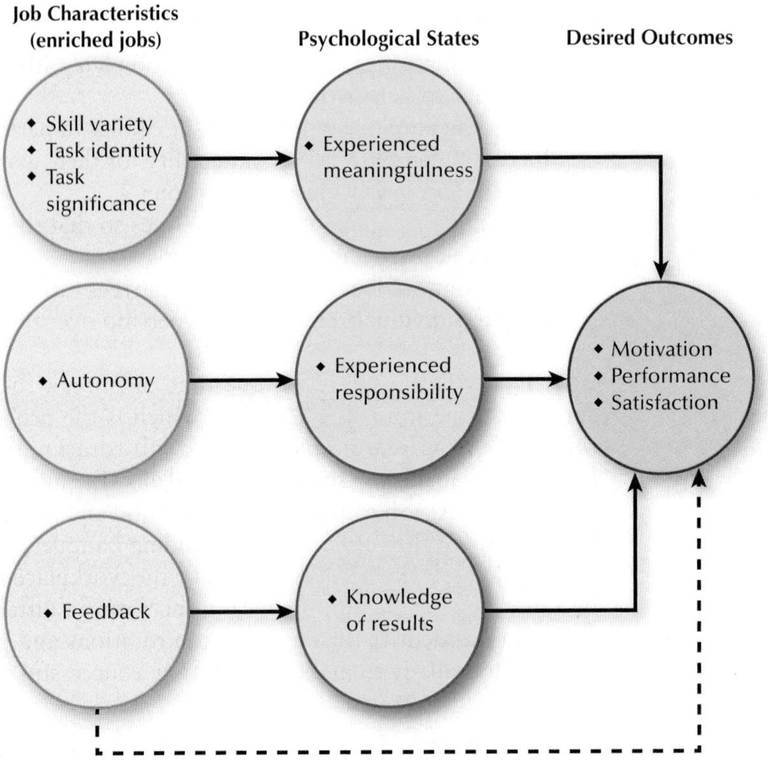

For example, when a customer calls with a problem, a customer specialist can handle the stages from maintenance to repair in order to resolve the problem.

- **Task significance** is the impact the job has on other people and the organization as a whole. A job is more meaningful if it is important to other individuals and the company. For instance, police officers may experience more job fulfillment when dealing with a real threat, rather than merely training to be ready in case a threat arises.[27] The position of culture officer is also becoming an important job in companies because the work requires an individual to develop and institutionalize a positive work environment throughout an organization.[28]

- **Autonomy** is the extent of individual freedom and discretion in the work and its scheduling. More autonomy leads to a greater feeling of personal responsibility for the work. For example, college professors are given a significant amount of autonomy to develop and teach courses and to pursue their research interests, which can make the work more satisfying.

- **Feedback** is the amount of information employees receive about how well or how poorly they have performed. When an organization uses multiple raters and forms to determine employee performance (e.g., customer ratings, peer evaluations, self appraisals, manager evaluations), the level of feedback increases because information is being provided by many individuals. The advantage of feedback is that it helps employees understand the effectiveness of their performance, which contributes to their overall knowledge of work.

Task significance
Impact the job has on other people and the organization as a whole

Autonomy
Extent of individual freedom and discretion in the work and its scheduling

Feedback
The amount of information employees receive about how well or how poorly they have performed

Motivation, performance, and satisfaction can be influenced by the level of each job characteristic. In other words, as one or more factor increases, employees should become more engaged with their work duties and responsibilities. Autonomy and feedback are especially powerful because they can magnify the effects of the other job characteristics.

4-2f Using Teams in Job Design

Typically, a job is thought of as a series of activities that are performed by just one person. However, where appropriate, jobs may be designed for teams to take advantage of the increased productivity, synergy, and commitment that often follow such design efforts. For these reasons, a number of organizations assign jobs to teams of employees instead of just assigning work to individuals. Some firms have gone as far as dropping such terms as *workers* and *employees* and have replaced them with titles such as *teammates*, *crew members*, and *associates* to emphasize teamwork.

As organizations have changed, the types of teams have changed as well. Having global operations with diverse individuals and using technology have affected the nature of how teams contribute to organizational projects. Mergers and acquisitions have also affected the development of leadership teams in organizations. For instance, an acquisition that occurred at Faurecia, a French-based provider of automotive components such as seats and interior/exterior parts, required a group of managers to assess themselves with online leadership diagnostic tools to determine how they could better interact with each other.[29]

Special Types of Teams   Several types of teams may periodically function outside the scope of members' normal jobs.[30] One is the special-purpose team, which is formed to address specific problems, improve work processes, and enhance the overall quality of products and services. Special-purpose teams are often a mixture of employees, supervisors, and managers so that diverse perspectives can be provided.

The self-directed team is comprised of individuals who are assigned a cluster of tasks, duties, and responsibilities to be accomplished. Unlike special-purpose teams, self-directed work teams become entities that use regular internal decision-making processes. The use of self-directed work teams in companies must be planned well and fit the underlying culture of the organization if the endeavor is to be successful.

The virtual team includes individuals who are separated geographically but who are linked by communications technology. The success of virtual work teams depends on a number of factors, including training of team members on virtual interaction, planning and managing virtual tasks and projects, and using technology to enhance teamwork. Leaders of virtual teams should also be given training so that they have the skills needed to be effective in the online, geographically dispersed work environment.[31]

Global Teams   Global operations have resulted in the increasing use of virtual teams in a variety of organizations. Members of these teams seldom or never meet in person; instead, they "meet" electronically via web-based systems. With global teams, it is important for managers and human resource departments to address various issues, including who is to be chosen for the teams, how they are to

---

Special-purpose team
Organizational team formed to address specific problems, improve work processes, and enhance the overall quality of products and services

Self-directed team
Organizational team composed of individuals who are assigned a cluster of tasks, duties, and responsibilities to be accomplished

Virtual team
Organizational team that includes individuals who are separated geographically but who are linked by communications technology

LO4 Discuss how flexible work arrangements are linked to work–life balancing efforts.

GLOBAL

communicate and collaborate online and in person (if at all), and what tasks and work efforts may be done with these teams. The "HR Competencies & Applications: Telecommuting in the Global Business Environment" feature explores important issues that human resource professionals should consider then working with individuals and teams in the virtual environment.

COMPETENCIES & APPLICATIONS

Telecommuting in the Global Business Environment

International telecommuting has become an important human resource issue in global business organizations. In the past, it was difficult for employees to telecommute from foreign locations because the technology was not sophisticated enough to facilitate good communication and coordination with team members and managers. However, the availability of smartphones, high-speed Internet access, advanced computers, and interactive software enables individuals who are employed at different worksites to complete their work interactively. These tools have helped companies better retain employees and more effectively utilize the talents that they bring to the workplace.

Companies may face a number of challenging situations related to international telecommuting. For instance, an employee may move to a country where an employer has a foreign site and telecommute back to the home office, or an employee may relocate to a country outside of the organization's footprint and telecommute from there. A company may also elect to create a mandatory telecommuting policy in a foreign country to save money, or it may create a more unified telecommuting policy for its global employees.

Regardless of the circumstances, companies should consider the following issues when creating global telecommuting strategies:

- Keep track of where employees reside in order to avoid complicated legal and payroll issues.
- Consider how telecommuting will affect employees who must get accustomed to working in a more solitary work environment.
- Develop a plan that indicates how employees are expected to interact with local worksites, communicate with other employees, and get their work done.
- Identify what resources will be provided by the organization to help employees telecommute.
- Fully consider the legal issues associated with global compensation, safety, and licensing.
- Develop a plan for ensuring data security as information is shared across borders.[32]

Many companies rely on global telecommuting to enhance worker engagement, and human resource professionals need to understand the inherent opportunities and challenges. If you were involved in this process:

1. What kinds of issues would you consider when developing global telecommuting strategies? What issues do you think are the most important?

2. What do think companies can do to make global telecommuting more successful?

KEY COMPETENCIES: Communication (Behavioral Competency) and People (Technical Competency)

GLOBAL

4-2g Teams and Work Efforts

The use of work teams has been a popular job redesign strategy in many companies. Improved productivity, increased employee involvement, greater coworker trust, more widespread individual learning, and greater individual diversity in knowledge, skills, and abilities are among the potential benefits. When transitioning to work teams, it is important to define the areas of work, scope of authority, and goals of the teams. Also, teams must recognize and address dissent, conflict, and other problems.[33]

The role of supervisors and managers changes with use of teams because of the presence of team leaders. Rather than giving orders, the team leader often becomes a facilitator to assist the team. Team leaders also mediate and resolve conflicts when they occur among team members, and it is common for them to interact with other teams and managers elsewhere in the company. Consequently, managers may need to be given special training to prepare them for the challenges associated with team leadership.

4-3 Designing Flexible Jobs

Flexibility can be designed into a job in several different ways, such as by changing *where* or *when* the work can be performed. A recent Families and Work Institute survey indicated that a majority of the companies sampled offer some type of flexible work arrangement (flextime, flexible breaks, completing work at home, etc.) to employees.[34] It is important for employers to consider these arrangements when designing jobs because flexible work opportunities are generally viewed by employees as being more attractive.

Flexible work is often spearheaded by using technology to enhance collaboration among employees, enabling them to accomplish work more efficiently and effectively. There is also growing interest in creating *flexible workspaces* that complement flexwork by eliminating cubicles and adding open work areas and shared offices and lounges. Accenture adopted this approach (in conjunction with telecommuting) over a decade ago, and the results have been promising, with higher employee satisfaction and engagement along with reduced office space needs. The company's managers and employees do not have their own offices; instead, they share workspaces to communicate and collaborate.[35]

Despite all the benefits provided by flexible work arrangements and the technology used to support these approaches, there are some inherent challenges such as information overload and attention fragmentation. Too much technological flexibility and connectivity without some consideration to how these factors influence the completion of work can cause problems for some employees. The need for uninterrupted time to synthesize information, reflect, apply judgment, and make good decisions is an important requirement in many professional jobs, but it can be difficult to find in a 24/7, on-call, flexible workplace. Some organizations prefer to have employees work in traditional office environments because it is believed that direct employee interactions benefit creativity and decision making. For instance, to help foster innovation, Yahoo suspended all of its flexible work arrangements and telecommuting in favor of requiring employees to work at Yahoo worksites.[36]

Flexible work arrangements enable employees to work at places other than their usual worksites. These approaches are collectively referred to as *telework* or *telecommuting.*

4-3a Place Flexibility: Telework

Telework
Employees complete work through electronic interactions, telecommunications, and Internet technology.

Individuals who work at home or places other than an organization's official worksite illustrate telework, which means that employees complete work through electronic interactions, telecommunications, and Internet technology. Twenty-four percent of Americans report that they work at least some hours at home each week.[37] Employees with higher education levels frequently have more opportunity for telework (see Figure 4-7).

Benefits and Disadvantages Some benefits of telework are environmental in nature and address problems caused by traffic, vehicle emissions, and overbuilding. Employees often find that they spend less for gasoline, vehicle maintenance, lunches, and dry cleaning. Not traveling to work saves employees time that can be used for other activities. Employees can also be more productive due to higher morale and decreased stress. The ability to telecommute can help attract new employees and retain current employees because they are more satisfied and committed to the employer.[38] Telecommuting can be especially useful during bad weather or widespread health issues such as pandemic flu.

However, some disadvantages are associated with telework. Some typical concerns include the following:

* Employees may not enjoy telework beyond a certain number of hours worked (such as 15 hours per week).
* Employees can feel like they are isolated socially from their coworkers.
* The electronic media used to facilitate telework may limit how well employees can interact with each other.

FIGURE 4-7   Education Level and Employed Persons Who Perform Work at Home

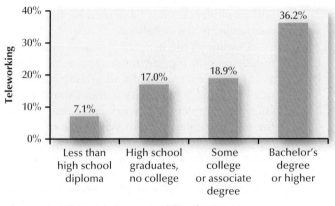

Source: American Time Use Survey, Bureau of Labor Statistics, 2013.

- Employees who have children and other responsibilities at home may face role conflict when work gets in the way.
- When telework teams include employees who have significant responsibilities at home, individuals might allow poor performance because they feel sorry for team members.
- Some employees may prefer to have more of a boundary between work and home.[39]

Managing Telework The nature of the employment relationship with teleworkers should be outlined in a policy that establishes clear work expectations, as well as the boundaries between work and home. For instance, working long hours and being available 24/7 while having to balance home and work requirements can be stressful for employees and may lead to burnout.[40] Maintaining employee motivation when individuals are not physically present at company facilities can also be challenging, particularly for international employees. Also, time zone differences between the United States and other countries may make it difficult for global employees to participate in conference calls or travel extensively for meetings. Calculating pay for nonexempt employees can also be complicated if they are allowed to telework.

After careful consideration of these issues, companies can develop telework in several ways:

- *Regular*: Employees may spend scheduled days or every day at an office at home
- *Brief occasional*: Employees may use a home office on weekends or at night to do a project
- *Temporary/emergency*: During bad weather, a natural disaster, or other events causing disruption, employees work from home

4-3b Time Flexibility: Work Scheduling

Considering different work schedules can be part of designing jobs, nonstandard schedules have been developed for employees in various occupations. The traditional work schedule in the United States of eight hours a day, five days a week is in transition. Workers may work fewer or more than eight hours at a workplace, and they may work additional hours at home.

The work schedules associated with jobs vary, as some jobs must be performed during "normal" daily work hours and on weekdays, while others require employees to work nights, weekends, and extended hours. There are significant differences in the hours worked in different countries as well. Given the global nature of many organizations, human resource practices must adjust to different locations. Organizations are using many work scheduling arrangements, including shift work, the compressed workweek, part-time schedules, job sharing, and flextime.

Shift Work A common work schedule design is shift work, which requires employees to work on various schedules that function at different times throughout a workday. Many organizations need 24-hour coverage and therefore may schedule three shifts per day, each eight hours long. Most employers provide some form of additional pay, called a *shift differential*, for working the evening or night shifts. Some types of shift work have been known to cause difficulties for some employees, such as weariness, irritability, lack of motivation, and illness. Although shift work is not universally popular, some employers must rely on 24/7 coverage; consequently, shift work is likely to continue to be utilized by some organizations.

Compressed Workweek Another type of work schedule design is the compressed workweek, which involves accomplishing a full week's work in fewer than five days of eight working hours each. Compression usually results in more work hours each day and fewer workdays each week, such as a four-day week with 10-hour days or a three-day week with 12-hour shifts. Workers who shift to 12-hour schedules often do not wish to return to eight-hour schedules because they have four days off each week, which provides a longer block of time off from work. However, 12-hour schedules can lead to sleep difficulties, fatigue, and an increased number of injuries, so companies should be aware of these inherent physical challenges.

Part-Time Schedules Part-time jobs are used when less than 40 hours per week are required for some workers to perform their work in an organization. Part-time jobs are attractive to those who may not want to work 40 hours per week, including older employees, parents of small children, and students. In some cases, professionals may choose part-time work because it fits their personal and occupational preferences.

Job Sharing Another alternative used is job sharing, which involves two employees performing the work of one full-time job. For instance, a hospital allows two radiological technicians to fill one job, and each individual works every other week. Such arrangements are beneficial for employees who may not want or be able to work full time because of family responsibilities, school schedules, or other personal and professional reasons.

Flextime In flextime, employees work a set number of hours a day but vary starting and ending times to get more scheduling flexibility. In another variation on this theme, employees may work 30 minutes longer Monday through Thursday, take short lunch breaks, and leave work at 1 p.m. or 2 p.m. on Friday. A study found that women who ask for flextime arrangements are thought by their (male and female) managers to be using these arrangements to take care of their personal responsibilities rather than work requirements.[41]

4-3c Managing Flexible Work

Flexible scheduling allows management to relax some of the traditional "time clock" control of employees, while still covering workloads.[42] In some cases, electronic monitoring may be used to facilitate the management of flexible work. For example, to get some measure of work activity and completion, a call-service firm can electronically monitor home-based employees on their use of phones, breaks, and production. Managers can also increase ongoing communication with employees to determine whether work requirements are being addressed.

4-3d Flexibility and Work–Life Balance

For many employees, balancing their work and personal lives is a significant concern. Work–life balance involves employer-sponsored programs designed to help employees balance work and personal responsibilities. For instance, Simon Wood-Fleming, the

---

compressed workweek
A workweek in which a full week's work is accomplished in fewer than five days of eight working hours each

Job sharing
Scheduling arrangement in which two employees perform the work of one full-time job

Work–life balance
Employer-sponsored programs designed to help employees balance work and personal life

chief marketing officer for the music service firm Pandora Media, enjoys running and working out during the workday, and other employees are encouraged to take time away from the office to exercise.[43] Research indicates that certain flexible work policies are associated with reduced conflicts between work and family.[44] Consequently, these efforts should enhance recruiting and retention efforts by attracting and keeping people who want flexibility in their jobs. Finally, having a PEP plan (or personal, energy, and professional vision) that focuses on balancing personal pursuits and professional objectives can also be beneficial.[45]

PERSPECTIVE

Convention and Visitors Bureau Keeps Flexwork in Perspective

The use of smart technology, computers, and the Internet in the workplace have enabled employees to stay better connected with their managers and colleagues, something that has provided them with more opportunities to get their work done. On the flipside, however, there is concern that this newfound flexibility may actually hurt employees when they are expected to always be "on the clock." In other words, a 24/7 mind-set can be perpetuated at work that negatively impacts employees' work–life balance. A recent study of business leaders and other professionals indeed found that individuals used their smartphones for work over 13 hours a day on weekdays, as well as around 5 hours during weekends (total weekly use was 72 hours). Participants in the survey claimed that management and communication problems were to blame for their extensive use of technology. This highlights the fact that managers must create reasonable expectations about technology use, and proper policies must be developed so that employees don't feel the need to stay constantly connected to the workplace.

Many organizations are trying to address these challenges in ways that are beneficial for all parties. The ideal situation is to use technology in a way that enhances productivity without having it intrude too much on employees' personal lives. The Durham, North Carolina, Convention and Visitors Bureau (CVB) has developed policies that keep flexible work in perspective so that a better balance between work and the home is achieved. The organization was recently given the Alfred P. Sloan Award for Excellence in Workplace Effectiveness and Flexibility for its efforts. E'Vonne Coleman-Cook, the Durham CVB's chief operating officer, provides the following recommendations that should assist companies as they develop such policies:

- Organizations need to set policies and values, and then back them up by living by the company's words.
- Managers' interactions with employees should be monitored to ensure reasonable standards are being enforced.
- The goals and expectations for each employee need to be identified so that the "rules of the game" are understood by all individuals.[46]

Keep in mind the practices used by the Durham CVB as you consider the following questions:

1. How could flexwork be better managed in the workplace given the inherent challenges and opportunities of this approach? How could HR professionals provide assistance?

2. How do you recommend organizations use technology so that work–life balance is not adversely impacted?

Managers should consider some challenges associated with managing work–life balance programs. Employees may lose faith in such programs if they are not applied consistently, and since it is not uncommon to have such policies identified and available but not actually practiced in some organizations, employees may dismiss them as "window dressing." In addition, companies have to develop reasonable work standards to avoid creating conflicts between work and home. The preceding "HR Perspective: Convention and Visitors Bureau Keeps Flex-Work in Perspective" feature explores some of the challenges related to flexible work and work–family balance.

Women may have negative experiences when it comes to balancing work and home life. A large global study found that supervisors believe men are better at managing work–life balance than are women.[47] Other research shows that men are more likely to feel comfortable about missing family activities than are women,[48] which potentially increases women's perceptions of work–family conflict.

4-4 Understanding Job Analysis

Creating and developing interesting jobs that fit effectively into the flow of an organization's work is called job design. The more narrow focus of job analysis involves using a formal system to gather information about what people actually do in their jobs. A basic building block of human resource management, job analysis is a systematic way of gathering and analyzing information about the content, context, and human requirements of jobs. Job analysis is the basis for all human resource practices because the process sets up how employees are hired, trained and developed, evaluated, and compensated. A Society for Human Resource Management survey found that of the companies that relied on job analysis, a majority used the process to help improve the recruitment of employees.[49]

A basic overview of the job analysis process is summarized graphically in Figure 4-8. The resulting information from job analysis is compiled into *job descriptions* and *job specifications* for use in many human resource activities.

Job analysis
Systematic way of gathering and analyzing information about the content, context, and human requirements of jobs

4-4a Purposes of Job Analysis

Job analysis, or work analysis, has grown in importance as the workforce and jobs have changed.[50] To be effective, human resource planning, recruiting, and hiring all should be based on job requirements identified through job analysis and the capabilities of individuals. In equal employment opportunity matters, accurate details on job requirements are needed because the credentials provided in job descriptions can affect court decisions. Additionally, compensation, training, and employee performance appraisals should be based on the specific needs of the jobs. Job analysis is also useful in identifying job factors and duties that may contribute to workplace health and safety as well as employee and labor relations issues. Information from job analyses that can be helpful in making a distinction among jobs includes the following:

- Work activities and behaviors
- Interactions with others
- Performance standards
- Financial and budgeting impact

FIGURE 4-8 Job Analysis in Perspective

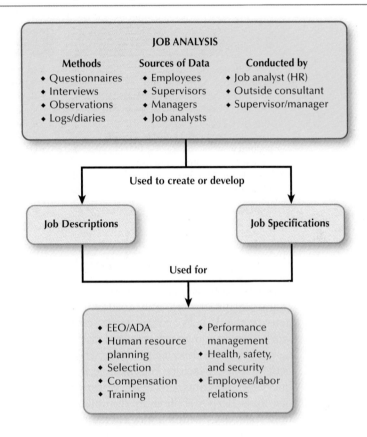

- Machines and equipment used
- Working conditions
- Supervision given and received
- Knowledge, skills, and abilities needed

4-4b Job Analysis Responsibilities

To be successful, job analysis requires a high degree of coordination and cooperation between the human resources unit and operating managers, and assigning responsibility for job analysis depends on who can best perform various parts of the process. In larger companies, the HR unit supervises the process to maintain its integrity and writes job descriptions and specifications for uniformity. Managers review the efforts of the HR unit to ensure accuracy and completeness; they may also request new job analyses when jobs change significantly. In smaller organizations, managers may perform all job analysis responsibilities. Figure 4-9 summarizes the typical division of job analysis responsibilities that occurs in organizations between the HR unit and managers.

Different types of job analysis can be used to secure information about jobs. The most traditional and widely used method is task-based job analysis; however, some organizations have emphasized the need for a competency-based approach. Both of these job analysis types are discussed in more detail in the following sections.

FIGURE 4-9 Typical Division of Human Resource Responsibilities: Job Analysis

HR Unit	Managers
• Coordinates job analysis • Writes job descriptions and specifications for review by managers • Periodically reviews job descriptions and specifications • Reviews managerial input to ensure accuracy • May seek assistance from outside experts for difficult or unusual analyses	• Complete or help complete job analysis information • Review job descriptions and specifications and maintain their accuracy • Request new analyses as jobs change • Use job analysis information to identify performance standards • Provide information to outside experts

4-4c Task-Based Job Analysis

Task-based job analysis is the most common type and focuses on the components and characteristics of work embedded within a job. A task is a distinct, identifiable work activity comprised of motions that employees perform, whereas a duty is a larger work segment comprised of several tasks that are performed by individuals. Since both tasks and duties describe activities, it is not always easy or necessary to distinguish between the two factors. For example, if one of the employment supervisor's duties is to interview applicants, one task associated with that duty would be asking job-related questions. Responsibilities are the obligations that individuals have to perform certain tasks and duties within a job. Therefore, the overall goal of task-based job analysis is to identify all the tasks, duties, and responsibilities that are part of a job.

4-4d Competency-Based Job Analysis

Unlike the traditional task-based approach to analyzing jobs, the competency approach considers how knowledge and skills are used. Competencies are individual capabilities that can be linked to enhanced performance by individuals or teams.

The concept of competencies varies widely from organization to organization because of the different types of work that can be performed. The term *technical competencies* is often used to refer to employees' specific knowledge and skills. *Behavioral competencies* are a different set of competencies, and some examples of these competencies include:

- Customer focus
- Team orientation
- Technical expertise
- Results orientation
- Communication effectiveness
- Leadership
- Conflict resolution
- Innovation
- Adaptability
- Decisiveness

Task
Distinct, identifiable work activity comprised of motions that employees perform

Duty
Larger work segment comprised of several tasks that are performed by individuals

Responsibilities
Obligations that individuals have to perform certain tasks and duties within a job

Competencies
Individual capabilities that can be linked to enhanced performance by individuals or teams

The competency approach to job analysis focuses on identifying the key individual characteristics that make employees successful on the job, and unlike task-based job analysis, one of the main purposes is to influence future job performance. As such, the competency approach may be more broadly focused on behaviors, rather than just on tasks, duties, and responsibilities. For instance, many supervisors talk about employees' attitudes, but they have difficulty identifying exactly what they mean by *attitude*. Using different approaches, supervisors can attempt to isolate the competencies that they consider to be part of employees' attitudes (perhaps team orientation, selfless service, and conflict resolution), as well as how these factors may affect performance.

Integrating Technology and Competency-Based Job Analysis As the workplace continues to evolve, there may be a more integrated use of task-based and competency-based job analyses. Another factor that will contribute to the use of both approaches is that in addition to the performance of job tasks and duties, strategic competencies are identified for some jobs. Consequently, human resource professionals (or whoever is conducting job analyses) are more likely to need a more integrated and comprehensive process. The decision about whether to use a task-based or competency-based approach to job analysis is affected by the nature of jobs; however, task-based analysis is likely to remain more widely used because it is the most defensible legally,[51] and it is the primary focus of the remainder of this chapter.

4-5 Implementing Job Analysis

The process of job analysis must be conducted in a logical manner, following appropriate management and professional psychometric practices.[52] Analysts usually follow a multistage process, regardless of the specific job analysis methods used. The stages for a typical job analysis, as outlined in Figure 4-10, may vary somewhat with the number of jobs included.

4-5a Plan the Job Analysis

Prior to the job analysis process itself, planning should be done to gather information about jobs from managers and employees. Probably the most important consideration is to identify the objectives of the job analysis, which might be as simple as updating job descriptions or as comprehensive as revising the organization's compensation programs. Whatever the purpose identified, the effort needs the support of top management.

FIGURE 4-10 Stages in the Job Analysis Process

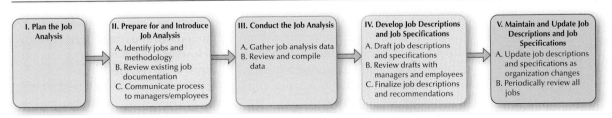

4-5b Prepare for and Introduce the Job Analysis

Preparing for job analysis includes identifying the jobs to be analyzed. Organization charts, existing job descriptions, previous job analysis information, and other resources are reviewed next. This includes identifying who will be involved in conducting the job analysis and the methods to be used. A key part is identifying and communicating the process to appropriate managers, affected employees, and others.

4-5c Conduct the Job Analysis

Data about jobs are collected using various methods; the methods used are based on time and the available resources. Once data from job analyses are compiled, the information can be sorted by job, organizational unit, and job family.

4-5d Develop Job Descriptions and Job Specifications

At this stage, the job analyst drafts job descriptions and job specifications. Generally, organizations do not recommend having managers and employees write job descriptions for several reasons. First, it reduces consistency in format and details, both of which are important given the legal consequences of job descriptions. Second, managers and employees vary in their writing skills, and they may write the job descriptions and job specifications to reflect what they do and what their personal qualifications are, instead of what the job requires. However, completed drafts should be reviewed by managers and supervisors, and then with employees, before they are finalized.

4-5e Maintain and Update Job Descriptions and Job Specifications

Once job descriptions and specifications have been completed and reviewed by all appropriate individuals, a system must be developed for keeping them current and posted on a firm's intranet source. One effective way to ensure that appropriate reviews occur is to use current job descriptions and job specifications as part of other human resource activities. For example, each time a vacancy occurs, the job description and specifications should be reviewed and revised as necessary before recruiting and hiring efforts begin. Similarly, in some organizations, managers and employees review job descriptions during performance appraisal interviews.

4-6 Job Analysis Methods

Job analysis information about what people are doing in their jobs can be gathered in a variety of ways. Traditionally, the most common methods have been (1) observations, (2) interviews, and (3) questionnaires. However, the expansion of technology has led to computerization and web-based job analysis information gathering methods. Sometimes a combination of these approaches is used depending on the situation and the organization.

4-6a Observation

With the observation method, a manager, job analyst, or industrial engineer watches an employee perform the job and takes notes that describe the tasks and duties performed. The observation method is limited because many jobs do not have complete and easily observed job duties or job cycles. Thus, observation may be more useful for repetitive jobs and in conjunction with other methods; or it can be used to verify information.

Work Sampling One type of observation, work sampling, does not require attention to each detailed action throughout an entire work cycle. This method allows a job analyst to determine the content and pace of a typical workday through statistical sampling of certain actions rather than through continuous observation and timing of all actions. Work sampling is particularly useful for routine and repetitive jobs because the factors of work do not change significantly from one day to the next.

Employee Diary/Log Another observation method requires employees to "observe" their own performance by keeping a diary/log of their job duties, noting how frequently those duties are performed and the time required for each one. Although this approach can generate useful information, it can be burdensome for employees to compile an accurate log while still performing their jobs. Technology can facilitate the logging or diary approach, reducing some of the problems associated with balancing data collection and work completion.

4-6b Interviewing

The interview method requires a manager, job analyst, or human resource specialist to talk with the employees performing each job. A standardized interview form is often used to record the information and ensure greater consistency. Both the employee and the employee's supervisor should be interviewed to obtain complete details about the job.

Sometimes group or panel interviews are used to collect information about jobs. A team of subject matter experts (SMEs) who have varying insights about a group of jobs is assembled to provide job analysis information. This option may be particularly useful for highly technical or complicated jobs because a great deal of complex information can be collected from groups of employees who work in these jobs. Since the interview method alone can be quite time consuming, combining it with one of the other methods is a common practice.

4-6c Questionnaires

The questionnaire is a widely used method of gathering job data because of its ease of use and convenience. A survey instrument that identifies job factors is developed ahead of time by human resource professionals and/or other managers, and this questionnaire is given to employees and managers to complete. The typical job questionnaire often covers the areas shown in Figure 4-11.

The questionnaire method offers a major advantage in that information about a large number of jobs can be collected inexpensively in a relatively short period of time. However, the questionnaire method assumes that employees can accurately analyze and communicate information about their jobs, which may not be the case in all situations.

FIGURE 4-11   Typical Areas Covered in a Job Analysis Questionnaire

Duties and Percentage of Time Spent on Each	Contact with Other People
• Regular duties • Special duties performed less frequently	• Internal contacts • External contacts
Supervision	**Physical Dimensions**
• Supervision given to others • Supervision received from others	• Physical demands • Working conditions
Decisions Made	**Jobholder Characteristics**
• Records and reports prepared • Materials and equipment used • Financial/budget responsibilities	• Knowledge • Skills • Abilities • Training/experience needed

Using interviews and observations in combination with the questionnaire method allows analysts to clarify and verify the information gathered in questionnaires.

Managerial Job Analysis Questionnaire   Since managerial jobs often differ from jobs with more clearly observable routines and procedures, some specialized job analysis methods exist for management jobs. One well-known method is the Management Position Description Questionnaire (MPDQ), an instrument that taps important elements of managerial/supervisory work. Comprised of more than 200 statements, the MPDQ examines a variety of management dimensions, including decision making and supervising.

4-6d Job Analysis and O*Net

A variety of resources to help with job analysis are available from the U.S. Department of Labor (DOL), and these resources have been developed and used over many years by a variety of entities. *Functional job analysis* uses a competency approach to job analysis, and a functional definition of what is done in a job can be generated by examining the three components of *data*, *people*, and *things*. The levels of these components traditionally have been used to identify and compare important elements of more than 120 jobs in the *Dictionary of Occupational Titles (DOT)*. O*Net is currently the main DOL resource available and provides employers with a wide range of useful items.

The O*Net database now contains data on more than 800 occupations, classified by industry. Included in the occupational categories are the following factors:

• Task statements of importance, relevance, and frequency
• Abilities (work activities, knowledge, skills, and work content)
• Training, work experiences, and education
• Interests and work values, work styles, and job zones

O*Net can be used in many ways that are highly beneficial to organizations. For example, one way is to see what abilities will be needed in certain jobs; more than 50 abilities are listed, including arm-hand steadiness, fluency of ideas, time sharing, visualization, written and oral comprehension, and speech clarity. Employers can use the abilities and the other components to generate data for some parts of job analysis and for developing job descriptions.

O*Net also now contains the *Dictionary of Occupational Titles (DOT)* and has hundreds of jobs descriptions already written and available. For example, on human resource jobs, the DOT and O*Net have listed details on occupations such as Employee Relations Specialist and Human Resource Advisor. For these and all other types of jobs, an extensive list of tasks and detailed work activities is provided. These details provided by O*Net give supervisors, managers, and human resource professionals a valuable resource as they develop or revise job descriptions, compare recruiting advertisements, develop training components, and perform other human resource activities. In summary, O*Net is a database of worker attributes and job characteristics to describe jobs and the skills workers will need to perform them,[53] and the database can be accessed at www.onetcenter.org.

4-7 Behavioral and Legal Aspects of Job Analysis

Job analysis involves determining what the core job involves, as well as what employees do (or are expected to do) while working in a job. A detailed examination of jobs, although necessary, can sometimes be a demanding and disruptive experience for both managers and employees, in part because job analysis can identify the difference between what currently is being performed in a job and what should be done. This is a major job analysis–related issue for some employees, but it is not the only concern. Other behavioral factors can affect job analysis and make the process more challenging.

4-7a Current Incumbent Emphasis

A job analysis and the resulting job description and job specifications should not just describe what the person currently in the job does and that person's qualifications. The incumbent may have unique capabilities and the ability to expand the scope of the job to assume more responsibilities, but the employer might have difficulty finding a suitable replacement if the person were to leave. Consequently, it is useful to focus on core duties and necessary knowledge, skills, and abilities by determining what the job would be if the incumbent were to quit or be moved to a different job.

4-7b "Inflation" of Jobs and Job Titles

People have a tendency to inflate the importance and significance of their jobs because they are not completely objective. Since job analysis information is used for compensation purposes, both managers and employees may hope that "puffing up" jobs will result in higher pay levels, greater "status" for résumés, and more promotional opportunities. Doing so often convolutes the job analysis process and results in inaccurate and/or confusing job descriptions.

Inflated job titles also can be used to make jobs sound better (and subsequently increase employee pride) without making major job changes or pay adjustments. For instance, banking and financial institutions often use officer designations to enhance status. In one small Midwestern bank, an employee who had three years' experience as a teller was "promoted" with no pay increase to Second Vice President of Customer Service. In effect, she became the lead teller when her supervisor was out of the bank and could subsequently sign more customer account forms, but her duties and compensation were basically the same.

An additional concern is the use of offbeat and unusual titles to describe jobs. For example, what is a Group idea Management Director, Chief Transformation Officer, or Marketing Evangelist? What does a Human Character Manager really do? These examples illustrate how job titles may be misleading, both inside and outside the place of employment; titles should convey a clear picture of what a job involves.

4-7c Employee and Managerial Concerns

Both employees and managers may have concerns about the job analysis process. If done correctly, the resulting job description should identify the activities performed in a job. However, it is difficult to capture all facets of a job in which employees perform a variety of duties and operate with a high degree of independence.

Employee Fears One concern that employees may have involves the purpose of a detailed investigation of their jobs. Some employees fear that an analysis of their jobs will limit their creativity and flexibility by overly formalizing their duties. They may also be concerned about pay deductions or even layoffs as a result of job analysis. However, having accurate, well-communicated job descriptions can assist employees by clarifying their roles and the expectations within those roles. One effective way to handle anxieties is to involve employees in the revision process so that there is some employee input and ownership of the compiled information.

Job Incumbent Influence The content of a job may also reflect the desires and skills of the incumbent employee, which can affect the content of the job analysis. For example, in one firm, an employee promoted to customer service supervisor continued to spend considerable time answering customer calls, rather than supervising employees taking the calls. As part of job analysis discussions, the operations manager discussed the need for the supervisor to train the employees on handling special customer requests and to delegate more routine duties to others.

Managerial Straitjacket Another concern of managers and supervisors is that the job analysis and job descriptions will unrealistically limit managerial flexibility. Since workloads and demands change rapidly, managers and supervisors may elect to move duties to other employees, cross-train employees, and have flexible means available to accomplish work. If job descriptions are written or used restrictively, employees may argue that a change or omission to a job description should limit management's flexibility to require that work. In organizations with unionized workforces, some very restrictive job descriptions may exist.

Because of such difficulties, the final statement in many job descriptions is a miscellaneous clause that consists of a phrase similar to "Performs other duties as needed upon request by immediate supervisor." This statement covers unusual situations in an employee's job that cannot all be highlighted in a job description. However, duties covered by this phrase cannot be considered essential functions under legal provisions, including the Americans with Disabilities Act, which is discussed in the next section.

4-7d Legal Aspects of Job Analysis

The *Uniform Guidelines on Employee Selection Procedures* (in Appendix E) make it clear that human resource requirements must be tied to specific job-related factors if employers are to defend their actions as a business necessity. Job descriptions are frequently the link to these job-related factors because they describe important tasks, duties, and responsibilities, and they often provide a basic overview of the individual characteristics needed to perform work.

Job Analysis and the Americans with Disabilities Act One result of the Americans with Disabilities Act (ADA) is increased emphasis by employers on conducting job analyses, as well as developing and maintaining current and accurate job descriptions and job specifications. The ADA requires that organizations identify the *essential job functions*, which are the fundamental duties of a job. These do not include the marginal functions of the positions. Marginal job functions are duties that are part of a job but are incidental or ancillary to the purpose and nature of the job. As covered in Chapter 3, the three major considerations used in determining essential functions and marginal functions are the following:

Marginal job functions
Duties that are part of a job but are incidental or ancillary to the purpose and nature of the job

* Percentage of time spent on tasks
* Frequency of tasks performed on the job
* Importance of tasks performed

Job analysis should also identify the physical demands of jobs. For example, the important physical skills and capabilities used on the job of a nursing professional could include being able to hear well enough to aid clients and doctors. However, hearing might be less essential for a heavy equipment operator working in a quarry.

Job Analysis and Wage/Hour Regulations As will be explained in Chapter 11, the federal Fair Labor Standards Act (FLSA) and most state wage/hour laws require that the percentage of time employees spend on manual, routine, or clerical duties affects whether they must be paid overtime for hours worked in excess of 40 hours a week. To be exempt from overtime, employees must perform their primary duties as executive, administrative, professional, or outside sales employees. *Primary* has been interpreted to mean occurring at least 50% of the time.

Other legal compliance efforts, such as those involving workplace safety and health, can also be facilitated and enhanced by the data provided by job analysis and job descriptions. It is difficult for an employer to have a legal staffing system without performing job analysis. Job analysis is truly the most basic human resource activity and the foundation for most other personnel decision and efforts.

LO6 List the components of job descriptions.

4-8 Job Descriptions and Job Specifications

The output from a job analysis is used to develop a job description and its job specifications. Together, these two documents summarize job analysis information in a readable format and provide the basis for defensible job-related actions.

4-8a Job Descriptions

Job description
Identifies a job's tasks, duties, and responsibilities

In most cases, a job description and a job specification are combined into one document that contains several sections. A job description identifies a job's tasks, duties, and responsibilities. It describes what is done, why it is done, where it is done, and, briefly, how it is done. Writing job descriptions can be challenging because identifying the necessary soft skills needed to perform a job, as well as the typical duties, can be difficult.[55] The following "HR Competencies & Applications: Writing Appropriate Job Descriptions" feature has suggestions for writing job descriptions.

4-8b Job Specifications

Job specifications
The knowledge, skills, and abilities (KSAs) an individual needs to perform a job satisfactorily

While the job description outlines activities to be done, the job specifications list the knowledge, skills, and abilities (KSAs) an individual needs to perform a job satisfactorily. KSAs might include the education, experience, work skill requirements, personal abilities, and mental and physical requirements a person needs to do the job, not necessarily the current employee's qualifications.[56]

4-8c Performance Standards

Performance standards
Indicators of what the job accomplishes and how performance is measured in key areas of the job description

Performance standards flow directly from a job description and indicate what the job accomplishes and how performance is measured in key areas of the job description. If employees know what is expected and how performance is to be measured, they have a much better chance of performing satisfactorily. Unfortunately, performance standards are often not developed as supplemental items in job descriptions. Even if performance standards have been identified and matched to job descriptions, they must be communicated to employees if the job descriptions are to be effective tools.

4-8d Job Description Components

A typical job description contains several major parts. The following sections present an overview of the most common components. Each organization formats job descriptions in a way best suited to its inherent culture and management practices. Consistency of information and formatting across all the organization's jobs ensures uniformity.

Identification The first part of the job description is the identification section, which includes the job title, department, reporting relationships, location, and date of analysis. It is advisable to note other information that is useful in tracking jobs and employees through HR systems. Additional items commonly noted in the identification section are job code, pay grade, exempt/nonexempt status under the Fair Labor Standards Act (FLSA), and the EEOC classification (from the EEO-1 form).

COMPETENCIES & APPLICATIONS

Writing Appropriate Job Descriptions

Developing and maintaining current job descriptions are important activities in human resource management because these documents affect so many other important personnel functions, including staffing, training, and compensation. Some key suggestions for writing job descriptions that include the essential functions and duties of a job are:

- *Compose specific duty statements*:
    1. A precise action verb and its object
    2. The frequency of the duties and the expected outcomes
    3. The tools, equipment, aids, and processes to be used
- *Be logical*. If the job is repetitive, describe the tasks as they occur in the work cycle. For varied jobs, list the major tasks first and follow these activities with the less frequent and/or less important tasks (in order).
- *Use proper details*. Make sure the description covers the meaningful duties of the job.
- *Be specific*. For example, instead of saying "Lifts heavy packages," say, "Frequently lifts heavy packages weighing up to 50 pounds."
- *Use the active voice*. Start each statement with a functional verb in the present tense (third-person singular). For instance, *Compiles, Approves,* or *Analyzes*. Avoid terms like *handles, maintains*, and *processes*.
- *Describe, do not prescribe*. Say, "Operates electronic imaging machine," not "Must

know how to operate electronic image machine." (The latter is a job specification, not a job description.)
- *Be consistent*. Define terms *like may, occasionally*, and periodically.
- *Include a miscellaneous clause*. This clause provides flexibility and may be phrased as follows: "Performs other related duties as assigned by supervisory personnel."

Several other factors should be considered when writing appropriate job descriptions:

- *Think about the future*. Consider how jobs may change over time, as well as the impact these changes might have on needed skills.
- *Have some priorities*. To reduce unneeded complexity, avoid discussing too many duties.
- *Limit critical characteristics*. Specify only five or six characteristics that candidates need to have to work in a job.
- *Talk about culture*. Describe the company's culture to let others know what it's like to work there.
- *Focus on continuous improvement*. Keep revising the job description to make it better.[54]

Based on these suggestions, consider the following questions:

1. What do you think are the most important characteristics of good job descriptions?
2. What kinds of issues would you consider when writing job descriptions?

KEY COMPETENCIES: Critical Evaluation (Behavioral Competency) and People (Technical Competency)

General Summary The general summary is a concise statement of the general responsibilities and components that make the job different from others. One human resource specialist has characterized the general summary statement as follows: "In thirty words or less, describe the essence of the job." Often, the summary is written after all other sections are completed so that a more complete overview is prepared.

FIGURE 4-12   Sample Job Description and Job Specifications

Identification Section

Position Title: Customer Service Supervisor

Department: Marketing/Customer Service   EEOC Class: O/M
Reports To: Marketing Director   FLSA Status: Exempt

General Summary

Supervises, coordinates, and assigns work of employees to ensure customer service department goals and customer needs are met.

Essential Job Functions

1. Supervises the work of customer service representatives to enhance performance by coordinating duties, advising on issues or problems, and checking work. (55%)
2. Provides customer service training for company employees in all departments. (15%)
3. Creates and reviews reports for service orders for new and existing customers. (10%)
4. Performs employee performance evaluations, training, and discipline. (10%)
5. Follows up with customer complaints and issues and provides resolutions. (10%)
6. Conducts other duties as needed guided by marketing director and executives.

Knowledge, Skills, and Abilities

- Knowledge of company products, services, policies, and procedures.
- Knowledge of marketing and customer programs, data, and results.
- Knowledge of supervisory requirements and practices.
- Skill in completing multiple tasks at once.
- Skill in identifying and resolving customer problems.
- Skill in oral and written communication, including Spanish communications.
- Skill in coaching, training, and performance evaluating employees.
- Skill in operating office and technological equipment and software.
- Ability to communicate professionally with coworkers, customers, and vendors.
- Ability to work independently and meet managerial goals.
- Ability to follow oral and written instructions.
- Ability to organize daily activities of self and others and to work as a team player.

Education and Experience

Bachelor's degree in business or marketing, plus 3–5 years of industry experience. Supervisory, marketing, and customer service experience helpful.

Physical Requirements	Percentage of Work Time Spent on Activity			
	0–24	25–49	50–74	75–100
Seeing: Must be able to see well enough to read reports.				X
Hearing: Must be able to hear well enough to communicate with customers, vendors, and employees.				X
Standing/Walking: Must be able to move about department.			X	
Climbing/Stooping/Kneeling: Must be able to stoop or kneel to pick up paper products or directories.	X			
Lifting/Pulling/Pushing: Must be able to lift up to 50 pounds.	X			
Fingering/Grasping/Feeling: Must be able to type and use technical sources.				X

Working Conditions: Normal working conditions absent extreme factors.

Note: *The statements herein are intended to describe the general nature and level of work being performed, but are not to be seen as a complete list of responsibilities, duties, and skills required of personnel so classified. Also, they do not establish a contract for employment and are subject to change at the discretion of the employer.*

Essential Job Functions and Duties The essential functions and duties are generally listed in order of importance in this component of the job description. It contains clear, precise statements on the major tasks, duties, and responsibilities performed in a job. Writing this section is often the most time-consuming aspect of preparing job descriptions because of the amount and detail of the information reported.

Job Specifications The qualifications needed to perform the job satisfactorily are identified in the job specifications section. The job specifications typically are stated as: (1) knowledge, skills, and abilities; (2) education and experience; and (3) physical requirements and/or working conditions. The components of the job specifications provide information necessary to determine what accommodations might and might not be possible under the Americans with Disabilities Act.

Disclaimers and Approvals Many job descriptions include approval signatures by appropriate managers and a legal disclaimer. This disclaimer allows employers to change employees' job duties or to request employees to perform duties not listed so that the job description is not viewed as a contract between the employer and the employee. Figure 4-12 contains a sample job description and job specifications for a customer service supervisor. Also, Appendix H has sample job descriptions and job specifications for human resource management jobs.

SUMMARY

- The workforce is changing but not entirely in the predicted ways.
- The workforce participation rate has declined, reducing the percentage of people in certain groups who are in the workforce.
- Work-ready credentials are ways to determine skills rather than assume that a degree grants specific skills to all who hold it.
- Work in an organization is divided into jobs, and workflow analysis shows how work flows through the organization.
- Job design involves developing jobs that people can do well. It may include simplification, enlargement, enrichment, or rotation.
- Designing jobs so that they incorporate skill variety, task identity and significance, autonomy, and feedback can improve jobs for employees.
- Work teams can be used when designing jobs.
- Jobs can be designed for place and/or time flexibility.
- Telework is leading to more place flexibility and can be regular, brief occasional, or temporary/emergency.

- Shift work, compressed work weeks, part-time positions, job sharing, and flextime can provide time and other schedule flexibility.
- Job analysis is a systematic investigation of the content, context, and human requirements of a job.
- Task-based job analysis focuses on the tasks, duties, and responsibilities associated with jobs.
- Competency-based job analysis focuses on basic characteristics of performance such as technical and behavioral competencies.
- A number of methods of job analysis are used, with interviews and questionnaires being the most popular.
- The behavioral reactions of employees and managers along with legal compliance issues must be considered as part of job analysis.
- The end products of a job analysis are job descriptions, which identify the tasks, duties, and responsibilities of jobs, and job specifications, which list the knowledge, skills, and abilities needed to perform a job satisfactorily.

CRITICAL THINKING CHALLENGES

1. Describe how changes in the workforce have been impacting organizations, including organizations for which you have recently worked.

2. For many individuals, the nature of work and jobs is changing. Describe these changes, some reasons for them, and how they are affecting both human resource management and individuals.

3. Explain how you would conduct a job analysis in a company that has never had job descriptions. Utilize the O*Net as a resource for your information.

4. You have recently assumed the role of Human Resource Manager in your company. In reviewing the company records, you note that the job descriptions were last updated five years ago.

The company's President has taken the position that there is no need to update the job descriptions. However, you also note that the company has grown by 50% during the past five years, resulting in many changes, including some in job functions. You want to build a business case to convince the President of the need to update the job descriptions. To help you build your case, use the information on the purpose of job descriptions at www.hrtools.com.

A. How can job descriptions be used as a management tool?
B. What role do job descriptions have in helping companies comply with various legal issues?

CASE — Unilever Jumps on the Flexible Work Bandwagon

In an effort to stay on the cutting edge of positive employment practices, the Anglo-Dutch consumer products firm Unilever recently created a new policy that grants flexible work arrangements to 100,000 individuals. This number represents almost all of the company's employees, minus some production workers who operate in factories. A trial run of the Agile Working program was conducted at one worksite, which led to the introduction of the process to many thousands of other employees several years later. There are plans to offer the program to select factory workers. Unilever also purchased equipment such as laptops, webcams, and smartphones to help individuals complete their work outside of the office. Employees have responded favorably to the technology, indicating that it helps them function effectively from remote locations.

These changes required a whole new way of thinking in the company, and the leadership approach that was used to guide human resources was changed dramatically. For example, managers pay less attention to some of the more traditional requirements and standards of work, such as looking good, working long hours, and having good attendance. Instead, they focus on how well employees complete their work based on expected results.

The managers at Unilever sold the idea of Agile Working by focusing on a number of points:

- Videoconferencing and other distance communication would cut travel costs.
- Technology enhancements would help improve workplace efficiency and effectiveness.
- The physical office requirements in different facilities would be decreased significantly.
- Employee job satisfaction should increase based on a more concerted focus on work–life balance.
- Flexible work opportunities should enhance worker engagement and retention.

The results of the program have been positive overall. Employees claim to be more satisfied on the job, and the company has enjoyed stronger hiring trends. Workers also report being healthier and less stressed out about their employment situations.[57]

QUESTIONS

1. Based on Unilever's Agile Working program, what else can human resource professionals do to facilitate work–life balance in organizations?

What other opportunities could Unilever offer its employees to enhance work–life balance?

2. What is your opinion of Agile Working? Do you think there are any disadvantages associated with this flexible work arrangement?

SUPPLEMENTAL CASES

Bon Secours Health Care

This case shows how a health care organization uses flexible work arrangements to provide care for patients, as well as to attract and keep employees. (For the case, go to www.cengage.com/management/mathis.)

The Reluctant Receptionist

This case illustrates how incomplete job analysis and job descriptions create both managerial and employee problems. (For the case, go to www.cengage .com/management/mathis.)

Jobs and Work at R. R. Donnelley

This case describes how a printing firm had to increase productivity and redesign jobs. (For the case, go to www.cengage.com/management/mathis.)

Flexible Work and Success at Best Buy

This case illustrates flexible scheduling at Best Buy. (For the case, go to www.cengage.com/management/ mathis.)

END NOTES

1. Adapted from Julie Bennett, "Balancing Work and Home Life Is Not Only a Woman's Issue," *Wall Street Journal*, June 20, 2012, p. B9.
2. Mitra Toossi, "Labor Force Projections to 2020: A More Slowly Growing Workforce," *Monthly Labor Review*, January 2012, pp. 43–64.
3. Mitra Toossi, "Labor Force Projections to 2020: A More Slowly Growing Workforce," *Monthly Labor Review*, January 2012, p. 46.
4. Henry G. Jackson, "Millennials @ Work," *HR Magazine*, May 2014, p. 8.
5. "Managing Through the Ages," *T+D*, January 2014, p. 15.
6. Dana Wilkie, "Collision Course: The Multigenerational Workforce," *SHRM Online*, February 19, 2014,

http://www.shrm.org/hrdisciplines /diversity/articles/pages/multigenera- tional-workforce.aspx.
7. Jennifer Schramm, "The Evolving Workplace," *HR Magazine*, May 2014, p. 72; Dana Wilkie, "Collision Course: The Multigenerational Workforce," *SHRM Online*, February 19, 2014, http://www.shrm.org/ hrdisciplines/diversity/articles/pages/ multigenerational-workforce.aspx.
8. Susan G. Hauser, "'Mindfulness' Is Being Incorporated into Employer Strategies to Combat Multitask- ing," *Workforce*, September 6, 2012, http://www.workforce.com/ articles/856-mindfulness-is-being -incorporated-into-employer- strategies-to-combat-multitasking.

9. Kathryn Tyler, "Listening Skills," *HR Magazine*, February 2014, p. 42.
10. Adapted from Donna M. Owens, "Quiet Time," *HR Magazine*, December 2013, pp. 26–27.
11. Patty Gaul, "Nearly Half of U.S. Ex- ecutives Are Concerned about Skills Gap," *T+D*, February 2014, p. 18.
12. Charles Kenny, "Factory Jobs Are Gone: Get Over It," *Bloomberg- Businessweek*, January 23, 2014, http://www.businessweek.com /articles/2014-01-23/manufacturing- jobs-may-not-be-cure-for- unemployment-inequality.
13. Susan R. Meisinger, "The Good News and the Bad News," *Human Resource Executive Online*, May 14, 2012, pp. 1–2.

14. Dori Meinert, "HR Teams Rank Low in Analytical Skills," *HR Magazine,* December 2013, p. 14.

15. Catherine Skrzypinski, "Study: Workers Head North to Bridge Skills Gap," *SHRM Online,* November 18, 2013, http://www.shrm.org/hrdisciplines/global/articles/pages/us-canada-skills-gap.aspx.

16. Theresa Minton-Eversole, "Skills Gaps Often Very Basic: Critical Thinking, Solving Problems," *HR Magazine,* May 2013, p. 20.

17. Antonio Franquiz, "All the Right Moves," *HR Magazine,* October 2013, pp. 59–61.

18. Ed Frauenheim, "Workforce Analytics: Disney's Real-Life Fairly Tale," *Workforce,* October 9, 2013.

19. Jeanna Smialek, "Home Is where the Jobs Are," *BloombergBusinessweek,* January 3, 2014, http://www.businessweek.com/articles/2014-01-03/for-jobs-revival-rural-towns-work-with-business.

20. C. Michael Ferraro and Jennifer Homer, "Workforce Investment Act Gained Momentum in 2013," *T+D,* January 2014, p. 17.

21. Lauren Weber, "Colleges Get Career-Minded," *Wall Street Journal,* May 22, 2013, p. A3.

22. Julian L. Alssid and Patricia Shields, "College in the Call Center," *T+D,* February 2014, pp. 50–54; Andrew Morse, "Online Education for Boomers," *Wall Street Journal,* July 5, 2012.

23. Garry Kranz, "Online Learning Gets Massive, Open," *Workforce,* August 13, 2013, http://www.workforce.com/articles/9295-online-learning-gets-massive-open.

24. Patty Gaul, "Nearly Half of U.S. Executives Are Concerned about Skills Gap," *T+D,* February 2014, p. 18.

25. "Badge Me," *T+D,* January 2014, p. 13.

26. Wan-Jing April Chang, Yung-Shui Wang, and Tung-Chun Huang, "Work Design–Related Antecedents of Turnover Intention: A Multilevel Approach," *Human Resource Management* 52 (January–February 2013), 1–26.

27. Teresa Amabile and Steven Kramer, "How Leaders Kill Meaning at Work," *McKinsey Quarterly,* January 2012, pp. 1–8.

28. Kathy Gurchiek, "Culture Officers Protect, Maintain Essence of Company,"

SHRM Online, December 6, 2013, http://www.shrm.org/hrdisciplines/orgempdev/articles/pages/corporate-culture-officers.aspx.

29. Julie Straw, "New Team, New Rules," *T+D,* September 2013, pp. 70–71.

30. Jessica L. Wildman, "Task Types and Team Level/Attributes: Synthesis of Team Classification Literature," *Human Resource Development Review* 11 (2012), 97–129.

31. Christina Mandzuk, "Challenges of Leading a Virtual Team: More Than Meets the Eye," *T+D,* January 2014, p. 20.

32. Adapted from Donald C. Dowling Jr. "Global Telecommuting Brings a Host of Issues," *SHRM Online,* November 20, 2013, http://www.shrm.org/hrdisciplines/global/articles/pages/global-telecommuting-issues.aspx.

33. Wharton School, "The Dark Side of Teamwork," *Human Resource Executive Online,* April 13, 2012, pp. 1–2.

34. Robert J. Grossman, "Phasing Out Face Time," *HR Magazine,* April 2013, pp. 32–38.

35. Sarah Fister Gale, "Some Companies Replace Cubicles with Flex Spaces," *Workforce,* November 20, 2013, http://www.workforce.com/articles/some-companies-replace-cubicles-with-flex-spaces.

36. Sarah Fister Gale, "Some Companies Replace Cubicles with Flex Spaces," *Workforce,* November 20, 2013, http://www.workforce.com/articles/some-companies-replace-cubicles-with-flex-spaces; Aliah D. Wright, "Yahoo Retrenches on Telecommuting," *HR Magazine,* April 2013, p. 11.

37. Marg C. Noonan and Jennifer L. Glass, "The Hard Truth about Telecommuting," *Monthly Labor Review Online* 135 (June 2012), 1.

38. Ed Frauenheim, "Research Backs Benefits of Flex Work for Workers—and Companies," *Workforce,* May 29, 2013; Angela Stone, "How Can Telecommuting for Telework Have an Impact on a Company's Sustainability?" *HR Magazine,* March 2013, p. 23.

39. Ed Frauenheim, "Research Backs Benefits of Flex Work for Workers—and Companies," *Workforce,* May 29,

2013; Kathy Gurchiek, "Still Room for Improvement in Work Flex, *SHRM Online,* October 7, 2013, http://www.shrm.org/publications/hrnews/pages/workflex-survey-october-national-work-and-family-life-month.aspx.

40. Bill Leonard, "Is Flex Work Blurring the Boundaries between Office and Home?" *SHRM Online,* October 16, 2013, http://www.shrm.org/publications/hrnews/pages/flex-work-overtime.aspx.

41. Dana Wilkie, "Managers Distrust Women Who Ask for Flextime More Than Men," *SHRM Online,* August 22, 2013, http://www.shrm.org/hrdisciplines/diversity/articles/pages/managers-distrust-women-flextime.aspx.

42. Jim Fickness, "Build Your Company's Flexibility Muscles Now," *Workspan,* May 2011, pp. 72–77; Sayed Sadjady, "Find the Right Balance with Flexibility," *Workspan,* June 2012, pp. 62–66.

43. Jen Murphy, "Finding Exercise That's in Tune with Work," *Wall Street Journal,* July 24, 2012, p. D4.

44. Tammy D. Allen, Ryan C. Johnson, Kaitlin M. Kiburz, and Kristen M. Shockley, "Work-Family Conflict and Flexible Work Arrangements: Deconstructing Flexibility," *Personnel Psychology* 66 (2013), 345–376.

45. Beverly Crowell, "PEP Buoys," *Workforce,* June 3, 2014, http://www.workforce.com/articles/20495-pep-buoys.

46. Adapted from Bill Leonard, "Is Flex Work Blurring the Boundaries between Office and Home?" *SHRM Online,* October 16, 2013, http://www.shrm.org/publications/hrnews/pages/flex-work-overtime.aspx.

47. Antonio Franquiz, "Managers Show Gender Bias in Views on Work/Life Balance," *HR Magazine,* October 2013, p. 16.

48. Aliah D. Wright, "Male Executives: Work/Life Balance is a Women's Issue," *SHRM Online,* April 4, 2014, http://www.shrm.org/hrdisciplines/businessleadership/articles/pages/male-execs-work-life-balance-a-womens-issue.aspx.

49. Bill Leonard, "Survey: HR Using Job Analyses to Hone, Focus Recruiting Efforts," *SHRM Online,* December 18, 2014, http://www.shrm.org/publications/hrnews/pages/hr-job-analyses-recruiting-efforts-survey.aspx.

50. FrederickP. Morgeson and Erich C. Dierdorff, "Work Analysis: From Technique to Theory," *APA Handbook of Industrial and Organizational Psychology* 2 (2011), 3–41.

51. Michael M. McDaniel et al., "The Uniform Guidelines Are a Detriment to the Field of Personnel Selection," *Industrial and Organizational Psychology* 4 (December 2011), 494–514.

52. R. B. Briner and D. M. Rousseau, "Evidence-Based 1-0 Psychology: Not There Yet," *Industrial and Organizational Psychology* 4 (March 2011), 3–22.

53. Frederick P. Morgeson and Erich C. Dierdorff, "Work Analysis: From Technique to Theory," *APA Handbook of Industrial and Organizational Psychology* 2 (2011), 15.

54. Stephanie Castellano, "What's in a Job," *T+D,* January 2014, p. 14.

55. Chad H. Van Iddekinge et al., "An Examination of the Validity and Incremental Value of Needed-at-Entry Ratings," *Applied Psychology: An International Review* 60 (2011), 24–45.

56. Adapted partly from Stephanie Castellano, "What's in a Job," *T+D,* January 2014, p. 14.

57. Based on Robert J. Grossman, "Phasing Out Face Time," *HR Magazine,* April 2013, pp. 32–38.

CHAPTER

5

Individual/ Organization Relations and Retention

Learning Objectives

After you have read this chapter, you should be able to:

LO1 Discuss four different views of motivation at work.

LO2 Explain the nature of the psychological contract.

LO3 Define the difference between job satisfaction and engagement.

LO4 Identify a system for controlling absenteeism.

LO5 Describe different kinds of turnover and how turnover can be measured.

LO6 Summarize various ways to manage retention.

WHAT'S TRENDING IN

INDIVIDUAL/ORGANIZATION RELATIONS AND RETENTION

HR professionals should develop workplace approaches that build stronger connections with employees. They must also be aware that organizational characteristics directly affect employee motivation, work attitudes, and engagement. Absenteeism and turnover often occur when organizations are not managed well, while high retention results when a satisfying work environment is created. Given these issues, here's what's currently trending in the area of individual/organization relations and retention:

1. Fostering employee motivation is always an ongoing concern for HR professionals. Companies are finding ways to enhance employees' work attitudes so that they are motivated to perform at high levels on the job.
2. Employee engagement often leads to greater loyalty and job performance. HR departments are trying to develop programs that get workers involved in ways that help organizations improve.
3. Employee withdrawal is a constant challenge for companies in a variety of industries, particularly those in the service sector. Unfortunately, such withdrawal, which is often precipitated by an undesirable work environment, can lead to excessive absenteeism and turnover. By partnering with line managers and senior leaders, HR professionals can focus their efforts on creating a workplace that discourages employees to leave their jobs.
4. The retention of employees is something that all organizations want to improve in both the short term and long term. Psychological contracts, work requirements, and other employment arrangements are being developed in different ways to enhance retention.

HEADLINE

Networking Engagement at Google and Yahoo

A network-based culture can be used to build greater employee engagement in organizations. Companies must therefore develop the right conditions that motivate employees to network more effectively with each other so that innovation, creativity, and positive decision making is fostered. In particular, by cultivating trust in the workplace, employees can build critical relationships and reach out to their colleagues in an effort to improve the organization.

The following strategies can be used to increase positive networking in companies:

- Get employees to feel comfortable about networking by emphasizing how learning is enhanced when it occurs. In this sense, networking is viewed as an individual competence that can help improve people *and* the workplace.
- Encourage employees to self-assess their own networking proficiencies. Once they know where they stand, help them determine how they can better engage with others through positive networking.
- Teach people to recognize defining moments that call for networking. These situations can make a difference in employees' successes.
- Help employees understand that networking can benefit the entire company, not just the individuals doing the networking.

A number of companies are capitalizing on some of these ideas and opportunities. For instance, the layout of Google's new worksite is designed so that people can interact more

Erin Siegal/Reuters

freely and randomly, which creates opportunities for innovative decision making in a more casual setting. Yahoo also buys into this kind of thinking; the company recently dropped its work-at-home programs in favor of requiring all employees to report to corporate offices to have more "face time" with each other. The basic idea is to create networking opportunities in a traditional workplace that enable workers to share more ideas and be more creative.[1]

Ideally, organizations are comprised of employees who have the ability to keep the company successfully moving forward. However, the value of employees is based on the level of their job performance. This performance depends on the effort these employees put into work, their ability, and employer support. Effort is in part determined by motivation, a topic that is worthy of consideration here. An individual's expectations about work, job satisfaction, commitment, engagement, and loyalty are some of the variables that can influence motivation, effort, and job performance.

These factors can also influence two potentially expensive HR challenges, absenteeism and turnover. Both factors represent withdrawal from the organization, which involves employees' feelings of separation. Understanding why people stay with an organization (called retention) or choose to withdraw requires organizational leaders to consider how companies treat employees. Desirable rewards, opportunities for development, reasonable HR policies, effective management of job and work–life issues, and workplace collegiality can enhance such treatment. The basics for understanding the relationships between employees and employers, as well as the associated consequences, are covered in this chapter.

LO1 Discuss four different views of motivation at work.

5-1 Individuals at Work

The relationship between individuals and their employers helps explain why people might choose to leave particular jobs or stay. For an employer to want to keep an employee, the individual must be performing well and making valuable contributions to the workplace.[2] Several factors affect the performance of employees, including individual abilities, the amount of effort expended, and the organizational support received. The HR unit exists in part to analyze and address these areas so that performance is enhanced and retention is increased. Exactly what the role of the HR unit "should be" often depends on the expectations of upper management, as well as the culture of the organization. As with any management function, HR management activities should be developed, evaluated, and changed as necessary so that they can contribute positively to the performance of individuals in their jobs, as well as enhance organizational performance overall.

5-1a Individual Performance Factors

The three major factors that affect how a given individual performs are illustrated in Figure 5-1. They are (1) individual ability to do the work, (2) effort expended, and (3) organizational support. The relationship of those factors is broadly defined in management literature as follows:

$$\text{Performance } (P) = \text{Ability } (A) \times \text{Effort } (E) \times \text{Support } (S)$$

Individual performance is enhanced to the degree that all three elements are present within an individual employee, but performance can be diminished if any factor is reduced or absent. For instance, assume that several production workers have the ability to do their jobs well and work productively, but the organization provides outdated equipment and/or the supervisors' management style causes negative reactions among the workers. These conditions would likely result in low job performance because the work environment is managed ineffectively.

FIGURE 5-1 Components of Individual Performance

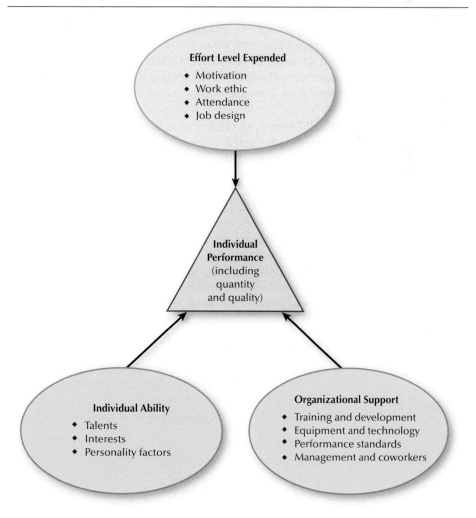

Effort Level Expended
- Motivation
- Work ethic
- Attendance
- Job design

Individual Performance (including quantity and quality)

Individual Ability
- Talents
- Interests
- Personality factors

Organizational Support
- Training and development
- Equipment and technology
- Performance standards
- Management and coworkers

Another example involves a customer service representative in a call center who has both excellent abilities and support. However, the individual dislikes "being tied to a telephone cord" all day and is frequently absent because of low satisfaction with the requirements of the job, even though the position pays well. In both cases, individual performance is likely to be lower compared to employment situations where all three components are present in a positive manner. Individual motivation is often a predictor of effort expended, so a brief overview of motivation as it affects performance is presented next.

5-1b Individual Motivation

Motivation
The desire that exists within a person that causes that individual to act

Motivation is the desire that exists within a person that causes that individual to act. People usually act for a number of reasons, but they are often tied to goals that have been set by themselves or by others around them. Thus, motivation is a goal-directed drive, and the process seldom occurs in a void. The words *need, want, desire,* and *drive* are all similar to *motive,* from which the word *motivation* is derived. Understanding motivation is important because compensation, turnover, and other HR concerns are related to it.

Approaches to understanding motivation vary because many theorists have developed their own views and models. Some approaches focus on intrinsic motivators that are inside an individual, while others concentrate on extrinsic factors that enhance motivation externally. Each approach has contributed to the understanding of human motivation. Four approaches are examined briefly in the following sections.

Need Theory   The theory of human motivation developed by Abraham Maslow has received a great deal of attention in academic and practitioner settings. This need theory of motivation assumes that only unsatisfied needs motivate individuals. Maslow classified human needs into five categories that ascend in a definite order. Until the more basic needs are adequately met, a person will not fully strive to meet higher needs. Maslow's well-known hierarchy is comprised of (1) *physiological needs,* (2) *safety and security needs,* (3) *belonging and love needs,* (4) *esteem needs,* and (5) *self-actualization needs.*

An assumption often made by those using Maslow's hierarchy is that workers in modern, technologically advanced societies have basically satisfied their physiological, safety, and belonging needs. Therefore, they will be motivated first by the needs for self-esteem and the esteem of others, and then by self-actualization. Conditions to satisfy these needs should therefore be present in the workplace to enable the job itself to be meaningful and motivating to employees.

Two-Factor Theory   Frederick Herzberg's motivation/hygiene theory assumes that one group of factors, *motivators,* accounts for increases in individual motivation because of enrichment and other positive work characteristics. Alternatively, *hygiene factors* can cause employees to become dissatisfied with work if these basic expectations are not adequately addressed; however, hygiene factors do not directly motivate employees.

Motivators	Hygiene Factors
• Achievement	• Interpersonal relationships
• Recognition	• Company policy/administration
• Work itself	• Supervision
• Responsibility	• Salary
• Advancement	• Working conditions

FIGURE 5-2   Need Theory and Two-Factor Theory Compared

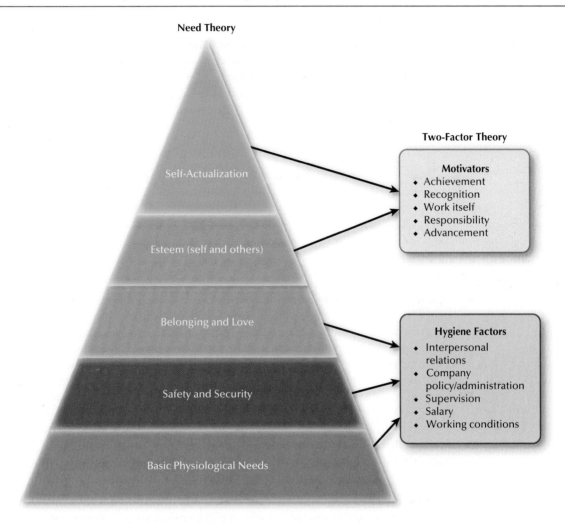

The implication of Herzberg's research for management and HR practices is that even when managers carefully consider and address hygiene factors to avoid employee dissatisfaction, employees may not be motivated to work harder. The two-factor theory suggests that only motivators cause employees to exert more effort and thereby enhance employee performance. Subsequent research has questioned whether the two groups of factors are really as distinct as Herzberg thought. Figure 5-2 shows a comparison of needs theory and two-factor theory.

Equity Theory   People want to be treated fairly at work, which is the basic underlying theme embedded within equity theory. Equity is defined as the perceived fairness of what the person does compared with what the person receives for doing it. *Inputs* are what a person brings to the organization, including educational level, age, experience, productivity, and other skills or efforts. *Outcomes* received by a person are the rewards obtained in exchange for all these inputs. Outcomes include pay, benefits, recognition of achievement, prestige, and any other rewards received.

Equity
The perceived fairness of what the person does compared with what the person receives for doing it

FIGURE 5-3 Simplified Expectancy Model of Motivation

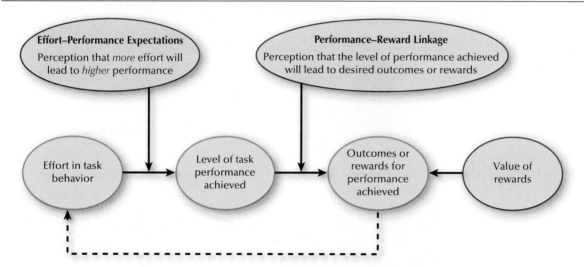

An outcome can be either tangible, which can include economic benefits (such as money) or intangible (such as recognition or achievement).

The employee's view of fair value is critical to the relationship between performance and job satisfaction because one's sense of equity is an exchange-based and comparative process. Assume an employee is an information technology (IT) specialist who exchanges talents and efforts (inputs) for the tangible and intangible rewards (outcomes) the employer provides. To determine perceived equity, the employee compares his or her talents, skills, and efforts to those of other IT specialists, both internally and at other firms. That perception, whether it is correct or incorrect, significantly affects that person's evaluation of the inputs and outcomes. A sense of inequity occurs when the comparison process results in an imbalance between inputs and outcomes, which can lead to negative results at work.

Expectancy Theory Lyman Porter and E. E. Lawler suggest that motivation is also influenced by what people expect. If expectations are not met, people may feel that they have been treated unfairly and consequently become dissatisfied. This theory states that individuals base decisions about their behaviors on their expectations that one or another alternate behavior is more likely to lead to desired outcomes. Figure 5-3 shows the three aspects of the behavior-outcome relationships.

- *Effort–performance expectations* refer to employees' beliefs that working harder will lead to high performance. If people do not believe that working harder leads to high performance, then their efforts may diminish.
- *Performance–reward linkage* considers individuals' expectations that high performance will actually lead to rewards. The performance–reward relationship indicates how instrumental or important effective performance is in producing desired results.
- *Value of rewards* refers to how valuable the rewards are to the employee. One determinant of employees' willingness to exert effort is the degree to which they value the rewards offered by the organization.

This model of motivation suggests that employees' levels of effort (motivation) are not simply a function of rewards. Employees must believe that they have the *ability to perform the tasks well*; they must expect that *high performance will result in receiving rewards*; and they must *value those rewards*. If all three conditions are met, employees will be motivated to exert greater effort on the job.[3]

5-1c Management Implications for Motivating Individual Performance

There is a motivating effect associated with making successful progress in meaningful work. Some would argue that this is the most powerful basis for motivation.

ETHICS

Working with Slackers Hurts Motivation

Research suggests that a large majority of employees report having to deal with slackers who intentionally don't work hard enough, making this issue a key ethical concern that relates to both workplace justice and fairness. Unfortunately, only a small percentage of individuals actually "cry foul" on colleagues who shirk their work responsibilities, which can perpetuate the problem and harm the motivation, satisfaction, and performance of other workers. Coworkers also end up working about four to six more hours each week to make up for the allocation of work that slackers don't complete, which can harm their own ability to perform at high levels.

But why don't people report slackers so that something can be done? At a minimum, employees should confront individuals who don't do their assigned work. Quite often, it's just easier for people to look the other way because they believe confrontation isn't worth the hassle. Unfortunately, most hardworking employees overlook all the risks associated with letting slackers get away with their selfishness and poor performance.

Companies much teach employees how to respond to workplace loafing. Situations should be handled diplomatically, but shirkers need to be "called on the carpet" for their lack of conscientiousness. In particular, training can be provided to help workers address slacking so that their motivation remains high. Companies should consider the following issues as they provide training to help employees deal with slackers: coworkers:

- *Don't be judgmental.* Start talking to your slacking coworker with an open mind and a curious demeanor. The individual might not understand how his or her slacking negatively affects you.
- *Make you coworker feel comfortable.* Show respect and describe how there are work objectives that you share in common.
- *Share your perceptions.* Talk about the behaviors you are witnessing in an impersonal way and convey how such conduct is not meeting expectations.
- *Talk about the challenges.* Describe how the slacking behavior is adversely impacting your own efforts and productivity.
- *Ask for feedback.* Determine if your coworker views the situation in a different light. You may not fully understand some of the circumstances that lead to the slacking behavior.[4]

Slacking is a common problem in business, and HR professionals should be sensitive to the inherent challenges so that these issues can be effectively addressed. Consider the following questions:

1. What kinds of signs might you look for when determining whether slacking is a problem? How should you encourage employees to report such poor performance?

2. Besides the training already discussed, what do think companies and HR departments can do to reduce the likelihood of coworker slacking?

Managers can undermine the meaningfulness of a person's work and therefore motivation by dismissing its importance, moving people off work before they finish it, shifting goals constantly, or neglecting to keep people updated on changing priorities. All these can diminish the motivation associated with meaningful work.[5] The behaviors of coworkers can also harm motivation. The preceding "HR Ethics: Working with Slackers Hurts Motivation" feature explores how employee loafing/shirking is a critical concern that can negatively affect individual motivation.

Organizational values, or the particular issues that companies address, may be important tools that can be used to motivate employees. A recent survey determined that being appreciated and respected in the workplace, being able to utilize personal capabilities, and liking the job were the top values that motivated workers. Other motivational issues included pay, employment security, good managers/leaders, and positive HR practices such as performance feedback, training, and benefits.[6] This research suggests that companies should improve these areas to increase employee motivation.

Many organizations spend considerable money to "motivate" their employees by using a wide range of tactics. For example, some firms use motivational speakers to inspire employees. Other employers give T-shirts, mugs, books, and videos to employees as motivators. However, the effectiveness of these expenditures has been questioned, particularly given the short-term nature of many of these programs and rewards. Managers and HR professionals would be better served by focusing on more substantive employment factors that have the capacity to increase individual motivation in the long term. Whatever issues are considered, answering a question often asked by managers,—How do I motivate my employees?—requires diagnosing employees' efforts, abilities, and expectations, as well of those of the organization.

LO2 Explain the nature of the psychological contract.

5-2 Individual Workers and Organizational Relationships

The relationship between individuals and their employers can be affected by HR practices and can vary widely from favorable to unfavorable. Important elements of these relationships include the psychological contract, job satisfaction, commitment, engagement, and loyalty (see Figure 5-4). Understanding these factors is more than just academically interesting. The economic health of organizations depends on the

FIGURE 5-4 The Individual–Organizational Relationship

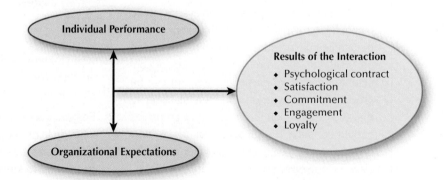

efforts of employees, which are driven by their ability and motivation to perform well. Employers must find ways to positively affect elements of individual–organization relationships so that work gets done.

5-2a Psychological Contract

Psychological contract
The unwritten expectations employees and employers have about the nature of their work relationships

A concept that has been useful in understanding individuals' relationships with their employers is the psychological contract, which refers to the unwritten expectations employees and employers have about the nature of their work relationships. Psychological contracts can create either positive or negative relationships between employers and individuals, so companies have a vested interest in cultivating appropriate and reasonable expectations to improve these ties. Psychological contracts are based on developing trust, building commitment, and improving loyalty with the ultimate goal of meeting both the employer's and employee's needs.

Unwritten psychological contracts between employers and employees encompass expectations about both tangible items (e.g., wages, benefits, employee productivity, and attendance) and intangible items (e.g., loyalty, fair treatment, and job security). Employers may attempt to detail their expectations through employee handbooks and policy manuals, but those materials are only part of the total "contractual" relationship. It is important to understand that significant parts of psychological contracts are often perceived rather than explicitly stated.

The Changing Psychological Contract Employees usually expect to exchange their efforts and capabilities for secure jobs that offer competitive pay, desirable benefits, opportunities to learn and develop, and career progression, among many other positive factors. But as some organizations have changed economically, in an effort to be more efficient, they have downsized and eliminated workers who had given long and loyal service. Consequently, a number of remaining employees in these firms question whether they should remain loyal to and stay with their employers. In other words, the contract has been altered in many organizations.

Despite these changes, employers must still make efforts to strengthen psychological contracts. Doing so requires HR professionals and line managers to focus on several elements of these arrangements. A psychological contract often involves the following expectations:

Employers Will Provide

- Competitive compensation and benefits
- Flexibility to balance work and home life
- Career development opportunities

Employees Will Contribute

- Continuous skill improvement and increased productivity
- Reasonable length of service
- Extra efforts and results when needed

Psychological contracts can be strengthened and employee commitment enhanced when the organization is involved in a cause that is important to the employee. Companies may also improve employment relationships by focusing on developing altruism in the workplace. This can be done by creating positive work norms, focusing on fairness and responsibility, and offering employees more autonomy.[7] Leadership styles also need to be better matched with HR strategies to help craft positive psychological contracts among employees.[8] Finally, the results of a recent study of science-oriented university faculty members working for a Latin American institution suggest that managers should build more positive social networks among employees so that they perceive psychological contracts more favorably. Better communication about rewards and more recognition in the workplace should also help.[9]

ETHICS

Conversely, psychological contracts can be violated—not only by personal mistreatment but also by a perception that the organization has abandoned an important principle or cause. For instance, when unethical or illegal behavior is committed by upper management, the psychological contract is violated and employees may feel anger, distrust, reduced loyalty and commitment, and increased willingness to leave. Serious ethical scandals may be particularly damaging to psychological contracts because awareness of unethical behavior is so widespread.

GLOBAL

Global Psychological Contract Concerns With many organizations having global operations, the psychological contract becomes more complicated. Employees in foreign countries and expatriate employees from the United States have varying psychological contract expectations. If organizational expectations are not made clear prior to relocation of expatriates, there is a greater chance that the assignment will be cut short or the employee will quit upon returning home.[10]

An additional concern for multinational firms is the need to meet the diverse psychological contract expectations of individuals in different cultures and countries. Consider the number of jobs that have been shifted from the United States and Europe to China, India, Romania, Mexico, the Philippines, Brazil, and other countries with different cultures. Being aware of varying psychological contract issues with international employees is important if global HR efforts are to succeed.

5-2b Job Satisfaction and Commitment

LO3 Define the difference between job satisfaction and engagement.

Job satisfaction
The positive feelings and evaluations derived from an individual's employment in a job

In its most basic sense, job satisfaction involves the positive feelings and evaluations derived from an individual's employment in a job. For example, recognizing an employee for a job well done by providing time off from work is likely to promote job satisfaction. There are many things a company can do from an HR perspective to increase employee job satisfaction such as providing fair pay and benefits, offering opportunities for promotion, training and developing workers, and communicating work expectations with regular performance appraisals. Figure 5-5 shows some of the most commonly recognized components of job satisfaction.

Alternatively, job *dissatisfaction* occurs when work experiences are negative and expectations are not met. An employee who expects clean and safe working conditions will likely be dissatisfied if the workplace is dirty and dangerous. The different

FIGURE 5-5 Components of Job Satisfaction

> **Job Satisfaction**
> - Adequacy of the pay
> - Opportunity for advancement
> - Supervision
> - Coworkers
> - Nature of the work

ideas managers and workers have about career development can also lead to job dissatisfaction among employees because work assignments don't always meet their income and growth expectations.[11] Employee job satisfaction is declining due to the changing nature of employment in companies, a shift that is often driven by global commerce, corporate restructuring, the growth in service-sector jobs, and decreased union presence. Employees are also pessimistic about government and business being able to address economic problems, among other issues.[12]

Many organizations and researchers study job dissatisfaction. At any one time, from 15% to 40% of working people across the nation are dissatisfied with their jobs. Higher unemployment rates usually mean more dissatisfied workers in the workforce because it is more difficult to change jobs, and people stay longer with jobs they do not like. Managers directly impact job satisfaction, and younger employees tend to have lower job satisfaction than older employees.[13]

Sometimes job satisfaction is called *morale*, a term usually used to describe the job satisfaction of a group or organization. A workplace that develops and emphasizes fair policies, organizational justice, ethical practices, teamwork, and a positive culture is in a good position to improve employee morale. Factors that can decrease morale include demanding and stressful work, poor management–employee interactions, undesirable rewards, work–life conflicts, and a lack of enrichment at work. It is also speculated that declines in overall earnings and the increasing income growth differences between the middle class and wealthy will erode morale. HR professionals need to ensure that profits are distributed to managers and employees in a fair manner.[14]

Poor morale and job satisfaction among employees often lead to attendance problems, low work performance, and retention issues. This is why HR professionals and operating managers must properly evaluate and manage employee work attitudes to ensure good retention. One way employers do this is by regularly surveying employees. One specific type of survey used by many organizations is an attitude survey, which focuses on employees' feelings and beliefs about their jobs and the organization. An annual employee survey of federal workers determined that 80% claimed they liked their job situations, and 60% felt engaged at work. However, only 67% of them would recommend their agency to others, down from the previous year. In addition, only 68% were satisfied with their jobs, and 59% were satisfied with the organization, both down from the previous year.[15]

> **Attitude survey**
> A survey that focuses on employees' feelings and beliefs about their jobs and the organization

Management can respond to survey results after they are compiled. If the employer takes responsive actions, employees may view the employer more positively. However, if management ignores the survey results, such inaction can lead to lower job satisfaction. This is why HR professionals must be proactive about partnering with managers to address the opportunities and challenges identified in employee surveys.

> **Organizational commitment**
> The degree to which workers believe in and accept organizational objectives and want to remain employed at a company

The degree to which workers believe in and accept organizational objectives and want to remain employed at a company is called organizational commitment. Job satisfaction influences organizational commitment, and both of these factors can in turn affect employee retention and turnover. It is the interaction of the individual and the immediate work context that determines levels of job satisfaction and organizational commitment. Managers and HR professionals must therefore create employment situations that prompt positive work attitudes and get employees engaged in the workplace.

5-2c Employee Engagement, Loyalty, and Organizational Citizenship

Employee engagement
The extent to which an employee's thoughts and behaviors are focused on his or her work and their employer's success

Employee engagement is the extent to which an employee's thoughts and behaviors are focused on his or her work and their employer's success. Interest in employee engagement has been growing in the field of HR management because the process can affect many important performance outcomes. For instance, engaged workers are more productive, exhibit greater dedication, perform at higher levels, and show higher retention than do unengaged workers.[16] Descriptions of engaged employees and disengaged employees are shown in Figure 5-6.

The concept of engagement is positive because it suggests that workers can contribute much more effectively to organizational results if there are attempts made to better connect them to the workplace.[17] Unfortunately, recent Gallup research suggests that employee engagement is a challenge in many firms, with only 31.5% of employees being engaged with their work, 51% not being engaged, and 17.5% being activity disengaged.[18] An HR department should therefore work with managers and employees to find better ways to improve engagement levels throughout an organization. Engagement can be enhanced by emphasizing the company's culture and practices during interviews, having managers support this culture in a consistent manner (such as during orientation), and providing employees with a supportive group of coworkers who make them feel part of the team. Providing challenging and dynamic employment opportunities, a respectful work environment, chances for promotion, and monetary incentives are also ways that employers can increase employee engagement.[19] Encouraging more idea entrepreneurship can be another way to enhance engagement. Idea entrepreneurs have a passion for certain issues, and they become highly involved in the workplace (they invest time, get others on board, etc.) to create positive change in firms.[20] The following "HR Competencies & Applications: Defeating Unengaged Employee Zombies" feature investigates other ways companies can prevent unengaged employees from acting like the zombies found in Hollywood movies.

Loyalty Many employees still want security, stability, a supervisor they respect, competitive pay and benefits, and the opportunity to advance. But competition and increasing costs of doing business have led companies to trim payrolls and to no longer offer some employment opportunities. As a result, the era of company loyalty might have passed, as people are more inclined to move between companies.[21]

FIGURE 5-6 Engaged and Disengaged Employees

Engaged Employees	Disengaged Employees
◆ Put in extra effort	◆ Simply put in time
◆ Are highly involved in their jobs	◆ Do not do best work
◆ Employ both effort and thought	◆ Are "checked out"/apathetic
◆ Are active/busy	◆ Do only their basic jobs
◆ Are fully invested in their jobs	◆ React only to pay

Loyalty
Being faithful to an institution or employer

Loyalty can be defined as being faithful to an institution or employer. Loyalty is a reciprocal exchange between organizations and their workers. Employees' loyalty to a company depends on their perceptions of the company's loyalty to them. The trend toward employees bearing more of the financial risk for retirement savings, health insurance, and career development has sent a clear message that the employee must control his or her own future because the employer is not loyal.[22] Evidence suggests that some employees unfortunately don't believe that their companies reciprocate the loyalty that they show.[23]

ETHICS

But there may be unique ways for managers to improve loyalty in organizations, as well as engagement. Employees are more loyal when their managers are humble, reserved, and trustworthy. For instance, apologizing to employees when mistakes are made can build trust in the workplace. A recent Forum Corporation survey found that managers claimed that they apologize much more frequently at work than their employees indicated. The results also showed that a majority of employees believed that trust in management was very important, while a little less than half of managers believed that it was important for management to be trusted by employees. Finally, the survey determined that lying, stealing the ideas of others, gossiping, and other communication problems were considered to be significant concerns about management, and such misbehavior is arguably caused by a low regard for trust.[24] Managers should be proactive about apologizing to employees when they make mistakes in order to build trust, loyalty, and engagement.

Organizational Citizenship Related to both engagement and loyalty is the concept of organizational citizenship. Organizational citizenship behavior (OCB) occurs when an employee acts in a way that improves the psychological well-being and social environment of an organization. Research suggests that individuals have many different motives that may encourage them to exhibit OCBs at work, some of which focus on employers and some of which focus on coworkers.[25] One study determined that Confucian Asians believe more strongly than do Anglos that OCBs are part of their jobs, and that OCBs benefiting others are considered part of work more so than are OCBs prompting organizational change. In addition, the more individuals think that OCBs are part of work, the more they act as citizens on the job.[26] Examples of citizenship include helping a coworker complete a work activity so that a deadline is reached and cheering on a colleague for receiving a reward. Other examples are getting involved and engaged in a project that helps the company's bottom line and volunteering to be on a committee that creates positive organizational policies. Organizational citizenship behavior generally leads to a more desirable workplace, more positive social interactions, and higher job performance.[27]

Organizational citizenship behavior
Occurs when an employee acts in a way that improves the psychological well-being and social environment of an organization

Employers might be able to encourage OCBs with the proper work characteristics and approaches. One study found that gratitude is positively related to OCB, which suggests that companies can treat employees in a manner that builds greater appreciation and recognition and prompts citizenship.[28] Citizenship fatigue may be another issue in companies, so HR professionals should focus efforts on developing a work context that supports employees, builds teamwork, and avoids pressuring individuals to exhibit OCBs.[29]

Work attitudes, engagement, loyalty, and citizenship are all factors that can influence decisions to remain with or leave an organization, and ultimately they are reflected in employee retention and turnover statistics. Individuals who are dissatisfied with their jobs or not committed to a company are more likely to withdraw from an organization. Disengaged and disloyal employees who are not citizens are also unlikely to perform well or be recognized in their jobs, also leading to withdrawal. One kind of withdrawal is turnover, which means an individual leaves an organization. Another kind of withdrawal is absenteeism, which involves failing to report to work when scheduled. Absenteeism is covered in the next section.

COMPETENCIES & APPLICATIONS

Defeating Unengaged Employee Zombies

For many reasons, employees can act like zombies in organizations that do not take the proper steps to increase engagement. A big part of this stems from the technology used by workers today, which encourages them to act in a brainless way when it comes to decision making, interpersonal communication, and group processes. There are several things that leaders can do to reduce these trends, but in particular, they need to find creative ways to engage individuals in the workplace. Like in a Hollywood movie, both leaders and employees have to work together to defeat the zombie hoards of the unengaged.

What makes unengaged employees act like zombies? First, unengaged workers have limited vision because they tend not to be future oriented, and they lack a clear focus, very similar to zombies. Second, they often lack a higher degree of coordinated effort in the workplace, so the left hand doesn't know what the right hand is doing. Once again, this mimics the behavior of zombies. Third, unengaged workers have the ability to slow down the work and movements of other productive coworkers, one more thing that people do to others when they change into zombies. Finally, they can distract employees from focusing on more promising endeavors at work by creating roadblocks to success (e.g., lots of meetings, bureaucratic processes, too much communication), much in the same way that fighting zombies takes time and resources away from other important survival needs.

How can employers effectively battle unengaged zombies? There are several things companies can do, including the following actions:

- Company leaders need to create a proper vision for success.
- Empower employees to implement the vision in a way that fits their preferences.
- Don't worry if you don't get everyone onboard with the new vision.
- Get managers involved in implementing any new strategies developed to support the vision.
- Managers need to develop meaningful communication about the company's strategy without overdoing it.
- Keep people up to date about the progress of planning and implementing the strategies.
- Support the people who are behind the vision by making sure that they have the tools to help each other.[30]

As an HR leader, you will likely be given the opportunity to help unengaged employees. Consequently, consider the following questions:

1. As an HR professional, how would you encourage workers to be more engaged in the workplace instead of acting like zombies?

2. What if your initial efforts didn't work? How would you improvise and strategize to make the situation at work better? Who could you turn to for assistance?

KEY COMPETENCIES: Leadership and Navigation (Behavioral Competency) and People (Technical Competency)

LO4 Identify a
system for controlling
absenteeism.

Absenteeism
Any failure by an
employee to report
for work as scheduled
or to stay at work
when scheduled

5-3 Employee Absenteeism

Employees who are absent from their work and job responsibilities create major
issues in the relationship between an employee and employer. Absenteeism is any failure
by an employee to report for work as scheduled or to stay at work when scheduled.
Being absent from work may seem like an insignificant matter to an employee. But if a
manager needs 12 people in a unit to get the work done, and 4 of the 12 are frequently
absent, either the output of the unit will decrease or additional workers will have to be
hired to meet needs. For some employers, productivity losses due to absenteeism can
be very expensive. The average daily cost is 1.3 times the wages of the absent worker.[31]
Some people are also not concerned about arriving at work on time. Tardiness can be
closely related to absenteeism.

5-3a Types of Absenteeism

Employees can be absent from work or tardy for several reasons. Clearly, some
absenteeism is inevitable because of illness, death in the family, and other personal
reasons. Though absences such as those that are health related are unavoidable
and understandable, they are still very costly. Many employers have sick leave policies that allow employees a certain number of paid days each year for *involuntary*
absences. However, much absenteeism is avoidable, or *voluntary*. Absence can also be
planned (the least disruptive), unplanned, incidental (less than a week), or extended
(lasting beyond a week).

Many employees see no real concern about being absent or late to work because
they feel that they are "entitled" to some absenteeism. In many firms, a relatively
small number of individuals are responsible for a large share of the organization's
total absenteeism. Regardless of the reason, employers need to know if someone is
going to be absent so that they can make adjustments. Organizations have developed
different ways for employees to report their absences. Some companies have established automated systems in which employees can call a special phone number and
alert managers about their possible absences. Special electronic notification email
accounts could also be used.

5-3b Controlling Absenteeism

Effective absence management involves striking a balance between supporting
employees who are legitimately unable to work and meeting operational needs.
Voluntary absenteeism can be more effectively controlled if managers understand its
causes and the associated costs. Figure 5-7 shows some of the direct and indirect costs
associated with absenteeism. Once the causes and costs are understood, managers can
use a variety of approaches to reduce it, including attendance rewards, paid time-off
programs, unused leave buyback policies, illness verification, and disciplinary actions.
Other more general approaches can be used to improve the workplace and reduce
absenteeism, for example, improving the availability of employment opportunities,
providing more generous compensation, and promoting work–life balance. A study
found that meaningful work was associated with increased engagement, which led
to reduced absenteeism.[32] Regardless of the strategies utilized, organizational policies
on absenteeism should be stated clearly in an employee handbook and consistently
enforced by supervisors and managers.

FIGURE 5-7 Sources of Direct and Indirect Costs of Absenteeism

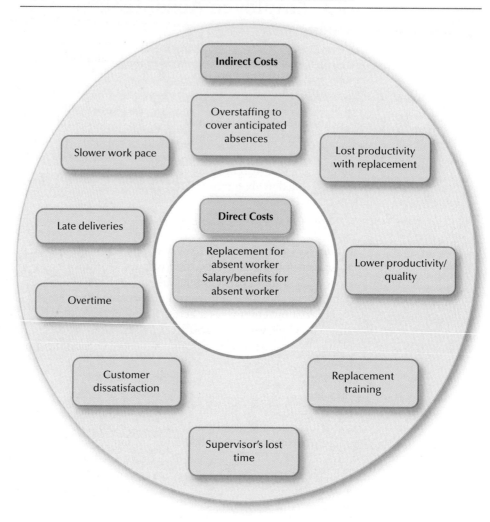

Employers use methods such as the following to address absenteeism:

- *Disciplinary approach:* Many employers use this approach. People who are absent the first time receive a verbal warning and subsequent absences result in written warnings, suspension, and finally dismissal.
- *Positive reinforcement:* Positive reinforcement includes actions such as giving employees cash, recognition, time off, and other rewards for meeting attendance standards. Offering rewards for consistent attendance, giving bonuses for missing fewer than a certain number of days, and "buying back" unused sick leave are all positive reinforcement methods of reducing absenteeism.
- *Combination approach:* A combination approach ideally rewards desired behaviors and punishes undesired behaviors. This carrot-and-stick approach uses policies and discipline to punish offenders and various programs and rewards to recognize employees with outstanding attendance. For instance, employees with perfect attendance may receive incentives of travel and other rewards. Those with excessive absenteeism would be terminated.

- *No-fault policy:* With a no-fault policy, the reasons for absences do not matter, and the employees must manage their own attendance unless they abuse that freedom. Once absenteeism exceeds normal limits, then disciplinary action up to and including termination of employment can occur. The advantages of the no-fault approach are that there is uniformity in the ways absence is handled, and supervisors and HR staff do not have to judge whether absences count as excused or unexcused.
- *Paid-time-off (PTO) programs:* Some employers have paid-time-off programs, in which vacation time, holidays, and sick leave for each employee are combined into a paid-time-off (PTO) account. Employees use days from their accounts at their discretion for illness, personal time, or vacation. If employees run out of days in their accounts, they are not paid for any additional days missed. PTO programs generally reduce absenteeism, particularly one-day absences, but they often increase overall time away from work because employees use all of "their" time off by taking unused days as vacation days.

MEASURE

5-3c Measuring Absenteeism

A major step in reducing absenteeism is to decide how the organization will calculate and record absences and then how to benchmark those rates. Controlling or reducing absenteeism must begin with continuous monitoring of the absenteeism statistics in work units. Such monitoring helps managers pinpoint employees who are frequently absent and departments that have excessive absenteeism. Various methods of measuring or computing absenteeism exist. One formula suggested by the U.S. Department of Labor is as follows:

$$\frac{\text{number of persons} - \text{days lost through job absence during period}}{(\text{average number of employees}) \times (\text{number of workdays})} \times 100$$

The absenteeism rate can also be based on number of hours instead of number of days.

One set of metrics that can be calculated is the rate of absenteeism, which can be based on annual, monthly, quarterly, or other periods of time. Other useful measures of absenteeism might include the following:

- *Incidence rate:* The number of absences per 100 employees each day
- *Inactivity rate:* The percentage of time lost to absenteeism
- *Severity rate:* The average time lost per absent employee during a specified period of time (a month or a year)

Additional information can be gained by separating absenteeism data into short-term and long-term categories. Different problems are caused by employees who are absent for one day 10 times during a year and employees who are absent one time for 10 days.

Turnover
The process in which employees leave an organization and have to be replaced

LO5 Describe different kinds of turnover and how turnover can be measured.

5-4 Employee Turnover

Turnover is the process in which employees leave an organization and have to be replaced. Many organizations have found that turnover is a very costly problem. For instance, health care firms in one state experienced over 30% turnover annually. The turnover cost in the state for nursing jobs alone was more than $125 million per year, with individual nurse turnover costs being $32,000 per person who left.[33]

The extent to which employers face high turnover rates and costs often varies by organization and industry. For example, the Society for Human Resource Management (SHRM) calculates that the average for all industries is 15% annual turnover. But companies in service industries such as restaurants have an average annual rate of 35%. Entertainment and recreation has 27% turnover and retail 22%. Health care and social assistance have 20% annual turnover.[34]

Research shows that many factors can lead to turnover. For instance, job dissatisfaction, low levels of various kinds of work commitment, work–life conflict, and decreased justice can encourage people to quit their jobs. Forces such as the availability of other employment opportunities and unemployment rates are also tied to employee turnover.[35] Turnover typically goes up as unemployment rates drop and dissatisfied employees can find other jobs.[36] Research also indicates that individuals who provide advice to their colleagues believe that they are not appropriately compensated for doing so, which results in stronger intentions to leave.[37] The means that companies need to pay close attention to how they recognize and compensate employees who help their coworkers. Another study determined that *boomerang employees* (individuals who leave a firm but are reemployed later) often quit because of personal reasons or events, while alumni (individuals who leave for good) often quit because of negative work experiences; boomerang employees also quit their jobs sooner in their employment tenure than do alumni employees.[38]

Organizations must be proactive about managing turnover so that the work environment is not adversely impacted. In particular, HR professionals and line managers must look for signs that point to possible turnover among employees. Some of these signs include:

- Low interest in getting promoted within the firm
- Low motivation to keep managers happy
- A reluctance to be involved in long-term work opportunities
- Decreased motivation to be enrolled in training and development opportunities
- Fewer contributions in meetings
- Just getting by or working only enough to get work done[39]

A good example of how turnover can be effectively managed involves the Atlanta-based Boys & Girls Clubs of America, which has almost 400 corporate employees. The organization determined that turnover is highest among employees with one to three years of service. Through exit interviews the organization determined that the most frequent reasons people left were bad job fit and poor job experiences (i.e., expectations were not met). As a result of its analysis, the HR department implemented a "more high-touch" recruiting system to reduce the number of poor hires. This included multiple on-site interviews. Further, recruiters changed how they measure recruiting success to include finding a *good* candidate, rather than just any candidate. Historically, they looked at time to fill vacancy but now focus on quality of hire. Supervisors evaluate quality of hire, and HR looks at performance reviews of new hires. Among 82 new hires, the organization kept 93% in the first two years of the new approach, and the overall turnover rate dropped from 11% to 9%.[40] For another example of how turnover can be managing effectively, see the following "HR Perspective: Rosemont Center Takes Care of Turnover" feature.

PERSPECTIVE

Rosemont Center Takes Care of Turnover

Rosemont Center, Inc., in Columbus, Ohio, is an agency that provides mental health and social services to youths and low-income families. These include outpatient therapy, foster care, day treatment, and mental health services.

At one point, annual employee turnover had reached 72%. The 62 employees included therapists, counselors, and social workers. At its peak, the staff numbered 150, but funding cuts led to elimination of some programs. During the ensuing layoffs, voluntary turnover jumped. Low morale and motivation became a problem for the survivors, and the quality of services was affected.

The HR Director checked the turnover metrics and put together a task force to identify causes. They identified the following issues:

- Demanding work
- Work–life balance: night work and weekends
- Low salaries
- On-call responsibilities without compensation

Exit interviews and employee satisfaction surveys were reviewed, and managers of similar agencies in Ohio were interviewed. These interviews were conducted to help improve employee satisfaction and reduce turnover. The task force's recommendations to the board included:

- *Career development*: Internal job bidding for promotions and transfers; create an internal list of people who would consider jobs at Rosemont
- *Rewards*: A salary study to make sure salaries were competitive

- *Management and organization*: Develop a system of support for directors and supervisors to reduce recruiting and orientation costs for new employees; encourage open communication with employees
- *Work–life balance*: Promote employee assistance programs and provide work–life balance training

With backing from the board of directors, the resulting program reduced turnover to 48%, and morale and service improved. The job bidding process was key to this success. Compensation was increased based on the salary study, and employees were given more benefit choices. Rosemont generated a list of candidates who wanted to work at the agency. When a position opened, several candidates were available. Formal training for managers had a positive effect on staff, who felt more supported by their supervisors. The company developed a training agenda that received funding. Finally, quarterly all-staff meetings and other events fostered a more open culture.[41]

Based on these approaches, consider the following questions:

1. Did the social services nature of this organization make the turnover situation any different compared to in a private company? Why or why not?

2. Have you seen similar efforts occur in places where you have worked? Describe them and comment on their success.

5-4a Types of Employee Turnover

Turnover is classified in many ways. One classification uses the following categories, although the two types are not mutually exclusive:

- **Involuntary Turnover**

  Employees are terminated for poor performance or work rule violations, or through layoffs

- **Voluntary Turnover**

  Employees leave by choice

Involuntary turnover is triggered at all levels by employers terminating workers because of organizational policies and work rule violations, excessive absenteeism, performance standards that are not met by employees, and other issues. Voluntary turnover can be caused by many factors, some of which are not employer controlled. Common voluntary turnover causes include job dissatisfaction, pay and benefits levels, supervision, geography, and personal/family reasons. Career opportunities in other firms, when employees receive unsolicited contacts, may lead to turnover for individuals, especially those in highly specialized jobs such as IT. Voluntary turnover may increase with the size of the organization, most likely because larger firms are less effective in preventing turnover.

Another view of turnover classifies it on the basis of whether it is good or bad for the organization:

- **Functional Turnover**

  Lower-performing or disruptive employees leave

- **Dysfunctional Turnover**

  Key individuals and high performers leave

Not all turnover in organizations is negative. On the contrary, functional turnover represents a positive change. Some workforce losses are desirable, especially if those who leave are lower-performing, less reliable, and/or disruptive individuals. Of course, dysfunctional turnover also occurs. That happens when key individuals leave, often at crucial times. For example, a software project leader leaves in the middle of a system upgrade to take a promotion at another firm. His departure causes the time line to slip because of the difficulty of replacing him. Further, other software specialists in the firm begin to seek out and accept jobs at competitive firms because he left. This is truly dysfunctional turnover.

Employees quit for many reasons, only some of which can be controlled by the organization. Another classification uses the following terms to differentiate types of turnover:

- **Uncontrollable Turnover**

  Employees leave for reasons outside the control of the employer

- **Controllable Turnover**

  Employees leave for reasons that could be influenced by the employer

Some examples of reasons for turnover the employer cannot control include: (1) the employee moves out of the geographic area, (2) the employee decides to stay home with young children or an older relative, (3) the employee's spouse is transferred, or (4) the employee is a student worker who graduates from college. Even though some turnover is inevitable, employers recognize that reducing turnover saves money, and they must address turnover that is controllable. Organizations are better able to keep employees if they address the concerns of those individuals that might lead to controllable turnover.

Churn
Hiring new workers while laying off others

Turnover and "Churn" Hiring new workers while laying off others is called churn. This practice raises a paradox in which employers sometimes complain about not being able to find workers with the right skills while they are laying off other employees.

As organizations face economic and financial problems that result in layoffs, the remaining employees are more likely to consider jobs at other firms. In this situation, turnover is more likely to occur, and efforts are needed to retain existing employees. HR actions such as information sharing, opportunities for more training/learning, and emphasis on job significance can be helpful in lowering individuals' turnover intentions.

MEASURE

5-4b Measuring Employee Turnover

Turnover is a considerable challenge for organizations, and to make matters worse, many companies do not formally measure employee separations. A survey conducted by a division of the American Management Association determined that 42% of the 977 business professionals sampled claimed that their companies had a formal approach for assessing employee turnover. Almost 30% claimed to have an informal approach in place for evaluating turnover, 12% indicated that their employers do not monitor quitting, and 17% didn't know if turnover was monitored at all.[42] This is a serious concern given that the U.S. Department of Labor estimates that the cost of replacing an employee ranges from one-half to five times the person's annual salary, depending on the position.[43]

The turnover rate for an organization can be computed on a monthly or yearly basis. The following formula, in which *separations* means departures from the organization, is widely used:

$$\frac{\textit{number of employee separations during the year}}{\textit{total number of employees at midyear}} \times 100$$

Turnover rates vary widely among industries and organizations, ranging from almost 0% to more than 100% a year. As a part of HR management information, turnover data can be gathered and analyzed in many ways, including the following categories:

- Job and job level
- Department, unit, and location
- Reason for leaving
- Length of service
- Demographic characteristics
- Education and training
- Knowledge, skills, and abilities
- Performance ratings/levels

Two examples illustrate why detailed analyses of turnover are important. A manufacturing organization had a companywide turnover rate that was not severe, but 80% of the turnover occurred within one department. Specific actions such as training supervisors and revising pay levels were needed to resolve problems in that unit. In a different organization, a global shipping/delivery firm identified reasons for turnover of sales and service employees and was able to focus on those reasons and reduce turnover in that group. The actions taken reduced turnover significantly, which contributed to an annual savings of several million dollars in direct and indirect costs. In both of these examples, the targeted turnover rates declined as a result of employer actions taken in response to turnover analyses.

5-5 HR Metrics: Determining Turnover Costs

A major step in reducing the expense of turnover is to decide how the organization will calculate and record employee departures, as well as how to benchmark the turnover rates. Determining turnover costs can be relatively simple or very complex, depending on the nature of the efforts made and the data used.

Figure 5-8 shows a model for calculating the cost of productivity lost to turnover. Of course, this is only one cost associated with turnover. But it is one that is more difficult to conceptualize. If a job pays $20,000 (A) and benefits cost 40% (B), then the total annual cost for one employee is $28,000 (C). Assuming that 20 employees have quit in the previous year (D) and that it takes three months for one employee to become fully productive (E), the calculation results in a per-person turnover cost of $3,500 (F). Overall, the annual lost productivity would be $70,000 for the 20 individuals who have left (G). In spite of the conservative and simple nature of this model, it easily makes the point that productivity lost to turnover is costly.

MEASURE

5-5a Detailing Turnover Cost

In addition to lost productivity, other factors to be included in calculating detailed turnover costs include the following:

- *Separation costs*: HR staff and supervisory time, pay rates to prevent separations, exit interview time, unemployment expenses, legal fees for challenged separations, accrued vacation expenditures, continued health benefits, and others
- *Vacancy costs*: Temporary help, contract and consulting firm usage, existing employee overtime, and other costs until the person is replaced
- *Replacement costs*: Recruiting and advertising expenses, search fees, HR interviewer and staff time and salaries, employee referral fees, relocation and moving costs, supervisor and managerial time and salaries, employment testing costs, reference checking fees, pre-employment medical expenses, relocation costs, and others

FIGURE 5-8 Model for Costing Lost Productivity

Job Title: _____

A. Typical annual pay for this job
B. Percentage of pay for benefits multiplied by annual pay
C. Total employee annual cost (A + B)
D. Number of employees who voluntarily quit the job in the past 12 months
E. Number of months it takes for one employee to become fully productive
F. Per person turnover cost ([E ÷ 12] × C × 50%)*
G. Annual turnover cost for this job (F × D)

*Assumes 50% productivity throughout the learning period (E).

FIGURE 5-9 Components of Turnover Cost

- *Training costs for the new person*: Paid orientation time, training staff time and pay, costs of training materials, supervisor and manager time and salaries, coworker "coaching" time and pay, and others
- *Hidden/indirect costs*: Costs that are less obvious, such as reduced productivity (calculated above), decreased customer service, lower quality, additional unexpected employee turnover, missed project deadlines, and others

Turnover metrics illustrate that turnover is an expensive HR and managerial issue that must be constantly evaluated and addressed. Figure 5-9 summarizes the costs of turnover.

As noted, not all turnover is negative. Losing low performers should be considered positive. There may be an "optimal" amount of useful turnover necessary to replace low performers and add part-time or contract workers with special capabilities to improve workforce performance.

MEASURE

5-5b Optimal Turnover

Even though turnover is a key concern for companies, some managers don't know how much turnover is optimal for their particular workgroups. A survey showed that nearly one-third of managers didn't have an idea about optimal turnover. Almost half believed that optimal turnover should be 10% or less.[44] This means that HR departments should partner with managers to help them determine what their optimal turnover rates really are.

Turnover costs and benefits can be calculated separately for various organizational segments. HR departments frequently strive to minimize all types of turnover, but in some cases, more turnover activity can be better. For example, reducing turnover makes sense when it is very expensive, when those leaving are more valuable than their replacements, or when there may not be suitable replacements. However, more turnover activity in certain segments of the organization may make sense if it costs very little, those leaving are less valuable than their replacements, or there is certainty that good replacements are available.[45] Another solution is to calculate the financial impact of different types of turnover and attach a dollar cost to it to determine the optimum level.[46]

5-6 Retaining Talent

In one sense, retention is the opposite of turnover. However, the reasons key people choose to stay with an employer may not be the opposite of those that compel others to quit. Retaining top talent is a concern for many employers, and understanding retention is the key to keeping more of those top performers.

5-6a Myths and Realities about Retention

Keeping good employees is a challenge for all organizations and becomes even more difficult as labor markets change. Unfortunately, some myths have arisen about what it takes to retain employees. Some of the most prevalent myths and realities that exist are as follows:

1. *Money is the main reason people leave.* Money is certainly a powerful recruiting tool, and if people feel they are being paid inadequately, they may be more likely to leave. But if they are paid close to the competitive level they expect, other aspects of the job become more important than the pay they receive.
2. *Hiring has little to do with retention.* This is not true. Recruiting and selecting the people who fit the jobs and who are less likely to leave in the first place, and then orienting them to the company, can greatly increase retention. It is important to select for retention. Do not hire people with a history of high turnover.
3. *If you train people, you are only training them for another employer.* Developing skills in employees may indeed make them more marketable, but it also tends to improve retention. When an employer provides employees with training and development assistance, job satisfaction may increase, and employees may be more likely to stay, particularly if they see more future opportunities internally.
4. *Do not be concerned about retention during organizational change.* The time when organizational change takes place is exactly when employees worry about their future. Although some people's jobs may have to be cut because of organizational factors, the remaining employees that the company *would like to keep* may have the most opportunity and reason to leave voluntarily. For example, during a merger or acquisition, most workers are concerned about job security and their employer's future. If they are not made to feel a part of the new organization early on, many may leave or evaluate other alternatives.
5. *If high performers want to leave, the company cannot hold them.* Employees are "free agents," who can indeed leave when they choose. The key to keeping high-performing employees is to create an environment in which they want to stay, grow, and contribute.

5-6b Drivers of Retention

Employee retention can be affected by a variety of job-related and personal factors. For instance, if employees choose to leave an organization for family reasons (e.g., because a spouse is transferring or to raise children), there may be a limited number of actions the employer can take to keep them on the job. However, there are significant actions that an employer can take to retain employees in many other circumstances. If employees want work–life balance in their careers or opportunities for training and development (i.e., personal growth), there are steps companies can take to address these preferences.

The actual reasons that people stay or leave may also vary by job, industry and organizational issues, geography, and other factors. Yet, many of these factors are within the employer's control. Figure 5-10 illustrates some of the drivers of retention, or areas in which employers can take action to increase the probability of keeping employees.

Organizational and Management Factors Many organizational and management factors influence individuals' job satisfaction and their decisions to stay with or leave their employers. Organizations that have clearly established goals and

FIGURE 5-10 Drivers of Retention

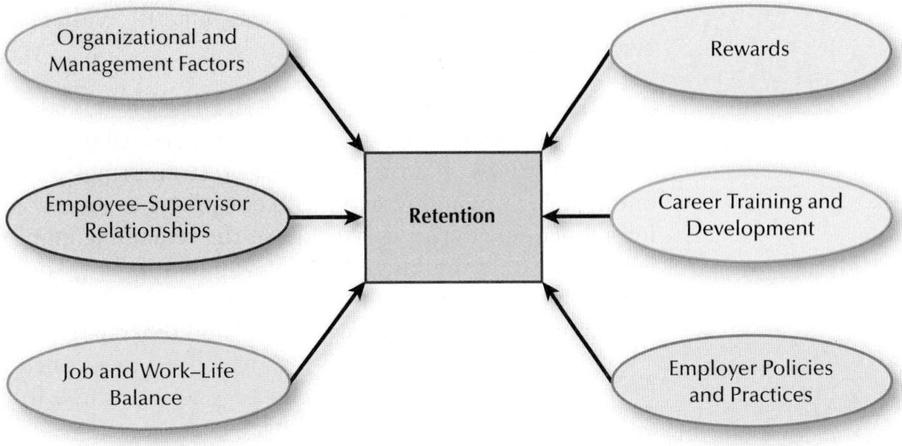

hold managers and employees accountable for accomplishing results are viewed as better places to work, especially by individuals wishing to progress both financially and professionally. Further, effective management provides the resources necessary for employees to perform their jobs well.

Other organizational attributes that affect employee retention are related to the management of the organization. In some organizations, external events are seen as threatening, whereas in others, they are seen as challenges requiring responses. The latter approach can be a source of competitive advantage, especially if an organization is in a growing, dynamic industry. Another organizational factor that can affect employee job performance and potential turnover intentions is "organizational politics." This can include managerial favoritism, having to be involved in undesirable activities, taking credit for what others do, and other actions that occur in many departments and organizational settings.

A final factor affecting how employees view their organizations is the quality of organizational leadership. Evidence suggests that the degree to which supervisors treat employees fairly can have a significant impact on retention.[47] A study of first-time mothers found that breaches of family-based psychological contracts increased women's intentions to quit, but that supervisors' management of fairness could weaken this desire.[48]

Employee–Supervisor Relationships Work relationships that affect employee retention include *supervisory/management support* and *coworker relations*. A supervisor or manager builds positive relationships and aids retention by being fair and nondiscriminatory, allowing work flexibility and work–family balancing, giving feedback that recognizes employee efforts and performance, and supporting career planning and development. One study found that servant leadership as well as a climate that allows workers to share concerns about family could be used to improve identification with a company and the degree to which work enhances family roles,[49] factors that could also encourage retention.

Additionally, many individuals build close relationships with coworkers. Such work-related friendships do not appear on employee records, but these relationships can be an important signal that a workplace is positive. Various survey results show that the development of friendships may be an important consideration when managing worker retention, particularly among Millennials.[50] Overall, what this means is that it is not just *where* people work but also with *whom* they work that affects employee retention.

Job Security and Work–Life Balance Many individuals have experienced a decline in job security during the past decades. All the downsizings, layoffs, mergers and acquisitions, and organizational restructurings have affected employee commitment, loyalty, and retention. As coworkers encounter and cope with layoffs and job reductions, the anxiety levels of the remaining employees rise. Consequently, employees start thinking about leaving before they also get laid off. Companies that focus on job continuity and security tend to have higher retention rates.

Some jobs are considered "good" and others are thought to be "bad," but not all people agree on which jobs are which. As mentioned previously, the design of jobs and peoples' preferences can vary significantly. Job design factors that can impact retention include the following:

- A knowledge, skills, and abilities mismatch, either through overqualification or underqualification, can lead to turnover.
- Job accomplishments and workload demands that are dissatisfying or excessively stressful may impact performance and lead to turnover.
- Both timing of work schedules and geographic locations may contribute to burnout in some individuals but not others.
- The ability of employees to balance work and life requirements affects their job performance and retention.

Rewards The tangible rewards that people receive for working come in the form of pay, incentives, and benefits. Employees often cite better pay or benefits as the reason for leaving one employer for another. Employers do best with retention if they offer *competitive pay and benefits,* which means they must be close to what other employers are providing and what individuals believe to be consistent with their capabilities, experience, and performance. If compensation levels are not close to market, often defined as 10% to 15% of the market rate, turnover is often higher. Some companies also use retention bonuses to encourage employees to stay; flat dollar amounts that are given in lump-sum payments are the most common forms.[51]

Another reward is *employee recognition,* which can be both tangible and intangible. Tangible recognition comes in many forms, such as "employee of the month" plaques and certificates for perfect attendance. Intangible and psychological recognition includes feedback from managers and supervisors acknowledging extra effort and performance even if monetary rewards are not given. Other kinds of rewards include perks of different types—usually used to retain employees with skill sets in short supply. For examples, see the following "HR Perspective: Aspenware Uses Perks to Help Retention" feature.

Career Training and Development Many employees in all types of jobs consistently indicate that organizational efforts to aid their career training and development can significantly affect employee retention. *Opportunities for personal growth* lead the list of reasons individuals took their current jobs and why they stay there. Personal growth might include personal rebooting as well for software developers. A software firm developed a "paid, paid vacation." Employees get $7,500 extra pay to take their paid vacations. The only catch is that they must unplug and actually go on vacation. The company received 2,500 applications for eight positions since the

Aspenware Uses Perks to Help Retention

Aspenware, a software developer in Denver, goes beyond free lunches and days off for skiing. It offers employees free time to pursue projects that have potential as a startup, subsidiary, or new line of business. Janet McIllece recently spent 10 to 20 hours per week for six months trying to find ways to explain complex data on the health of a stream to nontechnical audiences. Aspenware freed her to work on the project with her brother, a biologist with the U.S. Fish and Wildlife Service. They also paid for a three-day visit to Spokane for the project. Financing would have been available had the project turned into a business, with ownership stakes for McIllece. But that did not occur.

The market for software developers is very tight, forcing employers to devise ways to retain them. Some notable perks include pet-sitting services, in-house chefs, and a lifetime supply of Pabst Blue Ribbon beer. But the in-house incubation program at Aspenware goes beyond that, allowing employees to discover

their entrepreneurial and creative nature. The company carves out time and provides financing for ideas that may lead to a new line of business or a spin-off start-up.

Aspenware's founder stated, "Any of our people can get a job anywhere given their talent. ... There are lots of things we have to try to make sure this is an environment people want to be in."[52]

These words highlight how companies must provide the kinds of perks people want to improve employee retention. Based on these ideas, consider the following questions:

1. How would you evaluate Aspenware's use of perks to help improve retention? Is there anything you would do differently?

2. What other perks could be used to drive employee satisfaction and retention? Could these perks be offered in companies that are different from Aspenware?

"paid, paid vacation" idea went viral. The CEO says the perk was driven by competitive demand for software developers, but he had no idea the reaction would be so strong.

Training and development efforts can be designed to demonstrate an employer's commitment to keeping employees' knowledge, skills, and abilities current. Also, training and development can help underused employees attain new capabilities. Such programs have been used successfully in many different organizations such as Southwest Airlines, Hyatt Hotels and Resorts, and the U.S. armed forces.

Organizations address training and development in many ways. Tuition aid programs, typically offered as a benefit by many employers, allow employees to pursue additional educational and training opportunities. These programs may contribute to higher employee retention rates because the employees' new knowledge and capabilities can aid the employer. Also, through formal career planning efforts, employees and their managers discuss career opportunities in the organization and career development activities that will help them grow.

Career development and planning efforts can include formal mentoring programs. The efforts should also focus on providing professionals with the right opportunities that help advance their careers, opportunities like working in other areas of the firm or getting promoted.[53] For instance, IT organizations are using career development programs so that technology-savvy employees can expand their skills outside of technical areas. Programs in some firms focus on developing the competencies that employees need in managerial jobs.

ETHICS

Employer Policies and Practices Other factors found to affect retention are employer policies. For instance, the reasonableness of HR policies, the fairness of disciplinary actions, and the means used to allocate work assignments and opportunities all affect employee retention. If individuals feel that policies are unreasonably restrictive, are unethical, or are applied inconsistently, they may be more likely to look at jobs offered by other employers.

The increasing demographic diversity of U.S. workplaces makes the *nondiscriminatory treatment* of employees important, regardless of gender, age, and other characteristics. The organizational commitment and job satisfaction of ethnically diverse individuals are affected by perceived discriminatory treatment. Many firms have recognized that proactive management of diversity issues affects individuals of all backgrounds. Companies should also consider the unique needs of diverse employees. For instance, employers can better retain Millennials by providing a more flexible workplace, as well as focusing on opportunities that allow the company to give back to various stakeholders.[54] The cultural diversity found in global workplaces also requires special consideration when developing retention policies. A study found that expatriates' retention was affected by adjustment to the new work environment and by being embedded in the workplace, which were in turn influenced by different demands and tactics. The implications of these findings is that HR professionals should provide language, cultural, and relationship training so that expatriate retention is improved.[55]

5-6c Retention of Top Performers

Organizations that cannot consistently retain their top performers have a less qualified workforce, and perhaps are understaffed as well. Consequently, HR professionals must develop creative ways to retain high-performing employees. Just as Figure 5-11 indicates, HR professionals can focus on providing work opportunities that position high-performers to move up in the company. These opportunities can include mentoring with executives, challenging job assignments, development opportunities that build managerial competencies, and regular performance feedback. Organizations should also consider using *rerecruiting* to enhance retention. Rerecruiting is a strategic HR approach that involves getting outstanding employees to further connect with employers by focusing on the opportunities that initially attracted them to the organization.[56] Such discussions can encourage high performers to commit to the organization in a long-term capacity.

FIGURE 5-11   Retaining Top Performers

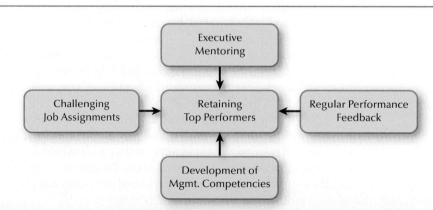

MEASURE

5-7 Managing Retention

The foregoing sections have summarized the results of many studies and popular HR practices to identify factors that can affect retention. Retention is important because turnover can cause poor performance in otherwise productive units. The focus now turns toward the keys to managing retention as part of effective HR management.

5-7a Retention Assessment and Metrics

Calculating both turnover and retention statistics provides a better picture of the movements of employees. The turnover formula was discussed previously. Retention rates can be calculated as the percentage of workers who remain in the firm from one point in time to another point in time.[57]

To ensure that appropriate actions are taken to enhance retention, management decisions require data and analyses rather than subjective impressions, anecdotes of selected individual situations, or panic reactions to the loss of key people. Examples of a process for managing retention are highlighted in Figure 5-12.

Analysis of turnover data is an attempt to get at the cause of retention problems. Managers should recognize that turnover is only a symptom of other factors that may be causing problems. When the causes are treated, the symptoms may be eliminated. Some of the first areas to consider when analyzing data about retention include the work, pay and benefits, supervision, occupations, departments, and demographics of

FIGURE 5-12 Process for Managing Retention

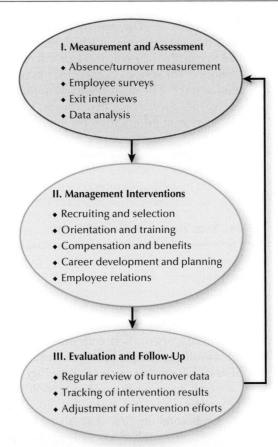

I. Measurement and Assessment

- Absence/turnover measurement
- Employee surveys
- Exit interviews
- Data analysis

II. Management Interventions

- Recruiting and selection
- Orientation and training
- Compensation and benefits
- Career development and planning
- Employee relations

III. Evaluation and Follow-Up

- Regular review of turnover data
- Tracking of intervention results
- Adjustment of intervention efforts

those leaving and those who stay. Common methods of obtaining useful perspectives are employee surveys, exit interviews, and first-year turnover evaluations.

Employee Surveys As previously mentioned in this chapter, employee surveys can be used to diagnose specific problem areas, identify employee needs or preferences, and reveal areas in which HR activities are well received or viewed negatively. Considering that morale does not necessarily equate to positive employee retention, companies can use surveys to evaluate the attitudes of employees so that the proper steps can be taken to keep workers satisfied.[58] Whether the surveys cover general employee attitudes, job satisfaction, or specific issues, the survey results must be examined as part of retention measurement efforts. For example, a growing number of "mini-surveys" on specific topics are being sent via email questionnaires, blogs, and other means.

Regardless of the topics in a survey, employee input provides data on the "retention climate" in an organization. By obtaining data on how employees view their jobs, their coworkers, their supervisors, and organizational policies and practices, these surveys can be starting points for reducing turnover and increasing the length of time that employees are retained. Some employers conduct attitude surveys annually, while others do so intermittently.

By asking employees to respond candidly to an attitude survey, management builds employees' expectations that actions will be taken on the concerns identified. Therefore, a crucial part of conducting an attitude survey is providing feedback to those who participated in it. It is especially important that even negative survey results be communicated to avoid fostering the appearance of hiding the results or placing blame. Also, leaders should develop actions plans for how results can be used in a strategic manner to positively change how organizations function.[59]

Exit Interviews One widely used means for assisting retention assessment efforts is the exit interview, in which individuals who are leaving the organization are asked to explain their reasons. Exit interviews can also be used to identify the types of "shocks" (or serious events) that may have encouraged employees to quit an organization.[60] HR must regularly summarize and analyze the data by category (e.g., reasons for leaving, department, length of service) to provide managers and supervisors with information for improving company efforts.[61] As described in the following "HR Competencies & Applications: Conducting Exit Interviews" feature, the exit interview process should include certain elements. Some HR departments contact former employees who were valuable contributors, as they may be willing to provide more information on email questionnaires or in telephone conversations conducted some time after they have left the organization.

First-Year Turnover Evaluations A special type of retention assessment focuses on first-year employees. It is not unusual for turnover to be high among employees during their first year. Sometimes, the cause of departure is voluntary; for example, individuals may identify a mismatch between what they expected in their jobs and managers and what actually occurs, or between their perceptions of the new job and its reality. Other times, individuals are involuntarily removed for poor performance in the first year. Some causes can be excessive absenteeism and mismatches with job requirements, or conflicts with other employees and managers. If these situations occur too often, HR may need to reevaluate recruiting and selection processes, as well as its job previews to make sure they are realistic.

Overall, focus on first-year retention and turnover is useful because individuals who stay for a year are more likely to extend their employment and have greater retention beyond the first year. Also, effective first-year efforts may lead to future career development, higher performance, and other positive retention factors.

Exit interview
An interview in which individuals who are leaving an organization are asked to explain their reasons

COMPETENCIES & APPLICATIONS

Conducting Exit Interviews

Departing employees may be reluctant to divulge their real reasons for leaving. A skilled HR interviewer may be able to gain useful information that departing employees do not wish to share with managers and supervisors. The following suggestions may be useful when conducting exit interviews:

- Decide who will conduct the exit interview and when the discussion will occur. These interviews can occur on the last day or so of a departing individual's employment, but it might be better to conduct them a few days before because an employee will be less distracted by the upcoming change.
- Emphasize that the information provided by the departing employee will be treated confidentially and used to make improvements.
- Utilize a checklist or a set of standard questions so that the information can be summarized. Typical areas covered include reasons for leaving, supervision, pay, training, liked and disliked aspects of the job, and details on the organization to which the employee is moving.

 When doing the actual exit interview, numerous questions can be asked. Those typically asked include the following:

[Q]: Why are you leaving?

[Q]: What have you liked and disliked about your job and managers?

[Q]: What company actions have made you and other employees more or less positive?

[Q]: What would or would not lead you to recommend this employer to future possible hires?

[Q]: Did you receive adequate training and support? Please explain.

[Q]: Did the job match your expectations when you were hired? If not, what failed to meet your expectations?

[Q]: What was frustrating about working here?

[Q]: What suggestions do you have to improve working conditions?

[Q]: Do you believe that any decisions or actions regarding your employment were discriminatory or unfair? Please explain.

Based on these suggestions, consider the following questions:

1. How would you conduct useful exit interviews?

2. What of kinds of questions would you ask?

KEY COMPETENCIES: Communication (Behavioral Competency) and Organization (Technical Competency)

5-7b Retention Evaluation and Follow-Up

Management can take numerous actions to deal with retention issues. The choice of a particular action depends on the analysis of the turnover and retention problems in a particular organization and should be custom-tailored for that organization.

 Tracking of intervention results and *adjustment of intervention efforts* should be part of retention evaluation and follow-up. Some firms use pilot programs to see how changes affect retention before extending them to the entire organization. For instance, to test the effect of flextime scheduling on employee turnover, a firm might try flexible scheduling in one department. If the turnover rate in that department drops in comparison to the turnover rates in other departments still working with set schedules, the firm might extend the use of flexible scheduling to other departments.

SUMMARY

- Individual performance is captured by the formula:
  performance = ability × effort × support.
- Motivation is explained by many theories—some of the most commonly used are needs theory, two-factor theory, equity theory, and expectancy theory.
- Psychological contracts are unwritten expectations that employees and employers have about the nature of their work relationships.
- The interaction between individuals and their jobs affects both job satisfaction and organizational commitment. The extent to which employees feel linked to organizational success can affect employee engagement and loyalty.
- Employee engagement is the extent to which an employee's thoughts and behaviors are focused on the employer's success.
- Loyalty to an employer depends on the employee's perception that the employer is loyal in return.
- Absenteeism and tardiness are related, and both require analysis and management.

- Absenteeism has both direct and indirect costs that add up to an expensive problem.
- Getting accurate measures on absenteeism is the beginning of solving the problem.
- Turnover occurs when employees leave an organization and must be replaced. It can be classified in many ways, but it should be measured and its costs determined.
- There is an optimum level of turnover that is likely *not* zero.
- Drivers of retention include organizational, managerial, and job factors that may affect employees' work–life balance, compensation and other rewards, career training and development, and employer policies and practices.
- Retention of employees is a major focus of HR management efforts in organizations.
- Retention is assisted by the use of retention measures, including employee surveys and exit interviews.
- Managing retention should include evaluation and tracking of both retention actions and turnover follow-up.

CRITICAL THINKING CHALLENGES

1. Describe your expectations for a job. How well does your employer meet the expectations you hold about the psychological contract?

2. If you became the new manager at a restaurant with high employee turnover, what actions would you take to increase retention of employees?

3. As the HR Manager, you must provide the senior management team with turnover costs for the following high-turnover position. Use websites such as www.talentkeepers.com and www.keepemployees.com, to calculate turnover and analyze the variables involved. Also identify any other data that might be relevant and then discuss how you would reduce the turnover.

   Position: Machine operator

   Number of employees: 250

   Number of turnovers: 85

   Average wage: $11.50/hour

   Cost of benefits: 35% of payroll

4. Your company has reaped the benefits of having long-term, tenured employees, but many of them are now approaching retirement. It is anticipated that approximately 20% of the company's workforce will retire in the next three to five years. In reviewing the remaining workforce through HR planning efforts, you have become aware of work–life balance issues that need to be reviewed and addressed. The company president has requested that you prepare a retention plan outlining these issues as well as ways to address them. Resources to help you address the issues in the retention plan can be found at www.workfamily.com.

   A. What steps will you take to identify key priorities in the work–life balance issues?

   B. How will you present a business case to gain management support for addressing those issues to help retain existing workers and to fill the positions vacated by retiring employees?

CASE — Carolina Biological Uses Survey to Assess Worker Engagement

Carolina Biological Supply, a Burlington, North Carolina provider of science and math educational products, uses a survey platform called Net Promoter System to track customers' impressions of the service provided by the company. However, the system has also enabled Carolina Biological Supply to assess the degree to which employees are engaged with workplace processes and activities. According to Katina Richmond, PHR, the information provided by the survey enables company leaders to identify key challenges associated with certain positions and work areas, which helps them develop useful solutions to problems. The instrument is anonymous and does not use the typical items and rating scales that are found on many other surveys. Even more importantly, it takes only about five minutes to answer the survey, which has driven the response rate up to around 80%.

The Net Promoter System is anchored by the question, "How likely would you be to recommend this company to a friend or family member?" Customer responses are provided on a 10-point scale, and individuals are placed into one of three groups: Promoters score a 9 to 10, Passives score a 7 to 8, and Detractors score a 0 to 6. The overall classifications enable companies to develop what are called Net Promoter Scores. HR professionals can use a variation of this question to evaluate employee engagement. The question is, "How likely would you be to recommend working at this company to a friend or family member?" There are other questions that can be used to measure both customer and employee satisfaction with a particular company. Survey participants can also provide written comments that provide richer data that can be analyzed.

Katina Richmond supervises the survey policy at Carolina Biological, including coordinating some of the administration, developing time lines, designing the survey, and communicating the purpose and expectations. This shows that it is typical for HR professionals to be highly engaged in the survey process, despite the involvement of a third-party provider. HR is also involved in developing plans that address any challenges highlighted in the survey data. A program called Carolina Cash was developed to reward employees for providing excellent ideas that benefit the organization.[62]

QUESTIONS

1. Since surveys can be important tools for obtaining employee feedback, how can HR professionals use them more effectively? What else could Carolina Biological do to get useful feedback from its employees?

2. What is your opinion of the Net Promoter System? What do you think are the advantages associated with this survey system? What are the potential disadvantages?

SUPPLEMENTAL CASES

The Clothing Store

This case describes one firm's approach to improving employee retention. (For the case, go to http://www.cengage.com/management/mathis.)

Accenture: Retaining for Itself

This case describes what a large consulting company does to help retain a virtual workforce. (For the case, go to http://www.cengage.com/management/mathis.)

Alegent Health

This case discusses how Alegent, a large nonprofit health care system, improved employee retention and reduced turnover. (For the case, go to http://www.cengage.com/management/mathis.)

END NOTES

1. Adapted from Lynn Waymon, Andre Alphonso, and Will Kitchen, "Internal Networking: Time–Waster or Value Creator?" *T+D*, October 2013, pp. 86–88.

2. John C. Dencker, "Who Do Firms Lay Off and Why?" *Industrial Relations: A Journal of Economy and Society* 51 (2012), 152–169.

3. Denny Strigl, "Results Drive Happiness," *HR Magazine*, October 2011, p. 113.

4. Adapted from Joseph Grenny, "Advancing Accountability in Your Organization," *T+D*, May 2013, p. 14.

5. Teresa Amabile and Steen Kramer, "How Leaders Kill Meaning at Work," *McKinsey Quarterly*, January 2012, pp. 1–8.

6. "What Motivates Employees?" *T+D*, October 2013, p. 16.

7. Gail Clarkson, "Twenty-First Century Employment Relationships: The Case for an Altruistic Model," *Human Resource Management* 53 (March–April 2014), 253–269.

8. Aoife M. McDermott, Edel Conway, Denise M. Rousseau, and Patrick C. Flood, "Promoting Effective Psychological Contracts through Leadership: The Missing Link between HR Strategy and Performance," *Human Resource Management* 52 (March–April 2013), 289–310.

9. Guillermo E. Dabos and Denise M. Rousseau, "Psychological Contracts and Informal Networks in Organizations: The Effects of Social Status and Local Ties," *Human Resource Management* 52 (July–August 2013), 485–510.

10. J. W. Beck and P. T. Walmshey, "Selection Ratio and Employee Retention as Antecedents of Competitive Advantage," *Industrial and Organizational Psychology* (2012), 92–95.

11. John Sullivan, "How Do We Develop a Solid Career Development Plan?" *Workforce*, June, 5, 2013, http://www.workforce.com/roadmaps/515-learning-development/516-plan/how-do-we-develop-a-solid-career-development-plan.

12. Carl E. Van Horn, "What Workers Really Want and Need," October 2013, pp. 45–51.

13. Paola Spagnoli et al., "Satisfaction with Job Aspects: Do Patterns Change over Time?" *Journal of Business Research* 65 (2012), 609–616.

14. Danna M. Owens, "Why Care about Income Disparity?" *HR Magazine*, March 2013, p. 53.

15. Phaedra Brotherton, "Federal Employees Report a Slight Decline in Job Satisfaction," *T+D*, May 2013, p. 20.

16. Patty Gaul, "The Magic Triangle of Employee Engagement," *T+D*, November 2013, p. 20.

17. Kristen B. Frasch, "The 'Virtuous Cycle' of Engagement and Productivity," *Human Resource Executive Online*, August 22, 2011, pp. 1–2; Lynn Gresham, "SHRM Survey Finds Engagement, Retention Top HR Concerns," *Employee Benefit News*, July 6, 2011, pp. 1–4; Andrew R. McIlvaine, "The Human Risk Factor," *Human Resource Executive Online*, February 6, 2012, pp. 1–5.

18. Amy Adkins, "Majority of U.S. Employees Not Engaged Despite Gains in 2014," Gallup.com, http://www.gallup.com/poll/181289/majority-employees-not-engaged-despite-gains-2014.aspx.

19. Patty Gaul, "The Magic Triangle of Employee Engagement," *T+D*, November 2013, p. 20; Mark Lukens, "Getting Engagement from the Get-Go," *HR Magazine*, February 2014, pp. 54–55.

20. "Idea Entrepreneur," *T+D*, November 2013, p. 15.

21. Bob Pike, "Who Else Values Loyalty?" *Training*, November–December 2011, p. 69.

22. Wharton School, "Declining Employee Loyalty: A Casualty of the New Workplace," *Human Resource Executive Online*, July 16, 2012, pp. 1–5.

23. Carl E. Van Horn, "What Workers Really Want and Need," October 2013, pp. 45–51.

24. "Apology and Trust in the Workplace," *T+D*, February 2014, p. 15.

25. Riki Takeuchi, Mark C. Bolino, and Cheng-Chen Lin, "Too Many Motives? The Interactive Effects of Multiple Motives on Organizational Citizenship Behavior," *Journal of Applied Psychology*, 2014, published online, 1–10.

26. Changquan Jiao, David A. Richards, and Rick D. Hackett, "Organizational Citizenship Behavior and Role Breadth: A Meta-Analytic and Cross-Cultural Analysis," *Human Resource Management* 52 (September–October 2013), 697–714.

27. Mark C. Bolino, Hsin-Hua Hsiung, Jaron Harvey, and Jeffrey A. LePine, "'Well, I'm Tired of Tryin'! Organizational Citizenship Behavior and Citizenship Fatigue," *Journal of Applied Psychology* 100, no. 1 (2015), 56–74.

28. Jeffrey R. Spence, Douglas J. Brown, Lisa M. Keeping, and Huiwen Lian, "Helpful Today, but Not Tomorrow? Feeling Grateful as a Predictor of Daily Organizational Citizenship Behaviors," *Personnel Psychology*, 2–14, 67, 705–738.

29. Mark C. Bolino, Hsin-Hua Hsiung, Jaron Harvey, and Jeffrey A. LePine, "'Well, I'm Tired of Tryin'! Organizational Citizenship Behavior and Citizenship Fatigue," *Journal of Applied Psychology*, 2–14, published online, 1–19.

30. Adapted from Ken Perlman and Jimmy Leppert, "Engage the Unengaged," *T+D*, May 2013, pp. 58–63.

31. Michael Klachefsky, "Health Related Cost Productivity: The Full Cost of Absence," *Productivity Insight #2*, Standard Insurance Company, August 2012, p. 1.

32. Emma Soane, Amanda Shantz, Kerstin Alfes, Catherine Truss, Chris Rees, and Mark Gatenby, "The Association of Meaningfulness, Well-Being, and Engagement with Absenteeism: A Moderated Mediation Model," *Human Resource Management* 52 (May–June 2013), 441–456.

33. "Estimating Turnover Costs," www.workforce.com.

34. Eric Krell, "5 Ways to Manage High Turnover," *HR Magazine*, April 2012, pp. 63–65.

35. Carl P. Maertz Jr. and Scott L. Boyar, "Theory-Driven Development of a Comprehensive Turnover-Attachment Motive Survey," *Human Resource Management* 51 (January–February 2012), 71–98.

36. David Shadovitz, "Talent Turnover Going Up … Again," *Human Resource Executive*, July–August 2012, p. 10.

37. Scott M. Soltis, Filip Agneessens, Zuzana Sasovova, and Giuseppe

(Joe) Labianca, "A Social Network Perspective on Turnover Intentions: The Role of Distributive Justice and Social Support," *Human Resource Management* 52 (July–August 2013), 561–584.

38. Abbie J. Shipp, Stacie Furst-Holloway, T. Brad Harris, and Benson Rosen, "Gone Today but Here Tomorrow: Extending the Unfolding Model of Turnover to Consider Boomerang Employees," *Personnel Psychology* 67 (2014), 421–462.

39. Kathy Gurchiek, "Study: Workers 'Leak' Turnover Cues," *SHRM Online*, March 6, 2014, http://www .shrm.org/hrdisciplines/staffingman- agement/articles/pages/workers-leak- turnover-cues.aspx; Kathy Gurchiek, "Recognizing the Clues to Imminent Employee Departure," *HR Magazine*, May 2014, p. 17.

40. Adrienne Fox, "Drive Turnover Down," *HR Magazine*, July 2012, pp. 23–27.

41. Adapted from Sonya M. Latta, "Save Your Staff, Improve Your Business," *HR Magazine*, January 2012, pp. 30–32.

42. Dori Meinert, "Measuring Turnover," *HR Magazine*, July 2013, p. 16.

43. For details on industries, types of jobs, and other components, go to www.dol.gov.

44. Dori Meinert, "Measuring Turnover," *HR Magazine*, July 2013, p. 16.

45. Wayne F. Cascio, "Be a Ringmaster of Risk," *HR Magazine*, April 2012, pp. 38–43.

46. Gary Kranz, "Keeping the Keepers," *Workforce Management*, April 2012, pp. 34–37.

47. Teresa A. Daniel, "Managing for Employee Retention," *SHRM Online*, February 27, 2012, http://www.shrm .org/templatestools/toolkits/pages/ managingforemployeeretention.aspx.

48. Whitney Botsford Morgan and Eden B. King, "Mothers' Psychological Contracts: Does Supervisor Breach Explain Intention to Leave the Organization?" *Human Resource Management* 51 (September–October 2012), 629–650.

49. Haina Zhang, Ho Kwong Kwan, Andre M. Everett, and Zhaoquan Jian, "Servant Leadership, Organiza- tional Identification, and Work-to- Family Enrichment: The Moderating Role of Work Climate for Sharing Family Concerns," *Human Resource Management* 51 (September–October 2012), 747–768.

50. Kathy Gurchiek, "Survey: Workplace Friends Important Retention Factor," *SHRM Online*, December 16, 2014, http://www.shrm.org/hrdisciplines/ employeerelations/articles/pages/ workplace-friendships.aspx.

51. Stephen Miller, "Sign-On, Retention and Spot Bonuses Show Upswing," *SHRM Online*, June 20, 2014, http://www.shrm.org/hrdisciplines/ compensation/articles/pages/ bonuses-upswing.aspx.

52. Based on Andy Vuong, "Ideas Un- leashed," *Denver Post*, July 22, 2012, p. K1.

53. Aliah D. Wright, "Sheahan: Rethink Retention, Promotion," *SHRM On- line*, October 2, 2013, http://www .shrm.org/publications/hrnews/pages/ peter-sheahan-retention-promotion- strategy-conference.aspx.

54. Mike Prokopeak, "Interview with Dan Schwabel: How to Retain Your Millennial Workers," *Workforce*, September 16, 2013, http://www .workforce.com/articles/9338-inter- view-with-dan-schwabel-how-to- retain-your-millennial-workers.

55. Hong Ren, Margaret A. Shaffer, David A. Harrison, Carmen Fu, and Katherine M. Fodchuk, "Reactive Adjustment or Proactive Embedding? Multistudy, Multiwave, Evidence for Dual Pathways to Expatriate Retention," *Personnel Psychology* 67 (2014), 203–239.

56. Adrienne Fox, "Keep Your Top Talent: The Return of Retention," *SHRM Online*, April 1, 2014, http:// www.shrm.org/publications/hrma- gazine/editorialcontent/2014/0414/ pages/0414-retention.aspx.

57. "How Do I Calculate Retention?" *SHRM Online*, December 4, 2012, http://www.shrm.org/india/ hr-topics-and-strategy/human- capital-standards-and-analytics/ pages/how%20do%20i%20cal- culate%20retention_%20is%20 retention%20related%20to%20 turnover_.aspx.

58. Rebecca R. Hastings, "High Morale Doesn't Guarantee Retention," *SHRM Online*, December 13, 2012, http://www.shrm.org/hrdisciplines/ employeerelations/articles/pages/ employee-morale-retention.aspx.

59. David L. Van Rooy and Ken Oehler, "The Evolution of Employee Opin- ion Surveys: The Voice of Employee as a Strategic Management Tool," September 2013, SIOP White Paper Series, SHRM.

60. Carol T. Kulik, Gerry Treuren, and Prashant Bordia, "Shocks and Final Straws: Using Exit-Interview Data to Examine the Unfolding Model's Decision Paths," *Human Resource Management* 51 (January–February 2012), 25–46.

61. Robert A. Giacalone, "Researching Exit Interviews," *Human Resource Execu- tive Online*, March 1, 2012, pp. 1–3.

62. Based on Kathryn Tyler, "Keeping Employees in the Net," *HR Magazine*, March 2013, pp. 55–57.

CHAPTER

6

Recruiting High-Quality Talent

Learning Objectives

After you have read this chapter, you should be able to:

LO1 Explain strategic recruiting decisions regarding employment branding, outsourcing, and other related issues.

LO2 Identify distinct labor markets and describe their unique characteristics.

LO3 Explain how technology and social networking affect recruiting processes for employers and candidates.

LO4 Identify three internal recruiting sources and issues associated with their use.

LO5 Highlight five external recruiting sources.

LO6 Define recruiting measurement and metrics and illustrate how analytics can be used to improve talent acquisition.

WHAT'S TRENDING IN

RECRUITING

Employment recruiting is undergoing major renovations and updates. The traditional posting of "want ads" in the newspaper and submitting paper resumes has given way to a nimble, technology-enhanced process that makes information more accessible and available more quickly for candidates and companies. Here's what's trending regarding technology and economic factors that impact how organizations source talent.[1]

1. The mass retirement of Baby Boomers and the smaller generation that follows puts candidates in the driver's seat. Organizations will need to "woo" prospective employees and manage the candidate experience to attract those with valued skills and experience.

2. Just-in-time staffing will become more common, with organizations using freelancers, temporary workers, and contractors with far greater frequency than in the past.

3. Business intelligence systems and Big Data will allow companies to track the success of recruiting from various sources to find the best and most cost-effective ways of identifying qualified workers. Use of data and assessment science will lead to more automated pre-screening.

4. "Social" sourcing and corporate talent networks help companies connect with potential employees in real time through viral communities. Promoting an employment brand will be more important in these online networks.

And the Winner ... Gets the Job

When the feature film *The Last Starfighter* was released in 1984, the thought of using a video game to identify the next pilot for interstellar combat seemed like futuristic science fiction. Fast forward a few decades, and you'll see that "gamification" is taking over the world of employment recruiting.

App development company Quixey uses the Quixey Challenge, a series of timed online puzzles, to identify engineers to hire. The company has created an entire game using crowdsourcing to generate questions. Users are invited to submit sample questions, which may be used in the game. An online leaderboard displays the names of winners and runners-up.

College students competed in Auberge Resorts' challenge to boost energy efficiency at its Esperanza Resort in Los Cabos. Proposals were submitted from across the United States, and the winning suggestion is under consideration for adoption by the hotel chain. PricewaterhouseCoopers created the xTREME Games to teach students about tax policy issues. Over 4,000 students from 84 colleges joined in the online competition and connected with PwC professionals to learn about employment opportunities. The companies can review game results to see students in action and filter out the best candidates. These online competitions are especially beneficial to students at lesser-known universities that companies might not visit.

The U.S. Army has taken what it learned in soldier training and uses games and simulations to make the recruiting experience engaging and useful to evaluate potential recruits and build brand awareness for the U.S. military. America's Army is a free downloadable game that places recruits in a very realistic multiplayer tactical shooting game. Players can

magicinfoto/Shutterstock.com

put themselves in the boots of a soldier and determine whether they are suited for combat. The $7 million investment has become the U.S. Army's top recruitment tool, attracting millions of potential new recruits.

So, games aren't just for fun anymore. They could very well be the new best way to recruit employees and companies are beginning to take notice.[2]

Talent acquisition
Process of finding and hiring high-quality talent needed to meet the organization's workforce needs

Recruiting
Process of generating a pool of qualified applicants for organizational jobs

The next two chapters explain the process of talent acquisition, the process of finding and hiring high-quality talent needed to meet the organization's workforce needs. There are two primary stages of acquiring talent—recruiting and selection. In this chapter, we discuss recruiting, the process of generating a pool of qualified candidates. In Chapter 7, we discuss selection, the process of choosing among candidates. Think of talent acquisition in terms of managing a supply chain of capable and motivated workers rather than as individual tasks or processes. The recruiting process connects companies to sources of potential employees, while selection involves picking the best "supplier" of talent. Consider how the talent supply chain must be managed to ensure an adequate supply of qualified employees. Planning ahead, building relationships with suppliers, ensuring quality, and creating efficiency are supply chain processes that can improve the quantity and quality of talent.[3]

Talent acquisition depends on workforce planning (Chapter 2) and general economic and labor market conditions. On the one hand, in a "buyers' market" companies have more freedom and bargaining power when hiring employees. On the other hand, when labor markets are tight (called a "sellers' market"), talent acquisition can be challenging. Hiring authorities report that many applicants lack basic skills, which makes it difficult to find qualified people to fill jobs.[4] Consider how organizations try to improve the supply of talent by targeting their recruiting efforts.

6-1 Recruiting

Recruiting becomes more important and complex as labor markets evolve. Although recruiting can be expensive, think about the cost of unfilled jobs. For example, consider a retail company where there are three vacant checker positions. Assume these three vacancies cost the company $300 for each business day the jobs remain vacant. If the jobs are not filled for four months, the cost of this failure to recruit in a timely fashion will be about $26,000. That is a lot of business lost due to inadequate staffing.

Although cost is certainly an issue—averaging $3,500 per hire—the *quality* of recruits is equally important.[5] For example, if an organizational strategy focuses on service quality as a competitive advantage, a company might hire only from the top 15% of candidates for critical customer-facing jobs and from the top 30% of candidates for all other positions. While this approach may raise the cost per hire, it will improve workforce quality and allow the organization to maintain its competitive edge.

FIGURE 6-1 Strategic Components of Effective Recruiting

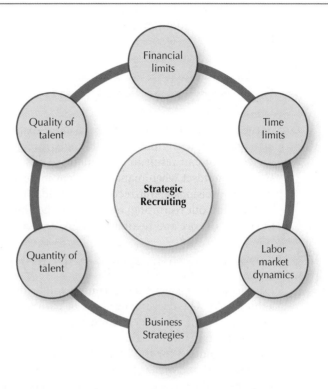

These examples illustrate how recruiting can be an important part of an organization's overall strategy and not simply an expense to be minimized. To be effective, recruiters need to understand competitors' business strategies and practices, labor market dynamics, the importance of both quality and quantity of talent, and time and money limits. Figure 6-1 highlights these components of effective strategic recruiting.

6-1a Strategic Recruiting and Human Resources Planning

LO1 Explain strategic recruiting decisions regarding employment branding, outsourcing, and other related issues.

Since talent is a key to ensure the production of the organization's goods and services, strategic planning for the business should include planning for workforce needs and recruiting. Strategic recruiting involves:

- Understanding how the business strategies impact how and where to successfully recruit qualified employees
- Identifying keys to success in the labor market, including competitors' recruiting efforts
- Determining the appropriate balance between quality and quantity of workers needed
- Recognizing the resource limits of time and money related to fulfilling recruiting activities
- Measuring the effectiveness of recruiting efforts

Recruitment planning can pinpoint not only the kinds and numbers of applicants but also how difficult recruiting efforts may be depending on the type of jobs being filled. In addition, effective recruiting focuses on discovering talent before it is needed.

6-2 Strategic Recruiting Decisions

Top executives and line managers share responsibility with human resources to manage the talent pipeline. Thinking strategically about how to acquire and optimize talent can result in a competitive advantage for the company.[6] Adopting a systemic mindset when managing talent involves several issues related to recruiting. Strategic decisions about recruiting consider factors such as assigning responsibility for carrying out recruiting, establishing the employment brand, determining the optimal mix of core and flexible workers, and considering diversity.

6-2a Assigning Responsibility for Recruiting

A basic decision is whether recruiting will be done by the employer or outsourced to a third party. This decision need not be entirely an either/or situation. In most organizations, HR staff members handle much of the recruiting. Since they understand the organization's culture, values, and strategies, inside recruiters may be better able to match candidates for the best job fit. However, recruiting can be time-consuming, and HR staff and managers have many other responsibilities. Outsourcing is a way to decrease the burden on internal recruiters. There are a number of ways in which recruiting can be outsourced.

Outsourcing the Recruiting Function Recruitment process outsourcing (RPO) is a rapidly growing option that streamlines recruiting and reduces recruiting costs. RPO firms can offer a menu of recruiting services from placing advertisements

FIGURE 6-2 Ways to Evaluate RPO Firm Performance

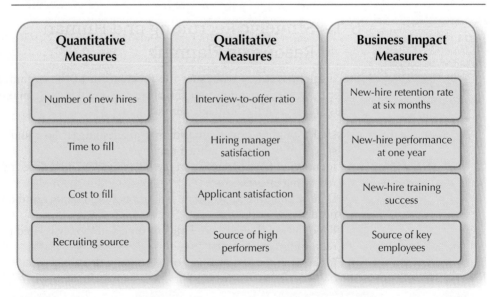

Quantitative Measures	Qualitative Measures	Business Impact Measures
Number of new hires	Interview-to-offer ratio	New-hire retention rate at six months
Time to fill	Hiring manager satisfaction	New-hire performance at one year
Cost to fill	Applicant satisfaction	New-hire training success
Recruiting source	Source of high performers	Source of key employees

to initial screening of applicants. RPO firms may serve a broad range of industries or specialize in particular sectors such as health care or financial services.[7] As with all outsourcing activities, companies should carefully research RPOs and ensure high-quality performance. Figure 6-2 shows various performance criteria that organization leaders can use to assess an RPO vendor.[8]

While RPOs can save the company time and money, care must be taken to preserve goodwill with applicants. Applicants may react negatively to outsourced recruiting and feel that it reduces their personal contact with the hiring organization. They may also have concerns about the privacy of information they provide during the screening process. These negative reactions can be minimized if the RPO operates in a professional manner and if the employer has a positive image.[9]

Professional Employer Organizations and Employee Leasing Another type of outsourcing is professional employer organizations (PEOs) and employee leasing. The employee leasing process is simple: An employer signs an agreement with the PEO, after which the employer's staff is hired by the leasing firm and leased back to the company for a fee. In turn, the leasing firm writes paychecks, pays taxes, prepares and implements HR policies, keeps all the required HR records for the employer, and bears legal liability.

One advantage of leasing employees is that they may receive better benefits than they otherwise would get in many small businesses. But all this service comes at a cost to employers. Leasing companies often charge employers between 4% and 6% of employees' monthly salaries. Thus, while leasing may save employers money on benefits and HR administration, it also may increase total payroll costs.

Whether recruiting is carried out by internal recruiting staff or outsourced to a third-party vendor, a primary consideration is presenting an attractive employment opportunity to a prospective employee. Developing a positive employment brand is critical for enticing high-quality talent to consider employment with the company.

6-2b Employment Branding and Employer of Choice

Employment brand
Distinct image of the organization that captures the essence of the company to engage employees and outsiders

The employment brand is the distinct image of the organization that captures the essence of the company to engage employees and outsiders. The brand is a set of qualities that promises a unique employment experience. Organizations strive to develop reputations as employers of choice. Those seen as desirable places to work are better able to attract qualified applicants compared to those that have poor reputations.

There are many "best employer survey" lists that rank organizations in terms of employee engagement, job satisfaction, pay, benefits, flexible schedules, corporate social responsibility, and other employee-friendly characteristics. Companies identified as the best places to work receive significantly more applicants than those that don't make the grade. Achieving that coveted status requires a focused effort and investment, much like developing a brand for the company's products.[10] Managing the employment brand is best achieved through a partnership between HR and marketing staffs. The following "HR Competencies & Applications: Manage Your Employment Brand" feature explains important elements of the employment brand.

Companies often spend considerable effort and money establishing brand images for their products. The same attention must be spent on developing an employment brand based on the benefits and opportunities offered to employees. The brand can create positive perceptions if the company also highlights the employee value

Manage Your Employment Brand

Successfully managing an employment brand doesn't happen by accident. To create and advertise the compelling story behind your company, take time to identify your employment brand and determine what makes your company unique. The following tips may help you get the most out of your branding efforts.[11]

- *Leverage your corporate brand.* Your company may already be well known for its products and services. Use that name recognition to connect with prospective employees.
- *Use the 80/20 rule.* When advertising jobs, be sure to spend most of the time talking about the job (80%) and less time promoting your brand (20%).
- *Engage visitors.* Use videos of employees rather than text to deliver the brand message.

- *Encourage current employees to spread the word.* Get employees to talk to others in their personal and professional networks.
- *"Mobilize" your message.* Create an easy-to-use mobile career site that allows users to connect on the go.

Recruiting and employer branding should be seen as part of an organizational marketing effort that is linked to the overall image and reputation of the organization and its industry. If you were responsible for enhancing your organization's employment brand:

1. How would you convince senior leaders that the investment would be worthwhile?

2. Who would you partner with inside and outside your organization to develop and convey your brand message?

KEY COMPETENCIES: Business Acumen; HR Expertise: People/Talent Acquisition

proposition, which is developed by focusing on the company's commitment to employee excellence and development. Keep in mind that the employment brand must reflect the genuine work environment and not simply be a marketing creation that doesn't match the true experience of life inside the organization.

6-2c Core versus Flexible Staffing

Another strategic decision involves how much recruiting will be done to fill staffing needs with core and flexible workers. Core workers are those employees that are foundational to the business; they typically work year-round, and the organization invests in their development. Flexible workers are hired as needed. Thinking of the supply chain, they are just-in-time workers who are employed for specific projects or periods of time.

Decisions as to who should be recruited hinge on whether to seek core employees or to use more flexible approaches, which might include temporary workers or independent contractors. Figure 6-3 shows how a company's workforce might be divided among different types of workers. Many employers have determined that keeping a large core workforce is too costly and limits flexibility. The large number of employment regulations also constrains the employment relationship, making many employers reluctant to hire new full-time core employees. Using flexible

Core workers
Employees that are foundational to the business

Flexible workers
Employees that are hired on an "as-needed" basis

FIGURE 6-3 Combination of Core and Flexible Workers

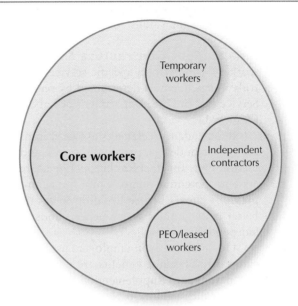

workers means that labor costs go from being a fixed expense to one that is variable, based on product demand and other economic conditions.

Flexible staffing involves workers who are not traditional employees. Alternative employment is becoming much more common in the United States as well as around the world. Over one-fifth of U.S. workers are considered part of the flexible workforce.[12] Using flexible staffing arrangements allows an employer to avoid some of the costs of full-time benefits such as vacation pay, health care, and pension plans. Flexible staffing may lead to recruiting in different markets, since it includes using temporary workers and independent contractors. Despite the many benefits, there are also many challenges associated with using flexible staffing, including low motivation, low performance, and increased costs.

Temporary Workers Over 3 million workers per day are employed as temporary workers.[13] Employers can hire their own temporary staff members or contract with agencies that supply temporary workers on an hourly, daily, or weekly basis. Originally developed to provide clerical and office workers to employers, temporary workers in professional, technical, and even managerial jobs are becoming more common. This reality is driven by the many benefits that these workers provide organizations.

Some employers hire temporary workers as a way to screen individuals to move into full-time, regular employment. Better-performing workers may move to regular positions when these positions become available. This "try before you buy" approach is potentially beneficial to both employers and employees. In addition, companies hire temporary workers because matching the firm's needs with the right workers can be easier, the costs associated with benefits can be avoided, and staffing flexibility is often greatly enhanced. However, if individuals come through temporary service firms, those firms typically bill client companies a placement charge if a temporary worker is hired for a full-time position. Also, employing temporary workers as opposed to full-time workers can have implications regarding federal laws such as the Family Medical Leave Act and the Fair Labor Standards Act.[14]

Independent Contractors Some firms employ independent contractors as workers who perform specific services on a contract basis. These workers must be truly independent as determined by regulations used by the U.S. Internal Revenue Service and the U.S. Department of Labor. This information is discussed further in Chapter 11.

Independent freelancers are used in many areas, including software programming, system design, personal services, and others. Online digital marketplaces like Elance, Lyft, and TaskRabbit operate as matchmaking services to connect freelancers with potential clients. Employers can see candidate profiles and reviews from previous clients before deciding to contract with the freelancer. Freelancers can better manage their assignments, choose their own work hours, and enjoy career independence.[15]

One major reason employers use independent contractors is to obtain significant savings because benefits are not provided to these individuals. Many freelancers "moonlight," supplementing their income from a traditional job with contract work, or they have multiple sources of income, including contract assignments. The freelance workforce is large and growing, and organizations like the Freelancers Insurance Company sell insurance and retirement plans to this employee group.[16]

Companies can mix and match the core workforce with temporary and contract workers as their business needs change. There may be conflicts between these various workforce segments, and managers should tune in and work hard to integrate the efforts from all workers to produce goods and services for customers. For example, core workers may view temporary workers as competitors and may treat them poorly to discourage them from performing above standards. Temporary workers have fewer ties to the company and may be less engaged which can upset the full-time workers. Figure 6-4 shows the advantages and disadvantages of using flexible staffing alternatives.

FIGURE 6-4 Advantages and Disadvantages of Using Flexible Staffing Alternatives

Advantages	Disadvantages
• Organizations can hire workers without incurring high costs.	• Flexible workers may perform less effectively than core workers.
• Reduces time spent on recruiting efforts such as screening and initial training of workers.	• Flexible workers may lack motivation because there are few opportunities for long-term employment and job advancement.
• Gives the organization staffing flexibility.	• Time limits on temporary work contracts prevent significant enhancements in individual skills and knowledge.
• Reduces the organization's legal compliance requirements.	
• Organization saves money by not providing employee benefits.	• Flexible workers in high demand fields may command premium wages.

6-2d Recruiting and EEO: Diversity Considerations

Recruiting strategies take into account a number of equal employment opportunity (EEO) and diversity considerations. Figure 6-5 shows the major issues companies face when proactively addressing a diverse applicant pool.

EEO and Recruiting Efforts Recruiting activities are subject to various equal employment laws and regulations. As part of legal compliance in the recruiting process, organizations may work to reduce disparate impact, or underrepresentation of protected-class members compared to the labor markets utilized by the employer. If disparate impact exists the employer may need to make special efforts to attract protected-class individuals. For employers with affirmative action programs (AAPs), special ways to reduce disparate impact can be identified as goals listed in those plans. Also, many employers who emphasize internal recruiting should take steps to attract minority applicants externally if disparate impact exists in the current workforce.

Equal Employment Opportunity Commission (EEOC) guidelines state that no direct or indirect statements of protected characteristics are permitted in recruiting materials or advertisements. These guidelines affect interviews, advertisements, and other recruiting activities. Some examples of impermissible terminology are *young and enthusiastic, Christian values,* and *journeyman lineman.* Also, advertisements should contain wording about being an equal opportunity employer, or even more specific designations such as EEO/M-F/AA/ADA. Employers demonstrate inclusive recruiting by having diverse individuals represented in company materials, in advertisements, and as recruiters.

Applicants pay attention to the diversity message in recruiting materials. When workforce diversity is showcased in recruiting ads, applicants of all races are more likely to pursue employment with the organization. Further, people who value diversity will be attracted by HR policies that support their own personal beliefs.

FIGURE 6-5 Recruiting and Diversity Considerations

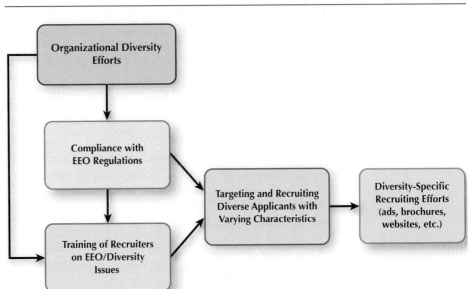

Organizations can increase the number of applicants by including diversity as a key element of the employment brand.[17]

Recruiting Diversity A broad range of factors can be considered when recruiting for diversity. Many employers have expanded efforts to recruit workers from nontraditional labor pools. These recruits for certain jobs may include the following:

- Persons with different racial/ethnic backgrounds
- Workers over 40 years of age, particularly retirees
- Single parents
- Workers with disabilities
- Welfare-to-work workers
- Long-term unemployed

The growth in racial/ethnic workforce diversity means that a wider range of potential employment sources should be utilized. Changes in diversity also need to be monitored and evaluated to ensure that the workplace, through properly managed recruiting strategies, is representative of these population demographics. For example, the growth in Hispanics in the United States means that specialized recruiting programs might be needed to identify and attract qualified individuals from this group for employment. Other potential employees may include older workers and retirees who are interested in seeking new employment opportunities. Single parents may be attracted to a family-friendly employer that offers flexibility, including part-time work, because balancing job and family life is often difficult. Some firms also recruit stay-at-home parents by using flexibility and work-at-home technology. Finally, individuals with disabilities are often overlooked despite their education and skill qualifications.

Gender-Neutral Recruiting Studies have shown that women are less likely to apply when job ads contain masculine sounding words such as *determined*, *assertive*, or *aggressive*. Women are more likely to apply when words like *dedicated*, *responsible*, or *conscientious* are used in advertisements. Men don't seem to be influenced one way or the other. So, there is little downside to using gender-balanced adjectives in recruiting ads. IT companies are also stepping up efforts to recruit qualified female candidates due to the overall shortage of technology workers. The Girl Scouts and other organizations have been working to introduce young women to science, technology, engineering, and math (STEM) fields of study from an early age, to encourage them to consider careers in these in-demand areas.[18]

Generational Differences in Recruiting The work values and preferences found among different generations can impact every aspect of the employment experience. In terms of recruiting, distinct approaches may be needed to connect with members of different generations. Baby Boomers (born between 1946 and 1964) may be more comfortable with traditional job posting methods and less inclined to use mobile technology to find a job. Generation X (born between 1965 and 1980) workers may value flexible work arrangements, child care, and other work-life balance programs. People in Generation Y (born between 1980 and 2000) utilize mobile technology extensively and value meaningful work and an opportunity to actively contribute to work policies and arrangements.

COMPETENCIES & APPLICATIONS

Getting Helicopter Parents into the Hangar

A growing issue in today's workplace is the appearance of *helicopter parents*. Helicopter parents are overinvolved, overcontrolling mothers and fathers who don't let their children live independently. They tend to navigate their children's lives and participate in everything from choosing college courses to joining their sons and daughters at job interviews.

Text messaging and other mobile technologies foster a world where parents and their adult children can stay in constant contact, sharing all the ups and downs of daily life. Adult children may appreciate the support and cheerleading offered by mom or dad, especially when the day hasn't gone well. Likewise, parents can continuously guide their children and assist them as they make decisions about many aspects of life.

Some organizations welcome the involvement of parents and actively encourage their participation in job search and employment decisions. Northwest Mutual embraces parents and invites them to be part of the interviewing process. Managers send notes home to mom when an employee hits or exceeds sales targets. Other organizations frown upon parents' involvement in the workplace and have withdrawn job offers when parents call to negotiate starting pay or other terms of employment for their children.[20]

The emergence of helicopter parents is something that can't be ignored. How would you handle this in the workplace?

1. How might an organization establish boundaries for parental involvement in their children's work life that is respectful of all parties involved? How would an HR department be involved in this process?

2. How might hosting a Take Your Parents to Work Day benefit the organization's talent management program?

COMPETENCIES: Global and Cultural Effectiveness; HR Expertise: Workplace/Diversity & Inclusion; People/Employee Engagement

When crafting recruiting messages and choosing the best media for recruiting, one consideration should be finding ways to connect with members of all generations. While members of a generation may share many similarities, it's also important to avoid letting stereotypes rule decisions about who to hire or how to reach them.[19] The preceding "HR Competencies & Applications: Getting Helicopter Parents into the Hangar" feature presents an emerging trend in the workplace.

LO2 Identify distinct labor markets and describe their unique characteristics.

Labor markets
The supply pool from which employers attract employees

6-3 Understanding Labor Markets

Learning some basics about labor markets aids in understanding recruiting. **Labor markets** are the supply pool from which employers attract employees. As with any supply chain, there are a variety of markets from which a buyer can obtain needed resources. Figure 6-6 depicts how the sourcing process is like the funnel in which the broad scope of labor markets narrows progressively to the point of selecting the best applicants. Of course, if the selected applicants reject the offers, then HR staff members must reach back into the supply chain, or applicant pool, for other candidates, and in extreme cases, may need to reopen the recruiting process.

FIGURE 6-6 Elements of the Labor Market

Labor Force Population

Applicant Population

Applicant Pool

Selected Applicants

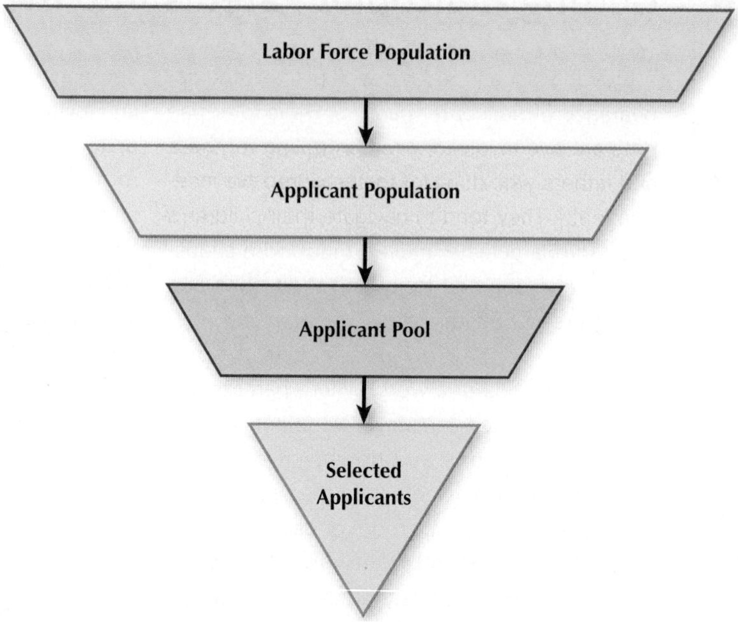

6-3a Elements of the Labor Market

Several methods can be used to identify labor markets. One useful approach is to take a broad view of labor markets and then narrow them down to specific recruiting sources. The broadest labor market component and measure is the labor force population, which is made up of all individuals who are available for selection if all possible recruitment strategies are used. For firms with operations in multiple countries, the labor force population can be much larger than that of a business operating in only one country. For example, some U.S.-based airlines have customer service centers located in the Philippines, India, and other countries as well as the United States. The labor force population for such businesses is much broader than that of a business operating in only one of these countries.

The applicant population is a subset of the labor force population that is available for selection if a particular recruiting approach is used. This population can be broad or narrow depending on the jobs needing to be filled and the approaches used by the employer. For example, if a firm is recruiting highly specialized engineers for multiple geographic locations, the recruiting methods may involve a broad range of approaches and sources, such as contacting professional associations, attending conventions, utilizing general and specialized websites, using recruiting consulting firms, and offering recruitment incentives to existing employees.

However, a smaller firm in a limited geographic location might limit its recruiting for management trainees to MBA graduates from major universities in the area. This recruiting method would result in a different group of applicants from those who might apply if the employer were to advertise the openings for management trainees on a local radio station, post a listing on Internet job boards, or encourage current employee referrals and applications.

Labor force population
All individuals who are available for selection if all possible recruitment strategies are used

Applicant population
A subset of the labor force population that is available for selection using a particular recruiting approach

Applicant pool
All persons who are actually evaluated for selection

The applicant pool consists of all persons who are actually evaluated for selection. Many factors can affect the size of the applicant pool, including the reputation of the organization and industry, a company's screening efforts, the job specifications, and the information available.

6-3b Recordkeeping of Applications

It is important to carefully define exactly who is an applicant and who is not because many employers are required to track and report applicant information to comply with equal employment and affirmative action plans. It is also important because employers may need this documentation if an applicant files a lawsuit. Any minimally qualified person who is interested in a position should be considered an applicant even if no formal posting of the job opening in question has been made or the person has not filed any sort of formal application. Figure 6-7 provides the definition of *Internet applicant* established by the EEOC and Office of Federal Contract Compliance Programs (OFCCP).[21]

Documenting Applicant Flow It is useful to develop an *applicant tracking system* when considering the applicant pool. Using such a system can make the recruiting process more effective. For example, when the size of the applicant pool increases, recruiters can identify the most effective future employees for several jobs, not just fill current jobs.[22]

Employers must collect data on applicant race, sex, and other demographics to fulfill EEO reporting requirements. Many employers ask applicants to provide EEOC reporting data on a separate form that may be attached to the application form. To avoid claims of impropriety, it is important that employers review and store this information separately and not use it in any selection decision. Since completing the form is voluntary, employers can demonstrate that they tried to obtain the data.

Unemployment Rates and Labor Markets The labor market follows the laws of economic supply and demand, and the unemployment rate varies with the business cycle. When the unemployment rate is high, many people are looking for jobs. When the unemployment rate is low, there are fewer applicants. As the economy

FIGURE 6-7 EEOC and OFCCP Definition of *Internet Applicant*

> **An "Internet Applicant" is an individual who satisfies all four of the following criteria:**
>
> - The individual submitted an expression of interest in employment through the Internet or related electronic data technologies;
> - The contractor considered the individual for employment in a particular position;
> - The individual's expression of interest indicated that the individual possesses the basic qualifications for the position; and
> - The individual, at no point in the contractor's selection process prior to receiving an offer of employment from the contractor, removed himself or herself from further consideration or otherwise indicated that he/she was no longer interested in the position.

recovers from the recent recession, firms are beginning to hire more employees. But they are being cautious out of concern that the improved economy will not last.[23]

Unemployment rates also vary depending on particular skill needs. Recruiting for jobs that require few specialized skills is quite different than recruiting for highly skilled workers. The federal government is struggling to attract younger technology-savvy workers because many people have a negative impression of working for bureaucratic agencies.[24] Trucking companies like U.S. Xpress, residential housing construction firms such as Van Dyk Construction, and libraries are all experiencing difficulty finding qualified workers to fill vacancies.[25] Talent shortages in high-technology jobs are so severe that companies like Google and Apple have begun courting kids in junior high school to develop apps for their smart phones.[26] Companies adopt creative solutions to help develop the skilled workers needed to fill jobs.

6-3c Different Labor Markets and Recruiting

The supply of workers in various labor markets differs substantially and affects staffing. To provide information that is useful for recruiting, labor markets can be viewed in several ways. These labor markets can include both internal and external sources. Organizations recruit in many labor markets, including:

- Industry-specific and occupational
- Educational and technical
- Geographic

Industry and Occupational Labor Markets Labor markets can be classified by industry and occupation. For example, the biggest increases in U.S. jobs until the year 2022 will be in the fields of healthcare, healthcare support, construction, and personal care fields.[27] These jobs represent the health care, retail, and education industries. A shortage of qualified applicants will make filling these jobs more difficult during the next few years.

Recruiting for smaller firms can also be challenging. For instance, a small landscaping company had to turn away business because the owner was unable to find individuals who had both managerial and landscaping experience. Despite offering a salary of $75,000 and retirement benefits, he couldn't fill the job. His experience is not unique, as over 40% of small firms are hampered in their efforts to grow and expand because they cannot find enough skilled workers.[28]

Educational and Technical Labor Markets Another way to look at labor markets is by considering the educational and technical qualifications that define the people being recruited. Employers may need individuals with specific licenses, certifications, or educational backgrounds. For instance, recruiting physician leaders for a medical organization led to the establishment of a special search committee to set goals for the organization. Then, as part of recruitment and selection, the top candidates were asked to develop departmental vision statements and three-year goals. That information made the recruitment and selection process more effective.[29] By networking extensively with executives, alumni, and recruiters, business schools are also taking active steps to ensure that MBA students are getting the kinds of experiences that make them attractive to organizations.[30]

Another special labor market is suppliers and contractors for U.S. military forces. Firms such as Cintas Corporation, with more than 34,000 employees, and Raytheon, with 77,000 employees, serve as federal government defense contractors.

The need to recruit for specialty jobs in engineering and technology by such firms illustrates why considering different types of technical labor markets is necessary. The following "HR Perspective: Decoding Military Resumes" feature highlights the challenges of recruiting former members of the military.

A prominent labor market that is expected to be in high demand over the next decade is bilingual and multilingual employees, particularly those individuals who can speak Spanish or Chinese.[32] With some research showing a lack of motivation among workers to learn these languages, this educational/technical area should be in high demand with good work opportunities. Similarly, third-culture children, or individuals who have spent considerable time in geographic/cultural regions different from those of their parents, will also be in demand because of their flexibility and knowledge of diverse cultural environments.

PERSPECTIVE

Decoding Military Resumes

Members of the armed forces face particular challenges when they try to reenter civilian life and careers. In general, they are hardworking, resilient, and adaptable team players. Despite the fact that many were quickly forced into leadership and decision-making roles during their active duty years, stereotypes can work against them outside of the military. Many employers have inaccurate beliefs that service members are rigid, bureaucratic, and out of touch with the needs of business.

Translating the military experience into terms that nonmilitary hiring authorities can understand is critical to help former service members find employment after their service obligations are fulfilled. While veterans must learn how to convey their skills and experience in terms that employers can understand, companies can also take the initiative to learn more about military career demands.

HR professionals can take proactive steps to increase hiring of veterans, including:

- Ask for help from current employees who served in the military. They can explain terminology used and certifications or knowledge designations. Since they know your organization's structure and culture,

they can help hiring managers see how the military experience would best fit within the company.

- Do a little legwork and research by reviewing military websites. This helps individuals understand the military's core values and how they might reflect the organization's value system.

- Be aware that many automated resume screening programs screen out veterans because they don't use *management-speak* on their resumes.

Consider adding keywords like *veteran* or *military* to widen the search criteria. Hiring veterans can be a win-win situation, as the organization might access a highly qualified and dedicated worker while doing a great public service. You can find more information at http://content.gijobs.com/hotjobs.[31]

Questions to consider:

1. What might hiring managers do to create a welcoming environment for military veterans?

2. What attributes of military veterans would lead to success in business?

KEY COMPETENCIES: Relationship Management, Global/Cultural Effectiveness; HR Expertise: People/Talent Acquisition

Geographic Labor Markets One common way to classify labor markets is based on geographic location. Markets can be local, area or regional, national, or international. Local and area labor markets vary significantly in terms of workforce availability and quality, and changes in a geographic labor market may force changes in recruiting efforts. For instance, if a new major employer locates in a region, existing area employers may see a decline in their numbers of applicants.

Geographic markets require different recruiting considerations. For example, attempting to recruit locally for a job market that is a national competitive market will likely result in disappointing applicant rates. A catalog retailer that tries to recruit a senior merchandising manager from the small town where the firm is located may encounter difficulties, although it may not need to recruit nationally for workers to fill administrative support jobs. Varying geographic labor markets must be evaluated as part of recruiting. It is often a function of how much the jobs pay in addition to the quantity of available talent.

GLOBAL

Global Labor Markets Employers in the United States are tapping global labor markets when necessary and offshoring when doing so is advantageous. Firms in different industries are expanding in India, China, Indonesia, Romania, Poland, and other countries. This expansion has caused an increase in the number of host country nationals hired to fill positions in foreign operations.

The migration of U.S. work overseas has been controversial. While many decry the loss of American jobs, some employers respond that they cannot be competitive in a global market if they fail to take advantage of labor savings. For example, at some operations in India and China, U.S. employers pay less than half of what they would pay for comparable jobs to be performed in U.S. facilities. However, advancements in American worker productivity have made it possible to have fewer U.S. employees to produce certain items, resulting in cost savings, even at higher wage rates. Hence, those jobs are not being exported to other countries.

The use of the Internet has resulted in recruiting in more varied geographic regions. But recruiting employees for global assignments may present problems that require different approaches from those used in the home country. Companies should be clear about foreign travel requirements when recruiting employees because applicants take this into consideration when deciding to pursue employment opportunities. Applicants may self-select out of the hiring process if they are not willing to travel globally for the job.[33] Recruiting processes must also account for variations in culture, laws, and language, as well as the individual preferences of potential workers. Dealing with foreign labor markets can be challenging because recruiting may be regulated and require government approval. Hiring foreign employees in the United States is subject to certain legal requirements, including visa requirements, and organizations must be concerned about hiring illegal immigrants.

6-3d Recruiting Source Choices: Internal versus External

Most employers use both internal and external recruiting sources. Both promoting from within the organization (internal recruitment) and hiring from outside the organization (external recruitment) come with advantages and disadvantages.

Organizations that face rapidly changing competitive environments and conditions may need to place a heavier emphasis on external sources. A possible strategy might be to promote from within if a qualified applicant exists and to go to external sources if not. However, for organizations operating in environments that change slowly, emphasis on promotion from within may be more suitable. An organization's goals for time to hire and the number of qualified applicants factor into the decision of whether to focus on internal or external recruiting.

Organizations differ in terms of the sequencing of recruiting internally or externally. Some exhaust internal sources before searching outside of the company. Others recruit in both labor markets at the same time to fill jobs faster. Recent evidence suggests that internal recruiting might produce the best results overall because existing employees who are given new work opportunities tend to perform considerably better than external hires, at least in the first three years of employment in a new job.[34] Once the various recruiting policy decisions have been addressed, the actual recruiting methods can be identified and used for both internal and external recruiting.

LO3 Explain how technology and social networking affect recruiting processes for employers and candidates.

6-4 Technology for Recruiting

Technological advances have led to dramatic changes in the way people find jobs. Mobile technology is becoming the hottest trend in employment recruiting, allowing many jobseekers to use their smartphones to find job opportunities.[35] The growth in the Internet has led both employers and employees to use Internet recruiting tools. Internet links, Web 2.0 sites, blogs, tweets, and other types of Internet/web-based applications have become vital elements of every company's recruiting strategy.

6-4a Social Media and Networking

Passive job candidates
Qualified individuals who aren't actively looking for work but might be interested if the right job comes along

Virtual online communities are a goldmine of networking opportunities for companies looking to identify talent, particularly passive job candidates, qualified individuals who aren't actively looking for work but might be interested if the right job comes along. Figure 6-8 shows the number of users on popular social networking sites. With millions of users, companies ignore social networks at their own peril.

FIGURE 6-8 Number of Users on Popular Social Networking Websites as of January 2014

Website	Users
◆ Facebook	◆ 1.15 billion
◆ Google+	◆ 359 million
◆ LinkedIn	◆ 313 million
◆ Twitter	◆ 215 million
◆ Instagram	◆ 150 million
◆ Pinterest	◆ 20 million

Source: Adapted from Pew Research

An important new skill for recruiters is building and accessing connections via social media. Sought-after recruiters will be those with high Klout scores, an algorithmic measure of the breadth of their online network.[36] Recruiters should develop their own networks, but they must also find ways to engage current employees and "share" their networks. Hard Rock Café did just that when it used Facebook to hire 120 people for a new restaurant in Florence, Italy—in 30 days![37]

Employers have a wide variety of options for using social networking to build their employment brand and find employees. For example, matchmaking website eHarmony plans to launch a job-search website using experience gained through years of matching individuals to their "ideal companion." Rather than using third-party websites, online retailer Zappos is establishing its own social network called Zappos Insiders to speed up hiring and develop a pool of candidates in the pipeline. Creating an exciting online image on Pinterest and Instagram is helping companies like Sodexo, Aon, and Pizza Hut attract followers who then become job candidates. And job candidates can use these websites to showcase their personalities and creativity.[38]

LinkedIn A well-known professional social networking website is LinkedIn. Individuals create a professional profile and can link to other users as well as to companies they might like to work for. LinkedIn's focus is professional networking, and therefore it can be a powerful way to expand candidates' job-search options. Likewise, companies can create employer branding content and invite users to "link in" with them. This identifies potential employees and helps spread the word on job vacancies.[39]

Twitter Social, legal, and employment-related messages can be transmitted using Twitter. -a fast-growing social networking site that has added 240 million users since 2010. Although messages are limited to 140 characters, tweeting has rapidly become a social network recruiting method. Recruiters tweet messages to both active and passive job candidates and then follow up with longer emails to facilitate recruiting. For example, Twitter has been used by bank recruiters for college recruiting and to hire bank tellers.[40]

Technology-enabled social networking continues to evolve. Job seekers and employers will continue to find new ways to connect, share information, and match the best applicants to jobs.

6-4b Web-Based Recruiting Options

Whether an organization is recruiting internally or externally, web-based recruiting is a primary way to advertise job vacancies. Of the many recruiting sites available to companies, the most common are Internet job boards, professional/career websites, and employer websites. While social networking sites and other technologies are gaining in popularity, these web-based methods are still heavily used.

Internet Job Boards Many Internet job boards, such as Indeed, Monster, Glass-Door, and CareerBuilder, provide places for employers to post jobs or search for candidates. These broad-based job boards offer access to numerous candidates across a wide range of professions and jobs. Niche websites like JobsinTrucks, HealthCareJobsite, and eFinancialCareers target specific occupations and make it more efficient for job seekers and employers to find each other.[41] Applicants can use these websites to establish a profile and upload their resume, which is made available to all employers that use the website. Combining an easy-to-use applicant experience and search capabilities for employers makes these websites a robust and productive choice for recruiters and job seekers.

Professional/Career Websites Many professional associations have employment links on their websites. As an illustration, for HR jobs, see the Society for Human Resource Management site (www.shrm.org) or the Association for Talent Development site (http://jobs.astd.org). Many professional associations provide job links to their members as a benefit of membership. Many private corporations maintain specialized career or industry websites that focus on IT, telecommunications, engineering, medicine, and other areas. Use of these targeted websites may reduce recruiters' search time and efforts. Also, posting jobs on such websites is likely to target applicants specifically interested in the job field and may reduce the number of less-qualified applicants.

Employer Websites Despite the popularity of job boards and association job sites, many employers have learned that their own company websites can be very useful when recruiting candidates and reinforcing the employer brand. Employers include employment and career information on their websites under headings such as *Employment* or *Careers*. This is the place where recruiting (both internal and external) is often conducted. On many of these sites, job seekers are encouraged to email résumés or complete online applications.

Since a website can be an effective tool for marketing the company, the formatting of the employment section of an organization's website must be creative and attractive enough to effectively market jobs and careers. A company website should present a favorable image of the employer by outlining information on the organization, including its products and services, organizational and industry growth potential, and organizational operations. Including positive employee testimonials on recruiting websites may make the employer more desirable and credible to job candidates; thus, HR departments and other hiring managers should consider incorporating such statements into the online recruiting process.

6-4c E-Video and Recruiting

With video capabilities of all types available, employers are using videos in several ways. Some firms use videos to describe their company characteristics, job opportunities, and recruiting means. Suppliers such as Monster and CareerTV have worked with employer clients to produce online recruitment videos. As the saying goes, "A picture is worth a thousand words." That is one reason videos can so effectively engage candidates and provide a realistic image of the company. Video interviews can save time and money for candidates who are not near the hiring location. Recent research shows that over one-third of organizations are using some type of video for talent acquisition.[42]

6-4d Gamification

Gamification
Using game thinking and software to engage people in solving problems

As described in this chapter's HR Headline feature, organizations are using scavenger hunts, trivia contests, games, puzzles, and other interactive competitions to interject excitement into the hiring process. Gamification uses game thinking and software to engage people in solving problems. It leverages our natural desire to compete and achieve, and many people entering the workforce have grown up with video games and are very comfortable with these programs.

Companies might use industry-related quizzes, company knowledge trivia contests, or information "hunts" to get potential candidates to investigate the company and uncover job opportunities. Games may be hosted online or might be incorporated into on-campus visits or job fair booth activities.[43] Candidates are beginning to expect a level of interaction and participation during the recruitment process. To attract the best candidates, recruiters should work to differentiate their organizations through gamification.

ETHICS

6-4e Legal Issues in Internet Recruiting

With the expansion of Internet recruiting, new and different concerns have arisen. Several of these issues have ethical and moral as well as legal implications. The following examples illustrate some of these concerns:

- When companies use screening software to avoid looking at the thousands of résumés they receive, are rejections really based on the qualifications needed for the job?
- How can data about an individual's protected characteristics be collected and analyzed for reports?
- Are too many individuals being excluded from the later phases of the Internet recruiting process based on unlawful information?
- Which applicants really want jobs? If someone has accessed a job board and sent an email asking an employer about a job opening, does the person actually want to be an applicant?
- What are the implications of Internet recruiting in terms of confidentiality and privacy?

Loss of privacy is a potential disadvantage with Internet recruiting. Sharing information gleaned from people who apply to job boards or even company websites has become common. As a company receives résumés from applicants, it is required to track those applicants and file its EEO report. But the personal information that can be seen by employers on websites such as Facebook, LinkedIn, and others may be inappropriate, and when employers access it, they may be violating legal provisions.

Employment lawyers are issuing warnings to employers about considering photos or comments posted on LinkedIn, Facebook, and Twitter in the hiring process. Information posted on social media may not be accurate or representative of the candidate and may not relate to job requirements or demands.[44] Some of the concerns raised have included postings of confidential details about an employee's termination, racial/ethnic background or gender, and the making of discriminatory comments.

A number of states have enacted social media privacy laws that restrict employers from inappropriately using online networks to screen applicants. Hiring managers and HR staff should proceed cautiously when they are considering checking candidates' social media profiles. It's important to find a balance between invading candidates' privacy and trying to reduce the risk of making a bad hire.[45] Since Internet usage has legal implications for recruiting, HR employment-related policies, training, and enforcement should be based on legal advice. In addition to various legal challenges, there are many ethical concerns related to hiring and social media.

6-4f Advantages of Using Technology in Recruiting

Employers have found many advantages to using technology to support recruiting. Compared to traditional recruiting methods such as newspaper advertising, employment agencies, and search firms, technology-enhanced recruiting can save the company money. Web-based job postings and social media are less expensive than newspapers or job fairs. In addition, web postings can be updated frequently and can be accessed by candidates at any hour of the day or night.

Another major advantage is that by reaching out to so many people who potentially represent diverse backgrounds and regions, a very large pool of applicants can be generated. The ability to find passive jobseekers is enhanced with web postings and social media. Technology-enhanced recruiting can also save time. Applicants can respond quickly to job postings by sending electronic responses, instead of using snail mail. Recruiters can respond more rapidly to qualified candidates to obtain additional information, request additional details, and establish times for further communication, including interviews.

The use of technology can enhance the employment brand through consistent messaging that reinforces the company's product brand. Videos, employee testimonials, and interactive games and contests all create an experience that is impossible to duplicate in a newspaper ad.

6-4g Disadvantages of Using Technology in Recruiting

The advantages of Internet recruiting should be balanced against disadvantages, some of which have already been suggested. Since more people will see job postings, technology-enhanced recruiting often creates additional work for HR staff members and others internally. More online job postings must be sent, many more résumés must be reviewed, and more emails, blogs, and tweets need to be dealt with. Expensive specialized software may also be needed to track the high volume of applicants resulting from the recruiting efforts.

In addition, many online applicants might not be qualified for open jobs, and some companies are shying away from web-based job boards in favor of social networking websites that provide better leads. Further, while some social networking websites such as LinkedIn and Twitter can be viable sources of leads, some applicants still prefer to use traditional search methods. And employers may find that applicants become wary of online hiring practices if the trend of accessing social medial persists.[46]

Another issue with Internet recruiting is that some applicants may have limited Internet access, especially individuals from lower socioeconomic groups and from certain racial/ethnic groups, raising issues of fairness in hiring. In addition, it is easy to access Internet recruiting sources, but not all who do so are actively looking for new jobs. However, these applicants require much employer time to process.

Technology-enhanced recruiting is here to stay, but it should be used in combination with traditional methods to ensure that qualified applicants from all walks of life are aware of job vacancies and are able to respond effectively.

LO4 Identify three internal recruiting sources and issues associated with their use.

6-5 Internal Recruiting Methods

Filling openings internally may motivate employees to stay and grow in the organization rather than pursuing career opportunities elsewhere. The most common internal recruiting methods include organizational databases, job postings, career plans,

FIGURE 6-9 Pros and Cons of Internal Recruiting

Pros	Cons
• Improves morale of promotee	• "Inbreeding" may lead to less diverse workforce
• Provides more accurate performance history	• Tunnel vision thinking may lead to a lack of new ideas
• Lowers recruiting costs	• May lower morale for individuals not promoted
• Offers hope and motivation to employees	• Employees may engage in "political" infighting for promotions
• Facilitates succession planning, future promotions, and career development	• Employees promoted may need to be trained or developed
• Improves organization fit because current employees understand the company's culture, hierarchy, and policies/practices	• Some managers may block the internal movement of good performers

current employee referrals, and rerecruiting of former employees and applicants. Some of the common pros and cons of internal recruiting are highlighted in Figure 6-9.

6-5a Organizational Databases

HR information systems (HRIS) allow HR staff to maintain background and knowledge, skills, and abilities (KSA) information on existing employees. As openings arise, HR can access databases by doing a keyword search and receiving a listing of current employees meeting the requirements. Software can sort employee data by occupational fields, areas of career interests, previous work histories, and other variables. For instance, if a firm has an opening for someone with an engineering degree and fluency in Mandarin Chinese, the key words *engineering* and *Mandarin* can be entered in a search field, and the program displays a list of all current employees with these two qualifications. Online and electronic talent profiles can also be developed to identify good talent.

The advantage of such talent databases is that they can be linked to other HR activities. Opportunities for career development and advancement are major reasons individuals stay with or leave their employers. With talent databases, internal opportunities for individuals can be identified. Employee profiles are continually updated to include items such as additional training and education completed, special projects handled, and career plans and desires noted during performance appraisals and career-mentoring discussions.

6-5b Job Posting

Job posting
System in which the employer provides notices of job openings, and employees respond by applying for specific openings

A primary way to recruit current employees for other jobs within the organization is job posting, a system in which the employer provides notices of job openings, and employees respond by applying for specific openings. Without some sort of job posting system, it is difficult for many employees to find out what jobs are open elsewhere in the organization. In many unionized organizations, job posting and bidding can be quite formal because the procedures are often spelled out in labor agreements. Seniority lists may be used by organizations that make promotion decisions based strictly on seniority.

Job postings have moved from flyers on the bulletin board to real-time job listings on the company's intranet. The purpose of the job posting system is to provide employees with more opportunities to move within the organization. Jobs are generally posted internally before any external recruiting is done. The organization should allow a reasonable period of time for current employees to check notices of available jobs before it considers external applicants.

Employees whose bids are turned down should discuss with their supervisors or HR department representatives what knowledge, skills, and abilities are needed to improve their opportunities in the future. In the end, only one individual can receive the promotion or transfer. To maintain harmony and motivation in the organization, it's important to explain to each unsuccessful bidder where his or her qualifications fell short. This is an ideal opportunity to reinforce the company's commitment to offer training and development to assist these employees.

When establishing and managing a job posting system, it is useful to consider how the organization might deal with the following issues:

- What happens if no qualified candidates respond to postings?
- Must employees inform their supervisors that they are applying for another job?
- Are there restrictions on how long an employee must stay in a job before applying for another internal one?
- What types of or levels of jobs will not be posted?

Career Plans Many organizations try to fill vacancies through promotions or transfers from within whenever possible. Software provider SAP actively promotes internal positions to the existing workforce through monthly email notifications listing "hot" jobs. This has resulted in a low attrition rate of 6% to 8%, well below the 10% industry average. Integrating employee career plans with internal job opportunities can reduce employee turnover, enhance individuals' skills and talent, and improve productivity.[47]

Although often successful, internal transfer and promotion of current employees may have some drawbacks. For instance, a person's performance on one job may not be a good predictor of performance on another because different skills may be required on the new job. Consider that the best candidate for Sales Manager may not be the top salesperson because the manager's job requires a very different skill set. Also, as employees transfer or are promoted to other jobs, individuals must be recruited to fill the vacated jobs. Planning on how to fill those openings should occur before the job transfers or promotions, not after.

6-5c Employee-Focused Recruiting

One commonly used source of potential recruits is suggestions from current or former employees. Since current and former employees are familiar with the employer, most of them will not refer individuals who are likely to be unqualified or who will make them look bad. Also, follow-up with former employees is likely to be done only with individuals who were good performers. Companies are also staying in touch with former employees through online networking websites so that they may be encouraged to work for the organization again.

Referrals from Current Employee A reliable source of people to fill vacancies is colleagues, friends, and family members of current employees. Current employees can acquaint potential applicants with the advantages of a job with the company, furnish emails and other means of introduction, and encourage candidates to apply. Compared to other methods, employee referrals often lead to higher-quality hires made in less time. Software programs can automate the process for even greater efficiency.[48] However, relying too heavily on them as an exclusive recruiting method may cause problems regarding equal employment regulations if diverse applicants are underrepresented in the organization's current workforce. Therefore, some external recruiting might be necessary to avoid legal problems in this area.

Employers in many geographic areas and occupational fields have established employee referral incentive programs. Midsized and larger employers are more likely to use employee referral bonuses. Referral programs typically provide a bonus to the referring employee. Health care software firm Aquilent pays a $2,000 referral bonus after the referred candidate meets his or her six-month anniversary. In addition, the referring employee receives a $100 restaurant gift card and is entered into a grand prize drawing.[49] The "HR Perspective: Employee Referrals Go 'Social'"

PERSPECTIVE

Employee Referrals Go "Social"

Many managers dream of taking a good idea and making it better through the use of technology. Chicago-based data security firm Trustwave has put its employee referral program on steroids by making it easy for employees to refer connections from their social networks. The HR department's weekly broadcast to its 1,100 employees highlights four featured job vacancies. Employees are encouraged to pass along these job leads to qualified network connections on LinkedIn, Facebook, Twitter, and other social medial platforms.

Employees who refer an individual who is eventually hired score a referral bonus of $5,000. Employees who refer the most new hires are recognized within the company and earn other awards. At one point, this partnership between employees and the company helped Trustwave fill 25% of its 399 new hires through employee referrals. Their results are consistent with industry averages of approximately 30% hires by referral.

Social networks are especially valuable because employees often remain in contact with former coworkers, professional associates, and classmates from college or trade school. New-generation referral software allows employees to share their networks with the company. Then, when job vacancies match someone in the employee's network, the software notifies the employee and suggests that the employee get in touch with that connection. Because it is voluntary, only those employees who wish to share their networks are included in the automated process.

Employee referrals can save time and money, and they can result in better hires for the organization. Leveraging employees' social networks can speed up the process and help companies find hidden talent.[50]

Given these practices, consider the following questions:

1. What incentive might you offer to employees to entice them to share their social network contact lists with referral software programs?

2. How would you determine the appropriate financial bonus for employee referrals?

KEY COMPETENCIES: Ethical Practice; HR Expertise: Organization/Technology & Data feature explains how companies are using employees' connections to expand their recruitment efforts.

Rerecruiting of Former Employees and Applicants Former employees and applicants are another source for recruitment. Both groups offer a time-saving advantage because something is already known about them. Seeking them out as candidates is known as rerecruiting because they were recruited previously.

Rerecruiting
Seeking out former employees and recruiting them again to work for an organization

Boomerangs Commonly known as boomerangs, individuals who have left an organization for other jobs are sometimes willing to return because the other positions and employers turned out to be less attractive than initially thought. Some organizations welcome them back, while others turn a cold shoulder. Annese & Associates, a New York–based communications provider, strongly encourages boomerangs to come back. Alternatively, Bloomberg shuns anyone who leaves the company and views them as traitors who are not treated warmly if they try to return.[51]

Exit interviews can be a key recruiting tactic to let good performers know that they would be welcomed back in the future. The key to getting boomerangs to return is connections with their former managers. Organizations with a favorable view toward boomerangs should encourage managers to maintain contact with good performers who leave the organization.[52]

Alumni Networks To enhance such efforts, some firms have established alumni networks to keep in contact with individuals who have left and also to allow the companies to rerecruit individuals as appropriate openings arise. The idea of these networks began in the consulting industry but has spread to financial services, technology, manufacturing, and other industries. Some of the alumni networks are established by the company, while others are created by the alumni themselves. In either case, they can be a valuable source of candidates who are familiar with the organization and might be great rehires.[53]

Another potential source consists of former applicants. Although they are not entirely an internal source, information about them can be found in the organization's files or an applicant database. Recontacting those who have previously applied for jobs and had good qualifications can be a quick and inexpensive way to fill unexpected openings. For instance, one firm that needed two cost accountants immediately contacted qualified previous applicants and was able to hire two individuals who were disenchanted with their current jobs at other companies.

LO5 Highlight five external recruiting sources.

6-6 External Recruiting Sources

External recruiting is part of effective talent acquisition. Regardless of the methods used, external recruiting involves some common advantages and disadvantages, which are highlighted in Figure 6-10. Some prominent traditional and evolving recruiting methods are highlighted next.

6-6a Media Sources

Media sources such as newspapers, magazines, television, radio, and billboards have been used widely in external recruiting. Some firms have sent direct mail using purchased lists of individuals in certain fields or industries. Internet usage has led to media sources being available online, including postings, ads, videos, webinars, and

FIGURE 6-10 Advantages and Disadvantages of External Recruiting

Advantages	Disadvantages
• New employees bring new perspectives that can be applied to business opportunities and challenges. • Training new hires may be cheaper and faster because of prior external experience. • New hires are likely to have fewer internal political issues/challenges in the firm. • New hires may bring new industry insights and expertise. • Potentially larger applicant pool generated by search efforts.	• The firm may not select someone who will fit well with the job and the organization. • The process may cause morale problems for internal candidates not selected. • New employees may require longer adjustment periods and orientation efforts. • The recruiting process may take more time and resources. • Recruiters often must evaluate more applications.

many other expanding media services. In some cities and towns, newspaper ads are still very prominent, though they may trigger job searchers to go to an Internet source for more details.

Recruiting patterns differ depending on company and location; for instance, different types of recruiting might be used to fill jobs at community banks in rural areas than those used to fill jobs in larger urban banks. Whatever medium is used, it should be tied to the relevant labor market, the job, and the company, and it should provide sufficient, easy-to-understand information.

Effectiveness of Evaluating Media Ads HR recruiters should measure the responses that different ads generate to evaluate the effectiveness of various sources. The easiest way to track responses to ads is to use different contact names, email addresses, or phone number codes in each ad so that the employer can identify which advertisement has prompted each applicant response that is received.

Although the total number of responses to each ad should be tracked, judging the success of an ad only by this number is a mistake. For example, it is better to have 10 responses with two qualified applicants than 30 responses with only one qualified applicant. Therefore, after individuals are hired, follow-up should be done to see which sources produced longer-lasting and better-performing employees.

Another consideration is the cost of using each type of media. If an Internet posting that cost $500 leads to one hirable candidate, the cost per hire is quite high compared to a television advertisement that cost $5,000 and resulted in 20 hirable candidates.

6-6b Competitive Recruiting Sources

Other sources for recruiting include professional and trade associations, trade publications, and competitors. Many professional societies and trade associations have websites or publications that provide job ads to their members. Such sources may be useful for recruiting specialized professionals.

Some employers have extended recruiting to customers. Some retailers such as Walmart and Best Buy have aggressive programs to recruit customers to become employees in stores. While in the store, customers can pick up applications, apply online using kiosks, and even schedule interviews with managers or HR staff members. Other firms have included employment announcements when sending out customer bills or newsletters.

6-6c Employment Agencies

Employment agencies, both public and private, are a recruiting source. Every U.S. state has its own state-sponsored employment agency. These agencies operate branch offices in cities throughout the state and do not charge fees to applicants or employers. They also have websites that potential applicants can use without having to go to the offices.

Private employment agencies operate in most cities. For a fee collected from either the employee or the employer, these agencies do some preliminary screening and put employers in touch with applicants. Private employment agencies differ considerably in the levels of service, costs, policies, and types of applicants they provide.

Headhunters The size of the fees and the aggressiveness with which some employment agencies pursue candidates for executive and other openings have led to such firms being called headhunters. These employment agencies focus their efforts on executive, managerial, and professional positions. Executive search firms are split into two groups: (1) *contingency firms* that charge a fee only after a candidate has been hired by a client company and (2) *retainer firms* that charge the client a set fee whether or not the contracted search is successful. Most larger firms work on a retainer basis. However, search firms are generally ethically bound not to approach employees of client companies in their search for job candidates for another employer.

Headhunters
Employment agencies that focus their efforts on executive, managerial, and professional positions

6-6d Labor Unions

Labor unions may be a useful source of certain types of workers. For example, in the electrical and construction industries, unions traditionally have supplied workers to employers. A labor pool is generally available through a union, and workers can be dispatched from the hiring hall to particular jobs in order to meet the needs of employers.

In some instances, labor unions can control or influence recruiting and staffing activity. An organization with a strong union may have less flexibility than a nonunion company in deciding who will be hired and where those people will be placed. Unions can benefit employers through apprenticeship and cooperative staffing programs, as they do in the building and printing industries.

6-6e Job Fairs and Creative Recruiting

Employers that need to fill a large number of jobs quickly may participate in job fairs and special recruiting events. Job fairs have been held by economic development entities, employer and HR associations, and other community groups to help bring employers and potential job candidates together. For instance, the SHRM chapter in a Midwestern metropolitan area annually sponsors a job fair at which 75 to 100 employers can meet applicants. Publicity in the city draws several hundred potential recruits for different types of jobs.

Job fairs can give participating companies access to a very large pool of applicants. However, many of those applicants may be unqualified or unsuitable for hiring. In addition, well-known employers are likely to have a lot of traffic at their booths, while smaller and/or unfamiliar firms may struggle to get noticed.

Industry- or skill-specific events usually have more qualified candidates. Such job fairs can also attract employed candidates who are casually looking around but may not put their résumés on the Internet.

Job fair coordinators work hard to make the experience fun and interactive by adding amenities such as food, music, live art shows, and contests to combat the stigma of "boring" employment events.[54] Virtual job fairs are becoming more common to recruit college students. Collegefeed is a third party that sets up virtual job fairs at schools such as Stanford and Carnegie Mellon. The university placement staff does not have to deal with administrative details or worry about hosting the virtual job fair on its own website. Although employers and students do not meet face-to-face, the convenience of virtual job fairs helps busy candidates learn about job opportunities.[55]

6-6f Educational Institutions and Recruiting

College and university students are a significant source of entry-level professional and technical employees. Most universities maintain career placement offices where employers and applicants can meet. Many considerations affect an employer's choice of colleges and universities at which to conduct interviews, as Figure 6-11 indicates.

Since college/university recruiting can be expensive and require significant time and effort, employers need to determine whether current and future jobs require individuals with college degrees in specific fields. They should also carefully select the colleges where they are likely to find the greatest hiring success.

Numerous factors determine success in college recruiting. Some employers actively build continuing relationships with individual faculty members and career staff at designated colleges and universities. Maintaining a presence on campus by providing guest speakers for classes and student groups increases an employer's contacts. Employers with a continuing presence and support on a campus are more likely to see positive college recruiting results. Students are more likely to pursue employment with companies that have a reputation for providing benefits and programs that address work-family balance, diversity, and competitive compensation.

FIGURE 6-11   College Recruiting: Considerations for Employers

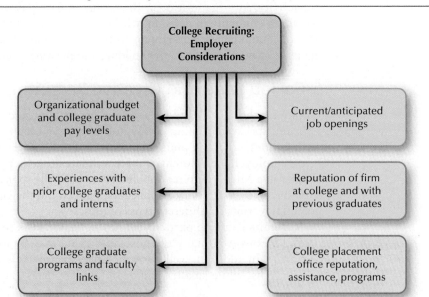

These firms are seen as prestigious and supportive, and students believe that their future success is important to the company.[56]

Desirable Attributes of College Recruits For many employers, grade point average (GPA) is a key criterion for evaluating job candidates during on-campus interviews. Some employers are beginning to put less emphasis on the name of the university and more focus on the student's experience as it relates to the job requirements. Hiring managers are asking students to show off projects they worked on, explain how they have developed skills, and highlight their interpersonal skills. Real-world experience can outweigh attending an elite university.[57]

Internships Since employers are more likely to hire college candidates with related employment experience, internships can critically enhance résumés. Internship experience is very important to employers, candidates, and college/university efforts. Internships give college students the opportunity to work for different companies and gain important career exposure. The relationship between an intern and his or her supervisor has a major impact on the quality of the experience, so companies should assign supportive managers who are able to offer a positive experience.[58] These work arrangements often lead to full-time employment after graduation, benefiting both the intern and the hiring organization. Recent changes in compensation regulations have severely restricted unpaid internships. The Department of Labor provides guidelines for determining private-sector unpaid internship criteria. All six of the criteria in Figure 6-12 must be met before an intern can work without compensation. Nonprofit and government employers are not subject to these guidelines.

School Recruiting High schools and vocational/technical schools may be valuable sources of new employees for some organizations. Many schools have a centralized guidance or placement office. Participating in career days and giving company tours to school groups are ways to maintain good contact with school sources. Cooperative programs, in which students work part-time while attending school, may also generate qualified future applicants for full-time positions.

Employers recognize that they may need to begin attracting capable students while they are in high school. For example, GE, IBM, and other corporations fund programs

FIGURE 6-12 Criteria for Allowable Unpaid Internships

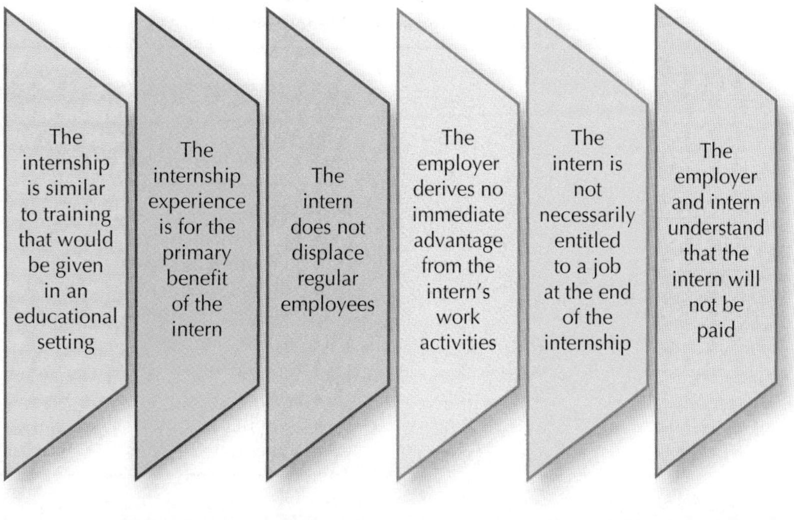

The internship is similar to training that would be given in an educational setting

The internship experience is for the primary benefit of the intern

The intern does not displace regular employees

The employer derives no immediate advantage from the intern's work activities

The intern is not necessarily entitled to a job at the end of the internship

The employer and intern understand that the intern will not be paid to encourage students with science and math skills to participate in summer engineering internships. Some employers specifically target talented members of minority racial/ethnic groups in high schools and provide them with career encouragement, summer internships, and mentoring programs as part of workforce diversity efforts.

MEASURE

LO6 Define recruiting measurement and metrics and illustrate how analytics can be used to improve talent acquisition

6-7 Recruiting Evaluation and Metrics

To determine the effectiveness of various recruiting sources and methods, it is important to evaluate recruiting efforts. The primary way to discover whether recruiting efforts are financially effective is to conduct formal analyses as part of recruiting evaluation. The emergence of Big Data and analytics is making this process easier than it was in the past.[59] Various other factors can be measured when evaluating recruiting. Figure 6-13 indicates many key recruiting measurement areas in which employers frequently conduct evaluations.

6-7a Evaluating Recruiting Quantity and Quality

Organizations evaluate recruiting effectiveness to see how their recruiting efforts compare with their goals and budget, past patterns, and the recruiting performance of other organizations. Measures of recruiting effectiveness can be used to see whether sufficient numbers of targeted population groups are being attracted and to determine the best sources of applicants.

Information about job performance, absenteeism, cost of training, and turnover by recruiting source helps adjust future recruiting efforts. For example, some companies find that recruiting at certain colleges or universities furnishes stable high performers, whereas recruiting at other schools provides employees who are more prone to leave the organization. General metrics for evaluating recruiting include quantity and quality of applicants.

Quantity of Applicants Since the goal of a good recruiting program is to generate a large pool of applicants from which to choose, *quantity* is a natural place to begin evaluation. The basic measure here considers whether the quantity of recruits is sufficient to fill job vacancies. A related question is: Does recruiting at this source provide enough qualified applicants with an appropriate mix of diverse individuals?

FIGURE 6-13 Recruiting Measurement Areas

Recruiting Measurement Metric Areas

Recruits:
- Quantity/Quality
- Recruitment satisfaction analyses
- Time to fill openings
- Cost per recruiting method
- Process metrics
- Yield ratios
- Selection rates
- Acceptance rates
- Success base rates

Quality of Applicants In addition to quantity, a key issue is whether the applicants' qualifications are sufficient to enable the organization to fill the job openings. Do the applicants meet job specifications, and do they perform the jobs well after hire? What is each recruiter's failure rate for new hires? Measures that can be used include performance appraisal scores, months until promotion, production quantity, and sales volume for each hire.

6-7b Evaluating Recruiting Satisfaction

The satisfaction of two groups is useful in evaluating recruiting. Certainly the views of managers with openings to fill are important because they are HR "customers" in a very real sense. But the applicants (those hired and those not hired) are also an important part of the process and can provide useful input.

Managers can respond to questions about the quality of the applicant pool, the recruiter's service, the timeliness of the process, and any problems that they experienced. Applicants might provide input on how they were treated, their perceptions of the company, the length of the recruiting process, and other aspects. Organizational characteristics, job attributes, and recruiter behavior all impact applicants' perceptions throughout the recruiting experience. Applicants with positive impressions of the organization tend to persist in the pursuit of employment with the firm, while those who develop a negative perception of the company drop out of the process. Positive impressions can also lead to a better corporate reputation and more referrals, which helps the recruiting process. [60]

6-7c Evaluating the Time Required to Fill Openings

Looking at the length of time it takes to fill openings is a common means of evaluating recruiting efforts. If openings are not filled quickly with qualified candidates, the organization's work and productivity are likely to suffer. If it takes 45 days to fill vacant positions, managers who need those employees will be unhappy, and unfilled positions cost money. Further, it may tarnish customer relationships if the company cannot deliver as promised.

Generally, it is useful to calculate the average amount of time it takes from contact to hire for each source of applicants because some sources may produce recruits faster than others. For example, one firm calculated the following averages for non-exempt, warehouse, and manufacturing jobs:

Source	Average Time from Contact to Hire (days)
Internet applicants	32
Employment agencies	25
Walk-in candidates	17
Employee referrals	12

These data reveal that when this firm used the Internet and employment agencies, it took significantly longer to fill the openings than when it relied on walk-in candidates and employee referrals. Matching sources used to the time available showed that employee referrals resulted in the fastest recruiting results for this particular group of jobs. However, different results might occur when filling executive jobs or highly skilled network technician jobs. Overall, analyses need to be made across the organization, by geographic region, and by different types of jobs.

6-7d Evaluating the Cost of Recruiting

Different formulas can be used to evaluate recruiting costs. The calculation most often used to measure such costs divides total recruiting expenses for the year by the number of hires for the year:

$$\frac{\text{total recruiting expenses}}{\text{number of recruits hired}}$$

The problem with this approach is accurately identifying items that should be included in recruiting expenses. Should expenses for testing, background checks, relocations, or signing bonuses be included, or are they more properly excluded?

Once such questions are answered, the costs can be allocated to various sources to determine how much each hire from each source costs. It is logical for employers to evaluate the cost of recruiting as a primary metric. Recruiting costs might include employment agencies, advertising, internal sources, and external means. The costs can also be sorted by type of job—costs for hiring managers, administrative assistants, bookkeepers, and sales personnel will all be different.

Certainly cost is an issue and some employers are quite concerned about cost per hire, but quality might be the trade-off. If an organization rushes the hiring process, it is possible that less-qualified candidates will be hired. Then time will be spent in dealing with mismatched or underperforming employees. And the organization will incur more costs as it works to hire a replacement.

6-7e General Recruiting Process Metrics

Because recruiting activities are important, the costs and benefits associated with them should be analyzed. A cost–benefit analysis of recruiting efforts may include both direct costs (advertising, recruiters' salaries, travel, agency fees, etc.) and indirect costs (involvement of operating managers, public relations, image, etc.). Cost–benefit information on each recruiting source can be calculated. Comparing the length of time that applicants hired from each source stay in the organization with the cost of hiring from that source also offers a useful perspective.

Yield ratio
Comparison of the number of applicants at one stage of the recruiting process with the number at the next stage

Yield Ratios One means for evaluating recruiting efforts is yield ratios, which compare the number of applicants at one stage of the recruiting process with the number at the next stage. The result is a tool for approximating the required size of the initial applicant pool. It is useful to visualize yield ratios as a pyramid in which the employer starts with a broad base of applicants that progressively narrows. As Figure 6-14 depicts, to end up with five hires for the job in question, the example company must begin with 100 applicants in the pool, as long as yield ratios remain as shown.

A different approach to using yield ratios suggests that over a specific length of time, organizations can develop ranges for crucial ratios. When a given indicator ratio falls outside that range, it may indicate problems in the recruiting process. As an example, in recruiting at colleges, the following ratios might be useful:

$$\frac{\text{college seniors given second interviews}}{\text{total number of seniors interviewed}} = \text{range of 30\% to 50\%}$$

FIGURE 6-14   Sample Recruiting Evaluation Pyramid

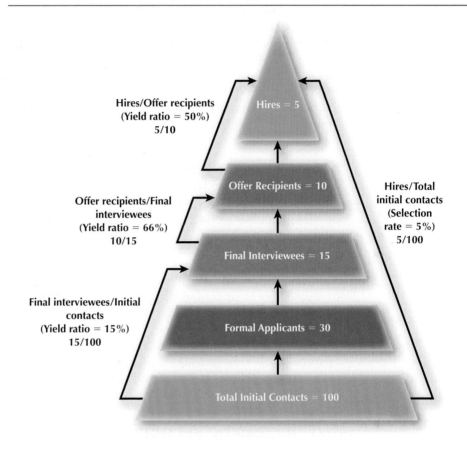

$$\frac{\text{number who accept offer}}{\text{number invited to the company to visit}} = \text{range of 50\% to 70\%}$$

$$\frac{\text{number hired}}{\text{number offered a job}} = \text{range of 70\% to 80\%}$$

$$\frac{\text{number finally hired}}{\text{total number interviewed on campus}} = \text{range of 10\% to 20\%}$$

Selection rate
Percentage hired from a
given group of candidates

Selection Rate   Another useful calculation is the selection rate, which is the percentage hired from a given group of candidates. It equals the number hired divided by the number of applicants; for example, a rate of 30% indicates that three out of 10 applicants were hired. The selection rate is also affected by the validity of the selection process. A relatively unsophisticated selection program might pick eight out of 10 applicants for the job. Four of those might turn out to be good employees. A more valid selection process might pick five out of 10 applicants, but four of five perform well. Selection rate measures not just recruiting but selection issues as well. So do acceptance rate and success base rate.

Acceptance rate
Percentage of applicants hired divided by total number of applicants offered jobs

Acceptance Rate Calculating the acceptance rate helps identify how successful the organization is at hiring candidates. The acceptance rate is the percentage of applicants hired divided by the total number of applicants offered jobs. After the company goes through all the effort to screen, interview, and make job offers, most of those offered jobs will hopefully accept them. If they do not, HR can investigate why managers and HR staff cannot "close the deal." It is common for HR staff to track the reasons candidates turn down job offers. That analysis helps explain the rejection rate by learning how competitive the employer is compared with other employers and highlighting what factors are causing candidates to choose employment elsewhere.

Success Base Rate A longer-term measure of recruiting effectiveness is the applicants' success base rate. The success base rate can be determined by comparing the number of past applicants who have become successful employees against the number of applicants they competed against for their jobs, using historical data within the organization. Also, benchmarking data can be used to compare the success base rate with the success rates of other employers in the geographic area or industry. This rate indicates whether the quality of the employees hired results in employees who perform well and have low turnover. For example, assume that if 10 people were hired at random, four of them would perform satisfactorily. Thus, a successful recruiting program should aim to attract the four in 10 who are capable of doing well at the particular job.

Realistically, no recruiting program will attract only people who will succeed in a particular job. However, efforts to make the recruiting program attract the largest proportion possible of those in the base rate group can make recruiting efforts more productive in both the short and long term.

6-7f Increasing Recruiting Effectiveness

To make recruiting more effective, consider the following recruiting activities:

- *Mining résumés*—A software approach to getting the best-fitting résumés from a big database
- *Tracking applicants:* An approach that takes an applicant all the way from a job listing to performance appraisal results
- *Using an employer career website:* A convenient recruiting place on an employer's website where applicants can see what jobs are available and apply
- *Providing an internal mobility system:* A system that tracks prospects in the company and matches them with jobs as they become available
- *Providing realistic job previews:* A process that individuals can use to get details on the employer and the jobs
- *Responsive recruiting:* An approach whereby applicants receive timely responses

Recruiting effectiveness can be increased by using evaluation data to target different applicant pools, tap broader labor markets, change recruiting methods, improve internal handling and interviewing of applicants, and train recruiters and managers.

Another key way to increase recruiting effectiveness rests with the recruiters themselves. Those involved in the recruiting process can either turn off recruits or create excitement. For instance, recruiters who emphasize positive aspects of the jobs and their employers can enhance recruiting effectiveness. Thus, it is important that recruiters communicate well with applicants and treat them fairly and professionally. Effective recruiting is crucial for every company, as it leads to the opportunity to select individuals for employment who will enhance organizational success.

SUMMARY

- Talent acquisition is the process of finding and hiring the high-quality talent needed to meet the organization's workforce needs.
- Talent acquisition involves recruitment and selection—much like managing the supply chain.
- Recruiting is the process of generating a pool of qualified applicants for an organization's jobs through a series of activities.
- Recruiting must be viewed strategically and tied to HR planning.
- Recruiting is a shared responsibility between HR and line managers, and each group contributes specific expertise to the process.
- Developing and managing the employment brand is an important aspect of attracting the most appropriate individuals to the organization.
- Organizations utilize both core and flexible workers to produce goods and services.
- The decision to use internal or external recruiting sources should take into account the advantages and disadvantages of each source. Efforts should be made to recruit a diverse workforce, including older workers, individuals with disabilities, women, and members of various racial/ethnic groups.

- Elements of the labor market are labor force population, applicant population, and applicant pool.
- Labor markets can be categorized by geographic area, industry, occupation, qualifications, and other characteristics.
- Technology has had a major impact on recruiting, and social media and other Internet platforms are important sources of applicants.
- While Internet recruiting may save money and time, it may also generate more unqualified applicants and may not reach certain groups of potential applicants.
- The most common methods of internal recruiting include organizational databases, job postings, career plans, employee-focused recruiting, and rerecruiting of former employees and applicants.
- The most common external recruiting sources are media, competitors, labor unions, employment agencies, job fairs and other special events, and educational institutions.
- Recruiting efforts should be evaluated to assess the effectiveness of the methods and approaches.

CRITICAL THINKING CHALLENGES

1. What labor markets should be considered when recruiting to fill an opening for a housekeeping staff at a local hospital? What labor markets should be considered for staffing the chief surgeon for the local hospital?

2. Discuss ways a regional bank could effectively use the Internet to recruit bank tellers.

3. Describe how a local firm might be able to utilize college/university interns to generate

future applicants for anticipated job openings within the next one to two years.

4. Assume you are going to look for a current job of interest to you. Utilize general job websites such as Monster, Taleo, Job, Yahoo!, and Indeed to learn about job possibilities for yourself.

5. Your small home health care service company of about 50 workers has traditionally

recruited employees using newspaper print advertisements. Applications have been decreasing from these ads, so you are looking for alternative ways to generate more applicant flow. The company president has requested that you, as HR manager, prepare an overview of how educational/academic and Internet recruiting efforts might improve the recruiting traffic. Present pros and cons of these new methods and compare them to newspaper recruiting.

A. What will your company need to do differently to actively use educational/ academic and Internet recruiting as you compete with other employers for qualified applicants?

B. As you recruit home health care professionals, identify the niche websites that you recommend be used for your Internet postings and the reasons for your recommendations. Identify possible educational/academic sources in your region.

CASE Finding Employees in the Customer Database

The winter holiday hiring season poses special challenges for many retailers. Knowing that jobs are likely to be short-term, temporary spots, serious job seekers typically don't respond to advertisements or job postings. However, retailers usually need to ramp up hiring in a major way during the last quarter of the year. Employment needs extend well beyond retail clerk positions, with companies looking to hire in package delivery, cybersecurity, and party planning. Trying to fill over 800,000 jobs in the United States in the short time before the holiday season demands creativity and stamina from recruiting experts.

Using contacts developed from customer loyalty programs and online shopping databases, retailers are reaching out directly to individuals who know and (hopefully!) like their companies. Advertising through social media can expand the candidate pool by attracting passive applicants or people who might not have considered seasonal work opportunities. But retailers are using social media in new ways, not simply for traditional job postings.

Crate & Barrel tweeted about job open houses for seasonal workers on the same feed that showed customers new product offerings. The Container Store, famous for its loyal customer base, sent nearly 2 million emails to customers who live within 20 miles of any of its stores. Knowing that customers are huge fans of its products, The Container Store hopes that even if the customer is not

looking for a new or additional job, perhaps he or she will pass along the email solicitation to friends. Children's clothing chain Carter's blasted emails to its customers inviting them to become "holiday helpers." Beverages and More (BevMo) capitalized on visits to its website as customers looked for cocktail recipes. The company posted job advertisements on the same page as the recipes and increased applications by 66%. One of BevMo's recruiters says that customers tend to be passionate about the company's products, and the hope is that employees will demonstrate that same level of dedication and passion for their work.

Staffing up for the holiday season is typically limited to a few months out of the year; thus, it is highly competitive as many retailers compete for the same talent. Tapping into databases of customers who already know the products can be an effective way to target people more likely to apply and become successful employees. And a common advantage for employees is an employee discount that makes it even easier and cheaper to continue shopping at their favorite store![61]

QUESTIONS

1. What are the advantages and disadvantages of using customer databases to recruit employees?

2. What unique benefits might a company consider providing to seasonal workers that would make the jobs more attractive?

SUPPLEMENTAL CASES

Is FedEx Recruiting Employees or Independent Contractors?

This case shows that to be able to define workers as independent contractors, an organization must meet several legal requirements that distinguish independent contractors from employees. (For the case, go to www.cengage.com/management/mathis.)

Recruiting at Kia

This case highlights how the car manufacturer Kia utilized an extensive recruiting process to hire good employees at a facility in Georgia. (For the case, go to www.cengage.com/management/mathis.)

Northwest State College

This case shows how recruiting policies can work against successful recruiting in a tight labor market. (For the case, go to www.cengage.com/management/mathis.)

Enterprise Recruiting

This case highlights how a large car rental firm successfully uses a range of recruiting approaches. (For the case, go to www.cengage.com/management/mathis.)

END NOTES

1. Josh Bersin, "The 9 Hottest Trends in Corporate Recruiting," *Forbes.com*, July 4, 2013, http://www.forbes.com/sites/joshbersin/2013/07/04/the-9-hottest-trends-in-corporate-recruiting; "2014 Recruiting Trends: A Look Back and a Look Ahead," *Zip Recruiter*, June 16, 2014, www.ziprecruiter.com/blog/2014/06/16/2014-recruiting-trends-a-look-back-and-a-look-ahead.

2. Based on Ellen Lee, "How to Try before You Buy when Hiring," *Forbes.com*, February 2, 2013, http://www.forbes.com/sites/bmoharrisbank/2013/02/04/how-to-try-before-you-buy-when-hiring/print; "6 Inspiring Examples of Gamification," *Userlike Blog*, February 28, 2014, https://www.userlike.com/en/blog/2014/02/28/6-inspiring-examples-of-gamification; Gabe Zicherman, "Beyond the Hype: 5 Ways That Big Companies Are Using Gamification," *Gigaom*, January 27, 2013, https://gigaom.com/2013/01/27/beyond-the-hype-5-ways-that-big-companies-are-using-gamificaton.

3. Mark Lengnick-Hall and Carolee Rigsbee, "Strategic Human Resource Management and Supply Chain Orientation," *Human Resource Management Review* 23 (2013): 366–377; Jim Rice and Daniel Stanton, "Is Talent Management the Next Frontier for S & OP?" *Supply Chain Management Review*, March/April 2012, 8–9.

4. SHRM, "The Ongoing Impact of the Recession: Recruiting and Skill Gaps," *SHRM online*, March 12, 2013, http://www.shrm.org/research/surveyfindings/articles/pages/shrm-recession-recruiting-skill-gaps-technology.aspx; Elaine Orler, "Finding People Has Never Been Easier, but Recruiting Has Never Been Harder," *TalentManagement.com*, May 30, 2014, http://blog.talentmgt.com/2014/05/30/finding-people-has-never-been-easier.

5. Bersin & Associates, "New U.S. Research Finds Dramatic Shift in Recruitment Spending towards Professional and Social Networks and away from Agencies and Job Boards," *Bersin by Deloitte*, November 17, 2011, http://www.bersin.com/News/Content.aspx?id=14998.

6. KPMG International, "Time for a More Holistic Approach to Talent Risk," November 2013.

7. Max Mihelich, "RPO Is on the Go," *Workforce*, February 2014, 44–47; Larry Heckathorn, "RPO's Value Proposition," *Human Resource Executive*, March 2014, pp. 30–32.

8. Eric Krell, "Results-Oriented Outsourcing," *HR Magazine*, July 2014, pp. 47–49.

9. Marius Wehner, Angelo Giardini, and Rudiger Kabst, "Graduates' Reactions to Recruitment Process Outsourcing: A Scenario-Based Study," *Human Resource Management* 51 no. 4 (July–August 2012): 601–624.

10. Valentina Franca and Marko Pahor, "The Strength of the Employer Brand: Influences and Implications for Recruiting," *Journal of Marketing & Management* 3, no. 1 (May 2012): 78–122; Gordham Saini, Purvi, Rai, and Manoj Chaudhary, "What Do Best Employer Surveys Reveal about Employer Branding and Intention to Apply," *Journal of Brand Management* 21, no. 2 (February–March 2014): 95–111; Kanika Sehgal and N. Malati, "Employer Branding: A Potent Organizational Tool for Enhancing Competitive Advantage," *IUP Journal of Brand Management* 10, no. 1 (March 2013): 51–65; Martin Edwards and Tony Edwards, "Employee Responses to Changing Aspects of the Employer Brand following a Multinational Acquisition: A Longitudinal Study," *Human Resource Management* 52, no. 1 (January–February 2013): 27–54.

11. Adapted from Success Factors, "Best Practices: Employer Branding. Five Tips to Make Your Career Site Your #1 Recruiting Asset," http://www.successfactors.com/content/dam/successfactors/en_us/resources/brochures/best-practices-employer-branding.pdf; David Spark, "18 Innovative Ways to Build Employer Brand," http://resources.dice.com/2013/01/14/18-innovative-ways-to-build-employer-brand; Todd Henneman, "Best Lists Best Bets?" *Workforce*, October 2014, pp. 29–31.

12. Peter Cappeli and J. R. Keller, "Classifying Work in the New Economy," *Academy of Management Review* 38, no. 4 (October 2013): 575–596; Max Mihelich, "Staffing Still Soaring," *Workforce*, October 2014, pp. 48–51.

13. "3 Million Temporary Help Workers Employed Daily in 2013, Most Since 2007," *HR Focus* 91, no. 4 (April 2014): 16.

14. Andrew McIlvaine, "Trying before Buying," *HREonline*, July 31, 2014; Dan Campbell, "Try before You Buy: Temp Talent That Goes Perm," *Talent Management*, July 1, 2014, http://www.talentmgt.com/blogs/7-the-recruitment-revolution/post/try-before-you-buy-temp-talent-that-goes-perm.

15. Geoffrey Fowler and Brenda Cronin, "Freelancers Get Jobs via Web Services," *Wall Street Journal*, May 29, 2013, p. B5.

16. Susan Adams, "More Than a Third of U.S. Workers Are Freelancers Now, but Is That Good for Them?" *Forbes.com*, September 5, 2014, http://timeli.info/item/2406376/Forbes_Leadership/More_Than_A_Third_Of_U_S_Workers_Are_Freelancers_Now_But_Is_That_Good_For_Them_Forbes.

17. H. Jack Walker, Hubert Field, Jeremy Bernerth, and J. Bret Becton, "Diversity Cues on Recruitment Websites: Investigating the Effects on Job Seekers' Information Processing," *Journal of Applied Psychology* 97, no. 1 (2012): 214–224; Derek Avery, Sabrina Volpone, Robert Stewart, Aleksandra Luksyte, Morela Hernandez, Patrick McKay, and Michelle Hebl, "Examining the Draw of Diversity: How Diversity Climate Perceptions Affect Job-Pursuit Intentions," *Human Resource Management* 52, no. 2 (March–April 2013): 175–194; Wendy Casper, Julie Wayne, and Jennifer Manegold, "Who Will We Recruit? Targeting Deep- and Surface-Level Diversity with Human Resource Policy Advertising," *Human Resource Management* 52, no. 3 (May–June 2013): 311–332.

18. Dori Meinert, "Are Your Job Ads Too 'Male-Sounding'?" *HR Magazine*, June 2014, p. 22; Andrea Park, "The IT Factor: Making Tech Jobs Female-Friendly," *Workforce*, July 2, 2014, http://www.workforce.com/articles/print/20614-women-and-IT.

19. Christina Duquette, Kevin Manuel, Diane Harvey, and Susan Bosco, "Generational Effects on Recruitment and Workplace Productivity," Proceedings of the Northeast Region Decision Sciences Institute, 2013; SHRM, "Generations: What Should Employers Consider when Recruiting from Different Generations. Baby Boomers, Generation X, and Generation Y?" *SHRM online*, September 20, 2012, http://www.shrm.org/templatestools/hrqa/pages/recruitingdifferentgenerations.aspx.

20. Based on Susan Lantz, "Getting on Board with Helicopter Parents," *HR Magazine*, December 2013, pp. 34–36; CNN, "How Helicopter Parents Can Ruin Kids' Job Prospects," *CNN.com*, July 2, 2013, http://www.cnn.com/2013/07/02/living/cnn-parents-helicopter-parenting-job-search; Anita Hofschneider, "Should You Bring Mom and Dad to the Office?" *Wall Street Journal*, September 10, 2013.

21. OFCCP, "What Is the Definition of an Internet Applicant?" http://www.dol.gov/ofccp/regs/compliance/faqs/iapp-faqs.htm#Q2GI; SHRM, "Affirmative Action: Definition of Applicant: Does OFCCP's Recent Rule on the Definition of Internet Applicant Mean All Electronic Submissions of Interest Are Applicants?" April 22, 2014, http://www.shrm.org/templatestools/hrqa/pages/cms_014915.aspx#sthash.8CNQcPj8.dpuf.

22. Joshua Ramey-Renk, "The Ins and Outs of Applicant Tracking," *HR Magazine* 58, no. 5 (May 2013): 50–52.

23. Joseph Coombs, "Labor Market Could Be back to Normal in 2018, CBO Predicts," *SHRM online*, March 6, 2014; Nick Otto, "As Job Market Grows, Employers Are Beginning to Put More Emphasis on Talent when Hiring," *Employee Benefit News*, August 5, 2014.

24. Rachel Feintzeig, "U.S. Government Struggles to Draw Young, Savvy Staff," *Wall Street Journal*, June 11, 2014, p. B1.

25. Brenda Cronin, "Help Wanted: In Truck Cabs," *Wall Street Journal*, July 8, 2014, p. A2; Kris Hudson, "Labor Pains Beset Builders," *Wall Street Journal*, May 2, 2014, p. A3; Lauren Weber, "Help Wanted: Librarians, Captains," *Wall Street Journal*, September 2, 2014, p. B3.

26. Daisuke Wakabayashi, "Tech Talent Hunt Tries New Venue: Middle School," *Wall Street Journal*, August 30–31, 2014, p. A1.

27. U.S. Bureau of Labor Statistics, "Employment Projections: 2012–2022," http://www.bls.gov/news.release/pdf/ecopro.pdf.

28. Sarah Needleman, "Skills Shortage Means Many Jobs Go Begging," *Wall Street Journal*, July 10, 2014, p. B1.

29. Kurt Scott, "The Search for Effective Physician Leaders," *Physician Executive*, March–April, 2009, pp. 44–48.

30. Melissa Korn, "Job Search Meets Fundraising," *Wall Street Journal*, May 28, 2014, p. D3; Alina Dizik, "Jointing the MBA Chase," *Wall Street Journal*, May 21, 2012, p. R12.

31. Based on Marylene Delbourg-Delphis, "A Relational Approach to Hiring Veterans," *Employment Relations Today* 41, no. 1 (Spring 2014): 11–17; Lin Grensing-Pophal, "Cracking the Code on Military Resumes," *HRE Online*, March 31, 2014, http://www.hreonline.com/HRE/view/story.jhtml?id=534356840; "Top 10 Jobs for Military Veterans," *T+D*, May 2013, p. 13.

32. Jennifer Smith, "Wanted: Temp Attorneys with Foreign-Language Skills," *Wall Street Journal*, July 21, 2012, p. B1.

33. Jean Phillips, Stanley Gully, John McCarth, William Castellano, and Mee Sook Kim, "Recruiting Global Travelers: The Role of Global Travel Recruitment Messages and Individual Differences in Perceived Fit, Attraction, and Job Pursuit Intentions," *Personnel Psychology* 67 (2014): 153–201.

34. Matthew Bidwell and J. R. Keller, "Within or Without? How Firms Combine Internal and External Labor Markets to Fill Jobs," *Academy of Management Journal* 57, no. 4 (2014): 1035–1055; Peter Cappeli, "Do Outside Hires Perform Better?" *Human Resource Executive Online*, April 23, 2012, www.hreonline.com; Todd Henneman, "The Insiders or the Outsiders?" *Workforce.com*, March 10, 2014.

35. Courtney Shelton Hunt, "Managing Human Capital in the Digital Era," *People & Strategy* 37, no. 2 (Summer 2014): 36–41; Luke Siuty, "Applying on the Go," *Workforce*, September 2014, p. 14.

36. Max Mihelich, "E-Recruiting: Dead and Alive," *Workforce*, May 2014, pp. 44–48; Andrew McIlvaine, "Social-Media Influence and HR," *Human*

Resource Executive, May 2013, p. 14; John Boudreau, "Rewarding the Right Connections," *Talent Management*, April 8, 2014, http://www.talentmgt.com/articles/view/rewarding-the-right-connections/.

37. Suzanne Lucas, "Hard Rock Café Hired 120 People in 30 Days Using Facebook (And You Can Too)," *Inc.*, June 7, 2014.

38. Max Mihelich, "I Am a Worker Seeking an Employer: eHarmony and the Job Search Industry," *Workforce.com*, May 20, 2013; Adam Auriemma, "Zappos Zaps Job Postings, Seeks Hires on Social Media," *Wall Street Journal*, May 27, 2014, p. B5; Pete Wolfinger, "Take an Interest in Pinterest," *HR Magazine*, April 2013, pp. 71–73; Rebecca Borison, "This Woman's Instagram Feed Was So Cool It Got Her a New Job," *Business Insider*, April 14, 2014, http://www.businessinsider.com/how-to-instagram-helps-landing-a-job.

39. Liz Ryan, "Ten Ways to Use LinkedIn in Your Job Search," Forbes.com, May 19, 2014; Hiranya Fernanco, "A Step-by-Step Guide to Getting a Job through LinkedIn," *Business Insider*, March 26, 2014.

40. Mary Wisniewski, "Tweeting for Talent: Bank Recruiters Try Social Media," *American Banker*, September 7, 2012, pp. 1–6.

41. Ken Sundheim, "35 Of the Most Influential Career Sites for 2014," Forbes.com, December 18, 2013, http://www.forbes.com/sites/kensundheim/2013/12/18/35-of-the-most-influential-career-sites-for-2014/; eBizMBA Rank, "The 15 Most Popular Job Websites: September, 2014," http://www.ebizmba.com/articles/job-websites.

42. Sarah Fister Gale, "Caught on Video: Companies Use Audiovisual Methods to Reel in Candidates," *Workforce.com*, July 22, 2014.

43. Tom Starner, "The Recruiting Game," *Human Resource Executive*, May 2014, pp. 17–20; Maura Ciccarelli, "Beyond the Job Fair," *Human Resource Executive*, June 2013, pp. 60–62; Ryan Phillips, "Gamification and its Place in Recruiting," *Sourcecon.com*, April 17, 2014, http://www.sourcecon.com/news/2014/04/17/gamification-and-its-place-in-recruiting.

44. Susan Jennings, Justin Blount, and M. Gail Weatherly, "Social Media: A Virtual Pandora's Box. Prevalence, Possible Legal Liabilities, and Policies," *Business Communication Quarterly* 77, no. 1 (March 2014): 96–113; Kathleen Hiday and Mary E. McDonald, "Risky Business: The Legal Implications of Social Media's Increasing Role in Employment Decisions," *Journal of Legal Studies in Business* 18 (2013): 69–107; Jeffrey Mello, "Social Media, Employee Privacy and Concerted Activity: Brave New World or Big Brother?" *Labor Law Journal* 63, no. 3 (Fall 2012): 165–173.

45. Aliah Wright, "More States Ban Social Media Snooping," *SHRM Online*, August 12, 2014; Jonathan Segal, "The Law and Social Media in Hiring," *HR Magazine*, September 2014, pp. 70–72.

46. Joshua Herbold and Bambi Douma, "Students' Use of Social Media for Job Seeking," *CPA Journal* 83, no. 4 (April 2013): 68–71; Teri Root and Sandra McKay, "Student Awareness of the Use of Social Media Screening by Prospective Employers," *Journal of Education for Business* 89, no. 4 (July–August 2014): 202–206.

47. Carol Patton, "Promoting Inside Jobs," *Human Resource Executive*, May 2013, pp. 28–30; Rhett Bryner, Janice Molloy, and Brett Gilbert, "Human Capital Pipelines: Competitive Implications of Repeated Interorganizational Hiring," *Journal of Management* 40, no. 2 (February 2014): 438–508.

48. Sarah Fister Gale, "It's Who You Know: Readying for Referrals," *Workforce*, July 2014, pp. 12.

49. Aquilent, Employee Referral Program, http://www/aquilent.com/careers/employee-referral-program.

50. Based on Dave Zielinski, "Referral Booster," *HR Magazine*, March 2013, pp. 63–66.

51. Kristen Frasch, "To (Outside) Hire or Re-Hire, *HR Online*, April 2, 2014; Kecia Bal, "Reaping a Return from Boomerangs," *HRE Online*, July 24, 2014; Julie Cook Ramirez, "Coming Home," *Human Resource Executive*, October 2, 2014, pp. 13–16.

52. Abbie Shipp, Stacie Furst-Holloway, Brad Harris, and Benson Rosen, "Gone Today but here Tomorrow: Extending the Unfolding Model of Turnover to Consider Boomerang Employees," *Personnel Psychology* 67, no. 2 (Summer 2014): 421–462.

53. The Economist, "Gone but Not Forgotten," *The Economist*, March 1, 2014.

54. Sarah Fister Gale, "Cocktails, Puppies and the New Job Fair," *Workforce*, September 2014, p. 12.

55. Melissa Korn, "College Job Fairs Go Virtual," *Wall Street Journal*, April 3, 2014, p. B4.

56. Julie Wayne and Wendy Casper, "Why Does Firm Reputation in Human Resource Policies Influence College Students? The Mechanisms Underlying Job Pursuit Intentions," *Human Resource Management* 51, no. 1 (January–February 2012): 121–142.

57. Robert Half Technology, "Does Alma Mater Matter? Not So Much, Say CIOs," August 20, 2014, http://www.newswire.ca/en/story/1400428/does-al-ma-mater-matter-not-so-much-say-cios; Melissa Korn, "The Amazon Interview," *Wall Street Journal*, May 2, 2013.

58. Jessisa Hurst, Linda Good, and Phil Gardner, "Conversion Intentions of Interns: What Are the Motivating Factors?" *Education & Training* 54, no. 6 (2012): 504–522; Philip Rose, Stephen Teo, and Julia Connell, "Converting Interns into Regular Employees: The Role of Intern-Supervisor Exchange," *Journal of Vocational Behavior* 84, no. 20 (April 2014): 153–163; Elizabeth Shoenfelt, Nancy Stone, and Janet Kottke, "Internships: An Established Mechanism for Increasing Employability," *Industrial and Organizational Psychology: Perspectives on Science and Practice* 6, no. 1 (March 2013): 24–28.

59. Kris Dunn, "Moneyball: It's One for the Ages," *Workforce*, May 2014, p. 13; Ranjan Dutta, "Using Predictive Analytics to Improve Hire Quality," *Talent Management*, August 12, 2014.

60. Krista Uggerslev, Neil Fassina, and David Kraichy, "Recruiting through the Stages: A Meta-Analytic Test of Predicators of Application Attraction at Different Stages of the Recruiting Process," *Personnel Psychology* 65 (2012): 597–660.

61. Adapted from Eric Morath, "Stores Try Filling Jobs for Holiday via Tweets," *Wall Street Journal*, October 27, 2014, p. B1; Steve Bates, "Seasonal Hiring Means Jobs for More Than Retail Clerks," *SHRM Online*, October 28, 2014, http://www.shrm.org/hrdisciplines/staffing-management/articles/pages/seasonal-hiring.aspx.

CHAPTER

7

Selecting Human Resources

Learning Objectives

After you have read this chapter, you should be able to:

LO1 Understand selection and placement and the levels of person/environment fit.

LO2 Explain two important qualities of selection predictors—reliability and validity.

LO3 Discuss the steps of a typical selection process.

LO4 Identify three types of selection tests and legal concerns about their uses.

LO5 Contrast several types of selection interviews and some key considerations in conducting these interviews.

LO6 Specify how legal concerns affect background investigations of applicants and use of medical examinations in the selection process.

LO7 Describe the major issues to be considered when selecting candidates for global assignments.

WHAT'S TRENDING IN
EMPLOYEE SELECTION

The process of selecting employees continues to evolve as economic, legal, technical, global, and demographic conditions change. As companies and applicants become more informed and sophisticated, their expectations and demands in the employment market change. Here's what's trending in employee selection:

1. Stepped up legal oversight of the selection process means that employers must be even more cautious about how they carry out hiring activities. Federal agencies have become more aggressive about enforcing nondiscrimination laws and are expanding protection for applicants and employees.
2. Readily accessible, "free-range" data on applicants that is posted on social media websites creates a digital fingerprint that follows people throughout their careers and lives. Companies may be tempted to use such information in hiring without truly understanding how it predicts job performance and any other associated selection decisions.
3. Automated pre-screening to quickly and efficiently narrow the applicant pool may lead to some qualified applicants being overlooked because of rigid formulas in the assessment software. Companies may revert to manual screening if too many good applicants slip through the cracks.
4. Higher-quality data on the performance of employees allows companies to better validate their selection process by connecting hiring decisions to outcomes.

Do Creative Job Seekers Score?

The job market is a competitive place, and those looking for a job may be tempted to consider some unusual gimmicks to get the attention of hiring managers. But does it pay to be different when applying for a job?

Some organizations receive over 350 applications for every job opening, and the use of automated applicant screening software can eliminate individuals from consideration in a nanosecond. This has resulted in some applicants adopting novel ways to get their résumé noticed. Some of these ploys succeed at getting the recruiter's attention and may show that the applicant has researched the company and is trying to fit in with the employer brand or company culture. In most cases, these tactics serve only to amuse hiring authorities or at worst, can irritate those making selection decisions.

Crafty or artistic companies tend to attract more creative applicants because it seems consistent with the company's business. Recruiters at Etsy have received everything from embroidered cover letters to résumés on potholders. Applicants may incorrectly assume that the only skill needed is creativity, while the company needs people with business and technology skills.

Applicants have used stunts like walking around with a sandwich board listing their credentials, renting a billboard on which they advertise their desire to find a job, or baking cookies or cupcakes and delivering them in person to the company. While these attention-grabbing incidents might get people to look, they rarely result in an interview or job offer.

What many applicants fail to realize is that companies establish selection protocols for a reason. Requiring all applicants to follow these protocols helps the company maintain legal hiring practices and ensures that candidates don't simply

Goodluz/Shutterstock.com

239

use charm to advance in the process. Applicants who try to end run around these procedures may look desperate, unusual, or even clueless. They may also be viewed as lacking social awareness of business norms or even unable to follow directions.

Rather than trying to impress with a dash of novelty, more successful candidates follow the standard recipe. Make sure your résumé doesn't have any mistakes or typos. Use a compelling, personalized cover letter to explain why you are interested in the particular company. Point out how your knowledge and skills would benefit the employer. And by all means, capitalize on any personal connections you have at the company. Being authentic, excited, passionate, and a good match for the job will trump being eccentric any day.[1]

These trends and many additional topics will be addressed in this chapter. The selection of high-quality employees depends on effective recruiting to generate applicants from which you can choose. And the success of each new employee also depends on the ability of first-line managers to ensure appropriate training and performance.

7-1 Selection and Placement

LO1 Understand selection and placement and the levels of person/ environment fit.

Selection is the second phase of the talent acquisition process. It involves choosing individuals with the correct qualifications to fill jobs in an organization. When looking at selection as part of the supply chain, think about recruiting as putting out the "request for proposals" and selection as narrowing down to the best "supplier" of talent. Without qualified employees, an organization is far less likely to succeed.

7-1a Placement

Selection
The process of choosing individuals with the correct qualifications needed to fill jobs in an organization

Placement
Fitting a person to the right job

The ultimate purpose of selection is **placement**, or fitting a person to the right job. Placement of people can be seen primarily as a matching process. How well an employee is matched to a job can affect the amount and quality of the employee's work, as well as the training and operating costs required to prepare the individual to perform. Further, employee morale is often enhanced because good fit encourages individuals to be positive about their jobs and what they accomplish.[2]

Selection and placement activities typically focus on applicants' knowledge, skills, and abilities (KSAs), but they should also include the candidate's motivation and needs. Psychologists label this *person/environment fit (P/E fit)*. P/E fit is vitally important to create a good match for both the employee and the organization. For maximum job performance and satisfaction, employees should be a good fit at all levels of the organization, as shown in Figure 7-1.

Person/organization fit
The congruence between individuals and organizational factors

Employers are concerned about the congruence between people and companies, or the **person/organization fit**. Person/organization fit is important from a *values and culture* perspective, with many organizations trying to positively link a person's principles to the values of the company. Organizations tend to favor job applicants who effectively blend into how business is conducted.

FIGURE 7-1 Person/Environment Fit (P/E Fit)

Organization Level	Fit Category	Fit Elements
◆ Organization (macro)	◆ Person/organization fit	◆ Values, culture
◆ Group/work unit (meso)	◆ Person/group fit	◆ Interpersonal, team skills
◆ Job (micro)	◆ Person/job fit	◆ Knowledge, skills, abilities, and motivation

Person/group fit
The congruence between individuals and group or work unit dynamics

Person/job fit
Matching the knowledge, skills, abilities, and motivations of individuals with the requirements of the job

Attraction-selection-attrition (ASA) theory
Job candidates are attracted to and selected by firms where similar types of individuals are employed, and individuals who are very different quit their jobs to work elsewhere

In addition to being a good match for the organization, it is also important that each individual works well with others in the work unit or department. Thus, person/group fit is the congruence between individuals and group or work unit dynamics. A qualified employee who does not communicate well, share information, or otherwise act as an effective team member can drag down the group's performance. Companies are structured into teams or groups that operate as a coordinated unit; therefore, getting the right people on the team is especially important.[3]

Selection decisions often begin with establishing person/job fit, that is, matching the knowledge, skills, abilities, and motivations of individuals with the requirements of the job. Fit is related not only to work satisfaction but also to company commitment and intentions to quit work.

Job analysis (Chapter 4) is conducted to help identify the most important KSAs for success on the job. Lack of fit between a person's KSAs and job requirements can be classified as a *mismatch*. A mismatch results from poor pairing of a person's needs, interests, abilities, personality, and expectations with characteristics of the job, available rewards, coworker relationships, and the organization. If an individual is poorly suited for a job, it is difficult to achieve acceptable performance.[4] Placement decisions are complex because of the many ways in which people must be a good fit for the work environment. As a result, the attraction-selection-attrition (ASA) theory is often used to better understand the concept of fit in companies. The ASA theory proposes that job candidates are attracted to and selected by firms where similar types of individuals are employed, and individuals who are very different quit their jobs to work elsewhere. Based on these ideas, it is easy to see why person/environment fit is important for long-term selection and placement strategies. If positive fit is established, organizations should have a more motivated and committed workforce that is more likely to stay and perform.[5]

7-1b Selection Responsibilities

Selection is a key responsibility for all managers in a company. Organizations vary in how they allocate selection responsibilities between HR specialists and operating managers. Meeting Equal Employment Opportunity Commission (EEOC) requirements and the strategic implications of staffing have encouraged many companies to place greater emphasis on hiring procedures and techniques and to centralize selection within the HR department. In other companies, each department (or its management team) screens and hires its own staff. Managers, especially those working in smaller firms, often select their own employees because these individuals directly impact their work, and there is often no HR staff to help make these decisions. But the validity and effectiveness of this approach may be questionable because managers may lack training in selection procedures and regulations.

FIGURE 7-2   Talent Acquisition Functions

Pre-Hire	Post-Hire
• Receive applications	• Place and assign new hires
• Interview applicants	• Orient and onboard new hires
• Administer pre-employment tests	• Conduct follow-up evaluations on new employees
• Conduct background screening	• Conduct exit interviews with departing employees
• Schedule physical examination	• Maintain appropriate records and reports

Another approach is to have HR professionals initially screen job candidates, and then managers or supervisors make the final selection decisions from the qualified applicant pool. Generally, the higher the position being filled, the greater the likelihood that the ultimate hiring decisions will be made by operating managers rather than HR professionals. The talent acquisition function in any organization may involve some or all of the activities shown in Figure 7-2.

Selection responsibilities are influenced by the existence of a central employment office, which is usually housed the Human Resources function. In smaller organizations, there is not enough staffing activity to justify a full-time employment specialist. But for larger firms, centralizing activities in an employment office might be appropriate. Centralized HR can improve legal compliance and ensure consistency in selection procedures. Further, HR staff is more likely to be aware of best practices and current trends that can be adopted by the company.

7-1c Selection, Criteria, Predictors, and Job Performance

Selection decisions are all about predicting which applicants will be the most successful on the job. Since no two individuals are exactly the same, the selection process is used to determine how those differences might affect job performance. There is a great deal of science and a little bit of art to these decisions.

Humans tend to be creatures of habit; therefore, the best predictor of future behavior is past behavior. Of course, past behavior is not an absolute predictor, but it tends to be a good indicator of how an individual will respond in the future. Selection methods and measures attempt to capture past behavior to help predict the future.[6]

Regardless of whether an employer uses job-specific KSAs or a more general skill set approach, effective selection of employees involves using selection criteria to predict future employee behavior. The heart of an effective selection system is an understanding of what constitutes good job performance. Knowing what good performance looks like in a particular job helps identify the qualities an employee must have to achieve successful performance. These are called selection criteria.

A selection criterion is a characteristic that a person must possess to successfully perform job duties. Figure 7-3 shows that ability, motivation, intelligence,

Selection criterion
Characteristic that a person must possess to successfully perform job duties

FIGURE 7-3 Job Performance, Selection Criteria, and Predictors

What constitutes good job performance on this job?	What does it take for a person to achieve good job performance?	What can be seen or measured to predict the selection criteria?
Elements of Good Job Performance	**Characteristics Necessary to Achieve Good Job Performance (Selection Criteria)**	**Predictors of Selection Criteria**
◆ Quantity of work ◆ Quality of work ◆ Compatibility with others ◆ Presence at work ◆ Length of service ◆ Flexibility	◆ Ability ◆ Motivation ◆ Intelligence ◆ Conscientiousness ◆ Appropriate risk for employer ◆ Appropriate permanence	◆ Experience ◆ Past performance ◆ Physical skills ◆ Education ◆ Interests ◆ Salary requirements ◆ Certificates/degrees ◆ Test scores ◆ Personality measures ◆ Work references ◆ Previous jobs and tenure

conscientiousness, appropriate risk, emotional control, communication skills, and permanence might be the selection criteria for many jobs. Selection criteria that might be more specific to managerial jobs include leading and deciding, supporting and cooperating, organizing and executing, and enterprising and performing.

To determine whether candidates possess certain selection criteria (such as ability and motivation), employers use predictors of selection criteria, which are measurable or visible indicators of those characteristics (or criteria). Figure 7-3 shows how job performance, selection criteria, and predictors are interrelated. Candidates who possess higher levels of these predictors would be expected to be better performers. Choosing appropriate predictors is not an easy task, but if done well, the organization can make better hiring decisions and improve overall performance. Prediction decisions aren't perfect, so we try to reduce the number of errors by using high-quality predictors. See the following "HR Competencies & Applications: Understanding Errors in Selection Decision Making" feature for an explanation of errors in decision making.

Predictors of selection criteria
Measurable or visible indicators of selection criteria

7-1d Reliability and Validity

LO2 Explain two important qualities of selection predictors—reliability and validity.

There are several indicators that are used to determine how free of errors decisions will be if we use specific predictors. Reliability and validity are two very important qualities of predictors, which are discussed in the following sections. See Appendix D for a more detailed explanation of these concepts.

COMPETENCIES & APPLICATIONS

Understanding Errors in Selection Decision Making

When using any kind of test, both test administrators and test takers want to in believe the results and rely on them when making decisions. Think about a medical test, for example. If a patient has taken a screening test for diabetes, a result that is accurate will help the patient and physician determine what to do. If the test results are negative, the patient would believe that he does not have diabetes and would go on living life as before. Alternatively, if the results are positive, the patient would consult with his physician to plan out a course of treatment. The decision made by the patient clearly depends on the results of the test—which he trusts are accurate. The same thing occurs when we use tests to help us make hiring decisions.

Errors in testing can and do occur. Two different types of errors in particular can happen—false positive and false negative. In the preceding example, how would things change for our patient if the test results were inaccurate? If the results of the test are negative but in fact the patient does have diabetes, then his health will suffer because of lack of treatment. This is a false negative, when the test results incorrectly indicate that the individual does not have some condition. Conversely, if the results of the test are positive but the patient does not really have diabetes, he will treat a condition that he does not have and perhaps become ill. This is a false positive, when the test results incorrectly indicate that the individual does have some condition.

Think about this in terms of employment testing. If a company administers a test that results in inaccurate assessment of applicants, then some unqualified people might be hired, and some qualified people might not be hired. In either case, the company would not be making the best hiring decisions, and employee performance would probably be lower than if the test were more accurate. Look at the graph below. There are four quadrants titled A, B, C, and D.

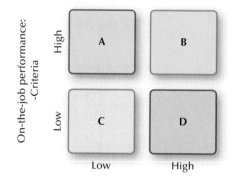

Results of selection test:
-Predictor

In quadrant A, the results of the selection test indicate that the applicant will not perform well on the job. However, if the person were hired anyway, he would turn out to be a high performer. That's the false negative. In quadrant B, the results of the selection test indicate that the applicant will be a high performer. The person is hired and he is, in fact, a high performer. That's a correct decision, a true positive. Now it's your turn, so answer the following questions:

1. Can you explain the results in quadrants C and D?

2. What are the implications to those making selection decisions? How can we reduce the number of false positive and false negative results?

KEY COMPETENCIES: Critical Evaluation, HR Expertise: People/Talent Acquisition & Retention; Organization/Technology & Data

Reliability
The extent to which a test or measure repeatedly produces the same results over time

Reliability The extent to which it repeatedly or consistently produces the same results over time reflects a predictor's reliability. For example, if a person took a test in December and scored 75 and then took the same test again in March and scored 76, the exam is probably reliable. Reliability can be increased by using the same testing procedure and conditions every time a test is administered. When using a 10-minute keyboarding test, it is important to use the same stopwatch, keyboard, and sample text for all candidates. It is also important to provide the same testing conditions for all applicants. Avoid putting one candidate in a noisy open office for the test and testing another candidate in a quiet isolated office. It would be unfair to compare results of tests given this way because the reliability would be low. A predictor that is not reliable is of no value in selection. Further, a test that has low reliability is unlikely to be valid.

Validity
The extent to which a test measures what it claims to measure

The second quality of predictors that we evaluate is validity, or accuracy. Validity refers to how well a test measures what it claims to measure. That sounds like circular logic, doesn't it? Think of a rain gauge. A rain gauge may be an accurate tool to measure the amount of rain that falls but not to measure air temperature. This emphasizes the idea that a test's validity is not assessed in the abstract. Rather, when a test is validated, it is assessed for accuracy in a specific context. Several types of validity are used in selection.[7]

Criterion-related validity is one method for establishing the validity associated with a predictor. Criterion-related validity involves obtaining scores on a selection predictor like a driving test and then later measuring the job performance of each employee. Then statistical analysis is used to identify a relationship between the two scores.

Concurrent validity
Measured when an employer tests current employees and correlates the scores with their performance ratings

A criterion-related validity study can be conducted in two different ways—using current employees or using applicants. Concurrent validity uses current employees to validate a predictor or "test." As shown in Figure 7-4, concurrent validity is measured when an employer tests current employees and correlates the scores with their performance ratings on appraisals.

Concurrent validity may be easier to assess because employees are readily available and can take the predictor test immediately. This shortens the time needed to complete the validation study. A disadvantage of the concurrent validity approach is that employees who have not performed satisfactorily at work are probably no longer with the firm and therefore cannot be tested. Also, extremely good employees may have been promoted or may have left the company for better work situations. Any learning on the job might also confound test scores.

Predictive validity
Measured when applicants' test results are compared with subsequent job performance

Another method for establishing criterion-related validity is predictive validity. To calculate predictive validity, applicants' test results are compared with their subsequent job performance (see Figure 7-4). Conducting the predictive validity study involves administering a predictor test to applicants but not using the results to make hiring decisions. That allows a company to hire people with a wide range of scores on the predictor and assess whether their subsequent job performance differs. Job success is then measured by assessing factors such as absenteeism, accidents, errors, and performance appraisal ratings. For example, if the employees who scored high on the driving test end up being better performers than those who scored poorly on the test, then the driving test can be considered a valid predictor of job performance. The driving test could then be used for future hiring decisions with some level of confidence that better employees would be selected.

7-1e Combining Predictors

If an employer chooses to use only one predictor, such as a pencil-and-paper test, to select individuals, the decision becomes straightforward. If the test is valid,

FIGURE 7-4 Concurrent and Predictive Validity

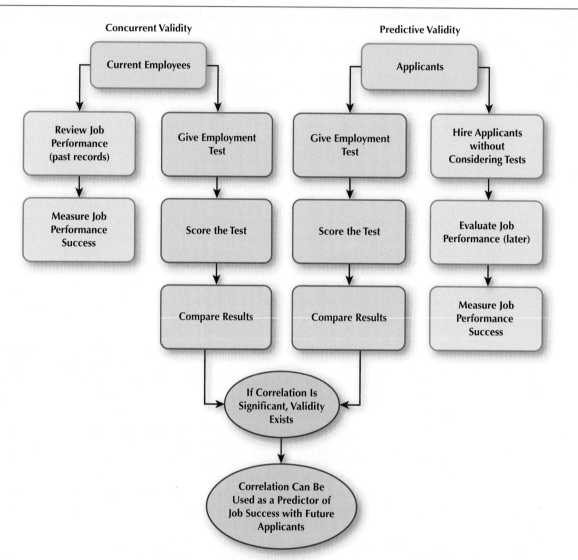

encompasses a major dimension of a job, and an applicant does well on the test, then that person could be given a job offer. When an employer uses predictors such as three years of experience, a college degree, and acceptable aptitude test score, job applicants are evaluated on all of these requirements and the multiple predictors must be combined in some way.[8] Two approaches for combining predictors are as follows:

- *Multiple hurdles*: A minimum cutoff is set on each predictor, and each minimum level must be "passed." For example, to be hired, a candidate for a sales representative job must achieve a minimum education level, a certain score on a sales aptitude test, and a minimum score on a structured interview.
- *Compensatory approach*: Scores from individual predictors are added and combined into an overall score, thereby allowing a higher score on one predictor to offset, or compensate for, a lower score on another. The combined index takes into consideration performance on all predictors. For

FIGURE 7-5   Comprehensive Selection Process

example, when making decisions about admitting students into graduate business programs, a higher overall score on an admissions test might offset a lower undergraduate grade point average.

A key concept in selection is obtaining a comprehensive profile of each applicant. It is like putting together a puzzle, as shown in Figure 7-5. Companies use various methods to collect information about applicants that help them select the best person for the job. In the interest of time and cost efficiency, it is best to use several methods that each add to the overall candidate record without duplicating too much information. Each step in the selection process should provide unique information to fill in the blanks. It is generally not advisable to rely on only one or two methods (such as applications and interviews) in making hiring decisions.

LO3 Discuss the steps of a typical selection process.

7-2 The Selection Process

Most organizations follow a series of consistent steps to process and select job applicants. Company size, job characteristics, the number of people needed, the use of electronic technology, and other factors lead to variations in the basic process. Selection can take place in a day or over a much longer period of time, and certain phases of the process may be omitted or the order changed, depending on the employer and the job being filled. There is not "one best way" that works for all situations. Each company establishes a process that offers it the best results in terms of quality and quantity of applicants. Figure 7-6 shows steps in a typical selection process.

7-2a Legal Considerations in Selection

Job-relatedness
A qualification or requirement in selection is significantly related to successful performance of job duties

A number of federal regulations and guidelines influence the selection process. In particular, the Uniform Guidelines on Employee Selection Procedures define important concepts and practices that companies must follow.

Job-relatedness means that a selection qualification or requirement is significantly related to successful performance of job duties. A thorough job analysis is conducted

FIGURE 7-6   Selection Process Flowchart

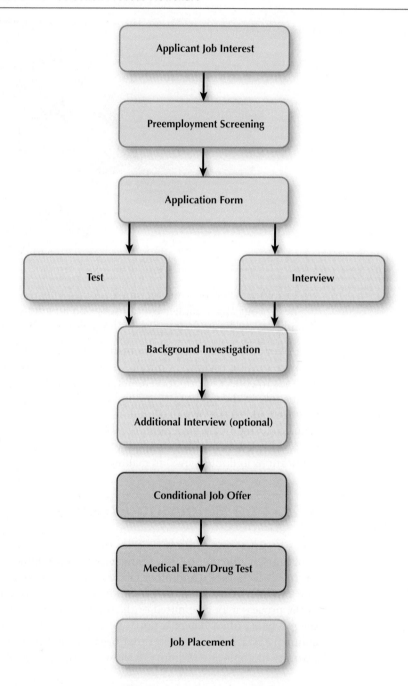

to establish that every qualification, such as high school education or nursing certification, is important for jobholders to perform assigned tasks. For example, requiring
taxi drivers to hold a valid driver's license is a job-related qualification.

Business necessity relates to a practice that is necessary for safe and efficient operations, such as restricting employees from wearing garments that might get caught
in machinery even though the attire may be required by the employee's religion. To

Business necessity
A practice that is
necessary for safe and
efficient operations

protect the safety of employees, customers, clients, and/or patients, employers may institute particular selection criteria as a business necessity.

What is a *test*? Under federal guidelines, any method of collecting information about job applicants that is used to make hiring decisions is considered a test. This definition is very broad, covering everything from looking at applicants' Facebook profiles to informal conversations during dinner. The standards of reliability and validity apply to all such tests, and hiring authorities should carefully consider all sources of information used in making selection decisions.

These concepts are incorporated into the selection process to keep the company in compliance with legal requirements and to aid in high-quality hiring practices.

7-2b Applicant Job Interest

Individuals seeking employment can indicate interest in many ways. Historically, individuals have submitted résumés by mail or fax, or they have applied in person at an employer's location. But with the growth in Internet recruiting, most individuals now complete applications online or submit résumés electronically.

Regardless of how individuals express interest in employment, the selection process has an important public relations dimension. Discriminatory hiring practices, impolite interviewers, unnecessarily long waits, unreturned telephone inquiries, inappropriate testing procedures, and lack of follow-up responses can produce unfavorable impressions of an employer. Job applicants' perceptions of the organization will be influenced by how they are treated.

Realistic job previews
Process through which a job applicant receives an accurate picture of a job

Realistic Job Previews Many individuals know little about companies before applying for employment. Consequently, when deciding whether to accept a job offer, they seek out information during the selection process, including compensation data, work characteristics, job location, and promotion opportunities. Unfortunately, some employers make jobs appear better than they really are. Realistic job previews provide potential employees with an accurate introduction to a job so that they can better evaluate the employment situation. Indeed, a realistic job preview can directly identify necessary training and clarify a job role.

Companies can use videos, employee testimonials, and job shadowing to provide a realistic snapshot of the work environment for applicants. A real benefit of realistic job previews is that applicants may withdraw from consideration if they don't think the job will be a good fit. This saves the company time invested in wooing a candidate who will end up turning down the job offer.[9]

7-2c Pre-Employment Screening

Many employers conduct pre-employment screening to determine if individuals meet the minimum qualifications for open jobs before they are allowed to fill out an application.

Electronic Assessment Screening The use of electronic pre-employment screening or assessment has grown. Computer software is often used to review résumés and application forms received during the recruiting and application process. Large companies often use software to receive, evaluate, and track the applications of many potential employees in order to save time during the screening process.

When a job posting generates 1,000 or more applications (which is not unusual for large companies or in difficult economic times), responding to each would be a full-time job. Electronic screening can speed up the process by using disqualification questions; screening questions to get at KSAs and experience; administering valid assessment tests; and performing background, drug, and financial screening. Some of the assessments might include auditions for the job that are conducted on the basis of simulations of specific job-related tasks. A good strategy is to use simple electronic assessment early to reduce the number of applicants before requiring applications or interviews, which leaves a much more qualified pool of remaining applicants with which to work. However, the trade-off to increased efficiency is often the elimination of individuals who might be qualified who do not make it through the screening process.[10]

A controversial trend is screening candidates based on information obtained from their social networking profiles. Doing so can have negative consequences for applicants and companies. The legality and appropriateness of such screening is highly questionable because most managers simply access available information without consistency or regard to job demands. The information found on Facebook or other online platforms can lead to discrimination against applicants due to their religion or sexual orientation.[11] Although it may be tempting to just click on an applicant's profile, top candidates may develop a negative opinion of the organization or, even worse, take legal action if they are not hired because of the information found on social networking sites.[12] Companies must walk a fine line and realize that random, haphazard screening in this manner is likely to attract attention from lawmakers who will no doubt restrict the practice if it becomes too prevalent.[13]

7-2d Applications and Résumés

Some employers do not use pre-employment screening prior to having applicants fill out an application form. Instead, they have every interested individual complete an application first. These completed application forms then become the basis for pre-screening information. Properly prepared, the application form serves five purposes:

1. It is a record of the applicant's desire to obtain a position.
2. It provides the interviewer with an applicant profile that can be addressed during the interview.
3. It is a basic employee record for applicants who are hired.
4. It can be used for research on the effectiveness of the selection process.
5. It is a formal document on which the applicant attests to the truthfulness of all information provided.

Many employers use only one application form for all jobs, but others use several forms depending on the position. For example, a hotel might use one form for management and supervisory staff and another for line employees. High-tech and other technology-based companies also staff many different kinds of administrative, managerial, and technical jobs, which can result in the use of multiple application forms.

Application Disclaimers Application forms typically include disclaimers and notices so that appropriate legal protections are clearly stated. Recommended disclosures include the following:

- *At-will employment*: Indicates the right of the employer or the employee to terminate employment at any time with or without notice or cause (where applicable by state law)
- *Reference contacts*: Requests permission to contact previous employers listed by the applicant on the application form or résumé

- *Employment testing*: Notifies applicants of required drug tests, pencil-and-paper tests, physical exams, or electronic or other tests that will be used in the employment decision
- *Application time limit*: Indicates how long application forms are active (typically six months) and that individuals must reapply or reactivate their applications after that period
- *Information falsification*: Conveys to an applicant that falsification of application information can be grounds for serious reprimand or termination

EEOC Considerations and Application Forms An organization should retain all applications and hiring-related documents and records for three years. Guidelines from the EEOC and court decisions require that the data requested on application forms must be job-related. Though frequently found on application forms, questions that ask for the following information are illegal:

- Marital status
- Height and weight
- Number and ages of dependents
- Information on spouse
- Date of high school graduation
- Emergency contact information
- Social Security number

Most of the litigation surrounding application forms has involved questions regarding the gender and age of a potential employee, so special attention should be given to removing any items that relate to these personal characteristics. Concerns about inappropriate questions stem from their potential to elicit information that should not be used in hiring decisions. Figure 7-7 shows a sample application form containing questions that generally are legal.

Résumés as Applications Applicants commonly provide background information through résumés. When the situation arises, EEOC standards require that an employer treat a résumé as an application form. If an applicant voluntarily furnishes some information on a résumé that cannot be legally obtained, the employer should not use that information during the selection process. Some employers require those who submit résumés to complete an application form as well so that there is consistent information on every applicant and appropriate comparisons can be made.

Regardless of how the background information is collected, there are several issues that should be considered when screening applications. Applications are better than résumés because all candidates must furnish the same information. Résumés are a marketing tool in which applicants present information they want employers to know but may omit negative information. Candidates need to consider that the typical résumé review takes less than five minutes; therefore, an easy to read, well-organized résumé can promote pre-screening success.[14]

To avoid problems with negligent hiring, companies should dutifully check the truthfulness of the information presented on résumés and application forms. Research from CareerBuilder suggests that over half of all applicants knowingly embellish their past work experiences.[15] An emerging trend to combat this problem is the pre-verified résumé. Job seekers submit their résumés to a third party that conducts a background screening and certifies the individual's credentials. The following "HR Perspective: The Good Housekeeping Seal of Approval?" feature explains this process.

FIGURE 7-7 Sample Application Form

Application for Employment
An Equal Opportunity Employer*   Today's Date _____

PERSONAL INFORMATION   Please Print or Type

Name	(Last)	(First)	(Full middle name)	

Current address	City	State	Zip code	Phone number ( )

What position are you applying for?	Date available for employment?	E-mail address

Are you willing to relocate? ☐ Yes ☐ No	Are you willing to travel if required? ☐ Yes ☐ No

Have you ever been employed by this Company or any of its subsidiaries before? ☐ Yes ☐ No	Indicate location and dates

Can you, after employment, submit verification of your legal right to work in the United States? ☐ Yes ☐ No	Have you ever been convicted of a felony? ☐ Yes ☐ No	*Convictions will not automatically disqualify job candidates. The seriousness of the crime and the date of conviction will be considered.*

PERFORMANCE OF JOB FUNCTIONS

Are you able to perform all the functions of the job for which you are applying, with or without accommodation?
☐ Yes, without accommodation   ☐ Yes, with accommodation   ☐ No

If you indicated you can perform all the functions with an accommodation, please explain how you would perform the tasks and with what accommodation.

EDUCATION

School level	School name and address	No. of years attended	Did you graduate?	Course of study
High school				
Vo-tech, business, or trade school				
College				
Graduate school				

PERSONAL DRIVING RECORD

This section is to be completed ONLY if the operation of a motor vehicle will be required in the course of the applicant's employment.

How long have you been a licensed driver?	Driver's license number	Expiration date	Issuing State

List any other state(s) in which you have had a driver's license(s) in the past:

Within the past five years, have you had a vehicle accident? ☐ Yes ☐ No	Been convicted of reckless operation? If yes, give dates: or drunken driving? ☐ Yes ☐ No	Been cited for moving violations? If yes, give dates: ☐ Yes ☐ No

Has your driver's license ever been revoked or suspended? ☐ Yes ☐ No If yes, explain:	Is your driver's license restricted? If yes, explain: ☐ Yes ☐ No

*We are an Equal Opportunity Employer. We do not discriminate on the basis of race, religion, color, gender, age, national origin, or disability.

PERSPECTIVE

The Good Housekeeping Seal of Approval?

With over half of all job candidates exaggerating information on their résumés, honest candidates are trying to find a way to stand out and let employers know that their résumés are truthful. Much like the Good Housekeeping Seal of Approval, which promises customers that they will receive a product as advertised, the pre-verified résumé assures employers that a job candidate's credentials check out.

Job seekers can purchase verification services from a number of third-party vendors. Background screening companies such as Employment Screening Resources and TalentWise offer a menu of options to users. Users can pay a small fee to have details about their education, work history, professional licenses, or criminal history verified by these agencies. Then when they submit their résumé to the employer, it has already been screened and verified.

These screening services are well regarded within the professional community. Employment Screening Resources is accredited by the National Association of Professional Background Screeners and TalentWise was named as a top provider by *HRO Today*.

Employer reactions are mixed because the quality of the screener must be established, and some companies have their own standards and processes to verify candidates. There is also a potential disparate impact issue if pre-verified résumés are given preference and those without them are members of a protected group.

Job candidates might want to conduct the screen to get peace of mind of knowing that a background screen run by an employer won't turn up anything unexpected. However, it is not likely that offering a pre-verified résumé will improve an applicant's chances of advancing through the hiring process. Companies still need to hire individuals with all the necessary knowledge, skills, and abilities. The pre-verified résumé may demonstrate that you are honest and truthful, but don't expect employers to show you any preference because of the "seal of approval."[16]

Consider the following questions about the pre-verification of resumes:

1. Would you consider using a service to pre-verify your résumé before you begin a job search? Why or why not?

2. If you were the HR manager for a small company with a limited budget, what would you consider to be the pros and cons of considering pre-verified résumés? Would you change the selection process for candidates who provide them?

7-2e Security Concerns and Immigration Verification

Businesses need to be proactive about verifying the identities and credentials of job applicants. Part of these efforts rest on careful examination of the accuracy of the details included on résumés and applications. Because it is illegal to knowingly hire employees who are not in the country legally, businesses are required to review and record identity documents, such as Social Security cards, passports, and visas, and to determine if they appear genuine. If HR personnel knowingly accept fraudulent documents, it may create legal liability. Company assets may be seized, and top managers may be prosecuted. U.S. Immigration and Customs Enforcement (ICE) can also audit the records of a business to ensure that it is compliant with employment eligibility laws and rules.

Employers must use the revised form I-9 for each employee hired and must determine within 72 hours whether an applicant is a U.S. citizen, registered alien, or illegal alien. A government program called E-Verify, run by the Department of Homeland Security, helps with this process. The use of E-Verify is mandatory for government contractors and subcontractors, and several states now require all public and private employers to use this service.[17] E-verify has improved the security of its website and now offers a service called Self Lock to allow users to protect their personal information.[18]

An employer should have policies in place to ensure compliance with immigration requirements and to avoid knowingly hiring or retaining illegal workers. I-9s should be completed, updated, audited, and stored. Some companies use paperless I-9 systems to better manage employment eligibility verification because electronic processing reduces errors, incompleteness, and illegibility; it also improves overall documentation management.

LO4 Identify three types of selection tests and legal concerns about their uses.

7-3 Selection Testing

Many kinds of tests can be used to help select qualified employees. Literacy tests, skill-based tests, personality tests, physical ability tests, and honesty tests can be used to assess various individual factors that are important to determine P/E fit. Valid employment tests help companies predict before hiring which applicants will likely be the most successful. For example, stockbrokers who failed a basic exam required to sell securities at least one time have worse disciplinary records than those that pass the exam on the first try.[19] While federal guidelines define all data collection methods as tests, this section specifically addresses traditional employment tests.

Selection tests must be evaluated extensively before being utilized for hiring decisions. The development of test items should be linked to a thorough job analysis, which is covered in Chapter 4. Also, initial review of the items should include an evaluation by knowledge experts, and statistical and validity assessments of the items should be conducted. Furthermore, applicant reactions to testing can impact future performance, so companies should consider how job seekers will feel about testing requirements.[20] In most instances, tests are not used as an "up or down" decision; rather, they provide valuable information about particular aspects of candidate suitability.

7-3a Ability Tests

Tests that assess an individual's ability to perform in a specific manner are grouped as ability tests. These are sometimes further categorized into *aptitude tests* and *achievement tests*. Aptitude tests attempt to measure potential, while achievement tests attempt to measure demonstrated skill or competence. For example, an individual may have a high level of math aptitude but until he studies algebra, he will not have mathematical achievement.

Cognitive ability tests
Tests that measure an individual's thinking, memory, reasoning, verbal, and mathematical abilities

Cognitive ability tests measure an individual's thinking, memory, reasoning, verbal, and mathematical abilities. Valid tests such as the Wonderlic Personnel Test and the General Aptitude Test Battery (GATB) can be used to determine applicants' basic knowledge of terminology and concepts, word fluency, spatial orientation, comprehension and retention span, general and mental ability, and conceptual reasoning. Some companies are considering using the Graduate Management Admission Test (GMAT) to assess candidates' cognitive ability.[21]

General mental ability testing is well established as a valid predictor for many jobs, but since some minority groups tend to score lower on such exams, there is considerable controversy over whether such tests *ought* to be used. When these tests are used, the case for business necessity must be made, and the instrument used should be validated for the organization using it. If a company can find a better way of assessing candidates than using a cognitive ability test, it may avoid problems of disparate impact.[22]

Physical ability tests
Tests that measure an individual's physical abilities such as strength, endurance, and muscular movement

Physical ability tests measure an individual's physical abilities such as strength, endurance, and muscular movement. At an electric utility, line workers must regularly lift and carry equipment, climb ladders, and perform other physical tasks; therefore, testing applicants' mobility, strength, and other physical attributes is job-related. Physical ability tests that assess muscular strength and endurance are likely to result in disparate impact against female applicants. But business necessity makes it acceptable to use such tests when they reflect essential job duties and requirements.[23]

Psychomotor tests
Tests that measure dexterity, hand–eye coordination, arm–hand steadiness, and other factors

Various skill-based tests can be used, including psychomotor tests, which measure a person's dexterity, hand–eye coordination, arm–hand steadiness, and other factors. Tests such as the MacQuarie Test for Mechanical Ability can measure manual dexterity for assembly line workers and others who regularly use psychomotor skills.

Work sample tests
Tests that require an applicant to perform a simulated task that is a specified part of the target job

Many organizations use situational tests, or work sample tests, which require an applicant to perform a simulated task that is a specified part of the target job. Requiring an applicant for an administrative assistant's job to type a business letter as quickly as possible would be one such test. Examples of work samples include an audition for someone seeking a role in a drama group's play or a tryout for a sports team. Work samples are among the most valid and appropriate tests because they are highly relevant and job-related.[24]

Situational judgment tests
Tests that measure a person's judgment in work settings

Situational judgment tests are designed to measure a person's judgment in work settings.[25] The candidate is given a scenario and a list of possible solutions to the problem and is required to make judgments about how to deal with the situation. For example, medical students who performed well on a video-based situational judgment test of interpersonal skills performed better during their internship experience and as physicians.[26] Situational judgment tests are a form of job simulation.

Assessment Centers An assessment center is not a place but a selection process composed of a series of evaluative tests during which candidates are assessed by multiple raters. In one assessment center, candidates go through a comprehensive interview, a pencil-and-paper test, individual and group simulations, and work exercises. Individual performance is then evaluated by a panel of trained raters.

The tests and exercises in an assessment center must reflect the content of the job for which individuals are being screened and the types of problems faced on that job. For example, a technology communications organization used a series of assessment centers to hire employees who would interact with clients. The company found that these centers improved the selection process and also provided new employees with a good road map for individual development. Consequently, while assessment centers are often expensive to develop and conduct they often reduce the potential for disparate impact and result in better staffing decisions.[27]

7-3b Personality Tests

Personality is a unique blend of individual characteristics that can affect how people interact with their work environment. Although many personality characteristics

FIGURE 7-8 Big Five Personality Characteristics

Big Five	Low Scorers	High Scorers
1 Extroversion	Loner Quiet Passive Reserved	Joiner Talkative Active Affectionate
2 Agreeableness	Suspicious Critical Ruthless Irritable	Trusting Lenient Soft-hearted Good-natured
3 Conscientiousness	Negligent Lazy Disorganized Late	Conscientious Hard-working Well-organized Punctual
4 Neuroticism	Calm Even-tempered Comfortable Unemotional	Worried Temperamental Self-conscious Emotional
5 Openness to experience	Down-to-earth Uncreative Conventional Uncurious	Imaginative Creative Original Curious

Source: http://blog.lib.umn.edu/paldr001/myblog/2011/11/ocean-or-canoe-the-model-of-personality.html

exist, some experts believe that there are a relatively small number of underlying major traits. The most widely accepted approach to studying personality traits is the "Big Five" personality framework.[28] The Big Five traits are generally considered to be useful predictors of various types of job performance in different occupations. The factors are shown in Figure 7-8. In particular, conscientiousness is a good predictor of successful job performance.[29] However, there is not one general "ideal" personality profile. Different jobs such as sale representative and financial auditor often require different personality types.

Organizations use various personality tests that assess the degree to which candidates' attributes match specific job criteria. In a world where eHarmony, Match.com, and others claim to assess individuals on a number of personality traits, it is critical that hiring authorities use only reliable, valid, job-related personality assessments. The first step in using such a test is to determine the desired personality profile on a job-specific basis through job analysis and evaluation of successful jobholders.[30]

Potential Issues with Personality Tests Faking is a major concern for employers using personality tests. Many test publishers admit that test profiles can be falsified, and they try to reduce faking by including questions that can be used to compute a social desirability or "lie" score. Researchers also favor the use of "corrections" based on components of the test to account for faking—a preference that also constitutes a strong argument for professional scoring of personality tests.

Another possibility is use of a fake warning, which instructs applicants that faking can be detected and can result in a negative hiring impression.[31]

An additional issue is the possibility that personality tests might inadvertently measure disabilities or mental health concerns such as depression or bipolar disorder. Automated personality tests may screen out applicants who have the skills but may not meet a particular personality profile. Kroger and CVS have both begun to look more carefully at how personality tests are affecting hiring decisions. To ensure fair evaluation of all applicants, the companies are modifying the questions on their tests to eliminate inquiries that might expose mental health issues.[32]

7-3c Emotional Intelligence Tests

Emotional intelligence
The ability to recognize and manage our own feelings and the feelings of others

Emotional intelligence reflects the soft skills that are critical for establishing good working relationships within the work unit and organization. Emotional intelligence is the ability to recognize our own feelings and the feelings of others and to effectively manage our own and others' emotions.[33] Figure 7-9 details the four dimensions of emotional intelligence.

As organizations use more teams and collaborative methods to accomplish tasks, selecting individuals who are aware of emotions in the workplace becomes more important. In particular, leaders who have a high level of emotional intelligence perform better and achieve superior outcomes than leaders with less of this competence. The concept of emotional intelligence is relatively common across countries, which means that as company operations span the globe, similar qualities lead to better results.[34]

FIGURE 7-9   Dimensions of Emotional Intelligence

Source: Adapted from http://coachingleaders.emotional-climate.com/emotional-intelligence/.

Leaders and employees who have a high level of emotional intelligence tend to be more creative and perform better on the job. They also may be more effective in team settings and handle stress better than employees lower in emotional intelligence.[35] As with all tests, a thorough job analysis can help establish the appropriate level of emotional intelligence needed for success on a particular job.

The use of behavioral assessments is an emerging trend in the selection practices of many organizations. These assessments focus on determining candidates' suitability for jobs based on a range of attributes. The following "HR Perspective: Behavioral Assessments" feature explains how several companies are benefiting from their use.

PERSPECTIVE

Behavioral Assessments

Companies attempt to assess job candidates on a wide range of attributes to improve P/E fit. Testing knowledge or hard skills can often be done in a relatively straightforward and easy way by asking candidates questions about the job content area or having them perform a sample of the job duties. Such ability tests help ensure that those hired will be capable of successfully performing the tasks involved in the job.

But there is much more to P/E fit than a good match between the applicant and the job requirements. Employers also need to determine whether applicants will work well with their designated teams or work units and if they will be a good long-term fit for the organization as a whole. Assessing the applicant's fit with the organization's culture, their work style, and their potential are much more difficult.

That's where behavioral assessments come into play. A company usually works with experts in Industrial/Organization Psychology to identify the competencies that have proven to lead to successful job performance. This often involves studying top performers to see what differentiates them from average or poor performers. Those qualities are then built into an assessment tool, which is often administered online early in the screening process. Each company can customize its assessment to measure employee performance elements that are most critical to success. Two companies in the same industry may value different aspects of employee performance.

AMC Theaters found that using a behavioral assessment to determine applicants' friendliness, service orientation, and dependability reduced turnover to well below industry averages and improved employee engagement by 40%. This led to increased customer satisfaction scores, which in turn resulted in higher revenue at its theaters. Seaport Hotel & World Trade Center, Inc. in Boston instituted a 20-minute behavioral assessment in its online screening process and reduced turnover to single-digit levels. The assessment focused on determining each job candidate's cultural fit for a particular job in the hotel.

These powerful results have led to an uptick in the use of behavioral assessments. While skill and knowledge tests are used by over half of U.S. companies, over a third are now using behavioral assessments to refine their selection process and generate better organization results.[38] Considering the popularity of behavioral assessments, discuss the following questions:

1. What ethical and legal concerns does the use of behavioral assessments raise? Do you believe that these assessments might be more subject to bias than skill and knowledge tests might be?

2. How do you think applicants might react to being asked to complete a behavioral assessment? Would you personally hesitate to participate in this type of screening for a job?

ETHICS

7-3d Honesty and Integrity Tests

Companies use different tests to assess the honesty and integrity of applicants and employees to prevent hiring dishonest employees, to reduce the frequency of lying and theft on the job, to communicate to applicants and employees alike that dishonesty will not be tolerated, and to reduce accidents. If used properly, honesty and integrity tests can be valid as broad screening devices for organizations. Research also indicates that even though honesty tests can be expensive to administer, they may reduce workers' compensation claims and save the company money.[36]

However, these instruments have limitations. For instance, socially desirable responses are a key concern, and some questions can be considered overly invasive, insulting, and not job-related. Sometimes false positives are generated (or an honest person is scored as dishonest). Test scores might be affected by individual demographic factors such as gender and race. Research is inconclusive regarding the usefulness of integrity tests. Further, applicants may react negatively to taking such a test. Selecting an appropriate test, training HR staff and mangers, and incorporating results into a broader selection process can mitigate some of the issues with integrity tests.[37]

Polygraphs The polygraph, more generally and incorrectly referred to as a lie detector, is a mechanical device that measures a person's galvanic skin response, heart rate, and breathing rate. The idea behind the polygraph is that if a person answers a question deliberately incorrectly, the body's physiological responses will "reveal" the falsification through the recording mechanisms of the polygraph. As a result of concerns about polygraph validity, Congress passed the Employee Polygraph Protection Act, which prohibits most private-sector employers from using polygraphs for pre-employment screening purposes. Federal, state, and local government agencies are exempt from the act, as are certain private-sector employers such as security companies and pharmaceutical companies. The act permits employers to use polygraphs as part of internal investigations of theft or loss. But in those situations, the polygraph test should be taken voluntarily, and the employee should be allowed to end the test at any time.

7-4 Selection Interviews

LO5 Contrast several types of selection interviews and some key considerations in conducting these interviews.

Interviews are one of the most common methods used for selection. Interviews are conducted both to obtain information about candidates and to provide information and reinforce the employer brand. They are an important part of "selling" the job opportunity to qualified applicants and of applicants "selling" themselves as the best choice.[39]

Interviews are often conducted at two levels: first, as an initial screening interview to determine if the person has met minimum qualifications, and then later, as an in-depth interview with HR staff members and/or operating managers to determine if the person will fit the designated job. Advance preparation is critical to get the most out of a pre-screening interview.[40] Before the in-depth interview, information from all available sources is pooled so that the interviewers can reconcile conflicting information that may have emerged from tests, application forms, and references.

FIGURE 7-10   Comparison of Structured and Unstructured Selection Interviews

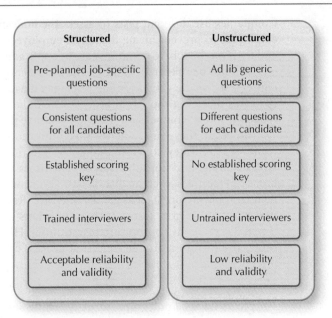

Structured	Unstructured
Pre-planned job-specific questions	Ad lib generic questions
Consistent questions for all candidates	Different questions for each candidate
Established scoring key	No established scoring key
Trained interviewers	Untrained interviewers
Acceptable reliability and validity	Low reliability and validity

7-4a Interview Quality

Selection interviews must meet the same standards for reliability and validity as all selection methods. In general, interviews are really quite poor predictors because many interviewers are not skilled at the process and rely too much on gut instinct. Establishing both high *intra-rater reliability* (within the same interviewer) and *inter-rater reliability* (across different interviewers) is difficult but can be achieved through the use of structured interviews. Inter-rater reliability becomes important because several interviewers are often involved in selecting employees from a pool of applicants.

Interviews must also be valid to enable useful selection. To be valid, interviews must accurately assess specific candidate qualities such as leadership ability, communication skills, or collaboration. Validity can vary depending on the degree of structure that is utilized in an interview format. Basically, an unstructured interview does not usually provide much actual validity, leading to growth in the popularity of structured interviews. The differences between structured and unstructured interviews are shown in Figure 7-10.

7-4b Structured Interviews

Structured interview
Interview that uses a set of prepared job-related questions that are asked of all applicants

A structured interview involves a set of prepared job-related questions that are asked of all applicants so that comparisons can be made more easily, resulting in better selection decisions. The structured interview is useful in the initial screening process because many applicants can be effectively evaluated and compared. However, the structured interview does not have to be rigid. The pre-determined questions should be asked in a logical manner but should not be read word for word. Applicants should be allowed adequate opportunity to explain their answers, and interviewers should probe with additional questions until they fully understand the responses. A standardized scoring key helps improve inter-rater reliability, as all interviewers score answers based on the same criteria. This process can make the structured interview more reliable and valid than other interview approaches.[41]

Structured interviews, including biographical, behavioral, and situational types, are useful when making selection decisions. The structured format ensures that a given interviewer has similar information on each candidate. It also ensures greater consistency in the subsequent evaluation of those candidates when several interviewers ask the same questions of applicants. Companies should train all interviewers so that they can conduct effective interviews using a structured interview format. Interview questions and possible responses are based on job analysis and checked by job experts to ensure content validity. The interviewer typically codes the suitability of the answer, assigns point values, and adds up the total number of points each interviewee has received.

Biographical Interview A *biographical interview* focuses on a chronological assessment of the candidate's past experiences. This type of interview is widely used and is often combined with other interview techniques. Overall, the process provides a sketch of past experiences.

Behavioral interview
Interview in which applicants give specific examples of how they have performed a certain task or handled a problem in the past

Behavioral Interview In the behavioral interview format, applicants are asked to describe how they have behaved or performed a certain task or handled a problem in the past, which may predict future actions and show how well applicants are suited for current jobs. An example of a behavioral interview line of questioning might be: "Tell me about a time when you initiated a project. What was the situation? What did you do? What were the results?" Questions such as these can be useful because candidates must describe what they have done to complete job requirements.

Situational interview
Structured interview that contains questions about how applicants might handle specific job situations

Situational Interview The situational interview invovles questions about how applicants might handle specific job situations. A variation is termed the *case study interview,* which requires a job candidate to diagnose and correct organizational challenges during the interview. Situational interviews assess what the interviewee would consider to be the best option, not necessarily what he or she did in a similar situation.[42] A useful technique for prompting high-quality responses is the STAR method, which is described in the following "HR Competencies & Applications: Catching STAR Employees" feature.

7-4c Less-Structured Interviews

Some interviews are unplanned and are not structured at all. Such interviewing techniques may be appropriate for fact finding or for counseling interviews but are not good for selection interviewing. These interviews may be conducted by operating managers or supervisors who have had little interview training. An *unstructured interview* occurs when the interviewer improvises by asking questions that are not pre-determined. A *semistructured interview* is a guided conversation in which broad questions are asked and new questions arise as a result of the discussion, for example, "What would you do differently if you could start over again?"

Some interviewers ask unusual questions such as "If you were a cartoon character, who would you be and why?" While such questions seem entertaining, unless creativity is an essential part of the job being filled, answers may be meaningless, and candidates may become confused or turned off. The use of offbeat questions is appropriate only if a job-related attribute is being assessed and responses are evaluated according to a scoring rubric. When posing any interview question, always ask yourself, "What am I trying to learn about a candidate's ability to do the job?"

COMPETENCIES & APPLICATIONS

Catching STAR Employees

Nobody wants to hire an underperformer or employee who will create problems within the work group. Most hiring managers hope to "catch a star employee" who will perform well and contribute to the success of the organization. Hiring stars makes the manager's job simpler and more rewarding. So, what's a manager to do?

Adopting the STAR method during employment interviews helps separate out the great applicants from the rest of the pack. Managers who are trained in this interviewing method can better determine the quality of each applicant's experience as it relates to the job. STAR is an acronym that stands for:

- **S**ituation
- **T**ask
- **A**ction
- **R**esult

The *situation or task* is the challenge that applicants faced or needed to accomplish. Applicants will explain the context in a succinct, informative way. For example, if you ask applicants to talk about how they handled a crisis in the past, they would provide specific details about the particular crisis and what was needed to overcome it.

The *action* is the essence of this interviewing method. Applicants should explain in detail what steps they took and the skills and resources used to accomplish the task. Applicants should demonstrate how they leveraged their skills to achieve particular results. They may also explain why they took certain actions and did not do other things. This analytical approach demonstrates that the candidate is able to critically assess actions and link them to outcomes.

The *result* is, of course, the final outcome. How did things turn out? Applicants who can reflect on what went well and what they might do differently if facing a similar situation show maturity and self-awareness, qualities that organizations value.

Star applicants will provide responses in this format to show how their knowledge and skills can benefit the organization. Hiring managers can prompt applicants to follow this approach by simply asking each applicant to explain the situation/task, action, and result.[43]

The STAR method is a formal process for evaluating job interview responses. Respond to the following questions that explore this approach:

1. Compare the pros and cons of using a technique like the STAR method to conduct employment interviews.

2. Would you anticipate that managers might resist using a formal method such as the STAR system? Might they perceive that it would limit their discretion in the hiring process?

KEY COMPETENCIES: Communication, Ethical Practice; HR Expertise: People/Talent Acquisition & Retention

Group interview
Several job candidates are interviewed together by a hiring authority

Group Interview A group interview occurs when several job candidates are interviewed together by a hiring authority. They may be especially useful when hiring for entry-level jobs when skill requirements are low and job fit involves factors such as scheduled work hours, availability of transportation to the work site, and other practical details. They can also be beneficial to assess interpersonal skills and teamwork. When a company must hire a high volume of low-skilled workers, it may not need or have time for individual interviews. However, recognize that candidates know they are competing for a limited number of jobs, and group interviews can therefore become disagreeable.[44]

Nondirective interview
Interview that uses questions developed from the answers to previous questions

A nondirective interview uses questions that are developed from the answers to previous questions. The interviewer asks general questions designed to prompt applicants to describe themselves. The interviewer then uses applicants' responses to shape the next question. With a nondirective interview, as with any less-structured interview, difficulties related to selection decisions include keeping the conversation job-related and obtaining comparable data on various applicants. Many nondirective interviews are only partly organized; as a result, a combination of general and specific questions is asked in no set order, and different questions are asked of different applicants for the same job. Comparing and ranking candidates is thus more open to subjective judgments and legal challenges, so this type of interview is best used for selection sparingly, if at all.

7-4d Who Conducts Interviews?

Job interviews can be conducted by an individual, by several individuals sequentially, or by panels or teams. For some jobs, such as entry-level positions requiring few skills, applicants might be interviewed solely by an HR professional. For other jobs, employers screen applicants via multiple interviews, beginning with an HR professional and followed by the appropriate supervisors and managers. Then a selection decision is made collectively. Managers need to ensure that multiple interviews are not redundant.

Panel interview
Interview in which several interviewers meet with the candidate at the same time

Team interview
Interview in which applicants are interviewed by the team members with whom they will work

Other interview formats are also utilized. In a panel interview, several interviewers meet with the candidate at the same time so that the responses are heard by all. Panel interviews may be combined with individual interviews. In a team interview, applicants are interviewed by the team members with whom they will work. However, without proper planning, an unstructured interview can occur during these group sessions, and applicants are sometimes uncomfortable with the format.

7-4e Effective Interviewing

Many people think that the ability to interview is an innate talent, but this is simply not the case. Just being personable and liking to talk is no guarantee that someone will be an effective interviewer. In fact, there are many factors related to interviewers that can influence how well interviewees perform, including the ability to prompt good social interaction, personality, and the design and structure of the interview itself. Even the questions that are asked of individuals can arguably affect the quality of interview sessions. Figure 7-11 provides a variety of questions commonly used in selection interviews and what they are attempting to predict.

Interviewing skills are developed through training and practice.[45] Suggestions for making interviewing more effective are as follows:

- *Plan the interview.* Interviewers should review all information before the interview and then identify specific areas for questioning.
- *Control the interview.* This includes knowing in advance what information must be collected, systematically collecting it during the interview, and stopping when that information has been collected. An interviewer should not monopolize the conversation.
- *Use effective questioning techniques.* Use questions that will produce full and complete answers that can be evaluated on the basis of job-relatedness.
- *Get a balanced view.* To enable informed hiring decisions, interviews should consider both the positive and negative attributes of job candidates.

FIGURE 7-11   Questions Commonly Asked in Selection Interviews

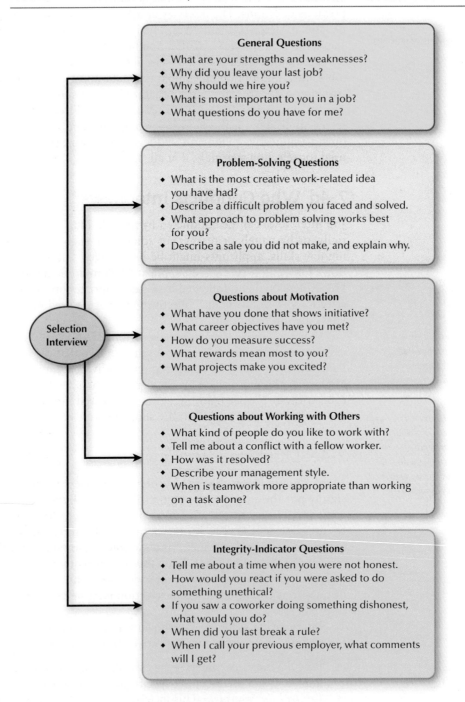

General Questions
- What are your strengths and weaknesses?
- Why did you leave your last job?
- Why should we hire you?
- What is most important to you in a job?
- What questions do you have for me?

Problem-Solving Questions
- What is the most creative work-related idea you have had?
- Describe a difficult problem you faced and solved.
- What approach to problem solving works best for you?
- Describe a sale you did not make, and explain why.

Questions about Motivation
- What have you done that shows initiative?
- What career objectives have you met?
- How do you measure success?
- What rewards mean most to you?
- What projects make you excited?

Questions about Working with Others
- What kind of people do you like to work with?
- Tell me about a conflict with a fellow worker.
- How was it resolved?
- Describe your management style.
- When is teamwork more appropriate than working on a task alone?

Integrity-Indicator Questions
- Tell me about a time when you were not honest.
- How would you react if you were asked to do something unethical?
- If you saw a coworker doing something dishonest, what would you do?
- When did you last break a rule?
- When I call your previous employer, what comments will I get?

Selection Interview

Questions to Avoid   The following types of questions should be avoided in selection interviews:

- *Yes/no questions*: Unless verifying specific information, the interviewer should avoid questions that can be answered "yes" or "no." For example, "Did you have good attendance on your last job?" will probably be answered simply "yes."

- *Obvious questions*: An obvious question is one for which the interviewer already has the answer and the applicant knows it.
- *Questions that rarely produce a true answer*: Avoid questions that prompt a less-than-honest response, for example, "How did you get along with your coworkers?" The likely answer is "Just fine."
- *Leading questions*: A leading question is one to which the answer is obvious from the way the question is asked. For example, "How do you like working with other people?" suggests the answer "I like it."
- *Illegal/inappropriate questions*: Questions that involve information such as race, age, gender, national origin, marital status, number of children, and other family-related issues are illegal. They are just as inappropriate in the interview as on the application form.
- *Questions that are not job-related*: All questions should be directly related to the job.

Listening Responses to Avoid Effective interviewers avoid listening responses such as nodding, pausing, making casual remarks, echoing, and mirroring. The applicant might try to please the interviewers by observing the feedback provided. However, giving no response to an applicant's answers may imply boredom or inattention. Therefore, interviewers should use friendly but neutral comments and gestures during the interview.

7-4f Problems in the Interview

Operating managers and supervisors are more likely than HR personnel to use poor interviewing techniques because they lack training or do not interview often. Several problems include the following:

- *Snap judgments*. Some interviewers decide whether an applicant is suitable within the first two to four minutes of the interview and spend the rest of the time looking for evidence to support their judgment.
- *Negative emphasis*. When evaluating suitability, unfavorable information about an applicant is often emphasized more than favorable information.
- *Halo effect*. The *halo effect* occurs when an interviewer allows a positive characteristic, such as agreeableness, to overshadow other evidence. The phrase *devil's horns* describes the reverse of the halo effect; this occurs when a negative characteristic, such as inappropriate dress, overshadows other traits.
- *Biases and stereotyping*. "Similarity" bias occurs when interviewers favor or select people whom they believe to be like themselves on the basis of a variety of personal factors. Interviewers should also avoid any personal tendencies to stereotype individuals because of demographic characteristics and differences.
- *Cultural noise*. Interviewers must learn to recognize and handle cultural noise, which results from social mores and cultural values and leads to responses that applicants believe are socially acceptable rather than factual.

Managers and others involved in the selection process frequently fall victim to their own unconscious biases. Without realizing it, many interviewers discount candidates whose religions or cultures differ from their own. To combat the problem of hidden biases, BAE Systems offers training to its employees. Since it trained its managers, the company has increased the number of women and minorities targeted for advancement. Helping people recognize and manage their biases is important for fair assessment of all candidates.[46]

LO6 Specify
how legal concerns
affect background
investigations of
applicants and use of
medical examinations in
the selection process.

7-5 Background Investigations

Background checking is critical for a wide range of positions, including schoolteachers, janitors, bank tellers, and many others. Background information can be obtained from a variety of sources, including past job records, credit history, testing records, educational and certification records, drug tests, criminal history, sex offender lists, motor vehicle records, and military records. Advancements in technology and access to information online have made it simpler for employers of all sizes to conduct background checks.

Failure to check the backgrounds of people who are hired can lead to embarrassment and legal liability.[47] Hiring workers who commit violent acts on the job is one example. For jobs in certain industries, such as those that provide services to children, services to vulnerable adults, security, in-home services, and financial services, background checks are mandated in some states. Federal regulations mandate background checks for people with commercial drivers' licenses who drive tractor-trailer rigs and buses interstate.

7-5a Negligent Hiring and Retention

An employer's liability hinges on how well it investigates an applicant's background. Consequently, information provided on the application form should be investigated, verified, and documented.

Negligent hiring
Occurs when an employer fails to check an employee's background and the employee injures someone on the job

Negligent hiring occurs when an employer fails to check an employee's background and the employee later injures or harms someone while performing job duties. There is a potential negligent hiring problem when an employer hires an unfit employee, a background check is insufficient, or an employer does not research potential risk factors that would prevent a positive hire decision. Similarly, negligent retention occurs when an employer becomes aware that an employee may be unfit for employment but continues to employ the person, and the person injures someone.

Negligent retention
Occurs when an employer becomes aware that an employee may be unfit for work but continues to employ the person, and the person injures someone

To reduce the probability of negligent hiring, companies verify applicant information and conduct background screening. Many organizations use outside vendors that specialize in conducting background checks because these firms can provide such services much more efficiently and effectively. Before contracting with a background screening company, it is advisable to verify the agency's reputation and licensure.[48]

ETHICS

Some employers use social media websites and the Internet to conduct background checks on employees. Many believe that websites provide extra insight into a job candidate's individual characteristics regardless of the information that has been provided to the company through the application form or résumé. Employers also use online network sites such as Facebook to obtain a variety of personal information about applicants. Anyone on the Internet can post damaging information about individuals, further complicating the process of performing fair and legitimate background checks if this information is utilized in job selection.

7-5b Legal Constraints on Background Investigations

Various federal and state laws protect the rights of individuals whose backgrounds may be investigated during pre-employment screening. One important step when conducting a background investigation is to obtain a signed release from the applicant authorizing the employer to conduct the investigation. Another requirement is making sure that background investigations are relevant to the jobs being performed and a business necessity.[49]

Credit History and Criminal Background Checks Many employers check applicants' credit histories. The logic is that poor credit histories may signal, either correctly or incorrectly, a certain level of responsibility. Firms that check applicants' credit records must comply with the federal Fair Credit Reporting Act, which requires:

- Disclosing that a credit check is being conducted
- Obtaining written consent from the person being checked
- Furnishing the applicant with a copy of the report

Some state laws also prohibit employers from obtaining certain credit information. Credit history should be checked on applicants for jobs in which use of, access to, or management of money is an essential job function. For example, financial institutions have a vested interest in checking the credit histories of employees who handle money, and retailers might conduct credit checks on cashiers and managerial staff who also deal directly with money. Credit scores may be acceptable predictors of job performance but are not valid for assessing the potential for workplace deviance. Mismanaged credit checks might violate the Fair Credit Reporting Act and prompt complaints to the EEOC. Companies should use these assessments only when needed, such as hiring for a job that involves financial responsibility.[50]

Employers conduct criminal background checks to prevent negligent hiring lawsuits. However, they must make sure that these checks are performed consistently and fairly across different employees applying for similar types of positions. Lawmakers have taken an interest in the examination of an applicant's criminal history because it often results in disparate impact. The following "HR Competencies & Applications: Ban-the-Box Legislation Proposed" feature explains legislative restrictions on employers' ability to use applicants' criminal history in selection decisions.

7-5c Medical Examinations and Inquiries

Medical information about applicants may be used to determine their physical and mental abilities to perform jobs. Physical standards for jobs should be realistic, justifiable, and linked to essential job requirements.

ADA and Medical Inquiries The Americans with Disabilities Act (ADA) prohibits the use of pre-employment medical exams, except for drug tests, until a job has been conditionally offered. Also, the ADA prohibits a company from rejecting an individual because of a disability and from asking job applicants any question related to current or past medical history until a conditional job offer has been made. Even though workers with disabilities can competently perform many jobs, they may sometimes be rejected because of their physical or mental limitations.[52] Once a conditional offer of employment has been made, some organizations ask the applicant to complete a pre-employment health checklist, or the employer pays for a physical examination of the applicant. It should be made clear that the applicant who has been offered the job is not really hired until the physical inquiry is successfully completed.

Drug Testing Drug testing, a widely-used selection tool, may be conducted as part of a medical exam, or it may be done separately. If drug tests are used, employers should remember that the accuracy of tests varies according to the type of test used, the drug tested, and the quality of the laboratory where the test samples are sent. Because of the potential impact of prescription drugs on test results, applicants should complete a detailed questionnaire on this matter before the testing.

COMPETENCIES & APPLICATIONS

Ban-the-Box Legislation Proposed

Checking one small box on an employment application might mean an applicant is eliminated from consideration regardless of skills or qualifications. That small box is the question on most applications that asks about criminal convictions. Most HR professionals indicate that a nonviolent felony conviction would be heavily weighted in a decision regarding an applicant, and a violent felony would be even more difficult to overcome in the hiring process.

Individuals with a criminal past face high hurdles to find gainful employment after serving their time in prison. However, being employed is one of the things that can help prevent former convicts from returning to a life of crime. Companies find themselves in a no-win situation trying to navigate between two conflicting obligations—(1) to provide a safe work environment and (2) to provide equal opportunity for all qualified applicants. Dollar General and BMW are two employers who found themselves at odds with the EEOC over their blanket disqualification policies.

Since a higher percentage of black and Hispanic men and women are imprisoned sometime during their lives than are white individuals, the EEOC took action to improve chances for former convicts. The agency issued guidelines that essentially prohibit companies from a blanket policy of disqualifying candidates with a criminal history, that is, they "banned the box." Instead, any screening policy must link the specific criminal conduct with the risks associated with a specific position in the company. Employers need to consider:

- Nature or gravity of the offense
- Time elapsed since the conviction and/or release from prison
- Nature of the job being sought

Ban-the-box laws have now been enacted in 11 states and many cities around the country. State and federal laws frequently conflict on this issue, and the EEOC has not helped employers reconcile differences between the two. In many cases, federal regulations are more strict than any imposed by states. HR professionals should consult with their legal counsel to ensure that any consideration of criminal background meets all requirements across states and federal jurisdictions.[51] Changing the use of criminal background checks presents some challenges to an organization's practices. Discuss these questions that relate to such screening:

1. What are the potential consequences (both positive and negative) of limiting the impact of criminal history on employment decisions?

2. For what types of jobs would you recommend companies utilize criminal background checks? For what types of jobs would they be unnecessary?

KEY COMPETENCIES: Ethical Practice; HR Expertise: Workplace/Employment Law Regulations

Safety-sensitive jobs may require a more stringent screening process than jobs with limited safety concerns.[53]

If an individual tests positive for drug use, an independent medical laboratory should administer a second—more detailed—analysis. Whether urine, blood, saliva, or hair samples are used, the process of obtaining, labeling, and transferring the samples to the testing lab should be outlined clearly, and definite policies and procedures should be established and followed.

FIGURE 7-12   Why Conduct Previous Employment Checks

7-5d Previous Employment Checks and Personal References

Work-related references from previous employers and supervisors can provide a valuable snapshot of a candidate's background and characteristics. Previous employment checks protect the company from negligent hiring claims, provide an overview of job candidates' past performance and honesty, and verify work credentials. Figure 7-12 outlines some of the important reasons for contacting applicant references.[54]

Personal references provided by job candidates are often of limited predictive value because individuals knowingly pick references who will speak highly of them. Previous supervisors and employers can often provide more useful information that can be utilized to more effectively evaluate job candidates. Good questions to ask previous supervisors or employers include the following:

- What were the dates of employment?
- What was the position held?
- What were the job duties?
- What strengths and weaknesses did you observe?
- Why did the individual leave employment?
- Would you rehire?

There are many ways to conduct employment checks, and one of the most common methods involves obtaining information via telephone. Managers should consider using an approach that attempts to verify the factual information given by the applicant. Some organizations send pre-printed reference forms to individuals who are giving references for applicants. These forms often include a release statement signed by the applicant so that those providing references can see they have been released from liability on the information they furnish.

7-5e Additional Selection Criteria

In the quest to find the best person for the job, hiring authorities sometimes consider additional indicators such as previous job tenure, time gaps between jobs, and educational credentials. Using this information should follow the basic guidelines of job-relatedness, business necessity, and P/E fit.

Previous job tenure is a measure of how long the applicant has stayed on jobs held in the past. For jobs requiring very little training, short tenure may not be as big a concern as for jobs that require substantial training. Employers that must invest a

Previous job tenure
A measure of how long the applicant has stayed on jobs held in the past

great deal of time training new hires to master job duties may be legitimately interested in assessing applicants' service tenure.

Criticism of *job hoppers* has decreased in recent years, and many hiring managers now expect that workers will leave the organization in a few years. In fact, a survey of HR managers showed that to be considered a job hopper, an applicant would have to change jobs six times in a 10-year period. Recent studies have shown that the average worker stays on the job for about five years.[55] So, it's helpful to be realistic about what to expect from newly hired employees.

Long-Term Unemployed Some hiring managers view long gaps between jobs as a red flag on an applicant's profile. Time gaps between jobs may be caused by a number of factors, many of which are not related to the applicant's suitability for employment. Individuals who have been laid off in economic downturns may face bias or discrimination, which makes it more difficult to find a new job. Since skills may erode during periods of unemployment, some companies hesitate to give these individuals an opportunity.

To combat this problem, the federal government enlisted support from over 300 business leaders, who pledged to adopt the following best practices when assessing long-term unemployed applicants:

1. Ensure that job advertisements do not discourage or discriminate against unemployed people.
2. Review screening procedures to ensure that unemployment status is not given inappropriate weight in hiring decisions.
3. Proactively reach out to agencies and other groups that work with long-term unemployed candidates.
4. Share best practices within the employer community.[56]

Educational Credentials Hiring managers frequently use attainment of a college degree to assess applicant commitment and intelligence. However, there is some question as to the validity of this credential, as a recent study has shown that merely possessing a college degree does not predict subsequent job performance. In any case, a college degree may indicate that an applicant has mastered specific subject matter that is critical to job duties.[57]

Some companies, like Boston Consulting Group, have recently begun to require applicants to report their scores on the SAT college entrance exam as a selection criterion. The SAT score is easy for hiring managers to understand as an indicator of cognitive ability. Because this request is becoming more common, some college students and recent graduates are including their score on their résumé. However, some hiring managers dismiss the SAT as a useful predictor and might actually be annoyed when candidates voluntarily provide it.[58]

Hiring managers are also less impressed with the prestige or pedigree of an applicant's college alma mater than they are with knowledge and skills related to the job field. Industry experience and expertise outweigh the name of the college on a candidate's degree.[59]

7-5f Making the Job Offer

The final step of the selection process involves extending an offer. Offers are made to job candidates whose skill and attribute profiles demonstrate that they will be a good fit for the job. A threshold selection approach that evaluates job candidates

FIGURE 7-13 Elements of an Employment Offer Letter

Job Details	Pay-Related Items	Employee Benefits	Working Conditions
◆ Title	◆ Pay grade or level	◆ Health insurance	◆ Start date
◆ Overview of job duties	◆ FLSA-exempt status	◆ Retirement or pension plan	◆ Days and hours of work
◆ Key responsibilities	◆ Incentive pay details	◆ Paid time off	◆ Work location
◆ Reporting relationships	◆ Pay period and pay dates	◆ Eligibility dates for all plans	◆ Employment-at-will statement
◆ Full- or part-time status		◆ Employee costs	

across different tests and evaluative procedures on the basis of clear benchmarks can be an effective tool for identifying top individuals for job offers.[60]

Job offers are often given over the telephone. Many companies then formalize the offer in a letter that is sent to the applicant. Some believe that the offer document should be reviewed by the employer's legal counsel and that the terms and conditions of employment should be clearly identified. Care should be taken to avoid vague, general statements and promises about bonuses, work schedules, or other matters that might change later. These documents should also allow the selected candidate to sign an acceptance of the offer and return it to the employer, where it becomes part of the candidate's personnel file. Figure 7-13 details information that should be included in an employment offer letter.

LO7 Describe the major issues to be considered when selecting candidates for global assignments.

GLOBAL

7-6 Global Staffing

Staffing global assignments involves making selection decisions that impact (or take place in) other countries. Cost is a major consideration when staffing global assignments, because establishing a business professional in another country can run as high as $1 million for a three-year job assignment. Further, if a business professional quits an international assignment prematurely or wants to transfer home, associated costs can be even greater. Failure rates for global assignments can run as high as 50% of those sent overseas.

7-6a Types of Global Employees

Global organizations can be staffed in many ways, including with expatriates, host-country nationals, and third-country nationals. Each staffing option presents some unique HR management challenges. Tax laws, employment regulations, and local customs all impact hiring in the international market. HR professionals need to be knowledgeable about the laws and customs of each country represented in their workforce. Experienced expatriates can provide a pool of talent that can be used as the firm expands operations into other countries.

7-6b Selection Process for Global Assignments

The fit between the individual and job characteristics is particularly important when dealing with overseas assignments because employees must have the proper

FIGURE 7-14   Selection Factors for Global Employees

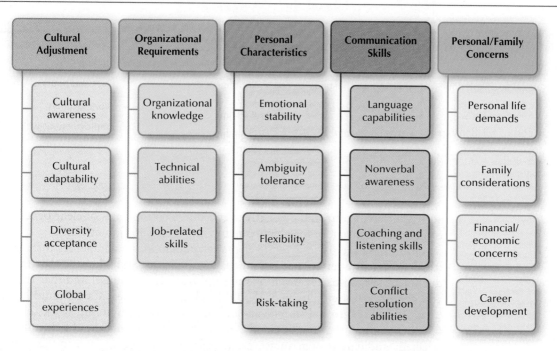

personalities, skills, and interpersonal abilities to be effective in the international environment.[61] The selection process for an international assignment should provide a realistic picture of the life, work, and culture to which the employee may be sent. In addition, assessing the candidates' ability to adjust to a new culture, environment, and job assignment are important to achieve good P/E fit for expatriate assignments.[62] HR managers start by preparing a comprehensive description of the job to be done such as typical responsibilities and work duties. Figure 7-14 shows many key competencies for successful global employees, which include the following:

- *Cultural adjustment*: Individuals who accept foreign job assignments need to be able to successfully adjust to cultural differences.
- *Organizational requirements*: Many global employers find that knowledge of the organization and how it operates is important.
- *Personal characteristics*: The experiences of many global firms demonstrate that the best employees in the home country may not be the best employees in a global assignment, primarily because of individuals' personal characteristics.
- *Communication skills*: Expatriate employees should be able to communicate in the host-country language, both verbally and in writing.
- *Personal and family concerns*: The preferences and attitudes of spouses and other family members can influence the success of expatriate assignments.

There are many issues that organizations face when making global selection decisions. A growing issue for U.S. firms that hire individuals to fill jobs in other countries is adequate background checks.[63] Global companies want to ensure that their employees have acceptable work histories and personal characteristics. To satisfy this demand, many firms have begun to specialize in pre-employment screening of global employees. Some countries have government-controlled employment processes that require foreign employers to obtain government approval before hiring local employees. Many countries, such as the United States and Australia, require foreign workers to obtain work permits or visas.

For U.S.-based firms, the assignment of women and members of racial/ethnic minorities to international posts involves complying with U.S. EEOC regulations and laws. Also, most U.S. EEOC regulations and laws apply to foreign-owned firms operating in the United States.

SUMMARY

- Selection is the process that matches individuals and their qualifications to jobs in an organization.
- Placement of people should consider person/job fit, person/group fit, and person/organization fit.
- Mismatches in fit can occur because of skills, geography, poor interpersonal skills, earning expectations, and work-family issues.
- Predictors linked to criteria are used to identify applicants who are most likely to perform jobs successfully.
- To comply with various legal requirements, selection decisions must be based on job-related criteria.
- To produce fair, legal selection decisions, predictors must be reliable and valid.
- The selection process—from applicant interest through pre-employment screening, application, testing, interviewing, and investigating backgrounds—must be handled by trained, knowledgeable individuals.
- Federal guidelines define the term *test* very broadly to include all forms of collecting information on job applicants.
- Application forms must meet EEO guidelines and ask only for job-related information.

- Selection tests include ability tests, assessment centers, personality tests, emotional intelligence tests, and honesty/integrity tests. Some are controversial.
- Structured interviews, including behavioral and situational types, are more effective and face fewer EEO compliance concerns than do unstructured and nondirective interviews.
- Interviews can be conducted individually, by multiple individuals, or using technology. Regardless of the method, effective job-related questioning techniques should be used.
- A candidate's background can be investigated in a variety of areas. Employers must take care to avoid potential legal concerns such as negligent hiring and negligent retention both when requesting and giving reference information.
- Checking credit history should be done only for jobs that involve handling money or finances.
- Global organizations can be staffed by individuals who are expatriates, host-country nationals, or third-country nationals.
- Selection factors for global employees include cultural adjustment, personal characteristics, communication skills, personal and family concerns, and organizational requirements.

CRITICAL THINKING CHALLENGES

1. You are the HR manager for a commercial airline. You have been assigned to develop a realistic job preview for flight attendants. Your objective is to give a balanced picture of the job so that applicants will better understand what they will be asked to do. Job duties, schedules, and other facets of the job should all be well understood early in the recruiting process to avoid poor P/E fit later on.

   A. How would you gather information about the job context and environment? Explain what sources you would use and why.

   B. How could you use technology to show the positive and negative aspects of the job?

2. Develop a work sample test to screen applicants for a college professor's job.

3. Develop a slate of six to eight behavioral interview questions to use for hiring a server for a restaurant. Review the job description on http://www.onetonline.org/ to identify essential job functions and qualifications.

4. You are preparing to train managers to recognize and overcome their inherent biases.

To prepare for this session, take the online Implicit Association Test to determine if you have any unconscious biases. You can find the test at: https://implicit.harvard.edu/implicit/.

5. How would you conduct a complete background investigation on applicants for the job of school bus driver to minimize concerns about negligent hiring?

CASE   It's All in the Family

What company wouldn't want a "leg up" in obtaining contracts for lucrative new business? Seeking to gain an advantage in the competitive world of investment banking led J.P. Morgan Chase & Company officials to seek out and hire the children of prominent Chinese officials. The individuals hired may have had the knowledge or skills needed to fulfill the jobs for which they were hired. But their most valuable qualification was something in their genes—being related to an influential member of the political or business elite in China. Having a connection to someone with decision-making authority to grant business opportunities to J.P. Morgan might have been the distinct factor that resulted in them getting the job.

The purposeful targeting of well-connected sons and daughters with the express purpose of driving business contracts might be considered bribery under federal law. The U.S. Justice Department has launched an investigation to determine if these hiring decisions violate the Foreign Corrupt Practices Act. In fact, the chief executive of J.P. Morgan's China operations voluntarily resigned. J.P. Morgan isn't alone in using such a practice. Citigroup, Goldman Sachs, Morgan Stanley, UBS, and others are also said to have done so.

Company executives at J.P. Morgan were aware of the program as well as broad anticorruption measures several years before the Securities and Exchange Commission began its investigation. Claiming that this preferential hiring is "the norm of business" in China, J.P. Morgan's top leaders believe they acted according to accepted standards. J.P. Morgan's business acquisition in China did indeed improve after it launched the selective hiring program.

The bank developed a spreadsheet detailing potential recruits along with their "valued" connections or business-enhancing prospects. They also created a special internship to accommodate some applicants who were screened less stringently than other job applicants. So, the candidates were given particular attention and a smooth path to employment. Government officials aren't stating that the employees are not qualified. They are more interested in the reason each was selected from the applicant pool. A finding that any of the banks involved intentionally hired the sons and daughters to win business might result in bribery charges.

The banks are scrutinizing their hiring practices as they respond to the government investigators' inquiries. This practice highlights differences in cultures, norms, and laws among nations. What might be considered an expected and completely acceptable practice in China might be deemed illegal—or at the very least, unethical—in the United States.[64]

QUESTIONS

1. Explain why it is or is not a good practice to consider the connections a job applicant might have that could enhance an employer's business portfolio.

2. Discuss whether targeting the children of well-connected political or business leaders is ethical.

3. Imagine that you are the Chief HR Officer for a company considering doing business in China. You have been informed that many of your competitors have implemented programs to hire the sons and daughters of influential Chinese leaders. What advice do you give to your executive leadership team? Whose interests would be most important in your policy decision?

SUPPLEMENTAL CASES

Using Data to Enhance Hiring Decisions

This case demonstrates the power of using data and statistical analysis to recruit high-quality workers who will perform well and stay with the company for a long time. (For the case, go to www.cengage .com/management/mathis.)

Strategic Selection: A Review of Two Companies

This case shows how Hallmark and United Health Group use selection as part of their strategic approach to HR. (For the case, go to www.cengage.com/management/ mathis.)

Full Disclosure on Sex Offenders?

This case investigates how Megan's Law, which specifies that all states must register all convicted sex offenders so that residents are aware of their presence in a neighborhood, generates implications about the use of criminal registries in hiring and employee management. (For the case, go to www .cengage.com/management/mathis.)

Selecting a Programmer

This case demonstrates how using a test after a pool of candidates has already been interviewed can present some difficulties. (For the case, go to www.cengage .com/management/mathis.)

END NOTES

1. Based on Lauren Weber, "When the Going Gets Tough, Job Hunters Call in the Stunt Resume," *Wall Street Journal*, January 24, 2014; Allison Linn, "Job Search Gimmicks Get Attention, Maybe Not Jobs," *Today.com*, January 30, 2013, http://www.today.com/ money/job-search-gimmicks-get-attention-maybe-not-jobs; Allison Green, "Could a Gimmick Get You a Job?" *U.S. News*, July 16, 2012, http:// www.money.usnews.com/money/blogs/ outside-voices-careers/2012/07/16/ could-a-gimmick-get-you-a-job

2. Allison Gabriel, James Diefendorff, Megan Chandler, Christina Moran, and Gary Greguras, "The Dynamic Relationships of Work Affect and Job Satisfaction with Perceptions of Fit," *Personnel Psychology* 67, no. 2 (Summer 2014), 389–420.

3. Amy Kristof-Brown, Jee Seong, David Degeest, Won-Woo Park, and Doo-Seung Hong, "Collective Fit Perceptions: A Multilevel Investigation of Person-Group Fit with Individual-Level and Team-Level Outcomes," *Journal of Organizational Behavior* 35, no. 7 (October 2014), 969–989; Jee Seong and Amy Kristof-Brown, "Testing Multidimensional Models of Person-Group Fit," *Journal of Manage-*

rial Psychology 27, no. 6 (2012), 536–556.

4. Helena Cooper-Thomas and Sarah Wright, "Person-Environment Misfit: The Neglected Role of Social Context," *Journal of Managerial Psychology* 28, no. 10 (2013), 21–37.

5. Annelies Van Vianen, J. W. Stoelhorts, and Marije DeGoede, "The Construal of Person-Organization Fit during the ASA Stages: Content, Source, and Focus of Comparison," in *Organizational Fit: Key Issues and New Directions*, edited by A. Kristof-Brown and J. Billsberry, John Wiley & Sons, 2012.

6. Ann-Kristina Lokke, "Past Absence as a Predictor of Present Absence: The Case of a Large Danish Municipality," *International Journal of Human Resource Management*, 25, no. 9 (May 2014), 1267–1280.

7. Paul Sackett, Dan Putka, and Rodney McCloy, "The Concept of Validity and the Process of Validation," in *Oxford Handbook of Personnel Assessment and Selection*, edited by Neal Schmitt, Oxford University Press, 2012.

8. Nathan Kuncel, David Klieger, Brian Connely, and Deniz Ones, "Mechanical versus Clinical Data Combination in Selection and

Admissions Decisions: A Meta-Analysis," *Journal of Applied Psychology* 98, no. 6 (2013), 1060–1072; Kate Hattrup, "Using Composite Predictors in Personnel Selection," in *Oxford Handbook of Personnel Assessment and Selection*, edited by Neal Schmitt, Oxford University Press, 2012.

9. Jesse Sostrin, "Avoid Costly Churn: Provide Candidates a Realistic Job Preview," *Entrepreneur.com*, March 28, 2014, http://www.entrepreneur .com/article/232594.

10. Dianna Stone, Kimberly Kukaszewski, Eugene Stone-Romero, and Teresa Johnson, "Factors Affecting the Effectiveness and Acceptance of Electronic Selection Systems," *Human Resource Management Review* 23 (2013), 50–70.

11. H. Kristl Davison, Catherine Maraist, R. H. Hamilton, and Mark Bing, "To Screen or Not to Screen? Using the Internet for Selection Decisions," *Employee Responsibilities and Rights Journal* 24, no. 1 (March 2012), 1–21; Jennifer Valentino-Devries, "Social Media and Bias in Hiring," *Wall Street Journal*, November 21, 2013; Dori Meinert, "Social Media Screening Leads to Hiring Discrimination," *HR Magazine*, January, 2014, p. 14.

12. David Shadovitz, "Dangers of Social-Media Screening," *HR Executive*, April 2014, p. 11; Tom Starner, "Risky Business," *HRE Online*, July 16, 2014, http://www.hreonline.com/HRE/view/story.jht ml?id=534357299&ss=tom+starner; J. William Stoughton, Lori Thompson, and Adam Meade, "Examining Applicant Reactions to the Use of Social Networking Websites in Pre-Employment Screening," *Journal of Business and Psychology*, November 2013, pp. 1–16.

13. Dana Wilkie and Alia Wright, "Balance Risks of Screening Social Media Activity," *HR Magazine*, May 2014, p. 14; Melanie Trottman, "Agency Looks Into Effect of Social Media on Jobs," *Wall Street Journal*, March 19, 2014, p. B7.

14. *HR Magazine*, "Your Resume," June 2014, p. 18.

15. Bruce Kennedy, "Don't Even Think about Lying on Your Resume," *CBSnews.com*, August 7, 2014, http://www.cbsnews.com/news/dont-even-think-about-lying-on-your-resume; Lara Walsh, "To Tell the Truth: Tales on Catching Tall Tales on Resumes," *Workforce.com*, September 30, 2014, http://www.workforce.com/articles/20813-to-tell-the-truth-tales-on-catching-tall-tales-on-rsums?v=preview.

16. Adapted from Toni Vranjes, "Pre-Verified Resumes: How Useful?" *HR Magazine*, January 2014, pp. 43–45.

17. Roy Maurer, "E-Verify Use Hits Half-Million Mark," *SHRM online*, January 27, 2014, http://www.shrm.org/hrdisciplines/global/Articles/Pages/E-Verify-Half-Million-Users.aspx; U.S. Citizenship and Immigration Services, "What's New: mE-Verify website for Workers and Jobseekers!" October 7, 2014, http://www.ucis.gov/e-verify/about-program/whatsnew.

18. Roy Maurer, "Suspect SSNs Can Now Be Locked in E-Verify," *SHRM online*, November 19, 2013, http://www.shrm.org/hrdisciplines/safetysecurity/articles/Pages/SSN-Lock-EVerify.aspx; Roy Maurer, "Employees to Be Notified of E-Verify Mismatches," *HR Magazine*, September 2013, p. 14.

19. Jean Eaglesham and Rob Barry, "Brokers Who Fail Test Have Checkered Records," *Wall Street Journal*, April 15, 2014, p. A1; Jean Eaglesham and Rob Barry, "Plan to Fix Cracks in Broker Record," *Wall Street Journal*, April 16, 2014, p. C1.

20. Jac Fitz-Enz, "Eye on Assessments," *Human Resource Executive*, November 2012, pp. 19–21; Julie McCarthy, Chad Van Iddekinge, Filip Lievens, Mei-Chuan Kung, Evan Sinar, and Michael Campion, "Do Candidate Reactions Relate to Job Performance of Affect Criterion-Related Validity? A Multistudy Investigation of Relations among Reactions, Test Scores, and Job Performance," *Journal of Applied Psychology* 98, no. 5 (2013), 701–719.

21. Melissa Korn, "Can GMAC Be More Than a B-School Exam?" *Wall Street Journal*, April 3, 2014, p. B4.

22. Philip Roth, Oh In-Sure, Maury Buster, Le Huy, Chad Van Iddekinge, Steve Robbins, and Michael Campion, "Differential Validity for Cognitive Ability Tests in Employment and Educational Settings: Not Much More Than Range Restriction?" *Journal of Applied Psychology* 99, no. 1 (January 2014), 1–20; Christopher Berry, Michael Cullen, and Jolene Meyer, "Racial/Ethnic Subgroup Differences in Cognitive Ability Test Range Restriction: Implications for Differential Validity," *Journal of Applied Psychology* 99, no. 1 (January 2014), 21–37.

23. Stephen Courtright, Brian McCormick, Bennett Postlethwaite, Cody Reeves, and Michael Mount, "A Meta-Analysis of Sex Differences in Physical Ability: Revised Estimates and Strategies for Reducing Differences in Selection Contexts," *Journal of Applied Psychology* 98, no. 4 (2013), 623–641; Michael Phillips, "Marine Corps Puts Women to the Test," *Wall Street Journal*, November 8–9, 2014, p. A1.

24. Mei-Chuan Kung, Matthew O'Connell, Esteban Trisatn, and Brian Dishman, "Simulate the Job: Predicting Accidents Using a Work Sample. *Journal of Organizational Psychology* 12, no. 3–4 (2012), 145–154; Deborah Whetzel, Michael McDaniel, and Jeffrey Pollack, *The Handbook of Work Analysis: Methods, Systems, Applications and Science of Work Measurement in Organizations*, 2012, 401–418.

25. Stefan Krumm, Filip Lievens, Joachim Huffmeier, and Anastasiya Lipnevich, "How 'Situational' is Judgment in Situational Judgment Tests?" *Journal of Applied Psychology*, August 2014, 1–18.

26. Filip Lievens and Paul Sacket, "The Validity of Interpersonal Skills Assessment via Situational Judgment Tests for Predicting Academic Success and Job Performance," *Journal of Applied Psychology* 97, no. 2 (2012), 460–468.

27. Andrew Speer, Neil Christiansen, Richard Goffin, and Maynard Goff, "Situational Bandwidth and the Criterion-Related Validity of Assessment Center Ratings: Is Cross-Exercise Convergence Always Desirable?" *Journal of Applied Psychology* 99, no. 2 (2014), 282–295; Nathan Kuncel and Paul Sackett, "Resolving the Assessment Center Construct Validity Problem (As We Know It)," *Journal of Applied Psychology* 99, no. 1 (2013), 38–47; Dan Putka and Brian Hoffman, "Clarifying the Contribution of Assessee-, Dimension-, Exercise-, and Assessor-Related Effects to Reliable and Unreliable Variance in Assessment Center Ratings," *Journal of Applied Psychology* 98, no. 1 (2013), 114–133; Elizabeth Monahan, Brian Hoffman, Charles Lance, Duncan Jackson, and Mark Foster, "Now You See Them, Now You Do Not: The Influence of Indicator-Factor Ratio on Support for Assessment Center Dimensions," *Personnel Psychology* 66 (2013), 1009–1047.

28. Bart Wille and Filip De Fruyt, "Vocations as a Source of Identity: Reciprocal Relations Between Big Five Personality Traits and RIASEC Characteristics over 15 Years," *Journal of Applied Psychology* 99, no. 2 (2014), 260–281; Bart Wille, Filip De Fruyt, and Barbara De Clercq, "Expanding and Reconceptualizing Aberrant Personality at Work: Validity of Five-Factor Model Aberrant Personality Tendencies to Predict Career Outcomes," *Personnel Psychology* 66 (2013), 173–223.

29. Jesus Sagado, Silvia Moscoso, and Alfredo Berges, "Conscientiousness, Its Facets, and the Prediction of Job Performance Ratings: Evidence of the Narrow Measures," *International Journal of Selection and Assessment*

21, no. 1 (March 2013), 74–84; Timothy Judge, Jessica Rodell, Ryan Klinger, and Lauren Simon, "Hierarchical Representations of the Five-Factor Model of Personality in Predicting Job Performance: Integrating Three Organizing Frameworks with Two Theoretical Perspectives," *Journal of Applied Psychology* 98, no. 6 (2013), 875–925.

30. Christopher Berry, Anita Kim, Ying Wang, Rebecca Thompson, and William Mobley, "Five-Factor Model Personality Measures and Sex-Based Differential Prediction of Performance," *Applied Psychology: An International Review* 62, no. 1 (January 2013), 13–43; Jonathan Shaffer and Bennett Postlethwaite, "A Matter of Context: A Meta-Analytic Investigation of the Relative Validity of Contextualized and Noncontextualized Personality Measures," *Personnel Psychology* 65 (2012), 445–494.

31. Jinyan Fan, Dingguo Gao, Sarah Carroll, Felix Lopez, T. Siva Tian, and Hui Meng, "Testing the Efficacy of a New Procedure for Reducing Faking on Personality Tests Within Selection Contexts," *Journal of Applied Psychology* 97, no. 4 (2012), 866–880; Edwin van Hooft and Marise Ph. Born, "Intentional Response Distortion on Personality Tests: Using Eye-Tracking to Understand Response Processes when Faking," *Journal of Applied Psychology* 97, no. 2 (2012), 301–316.

32. Lauren Weber and Elizabeth Dwoskin, "As Personality Tests Multiply, Employers Are Split," *Wall Street Journal*, September 30, 2014, p. A1.

33. Andrew Maul, "Examining the Structure of Emotional Intelligence at the Item Level: New Perspectives, New Conclusions," *Cognition & Emotion* 26, no. 3 (March 2012), 503–520; Oscar Ybarra, Ethan Kross, and Jeffrey Sanchez-Burks, "The 'Big Idea' That Is Yet to Be: Toward a More Motivated, Contextual, and Dynamic Model of Emotional Intelligence," *Academy of Management Perspectives* 28, no. 2 (May 2014), 98–107.

34. Nele Libbrecht, Alain de Beuckelaer, Filip Lievens, and Thomas Rockstuhl, "Measurement Invariance of the Wong and Law Emotional Intelligence Scale Scores: Does the Measurement Structure Hold across Far Eastern

and European Countries?" *Applied Psychology: An International Review* 63, no. 2 (April 2014), 223–2367.

35. Crystal Farh, Seo Myeong-Gu, and Paul Tesluk, "Emotional Intelligence, Teamwork Effectiveness, and Job Performance: The Moderating Role of Job Context," *Journal of Applied Psychology* 97, no. 4 (July 2012), 890–900; Felicia Lassk and David Shepherd, "Exploring the Relationship between Emotional Intelligence and Salesperson Creativity," *Journal of Personal Selling & Sales Management* 33, no. 1 (Winter 2013), 25–38; Ebru Aykan, "Relationships between Emotional Competence and Task-Contextual Performance of Employees," *Problems of Management in the 21st Century* 991 (2014), 8–17; Shane Nicholls, Matt Wegener, Darlene Bay, and Gail Cook, "Emotional Intelligence Tests: Potential Impacts on the Hiring Process for Accounting Students," *Accounting Education* 21, no. 1 (February 2012), 75–95.

36. Saul Fine, "Practical Guidelines for Implementing Preemployment Integrity Tests," *Public Personnel Management* 42, no. 2 (June 2013), 281–292.

37. Chad Van Iddekinge, Philip Roth, Patrick Raymark, and Heather Odle-Dusseau, "The Criterion-Related Validity of Integrity Tests: An Updated Meta-Analysis," *Journal of Applied Psychology* 97, no. 3 (2012), 499–530; Deniz Ones, Chockalingam Viswesvaran, and Frank Schmidt, "Integrity Tests Predict Counterproductive Work Behaviors and Job Performance Well: Comment on Van Iddekinge, Roth, Raymark, and Odle-Dusseau (2012)," *Journal of Applied Psychology* 97, no. 3 (2012), 537–542.

38. Adapted from Bill Roberts, "Most Likely to Succeed," *HR Magazine*, April 2014, pp. 69–71.

39. Adrian Bangerter, Nicolas Roulin, and Cornelius Konig, "Personnel Selection as a Signaling Game," *Journal of Applied Psychology* 97, no. 4 (2012), 719–738.

40. Kathryn Tyler, "Who You Gonna Call?" *HR Magazine*, April 2014, pp. 65–67.

41. Julia Levashina, Christopher Hartwell, Frederick Morgeson, and Michael Campion, "The Structured Employment Interview: Narrative and Quantitative Review of the Research

Literature," *Personnel Psychology* 67 (2014), 241–293.

42. Anne Jansen, Klaus Melchers, Filip Lievens, Martin Kleinmann, Michael Brandli, and Laura Fraeful, "Situation Assessment as an Ignored Factor in the Behavioral Consistency Paradigm underlying the Validity of Personnel Selection Procedures," *Journal of Applied Psychology* 98, no. 2 (2013), 326–341; Allen Smith, "Project-Based Interviews Spread beyond IT Industry," *SHRM online*, April 16, 2014, http://www.shrm.org/legalissues/federalresources/pages/project-based-interviews.aspx.

43. Adapted from Karla Ahern and Naomi Keller, "How to Prepare for a Job Interview," *Marketing News* 48, no. 8 (August 2014), 87; ISC Professional, "Competency-Based Interviews: The STAR Approach," http://www.interview-skills.co.uk/competency-based-interviews-STAR.aspx; Alan Carniol, "Inside the STAR Interview Approach: What You Need to Know," *Huffington Post.com*, May 21, 2013, http://www.huffingtonpost.com/alan-carniol/inside-the-star-interview_b_3310122.html.

44. SHRM, "Interviewing: When Would an Employer Use a Group Interview Technique?" *SHRM Online*, December 12, 2013, http://www.shrm.org/templatestools/hrqa/pages/whenwouldanemployeruseagroupinterviewtechnique.aspx.

45. Allen Smith, "Top Interview Do's and Don'ts," *SHRM online*, March 13, 2014, http://www.shrm.org/legalissues/federalresources/pages/interview.aspx.

46. Joann Lublin, "Do You Know Your Hidden Work Biases?" *Wall Street Journal*, January 10, 2014; Mark McGraw, "Religion on Display," *HRE Online*, July 2, 2014, http://www.hreonline.com/HRE/view/story.jhtml?id=534357282&ss=Mark+McGraw; Dana Wilkie, "Bringing Bias into the Light," *HR Magazine*, December 2014, pp. 22–27; Todd Henneman, "You, Biased? No, It's Your Brain," *Workforce*, February 2014, pp. 28–48.

47. Max Mihelich, "More 'Background' Noise," *Workforce*, September 2014, pp. 52–55.

48. Roy Maurer, "Screening the Screeners," *HR Magazine*, March 2013, p. 16.

49. Richard Brody, "Beyond the Basic Background Check: Hiring the 'Right' Employees," *Management Research Review* 33, no. 3 (2010), 210–223.

50. Jeremy Bernerth, Shannon Taylor, H. Jack Walker, and Daniel Whitman, "An Empirical Investigation of Dispositional Antecedents and Performance-Related Outcomes of Credit Scores," *Journal of Applied Psychology* 97, no. 2 (2012), 469–478; Laura Koppes Bryn and Jerry Palmer, "Do Job Applicant Credit Histories Predict Performance Appraisal Ratings or Termination Decisions?" *Psychologist-Manager Journal* 15 (2012), 106–127; Angela Preston, "Disney Sued for Misusing Background Checks," *SHRM Online*, November 20, 2013, http://www.shrm.org/hrdisciplines/safetysecurity/articles/pages/disney-sued-background-checks.aspx.

51. Adapted from Rita Zeidner, "Choices and Chances: The Dilemma of Criminal Background Screening," *HR Magazine*, June 2014, pp. 51–56; Roy Maurer, "Ban-the-Box Movement Goes Viral," *SHRM Online*, August 22, 2014, http://www.shrm.org/hrdisciplines/safetysecurity/articles/pages/ban-the-box-movement-viral.aspx; Allen Smith, "Critics of Criminal Background Check Guidance Speak at House Hearing," *SHRM Online*, June 12, 2014, http://www.shrm.org/legalissues/federalresources/pages/eeoc-oversight-hearing.aspx; Dana Wilkie, "Grants to Help Expunge Juvenile Criminal Records," *HR Magazine*, September, 2013, p. 11.

52. Stefan Groschl, "Presumed Incapable: Exploring the Validity of Negative Judgments about Persons with Disabilities and Their Employability in Hotel Operations," *Cornell Hospitality Quarterly* 54, no. 2 (May 2013), 114–123.

53. Patrick Schwedler, "Prescription Drugs and Dangerous Jobs: When Can Disclosure Be Required for Public Safety under the ADA?" *Employee Rights and Employment Policy Journal* 17, no. 1 (2013), 93–124;

Miranda Kitterlin, "Employee Attitudes Toward Pre-Employment Drug Testing in the Full-Service Restaurant Industry," *Journal of Foodservice Business Research* 16, no. 3 (July 2013), 313–326.

54. Dori Meinert, "Seeing behind the Mask," *HR Magazine*, February 2011, pp. 31–37. http://www.shrm.org/publications/hrmagazine/editorialcontent/2011/0211/pages/0211meinert.aspx.

55. Human Resource Executive, "Too Much Job-Hopping?" March 2014, p. 42; Bettina Wolf, "Is Job Hopping the New Normal?" *TD*, August 2014, p. 20; Tristan Lejeune, "Average U.S. Job Tenure Rises Slightly," *Employee Benefit News*, February 2013, p. 14.

56. Bill Leonard, "Obama Urges Employers to Hire the Long-Term Unemployed," *SHRM Online*, January 31, 2014, http://www.shrm.org/publications/hrnews/pages/obama-hire-long-term-unemployed.aspx; Bill Leonard, "Removing Barriers to Hiring the Long-Term Unemployed," *HR Magazine*, June 2014, pp. 34–40.

57. Ernie Stark and Paul Poppler, "Revisiting College Credentials as Employment Hurdles and Claims about Building Human Capital," *People & Strategy* 35, no. 3 (2012), 24–29.

58. Melissa Korn, "Job Hunt? Dig up Those SAT Scores," *Wall Street Journal*, February 26, 2014, p. B1.

59. T+D, "Employers Place Less Value on College Pedigrees," May 2014, p. 19.

60. Mike Noon, "Simply the Best? The Case for Using Threshold Selection in Hiring Decisions," *Human Resource Management Journal*, 22 (2012), 76–88.

61. In-Sue Oh, Russell Guay, Kwanghyun Kim, Crystal Harold, Jong-Hyun Lee, Chang-Goo Heo, and Kang-Hyun Shin, "Fit Happens Globally: A Meta-Analytic Comparison of the Relationships of Person-Environment Fit Dimensions with Work Attitudes and Performance across East Asia, Europe, and

North America," *Personnel Psychology* 67, no. 1 (Spring 2014), 99–152.

62. Thomas Hippler, Paula Caligiuri, Johanna Johnson, and Nataliya Baytalskaya, "The Development and Validation of a Theory-Based Expatriate Adjustment Scale," *International Journal of Human Resource Management* 25, no. 14 (2014), 1938–1959.

63. Colleen McCain Nelson, "Embassy Vetting Lapses Cited," *Wall Street Journal*, June 14–15, 2014, p. A5; Roy Maurer, "Benefits of Global Employment Screening Outweigh the Costs," *SHRM Online*, October 20, 2013, http://www.shrm.org/hrdisciplines/global/articles/pages/global-employment-screening.aspx. Eric Krell, "Forecast for Global Background Checks," *HR Magazine*, April 2013, pp. 67–69.

64. Based on Emily Glazer, Dan Fitzpatrick, and Jean Eaglesham, "J.P. Morgan Was Warned on Hiring," *Wall Street Journal*, October 23, 2014, p. C1; Dominic Rushe, "J.P. Morgan China Chief Executive Leaves as U.S. Investigation Continues," *Guardian*, March 24, 2014, http://www.theguardian.com/business/2014/mar/24/jp-morgan-china-chief-executive-investigation; Jessica Silver-Greenberg and Ben Protess, "Chinese Official Made Job Plea to J.P. Morgan Chase Chief," *New York Times*, February 9, 2014, http://dealbook.nytimes.com/2014/02/09/chinese-official-made-job-plea-to-jpmorgan-chase-chief/; Dan Ritter, "J.P. Morgan's Sons and Daughters Program: Corrupt or Just Competitive?" *Wall Street Cheat Sheet*, December 30, 2013, http://dealbook.nytimes.com/2014/02/09/chinese-official-made-job-plea-to-jpmorgan-chase-chief/; Neil Irwin, "Did J.P. Morgan Commit Bribery by Hiring the Kids of Chinese Politicians?" *Washington Post*, August 19, 2013, http://www.washingtonpost.com/blogs/wonkblog/wp/2013/08/19/did-jpmorgan-commit-bribery-by-hiring-the-kids-of-chinese-politicians/.

Talent Development

CHAPTER

8

Training Human Resources

Learning Objectives

After you have read this chapter, you should be able to:

LO1 Define training and discuss why a strategic approach is important.

LO2 Explain the major categories of training and describe instructional systems design.

LO3 Identify three types of analyses used to determine training needs.

LO4 Specify how to design a training program for adult learners.

LO5 Explain different means of internal and external training delivery.

LO6 Provide an example for each of the four levels of training evaluation.

WHAT'S TRENDING IN

TRAINING

Ensuring that workers are capable of fulfilling job responsibilities and contributing to the organization's success is a major focus of training initiatives. The ever-changing business environment creates some exciting challenges regarding how companies maintain and upgrade workers' knowledge and skills. Current aspects of the business environment impact training in the following ways.

1. The explosion in technology has led to dramatic changes in how companies deliver training. The process of learning "on the go" in brief, accessible modules is starting to replace more traditional methods.
2. Viewing training as an investment rather than a cost changes what leaders and executives expect from training programs. The introduction of data analytics offers trainers the opportunity to prove the value of training with solid data and metrics.
3. Ongoing skill gaps are being identified between what is needed to perform today's jobs and the lack of qualified people to fill them. Nearly half of the executives of U.S. firms cite skill gaps as a major source of concern for their organization.
4. Tracking and recognizing employees' learning achievements highlights the importance of skill and knowledge acquisition to both employers and employees. Companies are finding ways to reward employees with virtual badges and other forms of recognition for completing training programs.[1]

Training Impacts Bottom Line

WakeMed health system in North Carolina is a shining example of how training can deliver mission-critical skills and positively impact the bottom line. The organization's four education departments provide over 160,000 hours of training annually, which represents an investment of over $2 million. This commitment starts with the board of directors, who specify learning needs during the annual strategic planning process.

A critical business issue facing many health care providers has been the transition from paper to electronic patient records. At WakeMed, this involves over 230,000 patients in the emergency department, 7,700 babies delivered, and over 327,000 patients treated by specialty care physicians. This obviously creates an immense volume of records. To successfully transfer all the records required training for both clinical and nonclinical staff. The solution was to utilize multiple methods—including online modules, instructor-led classes, self-paced learning, and computer-based training—that were delivered 24/7 to accommodate workers' schedules. The system will go live in the near future, but WakeMed is confident that up-front training will ease the transition.

In further pursuit of continuous improvement, WakeMed tackled a key patient care need—transporting critically ill heart patients from rural areas to city-based emergency centers. The training team created a simulation-based learning program that uses a patient simulator named Sam. Sam weighs 160 pounds and costs $75,000. He is capable of breathing, blinking, and dying, and he can be given a wide variety of treatments. During the simulation, the care team assesses Sam's condition based on over 1,000 data points. They order helicopter transport since it reduces the two-hour ambulance trip to a half hour. En route to the hospital, the simulator

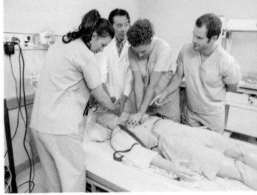
Tyler Olson/Shutterstock.com

provides scenarios to which the care team must respond in order to stabilize and save Sam. During a post-simulation debrief, the care team identifies areas where additional education and training were needed to keep Sam alive.

WakeMed's training initiatives have helped the health care system decrease patient mortality rates, prevent delays in care, and improve efficiency. They also address a business goal of increasing the number of cardiac patients who come to WakeMed for treatment. Now that's the way to show that training pays off.[2]

Businesses rely on capable, energized workers to survive because the environment in which they must compete changes. Talent development efforts are critical activities focused on building employee competence and commitment. If employees stagnate, their skills become obsolete, and companies can lose their competitive edge. Taking both a short- and long-term approach, talent development programs help employees succeed in their present jobs and prepare for growth opportunities in the future. In this chapter, we focus on training, the short-term focus. In Chapter 9, we take the long-term view and address development programs. Chapter 10 discusses the critical role of performance management. These three elements of talent development work together to provide the competencies needed for individual and organization success.

Training
Process whereby people acquire capabilities to perform jobs

Training is the process whereby people acquire capabilities to perform jobs. Training provides employees with specific, identifiable knowledge and skills for use in their present jobs. Organizational training may include "hard" skills, such as teaching sales representatives how to use intranet resources, showing a branch manager how to review an income statement, or helping a machinist apprentice learn how to set up a drill press. "Soft" skills are critical in many instances and can be taught as well. These skills include communicating, mentoring, managing a meeting, and working as part of a team.

Companies use a wide range of delivery methods to build workers' skills. As with many human resource programs, there is rarely one best way to deliver training. Hands-on approaches along with technology-based solutions can work effectively based on the content to be learned, the learner's current skill level, budget considerations, and many other factors. Each organization tries to obtain the greatest value for its training investment. This has led to many innovations and changes in the training arena. Training and development is a specialty field within the human resource discipline. There is a specific professional association, the Association for Talent Development, devoted to the practice of developing employees. The organization recently changed its name from the American Society for Training and Development to reflect the broader scope of activities within the field of talent development.[3]

LO1 Define training and discuss why a strategic approach is important.

8-1 Organizational Strategy and Training

Training represents a significant expenditure for most employers. However, it has historically been viewed tactically rather than strategically, which means that training is seen as a short-term activity rather than one that has longer-term effects on organizational success. There was some shift in the perceptions of training's value during the last recession. For example, some companies continued to provide training that was necessary for long-term strategic goals rather than simply eliminating all training commitments.

8-1a Strategic Training

Training can indeed help an organization accomplish its goals. For example, if increasing sales revenue is a critical part of the company's strategy, appropriate training would identify what is causing lower sales and recommend a solution. For maximum impact, HR and training professionals should get involved with the business and partner with operating managers to help solve their problems. Addressing strategic issues and helping the company develop business-critical skills, competencies, and processes will add value in a way that simply training to "run the business as usual" cannot.[4] Additionally, treating training strategically can help reduce the tendency of managers to think that training alone can solve most employee or organizational problems. With a strategic focus, the organization is more likely to assess whether training can actually address these issues and what else might be done. Training alone cannot fix all organizational problems.

A strategic decision by Walt Disney Company exemplifies how to use training strategically. Recognizing that animation artists were exceptionally difficult to find, Disney managers created the Character Animation Program World. Aspiring animators could study under the guidance of retired animation experts. Thus, the program created the sustainability Disney needed to continue producing the animation feature films that made it famous.[5] Only a long-term outlook on training leads managers to such solutions.

However, not *all* training is effective. Only one-quarter of respondents to a McKinsey survey said their training programs measurably improved business performance, and most companies don't measure training effectiveness. Most simply ask whether participants liked the training or not.[6] To be a strategic investment, training must align with company goals and contribute to the achievement of key performance indicators. In other words, it must produce positive results.

8-1b Investing in Training

Investment in employee training is significant. Recent research shows that workers receive an average of 31.5 hours per year in training, an investment valued at $1,208 per employee. Training costs typically make up about 2% of the cost of payroll. Figure 8-1 shows that companies are investing more now than in years past. Surprisingly, companies with fewer than 500 employees invest more per employee than larger companies do. This is likely because the significant fixed costs of developing training programs are spread across fewer employees.[7]

Training investments vary by industry, as well as by company size. Highly regulated industries like finance, insurance, banking, real estate, and health care all tend to invest more in training than manufacturing companies. This is also reflected in the content areas for training investments. Mandatory and compliance training is the number one content domain companies provide.[8]

Companies invest in training with the expectation that results will improve. Training focused on individual performance and capability should lead to enhanced skills, greater ability to adapt and innovate, better self-management, and performance improvement. Organization-wide improvements should be

FIGURE 8-1 Annual Training Expenditure per Employee, 2006–2013

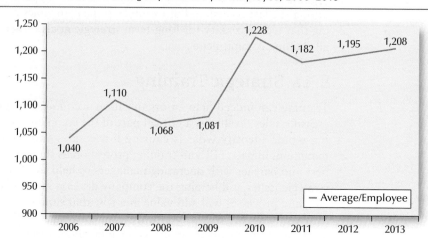

Source: Adapted from Association for Talent Development (ASTD), 2014 State of the Industry Report.

seen in lower employee turnover, improvements in effectiveness and productivity, more profitability and reduced costs, improved quality and customer service, and increased human capital.[9]

8-1c Organizational Competitiveness and Training

AT&T, General Mills, Accenture, McDonald's, IBM, and Procter & Gamble all emphasize the importance of training employees and managers. These companies and others recognize that training efforts can be integral to business success because it is similar to the continuous improvement process utilized in some manufacturing firms. The assumption is that training allows an organization to improve over time by increasing employees' knowledge and skills.

The nature of technological innovation and change is such that if employees are not continually trained, they may fall behind, and the company could become less competitive. Without ongoing training, organizations may not have staff members with the knowledge, skills, and abilities (KSAs) needed to compete effectively.[10]

Training can also affect organizational competitiveness by boosting retention of employees. One reason many individuals choose to stay with or leave organizations is the availability of career training and development opportunities. Employers who invest in training and developing their employees may enhance employee retention.[11] Figure 8-2 shows how training may help accomplish certain organizational strategies.

Knowledge Management For much of history, competitive advantage among organizations was measured in terms of physical capital. However, as the information age has evolved, knowledge and information have become the raw material that many organizations make and sell through their workers. Knowledge management is the way an organization identifies and leverages knowledge to be competitive.[12] It is the art of creating value by using intellectual capital, which is what the organization (or, more exactly, the people in the organization) knows. Knowledge management is a conscious effort to capture the explicit and tacit knowledge of the workers in the organization so that it can be shared and enhanced. Gathering, storing, and

Knowledge management
The way an organization identifies and leverages knowledge to be competitive

FIGURE 8-2 Linking Strategies and Training

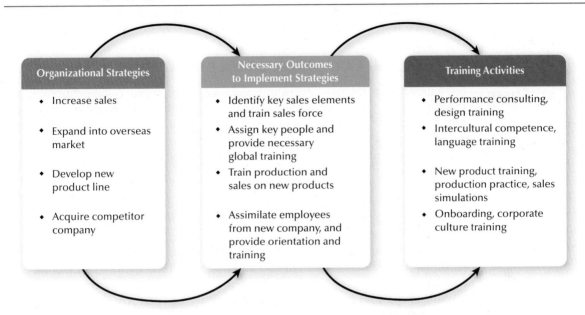

using the collective knowledge of employees is especially important in global companies. Sharing the nuances of intercultural business practices can save money and improve customer relationships.[13]

Integration of Performance with Training Job performance, training, and employee learning must be integrated to be effective. Organizations find that training experiences that use real business problems to advance employee learning are better than approaches that do not. Rather than separating the training experience from the context of actual job performance, trainers can incorporate everyday business issues as learning examples, thus increasing the realism of training exercises and scenarios. For example, as part of management training at General Electric, managers are given actual business problems to solve, and they must present their solutions to business leaders. Using real situations for practice is yet another way of merging the lines between training, learning, and job performance.

Sales Training Organizational competitiveness in many industries hinges on the success of the sales function. Innovative products or services do not magically find customers—they require well-trained professional salespeople to inform the appropriate audience. A key element in sales force success is often the training opportunities available. While over $5 billion is spent each year on sales training, the average learner retains only 20% of the content one month after training.[14]

Organizations frequently conduct their primary sales training efforts as large annual or biannual events. This is an expensive method of training because of travel costs, instruction costs, and reduced sales hours during training. Salespeople are often social beings, and an event that provides for sharing experiences with peers is usually well received. However, a mix of other approaches can cut costs and can also be effective. Mobile technologies, simulations, podcasts, e-learning, self-paced learning, and virtual coaching can all be used to leverage sales training. Using such technologies presents some challenges to trainers who must develop them but offers flexibility and opportunity if done well.[15] Salespeople need a mix of product training and interpersonal sales training to be successful.

GLOBAL

8-1d Global Competitiveness and Training

For a global firm, the most brilliant strategies will not improve competitiveness unless the company has well-trained employees throughout the world to carry them out. A global look at training is important as firms establish and expand operations worldwide. For U.S. employers, the challenge has increased because of the decline in specialized skilled and technical workers. Considering the number of global employees with international assignments, training is part of global competitive success.[16]

Global Assignment Training The orientation and training that expatriates and their families receive before departure significantly affect the success of an overseas assignment. When these programs are offered, most expatriates participate in them, which usually positively affects cross-cultural adjustment. Also, training helps expatriates and their families adjust to and deal with their counterparts in the host country. A recent survey showed that when companies provide generous expatriate training, those who participate adjust more easily and perform better when placed on assignment in the workplace.[17]

A related issue is the promotion and transfer of foreign citizens to positions in the United States. For example, many Japanese firms operating in the United States conduct training programs to prepare Japanese employees and their families for the food, customs, labor and HR practices, and other facets of working and living in the United States. Companies around the globe are recognizing the importance of preparing workers for overseas assignments and are offering training to smooth the transition.

Intercultural Competence Training Global employers are providing intercultural competence training for employees sent abroad and those who manage workers in multiple countries. Intercultural competence incorporates a wide range of human social skills and personality characteristics. As noted in Figure 8-3, three

FIGURE 8-3 Intercultural Competence Training

Component	Possible Training
Cognitive	• Culture-specific training (traditions, history, cultural customs, etc.) • Language course
Emotional	• *Uneasiness:* Social skills training focusing on new, unclear, and intercultural situations • *Prejudices:* Coaching may be clarifying • *Sensitivity:* Communication skills course (active listening, verbal/nonverbal cues, empathy)
Behavioral	• Culture Assimilator method • International projects • Social skills training focusing on intercultural situations

Source: Developed by Andrea Graf, PhD, and Robert L. Mathis, PhD, SPHR.

components of intercultural competence require attention when training expatriates for global assignments:

- *Cognitive*: What does the person know about other cultures?
- *Emotional*: How does the person view other cultures, and how sensitive is the person to cultural customs and issues?
- *Behavioral*: How does the person act in intercultural situations?

Of particular importance is providing training to managers who oversee workers in several countries. Training includes educating managers to recognize how the various laws, customs, and practices in each nation impact manager–employee relationships. There are a number of assessments that help managers obtain a personal profile of their approach to other cultures. The following "HR Competencies & Applications: Assessing Cultural Competence" feature explains several ways that companies measure the level of skills managers have when managing across cultures.

The complexities of multinational operations mean that companies large and small are likely to be dealing with workers, customers, and suppliers from different cultures. Building the capacity for all employees to work smoothly with diverse individuals is frequently done through diversity training, which is discussed in Chapter 3.

LO2 Explain the major categories of training and describe instructional systems design.

8-2 Training and Human Resources

There are several driving forces behind training initiatives. For instance, some training is done to comply with legal mandates. Other training is not required by law but is necessary for efficient operation of an organization. A particular type of training, orientation and onboarding, is becoming more critical to get new employees integrated into the organization and working productively as quickly as possible.

8-2a Legal Issues and Training

Some legal issues must be considered when designing and delivering training. One concern centers on the criteria and practices used to select individuals for inclusion in training programs. Since training can be an opportunity to advance in the organization, considering only job-related factors that do not result in disparate impact is important. Also, failure to accommodate individuals with disabilities in training can expose organizations to equal employment opportunity (EEO) lawsuits. Using psychological assessments to identify soft skills like emotional intelligence falls under the Uniform Guidelines and must be validated.[18]

Another legal issue involves requiring employees to sign *training contracts* to protect the costs and time invested in specialized employee training. For instance, an employee of Wells Fargo recently filed suit when the company tried to recoup more than $50,000 in training costs after she resigned. She had not completed the five-year program when she left. To encourage retention, it is common practice for large brokerage firms to include "clawback" provisions in their adviser training programs. In this case, the employee was earning less than the demanded amount, which she claims is a violation of wage laws. The case is being watched for its impact on training contracts.[19]

COMPETENCIES & APPLICATIONS

Assessing Cultural Competence

To help managers understand their present levels of cultural competence, many organizations use assessment questionnaires. After a manager completes the questionnaire, feedback is provided along with helpful resources and tips for improving areas that are weak. There are a variety of instruments, each with its own framework for elements of cultural competence. HR and training professionals can select the instrument that most appropriately measures what is important to the organization. Here are brief descriptions of four instruments.

One useful tool is the Multicultural Personality Questionnaire, which measures individuals on intercultural sensitivity, intercultural communication, intercultural relationship building, conflict management, leadership, and tolerance of ambiguity. Employees can complete the survey and learn how well-suited they are for international assignments. They can then create an action plan to strengthen areas of weakness so that they are better able to handle work in a global setting.[20]

There are alternative assessments that measure cultural awareness and adjustment. The International Profiler measures 10 competencies, including openness, flexibility, perceptiveness, and cultural knowledge. The Profiler is specifically designed as a development tool. With 10 competencies, it can become overwhelming to understand. Therefore, good coaching and interpretation are important for maximum benefit.

The Cultural Intelligence Scale looks at four factors: drive, knowledge, strategy, and action that relate to an individual's ability to manage within diverse cultures. The questions measure "cultural intelligence," or what the developers consider an individual's ability to function effectively in various cultural situations. The Scale helps employees understand how well they would adjust to new situations and function in unfamiliar settings.

Last, the Cross-Cultural Kaleidoscope is an awareness-building tool that helps employees evaluate the internal and external factors that form their cultural understanding. The instrument measures the individual's thoughts, feelings, and emotions related to cultural identity. This is followed with an assessment of the legal, political, economic, geographic, climate, and history factors related to the country where one lives. Reconciling one's personal sense of culture and seeing how it is influenced by outside forces can help employees put culture into perspective.

Clearly, there are many techniques organizations can use to identify the cultural profile of managers and other employees. The costs of assigning an individual who is not culturally ready to deal with diverse employee groups are significant. Training and coaching are important add-ons after an employee has completed an assessment. Assessments are a starting point, not the end of cultural awareness.[21] Consider the following questions about assessing cultural competence:

1. How would you recommend that organization leaders select from among the various assessment choices? What criteria would you use to evaluate each instrument?

2. What steps would you take to get the maximum benefit from cultural assessments? Do you believe that there is more to it than administering the instrument and providing results to each respondent?

KEY COMPETENCIES: Global & Cultural Effectiveness, Consultation; HR Expertise: Workplace/HR In the Global Context, Diversity & Inclusion

Finally, the Department of Labor has ruled that nonexempt employees who are training outside normal working hours (e.g., at home by completing web-based classes) must be compensated for their time. This is particularly challenging if employees access online training courses during off-duty hours.

A number of industries mandate extensive and ongoing training for employees. For example, the health care industry must train employees in confidentiality practices in addition to changes brought about by the Affordable Care Act.[22] The insurance and financial services industries also require employers to provide training specific to industry regulations.

Several federal laws either explicitly or implicitly require companies to train their employees. The Occupational Safety and Health Administration (OSHA) has extensive mandates for employee safety training. EEO laws strongly urge employers to provide training regarding harassment prevention, diversity, and inclusion. Supervisory staff should receive training to ensure that their decisions and actions comply with the complex array of employment laws. Accurate recordkeeping related to required training is important to demonstrate that the company is meeting its obligations.

8-2b Training Categories

Training can be designed to meet many objectives and can be classified in various ways. As Figure 8-4 shows, some common groupings of training include the following:

- *Legally required training*: Complies with various mandated legal requirements (e.g., OSHA and EEO) and is given to all employees upon hire along with periodic refreshers

FIGURE 8-4 Types of Training

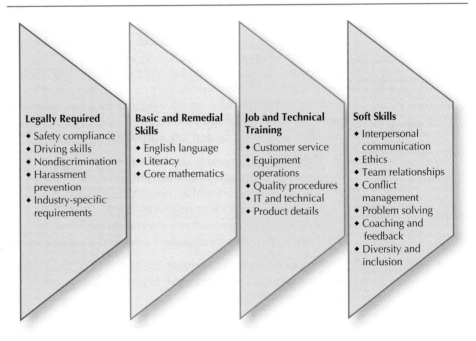

Legally Required
- Safety compliance
- Driving skills
- Nondiscrimination
- Harassment prevention
- Industry-specific requirements

Basic and Remedial Skills
- English language
- Literacy
- Core mathematics

Job and Technical Training
- Customer service
- Equipment operations
- Quality procedures
- IT and technical
- Product details

Soft Skills
- Interpersonal communication
- Ethics
- Team relationships
- Conflict management
- Problem solving
- Coaching and feedback
- Diversity and inclusion

- *Basic and remedial skills training*: Provides foundation skills that new employees may lack (e.g., literacy, English language proficiency)
- *Job and technical training*: Enables employees to perform their jobs better (e.g., product knowledge, technical processes and procedures, customer relations)
- *Soft skills training*: Improves organizational working relationships (e.g., interpersonal communication, conflict resolution) and the organization's culture (e.g., ethics)

Companies typically provide training in each of these categories. Training dollars are allocated based on what each organization determines are its greatest needs. For companies with many low-skill, low-wage jobs, fluency in English and basic literacy may be primary needs.[23] Basic job skills frequently are a high priority to ensure that employees are competent in critical thinking, listening, financial literacy, time management, and decision-making skills.[24] Finally, the future workplace will demand greater proficiency with soft skills such as adaptability, innovation, creativity, and emotional intelligence. Companies seeking to remain competitive are now providing training in these vital skills.[25]

8-2c New Employee Orientation/Onboarding

Orienting new employees is essential to prepare them to perform on the job as quickly as possible. Also called *onboarding*, orientation is the most important and widely conducted type of regular training provided for new employees.

Orientation

Planned introduction of new employees to their jobs, coworkers, and the organization

Orientation, which is the planned introduction of new employees to their jobs, coworkers, and the organization, is offered by most employers. It requires cooperation between the HR unit and operating managers and supervisors.[26] In a small organization without an HR department, the new employee's supervisor or manager usually assumes most of the responsibility for orientation.[27] In large organizations, managers and supervisors, as well as the HR department, often work as a team to orient new employees. Unfortunately, without good planning, new employee orientation sessions can come across as boring, irrelevant, and a waste of time to both new employees and their department supervisors and managers. But well-designed and delivered orientation can be very effective.

Among the decisions to be made when planning for new employee orientation are *what* to present and *when* to present it. Too much information on the first day leads to perceptions of ineffective onboarding. Several shorter sessions over a longer period of time, bringing in information as it is needed, are more effective. Effective orientation achieves several key purposes:

- Establishes a favorable employee impression of the organization and the job
- Provides organization and job information
- Enhances interpersonal acceptance by coworkers and builds the new employee's network of resources
- Accelerates socialization and integration of the new employee into the organization
- Ensures that employee performance and productivity begin more quickly

Since employers and employees both benefit from a successful onboarding process, it's important to get it right. Figure 8-5 shows key principles related to creating an effective onboarding process.

FIGURE 8-5 Elements of Effective Onboarding

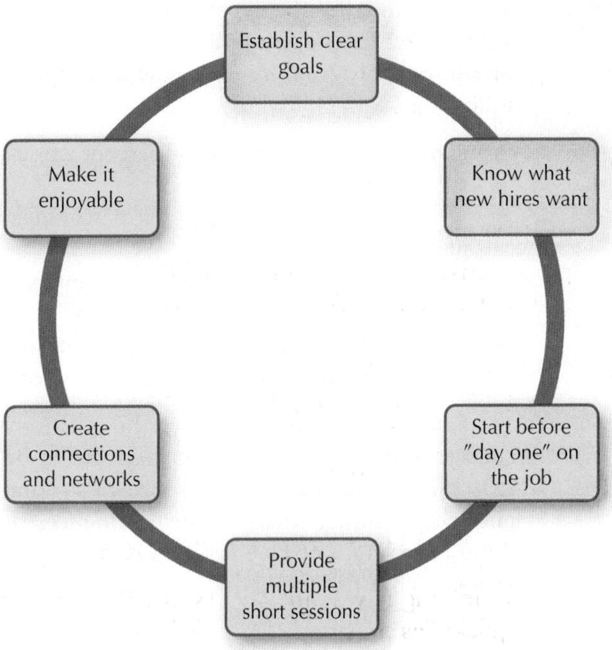

Source: Adapted from Dan Steer, "Onboard with It All," *T+D*, November 2013, pp. 26–29; Carmen Nobel, "First Minutes Are Critical in New-Employee Orientation," *HBS Working Knowledge*, April 1, 2013, http://hbswk.hbs.edu/item/7193.html.

Electronic Orientation Resources One way to improve the efficiency of orientation is to use electronic resources. Most employers have implemented some kind of electronic onboarding activities to improve their employee orientation efforts.[28] Employers can place general employee orientation information on company intranets or corporate websites. New employees log on and review much of the general material on organizational history, structure, products and services, mission, and other background information, instead of sitting in a classroom where the information is delivered in person or by video. Questions and concerns can be addressed by HR staff and others after employees have reviewed the web-based information.

Other organizations may use electronic resources a bit differently. At one company, when candidates accept an offer, they get an email with a link to a password-protected website that welcomes them. From home, they fill out their I-9, W-2, and other forms on that website. Before reporting to work, they get daily emails explaining where to park, where to get uniforms, and where to drop off their dry cleaning. Assigning a desk, getting a computer and security clearance, and many other orientation tasks are all done before the first day on the job by electronic onboarding. Using the interactive features of digital onboarding can make the process more engaging and informative. It can also create excitement for new employees.

MEASURE

8-2d Orientation: Evaluation and Metrics

To determine the effectiveness of an orientation training program, evaluation using specific metrics is appropriate. Measurement should address the success of both the orientation program *and* the new hires themselves. Suggested metrics include the following:[29]

- *Tenure turnover rate*: What percentage of new hires left the organization in six months or less?
- *New hires failure factor*: What percentage of the total annual turnover was new hires?
- *Employee upgrade rate*: What percentage of new employees received a high performance rating?
- *Development program participation rate*: What percentage of new employees have moved on to training for or promotion to higher jobs?

Successfully integrating new hires is important, and measuring the degree of success allows the orientation program to be managed well. The way in which a firm plans, organizes, and structures its training affects the way employees experience the training, which in turn influences the effectiveness of the training. After good planning, effective training requires the use of a systematic training process. Using such a process reduces the likelihood that unplanned, uncoordinated, and haphazard training efforts will occur without wasting valuable resources.

8-3 Instructional Systems Design

The overall goal of training efforts is to change and/or improve employee behavior. Employees may participate in training because of a knowledge or skill gap, changes in company processes, or performance problems. In all cases, the hope is that after completing the training, employees will perform their jobs better than they did before the training. To ensure that training delivers the hoped-for behavior changes, it is critical to systematically create and deliver training.[30]

Effective training does not begin the minute trainees walk into the training center and take their seats. Good training includes focused activities before, during, and after the actual training session. The better the upfront planning is, the better the actual training is likely to be. This planning helps the organization identify what is needed for employee performance *before* training begins so that there is better alignment between training and strategic needs. Then the follow-up after training brings the process full circle to determine how performance has been impacted.[31]

An orderly approach to training follows a purposeful process called instructional systems design. Instructional systems design (ISD) is a step-by-step process to ensure that the right learning materials are provided to the right people at the right time.[32] A popular model called the ADDIE framework (see Figure 8-6) is often used to explain this process. The ADDIE model includes five key phases:[33]

Instructional systems design (ISD)
A step-by-step process to ensure that the right learning materials are provided to the right people at the right time

- *Assessment*: The performance problem or issue is clarified, resource budgets are determined, and the learning environment and learner's existing knowledge and skills are identified.
- *Design*: Macro-level phase where learning objectives and media selection are determined.

FIGURE 8-6 ADDIE Model of Systematic Instructional Design Process

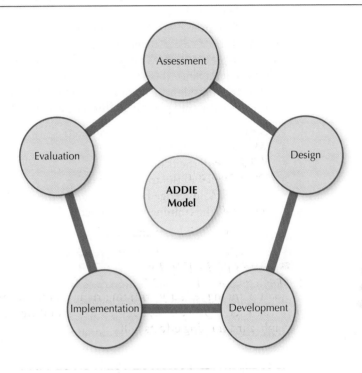

- *Development*: Micro-level phase where content is solidified, instructional materials are created, and pilot tested.
- *Implementation/Delivery*: Training is delivered to target audience.
- *Evaluation*: Assessments and measures are taken to determine the effectiveness of the training.

Each of the important phases of the model is presented in the following sections. While there are five distinct phases to the ISD process, in most cases, the phases overlap. Although the process appears to be linear, it is actually iterative. It is common to recycle back to an earlier phase when information is uncovered at later stages. For example, during the implementation phase, a trainer may discover that the needs assessment did not properly identify the specific content learners need to know. Then a brief reassessment might occur to get the training back on track.[34]

LO3 Identify three types of analyses used to determine training needs.

8-4 Training Needs Assessment

Assessing organizational training needs is the diagnostic phase of a training plan. This assessment includes issues related to employee and organizational performance to determine if training can help. Needs assessment measures the competencies of a company, a group, or an individual as they relate to what is required. It is necessary to find out what is happening and what should be happening before deciding if training will help, and if so, what kind of training is needed. Identifying gaps in performance is key to the assessment process. For instance, suppose the frequency of accidents in a manufacturing plant has increased from previous levels. Managers might review a wide range of possible causes such as changes in procedures, equipment malfunctions, increased production requirements, and worker capabilities. A thorough needs assessment will help managers zero in on the specific reasons for the increase in accidents. Training may be identified as one of the possible solutions to the problem. Since the organization has historical records of accident frequency, it will be fairly straightforward to determine the impact of the training.

Effective training planning efforts consider the following questions:

- Is there really a need for the training?
- Who needs to be trained?
- Who will do the training?
- What form will the training take?
- How will knowledge be transferred to the job?
- How will the training be evaluated?

8-4a Analysis of Training Needs

The first step in assessing training needs is analyzing what training might be necessary. Figure 8-7 shows the three sources used to analyze training needs.

Organizational Analysis Training needs can be diagnosed by analyzing organizational outcomes and looking at future organizational needs. A part of planning for training is identifying the KSAs that will be needed now and in the future as both jobs and the organization change. Both internal and external forces will influence training and must be considered when doing organizational analysis. For instance, the problems posed by the technical obsolescence of current employees and an insufficiently educated labor pool from which to draw new workers should be confronted and incorporated into the training design.

Organizational analysis comes from various measures of organizational performance. Departments or areas with high turnover, customer complaints, high grievance rates, high absenteeism, low performance, and other deficiencies can be pinpointed. Following the identification of problems, objectives can be developed if training is a solution. During organizational analysis, managerial focus groups can be conducted to evaluate changes and performance that might require training.

Job/Task Analysis A second level of analyzing training needs involves reviewing the jobs and tasks performed. Comparing worker skills in a job category to the skills

FIGURE 8-7 Sources of Information for Needs Assessment

Organization Analysis	Job/Task Analysis	Individual Analysis

• Grievances   • Observations
• Accidents   • Customer
• Waste/scrap   complaints
• Training   • Exit interviews
  observations • Equipment use
  • Attitude surveys
	• Employee • Job
	  KSAs specifications
	• Benchmarks • Efficiency data
	• Effectiveness • Employees
	    surveys
		• Performance • Questionnaires
		  appraisals • Surveys
		• Tests • Job knowledge
		• Records tools
		• Assessment
		  centers

needed for successful job performance can identify gaps that can be filled by training. For example, at a manufacturing firm, analysis identified the tasks performed by engineers who served as technical instructors for other employees. By listing the tasks required of a technical instructor, HR established a program to teach specific instructional skills, and the engineers were able to become more successful instructors.

Another way to pinpoint training gaps in the job or task being done is to survey employees and have them anonymously evaluate the current skill levels of themselves and their peers. This not only identifies job needs but also heightens employees' awareness of their own learning needs. A training needs survey can take the form of questionnaires or interviews with supervisors and employees individually or in groups. Web-based surveys, requests, and other inputs from managers and employees can be used to identify training needs for jobs.

A good example of needs assessment for a particular job occurred in the construction industry where there was a rash of accidents among Spanish-speaking construction workers. Construction companies recognized the need for training in English as a second language for many people. Restaurants, hospitals, and hotels have faced the same issue for a variety of jobs that employ diverse individuals.

Individual Analysis The third means of diagnosing training needs focuses on individuals and how they perform their jobs. The most common approach for making individual analysis involves using performance appraisal data. In some instances, a good HR information system can be used to identify individuals who require training in specific areas to be eligible for promotion. To assess training needs through the performance appraisal process, a supervisor first determines an employee's performance strengths and inadequacies in a formal review. Then the supervisor can design training to help the employee overcome the weaknesses and enhance the strengths. Tests can be a good means of individual-level analysis. For example, a police officer might take a qualification test with his or her service pistol every six months to indicate his or her current skill level. If an officer cannot qualify, training would certainly be necessary.

Another way of assessing individual training needs is to use both managerial and nonmanagerial (or peer) input about the kind of training that is needed. Individuals can also identify their own training needs.[35] Obtaining this kind of input can be useful in building support for the training from those who will be trained, particularly because they are well positioned to help identify training needs.

8-4b Establishing Training Objectives and Priorities

Once training requirements have been identified using needs analyses, training objectives and priorities can be established by a "gap analysis," which indicates the distance between where an organization is with its employee capabilities and where it needs to be. To close the gap, training objectives and priorities are then determined.[36] Three possible focuses for training objectives can be

- *Knowledge*: Imparting cognitive information and details to trainees (e.g., understanding how a new product works)
- *Skill*: Developing behavioral changes in how jobs and various task requirements are performed (e.g., improving speed on an installation)
- *Attitude*: Creating interest in and awareness of the importance of something (e.g., sexual harassment training)

The success of training should be measured in terms of the objectives that were set before it took place. When creating learning objectives, it is helpful to start at the end by specifying what a learner should be able to do after completing the training. This type of thinking guides the design and development of the training. Another key consideration is that useful objectives are measurable. For example, an objective for a new sales clerk might be to *demonstrate the ability to explain the function of each product in the department within two weeks*. This objective is specific and can be evaluated by the trainer or the employee's supervisor.

Most organizations do not have an unlimited amount of valuable resources such as time and money. Training competes with other HR and non-HR programs to secure financial and time support from the organization's leaders.[37] Since training is seldom an unlimited budget item and because organizations have multiple training needs, prioritization is necessary. Ideally, management looks at training needs in relation to strategic plans and as part of the organizational change process. Then training needs can be prioritized on the basis of objectives. Conducting the training most needed to improve organizational performance will produce visible results more quickly.

LO4 Specify how to design a training program for adult learners.

8-5 Training Design

Once training objectives have been established, the design of training can begin. Whether job-specific or broader in nature, training must be established to address the specific objectives. Effective training design considers the learners and instructional strategies, as well as how to maximize the transfer of training from class to the job site.

Working in organizations should be a continual learning process. Different approaches are possible because learning is a complex psychological process. For the training design to be effective and produce learning, each of the elements shown in Figure 8-8 must be considered.

FIGURE 8-8 Training Design Elements

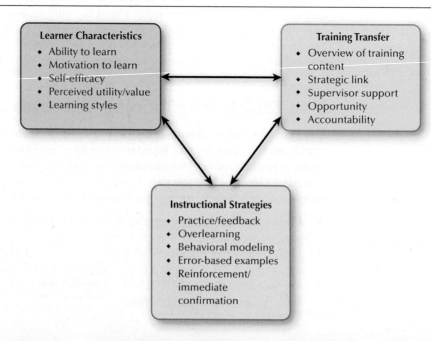

8-5a Learner Characteristics

For training to be successful, learners must be ready and able to learn. Learner readiness means that individuals have the ability to learn. However, individuals also must have the motivation to learn, have high confidence, see value in learning, and have a learning style that fits the training.

Ability to Learn Learners must possess basic skills, such as fundamental reading or math proficiency, and sufficient cognitive abilities. Companies may discover that some workers lack the cognitive ability to comprehend their training. Some have found that a significant number of job applicants and current employees lack the reading, writing, and math skills needed to learn the jobs. Employers might deal with the lack of basic employee skills in several ways:

- Offer remedial training to existing employees who need it.
- Test and hire workers who already have the necessary skills.
- Work with local schools to help better educate potential hires for jobs.

When designing training, it is important to identify the foundation skills needed for learners to grasp the material. Learners who lack the basic skills will be frustrated during training and are likely to retain little, if any, of the content. Therefore, it is critical to specify the entry level KSAs for success in the training program.

Motivation A person's desire to learn training content, referred to as *motivation to learn*, is influenced by multiple factors. For example, differences in gender and ethnicity, and the resulting experiences, may affect the motivation of adult learners. Some learners approach learning from an achievement perspective. Their primary goal is to "pass the test" or earn a certificate of completion. Their outlook is short term and is focused on completing the training and moving on. Other learners adopt a learning perspective. Their primary objective is to master the training content. They may not earn the highest grade in a course, but they are likely to retain more of the content. They will practice, seek feedback, and take other steps to truly learn the material.[38] Regardless of their motivations, without some drive to learn, those in a training program will not put forth the effort to succeed in training.

Some companies offer incentives to workers who complete training. Hudson Trail Outfitters, an outdoor gear retailer, discovered that employees are more motivated to complete training when they receive gear or clothing instead of monetary rewards. Dunkin' Donuts awards its employees points that can be traded in for merchandise. JetBlue and Deloitte use digital "badges" similar to Girl Scout and Boy Scout badges to designate employees who have mastered specific training content. The success of these programs is due to their alignment with each organization's culture and philosophy. Finding rewards or incentives that fit an organization's way of doing business is the secret to motivating employees to learn.[39]

Self-efficacy
People's belief that they can successfully learn the training program content

Self-Efficacy Learners must possess self-efficacy, which refers to people's belief that they can successfully learn the training program content. For learners to be ready for and receptive to the training content, they must believe that it is possible for them to learn the material. As an example, many college students have varying levels of self-efficacy depending on the domain being studied. Self-efficacy is a perception that may have nothing to do with one's actual ability to learn; rather, it reflects the way we see ourselves and our abilities.[40] Since people who believe strongly that they can learn perform better and are more satisfied with the training they receive, instructors and trainers must find appropriate ways to boost the confidence of trainees who are unsure of their learning abilities.

Perceived Utility/Value Training that is viewed as useful is more likely to be used on the job. Perceived utility or value of training is affected by a need to improve, the likelihood that training will lead to improvement, and the practicality of the training for use on the job. For training to be used on the job, learners must perceive a close relationship between the training and things they want in their work performance.

Learning Styles People learn in different ways. For example, *auditory* learners learn best by listening to someone else tell them about the training content. *Visual* learners think in pictures and figures, and they need to see the purpose and process of the training. *Tactile* learners must get their hands on the training resources and use them. Trainers who address all these styles by using multiple training methods can present more effective training.

In addition, training design must sometimes address special issues presented by adult learning, which involves the ways in which adults learn differently than do younger people. Certainly, the training design considers that all the trainees are adults, but adults come with widely varying learning styles, experiences, and personal goals. For example, training older adults in technology may require greater attention to explaining the need for changes and enhancing the older trainees' confidence and abilities when learning new technologies. In contrast, younger adults are more likely to be familiar with new technology because of their earlier exposure to computers and technology, but they may be less able to work alone to learn skills.

Malcolm Knowles's classic work on adult learning suggests five principles for designing training for adults.[41] According to that work and subsequent work by others, adults

- need to know why they are learning something;
- need to be self-directed;
- bring more work-related experiences into the learning process;
- enter into a learning experience with a problem-centered approach to learning; and
- are motivated to learn by *both* extrinsic and intrinsic factors.

The multigenerational workforce poses particular challenges in the design and delivery of training. While it is not advisable to simply lump everyone born within a generation into a box and assume that they will all respond in the same way, some understanding of the different generations is helpful when working to create useful training. The following "HR Competencies & Applications: Training a Multi-generational Workforce" feature identifies strategies that can help all learners get the most from training.

8-5b Instructional Strategies

An important part of designing training is to select the right mix of teaching strategies to fit learner needs and styles. Practice/feedback, overlearning, behavioral modeling, error-based examples, and reinforcement/immediate confirmation are strategies that are frequently used when designing a training experience.

Adult learning
(also known as andragogy) Ways in which adults learn differently than do younger people

COMPETENCIES & APPLICATIONS

Training a Multi-generational Workforce

There is more generational diversity in today's workplace than at any time in the past. Making sure that all employees are capable and ready to handle ever-changing tasks means that training is often an ongoing part of life in companies. Recognizing and embracing the differences brought by workers from each generation can lead to more engaging and effective training.

Each generation spans approximately a 20-year time period. Frequently, individuals in each generational cohort have similar values and behaviors based on shared experiences during their lifetime. While two people in the same generation are not carbon copies of each other, they often approach work in a similar way. Knowing a little about how each generation's workers view training helps trainers do a better job of connecting with each learner.

Baby Boomers (1946–1964) see the trainer as a knowledgeable partner in the learning process. They value qualifications and reputation, and they will seek to validate the trainer's credibility. Experience-based learning is highly effective for this group, and using audio methods tends to improve retention. Continual feedback can annoy them, but asking for their opinions during training keeps them engaged.

Generation X (1965–1980) learners view the trainer as a subject matter expert who can demonstrate proficiency on the spot. They value frequent feedback to help them gauge their performance level. Using multimedia delivery methods and letting them get their "hands dirty" by doing rather than watching enhances their learning retention and engagement.

Millennials (1981–2000) look for trainers who are knowledgeable mentors with deep real-world experience to share. They value practical training that can be used immediately. Many are visual learners who prefer image-dense material to solidify the learning moment. Teamwork and diversity in the training environment are crucial elements for optimal learning.

These differences are complemented by some similarities. Workers from all generations need to see how the training is relevant to their jobs. To gain trust and acceptance, trainers need to highlight what is in it for the learners. All learners appreciate knowing what is expected of them during the training and what they can expect to get from the training. Address differences in communication and work styles at the beginning of a training session to help everyone understand and appreciate how they are alike and different. Use a variety of learning methods to present content and provide a hands-on experience to satisfy diverse learning styles and preferences. Fostering a setting in which all participants learn from and teach each other creates a rich learning environment for everyone.[42] Consider how the mix of employees from different generations impacts the workplace and answer the following questions:

1. What are the rewards and challenges of managing a workforce composed of workers from different generations?

2. How can HR professionals assist line managers in dealing with workers from different generations? What HR programs should be customized to meet the diverse needs of workers from each generation?

KEY COMPETENCIES: Consultation, Global & Cultural Effectiveness; HR Expertise: Workplace/Diversity & Inclusion, Organization/Workforce Management, People/Employee Engagement

Practice/Feedback For some training, it is important that learners practice what they have learned and get feedback on how they have done so that they can improve. Active practice occurs when trainees perform job-related tasks and duties during training. This is more effective than simply reading or passively listening. For instance, assume a person is being trained as a customer service representative. After being given some basic selling instructions and product details, the trainee calls a customer and uses the skills mastered during training.

Feedback is crucial to help learners establish their competence level and adjust their effort. There are numerous sources of performance feedback during training. Trainers, fellow trainees, gauges on equipment or tools (like a speedometer), and the trainees themselves are all possible ways to provide information to the trainee. Feedback after training is also necessary to reinforce the training content. On the job, the trainee's supervisor or coworkers can observe the trainee and provide feedback to help the trainee improve performance.[43]

Active practice
Trainees perform job-related tasks and duties during training

Overlearning Repeated practice even after a learner has mastered the training content is referred to as overlearning. It may be best used to instill "muscle memory" for a physical activity to reduce the amount of thinking necessary and make responses automatic. Consider how most adults who drive perform many functions without consciously thinking about them as a result of constant repetition and practice. Overlearning produces improvement in learner retention. Even with overlearning, refreshers are still sometimes necessary to maintain proficiency.

Behavioral Modeling The most elementary way in which people learn and one of the best is through behavioral modeling, which involves copying someone else's behavior. The use of behavioral modeling is particularly appropriate for skill training in which the trainees must use both knowledge and practice. It can aid in the transfer of skills and the use of those skills by those who are trained. For example, a new supervisor can receive training and mentoring on how to handle disciplinary discussions with employees by observing as the HR director or department manager deals with such problems. Behavioral modeling is particularly effective for training supervisors and managers in interpersonal skills.[44] Fortunately or unfortunately, many supervisors and managers model behaviors they see their bosses exhibit. For that reason, supervisor training should include good role models to show learners how to properly handle interpersonal interactions with employees.

Behavioral modeling
Copying someone else's behavior

Error-Based Examples The error-based examples method involves sharing with learners what can go wrong when they do not use the training properly. A good example is discussing with pilots what can happen when they are not aware of a harmful situation that occurs while in flight. Training that includes relevant error-based examples improves air crew situational awareness. Error-based examples have been incorporated in medical, military, firefighting, police, and aviation training and have wide potential uses in other situations. The *after-action review* process is a powerful method of identifying decisions and actions taken during an event and evaluating their effectiveness. This type of training uses real cases to emphasize the importance of appropriate decision making.[45]

Reinforcement and Immediate Confirmation The concept of reinforcement is based on the *law of effect*, which states that people tend to repeat responses that give them a positive reward and to avoid actions associated with negative consequences. Using classic operant conditioning such as positive reinforcement for

Reinforcement
Based on the idea that people tend to repeat responses that give them some type of positive reward and to avoid actions associated with negative consequences

Immediate confirmation
Based on the idea that people learn best if they receive reinforcement and feedback as soon as possible after training

correct learned responses and negative consequences for incorrect responses can change learner behavior. Closely related is an instructional strategy called immediate confirmation, which is based on the idea that people learn best if they receive reinforcement and feedback as soon as possible after exhibiting a response. Immediate confirmation corrects errors that, if made and not corrected throughout the training, might establish an undesirable pattern that would need to be unlearned. It also aids with the transfer of training to the job.

8-5c Training Transfer

The best training in the world is of little use if trainees are not able to utilize the new knowledge and skills on the job. Training should be designed for maximum transfer from the classroom to the job. Transfer occurs when trainees actually use knowledge and information they learned in training once they are back on the job. The amount of training that effectively gets transferred to the job is estimated to be relatively low, especially given all the time and money spent on training.[46] Figure 8-9 shows important considerations before, during, and after training that lead to successful transfer of training.

Effective transfer of training meets two conditions. First, the trainees can take the material learned in training and apply it to the job context in which they work. Second, employees maintain their use of the learned material over time. Transfer of training is influenced by many things done before, during, and after training.[47] Offering trainees an *overview of the training content* and *how it links to the strategy* of the organization seems to help with both short-term and longer-term training transfer. Another helpful approach is to ensure that the *training mirrors the job* context as much as possible. For example, training managers to be better selection interviewers could include role-playing with "applicants" who respond in the same way that real applicants would.

FIGURE 8-9 Transfer of Training Factors

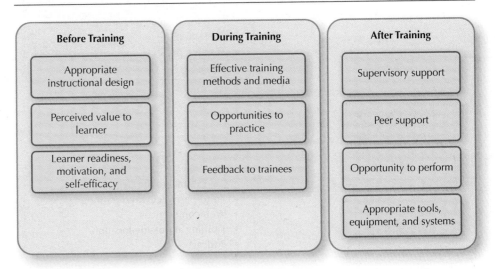

Source: Adapted from Muhammad Bhatti, Sharrifah Ali, Mohd Isa, and Mohamed Battour, "Training Transfer and Transfer Motivation: The Influence of Individual, Environmental, Situational, Training Design and Affective Reaction Factors," *Performance Improvement Quarterly* 27, no. 1 (2014), 51–82.

One of the most consistent factors in training transfer is the *support* new trainees receive *from their supervisors and peers* to use their new skills when they return to the job.[48] Supervisor support of the training, feedback from the supervisor, and supervisor involvement in training are powerful influences in transfer. *Opportunity to use the training* is also important. Transfer is obviously limited when someone is trained on something but then does not have the opportunity to use it. Learners need the opportunity to use new skills on the job if they are to retain those skills. Transfer of training is higher when, implementing a *just-in-time* philosophy, the trainee uses the new skills immediately after training.[49]

Finally, *accountability* helps transfer training from class to job. Accountability is the extent to which someone expects the learner to use the new skills on the job and holds them responsible for doing so.[50] It may require supervisory praise for doing the task correctly and sanctions for not showing proper trained behavior, but making people accountable for their own trained behavior is effective.

8-6 Training Delivery

Once training has been designed, the actual delivery of training can begin. Regardless of the type of training, many approaches and methods can be used to deliver it. The growth of training technology continues to expand the available choices, as shown in Figure 8-10.

FIGURE 8-10 Training Delivery Options

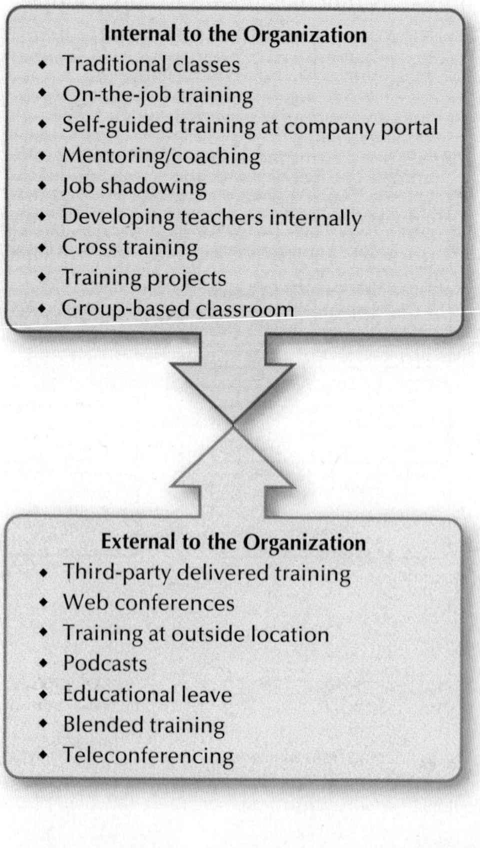

Internal to the Organization
- Traditional classes
- On-the-job training
- Self-guided training at company portal
- Mentoring/coaching
- Job shadowing
- Developing teachers internally
- Cross training
- Training projects
- Group-based classroom

External to the Organization
- Third-party delivered training
- Web conferences
- Training at outside location
- Podcasts
- Educational leave
- Blended training
- Teleconferencing

Whatever the approach used, a variety of factors must be balanced when selecting training delivery methods. Some common variables considered are:

- Nature of training
- Subject matter
- Number of trainees
- Individual versus team
- Self-paced versus guided
- Training resources/costs
- E-learning versus traditional learning
- Geographic locations involved
- Time allotted
- Completion timeline

To illustrate, a large firm with many new hires may be able to use the Internet, videos, and specific HR staff members to conduct employee orientation, while a small firm with few new hires may have an HR staff member meet individually with the new hires for several hours. A medium-sized company with three locations in the same geographic area may bring supervisors together for a two-day training workshop once a quarter. However, a large global firm may use web-based courses to reach supervisors throughout the world, with content available in several languages. Frequently, training is conducted internally to the organization, but some types of training use external resources.

Training occurs on both a planned (formal) and unplanned (informal) basis. Formal training is a deliberate planned process of learning activities. Informal training takes place when learning may not even be the primary focus, but it occurs anyway. Informal learning may be the result of self-initiated effort or serendipity, but it often occurs "in the moment" as needed.[51]

8-6a Internal Training

LO5 Explain different means of internal and external training delivery.

Internal training generally addresses topics specific to the organization and its jobs. Such training is popular because it saves the cost of sending employees away or paying outside instructors. Skills-based technical training is frequently conducted within organizations, and training materials are often created internally. Because of rapid changes in technology, building and updating technical skills may become crucial internal training needs. Basic training that focuses on technical skills is also being mandated by federal regulations in areas where the Occupational Safety and Health Administration (OSHA), the Environmental Protection Agency (EPA), and other agencies have jurisdiction. Three specific types of internal delivery options will be discussed here: informal training, on-the-job training, and cross-training.

Informal training
Training that occurs through interactions and feedback among employees

Informal Training One source of instruction is informal training, which occurs through interactions and feedback among employees. Much of what employees know about their jobs they learn informally from asking questions and getting advice from other employees and their supervisors, rather than from formal training programs.

Informal learning often occurs spontaneously when an employee identifies a need for knowledge or skills and seeks out training on the spot from an internal "guru." It may involve group problem solving, job shadowing, coaching, or mentoring; or it may evolve from employees seeking out other people who have the

FIGURE 8-11   Steps for On-the-Job Training

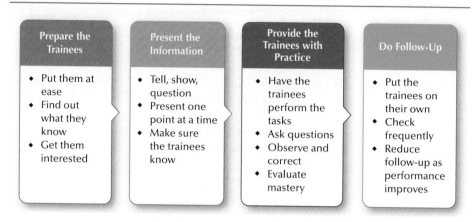

necessary knowledge. Although "informal training" may seem to be a misnomer, a great deal of learning occurs informally in work organizations, and some of it happens by design. Some organizations create learning communities, expert panels, social networks, and other ways for employees to connect on an as-needed basis with expert resources.[52]

On-the-job training
The most common training because it is flexible and relevant

On-the-Job Training The most common type of training at all levels in an organization is on-the-job training (OJT) because it is flexible and relevant to what employees do. Well-planned and well-executed OJT can be very effective. OJT, which is based on a guided form of training known as job instruction training (JIT), is most effective if a logical progression of steps is used, as shown in Figure 8-11. In contrast with informal training, which often occurs spontaneously, OJT should be planned. The trainer must be able to both teach and show the employees what to do.

However, effective OJT is not easy to achieve. Those doing the training may have no experience in training, no time to do it, or no desire to participate in it. Under such conditions, learners are essentially on their own, and training likely will not be successful. Another problem is that OJT can disrupt regular work. Unfortunately, OJT can sometimes amount to no training at all, especially if the trainers simply allow the trainees to learn the job on their own. Bad habits or incorrect information from the supervisor or manager can also be transferred to the trainees.

Cross-training
Training people to do more than one job

Cross-Training When people are trained to do more than one job—theirs and someone else's—cross-training is occurring. Cross-training offers the company more flexibility in assigning workers to tasks and can ensure uninterrupted production. Even though cross-training is attractive to the employer, it is not always appreciated by employees, who may feel that once they are cross-trained, they are required to do more work for the same pay. To counteract such responses and to make it more appealing to employees, learning "bonuses" can be awarded for successfully completing cross-training. Further, organizations can highlight how cross-training can help employees prepare for a future job transfer or promotion. Cross-training can also provide employees with a greater variety of tasks to perform on the job, keeping them more interested and engaged.

Unions typically are not in favor of cross-training because it threatens job jurisdiction and broadens jobs. Cross-training may require scheduling work differently during training, and temporary decreases in productivity may result as people learn. Overall, an effective cross-training program can overcome the concerns mentioned and has the potential to be good for both employer and employee.

8-6b External Training

External training, or training that takes place outside the organization, is used extensively by organizations of all sizes. Organizations use external training if they lack the capability to train workers internally or when many people need to be trained quickly. External training may be the best option in smaller firms because of limitations in the size of training staffs and in the number of employees who need various types of specialized training. Whatever the size of the organization, external training provides these advantages:

- It may be less expensive for an employer to have an outside trainer conduct training in areas where internal training resources are limited.
- The organization may have insufficient time to develop internal training materials.
- The staff may not have the necessary level of expertise for the subject matter in which training is needed.
- Employees can learn from participants from other companies.

Outsourcing of Training Many employers of all sizes outsource training to external training firms, consultants, and other entities. Perhaps one-third of training expenditures go to outside training sources. The reasons more outside training is not used may be related to cost concerns and a greater desire to link training to the specific organization's strategies.

When a company buys equipment or software, the purchase often includes training for its employees. Several computer software vendors offer technical certifications on their software. For example, being a Microsoft Certified Product Specialist gives employees credentials that show their level of technical expertise. Employees can include these certifications on their résumés, which may help if they decide to change jobs. These certifications also benefit employers, who can use them as job specifications for hiring and promotion.

Many suppliers host users' conferences, at which employees from different firms receive detailed training on using products, services, and features that are new to the employees. Some vendors conduct the training inside an organization as well if sufficient numbers of employees need training.

Government-Supported Job Training Funds for job training are often provided by federal, state, and local governments. The Trade Adjustment Assistance Community College and Career Training (TAACCCT) competitive grant program is a joint effort by the U.S. Departments of Labor and Education to target adult education. Educational institutions partner with employers to expand and improve their ability to deliver education and career training programs that will help job seekers get the skills they need for in-demand jobs. This federal program seeks to close the skills gap and enhance opportunities for workers and companies.[53]

At state and local levels, employers who add to their workforces can take advantage of programs that provide funding assistance to offset training costs.

As an example, many states offer workforce training assistance for employers. Skilled Trades Training Fund (Michigan) and NCWorks Incumbent Worker Training Grant (North Carolina) are two such training support efforts. Receiving these training grants is often linked to employers creating or retaining jobs.

Educational Assistance Programs Some employers pay for additional education for their employees. Typically, the employee pays for a course that is part of attainment of a college degree and is reimbursed upon successful completion of the course. The funds paid by the employer are considered nontaxable income for the employee up to amounts set by federal laws.

One concern about traditional forms of employee educational programs is that they may pose risks for the employer. Upon completion of the degree, the employee may choose to take the new skills and go elsewhere. To improve retention, employers must plan to help the employee use the new skills immediately following graduation. This concern has led to a common feature in these programs, the clawback provision. Companies frequently require that employees remain with the company for some period of time after receiving tuition assistance.

Policies regarding educational assistance should match the organization's objectives and employee relations philosophy. Some organizations select preferred colleges or universities where employees are encouraged to study, and some restrict courses to those that are relevant to the job or business. In any case, good follow-up and evaluation are important to verify that the program is building talent for the company.[54]

8-6c Combination Training Approaches

Whether training is delivered internally or externally, appropriate training must be chosen. The following section identifies two common training approaches that often integrate internal and external means. Both types of combination training programs rely on a partnership between a school and a company.

Cooperative/Apprentice Training Cooperative training approaches mix classroom training and on-the-job experiences. This training can take several forms. One form, generally referred to as *school-to-work transition*, helps individuals move into jobs while still in school or upon completion of formal schooling. Such efforts may be arranged with high schools, community colleges, or universities.

Another form of cooperative training used by employers, trade unions, and government agencies is *apprentice training*. An apprenticeship program provides an employee with on-the-job experience under the guidance of a skilled and certified worker. Certain requirements for training, equipment, duration, and proficiency levels may be monitored by a unit of the U.S. Department of Labor. Apprenticeships usually last two to five years, depending on the occupation. During this time, the apprentice usually receives lower wages than do certified individuals. The following "HR Perspective: Building Talent" feature describes several apprenticeship initiatives that are helping manufacturing firms fill critical skill needs.

Internships usually combine job training with classroom instruction from high schools, technical schools, colleges, and universities.[55] Internships benefit both employers and interns. Interns get real-world exposure, a line on their résumés, and a chance to closely examine a possible employer. Employers get a cost-effective source of labor and a chance to see the intern work before making a final hiring decision.

Building Talent

Vocational training programs have been a mainstay in Germany for decades. German youths enjoy the lowest unemployment rate in the world thanks to training programs that closely fit employers' skill needs. Many of these workers are hired for jobs in high-tech manufacturing. Conversely, in the United States, many parents and educators hold a low opinion of jobs in manufacturing and push young people into traditional college degree programs. This has made it difficult for manufacturers to find needed talent.

With a little financial help from Uncle Sam, apprenticeship programs are beginning to take root in American workplaces. President Obama pledged over $100 million for apprenticeship training. Although most of the companies that are signing on are German transplant operations, U.S. firms like Timken, ArcelorMittal, and Swagelok are starting programs. The changing nature of jobs in manufacturing is forcing these companies to "build" their own workforces.

The increased use of robotics and other technologies in these firms means that routine manual labor is often performed by machines. But jobs that are still done by people are much more technical than in the past. Through collaboration with vocational high schools and community colleges, these companies are helping to design courses specific to their industry needs. Some labor unions—such as those involved with construction trades like electrical or plumbing work—also provide vocational training related to their specific craft.

Apprenticeships are "real" jobs, and students spend time in the classroom learning theory and underlying foundational content. Then on the job site, they are guided by highly qualified experienced workers. An apprenticeship typically takes three years. High school students who enter apprenticeship programs can earn well above average pay and begin careers immediately after graduation. In addition to manufacturing, apprenticeships are becoming more popular in fields such as health care, child care, supply chain management, and information technology.

Rather than waiting for talent to come to them, Timken, ArcelorMittal, and Swagelock are building their own talent. This long-term perspective on talent development can provide these employers with a dedicated and capable workforce for today and into the future.[57] After reading this explanation of apprenticeship programs, answer the following questions:

1. Why do you think many U.S. companies are reluctant to implement apprenticeship programs? What arguments would you make to overcome their hesitance?

2. What types of jobs would be most appropriate for apprenticeship programs?

Recent court rulings and guidelines from the Department of Labor indicate that in most cases, interns must be paid. Companies must exercise extreme caution when utilizing unpaid interns.[56]

8-7 Technology in Training Delivery

The availability of tablet computers, mobile devices, virtual reality gear, and other technologies offers a tantalizing opportunity for trainers. However, hoping to connect with trainees through high-tech methods, companies sometimes don't plan properly to effectively deliver training. Using the proper technology for the proper content is key to making technology-based training pay off. Good training design and understanding learner preferences are important steps in capitalizing on technology in training.[58]

8-7a E-Learning: Online Training

E-learning is the use of web-based technology to conduct training online. E-learning is popular with employers because it offers cost savings and access to more employees. Training conducted with some kind of learning technology is likely to continue to increase. Almost 30% of learning hours today are totally technology based, according to an Association for Talent Development (ATD) report, and e-learning is preferred by workers under the age of 30.[59]

Online training should be designed to overcome common problems such as low usage rates and high attrition. In general, if learners believe that the training will be useful and easy to use, they are more likely to enroll and complete online courses.[60] Online training is particularly useful in a model called the *flipped classroom*. Before meeting for a face-to-face session, all trainees complete an online learning module. The classroom session is then devoted to hands-on activities, questions and answers about content, and project work. Companies as diverse as nuclear power plant operators and hair styling salons are using flipped classrooms to better utilize instructor and trainee time. The trainer's role shifts from teacher to facilitator, and trainees are accountable to the trainer and fellow learners for a productive training session.[61]

MOOCs Massive open enrollment online courses (MOOCs) are the latest version of online learning platforms. Some prestigious universities offer courses free of charge as MOOCs. Completion of the course does not earn the student a degree, but individuals seeking specific content may find them sufficient. Other universities have developed full MOOC degree programs. For example, AT&T partnered with Georgia Tech University to offer an online master's program in computer science. Over 200 AT&T employees have enrolled. The tuition is substantially lower than if the employees attended classes on the campus. Further, employees from across the country can participate in this program.

MOOCs are an evolving training solution and are likely to morph in the coming years. Websites like Khan Academy and TED Talks provide free, on-the-spot lectures and demonstrations on a wide range of topics. Trainers are looking for ways to validate MOOC training programs to determine if participants have mastered important content. Some companies welcome MOOC study, while others dismiss its value. As with all emerging technologies, careful assessment based on learning objectives is key to making MOOCs succeed.[62]

Distance Training/Learning Many college and university classes use some form of Internet-based course support. Hundreds of college professors use various packages to make their lecture content available to students. These packages enable virtual chat and electronic file exchange among course participants and enhance instructor–student contact.

Similarly, many large employers similarly use interactive two-way television to present classes. The medium allows an instructor in one place to see and respond to a "class" in any number of other locations. With a fully configured system, employees can take courses from anywhere in the world. Webinars are becoming a popular type of web-based training.

8-7b Simulations and Games

Training that incorporates simulations and games can engage learners while presenting a realistic portrayal of work-related tasks or challenges. Simulations and games are not the same, although the distinction gets fuzzy at times. Simulations seek to reproduce parts of the real world so that they can be experienced and manipulated, and learning can occur. Games are exercises that entertain and engage. They may or may not resemble the real world of work but can sometimes be used to illustrate points in training.

From highly complicated systems that replicate difficult landing scenarios for pilots to programs that help medical trainees learn to sew sutures, simulations allow for safe training when the risks associated with failure are high. For example, health care aides were given mobile tablets that allowed them to practice a simulated interaction with a patient. Health-related questions and a graphic of the human body helped the workers pinpoint and address patient issues. The simulation trained them to thoroughly investigate and record all issues presented by a patient.[63]

Certain industries are on the cutting edge of simulation for training, for example, aviation, military, and transportation. Flight simulators allow a fledgling pilot to practice without crashing an expensive plane. Military simulations allow use of large weapons systems without killing anyone. A 3-D virtual marine port emulates a real container terminal environment and helps operators safely train for the complex activities involved in moving cargo containers. These and other simulators reduce risk to trainees and others who might be injured or killed if training were to take place in the real world rather than virtually.[64]

The future for workplace games is bright, with Gartner predicting that over 70% of companies will have at least one gamified application in the near future.[65] Games are used to motivate and engage learners, and they often use achievement badges, levels that must be cleared, and other rewards. At Evault, new hire onboarding is a "game." New employees are sent on five "missions" that have learning objectives related to mastering some company-relevant content. The game is tablet based, and employees complete it at their own pace. New hires are now better informed and networked than in the past, thanks to the onboarding game.[66]

8-7c Mobile Learning

Incorporating mobile devices such as smartphones, tablets, or netbooks into training holds seemingly endless potential. However, m-learning, the use of mobile technology to conduct training, requires a sound strategy. Three key strategic decisions are:

1. *Target market*: Who are the learners you hope to reach with m-learning? Determine the learners' goals, work environment (e.g., remote, lots of travel), and technology competence level.
2. *Learning content*: What material or information do learners need to have on mobile devices? Are videos or are audio lessons better? What metrics will you use to measure mobile learning success?
3. *System architecture*: What operating system will be used? Will employees be permitted to use their own devices? Consider security issues related to access.[67]

Employees can use mobile devices to access instruction manuals for hardware and software. For instance, repair personnel can retrieve product manuals and

Simulations
Reproduce parts of the real world so that they can be experienced and manipulated, and learning can occur

Games
Exercises that entertain and engage

M-learning
Use of mobile technology to conduct training

instructional videos when they are out in the field and need help completing a repair job. In classroom training, attendees can use text messaging and other mobile apps to complete short quizzes or surveys, pose questions to the instructor or other trainees, and take notes.[68]

Learning content should be designed specifically for m-learning applications. Short text messages, videos, and reminders are best for mobile phones. Tablets provide for a more immersive and richer user experience. Brief amounts of information that can be easily digested are most appropriate for mobile device users who are typically learning on the go. The learning content can be built by users who can snap photos of what they are doing or working on and share them in a learning platform. M-learning can be an interactive, learner-based process when it is well designed.[69]

Blended Learning Generally, technology that was once center stage is becoming embedded in the learning and training processes. As learning and work merge ever closer in the future, technology is likely to integrate seamlessly into the work environment of more employees.

However, e-learning does not work well as the sole method of training, according to employers. One solution is blended learning, which is a learning approach that combines short, fast-paced, interactive computer-based lessons and teleconferencing with traditional classroom instruction and simulation. A blended learning approach can use e-learning for building knowledge of certain basics and traditional instructor-facilitated in-person training sessions for deeper understanding and practice. Blended learning seeks to capitalize on using the most appropriate delivery mode for specific content.

Blended learning provides greater flexibility with multiple training methods and can deliver superior training outcomes. For example, DHL Express combined an intensive 1.5-day customer service training with stand-alone, interactive online training modules. The training was translated into 42 languages, and participant feedback scores were positive, averaging 5.8 out of 6.0.[70]

Blended learning
Learning approach that combines short, fast-paced, interactive computer-based lessons and teleconferencing with traditional classroom instruction and simulation

8-7d Pros and Cons of Technology-Supported E-Learning

There are both advantages and disadvantages that must be considered when utilizing technology to provide training experiences. The rapid growth of technology can result in adoption before an organization has planned for appropriate training design and delivery. Technology-supported training seems like a quick and easy way to keep employees' skills current. Some employers think that they can "set it and forget it." However, that is not the case, and many dollars can be wasted through inappropriate use of technology for training.

In addition to being concerned about employee access to technology and the desire to use it, some employers worry that trainees will complete courses quickly but will neither retain nor use much of what they have learned to help them carry out their work. Taking existing training materials, putting them on the Internet or mobile devices, and cutting the training budget does not usually deliver the desired results.[71] Figure 8-12 presents the most commonly cited pros and cons of using technology to support workforce learning.

Pros	Cons
• Self-paced—trainees can proceed at their own speed • Interactive—taps multiple trainee senses • Automated scoring of exercises and assessments • Quick, appropriate feedback to learners • Incorporates built-in guidance and help for trainees to use when needed • Updating content is relatively easy • Allows for training "on the go" and "just-in-time" • Learners can contribute content to learning platform	• May cause trainee anxiety • Trainees must have easy, reliable access to technology • Relies on user self-direction and motivation to complete training • Is not appropriate for some training content (leadership, cultural change, etc.) • Significant up-front investment of both time and money • Significant support from top management necessary for success • Security and access concerns

LO6 Provide an example for each of the four levels of training evaluation.

8-8 Training Evaluation

Training evaluation compares post-training results to the pre-training objectives of managers, trainers, and trainees. Too often, training is conducted with little thought toward measuring outcomes and then evaluating it to determine if it was effective. Since training is both time consuming and costly, it should be evaluated.[72]

8-8a Levels of Evaluation

It is best to consider—before it begins—how training is to be evaluated. Donald L. Kirkpatrick identified four levels at which training can be evaluated.[73] They are reaction, learning, behaviors, and results.

Reaction Organizations evaluate trainees' reaction levels by conducting interviews with or administering questionnaires to the trainees. Assume that 30 managers attend a two-day workshop on effective interviewing skills. A reaction-level measure could be gathered by having the managers complete a survey asking them to rate the value of the training, the style of the instructors, and their perceived usefulness of the training.

Learning Evaluating learning can be conducted by measuring how well trainees have learned facts, ideas, concepts, theories, and attitudes. Tests on the training material are commonly used for evaluating learning, and they can be given both before and after training to provide scores that can be compared. If test scores indicate learning problems, then instructors get feedback and courses can be redesigned so that the content can be delivered more effectively. Of course, learning enough to pass a test does not guarantee that trainees will remember the training content months later or that it will change job behaviors.

Behaviors Evaluating training at the behavioral level means measuring the effect of training on job performance through observing workers on the job. For instance, the managers who participated in an interviewing workshop might be observed conducting actual interviews of applicants for jobs in their departments. If the managers asked questions as they were trained to and used appropriate follow-up questions, then behavioral indicators of the effectiveness of the interviewing training exist.

Results Employers evaluate results by measuring the effect of training on the achievement of organizational objectives. Since results such as productivity, turnover, quality, time, sales, and costs are relatively concrete, this type of evaluation can be done by comparing records before and after training. For the managers who attended interviewing training, evaluators could gather records of the number of individuals hired compared with the number of employment offers made before and after the training.

The difficulty with measuring results is pinpointing whether changes were actually the result of training or of other major factors. For example, the managers who completed the interviewing training program can be measured on employee turnover before and after the training, but turnover also depends on the current economic situation, the demand for workers, and many other variables. Parsing out the role that training played in improving results can be a challenge.

MEASURE

8-8b Training Evaluation Metrics

Training is expensive, and it is an HR function that requires measuring and monitoring. Cost–benefit analysis and return-on-investment (ROI) analysis are commonly used to measure training results, as are various benchmarking approaches.

Cost–benefit analysis
Comparison of costs and benefits associated with training

Cost–Benefit Analysis Training results can be examined through cost–benefit analysis, which compares costs and benefits associated with training. There are four stages in calculating training costs and benefits:

1. *Determine training costs.* Consider direct costs such as design, trainer fees, materials, facilities, and other administrative activities and indirect costs such as trainee time away from work.
2. *Identify potential savings results.* Consider employee retention, better customer service, fewer work errors, quicker equipment changeovers, and other productivity factors.
3. *Compute potential savings.* Gather data on the performance results and assign dollar costs to each of them.
4. *Conduct costs and savings benefits comparisons.* Evaluate the costs per participant, the savings per participant, and how the costs and benefits relate to business performance numbers.

Figure 8-13 shows some typical costs and benefits that may result from training. Even though some benefits (such as attitude changes) are hard to quantify, comparing costs and benefits associated with training remains a way to determine whether training is cost effective. All training should be evaluated regardless of delivery method. For example, one firm evaluated a traditional safety training program and found that the program did not lead to fewer accidents. Therefore, the safety training was redesigned, and better safety practices resulted.

FIGURE 8-13 Possible Costs and Benefits Related to Training

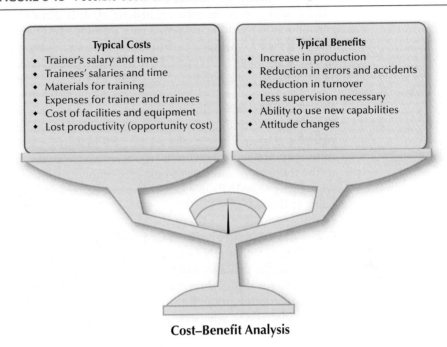

Typical Costs
• Trainer's salary and time
• Trainees' salaries and time
• Materials for training
• Expenses for trainer and trainees
• Cost of facilities and equipment
• Lost productivity (opportunity cost)

Typical Benefits
• Increase in production
• Reduction in errors and accidents
• Reduction in turnover
• Less supervision necessary
• Ability to use new capabilities
• Attitude changes

Cost–Benefit Analysis

Return-on-Investment Analysis and Benchmarking Training is often expected to produce a return on investment (ROI). Too often, though, a particular training regimen is justified because someone liked it rather than on the basis of resource accountability.[74] ROI simply divides the return produced because of the training by the cost (or investment) of the training.

In addition to evaluating training internally, some organizations use benchmark measures to compare it with training done in other organizations. To do benchmarking, HR professionals gather data on training in their organization and compare them with data on training at other organizations in the same industry and in companies of a similar size. Comparison data are available through the Association for Talent Development and its Benchmarking Service. This service has training-related data from more than 1,000 participating employers who complete detailed questionnaires annually. Training can also be benchmarked against data from the American Productivity & Quality Center and the Saratoga Institute.

8-8c Training Evaluation Designs

With or without benchmarking data, internal evaluations of training programs can be designed in many ways. The rigor of the three designs discussed next increases with each level.

Post-Measure The most obvious way to evaluate training effectiveness is to determine whether the employees can perform according to standard after attending the training. Assume that a customer service manager has 20 representatives who need to improve their data-entry speed. After a one-day training session, they take a test to measure this speed. If the representatives can all type the required speed after training, was the training beneficial? It is difficult to say—perhaps most of them could have done as well before training. Tests after training do not always clearly indicate whether a performance is a result of the training or could have been achieved without the training. Post-measure results reflect the level of trainee competence at only one point in time—right after the training is finished.

Pre-/Post-Measure By designing the evaluation just discussed differently, the issue of pre-test skill levels can be considered. If the data-entry speed is measured before and after training, the results will indicate whether the training made any difference. However, a question would remain: Was any increase in speed a response to the training, or did these employees simply work faster because they knew they were being tested? People often perform better when they know their efforts are being evaluated.

Pre-/Post-Measure with a Control Group Another evaluation design can address the preceding problem. In addition to testing the 20 representatives who will be trained, the manager can test another group of representatives who will not be trained, to see if they do as well as those who are to be trained. This second group is called a control group. If the trained representatives work significantly faster after training than those who were not trained, the manager can be reasonably sure that the training was effective.

Organizations invest billions of dollars and countless hours in training employees. These investments should support the goals of the organization and result in benefits to both the employees and the company. Thoughtful design, delivery, and evaluation of training offer the greatest probability of achieving success.

SUMMARY

- Training is a process that provides people with the capabilities they need to do their jobs.
- A strategic approach to training links organizational strategies and HR planning to various training efforts.
- Training affects factors such as organizational competitiveness, knowledge management, revenue, and performance.
- Global strategies must consider training as a key component, including intercultural competence training to prepare employees to respond more appropriately to situations encountered during global assignments.
- Four types of training are regular, basic/remedial skills, job/technical, and soft skills.
- The instructional systems design process consists of five phases: assessment, design, development, implementation, and evaluation.
- Training needs can be assessed using organizational, job/task, and individual analyses, and then training objectives can be set to help the organization meet those needs.
- Training design must consider learner readiness, learning styles, and learning transfer.
- Training can be delivered internally, through external means, or via a combination of both.
- Use of technology in training is increasing, and organizations should assess the pros and cons before adopting new technologies.
- Various organizations are taking advantage of training that uses technology such as web-based multimedia, mobile devices, MOOCs, simulation, and games.
- Training can be evaluated at four levels: reaction, learning, behavior, and results.
- Training evaluation metrics may include cost–benefit analysis, ROI analysis, and benchmarking.

CRITICAL THINKING CHALLENGES

1. Identify training needs for a group of entry-level workers in a fast food restaurant.

2. Why is evaluating training an important part of strategic training?

3. Develop an orientation checklist on the basis of one first-day session and a second session of four hours 30 days later.

4. Create a briefing for division managers showing the advantages and disadvantages of using MOOCs. Use websites, including www.td.org, www.coursera.org, and www.mooc-list.com.

5. Because of the rapid growth of your technology company, the executive team has asked HR to develop an internal training program. The purpose of the program is to help employees recently promoted to supervisory positions develop the leadership skill sets they need to be successful as supervisors. This will be the first formal training program for your small company. As part of the process, you want to consider the learning styles of the new supervisors. To help you develop a successful, results-oriented program, review various training websites, including www.agelesslearner.com.

   A. What training techniques should be implemented to meet the needs of the varied learning styles and maximize the learning potential of the participants.

   B. Identify the content topics that you will recommend be included in the program to ensure the development of successful leaders.

CASE   Saving Lives through Effective Training

Imagine employees in your company saving over 60 lives in one year. That's one result of training efforts at G4S, an integrated security solutions provider. With 46,000 employees operating in over 110 field locations across the country, delivering training with that kind of impact is a challenge.

Most of the security personnel at G4S don't have access to computers or are limited because of client firewalls. So, online training is not always practical. About 60% of the company's training is delivered via live instructor-led classroom sessions. In addition to providing training content, this delivery method reinforces the company's culture and allows employees to network and connect with their peers. In particular, all new managers participate in three week-long training events that teach them about company best practices, business operations, standards and practices, customer service, sales and marketing, and employee relations. The management training connects new managers to headquarters, shows them the "G4S Way," and gives them exposure to top leaders in the organization.

To supplement the classroom training, G4S established strategic partnerships with outside organizations such as the American Heart Association to deliver CPR and AED training. A partnership with the American Council on Education allows employees to earn college and continuing education credits. These collaborative programs extend the company's resources and help G4S's learning and development team focus on core training that is specific to the business. They also demonstrate the company's commitment to employee development and growth.

In addition to classroom and partner-delivered training, G4S created an intranet and social networking portal for employees. Corporate materials, policies and procedures, training manuals and workbooks, performance support tools, and industry news are all available to keep employees informed and up to date with practices in the industry and company. Employees can access the intranet from anywhere with an Internet connection. An especially innovative aspect of the site is that employees can create a personal profile that lists their skills, interests, accomplishments, and contact information. This makes it easy and convenient for anyone in the company to quickly identify individuals with specific skills or "know-how" who can be tapped for assistance on an as-needed basis.

Employee turnover at G4S is much lower than the industry average of 100%. More than 10,000 mangers have been trained since the program started. The training has helped the company reduce turnover by 8%, and complaints about supervisors have dropped by 10%. Implementing the distance learning intranet portal saved the company nearly $2 million in travel-related costs. So, saving both lives and dollars was made possible by a well-designed and well-delivered training strategy at G4S.[75]

QUESTIONS

1. How might the learning and development team determine which training content to create and deliver internally? How would you recommend evaluating potential external providers? What criteria would you use to decide which third-party providers to partner with?

2. What might motivate employees to share their skills and knowledge on a personal profile on the company's social networking intranet portal? What kind of incentives might you provide to encourage employees to share this information?

3. What measures in addition to turnover and employee complaints could be used to evaluate the effectiveness of G4S's training initiatives?

SUPPLEMENTAL CASES

Using Performance Support to Improve Learning

This case illustrates the process of performance support that employees use to improve their job performance. (For the case, go to www.cengage.com/management/mathis.)

Training Crucial for Hotels

This case illustrates the increased role training is playing in large U.S. hotel chains. (For the case, go to www.cengage.com/management/mathis.)

New Payroll Clerk

This case shows the frustration that often accompanies the first day at work and why orientation is important in reducing turnover. (For the case, go to www.cengage.com/management/mathis.)

Onboarding in the Twenty-First Century

This case outlines orientation efforts of Sun Microsystems, El Paso Corporation, and Zimmerman Advertising. (For this case, go to www.cengage.com/management/mathis.)

END NOTES

1. Patty Gaul, "Nearly Half of U.S. Executives Are Concerned about Skills Gap," T+D, February 2014, p. 18; Dinah Wisenberg Brin, "Report: Leaders Need to Help Bridge Middle-Skills Jobs Gap," SHRM Online, December 1, 2014, http://www.shrm.org/hrdisciplines/businessleadership/articles/pages/leaders-need-to-help-bridge-middle-skills-jobs-gap.aspx.

2. Based on Jennifer Salopek, "Tackling Business-Critical Issues through Training," TD: Talent Development, October 2014, pp. 65–67.

3. Kate Everson, "ASTD Reboots with New Name and Logo," Chief Learning Officer.com, May 6, 2014, http://www.clomedia.com/articles/5611-astd-reboots-with-new-name-and-logo.

4. Josh Bersin, "Where Is Your Money Going?" Chief Learning Officer, February 3, 2014, http://www.clomedia.com/articles/where-is-your-moning-going.

5. Peter Cappelli, "How Disney Solved Its Skills-Gap Problem." HRE Online.com, February 24, 2014, http://www.hreonline.com/HRE/view/story.jhtml?id=534356774.

6. Aaron DeMet et al., "Getting More from Your Training Programs," *McKinsey Quarterly*, October 2010, 1–6.

7. Laurie Miller, "2014 State of the Industry," *ATD Research: Connecting Research to Performance*, Association for Talent Development, November 2014, https://www.td.org/Publications/Research-Reports/2014/2014-State-of-the-Industry.

8. Laurie Miller, "2014 State of the Industry Report: Spending on Employee Training Remains a Priority," *TD: Talent Development*, November 2014, pp. 30–35.

9. Amit Mehra, Nishtha Langer, Ravi Bapna, and Ram Gopal, "Estimating Returns to Training in the Knowledge Economy: A Firm-Level Analysis of Small and Medium Enterprises," *MIS Quarterly* 38, no. 3 (September 2014), 757–771.

10. Accenture, "2013 Skills and Employment Trends Survey: Perspectives on Training," http://www.accenture.com/SiteCollectionDocuments/PDF/Accenture-2013-Sills-And-Employment-Trends-Survey-Perspectives-On-Otraining.pdf.

11. Andrea Davis, "Back to School," *Employee Benefit News*, September 15, 2012, pp. 26–28.

12. Stanley Slater, Eric Olson, and Hans Sorensen, "Creating and Exploiting Market Knowledge Assets," *Journal of Business Strategy* 33, no. 4 (2012), 18–27.

13. Neal Goodman, "Knowledge Management in a Global Enterprise," *TD: Talent Development*, December 2014, pp. 28–31; Geri McArdle and Salam Salamy, "Drilling to the Core of Training and Education," *T+D*, September 2013, pp. 48–52.

14. Kurt Andersen, "Sales Training That Keeps Reps Awake, Excited, and Learning," *TD: Talent Development*, December 2014, pp. 54–58.

15. Ann Pace, "Sales Training for the Virtual Interaction," *T+D*, June 2012, p. 18.

16. Shira Mor, Michael Morris, and Johann Joh, "Identifying and Training Adaptive Cross-Cultural Management Skills: The Crucial Role of Cultural Metacognition," *Academy of Management Learning & Education* 12, no. 3 (September 2013), 453–475.

17. Hyounae Min, Vincent Magnini, and Manisha Singal, "Perceived Corporate Training Investment as a Driver of Expatriate Adjustment," *International Journal of Contemporary Hospitality Management* 25, no. 5 (2013), 740–759; Michelle Sandlin, "Intercultural Training Important to Expats' Success," *Chron.com*, April 26, 2013, http://www.chron.com/jobs/articles/Intercultural-training-imporant-to-expats-4467195.php.

18. Gabrielle Wirth and Gary Gansle, "Jump toward Emotional Intelligence," *HR Magazine*, October 2012, 87–90.

19. Editor, "Wells Fargo Sued for Training Practices," *Chief Learning Officer*, March 21, 2014, http://www.clomedia.com/articles/wells-farg-sued-for-training-practices; Mason Braswell, "Trainee Lawsuit Could Clip Brokerages' Ability to Recoup Costs," *Investment News.com*, March 20, 2014, http://www.investmentnews.com/article/20140322/FREE/140329976/trainee-lawsuit-could-clip-brokerages-ability-to-recoup-costs.

20. Based on Karen van der Zee, Jan van Oudenhoven, Joseph Ponterotto, and Alexander Fietzer, "Multicultural Personality Questionnaire: Development of a Short Form," *Journal of Personality Assessment* 95, no. 1 (January–February 2013), 118–124.

21. Based on Jenny Plaiseter-Ten, "Cross-Cultural Competency Tools," *Training Journal*, February 2014, pp. 51–56.

22. Jennifer Salopek, "Ready for Change," *T+D*, October 2013, pp. 62–64.

23. Miriam Jordan, "Workers' English Skills Wane," *Wall Street Journal*, September 24, 2014, p. A2.

24. Carol Leaman, "Boost Basic Job Skills Training," *TD: Talent Development*, August 2014, pp. 35–39; Dori Meinert, "An Open Book," *HR Magazine*, April 2013, pp. 43–46; Stephanie Castellano, "Employers Are Now Providing Analytical Skills Training," *T+D*, April 2014, p. 16.

25. Ashley Slade, "Mind the Soft Skills Gap," *T+D*, April 2014, p. 20; Lisa Bodell, "Soft Skills for the Future," *T+D*, March 2014, pp. 35–38.

26. Talya Bauer, "Onboarding: The Power of Connection,"

SuccessFactors On-boarding White Paper Series, 2013, http://www.sap.com/bin/sapcon/en_us/downloadasset.2-14-05-may-29-01.onboarding-the-power-of-connection-pdf.bypassReg.html.

27. BambooHR, "Onboarding 101 for Small Business HR," 2014, http://www.bamboohr.com/resources/Onboarding101+Infographic.pdf.

28. Justin Mass, "Going Digital: Re-Imaging New Hire Orientation," *TD: Talent Development*, December 2014, pp. 61–64.

29. Kyle Lagunas, "Onboarding ROI: Metrics for Measuring the True Value," August 21, 2011, *SoftwareAdvice.com*, http://blog.softwareadvice.com/articles/hr/onboarding-roi-metrics-for-measuring-the-true-value/.

30. Kevin Lohan, "Back to Basics?" *TD: Talent Development*, October 2014, p. 33.

31. Robert Hewes, "Step By Step," *T+D*, February 2014, pp. 57–61.

32. Dawn Aziz, "What's in a Name? A Comparison of Instructional Systems Design, Organization Development, and Human Performance Technology/Improvement and Their Contributions to Performance Improvement," *Performance Improvement* 52, no. 6 (July 2013), 28–35.

33. Instructional Design Central, "Instructional Design Models," http://www.instructionaldesigncentral.com/htm/IDC_instructionaldesignmodels.htm.

34. David Defilippo and Lisa Shapiro, "Where Science Meets Art," *Chief Learning Officer*, December 2014, pp. 19–21.

35. Marty Buck and Mary Martin, "Leaders Teaching Leaders," *HR Magazine*, September 2012, pp. 60–62.

36. Lorri Freifeld, "Solving Today's Skill Gaps," *Training.com*, http://www.trainingmag.com/solving-todays-skill-gaps.

37. Emily Baumann and Greta Ballentine, "Estimate Training Resources with Precision," *T+D*, February 2014, pp. 20–22.

38. Norbani Che-Ha, Felix Mavondo, and Saad Mohd-Said, "Performance or Learning Goal Orientation: Implications for Business Performance," *Journal of Business Research* 67, no. 1 (January 2014), 2811–2820; Gera

Noordzij, Edwin Van Hooft, Heleen Van Mierlo, Arjan Van Dam, and Marise Ph. Born, "The Effects of a Learning-Goal Orientation Training on Self-Regulation: A Field Experiment Among Unemployed Job Seekers," *Personnel Psychology* 66 (2013), 723–755.

39. Eric Krell, "Get Sold on Training Incentives," *HR Magazine*, February 2013, pp. 57–60; Pat Galagan, "Playing Nice," *TD: Talent Development*, September 2014, pp. 24–27; T+D, "Badge Me," *T+D*, January 2014, p. 13.

40. Raymond Noe, Michael Tews, and Alena Marand, "Individual Differences and Informal Learning in the Workplace," *Journal of Vocational Behavior* 83, no. 3 (December 2013), 327–335.

41. Darlene McDonough, "Similarities and Differences between Adult and Child Learners as Participants in the Natural Learning Process," *Psychology*, March 4, no. 3A (2013), 345–348; Malcolm S. Knowles, Elwood F. Holton III, and Richard A. Swanson, *The Adult Learner*, 6th ed. (New York: Elsevier, 2005).

42. Based on April Ort, "Embrace Differences when Training Intergenerational Groups," *T+D*, April 2014, pp. 60–65; Shahron Williamsn Van Rooij, "Training Older Workers: Lessons Learned, Unlearned, and Relearned from the Field of Instructional Design,"*Human Resource Management* 51, no. 2 (March–April 2012), 281–298.

43. J. H. Stegeman, E. J. Schoten, and O. T. Terpstra, "Knowing and Acting in the Clinical Workplace: Trainees' Perspectives on Modelling and Feedback," *Advances in Health Sciences Education* 18, no. 4 (October 2013), 597–615.

44. Lucia Sigmar, Geraldine Hynes, and Kathy Hill, "Strategies for Teaching Social and Emotional Intelligence in Business Communications," *Business Communications Quarterly* 75, no. 3 (September 2012), 301–317.

45. Roni Reiter-Palmon, Victoria Kennel, Joseph Allen, Katherine Jones, and Anne Skinner, "Naturalistic Decision Making in After-Action Review Meetings: The Implementation of and Learning from Post-Fall

Huddles," *Journal of Occupational and Organizational Psychology* 88, no. 2 (June 2015), 322–340; Scott Clifton, Allen Joseph, Daniel Bonilla, Benjamin Baran, and Dave Murphy, "Ambiguity and Freedom of Dissent in Post-Incident Discussions," *Journal of Business Communication* 50, no. 4 (August 2013), 383–402.

46. Alan Saks and Lisa Burke-Smalley, "Is Transfer of Training Related to Firm Performance?" *International Journal of Training & Development* 18, no. 2 (June 2014), 104–115; Richard Kazbour and Lisa Kazbour, "Strategic Techniques to Enhance Training Transfer," *T+D*, October 2013, pp. 92–94.

47. Travor Brown, Martin McCracken, and Tara-Lynn Hillier, "Using Evidence-Based Practices to Enhance Transfer of Training: Assessing the Effectiveness of Goal Setting and Behavioural Observation Scales," *Human Resource Development International* 16, no. 4 (September 2013), 374–389; Amanda Shantz and Gary Latham, "Transfer of Training: Written Self-Guidance to Increase Self-Efficacy and Interviewing Performance of Job Seekers," *Human Resource Management* 51, no. 5 (September–October 2012), 733–746.

48. Eva Ellstrom and Per-Erik Ellstrom, "Learning Outcomes of a Work-Based Training Programme: The Significance of Managerial Support," *European Journal of Training & Development* 38, no. 5(2014), 180–197; Sue Lancaster, Lee Di Milia, and Roslyn Cameron, "Supervisor Behaviours That Facilitate Training Transfer," *Journal of Workplace Learning* 25, no. 1 (2013), 6–22; Ng Hua, "The Influence of Supervisory and Peer Support on the Transfer of Training," *Studies in Business & Economics* 8, no. 3 (December 2013), 82–97.

49. Peter Tiernan, "Examining the Use of Interactive Video to Enhance Just in Time Training in the Workplace," *Industrial & Commercial Training* 46, no. 3 (2014), 155–164.

50. Lisa M. Burke and Alan M. Saks, "Accountability in Training Transfer," *Human Resource Development Review* 8 (2009), 382–402.

51. Langevin Blog, "8 Benefits of Formal and Informal Learning," May 10, 2012, http://www.langevin.com/blog/2012/05/10/8-benefits-of-formal-and-informal-learning.

52. Barry Farber and Valery Hazanov, "Informal Sources of Supervision in Clinical Training," *Journal of Clinical Psychology* 70, no. 11 (November 2014), 1062–1072; Francisco Garcia-Penalvo, Ricardo Colomo-Palacios, and Miltiadis Lytras, "Informal Learning in Work Environments: Training with the Social Web in the Workplace," *Behaviour & Information Technology* 31, no. 8 (August 2012), 753–755.

53. White House Briefing Room, "Vice President Biden Announces Recipients of $450 Million of Job-Driven Training Grants," September 29, 2014, http://www.whitehouse.gov/the-press-office/2014/09/29/fact-sheet-vice-president-biden-announces-recipients-450-million-job-dri.

54. E. Faith Ivery, "Employee Education May Cost Too Much," *Chief Learning Officer*, January 22, 2014, http://www.clomedia.com/articles/employee-education-may-cost-too-much.

55. Stephanie Castellano, "Student Workers," *T+D*, February 2014, pp. 38–43; Brett Arends, "How Summer Can Change Your Future," *Wall Street Journal*, May 16, 2014; Tomika Greer, "Maximize the Internship Experience for Employers and Students," *T+D*, May 2013, pp. 70–72.

56. Max Mihelich, "Free Advice on Unpaid Internships," *Workforce*, August 2014, pp. 40–43; Laura O'Donnell, "Is Your Unpaid Intern Legit?" *HRMagazine*, April 2013, pp. 77–80.

57. Based on Sven Boll, "Skill Gap vs. Vocational Taboo," *Wall Street Journal*, September 12, 2014, p. A2; Olivera Perkins, "Job Training Takes Aim at Skills Gap," *Cleveland Plain Dealer*, August 3, 2014, p. F1; Lauren Weber, "Here's One Way to Solve the Skills Gap," *Wall Street Journal*, April 28, 2014, p. R3; Peter Downs, "Can't Find Skilled Workers? Start an Apprenticeship Program," *Wall Street Journal*, January 17, 2014.

58. Katie Kuehner-Hebert, "Special Report: Learning Technology," *Chief Learning Officer*, September 15,

2014, http://www.clomedia.com/articles/5764-special-report-learning-technology.

59. Laurie Miller, "2014 State of the Industry," *ATD Research: Connecting Research to Performance*, Association for Talent Development, November, 2014, https://www.td.org/Publications/Research-Reports/2014/2014-State-of-the-Industry.

60. Kenneth Brown and Steven Charlier, "An Integrative Model of e-Learning Use: Leveraging Theory to Understand and Increase Usage," *Human Resource Management Review* 23, no. 1 (March 2013), 37–49.

61. Jon Bergmann and Aaron Sams, "Flipped Learning: Maximizing Face Time," *T+D*, February 2014, pp. 28–31.

62. Dave Zielinski, "Massive Open Online Courses at Work," *SHRM Online*, April 7, 2014; http://www.shrm.org/hrdisciplines/orgempdev/articles/pages/massive-open-online-courses-at-work.aspx; Frank Kalman, "Here Come the MOOCs," *Chief Learning Officer*, January 24, 2014, http://www.clomedia.com/articles/here-come-the-moocs; Caroline Porter and Melissa Korn, "Can This Online Course Get Me a Job?" *Wall Street Journal*, March 4, 2014, p. B7; Sam Herring, "MOOCs Come of Age," *T+D*, January 2014, pp. 47–49.

63. Sharla King, Lili Liu, Eleni Stroulia, and Ioanis Nikolaidis, "Simulations in the Workplace: Integrating Technology into Health Care Aides' Workflow," *International Journal of Advanced Corporate Learning* 6, no. 2 (August 2013), 28–31.

64. Agostino Bruzzone and Francesco Longo, "3D Simulation as Training Tool in Container Terminals: The TRAINPORTS Simulator," *Journal of Manufacturing Systems* 32, no. 1 (January 2013), 85–98.

65. David Zinger, "Game On: A Primer on Gamification for Managers," *T+D*, May 2014, pp. 30–35; Karl Kapp, "Gamification: Separating Fact from Fiction," *Chief Learning Officer*, March 19, 2014, http://www.clomedia.com/articles/gamification-separating-fact-from-fiction; Michael Aumann, "Why Pay Attention to Games?" *Chief Learning Officer*, February 10, 2014, http://www.clomedia.com/articles/why-pay-attention-to-games.

66. Bill Roberts, "Gamification: Win, Lose, or Draw?" *HR Magazine*, May 2014, pp. 29–35.

67. J. P. Medved, "How to Create a Mobile Learning Strategy," *Chief Learning Officer*, April 4, 2014, http://www.clomedia.com/articles/how-to-create-a-mobile-learning-strategy; Chad Udell, "How to Create a Content Strategy for Mobile Learning," *ATD.org*, July 7, 2014, https://www.td.org/Publications/Blogs/Learning-Technologies-Blog/2014/07/How-to-Create-a-Content-Strategy-for-Mobile-Learning.

68. Michelle Baker, "Tech Tools for Training," *T+D*, July 2014, pp. 28–30, https://www.td.org/Publications/Magazines/TD/TD-Archive/2014/07/Tech-Tools-for-Training.

69. Katie Kuehner-Hebert, "Go Mobile?" *Chief Learning Officer*, February 26, 2014, http://www.clomedia.com/articles/go-mobile; Joanne Chan, "mLearning: The Way of Learning Tomorrow," *eLearningIndustry.com*, May 28, 2014, http://elearningindustry.com/mlearning-the-way-of-learning-tomorrow.

70. Rick Jackson and Sue Stoneman, "Engaging Global Training Program Delivers High-Performance Results," *Strategic HR Review* 12, no. 2(2013), 70–74.

71. Christine Keen and Zane Berge, "Beyond Cost Justification: Evaluation Frameworks in Corporate Distance Training," *Performance Improvement* 53, no. 10 (November 2014), 22–28; Natalie Wolfson, Thomas Cavanagh, and Kurt Kraiger, "Older Adults and Technology-Based Instruction: Optimizing Learning Outcomes and Transfer," *Academy of Management Learning & Education* 13, no. 1 (March 2014), 26–44; Jessica Li, "Web-Based Technology and the Changing Landscape of HRD," *Human Resource Development International* 16, no. 3 (July 2013), 247–250.

72. John Castaldi, "Constructing a Business Case for Training: Cause, Coincidence, or Correlation?" *T+D*, June 2012, pp. 32–34.

73. Alan Saks and Lisa Burke, "An Investigation into the Relationship between Training Evaluation and the Transfer of Training," *International Journal of Training & Development* 16, no. 2 (June 2012), 118–127; Perri Kennedy, Seung Chyung, Donald Winiecki, and Robert Brinkerhoff, "Training Professionals' Usage and Understanding of Kirkpatrick's Level 3 and Level 4 Evaluations," *International Journal of Training & Development* 18, no. 1 (March 2014), 1–21.

74. Kendra Lee, "Create a Simple Plan for ROI," *Training*, July–August 2011, p. 14; Phaedra Brotherton, "Organizations Lag behind in Measuring Learning's Value," *T+D*, February 2011, pp. 16–17.

75. Adapted from Jennifer Salopek, "Where Training Can Make the Difference between Life and Death," *TD: Talent Development*, October 2014, pp. 81–82.

CHAPTER

9

Talent, Careers, and Development

Learning Objectives

After you have read this chapter, you should be able to:

LO1 Identify the importance of talent management and discuss two reasons it may be difficult.

LO2 Explain the importance of succession planning and the steps involved in the process.

LO3 Differentiate between organization-centered and individual-centered career planning.

LO4 List options for development needs analyses.

LO5 Discuss three career issues that organizations and employees must address.

LO6 Identify several management development methods.

WHAT'S TRENDING IN
TALENT MANAGEMENT

Talent management practices have existed for a long time in organizations. However, the strategic impact of having the right talent is more apparent to organizations today as the economy becomes more global and high-quality employees become scarcer. The current trends in talent management include:

1. *Integrated talent management* is the new buzzword. Rather than considering each aspect of creating a talent pipeline as a separate process, companies are beginning to integrate all processes to ensure bench strength for the future.
2. Global leadership development is an important business activity. The globalization of business means that employees at all levels must be up-skilled to work effectively with colleagues around the world.
3. Succession planning is critical for organizational success. The need for developing leaders to step into roles made vacant by an ever-faster exodus of retiring workers highlights the need to proactively plan for an orderly transition.
4. Organizations are beginning to target and focus their investments in talent. They use data analytics to determine which workers and jobs require greater investment and will provide a greater payoff.

HEADLINE

Driven to Develop Employees

Fleet management company ARI supports vehicle fleets for more than 3,200 companies globally, managing over 1 million vehicles. The company's goal of promoting personal and professional employee growth led to the founding of ARI University. Creating a learning culture supports its most important competitive advantage—its people.

After assessing the learning needs of employees, the development team created three "schools" within ARI University. The Professional Development school builds core business skills like team building, software competence, and communication. The Fleet Management Expertise school focuses on keeping technicians' skills up to date with hands-on mechanical training. The Leadership Excellence school prepares employees for future roles in leadership and includes mentoring from executives, multiday offsite courses, and group projects addressing current business problems.

ARI's approach is to serve employees at every career stage, from entry level to leader-in-waiting. The company's executive team is closely involved in identifying high-potential employees and ensuring that they receive the training needed to advance in their careers. Courses at ARI University are limited to 20 participants to encourage a high level of interaction. Some courses are offered online, while others are classroom based. In-house subject matter experts create content for the courses to keep costs down and to provide internal development opportunities. These in-house experts serve as adjunct teachers who lead courses in collaboration with a learning team professional.

In addition to tapping into the company's wealth of knowledge to create courses, expert mentors are teamed up with new hires.

 HEADLINE

iStockphoto.com/vm

These mentoring pairs encourage peer-to-peer learning and get new hires up to speed rapidly. Each department head nominates a "learning champion" who is an ambassador for ARI University and other learning opportunities. ARI University uses employee-driven social media platforms like discussion forums and blogs to spread best practices throughout the organization. Employees post their profiles to identify themselves as subject matter experts who can be consulted by others within the company. ARI also offers a library of new and used books for employees to read at their convenience.

The ARI University Honor Society recognizes employees who complete 175 training hours in a two-year period. The company also offers 100% tuition reimbursement, and employees are eligible the moment they are hired. Employee engagement scores and internal promotion rates are tracked. Both measures have increased by more than 50% in the past three years. The learning culture at ARI is driven by the founder's belief that successful businesses must "train, employ, and reward" the best people.[1]

Talent management is quickly becoming a major concern to executives, boards of directors, investors, and employees. Organization sustainability rests on the skills and knowledge of workers. Instituting effective practices to ensure that workers are capable of fulfilling job requirements is a key strategic move for organizations. This is why leaders and HR professionals focus so much on developing the talent of employees.

Workforce planning is based on having the right talent in place as needed by the organization and its managers. Workforce planning works with talent management, which focuses on having the right individuals ready for jobs when needed. A significant part of talent management involves developing a pipeline of talented people. Additionally, talent management focuses on key positions and job families that will be required, skills that will be needed, and competency models, talent pools, and assessments of employees.

This chapter focuses on talent management as a strategy to enhance company performance. Much of this approach involves having a plan that effectively deals with employees' careers and provides for their developmental needs. In addition, talent management includes programs that cultivate important capabilities and competencies.

Strategic talent management
The process of identifying the most important jobs in a company that provide a long-term competitive advantage and then creating appropriate HR policies to develop employees so that they can effectively work in these jobs

LO1 Identify the importance of talent management and discuss two reasons it may be difficult.

9-1 Talent Management as Strategy

Successful talent management is strategic because employee development should be linked to the organization's objectives. Organizations must respond quickly to changes in environmental demands, and having the right talent helps them respond appropriately. Strategic talent management is the process of identifying the most important jobs in a company that provide a long-term advantage and then developing employees so that they can effectively work in these jobs.[2] Both talent and strategy are among the most important drivers of success in many organizations,

Integrated talent management (ITM)
A holistic approach to leveraging and building human capital.

which means that both issues are of primary concern to executive leaders. This suggests that companies should consider talent management when developing their business strategies.

Integrated talent management (ITM) is a holistic approach to leveraging and building human capital. Connecting multiple processes such as performance management, training and development, succession planning, and career management helps organizations to maximize HR practices.[3] Companies that adopt an integrated talent management perspective create processes that reinforce and support each other, and they utilize analytics and metrics to determine the value of these practices on organization outcomes. This evolving perspective highlights the importance of talent for an organization's success and sustainability.[4] Using ITM scorecards helps companies align talent management practices with critical business outcomes. By measuring the impact of these human capital processes on performance indicators such as revenue, operating costs, customer satisfaction, product/service quality, and employee turnover, the organization's leaders can determine how to invest organizational resources for maximum success. The major components in the employment life cycle (i.e., training/development, performance and succession management, etc.) should be integrated as one unit.[5]

One way to think of talent management is as a process that goes beyond simply recruitment and selection, and uses talent to meet the needs of the organization. Along the way, all the elements of talent management are encountered: training, succession planning, career planning, development, and performance management. Figure 9-1 shows the process. Training and performance management are covered in other chapters, while succession planning, career planning, and development are covered in this chapter.

Talent management practices related to growing talent within the organization are an investment in human capital rather than a short-term cost. Competitive advantage for the firm comes from deploying workers with high levels of competency and capability. Companies can maximize the value of talent management initiatives by following a supply chain approach that incorporates (1) developing current employees and hiring outside talent, (2) creating talent pools and broad competencies in employees, (3) using short-term talent forecasts that are likely more reliable than longer-term forecasts, and (4) establishing a balance between employees' and companies' ownership of career development.[6] Verizon embraces such an approach by requiring each employee to create an individual development

FIGURE 9-1   Integrated Talent Management

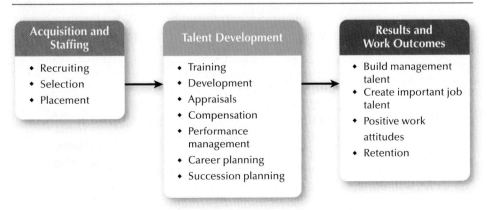

plan upon being hired. Through onboarding and subsequent assignments and feedback, the employee hones in on development activities to enhance the achievement of the individual plan.[7]

9-2 Talent Management in Perspective

The idea that human capital can be a source of competitive advantage for organizations is gaining ground, but many firms are not designed or managed to optimize talent performance.[8] The nature of the business and the environment in which it operates to some extent define appropriate strategies for talent management. The following "HR Competencies & Applications: Managing Talent for Success" feature details six key steps that companies can take to optimize investments in human capital.

Talent management can be challenging because of the nature of *talent* itself. Using a supply chain philosophy, one can think of a "deep bench" of talent as inventory. But unlike boxes full of empty bottles, talent does not necessarily remain available until needed—people may leave the company. The shelf life of promising managers and specialists is short if they do not have opportunities to grow with their current employer. Good inventory management therefore requires paying attention to employees' needs and goals.

Opportunities to learn and grow are attractive to job candidates as well as current employees. This highlights the importance of a successful talent management program. Attracting and retaining talent is only part of the equation—companies must also keep people engaged by looking for individual characteristics that lead to job success, providing good development opportunities for high-performing employees, and having a management team that builds confidence in the company's future prospects.[9]

9-2a Talent Management Information Systems

Talent management seems to lend itself to the use of various software-based systems that purport to integrate all the pieces of talent management into one manageable whole. For example, one company used a talent management system to

- document new employee orientation and training;
- automate registration of participants for training and development activities;
- track classroom training and certifications completed by all store employees;
- report on completions of training certifications for employees; and
- compile and report the training and development history of individuals for use with career planning and development.

However, research shows that while many companies recognize the value of using talent management technology, many still use a manual rather than automated approach.[11] The drive to automate talent management comes in part from the desire to pull together HR, finance, and operations data to get insights on talent that are otherwise difficult to obtain. Using a manual process makes it nearly impossible to accumulate all the information necessary to effectively manage the talent pool. Regardless of the current state of the art, there is great potential for automated talent management systems to aid decision making in the future, but these systems are certainly not the entire solution to talent management challenges.

COMPETENCIES & APPLICATIONS

Managing Talent for Success

Organization leaders can follow many paths to achieve the objectives established during the strategic planning process. Some leadership teams focus on products and services, while others may emphasize financial management techniques. Progressive organizations are beginning to see that human capital practices focused on talent management can go a long way toward delivering success toward goals. The following six pathways can be adopted in whole or in part to achieve success through managing talent:

1. *Embrace a decision science perspective.* Data about employees—including their knowledge, skills, and abilities (KSAs); interests; performance histories; and the like—can inform decisions about human capital practices that work or don't work. The evidence-based approach to managing people leverages what an organization knows about how to capitalize on this valued resource.

2. *Encourage informal learning.* Recognize the myriad ways in which employees obtain required knowledge and skills. Don't expect all training to occur in formal settings. Rather, establish networking and collaborative tools that foster peer-to-peer learning.

3. *Revolutionize stale processes.* Assess the effectiveness of current processes such as performance management. If they are not keeping pace with what employees need, don't apply band-aids. Instead, start from scratch to create systems that will be useful for managers and employees.

4. *Relinquish some control.* Allow employees autonomy and flexibility to determine work schedules and procedures. Hold employees accountable for results but don't dictate methods. Engagement increases when employees are offered the chance to make important decisions affecting their work environment.

5. *Align strategy, structure, and talent.* Determine which roles and individuals are critical to the organization's success. Invest more in those key components and address gaps in the rest of the workforce to bring them along.

6. *Establish a meaningful, enduring culture.* Identify and clearly articulate the organization's values and culture, and line up talent that supports these attributes. Hire, train, develop, and promote employees who embrace the culture and will perpetuate the organization's values.

Tackling all six of these paths can overwhelm leaders and employees. It's better to choose the particular pathways that can deliver the greatest impact in the quickest time frame. Taking a careful, measured approach should lead to more effective talent management without draining all of the organization's resources.[10] Consider how managing talent can address an organization's long-term objectives and answer the following questions:

1. What evidence would you use to convince top leaders that investing in talent can reap great rewards for the organization?

2. How would you prioritize among the six strategies offered in the text above? Which would you implement first, second, and so on?

KEY COMPETENCIES: Leadership & Navigation, Critical Evaluation, Consultation, Business Acumen; HR Expertise: Organization/Technology & Data, Organization/Workforce Management

9-2b Scope of Talent Management

As talent management has evolved, a variety of approaches and tools have also developed. The following sections describe the approaches that define talent management.

Target Jobs and Individuals The first issue is to identify the types of jobs that will be the focus of talent management efforts. In some organizations, talent management focuses on the CEO and other executive jobs, rather than more broadly. Other organizations target senior managers, mid-level managers, and other key employees. However, those groups represent only about one-third of the total workforce, which raises the question of whether talent management efforts would be more useful if they were more widely implemented within the workforce.

Some individual employees are considered critical to the organization's success. These critical employees do not necessarily occupy executive-level roles, but their KSAs and performance make them essential to the operation. For example, an IT employee who is responsible for maintaining the company's servers and other hardware may be mission-critical even though the job is not in the top echelon of the structure. Critical employees are frequently not told by their employers of their importance to the firm. Managers shy away from telling them out of fear that it might give them too much leverage and create expectations that cannot be met. However, not telling these employees how important they are puts the organization at risk for losing them to competitors.[12]

Competency Models What does a person who is ready to be promoted look like? What competencies should the person have? Competency models show KSAs for various jobs. An employer must ask, "What talent do we need to achieve this?" The answer can be found in a competency model. Competency models help identify talent and gaps. As explained in Chapter 1, the Society for Human Resource Management (SHRM) has developed a comprehensive competency model for the HR profession that identifies nine major categories.

Some companies maintain libraries of competency models. These libraries create a clear path for talent planning. Competency models might be created for executives, managers, supervisors, salespeople, technical professionals, and other key positions. One example of a competency is problem solving, which involves addressing complex organizational problems and developing solutions. Another example is multitasking, which involves effectively coordinating various work processes at the same time to get more work done. It is common for organizations to identify a small number of core competencies that apply to all job categories, along with job-specific competencies. Embedding the same competency framework during employee selection and subsequent performance management is the most powerful way to assess and develop talent.[13]

Managing Development Risks When developing talent, the employer always runs a risk that an employee who has been developed will choose to leave with the valuable skills gained. A way to reduce this risk is to have promising employees volunteer for development on their own time. Executive MBA programs that can be attended on evenings or weekends, extra projects outside a person's current assignment, volunteer projects with nonprofit organizations, and other paths can be used. The employer might contribute through tuition reimbursement or some selected time away from the job, but the risk is at least partly shared by the employee because he or she has invested time in the process.

The risk of losing employees in whom the company has invested should be weighed against the loss of talent if the company neglects development. The ability of employees to freely move in the labor market makes it important for firms to remain attractive to employees. Career growth opportunities are highly valued and can increase employee commitment and reduce turnover intentions.[14] Therefore, decisions about investing in talent should assess multiple risks.

Make-or-buy
Develop competitive human resources or hire individuals who are already developed from somewhere else

"Make or Buy" Talent? Employers face a make-or-buy choice: develop ("make") competitive human resources or hire ("buy") individuals who are already developed from somewhere else. In fact, some business acquisitions are made with the express purpose of acquiring rare talent. For example, PayPal bought StackMob to obtain engineering talent that would facilitate its entry into the mobile pay field.[15]

There are advantages and disadvantages to each approach.[16] If business conditions are relatively stable and predictable, an organization may do well to develop its own leaders through a make strategy. Doing so provides for continuity within the leadership ranks and creates leaders who are well versed in the specific drivers of the organization's success. However, developing leaders internally takes time and may result in tunnel vision from an overemphasis on organization-based intelligence.

A buy strategy shortens the development cycle and produces leaders quickly by hiring from the outside. In rapidly changing organizations or those that are growing quickly, this may be the better course of action. Buying talent can also provide the organization with fresh ideas and new approaches to business. However, buying talent can be costly, and there is greater risk when hiring externally. In addition, if an organization's culture is strong, an outside leader may have difficulty being effective. Like any financial decision, the make-or-buy decision can be quantified and calculated when assumptions are made about time, costs, availability, quality, and risk. Evidence suggests that certain situational characteristics should dictate whether to hire internal or external candidates. For instance, a recent study showed that when a company's culture is critical to its success, an internal candidate is better. Conversely, when the organization needs a new direction or particular skill set, hiring from outside is recommended. Consider that Microsoft tapped longtime insider Satya Nadella to serve as just its third CEO since the company's founding. On the other hand, Yahoo! drafted Marissa Mayer, a well-regarded technology expert from Google.[17] Every organization faces unique challenges, and whether to make or buy talent depends on many factors.

GLOBAL

Global Development Multinational organizations focus on developing employees who can manage people and operations in diverse environments. Competencies needed for global leadership are more complex than those focused on only one country. In addition to core leadership skills such as future orientation, empathy and concern for others, ethics and integrity, and team development, the global leader must also be able to work across cultures and contexts. Managers operating in a global setting need to manage paradoxes, appreciate the unique attributes of each context, and communicate effectively across time and geography.[18]

Global leadership programs seem to fall short of addressing a number of critical competencies. While the programs typically include managing change, critical thinking, and problem solving, they rarely include technology and competencies related to creativity and innovation. Comfort with and competence in using social networking technology is crucial in the global enterprise, since most work is done by virtual teams. However, many workers have not been formally trained in how to properly operate in this manner; learning by trial and error is costly and inefficient. Consulting company I4cp recommends incorporating the following elements into a global development plan:

1. Make global cultural fluency an organization-wide priority.
2. Tap into the best minds inside and outside of the organization to share knowledge and stories.
3. Offer a diverse slate of hard and soft skills development.
4. Leverage strategic workforce planning to determine skills gaps and to identify candidates for succession plans from the global workforce.[19]

Leadership development programs for diversified multinational enterprises should include participants from both developed and emerging economies. Managers from developed countries can learn firsthand about distinct cultural attributes from representatives working in less-developed countries. Likewise, those from emerging economies can interact with participants from developed nations and learn about the organization's sophisticated practices. Such cross-fertilization increases knowledge sharing and speeds up the development of all participants.[20]

9-2c High-Potential Individuals

HiPos
Individuals who show high promise for advancement in the organization

Some organizations focus talent management efforts primarily on "high-potential" individuals, often referred to as HiPos, which are individuals who show high promise for advancement in the organization. Attracting, retaining, and developing HiPos have become the main emphases for some talent management efforts. Targeting primarily HiPos may lead to many other employees seeing their career opportunities as being limited. The following "HR Ethics: HiPo or Non-HiPo?" feature poses some ethical challenges related to the identification and notification of employees with respect to organization high-potential development programs.

Determining *potential* is not a simple process. Figure 9-2 offers six attributes that constitute potential for growth and development. Clearly defining how the organization

FIGURE 9-2 HiPo Potential Assessment

Strong motivation to excel in pursuit of challenging goals

Humility to put group needs before personal needs

Insatiable curiosity to explore new ideas

Keen insight into connections that most people overlook

Strong engagement with work tasks and people

Determination to overcome obstacles

Source: Adapted from Claudio Fernandez-Araoz, "21st Century Talent Spotting," *Harvard Business Review* 92, no. 6 (June 2014), 46–56.

ETHICS

HiPo or Non-HiPo?

Identifying employees as having high potential and creating development programs tailored to their needs is not without controversy. Issues regarding the process used to identify HiPo employees, along with the process used to notify employees about their status, can pose ethical dilemmas for an organization.

The assessment of potential is part science and part art. Using methods such as manager nomination or evaluation is highly subjective. It is likely to result in some biased decisions about which employees will be enrolled into HiPo programs. In addition, relying on past performance evaluation ratings can lead to unfair choices as well. Unless the performance assessment process is valid and well grounded, too much personal discretion can influence ratings and render them ineffective for accurately measuring employee potential. To combat some problems with assessing potential, organizations are wise to adopt objective assessments administered by qualified professionals.

There is no clear best practice regarding notification and public identification of HiPo employees. In an era in which transparency is a key watchword, only a small percentage of executives describe their companies as open about how employees are selected for admission to HiPo and leadership programs. This secrecy seems to be driven by two factors—lack of management courage and concerns about managing HiPo employee expectations. Some executives worry about the fallout from broadcasting the criteria for selection around the organization. Further, they are concerned that once an employee is told that he or she is a HiPo, expectations for promotion or special treatment will exceed what the organization can fulfill.

Managing expectations of both HiPo and non-HiPo employees can best be accomplished by explaining and disseminating the selection standards. If employees understand how the decisions about entry into HiPo programs are made, they can better reconcile their own status. Mystery surrounding the process leads employees to question the fairness of decisions and suspect that the organization chooses these individuals arbitrarily.

Disclosing the names of those in HiPo programs can cut both ways. However, it is naïve to believe that employees will not figure out who is in the program and who isn't. Special training and networking opportunities, job assignments, and other obvious development practices will be offered to HiPo employees. It doesn't take others long to determine which list they are on. However, publicly acknowledging and identifying HiPos may lead to work-group dysfunction, envy, and other negative employee conduct.[26]

Establishing valid selection criteria, assessing potential using appropriate tools, and managing employee expectations all contribute to a HiPo program that effectively navigates the ethical issues inherent in these development opportunities. After reading the section on HiPo programs, consider the following questions:

1. How would you suggest communicating the names of those selected for HiPo programs? Should it be widely known in the organization, or should the list be kept "under wraps?"

2. How can managers deal with expectations HiPos might have regarding their career trajectory? What can be done to keep those expectations in check?

assesses potential helps demystify the selection process for HiPo programs. Identifying top performers may not be as difficult as trying to keep them satisfied and engaged. Assuming that all HiPos crave challenge and opportunity can lead to inferior results. A critical element is to discuss the future with these key players and discover their career aspirations. Offering high-profile assignments and face time with senior leaders are important aspects of HiPo development. Many prominent companies such as General Electric, Unilever North America, and IBM have established programs that effectively identify and cultivate talent in HiPos by linking corporate strategy to the development of leaders and providing learning opportunities that grow the business and the individual.[21] However, organizations should also be careful not to overwhelm these "stars" with intensive workloads that push them beyond reasonable limits.[22]

An important consideration of developing HiPos is recognizing that these programs typically involve about 10% of the organization's workforce. The organization still needs the full engagement and commitment of the remaining 90% of the workers. Investing in HiPos, while not undercutting universal growth opportunities for all, requires careful planning and execution.[23] For example, Fluor Corporation expects all employees to create and work on a career development plan, and all supervisors are held accountable for supporting employee growth. Promotions to higher levels in management are based in part on success at developing one's team.[24]

The public identification of HiPos is a delicate matter that rests on the level of trust employees have in the organization's commitment to overall worker growth and learning. Employees not identified as HiPos still seek advancement opportunities and assignments that will enhance their knowledge and skills. An organization is shortsighted if all development is focused on HiPos. Providing development initiatives to non-HiPos can foster engagement and job satisfaction in this vital core segment of the workforce.[25]

LO2 Explain the importance of succession planning and the steps involved in the process.

Succession planning
Preparing for inevitable vacancies in the organization hierarchy

9-3 Succession Planning

Succession planning is the basis for a company dealing successfully with staffing changes such as retirements, transfers, promotions, and turnover. **Succession planning** is the process of preparing for inevitable vacancies in the organization hierarchy. It involves more than simply replacement planning. Replacement planning usually involves creating a list of temporary replacements for important jobs, especially during crisis situations.[27] Succession planning should include a well-designed development system for employees since it takes an average of two to three years to develop a qualified successor.[28]

Despite the essential need for succession planning, it is all too often an afterthought. Many firms are negatively affected by a lack of succession planning. For example, the sudden departure of top executives at American Apparel, Pepsi, Sanofi, Target, and JCPenney left those companies flat-footed and without an obvious leader.[29] Stumbling through an unexpected leadership vacancy can make employees and investors feel uneasy or even anxious. Yet, many organizations fail to adequately plan for the loss of a key leader. The classic model of succession planning is the farm system in major league baseball. Talented young players are groomed through play in the minor leagues where they gain valuable experience and hone their skills. Those with superior results advance to the major league where their talents are utilized to help the team succeed.

9-3a Succession Planning Process

Succession planning follows logical steps, as shown in Figure 9-3. The process begins with defining key positions critical to the organization's strategy and then making certain top managers are personally involved in talent identification, mentoring, and coaching.[30] Some companies pay a bonus to encourage top executives to address succession planning.[31] The next step is to assess the talent available in the

FIGURE 9-3 Succession Planning Process

Integrate with Strategy
- What competencies will be needed?
- Which jobs will be critical?
- How should critical positions be filled?
- Are international assignments required?

Involve Top Management
- What is the CEO's role in succession planning?
- Are high-level executives involved in the process?
- Are top executives mentoring/coaching others?
- Is there authority/accountability for succession goals?

Assess Key Talent
- Does employee have important competencies? What's missing?
- Do assessments/evaluations provide useful information?
- Are results examined to determine individual talents?
- Are individuals and career goals/interests compatible?

Follow Development Practices
- How can important competencies be developed?
- Can an individual interact with executives and board members?
- Can talent pools be created for top-level jobs?
- What are the incentives for individual development?

Monitor and Evaluate
- Are multiple metrics used?
- Are successors effective after placement?
- Are positions filled internally?
- Are positions filled externally?
- Is the process viewed favorably?

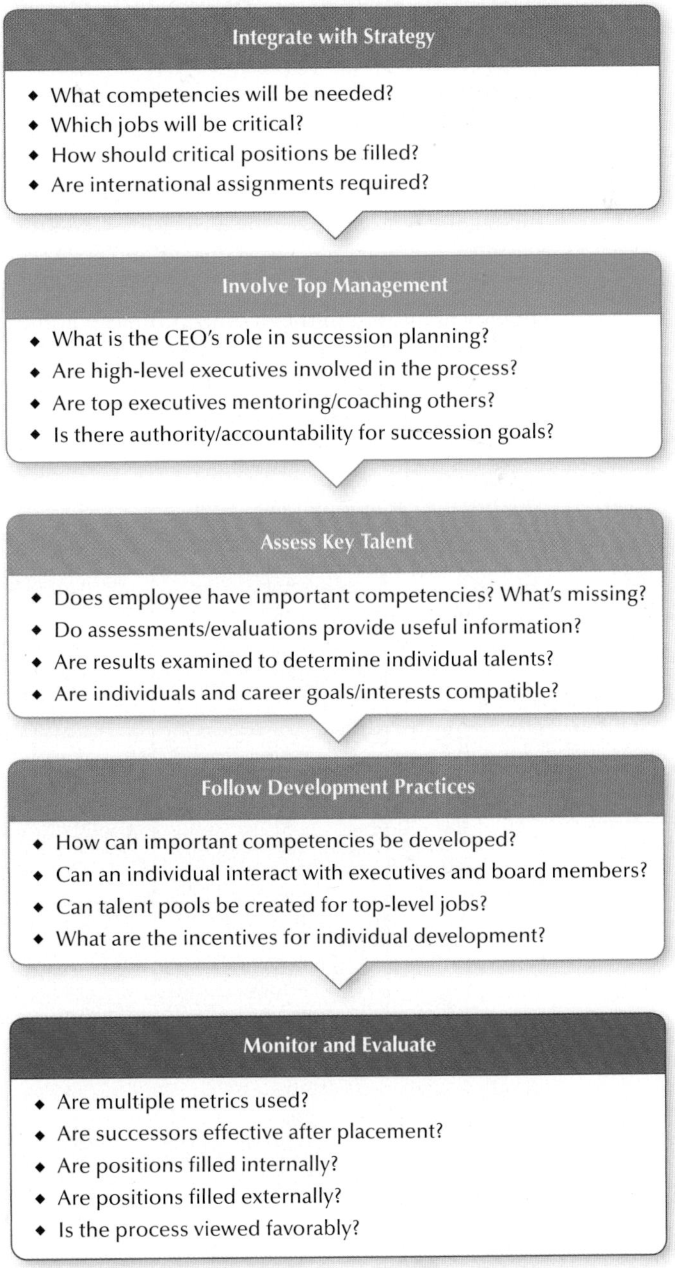

organization and determine who has the potential, who is ready now for promotion, and who needs additional development. Development practices can vary but should be aimed at specific needs in specific individuals. Finally, evaluating the success of the process is important, and appropriate measures are necessary to do so.[32]

All the work involved in the succession planning process should result in two outcomes: (1) identification of potential emergency replacements for critical positions and (2) other successors who will be ready with some additional development. The individuals identified as possible successors should be told what specific development they need and possible action steps to build their competencies.[33]

9-3b Succession Planning Decisions

Several decision are required as part of succession planning. These decisions require the following analysis: How can you identify and classify current talent? Should you make or buy talent? How can you measure systemic success?

Nine-Box Talent Grid
A matrix showing past performance and future potential of all employees

Identifying Current Talent Companies can be proactive in identifying the right managers and employees needed for successful succession planning. Managers determine if individuals are ready, willing, and able to perform duties at a higher level in the organization. Leaders should also take a current inventory of the talent that is already employed in the organization. A common framework is the Nine-Box Talent Grid, as shown in Figure 9-4. The Nine-Box Talent Grid[34] is a matrix showing past performance and future potential of all employees. Since focusing only on potential or performance may provide too narrow a view when developing succession plans

FIGURE 9-4 Nine-Box Talent Grid

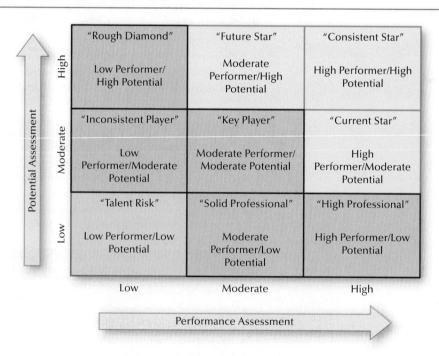

Source: http://www.smartmovescoach.com/how-do-i-make-sure-i-have-the-talent-to-grow-my-business/

for jobs and identifying candidates, a two-dimensional grid can outline individuals' potential to be promoted on one axis and current job performance on the other axis.

Such a talent inventory grid is particularly helpful in jobs that tend to be more complex. For example, assume that an Engineering Manager in a manufacturing company is creating a succession plan. The position requires individuals with extensive experience, industry contacts, technical expertise, project management skills, and other important competencies that suggest high potential. It is important to recognize that job demands for the Engineering Manager job differ substantially from those required of engineering professionals. Individuals who are outstanding engineers may excel at the technical aspects of the job but lack the abilities needed to manage others. The Nine-Box Talent Grid is therefore useful for assessing potential candidates on both important measures.

MEASURE

Metrics and Succession Planning Some organizations measure the impact of succession planning. A wide range of metrics are used depending on the company's priorities. The appropriate metric(s) should be selected early in the succession planning process. Key measures a company might consider are the reduced costs of turnover, higher performance, and organizational profitability. Organizations might also track how job vacancies are filled, the availability and readiness of candidates, and success rates of individuals who are promoted.

Computerized Succession Planning Models The expansion of information technology capabilities has resulted in employers being able to make succession planning data available electronically to staff members. Skills-tracking systems, performance appraisals, and other databases can be linked to succession plans. As employees complete training and development activities, their data can be updated and viewed as career openings become available in the company. Via intranet systems, employees can access and update their data, review job and career opportunities, and complete skill and career interest self-surveys. Software programs can facilitate integrated talent management practices.

9-3c Benefits of Succession Planning

Succession planning is a business imperative that provides for the organization's sustainability and success. The process can be conducted formally and informally. As companies become larger, the benefits of formal succession planning become greater, and for these larger companies, formal planning is recommended. Key benefits include the following:

- Having a supply of highly qualified individuals ready for future job openings
- Providing career opportunities and plans for individuals, which helps retention and performance motivation
- Providing a basis for the continual review of staffing requirements as organizational changes occur over time
- Enhancing the "brand" of the company and establishing the organization as a desirable place to work
- Generating confidence for investors and other stakeholders

Common Succession Planning Mistakes CEO succession should be primarily the responsibility of governing boards and top-level executives. One reason

COMPETENCIES & APPLICATIONS

Do's and Don'ts of Succession Planning

Many leaders readily acknowledge the importance of succession planning in companies. However, they often don't follow that philosophy with action. Research shows that less than half of executives believe that their organizations do an adequate job of grooming successors. Unplanned vacancies take about three months to fill, leaving a significant gap in the organization's leadership team. The following do's and don'ts represent best practices for effective succession planning:

- *DO be forward focused.* Look to the future and determine what competencies will be needed in five or ten years. Simply duplicating the leadership skills and style of current leaders is not likely to move the organization forward as times and demands change.
- *DO align compensation with succession planning.* Incentivize key leaders to create a working succession plan and mentor individuals identified as possible successors. Paying a bonus or other reward to executives who attend to this important task will get them to focus on getting it right. It is also advisable to offer deferred compensation (such as stock options) to those on the succession path. This keeps them invested in the organization and cuts down on turnover.
- *DO consider soft skills.* Development efforts should key in on interpersonal skills, emotional intelligence, problem-solving, creativity, and other vital leadership competencies. Investing too much time in functional, technical training will produce successors who are not effective at leading their team or organization.

- *DON'T wait until a vacancy occurs to begin succession planning.* At that point, it is a race to the finish, not an orderly, thoughtful development process. Every manager's number one priority should be identifying and preparing potential successors.
- *DON'T identify one individual for each role.* Putting all of your eggs in one basket is a risky proposition. The successor may leave the organization prematurely or may not develop successfully. Leading firms bring along multiple candidates with the understanding that choosing from among a pool is superior to having only one choice.
- *DON'T keep succession plans a secret.* Stakeholders have a vested interest in knowing that executives are planning for the future. Share the overall strategy with important parties. While specifically naming successors may not be necessary, assuring stakeholders that there is a living, working process calms their concerns.[35]

Considering the importance of succession planning, it is disappointing that so few organizations have implemented robust programs. Answer the following questions relative to succession planning best practices:

1. What are some possible reasons top leaders fail to create succession plans?

2. What role should the board of directors, HR, and executives each play to ensure effective succession planning?

KEY COMPETENCIES: Leadership & Navigation, Consultation; HR Expertise: People/Talent Acquisition & Retention, Strategy/Business & HR Strategy, Organization/Workforce Management boards have increased the priority of CEO succession is that it is required by the Sarbanes-Oxley Act.

But focusing only on CEO and top management succession is one of the most common mistakes made. Other mistakes include the following:

- Starting too late, when openings are already occurring
- Not effectively linking succession plans to strategic plans
- Allowing the CEO to direct the planning and make all succession decisions
- Looking only internally for succession candidates

Longer-term succession planning should include mid-level and lower-level managers, as well as other key nonmanagerial employees. Some firms target key technical, professional, and sales employees as part of succession planning. Others include customer service representatives, warehouse specialists, and other hourly employees who may be able to move up into other jobs or departments.

Actions such as planning careers and development follow from succession planning efforts. The preceding "HR Competencies & Applications: Do's and Don'ts of Succession Planning" feature describes how one organization conducts succession planning.

LO3 Differentiate between organization-centered and individual-centered career planning.

Career
Series of work-related positions a person occupies throughout life

9-4 Careers and Career Planning

A career is a series of work-related positions a person occupies throughout life. Employers and employees have different views of careers. Individuals pursue careers to satisfy their individual needs. Organizations see careers as an important part of talent management. Changes in employer approaches to career planning based on a less predictable business environment have put much of the responsibility for career management on the shoulders of individual employees.[36] However, companies need to take some responsibility in the career planning process by helping employees make good decisions and by providing positive work opportunities. Career management is therefore ideally a shared responsibility of employers and employees.

9-4a Changing Nature of Careers

The old model of a career in which a person worked up the ladder in one organization is becoming rarer. In a few industries, changing jobs and companies every few years is becoming more common. Many U.S. workers in high-demand jobs, such as information technologists and pharmacists, can dictate their own circumstances to some extent. The average 30- to 35-year-old in the United States may have already worked for up to seven different firms. The new career model involves more frequent job changes as well as changes in major vocational field. People rarely spend their entire working lives with the same firm doing the same type of work.[37]

Different Views of Careers The patterns of individuals' work lives are changing in many areas: more freelancing, more working at home, more frequent job changes, and more job opportunities but less security. Rather than letting jobs define their lives, more people set goals for the type of lives they want and then use jobs to meet those goals. Careers are transitioning from a traditional approach to a more contemporary one.[38] These changes are highlighted below.

- *Traditional career perspective*: Career success is represented by tangible things like title, money, power, and status. Individuals expect the employer to lead the way in terms of developing them and looking out for their career progression. Traditional career paths focus on upward moves to gain status and financial rewards.
- *Contemporary career perspective*: Career success is measured in terms of intrinsic satisfaction that comes from doing challenging work that increases the individual's skills and competencies. Intangibles like work–life balance, making an impact, working on projects you are passionate about, and long-term professional growth are highly valued. Individuals are more likely to be proactive about planning their careers rather than relying on their employer to take charge.

A particular framework, called the Protean career, defines the contemporary version of careers. The Protean career is a process whereby an individual makes conscious career plans to achieve self-fulfillment. Figure 9-5 shows elements of the Protean career. Protean workers embrace responsibility for managing their careers and seek life fulfillment through their work. They thoughtfully and proactively seek information to understand their own identity and plan career moves to gain skills and make an impact. Organizational support is still necessary, but Protean workers will take the steps necessary to achieve psychological success.[39]

Protean career
A process whereby an individual makes conscious career plans to achieve self-fulfillment

FIGURE 9-5 Elements of the Protean Career

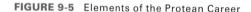
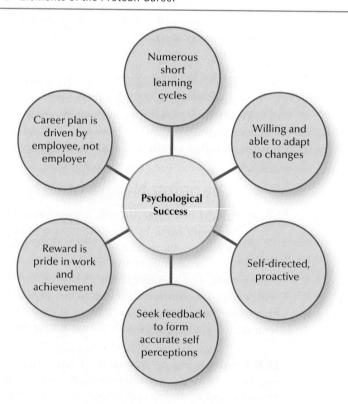

Source: Adapted from Martin Gubler, John Arnold, and Crispin Coombs, "Reassessing the Protean Career Concept: Empirical Findings, Conceptual Components, and Measurement," *Journal of Organizational Behavior* 35 (February 2014), S23–S40.

9-4b Organization-Centered Career Planning

Since careers are evolving, managing them puts a premium on career development by both employers and employees. Effective career planning considers both organization-centered and individual-centered perspectives. Figure 9-6 summarizes these perspectives to career planning.

Organization-centered career planning
Career planning that focuses on identifying career paths that provide for the logical progression of people between jobs in an organization

Organization-centered career planning focuses on identifying career paths that provide for the logical progression of people between jobs in an organization. Individuals follow these paths as they advance in organizations. For example, the right person might enter the sales department as a sales representative and then be promoted to account director, to district sales manager, and finally to vice president of sales.

A good career planning program includes elements of talent management, performance appraisals, development activities, transfer and promotion opportunities, and succession planning. To communicate with employees about opportunities and help with planning, employers frequently use career workshops, a career "center," and career counseling. Individual managers often play the role of coach and counselor in their direct contact with individual employees and within an HR-designed career management system.[40]

The approach an organization uses to enhance careers should provide opportunities for individual growth and development. For example, companies now favor using career lattices comprised of multidirectional job changes and lateral moves as mechanisms for providing employees important career experiences.[41] Another system for managing individual careers is the career path, or "map," which is created and shared with employees. MassMutual's career center includes four tools: career resource center, competency model and development guide, mentoring tool, and job

FIGURE 9-6 Organizational and Individual Career Planning Perspectives

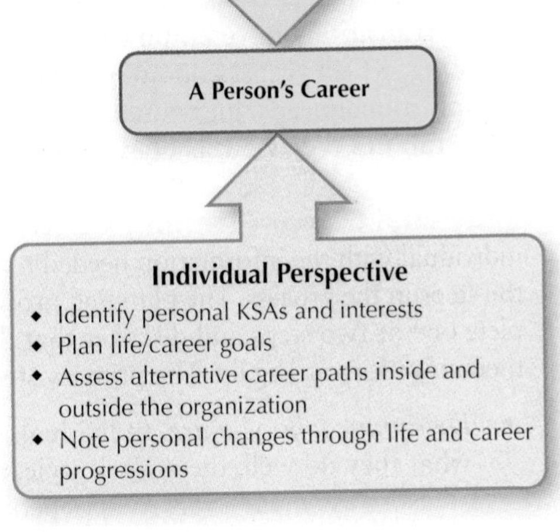

Organizational Perspective
- Identify future staffing needs
- Plan career ladders
- Assess individual potential and needs
- Match organizational needs to individual KSAs
- Develop and audit career system for success

A Person's Career

Individual Perspective
- Identify personal KSAs and interests
- Plan life/career goals
- Assess alternative career paths inside and outside the organization
- Note personal changes through life and career progressions

exploration tool. This toolkit helps employees find the information and resources needed to lay out a career path and helps the company retain valued talent.[42]

Career Paths Employees need to know their strengths and weakness, which they often discover through company-sponsored assessments. Then career paths to develop the weak areas and fine-tune the strengths are developed. Career paths represent employees' movements through opportunities over time. Although most career paths are thought of as leading upward, good opportunities also exist in cross-functional or horizontal directions.

Working with employees to develop career paths has helped employers retain key employees. For example, Hyatt Hotels Corp. actively promotes lattice career paths. Traditionally, General Managers were recruited only through two operational functions. The HR group questioned this limited recruiting approach and pushed for more cross-functional recruiting for these important roles. The philosophy has caught on, and recently an IT professional was internally recruited to join the HR department. The creativity in career paths is one reason Hyatt was named as a company most admired for HR on Fortune's annual "Most Admired Companies" list.[43]

Unfortunately, less than half of the respondents to a recent survey said that their employers outline career paths for them. An organization's career path tends to follow the hierarchical structure of the organization chart and not evolve to include more innovative ways for employees to move through jobs. Employees are too often left on their own, which can result in frustration and disappointment. Showing employees possible routes to fulfillment can lead to better retention and more satisfied workers.[44]

Employer Websites and Career Planning Many employers have careers sections on their websites to list open jobs. An employer's website is a link to the external world but should also be seen as a link to existing employee development. Sites can also be used for career assessment, information, and instruction. When designing websites, firms should consider the usefulness of the careers section for development as well as recruitment. For example, Spotify and Pepsi have engaging profiles of employees on their websites. Anyone inside or outside the company can review the profiles and learn about how the profiled employee's career path led to his or her current job.[45]

9-4c Individual-Centered Career Planning

Organizational changes have altered career plans for many people. Individuals have had to face "career transitions"—in other words, they have had to find new jobs.[46] These transitions have emphasized the importance of individual-centered career planning, which focuses on an individual's responsibility for a career rather than on organizational needs. Individuals behave more like "free agents" who move between opportunities they view as helping to further their own goals.[47]

Individual Career Planning Career planning involves several steps that provide an individual with the information needed to create a logical career path. Figure 9-7 shows the steps in the process. The planning process is not always linear. Individuals may complete one or two steps and discover that they need to cycle back to an earlier step and then move forward again. The primary steps in the career planning process are:

- *Determine who you are.* Individuals need to think about what interests them, what they do well, their work style, and what is important to them. Career advisors use many tools to help people understand themselves. Common

Career paths
Represent employees' movements through opportunities over time

Individual-centered career planning
Career planning that focuses on an individual's responsibility for a career rather than on organizational needs

FIGURE 9-7 Steps in Individual Career Planning

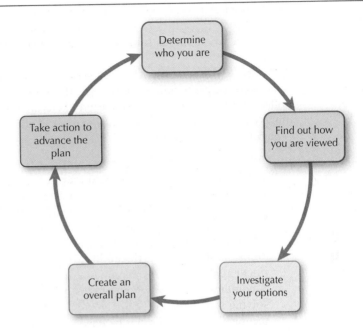

professional tests include the Holland Interest Inventory to determine preferences among vocational occupations and the Myers-Briggs Type Indicator of
personality. Whether professionally administered or taken on their own, the
essential first step is to understand the characteristics and attributes that an
individual possesses.

- *Find out how you are viewed.* Employees need feedback on how well they are
doing, how their bosses see their capabilities, and where they fit in organizational plans for the future. One source of this information is performance
appraisal feedback and career development discussions. Consulting with
trusted colleagues on and off the job can shed light on how others view the
individual's capabilities, strengths, and weaknesses.

- *Investigate your options.* Learning about the industry, the organization, and
the specific vocation are important so that career plans can be made within
the context of possibilities. The Bureau of Labor Statistics updates the Occupational Outlook Handbook and makes it available online. This is a helpful
resource that projects demand for particular skills and careers in the future.

- *Set a goal and create an overall plan.* After compiling all of the information
in the preceding steps, establish a long-term goal with interim short-term
milestones. Take into account current levels of competence and performance
along with interests and values. An important consideration is the demands
that a desired job may place on one's personal life, for example, relocation or a
hardship work schedule. Realistic goals are more practical than attractive but
unreachable goals. Determine what steps will be necessary to obtain the experiences and skills needed to advance.

- *Take action to advance the plan.* Taking action is the critical final step. Setting up
a career discussion with one's supervisor; enrolling in seminars, continuing education, or other types of programmed learning; or requesting to be assigned special projects or tasks are all proactive steps that get the career plan underway.[48]

Over time, as experience is gained and skills are mastered, the career plan should be revisited. A periodic evaluation of progress against goals along with a reassessment of the practicality of the plan help the individual stay on track and continuously focused on finding fulfillment through vocational and nonvocational activities.

Individual Career Profile A useful starting point in career planning is to assess interests, personality, skills, and values. The individual compiles a profile that reflects his or her unique constellation of characteristics. This profile will help determine what types of career options are most likely to lead to success and satisfaction. The following section provides brief explanations of each element of the profile.

- *Interests*: People tend to pursue careers that match their interests. Interests tend to be fairly stable over time, and they are reasonably valid as a predictor of job success and satisfaction. Interest assessments operate on the premise that individuals with similar interests are drawn to similar career fields. Identifying one's interests informs career decisions and focuses individuals on the types of jobs that would be most rewarding.[49]
- *Skills*: Skills represent the ability to do some task well. Individuals have distinct capabilities that make them especially well suited to particular jobs. A common categorization of skills includes basic skills, complex problem-solving skills, resource management skills, social skills, systems skills, and technical skills. Skills can be developed and improved over time with focus and practice.[50]
- *Personality*: An employee's personality includes that individual's personal orientation (e.g., extraversion, openness to experience, and conscientiousness) and personal needs (including affiliation, power, and achievement needs). Individuals with certain personality attributes find greater success in clusters of occupations that match their personality profile.[51]
- *Values*: Work values are an often underappreciated aspect of good career choices. Values act as an individual's "compass"; they guide behavior and focus effort. If an individual's values are poorly matched to the employer, then job dissatisfaction is likely to occur. Identifying beliefs and ideas that are personally important allows people to live and work authentically and in harmony with their true selves.[52]

Creating a career profile that includes interests, personality, skills, and values brings into focus the core of an individual's temperament and work style. Like assembling a jigsaw puzzle, the creation of the profile answers questions about what type of career will match the person's strengths, weaknesses, and natural tendencies. People are most productive and happy when their work lines up well with their overall makeup.

9-4d Career Progression Considerations

The typical career for individuals today includes more positions, transitions, and organizations than in the past, when employees were less mobile and organizations were more stable as long-term employers. But there remain general patterns in people's lives that affect their careers.

The first half of life is typically devoted to the quest for competence and for a way to make a mark in the world. Happiness during this time comes primarily from achievement and the acquisition of capabilities. The second half of life is different. The previous focus on skill mastery changes to the pursuit of integrity, values, and

FIGURE 9-8   General Career Phases

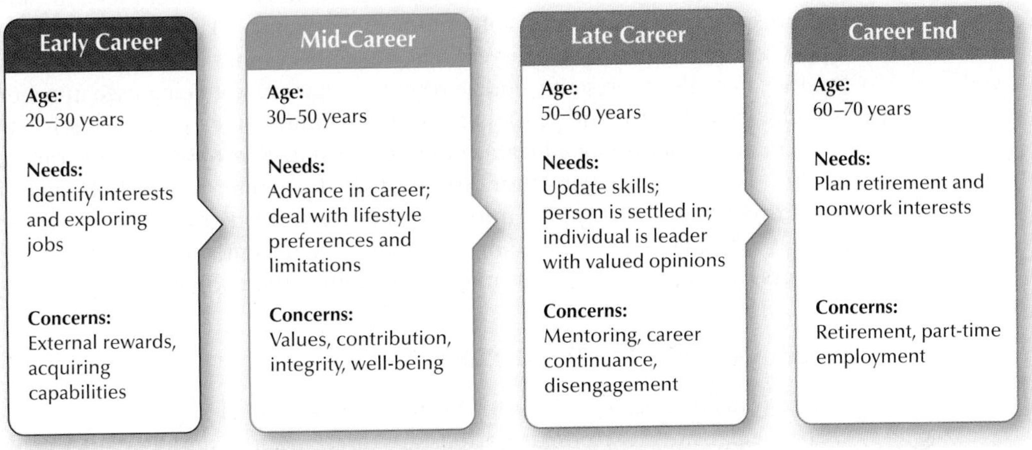

Early Career	Mid-Career	Late Career	Career End
Age: 20–30 years	**Age:** 30–50 years	**Age:** 50–60 years	**Age:** 60–70 years
Needs: Identify interests and exploring jobs	**Needs:** Advance in career; deal with lifestyle preferences and limitations	**Needs:** Update skills; person is settled in; individual is leader with valued opinions	**Needs:** Plan retirement and nonwork interests
Concerns: External rewards, acquiring capabilities	**Concerns:** Values, contribution, integrity, well-being	**Concerns:** Mentoring, career continuance, disengagement	**Concerns:** Retirement, part-time employment

well-being. For many people, internal values take precedence over external score-cards or accomplishments such as wealth and job title status. In addition, mature adults already possess certain skills, so their focus may shift to interests other than skills acquisition. Career-ending concerns, such as life after retirement, reflect additional shifts. Figure 9-8 shows a model that identifies general career and life periods.

Representative of this life pattern is the idea that careers and lives are not predictably linear; rather, they are cyclical. Individuals experience periods of high stability followed by transition periods of less stability that include inevitable discoveries, disappointments, and triumphs. These cycles of structure and transition occur throughout individuals' lives and careers. This cyclical view may be an especially useful perspective for individuals affected by downsizing or early career plateaus in large organizations. Such a perspective underscores the importance of flexibility in an individual's career. It also emphasizes the importance of individuals' continuing to acquire more and diverse KSAs.

Early Career Issues   Early career needs include finding interests, developing capabilities, and exploring jobs. Some organizations do a better job than others of providing those opportunities. Offering programs that satisfy the needs of individuals who are just starting their careers such as flexible work situations, alternative workplace arrangements, development activities, and opportunities to earn additional income are some approaches employers use to make jobs more attractive.

However, individuals in the early stages of their work in a profession need to take greater responsibility for their career planning. Such effort establishes greater ownership over individual development and facilitates empowerment. Being proactive about career planning also decreases the likelihood of sitting back and letting someone (or something) else manage the process.

Career Plateaus   Individuals who do not change jobs may face another problem—career plateaus. Many workers define career success in terms of upward mobility. As opportunities to move up decrease, some employers try to encourage employees to make lateral moves. These sideways moves can be beneficial if employees learn new skills that increase individual marketability and recharge their enthusiasm for their careers.

Plateaued employees are more likely to quit or retire early, possibly taking valuable knowledge with them. Further, employees who believe that they are "stuck in a rut" are less satisfied with their jobs and organizations.[53] Plateaued employees present a particular challenge for employers. They can affect morale if they become negative, but they may also represent valuable resources that are not being used appropriately.

One strategy for individuals to move beyond career plateaus is for them to participate in continuing education or take on special projects outside their normal field of expertise. Rotating workers to other departments is another way to deal with career plateaus. Tapping into the expertise and experience of longer-term employees who may be plateaued and engaging them as mentors for less experienced workers can improve their self-image and confirm their value to the organization.[54]

9-4e Career Transitions

Career transitions can be stressful for individuals who change employers and jobs. Of particular interest to organizations are three specific times of career transitions: organizational entry, job loss, and retirement.

Organizational Entry Starting as a new employee can be overwhelming. "Entry shock" is especially difficult for younger new hires who find the work world very different from school.[55] Entry shock includes the following concerns:

- *Supervisors*: The boss–employee relationship is different from the student–teacher relationship.
- *Feedback*: In school, feedback is frequent and measurable, but that is not true of most jobs.
- *Time*: School has short (quarter/semester) time cycles, whereas time horizons are longer at work.
- *The work*: Problems are more tightly defined at school; at work, the logistical and political aspects of solving work problems are often less certain.

Job Loss Job loss as a career transition has been most associated with downsizing, mergers, and acquisitions. Losing a job is a stressful event in one's career, frequently causing depression, anxiety, and nervousness. The financial implications and the effects on family can be extreme as well. Yet, many individuals do face the potential of job loss, and effectively addressing their concerns should be considered in career transition decision making. Unplanned job loss is one reason individuals should adopt a perspective of lifelong learning and maintain their skills.

Retirement Issues Whether retirement comes at age 50 or age 70, it requires a major adjustment for many people. Some areas of adjustment faced by retirees include self-direction, a need to belong, satisfying achievement needs, personal space, and goals. To help address concerns over these issues, as well as anxieties about finances, some employers offer preretirement planning seminars for employees.[56]

Career development for people at the end of their careers can be managed in many ways. Phased retirement, consulting arrangements, and callback of some retirees as needed all act as means for gradual disengagement between the organization and the individual. However, phased retirement is complicated by pension laws, which often restrict the number of hours employees who are receiving a pension can work.[57]

Early retirement often occurs as a result of downsizings and organizational restructurings. These events have required many managers and professionals to determine what is important to them while still active and healthy, with some deciding to remain employed in extended or second careers, and others electing to leave the workforce to enjoy leisure time and the pursuit of personal interests. To successfully encourage early retirement, management must avoid several legal issues, such as forced early retirement and pressuring older workers to resign.

9-5 Common Individual Career Problems

Four career issues are sufficiently common as to need individual treatment in this text: problems with technical and professional workers, women, dual-career couples, and individuals with global careers.

9-5a Technical and Professional Workers

Technical and professional workers, such as engineers, scientists, and IT systems experts, present a special challenge for organizations. Many of these individuals want to stay in their technical areas rather than enter management, yet advancement in many organizations requires a move into management. Most of these people like the idea of the responsibility and opportunity associated with advancement, but they do not want to leave the professional and technical activities at which they excel. Further, the skills required in management roles are very different than those needed in technical jobs.

Dual-career ladder
System that allows a person to advance through either a management or a technical/professional ladder

An attempt to solve this problem is the dual-career ladder, a system that allows a person to advance through either a management or a technical/professional ladder. Dual-career ladders are now used at many firms, most commonly in technology-driven industries such as pharmaceuticals, chemicals, computers, and electronics. For instance, a telecommunications firm created a dual-career ladder in its IT department to reward talented technical people who do not want to move into management. Different tracks, each with attractive job titles and pay opportunities, are provided.

9-5b Women and Careers

The percentage of working women has increased over the past several decades, with women today making up about half the workforce. Women are employed in all occupations and jobs, but their careers may have a different element than those of men. Since many women bear children and are often the primary caregiver, their career planning and advancement may be disrupted.

Work, Family, and Careers A common career approach for women is to work hard before children arrive, plateau or step off the career track when children are younger, and return to career-focused jobs that allow flexibility when the children are older. This approach is referred to as sequencing. But some women who sequence are concerned that the job market will not welcome them when they return or that the time away will hurt their advancement chances.

The interaction and conflicts among home, family, and career often affect women differently than they do men.[58] By the time men and women have been out of school for six years, on average, women have worked much less time than men. These and other career differences provide challenges for many women. Employers can tap into the female labor market by offering child care assistance, flexible work policies, and a general willingness to be accommodating.

Other approaches have been developed in companies to better utilize women's talents in the workplace. In particular, partnering women with senior executives, rather than less influential managers, can be useful because these individuals can function as strong advocates for competent female leaders.[59] Connecting women with the proper mentors who are willing to act as sponsors in getting them better, more high-profile positions is the key.[60] Some women are working well past the age of 60 due to financial needs created by divorce or caring for aging parents. Others continue to work to obtain intrinsic rewards and professional pride. Organizations benefit from utilizing this well-educated, highly skilled, dedicated workforce.[61]

Glass Ceiling Another concern specifically affecting women is the glass ceiling, the situation in which women fail to progress into top and senior management positions. Nationally, women hold about half of managerial/professional positions but only 10% to 15% of corporate officer positions.[62] Inflexible beliefs about women's roles and placement in the workplace are some of the possible causes of this gap.[63]

Glass ceiling
Situation in which women fail to progress into top and senior management positions

Some organizations provide leaves of absence but proactively keep women involved in the company during time off. Working Mother has named several companies as especially welcoming to working mothers. For example, CA Technologies pays 10 weeks of maternity leave and provides for job shadowing, mentoring, and leadership programs through its women's network. Management consulting firm Oliver Wyman pairs female high performers with senior sponsors to enhance their career progress.[64] Consequently, women are gradually making inroads into upper-level management positions.

9-5c Dual-Career Couples

As the number of women in the workforce continues to increase, particularly in professional careers, so does the number of dual-career couples. The U.S. Bureau of Labor Statistics estimates that more than 80% of all couples are dual-career couples. Many members of dual-career couples are both employed in management, professional, and technical jobs. Problem areas for dual-career couples include family issues and job transfers that require relocation.

For dual-career couples with children, family issues may conflict with career progression. It is important that such career development problems be recognized as early as possible. Whenever possible, involving both partners in planning, even when one is not employed by the company, may enhance the success of such efforts.

Traditionally, employees accepted transfers as part of upward mobility in organizations. However, both employees and companies often find relocation undesirable because of personal hardships such as leaving a support system and finding suitable work for a "trailing" spouse.

GLOBAL

9-5d Global Career Concerns

Global career management can be even more complex than domestic talent management. The movement of managers and employees can be challenging because corporate policies and cultural characteristics in different countries are often dissimilar, and individual expectations about the success of global assignments can vary greatly, thus affecting motivation and commitment. Successful companies develop a culture that facilitates the movement of talent globally and improves retention.

Further, they create sound mobility programs and processes that organize assignee information, effectively evaluate candidates, and provide coaching support during global assignments and repatriation efforts.[65]

Many global employees experience anxiety about their continued career progression. Therefore, employers should take steps to ensure that the experience gained overseas benefits the employee as well as the firm. Some companies address this issue by bringing expatriates back to the home country for development programs and interaction with other company managers and professionals during the assignment. Another potentially useful approach is to establish a mentoring system that matches an expatriate with a corporate executive at headquarters.

Repatriation
Process that involves planning and training for the reassignment of global employees back to their home countries

Repatriation The issue of repatriation is a process that involves planning and training for the reassignment of global employees back to their home countries. After expatriates return home, they often no longer receive the special compensation packages that had been available to them during their assignments. The result is that they may feel a net decrease in total income, even if they receive promotions and pay increases. In addition to dealing with concerns about personal finances, returning expatriates often must re-acclimate to U.S. lifestyles, transportation, and other cultural circumstances, especially if they have been living in less-developed countries.

Many expatriates enjoyed a greater degree of flexibility, autonomy, and independent decision making while living overseas than their counterparts in the United States. Back in the home organization, repatriated employees must readjust to closer working and reporting relationships with other corporate staff.

Another major concern focuses on the organizational status of expatriates when they return. Many expatriates wonder what jobs they will have, whether their international experiences will be valued, and how they will be accepted back into the organization. Unfortunately, many global employers do a poor job of repatriation. To counter this problem, companies should consider providing expatriates flexible assignments, mentoring efforts, meetings with key managers, career support, and guarantees of temporary employment if they complete their foreign assignments early.[66]

Development
Efforts to improve employees' abilities to handle a variety of assignments and to cultivate their capabilities beyond those required by the current job

Global Development Most global firms have learned that it is often a mistake to staff foreign operations with only personnel from headquarters, and they quickly hire local nationals. For this reason, global management development must focus on developing local managers as well as global executives. Global competencies should also be developed early in careers, instead of assigning domestic-based senior executives to international positions.[67] Development areas can include activities such as promoting cultural issues, running an international business, enhancing leadership and management skills, handling problematic people, and building personal qualities. Organizations might also recruit foreign graduate students into fast-track development programs to staff global positions, offer international assignments to leaders to improve their work experience, and utilize social networking to enhance training and development.[68]

LO4 List options for development needs analyses.

9-6 Developing Human Resources

Development involves efforts to improve employees' abilities to handle a variety of assignments and to cultivate their capabilities beyond those required by the current job. Development can benefit both organizations and employees. Employees and

FIGURE 9-9 Development versus Training

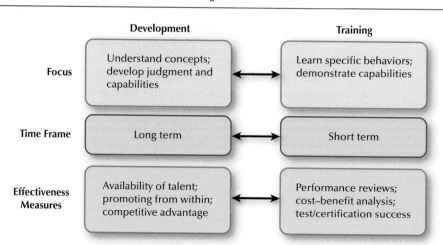

managers with appropriate experiences and abilities may enhance organizational competitiveness and the ability to adapt to a changing environment. In the development process, individuals' careers may also evolve and shift to new or different focuses. Hilton utilized a developmental program for executives that required them to work in various areas of different hotels to better understand how top-level business decisions influence the firm's properties.[69]

Development differs from training. It is possible to train people to answer customer service questions, drive a truck, enter data in a computer system, set up a drill press, or assemble a television. However, development in areas such as judgment, responsibility, decision making, and communication presents a bigger challenge. These areas may or may not develop through individuals' ordinary life experiences. A planned system of development experiences for all employees, not just managers, can help expand the overall level of capabilities in an organization. Figure 9-9 profiles development and compares it with training.

9-6a Possible Development Focuses

Some important and common management capabilities that may require development include emotional intelligence, critical thinking, strategic planning, learning agility, and ethical values.[70] For some technical specialists (tech support, database administration, network design, etc.), certain nontechnical abilities must be developed as well, such as the ability to work under pressure, work independently, solve problems quickly, and communicate clearly.

One point about development is completely clear. In numerous studies that asked employees what they want out of their jobs, training and development ranked at or near the top. The primary assets that individuals have are their knowledge, skills, and abilities (KSAs), and many people view the development of their KSAs as an important part of their jobs.

Lifelong Learning There is a close link between learning and development. For most people, lifelong learning and development are necessary and desirable.

For many professionals, lifelong learning may mean meeting continuing education requirements to retain certifications. For example, to keep their licenses to practice in most states, lawyers, CPAs, teachers, dentists, and nurses must complete continuing education requirements. For other employees, learning and development may involve training to expand existing skills and to prepare for different jobs, for promotions, or even for new jobs after retirement.

Assistance needed from employers for lifelong development typically comes through programs at work, including tuition reimbursement programs. However, much of lifelong learning is voluntary, takes place outside of work hours, and is not always formal. Although it may have no immediate relevance to a person's current job, learning often enhances an individual's confidence, ideas, and enthusiasm.

Reinvention Whether due to a desire for career change or because the employer needs different capabilities, people *reinvent* their careers in midlife or mid-career. These "jobshifters" need to develop capabilities in a new field that holds promise for a productive future. Commonly referred to as second acts, employees who make major changes from one career field to another often need some assistance from an employer to close the gap in their skills.[71] Upon discharge from active duty, military personnel frequently need to adapt their skills to civilian career opportunities. Safelite AutoGlass, Walmart, Capital One, and others have implemented programs targeting former military members who are transitioning. They offer assistance and development to bridge the skills learned in the military to those needed in their operations.[72]

9-6b Development Needs Analyses

Like employee training, employee development begins with an analysis of the needs of both the organization and the individuals within that organization. The goal, of course, is to identify strengths and weaknesses to determine the focus of development.[73] Methods that organizations use to assess development needs include assessment centers, psychological testing, and performance appraisals. Determining the best approach to individual development depends in part on the individual's level of development. The following "HR Competencies & Applications: Leveling Development Focus" feature describes four approaches managers can use.

Assessment centers
Collections of test instruments and exercises designed to diagnose an individual's development needs

Assessment Centers Collections of test instruments and exercises designed to diagnose an individual's development needs are referred to as assessment centers. Companies can use assessment centers for both developing and selecting managers. Employers use assessment centers for a wide variety of jobs.

In a typical assessment center experience, an individual spends two or three days away from the job performing many assessment activities. These activities might include role-plays, tests, cases, leaderless group discussions, computer-based simulations, and peer evaluations. Frequently they also include in-basket exercises in which the individual handles typical work and management problems. For the most part, the exercises represent situations that require the use of individual skills and behaviors. During the exercises, several specially trained judges observe the participants and later share their observations with the candidates.

Assessment centers provide an excellent means for determining individual potential in an unbiased manner.[74] Experience shows that key variables such as leadership, initiative, and supervisory skills cannot be measured with tests alone.

COMPETENCIES & APPLICATIONS

Leveling Development Focus

The classic book *Leadership and the One Minute Manager* by Ken Blanchard contains sage advice about how to work with employees who need development. Since most employees vary in the level of expertise they have on diverse job tasks, the author recommends that development needs analysis be conducted at the task level. For example, an entry-level accountant may be highly competent at posting journal entries but might need to learn how to create accurate, timely financial statements. The four development levels explained below help managers provide appropriate support to each employee on each task.

Level 1, *Enthusiastic beginner*. The employee is new to this task and has little to no working knowledge or expertise. Development should involve specific, detailed directions along with close monitoring and frequent feedback.

Level 2, *Disillusioned learner*. The employee may have tried and not succeeded at mastering the task at hand and has become discouraged. Self-efficacy starts to fall, and the individual is afraid to try again. Development should involve coaching and encouragement. Find novel ways to explain the task and provide plenty of positive reinforcement for even small successes.

Level 3, *Capable but cautious performer*. The individual has developed the necessary expertise and competence but is timid and lacks self-confidence. Offering support and publicly praising the employee can shore up motivation and self-image. Treat the employee as an expert and refer other employees to him or her as the "guru" of the task.

Level 4, *Self-reliant achiever*. The employee is now fully competent and confident when completing the task. He or she knows what to do, how to do it, and how to determine the quality of the work output. It's time to get out of the way and let the individual perform. Development should shift to skills that are at the level 1 stage.

Assessing each employee on a task-by-task basis can produce a rich development environment where energy is invested at the proper level. The employee will appreciate the personalized approach, and the manager will find that this type of development makes the most of time with the employee.[75] After considering these four development levels, answer the following questions:

1. How would you assess an individual's capabilities at the task level? What methods would be most appropriate to determine skill levels?

2. How would you prioritize the development of skills for a particular individual? Why would you work on some skills before others?

KEY COMPETENCIES: Consultation; HR Expertise: People/Learning & Development

---

Assessment centers also offer the advantage of helping identify employees with potential in large organizations. Supervisors may nominate people for the assessment center or employees may volunteer to participate.

Psychological Testing Psychological tests have been used for years to determine employees' developmental potential and needs. Intelligence tests, verbal and mathematical reasoning tests, and personality tests are often given. Psychological testing can provide useful information about individuals, motivation, reasoning abilities, leadership style, interpersonal response traits, and job preferences.

The biggest problem with psychological testing lies in interpretation because untrained managers, supervisors, and workers usually cannot accurately interpret

---

test results. After a professional scores the tests and reports the values to others in the organization, untrained managers may attach their own meanings to the findings. Also, some psychological tests are of limited validity, and test takers may fake desirable responses. Thus, psychological testing is appropriate only when the testing and feedback processes are administered by a qualified professional.

Performance Appraisals Well-done performance appraisals can be a source of development information. Performance data on productivity, employee relations, job knowledge, and other relevant dimensions can be gathered in such assessments. In this context, appraisals designed for development purposes (discussed in more detail in Chapter 10) may be different and more useful in aiding individual employee development than appraisals designed strictly for administrative purposes.

9-7 Talent Development Approaches

LO5 Discuss three career issues that organizations and employees must address.

Common development approaches can occur on or off the job. Figure 9-10 details these approaches. Employee development takes on added importance as knowledge work such as research skills and specialized technology expertise increases for almost all companies. Careful analysis of development needs results in selecting suitable methods.

9-7a Job-Site Development Approaches

All too often, unplanned and perhaps useless activities pass as development on the job. To ensure that the desired development actually occurs, managers must plan and coordinate their development efforts. Managers can choose from various job-site development methods.[76]

Coaching
A collaborative process focused on improving individual performance

Coaching The oldest on-the-job development technique is coaching, a collaborative process focused on improving individual performance. The coach and the person being coached create shared success through a series of ongoing conversations. The process relies on the coach serving as a facilitator rather than an evaluator. Questions that encourage the employee to self-reflect and assess his or her own performance are the basis for coaching interactions. Trust is the underlying foundation of coaching. A coach who demonstrates genuine interest and commitment to the employee creates an environment in which success can occur.[77]

Coaching is not done exclusively by managers. Junior employees are being paired with more senior workers to address the gap in technology skills. Social

FIGURE 9-10 HR Development Approaches

Job-Site Approaches	Off-Site Approaches
• Coaching	• Classroom courses
• Committees	• Seminars
• Job rotation	• Outdoor experiential activities
• Corporate universities	• Sabbaticals/leaves
• Career development centers	

media–savvy younger employees help older workers improve their digital competence. Peer coaches have helped Iron Mountain Sentinels reduce errors by 25% and
reduce turnover by 60%. Front-line employees learn from certified "peer coaches"
who are experts in the job they are doing every day.[78]

Unfortunately, organizations may be tempted to implement coaching without
sufficient planning. Even someone who is good at a job will not necessarily be able
to coach someone else to do it well. Coaches should receive training, feedback, and
recognition to ensure that they effectively work with employees for mutual success.

Committee Assignments Assigning promising employees to important committees may broaden their experiences and help them understand the personalities, issues, and processes governing the organization. For instance, employees on a
safety committee can gain a greater understanding of safety problems and management, which would help them become supervisors. They may also experience the
problems involved in maintaining employee safety awareness. However, managers
need to guard against committee assignments that turn into time-wasting activities.

Job Rotation The process of moving a person from job to job is called
job rotation, and it is widely used as a development technique. For example,
Johnson Controls rotates aspiring plant managers through a two-year program
during which they take on learning assignments in manufacturing, logistics, quality
control, and manufacturing engineering. They are exposed to operational challenges
along with business and leadership essentials.[79] When properly handled, such job
rotation fosters a greater understanding of the organization and improves employee
retention by making individuals more versatile, strengthening their skills, and reducing boredom. When opportunities for promotion within a smaller or medium-sized
organization are scarce, job rotation through lateral transfers may help rekindle
enthusiasm and develop employees' talents. Job rotation also prepares workers to
perform well in multiple jobs, which provides managers with some scheduling flexibility. A disadvantage of job rotation is that it can be expensive because a substantial amount of time is required to acquaint trainees with the different people and
techniques in each new work assignment.

Job rotation
Process of moving a
person from job to job

Corporate Universities and Career Development Centers Large
organizations may use corporate universities to develop managers and other employees.
For instance, for over 50 years, McDonald's has used Hamburger University to deliver
courses that prepare its managers for the challenges and opportunities associated with
managing the company.[80] Courses are designed to address company-specific knowledge and skills, and they can provide a competitive edge for the firm. Participation
does not usually result in a degree, accreditation, or graduation. A related alternative,
partnerships between companies and traditional universities, can occur where the universities design and teach specific courses for employers.[81]

Career development centers can also be set up to coordinate in-house programs
and programs provided by third parties. They may include assessment data for individuals, career goals and strategies, coaching, seminars, and online approaches.

9-7b Off-Site Development Approaches

Off-site development approaches give individuals opportunities to get away from
their jobs and concentrate solely on what is to be learned. Contact with others who

are concerned with slightly different problems and come from different organizations may provide employees with new and different perspectives. Various off-site methods can be used.

Classroom Courses and Seminars Most off-the-job development programs include some classroom instruction. People are familiar with classroom training, which gives it the advantage of being widely accepted. But the lecture system sometimes used in classroom instruction encourages passive listening and reduced learner participation, which is a distinct disadvantage. Sometimes trainees have little opportunity to question, clarify, and discuss the lecture material. The effectiveness of classroom instruction depends on multiple factors: group size, trainees' abilities, instructors' capabilities and styles, and subject matter.

Organizations often send employees to externally sponsored seminars or professional courses, such as those offered by numerous professional and consulting groups. Organizations also encourage continuing education by reimbursing employees for the costs of college courses. Tuition reimbursement programs provide incentives for employees to study for advanced degrees through evening and weekend classes they attend outside of their regular workdays and hours.

Outdoor Experiential Activities Some organizations send executives and managers to experiences held outdoors, called *outdoor training* or outdoor experiential activities. The rationale for using these wilderness excursions, which can last for several days, is that such experiences can increase self-confidence and help individuals reevaluate personal goals and efforts. For individuals in work groups or teams, shared risks and challenges outside the office environment can create a sense of teamwork. The challenges may include rock climbing in the California desert, whitewater rafting on a river, backpacking in the Rocky Mountains, or handling a longboat off the coast of Maine. Outfitters like Outward Bound offer programs tailored to corporate groups and custom design events to fit the organization's development goals.[82]

Survival-type management development courses may have more impact than many other management seminars. But companies must consider the inherent perils. Some participants have been unable to handle the physical and emotional challenges associated with rappelling down a cliff or climbing a 40-foot tower. The decision to sponsor such programs should depend on the capabilities of the employees involved and the learning objectives.

Sabbatical
Time off the job to
develop and rejuvenate

Sabbaticals and Leaves of Absence A sabbatical is an opportunity that some companies provide for employees to take time off the job to develop and rejuvenate, as well as to participate in activities that help others. Some employers provide paid sabbaticals, while others allow employees to take unpaid sabbaticals. The length of time away from work varies greatly.

Companies that offer sabbaticals speak well of the results. Positive reasons for sabbaticals are to help prevent employee burnout, offer advantages in recruiting and retention, and boost individual employee morale. Female employees have made use of sabbaticals or other types of leaves for family care reasons. The value of this time off to employees is seen in better retention of key female workers, who also often return more energized and enthusiastic about their work–life balancing act. The nature of the learning experience generally falls outside the control of the organization, leaving it somewhat to chance.

LO6 Identify several management development methods.

9-8 Management and Leader Development

Although development is important for all employees, it is essential for managers. Without appropriate development, managers may lack the capabilities to best deploy and manage resources (including employees) throughout the organization. While classroom training can be helpful, experience often leads to greater development of senior managers because much of it occurs in real-life, on-the-job situations.

Numerous approaches are used to mold and enhance the experiences that managers need to be effective.[83] The most widely used methods are supervisor development, leadership development, management modeling, management coaching, management mentoring, and executive education. Figure 9-11 shows experience-based sources of managers' learning and lists some important lessons for supervisors, middle managers, and senior-level executives that should be provided by development activities.

9-8a Problems with Management Development Efforts

Management development efforts are subject to certain common mistakes and problems. Many of the problems have resulted from inadequate HR planning and a lack of coordination of HR development efforts. Common problems include the following:

- Failing to conduct adequate needs analysis
- Trying out fad programs or training methods
- Substituting training for selecting qualified individuals

FIGURE 9-11 Management Lessons Learned from Job Experience

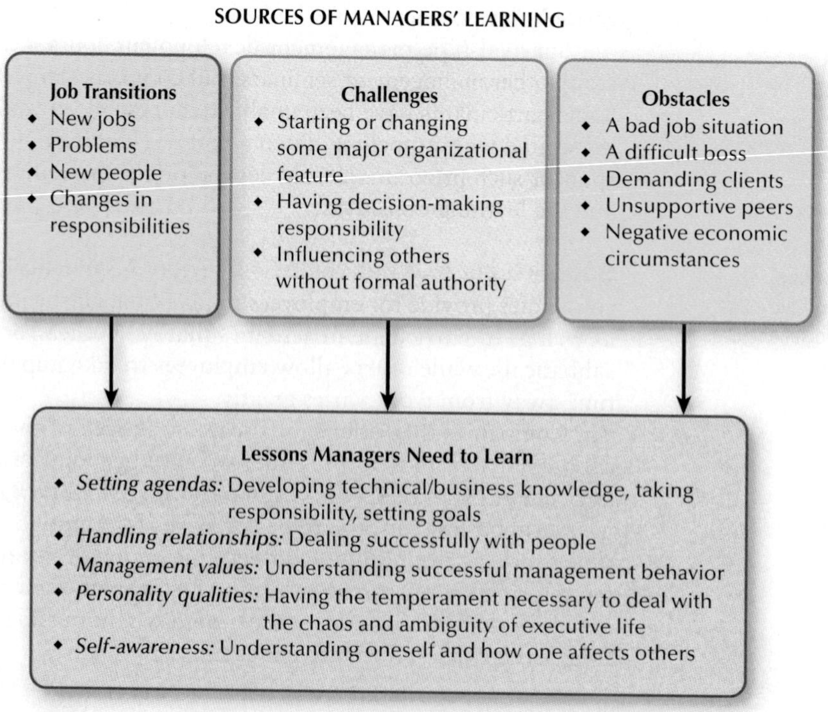

SOURCES OF MANAGERS' LEARNING

Job Transitions	Challenges	Obstacles
• New jobs • Problems • New people • Changes in responsibilities	• Starting or changing some major organizational feature • Having decision-making responsibility • Influencing others without formal authority	• A bad job situation • A difficult boss • Demanding clients • Unsupportive peers • Negative economic circumstances

Lessons Managers Need to Learn

- *Setting agendas:* Developing technical/business knowledge, taking responsibility, setting goals
- *Handling relationships:* Dealing successfully with people
- *Management values:* Understanding successful management behavior
- *Personality qualities:* Having the temperament necessary to deal with the chaos and ambiguity of executive life
- *Self-awareness:* Understanding oneself and how one affects others

Another common management development problem is *encapsulated development*, which occurs when an individual learns new methods and ideas but returns to a work unit that is still bound by old attitudes and methods. The development was "encapsulated" in the classroom and is essentially not used on the job. Consequently, individuals who participate in development programs paid for by their employers may become discouraged and move to new employers who allow them to use their newly developed capabilities more effectively.

9-8b Supervisor Development

The beginning level for managerial development is the first-line supervisory job. It is often difficult to move from being a member of the work group to being the boss. Therefore, new supervisors who are promoted from individual contributor roles often require new skills and mind-sets to be successful supervisors.

Employers may conduct *pre-supervisor training*. This is done to provide a realistic job preview of what supervisors will face and to convey to individuals that they cannot just rely on their current job skills and experience in their new positions. Development for supervisors may vary but usually includes some common elements such as basic management responsibilities, time management, and employee relations.

Employee relations training helps prepare supervisors to deal with "people problems" associated with overseeing employees. The training focuses on the development of the employee relations skills a person needs to work well with others. Most employee relations programs are aimed at new or relatively inexperienced first-line supervisors and middle managers. They cover motivation, leadership, employee communication, conflict resolution, performance management, team building, and other interpersonal topics.

9-8c Leadership Development

Executives are aware that effective leaders create positive change and are important for organizational success. Leadership development is expanding a person's capacity to be effective in leadership roles. Organizations such as Johnson & Johnson, General Electric, and 3M Company are among the top firms in leadership development. This development occurs in many ways: classroom programs, assessments, modeling, coaching, job assignments, mentoring, and executive education.

While universities may produce smart, ambitious graduates with good technical skills, many face a very steep learning curve when making the change from school into leadership positions.[85] Common ways to help individuals transition successfully into leadership roles include modeling, coaching, mentoring, and executive education. The following "HR Perspective: Playing the Leadership Game" feature describes a cutting-edge leadership program aimed at teaching future leaders valuable skills.

Modeling A common adage in management development says that managers tend to manage as they were managed. In other words, managers learn by behavior modeling, or copying someone else's behavior. Management development efforts can take advantage of natural human behavior by matching young or developing managers with positive models and then reinforcing the desirable behaviors exhibited by the learners.[86] The modeling process involves more than straightforward imitation or copying. For example, one can learn what not to do by observing a model who does something wrong. Thus, exposure to both positive and negative models can benefit a new manager as part of leadership development efforts.

Modeling
Copying someone else's behavior

Playing the Leadership Game

Financial services holding company BB&T has a passion for leadership. The company's leadership model is based on the idea that people act according to their beliefs and values. Leaders are successful when they can embed desirable beliefs and behaviors in their followers. A strong desire to spread the message about leadership led the company to develop outreach efforts to engage future leaders.

Reaching out to a target audience of 14- to 24-year-olds required a creative solution. BB&T found just the solution with a game that is accessed as a mobile app. LEGACY: A BB&T Leadership Challenge is an innovative, free gaming app that teaches users valuable leadership lessons. The game is a suite of 10 mini-games with 25 "quests" to save the village of Failburg. The medieval-themed role play challenges the player to help King Alpheus make the village successful. The king provides feedback and guidance to the player. The player must manage several village characters who are having difficulty handling their area of village operations. Using praise,

coaching, or scolding techniques, the player redirects each character. The village benefits when the player uses the proper strategy. A leadership meter tracks points earned during the game.

BB&T estimated that 3,000 to 4,000 users would download the app in the first two weeks. They were delighted when the number of downloads far exceeded that number, and over 15,000 people have accessed the app. While there is no direct tracking of users, the goal of spreading the leadership philosophy seems to be taking hold.[84] Based on these ideas, consider the following key questions for discussion:

1. Download the app from Google Play or the Apple Store and try it yourself. What is your evaluation of the usefulness of the LEGACY game to test leadership competence?

2. How can a game like LEGACY be used within a company to develop leaders? What type of competition and debriefing might be used in leadership development to promote use of the game?

Coaching Effective leadership coaching requires patience and good communication skills.[87] Like modeling, it complements the natural way humans learn. An outline of good coaching pointers will often include the following:

- Explain appropriate behaviors.
- Make clear why actions were taken.
- Accurately state observations.
- Provide possible alternatives/suggestions.
- Follow up and reinforce positive behaviors used.

Leadership coaching is a specific application of coaching. Companies may use outside experts as executive coaches to help managers improve leadership skills. Sometimes these experts help deal with problematic management styles. Consultants serving as executive coaches predominantly come from a psychology or counseling background and can serve many roles for a client by providing key questions and general directions. Sometimes they meet with employees in person, but many do their coaching by phone or electronically. Research on the effectiveness of leadership coaching suggests that coaching can be beneficial in dealing with chronic stress, psychological difficulties, and even physiological problems faced by executives and managers.[88]

FIGURE 9-12   Stages in Management Mentoring Relationships

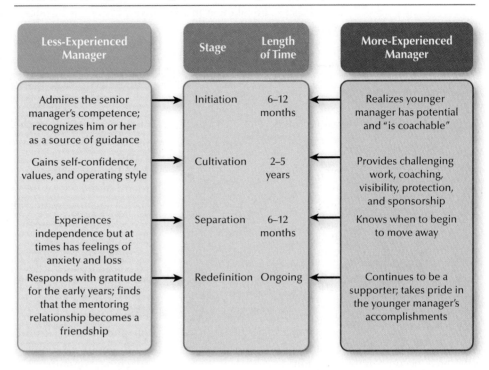

Less-Experienced Manager	Stage	Length of Time	More-Experienced Manager
Admires the senior manager's competence; recognizes him or her as a source of guidance	Initiation	6–12 months	Realizes younger manager has potential and "is coachable"
Gains self-confidence, values, and operating style	Cultivation	2–5 years	Provides challenging work, coaching, visibility, protection, and sponsorship
Experiences independence but at times has feelings of anxiety and loss	Separation	6–12 months	Knows when to begin to move away
Responds with gratitude for the early years; finds that the mentoring relationship becomes a friendship	Redefinition	Ongoing	Continues to be a supporter; takes pride in the younger manager's accomplishments

Management mentoring
A relationship in which experienced managers aid individuals in the earlier stages of their careers

Management Mentoring A method called management mentoring employs a relationship in which experienced managers aid individuals in the earlier stages of their careers. Such a relationship provides an environment for conveying technical, interpersonal, and organizational skills from a more experienced person to a designated less experienced person. Not only does the inexperienced employee benefit, but the mentor also may enjoy having the opportunity and challenge of sharing wisdom.[89]

Many individuals have a series of advisors or mentors during their careers and may find advantages in learning from the different mentors. Additionally, those being mentored may find previous mentors to be useful sources for networking. Figure 9-12 describes the four stages in most successful mentoring relationships.

In many countries around the world, the proportion of women holding management jobs is lower than the proportion of men holding such jobs. Similarly, the number of racial and ethnic minorities who fill senior management positions is low. Company mentoring programs that focus specifically on women and individuals of minority racial/ethnic backgrounds have been successful in some larger firms. On the basis of various narratives of successful female executives, breaking the glass ceiling requires developing political sophistication, building credibility, and refining management styles aided by mentoring.

Executive Education Executives in an organization often face difficult jobs because of changing and unknown circumstances. Churning at the top of organizations and the stresses of executive jobs contribute to increased turnover in these positions. In an effort to decrease turnover and increase management development capabilities, organizations are using specialized education for executives. This type of training includes executive education traditionally offered by university business schools and adds strategy formulation, financial models, logistics, alliances, and global issues. Enrollment in Executive Masters of Business Administration (EMBA) degree programs is also popular.

SUMMARY

- Talent management is important because it is concerned with the attraction, development, and retention of human resources.
- Training, succession planning, career planning, and performance management are crucial parts of talent management.
- Succession planning is the process that identifies how key employees are to be replaced, including deciding whether to make or buy talent and how to use electronic and web-based succession planning programs.
- Mistakes can occur in succession planning, including focusing only on CEO and senior management succession.
- The nature of careers is changing because retention of employees and work–life balance have become more important.
- Career planning may focus on organizational needs, individual needs, or both, and career paths and employer websites are part of career planning.
- A person chooses a career according to interests, personality, skills, values, and other factors.
- Several special individual career issues must be addressed, including those related to technical and professional workers.
- Career issues for women may include work–family balance and glass ceiling concerns, as well as being part of dual-career couples.

- Global career development has special challenges, including the necessity of relocating dual-career couples, global development, and repatriation.
- Development differs from training because it focuses on less tangible aspects of performance, such as attitudes and values.
- Developing specific competencies may require lifelong learning and redevelopment of employees.
- Needs analyses for development may include assessment centers, psychological testing, and performance appraisals.
- HR development approaches can involve job-site and off-site learning activities.
- On-the-job development methods include coaching, committee assignments, job rotation, and corporate universities and career centers.
- Off-site development means often include classroom courses, seminars, and degrees; outdoor experiences; and sabbaticals and other leaves of absence.
- Management development is a special focus in many organizations, including supervisor development and leadership development.
- Management modeling, coaching, and mentoring are valuable parts of management development efforts.

CRITICAL THINKING CHALLENGES

1. Discuss what talent management is and why it is a consideration addressed by a growing number of employers.

2. Visit the MindTap website and access the career development assessments. Complete one or several of the online assessments (interests, personality, skills, and values). Explain what you learned about yourself from each assessment that you completed. Visit the O*net website (http://www.onetonline. org) and follow the Advanced Search links to identify occupations that are a good match

for your profile. Discuss the attractiveness of the jobs presented and determine what developmental steps you would take to prepare for a career in one of the occupations.

3. How have the evolving business environment and the emergence of free agent workers affected make-or-buy talent decisions?

4. Design a management development program for first-level supervisors in a mass-market retail company. What courses and experiences do they need?

5. You are the HR Director of a large manufacturing company that is approximately 50 years old. The company has reaped the benefits of a mostly tenured workforce, and many of the key workers are now approaching retirement age. It is anticipated that approximately 20% of the company's workforce will retire in the next three to five years. To assist the company with the retirement transition process, you want to present a business case to the President for a succession plan for several key positions, including the Chief Financial Officer and Director of Operations.

   A. Which internal and external company advisors should be included in the succession planning process?
   B. The successor employee for the replacement of the Chief Financial Officer and Director of Operations positions should have an advanced level of work experience in what key essential functions? How can the company help candidates get these experiences?

CASE | Walmart's Boot Camp for Top Leaders

Mass retailer Walmart's executives realized that the company was capable of building and opening new stores faster than it could develop the leadership talent needed to operate them. To build that capability, the company launched a Leadership Academy that puts promising leaders through a 16-week boot camp.

Individuals with high potential are drafted into the program. They are reassigned from their normal job assignments and deployed to the academy. The boot camp training runs in two-week cycles beginning with in-depth training at the Bentonville, Arkansas, headquarters. After the initial training, participants return to their workplace and focus on specific projects that supplement their in-class learning. Their training combines theory and practice, and it uses business case scenarios and hands-on exercises. Recruits learn to think critically and make decisions under pressure.

Since the primary reason that newly promoted leaders fail is lack of soft skills, Walmart's Leadership Academy includes a significant amount of training on interpersonal skills such as listening, empathizing, building trust, and collaborating. A key element of the program is community involvement. Walmart stores are often one of the largest employers in the communities where they are located, and store managers serve as brand ambassadors and community leaders. Projects like building homes for low-income families or volunteering at children's and veterans' hospitals complement classroom and work-based training.

Participants in the program say that it is like military boot camp because the intensity is overwhelming and performance standards are rigorous. However, it prepares them for the challenges of running a store with many pressures and demands. There are similarities to planning a military strategy with logistics, resource constraints, and time pressures. The Leadership Academy is a natural extension of Walmart's commitment to hire military veterans. While not all of the participants are former service members, the program is particularly appealing to that segment of the workforce.

The program's ultimate objective is to promote graduates within one to three months of graduation. More than 500 leaders have completed the program since its inception.[90]

QUESTIONS

1. What are the pros and cons of rotating participants from in-class training back to the worksite every two weeks? What support would be needed at the worksite to ensure that the trainees get the most out of their hands-on assignments?

2. How would you evaluate the effectiveness of the Leadership Academy?

3. How does the overtone of military-style training impact Walmart's employment brand? Would this appeal to particular segments of the labor force? How might it impact the company's ability to recruit diverse employees and participants?

SUPPLEMENTAL CASES

Leadership Leverage

This case demonstrates how a health care company utilized talent to better manage the development of employees. (For the case, go to www.cengage.com/management/mathis.)

Developed Today, Gone Tomorrow

This case illustrates a serious concern some employers have about developing employees only to have them leave. (For the case, go to www.cengage.com/management/mathis.)

Equipping for the Future

This case shows how one company in the oil industry started a succession planning program. (For the case, go to www.cengage.com/management/mathis.)

END NOTES

1. Adapted from Katie-Jo Andreola, "Groom to Move," *HR Magazine*, May 2014, pp. 38–40.
2. Ilene Gochman and Paul Storfer, "Talent for Tomorrow: Four Secrets for HR Agility in an Uncertain World," *People & Strategy* 37, no. 2 (Summer 2014), 24–28.
3. Paula Ketter, "Defining Integrated Talent Management," *T+D*, September 2013, p. 6; Bersin and Associates, "Integrated Talent Management," http://www.bersin.com/Lexicon/Details.aspx?id=12860.
4. Shane Douthitt and Scott Mondore, "Creating a Business-Focused HR Function with Analytics and Integrated talent Management," *People & Strategy* 36, no. 4 (2013), 16–21; Maria Meyers and Marianne van Woerkom, "The Influence of Underlying Philosophies on Talent Management: Theory, Implications for Practice, and Research Agenda," *Journal of World Business* 49, no. 2 (April 2014), 192–203.
5. Toni Hodges Detuncq and Lynn Schmidt, "Examining Integrated Talent Management," *T+D*, September 2013, pp. 31–35.
6. Peter Cappelli, "A Supply Chain Model for Talent Management," *People & Strategy* 32, no. 3 (2009), 4–7.
7. Jennifer Salopek, "Good Connections," *TD*, October 2014, pp. 48–50.
8. David Collings, "Toward Mature Talent Management: Beyond Shareholder Value," *Human Resource Development Quarterly* 25, no. 3 (Fall 2014), 301–319.
9. Andrew R. McIlvaine, "The Human Risk Factor," *Human Resource Executive*, February 2012, 14–18.
10. Based on David Forman, "Stuck in Neutral," *T+D*, November 2013, pp. 46–50.
11. Darren Sprod, "Why Investing in Talent Management Software Is Smart Business," *Human Resources Magazine* 18, no. 6 (February–March 2014), 6–7.
12. Mark McGraw, "Critiquing Critical-Talent Practices," *Human Resource Executive*, April 14, 2014, http://www.hreonline.com/HRE/view/story.jhtml?id=534356938.
13. Anna Sutton and Sara Watson, "Can Competencies at Selection Predict Performance and Development Needs?" *Journal of Management Development* 32, no. 9 (2013), 1023–1035.
14. Hossein Nouri and Robert Parker, "Career Growth Opportunities and Employee Turnover Intentions in Public Accounting Firms," *British Accounting Review* 45, no. 2 (June 2013), 138–148; Wali Rahman and Zekeriya Nas, "Employee Development and Turnover Intentions: Theory Validation," *European Journal of Training and Development* 37, no. 6 (2013), 564–579.
15. Daniel Wolfe, "Global PayPal Buys StackMob to Add Engineering Talent," *Mergers & Acquisitions Report* 28, no. 51 (December 23, 2013), 14; Mary Wisniewski, "Need Tech Talent? BBVA's Answer Is Buy a Firm That Has It," *American Banker: Bank Technology News*, December 12, 2014, http://www.americanbanker.com/news/bank-technology/need-tech-talent-bbvas-answer-is-buy-a-firm-that-has-it-1071650-1.html.
16. American Management Association, "The Make or Buy Decision," June 3, 2014, http://www.amanet.org/training/articles/The-Make-or-Buy-Decision.aspx; Andrew R. McIlvaine, "Finding Talent: Buy It or Make It?" *HRE Online*, June 14, 2011, http://www.hreonline.com/HRE/print.jhtml?id=533339066.
17. Matthew Bidwell, "Paying More to Get Less: The Effects of External Hiring versus Internal Mobility," *Administrative Science Quarterly* 56, no. 3 (September 2011), 369–407; CEO World, "Are You Trying to Decide Whether to Hire an Internal or External Candidate?" *CEO World Magazine*, February 27, 2014, http://ceoworld.biz/ceo/2014/02/27/are-you-trying-to-decide-whether-to-hire-an-internal-or-external-candidate-9920976.
18. Katherine Holt and Kyoko Seki, "Global Leadership: A Developmental Shift for Everyone," *Industrial & Organizational Psychology* 5, no. 2 (June 2012), 196–215; Juliette Alban-Metcalfe and Beverly Alimo-Metcalfe, "Reliability and Validity of the Leadership Competencies and Engaging Leadership Scale," *International*

Journal of Public Sector Management 26, no. 1 (2013), 56–73.

19. Donna Parrey, "The Global Leadership Competencies We Aren't Teaching," *Talent Management*, June 13, 2014; Julie-Anne Sheppard, James Sarros, and Joseph Santora, "Twenty-First Century Leadership: International Imperatives," *Management Decision* 51, no. 2 (2013), 267–280.

20. Bjarne Espedal, Paul Gooderham, and Inger Stensaker, "Developing Organizational Social Capital or Prima Donnas in MNEs? The Role of Global Leadership Development Programs," *Human Resource Management* 52, no. 4 (July–August 2013), 607–625; Annimarie Neal and Karen Conway, "Executives, Take Charge," *T+D* 67, no. 11 (November 2013), 52–56; Roy Maurer, "Emerging Markets Drive Global Talent Strategy Shift," *SHRM Online*, November 5, 2013, http://www.shrm.org/hrdisciplines/global/articles/pages/emerging-markets-global-talent-strategy.aspx.

21. Maura C. Ciccarelli, "Perfecting the Hi-Po Process," *Human Resource Executive Online*, April 2, 2012, www.hreonline.com.

22. James Oldroyd and Shad Morris, "Catching Falling Stats: A Human Resource Response to Social Capital's Detrimental Effect of Information Overload on Star Employees," *Academy of Management Review* 37, no. 3 (2012), 396–418; Herman Aquinis and Ernest O'Boyle, "Star Performers in Twenty-First Century Organizations," *Personnel Psychology* 67, no. 2 (Summer 2014), 313–350; Donna Parrey, "Accelerating High Potential Development," *Chief Learning Officer* 13, no. 1 (October 2014), 26–47.

23. Roy Maurer, "Solely Focusing on High-Performers Puts Enterprise at Risk," *SHRM Online*, June 11, 2014, http://www.shrm.org/hrdisciplines/global/articles/pages/focus-high-performers-talent-risk.aspx; Amina Raza Malik, "High Potential Programs: Let's Hear It for 'B' Players," *Human Resource Management Review* 24, no. 4 (December 2014), 330–346; Sandi Edwards, "Maintaining the Delicate Balance when Developing High-Potential Programs," *T+D* 66, no. 4 (April 2012), 60–65.

24. Sarah Fister Gale, "Too High on High Potentials?" *Talent Management*, July 18, 2014.

25. Ingmar Bjorkman, Mats Ehrnrooth, Kristiina Makela, Adam Smale, and Jennie Sumelius, "Talent or Not? Employee Reactions to Talent Identification," *Human Resource Management* 52, no. 2 (March–April 2013), 195–214; Jolyn Gelens, Joeri Hofmans, Nicky Dries, and Roland Pepermans, "Talent Management and Organisational Justice: Employee Reactions to High Potential Identification," *Human Resource Management Journal* 24, no. 2 (April 2014), 159–175.

26. Based on Mark McGraw, "The Secrecy Surrounding Hi-Po Programs," *Human Resource Executive*, January–February 2013; Talent Management .com, "Majority of Companies Misidentify High Potentials," *TalentManagement.com*, March 25, 2014, http://www.talentmgt.com/articles/report-majority-of-companies-misidentify-high-potentials; Allan Church and Christopher Rotolo, "How Are Top Companies Assessing Their High-Potentials and Senior Executives? A Talent Management Benchmark Study," *Consulting Psychology Journal: Practice & Research* 65, no. 3 (September 2013), 199–223.

27. William J. Rothwell, "Replacement Planning: A Starting Point for Succession Planning and Talent Management," *International Journal of Training and Development* 15, no. 1 (2011), 87–99.

28. Frank Kalman, "Organizations Work to Bridge Succession Planning Gap," *Talent Management*, April 18, 2014, http://www.talentmgt.com/articles/organizations-work-to-bridge-succession-planning-gap.

29. Paul Ziobro and Joann Lublin, "Big Retailers Find It Hard Shopping for a CEO," *Wall Street Journal*, May 7, 2014, p. B1; Rachel Feintzeig, "You're Fired! And We Really Mean It," *Wall Street Journal*, November 5, 2014, p. B1; David Larker and Scott Saslow, "2014 Succession Planning and Talent Development Survey," http://www.gsb.stanford.edu/cldr/research/surveys/talent.html.

30. Theresa Minton-Eversole, "Will They Be Ready to Lead when You're Ready to Leave?" *SHRM Online*, June 22, 2014, http://www.shrm.org/hrdisciplines/orgempdev/articles/pages/succession-planning.aspx.

31. Mark McGraw, "Find Your Own Successor," *Wall Street Journal*, April 1, 2014.

32. Norma Davila and Wanda Pina-Ramirez, "Populate the Pipeline," *T+D*, February 2014, pp. 33–37.

33. Norma Davila and Wanda Pina-Ramirez, "Populate the Pipeline," *T+D*, February 2014, pp. 33–37.

34. SHRM Knowledge Center, "Succession Planning: What Is a 9-box Grid?" *SHRM Online*, December 3, 2012, http://www.shrm.org/templatestools/hrqa/pages/whatsa9boxgridandhowcananhrdepartmentuseit.aspx; Nicky Dries and Roland Pepermans, "How to Identify Leadership Potential: Development and Testing of a Consensus Model," *Human Resource Management* 51, no. 3 (May–June 2012), 361–385.

35. Based on Willa Plank, "Succession Do's and Don'ts," *Wall Street Journal*, April 28, 2014, p. R3; Doris Sims, "5 Ways to Increase Success in Succession Planning," *TD*, August 2014, pp. 60–65; Allan Church, "Succession Planning 2.0: Building Bench through Better Execution," *Strategic HR Review* 13, no. 6 (2014), 233–242.

36. Jill Cueni-Cohen, "Who's in Charge of Career Development?" *HRE Online*, March 19, 2014, http://www.hreonline.com/HRE/view/story.jhtml?id=534356842.

37. Larry Stevens, "Customizing Their Careers," *Human Resource Executive*, November 2013, pp. 18–20.

38. Edie Goldberg, "The Changing Tides of Careers," *People & Strategy* 35, no. 4 (2012), 52–58.

39. Martin Gubler, John Arnold, and Crispin Coombs, "Reassessing the Protean Career Concept: Empirical Findings, Conceptual Components, and Measurement," *Journal of Organizational Behavior* 35 (February 2014), S23–S40.

40. Jukka Vuori, Salla Toppinen-Tanner, and Pertti Mutanen, "Effects of Resource-Building Group Intervention on Career Management and Mental Health in Work Organizations: Randomized Controlled Field

Trial," *Journal of Applied Psychology* 97, no. 2 (2012), 273–286.

41. Eric Short, "Move around before Moving Up," *Chief Learning Officer*, July 2014, pp. 19–22; Eric Short, "Side Effects of Lateral Move," *Chief Learning Officer*, June 25, 2014, http://www.clomedia.com/articles/5700-side-effects-of-a-lateral-move.

42. Betsy Larson, "Custom Careers," *HR Magazine*, June 2013, pp. 54–56.

43. Mark McGraw, "Career Creativity," *Human Resource Executive*, December 2013, 12–16.

44. Tom Starner, "Career Path Conundrum," *HRE Online*, June 14, 2014, http://www.hreonline.com/HRE/view/story.jhtml?id=534357256.

45. Nick Leigh-Morgan, "10 Companies with Fantastic Career Sites and what You Can Learn from Them," *ERE.net*, November 20, 2012, http://www.ere.net/2012/11/20/10-companies-with-fantastic-career-sites-and-what-you-can-learn-from-them.

46. Scott Seibert, Maria Kraimer, Brooks Holtom, and Abigail Pierotti, "Even the Best Laid Plans Sometimes Go Askew: Career Self-Management Processes, Career Shocks, and the Decision to Pursue Graduate Education," *Journal of Applied Psychology* 98, no. 1 (2013), 169–182.

47. Katherine Jones, "New Faces, Changing Places: The Growth of the Free Agent Professional," *Workforce Solutions Review* 4, no. 5 (October–November 2013), 38–39; Jan Reuter, "Five Steps to a Recession Proof Career," *Industrial & Commercial Training* 45, no. 1 (2013), 60–63.

48. John Dudovskiy, "Career Planning and Personal Development Plan: Sample," *Research Methodology.net*, October 12, 2014, http://research-methodology.net/career-planning-and-personal-development-plan-sample/.

49. Thomas Harrington and Jennifer Long, "The History of Interest Inventories and Career Assessments in Career Counseling," *Career Development Quarterly* 61, no. 1 (March 2013), 83–92; Stephanie Burns, "Validity of Person Matching in Vocational Interest Inventories," *Career Development Quarterly* 62, no. 2 (June 2014), 114–127.

50. O*net.org, "Skills Search," http://www.onetonline.org/skills.

51. John Lounsbury, Nancy Foster, Jacob Levy, and Lucy Gibson, "Key Personality Traits of Sales Managers," *Work* 48, no. 2 (2014), 239–253; Stephen Woods, Filip Lievens, Filip DeFruyt, and Bart Wille, "Personality across Working Life: The Longitudinal and Reciprocal Influences of Personality on Work," *Journal of Organizational Behavior* 34 (July 2013), S7–S25.

52. Jacquelyn Smith, "How to Start Thinking about a Career Change," *Forbes.com*, November 12, 2012; Dawn Rosenberg McKay, "Identifying Your Work Values: Clarifying Your Work Values Leads to Job Satisfaction," *Aboutcareers.com*, http://careerplanning.about.com/od/selfassessment/a/work_values.htm; Malika Richards, Carolyn Egri, David Ralston, Irina Naoumova, Tania Casado, Florian Wangenheim, Thanh Hung Vu, Andre Pekerti, and Sylvia Schroll-Machl, "How Can We Better Understand Current and Future Workforce Values in the Global Business Environment?" *Thunderbird International Business Review* 54, no. 5 (September–October 2012), 609–623.

53. Hila Hofstetter and Aaron Cohen, "The Mediating Role of Job Content Plateau on the Relationship between Work Experience Characteristics and Early Retirement and Turnover Intentions," *Personnel Review* 43, no. 3 (2014), 350–376.

54. Yu-Hsuan Wang, Changya Hu, Carrie Hurst, and Chun-Chi Yang, "Antecedents and Outcomes of Career Plateaus: The Roles of Mentoring Others and Proactive Personality," *Journal of Vocational Behavior* 85, no. 3 (December 2014), 319–328; Veronica Godshalk and C. Melissa Fender, "External and Internal Reasons for Career Plateauing: Relationships with Work Outcomes," *Group & Organization Management*, November 14, 2014.

55. Becky Packard, Miki Leach, Yedalis Ruz, Consuelo Nelson, and Hannah DiCocco, "School-to-Work Transition of Career and Technical Education Graduates," *Career Development Quarterly* 60, no. 2 (June 2012), 134–144; Willibrord de Graaf

and Kaj van Zenderen, "School-Work Transition: The Interplay between Institutional and Individual Processes," *Journal of Education & Work* 26, no. 2 (April 2013), 121–142.

56. Anne Wohrmann, Jurgen Deller, and Mo Wang, "Postretirement Career Planning: Testing a Model Based on Social Cognitive Career Theory," *Journal of Career Development* 41, no. 5 (October 2014), 363–381.

57. Ameriprise Financial, "Working in Retirement," *Ameriprise.com*, https://www.ameriprise.com/retire/planning-for-retirement/retirement-saving/working-after-retirement.asp.

58. G. A. Maxwell and A. Broadbridge, "Generation Y Graduates and Career Transition: Perspectives by Gender," *European Management Journal* 32, no. 4 (August 2014), 547–553.

59. Lisa Cohen and Joseph Broschak, "Whose Jobs Are These? The Impact of the Proportion of Female Managers on the Number of New Management Jobs Filled by Women versus Men," *Administrative Science Quarterly* 58, no. 4 (December 2013), 509–541.

60. Dana Wilkie, "Women Know Mentors Are Key, so Why Don't They Have Them?" *SHRM Online*, March 31, 2014, http://www.shrm.org/hrdisciplines/diversity/articles/pages/women-few-mentors.aspx.

61. Kathryn Tyler, "Still on the Job," *HR Magazine*, May 2013, p. 42.

62. Jill Cueni-Cohen, "Empowering Hi-Po Women," *Human Resource Executive*, November 2014, pp. 47–49.

63. "How Women Can Contribute More to the US Economy," *McKinsey Quarterly*, April 2011, www.mckinseyquarterly.com.

64. Working Mother Magazine, "2014 Working Mother 100 Best Companies," http://www.workingmother.com/best-company-list/156592.

65. Eileen Mullaney, "Talent Mobility," *Workspan*, February 2012, pp. 32–36.

66. Pamela Cox, Raihan Khan, and Kimberly Armani, "Repatriate Adjustment and Turnover: The Role of Expectations and Perceptions," *Review of Business & Finance Studies* 4, no. 1 (2013), 1–15.

67. Kristen B. Frasch, "Defining Global Leadership Competencies," *Human*

Resource Executive Online, August 5, 2011, www.hreonline.com.

68. Neal Goodman, "Talent Development in a Global Economy," *Training*, July–August 2011, www.trainingmag.com.

69. Dori Meinert, "In the Trenches," *HR Magazine*, August 2011, p. 28.

70. Lauren Weber, "Here's what Boards Want in Executives," *Wall Street Journal*, December 10, 2014, p. B5.

71. Robert Grossman, "Encore!" *HR Magazine*, July 2014, pp. 27–31; Laurent Belsie, "The Job-Shifters: People Who Reinvent Themselves Mid-Career," *Christian Science Monitor.com*, February 5, 2012, http://www.csmonitor.com/Business/2012/0205/The-job-shifters-people-who-reinvent-themselves-mid-career; Richard Feloni, "Here's Why It's Never too Late to Reinvent Yourself," *Business Insider.com*, August 27, 2014, http://www.businessinsider.com/wireds-kevin-kelly-on-career-reinvention-2014-8.

72. TAOnline, "Featured Employers," *TAOnline.com*, http://www.taonline.com.

73. Michelle Hite and Amelia Nathanson, "How Do You Do?" *HR Magazine*, July 2014, pp. 40–42; Randall White, "Strength Is Not Enough," *Chief Learning Officer*, July 31, 2014, http://www.clomedia.com/articles/5744-strength-is-not-enough.

74. John Meriac, Brian Hoffman, and David Woehr, "A Conceptual and Empirical Review of the Structure of Assessment Center Dimensions," *Journal of Management* 40, no. 5 (July 2014), 1269–1296; Andrew Speer, Nell Christiansen, Richard Goffin, and Maynard Golf, "Situational Bandwidth and the Criterion-Related Validity of Assessment Center Ratings: Is Cross-Exercise Convergence Always Desirable?" *Journal of Applied Psychology* 99, no. 2 (March 2014), 282–295.

75. Based on Ken Blanchard, "What's Your Development Level?" *Chief Learning Officer*, March 10, 2014, http://www.clomedia.com/articles/what-s-your-development-level.

76. Candace House, "Custom-Made Employee Development," *Chief Learning Officer*, April 23, 2014, http://www.clomedia.com/articles/custom-made-employee-development; Jesse Segers and Ilke Inceoglu, "Exploring Supportive and Developmental Career Management through Business Strategies and Coaching," *Human Resource Management* 51, no. 1 (January–February 2012), 99–120.

77. Robyn Clark and Judah Kurtz, "Leading through Coaching: Tips for Fostering Success," *Chief Learning Officer*, January 15, 2014, http://www.clomedia.com/articles/leading-through-coaching-tips-for-fostering-success.

78. Sue Shellenbarger, "Tech-Impaired? Pair Up with a Younger Mentor," *Wall Street Journal*, May 28, 2014, p. D3; Wendy Marcinkus Murphy, "Reverse Mentoring at Work: Fostering Cross-Generational Learning and Developing Millennial Leaders," *Human Resource Management* 51, no. 4 (July–August 2012), 549–574; Katie Kuehner-Hebert, "Iron Mountain Sentinels; Certified Peer Coaches," *Chief Learning Officer*, March 3, 2014, http://www.clomedia.com/articles/iron-mountain-sentinels-certified-peer-coaches.

79. Johnson Controls, http://www.johnsoncontrols.com/content/us/en/about/our_people/leadership_development.html.

80. Pat Galagan and Jeanne Meister, "90,000 Served Hamburger University Turns 50," *T + D*, April 2011, p. 46; SHRM Knowledge Center, "Employee Development: Why Would a Company Institute a Corporate University?" *SHRM Online*, December 12, 2013, http://www.shrm.org/templatestools/hrqa/pages/employeedevelopmentwhywouldacompanyinstituteacorporateuniversity.aspx.

81. Jessica Li and Amy Lui, "Prioritizing + Maximizing the Impact of Corporate Universities," *T + D*, May 2011, p. 54.

82. Outward Bound, "Professional Programs," http://www.outwardbound.org/about-outward-bound/programs.

83. Adrienne Fox, "Help Managers Shine," *HR Magazine*, February 2013, pp. 43–48.

84. Based on Brittany Brown, "Future Leaders at Play," *T+D*, April 2014, pp. 24–27.

85. J. David Pincus and Harold Rudnick, "Leadership Blind Spot," *BizEd*, May–June 2013, pp. 41–45.

86. Lisa Dragoni, Haeseen Park, Jim Soltis, and Sheila Forte-Trammell, "Show and Tell: How Supervisors Facilitate Leader Development among Transitioning Leaders," *Journal of Applied Psychology* 99, no. 1 (2014), 66–86.

87. Sandi Maxey, "Putting the Focus on Coaching," *T+D*, April 2014, pp. 42–46; Sewon Kim, "Assessing the Influence of Managerial Coaching on Employee Outcomes," *Human Resource Development Quarterly* 25, no. 1 (Spring 2014), 59–85.

88. Kathryn Tyler, "Calling in a Coach," *HR Magazine*, September 2014, pp. 55–58.

89. Paul Thurston, Caroline D'Abate, and Erik Eddy, "Mentoring as an HRD Approach: Effects on Employee Attitudes and Contributions Independent of Core Self-Evaluation," *Human Resource Development Quarterly* 23, no. 2 (Summer 2012), 139–165; Wendy Axelrod, "Make Your Mentoring Program Memorable," *People & Strategy* 35, no. 4 (2012), 48–50.

90. Based on Garry Kranz, "Wal-Mart Drafts Leaders For Military-Style Training," *Workforce.com*, June 12, 2013, http://www.workforce.com/articles/wal-mart-drafts-leaders-for-military-style-training.

CHAPTER

10

Performance Management and Appraisal

Learning Objectives

After you have read this chapter, you should be able to:

LO1 Identify why performance management is necessary.

LO2 Distinguish among three types of performance information.

LO3 Explain the differences between administrative and developmental uses of performance appraisal.

LO4 Describe the advantages and disadvantages of multisource (360-degree) appraisals.

LO5 Discuss the importance of training managers and employees on performance appraisal and give examples of rater errors.

LO6 Identify several concerns about appraisal feedback and ways to make it more effective.

WHAT'S TRENDING IN
PERFORMANCE MANAGEMENT AND APPRAISAL

An organization's HR professionals and managers must work together to develop business approaches that bring out the best in employees. More specifically, they must create evaluation processes that enable managers to provide employees feedback so that they can improve their job performance. The management of employees' actions through these ongoing appraisals presents a number of challenges and opportunities, so organizational leaders must think strategically about performance management. Given these issues, here's what's currently trending in the area of performance management and appraisal:

1. Some managers consider performance management to be a useful tool, while others believe it is a waste of time. It is important for HR professionals to understand current opinions regarding this process so that useful partnerships can be developed in organizations. Some companies have eliminated formal appraisals in favor of ongoing feedback for employees.

2. The development of engaging performance appraisal policies is an opportunity to build excellence in companies. Gamification and multisource ratings are approaches that can be used to make performance evaluations more fun and accurate.

3. Ratings, rankings, and other approaches used to assess employees' job performance are always subject to discussion and debate. Managers need to understand the current applications associated with any one (or more) of these approaches.

4. Goal setting is an important part of managing employee performance. Organizations are using new paradigms to more effectively link corporate goals and employee objectives and to motivate employees to develop better goals.

HEADLINE

Gamification Makes Evaluations Fun at Persistent Systems

The managers at the international software and technology firm Persistent Solutions wanted to improve employee performance evaluations. They turned to the gamification company eMee to assist them in making performance management more fun. Given that the organization employs over 7,000 people across the globe, it was also important to make the act of conducting appraisals better. The resulting approach incorporated gamification to bring together group interaction, worker development, and individual recognition in a manner that enabled employees to be more involved in a transparent evaluation process.

The underlying premise of eMee's appraisal strategy is that employees are continuously provided information about their performance instead of just getting it at the end of the year. In addition, employees can manage the performance of peers, rather than simply relying on the feedback provided by supervisors. Performance is managed in a virtual environment, with avatars representing employees. Virtual rewards can be given to employees by supervisors and coworkers to recognize individuals for a job well done, and these rewards enable employees to accumulate points that are compared to performance targets and criteria. Reprimands can also be carried out in the virtual environment. The entire process is integrated into Persistent Systems' information management system, which streamlines the management of performance in the company.

As part of eMee's appraisal model, continual performance feedback is provided to Persistent Systems' employees from a variety of stakeholders and colleagues. This

 HEADLINE

 PERSPECTIVE

 COMPETENCIES & APPLICATIONS

Source: http://www.emee.co.in

363

ETHICS

Building
Ethics with
Multisource
Appraisals and
Coaching 382

has helped the company better manage performance even though people may move around in the company and have different bosses. The model has been so successful that it is estimated that the company saved over 28,000 hours of labor in a recent year by eliminating its old approach. Attrition has also declined, while job satisfaction and customer feedback have improved.[1]

Performance management identifies the work that individuals need to do to be effective and contribute to the mission and objectives of an organization. The process should also encourage, measure, and evaluate job performance so that improvements can be made. Finally, it seeks to communicate, improve, and reward performance.[2] Managers need to provide appropriate and useful feedback because employees don't always know exactly what they need to do to improve their performance. Properly designing and implementing the performance management and appraisal systems are key methods for increasing performance.

LO1 Identify why performance management is necessary.

10-1 The Nature of Performance Management

The performance management process starts by identifying the goals an organization should accomplish to remain competitive and profitable. Managers then identify how they and their employees can support these objectives by successfully completing work. Of course, the sum of the work completed in all jobs should advance the strategic plan. The following "HR Perspective: Goals Guide Performance at Mitchell International and Tornier" feature shows how business objectives should be linked to the management of individual job performance.

As Figure 10-1 shows, performance management links strategy to results. However, just having a strategic plan does not guarantee that results will be achieved. Strategies must be translated into department- or unit-level actions. Then these actions must be assigned to individuals who are held accountable for their accomplishment.

Performance management is often confused with one of its key components, the performance appraisal. Performance management is a series of activities designed to ensure that the organization gets the performance it needs from its employees. At a minimum, it should do the following:

Performance management
Series of activities designed to ensure that the organization gets the performance it needs from its employees

- Make clear what the organization expects.
- Document performance for personnel records.
- Identify areas of success and needed development.
- Provide performance information to employees.

Performance appraisal
Process of determining how well employees do their jobs relative to a standard and communicating that information to them

Performance appraisal is the process of determining how well employees do their jobs relative to a standard and communicating that information to them. This tool is a key part of performance management because it helps employees improve their job performance.

FIGURE 10-1 Performance Management Linkage

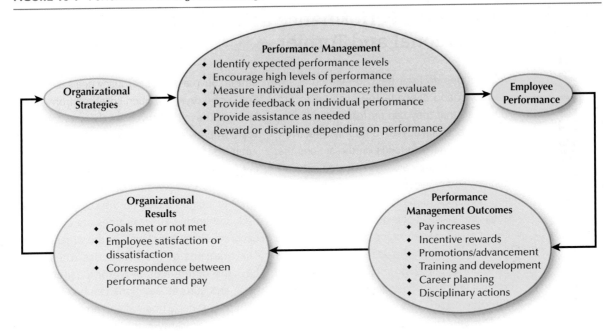

Successful performance management allows managers to prepare employees for work by focusing on the most important components of their jobs. This is often done by using evaluations to identify the level of performance and then providing feedback about how work can be improved. For example, in one company employees are rated on standardized job criteria by their supervisor, but they also complete self-evaluations. They receive the supervisor's completed evaluation forms several days ahead of appraisal meetings to consider the ratings. "Performance agreements" that follow explicitly connect individual actions to corporate goals, and the communication involved in forging those agreements ensures that managers and employees understand important performance issues. Based on information provided by a large group of business professionals and academics, the Society for Human Resource Management developed a new standard for performance management that can be used in a variety of organizations to better manage employees.[3]

However, the process is sometimes criticized for being outdated and/or ineffective. One report suggests that while 86% of firms actively use performance management, around 70% of those surveyed thought that the process was not positive, and 29% believed that is was unfair. A mere 3% of companies plan to alter their current approaches. Companies such as Adobe and REI are trying to change negative perceptions such as these by altering the way they manage performance. Adobe focuses on constant feedback and ownership with employees to help their performance, and REI has adopted a similar process that is more informal.[4]

GLOBAL

10-1a Global Cultural Differences in Performance Management

Performance management and appraisals are very common in the United States and some other countries. However, it can be challenging to institute U.S. practices in

PERSPECTIVE

Goals Guide Performance at Mitchell International and Tornier

Organizations do their best to take company-level goals and cascade them down to employees so that they can perform in ways that support these objectives. To do this effectively, organizations have to focus on the actions that will ensure that goals are implemented correctly. Adequate communication is a big part of this process, so managers need to learn to constantly discussing business objectives with employees, rather than simply relying on appraisal meetings that occur a few times a year. Good planning is also important so that employees understand the most important goals for which they will be held accountable.

The San Diego–based software service company Mitchell International uses technology to help communicate goals and manage employee job performance. Workers enter their goals into an interactive software package, and these goals become the source of frequent conversations that occur between managers and employees. Managers are provided templates that help provide direction to the one-on-one conversations with workers, some of which may occur as frequently as every two weeks. The HR department also communicates information about the company's strategic interests, which can be used to guide the performance management process.

The Amsterdam-based medical device organization Tornier also uses an innovative approach to link corporate goals to employees

efforts. Several select company goals are identified based on information collected from stakeholders. These objectives are then compared to the company's current situation to determine what needs to happen so that Tornier moves in the proper direction. A company-wide "success tree" (or a written game plan in outline form) is created based on the key goals identified, and unique success trees are created for each individual employed in the organization. The branches of these success trees show how the differences between desired situations and current situations can be reconciled with proper departmental and employee goals. This ensures clarity in the goal-setting process and increases personal accountability for goal accomplishment. In addition, Tornier assesses performance before and after actions are taken to support business goals, which provides measurement of progress.[5]

Based on the practices used by Mitchell International and Tornier, consider the following questions:

1. How should corporate goals be linked to employee objectives? How can HR professionals get involved in this process?

2. How do you recommend organizations use technology to enhance performance management? Does technology complicate goal-setting, and if so, what should be done to use technology more effectively?

countries that have dissimilar cultures. It can also be challenging when these practices are used to manage employees with diverse cultural backgrounds who are working in the United States.

In some countries and cultures, it is uncommon for managers to rate employees or to give direct feedback, particularly if some of the information is negative. For instance, in several countries, including China and Japan, there is great respect for authority and age. Consequently, the engagement of younger subordinates in joint discussions with their managers to conduct performance appraisals is uncommon. Use of programs such as multisource/360-degree feedback (discussed later in this chapter) might also be considered culturally inappropriate.

In some other cultures, employees may view criticism from superiors as negative rather than as useful feedback that highlights their training and development needs. Therefore, managers may not provide much feedback, and employees don't expect it. "Cultural customs" associated with formal meetings may need to be observed. For example, in some eastern European countries, it is common to have food and beverages before beginning any formal discussion. Performance management approaches might need to be modified in various global settings to accommodate different preferences.

10-1b Performance-Focused Organizational Cultures

Organizational cultures can vary on many dimensions, one of which involves the degree to which performance is emphasized. Some cultures are based on an *entitlement* approach, meaning that *adequate* performance and stability dominate the organization. Employee rewards vary little from person to person and have little to do with differences in individual performance. As a result, performance appraisal activities have few ties to performance and are primarily a "bureaucratic exercise."

At the other end of the spectrum is a *performance-driven* organizational culture, which focuses on the results and contributions made by employees. In this context, performance evaluations link results to employee compensation and development. There are benefits to developing a performance-focused culture throughout the organization. This approach can be particularly useful when assessing top leaders because they are required to improve the financial and operational performance of their organizations. Focusing on performance improvements through development activities can also help a company avoid interventions by activist investors who want to take over strategic planning and management through their ownership of shares.[6] Figure 10-2 shows the components of a successful performance-focused culture where pay depends on performance.

However, a pay-for-performance approach can present several challenges to organizations. For example, pay-for-performance plans used in organizations that usually have an entitlement philosophy are sometimes seen as creating inequity, particularly if some employees get bonuses and others receive no extra compensation. Tying bonuses to criteria such as employee performance may also be met with harsh criticism because some claim that the process prevents teamwork in the workplace.

Despite these issues, it appears that a performance-based-pay culture is desirable. It is sometimes argued that companies are not doing enough about low performers, and that failure to deal with poor performance is unfair to those who work hard. Employees who are not taking care of their work responsibilities can become combative

FIGURE 10-2 Components of a Performance-Focused Culture

| Clear Expectations, Goals, and Deadlines | Detailed Appraisal of Employee Performance | Clear Feedback on Performance | Manager and Employee Training as Needed | Consequences for Performance |

over their poor performance. Managers should address performance issues with a communication record that documents problems and holds individuals accountable.[7]

10-2 Identifying and Measuring Employee Performance

Performance criteria vary from job to job, but common employee performance measures include the following:

- Quantity of output
- Quality of output
- Timeliness of output
- Presence/attendance on the job
- Efficiency of work completed
- Effectiveness of work completed

Job duties
Important elements in a given job

Specific job duties from a job description should identify the important elements in a given job. For example, a front desk clerk must welcome guests to a hotel, understand the hotel's reservation system, and check guests in and out of their rooms. In other words, job duties define what the organization pays employees to do. Individuals' performance of their job duties should therefore be measured and compared against appropriate standards, and the results should be communicated to employees on a regular basis so that performance can be improved.

Given that most jobs have several elements and inherent complexities, multiple job duties are the rule rather than the exception. An individual might demonstrate better performance on some duties than others, and some duties might be more important than others to the organization. For example, professors are broadly required to conduct research, teach classes, serve on committees, be involved in professional groups, and provide assistance to outside university stakeholders. Some professors may focus heavily on one or two areas of work over the others because their universities value these particular aspects of the job.

Weights can be used to show the relative importance of different duties in a job. For example, in a management job at a company that wants to improve customer feedback, control operational costs, and encourage quality improvements, weights might be assigned as follows:

Weighting of Management Duties at Sample Firm	Weight
Improve customer feedback	50%
Control operational costs	30%
Encourage quality improvements	20%
Total Management Performance	**100%**

10-2a Types of Performance Information

LO2 Distinguish among three types of performance information.

Managers can use three different types of information about employee performance, as Figure 10-3 shows. *Trait-based information* identifies a character trait of the employee, such as attitude, initiative, or creativity, and may or may not be job related. For example, conscientiousness is often found to be a trait that is an important

FIGURE 10-3 Types of Performance Information

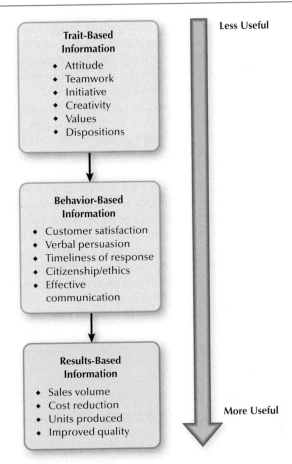

determinant of job performance. *Allophilia* is an important leadership trait that involves the degree to which employees are positive toward another group when they are not members of that group.[8] Other traits that are associated with star performers include modesty, a commitment to self-development, a willingness to express ideas, a fixation on customers, and the use of clear language (instead of jargon).[9] Yet, many of these traits tend to be ambiguous, and rater bias can affect how traits are viewed, so courts have generally held that trait-based performance appraisals are too vague to use when making HR decisions such as promotions or terminations. Also, focusing too much on trait characteristics such as "potential" can lead managers to ignore important behaviors and outcomes.

Behavior-based information focuses on specific behaviors that lead to job success. For a bartender, the behavior "drink up-selling" can be observed and used as performance information because a customer is encouraged to purchase a higher-quality beverage. Another example is an operations director who visits all the key work areas in a manufacturing plant during a morning walk-through behaves in a manner that increases visibility and communication with employees. Behavioral information can specify the behaviors management expects employees to exhibit. A potential problem arises when any of several behaviors can lead to successful performance, and employees rely on different behaviors to complete work. For example, because there is likely not one approach will make all salespersons effective at their jobs, one salesperson might successfully use one selling strategy with customers, while another might successfully use a different approach.

Results-based information considers employee accomplishments. For jobs in which measurement is easy and obvious, a results-based approach works well. For instance, a professor might receive extra compensation for securing grants or publishing papers in certain academic journals, or a salesperson in a retail outlet might receive extra commission pay based on how many products are sold. However, employers should recognize that the results that are measured are the ones that employees tend to emphasize, sometimes neglecting other important job activities. For example, a selling professional who works for an auto dealership and gets paid *only* for sales may be uninterested and/or unwilling to do paperwork and other activities not directly related to selling cars. Further, ethical or legal issues may arise when results alone are emphasized rather than *how* results are achieved, so care should be taken to balance the different types of information.

Performance measures can be viewed as objective or subjective. The *objective measures* can be observed. For example, the number of dinner specials sold or the number of tables serviced can be counted, which make them objective performance metrics. *Subjective measures* require judgment on the part of the evaluator and are more difficult to determine. One example of a subjective measure is a supervisor's ratings of an employee's "attitude," which can be difficult to evaluate based on varying ideas and preferences. Consequently, subjective measures should be used carefully and only when adequate support and/or documentation can be presented to support such evaluations.

10-2b Performance Standards

Performance standards
Define the expected levels of employee performance

Performance standards define the expected levels of employee performance. Sometimes they are labeled *benchmarks*, *goals*, or *targets*—depending on the approach taken. Realistic, measurable, clearly understood performance standards benefit both organizations and employees. Performance standards should be established *before* work is performed because they define the level of satisfactory job performance. Well-defined standards ensure that everyone involved knows the performance expectations.

Both numerical and non-numerical standards can be established. Sales quotas and production output are familiar numerical performance standards. A standard of performance can also be based on non-numerical criteria. Assessing whether someone has met a performance standard, especially a non-numerical one, can be difficult, but it can be done. For example, how would you measure a waitperson's ability to service a table? Figure 10-4 lists performance standards that facilitate such measurement and make assessment much more accurate, even though performance is non-numerical.

To make sure performance standards are applied uniformly, many organizations "calibrate" performances. Calibrating is often a group review conducted by managers to discuss the reasons behind each employee's rating. Ratings can be adjusted up or down by the group to ensure that they reflect similar performance standards.[10] This process can increase inter-rater reliability.

FIGURE 10-4 Example Performance Standards for Table Service of Waitperson

Performance Level	Demonstrated Ability
Superior	• Visits table quickly after guests are seated • Takes order exactly when guests are ready • Serves drinks and food immediately after items are prepared • Clears table and presents check immediately after meal is complete
Acceptable	• Visits table in a reasonable time after guest are seated • Takes order in a timely manner • Serves drinks and food after items are prepared • Clears table and presents check after meal is complete
Needs Improvement	• Visits table when there is time to do so • Takes order when ready • Serves drinks and food after other duties are completed • Clears tables and presents checks after servicing other tables

MEASURE

10-2c Performance Metrics in Service Businesses

Measuring service performance is difficult because services are often very individualized for customers. There is also typically great variation in the services that can be offered, and quality is often very subjective. Yet, the performance of people in service jobs is commonly evaluated with the basic productivity measures used in the industry. Some of the most useful sources of performance differences among managers in service businesses are as follows:

- Regional differences in labor costs
- Service agreement differences
- Equipment/infrastructure differences
- Work volume

On an individual level, common measures might include cost per employee, incidents per employee per day, number of calls per product, cost per call, sources of demand for services, and service calls per day. Many organizations also evaluate different measures of customer feedback that are provided on comment cards and surveys. Some companies even use "secret shoppers," individuals who are contracted to be customers and rate employees on the quality of services they provide, to obtain additional measures of customer service delivery. Once managers have determined appropriate measures of the service variance in their company, they can deal with waste, as well as service delivery and quality. Regardless of the approaches used, employers should remember that measuring performance in some way enables them to better manage performance.

10-3 Performance Appraisals

Performance appraisals are used to assess an employee's performance and create a mechanism for providing feedback about past, current, and future performance expectations. They are often viewed as a critical element of any performance management approach. Several terms can be used when referring to performance appraisals. These include *employee rating, employee evaluation, performance review, performance evaluation*, and *results appraisal.*

Performance appraisals are widely used for administering wages and salaries and identifying individual employee strengths and weaknesses. Most U.S. employers use performance appraisals for office, professional, technical, supervisory, middle management, and nonunion production workers, and there are many reasons for this widespread use. When designed well, performance appraisals can highlight and address many work-related issues, and by communicating a positive roadmap to employees, poor performance can often be successfully improved. Regardless of whether the feedback is positive or negative, employees benefit because the information helps them determine how to improve their job performance. In addition, appraisals can provide justification for many personnel actions such as promotions, pay raises, or terminations. It is therefore important for managers to be honest and objective in their appraisals of performance and to ensure that employees understand that the process is intended to help them. Managers should also praise employees when they do well at work and take into consideration their explanations for why their performance is not where it should be.[11]

But there are several challenges associated with performance appraisals. For instance, ratings night not adequately reflect the actual job performance exhibited by employees because of a rater's bias, misperceptions, or failure to watch employees work. This can even occur in a training situation. One study found that training participants may evaluate instruction more positively than expected because they think the instructor would like them to, they are sympathetic toward the instructor, or they are happy to be finished with the training.[12] Poorly done performance appraisals can also deflate motivation and harm workplace relationships, and some business professionals even think that performance evaluations are too subjective, political, and ultimately unnecessary because of these issues. An SHRM study found that more than half of HR professionals surveyed assigned their employers a B to C+ grade based on how they managed appraisals. Just over one-fifth assigned their employers a C grade for performance management (only 2% assigned an A grade for these efforts).[13]

Despite these challenges, having no formal performance appraisal can weaken discipline in a company and harm an employee's ability to improve. There are several ways employers can better manage performance appraisals. For instance, one study found that stronger trust in senior leadership can strengthen the positive relationship between employees' feelings about how fairly they are treated in performance evaluations given by their immediate bosses and their commitment to the company. Trust in leadership and justice should therefore be emphasized in companies.[14] Another study found that beliefs about HR's ability to convey what are considered to be successful behaviors to employees and the quality of appraisals provided can work together to enhance positive informal learning. This means that HR directives should be clear, consistent, and uniform to support the proper work environment, and that ongoing communication with employees should be emphasized to improve performance evaluations.[15]

Companies such as Air Products and Chemicals, Inc. and CareerBuilder.com are also using self-service online applications to better manage the administration of performance evaluations, as well as other important HR functions.[16] An SHRM survey also shows that HR professionals rate employers' management of appraisals higher when companies emphasize performance management.[17] Consequently, effective appraisals are entirely possible if the right issues are addressed and the proper approaches are used. See the "HR Perspective: Making Appraisals Work at Hilton Worldwide" feature for another example.

ETHICS

10-3a Performance Appraisals and Ethics

Performance appraisals may or may not focus on the ethics associated with how employees perform their jobs. Managers may be expected to take an active role in managing ethics in their area of responsibility but often do not understand the process. Many companies do not have a program to develop awareness of ethics, and some have no policies at all regarding ethical behavior. Discussing ethics in performance appraisals is one way to emphasize it to employees. Codes of conduct can provide useful company guidelines on ethical behavior, training can teach important workplace ethical values, and communication of ethical approaches to recurring workplace problems can help promote an ethical culture. Rewarding ethical behavior and punishing

PERSPECTIVE

Making Appraisals Work at Hilton Worldwide

The new chief HR officer at Hilton Worldwide found he had to create a performance management system from scratch when he arrived. Performance appraisals varied greatly, if they existed at all. In many companies (including Hilton), these processes are needlessly complex, are not connected to business goals, and are hated by managers and employees alike.

The fundamentals of performance management should be simple, reflected Matt Schuyler, the new CHRO at Hilton. Employees agree to goals at the start of the year, supervisors assess their progress at the end of the cycle, a good conversation takes place on how the employee is doing, and rewards are based on whether the goals were met. Fixing the overly complex process involves going back to the basics.

At Hilton, managers and employees now set objectives at the beginning of the year and check mid-way to see how things are going. The system documents individual accomplishments so that there are no surprises during the evaluation. The "mid-year check in" is designed to encourage continuous feedback during the rating period. The idea of keeping things simple, focusing on the conversation, and emphasizing two-way communication has been positive; in an employee survey, satisfaction with the process increased by 37%. "The goal of performance management is to give you feedback so you can get better, not to damage you or make you feel bad," says Schuyler.[18]

The use of goal setting and feedback has been beneficial at Hilton Worldwide. Answer the following questions about performance appraisals:

1. How would you evaluate Hilton's use of mid-year assessments of goal accomplishments? Do you think it should be done more frequently or less frequently?

2. How could an HR department help coordinate periodic goal setting and assessments of employee job performance?

undesirable behavior are also beneficial for improving ethical organizational practices. Doing so requires managers to include ethics metrics in performance measurement.

10-3b Uses of Performance Appraisals

LO3 Explain the differences between administrative and developmental uses of performance appraisal.

Organizations generally use performance appraisals in two potentially conflicting ways. One use is to provide a measure of performance for consideration in making pay or other administrative decisions about employees. This *administrative* role often creates stress for the managers doing the appraisals and the employees being evaluated because the rater is placed in the role of judge. The other use focuses on the *development* of individuals. In this role, the manager acts more as a counselor and coach than as a judge. The developmental performance appraisal emphasizes current training and development needs, as well as planning employees' future opportunities and career directions. Figure 10-5 shows both uses for performance appraisals.

Administrative Uses of Appraisals Three administrative uses of appraisal impact managers and employees the most: (1) determining pay adjustments; (2) making job placement decisions on promotions, transfers, and demotions; and (3) choosing employee disciplinary actions up to and including termination of employment.

A performance appraisal system is often the link between employee job performance and the additional pay and rewards they can receive. Performance-based compensation reinforces the idea that pay raises are based on performance accomplishments instead of length of service (seniority) or as part of automatic percentage raises granted to all employees. In pay-for-performance compensation systems, managers evaluate the performance of individuals and make compensation recommendations. If any part of the appraisal process fails, better-performing employees may not receive larger pay increases, and the result is perceived inequity in compensation.

Many U.S. workers say that due to flaws in performance appraisals, they see little connection between their performance and the size of their pay increases. Consequently, people argue that performance appraisals and pay discussions should be

FIGURE 10-5 Uses for Performance Appraisals

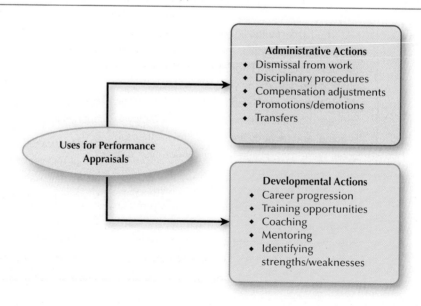

done separately. Two realities support this view. One is that employees often focus more on the pay received than on the developmental appraisal feedback. The other is that managers sometimes manipulate ratings to justify the pay they wish to give individuals. As a result, many employees view the appraisal process as a game because compensation increases have been predetermined before the appraisal is completed.

To address these issues, managers can first conduct performance appraisals and discuss the results with employees; then several weeks later, they can hold a shorter meeting to discuss pay issues. For example, one company created different performance appraisal and compensation forms that are considered separately at different times. By adopting such an approach, the results of the performance appraisal can be considered before the amount of the pay adjustment is determined. Also, the performance appraisal discussions between managers and employees can focus on issues for improvement—not just pay raises.

Employers are generally interested in the administrative uses of performance appraisals because the assessments and decisions made in these evaluations affect promotions, terminations, layoffs, and transfer assignments. Personnel actions based on performance appraisals must therefore be adequately documented to avoid legal concerns. Objective and fair criteria should be emphasized in the documentation used to support evaluations.

Developmental Uses of Appraisals For employees, appraisals can be a primary source of information and feedback to help them improve their performance. By identifying employees' strengths, weaknesses, needs, and potential, supervisors can provide employees with feedback about their progress at work, discuss areas in which additional training may be beneficial, and outline future developmental plans. Performance appraisal feedback is therefore well positioned to be a developmental tool.

Employees don't always know where and how to perform better, and managers cannot expect significant improvements if they do not provide enough developmental feedback. The purpose of performance feedback is to reinforce satisfactory contributions and to address work deficiencies. The developmental function of performance appraisals can also identify areas in which the employee might wish to grow. For example, in a performance appraisal interview focused exclusively on development, an employee found out that the only factor keeping her from being considered for a management job in her firm was inadequate working knowledge of cost accounting. Her supervisor suggested that she consider taking some night courses at the local college to help her develop these skills.

The use of teams provides a different set of circumstances for developmental appraisals. The manager may not see all of an employee's work, but the employee's team members do, therefore enabling them to provide important feedback. However, whether teams can handle administrative appraisals is still subject to debate, and clearly some cannot manage the additional responsibility. When team members participate in the appraisal process, they tend to avoid making judgments and shy away from differential rewards. Thus, group appraisals may be best suited for developmental purposes rather than administrative functions.

10-3c Decisions about the Performance Appraisal Process

A number of decisions must be made when designing performance appraisal systems. Some important ones involve identifying the appraisal responsibilities of the

FIGURE 10-6   Typical Division of HR Responsibilities: Performance Appraisal

HR Unit	Managers
• Designs and maintains appraisal system • Trains raters • Tracks timely receipt of appraisals • Reviews completed appraisals for consistency	• Typically rate performance of employees • Prepare formal appraisal documents • Review appraisals with employees • Identify development areas

HR unit and of the operating managers, selecting the type of appraisal system to use, and establishing the timing of appraisals.

Appraisal Responsibilities If done properly, the appraisal process can benefit both the organization and its employees. As Figure 10-6 shows, the HR unit typically designs an organization's performance appraisal system. Managers then use the appraisal system to evaluate employees. During development of the formal appraisal system, managers usually offer input about how the final system should work.

It is important for managers to understand that appraisals are *their* responsibility. Through the appraisal process, good employee performance can be made even better, poor employee performance can be improved, and poor performers can be removed from the organization. Performance appraisal must not simply be an HR requirement but should also be an important management process because guiding employees' performance is among the most important responsibilities of being a manager.

Type of Appraisals: Informal versus Systematic Performance appraisals can occur in two ways: informally and/or systematically. A supervisor conducts an *informal appraisal* whenever necessary. The day-to-day working relationship between a manager and an employee offers an opportunity for the evaluation of individual performance. A manager communicates this evaluation through various conversations on the job, or by on-the-spot discussion of specific occurrences. Although such informal feedback is useful and necessary, it should not replace formal appraisal.

Frequent informal feedback to employees can prevent surprises during a formal performance review. However, informal appraisal can become *too* informal. For example, a senior executive at a large firm so dreaded face-to-face evaluations that he delivered one manager's review while both sat in adjoining stalls in the men's room.

A *systematic appraisal* occurs when the contact between manager and employee is more formal, and a system is in place to report managerial impressions and observations on employee performance. This approach to appraisals is quite common. Systematic appraisals feature a regular time interval, which distinguishes them from informal appraisals. Both employees and managers know that performance will be reviewed on a regular basis, and they can plan for performance discussions.

Timing of Appraisals Most companies require managers to conduct appraisals once or twice a year, most often annually. Employees commonly receive an appraisal 60 to 90 days after hiring, again at six months, and annually thereafter. *Introductory employees*, who are new and are working in a trial period, should be informally evaluated often, perhaps weekly for the first month and monthly thereafter until the end of the introductory period. After that, annual reviews are typical. For employees in high demand, some employers use accelerated appraisals—every six months instead of every year. This is done to retain those employees since more feedback can be given and pay raises may occur more often. Meeting more frequently with employees may enhance individual performance. Organizations can require managers to meet with employees on a regular basis (e.g., quarterly), but if managers and employees want additional discussion, more meetings can be scheduled.

10-3d Legal Concerns and Performance Appraisals

Since appraisals are supposed to measure how well employees are doing their jobs, it may seem unnecessary to emphasize that performance appraisals must be job related. However, it is important for evaluations to adequately reflect the nature of work performed. Companies need to have appraisal systems that satisfy the courts and address corporate needs. The following "HR Competencies & Applications: Elements of a Legal Performance Appraisal System" feature shows the elements to consider.

10-4 Who Conducts Appraisals?

Performance appraisals can be conducted by anyone familiar with the performance of individual employees. Possible rating situations include the following:

- Supervisors rating their employees
- Employees rating their superiors
- Team members rating each other
- Employees rating themselves
- Outside sources rating employees
- A variety of parties providing multisource, or 360-degree, feedback

10-4a Supervisory Ratings of Subordinates

The most widely used means of rating employees is based on the assumption that the immediate supervisor is the person most qualified to evaluate an employee's performance realistically and fairly. To help provide accurate evaluations, some supervisors keep records of employees' performance so that they can reference these notes when rating performance. For instance, a sales manager might periodically observe a salesperson's interactions with clients and make notes so that constructive performance feedback can be provided.

However, relying on supervisor ratings can be problematic because of rating mistakes and biases. For instance, one study found that supervisors' ratings of employees can be affected by the typical times that employees start their workdays, with employees who start work later being viewed as less conscientious and lower performers compared to those who start work earlier. Supervisors' own preferences for evenings or mornings also affected their stereotypes of workers.[19]

COMPETENCIES & APPLICATIONS

Elements of a Legal Performance Appraisal System

The elements of a performance appraisal system that can survive court tests can be determined from existing case law. It is generally agreed that a legally defensible performance appraisal should include the following:

- Performance appraisal criteria based on job analysis
- Absence of disparate impact or disparate treatment
- Formal evaluation criteria that limit managerial discretion
- A rating instrument linked to job duties and responsibilities
- Documentation of the appraisal activities
- Personal knowledge of and contact with each appraised individual
- Training of supervisors in conducting appraisals
- A review process that prevents one manager, acting alone, from controlling an employee's career
- Counseling to help poor performers improve

Of course, having all these components is no guarantee against lawsuits. However, including them does improve the chance of winning lawsuits that might be filed. Based on these points, consider the following questions about the relevant legal aspects of a performance management system:

1. Based on the legal criteria outlined, which points do you think are the most important? Which ones would you focus on first as a practicing HR professional? Which legal criteria do you think might be the most challenging to implement?

2. Do you think there are other approaches (not listed) that could be used to enhance the legal defensibility of a performance appraisal system?

KEY COMPETENCIES: Business Acumen (Behavioral Competency) and Workplace (Technical Competency)

10-4b Employee Ratings of Managers

A number of organizations ask employees to rate the performance of their immediate managers. A variation of this type of rating takes place in colleges and universities, where students evaluate the teaching effectiveness of professors in the classroom. Another example is an Indian firm that requires employees to rate their bosses as part of a multi-source review process. All evaluations are then posted on the company's intranet. These performance appraisal ratings are generally used for management development purposes.

Asking employees to rate managers provides three primary advantages. First, in critical manager–employee relationships, employee ratings can be quite useful for identifying competent managers. The rating of leaders by combat soldiers is one example of such a use. Second, this type of rating program can help make a manager more responsive to employees. This advantage can quickly become a disadvantage if the manager focuses on being "nice" rather than on managing; people who are pleasant but have few other relevant qualifications may not be good managers in many situations. Finally, employee appraisals can contribute to career development efforts for managers by identifying areas for growth.

A major disadvantage of asking employees to rate managers is the negative reaction some may have to being evaluated by their subordinates. Also, the fear of reprisals may be too great for employees to give realistic ratings. This may prompt workers to rate their managers based solely on the way they are treated rather than on critical job requirements. Consequently, using these ratings for developmental purposes may be beneficial, but using them for administrative purposes may not be advisable.

10-4c Team/Peer Ratings

Having employees and team members rate each other is another type of appraisal. Peer and team ratings are especially useful when supervisors don't have the opportunity to observe each employee working, but work group members do. For instance, many training programs in the military use peer ratings to provide candidates extensive feedback about their leadership qualities and accomplishments. Using a sample of young Israeli military recruits, one study of peer evaluations found that ratings provided by individuals who were nominated for exhibiting positive behaviors, as well as ratings provided by those who were rated highly but who did not reciprocate these nominations, were stronger predictors of job performance compared to the total number of peer nominations.[20] Peer evaluations are also common in collegiate schools of business where professors commonly require students to conduct peer evaluations after the completion of group-based projects. Professors may also rate each other on their teaching efforts and activities.

It is possible that any performance appraisal, including team/peer ratings, can negatively affect teamwork and participative management efforts. Although team members have good information on one another's performance, they may choose not to share it in the interest of sparing feelings. Alternatively, they may unfairly attack other group members, thus using peer ratings as a way to punish others. Some organizations attempt to overcome such problems by using anonymous appraisals and/or having a consultant or HR manager interpret team/peer ratings.

10-4d Self-Ratings

A self-appraisal can be effective in certain situations. As a self-development tool, it requires employees to think about their strengths and weaknesses and set goals for improvement.[21] Employees working in isolation or possessing unique skills may be particularly suited for self-ratings because they are the only ones qualified to rate themselves.

However, employees may use different standards when rating themselves, so there may be differences between their ratings and those provided by their supervisors. Employees may be too lenient in self-evaluations by accentuating their positive contributions and minimizing the areas that need improvement. This may occur more frequently when companies use evaluations strictly for administrative purposes.

Despite these issues, the use of self-appraisals in organizations has increased. For instance, one organization successfully incorporated self-ratings into a traditional rating approach that previously did not generate enough dialogue and direction for individual development. The reactions from both workers and supervisors were favorable. Consequently, employee self-ratings can be a useful source of performance information for developmental purposes.

10-4e Outsider/Customer Ratings

People outside the immediate work group may be asked to participate in performance reviews. This "field review" approach can include someone from the

HR department as a reviewer, or completely independent reviewers from outside the organization. Examples include a review team evaluating a college president or a panel of division managers evaluating a supervisor's potential for advancement in the company. A disadvantage of this approach is that outsiders may not know the important demands within the work group or organization.

The customers or clients of an organization are good sources for outside appraisals. For sales and service jobs, customers may provide useful input on the performance behaviors of employees. For instance, many hospitality organizations such as restaurants and hotels use customer comment cards/surveys and secret shoppers to gather feedback about the service provided by customer contact personnel, and this information is commonly used for job development purposes. One study determined that the use of secret shoppers to facilitate coaching in several restaurants that were members of the same chain helped improve employee and organizational performance.[22]

10-4f Multisource/360-Degree Rating

Multisource rating, or 360-degree feedback, has grown in popularity. Multisource feedback recognizes that for many jobs, employee performance is multidimensional and crosses departmental, organizational, and even national boundaries. Therefore, information is needed from many sources to adequately and fairly evaluate an incumbent's performance in one of these jobs.

The major purpose of 360-degree feedback is *not* to increase uniformity by soliciting like-minded views. Instead, it is designed to capture evaluations of the employee's different roles to provide richer feedback during an evaluation. Figure 10-7 shows some of the parties who can be involved in 360-degree feedback. For example, an HR manager for an insurance firm deals with seven regional sales managers, HR administrators in five claims centers, and various corporate executives in finance, legal, and information technology. The Vice President of HR uses 360-degree feedback to gather data on all facets of the HR manager's job before completing a

FIGURE 10-7 Multisource Appraisal

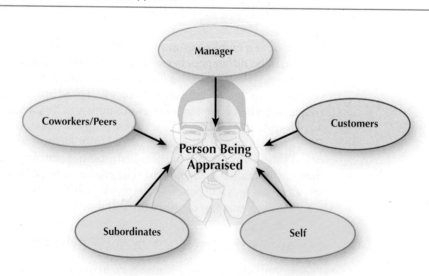

performance appraisal on the individual. Similar examples can be cited in numerous managerial, professional, technical, operational, and administrative jobs.

Significant administrative time and paperwork are required to request, obtain, and summarize feedback from multiple raters. Using electronic systems for the information can greatly reduce the administrative demands of multisource ratings and increase the effectiveness (i.e., privacy and expediency) of the process.

Developmental Use of Multisource Feedback As originally designed and used, multisource feedback focuses on the use of appraisals for the development of individuals. Conflict resolution skills, decision-making abilities, team effectiveness, communication skills, managerial styles, and technical capabilities are just some of the performance areas that can be evaluated. The manager remains the focal point in multisource feedback approaches, both to receive the feedback initially and to follow up with employees to provide an overview of the information provided. The following "HR Ethics: Building Ethics with Multisource Appraisals and Coaching" feature explores how sound performance management and 360-degree feedback can be used to develop leaders and reduce the chances for unethical behavior.

Administrative Use of Multisource Feedback The popularity of 360-degree feedback systems has led to the results being used for compensation, promotion, termination, and other administrative decisions. When using 360-degree feedback for administrative purposes, managers must anticipate several potential problems. Differences among raters can present a challenge, especially when using 360-degree ratings for discipline or pay decisions. Bias can just as easily be rooted in customers, subordinates, and peers as in a boss, and the lack of accountability of those sources can affect the ratings. "Inflation" of ratings is common when the sources know that their input will affect someone's pay or career. Also, issues of confidentiality and anonymity have led to lawsuits. Even though multisource approaches offer possible solutions to some of the well-documented dissatisfaction associated with performance appraisals, a number of other questions have arisen as multisource appraisals have become more common.

ETHICS

Evaluating Multisource Feedback Research on multisource/360-degree feedback has revealed both positives and negatives. More variability than expected may be seen in the ratings given by the different sources. Thus, supervisor ratings may need to carry more weight than peer or subordinate input to resolve the differences. One concern is that peers who rate poor-performing coworkers tend to inflate the ratings so that the peers themselves can get higher overall evaluation results in return.

Another concern is whether 360-degree appraisals improve evaluations or simply multiply the number of problems that occur by including more raters in the process. Also, some wonder whether multisource appraisals really create sufficiently better decisions to offset the additional time and investment required. These issues appear to be less threatening when the 360-degree feedback is used *only for development*. Companies should consider using multisource feedback primarily as a developmental tool to enhance future job performance, rather than using these appraisals for administrative decisions.

ETHICS

Building Ethics with Multisource Appraisals and Coaching

There are many successful business leaders who have stumbled due to ethical lapses. Some of these cases have involved violations of company policies and/or business laws, while others have been linked to poor decision making and improper behaviors. What's particularly troubling about many of the more high-profile ethical scandals is that the leaders were considered by many to be at the top of their game. Mark Hurd, who had an improper relationship with a contractor while he was CEO of Hewlett-Packard, Scott Thomson, the previous CEO of Yahoo who faked having a computer science degree, and Kathryn Abbate, the previous CEO who stole $7 million from a heath center located in Miami, are all examples of individuals who ignored their ethical compasses.

But why do these ethical failures occur? Evidence suggests that there are more opportunities for ethical transgressions as leaders get promoted up through the ranks of business. For instance, leaders often have more autonomy and more access to information, which can encourage them to do the wrong thing. Work–life imbalance can also be an issue for some executives, which can increase their stress levels. Greed, arrogance, and an entitlement mentality can be concerns. Finally, the culture of an organization, assuming it is unethical, can prompt leaders to behave in a risky manner.

So what can companies do to prevent the ethical lapses of business leaders? It should come as no surprise that many of the steps involve solid performance management. Here are some key considerations:

- Develop and promote an organizational culture that is ethical and stress this culture during onboarding so that leaders understand the importance of ethics at work.
- Use 360-degree evaluations to provide leaders a multitude of feedback from different raters who can identify performance issues.
- Apply coaching when necessary to help individuals negotiate job challenges and opportunities in a positive and productive way.
- Discuss the importance of ethical leadership when managing/affecting the careers of leaders (e.g., promoting individuals, changing their work roles).[23]

Ethical problems occur frequently in business, and HR professionals need to help prepare leaders for these challenges. Consider the following questions:

1. What kinds of approaches might you use to help leaders be more ethical? How could performance management processes be used to facilitate this aim?

2. Besides some of the ideas already discussed, what do you think companies can do to reduce the likelihood of leaders acting unethically?

10-5 Tools for Appraising Performance

A number of methods can be used to appraise performance. Some employers use one method for all jobs and employees, some use different methods for different groups of employees, and others use a combination of methods.[24] The following discussion highlights different tools that can be used, as well as some of the advantages and disadvantages of each approach.

10-5a Category Scaling Methods

The simplest methods for appraising performance are category scaling methods, which require a manager to mark an employee's level of performance on a specific form divided into categories of performance. A *checklist* uses a list of statements or words from which raters check statements that are most representative of the characteristics and performance of employees. Often, a scale indicating perceived level of accomplishment on each statement is included with the checklist, which then becomes a type of graphic rating scale.

10-5b Graphic Rating Scales

Graphic rating scale
Scale that allows the rater to mark an employee's performance on a continuum indicating low to high levels of a particular characteristic

The graphic rating scale allows the rater to mark an employee's performance on a continuum indicating low to high levels of a particular characteristic. Because of the straightforwardness of the process, graphic rating scales are common in performance evaluations. Figure 10-8 shows a sample appraisal form that combines graphic rating scales with essays. Three aspects of performance can be appraised using graphic rating scales: *descriptive categories* (such as quantity of work, attendance, and dependability), *job duties* (taken from the job description), and *behavioral dimensions* (such as decision making, employee development, and communication effectiveness).

Each of these types can be used for different jobs. How well employees meet established standards is often expressed either numerically (e.g., 5, 4, 3, 2, 1) or verbally (e.g., outstanding, meets standards, below standards). If two or more people are involved in the rating, they may find it difficult to agree on the exact level of performance achieved relative to the standard in evaluating employee performance. Notice that to reduce variation in interpretations of the standards by different supervisors and employees, each level specifies performance standards or expectations.

Concerns with Graphic Rating Scales Graphic rating scales in many forms are widely used because they are easy to develop and provide a uniform set of criteria to evaluate the job performance of different employees. However, the use of scales can cause rater error because the form might not accurately reflect the relative importance of certain job characteristics, and some factors might need to be added to the ratings for one employee, while others might need to be dropped. If they fit the person and the job, the scales work well. However, if they fit poorly, managers and employees who must use them might complain about the rating form.

Another concern is that regardless of the scales used, the focus should be on the job duties and responsibilities identified in job descriptions. The closer the link between the scales and what people actually do, as identified in current and complete job descriptions, the stronger the relationship between the ratings and the job, as viewed by employees and managers. Also, should the performance appraisal results be challenged legally, the closer performance appraisals measure what people actually do, the more likely employers are to prevail in a lawsuit.

An additional drawback to graphic rating scales is that separate traits or factors are often grouped, and the rater is given only one box to check. For example, *dependability* could refer to meeting deadlines for reports, or it could refer to attendance and tardiness. If a supervisor gives an employee a rating of 3, which aspect of dependability is being rated? One supervisor might rate employees on meeting deadlines, while another rates employees on attendance.

FIGURE 10-8 Sample Performance Appraisal Form

Date sent:	4/19/14	**Return by:**	5/01/2014
Name:	Joe Hernandez	**Job title:**	Receiving Clerk
Department:	Receiving	**Supervisor:**	Marian Williams

Employment status (check one): Full-time __X__ Part-time _____   **Date of hire:** 5/12/02

Rating period: From: 4/30/13   **To:** 4/30/14

Reason for appraisal (check one): Regular interval _X_   Introductory ___   Counseling only ___   Discharge ___

Using the following definitions, rate the performance as I, M, or E.

I—Performance is below job requirements and **improvement is needed.**

M—Performance **meets** job requirements and standards.

E—Performance **exceeds** job requirements and standards **most** of the time.

SPECIFIC JOB RESPONSIBILITIES: List the principal activities from the job summary, rate the performance on each job duty by placing an X on the rating scale at the appropriate location, and make appropriate comments to explain the rating.

```
I ————————————— M ————————————— E
```

Job Duty #1: Inventory receiving and checking
Explanation: _____

_____

```
I ————————————— M ————————————— E
```

Job Duty #2: Accurate record keeping
Explanation: _____

_____

```
I ————————————— M ————————————— E
```

Attendance (including absences and tardies):   Number of absences ___   Number of tardies ___
Explanation: _____

_____

Overall rating: In the box provided, place the letter—**I, M, or E**—that best describes the employee's overall performance.

Explanation: _____

_____

Another drawback is that the descriptive words sometimes used in scales may have different meanings to different raters. Terms such as *initiative* and *cooperation* are subject to many interpretations, especially if used in conjunction with words such as *outstanding, average*, and *poor*. As Figure 10-9 shows, scale points can be defined carefully to minimize misinterpretation.

FIGURE 10-9 Sample Terms for Defining Standards

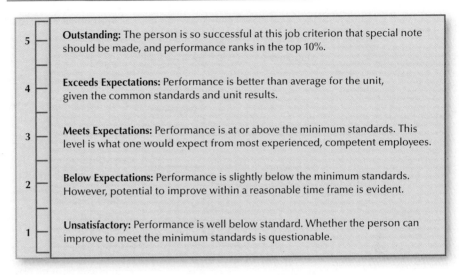

5 — **Outstanding:** The person is so successful at this job criterion that special note should be made, and performance ranks in the top 10%.

4 — **Exceeds Expectations:** Performance is better than average for the unit, given the common standards and unit results.

3 — **Meets Expectations:** Performance is at or above the minimum standards. This level is what one would expect from most experienced, competent employees.

2 — **Below Expectations:** Performance is slightly below the minimum standards. However, potential to improve within a reasonable time frame is evident.

1 — **Unsatisfactory:** Performance is well below standard. Whether the person can improve to meet the minimum standards is questionable.

Behavioral Rating Scales In an attempt to overcome some of the concerns with graphic rating scales, employers may use behavioral rating scales designed to assess individual actions instead of personal attributes and characteristics. Different approaches are used, but all describe specific examples of employee job behaviors. In a behaviorally anchored rating scale (BARS), these examples are "anchored" or measured against a scale of performance levels.

When creating a BARS system, identifying important *job dimensions*, which are the most important performance factors in a job description, is done first. Short statements describe both desirable and undesirable behaviors (anchors). These are then "translated," or assigned, to one of the job dimensions. Anchor statements are usually developed by a group of people familiar with the job. The group then assigns each anchor a number that represents the effectiveness of the behavior, and the anchors are fitted to a scale. Figure 10-10 contains an example that rates customer service skills for individuals taking orders for a national catalog retailer. Spelling out the behaviors associated with each level of performance helps minimize some of the problems related to graphic rating scales.

However, several problems are associated with the behavioral approach. First, creating and maintaining behaviorally anchored rating scales requires extensive time and effort. In addition, many appraisal forms are needed to accommodate different types of jobs in an organization. For instance, because nurses, dietitians, and admissions clerks in a hospital all have distinct job descriptions, a separate BARS form needs to be developed for each position.

Behaviorally anchored rating scale
Scale that describes specific examples of job behavior, which are then "anchored" or measured against a scale of performance levels

10-5c Comparative Methods

Comparative methods require that managers directly compare the performance levels of their employees against one another, and these comparisons can provide useful information for managing performance. An example would be an information systems supervisor who compares the performance of one programmer with that of other programmers. Comparative techniques include ranking and forced distribution.

FIGURE 10-10   Behaviorally Anchored Rating Scale for Customer Service Skills

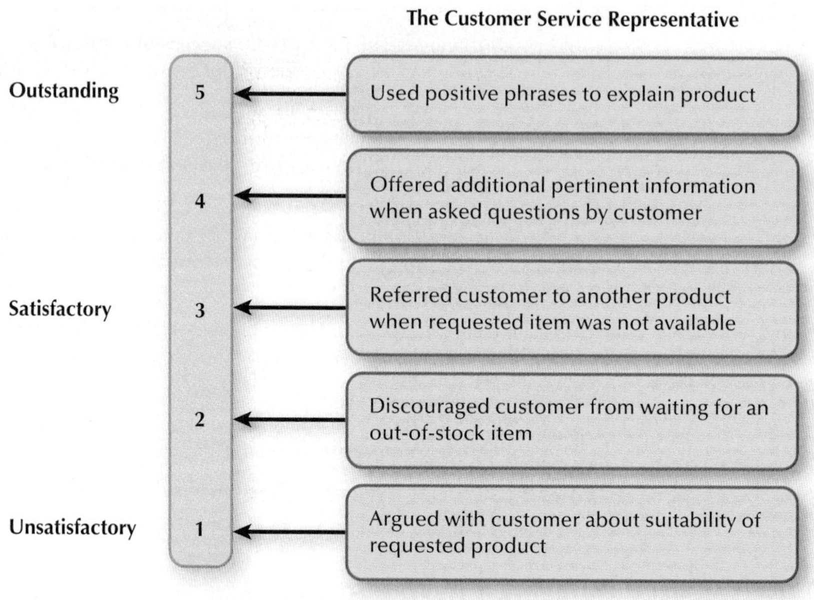

The Customer Service Representative

Outstanding	5	Used positive phrases to explain product
	4	Offered additional pertinent information when asked questions by customer
Satisfactory	3	Referred customer to another product when requested item was not available
	2	Discouraged customer from waiting for an out-of-stock item
Unsatisfactory	1	Argued with customer about suitability of requested product

Ranking
Performance appraisal method in which employees are listed from highest to lowest based on their performance levels and relative contributions

Ranking The ranking method lists the employees being rated from highest to lowest based on their performance levels and relative contributions. One disadvantage of this process is that the sizes of the performance differences between employees are often not clearly indicated. For example, the job performance of individuals ranked second and third may differ little, while the performance of those ranked third and fourth might differ a great deal. This limitation can be mitigated to some extent by assigning points to indicate performance differences. Ranking also means someone must be last, which ignores the possibility that the last-ranked individual in one group might be equal to the top-ranked employee in a different group. Further, the ranking task becomes unwieldy if the group of employees to be ranked is large.

Forced distribution
Performance appraisal method in which ratings of employees' performance levels are distributed along a bell-shaped curve

Forced Distribution Forced distribution is a technique for distributing ratings that are generated with any of the other appraisal methods and comparing the ratings of people in a work group. With the forced distribution method, the ratings of employees' performance levels are distributed along a bell-shaped curve similar to grading on a curve in school settings.[25] For example, a medical clinic administrator ranking employees on a 5-point scale would have to rate 10% of the employees as a 1 ("unsatisfactory"), 20% as a 2 ("below expectations"), 40% as a 3 ("meets expectations"), 20% as a 4 ("above expectations"), and 10% as a 5 ("outstanding").

Forced distribution or stack ranking has been used in some form by an estimated 30% of all firms with performance appraisal systems. At General Electric, the managers identified as the top 20% were rewarded richly so that few would leave. The bottom 10% of employees were given a chance to improve or leave. Yahoo has also adopted a stack ranking approach to help manage evaluations of the company's employees.[26]

FIGURE 10-11   Forced Distribution on a Bell-Shaped Curve

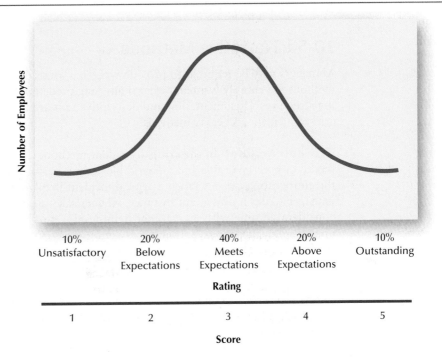

Advantages and Disadvantages of Forced Distribution   One reason firms have adopted forced distributions for appraisal ratings is to deal with "rater inflation." If employers do not require a forced distribution, performance appraisal ratings often do not match the normal distribution of a bell-shaped curve (see Figure 10-11).

The use of a forced distribution system forces managers to identify high, average, and low performers. Thus, high performers can be rewarded and developed, while low performers can be encouraged to improve or leave. Advocates of forced ranking argue that forced distribution ensures that compensation increases truly are differentiated by performance rather than being spread equally among all employees.

But the forced distribution method suffers from several drawbacks. Perhaps in a truly exceptional group of employees there are not 10% who are unsatisfactory. Another problem is that a supervisor may resist placing any individual in the lowest (or the highest) group. Difficulties also arise when the rater must explain to an employee why he or she was placed in one group while others were placed in higher groups. In some cases, the manager may make false distinctions between employees. By comparing people against each other, rather than against a standard of job performance, supervisors trying to fill the percentages may end up giving employees very subjective ratings.[27] Finally, forced ranking structures can increase anxiety in employees, promote conformity, and encourage gaming of the system. Consequently, a number of firms have been involved in lawsuits about forced distribution performance appraisal processes. In fact, one study found that the use of forced distribution rating approaches may result in more frequent adverse impact violations when managing company layoffs.[28] Microsoft recently dropped its use of stack rankings because it considered the practice to be controversial and thought it created unnecessary competition and broke down trust and teamwork.[29]

10-5d Narrative Methods

Managers may be required to provide written appraisal narratives. Some appraisal methods are entirely written, rather than using predetermined rating scales or ranking structures. Documentation and descriptive text are the basic components of the critical incident and essay methods.

Critical Incident In the critical incident method, the manager keeps a written record of both favorable and unfavorable actions performed by an employee during the entire rating period. When a critical incident involving an employee occurs, the manager writes it down. For instance, when a sales clerk at a clothing store spends considerable time with a customer helping him purchase a new suit, a manager might document this exceptional service for later review during an annual evaluation. The critical incident method can be used with other approaches to document the reasons an employee was given a certain rating.

Essay The essay method requires a manager to write a short essay describing each employee's performance during the rating period. Some free-form essays are written without guidelines; others are more structured, with prepared questions that must be answered. The rater usually categorizes comments under a few general headings. The essay method allows the rater more flexibility than other methods do, sometimes too much. As a result, appraisers often combine the essay with other methods.

The effectiveness of the essay approach often depends on a supervisor's writing and observation skills. Some supervisors do not express themselves well in writing and as a result produce poor descriptions of employee performance, whereas others have excellent writing skills and can create highly positive impressions of their employees. If well composed, essays can provide highly detailed and useful information about an employee's job performance.

10-5e Goal Setting and Management by Objectives

Goal setting is often viewed as one of the best approaches for enhancing performance management in general and the performance appraisal process in particular. Positive goal setting allows employees to be more directed in their work efforts, which can lead to higher job performance. A study of call center workers found that different internalized goals were associated with stronger achievement needs and job performance among individuals.[30] Managers can also give employees and work teams the responsibility to develop their own goals by helping them understand how their objectives are linked to company goals, overseeing the goal setting process, and making sure that all objectives are adequately connected.[31] The following "HR Competencies & Applications: Mentorships Require Dynamic Goal Setting" feature investigates how organizations can use mentoring as a mechanism for driving the goal-setting process among employees.

Management by objectives (MBO) is a specific performance appraisal method that highlights the performance goals that an individual and manager identify together. Each manager sets objectives derived from the overall goals and objectives of the organization; however, MBO should not be a disguised means for a superior to

Management by objectives (MBO)
A specific performance appraisal method that highlights the performance goals that an individual and manager identify together

Mentorships Require Dynamic Goal Setting

What makes goal setting such a perplexing process for mentors and mentees? First of all, goals must be SMART, meaning that they must be specific, measureable, action-based, realistic, and time-bound. If this isn't difficult enough, trying to figure out the roles that mentors and mentees should play in goal setting can be challenging as well. Mentors should help the process along, but mentees should be the ones who manage goal setting, particularly because the goals affect their job efforts. The overall objective in sound goal setting is to develop a learning partnership between both parties so that mentees can better set and work toward their professional objectives.

How can mentors help mentees take more responsibility for their goal setting? As a mentor, there are several things you can do to achieve these results:

- *Be a good listener.* Try to understand the mentee's current work situation to determine the contextual factors that may affect the goal-setting process. Also, try to determine an individual's strengths, weaknesses, opportunities, and threats (kind of like a personal SWOT analysis) so that goals can be developed based on the proper match between the work environment and the mentee's situation analysis.
- *Provide good examples.* Talk about your own positive work experiences to give mentees a model for success. You can also discuss other examples of successful people who were driven by positive goals.

- *Match all the important pieces together.* Be careful to help mentees connect their goals with the objectives of the organization. Also make sure that the goals established help mentees work effectively given their own work situations.
- *Brainstorm over different viewpoints.* Encourage mentees to view their characteristics and work situations in different ways to make sure that reasonable goals have been set.
- *Emphasize the importance of time.* Discuss which goals should be given priority and determine how well goals can be accomplished given the time lines established.

Evidence suggests that adopting these approaches will help build positive mentor–mentee relationships. At a minimum, this process can help encourage more communication among mentors and mentees, which is always productive when it comes to goal setting.[32]

As an HR professional or line manager, you will likely have to consider how to enhance mentorship arrangements. Consequently, consider the following questions:

1. How can mentorships be used to improve job performance?

2. How would you encourage mentors and mentees to be more engaged in the goal-setting process? How could you better prepare individuals for the challenges associated with mentorships?

KEY COMPETENCIES: Relationship Management (Behavioral Competency) and People (Technical Competency)

dictate the objectives of individual managers or employees. Other names for MBO include *appraisal by results, target coaching, work planning and review, performance objective setting,* and *mutual goal setting.* The goal setting that occurs as part of this process can be helpful in a variety of managerial functions.

MBO Process Implementing a guided self-appraisal system using MBO is a four-stage process. The stages are as follows:

1. *Job review and agreement:* The employee and the superior review the job description and the key activities that constitute the employee's job. The idea is to agree on the exact makeup of the job.
2. *Development of performance standards:* Together, the employee and his or her superior develop specific standards of performance and determine a satisfactory level of performance that is specific and measurable. For example, a quota of selling five cars a month may be an appropriate performance standard for a salesperson.
3. *Setting of objectives:* Together, the employee and the superior establish objectives that are realistically attainable.
4. *Continuing performance discussions:* The employee and the superior use the objectives as a basis for continuing discussions about the employee's performance. Although a formal review session may be scheduled, the employee and the supervisor do not necessarily wait until the appointed time to discuss performance. Objectives can be mutually modified as warranted.

The MBO process seems to be most useful with managerial personnel and employees who have adequate flexibility and control over their jobs. When imposed on a rigid and autocratic management system, MBO will often fail. Emphasizing penalties for not meeting objectives defeats the development and participative nature of MBO. Based on the results of one study, a strong MBO system can also help organizations generate a positive climate for goal setting.[33]

10-5f Combinations of Methods

No single appraisal method is best for all situations, so a performance measurement system that uses a combination of methods may be sensible. Using combinations may offset some of the advantages and disadvantages of individual methods. Category scaling methods are easy to develop, but they usually do little to measure strategic accomplishments. Further, they may make inter-rater reliability problems worse. Comparative approaches help reduce leniency and other errors, which makes them useful for administrative decisions such as determining pay raises. But comparative approaches do a poor job of linking performance to organizational goals and by themselves do not provide feedback for improvement as well as other methods do.

Narrative methods work well for development because they potentially generate more feedback information. However, without good definitions of performance criteria or standards, they can be so unstructured as to be of little value for administrative uses. The MBO approach works well to link performance to organizational goals, but it can require much effort and time for defining objectives and explaining the process to employees. Narrative and MBO approaches may not work as well for lower-level jobs as for positions with more varied duties and responsibilities.

When managers can articulate what they want a performance appraisal system to accomplish, they can choose and mix methods to realize advantages of each approach. For example, one combination might include a graphic rating scale of performance on major job criteria, a narrative for developmental needs, and an overall ranking of employees in a department. Different categories of employees (e.g., salaried exempt, salaried nonexempt, maintenance) might require different combinations of methods.

LO5 Discuss the importance of training managers and employees on performance appraisal and give examples of rater errors.

10-6 Training Managers and Employees in Performance Appraisal

Court decisions on the legality of performance appraisals and research on appraisal effectiveness both stress the importance of training managers and employees. For employees, performance appraisal training focuses on the purposes of appraisal, the appraisal process and timing, and how performance criteria and standards are linked to job duties and responsibilities. Most systems can be improved by training supervisors in how to conduct performance appraisals. Since conducting the appraisals is important, training should center around minimizing rater errors and providing raters with details on documenting performance information. Training is essential for those who have recently been promoted to managerial jobs and for whom conducting performance appraisals is a new experience. Managers with informed positive views of the performance appraisal system are more likely to use the system effectively. Unfortunately, such training occurs only sporadically or not at all in many organizations.

Without training, managers and supervisors often "repeat the past," meaning that they appraise others much as they have been appraised in the past. The following list is not comprehensive, but it does identify some topics to be covered in appraisal training for managers:

- Appraisal process and timing
- Performance criteria and job standards that should be considered
- How to communicate positive and negative feedback
- When and how to discuss training and development goals
- Conducting and discussing the compensation review
- How to avoid common rating errors

10-6a Rater Errors

There are many possible sources of error in the performance appraisal process. One of the major sources is the rater. Although completely eliminating errors is impossible, making raters aware of potential errors and biases helps to reduce them.

Varying Standards When appraising employees, a manager should avoid applying different standards and expectations to employees performing the same or similar jobs. Such problems often result from the use of ambiguous criteria and subjective weightings by supervisors.

Recency effect
Occurs when a rater gives greater weight to recent events when appraising an individual's performance

Primacy effect
Occurs when a rater gives greater weight to information received first when appraising an individual's performance

Recency and Primacy Effects The recency effect occurs when a rater gives greater weight to recent events when appraising an individual's performance. Examples include giving a customer service representative a rating based on phone calls taken during the week before the appraisal or giving a drill press operator a high rating even though the operator made the assigned quota only in the last two weeks of the rating period. Another time-related issue is the primary effect, which occurs when a rater gives greater weight to information received first when appraising an individual's performance.

Central Tendency, Leniency, and Strictness Errors Ask students, and they will tell you about professors who tend to grade easier or harder. A manager may develop a similar *rating pattern*. A rater who gives all employees a score within a narrow range in the middle of the scale (i.e., rate everyone as "average") commits a central tendency error, giving even outstanding and poor performers an "average" rating.

Rating patterns also may exhibit leniency or strictness. The leniency error occurs when ratings of all employees fall at the high end of the scale. To avoid conflict, managers often rate employees higher than they should. This "ratings boost" is especially likely when no manager or HR representative reviews the completed appraisals. The strictness error occurs when a manager uses only the lower end of the scale to rate employees.

Rater Bias When a rater's values or prejudices distort the rating, rater bias occurs. Such bias may be unconscious or quite intentional. For example, a manager's dislike of certain ethnic groups may cause distortion in appraisal information for some people. Use of age, religion, seniority, sex, appearance, or other "classification" may also skew appraisal ratings if the appraisal process is not properly designed. A review of appraisal ratings by higher-level managers may help correct this problem.

Halo and Horns Effects The halo effect occurs when a rater scores an employee high on all job criteria because of performance in one area of the assigned work responsibilities. For example, if a worker has few absences, the supervisor might give the worker a high rating in all other areas of work, including quantity and quality of output, without really thinking about the employee's other characteristics separately. The opposite is the horns effect, which occurs when a low rating on one characteristic leads to an overall low rating.

Contrast Error Rating should be done using established standards. One problem is the contrast error, which is the tendency to rate people relative to others rather than against performance standards. For example, if everyone else performs at a mediocre level, then a person performing only slightly better may be rated as "excellent" because of the contrast effect. But in a group where many employees are performing well, the same person might receive a lower rating. Although it may be appropriate to compare people at times, the performance rating usually should reflect comparison against performance standards, not against other people.

Similar-to-Me/Different-from-Me Errors Sometimes, raters are influenced by whether people possess characteristics that are the same as or different from their own qualities. For example, a manager with an MBA degree might give subordinates with MBAs higher appraisals than those who have only earned bachelor's degrees. The error reflects measuring an individual against another person (the rater) rather than measuring how well the individual fulfills the expectations of the job.

Sampling Error If the rater has seen only a small sample of the person's work, an appraisal may be subject to sampling error. For example, assume that 95% of

---

Central tendency error
Occurs when a rater gives all employees a score within a narrow range in the middle of the scale

Leniency error
Occurs when ratings of all employees fall at the high end of the scale

Strictness error
Occurs when a manager uses only the lower end of the scale to rate employees

Rater bias
Occurs when a rater's values or prejudices distort the rating

Halo effect
Occurs when a rater scores an employee high on all job criteria because of performance in one area of the assigned work responsibilities

Horns effect
Occurs when a low rating on one characteristic leads to an overall low rating

Contrast error
Tendency to rate people relative to others rather than against performance standards

the reports prepared by an employee have been satisfactory, but a manager has seen only the 5% that had errors. If the supervisor rates the person's performance as "poor," then a sampling error has occurred. Ideally, the work being rated should be a broad and representative sample of all the work completed by the employee.

LO6 Identify several concerns about appraisal feedback and ways to make it more effective.

10-7 Appraisal Feedback

After completing appraisals, managers need to communicate the results to employees to provide them with a clear understanding of how their performance compares to company standards and expectations. Organizations commonly require managers to discuss appraisals with employees. The appraisal feedback interview provides an opportunity to clear up any misunderstandings on both sides. In this interview, the manager should also focus on coaching and development.

10-7a The Appraisal Interview

The appraisal interview presents both an opportunity and a challenge. It can be an emotional experience for the manager and the employee because the manager must communicate both praise and constructive criticism. A major concern for managers is how to emphasize the positive aspects of the employee's performance while still discussing ways to make needed improvements. If the interview is handled poorly, the employee may feel resentment, which could lead to future performance problems. Consequently, a manager should clearly communicate how an employee's positive contributions have helped the organization perform well. When poor performance must be discussed, managers could use a series of questions and discussion points that enable employees to identify their own performance deficiencies and develop useful plans for performance improvement.

Employees often approach an appraisal interview with some concern. They may feel that discussions about performance are both personal and important to their continued job success. At the same time, they want to know how their managers view their performance. Figure 10-12 summarizes hints for an effective appraisal interview for supervisors and managers.

10-7b Reactions of Managers and Employees

Managers may feel some resistance about appraisals because they often have negative perceptions about the process. Many feel that their role requires them to assist, encourage, coach, and counsel employees to improve their performance. However, being a judge on one hand and a coach and a counselor on the other may cause some internal conflict.

Knowing that appraisals may affect employees' future careers may also cause altered or biased ratings. This problem is even more likely when managers know that they will have to communicate and defend their ratings to the employees, their bosses, and/or HR specialists. Managers can simply make the employee's ratings positive and avoid unpleasantness. But avoidance helps no one. A manager owes an

FIGURE 10-12 Appraisal Interview Hints for Appraisers

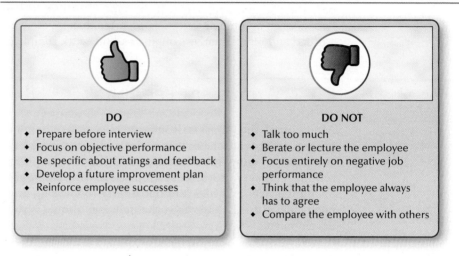

DO	DO NOT
◆ Prepare before interview ◆ Focus on objective performance ◆ Be specific about ratings and feedback ◆ Develop a future improvement plan ◆ Reinforce employee successes	◆ Talk too much ◆ Berate or lecture the employee ◆ Focus entirely on negative job performance ◆ Think that the employee always has to agree ◆ Compare the employee with others

employee a well-done appraisal, no matter how difficult an employee is or how difficult the conversation about performance might be.

Employees may well see the appraisal process as a threat and feel that the only way for them to get a higher rating is for someone else to receive a low rating. This win–lose perception is encouraged by the use of comparative rating methods. Emphasis on the self-improvement and developmental characteristics of appraisals may mitigate this reaction.

Another common employee reaction resembles students' response to tests. A professor may prepare a test that she perceives to be fair, but students may see it differently. Likewise, employees being appraised may not necessarily agree with the manager doing the appraising. However, in most cases, employees will view well-done appraisals as what they are meant to be—constructive feedback.

10-7c Effective Performance Management

Regardless of the approach used, managers should understand that performance management is important for companies to reach their strategic goals by working effectively with and through employees. When the process is used to truly develop employees as resources, it usually works. When the performance appraisal is used to help employees perform better at work, performance management is even more effective. In its simplest form, performance appraisal is the observation: "Here are your strengths and weaknesses, and here is a way to develop for the future."

Done well, performance management, working through the performance appraisal, can lead to higher employee motivation and satisfaction. To be effective, a system should be:

- Beneficial as a development tool
- Useful as an administrative tool
- Legal and job related
- Viewed as generally fair by employees
- Effective in documenting employee performance
- Clear about who are high, average, and low performers

SUMMARY

- Performance management systems attempt to identify, measure, communicate, develop, and reward employee performance.
- Performance management has a broad organizational focus, whereas performance appraisals are the processes used to evaluate how employees perform their jobs and then communicate that information to employees.
- Effective performance management has a number of components, beginning with a performance-focused organizational culture.
- Job criteria identify important elements of a job and affect the establishment of performance standards.
- Federal employment guidelines and court decisions influence the performance appraisal process.
- Appraising employee performance serves both administrative and developmental purposes.
- Performance appraisals can be done either informally or systematically.

- Appraisals can be conducted by superiors, employees (rating superiors or themselves), teams, outsiders, or other sources.
- Appraisal methods include category scaling, graphic rating scales, comparative, narrative, and management by objectives.
- Graphic rating scales and behavioral rating scales are widely used.
- Comparative methods include ranking and forced distribution, both of which raise methodological and legal concerns.
- Narrative methods include the critical incident technique and the essay approach.
- Training managers and employees on how to conduct performance appraisals can contribute to the effectiveness of a performance management system.
- Many performance appraisal problems are caused by a number of different rater errors.
- The appraisal feedback interview is a vital part of any appraisal system, and the reactions of both managers and employees must be considered when evaluating the system.

CRITICAL THINKING CHALLENGES

1. Describe how organizational culture and the use of performance criteria and standards affect the remaining components of a performance management system.

2. Suppose you are a supervisor. What errors might you make when preparing the performance appraisal on a clerical employee? How might you avoid those errors?

3. Based on your experiences, as well as the chapter information, what are some good "rules of thumb" for conducting successful performance appraisal interviews?

4. Review the performance appraisal process and appraisal form used by a current or former employer and compare it with those provided by other students. Also review other appraisal issues by going to www.workforce.com and searching for articles on *performance appraisals*. Develop a report suggesting changes to make the performance

appraisal form and process you reviewed more effective.

5. As the new HR Director of a company in the behavioral health industry, you have the responsibility to develop a performance management system. You need to present a business case to senior executives that the performance management system does not stand alone and must be integrated into the company's strategic plan, business needs, and measurements. For information on performance management best practices, review various publications in the articles tab at www.insala.com.

   A. Given several key practices for a successful performance management system, which ones should be implemented first?
   B. Identify key measurements to transition the company from the current system of looking at personality factors to a new system of looking at performance factors.

CASE   Microsoft Jettisons Stack Rankings

Microsoft has always been on the cutting edge of performance management and compensation. The firm has a reputation for hiring good employees and taking care of them by providing generous rewards and opportunities. In particular, paying workers based on their performance is an approach that the company has utilized for some time. Over the last several decades, Microsoft has given employees stock options, generous increases to base pay, and restricted stock units. A number of years ago, the flexible rewards program MyMicrosoft was offered, and it enabled workers to earn merit pay, bonuses, and restricted stock units.

In an effort to support this HR management philosophy, Microsoft introduced a stack rankings process more recently, which required managers to rate employees (on a scale of 1 to 5, with 1 being the highest) so that they could be ultimately ranked against each other. These rankings affected the amount of compensation (i.e., merit, bonuses, restricted stock units) employees would receive. The ranking process also forced managers to designate a certain percentage of their employees as poor performers.

This requirement makes stack ranking a controversial performance management approach because there are always losers, despite the fact that a company may be hiring and developing well. Critics also point out that the stack ranking process, or "rank and yank" as it is sometimes called, doesn't do much to create a sense of teamwork among employees. Despite these limitations, some managers, including the previous CEO of General Electric Jack Welch, defend the practice. They claim that it allows leaders to effectively differentiate varying levels of job performance among employees more effectively.

Given these concerns, Microsoft elected to drop its stack ranking system a few years after it was adopted. This means that managers do not have to use the scaling and ranking methods that were introduced several years earlier. In addition, managers do not have to indicate through the employee appraisals that a percentage of workers are not meeting standards. It will be interesting to see how managers continue to tweak the company's performance management system so that employees are rewarded fairly and accurately for their job performance.[34]

QUESTIONS

1. What is your overall opinion of the stack ranking system? Do you think this approach serves a purpose in modern organizations?

2. If you were to implement stack ranking in a company, how would you do it? What are the potential challenges associated with implementing this system? Would you use it, or would you elect to use an alternative approach?

SUPPLEMENTAL CASES

Performance Management at Netflix

This case provides an example of how a performance-oriented culture can be established to facilitate the performance management process. (For the case, go to www.cengage.com/management/mathis.)

Performance Management Improvements for Bristol-Myers Squibb

This case identifies how performance management systems might be redesigned. (For the case, go to www.cengage.com/management/mathis.)

Building Performance through Employee Participation

The case outlines what was done at Jewelers Mutual Insurance in allowing employees to have a say in performance management. (For the case, go to www.cengage.com/management/mathis.)

Unequal/Equal Supervisors

This case identifies the consequences of giving appraisal ratings that may not be accurate. (For the case, go to www.cengage.com/management/mathis.)

END NOTES

1. Adapted from David Zinger and Siddhesh Bhobe, "Game-Changing Performance Management," *T+D*, January 2014, p. 80.
2. Andrew R. McIlvaine, "There's Got to Be a Better Way," *Human Resource Executive*, July–August 2012, pp. 13–15; Samuel A. Culbert, "The Case for Killing Performance Reviews," *Human Resource Executive Online*, July 16, 2012, pp. 1–2.
3. Tom Starner, "SHRM Offers Performance Management Standard," *Human Resource Executive Online*, February 8, 2013, http://www.hreonline.com/HRE/view/story.jhtml?id=534354955.
4. Bettina Wolf, "No Change in Sight for Performance Management," *T+D*, February 2014, p. 12.
5. Adapted from Adrienne Fox, "Put Plans into Action," *HR Magazine*, April 2013, pp. 27–31.
6. Pat Galagan, "Before the Shark Strikes," *T+D*, November 2013, pp. 22–25.
7. Paul Falcone, "Winter 2013: Offense Is the Best Defense against Underperformers," *SHRM Online*, January 22, 2013, http://www.shrm.org/publications/managingsmart/pages/winter-2013-underperformers.aspx.
8. "Allophilia," *T+D*, January 2014, p. 13.
9. John R. Graham, "Winter 2013: Putting the 'Person' in Personnel Decisions," *SHRM Online*, January 22, 2013, http://www.shrm.org/publications/managingsmart/pages/winter-2013-put-person-in-personnel.aspx.
10. Rebecca R. Hastings, "Most Large Companies Calibrate Performance Pool Finds," *HR Magazine*, February 2012, p. 87.
11. Dana Wilkie, "Bracing for that Perennial Chore: Performance Reviews," *SHRM Online*, December 4, 2013, http://www.shrm.org/hrdisciplines/employeerelations/articles/pages/performance-reviews-evaluations.aspx.
12. Ben Locwin, "Psychological Biases May Influence Feedback on Evaluations," *T+D*, November 2013, p. 12.
13. "Effectiveness of Performance Appraisals Gets Mixed Reviews form HR Professionals in New SHRM Survey," *SHRM Online*, October 21, 2014, http://www.shrm.org/about/pressroom/pressreleases/pages/2014-performance-management-news-release.aspx.
14. Elaine Farndale and Clarke Kelliher, "Implementing Performance Appraisal: Exploring the Employee Experience," *Human Resource Management* 52 (November–December 2013), 879–897.
15. Timothy C. Bednall, Karin Sanders, and Piety Runhaar, "Stimulating Informal Learning Activities through Perceptions of Performance Appraisal Quality and Human Resource Management System Strength: A Two-Wave Study," *Academy of Management Learning & Education* 13 (2014), 45–61.
16. Dave Zielinski, "Making the Most of Manager Self-Service," *HR Magazine*, December 2013, pp. 51–55.
17. "Effectiveness of Performance Appraisals Gets Mixed Reviews from HR Professionals in New SHRM Survey," *SHRM Online*, October 21, 2014, http://www.shrm.org/about/pressroom/pressreleases/pages/2014-performance-management-news-release.aspx.
18. Based on Andrew McIlvaine, "There's Got to Be a Better Way," *Human Resource Executive*, July–August 2012, 14–18.
19. Kai Chi Yam, Ryan Fehr, and Christopher M. Barnes, "Morning Employees Are Perceived as Better Employees: Employees' Start Times Influence Supervisor Performance Ratings," *Journal of Applied Psychology* 99 (November 2014), 1288–1299.
20. Gil Luria and Yuval Kalish, "A Social Network Approach to Peer Assessment: Improving Predictive Validity," *Human Resource Management* 52 (July–August 2013), 537–560.
21. Lawrence C. Bassett, "No Such Things as Perfect Performance Management," *Human Resource Executive* 26 (September 16, 2012), 6.
22. Gary P. Latham, Robert C. Ford, and Danny Tzabbar, "Enhancing Employee and Organizational Performance through Coaching Based on Mystery Shopper Feedback: A Quasi-Experimental Study," *Human Resource Management* 51 (March–April 2012), 213–230.
23. Adapted from Teresa A. Daniel, "Executive Success and the Increased Potential for Ethical Failure," Legal Report, Society for Human Resource Management, July 2013, pp. 1–5.
24. James Smither and Manuel London (editors), *Performance Management: Putting Research into Action* (San Francisco: Jossey-Bass, 2009), 297–328.

25. Dori Meinert, "A Crack in the Bell Curve," *HR Magazine*, April 2012, p. 22.

26. Bill Leonard, "Announcements on 'Stack Rankings' Touch off Debate," *SHRM Online*, November 22, 2013, http://www.shrm.org/publications/hrnews/pages/announcements-on-stack-rankings-touch-off-debate.aspx.

27. Susan M. Steward, "Forced Distribution Performance Evaluation Systems: Advantages, Disadvantages, and Keys to Implementation," *e Content Management* 16 (March 2010), 168–179; E. O'Boyle Jr. and J. Arguinis, "The Best and the Rest: Revisiting the Norm of Normality of Individual Performance," *Personnel Psychology* 65 (2012), 79–119.

28. Gary W. Giumetti, Amber N. Schroeder, and Fred S. Switzer III, "Forced Distribution Rating Systems: When Does 'Rank and Yank' Lead to Adverse Impact?" *Journal of Applied Psychology* 100 (January 2015), 180–193.

29. Bill Leonard, "Announcements on 'Stack Rankings' Touch off Debate," *SHRM Online*, November 22, 2013, http://www.shrm.org/publications/hrnews/pages/announcements-on-stack-rankings-touch-off-debate.aspx.

30. Gary P. Latham and Ronald F. Piccolo, "The Effect of Context-Specific versus Nonspecific Subconscious Goals on Employee Performance," *Human Resource Management* 51 (July–August 2012), 511–524.

31. Robert Liddell, "Employee-Crafted Goals Pay Off," *HR Magazine*, July 2013, p. 63.

32. Adapted from Lois J. Zachary and Lory A. Fischler, "Facilitating Mentee-Driven Goal Setting," *T+D*, May 2013, pp. 76–77.

33. Eda Aksoy and Mahmut Bayazit, "The Relationship between MBO System Strength and Goal-Climate Quality and Strength," *Human Resource Management* 53 (July–August 2014), 505–525.

34. Based on Stephen Miller, "Integrating Performance Management and Rewards at Microsoft," *SHRM Online*, May 25, 2012, http://www.shrm.org/hrdisciplines/compensation/articles/pages/rewardsatmicrosoft.aspx; Stephen Miller, "'Stack Ranking' Ends at Microsoft," *SHRM Online*, November 20, 2013, http://www.shrm.org/hrdisciplines/compensation/articles/pages/stack-ranking-microsoft.aspx.

Compensation

CHAPTER

11

Total Rewards and Compensation

Learning Objectives

After you have read this chapter, you should be able to:

LO1 Identify the three general components of total rewards and give examples of each.

LO2 Explain the major laws governing employee compensation.

LO3 Outline strategic compensation decisions.

LO4 Understand the challenges of managing global compensation systems.

LO5 Illustrate the steps in developing a base pay system.

LO6 Describe how individual pay rates are set.

WHAT'S TRENDING IN
TOTAL REWARDS AND COMPENSATION

Employers should offer the types of compensation that recognize and motivate employees who work hard and contribute to the company's success. Organizations should offer competitive compensation that enables them to attract and retain good workers. Here's what's currently trending in the area of total rewards and compensation:

1. There are a number of ethical issues related to compensation. Higher-paid employees can sometimes misbehave, employers can work together to limit pay, and compensation itself can prompt worker greed.

2. When pay decisions are viewed as inappropriate or unfair, lawsuits can occur. There is growing concern about litigation targeting the misclassification of employees, overtime pay, and other wage violations.

3. Identifying situations that require employers to pay workers for their time is a challenge. Managers should understand the conditions that trigger payment of wages. These include shorter meal and rest breaks, donning required equipment and uniforms, and other work-related activities. In addition, proposed changes in overtime regulations may significantly impact employees and companies.

4. Setting reasonable pay to get competent employees is an important component of compensation management. To remain fair and competitive, employers have to use different sources of internal and external salary information to determine how much employees should be making. Some companies are paying employees above the traditional minimum amounts to attract competent workers; some states are even enacting laws that set minimum wage levels higher than the federal wage.

HEADLINE

Aztec Shops Uses Time-Tracking Software

O rganization leaders must understand a wide array of federal and state laws to appropriately pay their employees. For instance, managers need to know when workers are entitled to overtime, how much they should be paid for working overtime, what qualifies as "paid" activities, and how minimum wage for different jobs should be determined. What makes these issues particularly challenging is that federal and state wage mandates sometimes differ. Even though the Fair Labor Standards Act sets federal standards for proper wage administration, this does not prevent states from developing their own standards that must also be considered. For example, the state of Washington sets a higher minimum wage for a particular position compared to federal requirements, so workers there should receive the higher minimum wage.

Given these challenges, some organizations are turning to automated systems that track employees' time on the clock to better manage the administration of wages. This time-tracking technology provides increased efficiency when paying employees what they have earned by simplifying how employee work hours are monitored and reported. One such company is Aztec Shops located at San Diego State University, which utilizes its more than 650 full-time and part-time employees to sell books, clothing, and food on campus. The firm's payroll and project manager Leah Messenger relies on time-monitoring software called Kronos to track employees' work hours, as well as their meal and break times. Since workers in California are entitled to receive a meal break after working for five hours, Aztec's system automatically indicates that this time should be taken off. The system also has an "attestation" feature that allows employees to verify their time reports for errors and corrections. Use of Kronos has been a success story at Aztec Shops. Overtime and

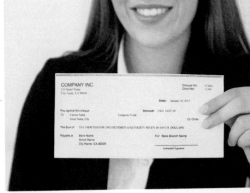

istockphoto.com/AndreyPopov

other compensation data can be accessed easily, and managers can generate reports that summarize employees' work times. While the system cost the company $500,000 over a two-year period, the investment appears to be well worth it.[1]

Total rewards
Monetary and nonmonetary rewards provided by companies to attract, motivate, and retain employees

To attract and retain high-quality talent, companies design reward packages that appeal to many different people. Companies do this by addressing pay and benefits with a total rewards approach. Such a philosophy includes all forms of compensation, that is, the monetary and nonmonetary rewards provided by a company to attract, motivate, and retain employees, as shown in Figure 11-1. The effectiveness of the reward system depends on how well compensation is linked to organizational strategies so that employees are encouraged to work in a manner that benefits the company. For example, General Motors tied a portion of salaried employees' bonus pay to customer loyalty ratings in new car sales and after-sales transactions. The company has focused on retaining customers and building on repeat business and is rewarding engineers, vehicle designers, field representatives, and other workers for improving this organizational metric.[2]

An effective total rewards approach balances the company's interests and costs with the needs and expectations of employees, which can be a difficult process. On one hand, costs related to compensation represent one of the largest portions of

FIGURE 11-1   Total Rewards Components

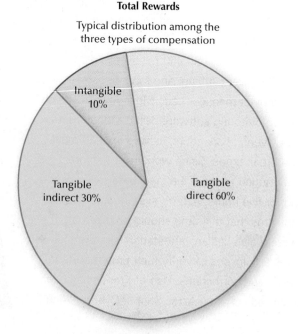

Total Rewards

Typical distribution among the three types of compensation

total operating expenses in most companies. On the other hand, employees want to be compensated fairly and have their individual needs met. They can choose to spend more time at work if compensation levels are desirable, or they can engage in more leisure activities when compensation is not attractive. The challenge then is for employers to achieve an optimal relationship between costs and employee impact while considering many financial and operational factors.[3]

The concept of total rewards requires a much broader understanding of pay or compensation than has traditionally been the case in organizations. A total rewards philosophy emphasizes how a company can use *both* direct and indirect (or relational) rewards to strengthen employee motivation and commitment. Economic conditions also require employers to make necessary adjustments to total rewards to reflect changing business environments. Broadly defining compensation should also help companies develop creative and competitive policies that keep employees motivated. For instance, startup companies that do not have extensive financial resources can offer employees time off from work, an enriched workplace, and ownership in the firm through stock options rather than giving them high pay.[4] Offering generous vacation leave, reimbursement of commuting costs, tuition assistance, access to a company car, coverage of moving expenses, and flexible work arrangements are other ways that companies can creatively reward their employees.[5]

LO1 Identify the three general components of total rewards and give examples of each.

11-1 Nature of Total Rewards and Compensation

Compensating employees is often a major cost item for employers, so top management and HR executives must work together toward aligning rewards with the strategic goals of the organization. This allows companies to offer compensation that leads to overall improvements to employee satisfaction and the bottom line. Several strategic decisions can guide the design of compensation practices:

- Compliance with all applicable laws and regulations
- Cost-effectiveness for the organization
- Internal and external equity for employees
- Optimal mix of compensation components
- Performance enhancement for the organization
- Performance recognition and talent management for employees
- Enhanced recruitment, involvement, and retention of employees

Employers strive to maintain their costs at a level that rewards employees fairly for their knowledge, skills, abilities, and performance accomplishments while allowing the firm to remain competitive and successful. WorldatWork is a leading professional association that focuses on compensation. The organization has developed a well-respected model of total rewards that includes tangible direct, tangible indirect, and intangible rewards.[6] Figure 11-2 identifies elements of three primary components of the total rewards package. It shows that total rewards can be broadly defined and also indicates that intangible rewards are an important aspect of the package.

Determining which rewards are valued by employees and applicants and finding affordable ways to provide those rewards can be challenging. Total reward

FIGURE 11-2 Elements of Total Rewards

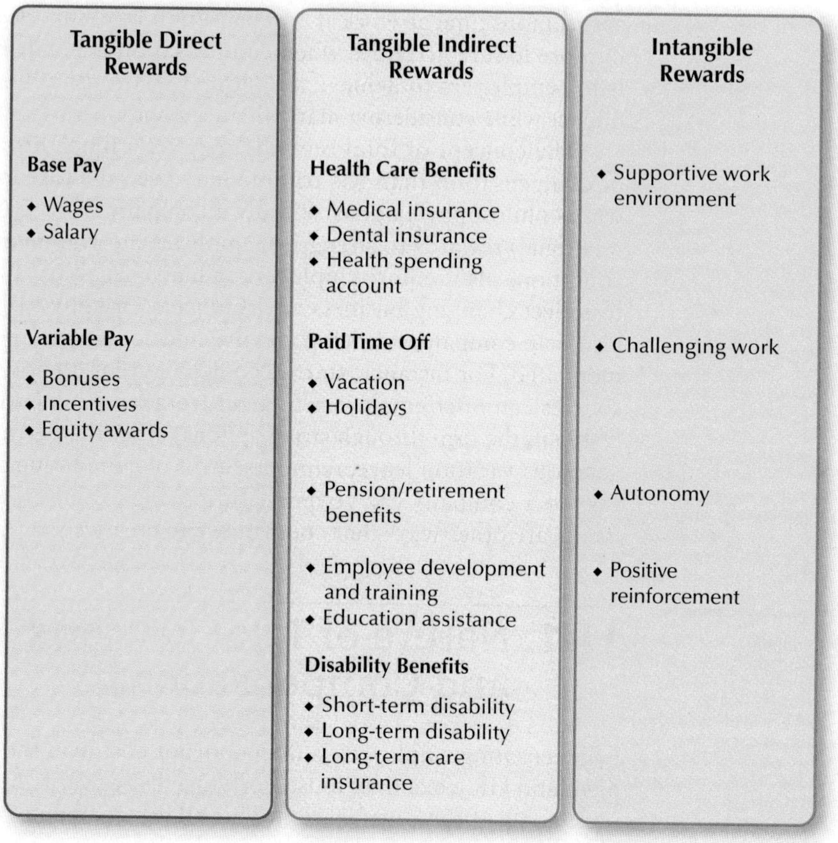

Tangible Direct Rewards	Tangible Indirect Rewards	Intangible Rewards
Base Pay ♦ Wages ♦ Salary	**Health Care Benefits** ♦ Medical insurance ♦ Dental insurance ♦ Health spending account	♦ Supportive work environment
Variable Pay ♦ Bonuses ♦ Incentives ♦ Equity awards	**Paid Time Off** ♦ Vacation ♦ Holidays	♦ Challenging work
	♦ Pension/retirement benefits	♦ Autonomy
	♦ Employee development and training ♦ Education assistance	♦ Positive reinforcement
	Disability Benefits ♦ Short-term disability ♦ Long-term disability ♦ Long-term care insurance	

Source: Adapted from *WorldatWork* (http://www.worldatwork.org).

programs should be evaluated on an ongoing basis to ensure that employees find them satisfying and that they are cost-effective and sustainable for the organization.[7] The organizational culture and pay policy should be complementary and consistent. For example, if the culture is a team-focused environment, total rewards might emphasize team/group rewards rather than individual rewards.

11-1a Components of Compensation

Tangible rewards
Elements of compensation that can be quantitatively measured and compared between different organizations

Intangible rewards
Elements of compensation that cannot be as easily measured or quantified

Tangible rewards are elements of compensation that can be quantitatively measured, so it is possible to calculate the monetary value of each reward. Consequently, employees can easily compare the tangible rewards offered by different organizations to determine relative compensation levels. Alternatively, intangible rewards are elements of compensation that cannot be as easily measured or quantified. How would an employee put a dollar value on having decision-making authority? How much is working in a positive and supportive office environment worth to an individual? What is the value of being offered enrichment and learning opportunities in the workplace? The perceived value of these intangible rewards can differ among employees, making the development and management of total rewards much more complex. Some employers may find that offering work-life balance opportunities and wellness programs can enhance employees' work satisfaction. Others may find that tangible rewards have a more immediate and positive impact on worker attitudes. This means that total rewards can vary greatly from company to company, and that employers should customize their approach to suit the needs and preferences of their workers.

One tangible component of a compensation program is *direct compensation*, the monetary rewards for work done and performance results achieved. *Base pay* and *variable pay* are the most common forms of direct compensation. The most common types of indirect compensation provided to employees are *benefits*.

Base pay
Basic compensation that an employee receives, often as an hourly wage or salary

Base Pay The basic compensation that an employee receives is called base pay. Organizations often provide basic compensation as either an hourly wage or as a salary. These two base pay categories are identified according to the way pay is determined and the nature of the jobs.

Wages
Payments calculated directly on the basis of time worked by employees

Hourly pay is most common and is based on the amount of time spent at work. Employees paid by the hour receive wages, or payments calculated directly on the basis of time worked. One report suggests that hourly pay in the United States for people employed in the private sector has increased by almost 5%, with pay increases for financial and construction employees; persons employed in the West; individuals making less than $50,000 a year; and those who are under the age of 35 experiencing larger increases.[8] Another report suggests that wages should grow by almost 2% in the near term.[9]

Salary
Consistent payments made each period regardless of the number of hours worked

In contrast, employees paid a salary receive the same consistent payments each period regardless of the number of hours worked. Even though the recent recession has slowed some pay growth, the outlook for salaried employees is moderately bright. Research suggests that salaries are trending up in some jobs, professions, and geographic regions. For instance, employees who receive high ratings on performance evaluations, as well as those who work in IT and medical occupations, have received higher salary increases.[10] Starting salaries for individuals hired into technology, accounting and finance, marketing, administrative, and legal jobs are also expected to increase.[11] In addition, increases to pay are expected to be slightly higher for salaried exempt employees compared to nonexempt workers. Individuals employed in the oil and gas sector might receive higher than average increases, while those employed in hospitals could receive lower than average increases.[12] Increases in budgets dedicated to salaries for companies located in Houston, Los Angeles, and San Francisco have been slightly above the average.[13]

Variable pay
Compensation linked directly to individual, team, or organizational performance

Variable Pay Another type of direct pay is variable pay, which is compensation linked directly to individual, team, or organizational performance. The most common types of variable pay are bonuses, incentive program payments, equity awards, and commissions. A recent survey indicated that 91% of firms provide variable pay to their employees and plan to dedicate almost 13% of pay for salaried individuals to variable compensation.[14] Employers are also using various bonuses and performance-based pay strategies to reward and retain their top performers.[15] Research shows that increases in total cash compensation for HR professionals, which includes salary and variable pay, are expected to remain at about 3% for the foreseeable future. HR executives who deal with legal matters, technology, talent management, and safety have received larger pay increases.[16] Variable pay, including executive compensation, is discussed in Chapter 12.

Benefit
Indirect reward given to an employee or group of employees as part of membership in the organization, regardless of performance

Benefits Many organizations provide indirect rewards in the form of employee benefits. With indirect compensation, employees receive financial rewards without receiving actual cash or other direct monetary payments. A benefit is an indirect reward given to an employee or group of employees as part of membership in the organization, regardless of performance. Examples of benefits are dental coverage, vacation leave, and retirement plans. The administration of benefits is discussed in Chapter 13.

LO2 Explain the major laws governing employee compensation.

11-2 Laws Governing Compensation

Pay practices are regulated by several federal laws that address issues such as overtime pay, minimum wage standards, hours of work, and pay equity. The following discussion examines the laws and regulations affecting base compensation. The laws and regulations that affect incentives and benefits are covered in Chapters 12 and 13.

11-2a Fair Labor Standards Act (FLSA)

The primary federal law affecting compensation is the Fair Labor Standards Act (FLSA), which was passed in 1938. Compliance with FLSA provisions is enforced by the Wage and Hour Division of the U.S. Department of Labor (DOL). Penalties for wage and hour violations often include awards of up to two years of back pay for affected current and former employees, along with a monetary penalty. Willful violations may be penalized by up to three years of back pay. For example, Walmart was assessed almost $5 million in back wages and penalties for overtime violations resulting from improperly classifying employees as exempt from overtime, and Staples was fined $42 million to settle similar claims.[17] In another case, the airport shuttle service at Baltimore-Washington International Thurgood Marshall Airport "Shuttle Express" was ordered to arbitrate with an individual who claimed that he was classified as an independent contractor or franchisee instead of an employee, which adversely affected his compensation.[18] The provisions of both the original act and subsequent revisions focus on the following major areas:

- Minimum wage
- Limits on the use of child labor
- Exempt and nonexempt status (overtime provisions)

Minimum Wage The FLSA sets a minimum wage to be paid to a broad spectrum of covered employees. The current minimum wage of $7.25 an hour was set as part of the Fair Minimum Wage Act of 2007. A lower minimum wage of $2.13 an hour is set for "tipped" employees, such as restaurant servers, but their compensation must equal or exceed the minimum wage when average tips are included. However, many states have minimum wage levels for both regular and tipped employees that are higher than the federal minimum wage, and employers must pay this higher wage.[19] A number of other states have enacted laws to increase the minimum wage for employees, while other states are exploring the possibility of increasing their minimum wages.[20] Given these variations in pay, employers that operate in multiple states should monitor minimum wage legislation that affects their operations.

Congressional action must be initiated before the minimum wage can be changed, and there is currently interest in raising the federal minimum wage.[21] This applies to both the regular minimum wage and the minimum wage for tipped positions. One report indicated that the tipped minimum wage has decreased by 40% and is a mere 29% of the standard minimum wage.[22] However, increasing the minimum wage could have a negative impact on job growth, and one report determined that such action could decrease total employment by an estimated 500,000 workers in the next several years.[23] A large-scale strike across seven cities in the United States was organized by thousands of fast food workers who demanded $15 an hour in wages, but meeting these demands would likely increase the cost of menu items and hurt demand.[24] Yet, unlike its competitors, Costco pays its employees well above minimum wage (an average of $21 an hour) and enjoys high profits driven by increased levels of worker engagement.[25]

There is often much legal speculation and litigation related to paying employees minimum wages. For instance, Marriott's announcement that it would encourage tipping of housekeepers (by leaving tip envelopes in guest rooms) has increased concern about the company paying these employees as tipped workers at the appropriate lower minimum wage.[26] A common FLSA violation involves not "topping off" employee wages when the tips collected added to the tipped minimum wage are lower than the standard minimum wage.[27] One lawsuit advances the argument that minor-league baseball players, who are not compensated for spring training or for participating in off-season leagues, are not provided enough pay to meet federal and state minimum wage and overtime requirements.[28] In another case, the mayor of Scranton, Pennsylvania, temporarily reduced the wages of city workers (including his pay) to the minimum wage of $7.25 an hour due to a budget crisis.[29]

Child Labor Provisions The child labor provisions of the FLSA set the minimum age for employment with unlimited hours at 16 years. For hazardous occupations, the minimum is 18 years of age. Individuals who are 14 to 15 years old may work outside school hours with certain limitations. Many employers require age certificates for employees because the FLSA makes the employer responsible for verifying an individual's age. Age certificates are supplied by high schools.

Exempt and Nonexempt Statuses Under the FLSA, employees are classified as exempt or nonexempt. Exempt employees hold positions for which they are not paid overtime. Nonexempt employees must be paid overtime. The current FLSA regulations used to establish whether a job qualifies for exempt status classify jobs into five categories, as shown in Figure 11-3. The regulations identify several factors to be considered when determining exempt status. To review the details for each exemption, go to the DOL's website at www.dol.gov.

When designing base pay, employers often categorize jobs into groupings that tie the FLSA status with the method of payment. Employers are required to pay overtime for *hourly* jobs to comply with the FLSA. Employees in positions classified as *salaried nonexempt* are also entitled to overtime pay. Salaried nonexempt positions sometimes include secretarial, clerical, and salaried blue-collar positions (like shift supervisor). The overtime can be calculated with a *standard method* that involves dividing a person's weekly salary by the total number of hours worked in a week and then providing the individual an additional payout of 1.5 times this rate for the number of hours worked over 40. An alternative method is the *fluctuating workweek*, which involves only paying one-third of the overtime rate because it is assumed that the base part of overtime pay has already been included in the salary that the individual has earned for that week. However, several criteria must be

Exempt employees
Employees who hold positions for which they are not paid overtime

Nonexempt employees
Employees who must be paid overtime

FIGURE 11-3   Determining Exempt Status under the FLSA

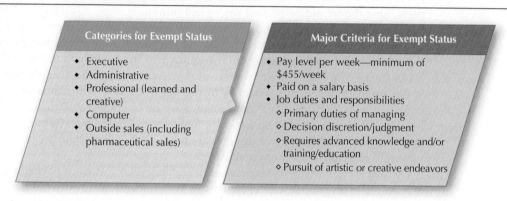

Categories for Exempt Status	Major Criteria for Exempt Status
• Executive • Administrative • Professional (learned and creative) • Computer • Outside sales (including pharmaceutical sales)	• Pay level per week—minimum of $455/week • Paid on a salary basis • Job duties and responsibilities ◇ Primary duties of managing ◇ Decision discretion/judgment ◇ Requires advanced knowledge and/or training/education ◇ Pursuit of artistic or creative endeavors

Source: Adapted from the DOL.gov.

met to use this method: (1) the hours that an individual works fluctuate weekly, (2) an individual gets a fixed salary that does not change based on hours worked, (3) the fixed salary is at least on par with the minimum wage, and (4) there must be a "clear mutual understanding" between the company and an individual that the fixed salary will be paid without regard for the hours worked.[30]

A common mistake employers make is not paying overtime to any salaried employees, even though some may qualify for nonexempt status. Exempt status is not necessarily granted to all salaried jobs; each job must be evaluated on a case-by-case basis. The FLSA does not require employers to pay overtime for *salaried exempt* jobs.

How to classify employees can be a challenge for organizations because the criteria used are outdated, confusing, and not always easily applied to the types of jobs currently found in modern companies. Some professionals believe that it is difficult for any organization to properly classify all jobs. There is even speculation that the FLSA regulations will be revised and rewritten to update their content, which unfortunately creates even more concern about misunderstandings and legal action.[31] Consequently, companies need to be proactive about preventing exemption litigation. One survey found that many organizations deal with employees who misrepresent their duties to show misclassification and earn overtime, are worried about lawsuits related to misclassifications, and are conducting audits to verify how jobs have been classified. Companies should also keep job descriptions current and use performance appraisals to help justify how jobs have been classified.[32]

Overtime   The FLSA established overtime pay requirements at 1.5 times the regular pay rate for all hours worked over 40 in a week, except for exempt employees. There are other exceptions to the overtime requirements, such as farm workers, but these exceptions are rare. There has been a recent push to expand the number of exempt employees who receive overtime, including managers in fast food outlets, loan officers, computer technicians, and individuals working in some other executive and professional jobs.[33] The salary basis would also be increased from $455 per week to a much higher amount (proposed to be $970 per week) that takes into consideration inflation and would include annual revising to keep pace with inflation. This would help prevent situations such as those where line workers make more than the salaried individuals who manage them.[34]

The workweek is defined as a consecutive period of 168 hours (24 hours × 7 days), and it does not have to be a calendar week. Hospitals and nursing homes are allowed a special definition of the workweek to accommodate their 24/7 scheduling demands. No daily number of hours requiring overtime is set, except for special provisions relating to hospitals and other specially designated organizations. Thus, if a manufacturing firm operates on a 4-day/10-hour schedule, no overtime pay is required by the act until the worker exceeds 40 hours worked in a week.

Companies need be careful about paying proper overtime to employees. For instance, employees' work schedules cannot be changed by an employer to avoid paying overtime, even when individuals are willing to go along with it.[35] The CEO of the New York City supermarket firm Gristede's Foods was held personally liable when the company failed to pay a settlement for various pay administration and overtime violations.[36]

Special Pay/Overtime Issues For individuals who are nonexempt, employers must consider many issues. These include the following:

- *Compensatory time off*: "Comp" hours are earned by public-sector nonexempt employees in lieu of payment for extra time worked at the rate of 1.5 times the number of hours over 40 that are worked in a week. Comp time is prohibited in the private sector and cannot be legally offered to employees working for private organizations.
- *Incentives for nonexempt employees*: Employers must add the amount of direct work-related incentives to an employee's base pay and then calculate overtime pay as 1.5 times the higher (adjusted) rate of pay.
- *Training time*: Time spent in training must be counted as time worked by nonexempt employees unless it is voluntary or not directly related to the job.
- *Security inspection time*: Some companies may have to count the time that employees spend going through security inspections after work as compensable. Claims related to security inspection time have been brought against organizations such as Amazon, Apple, and CVS Health.[37]
- *After-hours email time*: The increased use of email in organizations raises questions about whether employees can claim that responding to company emails after hours should count toward overtime. Organizations should consider adopting email curfew policies that discourage employees from reading and answering work-related emails off the clock.[38]
- *Travel time*: Travel time must be counted as work time if it occurs during normal work hours for the benefit of the employer. Travel to and from work is not considered compensable travel time.
- *Donning and doffing time*: Some jobs require employees to spend a significant amount of time donning protective equipment before they report for duty. This can also include clothing that is used for purposes of protection in a particular job.[39] Regulations regarding putting on and taking off such clothing and gear are complex. Questions regarding specific cases should be researched with the DOL.

The FLSA does not require employers to provide breaks or lunch periods, or to pay double-time for any hours worked. However, the FLSA does provide guidance when companies offer their employees breaks. The following "HR

Competencies & Applications: It's Break Time! Wait…Should I Get Paid?" feature explores situations that require companies to pay employees for their rest and meal breaks. A nurse employed at Genesis Healthcare advanced an FLSA collective action when the company started systematically reducing employees' time worked based on meal breaks, even when such breaks were not taken. Since no one else joined the lawsuit and a settlement was never challenged, it was eventually dismissed.[40] However, this case underscores how employers must properly manage payroll and breaks.

State laws also vary on many of these topics, and employers should research compliance requirements in all states in which they operate. The complexity of overtime determination and related matters can be confusing for managers, employees,

COMPETENCIES & APPLICATIONS

It's Break Time! Wait…Should I Get Paid?

The FLSA does not generally regulate whether organizations must provide their employees paid or unpaid breaks. However, it does indicate when employees should be paid when breaks are offered by an employer. For purposes of compensation, there are two different kinds of breaks that can be offered, rest breaks and meal breaks.

When workers take rest breaks that are 20 minutes or shorter in length, this time is compensable under the FLSA. This is the case because shorter breaks are often given by companies to improve how work gets done. When the time taken off from work for a meal break is shorter than 30 minutes, the time is compensable. Meal breaks can be shorter under certain situations, but it is up to the employer to show that these special conditions are legitimate. Another consideration is whether workers actually conduct business on their meal breaks. If individuals are asked to stay at the worksite during meal breaks, they may need to be paid even when the duration of the break is longer than 30 minutes. If employees are told to do work during their meal breaks, they likely need to be paid for their time off, which is not really "time off" anyway because they are really "on the clock."

Given these issues, a number of investigators with the U.S. Department of Labor believe that any break periods that are shorter than 30 minutes in duration count as compensable time. This is why some companies may elect to adopt such a policy, even though the law stipulates slightly different requirements for rest and meal breaks. Doing so enables organizations to avoid troublesome investigations, or even worse, lawsuits by disgruntled employees.[41]

HR professionals, and general managers make decisions about whether to pay employees for their rest and meal breaks. Consequently, consider the following questions:

1. Have you ever worked for an organization that did not honor the FLSA's pay requirements associated with rest and meal breaks? Were you aware of this issue, and did you do anything about it?

2. How can organizations encourage line managers to be more careful about paying (or not paying) employees for their breaks? What policies could be developed to help facilitate the process?

KEY COMPETENCIES: Business Acumen (Behavioral Competency) and People (Technical Competency) and HR professionals. The DOL has many informative publications on its website that clarify these issues.

11-2b Pay Equity Laws

Title VII of the Civil Rights Act of 1964 prohibits discrimination based on race, color, sex, religion, or national origin. However, prior to its passage, pay discrimination on the basis of sex was outlawed under the Equal Pay Act of 1963. Since then, additional laws have been proposed or enacted to counter wage discrimination on the basis of sex. For instance, the controversial Paycheck Fairness Act was proposed to provide income equality to women by requiring employers to show that pay differences exist due to business necessity, but the law could potentially result in greater government encroachment into business matters and increased lawsuits.[42]

Equal Pay Act of 1963 The act prohibits companies from using different wage scales for men and women performing substantially the same jobs. Pay differences can be justified on the basis of merit, seniority, quantity or quality of work, experience, or factors other than gender. Similar pay must be given for jobs requiring equal skills, equal responsibilities, or equal efforts, or for jobs done under similar working conditions.

Lilly Ledbetter Fair Pay Act This law was signed in 2009 in response to a U.S. Supreme Court decision restricting the statute of limitations allowed under the Equal Pay Act for claiming pay discrimination based on sex. Under the Equal Pay Act, an employee alleging discrimination had up to 300 days to file a claim. The Fair Pay Act essentially treats each paycheck as a new act of discrimination. Pay discrimination need not be intentional to be unlawful. Pay practices resulting in disparate impact are also actionable. Steps to reduce liability include conducting a periodic disparate impact analysis of compensation plans, properly documenting all compensation decisions, retaining complete pay records for an appropriate duration, and limiting discretion in pay decisions to higher levels in the organization.[43]

11-2c Independent Contractor Regulations

The growing use of contingent workers by many organizations raises questions about how to properly classify workers. For an employer, classifying someone as an independent contractor offers some significant advantages. The employer does not have to pay Social Security, unemployment, or workers' compensation costs. These additional payroll levies may add 10% or more to the costs of hiring the individual as an employee. However, these decisions can results in lawsuits. The Kansas Supreme Court decided that many of the FedEx drivers in the state were employees rather than independent contractors, which could result in the company paying payroll taxes and overtime expenses.[44]

Most federal and state entities rely on the criteria for independent contractor status established by the Internal Revenue Service (IRS). Figure 11-4 lists the factors the IRS uses to determine whether an individual can be classified as an independent contractor. A worker does not have to meet all 20 criteria, and no single factor is decisive in establishing the worker's status. Each case is analyzed, and the weight of evidence is used to make the final determination.[45] Key differences between an employee and an independent contractor are evaluated by reviewing behavioral control, financial control, and relationship-type factors.

FIGURE 11-4 IRS Guidelines for Independent Contractor Status

Behavioral Control/Instructions/Training That the Business Gives to the Worker

- When and where to do the work
- What tools and equipment to use
- What workers to hire or to assist with the work
- Where to purchase supplies and services
- What work must be performed by a specified individual
- What order or sequence to follow
- How work results are achieved

Financial Control

- Extent of the worker's investment
- Extent to which worker makes services available to a relevant market
- How the business pays the worker
- Whether or not the business reimburses travel expenses
- The extent to which the workers can realize a profit or loss

Type of Relationship

- Written contracts
- Whether the business provides employee-type benefits to the worker
- Permanency of the relationship
- Extent to which services provided by the worker are a key aspect of the regular business of the company

Source: IRS, Publication 15A, 2012.

Prevailing wage
An hourly wage determined by a formula that considers the rate paid for a job by a majority of the employers in the appropriate geographic area

Garnishment
A court order that directs an employer to set aside a portion of an employee's wages to pay a debt owed to a creditor

11-2d Additional Laws Affecting Compensation

Several compensation-related laws apply to firms that have contracts with the U.S. government. These laws require that federal contractors pay a prevailing wage, which is determined by a formula that considers the rate paid for a job by a majority of the employers in the appropriate geographic area. The Davis-Bacon Act of 1931, the Walsh-Healy Public Contracts Act, and the McNamara-O'Hara Service Contract Act include prevailing wage clauses that apply to firms engaged in federal construction projects or that work directly on federal government contracts.

Garnishment occurs when a creditor obtains a court order that directs an employer to set aside a portion of an employee's wages to pay a debt owed to the creditor. Regulations passed as a part of the Consumer Credit Protection Act limit the amount of wages that can be garnished. The act also restricts the right of employers to terminate employees whose pay is subject to a single garnishment order. All 50 states have laws applying to wage garnishments.

LO3 Outline strategic compensation decisions.

11-3 Strategic Compensation Decisions

When developing total rewards programs, managers should consider organizational climate and compensation philosophies, communication approaches, and the administrative responsibilities of a company's compensation approach. These decisions are related to how total reward programs are designed and managed. In addition, they affect how compensation information is shared with employees.

11-3a Organizational Climate and Compensation Philosophies

One important strategic objective of pay administration involves enhancing employees' satisfaction with the company's total rewards system, which can improve their overall work attitudes. This requires managers and HR professionals to consider a variety of organizational climate characteristics, some of which may seem unrelated to pay decisions. The goal is to create an organizational climate that reduces employee dissatisfaction with the current compensation. A recent study determined that a climate in which employees helped make decisions could be developed to reduce the negative effect of low pay satisfaction on employees' job satisfaction, commitment, and turnover intention. The results also showed that a climate in which information was shared directly improved employees' work attitudes.[46]

To motivate employees and direct their efforts toward organizational objectives, managers must also establish a guiding philosophy regarding total rewards and communicate this approach. Ideally, there is a good fit between the compensation philosophy implemented and the preferences of employees, which should increase their satisfaction with the pay they receive. Companies also need to properly manage the compensation philosophy to ensure that employees believe they are being treated fairly. For example, whatever approach is used should guide decisions about whether to give employees raises when they ask for them. Pay raise determinations need to be congruent with a firm's compensation philosophy.[47]

There are two basic compensation philosophies that are situated at opposite ends of a continuum, as shown in Figure 11-5. At one end of the continuum is the *entitlement* philosophy, and at the other end is the *performance* philosophy. Most compensation systems fall somewhere in between these two extremes.

Entitlement philosophy Assumes that individuals who have worked another year with the company are entitled to pay increases with little regard for performance differences

Entitlement Philosophy The entitlement philosophy assumes that individuals who have worked another year with the company are entitled to pay increases with little regard for performance differences. When organizations give automatic increases to their employees every year, they are using the entitlement philosophy. Most employees receive the same or nearly the same percentage increase. These automatic increases are often referred to as *cost-of-living raises*, even if they are not tied specifically to economic indicators.

FIGURE 11-5 Continuum of Compensation Philosophies

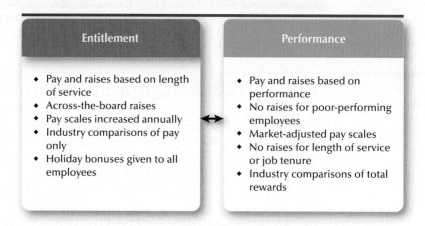

Entitlement	Performance
• Pay and raises based on length of service • Across-the-board raises • Pay scales increased annually • Industry comparisons of pay only • Holiday bonuses given to all employees	• Pay and raises based on performance • No raises for poor-performing employees • Market-adjusted pay scales • No raises for length of service or job tenure • Industry comparisons of total rewards

Pay-for-performance philosophy
Assumes that compensation decisions reflect performance differences

Performance Philosophy A pay-for-performance philosophy assumes that compensation decisions reflect performance differences. Organizations using this philosophy do not guarantee additional compensation for simply completing another year of service with the company. Instead, pay and incentives are structured to reward performance differences (quantity, quality, speed of work, customer satisfaction, and so forth) among employees. Outstanding performers are compensated with substantially greater pay increases and higher variable rewards than employees who perform at only a satisfactory level. Employees who perform below standards are denied pay increases and are often placed on performance-improvement plans that specify what they need to do to improve their contributions at work.

Few organizations follow an exclusively performance-oriented compensation philosophy, but the overall trend is toward greater use of pay-for-performance systems. For instance, the "say-on-pay" guidelines initiated by the Dodd-Frank Wall Street Reform and Consumer Protection Act require public companies to provide shareholders an opportunity to review (and participate in a nonbinding vote to approve) top management pay at least once over a three-year period, and these rules have encouraged companies to use more performance-based practices to compensate executives.[48] Given the increased focus on pay-for-performance philosophies, performance measures should reflect important outcomes to shareholders, customers, and employees.

11-3b Communicating Pay Philosophy

Sharing the organization's pay philosophy with employees helps them understand the total rewards package provided by the employer. In particular, such communication shows them how factors such as job tenure, raises, cost-of-living adjustments, and work performance can affect their compensation levels. Regularly communicating the details of compensation can improve employees' work attitudes because they understand more clearly how compensation is managed in the organization, thus enabling them to perform in ways that enhance their own pay. Compensation can be discussed during orientation, training sessions, and performance appraisal meetings. This information can also be included in company literature and on its website.

11-3c Compensation Responsibilities

HR specialists and line managers work together to administer compensation programs. HR specialists develop and administer the organizational compensation system and ensure that pay practices comply with all legal requirements. Because of the complexity involved, HR specialists typically conduct job evaluations and wage surveys, and they develop base pay programs and salary structures and policies. Line managers evaluate employee performance and participate in pay decisions. They are often the first point of contact for employees with questions about pay fairness. It is advisable to train managers about how the organization develops and administers its compensation program.

Payroll Administration Companies manage payroll administration in different ways. HR professionals may or may not do the actual processing of payroll. If they do, payroll staff may report to the company's HR function or the accounting function. However, this labor-intensive responsibility is often one of the first to be outsourced, so in some companies HR staff is not directly involved in processing payroll.

Calculating pay and ensuring timely, accurate payroll processing is important for maintaining a positive workplace. Record keeping is particularly critical, which is why many organizations use payroll systems to manage the process. Companies can use a variety of approaches to ensure accurate record keeping such as time clocks, time sheets, and automated processes. Managers and employees can work together to record work hours, but managers are responsible for the accuracy of payroll. As highlighted in the chapter opening Headline, many organizations use automated timekeeping systems to ensure accurate payroll processing. Managers can change time records, such as when an employee forgets to clock in or clock out, but these changes should be made carefully and for good reason.[49]

Companies also need to be careful that their payroll processes comply with compensation laws and do not encourage lawsuits. For instance, the medical products manufacturer Medline Industries was rounding the start times of hourly paid employees by 29 minutes, which resulted in problems for the company based on California law.[50] PetSmart paid a $1 million settlement on a class action lawsuit involving the mandatory use of ATM cards to pay individuals final wages after they were fired. Fees were incurred when the cards were used, cards were not accepted at all banks, and cards did not provide payment of full wages, which violated California law.[51]

MEASURE

11-3d Human Resource Metrics and Compensation

Employers spend a substantial amount of money on employee compensation. Just like any other area of cost, compensation expenditures should be evaluated to determine their effectiveness. Metrics can be tracked to assess the compensation program's internal performance and its external competitiveness.[52] A number of widely used measures are shown in Figure 11-6.

The raw data needed to calculate various measures may be found in many organizational functions. Wage rates, total payroll costs, and overtime information can be obtained from the payroll staff or vendor. Productivity numbers may be logged by the Operations Department. Tenure and pay range information may be recorded in the HRIS. Compiling all the information necessary to make proper assessments is complex and may require HR professionals to coordinate with other organizational functions. Ideally, compensation metrics should be computed each year and compared with historic results to show how the rate of compensation change compares

FIGURE 11-6 HR Metrics for Compensation

Metric	Calculation
Average hourly rate	◆ Add the individual hourly rates of pay for all employees. ◆ Divide by the number of employees.
Number of Full Time Equivalents (FTEs)	◆ Add the annual hours paid for all employees. ◆ Divide by the number of hours a full-time employee is scheduled to work. (This is frequently 2,080 hours.)
Average tenure	◆ Add the total years of service for all employees. ◆ Divide by the number of FTEs.
Average compa-ratio (comparative ratio)	◆ Calculate the compa-ratio for each employee. ◆ Add the compa-ratios. ◆ Divide by the number of employees.
Productivity	◆ Divide total revenue by the number of FTEs.
Average annual salary increase	◆ Calculate the salary increase for each employee. ◆ Add the increases. ◆ Divide by the number of FTEs.

with the rate of other financial change in the organization. The following "HR Perspectives: Using Predictive Analytics to Determine Pay" feature shows how progressive companies use metrics and analytics to improve their pay effectiveness.

11-4 Compensation System Design Issues

Depending on the compensation philosophies, strategies, and approaches used by an organization, many decisions are made that affect the design of the compensation system. Employee satisfaction with the compensation system can be influenced by how the organization manages these issues.

11-4a Motivation Theories and Compensation Philosophies

Research in the field of worker motivation was especially active during the 1960s, and many well-known theories emerged. Two theories of motivation in particular influence the design of compensation systems. Expectancy theory and equity theory are particularly relevant to the perceptions employees have of the total rewards provided by the organization.[53] The ideas behind these two theories were introduced in Chapter 5.

Expectancy theory
States that an employee's motivation is based on the probability that his or her efforts will lead to an expected level of performance that is linked to a valued reward

Expectancy Theory The expectancy theory of motivation was first introduced by Victor Vroom at Yale in 1964 and was later expanded by Porter and Lawler. Expectancy theory states that an employee's motivation is based on the probability

PERSPECTIVE

Using Predictive Analytics to Determine Pay

For many years, companies have collected information about compensation practices within their industry and geographic locations. This information helps ensure that the firm is paying competitively to attract and retain talented workers. In recent years, companies have started to use more sophisticated analytics to study employee turnover trends and determine how compensation might affect retention.

A large regional bank was experiencing high turnover among staff in front-facing positions. Before the use of predictive analytics, the bank might have simply raised the pay for these workers to reduce turnover. However, statistical modeling using a variety of metrics showed that workers were dissatisfied with career progress. Therefore, offering job changes and career development opportunities, even without additional pay, reduced employees' intentions to quit. The bank was able to use internal employee data to better direct investments in human resources. Using data more effectively led to better employee retention without increasing pay rates.

The Las Vegas casino chain Caesars Entertainment also discovered the power of analytics by carefully studying patterns in employee turnover. The company found that employees earning less than the midpoint of their salary range were 16% more likely to quit than those earning above the midpoint. Focusing on bringing employees' pay to the midpoint but not going beyond that amount had the greatest effect on reducing turnover. Zeroing in on compensation data along with other employment measures allows companies to more precisely determine how to best use total rewards to motivate and retain employees.[54]

Using analytics to manage compensation in organizations can be very useful and effective. Given this reality, consider the following questions:

1. In addition to providing more developmental opportunities, do you think the bank should have increased individuals' pay? Do you think Caesars should have increased employees' pay beyond the midpoint?

2. If you were an HR professional or general manager in charge of overseeing compensation in a company, what kinds of metrics and data would you use to determine how pay could better enhance retention?

that his or her efforts will lead to an expected level of performance that is linked to a valued reward. Figure 11-7 shows the important relationships in expectancy theory within the context of pay. In particular, this theory emphasizes the importance of finding valued rewards for the employee. Rewards that are not appreciated by the employee have little power to motivate performance. Additionally, a break between the promise and delivery of the reward will decrease motivation. For example, an employee who is promised a bonus to increase sales and achieves the desired result but who is then told that budget cuts prevent the company from giving the bonus will be much less likely to put extra effort into future performance. Managers who understand the key linkages in these expectations can better monitor employee motivation and adjust reward systems accordingly.[55]

Equity theory
States that individuals judge fairness (equity) in compensation by comparing their inputs and outcomes against the inputs and outcomes of referent others

Equity Theory The equity theory of motivation was first introduced by John Stacey Adams in 1963. This theory states that individuals judge fairness (equity) in

FIGURE 11-7   Expectancy Theory (example related to compensation)

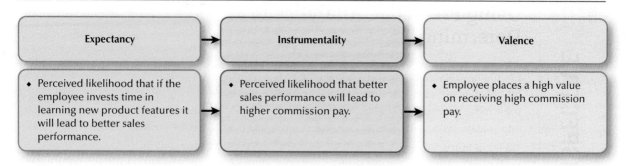

Source: Adapted from Victor Vroom, *Work and Motivation* (New York: McGraw Hill, 1964).

compensation by comparing their inputs and outcomes against the inputs and outcomes of referent others. These *referent others* are workers that the individual uses as a reference point to make these comparisons. Inputs include time, effort, loyalty, commitment, skill, knowledge, and enthusiasm. Outcomes include pay, job security, benefits, praise, recognition, and thanks. Figure 11-8 shows the important ratios in equity theory.

FIGURE 11-8   Equity Theory

Employee's Inputs / Employee's Outcomes		vs.	Referent Other's Inputs / Referent Other's Outcomes	

Inputs

Skills	Abilities	Knowledge	Effort
Loyalty	Commitment	Adaptability	Tolerance
Determination	Enthusiasm	Support of colleagues	Personal sacrifice

Outcomes

Wages	Salary	Benefits	Bonus
Recognition	Reputation	Praise	Thanks
Responsibility	Training	Sense of achievement	Advancement opportunities

Source: Adapted from John Stacey Adams, "Inequity in Social Exchange," *Advances in Experimental Social Psychology* 62 (1965), 335–343.

The comparisons are personal and are based on individual perceptions, not necessarily facts. Individuals who believe that they are not being rewarded fairly (such as getting lower outcomes than peers for the same inputs) can restore equity in two ways. They can reduce inputs or seek greater outcomes. Reducing inputs is a simple matter of investing less effort in work, refusing to work extra hours, or decreasing loyalty and commitment to the organization. For example, if Miranda feels that her pay is lower than that of her coworker Allan, she may refuse to work overtime or stop offering ideas and suggestions to improve company operations. Seeking additional outcomes is more difficult. The individual must request a pay increase or praise and recognition from a supervisor, who may or may not cooperate. Monitoring changes in employee behavior may help uncover perceptions of inequity. Managers should continually monitor equity relationships to identify areas that may harm employee motivation and retention.

11-4b Compensation Fairness and Equity

Most people work for monetary rewards. Whether they receive base pay or variable pay, the extent to which employees perceive their compensation to be fair often affects their performance and how they view their jobs and their employers. These perceptions can in turn affect other important work outcomes such as job satisfaction, organizational commitment, absenteeism, turnover, and retention. This is why HR professionals and other business leaders need to be particularly aware of both external and internal equity concerns if they want to effectively manage these outcomes.

External Equity If an employer's rewards are not viewed as equitable compared to other organizations, the employer is likely to experience higher turnover. This also creates greater difficulty in recruiting qualified and high-demand individuals. Depending on external labor markets, a lack of pay competitiveness from an external perspective can result in the employment of individuals who lack some of the knowledge, skills, and abilities (KSAs) necessary for them to do work effectively. It can also result in the employment of individuals who are less motivated to make valuable contributions to the organization, which can hurt firm performance. Organizations can track external equity by using pay surveys and looking at the compensation policies of competing employers.

Internal Equity Internal equity means that employees are compensated fairly within the organization with regard to the KSAs they use in their jobs, as well as their responsibilities, accomplishments, and job performance. Given how fairness is emphasized, employees evaluate their ratio of effort to reward in comparison to coworkers on an ongoing basis. These evaluations often affect how willing employees are to make valuable contributions to the organization. This is why the different pay levels of employees should be compared internally to make sure that compensation is fair, particularly when individuals ask for pay increases.[56] Internal equity can also relate to differences between the pay levels of managers and employees. The Securities and Exchange Commission has proposed a rule that would require public firms to indicate how their CEOs' compensation compares to the median levels received by workers.[57]

Perceptions of justice are also important managerial considerations because they indicate whether employees believe that workplace fairness is valued in a company. Two cocktail waitresses employed at Casino Queen pursued a racial discrimination and retaliation lawsuit because they believed that the way they were unfairly

FIGURE 11-9   Procedural Justice and Distributive Justice

Procedural Justice

Fair Processes

Fair Procedures

Distributive Justice

Fair Outcome
Distribution

assigned shifts and treated at work hurt their income levels and employment experiences.[58] Procedural justice and distributive justice are particularly important issues that are related to internal equity. Figure 11-9 illustrates these two types of justice.

Procedural justice
Perceived fairness of the process and procedures used to make decisions about employees, including their pay

Distributive justice
Perceived fairness of how rewards and other outcomes are distributed

Procedural justice is the perceived fairness of the processes and procedures used to make decisions about employees, including their pay. As it applies to compensation, the entire process of determining base pay for jobs, measuring performance, allocating pay increases, and determining incentives must be perceived as fair. If the processes used to allocate pay are considered to be fair, then employees should be more satisfied with the compensation that they receive.

A related issue is distributive justice, which is the perceived fairness of how rewards and other outcomes are distributed. For example, if a hard-working employee whose performance is outstanding receives the same across-the-board raise as an employee with attendance problems and mediocre performance, an inequity may be perceived. Likewise, if two employees have similar performance records but one receives a significantly greater pay raise, the other may perceive an inequity because of supervisory favoritism or other factors not related to the job.

To address concerns about both types of justice, some organizations establish compensation appeals procedures. Typically, employees are encouraged to contact the HR department after discussing their concerns with their immediate supervisors and managers.

Pay Secrecy   Another equity issue concerns the degree of secrecy organizations have regarding their pay systems. Pay information that may be kept secret in "closed" systems relates to information about individual pay amounts, pay raises, and incentive payouts. Some firms have policies that prohibit employees from discussing their pay with other employees, and violations of these policies can lead to disciplinary action. However, such policies may violate the National Labor Relations Act.

ETHICS

Beyond the legal issues, however, companies should examine the ethics of severely restricting employee discussion of pay. If an organization has implemented competitive pay practices and has a fair and reasonable pay structure, employee concerns about inequity can be reduced by sharing this information. Explaining pay grades and pay decision rules can enhance employee perceptions of fair and ethical treatment, as well as help them understand why different jobs are paid at different

ETHICS

High-Tech Firms Collude to Limit Employee Pay

Many Americans voluntarily place their names on a "do not call" list to prevent unsolicited telemarketing calls. But a conspiracy among high-tech employers in Silicon Valley led to software engineers being placed on a "do not cold call" list without their knowledge, a situation that potentially held down their compensation. In reality, the list didn't prevent telemarketers from calling—it actually prevented recruiters from calling to offer them potentially better jobs in the industry. It seems that to stabilize compensation and limit turnover of high-skilled employees, many prominent high-tech companies such as Apple, Google, Pixar, and Intel agreed to restrict poaching from each other. The companies shared the names of their employees with each other and placed them on the restricted list. Some agreements went so far as to ban hiring employees who had, on their own, applied for work at a rival firm.

These secret agreements were widely instituted to eliminate salary "bidding wars" among the companies. Employees receiving job offers from a rival tech firm could use that as leverage to request a pay increase with the current employer. And rivals might be able to learn about another company's pay practices by interviewing employees from the firm.

The courts view this employer practice as a violation of antitrust legislation and a restraint of trade. Top-level managers have been implicated in the agreements. The companies involved were connected with each other because many executives had overlapping board seats on other defendants' boards and worked closely with each other. While antitrust lawsuits usually involve the pricing and sale of products or services, it is important to remember that the labor market and compensation are also governed by these regulations. Companies are therefore forewarned that limiting employees' pay and opportunities to freely move in the job market can be a dangerous and costly way to retain talented workers.[59] Working together with competitors and other firms to limit free market adjustments to compensation is inappropriate. Based on these issues, consider the following questions:

1. How should companies address the possibility of bidding wars when trying to retain top talent? How should HR professionals or general managers help address this issue?

2. What compensation strategies would enable companies to attract and retain good employees without having to worry about bidding wars? How should the needs of employees be addressed in these strategies?

rates. Maintaining a cloak of secrecy invites curiosity and suspicion from employees, which may result in less trust about how they are being paid.

11-4c Market Competitive Compensation

Whether an organization's total reward practices are competitive has a significant impact on employees' views of compensation fairness. Consequently, providing competitive compensation to employees is a concern for all employers. Organizations face the challenge of whether to adopt practices common in an industry or to differentiate the firm by using novel or distinct compensation practices. They also

FIGURE 11-10 Compensation Quartile Strategies

Organization's Position in the Labor Marketplace	Quartile Position
Lead-the-Market Strategy (Company targets pay ranges so that 25% of other firms pay above and 75% pay below.)	Third Quartile
Match-the-Market Strategy (Company targets pay ranges so that 50% of other firms pay above and 50% pay below.)	Second Quartile
Lag-the-Market Strategy (Company targets pay ranges so that 75% of other firms pay above and 25% pay below.)	First Quartile

face the challenge of keeping their compensation levels competitive given what other firms are paying their employees, an issue that comes to the forefront when companies try to hire workers away from their current employers. The preceding "HR Ethics: High-Tech Firms Collude to Limit Employee Pay" feature discusses some of the ethical issues related to pay fairness and competitiveness.

Larger organizations may have higher compensation levels than smaller organizations because of higher productivity levels and economies of scale. The compensation mix is also affected by firm size, with larger organizations spending more on indirect compensation than small firms do.[60] Managers consider compensation mix and competitive position when developing their reward strategies. Many organizations use a *quartile strategy* to establish policies about where they wish to be positioned in the labor market, as illustrated in Figure 11-10. The quartile strategy reflects the overall market position where the organization sets its compensation levels.

Lag-the-Market Strategy An employer using a *first-quartile* strategy chooses to "lag the market" by paying below market levels for several reasons. If the employer is experiencing financial difficulties, it may be unable to pay more. Also, when an abundance of workers are available, particularly those with lower-level skills, a below-market approach can be used to attract sufficient workers at a lower cost. The downside of this strategy is that it increases the likelihood of higher worker turnover and lower employee morale. If the labor market supply tightens, then attracting and retaining workers becomes more difficult. Companies may adopt this strategy during recessionary times only to discover that when the economy gets better, turnover increases.

Lead-the-Market Strategy A *third-quartile* strategy uses an aggressive approach to "lead the market." This strategy generally enables a company to attract and retain sufficient workers with the required capabilities and be more selective when hiring. Since it is a higher-cost approach, organizations often look for ways to increase the productivity of employees who are receiving above-market wages.

Match-the-Market Strategy Most employers position themselves in the *second quartile* (median), the middle of the market, as determined by pay data from surveys of other employers' compensation plans. Choosing this level is an attempt to balance employer cost pressures and the need to attract and retain employees by providing compensation levels that "meet the market" for the company's jobs.

Selecting a Quartile Pay structures and levels can affect organizational performance and staffing quality. Deciding which quartile position to target is a function of many considerations—financial resources available, competitiveness pressures, and the market availability of employees with different capabilities. For instance, some employers with extensive benefits programs or broad-based incentive programs may choose a first-quartile strategy so that their overall compensation costs and levels are not excessive. The decisions about compensation mix and competitive position are related and should be addressed as part of a comprehensive total rewards strategy.

11-4d Competency-Based Pay

Most compensation programs are designed to reward employees for carrying out their tasks, duties, and responsibilities. The job requirements determine which employees have higher base rates. Employees receive more for doing jobs that require a greater variety of tasks, more knowledge and skills, greater physical effort, or more demanding working conditions. However, the design of some compensation programs emphasizes competencies rather than the tasks performed.

Competency-based pay
Rewards individuals for the capabilities they demonstrate and acquire

Competency-based pay rewards individuals for the capabilities they demonstrate and acquire. In knowledge-based pay (KBP) or skill-based pay (SBP) systems, employees start at a base level of pay and receive increases as they learn to do other jobs or gain additional skills and knowledge, and thus become more valuable to the employer. For example, a manufacturing firm operates plastic molding presses of various sizes. Operating larger presses requires more skills than smaller presses. Under a KBP or SBP system, press operators increase their pay as they learn how to operate the more complex presses, even though sometimes they may operate only smaller machines. Given the inherent advantages, these plans can lead to greater workforce flexibility and productivity.[61] Research also suggests that beneficial and fair competency approaches lead to increased work effort and organizational citizenship.[62]

11-4e Individual versus Team Rewards

As some organizations have shifted to using work teams, the concern is how to develop compensation programs that support the team concept. Determining how to compensate individuals whose performance may be a result of team efforts and achievements is complicated. For base pay, employers may compensate individuals on the basis of competencies, experience, and other job factors. Then they use team incentive rewards on top of base pay. Equity concerns are particularly challenging, and designing team rewards requires careful thought and planning.[63] Team-based incentives are discussed in Chapter 12.

GLOBAL

11-5 Global Compensation Issues

All of the issues discussed here can become confusing when dealing with global compensation. The growing world economy has led to an increase in the number of employees working internationally. Therefore, organizations with employees working throughout the world face some special compensation issues.

Variations in laws, living costs, tax policies, and other factors must be considered when designing the compensation for local employees and managers, as well as managers and professionals on international assignment. Fluctuations in the values of various currencies must be tracked and adjustments made as exchange rates rise or fall. With these and numerous other concerns, developing and managing a global compensation system becomes extremely complex.

One significant global issue in compensation design is how to compensate employees from different countries. Local wage scales vary significantly among countries, and there are differences between developed nations where employees earn a high level of pay and developing nations where compensation rates are a fraction of those in developed nations. Costs of living standards vary a great deal between nations and compensation differences may reflect differences in purchasing power among nations. These variations in compensation levels have led to significant offshoring, which involves moving jobs to lower-wage countries. The movement of call center and information technology (IT) jobs to India and manufacturing jobs to China, the Philippines, and Mexico are examples.[64] However, U.S. manufacturers have begun to *reshore* (return operations to the United States) production as wages in China and Mexico have risen.[65] This shows that compensation levels certainly play a role in helping companies decide where to locate their operations.

Offshoring
Moving jobs to lower-wage countries

Many organizations have started to globalize their pay policies to attract and retain employees from an international talent pool. This requires management to balance the desire for consistent practices throughout the company with the need for differentiating practices based on local input and customs. This also requires companies to monitor the pay level and policy trends in other countries. For instance, evidence suggests that the differences in top manager pay that have allegedly existed between the United States and many European countries are not as large as once thought.[66] Union-led agreements and political support in Germany have also encouraged wages in that country to steadily increase, while wages is Spain have decreased.[67] Finally, employees in Venezuela and Argentina are predicted to receive the highest pay hikes in the world, but inflationary pressures will eat away most or all of these gains. The most significant pay raises are expected to be experienced in Asian and Latin American countries, while some European countries such as Greece and Switzerland may experience the lowest increases in wages.[68]

GLOBAL

11-5a International Assignees

Multinational companies may staff their operations with a mixture of employees from around the world, and expatriates are often used to fill foreign positions. Regardless of how staffing is determined, compensation practices should be designed to maximize employee commitment and productivity. It has been estimated that the total employer costs for an expatriate, including all allowances, is three to four times the expatriate's salary, with the duration of a typical expatriate assignment at two or three years. The expense of sending expatriates abroad clearly warrants special attention in the global compensation approach.

Expatriate employees may have unique needs and preferences in terms of how the compensation package is structured. A married employee with children might have drastically different requirements than an unmarried employee. Because of the intricacies of devising an effective compensation plan for international assignees, companies often use consultants knowledgeable in this field.

A wide range of allowances and perquisites may be considered for inclusion in expatriate compensation. Hardship or hazard pay may be provided for expatriates assigned to dangerous or undesirable locations. Education assistance may be provided for the expatriate's dependents to make up for quality of education differences between the home and host country. Housing assistance in the form of free company-owned housing to make up for the difference in housing costs between locations may be granted. Multinational enterprises seek to find creative solutions that improve expatriate success while keeping costs under control.[69]

The two primary approaches to international compensation for expatriates are the home country–based approach and the host country–based approach.[70] The home country–based approach is the most commonly used method. The overall objective is to maintain the standard of living the expatriate had in the home country. Housing, taxes, and discretionary spending expenses are calculated based on those items in the home country. The company then pays the expatriate the difference so that he or she "remains whole." The home country approach can result in higher employer costs and more administrative complexity than other plans.

The host country–based approach compensates the expatriate at the same level as workers from the host country. The company might continue to cover the employee in its retirement plan and also provide a housing allowance. If the cost of living is substantially lower in the host country than in the home country, this approach might make sense because the expatriate can live comfortably while on assignment and can more effectively acclimate to the culture of the host country.

Home country–based approach
Maintains the standard of living the expatriate had in the home country

Host country–based approach
Compensates the expatriate at the same level as workers from the host country

LO5 Illustrate the steps in developing a base pay system.

11-6 Developing a Base Pay System

Figure 11-11 shows how a base compensation system is developed using the compensation philosophy and job analysis. The process incorporates information gathered while valuing jobs and analyzing pay surveys—activities designed to ensure that the pay system is both internally and externally equitable and in line with the organizational philosophy. The data compiled in these two activities are used to design pay structures, including pay grades and pay ranges. After pay structures are established, individual jobs are placed in the appropriate pay grades, and individual employee pay is determined. Finally, the pay system is monitored and updated.

Companies want their employees to perceive that they are being paid fairly in relation to pay for jobs performed by others within the organization, as well as individuals performing similar jobs in other companies. The two general approaches for valuing jobs are *job evaluation* and *market pricing*. Job evaluation looks at pay levels within the company, and market pricing looks outside the company. Both methods use relative comparisons to determine the worth of jobs in an organization. To comply with equal pay and nondiscrimination laws, companies should review the relative standing of each job to ensure that jobs held by women and minorities are not consistently ranked the lowest in the organization. Using valid methods and maintaining records regarding how ranking decisions are made can help a company defend its practices.[71]

FIGURE 11-11   Compensation Administration Process

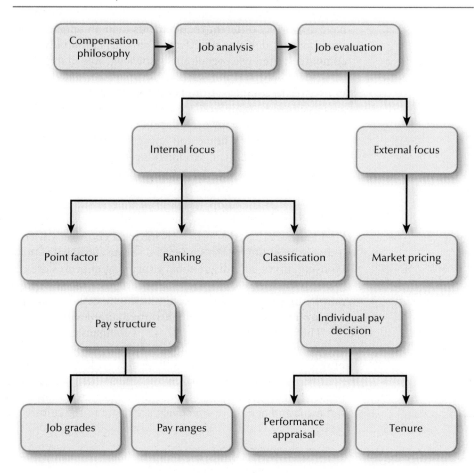

11-6a Job Evaluation Methods

Job evaluation
Formal, systematic
means to determine the
relative worth of jobs
within an organization

Job evaluation is a formal, systematic process to determine the relative worth of jobs within an organization. Employers can adopt one of several alternate methods.

The *ranking method* is a simple system that places jobs in order, from highest to lowest, by their value to the organization. This is a qualitative method in which the entire job is considered rather than individual components. The ranking method generally is more appropriate in a small organization that has relatively few jobs. For example, the ranking method might be used at a small family-owned dry cleaning shop with only two or three distinct job titles.

The *classification method* is often used in public-sector organizations. Descriptions of job classes are written, and then each job is put into a grade according to the class it best matches. A major difficulty with this method is that subjective judgments are used to develop the class descriptions and to place jobs accurately in them.

The *factor-comparison method* is a complex quantitative method that combines the ranking and point factor methods (explained below). Organizations that use this method must develop their own key jobs and factors. The factor-comparison method is time consuming and difficult to use, which accounts for its limited popularity in organizations.

Point Factor Method The most widely used job evaluation method, the point factor method, looks at compensable factors in a group of similar jobs and assigns weights, or *points*, to them. A compensable factor is a job dimension commonly present throughout a groups of jobs within an organization that can be rated for each job. For example, all jobs require some level of education and experience for successful performance.

The point factor method is the most popular job evaluation approach because it is relatively simple to use and considers the components of a job rather than the total

Compensable factor
Job dimension commonly present throughout a group of jobs within an organization that can be rated for each job

COMPETENCIES & APPLICATIONS

Point Factor Example

Job evaluation involves studying each position on a number of work dimensions and allows a job analyst to assess various aspects of each job to determine the job's relative value. Points are assigned to each compensable factor and then added to provide a total for each job. Jobs with similar point totals are considered to be relatively equal in importance.

A point factor system often uses compensable factors that reflect skill, responsibilities, social interaction, and working conditions. The skill dimension might be assessed on the basis of two compensable factors, the level of education and work experience needed for successful job performance, as illustrated in the following example. Each compensable factor is broken into degrees, and each factor may have a different number of degrees. In the example, there are five degrees for education but only four degrees for experience. Further, the point values are not universal for all compensable factors. The point values indicate the weight of each factor in the evaluation of each job.

The job analyst selects the appropriate levels of education and experience for each job and assigns the point value as the example shows. A similar chart is developed for each compensable

Degree	Level of Education	Point Value
1	High school diploma	20
2	Associate degree	25
3	Bachelor's degree	30
4	Master's degree	35
5	Doctoral degree	40

Degree	Years of Experience	Point Value
1	0–1	10
2	2–5	20
3	6–10	30
4	Over 10	40

factor such as responsibilities, social interaction, and working conditions. The job analyst rates each job on each compensable factor and calculates the total points. This process then leads to the placing of jobs in grades.

Consider the following questions:

1. How would you identify a job's compensable factors?

2. How would you determine what are appropriate levels for a job's compensable factors?

KEY COMPETENCIES: Critical Evaluation (Behavioral Competency) and Organization (Technical Competency) job. However, point factor systems have been criticized for reinforcing traditional organizational structures and job rigidity. Although not perfect, the point factor method is generally better than the ranking and classification methods because it quantifies job elements. Compensable factors are derived from job analysis and reflect the nature of different types of work performed in the organization, as explained in the preceding "HR Competencies & Applications: Point Factor Example" feature.

11-6b Market Pricing

While the point factor method has served employers well for many years, the trend is moving to a more externally focused approach. More companies are moving to market pricing, which uses market pay data to identify the relative value of jobs based on what other employers pay for similar jobs. A recent survey showed that 85% of companies use market pricing to figure out how to value different jobs, and 78% focused specifically on the market median values associated with total cash, which is calculated by adding together base pay and short-term variable compensation.[72]

Key to market pricing is identifying relevant market pay data for jobs that are good matches with the employer's jobs, geographic considerations, and company strategies and philosophies about desired market competitiveness levels. The switch to market pricing as part of strategic compensation decisions can ensure market competitiveness of compensation levels and practices. However, there will not always be a perfect match for each job in the external market. For example, compensation specialists at Crosstex Energy Services, a natural gas company with 500 employees, are able to match about 85% of the company's jobs. The remaining 15% can be quite challenging because these jobs are unique to Crosstex. Judgment and interpretation are needed to determine the appropriate pay levels for these jobs.[73]

Advantages of Market Pricing The primary advantage cited for the use of market pricing is that it closely ties organizational pay levels to what is actually occurring in the market, without distortion from "internal" job evaluation. An additional advantage of market pricing is that it allows an employer to communicate to employees that the compensation system is truly "market linked." Employees often see a compensation system that was developed using market pricing as having "face validity" and as being more objective than a compensation system that was developed using traditional job evaluation methods.

Disadvantages of Market Pricing The biggest disadvantage of market pricing is that pay survey data may be limited or may not be gathered in methodologically sound ways. It is also critical to understand the compensation mix that is common in the market. For example, one organization might allocate a much higher percentage of its compensation to variable pay than its competitors do. If so, then a comparison on base pay would result in the organization being out of step with the market when in fact, its employees might be more richly rewarded if they perform well.

Finally, tying pay levels to market data can lead to wide fluctuations on the basis of market conditions. Skills that are in great demand today can quickly become obsolete. Consider the IT job market during the past decade, when pay levels varied significantly. The "hot skills" of mobile app developers are likely to be replaced as technology evolves to its next version and mobile technology falls by the wayside. This is why it might be more effective to value jobs based on how well people employed in those jobs make valuable contributions to the organization, rather than providing rewards based on what employees earn in other companies.[74] The debate over the use of job evaluation versus market pricing is likely to continue because there are advantages and disadvantages to both approaches.

11-6c Pay Surveys

Pay survey
Collection of data on compensation rates for workers performing similar jobs in other organizations

Benchmark jobs
Jobs that are found in many other organizations that can be used for the purposes of comparison

A **pay survey** is a collection of data on compensation rates for workers performing similar jobs in other organizations. Pay surveys are an important element for establishing external pay equity. Both job evaluation and market pricing are tied to surveys of the pay that other organizations provide for similar jobs.

It is particularly important to identify common **benchmark jobs**—jobs that are found in many other organizations that can be used for the purposes of comparison. Often these jobs have stable content, are common across different employers, and are performed by a large number of employees. For example, benchmark jobs commonly used in the hospitality industry are housekeeper, front-desk clerk, concierge, and restaurant manager. Benchmark jobs are used because they provide "anchors" against which other jobs can be compared.

An employer may obtain surveys conducted by other organizations, access Internet data, or conduct its own survey. The make-or-buy decision regarding pay surveys is based on several factors such as the number of relevant competitors, the comparability of jobs, and time and budget issues. There are many vendors that provide general as well as custom surveys. National surveys on many jobs and industries are provided by the DOL's Bureau of Labor Statistics, professional and national trade associations, and various management consulting companies. Another common source of pay data is compensation surveys conducted by third parties that obtain data from employers.

Internet-Based Pay Information HR professionals can access a wide range of pay data online. Employment-related websites such as Salary.com and GlassDoor.com provide data gathered from companies and employees. Use of these sources requires caution because their accuracy and completeness may not be verifiable or may not be applicable to individual firms and employees.

Employees have also discovered online salary information and may bring Internet data to HR professionals or their managers after they determine their current pay is different from the pay reported on these websites. Responding to employee questions requires addressing many areas. Salary.com includes sample explanations on its website, including the following:

- *Job titles and responsibilities*: Compare the full job description, not just job titles and brief job summaries on the websites.
- *Experience, KSAs, and performance*: Most pay survey data on the Internet are averages of multiple companies and of multiple employees in those companies with varying experience, KSA levels, and performance.
- *Geographic differences*: Many pay survey sites on the Internet use geographic index numbers, not actual data from employers in a particular area.
- *Company size and industry*: Pay levels may vary significantly by company size, with smaller firms often offering lower pay. Also, pay levels may be lower in certain industries, such as retail and nonprofits.
- *Base pay versus total compensation*: Employers have different benefits and incentive compensation programs. However, Internet data usually reflect only base pay amounts.

Using Pay Surveys The proper use of pay surveys involves evaluating many factors to determine if the data are relevant and valid. The following questions should be answered for each survey:

- *Participants*: Does the survey cover a realistic sample of the employers with whom the organization competes for employees?
- *Broad based*: Does the survey include data from employers of different sizes, industries, and locales?
- *Timeliness*: How current are the data (when was the survey conducted)?
- *Methodology*: How established is the survey, and how qualified are those who conducted it?
- *Job matches*: Does the survey contain job summaries so that appropriate matches to job descriptions can be made?
- *Details provided*: Does the survey report on base pay, incentive pay, and other elements of compensation separately to allow comparison of the reward mix?

Pay Surveys and Legal Issues One reason employers use outside sources for pay surveys is to avoid charges that they are attempting to "price fix" wages. The concern is that employers might collude to set wages and restrict employees from earning a true market wage. One such case involved registered nurses in Detroit who claimed that local hospitals violated the Sherman Antitrust Act by sharing compensation data that artificially held wages down. Cases in other industries have alleged that by sharing wage data, the employers attempted to artificially hold wages down in violation of the law.[75]

Organizations participate in surveys if they meet the following conditions:

1. The survey must be administered by a third party such as a consultant or trade/professional association.
2. The data must be more than three months old.
3. A minimum of five employers must participate in the survey. No single employer's data may be worth more than 25% of the total.
4. All data must be aggregated and stripped of any identifying information.

In addition to antitrust considerations, companies participating in pay surveys must safeguard employee privacy and provide only de-identified data so that specific employee pay rates and names are not shared. Care must also be taken to avoid violating the National Labor Relations Act provisions that apply to disclosing wage and benefit information.

11-7 Pay Structures

After job evaluations and pay survey data are gathered, pay structures can be developed. Pay structures may be created for various types or categories of jobs such as hourly, salaried, technical, sales, and management. The nature, culture, and structure of the organization are considered when determining how many and which pay structures to have.

Developing sound pay structures also requires HR professionals to focus on several important considerations. Line managers should have some say in developing and revising pay/salary structures because they are familiar with employees' perceptions of pay, as well as their own staffing needs and challenges. Pay and salary structures also need to be linked to an organization's strategic initiatives and overall HR approach. Finally, they should be evaluated periodically using audits to determine whether adjustments are needed.[76]

11-7a Pay Grades

Pay grades
Groupings of individual jobs that have approximately the same value to the organization

When establishing a pay structure, organizations use pay grades, which are groupings of individual jobs that have approximately the same value to the organization. Although no set rules govern the establishment of pay grades, 11 to 17 grades are generally used in small and medium-sized companies. Two methods commonly used to establish pay grades are job evaluation data and job market banding.

Setting Pay Grades Using Job Evaluation Points One approach for determining pay grades uses job evaluation points or other data generated from the traditional job evaluation methods discussed earlier in the chapter. This process ties pay survey information to job evaluation data by plotting a market line, a graph line that shows the relationship between job value as determined by job evaluation points and job value as determined by pay survey rates. Market lines are developed by using statistical analysis techniques to calculate the regression equation. Figure 11-12 shows an example of a market line and regression equation used in setting a particular set of pay grades. A market line uses data to place jobs having similar point values into pay grades. Pay ranges can then be computed for each pay grade.

Market line
Graph line that shows the relationship between job value as determined by job evaluation points and job value as determined pay survey rates

Market banding
Grouping jobs into pay grades based on similar market survey amounts

Using Market Banding to Set Pay Grades Closely linked to the use of market pricing to value jobs, market banding groups jobs into pay grades based on

FIGURE 11-12   Market Pay Line and Job Evaluation Points

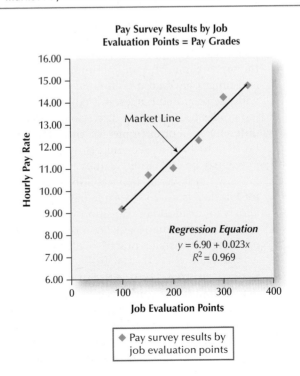

Pay Survey Results by Job Evaluation Points = Pay Grades

Regression Equation
$y = 6.90 + 0.023x$
$R^2 = 0.969$

◆ Pay survey results by job evaluation points

FIGURE 11-13 Market Bands for a Manufacturing Company

Grade	Job Title	Pay Survey Results	Minimum Pay	Midpoint Pay	Maximum Pay
1	Shipping Clerk	21,387	17,400	20,350	24,625
	Machine Operator	19,403			
	Utility Operator	20,723			
2	Quality Inspector	22,697	19,800	24,750	29,700
	Mechanic I	24,934			
	Scheduler	26,568			
3	Mechanic II	31,586	27,000	33,725	40,500
	Electrician I	35,914			
	Engineering Tech	33,685			

similar market survey amounts. Figure 11-13 shows three bands for jobs in a manufacturing company. The midpoint of the survey average is used to develop pay range minimums and maximums, the methods for which are discussed later in this chapter.

11-7b Pay Ranges

Once pay grades are determined, the pay range for each pay grade must be established. Using the market line as a starting point, the employer can determine minimum and maximum pay levels for each pay grade by making the market line the midpoint line of the new pay structure (see Figure 11-14). For example, in a particular pay grade, the maximum value may be 20% above the midpoint located on the market line, and the minimum value may be 20% below it. Once pay grades and ranges have been computed, then the current pay of employees is compared with the proposed ranges. It is common to have broader pay ranges for higher-level job grades because more discretion is needed to reflect capability and performance differences.[77] For example, for entry-level and production jobs, the pay range may be 10% to 15% above and below the midpoint. For executive-level positions, the range may be 40% to 60% above and below the midpoint.

Pay rates overlap between job grades. Notice in Figure 11-14 that the minimum for Grade 2 is not at the same pay rate as the maximum for Grade 1. This overlap allows for a smoother transition when an employee is promoted from one grade to the next. Some employers have reduced the number of pay grades and expanded pay ranges by using a practice called *broadbanding*.

Broadbanding
Practice of using fewer pay grades with much broader ranges than in traditional compensation systems

Broadbanding The practice of using fewer pay grades with much broader ranges than in traditional compensation systems is called broadbanding. Combining many grades into these broad bands is designed to encourage horizontal movement and therefore more skill acquisition. The main advantage of broadbanding is that it is more consistent with the flattening of organizational levels and the growing use of jobs that are multidimensional. A problem with broadbanding is that many

FIGURE 11-14 Example of Pay Grades and Pay Ranges

Grade	Point Range	Minimum Pay	Midpoint Pay	Maximum Pay
1	100–150	7.50	9.17	10.87
2	151–200	7.96	9.75	11.54
3	201–250	8.98	11.00	13.02
4	251–300	10.00	12.25	14.50
5	301–350	11.01	13.49	15.97
6	350–400	11.79	14.74	17.69

employees expect a promotion to be accompanied by a pay raise and movement to a new pay grade. By removing this grade progression, employees may feel that there are fewer promotional opportunities.

11-7c Individual Pay

Once pay grades and pay ranges have been established, pay can be set for each individual employee. Setting a range for each pay grade gives flexibility by allowing individuals to progress within a grade instead of having to move to a new grade each time they receive a raise. A pay range also allows managers to reward employees based on performance while maintaining the integrity of the pay system. Regardless of how well a pay structure is constructed, there can be occasions when an employee is paid outside of the range because of past pay practices, different levels of experience, or performance. There are risks in allowing these situations to persist, as they are evidence of poor pay administration and might lead to claims of pay inequities.

Red-circled employee
Incumbent who is paid above the range set for a job

Red-Circled Employees A red-circled employee is an incumbent who is paid above the range set for the job. For example, assume that an employee in Grade 3 has a current pay rate of $13.50 an hour, but the pay range for Grade 3 is $8.98 to $13.02 an hour. The person would be red-circled, and proper administration of the pay system would make the employee ineligible for a pay increase.

Several approaches can be used to bring a red-circled employee's pay into line. Although the fastest way would be to cut the employee's pay, that approach is not recommended and is seldom used. Instead, the employee's pay may be frozen until the pay range is adjusted upward. Another approach is to give the employee a small lump-sum payment but not adjust the pay rate when others are given raises. Of course, an employee being paid above the maximum range indicates that either the pay ranges are not keeping pace or the employee should be directed to development opportunities that will lead to a promotion to a job in a higher pay grade.

Green-circled employee
Incumbent who is paid below the range set for a job

Green-Circled Employees An incumbent who is paid below the range set for a job is considered to be a green-circled employee. Promotion is a major contributor to this situation. Green-circled problems might also result from opportunistic hiring when employees are earning below-market pay at their former employer. Generally, it is recommended that the satisfactory green-circled individual receive fairly rapid pay increases to reach the pay grade minimum. More frequent increases can be used if the minimum is a great deal above the incumbent's current pay.

Pay Compression and Salary Inversion One major problem many employers face is pay compression, which occurs when pay differences among individuals with different levels of experience and performance become small. Pay compression is frequently a result of labor market pay levels increasing faster than current employees' pay adjustments. Further contributing to the problem are pay freezes put in place during economic downturns. Salary inversion occurs when the pay given to new hires is higher than the compensation provided to more senior employees. When salary compression and inversion occur, they often negatively impact employee job satisfaction and morale. Companies can promote from within, hire people who are looking for promotions (rather than higher pay), and provide equity pay adjustments to address these issues.[78]

However, these strategies might not always work. In response to shortages of particular job skills in a highly competitive labor market, companies may have to pay higher amounts to hire people with those scarce skills. For instance, a shortage of skilled laborers and decreasing unemployment levels in states such as Texas have encouraged employers in the manufacturing sector to provide higher wages to hire and keep more employees.[79]

Pay compression
Occurs when the pay differences among individuals with different levels of experience and performance become small

Salary inversion
Occurs when the pay given to new hires is higher than the compensation provided to more senior employees

LO6 Describe how individual pay rates are set.

11-8 Determining Pay Increases

Decisions about pay increases are important in the relationships between employees, their managers, and the organization. Individuals express expectations about their pay and about how much of an increase is "fair," especially compared with increases other employees receive. Managers and HR professionals often work together to communicate pay increases and to help manage perceptions of any changes made to employee compensation.

Pay increases can be determined in several ways, including performance, seniority, cost-of-living adjustments, across-the-board increases, and lump-sum increases. These methods can be used separately or in combination.

11-8a Performance-Based Increases

As mentioned earlier, some employers have shifted to more pay-for-performance philosophies and strategies. Consequently, they have adopted the following means to provide employees with performance-based increases.

Targeting High Performers This approach focuses on providing the top-performing employees with significantly higher pay raises. One way to do this is to target the top employees for significantly greater increases, while providing standard increases to the remaining satisfactory performers. Recent reports indicate that raises given to top performers by their employers are higher than those provided to other employees.[80]

The primary reason for having such differentials is to reward and retain critical high-performing individuals. Key to rewarding exceptional performers is identifying how much their performance exceeds normal work expectations. Standard

ETHICS

High-Paid Employees Misbehave at Holiday Parties

You should probably exercise some caution when planning that next big holiday party at the office. A recent national survey conducted by the North Carolina–based organization Public Policy Polling highlighted some interesting findings. For instance, companies that employ many individuals who make greater than $100,000 a year are often more inclined to have holiday gatherings that have open bars and transportation for their employees who drink too much.

However, the study also determined that these companies were far less likely to establish rules about how employees should act at parties, as well as how to enforce these standards when individuals misbehave. Making matters even more challenging is the finding that high-paid employees are often the ones who behave in an unprofessional manner, with about 25% of them claiming that holiday parties serve to satisfy their romantic interests. Around 10% of employees who participated in the survey even claimed that they said or did things that they later regretted at these gatherings.

But why does this misbehavior occur? Some claim that the setting is to blame because people are in a social environment that encourages them to wear different clothing and to flirt with each other. The informal atmosphere and drinking also encourage them to drop their

guard and offer too many personal details to their colleagues.[81]

So what should organizations and their HR leaders do to prevent the misbehavior of their high-paid employees? Here are some key considerations:

- Develop basic codes of conduct for holiday parties so that some standards exist in the organization. Rules about consumption of alcohol, sexual harassment, and professional conduct can be outlined.
- Communicate the codes to employees before social gatherings. This can be done in meetings, through email messages, and in flyers posted on bulletin boards.
- Be sure to enforce standards when rules are broken. When employees misbehave, reasonable discipline should be applied to reinforce the importance of appropriate behavior at office functions.

These kinds of ethical issues are common in organizations, and HR professionals and managers need to think about these challenges. Consider the following questions about employee misbehavior:

1. What kinds of approaches might you use to prevent employees from misbehaving at office holiday parties?

2. How would you address incidences of employee misbehavior at office parties?

increases for average performers are usually aligned with labor market pay adjustments, which keeps those individuals at a competitive level. Lower performers receive less because of their performance issues, which "encourages" them to either improve their deficiencies or leave the organization. However, employees who perform exceptionally at work might feel entitled based on their high compensation, and managers should be aware that they might misbehave in the workplace as a result. The "HR Ethics: High-Paid Employees Misbehave at Holiday Parties"

ETHICS

feature investigates how high-performing and highly paid individuals may use office parties as a way to inappropriately fraternize with coworkers.

Pay Adjustment Matrix Integrating performance appraisal ratings with pay changes is done through a pay adjustment matrix, or merit-based performance matrix. A pay adjustment matrix reflects an employee's opportunity for pay increase.

The matrix considers two factors—the employee's level of performance as rated in an appraisal and the employee's position in the pay range (their current pay level quartile), which is often related to experience and tenure. An employee's placement on the chart determines his or her recommended pay increase. According to the matrix in Figure 11-15, if employee David is rated as exceeding expectations and is currently in the second quartile of the pay range, he is eligible for a raise of 3% to 5%.

Two elements of the sample matrix illustrate the emphasis on paying for performance. First, individuals whose performance is below expectations receive small to no raises. This approach sends a strong signal that poor performers will not continue to receive increases just by completing another year of service. In Figure 11-15, employees with "below expectations" ratings are eligible for 0% raises regardless of what quartile they are currently paid. Second, as employees move up the pay range, they must exhibit higher performance to earn the same percentage raise as those lower in the range performing at the same level. This approach is taken because the firm is paying above the market midpoint but receiving only satisfactory performance rather than above-market performance. Matrices can be constructed to reflect the specific pay-for-performance policies and philosophy in an organization and are typically revised based on the budgeted increase level.

The general objective is for all employees to be paid at approximately the pay range midpoint. To determine each individual employee's standing in relationship to the midpoint, many organizations use a value called the compa-ratio.

Compa-ratio
Pay level divided by the midpoint of the pay range

FIGURE 11-15 Pay Adjustment Matrix

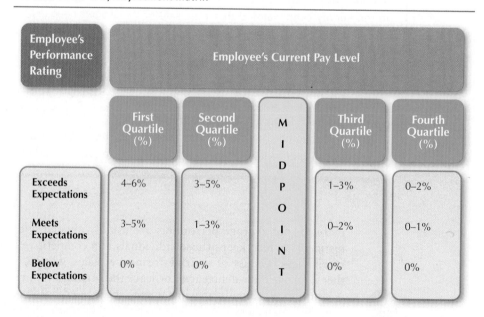

Employee's Performance Rating	Employee's Current Pay Level				
	First Quartile (%)	Second Quartile (%)	MIDPOINT	Third Quartile (%)	Fourth Quartile (%)
Exceeds Expectations	4–6%	3–5%		1–3%	0–2%
Meets Expectations	3–5%	1–3%		0–2%	0–1%
Below Expectations	0%	0%		0%	0%

Source: Adapted from Payscale's 2012 Compensation Best Practices report.

The compa-ratio is calculated by dividing the individual's pay level by the midpoint of the pay range. To illustrate, the following is an example of the compa-ratio for employee Jennifer:

Jennifer is an employee in Pay Grade 3. The pay range for Grade 3 is:

Minimum = 8.98; Midpoint = 11.00; Maximum = 13.02

Jennifer earns $9.90 per hour.

Jennifer's compa-ratio is (9.90/11) = 0.90

All employees whose compa-ratio is below 1.0 are paid below the pay range midpoint; all employees whose compa-ratio is over 1.0 are paid above the pay range midpoint. To ensure that the pay philosophy is enforced, pay administrators calculate the overall compa-ratio for the entire organization to determine the general pattern of pay rates relative to midpoint levels.

11-8b Standardized Pay Adjustments

Companies that have an entitlement philosophy rely more on standardized pay increases. Several methods can be used to provide standardized pay increases to employees.

Seniority
Time spent in an organization or working in a particular job

Seniority Time spent in an organization or working in a particular job, called seniority or tenure, can be used as the basis for pay increases. Many employers have policies that require an employee to work for a certain length of time before being eligible for pay increases. Pay adjustments based on seniority are often set as automatic steps depending on satisfactory performance during the required length of time. This is often used early in a person's employment. For example, the company may have automatic step increases at 30, 60, and 90 days to improve retention of new hires and to reward mastery of job skills.

Cost-of-Living Adjustments Another pay-raise practice is the use of a *cost-of-living adjustment (COLA)* whereby every employee's pay is increased to compensate for inflation and rising prices. Often, these adjustments are tied to changes in the Consumer Price Index (CPI) or some other general economic measure. However, the CPI may overstate the actual cost of living, and COLA increases do nothing to recognize employees for their relative contributions to the organization.

Across-the-Board Increases Unfortunately, some employers give across-the-board raises and call them *merit raises*, which they are not. They are usually given as a percentage raise based on standard market or financial budgeting determinations. If all employees get the same percentage pay increase, it is clearly not tied to merit or good performance. For this reason, employers should reserve the term *merit* for any amount above the standard raise, and they should state clearly which amount is for performance and which amount is the "automatic" portion.

Lump-Sum Increases Most employees who receive pay increases, either for merit or for seniority, receive an increase in the amount of their regular monthly or weekly paycheck. For example, an employee who makes $12.00 an hour and receives a 3% increase will move to $12.36 an hour.

Lump-sum increase (LSI)
One-time payment of all or part of a yearly pay increase

In contrast, a lump-sum increase (LSI) is a one-time payment of all or part of a yearly pay increase. The pure LSI approach does not increase the base pay. Therefore, in the example of a person making $12.00 an hour, if a 3% LSI is granted, the person receives a lump sum of $748.80 ($0.36 an hour × 2,080 working hours in the year). However, the base rate remains at $12.00 an hour, which slows down the progression of base wages.

The major advantage of an LSI plan is that it heightens employees' awareness of what their performance levels "merited." Another advantage is that the firm can use LSIs to slow down the increase of base pay and thus reduce or avoid the compounding effect on succeeding raises. One disadvantage of LSI plans is that workers who receive a lump-sum payment may become discouraged because their base pay does not change. Unions generally resist LSI programs because of their impact on pensions and benefits. And when calculating the employee's overtime pay, the LSI should be considered as part of the base wage calculation.

11-8c Compensation Challenges

A number of concerns for managers affect compensation planning and administration. Circumstances such as economic recessions and the gender pay gap that occur within and outside the organization can create employee dissatisfaction or turnover.

Economic Recessions During trying economic times, many organizations address shortfalls in revenue by reducing employment-related expenses. This may include reducing the quantities and amounts of raises given to employees. Layoffs and reductions in force may be other strategies used to lower costs. Managers and HR professionals should consider the potential negative impact of these approaches and use them sparingly because employee job dissatisfaction and turnover can occur if such strategies are implemented on a long-term basis.

Gender Pay Gap Despite laws prohibiting pay discrimination on the basis of sex (as discussed in Chapter 3), there is a persistent pay gap between men and women in the workplace. The wage gap is wider in some industries than others. However, women appear to have gained some ground in recent years. The pay differences between women and men seem to be decreasing generationally, with Millennials experiencing a greatly diminished pay gap. But the pay differences tend to increase in executive-level positions.[82] Continued monitoring of organizational pay levels and properly managing women's career progress are ways to address these concerns.

SUMMARY

- The concept of *total rewards* has become a crucial part of HR management and includes compensation, benefits, work-life balance practices, and performance and talent management.
- Compensation provided by an organization can come directly through base pay and variable pay and indirectly through benefits.
- The Fair Labor Standards Act (FLSA), as amended, is the major federal law that affects

pay systems. It requires most organizations to pay a minimum wage and to comply with overtime provisions, including appropriately classifying employees as exempt or nonexempt and as independent contractors or employees.

- A continuum of compensation philosophies exists, ranging from an entitlement philosophy to a performance philosophy.
- When designing and administering compensation programs, internal and external

equity, organizational justice, and pay openness all must be considered.
- Compensation practices for international employees can be designed using a variety of methods to ensure equity.
- A base pay system is developed using information from valuations of jobs and pay surveys, both of which are designed to ensure that the pay system is internally equitable and externally competitive.
- The valuation of jobs can be determined using either job evaluation or market pricing.

- Once a firm has collected pay survey data, it can develop a pay structure, which is composed of pay grades and pay ranges.
- Problems involving employees paid outside of the pay range can be addressed in many ways.
- Individual pay increases can be based on performance, seniority, cost-of-living adjustments, across-the-board increases, lump-sum increases, or a combination of different approaches.

CRITICAL THINKING CHALLENGES

1. Think of an organization where you have worked. What were its compensation policies, and how were they communicated to employees?

2. Congratulations! You have recently been promoted and are the company's new Human Resources Manager! You have offices in several countries, so how would you evaluate different compensation packages for employees who are located throughout the world?

3. Recently, larger companies have been in the news because of violations of overtime regulations. How should your Human Resources department protect itself from these devastating claims? Brainstorm some ideas on how to prevent these issues from occurring.

4. You are the HR Director for an insurance company with regional offices in several states. For each office, you want to be sure that the administrative assistants reporting to the regional manager are paid appropriately.

   A. Go to www.salary.com to find geographic pay survey data for this job in Hartford, Connecticut; Atlanta, Georgia; Omaha, Nebraska; and Phoenix, Arizona.
   B. Then recommend pay ranges, identifying the low, median, and high rates for each pay range.
   C. To present the data, list each of the offices in order from lowest median pay to highest median pay.

CASE | Establishing Pay at United Grinding Technologies Incorporated

Establishing pay in companies can be a tough task for HR professionals and general managers because doing it right is very important to the bottom line. Compensation is often one of the most expensive functions managed in organizations. The process can be particularly challenging when dealing with corporate jobs that function at the higher echelons of the hierarchy because of the inherent complexities of the work processes. HR leaders have to identify useful compensation data and appropriate benchmark

jobs so that the compensation amounts offered are competitive with comparative market levels. The compensation approaches employed also need to support a firm's overall pay ideas and philosophies.

One of the most important steps in developing reasonable pay involves securing sound salary data, information that is commonly collected through surveys. Luckily, HR professionals have many options for obtaining this information. The Bureau of Labor Statistics, various consulting firms, and many professional associations can provide companies with important pay survey data. There are many different types of free data that can be compiled from online sources, but HR departments should be cautious about using these data until the accuracy has been verified.

United Grinding Technologies, a grinding-machine firm located in Miamisburg, Ohio, had to deal with a number of these compensation issues. Christine Taylor, SPHR, the organization's Director of Corporate Human Resources, had to create a compensation plan to determine the pay rates for all 140 individuals employed with the company. However, there were problems—it was difficult to find appropriate benchmark jobs that enabled her to easily develop a pay structure. To make things work, she enlisted the help of line managers to create sound job descriptions, which were then used to match jobs with BLS and trade association pay survey data.

Multiple jobs with similar skills were used as benchmarks, since there were no exact matches in the databases. This enabled Taylor to get an idea of what to pay individuals working in these jobs based on positions that were reasonably comparable to the jobs found in United Grinding Technologies. According to Taylor, "It is more of an art than a science."[83]

QUESTIONS

1. How would you evaluate Taylor's approach for developing a pay structure at United Grinding Technologies? Would you have done anything differently?

2. If you were to develop a pay structure in a company where you have worked, how would you approach doing it? What are the potential challenges associated with implementing your approach?

SUPPLEMENTAL CASES

Is the FLSA a Dinosaur?

This case identifies how the Fair Labor Standards Act might need to be reformed because of restrictions caused by workweek definitions. (For the case, go to www.cengage.com/management/mathis.)

Compensation Changes at JC Penney

This case identifies how performance management systems might be redesigned. (For the case, go to www.cengage.com/management/mathis.)

Scientific Turmoil

This case discusses the concerns associated with having a formal base pay system and communication issues that occur. (For the case, go to www.cengage.com/management/mathis.)

Pay for Performance Enhances Employee Management at Scripps Health

This case discusses how a hospital uses pay for performance to improve employee productivity. (For the case, go to www.cengage.com/management/mathis.)

END NOTES

1. Adapted from David Zielinski, "Tech Support," *HR Magazine*, February 2013, pp. 34–38.
2. Mike Colias, "Employee Bonuses Driven by Customer Loyalty at General Motors," *Workforce.com*, June 8, 2012, http://www.workforce.com/ articles/employee-bonuses-driven-by-customer-loyalty-at-general-motors.
3. Vas Taras, "Direct versus Indirect Compensation: Balancing Value and Cost in Total Compensation," *Compensation & Benefits Review* 44 (2012), 24–28.
4. Dan King, "Creative Compensation," *Colorado Business Magazine (coloradobiz)*, June 3, 2013, https://www.cobizmag.com/articles/creative-compensation.
5. Laura Sweeney, "Creative Compensation: Beyond Salaries,"

Experience by Simplicity, https://www.experience.com/alumnus/article?channel_id=Salaries&source_page=home&article_id=article_1126286323673.

6. "WorldatWork," February 12, 2015, http://www.worldatwork.org/waw/aboutus/html/aboutus-waw.html; http://www.worldatwork.org/waw/adimLink?id=28330&nonav=y.

7. Joanne Sammer, "Measure Compensation's Impact," *HR Magazine*, September 2012, pp. 85–90; Eric Marquardt and Nick Dunlap "Compensation Risk Assessments: A Process for Active Plan Management and Continuous Improvement," *Compensation & Benefits Review* 44 (2012), 6–11.

8. Stephen Miller, "After-Inflation Wages Accelerating, Data Show," *SHRM Online*, October 15, 2014, http://www.shrm.org/hrdisciplines/compensation/articles/pages/wage-growth-accelerating.aspx.

9. Stephen Miller, "Forecast: Restrained Wage Growth Continues into 2015," *SHRM Online*, February 2, 2015, http://www.shrm.org/hrdisciplines/compensation/articles/pages/wage-growth-restraint.aspx.

10. Stephen Miller, "Pay Trends for 2014: Salary Increases Hold Steady," *SHRM Online*, October 8, 2013, http://www.shrm.org/hrdisciplines/compensation/articles/pages/2014-salary-increases-flat.aspx.

11. Stephen Miller, "Rise in Professionals' Starting Salaries Outpaces Wage Gains," *SHRM Online*, October 29, 2013, http://www.shrm.org/hrdisciplines/compensation/articles/pages/professionals-starting-salaries.aspx.

12. Jason Adwin, "2014 Salary-Increase Budgets Remain Stable; Range Adjustments Lag," *SHRM Online*, November 14, 2013, http://www.shrm.org/hrdisciplines/compensation/articles/pages/2014-salary-increase-budgets.aspx; Stephen Miller, "Base Salary Rise of 3% Forecast for 2015," July 9, 2014, http://www.shrm.org/hrdisciplines/compensation/articles/pages/2015-salary-budget-forecasts.aspx.

13. Stephen Miller, Salary Budget Increases Show Broad Consistency," *SHRM Online*, August 7, 2014, http://www.shrm.org/hrdisciplines/compensation/articles/pages/salary-budgets-consistent.aspx.

14. Stephen Miller, "Variable Pay Spending Spikes to Record High," *SHRM Online*, September 2, 2014, http://www.shrm.org/hrdisciplines/compensation/articles/pages/variable-pay-high.aspx.

15. Stephen Miller, "Salary Budget Increases Show Broad Consistency," *SHRM Online*, August 7, 2014, http://www.shrm.org/hrdisciplines/compensation/articles/pages/salary-budgets-consistent.aspx.

16. Joseph Combs, "A New Normal," *HR Magazine*, December 2013, pp. 28–32.

17. Shelley Banjo, "Wal-Mart to Pay $4.8 Million in Back Wages, Damages," *Wall Street Journal*, May 2, 2012; Allen Smith, "Wage and Hour Enforcement Ramps Up," *HR Magazine*, June 2012, p. 17.

18. Bryan J. Cohen, "Court Orders Arbitration of FLSA Wage Claims," *HR Magazine*, July 2013, p. 59.

19. United States Department of Labor website, http://www.dol.gov/elaws/faq/esa/flsa/001.htm; http://www.dol.gov/whd/minwage/america.htm; http://www.dol.gov/whd/state/tipped.htm.

20. Joanne Deschenaux, "Paid Leave, Minimum Wage, Marijuana Legalization on State Ballots," *SHRM* Online, October 23, 2014, http://www.shrm.org/legalissues/stateandlocalresources/pages/state-ballots-2014.aspx; Joanne Deschenaux, "Several States Raising Minimum Wage," *SHRM Online*, September 25, 2013, http://www.shrm.org/legalissues/stateandlocalresources/pages/states-raising-minimum-wage.aspx; Joanne Deschenaux, "States Vote for Paid Sick Leave, Higher Minimum Wages and Legalized Pot," *SHRM Online*, November 5, 2014, http://www.shrm.org/legalissues/stateandlocalresources/pages/state-ballot-initiatives-outcomes.aspx.

21. Bill Leonard, "2014 State of the Union Focuses on the Workplace," *SHRM Online*, January 29, 2014, http://www.shrm.org/publications/hrnews/pages/2014-state-of-the-union-workplace.aspx; Bill Leonard, "President Obama's 2015 Agenda to Focus on Key HR Issues," *SHRM Online*, January 21, 2015, http://www.shrm.org/publications/hrnews/pages/2015-state-of-the-union-hr-.aspx.

22. Allen Smith, "Report: Higher Tipped Minimum Wage Would Help Close Pay Gap," *SHRM Online*, April 4, 2014, http://www.shrm.org/legalissues/federalresources/pages/minimum-wage-gender-gap.aspx.

23. Bill Leonard, "2014 State of the Union Focuses on the Workplace," *SHRM Online*, January 29, 2014, http://www.shrm.org/publications/hrnews/pages/2014-state-of-the-union-workplace.aspx; Allen Smith, "CBO Report Examines Minimum-Wage-Increase Effect on Employment," *SHRM Online*, February 21, 2014, http://www.shrm.org/legalissues/federalresources/pages/cbo-minimum-wage-increase.aspx.

24. Venessa Wong, "This Is What Would Happen if Fast-Food Workers Got Raises" *Bloomberg Business*, August 2, 2013, http://www.bloomberg.com/bw/articles/2013-08-02/this-is-what-would-happen-if-fast-food-workers-got-raises.

25. Melissa Campeau, "'A Stick and a Carrot at the Same Time': Why Costco Pays Twice the Market Rate," *Financial Post*, October 30, 2014, http://business.financialpost.com/2014/10/30/a-stick-and-a-carrot-at-the-same-time-why-costco-pays-twice-the-market-rate/.

26. Allen Smith "Marriott's Maid-Tipping Campaign Raises Wage Questions," *SHRM Online*, September 19, 2014, http://www.shrm.org/legalissues/federalresources/pages/marriott-envelope-maids.aspx.

27. Allen Smith, "Report: Higher Tipped Minimum Wage Would Help Close Pay Gap," *SHRM Online*, April 4, 2014, http://www.shrm.org/legalissues/federalresources/pages/minimum-wage-gender-gap.aspx.

28. Ashby Jones, "Former Ballplayers Cry Foul," *Wall Street Journal*, September 20–21, 2014, p. A3.

29. Kris Maher, "Mayor Cuts Workers' Pay to Minimum Wage," *Wall Street Journal*, July 10, 2012, p. A2.

30. Jon Hyman, "The Fluctuating Rules for the Fluctuating Workweek," *Workforce*, November 20, 2013, http://www.workforce.com/blogs/3-the-practical-employer/post/20060-the-fluctuating-rules-for-the-fluctuating-workweek.

31. Allen Smith, "Uncertainty over FLSA Regulations Breeds Discontent," *SHRM Online*, April 1, 2014,

http://www.shrm.org/legalissues/federalresources/pages/flsa-regs-uncertainty.aspx.

32. Stephen Miller, "Safeguards Can Protect against Misclassification Lawsuits," *SHRM Online*, November 6, 2013, http://www.shrm.org/hrdisciplines/compensation/articles/pages/misclassification-lawsuits-safeguards.aspx.

33. Dara L. DeHaven and Margaret Santen Hanrahan, "Who Will Be Entitled to Overtime under Expected Rule Change?" *SHRM Online*, March 27, 2014, http://www.shrm.org/hrdisciplines/compensation/articles/pages/overtime-rule-change.aspx.

34. Allen Smith, "No Timeline for New Overtime Pay Rules," *HR Magazine*, May 2014, p. 11.

35. Amber Clayton, "Can Managers Change Employee Time Sheets?" *HR Magazine* (Solutions), May 2013, p. 26.

36. Matthew J. Cannova, "Supermarket CEO Found Personally Liable under FLSA," *HR Magazine*, October 2013, p. 63.

37. Brent Kendall, "Justices Weigh Pay for Amazon Security Checks," *Wall Street Journal*, October 9, 2014, p. B3.

38. Jon Hyman, "The Email Curfew for Wage-and-Hour Compliance," *Workforce*, November 20, 2013, http://www.workforce.com/blogs/3-the-practical-employer/post/20075-the-email-curfew-for-wage-and-hour-compliance.

39. Jon Hyman, "Clothes Make the Man, and the Wage-and-Hour Lawsuit," *Workforce*, November 11, 2013, http://www.workforce.com/blogs/3-the-practical-employer/post/20056-clothes-make-the-man-and-the-wage-and-hour-lawsuit.

40. Joanne Deschenaux, "Nurse's Collective Action Was Properly Dismissed," *HR Magazine*, June 2013, p. 20.

41. Adapted from Jonathan A. Segal, "Give Me a Break," *HR Magazine*, December 2013, pp. 58–60.

42. Bill Leonard, "Senate Hearing Previews Contentious Vote on Paycheck Fairness Act," *SHRM Online*, April 4, 2014, http://www.shrm.org/publications/hrnews/pages/paycheck-fairness-act.aspx; Bill Leonard, "Paycheck Fairness Act Stalls in Senate,"

SHRM Online, April 9, 2014, http://www.shrm.org/publications/hrnews/pages/paycheckfairnessactstallsinsenate.aspx.

43. Allen Smith, "Ledbetter Act Adds Lengthy To-Do List for HR," February 10, 2009, www.shrm.org; Brett A. Gorovsky, "Lilly Ledbetter Fair Pay Act of 2009: What's Next for Employers?" 2009, www.CCH.com.

44. Laura Stevens, "Court Sides with Kansas Drivers in Work Dispute," *Wall Street Journal*, October 6, 2014, p. B3.

45. "Employer's Supplemental Tax Guide," IRS.gov, Publication 15-A, 2012; "The IRS's 20-Factor Analysis," *US Chamber of Commerce Small Business Nation*, 2012.

46. Bert Schreurs, Hannes Guenter, Desiree Schumacher, I. J. Hetty Van Emmerik, and Guy Notelaers, "Pay-Level Satisfaction and Employee Outcomes: The Moderating Effect of Employee-Involvement Climate," *Human Resource Management* 52 (May–June 2013), 399–421.

47. Angela Collis, "What's the Best Way to Handle an Employee's Request for a Pay Increase?" *HR Magazine*, February 2013, p. 21.

48. Tamara Lytle, "Linking Executive Pay to Performance," *HR Magazine*, September 2013, pp. 59–61.

49. Amber Clayton, "Can Managers Change Employee Time Sheets?" *HR Magazine* (Solutions), May 2013, p. 26.

50. Roger S. Achille, "Damages Do Not Preclude Wage and Hour Class Action," *HR Magazine*, September 2013, p. 74.

51. Allen Smith, "Class Action over Final Wages Paid on ATM Card Settled for $1M," *SHRM Online*, February 11, 2015, http://shrm.org/legalissues/stateandlocalresources/pages/groomer-final-wages-atm.aspx.

52. Chris Ratajczyk, "A Primer on Base Pay Compensation Metrics," *Workspan Magazine*, July 2011, pp. 31–33; John Donney, "Benchmarking Human Capital Metrics," January 4, 2012, www.shrm.org.

53. Sefa Hayibor, "Equity and Expectancy Considerations in Stakeholder Action," *Business & Society* 51 (2012), 220–262.

54. Adapted from Rachel Emma Silver, "Big Data Upends the Way Workers Are Paid," *Wall Street Journal*, September 19, 2012, p. B1.

55. "Expectancy Theory of Motivation," 2012, www.managementstudyguide.com; Barry A. Friedman, Pamela L. Cox, and Larry E. Maher, "An Expectancy Theory Motivation Approach to Peer Assessment," *Journal of Management Education* 32 (2008), 580–612.

56. Angela Collis, "What's the Best Way to Handle an Employee's Request for a Pay Increase?" *HR Magazine*, February 2013, p. 21.

57. Stephen Miller, "SEC Proposes Rule to Disclose CEO-to-Worker Pay Ratios," *SHRM Online*, September 19, 2013, http://www.shrm.org/hrdisciplines/compensation/articles/pages/ceo-to-worker-pay-ratio-rule.aspx; "Regulatory Update: SHRM Comments on Challenges of Pay Ratio Disclosure," *SHRM Online*, January 29, 2014, http://www.shrm.org/advocacy/governmentaffairsnews/hrissuesupdatee-newsletter/pages/012914_3.aspx.

58. Kathryn P. Roberts, "Interference with Potential Gratuity Qualifies as Adverse Action," *SHRM Online*, February 3, 2014, http://www.shrm.org/legalissues/federalresources/pages/interference-potential-gratuity-adverse-action.aspx.

59. Based on Ted Olsen, "Agreements among Employers Not to Poach Others' Employees May Result in Antitrust Liability," *Sherman & Howard*, May 1, 2012; Jessica Guynn, "Apple, Google, Others to Face Antitrust Suit over Staff Poaching," *Los Angeles Times*, April 19, 2012; Marcus Wohlsen, "Suit Claims Tech Giants' Pacts on Poaching Held Down Pay," *Associated Press*, January 29, 2012; David M. Brown, "The 'No Poaching' Antitrust Litigation Case against Several High-Tech Companies Continues," *Abbey Spanier Blog*, June 19, 2012; Jonathan Stempel, "Apple, Google, Intel Fail to Dismiss Staff-Poaching Lawsuit," *Reuters*, April 19, 2012.

60. Kevin F. Hallock, "Go Big: The Firm-Size Pay (and Pay-Mix) Effect," *Workspan Magazine*, February 2012, 12–13.

61. Atual Mitra, Nina Gupta, and Jason D. Shaw, "A Comparative Examination of Traditional and Skill-Based Pay Plans," *Journal of Managerial Psychology* 26 (2011), 278–296;

Frank L. Giancola, "A Framework for Understanding New Concepts in Compensation Management," *Benefits & Compensation Digest* 46 (2009), 1–16; Frank L. Giancola, "Skill-Based Pay: Fad or Classic?" *Compensation & Benefits Review* 43 (2011), 220–226.

62. Elizabeth Redmond, "Competency Models at Work: The Value of Perceived Relevance and Fair Rewards for Employee Outcomes," *Human Resource Management* 52 (September–October 2013), 771–792.

63. Peter D. Jensen and Torben Pedersen, "The Economic Geography of Off-Shoring: The Fit between Activities and Local Context," *Journal of Management Studies* 48 (2011), 352–372; Arne Bigsten, Dick Durevall, and Farzana Munshi, "Off-Shoring and Occupational Wages: Some Empirical Evidence," *Journal of International Trade & Economic Development* 21 (2012), 253–269.

64. David Wessel and James R. Hagerty, "Flat U.S. Wages Help Fuel Rebound in Manufacturing," *Wall Street Journal*, May 29, 2012; Timothy Aeppel, "Detroit's Wages Take on China's," *Wall Street Journal*, May 23, 2012.

65. "International Pay and Benefits," Boeing.com, 2012, http://www.boeing.com/companyoffices/empinfo/benefits/global/index.html.

66. Dori Meinert, "U.S. vs. European Executive Pay Gap Narrow," *HR Magazine*, April 2013, p. 18.

67. Brian Blackstone and Vanessa Fuhrmans, "German Wages Are on the Upswing," *Wall Street Journal*, May 21, 2012, p. A10.

68. Roy Maurer, "Venezuelan Workers Set to Receive Highest Pay Raises in the World," *SHRM Online*, November 25, 2013, http://www.shrm.org/hrdisciplines/global/articles/pages/venezuela-highest-pay-raises-world.aspx.

69. "Cartus Survey Shows Employee Expectations Compete with Company Costs as Biggest Challenges for International Relocation Managers," *Yahoo Finance*, January 23, 2012.

70. Melissa Foss, "'I Owe the Company How Much?!' How to Manage the Tax Equalization Process to Avoid Surprises," *KPMG.com*, 2009–2010.

71. Angela Wright, "'Modernizing' Away Gender Pay Inequality? Some Evidence from the Local Government Sector on Using Job Evaluation," *Employee Relations* 33 (2011), 159–178; Kay Gilbert, "Promises and Practices: Job Evaluation and Equal Pay Forty Years On!" *Industrial Relations Journal* 43 (2012), 137–151.

72. Stephen Miller, "85% of Companies Targeted Market Median for Base Pay," *SHRM Online*, January 29, 2015, http://www.shrm.org/hrdisciplines/compensation/articles/pages/market-median-base-pay.aspx.

73. Nancy Hatch Woodward, "Matching Jobs with Pay," *HR Magazine*, May 2012, pp. 55–58.

74. Stephen Miller, "Tie Pay to Value, Not Market Data, Experts Advise," *SHRM Online*, May 2, 2013, http://www.shrm.org/hrdisciplines/compensation/articles/pages/pay-to-value.aspx.

75. Ted Olsen, "Antitrust Challenge to Employers' Exchange of Pay Information Continues," *Sherman & Howard*, May 1, 2012.

76. Joanne M. Sammer, "Updating Salary Structure: When, Why and How?" *SHRM Online*, May 21, 2013, http://www.shrm.org/compensation/articles/pages/updating-salary-structure.aspx; Sara D. Schmidt, "Keeping Salary Administration Programs Current," *SHRM Online*, June 17, 2913, http://www.shrm.org/hrdisciplines/compensation/articles/pages/salary-administration-programs.aspx.

77. "How to Establish Salary Ranges," *SHRM Online*, September 6, 2013, http://www.shrm.org/templatestools/howtoguides/pages/howtoestablishsalaryranges.aspx; Kerry Chou, "Making Your Salary Structure Work for You," *Worldatwork.org*, February 13, 2012, http://www.worldatwork.org/adimComment?id=58560.

78. Jim Kochanski and Yelena Stiles, "Put a Lid on Salary Compression before It Boils Over," *SHRM Online*, July 19, 2013, http://www.shrm.org/hrdisciplines/compensation/articles/pages/salary-compression-lid.aspx.

79. James R. Hagerty, "Help Wanted: Factory Pay Starts to Accelerate," *Wall Street Journal*, October 9, 2014, p. B1.

80. Stephen Miller, "Pay Raises Focus on Rewarding Top Performers," *SHRM Online*, August 12, 2914, http://www.shrm.org/hrdisciplines/compensation/articles/pages/pay-raises-2015.aspx; Stephen Miller, "Top Performers' Pay Differentiation Narrows for 2015," *SHRM Online*, September 10, 2014, http://www.shrm.org/hrdisciplines/compensation/articles/pages/pay-differentiation-narrows-2015.aspx.

81. Adapted from Dana Wilkie, "High-Income Workers Report Most 'Inappropriate' Behavior at Holiday Parties," *SHRM Online*, November 26, 2013, http://www.shrm.org/hrdisciplines/employeerelations/articles/pages/holiday-parties-inappropriate-behavior.aspx.

82. Dana Wilkie, "Millennials Closing Pay Gap, but Not Cutting Apron Strings," *SHRM Online*, December 4, 2014, http://www.shrm.org/hrdisciplines/diversity/articles/pages/millennials-pay-gap-.aspx.

83. Based on Joanne Sammer, "The Art of Setting Pay," *HR Magazine*, May 2013, pp. 65–67.

CHAPTER

12

Variable Pay and Executive Compensation

Learning Objectives

After you have read this chapter, you should be able to:

LO1 Define variable pay and identify three aspects of effective pay-for-performance plans.

LO2 Compare three types of individual incentives.

LO3 Identify key concerns that must be addressed when designing work unit/ team variable pay plans.

LO4 Specify why profit sharing and employee stock ownership are popular organizational incentive plans.

LO5 Explain three ways in which sales employees are typically compensated.

LO6 Identify the typical elements of executive compensation and discuss criticisms of executive compensation levels.

WHAT'S TRENDING IN

VARIABLE PAY?

Variable pay plans are being modified and updated to reflect changes in customer preferences, government oversight, and shareholder activism. Since variable pay can make up a significant portion of individual compensation, it is important to periodically review the organization's plan to ensure that it is driving employees to act in ways the organization wants. Current trends include:

1. A higher portion of pay is being tied to performance in more U.S. organizations. Companies are moving away from an entitlement mentality in response to workers looking for rewards tied to their contributions rather than their loyalty and tenure.

2. Greater transparency is being demanded regarding pay for executives. Several recently enacted laws demand greater disclosure of executive pay, and vocal investors are asking to be a part of the process for setting compensation. Public outcry led by the Occupy Wall Street movement has brought greater attention to the level of executive pay.

3. A reduction in the use of commissions for salespeople has occurred because more sales are taking place online with limited interaction with salespeople. This has changed the nature of pay given to sales professionals and has precipitated a reevaluation of their work.

4. Variable pay is becoming more common in companies located in a number of nations around the world. Targeting financial resources to recruit and retain high performers is achieved through pay for performance programs in these developing economies.

Applause! Applause!!

Employees at the professional services firm KPMG not only receive recognition for a job well done but are also involved in identifying peers who deserve awards. This creative program was launched at KPMG's facility in the United Kingdom. A critical element of the recognition awards is alignment with the company's core values. Employees and work teams that demonstrate outstanding performance in line with KPMG's core values and objectives can earn a "pat on the back" from their boss or from peers who notice the achievement. Management training and coaching programs now include a section on rewards and recognition to ensure that everyone understands the importance of peer-to-peer rewards.

These Encore! awards have broken through the traditional manager-operated programs at most companies. Since peers are more likely to see individuals or teams in action, everyone on the KPMG staff is involved in granting recognition awards. This reduces the temptation to perform above and beyond only when the boss is looking. It encourages all employees to always perform at their best.

Software allows staffers to rate and reward one another using a secure online portal. Guidelines that link levels of recognition to award values help employees choose the appropriate level for each award they give out. Recipients of the Encore! awards are given choices, primarily electronic gift cards from various local merchants. This way, the reward is more personalized and meaningful to the award-winner.

Since the program's implementation, KPMG has realized a 25% increase in the number of employees earning recognition awards and a 165% increase in the number of rewards given out. A new addition to the program is a "social recognition newsfeed" that broadcasts a stream of recent awards distributed. This makes it easy for peers to congratulate award recipients, and it further reinforces the

Vadym Drobot/Shutterstock.com

445

importance of going above expectations consistent with company values. Employees can earn and give "shout-outs" in recognition of a job well done.[1] You can see more about employee reactions to winning an Encore! award on this YouTube video: http://www.youtube.com/watch?v=lu22WQJN9oc.

Variable pay
Compensation that is tied to performance

Incentives
Tangible rewards that encourage or motivate action

Variable pay is compensation that is tied to performance. Better performance leads to greater rewards for employees. Performance may be evaluated and rewarded at the individual, group (a team or even a whole plant), or entire organization level. The term *pay for performance* is often used interchangeably with the term *variable pay* because this type of compensation moves pay from being a fixed cost to one that varies with employee performance. Incentives are tangible rewards that encourage or motivate action and therefore might be related to pay or be even broader. This chapter will deal with all three concepts and two special types of variable pay that include sales and executive compensation.

Do people work harder if their pay is tied to their performance? Yes, they do, *but* there are several caveats that make the relationship a bit less clear-cut. Employers apparently believe that pay based on performance can be used to tie business objectives to compensation because performance-based compensation is increasing for a large part of the workforce.[2] Variable pay plans in some form are used by the majority of companies. A survey by Aon Hewitt found that 91% of companies offer variable programs that amount to 12.7% of payroll for salaried exempt employees.[3]

Tying pay to performance can be attractive for both employers and employees. For employers, it can mean more output per employee (productivity), lower fixed costs, and shifting some risk to employees (because they must perform to get paid). For employees, it can mean more pay when they do their jobs well. But not everyone likes variable pay. For example, some employees don't like the risks associated with performance-based pay. Additionally, unions uniformly prefer that employees be paid for the amount of time they spend on the job rather than for the amount they produce.

12-1 Variable Pay: Incentive for Performance

A pay for performance philosophy differs from a traditional entitlement compensation philosophy in which difference in length of service is often the primary differentiating factor. Variable pay plans are designed to motivate employees to invest discretionary effort—the extra, over and above minimum needed to avoid getting fired. The philosophical foundation of variable pay rests on three basic assumptions:

- Some people or groups contribute more to organizational success than do others.
- Some people perform better and are more productive than are others.
- Employees or groups who perform better or contribute more should receive greater compensation.

There is evidence that variable pay broadly available to most employees does improve company performance.[4] However, not everyone wants to have their pay contingent on their performance. There is "self-selection," with incentive plans attracting different people with different characteristics such as gender and willingness to take risks.[5] In fact, some economic studies suggest that some of the variance in male wage rates versus female wage rates can be attributed to this self-selection regarding pay for performance. Men are more likely to take financial risks and choose jobs that pay for performance than are women.[6] Pay for performance has not been well received in the public sector or labor unions, where a philosophy of entitlement has dominated for many years.

Incentives can take many forms and may motivate some people but not others. For example, incentives might include simple praise, "recognition and reward" programs that award trips and merchandise, bonuses for performance accomplishments, money for successful team results, and profit sharing. A variety of possibilities are discussed throughout this chapter. A successful plan might include a combination of several types of incentives.

Extrinsic rewards
Rewards that are external to the individual

Figure 12-1 shows a wide variety of possible incentives for employees. Many of the rewards are extrinsic rewards, which are rewards that are external to the individual. Extrinsic rewards include base pay, monetary incentives, bonuses,

FIGURE 12-1   A Variety of Possible Incentives

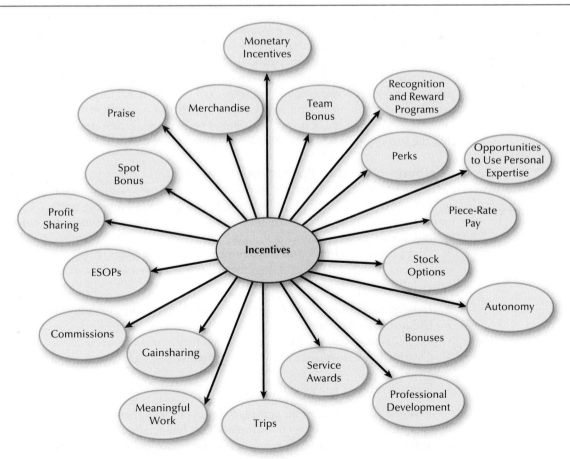

perquisites, and other measurable rewards. However, some research has shown that intrinsic rewards, or rewards that are internal to the individual, are more powerful in motivating workers to exercise discretionary effort to achieve their own and the organization's goals. Intrinsic rewards include meaningful work, autonomy, professional development, and opportunities to use their expertise.[7]

12-1a Effective Variable Pay

Employers adopt variable pay for many reasons, including the following:

- Link strategic business goals and employee performance
- Enhance organizational results and reward employees financially for their contributions
- Recognize different levels of employee performance through different rewards
- Achieve HR objectives such as increasing retention, reducing turnover, recognizing succession training, and rewarding safety
- Reduce fixed costs

As economic conditions and employee expectations have changed, the use of variable pay incentives has changed as well.[8] Under variable pay programs, employees may receive a greater share of the gains or declines in organizational performance results but also take greater risks. Even though variable pay has grown in use, some incentive programs have succeeded while others have not. Since they are complex and their success depends on multiple factors, incentives work, but they are not a panacea. If individuals see incentives as desirable, they are likely to put forth the extra effort to earn the incentive payouts. But not all employees believe that they are being rewarded for doing a good job, and not all individuals are motivated by their employers' incentive plans. Preferences for certain types of performance-based pay will also vary. Some employees prefer cash over noncash incentives, while noncash incentives can motivate some workers to perform better than cash rewards do. Organizations must make a variety of important compensation decisions to ensure that the variable pay offered will motivate a workforce with diverse needs.

Combating Variable Pay Complexity One factor that can lead to failure is having an incentive plan that is too complex for employees and management to understand. If the plan is too confusing or involves too many moving parts, the focus may not be on successful performance but on gaming the plan. Worse yet, employees may simply give up on trying to figure out how to earn the additional rewards.

Given these dynamics and the complexity of some plans, providing effective variable pay requires significant ongoing effort. Incentive plans are more successful if they follow these guidelines:

- Develop clear, understandable plans that are continually communicated.
- Use realistic performance measures.
- Keep the plans current and linked to organizational objectives.
- Clearly link performance results to payouts that recognize performance differences.
- Identify variable pay incentives separately from base pay on paychecks.

Variable pay plans can be considered successful if they fit the organization's objectives, culture, and financial resources. Both financial and nonfinancial rewards for performance can be useful in pay-for-performance plans. The manner in which

FIGURE 12-2 Factors for Effective Variable Pay Plans

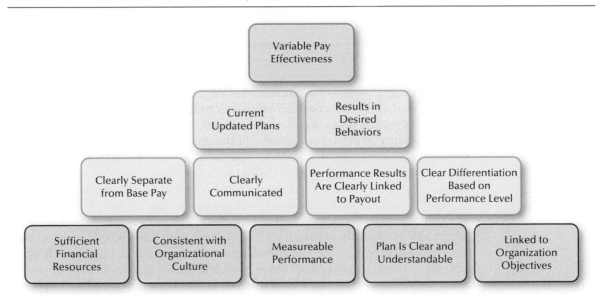

targets are set and measured is important.[9] Figure 12-2 shows many elements that can affect the success of a variable pay plan.

Does the Plan Fit the Organization? The effectiveness of any variable pay program relies on its consistency with the organization's culture.[10] For example, if an organization is family oriented and cooperative, an incentive system that focuses on individual rewards will likely fail. In such a case, the incentive plan has been "planted" in the wrong environment for it to grow.

When it comes to variable pay-for-performance plans, one size does not fit all situations. A plan that works well for one company will not necessarily work well for another. For instance, in professional service firms, performance measures such as client progress and productivity, new business development revenues, client satisfaction, and profit contributions are typically linked to pay-for-performance programs. These measures might not work as well in a different industry such as a retail company. Many companies find that variable pay plans make performance results a higher priority for employees. This may contribute to positive organizational results but also means that periodic review and adjustment of the variable pay plan is important to keep it relevant and effective.

Does the Plan Reward Appropriate Actions? Variable pay systems should be tied to desired performance. Employees must see a direct relationship between their efforts and results and financial and nonfinancial rewards. A key concept for variable pay is line of sight—the idea that employees can clearly see how their actions and decisions lead to desired outcomes. For example, front-line workers on the assembly line may have a clear line of sight to production output and product quality but would have difficulty seeing how their daily performance impacts corporate-wide profits. Top executives, on the other hand, have a clear line of sight to organization-wide results. Determining rewards at the appropriate level for each segment of the workforce is necessary to get maximum benefits from the pay plan.[11]

Line of sight
Idea that employees can clearly see how their actions and decisions lead to desired outcomes

Since people tend to produce what is measured and rewarded, organizations must make sure that what is being rewarded is clearly linked to what is needed and that rewards are distributed fairly.[12] For the programs to be effective, performance measures need to have appropriate emphasis and weights for calculating incentives. If incentive measures are perceived as manipulated or inappropriate, the variable pay system will not be effective. Using multiple measures helps ensure that important performance dimensions are not omitted. For example, assume a hotel reservation center wants to incentivize employees to increase productivity by lowering the time they spend on each call. If the amount of time spent is the only measure, then the quality of customer service and the number of reservations made might drop as employees rush callers to reduce call time. Therefore, the center should consider basing rewards on multiple measures such as call time, number of reservations booked, revenues generated, and the results of customer satisfaction surveys.

Linking pay to performance may not always be appropriate in all work situations. For instance, if output cannot be measured objectively, management might not be able to correctly reward higher performers with more pay. Managers might not even be able to accurately identify higher performers. For example, in a hospital emergency room, it may be impossible to identify the unique contributions of each team member and to reward each differently. Therefore, a group or work unit reward might be more preferable.

Employee misconduct such as accounting irregularities, churning customer accounts, giving inappropriate gifts to clients, and using company property for personal purposes can occur when employees try to meet expected pay for performance goals. The benefits to be gained from misconduct may exceed the fear of being caught. Performance-contingent compensation systems may unwittingly reinforce misconduct, especially if there is little base pay and much of the compensation is variable.[13]

A vital element of establishing a variable pay plan is determining appropriate performance measures to evaluate performance and the resulting rewards. Most organizations have a number of important targets to track results related to critical success factors.

12-1b Key Performance Indicators

Critical success factors are variables that have a strong influence on the results of the organization. Examples of critical success factors might include attracting and retaining profitable customers, generating profitable revenues, and leveraging talent for optimum results. Most organizations have a small number (between three and five) of critical success factors that truly drive all resource allocations and energy in the organization. Keeping this to a small number ensures that everyone remains focused on the really important things.[14]

Key performance indicators (KPIs) are the scorecard measures that tell managers how well the organization is performing relative to the critical success factors. For example, if attracting and retaining profitable customers is a critical success factor, then key performance indicators might include measures such as customer loyalty scores, repeat business, and customer referrals.

Key performance indicators (KPIs) Scorecard measures that tell managers how well the organization is performing relative to critical success factors

Key performance indicators can be determined at various levels of performance, the individual, work unit/group, or overall organization. Figure 12-3 shows an example of key performance indicators that a hospital might utilize in its variable pay plan. By selecting the most useful KPIs and tying them to rewards, an organization

FIGURE 12-3 Example of Key Performance Indicators: Hospital

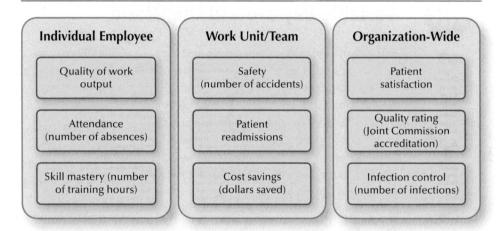

Individual Employee	Work Unit/Team	Organization-Wide
Quality of work output	Safety (number of accidents)	Patient satisfaction
Attendance (number of absences)	Patient readmissions	Quality rating (Joint Commission accreditation)
Skill mastery (number of training hours)	Cost savings (dollars saved)	Infection control (number of infections)

can best move employees toward performance that will really make a difference in outcomes.[15]

GLOBAL

12-1c Global Variable Pay

Variable pay is expanding in global firms, as well as among employers in other countries. In Europe, Asia, and Latin America, many management professionals and general staff are eligible for broad-based variable pay plans. Programs are similar to those at U.S.-based companies, but global programs must accommodate cultural, legal, and economic differences. Bonus programs are particularly important for retaining key staffers after global mergers and acquisitions.[16] For firms with operations in multiple countries, it is important to train managers in how to distribute rewards for maximum impact.

Although administering any incentive plan can be difficult, global incentive programs can be especially complex. A company may have an overarching strategy, such as growing market share or increasing the bottom line, but that strategy frequently results in different goals in different geographic regions. Also, laws and regulations differ from one country to the next. For example, in Latin America there are mandatory profit sharing regulations that must be reflected in variable plans. Team-based rewards are more common in collectivist cultures like Japan and Korea. Many nations and regions have very different perspectives on incentives, as the following "HR Competencies & Applications: Variable Pay around the World" feature shows.

12-1d Three Levels of Variable Pay

Variable pay plans can be classified into three levels or categories: individual, work unit/team, and organizational. Tying rewards to outcomes that employees can relate to (line of sight) means that rewards can reflect performance at each of these three levels. Ideally, having elements of each performance level gets employees thinking about their own performance, their group's performance, and the overall organization's performance. However, employees at different levels of the organization might receive different combinations of these rewards.

Individual incentives are given to reward the effort and performance of each employee. Some common means of providing individual variable pay are piece-rate

Variable Pay around the World

In the past, many global corporations built their variable pay plans around individual goals in a management by objectives (MBO) format. The trend in recent years, however, has been a move to a bottom-line results performance metric for incentive pay determination. Over 85% of global corporations have at least one variable pay plan, but plans are not identical across all countries in which a firm operates.

Variations in incentive plans are due to cultural differences as well as legal requirements. The following highlights some of the variances in different countries:

- France, Italy, Spain, Portugal, and Greece are very risk-averse nations; therefore, employees strongly prefer fixed to variable compensation. There are only small differences in payouts among employees.
- Japan and Korea emphasize team awards and have very minor differences in payouts among employees. Discussing performance is not culturally accepted or welcomed.
- China and India utilize variable pay to retain rather than reward employees. Rewards are based on effort rather than results.
- Argentina, Brazil, and Mexico have historically required profit sharing for all employees. High performers are singled out for particularly rich incentive payouts.
- Bahrain, Saudi Arabia, and the United Arab Emirates are relative newcomers to

incentive pay plans. Performance targets are not rigorous, and payouts are seen as an entitlement rather than earned rewards.

Managers attempting to find rewards to motivate discretionary effort in operations around the world clearly face challenges, as you can see by the information just presented. A one-size-fits-all approach might be unsuccessful without an extended transition period and significant training and coaching of employees and managers. Further, when transferring employees to operations outside of their home country, special consideration should be given to how rewards will translate.

Companies might work toward increasing the global focus on corporate results to drive all operations toward the common bottom line. Finding ways to improve employees' line of sight to the organization's outcomes will enhance the effectiveness of any global variable pay plan.[17] Respond to these questions about global pay:

1. How can a multinational enterprise design country-specific rewards that emphasize overall corporate performance rather than local operational performance?

2. What rewards would be most successful for intra-company transfers who relocate to various countries of operation?

KEY COMPETENCIES: Global and Cultural Effectiveness; HR Expertise: People/Total Rewards, Workplace/HR in the Global Context

systems, sales commissions, and individual bonuses. Others include special recognition rewards such as trips, merchandise, food, or gift cards. However, with individual incentives, employees may focus on what is best for them personally, which may harm the performance of other individuals with whom they are competing. The net result might be good for an individual but less than optimal for the organization. For this reason, group/team incentives may be more appropriate in some situations.

FIGURE 12-4 Levels of Variable Pay

	Individual Employee	Work Unit/Team	Organization-Wide
Best Used When	Output/results can be directly linked to specific employee	Interdependence and collaboration are critical to achieve results	Employees have solid line of sight to enterprise-level outcomes
Examples of Plan Design at This Level	◆ Piece-rate systems ◆ Bonuses ◆ Nonmonetary incentives ◆ Commissions	◆ Group/team results ◆ Gainsharing/goalsharing ◆ Quality improvement ◆ Cost reduction	◆ Profit sharing ◆ Employee stock plans ◆ Executive stock options

When an organization rewards an entire group for its performance, cooperation among the members may increase. The most common *work unit/team incentives* are gainsharing (or goalsharing) plans, whereby the employees in a work unit or group that meets certain performance goals share in the gains. Such programs often focus on quality improvement, cost reduction, and other measurable results.

Organizational incentives reward people based on the performance results of the entire organization. This approach assumes that all employees working together can generate improved organizational outcomes that lead to better financial performance. These programs often share some of the financial gains made by the firm with employees through payments calculated as a percentage of the employee's base pay. The most prevalent forms of organization-wide incentives are profit sharing plans and employee stock plans.

There are situations that are best suited to a particular level of incentive. Figure 12-4 shows the various incentive plans that fall under each category of variable pay and the optimal time to use each level of reward.[18] These different approaches are discussed individually in the sections that follow.

LO2 Compare three types of individual incentives.

12-2 Individual Incentives

Individual incentive systems tie personal effort to additional rewards for the individual employee. The conditions necessary to use individual incentive plans are as follows:

- *Individual performance must be identifiable.* The performance of each individual must be such that it can be identified and measured. Each employee must have job responsibilities and tasks that can be separated from those of other employees.
- *Individual competitiveness must be desirable.* Since individuals generally pursue the incentives for themselves, competition among employees may occur. Therefore, independent competition in which some individuals "win" and others do not must be something the employer can tolerate.
- *Individualism must be stressed in the organizational culture.* The culture of the organization must be one that emphasizes individual growth, achievements,

and rewards. If an organization emphasizes teamwork and cooperation, then individual incentives may be counterproductive.

- *Individuals must be in control of the pace of production.* Each employee should have the ability to increase or decrease effort and inputs to generate a particular level of performance.

12-2a Piece-Rate Systems

Piece-rate system
Pay system in which wages are determined by multiplying the number of units produced by the piece rate for one unit

The most basic individual incentive systems are piece-rate systems. Under a straight piece-rate system, wages are determined by multiplying the number of units produced (such as garments sewn or service calls handled) by the piece rate for one unit. Piece rate systems determine employee pay based on the level of output produced or work completed. Not everyone responds the same to piece-rate systems. Some work hard to make more money, others do the minimum. When workers are paid with a piece-rate system, inequality in pay naturally occurs. This inequality can lead to dysfunction within a work group, so training managers in the program specifics is helpful. The wage for each employee is easy to figure, and labor costs can be accurately predicted.

A *differential piece-rate system* pays employees one piece-rate wage for units produced up to a standard level of output and a higher piece-rate wage for units produced over the standard. Managers can determine the quotas or standards by using time and motion studies. For example, assume that the standard production quota for a worker is set at 300 units per day, and the standard rate is 25 cents per unit. In addition, for all units over the standard the employee receives 30 cents per unit. Under this system, the worker who produces 400 units in one day would earn $105 = (300 \times 25¢) + (100 \times 30¢)$. Many possible combinations of straight and differential piece-rate systems can be used.

Despite their incentive value, piece-rate systems can be difficult to apply because determining appropriate standards can be a complex and costly process for some types of jobs. In some instances, the cost of determining and maintaining the standards may be greater than the benefits derived. Also, jobs in which high standards of quality are necessary or individuals have limited control over output may be unsuited to piecework unless quality can be measured. Interestingly, although labor unions are usually not in favor of differential pay, piece-rate systems tend to be more accepted by union members and their leaders.[19] Typically, a time and motion study is conducted to establish the standard work pace and to determine what level of output leads to additional pay. The following "HR Competencies & Applications: Tracking Time and Motion" feature further explains how to conduct such a study.

12-2b Bonuses

Bonus
One-time payment that does not become part of the employee's base pay

Individual employees may receive additional compensation in the form of a bonus, which is a one-time payment that does not become part of the employee's base pay. Individual bonuses are used at all levels in firms and are a popular short-term incentive.

A bonus can recognize performance by an employee, a team, or the organization as a whole. When performance results are good, bonuses go up. When performance results are not met, bonuses go down or disappear. Many employers base part of an employee's bonus on individual performance and part on company results, as

COMPETENCIES & APPLICATIONS

Tracking Time and Motion

One of the most critical decisions managers make when implementing a piece-rate system is determining the base level of production that is required before additional output warrants incentive pay. Managers are inclined to demand a high level of production, while workers might be in favor of a much easier standard. The time and motion study process is a systematic analysis of the work that enables both managers and workers to feel confident when setting performance expectations.

A time and motion study is often conducted by an industrial engineer or job analyst who observes workers performing the job duties. A stopwatch is used to time each task, and detailed notes are taken to describe what the worker is doing. Using video can make the process much easier and faster. The job analyst usually observes a number of employees who perform the same job to get a balanced picture of how the job is done. It is important to note exceptions like machine breakdowns, out of stock materials, or other problems that the worker encounters, as this will affect the time on task.

After observing and recording the workers for several work cycles, the job analyst calculates the average time for each task in the operation and the average output produced by

each worker. In addition, the analysis typically involves reviewing historical production records to ensure that the time and motion study is accurately measuring expected output. Employees being studied for this purpose might otherwise be tempted to work slower in order to establish an easier standard of production.

A hospital in Michigan used time and motion studies to determine the percentage of time that health care providers spent on revenue-generating activities and those that did not generate revenue. This allowed the organization to determine clinical practice patterns, reassign work duties, and better utilize their skilled staffers for high-value work.[20] Consider the following questions now that you understand more about how time and motion studies are conducted:

1. If you were a worker being observed during a time and motion study, what possible reactions might you have to the process? How might your emotions impact your performance during the study?

2. What concerns would you have as a manager who was undertaking a time and motion study to establish incentive pay rates?

KEY COMPETENCIES: Critical Evaluation, Relationship Management, Business Acumen; HR Expertise: People/Total Rewards, Organization/Technology & Data

appropriate. However, according to recent research, 24% of companies award incentive payouts to employees who have not met performance expectations. Undermining the incentive potential of bonuses is a serious problem because it sends the wrong message to employees. Recommendations to reign in this counterproductive management behavior include the following:[21]

- Establish clear, metric-based employee reviews. Performance levels should be clearly stated and aligned with other reward and recognition programs.
- Ensure that employees who have not met performance criteria do not receive a payout. Instituting a review process and calibration session brings all the decisions into the open so that the managers' distribution of incentives is overseen by HR or upper management.

- Educate managers and employees about the incentive plan details. Make sure that employees understand how their performance will be evaluated and rewarded and that managers have clear guidelines for determining award levels.

Bonuses can also be used to reward employees for contributing new ideas, developing skills, or obtaining professional certifications. When an employee acquires valuable skills or certifications, a pay increase or a one-time learning bonus may follow. For example, Samsung financially rewards employees who submit applications for patents on the company's behalf. And at Genentech, a biotechnology firm, employees who are identified as MVPs for going above and beyond core job responsibilities receive a check for $1,000 to $2,500.[22]

"Spot" Bonuses A unique type of bonus is a spot bonus, so called because it can be awarded at any time. Spot bonuses are given for many reasons, perhaps for extra time worked, extra effort, or work on an especially demanding project. For instance, a spot bonus may be given to an information technology employee who installed a computer software upgrade that required extensive time and effort.

Often, spot bonuses are given in cash, although some firms allow managers to give gift cards, travel vouchers, or other noncash rewards. Noncash rewards vary in types and levels, but to be seen as desirable, they need to be visible and immediately useful. The keys to successful use of spot bonuses are to keep the amounts reasonable and to provide them only for exceptional performance accomplishments. The downside to their use is that they can create jealousy and resentment among other employees who believe that they deserved a spot bonus but did not get one.

Other Bonuses Employees may receive bonuses for almost anything noteworthy, but some common examples are referral bonuses (given for referring someone who is later hired), and hiring bonuses (given when someone agrees to hire on with a firm). Retention bonuses are used to keep a valuable employee with the company, and project completion bonuses are given upon completion of difficult projects.

12-2c Nonmonetary Incentives

Numerous nonmonetary incentives can be used to reward individuals, from one-time contests for meeting performance targets to awards for performance over time. For instance, safe-driving awards are given to truck drivers with no accidents or violations on their records during a year. Although such special programs can be developed for groups and for entire organizations, they often focus on rewarding individuals. Figure 12-5 shows several of the purposes for which nonmonetary incentives are used.

Advocates of nonmonetary incentives hold that there is a growing acceptance of noncash compensation for recognition purposes. In fact, they argue that recognition from an employee's manager may be highly valued, including a simple "Good morning" or "Thank you. I really appreciate the job you are doing."[23] However, research suggests that while nonmonetary incentives may have intrinsic motivating properties, employee perceptions of these rewards are influenced by several factors such as pay equity, organizational justice, and managerial discretion.

Performance Awards Merchandise, gift certificates, and travel are the most frequently used incentives for performance awards. Cash is still highly valued by

FIGURE 12-5 Purposes of Nonmonetary Incentives

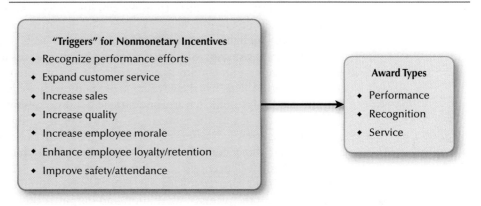

many employees because they can decide how to spend it. However, noncash incentives may be stronger motivators in some cases, according to a study that considered awards such as vacation cruises, home kitchen equipment, groceries, and other noncash items.[24] For instance, travel awards appeal to many U.S. employees, particularly trips to popular destinations such as Disney World, Las Vegas, Hawaii, and international locations. These examples show that many employees appreciate the trophy value of such awards and the variety they provide as much as the actual monetary value.

Recognition Awards Another type of program recognizes individual employees for their work. For instance, many organizations in industries such as hotels, restaurants, and retailers have established employee of the month and employee of the year awards. Hotels often use favorable guest comment cards as the basis for providing recognition awards to front-desk representatives, housekeepers, food and beverage workers, and other hourly employees.

Recognition awards often work best when given to acknowledge specific efforts and activities that the organization has identified as important. The criteria for selecting award winners may be determined subjectively in some situations. However, formally identified criteria provide greater objectivity and are more likely to be seen as rewarding performance rather than being based on favoritism. Companies often use factors such as new sales produced, customer service ratings, quality measures, or safety compliance. When giving recognition awards, organizations should use specific examples to clearly describe how those receiving the awards were selected.

Service Awards Another type of reward given to individual employees is the service award, typically given to recognize and reward longevity with the company. Many firms recognize length of service such as one year, five years, 10 years, and so on. The awards frequently increase in value as the length of service increases, and sometimes they are given as cash awards rather than as noncash gifts.

Some companies award gift cards to retail or restaurant locations, while others let qualifying employees select items from a range of merchandise choices (e.g., cameras or watches). The hottest new trend is to give iPads, televisions, and other technology gifts as part of service award programs. Firms can even offer employees special trips to resorts or social events. Sometimes, service awards are handed out at awards banquets or dinners to make employees feel special and to publicly acknowledge the value of long service.[25] Providing incentives at the individual level of performance highlights the unique contribution that each employee makes toward the organization's success. Since performance-based rewards are not integrated into employee base pay, an employee must continue to earn the incentive pay each year or reward period. This has the advantage of maintaining a high level of performance but can also lead to some tension and fatigue because employees are perpetually under the threat of losing the incremental pay. Using a combination of performance and entitlement rewards offers employees the possibility to earn additional rewards either through direct contributions or loyalty and commitment to the firm. [26]

Individual-level incentives are most effective when each employee's performance can be identified, isolated, measured, and rewarded. In many of today's organizations, teams are the primary work unit, and output is often accomplished through the combined efforts of several employees. Work unit/team reward plans are structured to address this issue.

12-3 Work Unit/Team Incentives

The use of teams in organizations has implications for incentive compensation. Although the use of teams has increased substantially in the past few years, the question of how to equitably compensate members remains a challenge. Studies have shown that while individuals who are incentivized increase their performance by 27%, teams that are incentivized increase their performance by 45%.[27] There are obviously substantial gains possible if team incentives are appropriately designed and administered.

Firms provide rewards for work units/teams for several reasons, as noted in Figure 12-6. Team incentives can take the form of cash bonuses for the members or noncash rewards such as paid time off, merchandise, or trips. Team incentive programs can place social pressure on members of the team because everyone in the group succeeds or fails together. Therefore, some argue that team incentives should be given to team members equally, although not everyone agrees.

12-3a Design of Work Unit/Team Variable Pay

LO3 Identify key concerns that must be addressed when designing work unit/team variable pay plans.

There are several key issues related to designing team variable pay plans. The main concerns are how and when to distribute the incentives and who will determine the incentive amounts.

Distribution of Work Unit/Team Incentives The two primary ways for distributing those rewards are as follows:

1. *Same size reward for each member*: All members receive the same payout, regardless of job level, current pay, seniority, or individual performance differences. This is the most common approach.
2. *Different size reward for each member*: Employers vary rewards given to team members depending on factors such as individual contribution to work unit/team results, current pay, years of experience, or skill levels of jobs performed.

FIGURE 12-6   Possible Reasons for Using Work Unit or Team Variable Pay

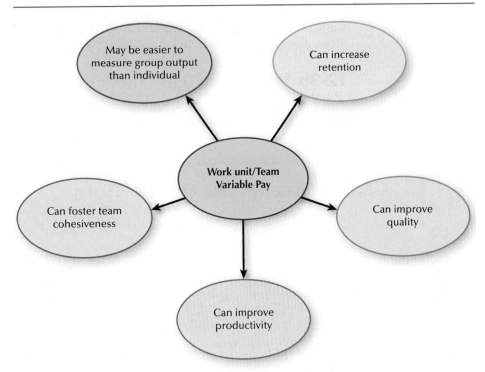

The size of the work unit/team incentive can be determined either by using a percentage of base pay for the individuals or the work unit/team as a whole, or by offering a specific dollar amount. For example, one firm pays members team bonuses based on a percentage of individual base rates that reflect years of experience and any additional training they have. Alternatively, the work unit/team reward could be distributed to all as an equal dollar amount.

Timing of Work Unit/Team Incentives The frequency of work unit/team incentive payouts is another important consideration. Payments may be made monthly, quarterly, semiannually, or annually, although the most common period used is annually. Shorter time periods increase the likelihood that employees will see a link between their efforts and the performance results that trigger award payouts, thus establishing a clear line of sight for team members. The nature of the teamwork, measurement criteria, and organizational results must all be considered when determining the appropriate time period.

Who Determines Work Unit/Team Incentive Amounts? To reinforce the effectiveness of working together, some work unit/team incentive programs allow members themselves to make decisions about how to allocate the rewards to individuals in the group. In some situations members vote, and in others a work unit/team leader decides. Of course, the incentive "pot" can be divided equally, thus avoiding conflict and recognizing that all members contributed equally to the team results. Many companies have found that team members are unwilling to make incentive decisions about coworkers. Consider the use of peer evaluations in many college classes. Team members are frequently reluctant to award minimal points to members who did not contribute out of concern for future encounters with fellow students. However, through training and coaching, team members can learn to better differentiate rewards among individuals on the team.[28]

12-3b Work Unit/Team Incentive Challenges

This difference between rewarding team members *equally* and rewarding them *equitably* triggers many of the problems associated with work unit/team incentives.

COMPETENCIES & APPLICATIONS

Getting Free Riders Off the Train

Working in teams can be a great experience when the camaraderie is high, team members are capable and motivated, and everyone pulls their share of the work load. Operating in teams can also be a terrible experience when some members don't give it their all and let others carry the burden.

Free riding, or social loafing, is a common problem in work teams. Since team results are often used to determine rewards for each member, negative feelings can occur when some members of the team don't contribute at the same level as others but still receive the team incentive award. High performers are the members most likely to quit in frustration, so managers can't ignore this toxic force on work teams.

How can managers avoid falling into the trap of allowing free riders on the train? Here are some guidelines for team structure that can reduce the chance that those free riders will receive undeserved rewards:

- Smaller teams are generally better, so limit the team to four or five members.
- Divide a complex task into manageable bits and make each team member accountable for specific portions of the overall task.
- Give every member of the team something personal to care about more than

themselves. Find out what matters most to each member of the team.
- Be transparent about how each member is doing on the tasks. Share feedback with all team members and provide coaching to those that are not working up to the required level.

Teams can be a powerful source of creativity, productivity, and innovation in organizations. Keeping all members focused and working toward team goals and incentive rewards means that managers have to engage each and every member and not allow free riders to sit idly by while everyone else performs well. Team dynamics will improve and the team will function more effectively if free riders get off the train.[31] Consider how social loafers impact work unit harmony and answer the following questions:

1. Consider a time when you worked on a class project or a project at work and some members of the team didn't pull their weight. How did you deal with it? What were the results?

2. What can work group leaders do to identify and deal with free riders on a work team?

KEY COMPETENCIES: Relationship Management, Ethical Practice; HR Expertise: People/Total Rewards, Organization/Organizational Effectiveness & Development

Rewards distributed in equal amounts to all members may be perceived as unfair by employees who work harder, have more capabilities, or perform more difficult jobs. This problem is compounded when an individual who is performing poorly prevents the work unit/team from meeting the goals needed to trigger the incentive payment.[29] Each organization should adopt a perspective that is consistent with the organization's core compensation philosophy.

Free rider
A member of the group who contributes little

A related challenge is that of "free riders" or "social loafers." A free rider is a member of the team who contributes little and rides on the efforts and success of the team. Further, some team members misrepresent their level of contribution because they believe it will not be easily detected. Such behavior can cause hard feelings and conflict in the group.[30] The preceding "HR Competencies & Applications: Getting Free Riders Off the Train" feature offers some recommendations to deal with free riders. Employee levels of trust in management and in the program design affect their perceptions of the fairness of how free riders are handled. Lack of trust can certainly reduce the value of any team variable pay plan. Social pressure from team members to hold down effort or results can also occur. Further, team agreement and pressure can result in cheating to dishonestly pad results.

Group size is another factor to consider when determining team incentives. If a group becomes too large, employees may feel that their individual efforts have little or no effect on the total performance of the group and the resulting rewards. But work unit/team incentive plans may also encourage cooperation in small work units where interdependence is high. Such plans have been used in many industries. Conditions for effective work unit/team incentives are shown in Figure 12-7. If these conditions cannot be met, then either individual or organizational incentives may be more appropriate.

FIGURE 12-7 Conditions for Effective Work Unit or Team Incentives

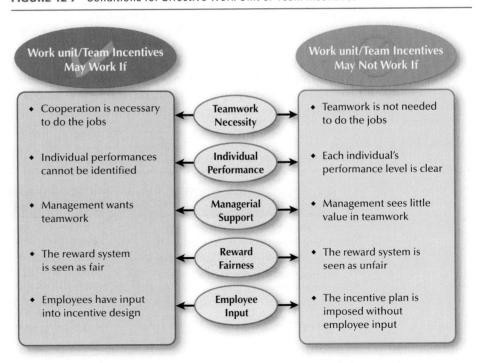

12-3c Types of Work Unit or Team Incentives

Work unit or team reward systems may compensate members in a number of ways. The two most common types of work unit or team incentives are team results and gainsharing.

Work Unit/Team Results Organizations may measure results such as group production, cost savings, customer satisfaction, or quality improvement. The work unit/team may be rewarded with cash bonuses, group awards, or some other incentive for exceeding expected results. The metrics chosen may be part of a balanced scorecard (as discussed in Chapter 2) that includes several important financial and nonfinancial measures deemed important for organization success.

Gainsharing
System of sharing with employees greater than expected gains in profits and/or productivity

Gainsharing The system of sharing greater than expected gains in profits and/or productivity with employees is gainsharing. To develop and implement a gainsharing plan, management establishes a baseline of expected performance based on historical standards. Then employees are involved with work teams to identify ways to improve productivity, quality, and/or financial performance above the baseline. These improvements lead to cost savings that are shared with employees. Managers and employees are trained in process assessment methods, and they share ideas and suggestions to create gains for the organization and the work team.

These group incentives may be based on a self-funding model, which means that the money used as rewards come from the improvement in organizational results (e.g., reduced costs). Measures such as productivity, spending, quality, and customer service benchmarks are often used.[32] Both organizational measures and departmental measures may be targeted, with the weights for gainsharing split between the two categories. Plans can also require that an individual in the group exhibit satisfactory performance to receive the gainsharing payments. Figure 12-8 outlines the pros and cons of using a gainsharing program.

Incentivizing employee performance efforts at the work unit or team level can certainly lead to cohesive teams that generate high productivity and innovation. However, the success of the organization as a whole rests on the contribution of each employee working toward important goals for the organization. Including an element of incentive pay based on organizational outcomes can ensure that every worker focuses on taking steps to fulfill those goals.

FIGURE 12-8 Pros and Cons of Gainsharing

Pros	Cons
• Leads to sustained improvements • Targets performance improvements • Aligns employees to organization goals • Fosters teamwork and continuous improvement	• Depends on participative management style • Requires open and transparent management communication • Measures must be carefully selected • Most successful when work context requires teamwork and collaboration

Source: Adapted from HR-Guide.com.

LO4 Specify why profit sharing and employee stock ownership are popular organizational incentive plans.

12-4 Organizational Incentives

An organizational incentive system compensates all employees according to how well the organization as a whole performs during the evaluation period. The basic concept behind organizational incentive plans is that overall results depend on organization-wide efforts and cooperation. The purpose of these plans is to produce better organizational results by rewarding cooperation. Organizational incentives get everyone in the company "rowing in the same direction." For example, the inherent conflict between marketing and production might be overcome if management uses an incentive system that emphasizes organization-wide profits and productivity.

To be effective, an organizational incentive program should include everyone from nonexempt employees to managers and executives. Two common organizational variable pay systems are profit sharing and employee stock plans.

12-4a Profit Sharing

Profit sharing
System to distribute a portion of an organization's profits to employees

As the name implies, profit sharing is a system to distribute a portion of organizational profits to employees. Giving employees a "piece of the action" can help enhance their commitment and increase job-related performance. The primary objectives of profit sharing plans can include the following:

- Improve organizational results
- Attract or retain employees
- Improve product/service quality
- Enhance employee morale
- Focus employees on organizational goals and objectives

Typically, the percentage of the profits distributed to employees is established by the end of the year before distribution, although both timing and payment levels might be determined later. In some profit sharing plans, employees receive their portions of the profits at the end of the year. In others, the payouts are deferred, placed in a fund, and made available to employees at retirement or at the time of their departure from the organization. In order to reward employees' loyalty and contributions to the company, Ikea recently started adding employees' profit sharing contributions to the company's existing 401(k) match.[33] Figure 12-9 shows how profit sharing plans can be funded and the money allocated. In recent years, some labor unions have supported profit sharing plans that tie employees' pay increases to improvements in broader organizational performance measures.

Challenges of Profit Sharing Plans While profit sharing plans can ensure that all employees pay attention to the organization's bottom line, there are some challenges associated with them. First, employees must trust that management will accurately disclose profit and other financial information. The definition and level of profit can depend on the accounting system used and on good and bad decisions made by those in top leadership roles. To be credible, management must be willing to disclose sufficient operational and financial information to alleviate the skepticism of employees, particularly if profit sharing levels fall from those of previous years. If profit sharing communication is done well, employee pay satisfaction and commitment can be improved.

FIGURE 12-9 Plan Design Choices for Profit Sharing Programs

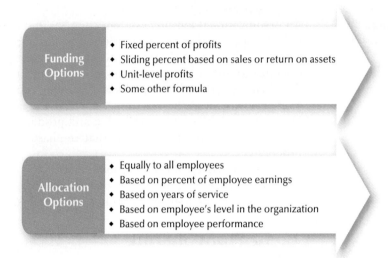

Funding Options
- Fixed percent of profits
- Sliding percent based on sales or return on assets
- Unit-level profits
- Some other formula

Allocation Options
- Equally to all employees
- Based on percent of employee earnings
- Based on years of service
- Based on employee's level in the organization
- Based on employee performance

Profits may vary a great deal from year to year, resulting in windfalls or losses beyond the employees' control. Payoffs are generally far removed in time from employees' individual efforts; therefore, higher rewards may not be obviously linked to better performance. Often the level of profits is influenced by factors not under the employees' control, such as accounting decisions, marketing efforts, competition, and elements of executive compensation. When implementing a profit sharing plan, companies should pay special attention to how it is explained to employees and how open leaders are about the organization's financial performance.

12-4b Employee Stock Plans

Organizational incentive plans include stock ownership in the organization to reward employees. The goal of these plans is to get employees to think and act like owners.

Stock option plan
Gives employees the right to purchase a fixed number of shares of company stock at a specified price for a limited period of time

A stock option plan gives employees the right to purchase a fixed number of shares of company stock at a specified exercise price for a limited period of time. If the market price of the stock exceeds the exercise price, employees can then exercise the option and buy the stock. The number of firms giving stock options to nonexecutives has declined in recent years, primarily because of changing laws, accounting regulations, and shareholder opposition.[34] In fact, top management at online gaming company Zynga actually clawed back stock options from employees when the company was preparing to go public. Fearing that some underperforming employees would own too great a share of the company, the CEO opted to take their shares back if their performance didn't improve.[35] Stock options can be difficult for employees to understand, and they often underestimate the real value of what they receive, which highlights the importance of providing financial education to employees, especially those who are new to stock options.[36]

Employee stock ownership plan (ESOP) Designed to give employees significant stock ownership in their organizations

Employee Stock Ownership Plans Firms in many industries have an employee stock ownership plan (ESOP), which is designed to give employees significant stock ownership in their organizations. According to the National Center for Employee Ownership, an estimated 7,000 companies in the United States offer broad employee-ownership programs, covering about 13 million workers.[37] Firms in many industries have ESOPs. The ESOP Association recognized 45 companies for continuously maintaining their plans for 25 years or more,[38] so ESOPs are not a passing trend. They are an important ownership structure in many, especially smaller, U.S. companies.

Establishing an ESOP creates several advantages. Primarily, the firm can receive favorable tax treatment on the earnings earmarked for use in the ESOP. Another is that an ESOP gives employees a sense of ownership so that they make decisions that will benefit not only themselves but also the company. This can result in employees feeling that they share in the growth and profitability of their firm. Employee ownership may motivate employees to be more productive and focused on organizational performance.

Many people approve of the concept of employee ownership because it provides employees with a voice in important matters regarding company operations and decisions. However, ownership can also be a disadvantage for employees because their wages, salaries and retirement benefits depend on the performance of the organization. This situation poses even greater risk for retirees because the value of pension fund assets may also depend on how well the company performs. Financial downturns, bankruptcies, and other travails of some firms during tough economic times have illustrated that an ESOP does not necessarily guarantee success for the employees who become investors.

12-4c Measuring the Effectiveness of Variable Pay Plans

Firms in the United States offer a wide range of incentive pay options and spend significant amounts on incentive payouts.[39] With incentive expenditures increasing each year, it is crucial that the results of variable pay plans be measured to determine their success.

Various metrics can be used, depending on the nature of the plan and the goals set for it. Figure 12-10 shows examples of metrics that can be used to evaluate variable pay plans.

FIGURE 12-10 Possible Metrics for Variable Pay Plans

Organizational Performance	Sales Programs	HR Related
• Actual vs. planned change • Revenue growth • Return on investment • Change in average employee productivity	• Increase in market share • Customer acquisition rate • Growth in sales to existing customers • Customer satisfaction	• Employee satisfaction • Turnover costs • Absenteeism costs • Accident rates and workers' compensation costs

MEASURE

A common metric for incentive plans is return on investment (ROI). To illustrate a general ROI example, suppose a company wants to reduce absenteeism and decides to use a program that provides rewards in the form of lottery chances each month for employees who were not absent during the month. An ROI metric would look at the dollar value of the improvement minus the cost of the program divided by the total cost. So, if the value of the reduction in absenteeism were $100,000 per year and the program cost $85,000 calculations would be (100,000 − 85,000) / 85,000, for just over a 17% return on the investment.

To help managers make decisions, other metrics can also be used to evaluate programs. Regardless of the variable pay plan, employers should collect and analyze data to determine if the expenditures are justified by increased organizational operating performance. If the measures and analyses show positive results, the plan truly represents pay for performance. If not, the plan should be changed to one that is more likely to succeed.

Salespeople and executives are two employee groups unique in many ways from other employees because of the nature of their jobs, and their pay is often different as well. Both of these types of employees are typically tied to variable pay incentives more than other employees. A consideration of sales and executive pay follows.

12-5 Sales Compensation

Given their boundary spanning roles, close interaction with customers, and work autonomy, the compensation paid to sales employees is frequently partially or entirely tied to individual sales performance. Salespeople who sell more products and services receive more total compensation than those who sell less. Sales incentives are perhaps the most widely used individual incentives. The intent is to stimulate more effort from salespeople so that they sell more, thus benefiting them and their employers.

Jobs in sales in many organizations have changed in the past two decades. While salespeople are still responsible for generating revenue for a company, today's customers have more choices and more information, and a great deal of product customization and ordering are done online directly by the customer.[40] The evolution in technology has changed the historical balance of power between salespeople and their customers. Compensation plans now have to take into account the different role expected of salespeople. See the following "HR Perspective: Sales Commissions Run out of Gas" feature for an explanation of how Internet sales are impacting the auto sales process.

Sales commission programs can effectively drive the behavior of sales representatives, especially if the sales performance measures are based wholly or mostly on sales volume and revenues. However, some sales incentive programs may encourage unethical behavior, particularly when compensation of sales representatives is based solely on commissions. For instance, there have been consistent reports that individuals in other countries who are buying major industrial equipment have received bribes or kickbacks from sales representatives. The bribes are paid from the incentives received by the sales representatives. This criticism may apply especially with major transactions that generate high revenues, such as aircraft contracts or major energy-related products.

PERSPECTIVE

Sales Commissions Run out of Gas

Traditionally, car salespeople earned a commission that was calculated as a percentage of the profit from a sale. Thus, they were highly motivated to upsell customers to more expensive vehicles or to add on features that the customers might not need or want. This, of course, created an image of the car salesperson as a pushy, aggressive individual whose own bank account was a higher priority than satisfying a customer.

Enter the Internet age, a time when customers can find detailed information about cars online. The previous leverage that the salesperson had in terms of better information seems to have vanished. Before online sales began to dominate, on average, customers spent over six hours researching cars in person. Now, they spend closer to three hours actually in showrooms and test-driving vehicles. Today's customers come to the showroom to test-drive a car, but they already have a lot of facts and figures along with competitive pricing information. Sales representatives are now called product specialists to convey the message that their function is to answer questions and offer detailed information about each vehicle on the lot. The majority of their time is now spent responding to online inquiries and selling in the virtual marketplace.

Profit margins on new cars have decreased over the past decade, leaving dealership managers a lot less money available to use as commissions. A new compensation model is emerging to pay car salespeople. Salespeople receive a more generous base salary, and rather than a commission tied to profitability of a car sale, a flat per-vehicle stipend is paid; bonuses are earned for hitting overall sales targets each month. This has led to a lower-stress environment for car shoppers and a more pleasant experience.

Naturally, hard-core commission-based salespeople are having some difficulty adjusting to the new pay schemes, and many are leaving the business. However, customers are happier and are more likely to return to the dealership for service needs and future car purchases. Technology is changing how cars are sold and how salespeople are paid. Who knows what the future holds for how people and cars will find each other.[41] Having read about the changes in how car salespeople are paid, answer the following questions:

1. What recommendations would you make to the owner of a car dealership to help her make a smooth transition from commission-only compensation to a system based on units sold?

2. How would you deal with a "star" salespeople who is against moving away from a commission-only compensation plan? What options might you consider if he or she threatened to leave your dealership to work for a competitor?

12-5a Types of Sales Compensation Plans

LO5 Explain three ways in which sales employees are typically compensated.

Sales compensation plans can be of three general types—salary only, straight commission, and salary plus commission. Each type of sales compensation has some associated challenges, which are discussed in the following sections.

Salary Only Some companies pay salespeople only a salary. The *salary-only approach* is useful when an organization emphasizes serving and retaining existing accounts over generating new sales and accounts. This approach is also frequently used to protect the income of new sales representatives for a period of time while they are building up their clientele. Generally, the employer extends the salary-only approach for new sales representatives for no more than six months, at which point a results-based approach is adopted. Salespeople who want additional rewards often function less effectively in salary-only plans because they are less motivated to sell without additional performance-related compensation.[42]

Commission

A percentage of the revenue that is generated by sales that is given to an agent or salesperson.

Commission Plans A commission is a percentage of the revenue that is generated by sales that is given to an agent or salesperson. As such, a commission represents a potential incentive for employees who qualify. Tips can be similar, even though they are paid by the customer rather than the employer. A straight salary has *no* additional commission incentive, while a straight commission has all compensation tied to the incentive. Determining the best mix of salary and commission to fit a situation is one of the decisions compensation managers must make. Commissions are integrated into the pay earned by sales workers in three common ways: straight commission, salary plus commission, and bonuses.

Straight Commission In the *straight commission system*, a sales representative earns a percentage of the value of the sales generated. Consider a real estate agent selling homes who receives no compensation if he or she doesn't sell a home but who receives a percentage of the selling price for a home that is sold. The advantage of this system is that it requires the sales representative to sell in order to earn. The disadvantage is that it offers no financial security or predictability for the sales staff.

Draw

Amount advanced against, and repaid from, future commissions earned by the employee

To offset this insecurity, some employers use a draw system in which sales representatives can draw advance payments against future commissions. The amounts drawn are then deducted from future commission checks. Arrangements must be made for repayment of drawn amounts if individuals leave the organization before earning their draws in commissions. The use of draws is influenced by the ratio of fixed to variable pay. When a small percentage of pay is fixed and a large percentage is variable, employees are more likely to take draws to provide needed funds until the next incentive payout occurs.

Salary plus commission

Combines the stability of a salary with a commission based on sales generated

Salary Plus Commission or Bonuses The form of sales compensation used most frequently is salary plus commission, which combines the stability of a salary with the performance aspect of a commission. A common salary to commission split is 80% to 20% or 70% to 30%, although the split varies according to industry and numerous other factors.[43] Some organizations also pay salespeople salaries and then offer bonuses (calculated as a percentage of the base pay) tied to how well each employee meets various sales targets or other criteria. A related method is using *lump sum bonuses*, which may lead to salespeople working more intensively to get higher sales results.

12-5b Sales Compensation Management Perspectives

Sales incentives work well, especially when they are tied to the broad strategic initiatives of the organization and its specific marketing and sales strategies.[44] However, as the economic and competitive environment has become more complex, employers in many industries have faced challenges in generating sales. Therefore, firms need to more thoroughly analyze their sales compensation costs, assess how sales pay is influencing employees' performance efforts, and then evaluate the extent to which sales and profit goals are being met.[45]

Administering Sales Compensation Programs Effective administration of compensation plans affects how well the plan drives the desired performance of salespeople. Many plans are multitiered and can be very complex. Selling over the Internet introduces additional challenges to incentive compensation. Some sales organizations combine individual and group sales bonus programs. In these programs, a portion of the sales incentive is linked to the attainment of group sales goals. The variable pay results can be difficult to calculate and administer.

Internet-based software has helped employers administer programs and post results daily, weekly, or monthly. Salespeople can use this information to track their results. Administering incentives globally is difficult, but HR technology has helped as incentive management software has become widespread.[46] These systems are advantageous because they can track the performance of numerous employees worldwide who may be covered by different incentive plans.

Consider a company that has different product lines, geographic locations, and company subsidiaries, and imagine tracking the performance of hundreds or thousands of sales representatives for a sales incentive program. Or imagine manually tracking attendance, safety, and training incentives for firms with employees worldwide. These scenarios definitely present a number of managerial challenges. The development of software systems to measure and record such factors has been important in helping support and manage global sales forces more effectively.

MEASURE

12-5c Measuring Effectiveness of Sales Compensation

Effective design of sales compensation requires establishing clear performance criteria and measures. Figure 12-11 shows some possible metrics for sales compensation plans. Generally, no more than three sales performance measures should be used in a sales compensation plan. Otherwise, the plans lose their effectiveness. Some plans may be too simple, focusing only on the salesperson's pay and not on wider organizational objectives such as profitability or customer satisfaction. These plans might motivate salespeople to sell products or services that results in financial loss to the firm or offends customers who will look for alternative suppliers in the future. Taking a balanced approach that considers multiple stakeholders can result in a win-win situation for all parties.

Considering that so many organizations utilize sales incentive plans, it is logical to think such plans are effective. However, many sales compensation plans are not seen as effective by either salespeople or managers and executives. One problem

FIGURE 12-11   Possible Metrics for Sales Compensation

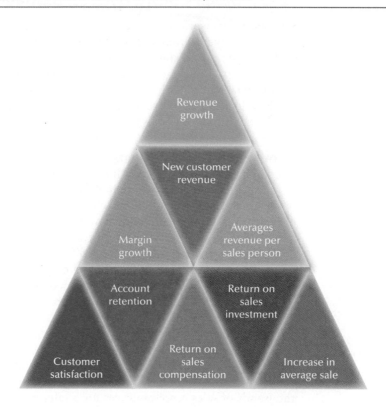

that can occur is when organizations make too many changes to sales incentives, which results in confusion. Excessive complexity also reduces the effectiveness of plans and creates problems with the sales representatives and managers. For example, a financial services company was not increasing revenues and was losing market share. Discussions with the sales staff revealed that none of them could explain how sales behaviors or making sales actually impacted their compensation. There were so many factors that entered into the equation that the salespeople just did the same thing each day because they could not figure out how their results actually drove their compensation.[47]

Effective sales incentives should ideally provide extra compensation for making sales, but sales managers warn that incentive systems will fail when a culture of entitlement takes hold in the salesforce. An entitlement culture can occur when employees come to see bonuses are *deferred salary* rather than extra pay for extra sales performance. When sales incentives designed to be extra pay for top performers become reliable paychecks on which everyone can count, entitlement has taken root and motivation drops.

Failure to deal with incentive programs that no longer motivate salespeople causes variable costs (pay for performance) to actually become fixed costs (salary) from the perspective of the employer. Pay without performance, poor quota setting, and little difference in pay between top and bottom performers cause these problems. Significant efforts are needed to establish and maintain effective sales incentive plans.

LO6 Identify the typical elements of executive compensation and discuss criticisms of executive compensation levels.

12-6 Executive Compensation

Executive compensation is handled differently from employee pay in most public companies, privately held companies, and even tax-exempt organizations.[48] The average CEO in the United States earns much less than those who head Fortune 100 companies. In fact, the Bureau of Labor Statistics reports that for the 250,000 CEOs in the United States, average annual salary was approximately $200,000. However, the pay packages of high-profile CEOs in large multinational firms overshadow this reality.[49] In the 300 largest U.S. companies, CEO pay averages over $10 million per year, which includes salary, bonuses, and stock options.[50] Stockholder activists argue that this pay is too high and is not tied closely enough to how well the company has performed—"pay for pulse," they call it. Corporate boards must work to preserve the reputation of the firm while also trying to create a compensation plan that will attract talented executives.[51]

From the 1940s through the 1970s there was little relationship between executive compensation and firm growth. However, the correlation has grown somewhat stronger in the past 30 years.[52] Ongoing outrage and dissatisfaction over executive pay is part of a mix of economic and social problems, including the growing gap between rich and poor. Defining what is wrong with C-suite (CEO, CFO, CHRO, etc.) pay is difficult, but it serves as a "hot button" for unions, corporate governance watchdogs, and lawmakers. In fact, the Dodd-Frank Wall Street Reform and Consumer Protection Act requires public companies to disclose the mathematical relationship between CEO total compensation and average employee total compensation. The Securities and Exchange Commission recently released rules regarding this reporting which will highlight the differences between executives' pay levels and that of lower-level workers.[53] What do CEOs do to earn all that money? Ideally, they should do three things well:

- Establish strategic direction for the organization
- Create shareholder value
- Ensure the sustainability of the enterprise

Establishing strategic direction requires good judgment, knowledge of the business and the industry, and a bit of a crystal ball view to accurately see what is coming. *Creating shareholder value* includes revenue growth, operating margins, net sales, earnings per share, and other financial measures valued by investors/owners. *Ensuring the sustainability of the enterprise* includes balancing social, environmental, and financial concerns with a focus on conscious deployment of resources to provide a sound future for the organization.[54] Clearly, being a successful CEO requires a complex set of skills and personal investment in the firm, and it is not a job everyone can do well.

12-6a Executive Compensation Controversy

At the heart of most executive compensation plans is the idea that executives should be rewarded if the organization grows in profitability and value over a period of years and be penalized if the executive fails to produce positive results. Variable pay distributed through different types of incentives is a significant part of executive compensation in organizations, both in the United States and around the world. Executive compensation, however—like business itself—should include an element of risk for the executive, and risk should be an integral part of an incentive plan. The executive suite should not provide an environment free of consequences. When the organization underperforms, senior managers should see their payouts and stock holdings fall.

Traditionally, companies have looked to other organizations in the same or a similar industry and of similar size as comparators to determine what the level of executive compensation should be. A potential downside of using this method is that CEO compensation tends to ratchet up as each company tries to pay its CEO above the average.[55] An additional complication is that many CEOs serve on the governing boards of other companies. They often have input on executive compensation plans and are inclined to provide pay similar to what they themselves receive. This approach has led to executive compensation that is perceived as excessive, and many outspoken opponents are making their opinions known.

12-6b Reigning in Executive Compensation

Shareholders and lawmakers are two groups that have pressed the hardest for some moderating of executive pay. Powerful and vocal shareholders may attempt to influence the process through the organization's governance process, while lawmakers enact statutes that include limits on executive compensation.

A provision of the Dodd-Frank Act requires public corporations to allow shareholders to vote on the presumed fairness of pay packages for the CEO and the other four highest-paid executives. The company's leadership team is not required to accept the shareholders' decision, so while it may seem that shareholders have a "say on pay," their opinions may fall on deaf ears. The main benefit of this law is increased transparency about how executives are compensated.[56]

The "clawback" provisions in the Sarbanes-Oxley and Dodd-Frank Acts allow for the recovery of incentive-based pay that was provided to executives and later determined to have been paid under false pretenses. For example, employee misconduct and restated earnings may be discovered some time after an incentive payment has been made. The Securities and Exchange Commission can demand repayment from an executive if such a case is proven. In reality, very few clawbacks have been invoked because establishing intentional misconduct can be quite difficult in complex cases, though perhaps the threat of clawbacks has decreased executive misconduct and earnings manipulation.[57] In any case, public corporations must now develop and share their policies on compensation clawbacks so that shareholders understand the process that has been adopted by the governance team.[58]

12-6c Elements of Executive Compensation

Many executives are in high tax brackets and receive many tax-favored compensation elements, so their total compensation packages often consist of much more than just their base pay. Executives are often interested in compensation and the mix of items in the total package because it affects the amount of actual value after taxes. Figure 12-12 illustrates common elements of executive compensation packages.

Executive Salaries The type of job, the size of the organization, the industry, and other factors all influence executive salaries. In some organizations, particularly nonprofits, salaries often make up 90% or more of total compensation. In contrast,

FIGURE 12-12 Elements of Executive Compensation Packages

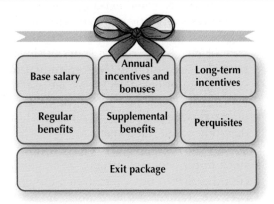

in large corporations, salaries may constitute less than half of a total executive compensation package. Executive salaries are reviewed by boards of directors to ensure that their organizations are competitive.

Executive Benefits Many executives are covered by *regular benefit plans* that are also available to nonexecutive employees, including retirement, health insurance, and vacation plans. In addition, executives may receive *supplemental benefits* that other employees do not receive. For example, corporate-owned insurance on the life of the executive is popular. This insurance pays both the executive's estate and the company in the event of death. Another supplemental benefit that has grown in popularity is company-paid financial planning for executives. Also, trusts of various kinds may be designed by the company to help executives deal with estate-planning and tax issues. *Deferred compensation* is another way of helping executives with tax liabilities created by incentive compensation plans.

Executive Perquisites (Perks) In addition to the regular benefits received by all employees, executives often also receive perquisites. Perquisites (perks) are special benefits—usually noncash items—for executives. Many executives value the status enhancement of these visible symbols, which allow the executives to be seen as "very important people" both inside and outside their organizations. Perks can offer substantial tax savings because some of them are not taxed as income.[59] Some popular executive perks are company cars, health club and country club memberships, first-class air travel, home security systems, use of private jets, stress counseling, and chauffeur services.

Perquisites (perks)
Special benefits—usually noncash items—for executives

Annual Executive Bonuses Annual bonuses for senior managers and executives can be determined in several ways. One way is to use a discretionary system whereby the CEO and the board of directors decide bonuses. The absence of formal, measurable targets may detract significantly from the pay for performance element of this approach. Another way is to tie bonuses to specific measures, such as return on investment, earnings per share, and net profit before taxes. More complex systems create bonus pools and thresholds above which bonuses are computed. Whatever method is used, it is important to describe it so that executives attempting to earn additional compensation understand the plan; otherwise, the incentive effect will be diminished.

Long-Term Incentives (LTI) To ensure that executives look beyond the immediate future when making critical decisions, executives' performance-based incentives should tie compensation to the long-term growth and success of the organization.[60] However, whether these incentives really emphasize the long term or merely represent a series of short-term successes is uncertain. Short-term rewards based on quarterly or annual performance may not result in the kind of long-run-oriented decisions necessary for the company to perform well over many years. As would be expected, the total amount of pay for performance incentives varies by management level, with CEOs receiving significantly more than other senior managers.

Executives frequently receive a stock option that gives them the right to buy stock in the company, usually at an advantageous price. Stock options were discussed earlier in this chapter. In addition to standard stock options, many executives are granted *restricted stock options*. A restricted stock option indicates that company stock shares will be paid as a grant of shares to individuals, usually linked to achieving specific performance criteria. The purpose of providing these equity awards is to encourage executives to "think like owners" and make business decisions that are in the firm's best interests.

Despite the prevalence of such plans, research has found little relationship between providing CEOs with stock options and subsequent firm performance. Recent corporate scandals involving executives who received outrageously high compensation due to backdating of stock options have led to a more measured approach to utilizing this form of incentive compensation.[61]

Restricted stock option
Indicates that company stock shares will be paid as a grant of shares to individuals, usually linked to achieving specific performance criteria

Exit Packages While severance packages and pension payments may not ordinarily make the headlines, special executive compensation for separation agreements and payouts as the executive is leaving are controversial. The payouts occur right at the time people are often unhappy with the executive and may appear unfair.[62] For example, a veteran executive at GE received over $25 million worth of benefits when he left and guaranteed that he would not compete with GE. His exit allowance represented "a generous severance package in exchange for his non-compete agreement," a consultant noted.[63] Controversy has also erupted over the "golden parachutes" provided to bank executives who leave to take jobs working for government agencies that oversee the financial industry. In a number of cases, vesting on long-term incentives was accelerated, and policies for stock options were bypassed. These exceptions call into question the fairness of pay policy application.[64]

GLOBAL

12-6d Global Executive Compensation

As firms based in both the United States and other countries expand globally, executive compensation issues are raised. Numerous executives have responsibilities for operations throughout the world, and they are compensated for those expanded responsibilities. However, senior executives in the United States continue to earn higher salaries than similar executives in other countries.

In the United States, critics of executive pay levels point out that many U.S. corporate CEOs have a ratio value of more than 350 times that of the average worker in their firms, while in Switzerland the ratio is 148, in the United Kingdom it is 84, and in Poland it is 28. When people around the world are asked to state the ideal ratio for CEO pay compared to the average worker, they generally state that a 5:1 ratio is desirable. So, actual and "ideal" ratios are quite far apart, which may explain why executive pay is typically seen as unreasonable.[65]

MEASURE

12-6e Measuring the Effectiveness of Executive Compensation

Executive bonuses and incentives. Customer satisfaction, employee satisfaction, market share, learning and development, productivity, and quality are other areas that can be measured to determine executive performance rewards.

Measurement of executive performance varies from one company to another. Some executive compensation packages use a short-term focus of one year, which may lead to large rewards for executive performance in a given year even though corporate performance over a multiyear period is mediocre, especially if the yearly measures are not carefully chosen. Executives may manipulate earnings per share by selling assets, liquidating inventories, or reducing research and development expenditures.[66] All of these actions may make organizational performance look better in the short run but impair the long-term growth of the organization.

Other executive compensation issues and concerns exist. Figure 12-13 highlights some of the criticisms and counterarguments related to executive compensation. One of the more controversial issues is that some executives seem to receive large awards for negative actions. Some people find it contradictory to reward executives who improve corporate results by cutting staff, laying off employees,

FIGURE 12-13 Point/Counterpoint Regarding Executive Compensation

Point	Counterpoint
Executive compensation often does not reflect company performance.	A competitive market for executives drives compensation package increases.
Boards give sizable rewards to both high- and low-performing executives.	The CEO is in charge and responsible for results.
Executives should not get rewards and bonuses for laying off much of the workforce.	Sports and entertainment stars earn as much as executives, or more, for playing games and acting.
Total compensation packages are excessive.	CEOs earn their money with endless hours, extraordinary stress, and major decisions.
Many people, not just the CEO, contribute to the success of a company.	Measuring company performance by short-term earnings and stock prices is insufficient.

negatively changing pension plans, or increasing health insurance deductibles, although sometimes cost-cutting measures are necessary to keep a company afloat.[67] However, a sense of reasonableness must be maintained. If rank-and-file employees are suffering, giving bonuses and large payouts to executives appears counterproductive and even hypocritical.

Incentives must be thoughtfully designed and carefully managed to produce the desired results. Employees from front-line workers to top executives pay attention to what behaviors and decisions will earn them the greatest rewards. Therefore, designing incentives to focus them on valued organization outcomes is central to effective incentive programs.

SUMMARY

- Variable pay, also called incentive pay, is compensation that can be linked to individual, work unit/team, and/or organizational performance.
- Effective variable pay plans fit both business strategies and organizational cultures, appropriately award actions, and are administered properly.
- Metrics for measuring the success of variable pay plans are available.
- Piece-rate and bonus plans are commonly used individual incentives.
- The design of work unit/team variable pay plans must consider how the incentives are to be distributed, the timing of the incentive payments, and who will make decisions about the variable payout.
- Organization-wide rewards include profit sharing and stock ownership plans.
- Sales employees may have their compensation tied to performance on several criteria. Sales

compensation can be provided as salary only, commission only, or salary plus commission or bonuses.
- Measuring the effectiveness of sales incentive plans is a challenge that may require the plans to be adjusted on the basis of success metrics.
- Executive compensation must be viewed as a total package composed of salaries, bonuses, benefits, perquisites (perks), and both short- and long-term performance-based incentives.
- Performance-based incentives often represent a significant portion of an executive's compensation package.
- A compensation committee, which is a subgroup of the board of directors, generally has authority over executive compensation plans. In addition, shareholders of public corporations have the right to vote on executive pay packages.

CRITICAL THINKING CHALLENGES

1. Discuss why variable pay-for-performance plans have become popular and what elements are needed to make them successful.
2. What are some key performance indicators that are used by organizations in which you have been employed? How did managers explain the importance of these KPIs, and were any rewards tied to them?
3. Describe how team rewards have been used in group projects you worked on in college classes or on the job. What challenges did you face when asked to give peer evaluations when there were "free riders" on your team, and how did you deal with them?
4. Suppose you have been asked to lead a task force to develop a sales incentive plan at

your firm. The task force is to generate a list of strategies and issues to be evaluated by upper management. Using details from www.salescompensation.org and other related websites, identify and develop preliminary materials for the task force.

5. Recent research has shown an inverse relationship between CEO pay and corporate performance. Read the article "The Highest-Paid CEOs Are the Worst Performers, New Study Says" at http://www.forbes.com/sites/susanadams/2014/06/16/the-highest-paid-ceos-are-the-worst-performers-new-study-says or related articles. Assume that you are the public

relations professional who must respond to recent inquiries from major investors regarding the compensation and performance of your company's CEO.

A. What information would you review as you prepare your statement? Would you share different information with the general public than you would with investors? If so, what information and why?

B. As a potential investor, how would the CEO's compensation affect your decision of whether to invest in a company? Why or why not?

CASE   Want to Earn a Bonus? Work for Uncle Sam

There is generally much criticism when it comes to compensating executives employed in for-profit business. But federal employees in a number of agencies also reaped generous incentive pay despite subpar performance, including when they made decisions contrary to their agency's mission and values.

The Internal Revenue Service (IRS) handed out nearly $3 million in performance bonuses to 2,800 employees who had recently been disciplined. The employees had committed a wide range of infractions, including fraud, failure to pay taxes, and misuse of government travel cards. Some of the employees had been disciplined with reprimands, suspension, and even termination. However, the IRS generally doesn't take into account such conduct issues when determining bonuses. IRS employees who are represented by a labor union are not prevented from receiving a performance bonus even if they are subject to disciplinary action.

The situation at the Veterans Administration was even more outrageous. Nearly $300 million in annual bonuses were distributed at this provider of health care to American military veterans. A scandal erupted when it was discovered that to meet agency performance metrics, treatment for many veterans

was delayed. To encourage higher productivity, the VA management team changed performance targets for claims processors between 2010 and 2012. VA claims processors would be rewarded for processing a high volume of claims. Difficult, complicated cases were set aside because they were time-consuming to process and would result in no bonus for the processor. The incentive system worked, but at what cost?

Incentives were not limited to claims processors. Executives at the VA earned performance bonuses as well—totaling $2.7 million. Allegations of misrepresenting patient wait times to make it appear that services were provided on a timely basis have spread throughout the VA system. Performance bonuses were paid to VA hospitals that had low backlogs for treatment. In an effort to earn the incentives, some employees were directed not to put veterans on wait lists, making it appear that wait times were short.

Federal officials took the agency's leadership to task and noted that there was an extreme reluctance to hold employees and executives accountable. Decisions made by many of these managers caused harm to veterans seeking health care. After a unanimous vote to eliminate all bonuses, lawmakers reversed themselves a few months later in 2014 when they reinstated the bonus program but capped it at $360 million per year.[68]

QUESTIONS

1. What dynamics at the IRS and VA may have contributed to actions employee took to earn a bonus?

2. What recommendations would you have for using incentive programs at these agencies in the future?

3. If you were able to vote on this pay package ("say on pay"), how would you vote and why?

SUPPLEMENTAL CASES

Best Buy Pays Big Bucks for CEO

This case deals with CEO pay for a newly hired executive at Best Buy. (For the case, go to www .cengage.com/management/mathis.)

Cash Is Good, Card Is Bad

Both positive and negative issues associated with the use of an incentive plan are discussed in this case. (For the case, go to www.cengage.com/management/mathis.)

Incentive Plans for Fun and Travel

This case discusses incentive plans that stimulate employee interest and motivate them to perform well. (For the case, go to www.cengage .com/management/mathis.)

Sodexo Incentives

This case shows how a large firm uses recognition and awards. (For the case, go to www.cengage.com/management/mathis.)

END NOTES

1. Based on Sara Turner, "KPMG's Employee Recognition Programme: Encore!" *People Management*, July 2012, p. 57.
2. Amy Lynn Flood, "High Hopes for Performance-Based Equity," *Workspan*, April 2012, pp. 27–32.
3. Stephen Miller, "Variable Pay Spending Spikes to Record-High Level," *SHRM Online*, September 2, 2014, http://www.shrm.org/hrdisciplines/compensation/articles/pages/variable-pay-high.aspx.
4. Anne C. Gielen et al., "How Performance Related Pay Affects Productivity and Employment," *Journal of Population Economics* 23 (2010), 291–301.
5. Thomas Dohmen and Armin Falk, "Performance Pay and Multidimensional Sorting: Productivity, Preferences, and Gender," *American Economic Review* 101 (2011), 556–590.
6. Gary Charness and Uri Gneezy, "Strong Evidence for Gender Differences in Risk Taking," *Journal of Economic Behavior & Organization* 83, no. 1 (June 2012), 50–58.
7. Christopher Cerasoli, Jessica Nicklin, and Michael Ford, "Intrinsic Motivation and Extrinsic Incentives Jointly Predict Performance: A 40-Year Meta-Analysis," *Psychological Bulletin* 140, no. 4 (July 2014), 980–1008.
8. Robert Greene, "Variable Compensation: Good Fit to Turbulent Environments," *Compensation & Benefits Review* 44, no. 6 (November 2012), 308–314.
9. Christopher Bergeron and Mark Szypko, "Aligning Goal Setting and Incentive Pay," *Workspan*, January 2012, pp. 44–47.
10. Pankaj Madhani, "Aligning Compensation Systems with Organization Culture," *Compensation & Benefits Review* 46, no. 2 (March 2014), 103–115.
11. Stephen Miller, "Make Way for Variable Pay," *SHRM Online*, June 27, 2012, http://www.shrm.org/hrdisciplines/compensation/

articles/pages/makewayforvariable-pay.aspx.

12. Terry Satterfield, "The Role of Merit Pay in Bonuses and Incentives," *Workspan*, February 2011, pp. 40–45.

13. David Gill, Victoria Prowse, and Michael Vlassopoulos, "Cheating in the Workplace: An Experimental Study of the Impact of Bonuses and Productivity," *Journal of Economic Behavior & Organization* 96 (December 2013), 120–134; Charlie Gilkey, "The Difference between Critical Success Factors and Key Performance Indicators," *ProductiveFlourishing.com*, September 12, 2012, http://www.productiveflourishing.com/the-difference-between-critical-success-factors-and-key-performance-indicators/#sthash.cFOeAetj.dpuf.

14. David Parmenter, "Setting KPIs That Genuinely Support Corporate Strategy," *Charter* 84, no. 6 (July 2013), 32.

15. Mindtools, "Performance Management and KPIs: Linking Activities to Vision and Strategy," http://www.mindtools.com/pages/article/newTMM_87.htm.

16. WorldatWork Newsline, "Cash Bonuses Important in Global M&As, Only Part of Equation to Retain Key Talent," October 8, 2014, http://www.worldatwork.org/adimComment?id=76052&from=Compensation%20News.

17. Based on Jacque Vilet, "Differences in Variable Pay Plans around the World," *Compensation Café*, November 11, 2011, http://www.compensationcafe.com/2011/11/differences-in-variable-pay-plans-around-the-world-and-trends-for-the-future.html.

18. Stephen Miller, "Incentive Compensation Tips and Pitfalls Shared," *SHRM Online*, June 1, 2012, http://www.shrm.org/hrdisciplines/compensation/articles/pages/incentivetips.aspx; WorldatWork, "Types of Compensation," http://www.worldatwork.org/home/html/compensation_home.jsp.

19. Patrick O'Halloran, "Union Coverage, Membership and Performance-Related Pay: Are Piece Rates Different?" *National Institute Economic Review* 226, no. 1 (November 2013), 30–41.

20. Based on Folusho Ogunfiditimi, Lisa Takis, Virginia Paige, Janet Wyman, and Elisa Marlow, "Assessing the Productivity of Advanced Practice Provides Using a Time and Motion Study," *Journal of Healthcare Management* 58, no. 3 (May–June 2013), 173–185; Puniavathi Puranam and Pramila Adavi, "Time and Motion Study, Analysis through Statistics," *NBM Media*, May 2012, http://www.nbmcw.com/articles/case-studies/28978-time-and-motion-study-analysis-through-statistics.html.

21. Joanne Sammer, "Not an Entitlement: Keep Bonuses Performance-Based," *SHRM Online*, June 2, 2014, http://www.shrm.org/hrdisciplines/compensation/articles/pages/performance-based-bonuses.aspx.

22. Lisa Bodell, "11 Non-Traditional Ways to Reward Innovative Employees," *TLNT Online*, September 2014, http://www.tlnt.com/2014/09/01/11-non-traditional-ways-to-reward-innovative-employees/.

23. Tom Starner, "The Value of Incentives," *Human Resource Executive Online*, April 18, 2012, http://www.hreonline.com/HRE/view/story.jhtml?id=533346834&ss=%22risk+management%22&s=18.

24. Melissa Van dyke and Mike Ryan, "Changing the Compensation Conversation and the Growing Utility of Noncash Rewards and Recognition," *Compensation & Benefits Review* 44, no. 5 (September 2012), 276–279.

25. Crawford, Robert, "Top Five Long-Service Awards for Employees," *Employee Benefits*, December 23, 2013, p. 1.

26. Barry Gerhart and Meiyu Fang, "Pay for (Individual) Performance Issues, Claims, Evidence and the Role of Sorting Effects," *Human Resource Management Review* 24, no. 1 (March 2014), 41–52.

27. Andrew Marshall, "Making Team Incentives Work," *SHRM Online*, August 9, 2013, http://www.shrm.org/hrdisciplines/compensation/articles/pages/team-incentives-work.aspx.

28. Terry Wagar and Wendy Carroll, "Examining Student Preferences of Group Work Evaluation Approaches: Evidence From Business Management Undergraduate Students," *Journal of Education for Business* 87, no. 6 (November–December, 2012), 358–362; Toni Vranjes, "Employers Embrace Peer-to-Peer Recognition," *HR Magazine*, November 2014, pp. 54–56.

29. Yvonne Garbers and Udo Konradt, "The Effect of Financial Incentives on Performance: A Quantitative Review of Individual and Team-Based Financial Incentives," *Journal of Occupational & Organizational Psychology* 87, no. 1 (March 2014), 102–137.

30. Julian Conrads, Bernd Irlenbusch, Rainer Rilke, and Gari Walkowitz, "Lying and Team Incentives," *Journal of Economic Psychology* 34 (February 2013), 1–7.

31. Based on Mark deRond, "Why Less Is More in Teams," *HBR Blog Net*, August 6, 2012, http://blogs.hbr.org/2012/08/why-less-is-more-in-teams/; Michaela Schippers, "Social Loafing Tendencies and Team Performance: The Compensating Effect of Agreeableness and Conscientiousness," *Academy of Management Learning & Education* 13, no. 1 (March 2014), 62–81; Joseph Ferrari and Timothy Pychyl, "If I Wait, My Partner Will Do It: The Role of Conscientiousness as a Mediator in the Relation of Academic Procrastination and Perceived Social Loafing," *North American Journal of Psychology* 14, no. 1 (2012), 13–24.

32. Robert Masternak, "Compensation: Incentive Plans. Gainsharing," *HR-Guide.com*, http://www.hr-guide.com/data/G443.htm.

33. Stephen Miller, "Ikea Initiates Annual 401(k) Profit Sharing Bonuses," *SHRM Online*, December 23, 2013, http://www.shrm.org/hrdisciplines/benefits/articles/pages/ikea-401k-profitsharing.aspx.

34. Valerie H. Diamond, "Global Plan Design and Compliance Strategies for ESPP," *Workspan*, September 2012, pp. 37–40; Daniel Gilbert, "Cheniere Withdraws Employee Stock Plan," *Wall Street Journal*, July 2, 2014, p. B11; Mike Esterl and Joann Lublin, "Coke Scales Back Stock Options," *Wall Street Journal*, October 2, 2014, p. B1.

35. Thomas Smith, "The Zynga Clawback: Shoring up the Central Pillar

of Innovation," *Santa Clara Law Review* 53, no. 2 (August 22, 2013), Article 4; Evelyn Rusli, "The Education of Zynga's Founder," *Wall Street Journal*, November 16, 2012, p. B1.

36. Meni Abudy and Efrat Shust, "Employees' Attitudes toward Equity-Based Compensation," *Compensation & Benefits Review* 44, no. 5 (September 2012), 246–253.

37. NCEO.org, "How an Employee Stock Ownership Plan (ESOP) Works," http://www.nceo.org/articles/esop-employee-stock-ownership-plan; Ruth Simon, "Firms Rethink ESOP Sale Practices," *Wall Street Journal*, November 20, 2014, p. B8.

38. The ESOP Association, "The ESOP Association Announces 2014 Silver ESOP Award Recipients," April 16, 2014, http://www.esopassociation.org/about-the-association/esop-awards/silver-esop-awards.

39. Stephen Miller, "Employers Award a Wider Variety of Incentive Pay," *SHRM Online*, March 21, 2014, http://www.shrm.org/hrdisciplines/compensation/articles/pages/incentive-pay-variety.aspx.

40. Scott Gillum, "The Disappearing Sales Process," *Forbes.com*, January 7, 2013, http://www.forbes.com/sites/gyro/2013/01/07/the-disappearing-sales-process/.

41. Based on Matt Jones, "Saying Good-Bye to Commission-Based Sales," *Edmunds.com*, February 27, 2014, http://www.edmunds.com/car-buying/saying-good-bye-to-commission-based-car-sales.html; Christina Rogers, "Saying Goodbye to the Car Salesman," *Wall Street Journal*, November 20, 2013, http://online.wsj.com/articles/SB10001424052702304672404579182061400578466.

42. Pankaj Madhani, "Realigning Fixed and Variable Pay in Sales Organizations: A Career Life Cycle Perspective," *Compensation & Benefits Review* 45, no. 4 (July 2013), 223–230.

43. Desmond Lo et al., "The Incentive and Selection Roles of Sales Force Compensation Contracts," *Journal of Marketing Research* 48 (2011), 781–798.

44. Pankaj Madhani, "Managing Sales Compensation: A Sales Force Configuration Approach," *Compensation & Benefits Review* 45, no. 2 (March 2013), 105–114.

45. Ines Küster and Pedro Canales, "Compensation and Control Sales Policies, and Sales Performance: The Field Sales Manager's Points of View," *Journal of Business and Industrial Marketing* 26 (2011), 273–285.

46. Justin Lane, "Challenges in Sales Compensation Administration," *Workspan*, August 2012, pp. 25–27.

47. Steven Slutsky, "Tips for Designing the Next Generation of Sales Compensation Programs," *Workspan*, October 2012, pp. 31–34.

48. Mark Stockwell and Eric Chapman, "Pay for Performance for Executives in Tax-Exempt Organizations," *Workspan*, October 2012, pp. 36–44.

49. Mark Perry and Michael Saltsman, "About That CEO/Employee Pay Gap," *Wall Street Journal*, October 13, 2014, p. A17.

50. Scott Thurm, "What's a CEO Worth? More Firms Say $10 Million," *Wall Street Journal*, May 15, 2013.

51. Scott Highhouse, Nicole Wood, Christopher Lake, and Sara Kirkendall, "Dispositional and Contextual Moderators of Public Outrage over Outsized Executive Bonuses," *Corporate Reputation Review* 17, no. 4 (October 2014), 290–299; Eric Hosken and Shaun Bisman, "The Key to Evaluating Executive Pay for Performance," *Workspan*, May 2013, pp. 35–38; Joann Lublin and Shira Ovide, "Discontent Mounts over CEO Pay at Oracle," *Wall Street Journal*, September 25, 2013; Theo Francis and Joann Lublin, "CEO Pay Keeps Rising, but Not as Quickly, Not for All," *Wall Street Journal*, March 27, 2014, p. B1.

52. Scott Olsen, "A New Perspective on the Executive Compensation Debate," *Workspan*, June 2013, pp. 47–52; Scott Thurm, "Pay for Performance No Longer a Punchline," *Wall Street Journal*, March 21, 2013, p. B1.

53. Donald Kalfen, "Comment on Proposed SEC Reporting Requirement: The CEO Pay Ratio," *Compensation & Benefits Review* 45, no. 5 (September 2013), 262–264; Joann Lublin, "The Boss Makes How Much More Than You?" *Wall Street Journal*, November 26, 2014, p. B9. Victoria McGrane and Joann Lublin,

"SEC Rule to Require Disclosure of Pay Gap," *Wall Street Journal*, August 5, 2015, B1-2.

54. Kimberly Merriman and Sagnika Sen, "Incenting Managers toward the Triple Bottom Line: An Agency and Social Norm Perspective," *Human Resource Management* 51, no. 6 (November–December, 2012), 851–872; Mark McGraw, "Getting CEO Appraisal Right," *Human Resource Executive*, July–August, 2013, pp. 38–39.

55. Charles Elson and Craig Ferrere, "Executive Superstars, Peer Groups, and Overcompensation: Cause, Effect, and Solution," *Journal of Corporation Law* 38, no. 3 (Spring 2013), 487–531; Todd Henneman, "A Bonus Onus: Peek at Peers," *Workforce*, June 2014, p. 14; Dan Lin, Kuo Hsien-Chang, and Wang Lie-Huey, "Chief Executive Compensation: An Empirical Study of Fat Cat CEOs," *International Journal of Business & Finance Research* 7, no. 2 (2013), 27–42.

56. Stephen Barlas, "Into the Say-on-Pay Foray," *Human Resource Executive*, October 2013, pp. 79–81; Ryan Krause, Kimberly Whitler, and Matthew Semadeni, "Power to the Principals! An Experimental Look at Shareholder Say-on-Pay Voting," *Academy of Management Journal* 57, no. 1 (February 2014), 94–115.

57. Gretchen Morgenson, "Clawbacks? They're Still a Rare Breed," *New York Times*, December 28, 2013, http://www.nytimes.com/2013/12/29/business/clawbacks-theyre-still-a-rare-breed.html?pagewanted=all.

58. Ken Stoler and Nicole Berman, "Executive Compensation: Clawbacks. 2013 Proxy Disclosure Study," *Pricewaterhousecoopers*, April 2014, http://www.pwc.com/en_US/us/hr-management/publications/assets/pwc-clawbacks-2013-proxy-disclosure-study.pdf.

59. Deborah Nielsen and Christopher Knize, "Executive Perquisites in the Spotlight," *Workspan*, July 2011, pp. 38–43.

60. Bruce Ellig, "Long-Term Plan Combinations," *Compensation & Benefits Review* 46, no. 1 (April 2014), 10–15; Daniel Moynihan, "Long-Term Incentives: Best Practice vs. Best Fit," *Workspan*, May 2013, pp. 59–61.

61. Don Nemerov, "Are Performance Based LTI Plans Effective?" *Workspan*, June 2012, pp. 32–38.

62. Knowledge@Wharton, "The End to Exorbitant CEO Exit Packages? Don't Hold Your Breath," July 18, 2012, http://knowledge.wharton.upenn.edu/article/the-end-of-exorbitant-ceo-exit-packages-dont-hold-your-breath.

63. Kate Linebaugh and Joann Lublin, "For Retired GE Executive, $89,000 a Month Not to Work," *Wall Street Journal*, August 2, 2012, p. A1.

64. Christina Rexrode, "Payouts for Government Job Takers under Fire," *Wall Street Journal*, November 20, 2014, p. C3.

65. Gretchen Gavett, "CEOs Get Paid Too Much, According to Pretty Much Everyone in the World," *HBR Blog Network*, September 23, 2014, http://blogs.hbr.org/2014/09/ceos-get-paid-too-much-according-to-pretty-much-everyone-in-the-world/.

66. Lee Dunham and Ken Washer, "The Ethics of Hedging by Executives," *Journal of Business Ethics* 111, no. 2 (December 2012), 1547–1164.

67. Kevin Hallock, "CEO Pay and Layoffs," *Workspan*, June 2013, pp. 12–13.

68. Based on John McKinnon, "Penalized IRS Workers Were Awarded Bonuses," *Wall Street Journal*, April 23, 2014, p. A4; Dustin Racioppi, "Report: VA Gave $100M in Bonuses as Vets Awaited Care," *USA Today*, June 11, 2014; Keith Rogers and Steve Tetreault, "VA Hospital Director Gets Bonus despite Problems," *Las Vegas Review-Journal*, July 7, 2014; Pete Kasperowicz, "VA Officials Will Get Millions of Dollars in Bonuses under House-Senate Agreement," *Blaze*, July 29, 2014; Mary Shinn, Daniel Moore, and Steven Rich, "Despite Backlogs, VA Disability Claims Processors Get Bonuses," *Washington Post*, August 25, 2013.

CHAPTER 13

Managing Employee Benefits

Learning Objectives

After you have read this chapter, you should be able to:

LO1 Define a benefit and identify four strategic benefit considerations.

LO2 Analyze the differences between employee benefits in the United States and those in other countries.

LO3 Distinguish between mandated and voluntary benefits and list three examples of each.

LO4 Discuss the trends in retirement plans and compare defined benefit and defined contribution plans.

LO5 Explain the importance of managing the costs of health benefits and identify some methods of doing so.

LO6 Describe the growth of financial, family-oriented, and time-off benefits and their importance to employees.

WHAT'S TRENDING IN
MANAGING EMPLOYEE BENEFITS

It is imperative from a strategic perspective that employers provide the types of benefits that motivate workers and encourage them to stay with a company. This is often difficult given that employees have very different needs and desires. Working with managers, HR professionals should identify the benefits that are the most desirable and then provide them to keep employees satisfied. To remain competitive in the long run, employers should also offer competitive benefits relative to other companies so that they can hire and keep competent workers. Given these concerns, here's what's currently trending in the management of employee benefits:

1. Benefits are being used to build a sustained competitive advantage and ultimately satisfy a company's strategic objectives. Employers that offer generous benefit packages are often viewed as "model" or "benchmark" organizations, making them desirable to job candidates when they choose where to work.

2. The costs associated with providing desirable benefits are increasing at a steady rate. This reality challenges companies to offer competitive benefits and also keep a close eye on the bottom line.

3. Effectively communicating benefits to employees is an ongoing concern for HR professionals. Employers are relying more on technology and social media to spread the good news to employees about the availability of benefits.

4. Companies are offering more unique benefits that satisfy the various needs of employees. Paid sick leave, adoption assistance, and retirement annuities are examples of some of these benefits. In addition, the Patient Protection and Affordable Care Act stands to greatly impact the health care benefits that companies offer employees.

Land O'Lakes Uses Benefits to Achieve Strategies

On a recent National Employee Benefits Day, the International Foundation of Employee Benefits Plans persuaded HR leaders who were involved in benefit management to celebrate their hard work by playing a tune called "Takin' Care of Benefits," which was based on the hit song "Takin' Care of Business" by Bachman-Turner Overdrive. This entertaining move was a way to congratulate these leaders for their contributions. But it also shows how much benefit administration has changed over the past several years. Benefits are now viewed as strategic tools that can help companies reach their objectives. Offering good benefits can indeed impact effective recruiting and retention of competent employees.

Land O'Lakes, the St. Paul, Minnesota food provider and agricultural organization, is one firm that has utilized benefits more strategically than many other companies. The senior director of benefits and HR operations, Pam Grove, has been instrumental in guiding the farmer-owned cooperative down the path of strategic benefit administration. Under her leadership, for instance, the organization now offers better benefits as a result of outsourcing and modifications made to health care coverage. These changes have resulted in long-term savings greater than $35 million. A high-deductible health care package that was offered in 2007 also resulted in high rates of employee participation that were far beyond expectations.

According to Grove, the money saved from these programs has been nice. But one of the primary motives for making these changes was to encourage the organization's benefit personnel to be much more oriented to managing business strategy. The resulting culture that has been established within the HR department is less focused on the

Ariana Lindquist/Bloomberg/Getty Images

administrative role of benefits. HR leaders and benefit specialists at Land O'Lakes want to be strategic partners. In this way, the benefits that are ultimately selected and offered by the firm can improve its ability to satisfy strategic objectives and improve the bottom line.[1]

Benefit
A tangible indirect reward provided to an employee or group of employees for organizational membership

Most companies provide benefits to workers as part of a total rewards package that ideally enhances their satisfaction with work. A benefit is a tangible indirect reward provided to an employee or group of employees for organizational membership. Benefits often include retirement plans, paid time off, health insurance, life and disability insurance, and many more. Benefits are not typically based on employee performance; rather, they are provided to all employees who meet certain eligibility requirements.

In the United States, employers often play a key role in providing benefits for workers. In many other nations, citizens and employers are taxed to pay for government-provided benefits, such as health care and retirement programs. Although federal and state regulations require U.S. employers to provide certain benefits, they voluntarily provide many others. A recent major change in how health care benefits are provided means that U.S. employers may be less involved in providing health insurance.

Benefits tend to be costly for the typical U.S. employer, often averaging at least one-third of payroll expenses. In highly unionized manufacturing and utility industries, they may represent well over half of payroll costs. Current trends and projections suggest that health care coverage will lead to increases in the costs associated with providing benefits to employees, with one survey of public and private employers showing that growth rates in health care expenses are expected to increase, despite recent modest growth rates.[2] Another survey found that health care expenses were ranked by CFOs as their primary business challenge. Findings also indicated that 53% of CFOs believe that labor costs will rise due to requirements of the Patient Protection and Affordable Care Act (PPACA), and 77% believe that employee contributions will also rise to help pay for these requirements.[3] Health care inflation steadily decreased from a rate of 6.3% in 2007 to a rate of 3.7% in 2012, but this trend is expected to reverse as ACA requirements such as mandatory health care benefits and additional related taxes/fees are implemented.[4] The increasing use of specialty drugs to treat serious illnesses is also expected to increase benefit costs. Many specialty drugs carry a price tag of over $600 a month, and the average expense of using these drugs is $10,000 a month for patients.[5]

Figure 13-1 shows employers' per-hour costs for typical benefits. The figure shows that there are differences between private- and public-sector employee compensation costs, especially concerning retirement benefits. Health insurance represents the largest percentage of benefit costs, followed by paid time off, legally required benefits, and retirement plans. Notice that of the average total compensation of $31.32 in the private sector, employers are paying $9.60 for benefits, a 30% add-on to the base pay.

FIGURE 13-1 Employer Compensation and Benefit Costs per Hour

Compensation Element	Private Industry Employers		State and Local Government Employers	
	Dollar ($)	Percentage (%)	Dollar ($)	Percentage (%)
Total compensation	31.32	100	43.95	100
Wages and salaries	21.72	69.4	28.17	64.1
Total benefits	9.60	30.6	15.78	35.9
Legally required benefits	2.50	8.0	2.59	5.9
Paid leave	2.16	6.9	3.20	7.3
Supplemental pay	1.10	3.5	0.35	0.8
Insurance	2.54	8.1	5.22	11.9
Retirement and savings	1.30	4.2	4.42	10.1

Source: U.S. Bureau of Labor Statistics, 2014.

LO1 Define a benefit and identify four strategic benefit considerations.

13-1 Benefits and HR Strategy

Some experts believe that companies will provide more voluntary benefits to employees such as dental, disability and life insurance plans, flexible spending accounts, membership discounts, and pet, identity-theft, and auto/home insurance programs.[6] A challenge for employers is how to balance the increasing costs of the benefits against their value to the organization and its employees. For instance, companies can choose to compete for or retain employees by providing different levels of base compensation, variable pay, and benefits. Similar to strategies targeted at improving pay, using a total rewards philosophy may mean putting greater emphasis on indirect rewards that can differentiate the company from its competitors. Exploring new benefit options that are desirable to employees and adopting a strategic approach to compensation that manages pay and benefits comprehensively can help organizations successfully recruit and retain quality employees. Overall, benefits should be a key consideration in the total rewards package when determining organizational strategies regarding compensation.[7]

The benefit approach adopted as part of total rewards depends on many factors, such as the size of the organization, workforce competition, organizational life cycle, employee demographics, financial circumstances, and corporate strategic approach. A family-owned hotel may focus on providing a generous benefits package that includes flexible working arrangements and an in-house cafeteria because it can't afford to pay employees as much as national lodging chains. Similarly, a high-tech company that employs a diverse workforce that includes many female employees may elect to offer more family-friendly benefits such as on-site daycare and adoption assistance. These examples illustrate how benefit choices are often influenced by many organizational factors that have strategic implications.

13-1a Benefits as a Competitive Advantage

Benefits can be used to create and maintain a competitive advantage for the organization. While they represent a significant cost, benefits are an important factor in employee commitment and retention. Attracting and retaining employees and increasing productivity are business objectives that can be enhanced through effective design of benefit programs. Surveys by Aflac and Towers Watson show that over 70% of employees regard employee benefits as an important factor in their decision to join or remain with an organization. There is also a strong connection between employee satisfaction with the benefits package and overall job satisfaction.[8] Unfortunately, one Society for Human Resource Management survey found that roughly 25% of employers focus on benefits to recruit workers, and only about 20% use them to retain current workers.[9] Evidence also suggests that benefits do not always meet the needs of both employers and workers and therefore do not lead to improved engagement or operational effectiveness.[10]

Employers may offer benefits to aid recruiting and retention, improve organizational performance, and meet legal requirements. Another Society for Human Resource Management survey found that 31% of companies utilize benefits as an effective way to recruit workers, and many HR professionals believe that providing benefits such as health care, retirement support, flexible work arrangements, employee development, and health/wellness initiatives will play a more prominent role in recruitment in the near future.[11] Some employers use benefits to reinforce the company philosophy of social and corporate citizenship. Firms that provide above average benefits are often viewed more positively within a community and the industry by customers, civic leaders, current employees, and individuals working for other firms. Conversely, employers who are seen as skimping on benefits, cutting benefits, or taking advantage of workers may be viewed more negatively.

Hilton Worldwide is a good example of how a company can utilize benefits to improve operating results. The company now uses benefits as an effective way to differentiate the organization from the competition. "Benefits are no longer about just providing employees with traditional plans," says Diane Heyman, SPHR, who works as Hilton's global compensation and benefits head. "Our team has become partners with the business in how to offer competitive packages." Based on the findings of various research programs and employee surveys, Hilton Worldwide started a comprehensive paid-time-off program to replace vacation and sick pay because it found that people wanted greater flexibility to manage their time off.[12] This is a prime example of how an organization can leverage benefits that are valued by employees.

Benefits can influence employees' decisions about which employer to work for, whether to stay with or leave an organization, and when to retire. What benefits are offered, the competitive level of benefits, and how those benefits are viewed by individuals all affect employee attraction and retention efforts. An additional concern is the changing composition of the U.S. workforce and how expectations about benefits by different generations of employees are affecting benefit decisions for employers. For instance, many Baby Boomers who are approaching retirement age are concerned about retirement benefits and health care, while younger workers are more interested in flexible and portable benefits as well as career development opportunities. Similarly, increased diversity in the workplace encourages companies to offer more voluntary benefits that satisfy different individual needs. Offering benefit plans that appeal to employees at different stages of life and with different needs and priorities is a way to attract and retain a diverse workforce.

13-1b Tax-Favored Status of Benefits

Providing employees benefits rather than wages can be advantageous for employees. Most benefits (except for paid time off) are not taxed as income to employees. During World War II, wage and price controls were instituted to ensure appropriate use of resources and to keep inflation rates low. Wishing to attract and reward hardworking employees, companies began to offer paid fringe benefits as added incentives. Since benefits were not paid in wages, they were never taxed as income to the employee, yet the company could deduct the cost as a business expense. This explains why the United States differs from many other countries in how benefits (especially health insurance) are provided to workers.

The tax-favored status means that a dollar in employee benefits is actually worth much more to an employee. For example, if Sally is an employee who is in the 25% tax bracket and earns an extra $400 as a special bonus, she will pay $100 in taxes on this amount (disregarding deductions). So, her special bonus increases Sally's total rewards by only $300. But if Sally's employer provides her with group legal insurance benefits worth $400, she receives the full value of $400 since it is not reduced by taxes. This feature makes benefits a desirable form of compensation to employees if they understand the value provided by the benefits. See the accompanying "HR Competencies & Applications: Gross Up Pay Calculation" feature to learn how to "gross-up" wages.

13-1c Global Benefits

LO2 Analyze the differences between employee benefits in the United States and those in other countries.

GLOBAL

There are significant differences in benefits across the globe. In many countries, a variety of benefits are provided through programs administered by the government. Employers and employees are taxed heavily to pay into government funds that cover these benefits. The costs of these benefits are often quite high due to generous retirement and health insurance plans, coupled with an aging workforce and increasing retiree populations. In Portugal, for example, the government was forced to drop a controversial plan to increase employee social security contributions from 11% to 18% of pay in an effort to address public deficits. An outcry by unions and workers put an end to the idea, and now the government will seek alternate ways to restore economic stability in the retirement system.[13] National pension programs in Germany, France, and Japan, among other countries, are facing significant financial pressures because of their aging workforces and populations. The Social Security and Medicare systems in the United States face similar challenges. In Mexico, legislators are considering programs that provide unemployment insurance and universal pensions to some individuals, and changes to social security contributions have also been approved.[14]

Health care benefits also differ significantly worldwide. Developed nations (with the exception of the United States until very recently) are far more likely to provide compulsory, government-sponsored health plans for all citizens, regardless of employment status. Countries including Great Britain, Chile, South Korea, Thailand, Brazil, and Canada have universal health care programs. These programs are financed either by employer contributions or from income taxes paid by employees, or a combination of both. In most countries, wealthier citizens can

COMPETENCIES & APPLICATIONS

Gross Up Pay Calculation

To determine the "true" value of employee benefits, HR professionals can calculate the "gross-up" amount that represents the equivalent pay to the employee. **Gross-up** means to increase the net amount of what the employee receives to include the taxes owed on the amount. Let's say that Harold is our employee and he is in the 38% tax bracket. His employer provides pet care insurance worth $200. Harold is given the choice of accepting the pet insurance benefit or taking the cash equivalent. To be fair, Harold should receive the grossed-up value of that benefit, not simply $200 in his paycheck. Remember that if he receives $200 in his pay, he will pay income taxes on that amount and will net $124 ($200 less taxes of $76).

To calculate how much the $200 is really worth to Harold, calculate the gross-up by following these steps:

1. 100% − tax% = net%
   (100% − 38%) = 62%

2. payment/net% = gross amount of earnings
   ($200/62%) = $322.58

3. Check by calculating Harold's gross-to-net pay
   (payment × net%) = net pay
   ($322.58 × 62%) = $200

Now, Harold can make an informed decision about which option to select, knowing that he is receiving the same value no matter which way he chooses. The $200 insurance benefit is really worth $322.58 to an employee in the 38% tax bracket (if he or she has a dog).

KEY COMPETENCIES: Critical Evaluation (Behavioral Competency) and People (Technical Competency)

Gross-up
To increase the net amount of what the employee receives to include the taxes owed on the amount

purchase private health insurance and seek treatment from private medical providers rather than using public medical providers. Recent legal changes mean that U.S. citizens will have universal access to health care in the coming years. This topic will be covered in greater detail later in this chapter. Figure 13-2 shows the percentage of gross domestic product (GDP) spent on health care in selected countries. Costs in the United States are the highest in the world at nearly 18% of 2010 GDP, while developing nations like Bangladesh spend less than 4% of GDP.

The amount of paid leave provided to employees also varies significantly in different countries. Paid time off for childbirth and medical disability are generous in Scandinavian and European countries, and they provide lengthy paid leave for new mothers. A number of countries also provide paid time off for new fathers as well. For example, mothers in Sweden receive 14 weeks of job-protected maternity leave with at least 80% salary paid, while fathers receive two weeks of paternity leave at 80% of salary. In addition, parents are eligible for up to 480 additional paid days off for parental leave until the child's first year of school. Few industrialized nations do not mandate such benefits for employees.[15] With regard to childbirth and sick leave, the United States is the only major developed nation that does not guarantee workers pay during such absences from work.

Given these various issues, companies that employ people in different countries face a number of challenges. Firms must provide generous benefits to be competitive in local labor markets, but finding equitable and practical solutions to the

FIGURE 13-2 Percentage of GDP Spent on Health Care in Select Countries

Country Name	2000	2012
United States	13.6	17.9
France	10.1	11.7
Austria	10.0	11.5
Germany	10.4	11.3
Canada	8.8	10.9
Belgium	8.1	10.8
Portugal	9.3	9.4
Brazil	7.2	9.3
Korea, Rep.	4.3	7.5
Mexico	5.1	6.1
China	4.6	5.4
India	4.3	4.0
Thailand	3.4	3.9
Philippines	3.2	4.6
Bangladesh	2.8	3.6

Source: World Bank, 2015.

differences among national requirements is complicated. For instance, some Latin American organizations offer more generous (and voluntary) benefits to increase employee motivation and morale. A survey of workers and employers in Mexico, Chile, and Brazil found that a majority of firms in each of these countries uses benefits to enhance employee performance. Findings also showed that companies focus on voluntary benefits such as health and wellness initiatives and different kinds of insurance (life, disability, etc.).[16] Multinational companies operating in various countries must determine how to compensate both host-country nationals and expatriates so that all employees will feel that they are being treated fairly. How they handle these decisions impacts global attraction and retention of employees among international employers.

13-1d Public-Sector Benefits

Workers in the public sector have for many years enjoyed more generous benefits than those in the private sector. Many states and cities face serious budget shortfalls because of the funding requirements for employee retirement and health care plans. Several state governments have deferred payments to pension funds because they are already in debt and do not have enough tax revenue to cover the costs. This has led to proposed and enacted legislation in several states to roll back the power of public-sector unions that have successfully bargained for these benefits.

Public-sector workers (police, firefighters, teachers, and other government workers) belong to labor unions at a much higher rate than do nongovernment workers. Their union contracts often include free health care and traditional defined benefit pension plans. These are costly benefits that many states and cities can no longer afford. However, because the benefits are part of negotiated labor agreements, both the union and the employer must agree on changes. Some states and their union workers are finding ways to modify benefits plans. Many others will be dealing with this issue in the coming years.

13-2 Managing Benefits

Benefit programs must be designed, administered, communicated, and measured. To maximize the impact that employee benefits have on employee satisfaction and retention, careful consideration must be given to designing benefit programs with the overall organizational philosophy and strategy in mind.

13-2a Benefits Design

Organizations design benefit plans with a goal of providing value for employees while remaining cost-effective for the company. Many key decisions must be made as part of benefits design as highlighted in Figure 13-3.

Flexible benefits plan
Program that allows employees to select the benefits they prefer from options established by the employer

Flexible Benefits As part of both benefits design and administration, employers may offer employees choices in benefits. A flexible benefits plan is a program that allows employees to select the benefits they prefer from options established by the employer. As a result of the changing composition of the workforce, flexible benefits plans have grown in popularity. Flexible benefits systems recognize that individual employee situations differ because of age, family status, and lifestyle. For instance, dual-career couples may not want to duplicate benefits from two different employers. Under a flex plan, one of them can forgo some benefits that are available in the partner's plan and take other benefits instead.

A problem with flexibility in benefit choice is that employees may choose an inappropriate benefits package. Younger employees may decide not to participate in the retirement plan because they believe retirement is decades away and that there is sufficient time to save in the future. However, this may result in inadequate retirement savings for the employee. Part of this problem can be overcome by requiring

FIGURE 13-3 Benefit Design Decisions

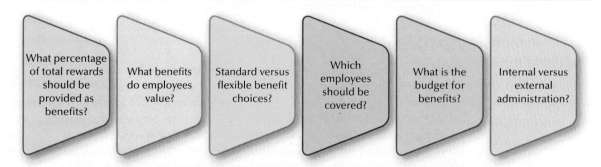

employees to select a core set of benefits (life, health, retirement, and disability insurance) and then offering options on other benefits.

Another problem can be adverse selection by employees, a situation in which only higher-risk employees select and use certain benefits. For example, employees with young children are far more likely to enroll in orthodontia benefit plans that provide braces than are older employees. Since insurance plans are based on a group rate, the premium rates might be higher because too few employees who do not need braces enroll in the plan.

Offering more choices leads to higher administrative costs for the organization. Since many flexible plans have become complex, they require more administrative time and information systems to track the choices made by employees. Despite the disadvantages, flex plans will likely continue to grow in popularity.

Part-Time Employee Benefits and Status Another key design issue is whether to provide benefits to part-time employees. Many employers do not provide part-time employee benefits, except some paid time off. Figure 13-4 shows the percentage of full-time and part-time employees in the private sector that have access to and participate in selected employee benefits. Part-time employees are most likely to receive retirement benefits and least likely to receive medical care and life insurance benefits. Benefits for part-time employees are often provided in proportion to the percentage of full-time work they provide.

Still another concern relates to whether employees are designated as part-time workers, which can affect their eligibility for benefits in a company. Besides what is specified in certain laws and regulations, companies can create their own hourly thresholds for part-time and full-time status, but once these standards are established, they must be honored or legal problems may arise. Based on generally accepted standards likely held by the Department of Labor and the Internal Revenue Service, "consistently working" 35 hours per week is a common threshold for the designation of employees as full time. Consequently, employers should evaluate jobs on a regular basis to determine part-time/full-time status and properly verify whether employees should receive benefits. Factors such as temporary increased hours and seasonal work should be considered.[17]

Adverse selection
Situation in which only higher-risk employees select and use certain benefits

FIGURE 13-4 Access to and Participation in Selected Employee Benefits for Private-Sector Workers

Benefit Category	Part-Time Employee		Full-Time Employee	
	Access (%)	Participation (%)	Access (%)	Participation (%)
Retirement	37	19	74	58
Medical care	23	12	86	63
Life insurance	13	11	72	71

Source: U.S. Bureau of Labor Statistics, 2014.

Note: Access means that the employee is offered the opportunity to enroll in the benefit plan. Participation means that the employee actually enrolls in the benefit plan or receives the benefit.

Domestic Partner Benefits There have been a number of challenges to how marriages are defined at different state and federal levels, with cases focusing on the Defense of Marriage Act (DOMA), as well as whether and how to recognize same-sex marriage.[18] The U.S. Supreme Court recently voted against DOMA, which changed the way terms such as *marriage* and *spouse* are defined and essentially treats same-sex spouses the same as opposite-sex married couples. This means that same-sex spouses may be entitled to certain benefit plans, and if same-sex couples get divorced, one partner may be entitled to a share of retirement benefits.[19]

In states where gay marriage is legal, companies have to consider whether to treat same-sex spouses in the same manner as traditional married couples with regard to benefits. This issue is made even more complicated when organizations have operations in multiple states with varying laws. While insurance issuers cannot deny coverage to same-sex married couples, even in states where same-sex marriage is not formally (or legally) recognized, employers can elect to offer benefits plans that do not cover these individuals. There is speculation these situations will result in increased litigation under Title VII of the Civil Rights Act.[20] However, employers must provide same-sex couples the benefits provided under federal law even if they are working and/or living in states that have not legalized same-sex marriage. An example would be allowing a legally married same-sex partner who is employed in a state that does not support same-sex marriage to take funds from a 401(k) retirement account to pay for a spouse's emergency medical treatments.[21] Overall, organizations can demonstrate that they are accommodating and respectful of all workers when they provide benefits to married same-sex couples, which can enhance recruiting, employee satisfaction, and retention.

Older Workers Benefit Needs Hiring and retaining older workers can be an important strategy for an organization seeking high-quality talent with a wealth of knowledge and experience. Modified work schedules, part-time benefits, and simplified seasonal travel can be attractive to older workers. For example, CVS Caremark instituted a snowbird program to allow pharmacists to migrate south for the winter months and transfer to pharmacies in those locations. The pharmacists return to their northern homes during the warmer months and work in pharmacies there for the summer.[22]

Phased retirement programs allow employees to work part time and withdraw some retirement funds at the same time. Wellness programs and annual financial planning counseling are also highly valued by older workers. Since many older workers plan to remain actively employed into their later years, organizations can offer benefits targeted to this employee population and retain skilled workers for the organization.

13-3 Benefits Administration, Technology, and Communication

Open enrollment
A time when employees can change their participation level in various benefit plans and switch between benefit options

Legal compliance, record keeping, enrollment, and participation issues result in a significant administrative responsibility for organizations. Organizations may elect to have internal benefits professionals handle these duties, or they may use employees and vendors to streamline many of the routine clerical tasks involved. Many organizations offer an open enrollment period once a year. Open enrollment is a time when employees can change their participation level in various benefit plans and switch between benefit options.

Outsourcing Benefits Administration With the myriad of benefits, it is easy to see why many organizations must make coordinated efforts to administer benefits programs. One significant trend is the outsourcing of benefits administration. Third-party administrators (TPAs) are vendors that provide enrollment, record keeping, and other administrative services to organizations. Outsourcing is on the rise, and many organizations use TPAs to help manage costs and to provide expertise and efficiency in plan administration. However, employers need to be aware of the terms of vendor contracts and do their best to negotiate reasonable terms. The following issues should be considered by HR professionals when trying to secure beneficial vendor contracts:

Third-party administrator (TPA)
A vendor that provides enrollment, record keeping, and other administrative services to an organization

- Examine contracts closely and be familiar with the terms to determine the best deal.
- Make sure that vendors and companies are protected from errors (that can lead to penalties/fees) made by either party, something called *mutual indemnification.*
- Get vendors to agree on prices that will not change in the short run.
- Specify all services provided by vendors in the contract.
- Secure any promises made by vendors in writing.
- Look out for excessive vendor fees, often paid by employees.
- Push to get a termination clause in vendor contracts and be cautious of termination penalties.[23]

Technology and Employee Self-Service The spread of HR technology, particularly web-based and mobile systems, has significantly changed the benefit administration burden on HR staff. Internet and computer-based systems are being used to communicate benefit information, conduct employee benefit surveys, and facilitate benefit administration. These systems can decrease expenses, increase positive communication, and effectively connect people across many HR functions, including benefit management.

Information technology makes it possible for companies to offer self-service to employees. Self-service is technology that allows employees to change their benefit choices, track their benefit balances, and submit questions to HR staff members and external benefit providers. However, not all employees can easily navigate the online system for benefit enrollment and maintenance. While the ideal self-service portal includes links to medical care providers, investment funds for retirement plans, and other important information, it can easily overwhelm employees. It is therefore important that assistance is available and that employees are provided with help screens, contact information for administrators, and access to HR experts.[24]

Self-service
Technology that allows employees to change their benefit choices, track their benefit balances, and submit questions to HR staff members and external benefit providers

MEASURE

13-3a Benefits Measurement

The significant costs associated with benefits require that analyses be conducted to determine the payoffs for the expenditures. Numerous HR metrics can be used to evaluate whether benefits are providing the expected results in terms of employee retention and satisfaction. Some examples are shown in Figure 13-5.

Other metrics are used to measure the return on the expenditures for various benefit programs provided by employers. Some common benefits that employers track using HR metrics are workers' compensation, wellness programs, prescription

FIGURE 13-5 Frequently Used Benefit Metrics

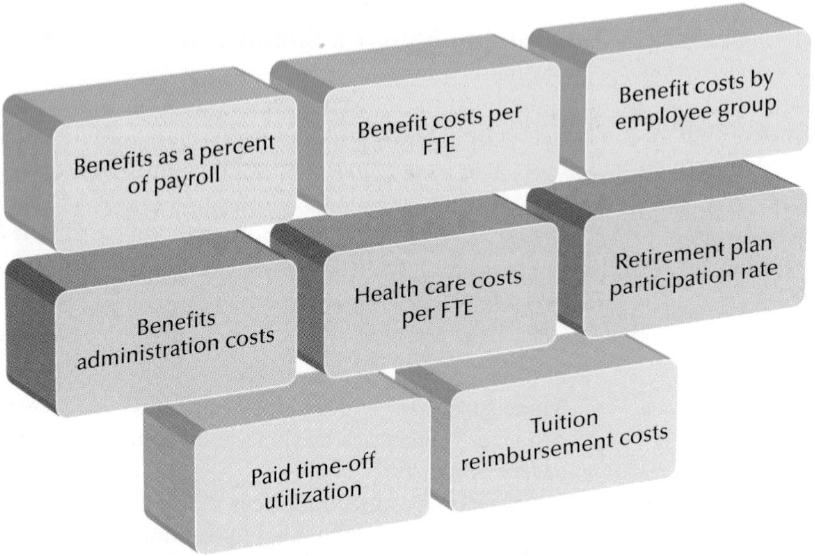

drug costs, leave time, tuition aid, and disability insurance. The point is that both benefit expenditures generally and costs for individual benefits need to be measured and evaluated as part of strategic benefits management.

13-3b Benefit Cost Control

Since benefit costs have risen significantly in the past several years, particularly for health care, employers are focusing more attention on measuring and controlling them, even reducing or dropping benefits offered to employees. Increases in employer expenditures for benefits are growing faster than increases in wages for employees.[25] For example, during economic downturns, many organizations stop contributing to the employee 401(k) plan, reduce education reimbursement, and cut training expenses. Companies are likely to wait until they are confident that they can afford the programs before benefits are reinstated. To soften the blow to employees, some companies add voluntary benefits such as group auto and home insurance programs at reduced group rates.

Another common means of benefit cost control is cost sharing, which refers to having employees pay for more of their benefit costs. The majority of firms use this strategy along with providing wellness programs, offering employee health education, and changing prescription drug programs. Companies might also consider consolidating benefit packages into more streamlined offerings so that costs can be minimized.

13-3c Benefit Communication

Employees are often not fully aware of the values and costs associated with the benefits provided by employers. This is in large measure due to ineffective communication by the company and the lack of a clear strategy for discussing benefits with employees. This means that the investments many companies make in benefits may not be helping them effectively attract and retain competent employees.

Benefit communication and employees' satisfaction with benefits are most definitely linked. For instance, employees often do not fully understand their health benefits, a situation that can cause dissatisfaction in the workplace. Consequently, many employers develop special benefit communication systems to inform employees about the monetary value of the benefits they provide. The findings of Bank of America Merrill Lynch's *Workplace Benefits Report,* which surveyed over 1,000 employers across the United States, showed that roughly one-third of HR professionals dedicate time to teaching workers about their benefits. These education efforts commonly focus on retirement, health care, and staffing issues such as downsizing.[26]

Employers can adopt some best practices when designing benefit communications. Companies can focus on developing communication policies that enable them to educate employees about their benefits and the associated costs, and the Internet and social media might help drive more effective communication with individuals and groups. A Society for Human Resource Management survey determined that the main approaches used by companies to communicate benefit information to employees included online/print materials, group sessions, and personal counseling. Only 3% of the companies relied on social media for benefit communication, but 8% of those that didn't claimed that they would do so in the near future.[27] The Xerox firm ACS uses a virtual fair to educate employees about benefit opportunities and enroll them in different programs.[28]

When planning benefit communication efforts, it is important to consider factors such as the timing and frequency, the communication methods, and any specialized content. Any significant changes to benefits, such as reduced 401(k) matches and increased employee health plan contributions, should be communicated by top managers in the organization. Providing the rationale for these actions helps employees understand why their benefits are being changed. This communication should be supported by HR professionals and other key managers who are well informed and can answer any questions.

Personal Benefit Statements Some companies give individual employees a personal statement that translates benefits into dollar amounts. These statements give employees a snapshot of the total compensation they receive. They help employees see the "hidden paycheck," that is, the value of their benefits. These statements can be shared with family members to emphasize the true package of rewards provided by the employer.

13-3d Types of Benefits

LO3 Distinguish between mandated and voluntary benefits and list three examples of each.

Employers offer a wide range of benefits. Some are mandated by laws and government regulations, while others are offered voluntarily by employers as part of their HR strategy. Figure 13-6 lists the major categories of benefits and highlights those that are legally required and those that are voluntarily provided by employers.

While there are many mandated benefits that employers in the United States must provide to employees, in general, the United States requires fewer employee benefits than many other nations. However, employers voluntarily offer a broad variety of other benefits to help them compete for and retain employees. By offering additional benefits, organizations provide greater security and support to workers with diverse personal circumstances. In addition, as jobs become more flexible and varied, both workers and employers recognize that choices among benefits are necessary, as evidenced by the growth in flexible benefits and cafeteria benefit plans.

FIGURE 13-6 Types of Benefits

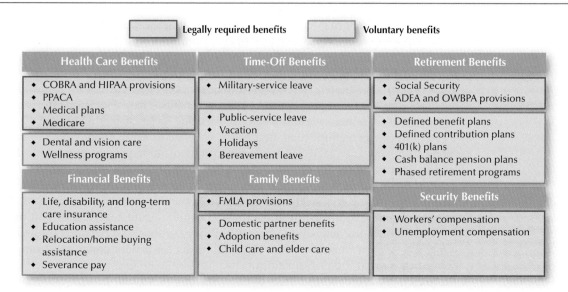

Cafeteria benefit plan
Employees are given a budget and can purchase the bundle of benefits most important to them from the "menu" of options offered by the employer

A cafeteria benefit plan is one in which employees are given a budget and can purchase the bundle of benefits most important to them from the "menu" of options offered by the employer.

13-4 Legally Required Benefits

The earliest benefit law was the Social Security Act, which was passed at the end of the Great Depression. Little was done on the federal level after that until the 1970s and later. Federal statutes have been enacted to address financial and employment security for workers, particularly those with medical problems.

13-4a Social Security and Medicare

The Social Security Act of 1935 and its later amendments established a system to provide *old-age, survivor's, disability,* and *retirement* benefits. Administered by the federal government through the Social Security Administration, this program provides benefits to individuals who were previously employed. Medicare was implemented in 1965 to provide medical care for people over the age of 65. The Federal Insurance Contributions Act (FICA) was passed to facilitate payroll contributions in support of both programs.

Social Security Employees and employers share in the cost of Social Security through a tax on employees' wages or salaries. When the law was first enacted, employers and employees each contributed 1% of worker wages to the fund. By 1990, the rate had increased to 6.2% paid by each party (for a total of 12.4%), which is the current rate of payroll tax contributions. The amount of wages subject to tax is reviewed and increased periodically. Starting in 2015, the taxable wage base was increased from $117,000 to $118,500, with earnings over that amount not being subject to Social Security tax.[29]

Social Security is a politically sensitive program. The U.S. Congress has responded to public pressure by raising payments and introducing cost-of-living adjustments. An increasing number of financial experts are also providing advice to individuals about the best times to start drawing Social Security based on variables such as work income, retirement account income, and spousal (Social Security) benefits, and a number of inexpensive or free online resources can assist with calculations and planning.[30] However, concerns persist about the long-term financial viability of the program. In response, the normal retirement age to receive maximum Social Security benefits has been steadily increased from 65 to 67, and it remains to been seen if further age increases will occur in the future. Figure 13-7 shows the retirement age for employees born in various years. Further legislative action will likely be required to address criticisms that the system is not sustainable in its current form.

Medicare Medicare is a government-operated health insurance program for older Americans (age 65 and above) and for some citizens with disabilities. Medicare is funded by a tax on employers and employees. Each party pays 1.45% of employee

FIGURE 13-7   Normal Retirement Age for Social Security Benefits

Year of Birth	Age
1937 and prior	65
1938	65 and 2 months
1939	65 and 4 months
1940	65 and 6 months
1941	65 and 8 months
1942	65 and 10 months
1943–54	66
1955	66 and 2 months
1956	66 and 4 months
1957	66 and 6 months
1958	66 and 8 months
1959	66 and 10 months
1960 and later	67

Source: U.S. Social Security Administration, http://www.ssa.gov/OACT/ProgData/nra.html.

earnings. Unlike the taxes paid for Social Security, there is no earnings limit on Medicare contributions. Therefore, all wages earned by workers are taxed at 2.9%. An additional Medicare tax of 0.9% for individuals who earn higher incomes was instituted in 2013; employers are expected to withhold this tax for compensation that exceeds $200,000 per year. The percentage that an employee pays increases to 2.35% (from 1.45%) on income that is earned above certain threshold levels, which are $250,000 for spouses filing jointly; $125,000 for spouses filing separately; and $200,000 for single wage earners. The portion of the tax that an employer pays remains unchanged at 1.45%.[31] The future financial solvency of the program has been questioned, and legislative action in the coming years is likely to be needed to address the program's continuation.

13-4b Workers' Compensation

Workers' compensation
Security benefits provided to workers who are injured on the job

Workers' compensation are security benefits provided to workers who are injured on the job. State laws require most employers to provide workers' compensation coverage by purchasing insurance from a private carrier, state insurance fund, or self-insuring.

Workers' compensation regulations require employers to provide cash benefits, medical care, and rehabilitation services to employees for injuries or illnesses that occur within the scope of their employment. In exchange, employees give up the right to pursue legal actions and awards. However, various circumstances may influence a company's obligation to pay workers' compensation. The following "HR Competencies & Applications: "'One Toke over the Line'—No Coverage for Medical Marijuana" feature explores how medical and recreational marijuana use by employees may impact such coverage.

No-fault insurance
An injured worker receives benefits even if the accident was the employees' fault

The concepts of no-fault insurance and exclusive remedy balance the rights of employers and employees under workers' compensation. No-fault insurance means that an injured worker receives benefits even if the accident was the employee's fault. For example, if an employee violates the safety rules and fails to wear safety shoes and drops a heavy object on his foot that causes a broken toe, his medical and disability expenses will still be paid by the employer's insurance coverage. Exclusive remedy means that workers' compensation benefits are the only benefits injured workers may receive from the employer to compensate for work-related injuries. In most instances, an injured worker cannot file a lawsuit for additional money.

Exclusive remedy
Workers' compensation benefits are the only benefits injured workers may receive from the employer to compensate for work-related injuries

Workers' compensation programs are funded at the employer's expense; workers cannot be required to make financial contributions for this coverage. Since each state operates independently, employers must be aware of various regulations if they operate in multiple states. The Bureau of Labor Statistics reports that, on average, private-sector employers spend about $0.42 per hour, or 1.5% of total payroll, in workers' compensation costs.[32] Costs in some states are much higher. Costs can vary a great deal based on the requirements in each state and the safety record for each company. One of the most effective cost-control mechanisms to keep premiums low involves focusing on accident prevention. The types of jobs in companies, the work that is performed, and employees' pay rates can also influence the expenses related to workers' compensation insurance. Given these many variables, there is also growing concern over "premium fraud" on the part of employers. Companies can distort the number of previous claims, misclassify employees, and disclose incorrect (lower) pay to reduce the costs associated with workers' compensation. These misrepresentations can lead to serious and costly legal action.[33]

COMPETENCIES & APPLICATIONS

"One Toke over the Line"—No Coverage for Medical Marijuana

A number of states have legalized the use of marijuana for medical purposes. Two other states, Colorado and Washington, have legalized marijuana for recreational use. These actions have fueled debates and clouded many issues about how to treat the drug for the purposes of workers' compensation. This is because the use of marijuana for any purpose, despite what state statutes allow, is still illegal under federal law.

One of the most pressing questions about medical use of the drug is who gets to pay for it in workers' compensation cases? States such as Michigan, Vermont, Colorado, and Montana have specified that insurers are not required to reimburse employees for medical marijuana, and many experts believe that this is currently the case in many others states as well, even in states that offer no legal precedence or have legalized the drug in some way. However, such an approach has been challenged and could be reviewed further in new court cases.

Employers with zero-tolerance drug policies appear to be particularly protected against reimbursement claims for medical marijuana. For instance, companies can still terminate the employment of individuals who use marijuana because federal law recognizes it as an illegal substance, even in states such as Colorado that have legalized the drug for recreational use. Courts have also generally supported an employer's right to fire employees who have used marijuana for

medical purposes when the company has a zero-tolerance drug policy. However, states such as New Mexico and Rhode Island have laws in place to protect the use of medical marijuana, so HR professionals and managers should become familiar with relevant state statues.

Another challenge involves situations where employees are injured on the job and test positive for marijuana use, but the drug did not lead to the injuries. A recent case in Oklahoma determined that a worker was still entitled to workers' compensation benefits even though it was determined that he had marijuana in his system—because the drug did not contribute to his being harmed.[34]

As a line manager or HR professional, you might have to make determinations about employee drug use and workers' compensation. You might also work for a company that has a zero-tolerance drug policy. Consequently, consider the following questions:

1. Have you ever worked for an organization that had a zero-tolerance drug policy? If so, how did the company manage this policy? If not, do you think your employer should have developed such a policy?

2. What should HR professionals and line managers do to better educate themselves about the impact of marijuana use on workers' compensation?

KEY COMPETENCIES: Ethical Practice (Behavioral Competency) and Workplace (Technical Competency)

13-4c Unemployment Compensation

Unemployment compensation was established as part of the Social Security Act of 1935 to provide a minimum level of benefits for workers who are out of work. Each U.S. state operates its own unemployment compensation system, and benefit levels and job-search provisions differ significantly from state to state. Each company pays an unemployment tax that is based on an "experience rate," which reflects the number of claims filed by workers who leave employment.

Under normal circumstances, an employee who is out of work and actively looking for employment can receive up to 26 weeks of pay at the rate of 50% to 80% of normal pay. Most employees are eligible. However, workers fired for misconduct or those not actively seeking employment are generally ineligible.

During times of widespread economic hardship, the government might increase the number of weeks during which eligible workers receive benefits. In recent years, unemployed workers could collect benefits for up to 99 weeks. The decision to extend benefits is often controversial, and legislators struggle to find a balance between providing income security to workers and reducing workers' motivation to seek employment.

13-4d Additional Legally Required Benefits

Besides workers' compensation and unemployment insurance, most companies must provide additional benefits. Continued group medical benefits under COBRA regulations are discussed in the section on health care. Health care portability and medical information privacy under HIPAA are also discussed in the health care section later in this chapter. Job-protected medical leave under FMLA is discussed in the section on time-off benefits.

LO4 Discuss the trend in retirement plans and compare defined benefit and defined contribution plans.

13-5 Retirement Benefits

The aging of the workforce in many countries is affecting retirement planning for individuals and retirement plan costs for employers and governments. In the United States, the number of citizens at least 55 years of age has increased significantly in recent years, and older citizens constitute a large portion of the population. More workers are delaying retirement because of financial difficulties and decreased value of retirement savings coupled with longer life spans. Approximately 30% of workers in one survey had no plans to stop working or did not know when they would retire.[35] There is speculation that senior employees' postponement of retirement is preventing some upwardly mobile younger employees from getting better jobs, but some recent evidence suggests that this might not be the case.[36] However, staffing "bottlenecks" can occur, and workplace management is more difficult when senior workers delay the move to retirement because they are concerned about their financial situations.[37] According to Eileen Timmins, who is Executive Vice President of HR at the financial services company Allston Trading, "Employers need to know that employees can retire when the time comes so that employees underneath them can develop and take on those roles."[38]

Unfortunately, most U.S. citizens have inadequate savings and retirement benefits to fund their retirements. According to a study by the Employee Benefit Research Institute, 60% of workers report that they have less than $25,000 in savings, excluding the value of their home.[39] Based on the findings of a joint study sponsored by the Transamerica Center for Retirement Studies and Aegon, it is also thought that Millennials in many countries will be less financially stable in retirement than the previous generation because many are not planning well enough for the move into retirement.[40] Several proposed presidential initiatives might address some of these issues by focusing on retirement planning equity (limiting the amount that can be saved in retirement accounts) and encouraging individuals to invest in a new type of savings bond.[41]

While traditional pension plans that provided a defined amount for retirement at a defined age were the norm for decades, since the early 1980s, fewer companies

FIGURE 13-8 The Three-Legged Stool of Retirement Income

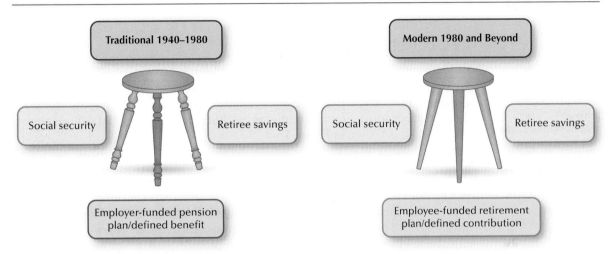

have provided these plans. Instead, employee-funded retirement accounts have become standard. Evidence provided by the Benefit Research Institute shows that in 1979, of all private-sector employees, 62% of those who had retirement benefits were enrolled solely in pension plans, 16% were enrolled solely in defined contribution plans, and 22% were utilizing both programs. In comparison, by 2011, a mere 7% had pension plans, 69% had defined contribution plans, and a percentage similar to the one reported in 1979 participated in both programs.[42] Given these realities, retired individuals must often rely on Social Security payments, which were not designed to provide full retirement income.

Three-legged stool
A model showing the three sources of income to fund an employee's retirement

Financial planners refer to these options as the three-legged stool of retirement income, which is a model showing the three sources of income to fund an employee's retirement. Figure 13-8 shows how the model has changed over time, with workers now carrying a greater financial burden to prepare for retirement. Employers emphasize that employees must take on more responsibility to plan and save for retirement.

Retirement benefits can be a valuable tool for attracting and retaining workers. Sixty percent of employees with less than two years of service at companies with traditional pension plans state that the pension plan is an important reason for their job choice. Further, 80% of workers at companies with traditional pensions plan to continue working for their employer until they retire. Over half of employees surveyed report that they would switch jobs to get better retirement benefits.[43] Therefore, the decisions a company makes about its retirement benefits can have an important and lasting impact on talent management.

13-5a Retirement Plan Concepts

Vesting
A benefit that cannot be taken away

Certain rights are associated with retirement plans. One such right, called vesting, gives employees a benefit that cannot be taken away. If employees resign or are terminated before they have been employed long enough to become vested, no pension rights accrue to them except the funds they have contributed. If employees work for the required number of years to be fully vested, they retain their pension rights and receive the amounts contributed by both the employer and themselves.

Portability
A retirement plan feature that allows employees to move their retirement benefits from one employer to another

Another feature of some retirement plans is portability. In a portable plan, employees can move their retirement benefits from one employer to another. Instead of requiring workers to wait until they retire to move their retirement plan benefits, once workers are vested in a plan, they can transfer their fund balances to other retirement plans if they change jobs.

13-5b Retirement Plans

Retirement plan
A program established
and funded by the em-
ployer and/or employees
to fund employees' retirement years

A retirement plan is a program established and funded by the employer and/or em-ployees to fund employees' retirement years. Organizations are not required to offer retirement plans to employees beyond contributions to Social Security. There are two broad categories of retirement plans: defined benefit plans and defined contri-bution plans, as shown in Figure 13-9.

Defined benefit plan
Retirement program in
which employees are
promised a pension
amount based on age and
years of service

Defined Benefit Pension Plans   A traditional pension plan is one in which the employer makes required contributions and the employee receives a defined amount each month upon retirement. A defined benefit plan is a retirement program in which employees are promised a pension amount based on age and years of service. A small percentage of companies in the private sector offer defined benefit plans to their employees, while public-sector employers still provide them. Based on data from the Pension Benefit Guarantee Corp., there has been a consistent decrease in defined benefit plans from 114,000 in 1985 to a current number of roughly 38,000.[44]

Contributions are based on actuarial calculations of the benefits to be paid to employees after retirement and the formula used to determine such benefits. A de-fined benefit plan gives employees greater assurance of benefits and greater predict-ability in the amount of benefits that will be available for retirement. These plans reward long service with a company.

Companies that provide defined benefit plans must comply with cumbersome and strict government rules regarding the funding of the plan. If the funding is inadequate to pay the benefits promised, the company must make up the shortfall. To reduce some of these risks, some employers have excluded new employees from these pro-grams and/or halted future accruals of benefits. Another option is called de-risking, which enables a company to (1) pay benefits to terminated workers in the form of lump sum payouts or (2) turn over their funds to another provider by purchasing an annuity.[45] Many employers have dropped defined benefit plans in favor of defined contribution plans (discussed next) so that their contribution liabilities are known.

FIGURE 13-9   Comparison of Defined Benefit and Defined Contribution Retirement Plans

Defined Benefit	Defined Contribution
• Typically funded at least in part by employer	• Typically funded by employee and employer
• Amount of benefit paid at retirement is predetermined	• Amount of benefit at retirement is determined on the basis of investment performance
• Investment risk borne by employer	• Investment risk borne by employee
• Benefit guaranteed by Pension Benefit Guaranty Corporation (PBGC)	• Benefit not guaranteed
• Amount of contribution changes on the basis of actuarial assumption	• Amount of contribution is defined by employee participation level and company match
• Common in public sector and unionized workforces	• Common in private sector and nonunion workforces

Defined benefit pension plans offer greater security to employees. The benefits are guaranteed by the Pension Benefit Guaranty Corporation (PBGC). The PBGC maintains a solvency fund to pay benefits if a company goes bankrupt and cannot pay its retiree benefits. The fund is supported by employer contributions of approximately $60 per participant per year.

Defined benefit plans may see a resurgence, but in a modified form. Since so few companies offer them to new employees, reintroducing these plans could be a source of differentiation in the labor market. However, funding risk and regulatory burdens make companies wary. Companies may create new hybrid plans that will be attractive to employees without creating too great a liability for the employer.[46]

Defined contribution plan
Retirement program in which the employer and/or employee makes an annual payment to an employee's retirement account

Defined Contribution Pension Plans A defined contribution plan is a retirement program in which the employer and/or employee makes an annual payment to an employee's retirement account. The key to this plan is the contribution rate; employee retirement benefits depend on fixed contributions and investment earnings. Profit-sharing plans, employee stock ownership plans (ESOPs), and 401(k) plans are common defined contribution plans. Because of their portability and other features, these plans are sometimes preferred by younger, shorter-term employees. When individuals retire or begin working for other employers, they can keep funds in the current account, withdraw the cash and use or reinvest it some other way, or do both to varying degrees. Research indicates that more employees who change jobs before retiring are leaving the funds in these accounts instead of withdrawing them.[47]

Since these plans hinge on the investment returns on previous contributions, employees' retirement benefits are somewhat less secure and predictable. Companies can also be held liable for their management of ESOPs when the performance of stock is below what it expected. The pharmaceutical firm Amgen was taken to court when it provided a program to its workers that provided stock that eventually underperformed as a result of two ineffective and potentially unsafe drugs that the company sold. Lawsuits by employees and nonemployees focused on the lack of transparency in the company's disclosure of its financial challenges, as well as the impact these challenges would likely have on stock prices.[48]

401(k) plan
Plan allows for a percentage of an employee's pay to be withheld and invested in a tax-deferred account

The 401(k) plan gets its name from section 401(k) of the federal tax code. This plan allows for a percentage of an employee's pay to be withheld and invested in a tax-deferred account. 401(k) plans now dominate the field of employment-based retirement programs.[49] These plans are attractive to employees because contributions are made on a tax-deferred basis, so the employee pays lower income taxes during working years. Of course, taxes must be paid when funds are withdrawn during retirement. The most common reason given by companies for offering 401(k) plans is a concern for employees' financial security.[50] However, with 401(k) plans, the employee becomes the manager of investment risk and the decision maker regarding investment options. The Department of Labor now requires companies to disclose to participants in quarterly and annual statements (which are available online) information about the fees, expenses, and investment alternatives associated with their 401(k) plans.[51] Another option that few employers offer is the use of annuities that pay certain fixed or variable amounts of money to individuals in retirement. For example, the high-tech products and services company United Technologies has such a program that eventually transfers employees' investments in 401(k) plans into annuities that provide guaranteed income in retirement.[52]

There are many features that companies may include in the 401(k) plan. A valuable characteristic of these plans is company matching contributions. Many employers match the employee's contribution up to a percentage of pay, which encourages employees to enroll in such plans and feel positive about making contributions themselves. Another option is allowing employees to obtain loans from their 401(k) accounts. Individuals are expected to pay back loans from these accounts with interest. However, if a loan cannot be repaid, it is classified as an early withdrawal for individuals below the age of 59.5 years, income taxes are paid on the amount withdrawn, and a 10% penalty is assessed. Evidence suggests that this loan feature can encourage more employees to participate in 401(k) programs.[53] Money can also be taken out of these accounts free of penalties to buy a home.[54]

Auto-enrollment
Process by which employee contributions to a 401(k) plan are started automatically when an employee is eligible to join the plan

There are other ways that employees can be encouraged to participate in 401(k) programs. One feature that can help is the use of automatic enrollment. Auto-enrollment is a process by which employee contributions to a 401(k) plan are started automatically when the employee is eligible to join the plan. Some companies set the initial contribution rate at around 3% of pay, but others are setting the initial rate higher, from 4% to 6%. The employee has the ability to increase that rate or to stop the contributions voluntarily. Some companies also use automatic increases of 1% a year to boost employee contribution levels unless employees voluntarily stop these increases.[55] Since smaller companies are less inclined than larger firms to offer 401(k) and other retirement programs to their employees, there is interest in offering tax incentives to help small businesses facilitate effective retirement planning.[56]

Financial education and counseling can be used to help employees understand how to manage their 401(k) and get the greatest value from the plan. People who use investment assistance earn better returns on their retirement funds than those who manage their own accounts. Employers can offer a variety of education programs designed for specific groups of employees. More than 75% of companies offer online education tools such as webinars, risk assessments, and retirement calculators.[57] Since companies have turned to 401(k) plans as their main retirement programs, educating employees is an important part of helping them achieve financial security in retirement. Overall, there are several approaches that companies should use to improve employee participation rates, which include:

- Use automatic enrollment and increases to get the ball rolling.
- Help workers roll over money from previous tax-deferred plans so that they dedicate more funds to retirement.
- Keep an eye out for employees who need help managing their current accounts and/or retirement planning.
- Custom-tailor retirement communications to fit the needs of the audience.
- Adopt a holistic approach to retirement planning that considers all investments and potential streams of money.[58]

Cash Balance Pension Plans Some employers have changed traditional pension plans to hybrids based on ideas from both defined benefit and defined contribution plans. One such plan is a cash balance plan, a retirement program in which benefits are based on accumulated annual company contributions, expressed as a percentage of pay, plus interest credited each year. With these plans, retirement benefits accumulate at the same annual rate until an employee retires. Since cash balance plans spread funding across a worker's entire career, these plans work better for mobile younger workers. The plans are gaining in popularity, especially among small businesses, which account for 84% of these plans.[59]

Cash balance plan
Retirement program in which benefits are based on accumulated annual company contributions, expressed as a percentage of pay, plus interest credited each year

13-6 Legal Regulation of Retirement Benefits

Numerous laws and regulations affect retirement plans. Key regulations govern plan communications, funding, and other important aspects of retirement programs. The laws have been enacted to ensure that workers understand their plans and are assured of receiving the full value of promised benefits.

13-6a Employee Retirement Income Security Act

Widespread criticism of many pension plans led to enactment of the Employee Retirement Income Security Act (ERISA) in 1974. The purpose of this law is to ensure that private pension plans and other plans governed by ERISA meet minimum standards. ERISA requires plans to periodically provide participants with information about plan features (such as vesting), funding, and benefit accrual amounts. It also gives participants the right to file lawsuits for violations of the law. Plans falling under ERISA can also establish statutes of limitation on the period of time that individuals can challenge denial of benefits (e.g., for long-term disability programs), as long as standards are considered reasonable and are allowed by law.[60]

Violations of ERISA can lead to costly lawsuits for employers. A U.S. Supreme Court case involving US Airways and an employee who was injured in a car accident determined that ERISA allows courts to modify the content of a health plan. This ruling highlights the idea that benefit plans should be clearly written and reasonable to implement.[61] In another case, a court found that Pactiv Corp. did not function as an ERISA fiduciary when it fired an employee who was previously injured on the job because he did not provide documentation showing that he could return to work.[62] These cases illustrate that employers should spend considerable time developing policies that comply with the provisions of the law.

13-6b Retirement Benefits and Age Discrimination

According to a 1986 amendment to the Age Discrimination in Employment Act (ADEA), most employees cannot be forced to retire at a specific age. In many employer pension plans, "normal retirement" is the age at which employees can retire and receive full pension benefits. Employers must decide whether individuals who continue to work past normal retirement age (typically 65) are eligible for the standard benefit package provided to active employees under age 65. Changes in Social Security regulations have increased the age for full benefits past age 65, so modifications in policies may occur.

Early Retirement Many pension plans include provisions for early retirement to allow workers to retire before the normal retirement age. Phased retirement is an alternative used by individuals and firms. Historically, employees either worked full time or were retired full time. Phased retirement allows employees to bridge between these two states while offering the company a chance to retain important knowledge and skills.

Some employers use early retirement buyout programs to cut back their workforces and reduce costs. Buyout programs often include incentives such as outplacement services, health care benefits, and a severance payment. There is, of course, a risk that too many employees will participate, thereby leaving the company shorthanded. Employers must take care to make these early retirement programs truly voluntary and to communicate them effectively.

Older Workers Benefit Protection Act The Older Workers Benefit Protection Act (OWBPA) was enacted in 1990 as an amendment to the ADEA. It requires equal treatment for older workers in early retirement or severance situations. It also sets specific criteria that must be met if older workers are asked to sign waivers promising not to sue for age discrimination in exchange for severance benefits during layoffs.

13-7 Health Care Benefits

LO5 Explain the importance of managing the costs of health benefits and identify some methods of doing so.

Employers provide a variety of health care and medical benefits, usually through insurance coverage. Major changes brought about by the Patient Protection and Affordable Care Act (PPACA), which is still evolving, may significantly alter the involvement of employers in providing these essential benefits. This legislation is discussed in the following section.

Employees often consider health plans to be one of the most important benefits that companies offer. The most common plans cover medical, dental, prescription drug, and vision care expenses for employees and their dependents. Unfortunately, a recent study of government survey data found that 11.5 million fewer Americans were covered by organization-sponsored health insurance plans in 2011 compared to those who were covered in 2000. Findings also showed that fewer private companies provided such plans over this time line, and fewer employees enrolled in them.[63]

13-7a Increases in Health Benefit Costs

Managing health care benefits can be challenging, time-consuming, and expensive for companies. For several decades, the costs associated with health care coverage have increased considerably in the United States. This raises a number of concerns for both employers and employees because they have to pay for this coverage.

Between 2000 and 2011, the average yearly premium for a single worker increased by approximately 100%, while the premiums for families rose approximately 125%. Yearly premiums have increased somewhat overall, but employees are now expected to pay much more of these premiums.[64] The average expenses associated with health care coverage are expected to increase to $11,304 per employee per year.[65] In California alone, there has been a 185% increase in the cost of health care premiums since 2002, and average premiums for single and family plans are all higher than national averages.[66] Once again, these increased expenses have led companies to require employees to shoulder some of the costs of premiums and benefits. On average, it is predicted that employees will pay 23.6% of premiums (or $2,664), while average out-of-pocket expenses are projected to be $2,487.[67]

Even though overall costs and spending have risen, the good news is that growth rates in health care spending in the United States have been relatively slow, likely driven by recessionary pressures. However, such spending might increase because of new health care legislation.[68] The following sections summarize this legislation and discuss the implications for organizations.

13-7b Health Care Reform Legislation

Landmark legislation enacted in 2010 changed health care in the United States, making insurance available to an additional 32 million people. Provisions of the Patient Protection and Affordable Care Act (PPACA) were phased in over several years, culminating in universal coverage in 2014. While the act was strongly opposed by many Americans,[69] the U.S. Supreme Court ruled in 2012 and 2015 that the provisions of the law were constitutional. Therefore, the landscape of employer-sponsored health benefits will continue to undergo many significant changes over the coming years.

There has been considerable debate over a number of the provisions outlined in the PPACA. The PPACA requires employer-provided plans to cover various contraceptive services and drugs such as the "morning-after pill," a mandate that may violate rights outlined in the Religious Freedom Restoration Act.[70] Organizations with religious affiliations such as Hobby Lobby, the Christian bookstore firm Mardel, Conestoga, and Hercules Industrials have challenged the law in court. The U.S. Supreme court determined that family-owned, private companies could not be forced to offer workers health insurance plans that cover contraceptive procedures that violate religious freedom and expression.[71]

Another area of concern involves the law's threshold for determining whether workers are considered full-time employees. The PPACA currently specifies that individuals who work 30 hours a week or more are considered full-time employees and should be included in the overall count used to determine if a company must provide workers health care coverage. Some business professionals suggest that this threshold be increased so that employers won't reduce employee hours to avoid having to comply with PPACA provisions.[72] Legislators are considering whether to change this work-hour threshold.[73] One Society for Human Resource Management study determined that 21% of member organizations have either decreased or plan to decrease the number of hours per week for part-time work below a cutoff of 30.[74]

Key Provisions The PPACA includes many important provisions intended to provide affordable health care for all citizens. To achieve this goal, enrollment in health coverage is now mandated for every citizen. Key elements of the law are highlighted in Figure 13-10, and more details are provided in the next sections.

13-7c Employer-Sponsored Plans

Employers face a decision about continuing to offer their own health insurance plans or to drop their plans in favor of government-sponsored coverage. Employers with at least 50 full-time or full-time equivalent (FTE) employees who work at least 30 hours per week are required to offer minimum essential health care coverage to these workers and their dependent children (until they are 26 years old).[75] Health care coverage needs to be affordable, and employee costs cannot exceed government-mandated levels.[76] Employers that fail to provide adequate health coverage will pay an annual penalty of $2,000 per employee beyond the first 30 full-time workers. As a result, some employers are considering whether to cut staff or reduce hours to avoid fines, while other companies have decided that it makes more sense to just pay the fines.[77] Employers that offer coverage could pay a $3,000 penalty per employee for those who receive a premium tax credit to buy insurance because the plan would be considered too costly, using a benchmark of 9.5% of a worker's household income.[78]

Dropping health insurance plans, or hiring more part-time staff and/or decreasing the number of hours employees work in order to avoid providing health care coverage, can have a negative effect on attracting, motivating, and retaining employees. Companies should also be aware of the potential for customer backlash over

FIGURE 13-10 Key Provisions of the Affordable Care Act

Requires most individuals to maintain minimum essential coverage or pay a penalty

Requires companies with 50 or more employees (who work 30 hours a week or more) to provide health care coverage or pay a penalty

Extends dependent coverage up to age 26

Eliminates lifetime and unreasonable annual benefit limits

Requires coverage for preventive services

Restricts insurance companies from setting rates based on an individual's health status, medical conditions, other health-related factors

Creates state-run health care exchanges through which insurance companies will offer competitive health plans

the use of these cost-cutting approaches. After experiencing weakened sales, companies such as Darden Restaurants and Papa John's International have tempered their publicly declared plans to reduce workers' hours and charge higher prices.[79] Also, a recent survey showed that only 3% of employers are likely to discontinue health care plans for active employees as a result of the change in law.[80]

Employers that provide high-cost ("Cadillac") health benefits to employees may face a 40% tax starting in 2018. The threshold for this tax is $10,200 for an individual plan and $27,500 for a family plan. Some employers offer high-cost plans because a generous plan is part of their attraction and retention strategy, and the inability to offer these top-tier programs might harm the ability to effectively manage talent.[81]

Employers must report the value of employer-paid health coverage on employees' W-2 forms. Additional rules have been developed regarding how and what information should be reported to the IRS and employees.[82]

13-7d Controlling Health Care Benefit Costs

Employers offering health care benefits are taking a number of approaches to control and reduce their costs. The most frequently used strategies include the following:[83]

- Increasing deductibles and copayments
- Instituting high-deductible plans
- Increasing employee contributions

- Using managed care
- Limiting family coverage; excluding spouses
- Switching to consumer-driven health plans
- Increasing health preventive and wellness efforts

Deductible
Money paid by an insured individual before a health plan pays for medical expenses

Increasing Employee Cost Sharing A deductible is money paid by an insured individual before the medical plan pays for medical expenses. Employers that raise the per-person deductible from $300 to $500 realize significant savings in health care expenses because employees use fewer health care services and prescription drugs.

The use of high-deductible plans is expected to increase as a result of the PPACA. Employers are trying to secure inexpensive programs that will enable them to comply with the law's stipulations, thus avoiding costly fines and taxes (such as the "Cadillac" tax). The programs are often relatively inexpensive, but patients must pay high deductibles that are often $1,000 or more before coverage begins. A Towers and Watson survey determined that 79% of large companies planned to provide employees with high-deductible plans; FedEx is one such company that is doing so for its 225,000 U.S. employees.[84]

Copayment
The portion of medical expenses paid by an insured individual for medical treatment

Copayments are the portion of medical expenses paid by an insured individual for medical treatment. For example, the health plan may require a fixed $20 copay for each physician visit. Alternatively, the copay may be based on a percentage, such as 20%, of medical treatment costs up to a set dollar amount. Companies can increase the fixed copay amount, increase the percentage, or increase the dollar amount that employees share for costs. For example, copays and deductibles for more high-cost drugs are up 25%, and some companies are even making employees pay from 10% to 30% of the prices of these drugs.[85]

13-7e Increasing Employee Contributions

Employees are usually required to pay a portion of the monthly premium to maintain health care insurance. On average, single employees pay 18% of premiums, while employees with family coverage pay 28% of premiums. Over 50% of employers plan to increase the percentage that employees contribute to health plan premiums.[86]

Managed care
Approaches that monitor and reduce medical costs through restrictions and market system alternatives

Using Managed Care Several other types of programs attempt to reduce health care costs paid by employers. Managed care consists of approaches that monitor and reduce medical costs through restrictions and market system alternatives. Managed care plans emphasize primary and preventive care, the use of specific providers that charge lower prices, restrictions on certain kinds of treatment, and prices negotiated with hospitals and physicians. Preferred provider organizations (PPO) and health maintenance organizations (HMO) are the most common forms of managed care.

Spousal Exclusions Spousal exclusion provisions limit access to a company's health plan when an employee's spouse works for another company that offers health insurance. Companies may charge a premium surcharge to enroll the spouse or require that the spouse enroll in his or her own employer's plan. Approximately 20% of employers have adopted these restrictions, and more companies are planning to do so.[87]

Consumer-driven health (CDH) plan
Health plan that provides employer financial contributions to employees to help cover their health-related expenses

13-7f Consumer-Driven Health Plans

Some employers are turning to health insurance plans that allow employees to choose their insurance. The most widely used is a consumer-driven health (CDH) plan, which is a health plan that provides employer financial contributions to employees to help cover their health-related expenses. For example, Sears Holdings Corporation and Darden Restaurants recently implemented these plans. The companies provide a fixed sum of money to employees and allow them to choose their medical coverage and insurer from an online marketplace. Any employee can buy up the benefit level by paying additional costs beyond what the employer contributes.[88] CDH plans may represent the wave of the future as they give employees ownership of their health care dollars. Many more large and small companies are indeed offering such programs.

13-7g Dental and Vision Coverage

Additional health benefits frequently include coverage for dental and vision care expenses. Employees typically pay a portion of the premium for dental and vision plans. These plans often emphasize preventive care. Semi-annual dental visits and annual optometry visits may be covered in full or at minimal cost to the employee.

13-7h Wellness Initiatives and Other Innovative Health Care Programs

Preventive measures and wellness efforts can take many forms in companies. Many employers offer programs to educate employees about health care costs and how to reduce them. Newsletters, formal classes, and many other approaches are designed to help employees understand why health care costs are increasing and what they can do to control them. A major strategy of cost reduction is wellness programs that focus on improving worker health. Employees receive incentives to use wellness facilities and to participate in health-related programs.

Almost 40% of employers are expected to encourage employees to enroll in wellness plans and to focus on cost savings when making decisions about their health care.[89] Nearly 75% of companies use incentives to engage employees in health improvement programs, with an average incentive of $430 per employee.[90] Creating a "culture of health" and involving workers' family members in wellness efforts can go a long way toward lowering health care costs and improving lives.

ETHICS

However, there are some challenges associated with the use of health and wellness programs to more effectively manage health care costs. For instance, several Equal Employment Opportunity Commission lawsuits involving companies such as Honeywell International that use significant incentives to motivate employees to sign up for wellness program has some top corporate leaders threatening to turn against the PPACA. The law allows organizations to offer incentives that equal up to half of health care costs, but some believe that the medical testing required to get these discounts is a violation of the Americans with Disabilities Act (ADA). Under the ADA, medical tests are permissible for voluntary wellness programs, but an argument can be made that large incentives essentially make such programs mandatory.[91] Although these initiatives are intended to save money, they pose some ethical issues because employees may feel that their employer is invading their personal privacy or putting cost savings before individual freedom. Another concern is that employees might not feel comfortable participating in workout sessions and wellness activities with their coworkers because these activities can be overly competitive and can invite individuals to judge each other.[92]

Employers are also relying on a constellation of innovative health care programs to promote interest and participation among employees. Such policies enable

PERSPECTIVE

Innovative Health Care Programs Beneficial

Some companies have started to offer a variety of innovative health care programs that provide better services to employees. These policies have enabled companies to encourage workers to focus more on health care matters and to participate in corporate programs. Employees are also more educated about health care issues and the available opportunities provided by their employers.

Numerous company examples can be highlighted. For instance, BMW created a large health care clinic staffed with almost 50 employees at its Greer, South Carolina facility. This center gives workers access to vision, dental, occupational, X-ray, and lab services, which has resulted in positive gains in the workplace. The Archdiocese of Indianapolis, Chrysler, and a number of other organizations have started using health advocates who provide employees and their dependents with guidance about health matters, including getting medical care, working with insurance companies, and attending educational sessions.

Other programs can also be beneficial. Partnering with Presbyterian Healthcare Services, Intel started Connected Care, a plan that provides workers and their dependents with access to quality services that ultimately reduce costs because of increased coordination and planning between the company and the provider (called an *accountable care organization*). Finally, United Food and Commercial Workers International Union & Employees Trust relies on a web-based tool to help retired grocery store workers make decisions about their health care plans.[93]

As evidenced by these examples, companies can promote health care with a number of programs that are innovative, interactive, and educational. HR professionals can take on a leadership role in the development in these policies, which positions HR as a key player in the promotion of health care matters in the workplace. Given these opportunities to enhance health awareness and program participation, consider the following questions:

1. How would you rate these innovative programs implemented in these companies? Is there anything these companies could have done better to promote health care among employees?

2. What kinds of innovative programs do you think organizations should offer employees? If you were an HR professional, what would you do to promote health care in your organization?

companies to offer better benefits to workers, thus improving their health. These polices have also helped employers better educate employees about health-related matters, thus promoting wellness more effectively in the workplace. The "HR Perspective: Innovative Health Care Programs Beneficial" feature discusses how different programs can be used to promote health care among employees.

13-7i Health Care Legislation

The importance of health care benefits to employers and employees has led to the creation of a variety of federal and state laws. Several laws have been enacted to provide protection for employees who leave their employers, either voluntarily or involuntarily. To date, the two most important laws that govern issues related to the protection of former workers are COBRA and HIPAA.

COBRA Provisions The Consolidated Omnibus Budget Reconciliation Act (COBRA) requires that most employers with 20 or more full-time and/or part-time employees offer extended health care coverage to certain groups of plan participants. The different groups are as follows:[94]

- Employees who voluntarily quit or are terminated
- Widowed or divorced spouses and dependent children of former or current employees
- Retirees and their spouses and dependent children whose health care coverage ends
- Any child who is born or adopted by a covered employee
- Other individuals involved in the plan such as independent contractors and agents/directors

Qualifying event
An event that causes a plan participant to lose group health benefits

A qualifying event is an event that causes a plan participant to lose group health benefits. Typically, reduction in work hours or loss of employment constitutes a qualifying event for employees. Divorce or death of an employee constitutes a qualifying event for covered family members. When a qualifying event occurs, a complex notification process begins. There are a number of deadlines that the company and the employee must meet to comply with COBRA requirements. Figure 13-11 shows the timeline regarding notification and important qualifying circumstances.

The individual no longer employed by the organization must pay the premiums, but the employer may charge the individual up to 102% of the premium costs. The extra 2% generally falls short of the true cost of providing this coverage.

Compliance with COBRA regulations can be very complicated, and noncompliance with the law can lead to lawsuits and substantial penalties. Consequently, COBRA requirements often mean additional paperwork and related costs for many

FIGURE 13-11 Timeline of COBRA Notification Requirements

Event	Notification Deadline
1. COBRA Initial Notice must be provided	1. Within *30 days* after the employee first becomes enrolled in the group health plan
2. Employer to notify plan administrator	2. Within *30 days* after the qualifying event date
3. COBRA Qualifying Event Notice	3. *14 days* from the date the plan administrator receives notification from employee
4. Qualified beneficiary has right to elect COBRA Coverage	4. *60 days* from the date of COBRA notice
5. Qualified beneficiary initial premium due	5. *45 days* from the date of electing COBRA
6. Monthly COBRA premium grace period	6. *30 days* after the first day of each month
7. Employee/qualified beneficiary to notify plan administrator of a qualifying event	7. *60 days*
8. Continuation period ends	8. *18 months* after qualifying event for terminated employees
	29 months after qualifying event for disabled terminated employees
	36 months after qualifying event for spouse and dependent children plan participants

Source: Adapted from https://www.goigoe.com/Employers/COBRATimelines.aspx.

employers. COBRA administration is frequently outsourced to a third-party administrator that has expertise and data processing capabilities.

HIPAA Provisions The Health Insurance Portability and Accountability Act (HIPAA) of 1996 allows employees to switch their health insurance plans when they change employers and to enroll in health coverage with the new company regardless of pre-existing health conditions. The statute also prohibits group insurance plans from dropping coverage for a sick employee and requires them to make individual coverage available to people who leave group plans.

One of the greatest impacts of HIPAA comes from its provisions regarding the privacy of employee medical records. These provisions require employers to provide privacy notices to employees. They also regulate the unauthorized disclosure of protected health information. In 2013, several revisions to HIPAA went into effect that call for companies to provide more training on new security and breach standards. One change is that any entity that handles personal health information is considered a business associate under the law. Another change is that any impermissible utilization or transfer of personal health information is considered a breach, even if there is no apparent risk of harming the person involved.[95]

LO6 Describe the growth of financial, family-oriented, and time-off benefits and their importance to employees.

13-8 Financial Benefits

Companies may offer employees a wide range of special benefits that provide financial support. Figure 13-12 illustrates some common financial benefits. Employers find that such benefits can be useful in attracting and retaining employees. Workers like receiving these benefits, which are often not taxed as income.

13-8a Insurance Benefits

In addition to health care insurance, some companies provide other types of insurance. These benefits offer major advantages for employees because employers may pay some or all of the costs. Even when employers do not pay any of the costs,

FIGURE 13-12 Common Types of Financial Benefits

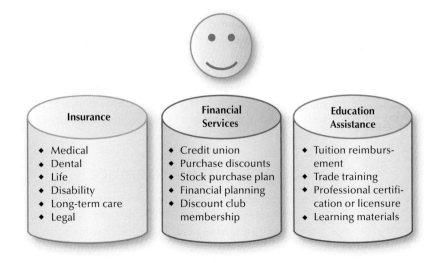

Insurance
- ◆ Medical
- ◆ Dental
- ◆ Life
- ◆ Disability
- ◆ Long-term care
- ◆ Legal

Financial Services
- ◆ Credit union
- ◆ Purchase discounts
- ◆ Stock purchase plan
- ◆ Financial planning
- ◆ Discount club membership

Education Assistance
- ◆ Tuition reimbursement
- ◆ Trade training
- ◆ Professional certification or licensure
- ◆ Learning materials

employees still benefit because of the lower rates available through group programs. The most common types of insurance benefits are the following:

- *Life insurance*: A typical level of coverage is one and one-half or two times an employee's annual salary.
- *Disability insurance*: Both *short-term* and *long-term disability insurance* provide continuing income protection for employees who become disabled and are unable to work.
- *Long-term care insurance*: Usually voluntary, these plans allow employees to purchase insurance to cover costs for long-term health care in a nursing home, in an assisted-living facility, or at home. Though employees usually pay for the premiums, they may get cheaper rates through employer-sponsored group plans.
- *Legal insurance*: In these plans, employees (or employers) pay a flat fee for a fixed number of hours of legal assistance each month. In return, they have the right to use the service of a network of lawyers to handle their legal problems.

13-8b Financial Services

Financial benefits include a wide variety of items. A *credit union* sponsored by the employer provides savings, checking, lending, and other financial services for employees. *Purchase discounts* allow employees to buy goods or services from their employers at reduced rates, often at a company store. *Discount programs* and *club memberships* may also be offered to allow employees to purchase goods from local vendors or "club" stores at lower rates. The programs are inexpensive for companies to implement and are viewed positively by employees.[96]

Employee thrift plans, savings plans, or *stock purchase plans* may be available. To illustrate, in a *stock purchase plan*, employees may buy shares in the company at a discount, or the company pays the brokerage fees. This type of plan allows employees to benefit from the future growth of the corporation with the intention of increasing employee loyalty to the organization and interest in its success.

Financial planning and *counseling* are especially valuable services for executives, many of whom may need information on investments and tax shelters, as well as comprehensive financial counseling because of their higher levels of compensation. The importance of these financial planning benefits will likely grow as a greater percentage of workers approach retirement age and need to plan for retirement. Many employees are also focused on saving for their children's college education, given the many concerns about rising student loan debt in the United States, so they are looking for assistance with this issue.[97]

Relocation Assistance Relocation benefits are offered by many firms. Companies may pay for temporary living expenses and moving expenses, and help a "trailing spouse" find a job. Numerous other financial-related benefits may be offered as well, including the use of a company car, company expense accounts, and assistance in buying or selling a house.

13-8c Education Assistance

Another benefit that is popular with employees is education assistance and tuition aid, which pays some or all of the costs associated with formal education courses and degree programs. Many employers offer some form of education assistance to their employees. Some employers reimburse the employee for a percentage of tuition based on grades earned, while others may require only a passing grade of C or above. Often, the course of study must be related to the employee's current job or a logical career path within the company. Unless the education paid for by the employer meets certain conditions, employees must count the cost of educational aid as taxable income.

13-8d Severance Pay

Companies may provide severance pay to individuals whose jobs are eliminated or who leave the company by mutual agreement. While the Worker Adjustment and Retraining Notification Act (WARN) of 1988 requires employers to give 60 days' notice of mass layoff or plant closings, it does not mandate severance pay. The amount of severance pay is often determined by an employee's level within the organization and years of service with the company. Some employers provide continued health insurance or outplacement assistance as part of the severance package.

There are some financial issues that should be considered when offering severance payments. A recent U.S. Supreme Court ruling specified that severance payments are considered taxable income for FICA calculations.[98] Severance pay may also affect the unemployment benefits received by former employees. Much of this is determined by how states treat severance payments, how the company specifies these payments, and the company policies are implemented.[99] HR professionals and managers should consult state guidelines when instituting severance pay.

13-9 Family-Oriented Benefits

The composition of families in the United States has changed significantly in the past few decades. Two-earner families and single-parent households are now the norm. Workers therefore seek out companies that balance work and nonwork obligations and offer family-friendly benefits. To enhance the recruiting and retention of high-quality talent, employers have established a variety of family-oriented benefits. The following "HR Perspective: Helping Employees Realize the American Dream" feature describes how some companies assist workers with home ownership. A major legal requirement regarding family-oriented benefits is the Family and Medical Leave Act (FMLA), which provides for unpaid leaves of absence.

13-9a Family and Medical Leave Act

The FMLA was enacted in 1993 and has been amended several times. It covers all federal, state, and private employers with 50 or more employees who live within 75 miles of the workplace. Only employees who have worked at least 12 months and 1,250 hours in the previous year are eligible for leave under the FMLA. The law provides for unpaid leave; however, some companies pay short-term disability benefits during FMLA leaves under certain conditions.

FMLA Leave Provisions The law requires employers to allow eligible employees to take a maximum of 12 weeks of unpaid, job-protected leave during any 12-month period for the following situations:[100]

- Birth of a child and care for the newborn within one year of birth
- Adoption or foster care placement of a child
- Caring for a spouse, child, or parent with a serious health condition
- Serious health condition of the employee

PERSPECTIVE

Helping Employees Realize the American Dream

Among the list of creative benefits some companies offer, a few have implemented programs that help their employees realize the dream of home ownership. These programs are a low-cost, high-reward way to increase employee commitment and retention.

CVS Caremark, Northrop Grumman Shipbuilding, and Loyola University have all found ways to assist their employees with buying a home. Elements of their programs include the following:

- Educating workers about home ownership
- Counseling workers on how to improve their credit score
- Steering them to affordable neighborhoods with dependable public transit
- Assisting with down payment or closing costs
- Forgiving loans if the employee stays with the company for a required number of years

The city of Chicago is a hotbed of this activity because of a program started by the Metropolitan Planning Council several years ago that offers free real estate and credit counseling to employees of local firms. The program was so successful that the state of Illinois now offers tax credits and matches incentives paid by companies to help with employee home purchases. Over 50 Illinois employers now take advantage of the state's program.

Of course, companies located outside of Illinois also offer these opportunities to their employees. Aurora Health Care, a Milwaukee-based hospital system with 29,000 employees, provides a $3,000 forgivable loan to employees

who buy homes in the city. Over 400 employees, including dieticians and nursing assistants, have purchased homes through the assistance program. The hospital has benefited by improved employee productivity and loyalty, along with a significant reduction in turnover.

CVS employees typically earn between $30,000 and $50,000 and are therefore very grateful for the counseling and financial help extended by the company. CVS uses a learning center staffed by a local faith-based organization because many of their employees don't trust banks and don't want the company to know too much about their personal finances. At Loyola University, to be eligible for help with buying a home, employees must buy near specific mass transit lines because the institution has a green initiative to reduce reliance on cars for commuting.

With or without government incentives, employers find that programs aimed at helping employees become homeowners provide win-win situations. This is an example of employers providing creative and useful benefits to employees who can really use them.[101]

Based on these issues, answer the following questions:

1. Do you think offering home ownership benefits will improve employees' work satisfaction? If so, why?

2. What other benefits could be offered by companies to encourage and facilitate employee home ownership?

- Military family members who must handle the affairs for military members called to active duty
- Twenty-six weeks leave to care for a military servicemember injured while on active duty

Serious health condition
An illness or injury that requires inpatient care or continuing treatment by a health care provider for medical problems that exist beyond three days

A serious health condition is an illness or injury that requires inpatient care or continuing treatment by a health care provider for medical problems that exist beyond three days. An employer may require a medical certificate from a health care provider to support the reason for the employee's leave. The Department of Labor has issued many guidelines regarding FMLA employee leaves, as shown in Figure 13-13.

FIGURE 13-13 Guidelines Regarding FMLA Administration

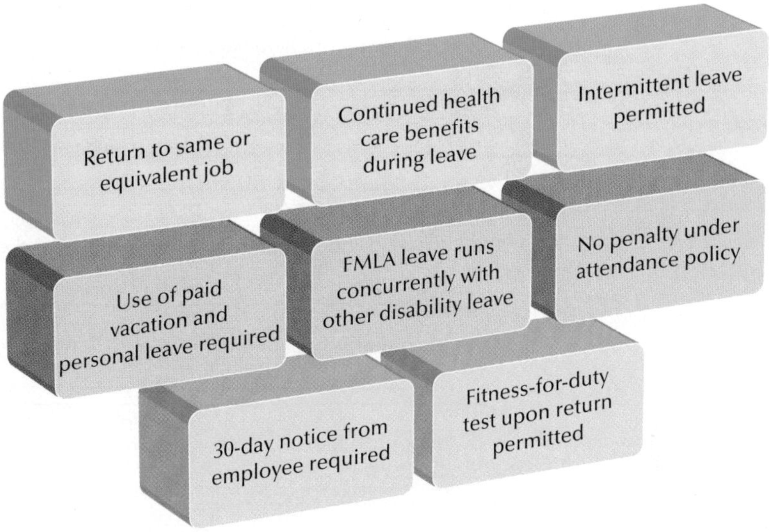

Source: http://www.dol.gov/whd/fmla.

The FMLA has been revised and/or reevaluated at various times. Noteworthy revisions were made in 2009 regarding military servicemembers and their families. Expanded coverage allows families of injured active military servicemembers to take caregiving leave for up to 26 weeks to assist servicemembers who were injured on active duty. The law was further expanded to help families of National Guard or Reserves personnel manage their affairs while the member is on active duty in support of a contingency operation. A recent interpretation by the Department of Labor suggests that employees will be able to request leave under the FMLA to take care of adult children who are suffering from a serious illness under certain conditions.[102]

Impact of the FMLA Since the enactment of the FMLA, a significant percentage of employees have taken family and medical leave. Although FMLA leave is unpaid, employers have to cover the workload for employees on family leave. There is sometimes concern that employees who use such leave might not be meeting work expectations or are negatively impacting company operations, so accommodation efforts, reasonable scheduling, and performance appraisals can be challenging.[103] As many employees seek to balance work demands with family and medical situations, significant demands have been placed on HR professionals to ensure compliance with FMLA provisions.

13-9b Family-Care Benefits

Family issues are important for many organizations and workers. Companies may offer work–life balance options to all employees regardless of family status. A variety of family benefits can be provided.

Adoption Benefits A number of employers provide maternity and paternity benefits to employees who give birth to children. Some employees adopt children, and in the interest of fairness and life enrichment, some organizations provide specific benefits to support adoption. The following "HR Perspective: Robins & Morton

FIGURE 13-14   Child-Care and Elder-Care Programs

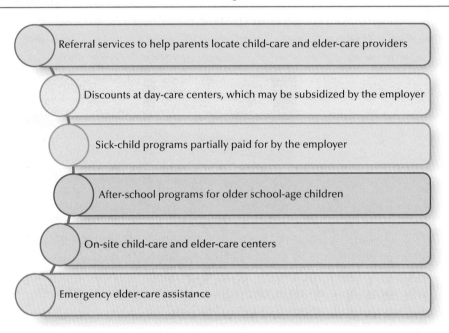

Referral services to help parents locate child-care and elder-care providers

Discounts at day-care centers, which may be subsidized by the employer

Sick-child programs partially paid for by the employer

After-school programs for older school-age children

On-site child-care and elder-care centers

Emergency elder-care assistance

Builds Morale with Adoption Assistance" feature discusses how adoption assistance can be used to enhance how individuals perceive their employers.

Child-Care and Elder-Care Assistance Balancing work and family responsibilities is a major challenge for many workers. Whether they are single parents or part of dual-career couples, employees often experience difficulty obtaining high-quality, affordable child care. Further, employees may be "sandwiched" between raising their own children and caring for aging parents. Figure 13-14 highlights programs to help employees deal with child-care and elder-care issues. These programs can be beneficial to companies because they can enhance employees' work attitudes and retention.

13-10 Paid-Time-Off Benefits

Time-off benefits represent a significant portion of total benefit costs. Employers give employees paid time off for a variety of circumstances. Paid lunch breaks and rest periods, holidays, and vacations are common. But time off is given for many other purposes as well, including various leaves of absence. Employees place high value on paid time off, and some prefer time off rather than extra pay.

13-10a Vacation Pay

Paid vacations are a common benefit. Employers often use graduated vacation time scales based on employees' lengths of service. Some companies have a "use it or lose it" policy whereby employees forfeit any vacation not used during the year. Other companies have policies to buy back unused vacation time, or they allow employees to donate unused vacation days to a pool that can be used by other workers.

PERSPECTIVE

Robins & Morton Builds Morale with Adoption Assistance

More and more companies are offering adoption assistance to their employees. About 39% of U.S. organizations offered adoption assistance just over a decade ago. However, a more recent survey indicated that over half of employers offer such services. It is more common for firms that are listed in *Working Mother* magazine's top 100 family-friendly companies to offer adoption services to their employees. A survey sponsored by the Society for Human Resource Management found that 11% of companies provided money to help with adoptions, and 16% even provided paid leave. Further, the number of organizations that report their adoption practices in association with the Dave Thomas Foundation has been steadily increasing each year. The foundation's leader, Rita Soronen, thinks that more companies would offer such benefits if they knew how much employee morale can be increased at very modest costs.

The Birmingham-based construction and engineering firm Robins & Morton, which employs over 1,000 individuals at multiple worksites located in the Southeast, is one company that has enjoyed these positive experiences. The company initially offered its employees financial support for fertility treatments to aid with pregnancy. However, Aimee Comer, the firm's HR Director, realized the company's

benefits could be improved by providing adoption support as an additional benefit. The company now provides up to $10,000 to its workers for assistance with adoption. Robins & Morton also provides employees with up to eight weeks of paid time off, as well as other leave options, to help with adoptions. It is expected that these additional benefits will cost much less than the expenses associated with a regular pregnancy.

Several families (an estimated 0.5% of the workforce at Robins & Morton) have used the adoption support. This number is similar to national rates of use identified by the Dave Thomas Foundation. These opportunities have increased employees' satisfaction with the company because they believe it cares about families. Consequently, other firms should consider offering similar benefits to improve employee loyalty.[104] Based on these issues, consider the following questions:

1. Do you think companies should be involved in family matters such as adoption? How should HR professionals be involved in this process?

2. What kind of adoption support do you think organizations should offer employees? What kinds of cost constraints do you think should be considered?

13-10b Holiday Pay

Most employers provide pay for a variety of holidays. Employers in the United States commonly offer fewer paid holidays than those in many other countries. The number of paid holidays can vary depending on state/provincial laws and union contracts.

As an abuse-control measure, employers can require employees to work the last scheduled day before a holiday and the first scheduled workday after a holiday to be eligible for holiday pay. Some employers pay time-and-a-half to hourly employees who must work on holidays.

13-10c Leaves of Absence

Employers grant *leaves of absence,* taken as time off with or without pay, for a variety of reasons. All the leaves discussed here add to employer costs even if they are unpaid because the missing employee's work must be covered, either by other employees doing extra work or by temporary employees working under contract.

Leaves are given for a variety of purposes. Some, such as *military leave, election leave,* and *jury leave,* are required by various state and federal laws. Employers can pay the difference between the employee's regular pay and the military, election, or jury pay. Federal law prohibits discriminating against military reservists by requiring them to take vacation time when deployed or in training.

Funeral leave, or *bereavement leave,* is another common type of leave offered. An absence of up to three days for the death of immediate family members is often granted. Some policies also allow unpaid time off for the death of more distant relatives.

Family Leave As mentioned earlier in the chapter, the FMLA guarantees unpaid leave for certain family and medical reasons. Even though *paternity leave* for male workers is available under the FMLA, a relatively low percentage of men take it. The primary reason for the low usage is a perception that it is not as socially acceptable for men to stay home for child-related reasons. This view has begun changing as Gen X fathers are participating more actively in childrearing duties.

Sick Leave Many employers allow employees to miss a limited number of days because of illness without losing pay. The majority of U.S. workers receive paid sick leave. Some employers allow employees to accumulate unused sick leave, which may be used in case of catastrophic illnesses. Others pay their employees for unused sick leave. If an organization does not pay workers for sick time, it might be encouraging them to come to work when they are ill, causing lower productivity, or spreading illness and disease.

13-10d Paid-Time-Off Plans

Paid-time-off (PTO) plans
Plans that combine all sick leave, vacation time, and holidays into a total number of hours or days that employees can take off with pay

A growing number of employers have made use of a paid-time-off (PTO) plans. These plans combine all sick leave, vacation time, and holidays into a total number of hours or days that employees can take off with pay. Many employers have found PTO plans to be more effective than other means of reducing absenteeism, scheduling time off, increasing employee understanding of leave policies, and assisting with recruiting and retention.

13-10e Employee-Paid Group Benefits

To combat the high cost of benefit programs, some companies offer employees the opportunity to purchase benefits through payroll deductions. The cost for these benefits is typically less than if the employee purchased them on his or her own. This occurs because the buying power of the group reduces the cost.

Adding employee-paid voluntary benefits is becoming a popular and cost-effective strategy for many companies. It is part of a trend that gives employees choices but also makes them responsible for selecting and funding the benefits they find valuable. In particular, employees are willing to pay for the cost of income protection insurance in the case of disability. Other employee-paid benefits include pet health care insurance, critical illness coverage (cancer care), and supplemental life insurance. Payroll deductions make employee participation in these plans convenient and simple.

SUMMARY

- Benefits provide additional compensation to employees as a reward for organizational membership.
- Because benefits generally are not taxed, they are highly desired by employees.
- Benefit design and cost-control actions are crucial to strategic benefit efforts.
- Companies in most nations outside the United States are required to provide more generous benefits for their employees than are companies in the United States.
- Public-sector employees in the United States frequently receive richer benefits than employees working in the private sector.
- Benefit administration is often outsourced to third-party administrators.
- Benefits can be viewed as mandatory or voluntary. The general types of benefits include security, health care, retirement, financial, family oriented, and time off.
- Major legally required benefits are Social Security, Medicare, workers' compensation, and unemployment compensation.
- Organizations provide retirement benefits through defined benefit or defined contribution plans. Use of defined contribution and cash balance retirement plans is growing.

- Retirement programs are governed by several federal laws, including ERISA and ADEA.
- Recent federal legislation requires employers to provide health care benefits to their employees.
- Because health care benefit costs have increased significantly, employers are managing their health benefit costs more aggressively by increasing employee copayments and employee contributions, limiting spousal coverage, using managed care, and switching to consumer-driven health (CDH) plans.
- Federal laws allow former employees to continue their group medical insurance after leaving employment and limit the use of pre-existing condition limits for new plan participants.
- Various types of financial services, insurance benefits, relocation assistance, education assistance, and other benefits enhance the appeal of an organization to employees.
- Family-oriented benefits include complying with the Family and Medical Leave Act (FMLA) of 1993 and offering adoption benefits, child-care assistance, and elder-care assistance.
- Holiday pay, vacation pay, various leaves of absence, and paid-time-off plans are another means of providing benefits to employees.

CRITICAL THINKING CHALLENGES

1. Why are benefits strategically important to employers, and what are some key strategic considerations?

2. Discuss the following statement: "Health care costs are out of control in the United States, and increasing conflicts between employers and employees are likely as employers try to reduce their health benefit costs."

3. Assume that as an HR staff member, you have been asked to research consumer-driven health plans because your employer is considering implementing one. Go to a leading benefits information resource, *Employee Benefit News*, at www.benefitnews.com, and identify elements of a successful CDH plan and some examples of firms that use such a plan.

4. Based on the information discussed in the chapter, how would you oversee the design (or redesign) of a benefits program in a large organization? What issues would you consider?

5. Your company now has more than 60 employees. The controller has been handling all of the HR functions, including administration of the company's benefits. You are considering outsourcing the benefit administration function to enable the controller to focus more on the company's accounting needs. Information to assist you in determining the type of services that would best meet the company's needs can be found at www.corbanone.com.

   A. What are the differences between the services offered by an HRO, ASO, and PEO?
   B. Based upon the company's size and the types of benefits offered, which service will best meet the needs of the company?

CASE | The Limited Taps Technology to Communicate Benefits

Employees' satisfaction with their benefits is driven in part by a company's ability to effectively communicate available services and opportunities. A number of companies are now relying on technology in the form of social media and employee blogs that provide employees with important information about their benefit options. These technology-based strategies can be further supported by reaching out to employees with more traditional forms of communication.

The Limited, a medium-sized women's apparel retailer located in the United States, is one company that has adopted these approaches. Since the firm has thousands of employees spread across many storefronts located in 42 states, it had to develop a way to communicate appropriately about benefits in a way that would be appreciated by its workforce, which tends to be young and female. It was decided that all communication content would be developed in house to minimize costs. Messages focus on how to develop healthy lifestyles such as eating better and minimizing stress, as well as how to improve financial well-being.

Another important part of The Limited's benefit strategy focused on using social media to enhance communication with employees. This was a practical approach since employees used blogs, Facebook, and other forms of online communication. The approach also enabled the company to contact individuals on a more frequent basis to provide them with up-to-date information about benefits, and it provided employees with instant access to benefit support. For instance, some of the available options included around-the-clock access to physicians, assigned health consultants, and support for child-related matters.

The Limited also created a program called Total Value of Health that educates employees about their benefits. A website, benefit guide, blogs, and newsletters were all offered to better inform individuals. These communication efforts have resulted in greater familiarization with, understanding of, and utilization of the company's benefits. They also demonstrate how well technology can help HR professionals promote benefits to employees.[105]

QUESTIONS

1. How would you evaluate The Limited's approach for communicating information about benefits to its employees? What might you have done differently if you were an HR professional in the company?

2. If you were to use technology to assist with communicating about benefits, how would you approach doing it? What are the potential challenges associated with your strategy?

SUPPLEMENTAL CASES

Creative Benefits Tie Employees to the Company

This case investigates how a number of companies offer creative benefits to employees to enhance their work engagement and job performance. (For the case, go to www.cengage.com/management/mathis.)

Benefiting Connie

This case describes the problems that can occur when trying to coordinate time-off leaves for employees. (For the case, go to www.cengage.com/management/mathis.)

Delivering Benefits

This case explores how FedEx provides benefits to its employees. (For the case, go to www.cengage.com/management/mathis.)

Strategic Benefits at KPMG Canada

This case explores how KPMG Canada updated its benefit program by involving employees in the design process. (For the case, go to www.cengage.com/management/mathis.)

END NOTES

1. Adapted from Susan Wells, "Benefits Strategies Grow," *HR Magazine,* March 2013, pp. 26–34.
2. Stephen Miller, "Health Benefit Costs Could Jump in 2014," *HR Magazine,* February 2014, p. 15.
3. Stephen Miller, "Health Care Costs Remain CFO's Top Concern," *HR Magazine*, February 2014, p. 17.
4. Susan J. Wells, "The Price of Health," *HR Magazine,* March 2014, pp. 22–28.
5. Tamara Lytle, "The Looming Rx Threat," *HR Magazine,* March 2014, pp. 30–34.
6. John Scorza, "Growth in Voluntary Benefits Expected in 2014," *SHRM Online,* December 3, 2013, http://www.shrm.org/hrdisciplines/benefits/articles/pages/voluntary-benefits-2014.aspx.
7. Les Richmond and Kimberly Fox, "Aligning Benefits Strategy with Total Rewards Philosophy," *WorldatWork.org,* 2012.
8. Lauren Weber, "Benefits Matter," *Wall Street Journal,* April 4, 2012; "Why a Healthy Workforce May Be the Next Great Employment Differentiator," *Aflac WorkForce Report,* 2012.
9. Stephen Miller, "Benefits Underused to Recruit and Retain, SHRM Finds," *HR Magazine,* February 2014, p. 57.
10. "2012 Total Rewards Survey: Transforming Potential into Value," *AON Hewitt,* 2012; Andrea Davis, "Choosing Better Benefits," *Employee Benefit News,* January 2012, p. 29.
11. Susan Wells, "Benefits Strategies Grow," *HR Magazine,* March 2013, pp. 26–34.
12. Susan Wells, "Benefits Strategies Grow," *HR Magazine,* March 2013, pp. 26–34.
13. Patricia Kowsmann, "Portugal Gives Ground on Worker Contributions," *Wall Street Journal,* September 24, 2012.
14. Maria Rosario Lombera-Gonzalez, "Significant Tax, Social Security Reforms to Impact Employment in Mexico," *SHRM Online,* April 2, 2014, http://www.shrm.org/hrdisciplines/global/articles/pages/tax-social-security-reforms-mexico.aspx.
15. "Family Leave: U.S., Canada, and Global," *Catalyst.org,* May 2012; Bernd Debusmann Jr., "U.S. behind the World on Parental Leave: Report," *Thomas Reuters,* February 23, 2011; Erin Killian, "Parental Leave: The Swedes Are the Most Generous," *NPR.org,* August 8, 2011; Jens Hansegard, "For Paternity Leave, Sweden Asks if Two Months Is Enough," *Wall Street Journal,* August 1, 2012.
16. Roy Maurer, "Latin American Companies Embracing Workplace Benefits," *SHRM Online,* December 9, 2013, http://www.shrm.org/hrdisciplines/global/articles/pages/latin-american-workplace-benefits.aspx.
17. Patricia Graves, "When Should a Part-Time Employee Be Re-Classified as Full-Time?" *HR Magazine,* February 2013, p. 21.
18. Stephen Miller, "Supreme Court Hears Same-Sex Marriage Cases," *HR Magazine,* May 2013, p. 11.
19. Allen Smith, "DOMA Decision Will Affect Thousands of Laws," *HR Magazine,* September 2013, p. 12.
20. Stephen Miller, "FAQ Addresses Health Coverage for Same-Sex Spouses," *SHRM Online,* March 31, 2014, http://www.shrm.org/hrdisciplines/benefits/articles/pages/same-sex-spouses-coverage.aspx.
21. Joanne Sammer, "Benefits after DOMA," *HR Magazine*, October 2013, pp. 53–55.
22. Tamara Lytle, "Benefits for Older Workers," *HR Magazine,* March 2012, pp. 53–58.
23. Andrea Gehman and Paul Lang, "Reduce Risks of Benefits Plan Contracting," *HR Magazine,* July 2013, pp. 61–62.
24. Virginia Eanes, "Goodbye, Yellow-Brick Road," *Employee Benefit News,* April 1, 2009.
25. Dennis Cauchon, "Job Benefits Growing Faster Than Wages," *USA Today,* October 19–21, 2012; Joe Light, "As Labor Costs Increase, Signs Point to Benefits," *Wall Street Journal,* May 2, 2011.
26. Stephen Miller, "HR Spends More Time Educating about Benefits," *HR Magazine,* February 2014, p. 10.

27. Stephen Miller, "HR Spends More Time Educating about Benefits," *HR Magazine*, February 2014, p. 10.

28. Eric Vidal, "Case Study: ACS Creates a Virtual Benefits Fair," *InterCall*, intercall.com.

29. Stephen Miller, "FICA Adjusts: Income Subject to Payroll Tax Increases in 2014," *SHRM Online*, October 30, 2013, http://www.shrm.org/hrdisciplines/compensation/articles/pages/fica-social-security-tax-2014.aspx.

30. Kelly Greene, "When to Take Social Security," *Wall Street Journal*, July 21–22, 2012, p. B8.

31. Stephen Miller, "FICA Adjusts: Income Subject to Payroll Tax Increases in 2014," *SHRM Online*, October 30, 2013, http://www.shrm.org/hrdisciplines/compensation/articles/pages/fica-social-security-tax-2014.aspx.

32. "BLS: Table 5. Private Industry, by Major Occupational Group and Bargaining Status," 2012, http://bls.gov/news.release/ecec.t05.htm.

33. Kevin M. Cruz, "Beware of Workers' Comp Premium Fraud," *HR Magazine*, February 2014, pp. 51–53.

34. Based on Kirk Rafdal, "Testing Positive for Marijuana Did Not Bar Workers' Comp," *HR Magazine*, March 2013, p. 18; David Tobenkin, "Workers' Comp and Pot: A Toke Too Many?" *HR Magazine*, July 2013, pp. 44–46.

35. "Changes to Retirement Benefits: What HR Professionals Need to Know in 2012," *Workplace Visions*, *SHRM*, Issue 1, 2012.

36. Dana Wilkie, "Older Workers' Employment Status Debated," *SHRM Online*, January 29, 2014, http://www.shrm.org/hrdisciplines/diversity/articles/pages/older-workers-stealing-jobs.aspx.

37. Joanne Sammer, "Steady Retirement Income Streams," *HR Magazine*, September 2013, pp. 41–46.

38. Joanne Sammer, "Paving the Road to Retirement," *HR Magazine*, March 2014, pp. 38–42.

39. Stephen Blakely and Jack VanDerhei, "EBRI's 2012 Retirement Confidence Survey: Job Insecurity, Debt Weigh on Retirement Confidence, Savings," *Employee Benefit Research Institute*, March 13, 2012.

40. Roy Maurer, "Millennials Worldwide Need Help Planning for Retirement," *SHRM Online*, November 25, 2013, http://www.shrm.org/hrdisciplines/global/articles/pages/millennials-planning-retirement.aspx.

41. Bill Leonard, "2014 State of the Union Focuses on the Workplace," *SHRM Online*, January 29, 2014, http://www.shrm.org/publications/hrnews/pages/2014-state-of-the-union-workplace.aspx; Stephen Miller, "President's Budget Would Cap Savings Breaks, Expand Enforcement," *SHRM Online*, March 6, 2014, http://www.shrm.org/hrdisciplines/benefits/articles/pages/budget-caps-savings-breaks.aspx.

42. Joanne Sammer, "Paving the Road to Retirement," *HR Magazine*, March 2014, pp. 38–42.

43. Stephen Miller, "Better Retirement Plans May Prompt Job Switching," *HR Magazine*, July 2012, p. 11; "Reeling Them in with Retirement Bait: Retirement Benefits Shown Effective to Attract and Retain," *Employee Benefit News*, February 2011, p. 58.

44. Joanne Sammer, "Steady Retirement Income Streams," *HR Magazine*, September 2013, pp. 41–46.

45. Kendall Daines, "De-Risking Pension Plans," *HR Magazine*, May 2013, pp. 79–82.

46. Joanne Sammer, "Are Defined Benefit Plans Dead?" *HR Magazine*, July 2012, pp. 29–32.

47. Stephen Miller, "Job Changers Hold on to Retirement Savings," *SHRM Online*, November 15, 2013, http://www.shrm.org/hrdisciplines/benefits/articles/pages/job-changers-401ks.aspx.

48. John P. Keil, "Faulty Securities Filings Can Lead to Benefits Liability," *SHRM Online*, November 22, 2013, http://www.shrm.org/legalissues/federalresources/pages/faulty-securities-filings-benefits-liability.aspx.

49. Christopher Farrell, "Fine-Tuning the 401(k)," *Bloomberg Businessweek*, April 5, 2012, p. 80.

50. "2012 Workplace Benefits Report," *Bank of America Merrill Lynch*, 2012.

51. Geoffrey Michael, "Saving Money on Your Savings," *Wall Street Journal*, July 16, 2012, p. R3.

52. Joanne Sammer, "Steady Retirement Income Streams," *HR Magazine*, September 2013, pp. 41–46.

53. Joanne Sammer, "Explain 401(k) Plan Loans' Upsides and Downsides," *SHRM Online*, February 21, 2014, http://www.shrm.org/hrdisciplines/benefits/articles/pages/explaining-401k-loans.aspx.

54. Joanne Sammer, "Paving the Road to Retirement," *HR Magazine*, March 2014, pp. 38–42.

55. Stephen Miller, "Employers Embrace Proactive Steps to Improve Savings Rates," *SHRM Online*, April 2, 2014, http://www.shrm.org/hrdisciplines/benefits/articles/pages/proactive-401k-features.aspx.

56. Bill Leonard, "Hearing Examines Barriers to Small Businesses' Retirement Plans," *SHRM Online*, October 8, 2013, http://www.shrm.org/publications/hrnews/pages/house-hearing-barriers-small-businesses-retirement-plans.aspx.

57. Kathleen Koster, "Online or Face Time?" *Employee Benefit News*, October 2012, pp. 20–22.

58. Joanne Sammer, "Paving the Road to Retirement," *HR Magazine*, March 2014, pp. 38–42.

59. "Annual Adoption of Cash Balance Plans Nearly Doubled," *SHRM.org*, July 26, 2012.

60. Joanne Deschenaux, "Supreme Court Upholds ERISA Contractual Limitations Periods," *HR Magazine*, February 2014, p. 14.

61. Stephen Miller, "Court Upholds Health Plan's Contract Language," *HR Magazine*, June 2013, p. 22.

62. Roger S. Achille, "Termination Did Not Breach ERISA Fiduciary Duty," *SHRM Online*, October 10, 2013, http://www.shrm.org/legalissues/federalresources/pages/termination-erisa-fiduciary-duty.aspx.

63. Stephen Miller, "Employer-Provided Health Coverage Declines across the Decade," *HR Magazine*, June 2013, p. 24.

64. Stephen Miller, "Employer-Provided Health Coverage Declines across the Decade," *HR Magazine*, June 2013, p. 24.

65. Stephen Miller, "Larger Increases in Health Premiums Expected," *SHRM Online*, November 17, 2014, http://www.shrm.org/hrdisciplines/benefits/articles/pages/health-cost-inflation.aspx.

66. Stephen Miller, "California's Group Health Premiums Outpace National

Average," *SHRM Online*, January 30, 2014, http://www.shrm.org/hrdisciplines/benefits/articles/pages/california-premiums-outpace.aspx.

67. Stephen Miller, "Larger Increases in Health Premiums Expected," *SHRM Online*, November 17, 2014, http://www.shrm.org/hrdisciplines/benefits/articles/pages/health-cost-inflation.aspx.

68. Stephen Miller, "Health Benefit Costs Could Jump in 2014," *SHRM Online*, November 25, 2013, http://www.shrm.org/hrdisciplines/benefits/articles/pages/health-costs-2014.aspx; David Wessel, "Why Health-Spending Trend Matters," *Wall Street Journal*, July 5, 2012.

69. Neil King Jr. and Daniel Lippman, "More Americans Favor Striking Down Health-Care Law," *Wall Street Journal*, June 27, 2013, p. A4.

70. Jason A. Rothman, "Government Enjoined from Enforcing ACA Contraceptive Mandate against Employer," *SHRM Online*, November 1, 2013, http://www.shrm.org/legalissues/federalresources/pages/government-enjoined-enforcing-aca-contraceptive-mandate.aspx; Allen Smith, "Contraceptive-Coverage Case Argued before Supreme Court," *SHRM Online*, March 25, 2014, http://www.shrm.org/legalissues/federalresources/pages/contraceptive-coverage-oral-argument.aspx.

71. Allen Smith, "HHS Loses Contraceptive Coverage Case," *SHRM Online*, June 30, 2014, http://www.shrm.org/legalissues/federalresources/pages/hobby-lobby.aspx.

72. Allen Smith, "Legislation to Change 30-Hour Full-Time Threshold Debated," *SHRM Online*, January 30, 2014, http://www.shrm.org/legalissues/federalresources/pages/30-hour-full-time-employee.aspx.

73. Allen Smith, "House Passes 40-Hour Workweek Threshold for PPACA," *SHRM Online*, January 7, 2015, http://www.shrm.org/legalissues/federalresources/pages/40-hour-workweek.aspx; Allen Smith, "Senate Hears Testimony on ACA's Definition of Full-Time," *SHRM Online*, January 23, 2015.

74. Allen Smith, "Senate Hears Testimony on ACA's Definition of Full-Time," *SHRM Online*, January 23, 2015.

75. Stephen Miller, "Health Care Reform's Employer-Mandate Calculations Clarified," *HR Magazine*, February 2013, p. 11; Stephen Miller, "Spousal-Coverage Shifts: What Goes Around Comes Around," *HR Magazine*, March 2014, p. 14.

76. Stephen Miller, "2014 Out-of-Pocket Cap on Costs May Exclude Stand-Alone Drug Plans," *HR Magazine*, October 2013, p. 10.

77. Angus Loten and Sarah E. Needleman, "For U.S. Firms, Insurance Deadline Looms," *Wall Street Journal*, October 2, 2014, p. B4.

78. Joanne Sammer, "The Mandate and Beyond," *HR Magazine*, March 2013, pp. 37–42.

79. Joanne Sammer, "The Mandate and Beyond," *HR Magazine*, March 2013, pp. 37–42.

80. "Employers Remain Committed to Benefits," *Employee Benefit News*, May 2012, p. 50.

81. Joanne Sammer, "The Mandate and Beyond," *HR Magazine*, March 2013, pp. 37–42.

82. Stephen Miller, "Final Rules Implement ACA Employer Reporting Requirements," *SHRM Online*, March 7, 2014, http://www.shrm.org/hrdisciplines/benefits/articles/pages/aca-employer-reporting-rules.aspx.

83. "Health-Care Costs Projected to Increase 5.3% in 2013," *Worldatwork.org*, August 29, 2012; "U.S. Employers Revamping Health Care Benefits," *HR Magazine*, HR Trendbook, 2012.

84. John Tozzi, "What the GOP Has to Love about Obamacare," *Bloomberg Businessweek*, September 9–15, 2013.

85. Stephen Miller, "Co-pays and Deductibles up Sharply for High-Cost Drugs," *SHRM Online*, March 10, 2014, http://www.shrm.org/hrdisciplines/benefits/articles/pages/rx-deductibles-copays.aspx.

86. Joanne Sammer, "Health Care Costs Likely to Jump in 2013," *Business Finance Magazine*, September 17, 2012; "Large Employers Plan Benefits Overhaul," *Employee Benefit News*, October 2011, p. 66.

87. David Tobenkin, "Spousal Exclusions on the Rise," *HR Magazine*, November 2011, pp. 55–60.

88. Anna Wilde Mathews, "Big Firms Overhaul Health Coverage," *Wall Street Journal*, September 27, 2012.

89. Stephen Miller, "Employers Foresee Big Health Benefit Changes Over 3–5 Years," *SHRM Online*, February 24, 2014, http://www.shrm.org/hrdisciplines/benefits/articles/pages/health-benefit-changes-foreseen.aspx.

90. "Dollar Value of Wellness Incentives on the Rise," *Employee Benefit News*, April 15, 2012.

91. Sharon Begley, "Exclusive: U.S. CEOs Threaten to Pull Tacit Obamacare Support over 'Wellness' Spat," *Yahoo News*, November 29, 2014, http://news.yahoo.com/exclusive-u-ceos-threaten-pull-tacit-obamacare-support-120556143--sector.html;_ylt=A0SO8w_qfyRVt7QA6ZVXNyoA;_ylu=X3oDMTEzN2Jma2tvBGNvbG8DZ3ExBHBvcwMxBHZ0aWQDU1dJTUMwXzEEc2VjA3Ny.

92. Kurt Soller, "Don't Exercise with Coworkers or Clients," *BloombergBusinessweek*, January 2, 2014, http://www.bloomberg.com/bw/articles/2014-01-02/dont-exercise-with-co-workers-or-clients.

93. Adapted from Bill Leonard, "A Holistic Approach to an Onsite Health Clinic," *HR Magazine*, April 2013, p. 14; Susan J. Wells, "Holding Health Care Accountable," *HR Magazine*, September 2013, pp. 24–30; Nancy Hatch Woodward, "My Advocate," *HR Magazine*, pp. 37–40; Dave Zielinski, "Help Retirees Manage Health Coverage," *HR Magazine*, May 2013, pp. 69–72.

94. "FAQs for Employees about COBRA Continuation Health Coverage," Employee Benefits Security Administration, *DOL.gov*.

95. Susan R. Heylman, "Coming: HIPAA Revisions, Greater Enforcement," *HR Magazine*, July 2013, p. 10.

96. Marli D. Riggs, "Everybody Loves a Deal," *Employee Benefit News*, October 2012, pp. 24–25.

97. Stephen Miller, "More Employees Saving for Kid's College," *HR Magazine*, October 2013, p. 14.

98. Allen Smith, "High Court Says Severance Is Taxable," *SHRM Online*,

March 25, 2014, http://www.shrm .org/legalissues/federalresources/ pages/supreme-court-severance-taxable.aspx; G. J. Stillson MacDonnell, "Supreme Court to Consider Tax Treatment of Severance Payments," *SHRM Online*, October 3, 2013, http:// www.shrm.org/hrdisciplines/ compensation/articles/pages/ tax-treatment-severance.aspx.

99. Edward Yost, "How Does a Lump-Sum Severance Payment Affect Unemployment Benefits Compared with Payments Spread

Out over a Few Pay Periods? What Are the Tax Implications?" *HR Magazine,* Solutions, March 2014, p. 20.

100. "Family and Medical Leave Act," 2012, http://www.dol.gov/whd .fmla.index.htm.

101. Based on James Warren, "It Pays to Help Workers Buy a Home," *Bloomberg Businessweek,* June 14–20, 2010, p. 28.

102. Allen Smith, "Guidance May Increase Leave Requests for Care of Adult Children," *HR Magazine,* March 2013, p. 14.

103. Deb Levine, "What Should an Employer Do when an Employee on Intermittent Leave under the Family and Medical Leave Act (FMLA) Is Not Getting the Job Done Well or on Time?" *HR Magazine,* Solutions, February 2014, p. 20.

104. Based on Dori Meinert, "Families First," *HR Magazine*, September 2013, pp. 33–38.

105. Adapted from Bruce Shutan, "Meet the 2013 I-COMM Award Winners," *Employee Benefit News,* September 15, 2013, pp. 49–51.

Employee Relations

CHAPTER

14

Risk Management and Worker Protection

Learning Objectives

After you have read this chapter, you should be able to:

LO1 Understand risk management and identify its components.

LO2 Discuss important legal areas regarding safety and health.

LO3 Outline the basic provisions of the Occupational Safety and Health Act of 1970 and recordkeeping and inspection requirements.

LO4 Recognize the activities that constitute effective safety management.

LO5 List three workplace health issues and highlight how employers are responding to them.

LO6 Define workplace security concerns and discuss some elements of an effective security program.

LO7 Describe the nature and importance of disaster preparation and recovery planning for HR.

WHAT'S TRENDING IN
RISK MANAGEMENT AND WORKER PROTECTION

Health, safety, and security issues are becoming more important to employers and their workers as threats from natural and manmade disasters continue to impact the workplace. Companies must remain vigilant to protect workers and other stakeholders from potential losses. Here are some leading trends in risk management and worker protection.

1. Activist federal safety agency actions include new accident reporting rules and attempts to publicize company safety records. The Occupational Health and Safety Administration (OSHA) is focused on making all safety reporting information easily and widely available, and on requiring injury prevention programs.

2. A spotlight has begun to show on global suppliers in developing countries where workers are subject to unsafe working conditions. Several highly publicized cases of fires and other disasters have highlighted the lack of proper safety standards in many nations.

3. Companies are introducing more wellness programs to decrease the costs of health care, especially in light of Patient Protection and Affordable Care Act requirements. Employers are becoming more proactive by using carrots and sticks to incentivize workers and their families to adopt healthy practices. Health concerns such as the popularity of e-cigarettes and legalized marijuana in several states pose new challenges for organizations that must determine how to control these substances in workplaces while complying with myriad laws and regulations.

4. Data security breaches at many large retailers, financial institutions, and government agencies highlight a need for extreme vigilance on the part of everyone who handles data for organizations. New employment policies, screening practices, and other measures are being taken to prevent large-scale data theft or misuse.

HEADLINE

Driven to Be the Best

Over 7,000 drivers at UPS have driven accident-free for 25 years or more in their careers. They have collectively driven over 5 billion miles, and their achievement represents over 198,000 years of safe driving. That is enough miles to drive round trip to Mars and back 19 times! The top driver has actually gone 52 years without an accident.

For these drivers, avoiding fender-benders on the road is no accident. It takes careful planning and attention while on the job. Plotting a course to avoid making left turns, fully stopping at red lights and stop signs, and driving at or below posted speed limits all add up to preventing avoidable accidents. And UPS considers nearly every accident avoidable.

How do drivers get started on a journey of safe driving? All new drivers attend an intensive mandatory weeklong training program that emphasizes safety and ethics. Award-winning UPS drivers are required to memorize more than 600 compulsory methods such as frequently checking their mirrors and leaving exactly one full car length of space in front of their vehicle when they stop. The drivers face a wide range of driving obstacles. For instance, in Alaska black bears and deer make regular appearances on the road, and snow and ice are common challenges. Drivers find ways to avoid these problems and still complete their deliveries on time, and that is no small feat. Drivers who drive for 25 years without an accident become members of the Circle of Honor, and they make up about 7% of all UPS drivers. They are rewarded with a coveted leather bomber jacket along with other accolades.

UPS is not alone in recognizing safe drivers. Frito-Lay honors those who drive 1 million miles without an accident, which typically takes 12 years to achieve. Con-way Freight gives drivers with 2 million accident-free miles an embroidered jacket along with a class ring.

Of course, these companies save untold amounts of money and time by fostering a culture of safe driving. Putting rewards behind

lightpoet/Shutterstock.com

safety programs shows employees that it really does matter, and that they can benefit from following safe practices. The next time you receive a package at your door, an "honored" driver might be delivering it.[1]

Organizations can take steps to anticipate threats to business assets and operations. Understanding and preparing for these challenges is the focus of *risk management*. Even though managers may realistically have a limited capacity to predict future events and plan ahead, it is important to consider the possibilities for losses and disruptions and to develop a game plan to respond to these issues.

Risk management
Involves the responsibility to consider physical, human, and financial factors to protect organizational and individual interests

Planning for risk helps mitigate negative impacts and enhances the capacity to realize possible opportunities. Managers can use various tools such as "heat maps" that compare risk factors and "traffic light" diagrams that convey levels of risk intensity (color-coded as red, yellow, and green).[2] Risk management involves the responsibility to consider physical, human, and financial factors to protect both organizational and individual interests.

Risk management involves these essential issues:

- How big is the threat to our organization?
- How likely is the threat to occur?
- What options do we have to reduce its impact?
- What is the preferred course of action to prevent a major loss?[3]

Even though risk management is often a distinct business function, there are specific and separate risks associated with employees. In the United States and other developed nations, HR departments are included in the prevention, minimization, and elimination of workplace risks. For example, there have been more workers' compensation and employment liability insurance payments because of rightsizing efforts and accusations of unfair employment practices.[4] These issues call for collaboration between risk managers and HR executives to develop plans that protect companies. When HR is involved in risk management, the organization may save both financial and human assets.

Health
General state of physical, mental, and emotional well-being

There are a variety of risk management issues linked to HR, including preventing accidents and health problems at work, protecting employees from workplace violence, and ensuring HR data security. Other issues can involve preparing for natural disasters, terrorist attacks, and global disease outbreaks. A major part of HR-based risk management in most organizations involves health, safety, and security, as shown in Figure 14-1. The terms *health, safety, and security* are closely related and—because they affect each other in practice—can often be considered together when policies are created. The broader and somewhat more nebulous term is health, which refers to a general state of physical, mental, and emotional well-being. A healthy person is free from illness, injury, or mental and emotional problems that impair normal human activity. Health management practices in organizations strive to maintain that overall well-being. For instance, a company might provide its workers and their families with preventive flu shots as part of a generalized health and wellness plan so that individuals are encouraged to be healthier.

FIGURE 14-1 Key Facets of HR-Based Risk Management

HR-Based Risk Management

Safety
Condition in which people's physical well-being is protected

Security
Protection of employees and organizational facilities from forces that may harm them

Typically, safety refers to a condition in which people's physical well-being is protected. The main purpose of effective safety programs in organizations is to prevent work-related injuries and accidents. For example, a manufacturing operation that involves saws and cutting tools would provide guards and devices to lessen the risk of harm to workers. Finally, the purpose of security is the protection of employees and organizational facilities from forces that may harm them. With the growth of workplace violence and issues such as data breaches, terrorism, and sabotage, security has become a concern for both employers and employees. Education can help; for instance, an insurance company could offer workplace violence seminars to educate its employees on the warning signs that often lead to danger to others on the job.

LO2 Discuss important legal areas regarding safety and health.

14-1 Safety and Health Regulations

Employers must comply with a variety of federal and state laws when developing and maintaining healthy, safe, and secure work environments. Major legal concerns are workers' compensation legislation, the Americans with Disabilities Act, child labor laws, civil rights nondiscrimination provisions, and collective bargaining laws.

14-1a Workers' Compensation

First enacted in the early 1900s, workers' compensation laws are on the books in all states today. As noted in Chapter 13, under these laws employers purchase insurance to compensate employees for injuries received while on the job. Experience-rated premiums reflect the company's accident rate. Employers that have higher accident rates pay higher premiums. Figure 14-2 shows the typical elements of benefits paid to injured workers or their survivors. Depending on the amount of lost time and the injured workers' wage level, these laws often require payments be made to an employee for the time away from work because of an injury, to cover medical bills, and

FIGURE 14-2   Elements of Workers' Compensation Benefits

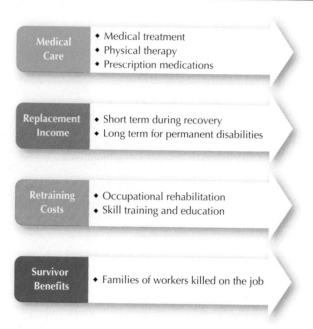

Source: Adapted from http://injury.findlaw.com/workers-compensation.html

for retraining if a new job is required as a result of the incident. Most state laws also set a maximum weekly amount for determining workers' compensation benefits. Frequently, workers' compensation benefits also make up for the permanent loss of some functionality or inability to perform the previous job.

Workers' compensation coverage in many states includes emotional impairment that may have resulted from physical injury, as well as job-related strain, stress, anxiety, and pressure. Some cases of suicide have also been determined to be job related in some states, with payments made under workers' compensation. Companies with operations in multiple states must pay particular attention to the specific requirements in each state, as they differ widely.

Another aspect of workers' compensation coverage relates to employees who telecommute. In most situations, while working at home for employers, individuals are covered under workers' compensation laws. Therefore, if an employee is injured while doing employer-related work at home, the employer is likely liable for the injury.

Controlling Workers' Compensation Costs   Workers' compensation costs have become a major issue and can represent from 2% to 10% of payroll for employers. Given these cost concerns, companies should focus on preventing injuries and accidents. An accident that doesn't happen saves a worker from physical and emotional trauma, and it saves the company financial and management resources. Accident prevention is the primary way to keep workers' compensation costs low. A number of detailed recommendations are presented in the "Safety Management" section later in this chapter.

Another key to reducing these expenses are *return to work plans*. These plans monitor employees who are off work because of injuries and illness with the goal of having them return to do *restricted duty work* that is less physically demanding until they are able to perform their full range of job duties. While restricted duty return to work programs can save workers' compensation costs, employers still incur the costs of lower productivity and workload distribution issues.[5] Human resource professionals work to integrate benefits from workers' compensation with requirements under the Family and Medical Leave Act (FMLA). Injured workers may be entitled to time off under the FMLA while recuperating from injuries sustained on the job.

ETHICS

Workers' compensation fraud is an expensive problem. It is estimated that about one-fourth of the workers' compensation claims filed are fraudulent. False and exaggerated claims make up the bulk of the fraud and cost employers billions of dollars annually. Employees may fabricate injuries or malinger on disability leave to obtain greater benefits. Employers must continually monitor their workers' compensation expenditures. Efforts to reduce workplace injuries, illnesses, and fraud can reduce workers' compensation premiums and claims costs. Many of the safety and health management suggestions discussed later in this chapter can help reduce workers' compensation costs.

Fraud may also be committed by employers who underreport injuries or misclassify employees to avoid paying high premiums. Line managers and HR staff may be tempted to deny claims in order to lower workers' compensation costs. However, the ethical treatment of workers means that legitimate injuries are appropriately investigated and handled according to established company standards. The organization's culture and reward programs should align to promote accurate recordkeeping related to safety and prompt treatment for injured workers.

14-1b Americans with Disabilities Act and Safety Issues

When employers try to return injured workers to restricted duty work to reduce workers' compensation costs, they may encounter issues with the Americans with Disabilities Act (ADA). When making accommodations for injured employees by offering restricted duty work, employers may undercut what are really essential job functions. Making such accommodations for injured employees for an extended period of time may require employers to make similar accommodations for job applicants with disabilities. Therefore, limiting the duration of restricted duty work may help the company avoid future ADA issues.

HR professionals understand ADA guidelines as they affect physical disabilities. However, it becomes more difficult when mental illness is at issue. Employees might not be aware of the extent to which their disabilities (such as depression) might be affecting their job performance. To the extent that workplace misconduct is an issue, management should follow normal procedures. If an employee shows signs of violence, managers should carefully assess the situation, and perhaps input from mental health professionals will assist in formulating a course of action that preserves the employee's dignity while providing for a safe work environment.

Navigating between workers' compensation, FMLA, ADA, and many other state laws can be a complex situation for the injured worker and the company. Sound policies and procedures established by human resources can make the process smoother and easier to manage.[6]

14-1c Child Labor Laws

Safety concerns affecting younger workers, especially those under the age of 18, have resulted in restrictions on the type of work they can perform and the schedules they can work. Child labor provisions in the Fair Labor Standards Act (FLSA) set the minimum age for most employment at 16 years, with some exceptions for individuals who are 14 or 15 years old. Figure 14-3 details the permissible and prohibited work schedules and duties for young workers. There are certain exceptions for family-owned businesses and particular restrictions for hazardous occupations. In fact, teens working for farms and family-owned firms may be exposed to fewer hazards and incur fewer injuries.[7]

Penalties for violating these provisions can be costly; a single charge may result in a minimum fine of $8,000. Therefore, companies need to be very careful in how they employ young workers.[8] Two grocery store chains in Iowa—Fareway and HyVee—were recently cited for allowing workers under the age of 18 to operate compactors and cardboard bailers, work that is considered dangerous. Both situations resulted in enforcement actions and fines for violating the FLSA.[9]

Employers with many young employees find that work-related injuries of teen-aged workers are a significant issue. The retail and restaurant sectors consistently face safety and health issues with these workers. Since many young workers take more risks at work, much like they do when they drive cars, they are more likely

FIGURE 14-3 Child Labor Law Restrictions

Age	Restrictions
Any age	◆ Permitted to deliver newspapers ◆ Permitted to work as an entertainer ◆ Permitted to work for a family-based farm or other business that is owned and operated by their parents ◆ Cannot work in manufacturing or mining jobs regardless of ownership
Ages 14 to 15	◆ Can work a maximum of 3 hours/day up to 18 hours/week when school is in session ◆ Can work between the hours of 7:00 a.m. and 7:00 p.m. when school is in session ◆ Can work a maximum of 8 hours/day up to 40 hours/week when school is not in session ◆ Can work until 9:00 p.m. when school is not in session
Ages 16 to 18	◆ Can work unlimited hours in permissible jobs ◆ May perform any farm job ◆ May perform any nonhazardous job ◆ May not drive on public roads or perform duties of a delivery driver
Age 18	◆ Minimum age for employment in hazardous occupations ◆ No longer subject to child labor provisions

Source: Adapted from Department of Labor, http://www.dol.gov/whd/childlabor.htm.

to get injured.[10] In response, OSHA has created a special section on its website that addresses teens and provides videos, photos, and text explanations of work-related hazards along with worker rights and responsibilities. Teenage workers might be less cautious than older employees on the job, so extra steps should be taken by managers to highlight workplace safety issues. In addition, properly training managers and employees in permissible tasks for younger workers and safe practices is critical in the effort to prevent injuries to these higher-risk workers.

14-1d Legal Issues Related to Work Assignments

The rights of employees in work assignments are addressed as part of various regulations. Two primary areas where work assignments and concerns about safety and health intersect are reproductive health and unsafe work.

Work Assignments and Reproductive Health Assigning employees to work in areas where their ability to have children may be affected by exposure to chemical hazards or radiation is an issue. Women who are able to bear children or are pregnant present the primary concerns, but in some situations, the possibility that men might become sterile is also an issue. Based on standards specified in the Civil Rights Act and the Pregnancy Discrimination Act, employers should not prevent women (or men) from working in hazardous jobs because of reproductive concerns. Although employers have no absolute protection from liability, the following actions can help:

- Maintain a safe workplace for all by seeking the safest working methods.
- Comply with all state and federal safety laws.
- Inform employees of any known risks.
- Document employee acceptance of any risks.

Refusing Unsafe Work Under labor laws, workers may challenge unsafe work assignments, whether or not they are members of a labor union. Both union and nonunion workers have refused to work when they considered the work unsafe, and several court cases support their actions. The conditions for refusing work because of safety concerns include the following:

- The employee's fear is objectively reasonable.
- The employee has tried to have the dangerous condition corrected.
- Using normal procedures to solve the problem has not worked.

GLOBAL

14-1e Global Safety, Health, and Security Issues

HR managers must also consider risk management when dealing with employees around the world. Safety and health laws and regulations vary from country to country, ranging from virtually nonexistent to more stringent than those in the United States. The importance placed on health, safety, and security relates somewhat to the level of regulation and other factors in each country.

When sending workers on international assignments, special care must be taken to protect them from personal assault, theft, natural disasters, disease, poor health care, and other issues.[11] Organizations in the United States and other nations such as Germany, Australia, and the United Kingdom have instituted duty-of-care requirements specifying that companies take active steps to protect the well-being of employees and their families when they are required to work and live overseas. In addition to concerns over security and logistics, HR departments must also be aware of the tax and immigration risks that individuals potentially face when they travel abroad for shorter periods to conduct business.[12]

ETHICS

A recent uptick in the number of well-publicized industrial accidents in developing countries has begun to shed light on dangerous working conditions common in other countries. Fires in Bangladeshi garment factories and suicides at Chinese electronics manufacturers show how lax safety standards and oppressive work environments can lead to tragedy. The following "HR Ethics: What Is the Real Cost of Your iPhone?" feature discusses the challenges for companies seeking to purchase low-cost products from suppliers in less-progressive countries.

HR

ETHICS

What Is the Real Cost of Your iPhone?

Consumers often look for products with unique features or those that are very inexpensive. In response, companies try to find suppliers that can produce these products at the lowest cost so that they can sell them at a profit. What many consumers may not realize is that often the real cost of the product is not dollars and cents, but human loss and suffering.

Most electronics, including the wildly popular iPhone, are produced primarily in China and other developing nations. Safety and health laws in these countries lag behind those in the United States, and workers there are subjected to strenuous work schedules and poor working conditions. Workers are often housed in overcrowded dormitories. They are frequently required to work excessive overtime schedules—they often work seven days a week—and may be required to handle toxic chemicals while producing the electronic devices. Worker suicides occurred with alarming regularity at Hon Hai's facilities in recent years. Workers have also staged walkouts and pickets to obtain higher wages.

Companies such as Apple, HP, and Samsung deal with these suppliers because doing so is cheaper than manufacturing in the United States. It can take years to develop a productive working relationship with a supplier to ensure product quality and that delivery schedules are met. The companies are naturally reluctant to drop a supplier unless violations are serious and ongoing. Samsung recently determined that the majority of its suppliers fail to comply with safety regulations such as providing adequate safety equipment, conducting evacuation drills, and maintaining reasonable overtime schedules.

Auditing suppliers is now a regular practice for U.S.-based companies, and they are making an effort to reduce safety problems and worker abuse around the world. However, the allure of low-cost products and consumer demand for constant innovation make it difficult to put worker safety first. As long as customers continue to buy iPhones and other electronics and do not object to hazardous work conditions at production facilities, companies are not likely to be motivated to change their practices.[13]

With worker safety issues in mind, consider the following questions:

1. How can consumers learn about supply chain issues and worker safety concerns when shopping for electronic devices? How could an HR department help?

2. What can companies do to ensure that their suppliers comply with worker safety and health regulations? How should HR professionals ensure that safety and health are key issues in the workplace?

In addition to complying with workers' compensation, ADA, and child labor laws, most employers must comply with the Occupational Safety and Health Act of 1970. This act, which is administered by the Occupational Safety and Health Administration, has had a tremendous impact on the workplace.

LO3 Outline the basic provisions of the Occupational Safety and Health Act of 1970 and recordkeeping and inspection requirements.

14-2 Occupational Safety and Health Act

The Occupational Safety and Health Act of 1970 was enacted to ensure that the health and safety of workers would be protected. Every employer that is engaged in commerce and has one or more employees must comply with the act. Farmers with fewer than 10 employees are exempt. Employers in specific industries, such as railroads and mining, are covered under other health and safety acts. Federal, state, and local governments are covered by separate statutes and provisions.

The Occupational Safety and Health Act of 1970 established three agencies within the Department of Labor to oversee various aspects of workplace safety:

1. The Occupational Safety and Health Administration, known as OSHA, administers the provisions of the law, conducts workplace inspections, and works with companies to improve worker safety.
2. The National Institute for Occupational Safety and Health (NIOSH) is a supporting body that conducts research and develops safety standards.
3. The Occupational Safety and Health Review Commission (OSHRC) reviews OSHA enforcement actions and addresses disputes between OSHA and employers that are cited by OSHA inspectors.

By making employers and employees more aware of safety and health considerations, OSHA has significantly affected organizations. OSHA regulations and its on-site presence appear to have contributed to reductions in the number of accidents and injuries. OSHA leaders recently announced plans for additional rules and guidelines regarding permissible exposure levels of certain hazardous chemicals and tougher whistleblower protection standards. On the other hand, they dropped a proposed requirement for employers to maintain injury and illness prevention programs. As priorities change in the federal administration, the emphasis OSHA places on various issues also changes.[14]

14-2a OSHA Enforcement Actions and Results

A major responsibility of OSHA is to enforce safety regulations in an effort to reduce injuries and illnesses in the workplace. Enforcement includes creating guidelines and rules, investigating, inspecting, and levying fines. Compliance officers have great discretion and authority to ensure worker safety.

The results of OSHA's enforcement process are evident in accident statistics since passage of the law. Since 2003, incidences of both fatal and nonfatal occupational injuries and illnesses have steadily declined.[15] Figures 14-4 and 14-5 show these positive trends. Specific accident and illness rates vary depending on the industry, type of job, and other factors. The number of workplace injuries and illnesses also varies by employer size, with medium-sized companies having the highest reported rates and small businesses having the lowest rates.[16]

Unfortunately, while occupational fatalities are at their lowest level in decades, Hispanic workers experience a much higher proportion of fatal injuries than their

FIGURE 14-4 Nonfatal Occupational Injury and Illness Incidence Rates, 2004–2013

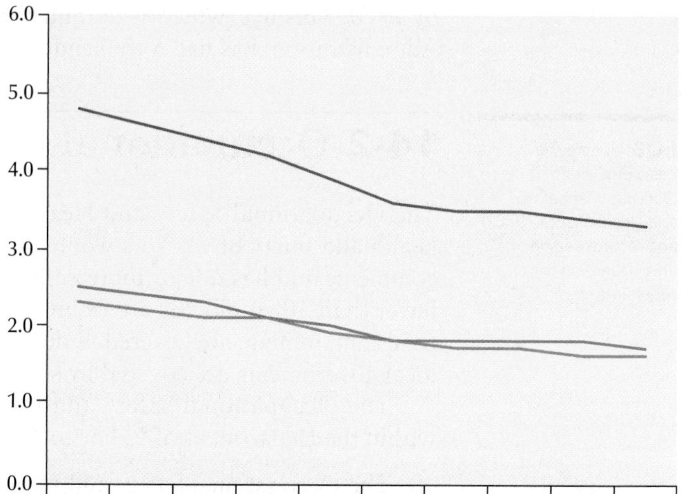

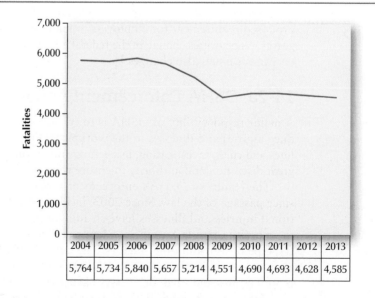

		2004	2005	2006	2007	2008	2009	2010	2011	2012	2013
——	Total Recordable Cases (TRC)	4.8	4.6	4.4	4.2	3.9	3.6	3.5	3.5	3.4	3.3
——	Days Away from Work and Transfers (DART)	2.5	2.4	2.3	2.1	2.0	1.8	1.8	1.8	1.8	1.7
——	Other Recordable Cases (ORC)	2.3	2.2	2.1	2.1	1.9	1.8	1.7	1.7	1.6	1.6

Source: Adapted from OSHA.gov.

FIGURE 14-5 Workplace Fatalities, 2004–2013

2004	2005	2006	2007	2008	2009	2010	2011	2012	2013
5,764	5,734	5,840	5,657	5,214	4,551	4,690	4,693	4,628	4,585

Source: Adapted from OSHA.gov.

numbers would warrant. This disturbing trend has continued for a number of years. Experts believe that language barriers, fear of speaking out, and working in more dangerous occupations (such as construction) all contribute to their higher rates of fatal injury.[17] Industries that employ a high percentage of Latinos should make extra efforts to ensure that workers understand safe practices and are equipped with proper protective gear.

Twenty percent of all workplace fatalities occur in the construction industry. Leading causes for those deaths include falls, being struck by an object, and electrocution. This has led OSHA to beef up requirements for fall protection, especially in the residential construction sector. Many building contractors believe that they provide adequate protection to workers, and they are opposing stricter regulations.[18]

OSHA has initiated stronger enforcement efforts on behalf of temporary workers. Temporary workers make up a significant share of the workforce and unfortunately, they have a much higher risk of occupational injury. Staffing agencies and the companies who employ temporary workers both bear some responsibility for ensuring that these individuals are properly trained and equipped for any workplace hazards that they may encounter.[19]

While national safety statistics show improvement, there are still noteworthy tragic accidents that result in significant human and financial loss. For example, Behr Iron & Steel in Illinois was cited for numerous violations and fined nearly $500,000 following the death of a worker at the company's scrap metal facility who sustained multiple injuries after his arm was caught in a conveyor belt. Similarly, Republic Steel was fined $2.4 million for failing to provide workers with adequate protection from falls on girders several stories above furnaces and failing to provide machine guards on hazardous machinery.[20, 21] These examples show that although workplace safety is improving overall, many companies and their employees continue to suffer due to unsafe conditions.

14-2b Workplace Safety Standards

To foster workplace safety, OSHA has established specific standards to regulate equipment and other aspects of the work environment. National standards developed by engineering and quality control groups are often used by OSHA to establish its own standards. OSHA rules and standards are frequently complicated and technical. While many industries, like construction and health care, have specific workplace requirements, all companies must adhere to two key provisions:

- *General duty*: The act requires that the employer has a general duty to provide safe and healthy working conditions, even in areas where OSHA standards have not been set. Employers that know or reasonably should know of unsafe or unhealthy conditions can be cited for violating the general duty clause.
- *Notification and posters*: Employers are required to inform their employees of OSHA safety and health standards. OSHA posters must also be displayed in prominent locations in workplaces.

Hazard Communication OSHA has established *process safety management* (PSM) standards that focus on hazardous chemicals. Hazard communication standards require manufacturers, importers, distributors, and users of hazardous chemicals to evaluate, classify, and label those substances using standardized symbols. Employers must make information about hazardous substances available to employees, their representatives, and health professionals. This information is contained in *material safety data sheets* (MSDSs), which must be readily accessible to those who work with chemicals and certain other dangerous substances. The MSDSs indicate antidotes or actions to be taken should someone be exposed to the substances. If the organization employs many workers for whom English is not the primary language, then the MSDSs should be available in the necessary languages. Also, workers should be trained in how to access and use the MSDS information.

Additional process safety management requirements include *lockout/tag-out regulations*. Firms must control hazardous energy such as electrical or hydraulic power by providing mechanics and tradespeople with locks and tags to make equipment inoperable during repair or adjustment to prevent accidental start-up of defective machinery. Strict procedures regarding removal of the device help ensure that equipment is safe to operate.

Personal Protective Equipment Standards for personal protective equipment (PPE) require that employers analyze job hazards, provide adequate PPE to employees in hazardous jobs, and train them in the use of PPE items. Common PPE items include safety glasses, hard hats, and safety shoes. Employers are required to provide PPE to all employees (at no cost) who work in an environment that presents hazards or who might have contact with hazardous chemicals and substances on the job. Some courts have ruled that employees are entitled to be paid for the time it takes to put on and take off protective equipment, while others have ruled that they are not entitled to pay. Claims of this nature are case specific, and no broad generalizations can be made. If a company requires significant "donning and doffing" for safety purposes, managers should work with HR to determine if payment is warranted.[22]

Bloodborne Pathogens and Infectious Diseases OSHA has established a standard regarding exposure to bloodborne pathogens such as the hepatitis B virus (HBV) and the human immunodeficiency virus (HIV). This regulation was developed to protect employees who are regularly exposed to blood and other such substances from contracting AIDS and other serious diseases. Obviously, health care laboratory workers, nurses, and medical technicians are at greatest risk. Providing workers with protective equipment such as gloves and masks along with training in proper handling of bodily fluids are important precautions that help avoid the spread of infectious diseases.

The recent outbreak of Ebola highlights that the requirements under this standard as universal precautions to prevent infection are important when facing this virus. Workers at particular risk may include those in the health care, mortuary and death care, airline, and other travel service industries. Training and protective equipment are important preventive measures for companies to implement.[23]

Pandemic Guidelines In addition to regulations, OSHA issues guidelines to protect people at work in matters of health and safety. One such set of guidelines can help employers prepare for a pandemic such as West Nile virus, bird flu, or swine flu. These guidelines provide information about how organizations can manage a serious disease outbreak with proper procedures and safety equipment. In addition, guidelines are provided to help a company continue operations with a depleted workforce.

Cumulative trauma disorders (CTDs) are muscle and skeletal injuries that occur when workers repetitively use the same muscles when performing tasks.

Cumulative trauma disorders (CTDs)
Muscle and skeletal injuries that occur when workers repetitively use the same motions when performing tasks

Carpal tunnel syndrome, a cumulative trauma disorder, is an injury common to people who put their hands through repetitive motions such as typing, playing certain musical instruments, cutting, and sewing.

Problems caused by repetitive and cumulative injuries occur in a variety of work settings. The meatpacking industry has a very high level of CTDs. Grocery cashiers experience CTDs from repetitively twisting their wrists when they scan bar codes on canned goods. Office workers experience CTDs too, primarily from doing extensive typing and data entry on computers and computer-related equipment. Workstation design that encourages proper posture, assistive devices, and job rotation may alleviate some of these repetitive motion injuries. Ergonomic studies and solutions are explored later in this chapter's "Safety Management" section.

14-2c OSHA Recordkeeping Requirements

Employers are generally required to maintain a detailed annual record of the various types of injuries, accidents, and fatalities for inspection by OSHA representatives and for submission to the agency. Most organizations must complete OSHA Form 300 to report workplace accidents and injuries and retain it for five years.

Reporting Injuries and Illnesses The OSHA 300 log is the primary reporting document that companies must prepare and maintain related to workplace injuries. The log is not sent to OSHA unless specifically requested by the agency. The required information recorded on the log includes:

- Employee's name and job title
- Date and place of injury
- Description of injury or illness
- Injury classification (as explained later in this discussion)

Employers must keep a log for each establishment on site. Employees have the right to review these records. Each year, employers are also required to summarize data from the log and post it in the workplace from February 1 through April 30. Injuries to direct and indirect (temporary, contract, and other contingent workers) workers must all be recorded.

Categories of recordable injury include:

- *Death*: Fatality at the workplace or caused by work-related actions
- *Injuries causing days away from work*: Job-related injuries or disabling occurrences that cause an employee to miss regularly scheduled work on the day following the accident
- *Injuries or illnesses causing job transfer or restricted duty*: Job-related injuries or illnesses that lead to an employee working in a job outside his or her normal assignment
- *Other recordable cases*: Injuries that require treatment by a physician but do not cause an employee to miss a regularly scheduled work turn[24]

The recordkeeping requirements for these injuries and illnesses are summarized in Figure 14-6. Notice that only very minor injuries (those requiring only first aid) do not have to be recorded for OSHA. For example, an employee who closes his hand in a door and is treated by a first aid responder with an ice pack but does not seek further medical treatment would not be considered to have a recordable injury.

FIGURE 14-6   Determining Recordability of Cases under the Occupational Safety
and Health Act

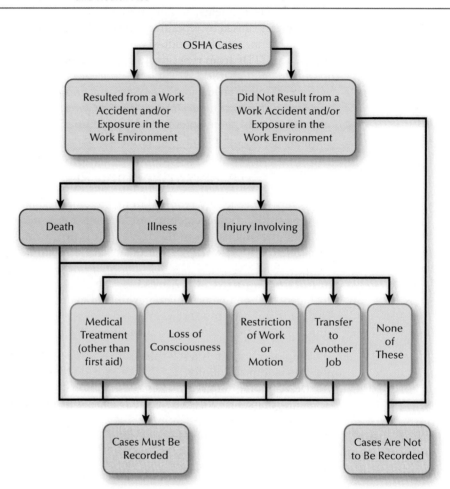

New reporting requirements effective in 2015 expanded the list of incidents
that must be reported directly to OSHA shortly after they occur. Occupational fatalities and hospitalizations of three or more employees must be reported directly to
OSHA within eight hours of the occurrence. In addition, injuries that result in am-
putation, loss of an eye, or one employee being hospitalized must also be reported
directly to OSHA within 24 hours of their occurrence. OSHA officials are focusing
on these severe incidents that lead to major human loss because they indicate that
serious hazards are likely to be found in such workplaces.[25]

OSHA dropped a proposed rule that would have made all OSHA 300 logs publicly available on its website. Safety experts expressed concern that such public disclosure might endanger the anonymity of injured workers. They were also worried
that it might drive employers to underreport accidents,[26] a concern that is not without merit, as there is reason to believe that some organizations misrepresent how
often injuries and illnesses occur in the workplace. Nearly half of employers investigated by OSHA for documentation problems failed to report every worker illness or
injury. Health care providers also claim that some companies have encouraged them

to deemphasize illnesses and injuries, as well as to give inadequate treatment to employees. Accurate reporting is more likely to occur in organizations with a positive safety climate and when supervisors consistently enforce safety behaviors. Managers must realize that companies can incur hefty fines—in the millions of dollars—for not properly disclosing incidents. In an effort to mitigate these concerns, companies should carefully review manager performance assessment and reward programs to ensure that managers are not motivated to inaccurately report accident occurrences in order to earn a bonus or other reward.[27]

14-2d OSHA Inspections

The Occupational Safety and Health Act provides for on-the-spot inspections by OSHA compliance officers or inspectors. Inspections may also occur as part of an investigation of a complaint or as part of targeted enforcement in high-hazard industries. In *Marshall vs. Barlow's, Inc.,* the U.S. Supreme Court held that safety inspectors must produce a search warrant if an employer refuses to voluntarily allow the inspectors into the facility. The Court also ruled that an inspector does not have to show probable cause to obtain a search warrant. A warrant can be obtained easily if a search is part of a general enforcement plan.[28]

Dealing with an Inspection When an OSHA compliance officer arrives, managers should ask to see the inspector's credentials. Next, the company HR representative or safety professional should insist on an initial conference with the compliance officer. The compliance officer may request that a union representative, an employee, and a company representative be present while the inspection is conducted. During the inspection, the officer checks organizational records to see if they are being maintained and to determine the number of accidents that have occurred. Following this review of the safety records, the officer conducts an on-the-spot inspection and may use a wide variety of equipment to verify compliance with standards. After the inspection, the compliance officer can issue citations for any violations of standards and provisions of the act.

Citations and Violations Although OSHA inspectors can issue citations for violations of the act, whether a citation is issued depends on the severity and extent of the problems, and on the employer's knowledge of them. In addition, depending on the nature and number of violations, monetary penalties can be assessed against employers. The nature and extent of the penalties depend on the type and severity of the violations as determined by OSHA officials.

Many types of violations are cited by OSHA. Ranging from the most severe to minimal, including a special category for repeated violations, the most common are as follows:

- *Imminent danger*: When there is reasonable certainty that the condition will cause death or serious physical harm if it is not corrected immediately, an imminent danger citation is issued, and the inspector posts a notice. Imminent danger situations are handled on the highest-priority basis. If the condition is serious enough and the employer does not cooperate, a representative of OSHA may obtain a federal injunction to close the worksite until the condition is corrected. The absence of guardrails to prevent employees from falling into heavy machinery is one example of an imminent danger.

- *Serious*: When a condition could probably cause death or serious physical harm, and the employer should know of the condition, OSHA issues a serious violation citation and may impose a fine up to $7,000 per violation. Examples of serious violations are the absence of a protective screen on a lathe and the lack of a blade guard on an electric saw.
- *Other than serious*: Violations that could impact employees' health or safety but probably would not cause death or serious harm are called other than serious. Violators may be fined up to $7,000 per violation. Having loose ropes in a work area might be classified as an other than serious violation.
- *De minimis*: A *de minimis* condition is one not directly and immediately related to employees' safety or health. No citation or fines are issued, but the condition is mentioned to the employer. Lack of doors on toilet stalls is a common example of a de minimis violation.
- *Willful and repeated*: Citations for willful and repeated violations are issued to employers that have been previously cited for violations. If an employer knows about a safety violation or has been warned of a violation and does not correct the problem, a second citation is issued. The penalty for a willful and repeated violation can be high, ranging from $5,000 to $70,000 per violation.

Federal OSHA compliance officers conducted over 39,000 inspections and found over 70,000 violations in a recent year. The most common violations are related to fall protection, hazard communication, scaffolding, respiratory protection, and powered industrial trucks. The construction industry is cited more often than any other industry.[29]

<table>
<tr><td>LO4 Recognize the activities that constitute effective safety management.</td></tr>
</table>

14-3 Safety Management

Accidents can be costly for organizations because there are direct, indirect, and immeasurable costs associated with occupational safety incidents. Figure 14-7 shows that the direct costs of accidents and illnesses are only a small part of the total costs, and organizations should estimate all the expenses associated with health and safety issues, particularly any indirect costs that might be overlooked.

Well-designed and effectively managed safety programs can result in reduced accidents and associated costs. Further, a variety of safety problems often decline as a result of management efforts that emphasize a safe work environment. Companies that proactively manage safety efforts tend to perform better financially than those that do not. Often, the difference between high-performing firms with good occupational safety records and other firms is that the former have effective safety management programs. The HR unit and operating managers share responsibility for coordinating health, safety, and security efforts.

Organizations with effective safety management programs take many of the following steps to reduce accidents:

- Organizational commitment to safety
- Safety policies, discipline, and recordkeeping
- Safety training and communication
- Effective safety committees
- Inspection, investigation, and evaluation
- Accident reduction using ergonomics

FIGURE 14-7 Examples of Direct, Indirect, and Immeasurable Costs of Accidents

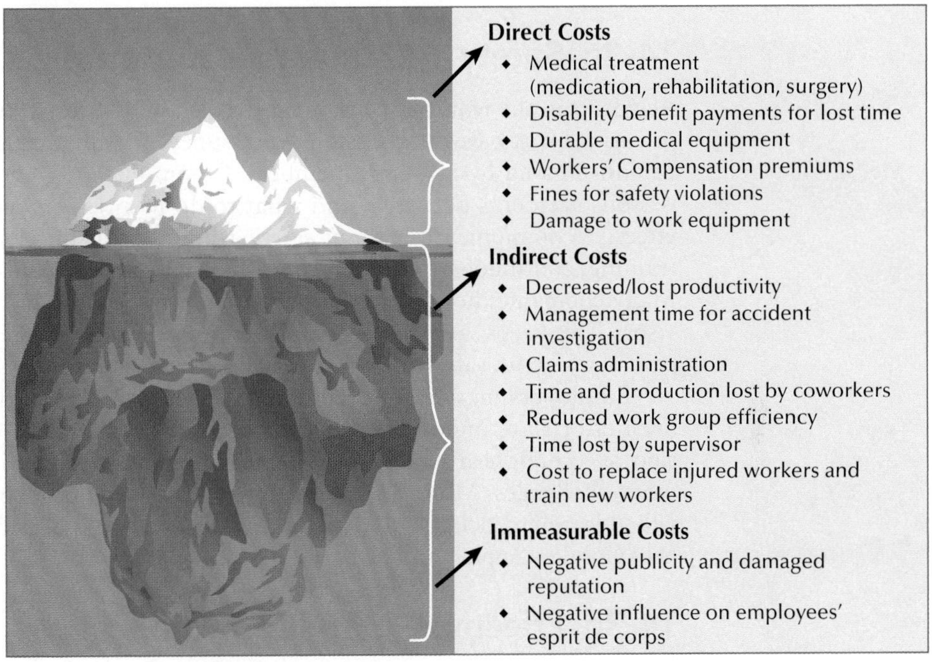

Direct Costs
- Medical treatment (medication, rehabilitation, surgery)
- Disability benefit payments for lost time
- Durable medical equipment
- Workers' Compensation premiums
- Fines for safety violations
- Damage to work equipment

Indirect Costs
- Decreased/lost productivity
- Management time for accident investigation
- Claims administration
- Time and production lost by coworkers
- Reduced work group efficiency
- Time lost by supervisor
- Cost to replace injured workers and train new workers

Immeasurable Costs
- Negative publicity and damaged reputation
- Negative influence on employees' esprit de corps

Source: Based partly on http://www.fit2wrk.com/_forms/ARTICLE_Fit2wrk_ClinicalEd_vol1-16.pdf.

14-3a Organizational Commitment to Safety

At the heart of safety management is an organizational commitment to a comprehensive safety effort that should be coordinated at the top level of management and include all members of the organization. The actions of managers should also support this effort. For instance, a manager in a metal stamping plant who fails to use hearing protection can hardly be surprised when employees neglect to wear earplugs or earmuffs.

Balancing the competing demands for safety and productivity can be difficult, especially for front-line supervisors. Executives must lead the effort by establishing a culture that emphasizes safety as the highest priority. Enlightened managers adopt a long-term view by recognizing that safe operations also result in higher productivity and better organizational outcomes.[30]

14-3b Safety Policies, Discipline, and Recordkeeping

Designing safety policies and rules along with disciplining violators are important components of safety efforts. Frequently reinforcing the need for safe behavior and frequently supplying feedback on positive safety practices are also effective ways of improving worker safety. Such safety-conscious efforts must involve employees, supervisors, managers, safety specialists, and HR personnel.

For policies about safety to be effective, good recordkeeping about accidents, causes, and other details is necessary. Without records, an employer cannot track safety performance or compare benchmarks against other employers, and the employer may not even realize the extent of the safety problems.

14-3c Safety Training and Communication

Accidents in the workplace are often reduced with safety training that is conducted in various ways. Regular sessions with supervisors, managers, and employees can be coordinated by HR staff members. Communicating about safety procedures, reasons accidents occurred, and what to do in an emergency is critical. Without effective communication about safety, training is insufficient. To reinforce safety training, continuous communication to develop safety consciousness is necessary. Many companies hold brief monthly safety meetings conducted by front-line supervisors. This keeps safety on everyone's mind and provides a regular forum to remind employees about safe work practices and accident prevention.[31]

Employers may need to communicate in a variety of media and languages. Such efforts are important to address the special needs of workers who have vision, speech, or hearing impairments; who are not proficient in English; or who face other challenges. Multiple training approaches might be needed to enhance individual learning, including the use of role-playing and other active practice exercises, behavioral examples, and extensive discussion.

14-3d Effective Safety Committees

Employees frequently participate in safety planning through safety committees, which are often composed of workers from a variety of levels and departments. A safety committee generally meets at regularly scheduled times, has specific responsibilities for conducting safety reviews, identifying risks, and making recommendations for changes necessary to avoid future accidents. At least one member of the committee usually comes from the HR department.

Some best practices for utilizing safety committees include:

- *Leadership involvement*: Senior leaders need to endorse and support safety committee efforts. Middle managers and front-line supervisors must actively assist the committee and address concerns.
- *Committee selection*: To ensure commitment, employees who are already safety advocates should be assigned to the committee. Member terms should be staggered to provide a fresh perspective and continuous energy.
- *Committee structure*: Typically, equal representation from management and employees keeps the committee in balance. Smaller committees (up to 12 members) normally function better than do larger committees.[32]

14-3e Inspection, Investigation, and Evaluation

It is not necessary to wait for an OSHA inspector to check the work area for safety hazards. Regular inspections can be performed by a safety committee or by a company safety coordinator. Problem areas should be addressed immediately to prevent accidents and keep work productivity at the highest possible levels. Also, OSHA inspects organizations with above-average rates of lost workdays more frequently. Therefore, reducing accidents can lower the frequency of on-site OSHA visits.

The accident investigation process is shown in Figure 14-8. Identifying why an accident occurred is extremely important to determine the workplace conditions

FIGURE 14-8 Accident Investigation Process

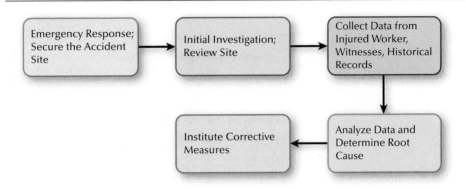

and worker behaviors that led to the incident. Talking with the injured worker and witnesses helps establish the facts and time line so that the root cause of the accident can be determined. This information is critical to prevent future occurrences.[33]

Closely related to accident investigation is research to determine ways of preventing accidents. Employing safety engineers or having outside experts evaluate the safety of working conditions may be useful. If many similar accidents seem to occur in an organizational unit, a safety training program may be necessary to emphasize safe working practices. As an example, a medical center reported a greater than average number of back injuries among employees who were lifting heavy patients. Installing patient-lifting devices and safety training on the proper way of using them was initiated. As a result, the number of worker injuries was reduced.

14-3f Accident Reduction Using Ergonomics

Ergonomics
Study and design of the work environment to address physical demands placed on individuals as they perform their jobs

Ergonomics is the study and design of the work environment to address physical demands placed on individuals as they perform their jobs. The primary goal is to make work more human friendly and to reduce work-related injuries, particularly repetitive motion problems. In a work setting, ergonomic studies look at factors such as fatigue, lighting, tools, equipment layout, and placement of controls. Ergonomics can provide economic value to employers by reducing injuries.

For specific problem industries and jobs, OSHA has voluntary guidelines that identify industries with serious ergonomic problems and give employers tools to help highlight and control ergonomics hazards. Among the industries receiving guidelines are nursing homes, poultry processors, and retail grocery stores.

Ergonomics analysis includes reviewing physical, environmental, and psychological stressors and finding ways to reduce their impact on workers. Management must commit to reducing injuries caused by repetition and cumulative trauma, along with poor workstation design and workflow.[34] Getting employees involved is the key to successfully implementing an ergonomics program.

14-3g Approaches for Effective Safety Management

Companies typically use elements from each of three basic approaches to manage safety. Figure 14-9 shows the organizational, engineering, and individual approaches and their components.

FIGURE 14-9   Approaches for Effective Safety Management

> **Organizational Approach**
>
> - Designing safe jobs.
> - Develop and implement safety policies.
> - Use safety committees.
> - Coordinate accident investigations.
> - Create a safety culture.
> - Establish reward and recognition programs.
>
> **Engineering Approach**
>
> - Design appropriate work settings and equipment.
> - Utilize proper guarding and alert systems.
> - Evaluate and use equipment and assistive devices.
> - Apply ergonomic principles.
> - Implement safety procedures in the workplace.
>
> **Individual Approach**
>
> - Reinforce safety motivation and attitudes.
> - Provide employee safety training.
> - Rewarding safety through incentive programs.
> - Discussing safety in meetings and at worksites.

Organizational Approach   Companies can effectively manage safety by designing safer jobs and creating policies that encourage safety. Safety committees can be used to increase awareness and involve employees in safety issues. Guidelines for accident investigations can help managers identify the causes of safety incidents. Finally, reward and recognition programs are a common method of keeping safety at the top of employees' priority list.[35]

Engineering Approach   Employers can prevent some accidents by designing machines, equipment, and work areas so that it is much more difficult for workers who perform potentially dangerous jobs to injure themselves and others. Providing safety equipment and guards on machinery, installing emergency switches and safety rails, keeping aisles clear, and installing adequate ventilation, lighting, heating, and air conditioning can all help make work environments safer. The use of ergonomic techniques further advances injury prevention through workstation design.

Individual Approach   Engineers approach safety from the perspective of redesigning the machinery or the work area. Industrial psychologists and human factors experts see safety differently. They address the proper match of individuals to jobs and emphasize employee training in safety methods, fatigue reduction, and health awareness. The results of many field studies involving thousands of workers show a definite relationship between human factors and occupational safety. Behavior-based safety (BBS) approaches are efforts to reduce *risky behavior* and increase safe behavior by defining unsafe behavior and attempting to change it. While BBS is beneficial, it does not constitute a complete approach to dealing with safety.

By combining organizational, engineering, and individual elements, companies can create an integrated approach to injury prevention. The most effective safety management program is one that is consistent with the organization's culture and management philosophy.

14-3h Measuring Safety Efforts

MEASURE

Organizations should monitor and evaluate their safety efforts. Just as organizational accounting records are audited, a firm's safety efforts should be audited

COMPETENCIES & APPLICATIONS

Calculating Incidence Rates

An organization's leaders frequently compare their safety results to other organizations in their industry and to their own organization over time. However, companies vary widely in size, making comparisons difficult and perhaps meaningless.

Take two manufacturing companies as an example:

- Company A has 2,500 employees and incurred 45 recordable accidents.
- Company B has 200 employees and incurred 7 recordable accidents.

Which company is running a safer operation? It looks like Company B because it had fewer injuries. But Company A employs a lot more workers. How can you compare the two?

There is a useful formula that easily determines the answer to this question. The incidence rate of injuries and illnesses can be computed as follows:

incidence rate
= (number of injuries and illnesses × 200,000)
÷ employee hours worked

The 200,000 hours in the formula represents the equivalent of 100 employees working 40 hours per week, 50 weeks per year and provides the standard base for the incidence rates. Therefore, no matter how many employees a company has, it is possible to compare incidence rates within an industry or over time.

So, which company is doing a better job? Let's calculate their incidence rates:

Company A	Company B
$\left(\dfrac{45 \times 200,000}{5,000,000}\right) = 1.8$	$\left(\dfrac{7 \times 200,000}{400,000}\right) = 3.5$

Now we can see that Company B is incurring injuries at the rate of 3.5 for every 100 workers, while Company A is incurring only 1.8 injuries for every 100 workers. So, Company A is keeping its workers safer. You can use the same formula to compute incidence rates for all recordable injuries, injuries with lost work days, and any other category of illnesses or injuries.

Each year, the Bureau of Labor Statistics publishes national incidence rates detailed by industry and employer size to help companies track their results against others in the same industry or of similar size. OSHA also uses this information to identify worksites with high incidence rates so that stepped-up enforcement and preventive action can be taken.[36]

Now that you understand how incidence rates can be computed, answer the following questions:

1. How might safety committees use this information when working on accident prevention programs? Could an HR department provide any assistance?

2. How might reward programs for managers take into account incidence rates for injuries and illnesses? What could HR professionals do to facilitate any changes made to the reward system?

KEY COMPETENCIES: Critical Evaluation, Business Acumen; HR Expertise: Organization/ Technology & Data, Workplace/Risk Management periodically as well. Accident and injury statistics should be compared with previous accident patterns to identify any significant changes. This analysis should be designed to measure progress in safety management.

Organizational safety efforts are measureable. Common metrics are workers' compensation costs per injury/illness; percentage of injuries/illnesses by department, work shifts, and job categories; and incident rate comparisons with industry and benchmark targets. Regardless of the specific measures used, it is critical to use relevant HR metrics to track and evaluate safety management efforts. The preceding "HR Competencies & Applications: Calculating Incidence Rates" feature explains how to determine the frequency of injuries to enable comparison.

Employers in a variety of industries have found that emphasizing health and safety pays off in many ways. Lower employee benefits costs for health care, fewer work-related accidents, lower workers' compensation costs, and more productive employees can all result from employer efforts to stress health and safety.

LO5 List three workplace health issues and highlight how employers are responding to them.

14-4 Employee Health and Wellness

Employee health problems are varied—and somewhat inevitable. They can range from minor illnesses such as colds to serious illnesses related to the jobs performed. Some employees have emotional health problems; others have alcohol or drug problems. Some problems are chronic; others are transitory. All may affect organizational operations and individual employee productivity.

Employers face a variety of workplace health issues. Previously in this chapter, cumulative trauma injuries and exposure to hazardous chemicals were discussed because OSHA has addressed these concerns through regulations or standards. Other concerns associated with employee health include substance abuse, emotional/mental health, older workers, smoking, and obesity.

14-4a Substance Abuse

Substance abuse
Use of illicit substances or misuse of controlled substances, alcohol, or other drugs

Use of illicit substances or misuse of controlled substances, alcohol, or other drugs is called substance abuse. The millions of substance abusers in the workforce cost global employers billions of dollars annually. Recent studies show confounding results regarding the trend in illegal drug use by employees. Drug testing companies report an overall decline; however, they also report a rise in the use of heroin and painkillers.[37]

Employers' concerns about substance abuse stem from the ways it alters work behaviors, causing increased tardiness and absenteeism, lower productivity, a higher rate of mistakes, and more industrial accidents. It can also cause an increase in withdrawal (physical and psychological) and antagonistic behaviors, which may lead to workplace violence.[38] Many companies have instituted drug screening programs that include pre-employment testing and testing after workplace accidents, along with zero-tolerance policies that address employees' use of alcohol and drugs.

A company should also consider utilizing an employee assistance program (EAP) for support and counseling related to substance abuse. EAPs assist troubled employees so that they can remain employed. HR professionals get involved in substance abuse issues by taking actions such as training supervisors to identify and help prevent problems. They also work with supervisors and managers to institute progressive discipline for substance abusers that provides them with a chance to seek assistance.

FIGURE 14-10 Common Signs of Substance Abuse

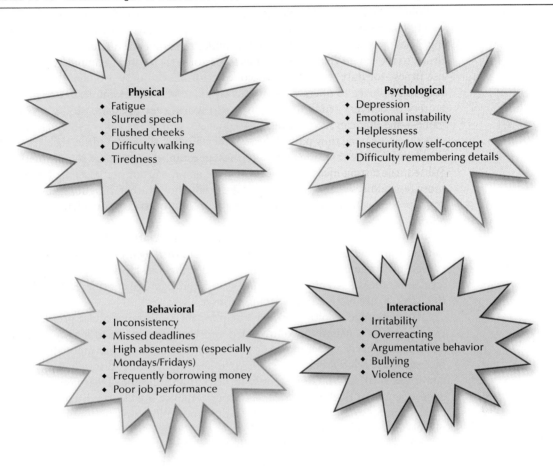

Physical
- Fatigue
- Slurred speech
- Flushed cheeks
- Difficulty walking
- Tiredness

Psychological
- Depression
- Emotional instability
- Helplessness
- Insecurity/low self-concept
- Difficulty remembering details

Behavioral
- Inconsistency
- Missed deadlines
- High absenteeism (especially Mondays/Fridays)
- Frequently borrowing money
- Poor job performance

Interactional
- Irritability
- Overreacting
- Argumentative behavior
- Bullying
- Violence

HR professionals and managers should refrain from diagnosing employees, as this is a task best left to those trained in mental health and substance abuse issues. Rather, all management actions should focus on work behaviors and job performance. Figure 14-10 shows common signs of substance abuse that HR professionals and managers can monitor. However, not all signs may manifest in any one case. A pattern that includes some of these behaviors should indicate the need to pay closer attention.

Many companies use alcohol and drug testing, especially following an accident or some other reasonable cause. A majority of companies require some or all applicants to take a drug test before they are hired. Using these tests can improve employee productivity and attendance, and reduce injuries and workers' compensation claim costs.[39] Some employers also use random testing programs.

The U.S. Department of Transportation requires drug testing for transportation workers in aviation, trucking, railroad, mass transit, pipeline, and commercial vessel operations. The U.S. Department of Labor provides extensive guidance on its website to help employers implement legal and effective drug testing programs. Key points include careful selection of a certified testing lab, proper policy and notification to applicants and employees, precise chain of custody, and confirmatory testing of positive results.

Types of Drug Tests There are several types of tests to detect drug use: urinalysis, radioimmunoassay of hair, surface swiping, and fitness-for-duty testing. The innovative fitness-for-duty tests can be used alone or in conjunction with focused drug testing. These tests can identify individuals under the influence of alcohol or prescription drugs to the extent that their abilities to perform their jobs are impaired. Some firms use fitness-for-duty tests to detect work performance safety problems before permitting an employee to operate dangerous equipment. As an example, in one firm when a crew of delivery truck drivers comes to work, they are asked to "play" a video game—one that can have serious consequences. Unless the video game machine presents receipts saying they passed the test, they are not allowed to drive their trucks that day. It works like this—the computer has an established baseline for each employee. Subsequent testing measures each employee against his or her baseline. Interestingly, most test failures are unrelated to drugs or alcohol. Rather, fatigue, illness, and personal problems more frequently render a person unfit to perform a hazardous job.

Handling Substance Abuse Cases The ADA affects how management can handle substance abuse cases. Currently, users of *illegal* drugs are specifically excluded from the definition of *disabled* under the act. However, those addicted to *legal* substances (e.g., alcohol and prescription drugs) are considered disabled under the ADA, as are recovering substance abusers.

To encourage employees to seek help for their substance abuse problems, a *firm choice option* is usually recommended and has been endorsed legally. In this procedure, a supervisor or a manager confronts the employee privately about unsatisfactory work-related behaviors. Then, in keeping with the disciplinary system, the employee is offered a choice between help and discipline. Treatment options and consequences of further unsatisfactory performance are clearly discussed, including what the employer will do. Confidentiality and follow-up are important when employers use the firm choice option.[40]

Legalized Marijuana The legal use of marijuana for medical reasons has been authorized in nearly half of the states in the United States. In addition, several states have also legalized the recreational use of marijuana. This poses some dilemmas for companies located in those states. However, even though consumption of alcohol is legal, employers are still permitted to limit its use in the workplace. Conflicting state and federal treatment of marijuana adds to the problem for employers as they work to maintain a safe work environment.[41]

An organization might consider developing a zero-tolerance policy if it is not currently required by state regulations to make accommodations for users of medical marijuana. Consumption of the drug is still illegal under federal law. Another option involves placing users of medical marijuana on disability leave (or time off associated with the Family and Medical Leave Act) so that these individuals can assess their current situation in the company. Finally, companies might utilize fitness-for-duty tests to ensure that workers can safely and effectively perform their job duties. There may be liability if an employee who is known by the employer to be using marijuana is involved in an accident. Employers should continue to monitor legal decisions regarding the legalization of marijuana and adapt their policies as needed.

14-4b Emotional/Mental Health

A variety of emotional/mental health issues arise at work that must be addressed by employers. Many individuals are facing work, family, and personal life pressures.

Although most people manage these pressures successfully, some individuals have difficulty handling the demands. Due to the stigma associated with such concerns, many employees conceal these illnesses and fail to get the help they need. This only makes the problem worse, and their work performance and overall well-being can suffer as a result.[42] Specific events, such as death of a spouse, divorce, or medical problems, can affect individuals who otherwise have been coping successfully with life's pressures. Depression is another common emotional/mental health concern. The effects of depression are seen at all organizational levels, from warehouses and accounting offices to executive suites.

Beyond trying to communicate with employees and relieving some workload pressures, it is generally recommended that supervisors and managers contact HR personnel, who can intervene and then refer affected employees to outside resources through employee assistance programs. It is also important to note that emotional/mental illnesses such as schizophrenia and depression are considered disabilities under the ADA, and employers may need to accommodate employees with these conditions.

14-4c Stress

Stress
The harmful physical or psychological reaction that occurs when people are subject to excessive demands or expectations

Individuals who feel that they lack control and resources to deal with the many pressures they face can experience stress and burnout. Stress is the harmful physical or psychological reaction that occurs when people are subject to excessive demands or expectations. In fact, the most common reason for long-term work absence is stress.[43] Health and safety professionals cite stress as the number one concern in modern workplaces.[44] Absenteeism, reduced productivity, interpersonal conflict, and employee turnover are just a few of the negative outcomes when stress is not resolved.[45] Figure 14-11 provides examples of sources of workplace stress and possible ways to address them.

14-4d Smoking at Work

In response to health studies, complaints by nonsmokers, and resulting state laws, many employers have instituted no-smoking policies throughout their workplaces. Some companies refuse to hire smokers or nicotine users because they want to improve job performance, reduce health-related expenses, and promote healthier lifestyles.

FIGURE 14-11 Workplace Stressors and Ways to Combat Workplace Stress

Workplace Stressors	Ways to Combat Workplace Stress
◆ Increased volume of work	◆ Learn coping strategies
◆ Longer work hours	◆ Get enough sleep
◆ Increased pace of work and tight deadlines	◆ Get Regular exercise
◆ Increased performance expectations and pressures	◆ Relax
	◆ Eat healthy, nutritious meals
	◆ Seek support from sympathetic colleagues

Source: Adapted from Donna Owens, "Stressed Out," *HR Magazine*, March 2014, pp. 44–45.

The emergence of e-cigarettes has complicated matters for employers. While e-cigarettes do not produce smoke, the vaporized liquids contain nicotine, and federal agencies have not yet agreed on their legal status. The Food and Drug Administration does not consider them a drug or medical device, and they are therefore not subject to FDA oversight. The Department of Transportation prohibits their use on airplanes. Several states (e.g., New Jersey, North Dakota, and Utah) and municipalities (e.g., Chicago) have banned e-cigarettes in public places and places of employment. Companies should develop appropriate polices in accordance with legal requirements and organizational culture and standards.[46]

14-4e Health Promotion

Health promotion
Supportive approach of facilitating and encouraging healthy actions and lifestyles among employees

Employers concerned about maintaining a healthy workforce try to move beyond simply providing healthy working conditions and promote employee health and wellness in other ways. Health promotion is a supportive approach of facilitating and encouraging healthy actions and lifestyles among employees. Health promotion efforts can range from providing information and increasing employee awareness of health issues to creating an organizational culture supportive of employee health enhancements, as Figure 14-12 indicates. Going beyond simple compliance with workplace safety and health regulations, organizations engage in health promotion by encouraging employees to make physiological, mental, and social choices that improve their health.

The first level of health promotion (information and awareness) leaves much to individual initiatives for following through and making changes in actions and behaviors. Employers provide information on topics such as weight control, stress management, nutrition, exercise, and smoking cessation. Even though such efforts may be beneficial for some employees, employers that wish to impact employees' health must also offer second-level efforts, such as more comprehensive programs and actions that focus on employees' lifestyle and wellness. The third level requires a commitment to wellness that is seldom seen in employers.

Obesity Nearly one-third of U.S. adults are obese, and another one-third are overweight.[47] Obesity is a fact of modern life and a concern to employers due to related economic costs, including doctor visits, diabetes, high blood pressure, higher health care premiums, and lost workdays. Obesity affects employees both mentally and

FIGURE 14-12 Health Promotion Levels

Level 1 **Information and Awareness**	Level 2 **Lifestyle/Wellness**	Level 3 **Health Emphasis**
• Brochures and materials • Health risk screenings • Health tests and measurements • Special events and classes	• Wellness education program • Regular health classes • Employee assistance programs • Support groups • Health incentives	• Benefits integrated with programs • Dedicated resources and facilities • Continuous health promotion • Health education curriculum

physically, so programs to combat it should address both aspects.[48] Companies can take steps to address the increasing problem of obese employees. Some firms offer incentives to workers who are involved in physical fitness programs and lose weight. In one firm with an active program focusing on obese employees, more than 2,000 employees lost over 61,000 pounds as part of the program.

Wellness Programs Companies' drive to improve productivity, decrease absenteeism, and control health care costs has merged into programs to improve employee well-being. Wellness programs are programs designed to maintain or improve employee health before problems arise. They encourage self-directed lifestyle changes, including reducing cholesterol and heart disease risks and implementing individualized exercise programs and follow-up. Employer-sponsored support groups have been established for individuals dealing with health issues such as weight loss, nutrition, and the need to break unhealthy habits.

Wellness programs
Programs designed to maintain or improve employee health before problems arise

Managing employee health may involve offering incentives to individuals who participate in wellness programs and meet or exceed various health targets and metrics. An alternative to incentives is penalizing employees who don't undergo screenings or fail to follow prescribed treatment regimens for chronic health problems. Employees far prefer "carrots" to "sticks," and there are some potential issues under the Affordable Care Act related to imposing penalties for health compliance.[49] Companies spend an average of $600 per employee on wellness-based incentives. Lifestyle management programs such as weight management, physical activity, and stress management are the most frequently used approaches.[50]

Wellness apps for mobile devices have become the latest trend, with employers using technology such as biometrics and personalized wellness plans. Redbox Automated Retail gave its employees trackers when they joined a company-sponsored walking challenge. They urged the employees to take selfies when they were wearing their trackers in unusual locations. Keeping wellness programs fresh and interesting helps maintain employee participation and success.[51]

Employee Assistance Programs As previously mentioned, organizations can respond to specific and difficult health issues with an employee assistance program (EAP), which is a program that provides counseling and other help to employees having emotional, physical, or other personal problems. An employer typically contracts with a third-party counseling agency for the service. Employees who have problems may then contact the agency, either voluntarily or by employer referral, for assistance with a broad range of problems. The employer or the health care plan pays for counseling costs.

Employee assistance program (EAP)
Program that provides counseling and other help to employees having emotional, physical, or other personal problems

EAPs ideally help improve employee performance (lower absenteeism/turnover and higher involvement), reduce expenses associated with benefits (decreased claims and workers' compensation costs), and enhance organizational well-being (better wellness, lower risk/security problems, drug testing follow-up).[52] These programs often provide help for troubled employees, identifying problems, allowing for short-term interventions, and referring employees who need more complex services. Employees' EAP utilization rates are under 5%. A high percentage of calls are related to child care and elder care.[53] Other areas commonly addressed by EAPs include mental health and substance abuse problems, relationship issues, legal and financial problems, and career advice. Companies can encourage employees to use these resources when needed and protect individuals' confidentiality so that they feel safe in using the EAP.

LO6 Define workplace security concerns and discuss some elements of an effective security program.

14-5 Workplace Security Concerns

Traditionally, when employers have addressed worker risk management, the main focus has been on reducing workplace accidents, improving safety practices, and reducing health hazards at work. However, providing security for employees is becoming more important. Threats can involve physical harm, financial damage, or data theft and misuse. Virtually all of these areas have significant HR implications.

14-5a Security Management

A comprehensive approach to security management is needed to address a wide range of possible threats to an organization's assets and workers. These threats may come from outside the organization or may be due to employee misbehavior. HR managers may be responsible for security programs or may work closely with security managers or consultants.

Security audit
Comprehensive review of organizational security

Security Audit A security audit is a comprehensive review of organizational security. Sometimes called a *vulnerability analysis,* such an audit uses managers inside the organization (e.g., the HR manager and the facilities manager) and outsiders (e.g., security consultants, police officers, fire officials, and computer security experts) to assess security issues and risks.

Typically, a security audit begins with a survey of the area around the facility. Factors that can be evaluated include lighting in parking lots, traffic flow, location of emergency response services, crime in the surrounding neighborhood, and the layout of the buildings and grounds. Vulnerabilities in data systems have become an ever-growing issue, and cybersecurity protections should be included in the security audit.[54] The audit may also include a review of the security available within the firm, including the capabilities of guards. Another part of the security audit reviews disaster plans, which address how to deal with events such as earthquakes, floods, tornadoes, hurricanes, and fires.

Controlled Physical Access A key part of security involves controlling access to the organization's physical facilities. Many workplace homicides occur during robberies. Therefore, employees who are most vulnerable, such as taxi drivers and convenience store clerks, can be protected with bulletproof partitions and restricted access areas.

Many organizations limit access to facilities and work areas by using electronic access or keycard systems. Although not foolproof, these systems can make it more difficult for an unauthorized person, such as an estranged spouse or a disgruntled former employee, to enter the premises. Access controls can also be used in elevators and stairwells to prevent unauthorized people from entering designated areas within a facility.

Access to HR Data Controlling computer access is an important part of safeguarding employees' personal data. Coordinating with information technology staff to change passwords and access codes, and otherwise protect company information are important steps to secure IT resources. Threats to business data include hackers breaching computer systems, remotely installed malware, theft of laptops and mobile storage devices, and insider threats. Preventing access and downloading capabilities decreases the chance of employees either intentionally or accidently exposing company data.[55] The following "HR Competencies & Applications: Dangers of BYOD" feature discusses issues related to employees using their personal devices to perform work-related tasks.

Since HR information systems are a treasure trove of valuable personal data, special precautions should be taken to secure these data. Using third-party vendors and cloud-based data storage increases the risk of data theft or breaches. For example, a recent breach of HR systems at the U.S. Postal Service compromised the

COMPETENCIES & APPLICATIONS

Dangers of BYOD

Bring your own device (BYOD) policies are becoming common in most workplaces because employees want to stay in touch using their smartphones, and companies save resources by not having to provide technology to all employees. However, this trend is not without risk. Nearly half of Generation Y employees admit that they don't follow corporate security guidelines, and over 10% wouldn't report an incident in which their device has been compromised.

Think about all of the photos, messages, and other data you might store on your personal mobile phone or tablet. If your employer enforces strict procedures when employees terminate, you might find that your device has been wiped clean, and all of your personal data is lost when you leave the company; to protect company data, some firms do just that. It sounds like a harsh solution, but what's a company to do?

Here are some things to consider as managers create policies to deal with the BYOD trend:

- Are employees' personal devices as secure as office-based equipment?
- How can companies protect corporate data when employees can access it from mobile devices?
- Are there procedures in place to promptly and effectively address breaches from mobile devices?

- Has the company established a protocol to wipe a compromised device clean of all data files?
- What controls are in place to manage employees' use of apps to protect against malware and other attacks?

Setting up security measures to restrict access to sensitive company data from mobile devices, training employees in data security procedures, and coordinating between HR and IT personnel when employees terminate their employment are critical steps in efforts to protect vital data resources. Ensuring that employees understand the implications of using their own devices to access company data can prevent loss of personal data.[56]

Consider the advantages and disadvantages of allowing employees to bring their own devices to work and answer the following questions:

1. How can companies encourage employees to report when their devices are compromised? How could HR departments assist with these efforts?

2. What is your opinion on using your own mobile phone or tablet to perform your job duties?

KEY COMPETENCIES: Communication, Consultation; HR Expertise: Organization/Technology & Data; Workplace/Risk Management personal data of over 800,000 employees, potentially disclosing their names, Social Security numbers, dates of birth, and other sensitive data.[57] Information security experts believe that data security is 20% technical and 80% managerial. This emphasizes the importance of policies, training, and employee awareness and vigilance for all who handle HR data.[58]

14-5b Employee Screening and Selection

A key facet of providing security is screening job applicants. Legal constraints somewhat limit what HR management can do, particularly regarding the use of psychological tests and checking references. However, firms that do not screen employees adequately may be subject to liability if an employee later commits crimes. For instance, an individual with a criminal record for assault was hired by a firm to maintain sound equipment in clients' homes. The employee used a passkey to enter a home and assaulted the owner; consequently, the employer was held responsible for not doing an adequate background check. Of course, when selecting employees, employers must be careful to use only valid, job-related screening means and to avoid violating federal equal employment opportunity (EEO) laws and ADA.

14-5c Security Personnel

Providing adequately trained security personnel in sufficient numbers is part of security management. Many employers contract with firms specializing in security. If security is provided in-house, security personnel must be selected and trained to handle a variety of workplace security problems, ranging from dealing with an employee's violent behavior to taking charge in natural disasters. Many states require security guards to be registered and often require ongoing training to maintain that status. Essential skills for a security guard include decision-making skills, patience, observation skills, and physical strength.[59]

14-5d Workplace Violence

Workplace violence consists of violent acts directed at someone who is at work or on duty. For example, physical assault, threats, harassment, intimidation, and bullying all qualify as violent behaviors at work. Workplace violence can be instigated by several categories of individuals:

- *Criminal*: A crime is committed in conjunction with the violence by a person with no legitimate relationship with the business (e.g., robber, arsonist, trespasser).
- *Customer*: A person with a legitimate relationship with the business becomes violent (e.g., patient, student, inmate, customer).
- *Coworker*: A current or past employee attacks or threatens another employee (e.g., contractor, temp).
- *Domestic*: A person who has no legitimate relationship with a business but has a personal relationship with the victim commits some form of violence against an employee (e.g., family member, boyfriend).

Since acts of violence in the workplace can be committed by employees inside the firm, as well as those outside the firm, all workers should be trained to identify signs that might indicate an impending violent act.

FIGURE 14-13 Levels of Workplace Violence Warning Signs

Level 1 Early Warning Signs
- Intimidating/bullying
- Discourteous/disrespectful
- Uncooperative
- Verbally abusive

Level 2 Escalating Situation
- Argumentative with customers, coworkers, and management
- Insubordination
- Sabotage of equipment or stealing property for revenge
- Verbal or written threats to hurt coworkers or managers

Level 3 Further Escalation
- Threats of suicide
- Physical altercation
- Destruction of property
- Extreme rage
- Brandishing weapons to harm others

Source: Adapted from DOL.gov, http://www.dol.gov/oasam/hrc/policies/dol-workplace-violence-program.htm.

Workplace Violence Warning Signs In many cases, the perpetrator of a violent act exhibits signs well before committing the act.[60] However, these signals are often given inadequate attention or dismissed. Fears of litigation cause some HR professionals and managers to wait for clearer evidence that an employee will act violently. Although a cautious approach may seem legally defendable, companies also have a duty to protect their workers from workplace danger. Taking threats seriously and acting proactively if an employee poses a threat are appropriate steps to take.[61]

Warning signs may be exhibited at various levels, as shown in Figure 14-13. All employees should receive awareness training to emphasize the shared responsibility for maintaining a safe workplace. Supervisors should observe and document odd behavior. Involving HR staff and mental health experts along with law enforcement personnel when situations escalate can help contain a potentially violent incident. Balancing the rights of individual employees with the right for all to work in a safe and secure worksite is not easy, and companies must work to establish policies and procedures that reduce threats of violence.[62]

Violence Prevention Training Managers, HR staff members, supervisors, and employees should be trained on how to recognize the signs of a potentially violent employee and what to do when violence occurs.[63] During training at many firms, participants learn the typical profile of potentially violent employees and are trained to notify the HR department and to refer employees to outside counseling professionals. Such training requires observers to notice individuals' verbal and nonverbal reactions that may indicate anger or hostility and to listen to individuals who are exhibiting such reactions.

Specific suggestions addressed in training for dealing with potentially violent employees typically include the following:

- Ask questions requiring explanations and longer answers that allow the individual to vent.
- Respond calmly and nonthreateningly to the individual's emotions, acknowledge concerns, and demonstrate understanding about how the individual feels.
- Get assistance from others, perhaps a manager not directly affected by the situation being discussed.
- Indicate the need for time to respond to the concerns voiced and then set up another time for follow-up.
- Notify security and HR personnel whenever an employee's behaviors change dramatically or when a job disciplinary action may provoke significant reactions from an employee.

Workplace Incivility and Bullying Dysfunctional workplace interactions can create a workplace filled with hostility and disrespect. Incivility occurs when rude behavior by ill-mannered coworkers or bosses makes the targets of incivility feel annoyed, frustrated, or offended. Most employees do not find incivility serious enough to file a formal complaint.[64] But incivility can escalate into bullying and lead to other destructive workplace behaviors that are likely to require action.[65]

Bullying is behavior that the victim perceives as oppressive, humiliating, threatening, or infringing on the target's human rights and that occurs over an extended period of time. Bullying, especially by supervisors, can result in damage to the employee and to the organization, leading to increased turnover.[66] Bullying can lead to serious physical and emotional damage to targets and result in lost time from work and lower productivity.[67] Both supervisors and coworkers have been found to bully, and targets typically quit their jobs rather than stay and attempt to work things out through the organization's complaint mechanisms.[68] Instituting effective policies, training employees and supervisors, and providing a confidential reporting process can help reduce workplace bullying.[69]

Dealing with Workplace Violence The increase in workplace violence has led many employers to develop policies and practices that aim to prevent and respond to it. Policies can specify how workplace violence is to be dealt with in conjunction with disciplinary actions and referrals to EAPs. Training managers and others is an important part of successful practice. Utilizing case studies and providing definitions and examples are more effective than simply training employees on the company's policy. Establishing a supportive, respectful organizational climate can also mitigate concerns about workplace bullying and other counterproductive behaviors.[70]

One application of these policies is a *violence response team*. Composed of security personnel, key managers, HR staff members, and selected employees, this team functions much like a safety committee, but with a different focus. Such a team conducts analyses, responds to and investigates employee threats, and may even help calm angry, volatile employees.

Employers must be careful because they may face legal action for discrimination if they discharge employees for behaviors that often precede violent acts. For example, in several cases, employees who were terminated or suspended for making threats or even engaging in physical actions against their coworkers then sued their employers, claiming they had mental disabilities covered under the ADA.

Post-violence response is another aspect of managing workplace violence. Whether the violence results in physical injuries or death, or just intense interpersonal conflicts, it is important that employers have plans to respond afterward. Their response must reassure employees who may be fearful of returning to work or who experience anxiety and sleeplessness, among other reactions. Providing referrals to EAP resources, allowing employees time to meet with HR staff, and arranging for on-site trained counselors are all possible elements of post-violence response efforts.

LO7 Describe the nature and importance of disaster preparation and recovery planning for HR.

14-6 Disaster Preparation and Recovery Planning

During the past several years, many significant disasters have occurred. Some have been natural disasters, such as hurricanes, major snowstorms, flooding in various states, tornadoes, and wild fires. There has also been concern about terrorism, and fires and explosions have damaged some firms. According to a SHRM study, the 9/11 attacks encouraged many organizations to revisit and update the plans used to prepare employees for various disasters, and while not every kind of problem can be foreseen, just having such a plan can be very beneficial for building confidence.[71] All of these issues have led to an expanded role for HR staff in disaster planning.

Crisis management has become important to prepare for any instance in which organizations and their employees are impacted by such events. Effectively managing a crisis that a company faces can be detailed in three basic steps:[72]

- *Pre-crisis:* Identify how crises can be avoided through proper preparation, risk assessment, and disaster prevention.
- *Crisis:* Craft a plan that enables the firm to adequately identify and respond to a crisis.
- *Post-crisis:* Identify how the organization can better respond to the same or a similar crisis if it were to happen again.

GLOBAL

Such planning and preparation is particularly important when sending employees abroad for overseas assignments. Proper planning should be conducted before individuals leave their home worksites. If possible, HR professionals should visit foreign locations and discuss security with employees, and the degree to which a security presence and personal weapons are needed for protection should be determined. An evaluation should be made to determine the potential risks to employees and families who are being sent abroad.

14-6a Disaster Planning

Effective disaster planning involves the three components shown in Figure 14-14. Imagine that a hurricane destroys a facility where employees work as well as many of the employees' homes. Or picture an explosion or terrorist attack that prohibits workers from getting to their workplaces. These situations demonstrate the human dimensions to natural and human-caused disasters. However, many employees

FIGURE 14-14   Elements of a Disaster Plan

report that their companies are not prepared to handle emergencies that might affect them.[73] Disaster planning should include consideration of organizational factors, human impact analysis, and disaster training.

Organizational Assessment   Organizational assessment includes establishing a disaster planning team, often composed of representatives from HR, security, information technology, operations, and other areas. The purpose of this team is to conduct an organizational assessment of how various disasters might affect the organization and its employees. Then a disaster recovery plan is developed to identify how the organization will respond to various situations.

Human Impact Planning   The impact of events on people should be assessed and contingency plans put in place. Issues such as having backup databases along with employee contact information are key considerations of such planning. Identifying who will take responsibility for various duties and how these efforts will be coordinated must also be determined.

Some organizations have done an effective job with such planning. For instance, after losing power and Internet service because of Hurricane Sandy, ICS Software, a New York–based provider of health administration programs, used cloud phone services offered by the firm 8×8 so that employees could continue talking to customers from their residences.[74]

Disaster Training   All planning efforts may be wasted if managers and employees are not trained on what to do when disasters occur. Training should take place regularly and reflect actual workplace conditions to simulate a real emergency as closely as possible. This training should cover a wide range of topics, including the following:

- First aid/CPR
- Hazardous materials containment
- Disaster escape means

- Employer contact methods
- Organizational restoration efforts

But this training is not sufficient without conducting exercises or simulations that allow managers and employees to use the training.[75] Much like public schools have fire evacuation exercises, employers may have site evacuation drills. Regular tests to ensure that information technology and databases are securely accessible away from the main location should occur. Responses observed during exercises or simulations may identify additional training needs or modifications needed within the organization.

SUMMARY

- The four components of risk management are workplace safety and health, employee health and wellness promotion, workplace and worker security, and disaster preparation and recover planning.
- Health is a general state of physical, mental, and emotional well-being. Safety is a condition in which the physical well-being of people is protected. Security is the protection of employees and organizational facilities.
- Workers' compensation coverage is provided by employers to compensate employees who suffer job-related injuries and illnesses.
- Both the Family and Medical Leave Act (FMLA) and the Americans with Disabilities Act (ADA) affect employer health and safety policies and practices.
- The Fair Labor Standards Act (FLSA) limits the types of work that younger employees, especially those under the age of 18, can perform.
- Global security is of growing importance, and employers must plan carefully for employees who are traveling and working abroad.
- Companies that operate in multiple countries must evaluate various requirements and safety standards, and they then must plan accordingly.
- The Occupational Safety and Health Act states that employers have a general duty to provide safe and healthy working conditions.
- The Occupational Safety and Health Administration (OSHA) has established safety standards to provide guidance in many areas, including hazard communication and personal protective equipment. OSHA requires employers to keep records of occupational illnesses and injuries, inspects workplaces,

and can issue citations for several levels of violations. Developing safety policies, disciplining violators, keeping safety records, conducting safety training, communicating on safety issues, establishing safety committees, inspecting work areas for safety concerns, investigating accidents, and evaluating safety efforts are all part of comprehensive safety management.
- Effective safety management requires integrating three approaches: organizational, engineering, and individual.
- Ergonomics looks at the physical demands of work. Employers can promote employee health at several levels to improve organizational operations and individual employee productivity.
- Substance abuse, emotional/mental health, and smoking at work are common health issues and thus a growing concerns for organizations and employees.
- Employers have responded to health problems by establishing and supporting wellness programs and employee assistance programs.
- Establishing and maintaining an organizational culture of health continues to pay off for many employers.
- Secure workplaces and corporate data are important, particularly as the frequency of computer hacking attacks increases.
- Employers can enhance security by conducting security audits, controlling access to workplaces and computer systems, screening employees adequately during the selection process, and providing security personnel.
- Disaster preparation and recovery planning have grown to be important HR concerns.

CRITICAL THINKING CHALLENGES

1. What can first-line supervisors do to help control workers' compensation costs, and how might they be rewarded for doing so?

2. What should an employer do when facing an OSHA inspection?

3. As the HR manager of a distribution and warehouse firm with 600 employees, you plan to discuss a company wellness program at an executive staff meeting next week. The topics to cover include what a wellness program is, how it can benefit the company and employees, and the process for establishing it. To aid in developing your presentation to the executives, consult the website www.welcoa.org and other applicable websites you can locate.

4. What should be included in disaster planning for a large employer in Annapolis, Maryland, that is concerned about natural disasters such as floods and snowstorms that might shut down the company and parts of the city?

5. The number and magnitude of data breaches have been increasing at retailers, banks, government agencies, and other institutions. The management team at your company has decided to develop plans for dealing with data security breaches. Because your company has many employees who telecommute and you employ a high percentage of contract and temporary employees, there are many factors to consider.

A. What policies would you recommend to help ensure that insiders (including direct and indirect workers) do not steal sensitive corporate data or compromise the integrity of the computer system?

B. Write a suggested procedure for dealing with computer and data access when an employee (including direct and indirect workers) terminates employment. What steps should be taken to protect the company's IT data?

CASE   Building a Culture of Safety

The construction industry accounts for the most workplace fatalities of any sector and is generally considered a high-risk environment. One construction firm, Messer Construction, decided to address this problem by implementing a comprehensive safety program called Safety4Site for its employees and subcontractors. A major focus of the program was creating a safety culture to improve safety awareness and prevent injuries.

Safety culture has three interdependent elements—behavior (actions taken by employees that are safe or unsafe), person (employee perceptions and attitudes about safety), and environment (organizational safety management systems). Messer Construction's approach included all three aspects and was aimed primarily at reducing incidents of the four major OSHA hazards in construction: falls, struck by, caught in or caught between, and electrocution.

The three key pieces of Messer's program were:

1. *Universal use of eye protection.* All employees were required to wear safety glasses when on a project site.

2. *Daily safety talks.* Called toolbox huddles, these daily briefings reminded employees of important safety precautions and discussed any incidents that had occurred.

3. *Employee accountability.* Based on 20 identified unsafe behaviors, all employees (managers as well as craftspeople) were expected to report any violations they witnessed on a project site.

Before the program was launched, managers participated in a three-hour implementation training session, and all employees received four hours of hazard training. To emphasize expected compliance, any employee who committed one of the 20 unsafe behaviors would be taken off the job site for a day and upon returning the following day would lead the toolbox huddle before beginning work again. Second violations would result in a 30-day unpaid suspension. Messer's management was obviously serious about ensuring that everyone worked safely.

Data collected four years after the program's introduction showed a 66% drop in violations over that time period. Managers identified and reported 60% of violations, 35% were reported by designated safety coordinators, and 5% were reported by front-line employees. Managers were actively involved in safety matters and committed to the program. Surveys taken after four years showed that 99% of workers were aware of the overall safety program. Most participants had positive views about Messer's safety culture and performance. An important outcome was that 99% of workers knew that they were accountable for their safety on the job site, and 79% felt responsible for their coworkers' safety.

Managers stated that safety measures were a higher priority than the operating budget or meeting scheduled build dates. In fact, they saw these safety efforts as a long-term program that would save money and reduce injuries. Further, the vast majority of workers stated that they would not take risks just to get a job done. The only change recommended by employees was to provide them with safety incentives or rewards.

Overall, Messer Construction instilled a safety culture that will give workers peace of mind knowing that their safety is nonnegotiable. They can build buildings with Safety4Site.[76]

QUESTIONS

1. What could be done to increase front-line workers' reports of violations? Why might they be reluctant to report violations they witness?

2. What rewards might be offered to front-line workers for working safely and preventing injuries? What rewards might be offered to job site managers who safely lead projects?

3. Visit the Messer Construction company website at http://messer.com/process/safety4site. How has the Safety4Site program impacted Messer's business outcomes? Has the company been awarded any recognition for its efforts?

SUPPLEMENTAL CASES

Wellness Programs Help the Bottom Line

This case explores the positive individual and organizational benefits of wellness programs. (For the case, go to www.cengage.com/management/mathis.)

Data Security

This case explores the different challenges associated with managing data security. (For the case, go to www.cengage.com/management/mathis.)

What's Happened to Bob?

This case concerns warning signs of possible alcohol use and the consequences at work. (For the case, go to www.cengage.com/management/mathis.)

Communicating Safety and Health Success

This case provides information on the success of safety and health efforts in the workplace. (For the case, go to www.cengage.com/management/mathis.)

END NOTES

1. Based on Laura Stevens, "For Those in UPS's 'Circle of Honor,' Safe Driving Is the Total Package," *Wall Street Journal*, June 5, 2014, p. A1; UPS.com, "This UPS Driver Has Not Had an Accident in 52 Years," Compass. UPS.com, http://compass.ups.com/UPS-driver-has-driven-50-years-accident-free.

2. Ravin Jesuthasan, Angel Hoover, and Towers Watson, "Exploiting Workforce Risks to Transform Your HR Function," *Workspan*, March 2012, pp. 39–42.

3. Elisabeth Pate-Cornell and Louis Cox, "Improving Risk Management: From Lame Excuses to Principled Practice," *Risk Analysis: An International Journal* 34, no. 7 (July 2014), 1228–1239.

4. Andrew Van Brimmer, "Risky Business: Human Resource and Risk Management Roles Complement Each Other," *HR Magazine*, March 2012, pp. 50–51.

5. Sophie Soklaridis, David Cassidy, Gabrielle Van der Velde, Emile Tompa, and Sheila Hogg-Johnson, "The Economic Cost of Return to Work: An Employer's Perspective," *Work* 43, no. 3 (2012), 255–262.

6. ERC.com, "When Workers Compensation Intersects with FMLA & ADA," *HR Insights Blog*, October 25, 2013, http://www.yourerc.com/blog/post/When-Workers-Compensation-Intersects-with-FMLA-ADA.aspx.

7. Kimberly Rauscher, Douglas Myers, Carol Runyan, and Michael Schulman, "Young Worker Safety in Construction: Do Family Ties and Workgroup Size Affect Hazard Exposures and Safety Practices?" *Work* 42, no. 4 (2012), 549–558. Bill Tomson and Mark Peters, "Injuries Fall for Young Who Work on Farms," *Wall Street Journal*, April 16, 2012.

8. U.S. Department of Labor Wage and Hour Division, "Child Labor," http//www.dol.gov.whd.childlabor.htm.

9. The Gazette [Iowa City], "Iowa Grocery Stores Cited for Child Labor Violations," March 28, 2014, http://thegazette.com/2013/08/01/iowa-grocery-stores-cited-for-child-labor-violations.

10. Ladan Nikravan, "Risky Business: Millennials at Work," *Chief Learning Officer*, August 1, 2014, http://www.clomedia.com/blogs/1-ask-a-gen-y/post/5746-risky-business-millennials-at-work.

11. Donald Dowling Jr., "Global Workplace Health and Safety Compliance: From the 'Micro' (Protecting the Individual Traveler) to the 'Macro' (Protecting the International Workforce)," *White and Case Online*, March 2011, http://www.internationalsosfoundation.org/?wpfb_dl=19.

12. Eric Krell, "Be a Global Risk Manager," *HR Magazine,* March 2012, pp. 81–84; Jay Sternberg and Brett Guiley, "Business Travelers," *Workspan,* April 2012, pp. 75–78.

13. Based on Junhah Lee, "Samsung Says 59 China Suppliers Failing Safety Rules," *Bloomberg.com*, June 30, 2014, http://www.bloomberg.com/news/2014-07-01/samsung-says-59-china-suppliers-failing-safety-rules.html; Lorraine Luk, "Hon Hai Confirms Employee Deaths," *Wall Street Journal*, May 20, 2013; Charles Duhigg and David Barboza, "In China, Human Costs Are Built into an iPad," *New York Times*, January 26, 2012, http://www.nytimes.com/2012/01/26/business/ieconomy-apples-ipad-and-the-human-costs-for-workers-in-china.html?pagewanted=all&_r=0.

14. Roy Maurer, "OSHA Shelves Proposed Rule on Injury, Illness Prevention," *HR Magazine*, July 2014, p. 13; Roy Maurer, "OSHA Releases Regulatory Plans for 2015," *SHRM Online*, December 2, 2014, http://www.shrm.org/hrdisciplines/safetysecurity/articles/pages/osha-regulatory-plans-2015.aspx; Roy Maurer, "Company Charged with Retaliation after Employees Participate in Inspection," *SHRM Online*, November 26, 2013, http://www.shrm.org/hrdisciplines/safetysecurity/articles/pages/gaines-retaliation-truckers-inspection.aspx; Alexandra Berzon, "Battle over Risky Chemicals," *Wall Street Journal*, November 21, 2013, p. B1.

15. U.S. Bureau of Labor Statistics, "Employer-Reported Workplace Injuries and Illnesses, 2012," November 7, 2013, *BLS.gov*; U.S. Bureau of Labor Statistics, "Number of Fatal Work Injuries, 1992–2012," 2014, BLS.gov.

16. Ron Maurer, "U.S. Workplace Fatalities Drop 5 Percent in 2013," *HR Online*, September 16, 2014, http://www.shrm.org/hrdisciplines/safetysecurity/articles/pages/us-workplace-fatalities-drop-2013.aspx; Roy Maurer, "2012 Workplace Injury Rate Continues Downward Trend," *SHRM Online*, November 15, 2013, http://www.shrm.org/hrdisciplines/safetysecurity/articles/pages/2012-workplace-injury-rate-decline.aspx.

17. Alexandra Berzon, "Workplace Fatality Rate Rises for Latinos," *Wall Street Journal*, September 12, 2014, p. B3; Peter Rousmaniere, "Translated Safety Training Key for Immigrant Workers," *SHRM Online*, December 1, 2014, http://www.shrm.org/hrdisciplines/safetysecurity/articles/pages/translated-safety-training-immigrant-workers.aspx.

18. Alexandra Berzon and Kris Hudson, "Builders, OSHA Square Off on Rooftop Safety," *Wall Street Journal*, September 29, 2014, p. B1.

19. Andrew McIlvaine, "Temporary Workers, Risky Situations," *HRE Online*, April 9, 2014, http://www.hreonline.com/HRE/view/story.jhtml?id=534356936; Kathryn Tyler, "Better Safe Than Sorry," *HR Magazine*, December, 2014, pp. 44–45; Roy Maurer, "OSHA Published Temp Worker Safety Best Practices," *SHRM Online*, August 26, 2014, http://www.shrm.org/hrdisciplines/safetysecurity/articles/pages/osha-temp-well-worker-safety-best-practices.aspx.

20. Olivera Perkins, "Republic Steel Fined $2.4 Million for OSHA Health and Safety Violations at Lorain Plant and 3 Other Facilities," *Cleveland Plain Dealer*, April 28, 2014.

21. Ben Stanley, "OSHA: Safety Violations Caused Death at Behr Iron & Steel's South Beloit Recycling Facility," *Rockford [IL] Register Star*, September 4, 2014. http://www.rrstar.com/article/20140904/News/140909728#ixzz3IF7zPEG8.

22. Jill Stanforth Tauber, "Donning and Doffing Claims Not Defeated by Absence of OSHA Standard," *SHRM Online*, December 2, 2013, http://www.shrm.org/legalissues/federal-resources/pages/donning-doffing-claims-osha.aspx.

23. OSHA, "Safety and Health Topics: Ebola," https://www.osha.gov/SLTC/ebola/standards.html.

24. U.S. Department of Labor, "OSHA Forms for Recording Work-Related Injuries and Illnesses," https://www.osha.gov/recordkeeping/new-osha300form1-1-04.pdf.

25. OSHA, "News Release: OSHA Announces New Requirements for Reporting Severe Injuries," September 11, 2014, https://www.osha.gov/pls/oshaweb/owadisp.show_document?p_table=NEWS_RELEASES&p_id=26673; Roy Maurer, "OSHA Announces New Injury Reporting Rules," *SHRM Online*, September 15, 2014, http://www.shrm.org/hrdisciplines/safetysecurity/articles/pages/osha-announces-new-injury-reporting-rules.aspx.

26. Roy Maurer, "Employers Debate Publication of Injury and Illness Data," *HR Magazine*, March, 2014, p. 15.

27. Dave Zielinski, "What's Safe? Employers Underreport Injuries and Illnesses," *HR Magazine*, February 2012, p. 12; Roy Maurer, "Safety Climate, Supervisory Behavior Linked to Accident Underreporting," *SHRM Online*, February 5, 2014, http://www.shrm.org/hrdisciplines/safetysecurity/articles/pages/safety-climate-accident-underreporting.aspx; Kecia Bal, "Linking Culture to Accident Reporting," *HRE Online*, March 20, 2014, http://www.hreonline.com/HRE/view/story.jhtml?id=534356841.

28. *Marshall v. Barlow's, Inc.*, 98 S. Ct. 1816 (1978).

29. OSHA.gov, "Commonly Used Statistics"; OSHA.gov, "Industry Profile for OSHA Standard ALL"; OSHA.gov, "Top 10 Most Frequently Cited Standards."

30. Mark Pagell, David Johnston, Anthony Veltri, Robert Klassen, and Markus Biehl, "Is Safe Production an Oxymoron?" *Production & Operations Management* 23, no. 7 (July 2014), 1161–1175.

31. Roy Maurer, "How to Make Your Safety Training Talks Effective," *SHRM Online*, June 1, 2014, http://www.shrm.org/hrdisciplines/safetysecurity/articles/pages/safety-toolbox-training-talks.aspx.

32. Richard Horan, "Safety Committees: Line Ownership & the SH&E Professional," *Professional Safety*, August 2013, p. 42.

33. Fred Manuele, "Preventing Serious Injuries & Fatalities," *Professional Safety* 58, no. 5 (May 2013), 51–59.

34. Professional Safety, "Overcoming Ergonomic Risks Improves Workplace Safety," September 2012, p. 16; Roy Maurer, "Does OSHA Regulate Ergonomic Hazards?" *SHRM Online*, November 5, 2014, http://www.shrm.org/hrdisciplines/safetysecurity/articles/pages/osha-regulate-ergonomic-hazards.aspx.

35. Jim Atten, "Building Workplace Safety with Rewards and Recognition," *OHS Online*, June 1, 2014, http://ohsonline.com/Articles/2014/06/01/Building-Workplace-Safety-with-Rewards-and-Recognition.aspx?p=1.

36. Based on U.S. Bureau of Labor Statistics, "Injuries, Illnesses, and Fatalities: How to Compute a Firm's Incidence Rate for Safety Management," November 7, 2013, http://data.bls.gov/cgi-bin/print.pl/iif/osheval.htm.

37. Arian Campo-Flores, "Drug Use at Work Roils Firms," *Wall Street Journal*, October 13, 2014, p. A3; Lauren Weber, "Drug Use on Decline at Work, Except Rx," *Wall Street Journal*, November 18, 2013; Allen Smith, "Drug Use up among Workers," *SHRM Online*, September 19, 2014, http://www.shrm.org/legalissues/stateandlocalresources/pages/drug-use-workers.aspx.

38. Melissa Richmond, Jennifer Shepherd, Fred Pampel, Randi Wood, Brie Reimann, and Leigh Fischer, "Association between Substance Use, Depression, and Work Outcomes: An Evaluation Study of Screening and Brief Intervention in a Large Employee Assistance Program," *Journal of Workplace Behavioral Health* 29, no. 1 (January–March, 2014), 1–18.

39. Ken Pidd and Ann Roche, "How Effective Is Drug Testing as a Workplace Safety Strategy? A Systematic Review of the Evidence," *Accident Analysis & Prevention* 71 (October 2014), 154–165.

40. Jonathan Segal, "Elephant in the Living Room," *HR Magazine*, March 2012, pp. 95–98.

41. Max Mihelich, "Where There's Smoke: The Hazy Issue of Marijuana in the Workplace," *Workforce*, July 2014, pp. 20–21; Tamara Lytle, "Marijuana Maelstrom," *HR Magazine*, June 2014, pp. 43–48; Joanne Deschenaus, "Do Marijuana Laws Leave Drug Policies Up in Smoke?" *HR Magazine*, May 2014, p. 15.

42. Rita Pyrillis, "A Monumental Problem," *Workforce*, September 2014, pp. 45–56.

43. Jennifer Schramm, "Manage Stress, Improve the Bottom Line," *HR Magazine*, February 2013, p. 80.

44. Editor@clomedia.com, "Report: Stress Neglected at Work," *Chief Learning Officer*, February 3, 2014, http://www.clomedia.com/articles/report-stress-neglected-at-work.

45. Alistair Dornan, "Why Employers Must Tackle Stress," *Occupational Health* 66, no. 7 (July 2014), 11.

46. Lauren Weber and Mike Esterl, "E-Cigarettes Spark Dilemma for Employers," *Wall Street Journal*, January 15, 2014; Ken Wassum, "What to Do about E-Cigarettes," *HRE Online*, August 22, 2014, http://www.hreonline.com/HRE/view/story.jhtml?id=534357474; Rita Pyrillis, "Care for a Smoke Controversy? Try Electronic Cigarettes," *Workforce*, December 2012, p. 16; Joanne Deschenaux, "Should Employers Ban E-Cigarettes in the Workplace?" *SHRM Online*, February 21, 2014, http://www.shrm.org/legalissues/stateandlocalresources/pages/should-employers-ban-e-cigarettes.aspx.

47. Max Mihelich, "The Dangers of Being Obtuse about Obesity," *Workforce.com*, March 11, 2014, http://www.workforce.com/articles/20303-the-dangers-of-being-obtuse-about-obesity.

48. Sarah Sipek, "Observations on Obesity in the Workforce," *Workforce*, September 2014, p. 18; Lauren Weber and Rachel Emma Silverman,

"Memo to Staff: Time to Lose a Few Pounds," *Wall Street Journal*, December 17, 2014, p. B1.

49. Lauren Weber, "A Health Check for Wellness Programs," *Wall Street Journal*, October 18, 2014, p. B1; Sharon Begley, "U.S. CEOs Threaten to Pull Tacit Obamacare Support over 'Wellness' Spat," *Reuters.com*, November 29, 2014, http://in.reuters.com/article/2014/11/29/us-usa-healthcare-wellness-exclusive-idINKCN0J-D0AC20141129; Stephen Miller, "EEOC's Third Wellness Lawsuit Targets Incentives, Sparks Criticism," *SHRM Online*, November 3, 2014, http://www.shrm.org/hrdisciplines/benefits/articles/pages/eeoc-sues-honeywell.aspx.

50. Stephen Miller, "Spending on Wellness Incentives up 15% in 2014," *SHRM Online*, February 24, 2014, http://www.shrm.org/hrdisciplines/benefits/articles/pages/wellness-spending-up.aspx; Beena Thomas, "Fifth Annual Wellness in the Workplace Study: An Optum Research Update," *Optum.com*, 2014, https://www.optum.com/content/dam/optum/resources/whitePapers/042313-ORC-wellness-in-the-workplace-WP.pdf.

51. Rita Pyrillis, "Wellness Apps for Workers Becoming More Apropos," *Workforce.com*, January 6, 2014, http://www.workforce.com/articles/20165-wellness-apps-for-workers-becoming-more-apropos; Dave Zielinski, "Help Employees Get Healthy," *HR Magazine*, July 2013, pp. 53–56.

52. Partnership for Workplace Mental Health, "Employee Assistance Programs," http://www.workplace-mentalhealth.org/Topics/Employee-Assistance-Programs.aspx; International EAP Association, "Definitions of an Employee Assistance Program (EAP) and EAP Core Technology," http://www.eapassn.org/i4a/pages/index.cfm?pageid=521.

53. Rebecca Vesely, "EAPs Modernize, but Employees Are Slow to Catch On," *Workforce.com*, February 21, 2012, http://www.workforce.com/articles/print/eaps-modernize-but-employees-are-slow-to-catch-on.

54. Roy Maurer, "Protect Your Business from Cyberthreats," *SHRM Online*, December 31, 2012, http://www.shrm.org/hrdisciplines/safetysecurity/articles/pages/protect-your-business-cyberthreats.aspx; Bill Leonard, "Are 'Inside Jobs' the Biggest Cybersecurity Threat to Employers?" *SHRM Online*, November 24, 2014, http://www.shrm.org/hrdisciplines/safetysecurity/articles/pages/biggest-cybersecurity-threat-employers.aspx.

55. Roy Maurer, "Corporate Fraud on the Rise Worldwide," *SHRM Online*, December 5, 2013, http://www.shrm.org/hrdisciplines/global/articles/pages/corporate-fraud-rise-worldwide.aspx.

56. Based on Sarah Fister Gale, "Data Dilemma: What to Do when BYOD Workers Say 'Bye'," *Workforce.com*, July 7, 2014, http://www.workforce.com/articles/20524-data-dilemma-what-to-do-when-byod-workers-say-bye; Leonard Webb, "Rethinking Mobile Security," *SHRM Online*, May 9, 2014, http://www.shrm.org/hrdisciplines/technology/articles/pages/rethinking-mobile-security.aspx; Lauren Weber, "Leaving a Job? Better Watch Your Cellphone," *Wall Street Journal*, January 22, 2014, p. B7; Joe Mullich, "A Delicate Balance: Employee-Owned Devices in the Workplace," *Wall Street Journal*, August 2, 2012, p. B7.

57. Doina, Chiacu, "U.S. Postal Service Data Breach May Compromise Staff, Customer Details," *Reuters*, November 10, 2014, http://www.reuters.com/article/2014/11/10/us-cybersecurity-usps-id-USKCN0IU1P420141110.

58. Drew Robb, "Could HR Be the Next Target?" *HR Magazine*, July 2014, pp. 50–52; Aliah Wright, "Keep Cyberspies Out," *HR Magazine*, July 2013, pp. 21–26.

59. Bureau of Labor Statistics, *Occupational Outlook Handbook*, http://www.bls.gov/ooh/protective-service/security-guards.htm#tab-4.

60. Cammie Menendez, "Workplace Violence: Impact, Causes, and Prevention," *Work* 42, no. 1 (2012), 15–20.

61. Barbara Hoey, "Defuse Workplace Violence," *HR Magazine*, November 2013, pp. 67–69.

62. Barbara Hoey, "Defuse Workplace Violence," *HR Magazine*, November 2013, pp. 67–69.

63. Rosalind Jackson, *Preventing Workplace Violence: A Training Guide for Managers and Supervisors. Proven Practices*, Elsevier, September 2014.

64. Larissa Beattie and Barbara Griffin, "Accounting for Within-Person Differences in How People Respond to Daily Incivility at Work," *Journal of Occupational & Organizational Psychology* 87, no. 3 (September 2014), 625–644.

65. Laurenz Meier and Paul Spector, "Reciprocal Effects of Work Stressors and Counterproductive Work Behavior: A Five-Wave Longitudinal Study," *Journal of Applied Psychology* 98, no. 3 (May 2013), 529–539.

66. Manuela Priesemuth, Marshall Schminke, Maureen Ambrose, and Robert Folger, "Abusive Supervision Climate: A Multiple-Mediation Model of its Impact on Group Outcomes," *Academy of Management Journal* 57, no. 5 (October 2014), 1513–1534.

67. Morten Birkeland and Stale Einarsen, "Outcomes of Exposure to Workplace Bullying: A Meta-Analytic Review," *Work & Stress* 26, no. 4 (October–December 2012), 309–332; Lin Grensing-Pophal, "Bullies Are (Still) in the Workplace," *HR Executive*, January–February 2013, p. 14.

68. Al-Karim Samnani, "The Early Stages of Workplace Bullying and How It Becomes Prolonged: The Role of Culture in Predicting Target Responses," *Journal of Business Ethics* 113, no. 1 (March 2013), 119–132.

69. Naomi Brown, "Filling in the Gaps: How Emotional Intelligence Training Can Combat Workplace Bullying," *HR Professional* 29, no. 8 (November–December 2012), 39–40.

70. Liu-Qin Yang, David Caughlin, Donald Truxillo, Michele Gazica, and Paul Spector, "Workplace Mistreatment Climate and Potential Employee and Organizational Outcomes: A Meta-Analytic Review from the Target's Perspective," *Journal of Occupational Health Psychology* 19, no. 3 (July 2014), 315–335.

71. Tamara Lytle, "Rising from the Rubble," *HR Magazine*, September 2011, pp. 64–69.

72. Daniel Laufer, "Charting a Course through Crisis," *BizEd,* September–October 2010, pp. 46–50.

73. Roy Maurer, "Half of Companies Not Prepared for Emergencies, Employees Say," *SHRM Online,* June 20, 2014, http://www.shrm.org/hrdisciplines/safetysecurity/articles/pages/companies-not-prepared-emergencies.

aspx#sthash.lFDp2Qir.dpuf.

74. "Businesses Affected by Hurricane Sandy Turn to 8x8 Cloud Communications Services to Enable Business Continuity," Yahoo Finance, November 12, 2012, http://uk.reuters.com/article/2012/11/12/idUS113274+12-Nov-2012+BW20121112

75. John Amann, "Planning for Workplace Emergencies," *Professional Safety,* January 2013, pp. 28–29.

76. Based on Ruoyu Jin and Qian Chen, "Safety Culture: Effects of Environment, Behavior, and Person," *Professional Safety,* May 2013, pp. 60–70.

CHAPTER 15

Employee Rights and Responsibilities

Learning Objectives

After you have read this chapter, you should be able to:

LO1 Explain elements of employment contracts, including noncompete and intellectual property agreements.

LO2 Define employment at will and discuss how wrongful discharge, just cause, and due process are interrelated.

LO3 Discuss issues associated with employee privacy, free speech, and whistle-blowing.

LO4 Analyze workplace monitoring, employer investigations, and other steps taken to ensure a safe and productive workplace.

LO5 Understand the use of policies, procedures, and employee handbooks to communicate workplace behavior and performance expectations.

LO6 Outline approaches to employee discipline and termination of employment.

WHAT'S TRENDING IN EMPLOYEE RIGHTS AND RESPONSIBILITIES

Today's workers expect their employers to provide a fair, safe workplace where they can perform rewarding work and attain personal fulfillment. Employees are more willing to assert themselves and demand to be treated with dignity and respect, so employers are changing their policies and practices to ensure that workers find the workplace welcoming and professional. The following trends in employee relations reflect these issues:

1. There is heightened awareness and concern in organizations about data security and privacy. Recent breaches of databases in many large retailers and government agencies have increased people's concerns about protecting their personal information. Compromises in databases put people at risk for identity theft and other negative outcomes.
2. Privacy issues are in the forefront as websites, marketers, and now employers begin to collect data on every move we make. While many people appreciate customized services, they don't approve of wide-scale tracking and collecting of information about their movements on the Internet or in their workplaces.
3. The decline in union representation in the workforce means that employees have a more direct relationship with their employer. Lacking the protection and advocacy provided by a labor union puts employees in a challenging position to negotiate their terms of employment and defend their employment rights. Individuals with in-demand skills may negotiate a personalized "deal," but the power of companies often dictate the terms of employment.
4. Increased activism in government agencies and legislatures has resulted in an expansion of worker protection laws and additional restrictions on employer conduct. These laws and restrictions greatly influence the nature of employment in companies.

HEADLINE

Sensing What Workers Are Doing

Dmitriy Shironosov/Shutterstock.com

Most companies are interested in improving productivity and maximizing the use of space in their facilities. A growing trend is to use Big Data collected from sensors worn by employees or attached to furniture. That sounds a little invasive, doesn't it? However, when managers are open about these studies and explain the purpose to employees, most workers cooperate willingly.

Cubist Pharmaceuticals in Lexington, Massachusetts asked its employees to wear iPhone-size badges for four weeks to collect details on their motions, whereabouts, voice levels, and conversation patterns. They combined this information with data from email and weekly employee surveys. The company found that face-to-face interactions led to higher productivity than emails. During lunchtime, personal interactions dropped substantially as people stayed at their desks to check email. In an effort to encourage more high-productive interactions, Cubist redesigned its cafeteria and set up a mid-afternoon coffee break.

Employees at Kimberly-Clark Corporation frequently complained about a shortage of meeting space. The company put sensors on conference room chairs and learned that rooms designed to hold a dozen people were routinely being used by only three or four individuals. In response to this situation, the company created more small conference spaces to allow more groups to meet and collaborate. Complaints from employees fell considerably as a result of these efforts.

Typically, data in these studies are aggregated to show patterns of group interactions or space utilization. Of course, managers have to make sense of all of the data and use it appropriately—not to "catch" employees loafing around or doing nonwork tasks.

Employee anonymity and privacy are critical to making this type of data collection and analysis useful. Legitimate use of sensor technology can improve the workplace for workers and their managers, but only if everyone acts in a trustworthy and professional manner.[1]

This chapter explores many interrelated issues that affect the management of human resources: *employee rights*, *HR policies*, and *discipline*. Employees have some basic rights as citizens, but those rights are further influenced by the HR policies and rules an employer establishes. For instance, disciplinary policies establish standards about how managers should deal with those who fail to follow organizational requirements. The variations in how these policies are managed illustrate how the concepts of rights, policies, and discipline evolve as legal, societal, and organizational values change. At one time, there were few restrictions on how employers could operate an organization. However, there are now a multitude of laws and employee rights that affect employer–employee relationships. HR professionals must help create a work environment that honors fairness, protects individual privacy, treats all workers with dignity and respect, while at the same time allowing the business to succeed.

15-1 Employer and Employee Rights and Responsibilities

Rights
Powers, privileges, or interests derived from law, nature, or tradition

Statutory rights
Rights based on specific laws or statutes passed by federal, state, or local governments

Responsibilities
Obligations to perform certain tasks and duties

Rights generally do not exist in the abstract. Instead, rights are powers, privileges, or interests derived from law, nature, or tradition. Of course, defining a right presents considerable potential for disagreement. For example, does an employee have a right to privacy of communication in personal matters when using the employer's computer on company time? Moreover, *legal rights* may or may not correspond to certain *moral rights*, which opens "rights" up to controversy and lawsuits.

Statutory rights are the result of specific laws or statutes passed by federal, state, or local governments. Various laws have granted employees certain rights at work, such as equal employment opportunity, collective bargaining, and workplace safety. These laws and their interpretations have also been the subjects of a considerable number of court cases because employers also have rights.

Rights are offset by responsibilities, which are obligations to perform certain tasks and duties. Employment is a reciprocal relationship in that both the employer and the employee have rights and obligations as depicted in Figure 15-1. For example, if an employee has the right to a safe working environment, then the employer has an obligation to provide a safe workplace. If the employer has a right to expect uninterrupted, high-quality work from the employee, then the worker has the responsibility to be on the job and to meet job performance standards. The reciprocal nature of rights and responsibilities suggests that each party in an employment

FIGURE 15-1   Balancing Employee and Employer Rights and Responsibilities

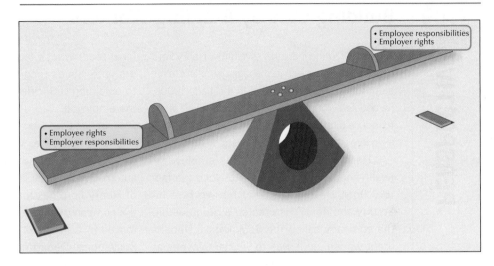

relationship should ideally regard the other as having rights and should treat others' rights with respect.

The relationship between employers and their employees has evolved over time. Some companies have assumed a paternalistic approach to their workers, while others keep a hands-off approach. The following "HR Perspective: Building Cars by Building Workers" feature provides an historical perspective on how Henry Ford treated his employees. Compared to modern-day employee expectations, it shows how very much the world of work can impact people's lives.

15-1a Contractual Rights

LO1 Explain elements of employment contracts, including noncompete and intellectual property agreements.

When individuals become employees, they take on both employment rights and responsibilities. Those obligations can be spelled out formally in a written employment contract or more likely in an employer handbook and policies disseminated to employees. Contracts formalize the employment relationship. An employee's contractual rights are based on a specific contract with an employer. For instance, a union and an employer negotiate a labor contract that specifies the terms, conditions, and rights that employees who are represented by the union have with the company. The contract also spells out the company's rights and obligations.

Contractual rights
Rights based on a specific contract between an employer and an employee

Employment Contracts Traditionally, executives and senior managers have negotiated individual employment contracts, but they are now becoming more common for highly specialized professional and technical employees who have scarce skills. An employment contract is a formal agreement that outlines the details of employment. An employment agreement should address all particulars of the employment relationship, including:

Employment contract
Formal agreement that outlines the details of employment

- Base pay and incentive compensation
- Basic and supplementary benefits and perquisites

PERSPECTIVE

Building Cars by Building Workers

As a leader in the industrial revolution, Henry Ford had a unique approach to managing workers in his automobile assembly plants. In the early 1900s, he doubled workers' pay to $5 per day in an effort to reduce turnover. He also did so because he had a sincere interest in their well-being.

Henry Ford's interest in his employees' health and security went well beyond the factory floor. He required that his workers be "thrifty and neat." He created a group within the company called the Sociological Department whose job it was to visit employees at home and help them manage their household finances and family health. Eventually, the department had over 200 agents who worked with Ford's 13,000 employees, many of whom were immigrants seeking to improve their lot in life.

Ford's assembly line workers had to obtain authorization from the Sociological Department if they wished to buy a car. They would be quizzed on their family status (whether they were married and had children), any outstanding debts, and whether they had life insurance. Only after proving their financial security were they granted permission to buy a car. Ford also provided the services of a legal team whose lawyers would help workers with issues ranging from buying a home to obtaining U.S. citizenship—all at no cost to the employee.

Jobs at Ford were highly coveted, and Ford Motor Company was viewed as an employer of choice because it paid the highest wages in the automotive industry. The paternalistic approach of Henry Ford has long since disappeared at the company, and the automotive industry has moved forward in the hundred years since the Sociological Department checked in on workers and helped them become good employees *and* good citizens in their communities. Consider Ford's humanitarian way of dealing with his employees as you answer the following questions:[2]

1. How did Ford's approach to employee relations impact employees? Do you think it was to their advantage or disadvantage for the company to take such an active interest in their lives?

2. What are some of the things Henry Ford did that you think have merit? If you were running a company, what practices of his might you adopt?

- Key job functions and performance criteria
- Contract term
- Terms and conditions for terminating employment

Companies are more likely to use a formal employment contract when employees are hired from outside the organization rather than being internally promoted, the employment situation is highly risky and uncertain, and compensation is unusually generous.

Noncompete Agreements Employment contracts may include noncompete agreements, which prohibit individuals who leave an organization from working with an employer in the same line of business for a specified period of time. A noncompete agreement may be presented as a separate contract or as a clause in an

Noncompete agreements
Agreements that prohibit individuals who leave an organization from working with an employer in the same line of business for a specified period of time

employment contract. Though primarily used with newly hired employees, some firms have required current employees to sign noncompete agreements. In the past, noncompetes were required only at top executive levels, but now they often apply to sales representatives, engineers, and others involved in research and innovation. The use of noncompete agreements can enhance manager stability, reduce employee costs, and encourage greater expenditures on human capital.[3]

Courts have ruled both for and against companies that have fired employees who refuse to sign noncompete agreements or violate them. Such lawsuits have increased tremendously in the past decade. Consider the founder of a small technology startup who was sued by his former employer. They settled the legal action after six months of negotiating. Startup firms often face greater financial issues when trying to recruit highly skilled talent. Restrictions imposed due to noncompete agreements make it very difficult for these companies to legally hire employees. A Cambridge, Massachusetts technology startup founder says that noncompete agreements have made it difficult for him to hire software engineers at his year-old firm. However, he also requires newly hired employees to sign a noncompete to protect the intellectual value created at the firm.[4]

To create enforceable noncompete agreements, the specified criteria must balance the interests of both employees and employers. Reasonable geographical and time limitations should be imposed, and the agreement should be confined to jobs of a similar type. Some states more aggressively enforce noncompete agreements than do others. The courts use the following guidelines to determine whether a particular noncompete agreement is acceptable:

- Sets reasonable limits on the expectations of employees not looking for work elsewhere
- Typical duration under two years
- Restricts activity to a logical geographic scope
- Grants employees additional "consideration" beyond regular employment
- Limits employees from working within the current area of specialization but does not prohibit employment in new fields[5]

Contracts may also include *nonpiracy agreements*, which bar former employees from soliciting business from former customers and clients for a specified period of time. Clauses requiring *nonsolicitation of current employees* can be incorporated into the employment agreement. These limitations are created to protect the company from former employees attempting to recruit former coworkers or clients, essentially poaching talent or business.

Intellectual Property An area often covered in employment contracts is protection of *intellectual property* and *trade secrets*. A 1996 law made theft of trade secrets a federal crime punishable by fines up to $5 million and 15 years in jail. Employer rights in this area include the following:

- The right to keep trade secrets confidential
- The right to have employees bring business opportunities to the employer first before pursuing them elsewhere
- A common-law copyright for works and other documents prepared by employees for their employers

The primary objectives of using employment contracts to help protect trade secrets are to notify workers that they will be privy to sensitive information on the job, to limit employees' discussion of trade secrets and competitive actions, and to indicate that innovations made by employees on the job fall under the management and control of the organization.[6]

15-1b Implied Contracts

The employment relationship is affected by both formal and informal agreements. The rights and responsibilities of the employee may be spelled out in a job description, an employment contract, HR policies, or a handbook, but often they are not. The rights and responsibilities of the employee may exist *only* as unwritten employer expectations about what is acceptable behavior or performance on the part of the employee. Some court decisions have held that if an employer hires someone for an indefinite period or promises job security, the employer has created an implied contract. An implied contract is an unwritten agreement created by the actions of the parties involved. Such promises establish employee expectations, especially if there has been a long-term business relationship.

When the employer fails to follow up on the implied promises, the employee may pursue remedies in court. Numerous federal and state court decisions have held that such implied promises, especially when contained in an employee handbook, constitute a contract between an employer and its employees, even without a signed contract document.

> **Implied contract**
> An unwritten agreement created by the actions of the parties involved

> **LO2** Define employment at will and discuss how wrongful discharge, just cause, and due process are interrelated.

15-2 Rights Affecting the Employment Relationship

As the power of labor unions has declined in the United Stated and employees increasingly regard themselves as free agents in the workplace, the struggle between individual employee and employer rights has become heightened. Several concepts from law and psychology influence rights in the employment relationship, including employment at will, wrongful or constructive discharge, just cause, due process, and organizational justice.

15-2a Employment at Will

> **Employment at will (EAW)**
> A common-law doctrine states that employers have the right to hire, fire, demote, or promote whomever they choose, unless there is a law or a contract to the contrary, and employees may quit at any time with or without notice

Employment at will (EAW) is a common-law doctrine stating that employers have the right to hire, fire, demote, or promote whomever they choose, unless there is a law or a contract to the contrary, and employees can quit at any time with or without notice. An EAW statement in an employee handbook usually contains wording such as the following:

> *The Company does not offer permanent or guaranteed employment. Either the Company or the employee can terminate the employment relationship at any time, with or without cause, with or without notice. This is called Employment at Will. This employment-at-will relationship exists regardless of any other written statements or policies contained in this Handbook or any other Company documents or any verbal statement to the contrary.*[7]

National restrictions on EAW include prohibitions against the use of race, age, sex, national origin, religion, and/or disabilities as bases for termination. Restrictions on other factors vary from state to state. Nearly all states have enacted one or more statutes to limit an employer's right to discharge employees.

EAW and the Courts The courts have recognized certain exceptions to EAW as follows:

- *Public policy exception*: This exception to EAW holds that employees can sue if fired for a reason that violates public policy. For example, an employee who was fired for filing a complaint with OSHA can sue the employer.
- *Implied contract exception*: This exception to EAW holds that employees should not be fired as long as they perform their jobs. Long service, promises of continued employment, and lack of criticism of job performance imply continuing employment.
- *Good-faith and fair-dealing exception*: This exception to EAW suggests that a covenant of good faith and fair dealing exists between employers and at-will employees. If an employer breaks this covenant by unreasonable behavior, the employee may seek legal recourse.

Over the past several decades, many state courts have revisited and revised EAW contractual provisions. Some courts have placed limits on the doctrine, including situations when employers act harmfully toward workers.

Wrongful discharge
Termination of an individual's employment for reasons that are illegal or improper

Wrongful Discharge Employers that run afoul of EAW restrictions may be guilty of wrongful discharge, which involves the termination of an individual's employment for reasons that are illegal or improper. Employers can take several precautions to reduce wrongful-discharge liabilities. Having a well-written employee handbook, training managers, and maintaining adequate documentation are key ways to prevent wrongful discharge.

A landmark court case regarding wrongful discharge was *Fortune vs. National Cash Register Company* (1977). The case involved the firing of a salesperson (Mr. Fortune) who had been with National Cash Register (NCR) for 25 years.[8] Mr. Fortune was terminated shortly after he sold a large customer order that would have earned him a substantial commission. After reviewing the evidence, the court concluded that he was wrongfully discharged because NCR dismissed him to avoid paying the commission, thus violating the covenant of good faith and fair dealing. Given the increase in wrongful-discharge lawsuits based on different interpretations of the law, companies are much more concerned today about the potential for litigation. Organizations need an appropriate defense against wrongful-discharge lawsuits, some of which are highlighted in Figure 15-2.

Constructive discharge
Process of deliberately making conditions intolerable to get an employee to quit

Constructive Discharge Closely related to wrongful discharge is constructive discharge, which is the process of deliberately making conditions intolerable to get an employee to quit. Under normal circumstances, an employee who resigns rather than being dismissed cannot later collect damages for violation of legal rights. An exception to this rule occurs when the courts find that the working conditions were made so intolerable as to *force* a reasonable employee to resign.[9] Then, the resignation is no longer considered voluntary, but is effectively an involuntary termination. Dangerous duties, insulting comments, and failure to provide reasonable work are examples of actions that can lead to a claim of constructive discharge.

FIGURE 15-2 Keys for Preparing a Defense against Wrongful Discharge

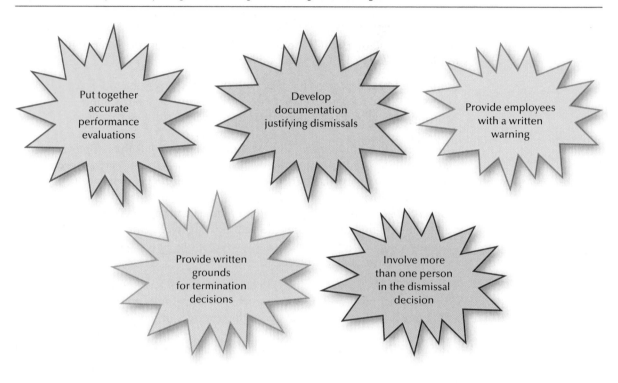

Put together accurate performance evaluations

Develop documentation justifying dismissals

Provide employees with a written warning

Provide written grounds for termination decisions

Involve more than one person in the dismissal decision

ETHICS

Just cause
Reasonable justification for taking employment-related action

15-2b Just Cause

Just cause is reasonable justification for taking employment-related action. Union contracts typically require an employer to provide a "good reason" for disciplinary actions such as dismissal, but this protection does not exist in at-will situations. Even though definitions of *just cause* vary, the overall concern is fairness. To be viewed by others as *just*, any disciplinary action must be based on facts in the individual case. Violations of these requirements can result in legal action. For instance, a court could easily rule that a high-performing worker was not fired for just cause if he had been terminated for poor performance after taking unpaid time off associated with the Family and Medical Leave Act to help a sick relative.

15-2c Due Process

Due process
Occurs when an employer is determining if there has been employee wrongdoing and uses a fair process to give an employee a chance to explain and defend his or her actions

Due process, like just cause, is about fairness. Due process protects employees from unjust or arbitrary discipline or termination. Due process occurs when an employer is determining if there has been employee wrongdoing and uses a fair process to give an employee a chance to explain and defend his or her actions. This typically involves thoroughly investigating all employment actions and giving individuals an opportunity to express their concerns to objective reviewers of the facts in the situation. Due process represents ethical and respectful treatment of employees, and companies that fail to utilize such a process risk being seen as unethical. Organizational justice is a key part of due process.

FIGURE 15-3 Criteria for Evaluating Just Cause and Due Process

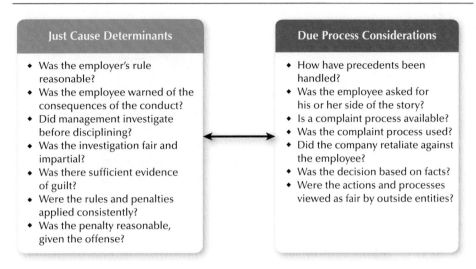

Just Cause Determinants	Due Process Considerations
• Was the employer's rule reasonable? • Was the employee warned of the consequences of the conduct? • Did management investigate before disciplining? • Was the investigation fair and impartial? • Was there sufficient evidence of guilt? • Were the rules and penalties applied consistently? • Was the penalty reasonable, given the offense?	• How have precedents been handled? • Was the employee asked for his or her side of the story? • Is a complaint process available? • Was the complaint process used? • Did the company retaliate against the employee? • Was the decision based on facts? • Were the actions and processes viewed as fair by outside entities?

Figure 15-3 shows some factors to be considered when evaluating just cause and due process. Courts determine if employers' actions are fair based on how managers address these factors.

15-2d Organizational Justice

Organizational justice
The fairness of decisions and resource allocations in an organization

Organizational justice is the fairness of decisions and resource allocations in an organization. Employees' perceptions of fairness and justice in the workplace influence their attitudes and behaviors. For example, employee job satisfaction and commitment are affected by how fairly they believe they are treated by the company.[10] A wide range of HR activities can affect these perceptions of justice, including selection processes, job performance reviews and appraisals, and disciplinary actions. A recent study showed that workers who are laid off are less likely to hold grudges if they understand how the decisions were made and believe they were treated fairly in the process.[11]

Individual perceptions of fairness or justice in the workplace depend on at least three different types of assessments—the process of decision making, the actual decision made, and how the decision is explained to an employee. The elements of organizational justice, as shown in Figure 15-4, are explained in the following sections.[12]

Procedural justice
Perceived fairness of the processes used to make decisions about employees

The first factor, procedural justice, focuses on whether the procedures that led to an action were appropriate and clearly understood, and whether they provided an opportunity for employee input. Procedural justice is the perceived fairness of the processes used to make decisions about employees. In other words, are the rules fair and fairly applied to everyone? Due process is a key part of procedural justice when making promotion, pay, discipline, and other HR decisions. If organizations provide procedural justice, employees may not always like a particular decision, but they tend to respond positively because they know it was reached in a fair way.

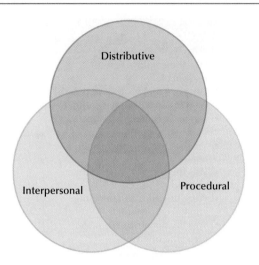

FIGURE 15-4   Interrelated Elements of Organizational Justice

Second, people obviously prefer favorable outcomes for themselves. They decide the favorability of their outcomes by comparing them with the outcomes of others, given their relative situations. This decision involves the concept of distributive justice, which is the perceived fairness in the distribution of outcomes. Disciplinary action based on favoritism—when some are punished and others are not—would likely be viewed as unfair. Fairness depends on employee perceptions and is ultimately a subjective determination.

Interactional justice is the extent to which a person affected by an employment decision feels treated with dignity and respect. Is an adequate explanation provided to explain the decision? Is the employee treated considerately and professionally? For example, if a manager gruffly delivers the news that an employee has not been selected for promotion and fails to explain why, the employee is likely to feel that the decision was unfair. In turn, the employee is more likely to treat coworkers negatively, and the perceived unfairness trickles down through the organization or work group.[13]

Employees who feel that they have not been treated fairly may respond in a number of ways, sometimes even counterproductively. For instance, some look for ways to "even the score" and seek revenge by acting destructively. Others may forgive a single unfair decision if their overall opinion is that the organization acts fairly. Managers should continuously work to foster a reputation as fair and just since employees maintain a fairly stable perception of the organization's level of justice and can excuse an exceptional episode of unfairness.[14]

Companies may improve perceptions of justice by providing procedures to deal with employee complaints. In union-free firms, the complaint procedures differ from those for unionized employees, who typically have a formal grievance procedure specified in the union contract. Due processes in union-free firms are more varied and may address a broader range of issues. Numerous employers use an open-door policy, which allows workers who have a complaint to talk directly to someone in management. However, this policy can be mishandled, so union-free firms benefit from having formal complaint procedures that are well defined to provide a more systematic due process for employees than do open-door policies.

Distributive justice
Perceived fairness in the distribution of outcomes

Interactional justice
The extent to which a person affected by an employment decision feels treated with dignity and respect

Open-door policy
A policy that allows workers with a complaint to talk with someone in management

15-2e Alternative Dispute Resolution

Disputes between management and employees about work issues are normal and inevitable, but how the parties resolve their disputes is important. Open-door policies, formal grievance procedures, and lawsuits provide several resolution methods. However, companies are looking to alternative means of settlement. High litigation costs, delays in the court system, and damage to employer–employee relationships have prompted growth in alternative dispute resolution (ADR) methods such as arbitration, peer review panels, ombuds, and mediation. For employees to trust these methods, companies should communicate decisions clearly and give employees an opportunity to provide input.[15]

Arbitration Disagreements between employers and employees can result in lawsuits that are costly and time-consuming. Consequently, to settle disputes, some companies use the process of arbitration.

Arbitration is a process that uses a neutral third party to make a binding decision, thereby eliminating the need to involve the court. Arbitration has been a common feature in union contracts. However, it must be set up carefully if employers want to use it in union-free situations. Since employers often select the arbitrators, and because arbitrators may not be required to issue written decisions and opinions, some see the use of arbitration in employment-related situations as unfair.

Some firms use *compulsory arbitration*, which requires employees to sign a pre-employment agreement stating that all disputes will be submitted to arbitration. These agreements require employees to waive their rights to pursue legal action until the completion of the arbitration process. A legal check of compulsory arbitration as part of ADR should be done before adopting the practice. In addition, companies should ensure that arbitrators function in an equitable manner, arbitration decisions and awards reflect the law, and proper attempts are made by the organization to communicate arbitration agreements to employees.[16]

Peer Review Panels Some companies allow their employees to appeal disciplinary actions to an internal committee of employees. This panel reviews the actions and makes recommendations or decisions. Peer review panels use fellow employees and perhaps a few managers to resolve employment disputes. Panel members are specially trained volunteers who sign confidentiality agreements, after which the company assigns them to hear appeals.

These panels have several advantages, including reduced lawsuits, provision of due process, decreased costs, and management and employee development. Also, peer review panels can complement a formal complaint process for at-will employees because solutions can be identified and implemented without court action. If an employee later files a lawsuit, the employer has a stronger case since a group of the employee's peers previously reviewed the employer's decision and found it to be appropriate.

Ombuds Some organizations ensure process fairness through ombuds—individuals outside the normal chain of command who act as independent problem solvers for both management and employees. At many large and medium-sized firms, ombuds have effectively addressed complaints about unfair treatment, employee–supervisor conflicts, and other workplace behavior issues. Ombuds address employees' complaints and operate with a high degree of confidentiality; they can also improve employee perceptions of procedural justice.[17]

Arbitration
Process that uses a neutral third party to make a binding decision, thereby eliminating the need to involve the court

Ombuds
Individuals outside the normal chain of command who act as independent problem solvers for both management and employees

Mediation Ombuds, as well as other individuals and groups who oversee disputes, will sometimes use *mediation* as a tool for developing appropriate and fair outcomes for all parties involved. Mediators may use either a facilitative or evaluative

COMPETENCIES & APPLICATIONS

Setting Up an Alternative Dispute Resolution Process

Creating an internal process to settle employment-related disputes and conflicts can benefit both the organization and its employees with faster resolution of complaints and issues. An alternative dispute resolution (ADR) process can address issues such as employee discipline matters, violations of policy, and employment termination decisions.

ADR can take a number of forms, including arbitration, peer review, ombuds, and mediation. It is not necessary to include all forms of ADR—managers can choose the approaches that make the most sense for the organization. Here are some suggested steps in developing an ADR process:

1. Determine the organization's readiness for ADR. Is ADR consistent with the organization's culture and other HR processes? There needs to be a good match between culture and process for ADR to work.

2. Identify key stakeholders among both formal and informal leaders. Top executives must support an ADR program. Don't ignore the informal leaders, since they can influence the rest of the employees, and their support is critical.

3. Research the various ADR options to determine which ones are the best fit for the organization. For example, peer review is most successful when there is a high level of trust within the workforce.

4. Design the program by using a cross-functional team that includes HR, line managers, and senior managers. This way, input from many different areas of the organizations is provided.

5. Get feedback from employees on the initial design. Use focus groups, town hall meetings, suggestion systems, or email polls. Share all the details so that employees can effectively evaluate the process.

6. Design the rollout strategy and communication plan. Determine whether to "go live" right from the start or to use a pilot test of the process first. Decide how to get the word out to managers and employees so that they understand how the process works and what types of disputes are appropriate to bring to the ADR process.

7. Remind employees about the process periodically, such as once a year, so that they know it is operational and effective.

ADR can be effective only if all managers and employees understand the process and trust it to resolve their issues. The benefits it can provide mean that employers and employees will not be tied up in a lengthy, drawn-out process of resolving problems. Speedy, fair resolution allows everyone to move on from a situation and get back to productive work.[18] As you consider the process of ADR, discuss these questions:

1. Have you worked at a job where ADR was used? If so, what type of ADR was there, and how effectively did it work?

2. If you were a manager, what would you see as the advantages and disadvantages of using the various forms of ADR to resolve employment disputes?

KEY COMPETENCIES: Relationship Management, Business Acumen; HR Expertise: Organization/Structure of the HR Function, Organization/Employee Relations approach to dispute resolution. Facilitative techniques foster communication among the parties to help uncover options for settling. Evaluative techniques, on the other hand, point out the potential weaknesses in each side's case and offer potential settlement options. Many mediators use a combination of those approaches depending on the circumstances of the dispute.[19]

The variety of ADR methods available to employers can be confusing. The preceding "HR Competencies & Applications: Setting Up an Alternative Dispute Resolution Process" feature offers a step-by-step process to establish an effective means of resolving employment disputes without the high cost of litigation.

15-3 Managing Individual Employee and Employer Rights Issues

Although the U.S. Constitution grants certain rights to citizens, over the years, laws and court decisions have limited their application in the workplace. Globally, laws and policies vary, which means employers with expatriates and local workers in different countries face a confusing array of obligations. Balancing both employers' and employees' rights is a growing HR concern because of increased litigation and an expanding global workforce. Employers have legitimate rights to ensure that employees are doing their jobs and working in a secure environment, while employees expect their rights, both on and off the job, to be protected.

Right to privacy
An individual's freedom from unauthorized and unreasonable intrusion into personal affairs

The **right to privacy** is defined in legal terms as an individual's freedom from unauthorized and unreasonable intrusion into personal affairs. Although the right to privacy is not specifically identified in the U.S. Constitution, past U.S. Supreme Court cases have established that such a right must be considered. Also, several states have enacted right-to-privacy statutes. A scope of privacy concerns exists in other countries as well.

The dramatic increase in Internet communications, social media, mobile devices, and telecommunications systems is changing the nature of privacy issues in many workplaces. The use of technology by employers to monitor employee actions also increases concerns that the privacy rights of employees are being threatened.

15-3a Privacy Rights and Employee Records

LO3 Discuss issues associated with employee privacy, free speech, and whistle-blowing.

The Privacy Act of 1974 was enacted to protect individual privacy rights in the United States. It includes provisions affecting HR recordkeeping systems. This law applies *only* to federal agencies and to organizations supplying services to the federal government. However, similar laws in some states, while somewhat broader in scope, have also been passed. For the most part, state rather than federal law regulates private employers on this issue.

Employee Medical Records Recordkeeping and retention practices have been affected by a provision in the Americans with Disabilities Act (ADA) requiring that all medical-related information be maintained separately from all other confidential files. The Health Insurance Portability and Accountability Act (HIPAA) also includes regulations designed to protect the privacy of employee medical records. Both paper and electronic files must be safeguarded. As a result of all the legal restrictions, many employers have established several separate files on each employee.

Security of Employee Records It is important to establish access restrictions and security procedures for employee records to protect the privacy of employees and protect employers from potential liability for improper disclosure of personal information. Individuals' Social Security numbers, personal addresses, and other contact information should be protected.

The Data Protection Act requires employers to keep personnel records up to date and keep only the details that are needed.[20] The following guidelines are offered regarding employer access and storage of employee records:

- Restrict access to records to a limited number of individuals.
- Use confidential passwords for accessing employee records in various HR databases.
- Set up separate files and restricted databases for particularly sensitive employee information.
- Inform employees about which types of data are retained.
- Purge employee records of outdated data.
- Release employee information only with employee consent.

Personnel files and records are usually maintained for three years. However, different types of records should be maintained for shorter or longer periods of time based on various legal and regulatory standards. Another concern is how electronic records are maintained and secured, especially given the advances in software, email, and mobile technology. Companies should establish an electronic records policy to ensure legal compliance and avoid violating individuals' personal rights. Employers must comply with federal, state, and international records retention laws.

Data privacy is becoming increasingly important with the growth of mobile technologies and the use of applications (apps) that offer various functions. A large number of apps collect information about users. It is vital to ensure that company policies accurately and completely identify all data being collected so that users are aware of how their personal information is being handled.[21]

15-3b Employees' Free Speech Rights

Individual right to freedom of speech is protected by the U.S. Constitution. However, that freedom is *not* unrestricted in the workplace, so employees and companies need to be aware of appropriate boundaries.[22] Three situations in which employees' freedom of speech might be restricted include expressing controversial views, whistle-blowing, and using the Internet and other communication-based technology.

Employee Advocacy of Controversial Views Questions of free speech can arise over the right of employees to advocate controversial viewpoints at work. Numerous examples can be cited. For instance, can an employee of a tobacco company join in antismoking demonstrations outside of work? Can a disgruntled employee at a union-free employer wear a union badge or a cap at work? Can an employer discipline employees in these situations? The answer is likely "yes" if the disciplinary actions can be justified by job-related reasons and the company follows a due process procedure. In one U.S. case, a court ruled against a white worker who displayed Confederate flags on his toolbox, which offended some African-American employees. The court said that the worker's free speech right was not violated when the employer fired him for refusing to remove the flags.[23]

However, simply because an employer *might be able* to punish employees who make inappropriate statements that embarrass the company, should the employer do so? Perhaps an employer shouldn't because employees may view this as heavy-handed and an overreaction. It may cause other employees to quit their jobs or to lose respect for the employer. The best way to handle these concerns is to (1) attempt informal resolution first, (2) clearly outline the boundaries and standards for appropriate behavior in a formalized policy that addresses work expectations, and (3) have a signed nondisclosure privacy agreement.

ETHICS

Whistle-blowers
Individuals who report real or perceived wrongs committed by their coworkers or employers

Whistle-Blowing and Employee Protection Individuals who report real or perceived wrongs committed by their coworkers or employers are called whistle-blowers. Many well-known whistle-blowing incidents have occurred in past years. A high-profile whistle-blowing case heard by the U.S. Supreme Court involved a former air marshal who disclosed to a journalist that the Transportation Security Administration (TSA) had reduced in-flight marshal protection due to budget reasons despite credible threats of possible terrorist hijacking plots.[24] The case shows the possible conflict between two legislative priorities—to prevent terrorist attacks and to encourage whistle-blowing. The Edward Snowden incident also exemplifies this conflict in national priorities.[25] Cases of whistle-blowing often involve controversial topics and are often very complex. No comprehensive whistle-blowing law fully protects the right to free speech of both public and private employees.

Several laws, such as the Sarbanes-Oxley Act and the Dodd-Frank Act, protect corporate whistle-blowers.[26] For instance, the Sarbanes-Oxley Act is intended to remedy companies' ethical breaches by requiring organizations to properly report financial results, encouraging ethical business practices, and providing protection for whistle-blowers.[27] The Dodd-Frank Act also protects whistle-blowers and provides financial incentives to individuals who report wrongdoing. In addition to paying fines, a company that is found guilty of retaliation is required to (1) reinstate the individual back to his or her job, (2) provide back pay or double back pay to make up for lost compensation, and (3) cover any costs associated with legal counsel.[28]

Employers need to address two key questions in regard to whistle-blowing: (1) When do employees have the right to speak out, with protection from retribution? (2) When do employees violate the confidentiality of their jobs by speaking out? Even though the answers may be difficult to determine, retaliation against whistle-blowers is clearly not appropriate or legal. Whistle-blowers are often treated poorly by their employers because they are seen as disloyal and as a significant threat to the stability of the organization. This is why an ethical culture that includes reporting mechanisms that encourage employees to tell managers about problems and retaliation policies that prevent mistreatment of whistle-blowers are beneficial.[29] The culture of the organization often affects the degree to which employees report inappropriate or illegal actions internally or resort to using outside contacts. Consequently, HR professionals should be actively involved in helping the company develop an ethical culture by creating fair and ethical policies.

15-3c Technology and Employer–Employee Issues

The extensive use of technology by employers and employees constantly creates new issues to be addressed.[30] For example, terminating workers for openly complaining about an employer on social media has come under scrutiny based on recent court rulings. The National Labor Relations Board has ruled that disciplining employees for posting negative comments about an employer's practices may not be acceptable if the posting amounts to protected activity. However, interpretation of the ruling suggests that it does not condone excessive disloyalty or communication of highly sensitive content.[31]

An emerging counterpart to employers monitoring employees is the practice of employees recording conversations in the workplace. The popularity of mobile phones and many company policies allowing personal devices in the workplace have led to employees covertly recording closed-door meetings during which employment matters are discussed. The legal status of such recordings is still being determined as various state and federal laws are considered along with specific facts in any case. Employers are wise to implement a no recording policy to address the issue up front.[32]

ETHICS

Monitoring Electronic Communications The use of email, social media, and text messaging has led to major issues regarding employee and workplace privacy. Employers have good reason to monitor what is said and transmitted through their Internet and voicemail systems despite employees' concerns about free speech. Organizations want to reduce employee misconduct, protect corporate resources, prevent hacking and virus attacks, ensure productivity, and follow federal guidelines.[33] Many employers have specialized software that can retrieve deleted email and other electronic communications, retrace web searches, and even record each keystroke made on employees' computers. Monitoring, while perhaps needed, can harm work unit cohesion and trust among employees.[34]

Employees have varying opinions about electronic monitoring based on different situational factors, which can present many challenges. They may understand the reasons companies monitor their electronic communications but also worry about their personal privacy and confidential data.[35] Further, the standards and acceptance of monitoring vary greatly in different nations (e.g., France versus the United Kingdom), so companies need to consider these factors and inform managers about what actions are considered appropriate.[36] Organizations need to consider such issues when developing policies regarding the monitoring of electronic communications.

The practice of employees using their own mobile devices such as smartphones and digital tablets in the workplace raises additional issues. Bring your own device (BYOD) is becoming increasingly common, and it presents both advantages and disadvantages for firms. Employees are already familiar with their own devices, which makes them more efficient and productive using this technology. However, concerns about data security, lost or stolen devices, and privacy should be addressed with a company policy.[37]

Bring your own device (BYOD)
The practice of employees using their own mobile devices such as smartphones and digital tablets in the workplace

HR Policies on Electronic Communications Since a great deal of work activity involves using technology, it is important for HR professionals to provide guidance to executives, managers, and employees. Many employers have developed and disseminated electronic communications policies. Figure 15-5 outlines recommended employer actions for such policies, including monitoring. These policies should describe to employees why monitoring is needed, the methods used, and the amount of monitoring planned. Employees should also sign off to indicate that they understand the purpose and scope. Inappropriate communication and material should be clearly discussed, and individuals should receive guidance about the company's standards for using communication systems to send and receive private

FIGURE 15-5 Recommended Employer Actions regarding Electronic Communications

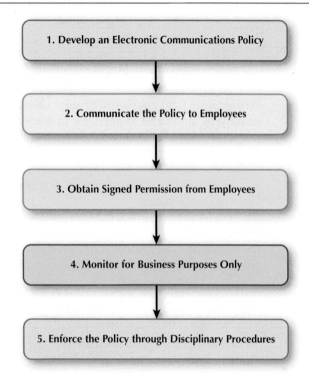

1. Develop an Electronic Communications Policy

2. Communicate the Policy to Employees

3. Obtain Signed Permission from Employees

4. Monitor for Business Purposes Only

5. Enforce the Policy through Disciplinary Procedures

messages. A proactive approach that attempts to balance the rights of the company with the privacy concerns of employees can preserve the dignity of all parties and lead to a professional and productive work environment.[38]

15-3d Employee Rights and Personal Behavior Issues

Another area employers should watch is employee personal behavior on or off the job. For example, an invasion of privacy claim might result if an employer investigates off-the-job charges of illegal behavior. Failure to conduct due diligence can jeopardize disciplinary actions that should be taken by employers or can result in liability for negligent retention. Some of the more prevalent concerns in this area are discussed next.

Counterproductive Behavior Employers may decide to review unusual behavior by employees both on and off the job. The occurrence of various counterproductive behaviors such as bullying, substance abuse, stealing, and sabotage can potentially hurt companies and their employees. Employees may commit some of these actions off the job site. For example, an employee may send threatening or harassing emails or text messages to a coworker's personal accounts. This situation might warrant employer involvement to protect the targeted employee and reduce the chance of litigation.

Organizations must also deal with employees and/or managers who are hostile, insulting, or extremely rude to customers, suppliers, and/or employees at different levels of the organization. To respond to such actions, managers and HR professionals should document inappropriate behaviors and meet privately with individuals to discuss concerns, give feedback, and explain expectations. Defining acceptable and unacceptable behaviors and communicating standards to all employees is also helpful. In an effort to reduce volatile behavior, companies can require employees to pass a fitness-for-duty test before reporting for work, particularly in occupations that are considered dangerous.[39]

Dress and Body Appearance Limitations Employers have put limits on employees' dress and appearance in some situations, including items such as visible tattoos, certain clothing and accessories, and body piercings. Having a written dress policy is recommended to ensure consistency, safety, and fair treatment. One industry in which dress and appearance codes and policies are important is the food and beverage industry. For instance, a pizza firm prohibits visible tattoos and many kinds of body piercing.

To comply with civil rights laws, special consideration should be given to assessing religious or ethnic attire. Job-related reasons for imposing specific dress requirements are typically supported by the courts. The key is to give adequate notice to employees and managers, consistently enforce restrictions, and answer concerns before a dress and appearance code is implemented.

Off-Duty Behavior An additional employee rights issue concerns personal behavior off the job. Employee misconduct off the job has the potential to seriously damage the reputation of the business, especially if individuals wear clothing or other identifying badges or logos that show the general public where they work. Employers encounter special difficulty in establishing just cause for disciplining employees for their off-the-job behavior. To protect intellectual property or trade secrets, some firms establish rules that restrict employees from dating or from "moonlighting" for a competitor.

Most people believe an organization should not control the lives of its employees off the job except when there are clear job-related consequences. For example, a company can take action if an employee who drives as part of his or her job is cited for drunk driving. But what should an employer do if an employee is an acknowledged transvestite, a member of an activist environmental group, a leader in a racist group, or an exotic dancer on weekends? In some of these cases, the employer should do nothing; in other cases, action might be taken. Employers must balance concerns about negligent retention with concerns for employee privacy.[40]

Weapons in the Workplace Companies face a vexing situation regarding employees who legally own firearms and believe they have the right to bring them to work. Highly publicized cases of employees who open fire in the workplace, especially in response to being terminated, make everyone aware of the dangers of weapons. Although U.S. citizens have a constitutional right to bear arms, does that right transfer to the workplace? In private-sector workplaces, it does not. However, 20 states have enacted legislation preserving the rights of employees to carry firearms, even on an employer's premises. Employers are legally obligated to provide a safe working environment for all employees. Balancing that obligation with employees' individual rights is still being decided in the courts. Suggestions for addressing this issue are presented in the following "HR Competencies & Applications: Caught in the Crosshairs" feature.

COMPETENCIES & APPLICATIONS

Caught in the Crosshairs

Finding a way to balance the individual right to bear arms with the requirement to create a safe workplace can challenge human resource professionals, and gun control is certainly a controversial political topic. However, employers have legitimate concerns about weapons in the workplace for practical and business reasons. Three-fourths of all workplace fatalities are related to guns, and many tragic incidents of worker-committed gun violence have occurred in recent years.

The Second Amendment of the U.S. Constitution protects a citizen's right to own and bear arms and, as mentioned earlier, 20 states have enacted laws that allow employees and others to carry firearms on an employer's premises. Some of these laws specifically address concealed weapons and affirmatively permit storing firearms in a privately owned vehicle in an employer's parking lot. The courts have found that such laws are not pre-empted by OSHA's general duty clause. This leaves employers to find a way to satisfy these competing mandates.

Important things to determine include:

1. How does the company define the term *weapon*? Is it only guns, or do other weapons such as knives or machetes also qualify as weapons?

2. How does the company define the term *workplace*? Does the workplace include an employer's parking lot?

3. If the company decides to permit firearms in employees' vehicles, what measures will be put in place to minimize risks? Must all weapons be locked in a vehicle's trunk? Must ammunition be kept separately from the firearm itself?

4. If security guards are authorized to carry weapons, what steps are taken to ensure that they are properly screened and trained?

This is an evolving and controversial issue. HR professionals should stay informed about legislation in all states in which the organization has employees and operations. The primary consideration should be for a safe workplace for everyone. Employers should continue to monitor court rulings and address the issue proactively.[41] Based on these issues, consider the following questions:

1. How do you feel about the right to bear arms and whether companies should be limited in restricting employees from having weapons on the premises?

2. What restrictions would you recommend to companies regarding weapons in the workplace?

KEY COMPETENCIES: Leadership & Navigation, Consultation; HR Expertise: Organization/Employee Relations, Workplace/Employment Law Regulations

15-4 Balancing Employer Security and Employee Rights

Balancing employer and employee rights is difficult. On one side, employers have a legitimate need to ensure that employees are performing their jobs properly in a safe, secure environment. On the other side, employees expect their rights to be protected.

Technology has made it easier and cheaper to monitor employees. It also increases the risks of data loss or other threats to companies' information or reputation. Social media is the new gathering place for people to share legitimate as well as harmful comments about their employers. Monitoring social media sites may uncover employee misconduct that an employer has a right to know about. For example, several hospital employees were caught discussing a patient on Facebook in clear violation of hospital policy and HIPAA privacy regulations. Employers can monitor social media when there is a job-related reason to do so. However, the sheer volume of data generated on social media makes this a practice best conducted by exception rather than as an ongoing procedure.[42]

15-4a Workplace Monitoring

LO4 Analyze workplace monitoring, employer investigations, and other steps taken to ensure a safe and productive workplace.

In the United States, the right of protection from unreasonable search and seizure concerns only such actions taken by government officials. Thus, employees of private-sector employers can be monitored, observed, and searched at work by representatives of the employer. Several court decisions have reaffirmed the principle that both private- and public-sector employers may search desks, files, lockers, and computer files without search warrants if they believe that work rules have been violated. Also, the terrorist attacks of September 11, 2001, led to passage of the USA PATRIOT Act, which expanded legislation to allow government investigators to engage in broader monitoring of individuals and workplaces, to protect national security.

Conducting Video Surveillance at Work Numerous employers have installed video surveillance systems in their workplaces. Some employers use these systems to ensure employee security, such as in parking lots, garages, and dimly lit exterior areas. Other employers have installed them on retail sales floors, in production areas, and parts and inventory rooms to reduce theft and shrinkage. When video surveillance is extended into employee restrooms, changing rooms, and other more private areas, employer rights and employee privacy collide. It is important that employers using such methods develop a video surveillance policy, inform employees about the policy, conduct the surveillance only for legitimate business purposes, and strictly limit those who view the surveillance results. Employee morale should be considered when developing policies because employees may see monitoring systems as a sign that they are not trusted, which can lower their commitment and positive impressions of the company.

Monitoring Employee Performance Employee activity may be monitored to measure performance, ensure performance quality and customer service, check for theft, and/or enforce company rules or laws. The common concerns in a monitored workplace usually center not on whether monitoring should be used but on how it should be conducted, how the information should be used, and how feedback should be communicated to employees. Companies should strive to collect information that is needed to manage business operations but not track every detail just because they *can*.[43] Research points to other considerations. A recent study determined that electronic monitoring processes that were utilized for employee development, that were adequately explained, and that provided good feedback resulted in more positive perceptions of organizational justice, which led to many positive work outcomes such as supervisor trust, work satisfaction, and work performance.[44]

At a minimum, employers should obtain a signed consent form indicating that the employee knows performance will be monitored and phone calls will regularly

ETHICS

Is Somebody Out There Watching Me?

Employers have a right to expect that employees who are on the clock are performing their job duties in a safe and efficient manner. Employees, on the other hand, prefer to work free from scrutiny and invasive management oversight. The two parties' expectations can put them on a collision course for employee relations problems.

Companies in trucking and service industries have started to utilize GPS technology to track drivers' movement and operating practices. Over 37% of service-related companies track their workers' locations using either handheld devices or their vehicles. Tracking can be used to improve customer service by notifying clients that a service technician is on the way or to verify that service was provided. It can also be used to uncover employee misconduct or unsafe driving practices.

Sophisticated tracking software can record if drivers brake too hard or speed. If a driver is too close to another vehicle, the software can intercede by slowing down the truck. In addition to using this type of tracking to discipline employees, some firms also use it to identify and reward drivers who demonstrate exemplary driving habits.

There are few regulations limiting employers' ability to track employees, and no federal laws prohibit employers from using GPS.

Further, with the exception of Delaware and Connecticut, there is no requirement that employers even tell workers that they are being tracked. However, keeping silent about tracking endangers the trust that employees have in their employers. There is also a benefit of letting workers know that they are being monitored, as it might deter them from breaking the rules. The owner of Accurid Pest Solutions says that since instituting monitoring, his drivers now call the dispatch center if they have to pull off the road or change their routing.

Employers and employees work hard to maintain a safe, productive work environment. Tracking worker activities should be done with consideration for both sides of the issue and using an approach of fairness and respect.[45] After reading about this practice, answer the following questions:

1. What are the costs and benefits of implementing a tracking program but not telling employees about it? Should companies tell employees that their actions are being tracked?

2. What are the possible reactions employees might have if they are advised up front that their activities will be tracked? What could be done to improve their reactions?

be taped. It is further recommended that employers provide employees with feedback on monitoring results to help employees improve their performance and to commend them for good performance.[46] For example, one call center allows employees to listen to their customer service calls and rate their own performance. Then the employees meet with their supervisors to discuss both positive and negative performance issues. The preceding "HR Ethics: Is Somebody Out There Watching Me?" feature presents details of employee monitoring in the trucking industry.

15-4b Employer Investigations

Another area of concern regarding employee rights involves workplace investigations. The U.S. Constitution protects public-sector employees in the areas of due process, search and seizure, and privacy at work, but private-sector employees are not protected. Whether it occurs on or off the job, employees' unethical or illegal behavior can be a serious problem for organizations. Examples of employee misconduct include illegal drug use, falsification of documents, misuse of company funds, disclosure of organizational secrets, workplace violence, employee harassment, and theft of corporate resources.

Conducting Work-Related Investigations Workplace investigations can be conducted by internal or external personnel. Often, HR staff and company security personnel lead internal investigations. In the past, the use of outside investigators such as the police, private investigators, or attorneys was restricted by the Fair Credit Reporting Act. However, passage of the Fair and Accurate Credit Transactions (FACT) Act changed the situation, and now employers can hire outside investigators without first notifying the individuals under investigation or getting their permission.

Technology is frequently used when workplace investigations are conducted. This allows employers to review emails, access computer logs, conduct video surveillance, and use other investigative tactics. When using audiotaping, wiretapping, and other electronic methods, care should be taken to avoid violating privacy and legal regulations. In addition to these considerations, the following best practices should be used when conducting workplace investigations:

- Develop a good working plan that outlines how the company should respond to crises before they occur. Confidentiality should be a high priority throughout investigations, and all important incidents should be properly documented.
- Specify whether HR or another party (e.g., an attorney or accountant) will conduct the actual investigation of workplace incidents. If possible, select an objective and impartial investigator who does not have any professional connections with the individuals being investigated.
- Investigate problems quickly before evidence can be tampered with or destroyed and begin interviewing key witnesses. Investigate wrongdoing within several days after being made aware of the incident and try to finish the investigation within two weeks.
- Assess the credibility of individuals providing information in an investigation by looking at the following factors: personal demeanor, reliability, chronology, credibility of answers provided, whether information can be corroborated, and past and present motives.
- Use the stories and information collected to conclude the investigation and recommend any remedial steps that should be taken. Present the results of investigations to key decision makers and make appropriate recommendations.[47]

ETHICS

Employee Theft and Fraud Employee theft of property and company secrets does occur, and white-collar theft through embezzling, accepting bribes, and stealing company property is also a concern. Evidence suggests that fraud is a significant challenge for businesses in the United States, with the average company losing 5% of its annual revenues to fraud. Not surprisingly, employees at higher levels in an organization commit more serious acts of fraud. For example, the average loss is $500,000 when an executive is involved compared to $75,000 when the fraud is committed by a lower-level employee.[48] If the organizational culture encourages or allows such questionable behavior, employees are more likely to see theft as acceptable. In addition, the more pressure there is to achieve, opportunities to act unethically, and ways to rationalize misconduct, the more likely organizations will experience fraud.[49]

There are a number of ways to address employee theft and other workplace misconduct. Typical methods include conducting thorough pre-hire applicant screening and background investigations. Honesty tests may also be used both before and after a person is hired. After hire, workplace monitoring can be used to review unusual behaviors. Developing an ethics code that outlines appropriate behaviors and encouraging managers and business owners to model desired behavior help highlight the organization's expectations. Ethics training that focuses on enhancing ethical decision making in the workplace can also prevent employee misconduct. Finally, internal checks and balances along with splitting up critical job functions across different positions and random audits of inventory can help reduce employee fraud.[50]

Honesty and Polygraph Tests Paper-and-pencil honesty tests are alternatives to polygraph testing, as mentioned in Chapter 7. These tests are widely used in pre-hire screening, particularly in the retail industry and others. Polygraph tests may be used as part of an internal investigation for employees who are *reasonably suspected of involvement in a workplace incident (theft, embezzlement, etc.) that resulted in specific economic loss or injury to the employer*. The Employee Polygraph Protection Act prohibits the use of polygraphs for most pre-employment screening and also requires that employees must

- be advised of their rights to refuse to take a polygraph exam;
- be allowed to stop the exam at any time; and
- not be terminated because they refuse to take a polygraph test or solely because of the exam results.

If private-sector employers administer polygraph tests to employees or applicants, they are required to use licensed, bonded examiners and to carefully guard the information obtained during the test.[51] Organizations should thoroughly evaluate the need for such tests and use them sparingly.

Substance Abuse, Drug Testing, and Employee Rights Employee substance abuse and drug testing have received a great deal of attention. Concern about substance abuse at work is appropriate, given that absenteeism, accident and damage rates, and theft and fraud are higher for workers using illegal substances or misusing legal substances such as prescription drugs and alcohol. The National Council on Alcohol and Drug Dependence (NCADD) estimates that 70% of people who illegally use drugs are employed.[52] Figure 15-6 identifies some of the negative effects of substance abuse in the workplace. Ways to address substance abuse problems were discussed in Chapter 14. Employee rights associated with substance abuse are discussed in the following sections.

Laws Addressing Drug Testing The ADA specifies that alcoholism is a disability but that dependency on illegal drugs is not. Individuals in treatment or in a recovery program for an addictive substance are protected by provisions in the ADA. However, employees who are not capable of working because they are under the influence, have poor attendance records, or are poor performers regardless of their drinking and/or drug problems are subject to disciplinary action.

The U.S. Supreme Court has ruled that certain drug-testing plans do not violate the Constitution. Private-sector programs are governed mainly by state laws, which can be a confusing hodgepodge. The Drug-Free Workplace Act of 1988 requires

FIGURE 15-6 Negative Impacts of Substance Abuse in the Workplace

Work Performance	Personal Behavior	Financial Costs
• Inconsistent work quality • Increased absenteeism • Carelessness; mistakes • Risky, unsafe acts	• Blaming coworkers for own errors • Complaints, excuses for time off • Deteriorating personal hygiene • Avoiding colleagues	• Inadequate production • Rework or replacement for poor quality production • Coverage for absences • Workers' compensation and health care

Source: Adapted from NCADD, https://ncadd.org/learn-about-drugs/workplace/242-drugs-and-the-workplace.

government contractors to take steps to eliminate employee drug use. Failure to do so can lead to disqualification for government contracts. Tobacco and alcohol do not qualify as controlled substances under the act, and off-the-job drug use is not included. The U.S. Department of Transportation (DOT) requires regular testing of truck and bus drivers, train crews, mass-transit employees, airline pilots and mechanics, pipeline workers, and licensed sailors. Firms that operate under DOT guidelines must use pre-employment, post-accident, and random drug exams to verify that individuals involved in transportation activities are fit for duty. Employees who fail an exam or refuse to participate are barred from working and must enroll in treatment. They must also pass a separate return-to-duty drug screen and be randomly tested six additional times over a 12-month period.

Drug Testing and Employee Rights Unless federal, state, or local law prohibits testing, employers have a right to require applicants and employees to submit to drug testing. Pre-employment drug tests are widely used. Employers generally use one of three policies when current employees are required to undergo drug testing: (1) random testing of everyone at periodic intervals, (2) testing only in cases of probable cause, or (3) testing after accidents. If testing is done for probable cause, it must be based on performance-related behaviors, such as excessive absenteeism or poor performance, not just the substance use itself. From a policy standpoint, it is most appropriate to test for drugs when the following conditions exist:

- Job-related consequences of the abuse are severe enough that they outweigh privacy concerns.
- Accurate test procedures are available.
- Written consent of the employee is obtained.
- Results are treated confidentially, as are any related medical records.
- Employer offers a complete drug rehabilitation program, including an employee assistance program.

The recent legalization of marijuana in some states adds additional complexity to this issue. However, employers are free to establish policies and work expectations to provide a safe and productive workplace. Employees reporting for duty who cannot perform their jobs properly are not immune from reprimand even in states where recreational marijuana use is legal.[53]

15-5 Human Resource Policies, Procedures, and Rules

Policies
General guidelines that help focus organizational actions

Procedures
Customary methods of handling activities

Rules
Specific guidelines that regulate and restrict individuals' behavior

HR policies, procedures, and rules greatly affect the employment relationship. Policies act as general guidelines that help focus organizational actions. Policies are general in nature, whereas procedures and rules are specific to various situations. The important role of all three requires that they be reviewed regularly.

Procedures provide customary methods of handling activities and are more specific than policies. For example, a policy may state that employees are awarded vacations according to years of service, and a procedure establishes the specific steps for authorizing vacation time.

Rules are specific guidelines that regulate and restrict individuals' behavior. They are similar to procedures in that they guide action and typically allow no discretion in their application. Rules reflect a management decision that action be taken—or not taken—in a given situation, and they provide more specific behavioral guidelines than do policies. An example of a rule might be that a vacation day may not be scheduled the day before or after a holiday.

Perhaps more than any other part of the organization, the HR function needs policies, procedures, and rules. People react strongly to differential treatment regarding time off, pay, vacation time, discipline, and other factors. New and smaller employers often start without many of these HR issues well defined. But as these companies grow, issues become more complex, with policy decisions being made on an as-needed basis. Before long, the inconsistency and resulting employee complaints bring on the need for clear policies, procedures, and rules that apply to everyone. Therefore, it is advisable to establish and enforce specific HR policies, procedures, and rules.

Coordination and shared responsibility between the HR unit and operating managers are necessary for HR policies, procedures, and rules to be effective. As Figure 15-7 shows, managers are the main users and enforcers of policies, procedures, and rules, and they should receive explanations about these topics and training in how to carry them out. The HR unit supports managers, reviews policies and disciplinary rules, and trains managers to use them. Often policies, procedures, and rules are provided in employee handbooks.

FIGURE 15-7   Shared Responsibility for Policies, Procedures, and Rules

HR Unit	Managers
• Designs formal mechanisms for coordinating HR policies • Assists in developing organization-wide HR policies, procedures, and rules • Provides information on application of HR policies, procedures, and rules • Trains managers to administer policies, procedures, and rules	• Help in developing HR policies and rules • Review policies and rules with all employees • Apply HR policies, procedures, and rules • Explain rules and policies to all employees • Give feedback on effectiveness of policies and rules

GLOBAL

Global Considerations Organizations that have employees in several countries face particular complexities regarding employment policies and practices. Some U.S. laws apply to all U.S. citizens regardless of where their workplace is located. When employing workers in the European Community (EC), regulations within the EC and each specific country (such as Austria or France) must be followed. An employment law audit is recommended to ensure full compliance with all requirements. Terminating employees is especially difficult in many countries (such as Italy). Some organizations adopt a comprehensive set of work rules that meet the standards of the most restrictive nation. However, this can be costly, as it imposes the highest standard as a universal. Other organizations comply with each individual nation's laws and requirements. This strategy can be costly to administer, as it entails managing a portfolio of legal mandates and policies. Typically, HR policy decisions should align with the organization's overall philosophy and global strategy.[54]

15-5a Employee Handbooks

> **LO5** Understand the use of policies, procedures, and employee handbooks to communicate workplace behavior and performance expectations.

> **Employee handbook**
> A physical or electronic manual that explains a company's essential policies, procedures, and employee benefits

An **employee handbook** is a physical or electronic manual that explains a company's essential policies, procedures, and employee benefits. It is an important tool for communicating information about workplace culture, benefits, attendance, pay practices, safety issues, discipline, and other critical information for employees, and it can help prevent employment lawsuits.[55] Handbooks are sometimes written in a formal legalistic fashion but are more effective when written so that employees can easily understand the contents. Using more common language can make the handbook more readable and usable. Even small organizations can use available computer software with sample policies to prepare handbooks relatively easily.

There are a number of best practices that a company should consider when developing an employee handbook. Managers should view handbooks as a mechanism that enables the firm to better communicate standards to workers. Given this viewpoint, handbooks should be customized to fit a company's current situation instead of being too generalized. Also, the more personalized, easy to understand, and well organized (with many headings and subheadings) a handbook is, the more likely it will be accepted and appreciated by employees. Figure 15-8 suggests a range of topics that might be included in a handbook. Each company will include those policies and subjects that are most important for their employees. Several recommendations on creating an employee handbook include:

- *Eliminate controversial phrases.* For example, the phrases *probationary* and *permanent employee* may be misinterpreted to imply that employees are no longer employed at will once they have passed a training period. This wording can lead to disagreement over what the parties meant by *permanent*. A more appropriate phrase is *regular employee*.
- *Use disclaimers.* Disclaimers should be prominently displayed, not hidden in small text where they are essentially overlooked and meaningless. For instance, many companies include a disclaimer to highlight the at-will status of employees. If a company wishes to convey information about important employment limitations, it is critical that employees are aware of the disclaimers.
- *Keep the handbook current.* The contents in employee handbooks must be revisited and revised when new issues are encountered or the conditions of the workplace change. Doing so helps prevent employee grievances and complaints. Consequently, employee handbooks and HR policies should be reviewed on an ongoing basis but at least once a year.[56]

FIGURE 15-8 Possible Topics for an Employee Handbook

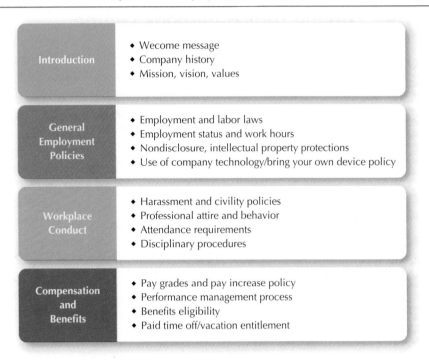

Introduction	• Wecome message • Company history • Mission, vision, values
General Employment Policies	• Employment and labor laws • Employment status and work hours • Nondisclosure, intellectual property protections • Use of company technology/bring your own device policy
Workplace Conduct	• Harassment and civility policies • Professional attire and behavior • Attendance requirements • Disciplinary procedures
Compensation and Benefits	• Pay grades and pay increase policy • Performance management process • Benefits eligibility • Paid time off/vacation entitlement

Sources: Based on Susan Heathfield, "Need to Know what Goes in an Employee Handbook";http://humanresources. about.com/od/handbookspolicies/a/sample_handbook.htm; Small Business Administration, "Employee Handbooks"; https://www.sba.gov/content/employee-handbooks.

To communicate and discuss HR information, a growing number of firms provide employee handbooks electronically using an intranet, which enables employees to access policies at any time. It also allows changes in policies to be made electronically rather than distributed as paper copies. Additionally, the handbook can be linked to related information that makes accessing details easier for employees. The following "HR Competencies & Applications: Taking Your Handbook Online" feature provides recommendations for moving from a paper to a digital handbook.

Legal Considerations and Best Practices The courts have used employee handbooks against employers in lawsuits by charging a broken "implied" contract. This should not eliminate the use of employee handbooks as a way of communicating policies to employees. In fact, not having an employee handbook with clear HR policies can leave an organization open to costly litigation as well. A sensible approach is to first develop sound HR policies and employee handbooks to communicate them and then have legal counsel review the language contained in the handbook.

15-5b Communicating Human Resource Information

HR communication focuses on the receipt and dissemination of HR data and information throughout the organization. *Downward communication* flows from top management to the rest of the organization, informing employees about what is and will be happening in the organization and what top management's expectations

COMPETENCIES & APPLICATIONS

Taking Your Handbook Online

Moving from a paper handbook to a digital one can help companies cut costs, make updates easier and quicker, and provide employees with a more interactive format. Before jumping in and simply copying all the content from paper to digital form, HR professionals and other managers should take some time to plan for a smooth transition. The following steps can help make the process go smoothly:

1. *Put the acknowledgment up front.* Set up the handbook so that employees must first read all disclaimers and complete an acknowledgment before gaining access to the handbook contents.

2. *Require employees to log in.* Required use of company passwords and sign-on credentials limits access to this internal document to those who have a legitimate right to read it. The handbook is not generally made available to those outside the company.

3. *Link handbook content to relevant information.* A powerful use of online handbooks is linking related documents and information for employees. For example, in the section that discusses payroll, link to tax withholding forms to make it easy for employees to find the correct documents.

4. *Include email and telephone contact information for HR staff.* Many employees prefer to contact HR to ask questions or get clarification of policies or benefits. Make HR easy to reach so that employees see the staff as supportive and available.

5. *Proofread everything before it goes "live."* Model good practice and verify spelling, grammar, and punctuation before releasing content. The handbook should represent the professional image of HR and the company. Test all the hyperlinks and keep them current if linked content is moved or changed.

6. *Notify employees of the change.* Announce the change to an online handbook in a way that ensures all employees will know about the new format. Consider a mandatory sign-on within the transition period and required acknowledgement. Check in with employees that don't respond so that you can answer any questions they may have.

7. *Immediately notify employees of changes.* Be sure to develop a process for maintaining the handbook and letting employees know when things change. While an online handbook can be easily updated, it is critical that employees are notified when important changes are made to policies and procedures.

8. *Keep a few printed copies available.* Some employees are not comfortable with technology and may prefer a hard copy of the handbook. Print a few and let employees know that they are available on an "as-requested" basis. Be sure that the printed copies always reflect the most up-to-date version of the handbook.[57]

Using technology to disseminate policies and other important employment information can be efficient and effective. Consider the following questions about online handbooks:

1. What are some of the interactive features that you would incorporate into an online employee handbook? How do you think these features would enhance employee use of the handbook?

2. How often would you determine if changes to an employee handbook were needed? How would you notify employees of changes to handbook contents?

KEY COMPETENCIES: Communication; HR Expertise: Organization/Employee Relations, Organization/Technology & Data and goals are. For instance, organizations communicate with employees through internal publications and media, including newsletters, company magazines, organizational social media websites, videos, Internet postings, and email announcements. Whatever the formal means used, managers should make an honest attempt to communicate information employees need to know.

Upward communication enables managers to learn about employees' ideas, concerns, and information needs. Companies use surveys and employee suggestion programs to encourage the upward communication of good ideas.[58] For instance, the creation of Amazon Prime was a suggestion from a software engineer. The Prime loyalty program provides members with free two-day shipping and has resulted in billions of dollars of additional sales for Amazon.[59] Companies also use frequent, short questionnaires called pulse surveys to solicit anonymous employee feedback. Often delivered as a mobile app, quick surveys are pushed out to employees who can safely inform company leaders about problems or concerns in the workplace. Canadian casual dining restaurant chain Earls discovered through a pulse survey that kitchen prep teams felt socially isolated from the rest of the workers due to their early starting time. With this information, Earls managers could then be more attentive to this group of workers and try to improve their commitment and engagement.[60]

Maintaining a healthy exchange in both top-down and bottom-up communication keeps all organization members informed and engaged with current initiatives and issues in the firm. Employees feel more connected to the organization and are more willing to offer their ideas when management supports and welcomes their input.[61]

Pulse surveys
Frequent, short questionnaires used to solicit anonymous employee feedback

LO6 Outline approaches to employee discipline and termination of employment.

Discipline
A process of corrective action used to enforce organizational rules

15-6 Employee Discipline

The previous sections about employee rights and organizational rules provide the backdrop for a discussion of employee discipline because employee rights often are a key issue in disciplinary cases. Discipline is a process of corrective action used to enforce organizational rules. Problem employees are most often affected by the discipline system. Common disciplinary issues caused by problem employees include absenteeism, tardiness, productivity and quality deficiencies, safety violations, and insubordination. Fortunately, problem employees represent a small percentage of the workforce in most companies. However, if managers fail to deal with problem employees promptly, work outcomes are often negatively affected, and work unit relationships can become strained. Identifying violations and other behavior problems and taking steps to correct them is a responsibility primarily borne by line managers, but HR staff assists in dealing with disciplinary action.

15-6a Effective Discipline

Because of legal concerns as well as justice perceptions, managers must understand discipline and know how to administer it properly. Effective discipline should be aimed at the problem behaviors, not at the employees personally, because the goal is to improve performance. If a manager tolerates or ignores unacceptable behavior, other employees will see this as tacit approval and may also misbehave. However, if selected employees are not reprimanded for violations, those who are punished may resent the unfairness of that action. These managerial decisions influence employees' sense of organizational justice and can lead to lowered commitment and engagement.[62]

Role of Human Resources HR professionals assist line managers in dealing with disciplinary matters. While enforcing rules and handling discipline is primarily the responsibility of line managers, HR managers oversee disciplinary procedures to ensure that remedial actions follow corporate and legal guidelines, are done appropriately, and are fair and consistent. A recent study conducted in the United Kingdom found that line managers were expected to handle discipline cases. HR was expected to function in a more objective, advisory role, performing activities such as assisting inexperienced line managers during hearings and guiding the actions of managers. However, evidence suggested that many managers were not capable of handling some disciplinary situations, which meant that HR had to step in and manage cases in a more formal manner.[63] These findings show that HR professionals must be adequately prepared to function as trainers and mediators in cases where discipline must be administered to employees.

Training of Supervisors Training supervisors and managers on when and how discipline should be used is crucial. Employees see disciplinary action as more fair when given by trained supervisors who base their actions on procedural justice than when discipline is carried out by untrained supervisors. Training in counseling and communication skills provides supervisors and managers with the tools necessary to deal with employee performance problems, regardless of the disciplinary approaches used.

15-6b Approaches to Discipline

The disciplinary system can be viewed as an application of behavior modification to a problem or unproductive employee. The best discipline is clearly self-discipline, and most people can be counted on to do their jobs effectively when they understand what is required at work. But for some people, the prospect of external discipline helps their self-discipline. The two most common approaches to discipline are *positive discipline* and *progressive discipline*.[64]

Positive Discipline Approach The positive discipline approach builds on the philosophy that violations are actions that usually can be corrected constructively without penalty. When using this approach, managers focus on fact finding and guidance to encourage desirable behaviors, rather than penalties to discourage undesirable behaviors. The four steps to positive discipline are as follows:

1. *Counseling*: The goal of this phase is to heighten employee awareness of organizational policies and rules. Often, people simply need to be made aware of rules, and knowledge of possible disciplinary actions may prevent violations.
2. *Written documentation*: If an employee fails to correct behavior, then a second conference becomes necessary. Whereas the first stage occurs as a conversation between supervisor and employee, this stage is documented in written form, and written solutions are identified with the aim of preventing further problems from occurring.

3. *Final warning*: If the employee does not follow the written solutions noted in the second step, a final warning conference is held. In that conference, the supervisor again emphasizes to the employee the importance of correcting the inappropriate actions. Some firms require the employee to take a day off with pay to develop a specific written action plan to remedy the problem behaviors. The decision day off emphasizes the seriousness of the problem and the manager's determination to see that the behavior is changed.
4. *Discharge*: If the employee fails to follow the action plan that was developed and problems continue, then the supervisor can discharge the employee.

The advantage of this positive approach to discipline is that it focuses on solving problems. The greatest difficulty with the positive approach to discipline is the extensive amount of training required for supervisors and managers to become effective counselors and the need for more supervisory time with this approach than with the progressive discipline approach. Utilizing a positive discipline approach must be an appropriate fit for an organization's culture and employment philosophy.

Progressive Discipline Approach Progressive discipline incorporates steps that become progressively more severe and are designed to change the employee's inappropriate behavior. Figure 15-9 shows a typical progressive discipline process; most progressive discipline procedures use verbal and written reprimands and suspension before resorting to dismissal. For example, at a manufacturing firm, an employee's failure to call in when absent from work might lead to a suspension without pay after the third offense in a year. Suspension sends employees a strong message that undesirable job behaviors must change, or termination is likely to follow.

Although it appears to be similar to positive discipline, progressive discipline is more administrative and process-oriented. Following the progressive sequence ensures that both the nature and the seriousness of the problem are clearly communicated to the employee. Not all steps in progressive discipline are followed in every case. Certain serious offenses are exempted from the progressive procedure

FIGURE 15-9 Progressive Discipline Process

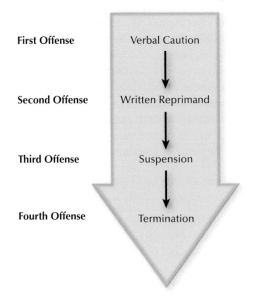

and may result in immediate termination. Some offenses that can lead to immediate termination include intoxication at work, alcohol or drug use at work, severe types of harassment, fighting, and theft. However, if a firm has a written progressive disciplinary policy, it should be followed when immediate termination is not appropriate; otherwise, an employee's dismissal could be considered outside the normal disciplinary procedures.

15-6c Challenges in Employee Discipline

At-Will Employment A disciplinary process can demonstrate to employees the organization's commitment to due process and just cause in employment actions. However, there is a potential for a formally stated discipline process to undercut an organization's at-will provisions. Conferring with legal counsel in the development of both an at-will provision and a discipline procedure can help an organization reconcile these two issues.[65]

Fairness and Consistency Fairness in disciplining employees is not a simple matter. Does fairness require that all employees who commit the same infraction receive the same punishment? Does it mean that companies are forever tied to past practices? An emphasis on equity is key. Consider two employees who both violate an attendance requirement to call in before the start time in case of absence. One employee has violated this rule numerous times, while it is the first offense for the other employee. Clearly, the repeat offender would receive a harsher punishment than the first-time offender.[66] Likewise, if work conditions have changed over the years, a company is not prevented from updating work rules and levels of reprimand simply because in the past different decisions were made. It is, however, very important to ensure that disciplinary action is taken without regard to employees' protected status characteristics such as age, gender, race, or religion.[67]

Documentation Problems While managers are typically advised to "document, document, document," there can be a downside if documentation is sloppy, inconsistent, or incomplete. Documenting employee conduct issues is critical to ensure that the process is done correctly. Documentation should include (1) company performance and behavior expectations, (2) the employee's specific failure to comply, (3) prior warnings or counseling with the employee, (4) expectations for future conduct, and (5) consequences for failure to correct the deficiencies. Managers sometimes get distracted when documenting issues and focus on the employee's intentions rather than results, include too much detail, fail to lay out specific consequences, or fail to provide any specific examples of the employee's behavior. Training for managers with regard to the discipline process should include detailed, hands-on practice in recording and documenting employee performance problems in addition to how to hold a disciplinary meeting.[68]

Reluctance to Discipline Managers may be reluctant to use discipline for many reasons. Some of the main reasons include the following:

- *Organizational culture of avoiding discipline*: If the organizational "norm" is to avoid penalizing problem employees, then managers are less likely to use discipline or to dismiss problem employees.
- *Lack of support*: Some managers do not want to use discipline because they fear that their decisions will not be supported by higher management. All levels

of management should be in agreement with respect to disciplinary actions. Reversing frontline supervisors' decisions can seriously undermine their authority and harm their effectiveness.

- *Guilt*: Managers realize that before they became managers, they may have committed the same violations as their employees, and therefore they do not discipline others for similar actions because of their previous conduct.
- *Fear of loss of friendship*: Managers may fear losing friendships or damaging personal relationships if they discipline employees.
- *Avoidance of time loss*: Discipline often requires considerable time and effort. Sometimes it is easier for managers to avoid taking the time required for proper discipline, especially if their actions may be overturned on review by higher management.
- *Fear of lawsuits*: Managers are sometimes concerned about being sued for disciplining an employee, particularly if the discipline leads to termination.

Support from HR can help reluctant managers promptly deal with employee performance and behavioral problems. As a part of their own performance expectations, managers should be held accountable for enforcing all organizational policies.

15-6d Termination: The Final Disciplinary Step

Termination
Occurs when an employee is removed from a job at an organization

The final stage in the disciplinary process may be called *discharge, firing, dismissal,* or *termination,* among other terms. Regardless of the word used, termination occurs when an employee is removed from a job at an organization. Both positive and progressive approaches to discipline clearly provide employees with warnings about the seriousness of their performance problems before dismissal occurs.

Terminating an individual's employment is a serious matter and one that should be taken only after conferring with HR and confirming that the decision is free of bias. Terminations should not take place in the heat of the moment. Even in cases that involve very serious infractions, such as an employee found drinking alcohol on the job, the employee should be suspended without pay pending an investigation. The time taken to thoroughly review the situation may save the company time and litigation costs in the end.[69]

Termination Issues Terminations occur for a wide range of reasons. For instance, excessive violations of attendance policies commonly lead to employee terminations. Other causes involve breaking company rules, behavioral issues such as sexual harassment and other unethical acts, and poor execution of work-related duties. Misconduct due to substance abuse and addiction can also lead to termination, particularly in jobs that require driving.

Terminating an employee should be done face-to-face. Using email or voicemail to terminate an employee is too impersonal but may be necessary when dealing with remote workers.[70] Another concern is when managers must terminate potentially violent employees. Managers must be careful not to move forward with these terminations too hastily, and they should get assistance from individuals in security, HR, and legal counsel when handling such cases. Utilizing an employee assistance program (EAP) professional can also help defuse a potentially violent situation.[71]

As previously mentioned, HR professionals and managers may face *wrongful termination* claims and lawsuits when they terminate employees. These legal challenges can be based on federal, state, and local laws. At face value, terminating workers because they do not keep their promises would seem equitable and defensible in many courts. However, to win wrongful termination lawsuits, employers need to follow appropriate HR processes and disciplinary procedures, as well as consistently document reasons for termination.

One difficult phase of employee termination is the removal of dismissed employees and their personal possessions from company facilities. The standard advice from legal experts is to physically remove the employee as quickly as possible. Ex-employees are often escorted out of the building by security guards. Some firms allow terminated employees to return to their desks, offices, or lockers to retrieve personal items under the observation of security personnel and the department supervisor/manager, but this means the ex-employee may be seen by and talk to coworkers while still upset or angry. It is unwise to give terminated employees access to computer systems or company databases after they are terminated, so HR should work closely with IT to immediately block ex-employees' sign-on credentials.

In all cases involving employee termination, treating the employee with dignity and respect is an ethical approach that may lead to fewer lawsuits and better perceptions of the company by employees. Harsh, inhumane treatment of employees being terminated can have a chilling effect throughout an organization and serves no legitimate business purpose.

Separation Agreements In some termination situations, formal contracts may be used. One type is a separation agreement, an agreement in which a terminated employee agrees not to sue the employer in exchange for specified benefits, such as additional severance pay or other consideration.

For such agreements to be legally enforceable, the consideration is usually additional benefits not part of a normal termination package. For example, a firm may provide more generous severance pay or extended outplacement as consideration. For international employees, different legal requirements may exist in various countries, including certain requirements for severance pay and benefits. When using separation agreements, care must be taken to avoid the appearance of constructive discharge of employees. These agreements should be reviewed by legal counsel and comply with all regulations, including the WARN Act and the Older Workers' Benefit Protection Act.

Separation agreement
Agreement in which a terminated employee agrees not to sue the employer in exchange for specified benefits

SUMMARY

- The employment relationship is a reciprocal one in which both employers and employees have statutory and contractual rights, as well as responsibilities.
- Contractual rights can be spelled out in an employment contract or be implied as a result of employer actions or promises.
- Employment at will gives employers the right to hire and terminate employees with or without notice or cause and gives employees the right to quit with or without notice.

- Court decisions have led to exceptions in employment-at-will relationships for violations of public policy, an implied contract, and good faith and fair dealing.
- Wrongful discharge occurs when an employer improperly or illegally terminates an individual's employment.
- Constructive discharge is the process of making conditions intolerable to get an employee to "voluntarily" quit a job.
- Just cause and due process are steps taken to protect employees from unfair employment-related actions.

- Organizational justice is based on assessment of three elements: procedural, distributive, and interactional justice.
- Alternative dispute resolution (ADR) approaches such as arbitration, peer review panels, ombuds, and mediation can be used to address employee complaints or disputes.
- Balancing employer and employee rights becomes an issue when dealing with privacy rights, access to employee records, free speech, and whistle-blowing situations.
- Employers are increasingly being called upon to safeguard employees' personal information, especially as the uses of technology and electronic records grows.
- The rights of employees for personal behavior must be balanced by employers' rights, particularly in regard to individuals' display of behaviors, unique dress or appearance, bringing weapons to work, and questionable off-duty actions.
- Companies have great latitude to monitor employee actions via technology and on the job site.
- Employer investigations, including drug testing, protect both employer and employee rights.
- HR policies, procedures, rules, and handbooks should be carefully developed and communicated to employees. Courts sometimes view employee handbooks as implied contracts.
- Disciplinary processes are used to enforce organizational rules and ensure a safe, productive workplace.
- The final disciplinary phase is termination of an individual's employment, which might include a separation agreement and severance benefits.

CRITICAL THINKING CHALLENGES

1. Identify how overreliance on the employment-at-will doctrine can create problems for supervisors and employees. What are the ramifications if companies default to EAW rather than dealing directly with employee conduct problems?

2. Discuss the impact on an individual employee and work unit if organizational justice is not honored by managers. Recall any past work experience you may have in which a supervisor "played favorites." How did that impact your job performance and commitment to the company? How did you react to the injustice?

3. Give some examples of how technology is creating employer–employee rights and policy issues. Then suggest some possible actions that may be needed.

4. Assume that as the HR manager, you have decided to prepare some guidelines for supervisors to use when they have to discipline employees. Gather the information needed, using Internet resources such as www.blr.com and www.workforce.com for sample policies and other details. Then prepare a guide for supervisors on implementing both positive and progressive discipline.

5. Management is developing a company workplace monitoring program to track compliance with safety procedures at an offshore oil rig platform in the Gulf of Mexico. The monitoring program is expected to help improve workplace safety compliance and reduce injuries to workers as well as possible environmental problems. To assist HR in developing the monitoring program, visit the SHRM website and conduct your own research to identify best practices regarding monitoring of workplace activity.

   A. What key components should be included in your company's employee monitoring program to best meet the needs of both employees and the company?

   B. Explain how you will introduce this program to workers. Provide your rationale for instituting monitoring equipment and reporting procedures. Convince workers that this program is for their benefit as well as for the benefit of the company.

CASE How Special Is That Sandwich?

Companies have every right to protect their intellectual property and trade secrets. In fact, they have a responsibility to shareholders to do so because this proprietary information is often the source of competitive advantage. Careful safeguarding of secrets is an important part of ensuring the sustainability of the firm.

But what exactly qualifies as a trade secret? For instance, one fast food company advertises its "secret sauce," and a producer of baked beans' "secret family recipe" has been widely featured in its television commercials. Would anyone argue that the search algorithm developed and used by Google is a trade secret? Probably not. Trade secrets are pretty broadly defined and can include things like customer lists, recipes, formulas, and software. So, is a sandwich recipe a trade secret? Jimmy John's management certainly thinks so. The recipe consisting of a quarter pound of roast beef with provolone cheese on a pita is a trade secret in the company's eyes.

The New Jersey–based sandwich company requires all of its workers—including entry-level workers who are earning starting wages—to sign a stringent "noncompetition" clause as part of the hiring process. When employees sign the agreement, they agree not to work "at any business which derives more than 10% of its revenue from selling submarine, hero-type, deli-style, pita and/or wrapped or rolled sandwiches." That would seem to cover an awful lot of establishments, from direct competitors in the food industry to the gas stations, convenience stores, and the neighborhood hospital cafeteria.

Former employees are prohibited from working in such a place for two years after they leave Jimmy John's employment. The geographic limit is set at three miles of either the Jimmy John's location where the individual previously worked or any other Jimmy John's shop (there are 2,000 U.S. store locations). That's a fairly broad swath of geography. Because Jimmy John's operates in 43 states, it is difficult to state without exception that the noncompete clause would not be upheld in a court proceeding. However, most legal experts believe that it is overly broad and the company would be unlikely to prevail in a lawsuit. It hasn't been tested in court yet.

Why would a company implement and require such a tough restriction on low-wage workers? That is anybody's guess, and the company's management wouldn't respond to reporters who uncovered the story. So, we can only speculate on why such a policy exists. Lawmakers have become interested in the case because it appears to almost border on intimidation and bullying of workers. Companies are certainly free to set policies and practices to protect legitimate business concerns. But it seems to be a stretch to consider meat, cheese, and bread as anything special that needs the special protection of a noncompete agreement.[72]

QUESTIONS

1. Based on your understanding of this case, what possible reasons could Jimmy John's management have for adopting this policy? If you were the HR manager at Jimmy John's, what pros and cons would you point out to management in terms of the effect of having this policy?

2. If you were an entry-level worker at Jimmy John's, how would the requirement to sign a noncompete agreement influence your opinion of the company? What likely steps might you take when you leave employment there?

SUPPLEMENTAL CASES

Dealing with Workplace Bullying

This case explores the problems that occur when "bullying" bosses or employees are present in the workplace. (For the case, go to www.cengage.com/management/mathis.)

Employer Liable for "Appearance Actions"

This case discusses a California court ruling on terminating a female for her personal appearance. (For the case, go to www.cengage.com/management/mathis.)

George Faces Challenges

This case describes the problem facing a new department supervisor when HR policies and discipline have been handled poorly in the past. (For the case, go to www.cengage.com/management/mathis.)

END NOTES

1. Based on Rachel Emma Silverman, "Tracking Sensors Invade the Workplace," *Wall Street Journal*, March 7, 2013, p. B1–2.
2. Based on Richard Snow, "Henry Ford's Experiment to Build a Better Worker," *Wall Street Journal*, May 10, 2013.
3. Mark J. Garmaise, "Ties That Truly Bind: Noncompetition Agreements, Executive Compensation, and Firm Investment," *Journal of Law, Economics, and Organization* 27, no. 2 (2011), 376–425.
4. Ruth Simon and Angus Loten, "When a New Job Leads to a Lawsuit: Litigation over Noncompete Clauses Is Rising. Does Entrepreneurship Suffer?" *Wall Street Journal*, August 15, 2013, p. B1.
5. Scott Oswald, "The Evolving Status of Non-Compete Agreements," *Compensation & Benefits Review* 44, no. 6 (November 2012), 336–339l; HR Specialist, "U.S. Supreme Court Addresses Arbitration of Noncompete Agreements," *HR Specialist: Texas Employment Law* 8, no. 2 (February 2013), 6.
6. Roger M. Milgram and Eric E. Benson, "Use of Agreements to Protect Trade Secrets in the Employment Relationship," *Milgram on Trade Secrets, Lexis Nexis*, 2015.
7. Susan Heathfield, "Employment at Will Sample Policy," http://humanresources.about.com/od/policysamples/p/at_will_policy.htm.
8. *Fortune v. National Cash Register Co.*, 373 Mass. 96, 36 N.E.2d 1251 (1977).
9. Myrtle Bell, Daphne Berry, Dennis Marquardt, and Tiffany Green, "Introducing Discriminatory Job Loss: Antecedents, Consequences, and Complexities," *Journal of Managerial Psychology* 28, no. 6 (2013), 584–605.
10. Marc Ohana, "A Multilevel Study of the Relationship between Organizational Justice and Affective Commitment: The Moderating Role of Organizational Size and Tenure," *Personnel Review* 43, no. 5 (2014), 654–671; Jolyn Gelens, Nicky Dries, Joeri Hofmans, and Roland Pepermans, "The Role of Perceived Organizational Justice in Shaping the Outcomes of Talent Management: A Research Agenda," *Human Resource Management Review* 23, no. 4 (December 2013), 341–353.
11. Gary Blau, Tony Petrucci, and John McClendon, "Effects of Layoff Victims' Justice Reactions and Emotional Responses on Attitudes toward Their Previous Employer," *Career Development International* 17, no. 6 (2012), 500–517.
12. Natalia Cuguero-Escofet and Marion Fortin, "One Justice or Two? A Model of Reconciliation of Normative Justice Theories and Empirical Research on Organizational Justice," *Journal of Business Ethics* 124, no. 3 (October 2014), 435–451.
13. Maureen Ambrose, Marshall Schminke, and David Mayer, "Trickle-Down Effects of Supervisor Perceptions of Interactional Justice: A Moderated Mediation Approach," *Journal of Applied Psychology* 98, no. 4 (2013), 678–689.
14. D. Ramona Bobocel, "Coping with Unfair Events Constructively or Destructively: The Effects of Overall Justice and Self–Other Orientation," *Journal of Applied Psychology* 98, no. 5 (2013), 720–731.
15. Alexander Colvin, "American Workplace Dispute Resolution in the Individual Rights Era," *International Journal of Human Resource Management* 23, no. 4 (February 2012), 459–475; William Roche and Paul Teague, "The Growing Importance of Workplace ADR," *International Journal of Human Resource Management* 23, no. 4 (February 2012), 447–458.
16. Michael Delikat, "Arbitrating Workplace Disputes," *Human Resource Executive Online*, June 16, 2010, www.hreonline.com.
17. Tyler Harrison, Paula Hopeck, Nathalie Desrayaud, and Kristen Imboden, "The Relationship between Conflict, Anticipatory Procedural Justice, and Design with Intentions to Use Ombudsman Processes," *International Journal of Conflict Management* 24, no. 1 (2013), 56–72.

18. Based on TheHRSpecialist.com, "Follow 6 Steps to Set Up Alternative Dispute Resolution Process," *Pennsylvania Employment Law* 9, no. 7 (July 2014), 4.

19. Jeffrey Grubman, "Employment Mediation Requires a Unique Touch," *JAMS ADR Blog at Mediate.com*, http://www.mediate.com/articles/GrubmanJbl20140905.cfm; Michael Rooni, "An Action Plan for Mediation," *Mediate.com*, http://www.mediate.com/articles/RooniM2.cfm.

20. For details on the retention of employee records and documents, go to www.hrcompliance.ceridian.com.

21. Al Saikali, "Failure to Match: The Next Wave of Data Privacy Litigation?" *SHRM Online*, November 27, 2013, http://www.shrm.org/hrdisciplines/safetysecurity/articles/pages/data-privacy-litigation.aspx.

22. Max Mihelich, "Free Speech Can Be Costly in the Workplace," *Workforce*, June 2014, pp. 18–19.

23. *Dixon v. Coburg Dairy Inc.*, No. 02-1266 (4th Cir., May 30, 2003).

24. Jess Bravin, "Supreme Court Weights Whistleblower Protections," *Wall Street Journal*, November 4, 2014.

25. Barton Gellman, "Edward Snowden, after Months of NSA Revelations, Says His Mission's Accomplished," *Washington Post*, December 23, 2013, http://www.washingtonpost.com/world/national-security/edward-snowden-after-months-of-nsa-revelations-says-his-missions-accomplished/2013/12/23/49fc36de-6c1c-11e3-a523-fe73f0ff6b8d_story.html.

26. Drew Harker and Matthew D. Keiser, "Whistleblower Incentives and Protections in the Financial Reform Act," *Advisory*, Arnold & Porter LLP, July 2010, pp. 1–3; Dori Meinert, "Whistle-Blowers: Threat or Asset?" *HR Magazine*, April 2011, pp. 27–32.

27. Joanne Deschenaux, "Justices Weigh Scope of SOX Whistleblower Protections," *SHRM Online*, November 13, 2013, http://www.shrm.org/legalissues/federalresources/pages/scope-sox-whistle-blower-protections.aspx.

28. Drew Harker and Matthew D. Keiser, "Whistleblower Incentives and Protections in the Financial Reform Act," *Advisory*, Arnold & Porter LLP, July 2010, pp. 1–3.

29. Dori Meinert, "Whistle-Blowers: Threat or Asset?" *HR Magazine*, April 2011, pp. 27–32.

30. Bernadine Van Gramberg, Julian Teicher, and Anne O'Rourke, "Managing Electronic Communications: A New Challenge for Human Resource Managers," *International Journal of Human Resource Management* 25, no. 16 (2014), 2234–2252.

31. Sam Hananel, "Facebook: Protected Speech," *Denver Post*, February 8, 2011, p. 7B.

32. Nina Massen, "Recorded Risk: Smartphones Make Capturing Conversations at Work a Cinch, and a Legal Headache," *HR Magazine*, November, 2014, pp. 66–68.

33. Jeffrey Mello, "Social Media, Employee Privacy and Concerted Activity: Brave New World or Big Brother?" *Labor Law Journal* 63, no. 3 (Fall 2012), 165–173; Vernon Francis, Thomas Johnson, and Kate Ericsson, "Social Media and Employee Monitoring: New Lessons for Employers," *Employee Relations Law Journal* 39, no. 2 (Autumn 2013), 59–70.

34. Aisling O'Donnell, Michelle Ryan, and Jolanda Jetten, "The Hidden Costs of Surveillance for Performance and Helping Behaviour," *Group Processes & Intergroup Relations* 16, no. 2 (March 2013), 246–256.

35. Jonathan Feldman, "Monitoring vs. Spying: Are Employers Going Too Far?" *Information Week*, March 18, 2013, http://www.informationweek.com/it-leadership/monitoring-vs-spying-are-employers-going-too-far/d/d-id/1109115?.

36. European Commission, "Data Protection at Work," http://ec.europa.eu/social/main.jsp?catId=708.

37. Jon Hyman, "Bring Your Own Policies," *Workforce*, December 2013, p. 25; Kathleen Koster, "BYOD Policies Broaden Engagement Possibilities," *Employee Benefit News*, August 2013, pp. 10–12.

38. Kathleen Koster, "Tattle-Tale Technology," *Employee Benefit News*, April 15, 2012, pp. 8–9.

39. Maria Greco Danaher, "Fitness-for-Duty Exam Can Be Based on Concern about Volatile Behavior," *HR Magazine*, November 2010, p. 72.

40. SHRM HR Knowledge Center, "Employee Conduct: Can We Consider Off-the-Job Conduct when We Make Employment Decisions Such as Hiring or Firing?" *SHRM Online*, December 3, 2012, http://www.shrm.org/templatestools/hrqa/pages/off-the-jobconduct.aspx.

41. Based on Jonathan Segal, "Employers in the Crossfire: Do You Have the Right to Ban Guns in Your Workplace?" *HR Magazine*, June 2013, pp. 105–107; William Martin, Helen Lavan, Yvette Lopez, Charles Naquin, and Marsha Katz, "An Ethical Analysis of the Second Amendment: The Right to Pack Heat at Work," *Business and Society Review* 119, no. 1 (March 2014), 1–36.

42. Nancy Flynn and Lewis Maltby, "Should Companies Monitor Their Employees' Social Media?" *Wall Street Journal*, May 12, 2014, p. R1.

43. Graham Sewell, James Barker, and Daniel Nyberg, "Working under Intense Surveillance: When Does 'Measuring Everything That Moves' Become Intolerable?" *Human Relations* 65, no. 2 (February 2012), 189–215.

44. Karin Mika, "The Benefit of Adopting Comprehensive Standards of Monitoring Employee Technology Use in the Workplace," *Cornell HR Review*, September 2014, pp. 1–7.

45. Based on Spencer Ante and Lauren Weber, "Memo to Workers: The Boss is Watching," *Wall Street Journal*, October 23, 2013, p. B1.

46. Devasheesh Bhave, "The Invisible Eye? Electronic Performance Monitoring and Employee Job Performance," *Personnel Psychology* 67 (2014), 605–635.

47. Dori Meinert, "Be a Super Sleuth," *HR Magazine*, December 2014, pp. 28–33; Jared Shelly, "To Find the Truth," *Human Resource Executive Online*, September 2, 2011, www.hreonline.com; David I. Weissman, "Proper Workplace Investigations," *HR Magazine*, May 2011, pp. 71–76.

48. Curtis Verschoor, "Fraud Continues to Cause Significant Losses," *Strategic Finance* 96, no. 8 (August 2014), 11–85.

49. Augustine Enofe, Pesi Amaria, and Man Hope, "Keeping Employees Honest: A Matter of Corporate Culture, Changes in Employee

Lifestyle, or Greed," *International Journal of Business, Accounting, & Finance* 6, no. 1 (Winter 2012), 92–123.

50. Kevin Kobelsky, "A Conceptual Model for Segregation of Duties: Integrating Theory and Practice for Manual and IT-Supported Processes," *International Journal of Accounting Information Systems* 15, no. 4 (December 2014), 304–322.

51. eLaws, "Other Workplace Standards: Lie Detector Tests," http://www.dol .gov/compliance/guide/eppa.htm.

52. National Council on Alcoholism and Drug Dependence, "Drugs and the Workplace," https://ncadd.org/learn -about-drugs/workplace/242-drugs -and-the-workplace.

53. Joanne Deschenaux, "Do Marijuana Laws Leave Drug Policies up in Smoke?" *HR Magazine*, May 2014, p. 15.

54. Stephen Hirschfeld, "Global Employee Handbooks Must Balance Compliance with Culture," *SHRM Online*, November 18, 2013, http: //www.shrm.org/hrdisciplines/global /articles/pages/global-employee -handbooks-compliance.aspx.

55. Kevin Smith and Lisa Harris, "Drafting an Effective Employee Handbook," *Employment Relations Today* 41, no. 1 (Spring 2014), 71–79; SHRM Online, "How to Develop an Employee Handbook," May 3, 2013, http://www.shrm.org /templatetools/howtoguides/pages /developemployeehandbook.aspx.

56. Susan Milligan, "The Employee Handbook: A Perennial Headache," *SHRM Online*, April 1, 2014, http: //www.shrm.org/hrdisciplines /employeerelations/articles/pages /employee-handbook-writing.aspx; Steve Taylor, "Employee Handbook Updates for 2013," *HR Magazine* 58, no. 2 (February 2013), 14.

57. Based on HR Specialist, "Take Your Employee Handbook Online: 8 Tips," *HR Specialist* 10, no. 9 (September 2012), 1–2; SHRM Online, "Employee Handbooks: What Issues Do We Need to Take into Consideration before Making a Transition to Electronic Handbooks?" November 30, 2012, http://www.shrm.org/templatetools /hrqa/pages/cms_015386.aspx.

58. Rachel Emma Silverman, "Are You Happy in Your Job? Bosses Push Weekly Surveys," *Wall Street Journal*, December 3, 2014, p. B1; Tamara Lytle, "Give Employees a Say," *HR Magazine*, October 2011, pp. 68–72; Michael O'Brien, "Beyond Engagement," *Human Resource Executive*, March 2012, pp. 40–42.

59. Leila Durmaz, "These 6 Ideas from Employee Suggestion Programs Boosted Company Performance," *IM Blog*, April 12, 2013, http://imblog .ideaglow.com/6-ideas-employee -suggestion-programs-boost-company/.

60. Christopher Mims, "Apps Tell Boss What Workers Really Think," *Wall Street Journal*, June 22, 2015, B1.

61. Karen Mishra, Lois Boynton, and Aneil Mishra, "Driving Employee Engagement: The Expanded Role of Internal Communications," *Journal of Business Communication* 51, no. 2 (April 2014), 183–202; Emma Karanges, Amanda Beatson, Kim Johnston, and Ian Lings, "Optimizing Employee Engagement with Internal Communication: A Social Exchange Perspective," *Journal of Business Market Management* 7, no. 2 (2014), 329–353.

62. Michel Tremblay, Christian Vandenberge, and Olivier Doucet, "Relationships between Leader-Contingent and Non-Contingent Reward and Punishment Behaviors and Subordinates' Perceptions of Justice and Satisfaction, and Evaluation of the Moderating Influence of Trust Propensity, Pay Level, and Role Ambiguity," *Journal of Business & Psychology* 28, no. 2 (June 2013), 233–249.

63. Carol Jones and Richard Saundry, "The Practice of Discipline: Evaluating the Roles and Relationship between Managers and HR Professionals," *Human Resource Management Journal* 22, no. 3 (2012), 252–266.

64. Margaret Bryant, "Managing Corrective Action," *SHRM Online*, February 13, 2014, http://www.shrm .org/templatetools/toolkits/pages /correctiveaction.aspx.

65. Paul Falcone, "Employment-at-Will vs. Progressive Discipline: Understanding the Legal Dichotomy," April 26, 2014, http://www.paulfalconehr .com/employment-at-will-vs

-progressive-discipline-understanding -the-legal-dichotomy/.

66. HR Specialist, "Two Employees Involved in Same Incident? Punishment Can Differ if It's Not Discriminatory," *HR Specialist: Ohio Employment Law* 69, no. 2 (February 2012), 3.

67. HR Specialist, "Track Discipline for Equitable Punishment," *HR Specialist: Texas Employment Law* 7, no. 7 (July 2012), 1–2.

68. Jonathan Segal, "Documentation Dangers: Don't Exaggerate or Soft-Pedal when Documenting Employee Problems," *HR Magazine*, October 2014, pp. 64–66.

69. Dana Wilkie, "Right and Wrong Ways to Terminate," *SHRM Online*, September 12, 2013, http://www.shrm .org/hrdisciplines/employeerelations /articles/pages/right-wrong-ways-to -terminate.aspx.

70. SHRM Online, "Termination: How Should We Terminate a Remote Employee?" December 27, 2012, http://www.shrm.org/templatestools /hrqa/pages/terminatingremoteworkers .aspx.

71. ESI Employee Assistance Group, "Planning Terminations That Involve Potentially Violent Employees," *HRWeb Café*, http://www .hrwebcafe.com/2013/02/planning_ terminations_that_inv.html.

72. Based on Clare O'Connor, "Does Jimmy John's Non-Compete Clause for Sandwich Makers Have Legal Legs?" *Forbes.com*, 2014, http://www.forbes .com/sites/clareoconnor/2014/10/15 /does-jimmy-johns-non-compete -clause-for-sandwich-makers-have -legal-legs/; Ben Rooney, "Jimmy John's under Fire for Worker Contracts," *CNN.com*, October 22, 2014, http://money.cnn.com/2014/10/22/news /jimmy-johns-non-compete/; Suzanne Lucas, "Jimmy John's Serves up Lessons on Terrible Management," *Inc .com*, October 15, 2014, http://www .inc.com/suzanne-lucas/jimmy-john-s -abominable-non-compete-clause.html; Neil Irwin, "When the Guy Making Your Sandwich Has a Noncompete Clause," *New York Times.com*, October 14, 2014, http://www.nytimes .com/2014/10/15/upshot/when-the -guy-making-your-sandwich-has-a -noncomplete-clause.html?_r=0.

CHAPTER

16

Union–Management Relations

Learning Objectives

After you have read this chapter, you should be able to:

LO1 Discuss what a union is and explain why employees join and employers resist unions.

LO2 Outline the current state of union activity in the United States and identify several reasons for the decline in union membership.

LO3 Explain the provisions of each of the major U.S. labor laws and recognize the impact of these laws and National Labor Relations Board (NLRB) rulings on nonunion workplaces.

LO4 Describe the phases of unionization and the typical collective bargaining process.

LO5 Define a grievance and identify the stages in a dispute resolution procedure.

LO6 Understand the differences in how unions operate in the global arena.

610

WHAT'S TRENDING IN LABOR RELATIONS?

Workers in union and nonunion workplaces are impacted by the existence of labor laws and decisions rendered by the National Labor Relations Board (NLRB). In particular, these factors influence how employers and employees interact with each other at work, whether unions are present or not. Support for unions also fluctuates among workers and lawmakers based on changing preferences. Several key trends in the labor relations field include the following:

1. There is a dilution of public employee union power in many states. Lawmakers in Wisconsin, Michigan, Indiana, and Ohio recently took steps to reduce the power of public-sector labor unions. Changes such as eliminating the automatic withdrawal of union dues have led to decreased support for public unions.
2. An activist labor board has extended its decisions to encompass more and more workers, both union and nonunion. The labor board's rulings modify the timing of representation elections and lead to additional changes in workplace practices.
3. Highly skilled workers in technology industries are rejecting union organizing attempts, preferring to negotiate their own terms and conditions of employment.
4. Right-to-work laws are becoming more prevalent in the United States, with 25 states now limiting the power of labor unions in the private and public sectors. Workers in those states now have greater freedom regarding membership in a union.

The landscape is constantly shifting with respect to regulations of workplace practices. Labor laws continue to evolve as workers and lawmakers respond to changes in how managers operate their companies and treat their workers. As labor board rulings and workforce dynamics evolve, managers and HR professionals need to remain current on how human resource practices must be modified.[1]

HEADLINE

Wildcat Union of NCAA Football Players

While no one would argue that college football is a big business on many campuses, a recent decision by the NLRB might have led to players being treated as employees first and students second. Athletes on scholarship at Northwestern University in Chicago asked the NLRB to determine their right to organize a labor union. The initiative was started by the Wildcat's former quarterback with help from the United Steelworkers and the College Athletes Players Association.

Football players' schedules are tightly controlled by coaching staff and National Collegiate Athletic Association (NCAA) regulations. Several weeks before the academic school year begins, players report for training camp and follow a rigid daily program that prepares them for the upcoming football season. The month-long training camp usually requires approximately 50 to 60 hours per week of activities devoted to conditioning and practicing plays and strategies. Once classes start, they typically spend 40 to 50 hours per week on sports-related obligations and 20 hours on their academic coursework. The players' contend that the majority of their time is spent on football "work" as opposed to schoolwork.

A decision by the regional director of the NLRB allowing these college athletes to organize applied only to players on scholarship. The athletes hoped to negotiate over the additional costs associated with attending Northwestern such as health benefits, travel for home visits, utility bills, mobile phone bills, and so forth.

The NLRB's decision would have applied only to private universities, not public institutions. However, the full labor board in Washington, DC, overturned the regional director's decision. For now,

John Gress/Getty Images

college football players remain students; not employees who are eligible to form a labor union make the final decision in this case. This issue brings a whole new meaning to Wildcat strikes.[2]

Union
Formal association of workers that promotes the interests of its members through collective action

A union is a formal association of workers that promotes the interests of its members through collective action. In the United States, unions typically try to increase compensation, improve working conditions, and influence workplace rules. When workers are represented by a union, these issues are decided through collective bargaining agreements and specified in formal contracts that have been negotiated by management and labor.

Unions did not seem to have a bright future in the 1930s when the National Labor Relations Act (NLRA) was passed, giving unions a legal right to exist. Then they grew to represent over one-third of workers in the 1950s, only to see their strength in the private sector drop to less than 8% recently. However, in the public sector, unions are more common. These trends illustrate the inherent political nature of unionization, particularly because government and public opinion play such prominent roles in union strength.

While many managers think that they do not need to understand labor laws because they work in union-free workplaces, this is simply not the case. In recent years, the government has broadened its interpretation and application of labor laws to include employees who are not represented by labor unions. Therefore, a basic understanding of labor laws and NLRB rulings is important for all managers and HR professionals.[3]

Exactly how political, economic, and workforce changes affect employers and unions will be factors in the future of the labor–management relationship. Even though fewer workers have chosen to join unions in recent years than in the past, employers and HR professionals still need to understand the system of laws, regulations, court decisions, and administrative rulings related to the nature of unions. This is important because unions remain a strong alternative for employees in the event of poor HR practices.

16-1 Perspectives on Unionization

Union representation has many advantages and disadvantages. For instance, unions give employees an opportunity to provide feedback to employers about their concerns and suggestions that would be difficult to express otherwise. Unions can provide a balance to the unchallenged decision-making power of management when needed. Increases in job tenure, performance, and employee earnings are often associated with unionization. Alternatively, unions can negatively impact the allocation of organizational resources, decrease profitability, and hurt productivity as a result of increased compensation and rigid work practices. These points should be considered when exploring why employees join unions and why employers resist unionization.

16-1a Why Employees Unionize

Over the years employees have joined unions for two general reasons: (1) they are dissatisfied with how they are treated by their employers, and (2) they believe that unions can improve their work situations. If employees believe they are being treated unfairly by their companies, they may turn to unions to get assistance with their concerns. As Figure 16-1 shows, the major factors that can trigger unionization are issues of compensation, working conditions, management style, and employee treatment.

One of the primary determinants of whether employees want to unionize is how well their companies are managed. Unions function as a watchdog for workplace equity and make sure that employees are treated fairly. Without union representation, employees may be paid unfairly and treated poorly. Employees expect to receive reasonably competitive compensation, a good working environment, effective management and supervision, and fair and responsive treatment. When these basic expectations are not met, employees may seek out a labor union. Unionization often occurs when employees feel disrespected, unsafe, underpaid, and unappreciated; they see a union as a viable option for change.

The opinions people have about unions in general along with the actions and decisions of managers influence whether they favor union representation.[4] This implies that general opinions of organized labor create a certain mind-set among workers either for or against unions, regardless of the practices they immediately experience on the job. Once unionization occurs, the ability of the union to foster commitment from members and to remain as their bargaining agent depends on how well the union succeeds in providing the services that its members want, which can further strengthen or weaken workers' perceptions of unions.

FIGURE 16-1 Factors Leading to Employee Unionization

Desirability of Unionization

1. Working Conditions
- Inadequate staffing
- Mandatory overtime
- Unsatisfactory work requirements
- Unrealistic expectations

2. Compensation
- Noncompetitive pay
- Inadequate benefits
- Inequitable pay raises
- Unfair allocation of resources

3. Management Style
- Arbitrary decision making
- Use of fear/intimidation
- Lack of recognition
- Autocratic leadership

4. Employee Treatment
- Job insecurity
- Unfair discipline/policies
- Lack of response to complaints
- Harassment/abusive behaviors

16-1b Why Employers Resist Unions

Some employers would rather not have to negotiate with unions because they affect how employees and workplaces are managed.[5] Unions are criticized for creating inefficiencies at work that cause waste and poor performance. For instance, the merger between American Airlines and US Airways has taken much longer than expected because the unions representing pilots and flight attendants cannot agree on a consistent set of work rules and compensation plans. Integrating the two companies requires approval from labor unions, and the company has not been able to finalize terms and conditions of employment. The matters are likely to move to mediation or arbitration for resolution.[6] The delays result in added costs and lower customer service as workers and managers face a standoff.

Union workers frequently receive higher compensation than nonunion workers, but on the flipside, higher pay and benefits might be related to longer job tenure and better job performance, if union leadership is aligned with company goals.[7] Despite this higher productivity, managers still try to identify labor-saving ways of doing work to offset increased expenses. For instance, performance-based compensation and profit sharing were explored at General Motors as a way of increasing productivity and reducing the risks associated with non-incentive-based raises.[8]

Some employers seek to build a cooperative relationship with labor unions, while others choose an aggressive, adversarial approach.[9] However, there are numerous strategies that can be employed to prevent unionization from occurring in the first place. As stated previously, employees become interested in organizing a union when they feel mistreated by their employers and/or operate in an unfair, undesirable, or even dangerous work environment. To remain union free, companies must be proactive and develop good employment practices; earn employee trust; encourage employee feedback; offer fair, competitive compensation; and build supportive supervisory relationships with workers. Both HR professionals and operating managers must be attentive and responsive to employees. Primary responsibility for dealing with labor unions may fall to HR or line managers depending on the organization's philosophy and history. For example, in the railroad industry, there is typically a separate function for labor relations since there are multiple unions representing various segments of the workforce and the contracts are quite complex.

LO2 Outline the current state of union activity in the United States and identify several reasons for the decline in union membership.

16-2 Union Membership in the United States

Unions played a critical role in improving the lives of American workers. Early forms of labor unions began in the eighteenth century with craft unions for skilled workers in jobs such as newspaper typesetters, boot makers, and shoemakers. With a focus on better wages, reasonable work hours, and safer working conditions, these organizations evolved as the Industrial Revolution took hold in the early twentieth century. Factories began springing up all across the nation, and demand for workers was high. Many jobs in factories were unskilled because assembly lines replaced the handwork of previous craftsmen.

Immigration was flourishing at the time, and countless individuals landed on our shores with limited English language skills but hearty souls and a strong work ethic.[10]

In many workplaces, conditions were deplorable, and workers were required to work long hours with few breaks for relatively little compensation. The "sweat-shop" was common, and unsafe worksites were typical. A tragic fire at the Triangle Shirtwaist Company in 1911 resulted in the deaths of 147 workers, mostly women and young girls. Employment of children was not unusual, and employees had few protections for their safety and security.

Company owners and managers did not take kindly to the perceived interference from labor unions. They resisted all attempts to organize workers and on several occasions the military, National Guard, and police were sent to help keep the peace. Impassioned workers rioted in New York, Chicago, and other industrial centers. In the West, miners were killed or arrested in response to a number of work stoppages. In 1914, the Ludlow Massacre led to the deaths of 5 men, 2 women, and 12 children. Company "guards" hired by the mine operators attacked a union tent camp with machine guns and then set it afire in an effort to persuade striking workers to return to the mine. These examples show that during the early part of the twentieth century, labor and management fought bitterly, with management often prevailing in the courts.[11]

The financial crisis of the Great Depression in 1929 and the resulting economic hardship on workers and their families led to enactment of legislation to provide for worker financial and physical safety and security. To counteract the power of company owners, labor union membership was encouraged and supported by law. Workers gained the right to form labor unions and to negotiate with their employers regarding terms and conditions of their employment. Although companies were not necessarily happy with this turn of events, the playing field was being leveled, and workers now had a voice protected by law.

In the years immediately following enactment of labor-friendly legislation, membership in unions was at an all-time high. More than 30% of the work-force was represented by unions from 1945 to 1960. However, as shown in Figure 16-2, since 1983, membership in unions has steadily declined, and unions in the United States now represent only 12.4% of eligible workers. Unions are more prevalent in the public sector; in recent years, public employees were more than five times more likely to be union members than employees in the private sector.[12]

Figure 16-3 shows the significant difference between the private and public sectors. Private-sector employees are far less likely to belong to labor unions, with only 6.7% represented in 2013. A very different story is seen in the public sector, with 35.3% of workers represented by labor unions. Of course, the public sector makes up a smaller proportion of the total workforce. Thus, the overall trend has been a decline for several decades.[13]

However, it's not all bad news for unions, with some of them prospering. In the past several years, unions have used publicity, pickets, boycotts, and strikes to organize thousands of janitors, health care workers, cleaners, and other low-paid workers. More women and black workers are now represented by unions than historically.[14]

FIGURE 16-2   Percentage of Employed U.S. Workers Belonging to Unions

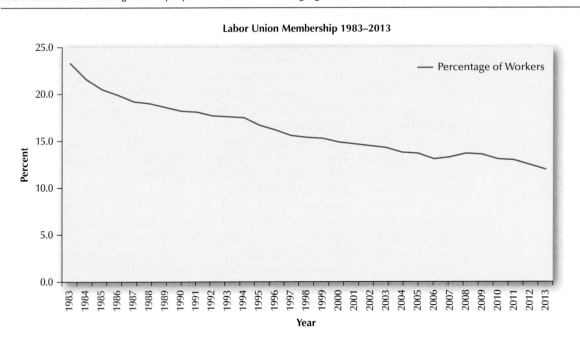

Source: Bureau of Labor Statistics.

FIGURE 16-3   Union Membership by Sector, 1983–2013

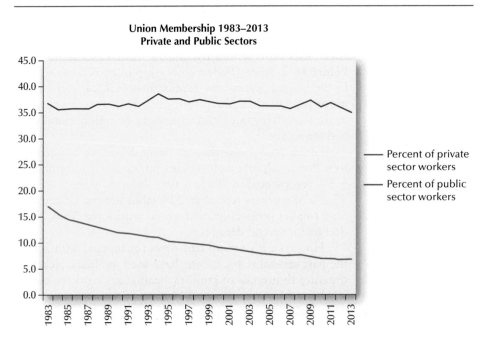

Source: Bureau of Labor Statistics.

16-2a Reasons for U.S. Union Membership Long-Term Decline

Several general trends have contributed to the decline of U.S. union membership, including deregulation, foreign competition, lack of individual support, increased right-to-work legislation, and an increasing use of temporary or contingent workers. Managers in many companies have become more proactive and aggressively work to counteract union arguments through improved workplace practices.[15]

To some extent, unions may be victims of their own successes. Unions in the United States have historically emphasized helping workers obtain higher wages and benefits, shorter working hours, job security, and safe working conditions from their employers. Some believe that one cause for the decline of unions has been their success in getting those important issues passed into law for everyone. Therefore, unions may no longer be seen as necessary by many workers, even though they enjoy the results of past union efforts to influence legislation that has benefited them.[16]

Geographic Changes During the past decade, job growth in the United States has been the greatest in states located in the South, the Southwest, and the Rocky Mountains, places traditionally less open to unions and more "employer friendly." For example, Ohio once ruled as the "rubber capital," but it has now been surpassed by Oklahoma and South Carolina, the two biggest producers of rubber tires in North America. Tire manufacturers moved south to take advantage of government-provided tax incentives and a right-to-work labor climate that offers greater latitude to management in running its operations.[17]

Another geographic issue involves the movement of many low-skill jobs outside the United States. Many manufacturers with heavily unionized U.S. workforces have moved a significant number of low-skill jobs to the Philippines, China, Thailand, and Mexico to take advantage of cheaper labor and fewer employment restrictions. However, recent worker protests in some developing countries have led to higher wages and increased labor regulations, which reduce the cost advantage of moving work offshore.[18]

Industrial Changes Much of the decline of union membership can be attributed to the shift in U.S. jobs from industries such as manufacturing, construction, and mining to service industries. Private-sector union membership is primarily concentrated in the shrinking part of the economy, and unions are not making significant progress in the fastest-growing segments of the U.S. economy. For example, there are small percentages of union members in wholesale/retail industries and financial services, the sectors in which many new jobs have been added, whereas the number of manufacturing jobs continues to shrink. A look at Figure 16-4 shows that nongovernmental union members are heavily concentrated in utilities, transportation and warehousing, and other industrial jobs.

Unions have had difficulties making inroads with the growing number of workers in service-related jobs. Amazon has aggressively opposed labor unions for years and uses the services of a law firm that specializes in fighting union organizing efforts when the situation gets serious. Managers at fulfillment centers have reacted quickly to labor organizers distributing union literature to Amazon workers. Until recently, no union efforts led to a representation election. However, employees in Delaware voted down union representation in a first-ever union election.[19] The union message and tactics seem less effective with workers in nonindustrial occupations.

FIGURE 16-4 Union Membership by Industry, 2013

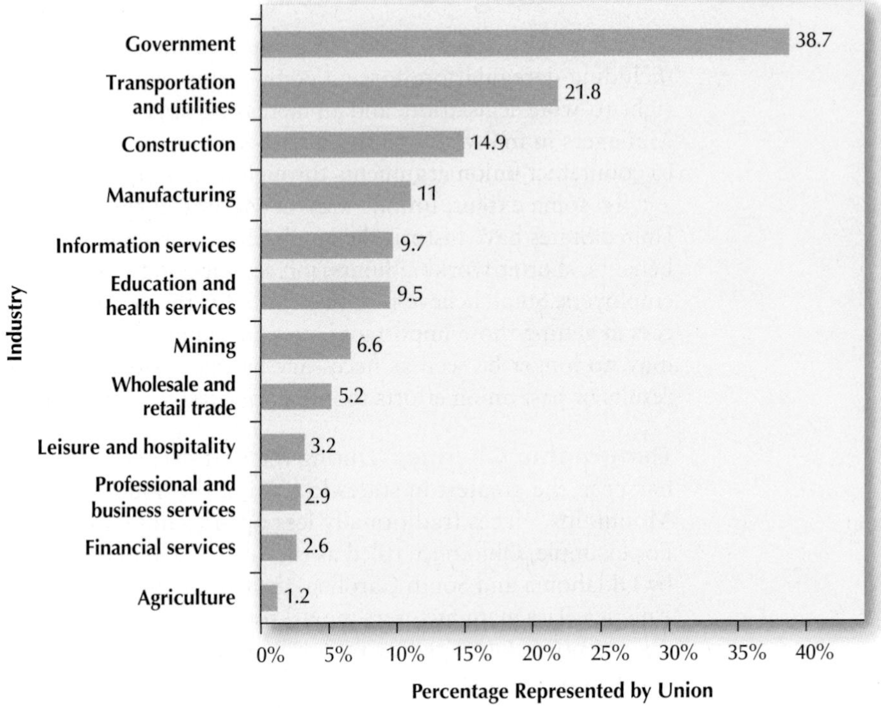

Source: Bureau of Labor Statistics.

Workforce Changes Many of the workforce changes discussed in earlier chapters have contributed to the decrease in union representation of the labor force. The decline in many blue-collar jobs in heavy industry has been especially significant. For example, the United Mine Workers of America was once one of the nation's most powerful unions with 800,000 members. Today, there are only 35,000 members and of those, only 20,000 work in coal mining.[20]

There are growing numbers of white-collar employees such as clerical workers, insurance claims representatives, data input processors, mental health aides, computer technicians, loan officers, auditors, and retail sales workers. Unions have increased efforts to organize white-collar workers because advances in technology have boosted their numbers in the workforce. However, unions have faced challenges in organizing these workers. Many white-collar workers see unions as resistant to change and not in touch with the concerns of the more educated workers in technical and professional jobs. In addition, many white-collar workers exhibit attitudes and preferences quite different from those held by blue-collar union members and they tend to view unions as being oriented primarily toward blue-collar workers.

The growing percentage of women in the U.S. workforce presents another challenge to unions. In the past, unions have not been as successful in organizing female workers as they have been in organizing male workers. Some unions are trying to focus more on recruiting female members, and unions have been in the forefront in the push for legislation on such family-related practices as child care, maternity and paternity leave, pay equity, and flexible work arrangements. Women in "pink-collar," low-skill service jobs have been somewhat more likely to join unions than women working in white-collar jobs. More women tend to work in pink-collar jobs, and women overall tend to have a lower opinion of unions than do men.[21]

16-2b Public-Sector Unionism

Unions have historically enjoyed significant success in the public sector. The public sector (federal, state, and local) is the most highly unionized segment of the U.S. workforce, with more than 35% of government workers represented by unions. Local (city and county) government workers have the highest unionization percentage of any group in the U.S. workforce.

Unionization of state and local government employees presents some unique challenges. First, some employees work in critical service areas such as police and firefighting. Granting these workers the right to strike endangers public health and safety. Consequently, more than 30 states have laws prohibiting work stoppages by public employees. These laws also specify a variety of ways to resolve negotiation impasses, including arbitration. But many government employees seem to believe that unions still give employees in these areas greater security and better ability to influence decisions on wages and benefits compared to nonunion workers.

Public-sector unions have come under attack in recent years.[22] The high cost of union benefits, particularly retirement plans, has become a flashpoint between lawmakers and labor representatives. Public unions have been slow to change from traditional defined benefit pensions to the more contemporary defined contribution (401[k]) plans. Serious issues with inadequately funded pensions are causing city and state officials to consider drastic changes to public employees' union rights.[23] Indiana, Wisconsin, and Michigan recently enacted right-to-work laws that reduce the bargaining power of unions. A key element of most union contracts is the automatic deduction of union dues from workers' paychecks. In Wisconsin, such deductions were outlawed, which led to a substantial drop in union membership there.[24] Controversy continues to plague public employee unions and their government employers. Finding common ground and mutually beneficial resolution will be a challenge for elected officials in the future.

16-2c Unions Fighting for Survival

The continuing losses have led to disagreements among unions about how to fight the decline. A number of unions have devised creative strategies to remain relevant and in the public eye. Some companies are more forceful in their attempts to combat these efforts, while others ignore them and go about their business.[25] Creating partnerships with outside organizations, protesting on behalf of low-wage workers, and holding work stoppages of short duration at selected employers are all attempts to show the impact of the collective worker voice. In addition, unions are targeting specific groups of workers who they believe will be most supportive of joining the cause.

Partnerships and Worker Centers By building ties to environmental advocacy groups, plaintiffs' attorneys, racial and feminist groups, and other liberal organizations, unions are working to develop a coalition that could hold sway in state legislatures as well as Washington, DC. Banding together to apply pressure to lawmakers on a variety of worker-centered issues keeps labor unions at the forefront of protecting rank-and-file employees' interests.[26]

Worker centers usually operate as nonprofit organizations that offer their members a variety of services. They often serve as a front for unions and provide worker advocacy, lobbying, legal advice, and training services. Over 230 such centers focus on immigrant populations and low-wage workers with the overall purpose of helping members achieve economic justice and obtain safer and overall better working conditions. The centers are not subject to labor board oversight because their activities are broad in scope and do not amount to formal collective bargaining. Some worker centers have staged work stoppages at fast food establishments and big-box retailers to highlight low wages and other unacceptable working conditions. Worker centers start by trying to influence the general public about workers' plight but primarily encourage workers to join organized labor unions.[27]

Protests and Work Stoppages Walmart is a perennial target of union organizers, and busy shopping times like Black Friday are designated as protest days at many stores. Protesters, who are often joined by union members from the United Food & Commercial Workers, picket outside stores to demand higher wages and better working conditions. Walmart has disciplined some protesting employees under its attendance policy. The issue is under review by the NLRB, and it is not certain if workers have the right to "strike" when they are not part of a labor union.[28]

Fast food chains have also been affected by employees walking out in an effort to secure higher pay. McDonald's, Wendy's, and Burger King establishments in major cities have been subjected to protests staged by the Service Employees International Union (SEIU). Restaurant workers joined SEIU members to picket fast food locations. Both fast food chains and big-box retailers experience high employee turnover, which makes union organizing difficult.

Low-Skilled Workers Unions also target low-skilled workers, many of whom have jobs that pay less and are less desirable. Janitors, building cleaners, nursing home aides, and meatpacking workers are examples of groups that unions have successfully targeted. For instance, in the health care industry, workers in nursing homes are a fast-growing segment of the workforce. Many employees in this industry are relatively dissatisfied. The industry is often noted for its low pay and difficult, heavy work, and many employees are women who work as nurses' aides, cooks, launderers, and other low-wage laborers.

Immigrant workers in low-skill jobs comprise another group of individuals targeted by unions. Some unions have also been politically active in supporting legislation to allow illegal immigrant workers to get work permits and citizenship over time. Although these efforts are not always successful, unions are likely to continue pursuing industries and employers with numerous low-skill jobs and low-skilled workers. The advantages of unionization are especially strong for these employees.

Contingent Workers and "Joint Employer" Status Since many employers have added contingent workers instead of full-time employees, unions have tried to target part-time, temporary, and other employees who are not standard full-time workers.[29] A controversial decision by the NLRB treats temporary or contract workers as part of a primary employer's workforce. This joint employer status means that a company that uses temporary workers bears as much responsibility for complying with employment laws as the temporary agency that actually employs the workers. If the primary employer's workforce is unionized, contingent workers are also eligible to become union members. Subcontracted employment is prevalent throughout the U.S. workforce, and this labor board decision would have far-reaching, unpredictable consequences. Labor advocates and employers are closely watching the decision to determine how it will impact union organizing and other employment practices.[30]

LO3 Explain the provisions of each of the major U.S. labor laws and recognize the impact of these laws and NLRB rulings on nonunion workplaces.

16-3 U.S. Labor Laws

Several key labor laws have been enacted in the United States over the years. The "pendulum" has swung from a highly union-friendly stance to a more employer-friendly one. Federal lawmakers have taken actions both to hamper unions and to protect them.

16-3a Early Labor Legislation

Early in the twentieth century, two important federal laws were passed that fostered employees' rights to form labor unions. These laws were intended to ensure economic prosperity in the United States and to provide workers with some basic rights and protections from unrestrained companies.

Railway Labor Act The Railway Labor Act (RLA) of 1926 represented a shift in government regulation of unions. The result of a joint effort between railroad management and unions to reduce transportation strikes, this act gave railroad employees "the right to organize and bargain collectively through representatives of their own choosing." In 1936, airlines and their employees were added to those covered by the RLA.

The RLA mandates a complex and cumbersome dispute resolution process. This process allows either the unions or the management to use the NLRB, a multistage dispute resolution process, and even the power of the president of the United States to appoint an emergency board. The end result of having a prolonged process that is subject to political interference has been that unions often work for two or more years after the expiration of their old contracts.

Norris-LaGuardia Act The stock market crash and the onset of the Great Depression in 1929 led to massive employer cutbacks. In some industries, employee resistance led to strikes and violence. Under laws at that time, employers could ask a federal judge to issue an injunction ordering workers to return to work. In 1932, Congress passed the Norris-LaGuardia Act, which guaranteed workers some rights to organize and restricted the issuance of court injunctions in labor disputes. An important provision of the law was to prohibit employers from asking employees to sign yellow dog contracts, which were pledges by workers not to join a labor union. Employees who joined a labor union after they signed such contracts were subject to discipline or termination. The Norris-LaGuardia Act thus freed employees from some of the constraints and punishments that employers had previously used to thwart their efforts to organize.[31]

Yellow dog contracts Pledges by workers not to join a labor union

Labor Law Foundation The economic crises of the early 1930s and the continuing restrictions on workers' ability to organize into unions led to the passage

FIGURE 16-5 Major National Labor Laws

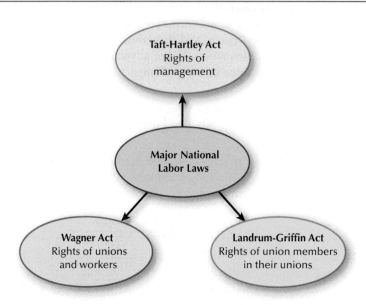

of landmark labor legislation, the Wagner Act, in 1935. Later acts reflected other pressures and issues that required legislative attention. Three acts—passed over a period of almost 25 years—constitute the core of U.S. labor law: (1) the Wagner Act, (2) the Taft-Hartley Act, and (3) the Landrum-Griffin Act. Figure 16-5 indicates the primary focus of each act.

16-3b Wagner Act (National Labor Relations Act)

The National Labor Relations Act, more commonly referred to as the Wagner Act, has been called the Magna Carta of labor and was, by anyone's standards, pro-union. Passed in 1935, the Wagner Act was an outgrowth of the Great Depression. With employers having to close or cut back their business operations, workers were left with little job security. However, the high rate of unemployment and the large percentage of workers who were recent immigrants allowed companies to hold down wages and pay little heed to workers' concerns. Workers were reluctant to speak out, as they could be easily replaced at a time when unemployment rates exceeded 20%.

Unions stepped in to provide a feeling of solidarity and strength for many workers. The Wagner Act declared, in effect, that the official policy of the U.S. government was to encourage collective bargaining. Specifically, it established the right of workers to organize free from management interference. Workers were provided with the right to participate *or not participate* in union membership. The basic provisions of the law, spelled out in Section 7, protect employees' rights as follows:

1. Employees shall have the right to self-organization, to form, join, or assist labor organizations,
2. To bargain collectively through representatives of their own choosing,

3. And to engage in other concerted activities for the purpose of collective bargaining or other mutual aid or protection.
4. Employees shall also have the right to refrain from any or all of such activities except to the extent that an agreement requires membership in a labor organization as a condition of employment.[32]

Protected concerted activities
Actions taken by employees working together to try to improve their pay and working conditions, with or without a union

Unfair labor practices
Actions that employers are legally prohibited from taking to prevent employees from unionizing

These Section 7 rights have broad application, in particular the right to engage in protected concerted activities, actions taken by employees working together to try to improve their pay and working conditions, with or without a union. This is discussed at greater length later in this chapter. In addition to these rights, Section 8 of the law defined a number of actions that employers are legally prohibited from taking to prevent employees from unionizing. These are called unfair labor practices. The following "HR Competencies & Applications: Unfair Labor Practices" feature explains this in detail.

National Labor Relations Board Enforcement of the Wagner Act was assigned to the newly created National Labor Relations Board (NLRB), and today, the NLRB administers all provisions of this and all subsequent labor laws. The primary functions of the NLRB include conducting union representation elections, investigating complaints by employers or unions through its fact-finding process, issuing opinions on its findings, and prosecuting violations in court. The five members of the NLRB are appointed by the president of the United States and are confirmed by the U.S. Senate. Significant decisions and activities of the NLRB are discussed at the end of this section.

16-3c Taft-Hartley Act (Labor Management Relations Act)

The Labor Management Relations Act, better known as the Taft-Hartley Act, was passed in 1947 as a means to offset the pro-union Wagner Act by limiting union actions. It was considered to be pro-management and became the second major labor law.

The new law amended or qualified in some respect major provisions of the Wagner Act and established an entirely new code of conduct for unions. The Taft-Hartley Act confirmed employees' Section 7 rights and further protected them from restraint by unions. Several changes were made to the process of representation elections, most notably excluding supervisors from inclusion in the bargaining unit. Congress also added new types of elections. Of note, union members were given the right to hold elections to deauthorize or decertify the union thus reversing the process of representation. The law allowed states to enact right-to-work laws that gave workers greater freedom to reject union membership.

A primary feature of the Taft-Hartley Act was the identification of unfair labor practices that might be committed by unions. Lawmakers recognized that companies may not be the only party that might violate workers' rights. The following "HR Competencies & Applications: Unfair Labor Practices" feature explains the illegal acts of unions that were defined as unfair labor practices. The act expanded the NLRB from three to five members and established the Federal Mediation and Conciliation Service (FMCS) as an agency to help management and labor settle labor contract disputes. The act required that the FMCS be notified of disputes over contract renewals or modifications if they were not settled within 30 days after the designated date.[33]

COMPETENCIES & APPLICATIONS

Unfair Labor Practices

Specific actions taken by employers and unions have been designated as illegal by various labor laws. These unfair labor practices (ULPs) typically work at cross-purposes to workers' interests for fair treatment and representation.

To protect union rights, the Wagner Act prohibited employers from committing unfair labor practices. Several of those practices were identified as follows:

- Interfering with, restraining, or coercing employees in the exercise of their right to organize or to bargain collectively
- Dominating or interfering with the formation or administration of any labor organization
- Encouraging or discouraging membership in any labor organization by discriminating with regard to hiring, tenure, or conditions of employment
- Discharging or otherwise discriminating against an employee because the employee filed charges or gave testimony under the act
- Refusing to bargain collectively with representatives of the employees

To protect workers and companies from inappropriate labor union actions, the Taft-Hartley Act prohibited the following unfair labor practices:

- Refusing to engage in good-faith negotiations with employers
- Engaging in activities that might cause employers to discriminate against employees because of their union or nonunion status
- Coercing or discriminating against members
- Charging members excessive membership fees
- Failing to adequately represent all those covered by a collective bargaining agreement
- Engaging in secondary boycotts with neutral parties if the company and union are in a labor dispute

Unions, companies, and employees can file a ULP charge with the NLRB depending upon the issue at hand. The NLRB investigates and resolves these charges. Over the past decade, the NLRB has handled an average of 22,000 complaints each year. Less than 10% typically result in a formal complaint being issued against the alleged wrongdoer.[34] Answer the following questions after reading the previous section on ULPs:

1. What should companies do to reduce the chance of ULPs? Who should receive training regarding these labor issues?

2. If the NLRB files a ULP charge against a company, what recourse does the company have? How can the company respond if it believes that the ULP is without merit?

KEY COMPETENCIES: Ethical Practice, Consultation; HR Expertise: Organization/Employee Relations, Workplace/Employment Law Regulations

National Emergency Strikes The Taft-Hartley Act allows the president of the United States to declare that a strike constitutes a national emergency. A national emergency strike is one that would impact an industry or a major part of it in such a way that the national economy would be significantly affected. The act allows the president to declare an 80-day cooling-off period during which the union and management continue negotiations. Only after that period can they strike if a settlement has not been reached.

Over the decades, national emergencies have been designated in the railroad, airline, and other industries. For example, the national emergency provisions were involved in a strike of transportation and dock workers throughout the U.S. West Coast states. During the 80-day period, a contract agreement was reached, so a strike was averted.

Right-to-Work Provision One provision of the Taft-Hartley Act, section 14(b), deserves special explanation. This section allows states to pass laws that restrict compulsory union membership. Accordingly, several states have passed right-to-work laws, which prohibit requiring employees to join unions as a condition of obtaining or continuing employment. The laws were so named because they allow a person the right to work without having to join a union.

While the majority of right-to-work state laws were enacted between 1947 and 1963, in the recent past, several union stronghold states have also joined the list. There are now 25 states with right-to-work laws in effect, as shown in Figure 16-6. Employment levels tend to be higher in right-to-work states, but wages tend to be lower. However, many right-to-work states have lower costs of living; therefore, wage differences may not be as great as they appear.[35] There is also some research showing that use of contingent workers is lower in right-to-work states.[36] The impact of right-to-work laws on state employment outcomes is complex and is determined by many factors in each state.

Right-to-work laws
State laws that prohibit requiring employees to join unions as a condition of obtaining or continuing employment

FIGURE 16-6 Right-to-Work States

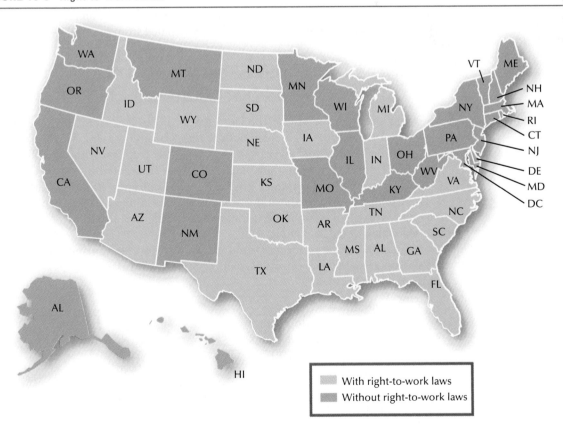

With right-to-work laws
Without right-to-work laws

Open shop
Employer in which workers are not required to join or pay dues to a union

In states with right-to-work laws, employers may have an open shop, which indicates workers cannot be required to join or pay dues to a union. Thus, even though a union may represent a group of employees at a company, individual workers cannot be required or coerced to join the union or pay dues. However, those workers are still subject to the terms and conditions negotiated by the union, and the union must represent them in any disputes. Consequently, in many right-to-work states, individual membership in union groups is significantly lower. The NLRB is considering overturning existing law and allowing unions to charge nonmembers a fee to process grievances in right-to-work states. Such a ruling would enhance the power of unions and reduce the impact of these state laws.[37]

The nature of union–management relations is affected by the right-to-work provisions of the Taft-Hartley Act. Right-to-work generally prohibits an employer from having a closed shop, which requires individuals to join a union before they can be hired. Because of concerns that a closed shop allows a union to control who may be considered for employment and who must be hired by an employer, section 14(b) prohibits closed shops except in construction-related occupations.

Closed shop
Employer that requires individuals to join a union before they can be hired

In states that do not have right-to-work laws, different types of arrangements exist. Three of the different types of "shops" are as follows:

- *Union shop*: Workers must join the union, usually 30 to 60 days after being hired.
- *Agency shop*: Workers who don't join the union must make payments equal to union dues and fees to get union representation services.
- *Maintenance-of-membership shop*: Workers must remain members of the union for the period of the labor contract.

The nature of the shop is negotiated between the union and the employer. Employees who fail to meet the requirements are often terminated from their jobs.

16-3d Landrum-Griffin Act (Labor Management Reporting and Disclosure Act)

The third major labor law in the United States, the Landrum-Griffin Act, was passed in 1959 to protect the democratic rights of union members. The need for these member protections grew from instances of corruption within the Teamsters and other unions. Some unethical union officials embezzled funds for their own use, basically stealing from their own members. Under the Landrum-Griffin Act, unions are required to establish bylaws, make financial reports, and provide union members with a bill of rights. The law appointed the U.S. secretary of labor to act as a watchdog of union conduct.[38]

As required by the Landrum-Griffin Act, unions must file a financial report detailing all receipts and disbursements of funds along with a breakdown of payments made for the following activities:

- Representational activities
- Political activity and lobbying
- Contributions, gifts, and grants
- General overhead
- Union administration

The Office of Labor-Management Standards within the Department of Labor collects and retains all reports. In addition to these annual financial reports, copies of collective bargaining agreements that cover more than 1,000 workers are publicly available on the agency's website.[39] This transparency is similar to the reporting that public corporations provide to government officials and other stakeholders.

16-3e Significant NLRB Activities and Rulings

The NLRB is an appointed body whose members are nominated by the president of the United States and confirmed by Senate. There are four board members who each serve a five-year term and one general counsel who serves a four-year term. The nomination process can be politically charged and in recent years, disagreement over the confirmation procedures led to a Supreme Court decision in *NLRB v. Noel Canning 134 S.Ct. 2550 (2014)* that overturned the appointment of several board members. The trickle-down impact of that decision is a possible rehearing of over 400 cases decided during the disputed period.[40]

The NLRB's position on workplace issues is often influenced by national politics and executive branch priorities. The current board has issued far-reaching decisions that impact many aspects of employment policies and practices, particularly in nonunion settings. Taking an expansive view of employees' Section 7 rights has resulted in several contentious rulings regarding language in employee handbooks and the definition of protected concerted activity. Key rulings by the labor board include company policies on employees' use of social media, company policies on courteous or respectful behavior, company confidentiality rules, and bargaining unit determination and elections.

Policies on Employees' Use of Social Media and Electronic Communications Employers' ability to limit what employees say about them on social media has been severely limited. While a company can restrict employees' use of its logo or trademarks, it cannot prohibit people from identifying where they work and posting derogatory comments about the company, as long as it is done with the intention of prompting coworkers to take group action. Such postings are considered protected concerted activity if their goal is collective action to improve workplace conditions. Employees are not permitted to "rant" online by posting inappropriate comments, but discussing workplace treatment, compensation, and other relevant issues is permissible. Companies can forbid employees from committing sexual harassment, threats of violence, sabotage, and abusive or malicious activity on social media. It is advisable to craft a narrow policy and include specific examples of what constitutes inappropriate verbiage or behavior.[41]

The NLRB recently ruled on how far employers can go in restricting use of email and other communications technology. Employees were granted the right to use company email systems to organize a union and communicate with coworkers about wages and working condition during nonworking hours. This is advantageous to labor unions since email is an efficient and easy way to broadly notify employees about union organizing activities. Companies may have policies that restrict the use of electronic communications to nonworking hours but, in reality, they are not rigidly enforced. Employers may choose to restrict overall use of email by employees in order to reduce congestion and traffic on their email systems. Union and nonunion employers are affected by any labor board ruling on this matter.[42]

Courteous or Respectful Behavior Many companies have created personal conduct policies to prohibit discourteous behavior or language in the workplace. The goal is typically to set expectations of professional demeanor. The labor board has called these policies overbroad and "chilling." For example, First Transit's policy that prohibited "discourteous or inappropriate attitude or behavior to passengers, other employees, or members of the public, as well as disorderly conduct during working hours" was called imprecise and ambiguous and as such could be considered to restrict employees' Section 7 rights. The labor board's ruling was issued to ensure that employees are free to express dissatisfaction with company policies and practices, and to disagree with management actions. Further board guidance has condoned the use of profanity by employees when talking to their bosses and even in front of customers. To comply with this ruling, companies should cite specific examples of prohibited behavior and clearly communicate these to employees.[43]

Company Confidentiality Rules The labor board has limited policies that restrict employees from sharing certain confidential information. Employers cannot ban employees from discussing personal or financial information (such as their individual pay rates) or other sensitive information. This is especially troubling with regard to a workplace investigation about misconduct. This ruling puts companies in a no-win situation, as the Equal Employment Opportunity Commission (EEOC) requires confidentiality during investigations. A blanket confidentiality policy will likely be outlawed by the NLRB. Companies can protect trade secrets and proprietary information. They should also state the right to conduct a confidential investigation if circumstances warrant it.[44]

Bargaining Unit Determination and Elections While union organizers typically attempt to create large bargaining units that will generate substantial dues revenue, in recent years, they have sought to establish labor unions within a microunit that includes only one job category or department within a company. Forty-one employees in Macy's Department Store working in the cosmetics and fragrances department were permitted to form a labor union, while the rest of the 150 store employees remained union-free. Taking on these microunits makes organizing easier because there are often pockets of discontent within an organization. Companies must show that additional employees or departments should be added to the bargaining unit because of shared common interests with those seeking to organize the union.[45]

> **Microunit**
> Bargaining unit that includes only one job category or department within a company

In addition to the definition of a bargaining unit, the labor board has also instituted rules and procedures to speed up representation elections. Commonly referred to as "ambush" or "quickie," these election rules give companies and employees as little as 10 days to campaign and educate workers from the time a petition is filed with the NLRB until a vote occurs. This strategy is favorable to unions since support for representation is often highest when the petition is filed, and managers are often caught off guard. Previous procedures usually provided a six-week campaign period. Aggressive union-free actions by employers were more successful with a longer time to convince employees not to support the union.[46]

Franchisors as Joint Employer A recent decision by the NLRB states that McDonald's USA and its franchisees are joint employers for the purposes of compliance with labor laws. The labor board's opinion is that the franchisor is liable for labor violations at all operations bearing the company's name, regardless of who owns the restaurant.[47] This aggregate workforce is far more attractive to a labor union seeking to organize workers. Previously, each franchise operated independently with relatively few employees, not usually enough to expend a lot of union resources to establish a local union.[48] The ruling certainly changes the nature of the franchise business model in the United States.

These rulings by the labor board highlight the need for companies to maintain effective two-way communication with their workers and to address workplace issues promptly and fairly. Companies that fail to establish good employee relations programs may find that their employees turn to labor unions to resolve their problems.

LO4 Describe the phases of the unionization process and the typical collective bargaining process.

16-4 The Union Organizing Process

The typical union organizing process is outlined in Figure 16-7. The process of unionizing workers may begin in one of two primary ways: (1) a union targets an industry, a region, or a company or (2) employees request union representation. In the first case, the local or national union identifies a firm, industry, or region in which it believes unionization can succeed. The logic for targeting is that if the union succeeds in one firm or a portion of an industry or a region, then many other workers in the industry or region will be more willing to consider unionizing. In the second case, the impetus for union organizing occurs when individual workers at an employer contact a union and express a desire to unionize. The employees themselves—and/or the union—may then begin to campaign to win support among the other employees. In these situations, the union knows that there is already some worker dissatisfaction, which makes organizing a bit easier.

16-4a Organizing Campaign

Like other entities seeking members, a union usually mounts a systematic campaign to persuade individuals to join. As would be expected, employers respond to unionization efforts by taking various steps to oppose the union.

Employers' Union Prevention Efforts Employers may make strategic decisions and take aggressive steps to remain union free. Such a choice is perfectly rational but may require some specific HR policies and philosophies. For example, "preventive" employee relations may emphasize good morale and loyalty based on concern for employees, competitive wages and benefits, a fair system for dealing with employee complaints, and safe working conditions. Other factors may also play a part in employees' decisions to remain union free, but if employers adequately address the points just listed, fewer workers are likely to feel the need for a union to represent them.[49] Some companies address the issue with a union-free statement in

FIGURE 16-7 Typical Unionization Process

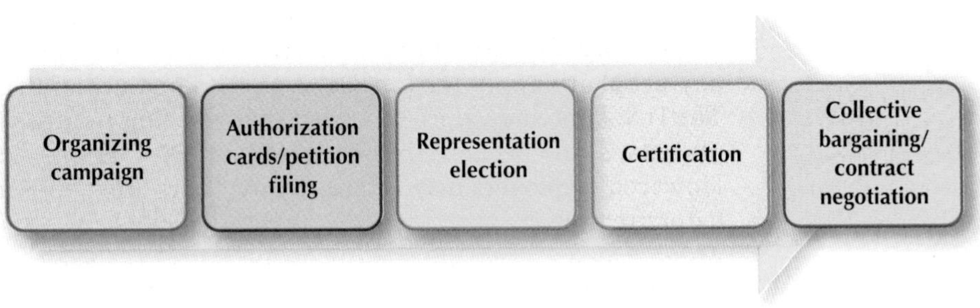

the employee handbook explaining to workers the company's employee relations philosophy. The newly enacted rules for "quickie" elections mean that companies that wish to remain union free should proactively engage with employees and maintain an ongoing dialogue about their union-free philosophy.

No-solicitation policy
Policy that restricts employees and outsiders from distributing literature or soliciting union membership on company premises

Many employers have created a no-solicitation policy to restrict employees and outsiders from distributing literature or soliciting union membership on company premises. Employers without such a policy may be unable to prevent those acts. A policy against solicitation must be a long-term, established approach, not a single action taken to counter a specific and immediate unionization attempt. Company no-solicitation rules must be applied uniformly such that all solicitations are treated alike. Therefore, employees who solicit coworkers to raise money for local charities should be treated the same as those who solicit coworkers to join a union. This issue is complex, and it is wise to obtain legal advice before creating a policy statement.[50]

Management representatives may use various tactics to defeat a union organizing attempt. The management campaign often begins when union literature appears or workers begin talking about unionizing. Some employers hire consultants who specialize in combating unionization efforts. Using these "union busters," as they are called by unions, appears to enhance employers' chances of winning the representation election. Companies should carefully confer with legal counsel before engaging these services. A pending NLRB rule would require disclosure of these arrangements.[51]

Unions' Organizing Efforts The organizing and negotiating successes of unions are tied to the economy and economic trends. Union persuasion efforts can take many forms, including personally contacting employees outside of work, mailing materials to employees' homes, emailing information about the union to employees, inviting employees to attend special meetings away from the company, and publicizing the advantages of union membership. Brochures and leaflets can be given to employees as they leave work, mailed to their homes, or even attached to their vehicles, as long as the union complies with the rules established by laws and the NLRB. The purpose of all this publicity is to encourage employees to sign authorization cards. Having union supporters inside the company is a powerful tool for organizing, particularly in instances where unhappy employees have initiated contact with the union.

To encourage individuals to become involved in unionization efforts, unions have adopted electronic approaches, such as establishing websites where interested workers can read about benefits of unionization. Virtually all labor unions have websites on which they explain how their efforts help workers. They discuss issues of interest to potential members to encourage them to join. Successes in unionizing groups of employees are described. Also, the differences between wages, benefits, and job security are contrasted before and after unionization occurred.

Salting
Practice in which unions hire and pay people to apply for jobs at certain companies to begin organizing efforts

Unions sometimes pay organizers to infiltrate a targeted employer and try to organize workers. In this practice, known as salting, the unions hire and pay people to apply for jobs at certain companies to begin organizing efforts. The U.S. Supreme Court has ruled that refusing to hire otherwise-qualified applicants, solely because they are also paid by a union, violates the Wagner Act. However, employers may refuse to hire "salts" for job-related and nondiscriminatory reasons.[52]

16-4b Authorization Cards

Union authorization card
Card signed by employees to designate a union as their collective bargaining agent

A union authorization card is signed by employees to designate a union as their collective bargaining agent. An example of a union authorization card is shown in Figure 16-8. At least 30% of the employees in the targeted group must sign authorization cards before a representation election can be scheduled.

Union advocates have lobbied for changing laws so that elections are not needed if more than 50% of the eligible employees sign authorization cards. Some states have enacted such laws for public-sector unionization. Also, some employers have taken a neutral approach and agree to recognize unions if a majority of workers sign authorization cards. During an organizing campaign, union supporters work hard to convince each coworker to sign an authorization card. It is critical that employees understand that an authorization card is not simply a request to hold a representation election. If enough employees sign cards, it is possible that the union will be designated as their representative without an election. The fact that an employee signs an authorization card does not necessarily mean that the employee is in favor of a union. Employees who do not want a union might sign authorization cards because they want management to know they are disgruntled or because they want to avoid upsetting coworkers who are advocating for unionization.

16-4c Representation Election

An election to determine if a union will represent the employees is supervised by the NLRB for private-sector organizations and by other agencies for public-sector organizations. If two unions are attempting to represent employees, the employees will have three choices: union A, union B, and no union.

FIGURE 16-8 Example of a Union Authorization Card

AUTHORIZATION FOR REPRESENTATION

I hereby authorize Teamsters Union Local No. 315, I.B.T., under the National Labor Relation Act. I, to be my exclusive collective bargaining representative in negotiations for better wages and working conditions.

Name_____ Print   Date Hired_____
Address_____ Telephones_____
City_____ State_____ Zip_____
Name of Company_____
Kind of Work_____ Dept._____ Salary_____
Date_____ Your Signature_____

This card is strictly confidential. Please remove tape and seal.

Source: Adapted from http://www.cintasfreedomtochoose.com/card-anatomy.asp.

Bargaining unit
Employees eligible to select a single union to represent and bargain collectively for them

Bargaining Unit Before any election, the appropriate bargaining unit must be determined. A bargaining unit is composed of all employees eligible to select a single union to represent and bargain collectively for them. If management and the union do not agree on who is and who is not included in the unit, the regional office of the NLRB must make the determination. A major criterion in deciding the composition of a bargaining unit is what the NLRB calls a community of interest. For example, at an airline, pilots, flight attendants, and mechanics would probably not be included in the same bargaining unit; these employees have widely varying jobs, areas of work, physical locations, and other differences that would likely negate a community of interest. As mentioned in the previous section, new smaller microunits may be formed rather than company-wide bargaining units. Employees who constitute a bargaining unit have mutual interests in the following areas:

- Wages, hours, and working conditions
- Traditional industry groupings for bargaining purposes
- Physical location and amount of interaction and working relationships between employee groups
- Supervision by similar levels of management

Supervisors and Union Ineligibility The Taft-Hartley Act excludes supervisors from voting for or joining unions. As a result, supervisors cannot be included in bargaining units for unionization purposes, except in industries covered by the RLA. But who qualifies as a supervisor is not always clear. The NLRB expanded its definition to classify a supervisor as any individual with authority to hire, transfer, discharge, discipline, and use independent judgment with employees. Numerous NLRB and court rulings have been issued regarding supervisory designation in various situations. A major case decided by the U.S. Supreme Court found that charge nurses with RN degrees were supervisors because they exercised independent judgment. This case and others have provided employers and unions with some guidance about who should be considered supervisors and thus excluded from bargaining units.[53]

Election Unfair Labor Practices Employers and unions engage in many activities before an election. Both the Wagner Act and the Taft-Hartley Act place restrictions on these activities. Once unionizing efforts begin, all activities must conform to the requirements established by applicable labor laws. Both management and the union must adhere to those requirements, or the results of the effort can be appealed to the NLRB and overturned. The following "HR Competencies & Applications: Unionization Do's and Don'ts" feature highlights some of the legal and illegal actions managers must be aware of during unionization efforts. Figure 16-9 shows a commonly used acronym, TIPS, that concisely represents the actions employers cannot engage in during a campaign.

Election Process If an election is held, the union must receive only a simple majority of the votes to win. For example, if a group of 200 employees is the identified bargaining unit, and only 50 people vote, only 26 (50% of those voting plus 1) need to vote yes for the union to be named as the representative of all 200 employees. Typically, with a smaller number of employees in the bargaining unit, there is a higher likelihood that the union will win.

FIGURE 16-9　TIPS: Unfair Labor Practices during Organizing Campaigns

T	Threaten	Threaten to reduce pay, fire workers, or take other negative steps to prevent workers from voting for a union.
I	Interrogate	Grill or quiz employees to learn the identity of the workers who initiated the organizing attempt. Question employees about how individual workers are planning to vote.
P	Promise	Promise pay raises, promotions, better working conditions, or other perks and benefits in exchange for employees rejecting the union.
S	Spy	Follow/tail employees, visit employee gathering places, write down license numbers, and investigate who is participating in union organizing activities.

If either side believes that the other side committed unfair labor practices, the election results can be appealed to the NLRB. If the NLRB finds evidence of unfair practices, it can order a new election. If no unfair practices were committed and the union obtains a majority in the election, the NLRB then certifies the union to serve as representative of employees in the bargaining unit.

16-4d　Certification and Decertification

Official certification of a union as the legal representative for designated private-sector employees is given by the NLRB, and for public-sector employees, it is given by an equivalent body. Once certified, the union attempts to negotiate a contract with the employer. The employer *must* bargain; refusing to bargain with a certified union constitutes an unfair labor practice.

Decertification
Process whereby a union is removed as the representative of a group of employees

If members no longer wish to be represented by the union, they can use the election process to sever the relationship between themselves and the union. Similar to the unionization process, decertification is a process whereby a union is removed as the representative of a group of employees. Employees attempting to oust a union must obtain decertification authorization cards signed by at least 30% of the employees in the bargaining unit before an election may be held. If a majority of those voting in the election vote to remove the union, the decertification effort succeeds. Some reasons that employees might decide to vote out a union are that the treatment provided by the employer has improved, the union has been unable to address the changing needs of the organizational workforce, or the image of the union has declined. Current regulations prohibit employers from initiating or supporting decertification because it is a matter between employees and unions, and employers must stay out of the process.

Unionization Do's and Don'ts

Employers can take numerous actions to prevent unionization. All managers and supervisors must adhere to NLRB and other requirements to avoid unfair labor practices. Listed below are some common do's and don'ts.[54]

✔ DO (LEGAL)

- Tell employees that the employer opposes unionization and explain why.
- Tell employees how current wages and benefits compare with those in other firms.
- Correct any inaccurate information presented by union supporters.
- Tell employees the disadvantages of having a union (dues, assessments, etc.).
- Show employees articles about unions and relate negative experiences elsewhere.
- Explain the unionization process to employees accurately.
- Forbid distribution of union literature during work hours in work areas.
- Enforce disciplinary policies and rules consistently and appropriately.

✘ DON'T (ILLEGAL)

- Tell employees that they will be given pay increases or promotions if they vote against the union.

- Suggest that the company will close down or move if a union is voted in.
- Monitor union meetings.
- Discriminate against employees who are taking part in union activities.
- Visit employees' homes to talk them out of voting for the union.
- Make a speech to employees or groups at work within 24 hours of the election.
- Ask employees how they plan to vote or if they have signed authorization cards.
- Encourage employees to persuade others to vote against the union.
- Tell employees that they will be terminated or disciplined if they advocate the union.

After you have read these Dos and Don'ts, consider the following questions:

1. What are the advantages and disadvantages of hiring a "union buster" expert to assist if a company is faced with a union organizing attempt?

2. What recommendations would you give to line managers who are dealing with the inevitable disagreements between employees who support the union and those who do not? How can work unit dynamics and performance be affected during a union organizing campaign?

KEY COMPETENCIES: Communication, Ethical Practice, Relationship Management; HR Expertise: Organization/Employee Relations, Workplace/Employment Law & Regulations

16-4e Contract Negotiation (Collective Bargaining)

Collective bargaining
Process whereby representatives of management and workers negotiate over wages, hours, and other terms and conditions of employment

Collective bargaining, the last step in unionization, is the process whereby representatives of management and workers negotiate over wages, hours, and other terms and conditions of employment. The goal of this give-and-take process between representatives of the two organizations is to establish conditions beneficial to both. A collective bargaining agreement will typically be in force for several years; therefore, both sides attempt to negotiate terms that they can live with for some time. The bargaining process balances the power between the parties.

Management–union relations in collective bargaining can follow one of several patterns. Figure 16-10 depicts them as a continuum, ranging from conflict to collusion.

FIGURE 16-10 Continuum of Collective Bargaining Relations

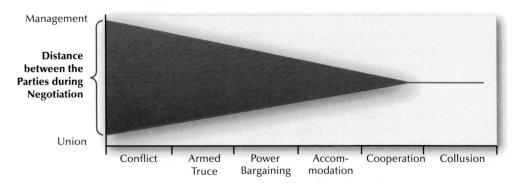

On the left side of the continuum, management and the union see each other as enemies. On the right side, the two entities join in collusion, which is relatively rare in U.S. labor history and is illegal. Most positions fall between these two extremes.

The power relationship in collective bargaining involves conflict, and the threat of conflict seems necessary to maintain the relationship. Perhaps the most significant aspect of collective bargaining is that it is a continuing relationship that does not end immediately after an agreement is reached. Instead, it continues for the life of the labor agreement and beyond.[55] Therefore, the more cooperative the parties are, the less hostility and conflict will carry over into the workplace. However, this cooperation does not mean that the either party agrees to all demands from the other.

16-5 Collective Bargaining Issues

A number of issues can be addressed during collective bargaining. Management rights, union security, and dues checkoff are important issues subject to collective bargaining. These and other issues common to collective bargaining are discussed next.

16-5a Management Rights

Management rights
Rights reserved so that the employer can manage, direct, and control its business

Virtually all labor contracts include management rights, which are rights reserved so that the employer can manage, direct, and control its business. By including such a provision, management attempts to preserve its unilateral right to make changes in areas not identified in a labor contract. Management naturally tries to retain as much latitude and freedom to run its operations as possible.

16-5b Union Security

Union security provisions
Contract clauses to help the union obtain and retain members and collect union dues

A major concern of union representatives when bargaining is the negotiation of union security provisions, contract clauses that help the union obtain and retain members and collect union dues. One type of union security clause in labor contracts is the *no-layoff policy*, or *job security guarantee*. Such a provision is especially important to many union workers because of all the mergers, downsizings, and job reductions taking place. However, management is often unwilling to consider this type of provision.

Types of Required Union Membership Another union security provision is *requiring union membership* of all employees, subject to state right-to-work laws. As mentioned earlier, a closed shop is illegal except in limited situations within the construction industry. But other types of arrangements can be developed, including union shops, agency shops, and maintenance-of-membership shops, which were discussed earlier.

Dues checkoff clause
Provides for the automatic deduction of union dues from the payroll checks of union members

Union Dues Issues A common union security provision is the dues checkoff clause, which provides for the automatic deduction of union dues from the payroll checks of union members. The dues checkoff provision makes it much easier for the union to collect its funds, and without it, the union must collect dues by billing each member separately. For instance, when the state of Wisconsin eliminated dues checkoff for public union members, participation in the union dropped dramatically and was accompanied by a substantial loss of dues revenue. Ironically, Wisconsin was the first state to grant public-sector unions the right to organize and collectively bargain in 1959.[56]

16-5c Classification of Bargaining Issues

The NLRB has classified collective bargaining issues into three categories: mandatory, permissive, and illegal.

Mandatory issues
Negotiation topics and collective bargaining issues identified specifically by labor laws or court decisions as subject to bargaining

Mandatory Issues Negotiating topics and collective bargaining issues identified specifically by labor laws or court decisions as subject to bargaining are mandatory issues. If either party demands to negotiate on these issues, then they must be included in bargaining. Generally, mandatory issues relate to wages, benefits, nature of jobs, and other work-related subjects. Mandatory subjects for bargaining are shown

FIGURE 16-11 Mandatory Subjects of Collective Bargaining

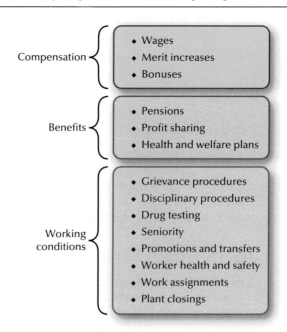

Compensation
- Wages
- Merit increases
- Bonuses

Benefits
- Pensions
- Profit sharing
- Health and welfare plans

Working conditions
- Grievance procedures
- Disciplinary procedures
- Drug testing
- Seniority
- Promotions and transfers
- Worker health and safety
- Work assignments
- Plant closings

Source: Adapted from SHRM.org, http://www.shrm.org/templatestools/hrqa/pages/collectivebargainingsubjects.aspx.

in Figure 16-11. Refusing to bargain over these issues by either management or the union constitutes an unfair labor practice.

Permissive issues
Collective bargaining issues that are not required but might relate to certain jobs or practices

Illegal issues
Collective bargaining issues that would require either party to take illegal action

Permissive Issues In addition to the mandatory subjects of bargaining, there are collective bargaining issues that are not required but might relate to certain jobs or practices. These are categorized as permissive issues, which can be negotiated if both parties agree. Examples of permissive issues include benefits for retired employees, internal union business, designation of negotiators, and use of union labels.[57]

Illegal Issues A final category, illegal issues, includes those collective bargaining issues that would require either party to take illegal action. Examples would be giving preference to union members when hiring employees or demanding a closed-shop provision in the contract. If one side wants to bargain over an illegal issue, the other side can refuse.

16-6 Collective Bargaining Process

The collective bargaining process involved in negotiating a contract consists of four possible stages: preparation and initial demands, negotiations, settlement or impasse, and strikes and lockouts. Throughout the process, management and labor representatives determine the terms and conditions for their ongoing relationship.

16-6a Preparation and Initial Demands

Management and union representatives have a great deal at stake; therefore, they spend substantial time and effort preparing for negotiations. Employer and industry data concerning wages, benefits, working conditions, management and union rights, productivity, safety, and absenteeism are gathered.

Each side presents its list of demands to the other to begin the bargaining process. If the organization argues that it cannot afford to pay what the union is asking, then it must provide evidence of its financial status. The primary focus of bargaining for both union and management is on the mandatory areas of wages, benefits, and working hours and conditions. The amount of rancor or calmness exhibited may set the tone for future negotiations between the parties.

16-6b Continuing Negotiations

After taking initial positions, each side attempts to determine what the other side values highly so that the best bargain can be struck. For example, the union may be asking the employer to pay for dental benefits as part of a package that also includes wage increases and retirement benefits. However, the union may be most interested in the retirement benefits and may be willing to trade the dental payments for better retirement benefits. Management must determine the union's priorities and then decide exactly what to trade in order to reach agreement.

Good Faith Provisions in federal law require that both employer and union bargaining representatives negotiate in good faith. In good-faith negotiations, the parties agree to send negotiators who can bargain and make decisions, rather than people who do not have the authority to commit either group to a decision. To be more effective, meetings between the parties should be conducted professionally and address issues, rather than being confrontational. Refusing to bargain, scheduling meetings at absurdly inconvenient hours, and/or using other conflicting tactics may lead to employers or unions filing complaints with the NLRB.

16-6c Settlement and Contract Agreement

After reaching an initial agreement, the bargaining parties usually return to their respective constituencies to determine if the informal agreement is acceptable. A particularly crucial stage is ratification of the labor agreement, which a process by which union members vote to accept the terms of a negotiated labor agreement. Before ratification, the union negotiating team explains the agreement to the union members and presents it for a vote. If the members approve the agreement, it is then formalized into a contract. Figure 16-12 lists the typical items in a labor agreement.

16-6d Bargaining Impasse

Regardless of the structure of the bargaining process, labor and management do not always reach agreement on the issues. If they reach an impasse, then the disputes can be taken to conciliation, mediation, or arbitration.

Conciliation and Mediation When an impasse occurs, an outside party such as the Federal Mediation and Conciliation Service may help the two deadlocked parties continue negotiations and arrive at a solution. In conciliation, the third party facilitates the dialogue between union and management negotiators to reach a voluntary settlement but makes no proposals for solutions. In mediation, the third party suggests ideas for solutions to help the negotiators reach a settlement.

Ratification
Process by which union members vote to accept the terms of a negotiated labor agreement

Conciliation
Process by which a third party facilitates the dialogue between union and management negotiators to reach a voluntary settlement

Mediation
Process by which a third party suggests ideas to help the negotiators reach a settlement

FIGURE 16-12 Typical Items in a Labor Agreement

Labor Agreement

1. Purpose of agreement
2. Nondiscrimination clause
3. Management rights
4. Recognition of the union
5. Dues checkoff
6. Wages
7. Incentives
8. Hours of work
9. Vacations
10. Sick/absence leaves
11. Discipline
12. Separation allowance
13. Seniority
14. Pension/insurance
15. Safety
16. Grievance procedure
17. No-strike or lockout clause
18. Definitions
19. Terms of contract (dates)
20. Appendices

In conciliation and mediation, the third party does not impose a solution. Sometimes fact finding helps clarify the issues of disagreement as an intermediate step between mediation and arbitration.

Arbitration
Process that uses a neutral third party to make a decision

Arbitration In arbitration, a neutral third party makes a decision. Arbitration can be conducted by an individual or a panel of individuals. "Interest" arbitration attempts to solve bargaining impasses, primarily in the public sector. This type of arbitration is uncommon in the private sector because companies generally do not want an outside party making decisions about their rights, wages, benefits, and other issues. Fortunately, in many situations, agreements are reached through negotiations without the need for arbitration. When disagreements continue, strikes or lockouts may occur.

16-6e Strikes and Lockouts

Lockout
Management shuts down company operations to prevent union members from working

Strike
Union members refuse to work in order to put pressure on an employer

If a deadlock cannot be resolved, an employer may revert to a lockout—or a union may revert to a strike. In a lockout, management shuts down company operations to prevent union members from working. This action may avert possible damage or sabotage to company facilities or injury to employees who continue to work. It also gives management leverage in negotiations.

During a strike, union members refuse to work in order to put pressure on an employer. Often, the striking union members picket or demonstrate against the employer outside the place of business by carrying placards and signs. Five types of strikes can occur, as shown in Figure 16-13.

Between 1947 and 1982, there were typically 200 to 300 work stoppages annually. In 1981, President Reagan ended the air traffic controllers' strike with replacement workers. Since that time, the annual number of work stoppages has dropped to

FIGURE 16-13 Types of Strikes

Economic Strikes	◆ The parties fail to reach agreement during collective bargaining.
Unfair Labor Practices Strikes	◆ Union members leave their jobs over what they feel are illegal employer actions, such as refusal to bargain.
Wildcat Strikes	◆ Occur during the life of the collective-bargaining agreement without approval of union leadership and violate a no-strike clause in a labor contract. Strikers can be discharged or disciplined.
Jurisdictional Strikes	◆ Members of one union walk out to force the employer to assign work to them instead of to members of another union.
Sympathy Strikes	◆ One union chooses to express support for another union involved in a dispute, even though the first union has no disagreement with the employer.

one-tenth of the previous rate.[58] Many unions are reluctant to go on strike because of the financial losses their members would incur or the fear that a strike would cause the employer to go bankrupt. In addition, management has shown its willingness to hire replacements, and some strikes have ended with union workers losing their jobs. See "HR Perspective: Labor Agreement Takes Flight" feature for details about contract negotiations at Boeing.

PERSPECTIVE

Labor Agreement Takes Flight

The threat of a work stoppage by the machinists' union at Boeing did not stop the company from demanding a labor contract that allows it to reduce costs and improve productivity. Boeing was determining where to produce the new version of its 777 long-range jet at the time of labor negotiations with its union workers in Everett, Washington. Company officials told workers that production of major sections of the new aircraft might be assigned to its facility in South Carolina, a right-to-work state, or possibly at a not-yet-established facility in the U.S. Southwest. Several states were wooing the company with tax incentives and other economic rewards to set up operations. The Washington State production facility is the company's oldest and has traditionally been the hub of manufacturing. But high labor costs are making alternate locations more attractive.

The company's threats to move production to a more labor-friendly location played against the union's threat to reject a contract offer and hit the picket lines. Striking is the union's most potent weapon to convince management that its demands are serious. The 32,000 employees represented by the International Association of Machinists (IAM) have had a contentious relationship with Boeing for many years. Labor peace is critical in an industry with long lead times and significant capital investments. Both the company and union understand the importance of good relations, yet somehow they manage to come to terms only after each side has wielded its power.

Initially, the union workers rejected the proposed contract, which included deep concessions on wages, seniority, and retirement benefits. A number of high-profile local and state civic leaders weighed in and urged the union members to accept the deal. After several additional rounds of proposals and counterproposals, the labor agreement was ratified in a 51% to 49% vote. The contract will run for eight years, giving both sides a long-term assurance of certainty. Likewise, the state also offered several financial incentives for Boeing to keep the work in Washington. The final contract delivered a critical element to the company, replacing an expensive defined benefit pension plan with a defined contribution 401(k) plan.

Despite the ability to withhold labor by striking against an employer, this tactic is rarely used because it is costly to employees as well as the company. Unions take to the streets only under circumstances that cannot be resolved in any other way. Boeing and the IAM can now work more cooperatively until the next contract in several years.[59] Answer the following questions about Boeing's business decision regarding the location of its operations:

1. How much weight do you think companies should put on tax and other incentives to locate their operations in a particular state or city? Is it a good thing for taxpayers?

2. If you were a member of the IAM, how would you feel about the company's threats to move the jobs elsewhere? After settling the contract disputes, what would be your level of loyalty and commitment to the company?

Replacement of Workers on Strike Management retains and sometimes uses its ability to simply replace workers who strike. Workers' rights vary depending on the type of strike that occurs. For example, in an economic strike, an employer is free to replace the striking workers. But in an unfair labor practices strike, the workers who want their jobs back at the end of the strike must be reinstated.

16-6f Trends in Union–Management Negotiations

A decline in membership, an increase in business competition, and the availability of more attractive options for handling employee issues have severely weakened interest in unions. These realities have encouraged unions in both the public and private sectors to make more concessions when negotiating with management. For example, the United Auto Workers agreed to a $1 billion reduction in employee benefits and other significant concessions to help American automotive companies after they were bailed out by the federal government.[60] There even has been interest in cooperative arrangements between labor organizers and companies so that both parties achieve success, which is discussed in the next section.

In addition, courts have played a prominent role in clarifying the parameters of collective bargaining arrangements. For example, the Second U.S. Court of Appeals determined that Pratt & Whitney Division's (of United Technology Corporation) plans to close two of its Connecticut-based airplane repair shops breached a collective bargaining arrangement made with the District Lodge 26 union. The ruling was based on the idea that the company had not fully considered labor issues when deciding to close the facilities.[61]

16-7 Union–Management Cooperation

The adversarial relationship that naturally exists between unions and management may lead to strikes and lockouts. However, such conflicts today are relatively rare. Even more encouraging is the recognition on the part of some union leaders and employer representatives that cooperation between management and labor unions offers a useful route if organizations are to compete effectively in the global economy.[62]

During the past decade, firms have engaged in organizational and workplace restructuring in response to competitive pressures in their industries. Restructurings have had significant effects such as lost jobs, changed work rules, and altered job responsibilities. When restructurings occur, unions can take a number of approaches, ranging from resistance to cooperation. More successful organizational restructurings occur when unions have been able to obtain information and share that information with their members to work constructively with the company management at various levels.

16-7a Employee-Involvement Programs

It seems somewhat illogical to suggest that union–management cooperation or involving employees in making suggestions and decisions could be bad, and yet some decisions by the NLRB appear to have done just that. Some historical perspective is required to understand the issues that surrounded the decisions.

In the 1930s, when the Wagner Act was enacted, some employers formed sham company unions, coercing workers into joining them to keep legitimate unions from organizing the employees. As a result, the Wagner Act prohibits employer-dominated labor organizations. These prohibitions were enforced, and company unions disappeared. But the use of employee-involvement programs in organizations today has raised new concerns along these lines.

Because of the Wagner Act, employee-involvement programs set up in past years may be illegal, according to an NLRB decision dealing with Electromation, an Elkhart, Indiana, firm. Electromation used teams of employees to solicit other employees' views about such issues as wages and working conditions. The NLRB labeled these teams *labor organizations,* in line with Wagner Act requirements. It further found that the teams were dominated by management, which had formed them, set their goals, and decided how they would operate. The results of this and other decisions have forced many employers to rethink and restructure their employee-involvement efforts.

Federal court decisions have upheld the NLRB position in some cases and reversed it in others. One key to decisions allowing employee-involvement committees and programs seems to be that these entities should not deal directly with traditional collective bargaining issues such as wages, hours, and working conditions. Other keys are that the committees should be composed primarily of workers and that they have broad authority to make operational suggestions and decisions.

Affinity groups
Groups for employees with a common interest or characteristic

Companies should keep these restrictions in mind when establishing affinity groups for employees with a common interest or characteristic. Affinity groups are usually built around protected status factors such as race, gender, or religion. While affinity groups can be established and encouraged to allow sharing among employees, companies should not seek recommendations about any workplace conditions from the group. It should also be clear that members of the group do not represent interests of other employees; they speak only for themselves.[63]

16-7b Unions and Employee Ownership

In some situations, unions have encouraged workers to become partial or full owners of the companies that employ them. These efforts were spurred by concerns that firms were preparing to shut down, merge, or be bought out. Such results were likely to cut the number of union jobs and workers.

Employee stock ownership plans (ESOPs) for union members have even become popular. Such programs have been successful in some situations because members have purchased all or part of an organization. However, such programs might undermine union support by creating a closer identification with the concerns and goals of employers, instead of union solidarity.

LO5 Define a grievance and identify the stages in a dispute resolution procedure.

16-8 Resolving Disputes

Complaint
Indication of employee dissatisfaction

Grievance
Complaint formally stated in writing

Employee dissatisfaction is a potential source of trouble for employers, whether it is expressed or not. Therefore, it is important that employees have an outlet to register dissatisfaction. A complaint, which is merely an indication of employee dissatisfaction, is one outlet. If an employee who is represented by a union believes that the company has taken an action contrary to the collective bargaining agreement, and submits it in writing, then that complaint becomes a grievance. A grievance is a complaint formally stated in writing.

Management should address both complaints and grievances because they highlight possible issues with workers and potential problems within the workforce. Without a grievance procedure, management may be unaware of employee concerns and unable to respond appropriately. Therefore, a formal grievance procedure provides a valuable communication tool for organizations, whether a union is present or not. A wide variety of grievance procedures and dispute resolution approaches are used to address employee dissatisfaction, particularly in union-free workplaces. For instance, alternative dispute resolution techniques such as mediation, panel assessments, open-door policies, and peer reviews can be effective. Those processes are discussed in Chapter 15. When employees are represented by a union, a formal grievance process, which usually ends in arbitration, is used to resolve problems.[64]

The typical division of responsibilities between the HR unit and operating managers for handling grievances varies considerably from one organization to another, even among unionized firms. The HR unit usually has more general responsibilities. Managers typically attempt to prevent and resolve grievances in order to maintain work unit harmony. Grievance resolutions may constrain future management decisions and actions, so it is important that managers actively participate in the process and handle grievances as quickly and professionally as possible.

16-8a Grievance Procedures

Grievance procedures
Specific steps used to resolve grievances

Grievance procedures are specific steps used to resolve grievances between employees and employers. Many times, first-line supervisors who are closest to a problem act as a primary problem solver in employee grievance cases. However, supervisors can be distracted by other work matters and may even be the subject of an employee's grievance. Consequently, grievances need to be handled with a specified resolution approach so that problems are appropriately resolved.

Union Representation in Grievance Procedures A unionized employee generally has a right to union representation if the employee is being questioned by management and if discipline may result. If these so-called *Weingarten rights* (named after the court case that established them) are violated and the employee is dismissed, he or she usually will be reinstated with back pay. Employers are not required to allow nonunion workers to have coworkers present in grievance procedure meetings. However, employers may voluntarily allow such presence.[65]

16-8b Steps in a Grievance Procedure

Grievance procedures can vary based on what is negotiated in the collective bargaining agreement. At each stage of the process, the goal is to resolve the issue and not proceed to the next step. Figure 16-14 shows a typical grievance procedure, which consists of the following steps:[66]

1. The employee discusses the grievance with the union steward (the representative of the union on the job) and the supervisor.
2. The union steward discusses the grievance with the supervisor's manager and/or the HR manager.
3. A committee of union officers discusses the grievance with appropriate company managers.

25

thorough

go

true

FIGURE 16-14   Steps in a Typical Grievance Procedure

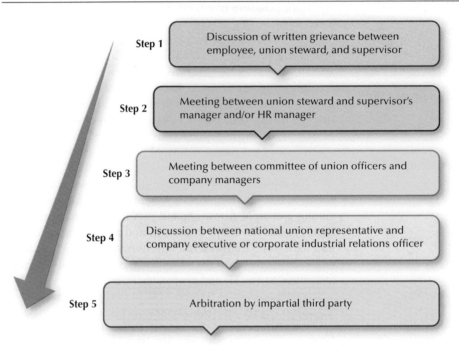

Step 1 — Discussion of written grievance between employee, union steward, and supervisor

Step 2 — Meeting between union steward and supervisor's manager and/or HR manager

Step 3 — Meeting between committee of union officers and company managers

Step 4 — Discussion between national union representative and company executive or corporate industrial relations officer

Step 5 — Arbitration by impartial third party

4. The representative of the national union discusses the grievance with designated company executives or the corporate industrial relations officer.
5. If the grievance is not solved at this stage, it goes to arbitration. An impartial third party may ultimately dispose of the grievance.

Grievance arbitration
Means by which a third party settles disputes arising from different or conflicting interpretations of a labor contract

Grievance arbitration is a means by which a third party settles disputes arising from different or conflicting interpretations of a labor contract.[67] This process should not be confused with contract or issues arbitration, discussed earlier, in which arbitration is used to determine how a contract will be written. The U.S. Supreme Court has ruled that grievance arbitration decisions issued under labor contract provisions are enforceable and generally may not be overturned by the courts. In essence, the arbitrator has the final word on the decision. Grievance arbitration includes many topic areas, with discipline and discharge, safety and health, and security being common concerns.

LO6 Understand the differences in how unions operate in the global arena.

GLOBAL

16-9 Unions in the Global Arena

Globalization increases the degree to which there is economic competition among workers, companies, and nations. As such, the ability of a country to remain competitive (i.e., increasing the availability of jobs and attracting foreign direct investment) is often influenced by its labor laws and attitude toward labor unions. In some nations, unions have relatively limited bargaining power compared to the bargaining power of employers. However, in other countries, this is not the case. Diverse legal requirements and social mores have created very different situations around the world, so HR professionals should be aware of these variations when operating globally.

Many developing nations are experiencing many of the same issues regarding treatment of workers as U.S. employers did during the Industrial Revolution in the early 1900s.[68] As the world economy becomes more integrated, unions worldwide are facing changes. The status of global unions is being affected in several ways.

16-9a International Union Issues

The percentage of union membership varies significantly from country to country. The highest is in the Scandinavian countries, followed by countries in continental Europe.[69] Collective bargaining is set in law as the way wages are to be determined in Europe. However, in many European countries, artificially high wages and generous benefits have kept the unemployment rate high. Given these realities, the pressures for change are increasing. The range of labor concerns is quite wide and varies from country to country, with some countries most concerned about child labor; others' most pressing issues involve safety practices or employee participation in decisions.

In some countries, unions do not exist at all, are relatively weak, or are closely tied to political parties. For instance, in Italy and France, national strikes occur regularly to protest proposed changes in government policy on retirement, pension programs, and regulations regarding dismissal of employees. In recent years, pilots at French and German airlines staged strikes to protest proposed reductions in their generous benefit packages.[70] Auto workers in South Africa have used work stoppages to demand higher pay, which has resulted in lower foreign investment in the country.[71] Spain's National Court invalidated the layoff of 800 Coca-Cola workers after the company cut back its operation due to decreasing revenues and overcapacity in its facilities.[72] Labor unrest is not uncommon, and work stoppages, protests, and strikes occur in many countries.

Codetermination
Practice in which union or worker representatives are given positions on a company's board of directors

Some countries require the practice of codetermination in which union or worker representatives are given positions on a company's board of directors. This practice is common in European countries, and it led to a clashing of cultures and practices at the Chattanooga, Tennessee, Volkswagen facility. Since the company is German owned and operated, management favored involving workers on the board of directors. This would have required that the employees form a labor union, a position that was supported by company managers. Workers disagreed and elected not to organize a union. The end-of-chapter case highlights the events at this facility.[73] Differences from country to country in how collective bargaining occurs are also quite noticeable. In the United States, local unions bargain with individual employers to set wages and working conditions. In Australia, unions argue their cases before arbitration tribunals. In Scandinavia, national agreements with associations of employers are the norm. In France and Germany, industry-wide or regional agreements are common. In Japan, local unions bargain but combine at some point to determine national wage patterns.

16-9b Global Labor Organizations

Several organizations address global labor relations standards. The International Labour Organization, based in Switzerland, coordinates the efforts of labor unions worldwide and has issued some principles about rights at work. Such coordination is occurring as unions deal with multinational firms with operations in multiple countries.

Throughout the world, unions are also linking up as part of global labor federations. The Union International Network (UIN) is an entity composed of unions from numerous countries. This organization and other international groups are working to establish international policies on child labor, worker safety and health, and training.

The UIN is also providing aid and guidance to unions in developing countries, such as those in Africa and Asia. Unions in the United States are very active in these global entities. In some situations, establishing agreements with employers based in the European Union has led to more U.S. union membership in multinational firms.

16-9c The United States and Global Differences

Union management relations in the United States addresses some issues differently from other countries. In the United States, the key union focuses have been the following:

- *Economic issues vs. other concerns*: In the United States, unions have typically focused on improving bread-and-butter issues for their members—wages, benefits, job security, and working conditions. In some other countries, integration with ruling governmental and political power and activism are equal concerns along with economic issues. In the United Kingdom, labor unions provide training programs that improve worker readiness and allow companies to hire a highly skilled workforce.
- *Organization by kind of job and employer*: In the United States, carpenters often belong to the carpenters' union, truck drivers to the Teamsters, teachers to the American Federation of Teachers or the National Education Association, and so on. Also, unionization can be done on a company-by-company basis. In other countries, national unions bargain with the government or with employer groups.
- *Collective agreements as "contracts"*: In the United States, collective bargaining contracts usually spell out compensation, work rules, and the conditions of employment for several years. In other countries, the agreements are made with the government and employers, sometimes for only one year because of political and social issues.
- *Competitive relations*: In the United States, management and labor traditionally take the roles of competing adversaries who often clash to reach agreement. In many other countries, tripartite bargaining occurs between the national government, employers' associations, and national labor federations with little conflict or obstruction.

Labor laws impact the relationship between companies and their workers, whether a union represents employees or not. Managers and HR professionals strive to create a work environment that is productive, fair, and respectful. Taking steps to identify and address worker concerns can set the stage for positive interactions and outcomes for employers and employees alike.

SUMMARY

- A union is a formal association of workers that promotes the interests of its members through collective action.
- Workers join unions primarily because of management's failure to address organizational and job-related concerns.
- In the early 1990s, unions fought difficult battles to overcome powerful companies and earned the right to organize.

- The history of unions in the United States indicates that they primarily focus on wages, hours, and working conditions.
- In the United States, current union membership as a percentage of the workforce is down dramatically, being less than 12% of the civilian workforce.
- Unions in general have experienced a decline in membership because of geographic, industrial, and workforce changes.

- In attempts to grow, unions are targeting professionals, low-skilled workers, and contingent and part-time workers.
- Public-sector unions have recently come under attack, and some states have limited their power.
- Three laws provide the foundation of labor law and the legal basis for labor relations today: the Wagner Act, the Taft-Hartley Act, and the Landrum-Griffin Act.
- The Wagner Act was designed to protect unions and workers; the Taft-Hartley Act restored some powers to management; and the Landrum-Griffin Act was passed to protect individual union members.
- Issues addressed by the different acts include unfair labor practices, national emergency strikes, and right-to-work provisions.
- The NLRB has issued a number of controversial rulings that impact both union and union-free workplaces.
- The unionization process includes an organizing campaign, authorization cards, a representation election, certification and decertification, and contract negotiation through collective bargaining.
- Collective bargaining occurs when management negotiates with representatives of workers over wages, hours, and working conditions.
- The issues subject to collective bargaining fall into three categories: mandatory, permissive, and illegal.
- The collective bargaining process includes preparation and initial demands, negotiations, and settlement and contract agreement.
- When an impasse occurs during bargaining, work stoppages through strikes or lockouts can be used to pressure the other party.
- Union–management cooperation has been beneficial in many situations, although care must be taken to avoid violations of NLRB provisions.
- Grievances express workers' written dissatisfactions or differences in contract interpretations.
- A grievance procedure begins with the first-level supervisor and may end—if the grievance is not resolved along the way—with arbitration by a third party.
- Unions are becoming more global as the world economy expands, and global labor federations are expanding, despite differences in approaches.

CRITICAL THINKING CHALLENGES

1. Discuss the following statement: If management gets a union, it deserves one.

2. Suppose a coworker just brought you a union leaflet urging employees to sign an authorization card. What questions would you ask of the union supporter? What may happen from this point on?

3. As the HR manager, you have heard rumors about potential efforts to unionize your warehouse employees. Use the Employment Law Information Network (www.elinfonet.com/human-resources/Union-Avoidance) website to develop a set of guidelines for supervisors if they are asked questions by employees about unionization as part of a "union prevention" approach.

4. Several states have limited public-sector union power. What are some reasons for lawmakers taking this stand? What are the advantages and disadvantages of workers in the public sector belonging to labor unions? How does this impact taxpayers?

5. There has been some discussion among the employees in your company's insurance claims processing unit about forming a union. Company management has asked you to research existing labor agreements in the industry. You utilize the Department of Labor's Office of Labor-Management Standards website and access a collective bargaining agreement from the Online Public Disclosure Room (http://www.dol.gov/olms/regs/compliance/rrlo/lmrda.htm). You find the contract between the American National Insurance Company and the United Food and Commercial Workers. The UFCW is the union your employees are talking to, so you want to see how they have

worked with other employers. You review the contract and highlight points that you think are interesting and notable.

A. Assess the Management Rights clause. Has the company retained important rights, or does it appear that the union has substantial power to direct business operations? Are there additional rights you think should be retained by the company?

Has the union included language to protect its own security and interests?

B. Evaluate the compensation and benefits that employees receive. Is paid time off adequate or overly generous? Do employees receive generous retirement benefits? What is your overall evaluation of how "tough" the union is likely to be if your employees elect it as a representative?

CASE Driving Away the UAW

Volkswagen (VW) Motors is a German-headquartered automobile manufacturer. A common practice in German companies is to utilize a "works council," a supervisory body made up of workers and managers who consult on business operations. U.S. labor laws strictly forbid such worker involvement without the official recognition of a labor union. So, the UAW saw an opportunity to organize workers at the VW Chattanooga, Tennessee, plant with the blessing of company management. Since the plant is overseen by German leadership, the union felt it would be supported in its efforts. However, workers at the plant would have the final say regarding union representation.

VW management did, in fact, seem to be on the UAW's side and had agreed to allow the union to be recognized based on a card check procedure rather than a representation election. The company allowed union organizers to campaign inside the plant, a highly unusual move. The labor union in Germany, a "cousin" of the UAW, had pushed for the welcoming posture to the U.S. union. Company and German union officials were highly committed to establishing a works council and felt that allowing the UAW to organize workers would allow that process to happen.

The company had pledged to remain neutral, but many of its actions appeared to strongly assist the union in its efforts. Not all employees at the plant favored representation by the union, but they were denied the right to hold meetings or campaign inside the plant. Such collusion between a company and union is potentially a violation of the Taft-Hartley Act. Workers insisted on the right to a secret ballot election, and the company eventually agreed.

In the highly contested battle, workers voted 712–626 not to join the UAW. With the undeniable support from the company, the UAW could hardly look for unfair labor practice violations. The vote was clear. Workers prefer dealing directly with plant management and working without labor union representation. In the weeks and months following the election, the UAW initially requested that the NLRB schedule a do-over election. Their contention was that local and state politicians had swayed workers with a promise of economic benefits if the workforce remained union free. They eventually dropped their request and accepted the no vote from the workers.

Since the election, the UAW has established an "American-style works council," a nonbargaining-unit local of the union. The group will meet with company representatives to discuss workplace issues but will not be empowered to negotiate a contract. The UAW remains hopeful that this works council will serve as a jumping off point for a full-fledged union in the future.[74]

QUESTIONS

1. Under what circumstances might a company side with a union in its attempt to organize employees? How would you, as an employee, feel if your employer supported you joining a union?

2. What role should politicians and lawmakers play in union votes such as the one in Chattanooga? Do lawmakers have a vested interest in the success of businesses within their legislative territory?

SUPPLEMENTAL CASES

Teamsters and the Fraternal Order of Police (FOP)

This case discusses how unions sometimes compete to represent workers and explores experiences at the Denver Sheriff's Department. (For the case, go to www.cengage.com/management/mathis.)

Walmart and Union Prevention

This case covers Walmart's efforts to stay nonunion. (For the case, go to www.cengage.com/management/mathis.)

The Wilson County Hospital

This case deals with labor disputes in a unionized hospital. (For the case, go to www.cengage.com/management/mathis.)

END NOTES

1. Based on Kate Everson, "Union Up and Fly Right," *Chief Learning Officer*, July 2014, p. 29.

2. Based on Allen Smith, "College Football Players Persuade NLRB They Are Employees," *SHRM Online*, March 27, 2014, http://www.shrm.org/legalissues/federalresources/pages/college-football-players.aspx; Alejandra Cancino, "Northwestern, Union Square off in Football Labor Filings," *Chicago Tribune*, August 1, 2014; Douglas Belkin, Melanie Trottman, and Rachel Bachman, "College's Football Team Can Unionize," *Wall Street Journal*, March 27, 2014, p. A2; Melanie Trottman, "NLRB Sacks Northwestern Football Players' Unionizing Drive," *Wall Street Journal*, August 17, 2015, http://www.wsj.com/articles/nlrb-declines-to-decide-whether-northwestern-football-players-can-unionize-1439828380; Ben Strauss, "NLRB Rejects Northwestern Football Players' Union Bid," *New York Times*, August 17, 2015, http://www.nytimes.com/2015/08/18/sports/ncaafootball/nlrb-says-northwestern-football-players-cannot-unionize.html?_r=0.

3. Joanne Deschenaux, "NLRB Not Just for Unionized Workforces, *SHRM Online*, June 19, 2013, http://www.shrm.org/publications/hrnews/pages/nlrb-not-just-for-unionized-workforces.aspx; Kate Everson, "Learning to Work with Unions," *Chief Learning Officer*, July 2014, pp. 26–29.

4. Pew Research, "Favorable Views of Business, Labor Rebound," *Pew Research Center for the People & the Press*, June 27, 2013, http://www.people-press.org/2013/06/27/favorable-views-of-business-labor-rebound.

5. Michele Campolieti, Rafael Gomez, and Morley Gunderson, "Managerial Hostility and Attitudes towards Unions: A Canada-US Comparison," *Journal of Labor Research* 34, no. 1 (March 2013), 99–119.

6. Susan Carey, "American Airlines Flight Attendants Reject Contract Offer," *Wall Street Journal*, November 10, 2014, p. B3; Susan Carey, "American, Pilots Continue to Talk," *Wall Street Journal*, November 24, 2014, p. B4; Kris Maher, "Unions Set Pact for US Airways-AMR Merger," *Wall Street Journal*, May 15, 2013, p. B7.

7. George Long, "Differences between Union and Nonunion Compensation, 2001–2011," *Monthly Labor Review* 136, no. 4 (April 2013), 16–23.

8. Sharon Terlep, "GM Rethinks Pay for Unionized Workers," *Wall Street Journal*, January 12, 2011, p. B6.

9. Kate Everson, "Learning to Work with Unions," *Chief Learning Officer*, July 3, 2014, http://www.clomedia.com/articles/5708-learning-to-work-with-unions.

10. History.com Staff, "Labor Movement," *History.com*, 2009, http://www.history.com/topics/labor.

11. Allen Lutins, "An Eclectic List of Events in U.S. Labor History," February 26, 2013, http://www.lutins.org/labor.html.

12. BLS.gov, "Union Members, 2013," January 24, 2014, http://www.bls.gov/news.release/pdf/union2.pdf.

13. BLS.gov, "Union Members, 2013," January 24, 2014, http://www.bls.gov/news.release/pdf/union2.pdf.

14. BLS.gov, "Union Members, 2013," January 24, 2014, http://www.bls.gov/news.release/pdf/union2.pdf.

15. Allen Smith, "Battle-Tested Big Labor Has Some Cause for Optimism," *SHRM Online*, August 29, 2014, http://www.shrm.org/legalissues/federalresources/pages/labor-2014.aspx; Drew Desilver, "American Unions Membership Declines as Public Support Fluctuates," *Pew Research Center*, February 20, 2014, http://www.pewresearch.org/fact-tank/2014/02/20/for-american-unions-membership-trails-far-behind-public-support/; Omer Turgrul Acikgoz and Baris Kaymak, "The Rising Skill Premium and Deunionization," *Journal of Monetary Economics* 63 (April 2014), 37–50.

16. Max Mihelich, "Labor Daze," *Workforce*, April 2014, pp. 22–31.

17. Jeff Bennett, "Tire Makers' New Home," *Wall Street Journal*, April 11, 2012.

18. Kyong-Ae Choi, "Worker Unrest Hits Hyundai," *Wall Street Journal*, August 8, 2012, p. B2; Han Yan Yuan, "Protests, Suicide: China's Labor Unrest Leads to Reform," *CNN World.com*, September 5, 2014, http://www.cnn.com/2014/09/05/world/asia/china-labor-union-reform/.

19. Brad Stone, "Amazon Employees Vote to Reject Union," *Bloomberg Businessweek*, November 23, 2014, http://www.businessweek.com/articles/2014-01-15/amazon-employees-vote-to-reject-union; Verne Kopytoff, "How Amazon Crushed the Union Movement," *Business.Time.com*, January 16, 2014, http://time.com/956/how-amazon-crushed-the-union-movement; Sarah Sloat, "Amazon Faces Further Strife," *Wall Street Journal*, December 17, 2013.

20. Kris Maher, "Mine Workers Union Shrinks but Boss Fights On," *Wall Street Journal*, January 9, 2014.

21. Benjamin Artz, "Does the Impact of Union Experience on Job Satisfaction Differ by Gender?" *Industrial & Labor Relations Review* 65, no. 2 (April 2012), 225–243.

22. Richard B. Freeman, "The War against Public Sector Collective Bargaining in the US," The Journal of Industrial Relations 54, no. 3 (June 2012), 386–408; Amity Shlaes, "Public Unions vs. the Public," *Wall Street Journal*, January 16, 2015, p. A11.

23. Allysia Finley, "The Democrat Who Took on the Unions," *Wall Street Journal*, March 24, 2012, p. A13; Daniel DiSalvo, "The Changing Politics of Public Sector Pensions," *Realclearpolicy.com*, October 23, 2013, http://www.realclearpolicy.com/articles/2013/10/23/the_changing_politics_of_public_sector_pensions_703.html; Mark Funkhouser, "The Reforms That Public Pensions Really Need," *Governing.com*, January 21, 2014, http://www.governing.com/gov-institute/funkhouser/col-rockefeller-institute-reform-public-pension-defined-benefit.html; Jennifer Hickey, "Coming Pension Meltdown: The 10 Most Troubled City Systems," *Newsmax.com*, November 11, 2013, http://www.newsmax.com/Newsfront/city-pension-shortfall-underfunded/2013/11/11/id/536027.

24. Editor, "A Keystone Paycheck Reform," *Wall Street Journal*, January 25, 2014; Akash Chougule, "It's Working in Wisconsin: High Court Upholds Act 10," *Forbes.com*, August 12, 2014, http://www.forbes.com/sites/realspin/2014/08/12/its-working-in-wisconsin-high-court-upholds-act-10.

25. Kevin Donovan, "Civil Litigation and Other Nontraditional Union Tactics in Labor-Management Disputes: Legal Protection Available to 'Secondary Targets'," *Employee Relations Law Journal* 40, no. 1 (Summer 2014), 16–21.

26. Editor, "Members Not Only," *Wall Street Journal*, September 16, 2013.

27. Richard Berman, "The Labor Movement's New Blood," *Wall Street Journal*, September 13, 2013, p. A15; Robert Grossman, "Leading from Behind?" *HR Magazine*, December 2013, pp. 37–41; Claire Zillman, "Amazon Union Push: Practically Built to Fail," *CNN Money.com*, January 17, 2014, http://fortune.com/2014/01/17/amazon-union-push-practically-built-to-fail.

28. Allen Smith, "Black Friday Will Bring More Protests at Wal-Mart," *SHRM Online*, November 19, 2014; Shelly Banjo and Melanie Trottman, "Wal-Mart Fights Back on Strikes," *Wall Street Journal*, February 3, 2014.

29. Erin Hatton, "Temporary Weapons: Employers' Use of Temps against Organized Labor," *Industrial & Labor Relations Review* 67, no. 1 (January 2014), 86–110.

30. Jill Cueni-Cohen, "Separate Companies, Joint Employers?" *HRE Online*, July 7, 2014, http://www.hreonline.com/HRE/view/story.jhtml?id=534357284; Allen Smith, "NLRB General Counsel: McDonald's Is Joint Employer with Franchisees," *SHRM Online*, July 30, 2014, http://www.shrm.org/legalissues/federalresources/pages/nlrb-joint-employers.aspx; Melanie Trottman, "NLRB Case Tests Who Employs Contract Workers," *Wall Street Journal*, August 27, 2014.

31. SHRM, "Norris-LaGuardia Act of 1932," *SHRM Online*, http://www.shrm.org/legalissues/federalresources/federalstatutesregulationsandguidanc/pages/norris-laguardiaactof1932.aspx.

32. Employment Laws.com, "Wagner Act," http://employment.laws.com/wagner-act; NLRB.gov, "National Labor Relations Act," *NLRB.gov*, http://www.nlrb.gov/resources/national-labor-relations-act.

33. NLRB.gov, "Charges and Complaints," http://www.nlrb.gov/news-outreach/graphs-data/charges-and-complaints/charges-and-complaints.

34. NLRB.gov, "1947 Taft-Hartley Substantive Provisions," http://www.nlrb.gov/who-we-are/our-history/1947-taft-hartley-substantive-provisions.

35. Neil Shah and Ben Casselman, "Right-to-Work Economics," *Wall Street Journal*, December 15, 2012.

36. Christopher Surfield, "Government Mandates and Atypical Work: An Investigation of Right-to-Work States," *Eastern Economic Journal* 40, no. 1 (Winter 2014), 26–55.

37. Allen Smith, "NLRB May Legitimize Union Fees in Right-to-Work States," *SHRM Online*, May 5, 2015. http://www.shrm.org/hrdisciplines/laborrelations/articles/pages/nlrb-union-fees.aspx.

38. Employment Laws.com, "Landrum-Griffin Act," http://employment.laws.com/landrum-griffin-act; NLRB.gov, "1959 Landrum-Griffin Act," http://www.nlrb.gov/who-we-are/our-history/1959-landrum-griffin-act.

39. U.S. DOL.gov, "Union Reports, Other Reports, and Collective Bargaining Agreements," *Online Public Disclosure Room*, http://www.dol.gov/olms/regs/compliance/rrlo/lmrda.htm.

40. Melanie Trottman, "Board Faces a Scramble to Revisit Cases," *Wall Street Journal*, June 27, 2014, p. A2; U.S. Chamber of Commerce, "Recess Appointments Litigation Resource Page," http://www.chamberlitigation.com/recess-appointments-litigation-resource-page; Joanne Deschenaux, "High Court Rules NLRB Appointments Unconstitutional," *SHRM Online*, June 26, 2014.

41. Margaret Lucero, Robert Allen, and Brian Elzweig, "Managing Employee Social Networking: Evolving Views from the National Labor Relations Board," *Employee Responsibilities & Rights Journal* 25, no. 3 (September 2013), 143–158; Denise Keyser and Mary Cate Gordon, "Good and Bad News for Your Social Media Policy," *Employee Benefit News*, March 2012, p. 25; Sheryl Halpern and Charles Gardner, "NLRB Offers Long-Awaited Guidance on Social Media," *Employee Benefit News*, February 2013, p. 12.

42. Melanie Trottman, "Labor Unions Win Key Email Ruling," *Wall Street Journal*, December 12, 2014, p. B3; Allen Smith, "NLRB Invites Input on Using Employers' E-mail for Organizing," *SHRM Online*, May 8,

2014, http://www.shrm.org/legalissues/federalresources/pages/nlrb–email–organizing.aspx.

43. Allen Smith, "Personal Conduct Policy Rules Overbroad," *SHRM Online*, April 8, 2014, http://www.shrm.org/legalissues/federalresources/pages/personal–conduct–policy.aspx; Melissa Gonzalez Boyce, "NLRB Actions Increasingly Target Nonunion-Employer Policy Provisions," *Employment Relations Today* 41, no. 1 (Spring 2014), 41–46; Editorial, "The Hooters Precedent," *Wall Street Journal*, September 23, 2014; Loren Forrest and Frederick Braid, "Recent NLRB Decisions Condone Workplace Profanity and Insubordination," September 16, 2014, *Mondaq.com*, http://www.mondaq.com/unitedstates/x/340472/employee+rights+labour+relations/Recent+NLRB+Decisions+Condone+Workplace+Profanity+and+Insubordination.

44. Melissa Gonzalez Boyce, "NLRB Actions Increasingly Target Nonunion-Employer Policy Provisions," *Employment Relations Today* 41, no. 1 (Spring 2014), 41–46; Jon Hyman, "Another One Bites the Dust: NLRB Invalidates Confidentiality Policy," *Workforce.com*, February 11, 2014, http://www.workforce.com/blogs/3-the-practical-employer/post/20257-another-one-bites-the-dust-nlrb-invalidates-confidentiality-policy.

45. Allen Smith, "NLRB Recognizes Departmental Micro Bargaining Unit at Macy's," *SHRM online*, July 31, 2014; Eric Stuart, "NLRB Decisions on 'Micro-Units' Provide Guidance for Employers Concerned with Union Organizing," August 7, 2014, *OgletreeDeakins.com*, http://blog.ogletreedeakins.com/nlrb-decisions-on-micro-units-provide-guidance-for-employers-concerned-with-union-organizing/#sthash.GTNSJqQ2.dpuf; Allen Smith, "Unions Get Green Light to Organize Microunits," *HR Magazine*, October 2013, p. 8.

46. Allen Smith, "Ambush Election Rule Catches Many Employers Flat-Footed," *SHRM Online*, April 13, 2015, http://www.shrm.org/hrdisciplines/laborrelations/articles/pages/ambush-effective.aspx; Harold P. Coxson, "Is an 'Ambush' the Best Way for Unions to Win Representation Elections?" *Ogletreedeakins.com*, February 6, 2014, http://blog.ogletreedeakins.com/is-an-ambush-the-best-way-for-unions-to-win-representation-elections/#sthash.QgHqCi6i.dpuf;

47. NLRB.gov, "McDonald's Fact Sheet," http://www.nlrb.gov/news-outreach/fact-sheets/mcdonalds-fact-sheet; Melanie Trottman and Julie Jargon, "NLRB Names McDonald's as 'Joint-Employer' at Its Franchises," *Wall Street Journal*, December 19, 2014; Kate Taylor, "Franchise Industry Strikes Back at NLRB's 'Joint Employer' Decision," *Entrepreneur*, September 23, 2014, http://www.entrepreneur.com/article/237759; Office of Public Affairs, "NLRB Office of the General Counsel Issues Consolidated Complaints against McDonald's Franchisees and their Franchisor McDonald's, USA, LLC as Joint Employers," *NLRB.gov*, December 19, 2014, http://www.nlrb.gov/news-outreach/news-story/nlrb-office-general-counsel-issues-consolidated-complaints-against.

48. Melanie Trottman, "Franchisees Buck Wage Push," *Wall Street Journal*, November 24, 2014, p. A3; Julie Jargon and Kris Maher, "Fast-Food Chains Face Protests," *Wall Street Journal*, August 30, 2013, p. B3; Harold Meyerson, "Unions Try New Models for Future Growth," *Cleveland Plain Dealer*, May 19, 2013, p. G6.

49. SHRM Knowledge Center, "How Can We Prevent a Union from Organizing in Our Company?" *SHRM Online*, May 11, 2012, http://www.shrm.org/templatestools/hrqa/pages/preventunionorganization.aspx.

50. Jon Hyman, "Soliciting Is One Tough Cookie," *Workforce*, July 2014, p. 22.

51. David Shadovitz, "Revamping the 'Advice Exemption'," *Human Resource Executive*, May 2014, p. 10.

52. *Toering Electric Co.*, 351 NLRB No. 18 (September 29, 2009).

53. Michael J. Burns, "'Supervisor': The Differences between the FLSA, NLRA and Title VII Definitions," *American Society of Employers*, April 2, 2014, https://www.aseonline.org/ArticleDetailsPage/tabid/7442/ArticleID/852/%E2%80%9CSupervisor%E2%80%9D-The-Differences-Between-the-FLSA-NLRA-and-Title-VII-Definitions.aspx.

54. SHRM Knowledge Center, "Union Organizing: What Can Management Do during a Union Campaign?" *SHRM Online*, June 1, 2012, http://www.shrm.org/templatestools/hrqa/pages/unioncampaigns.aspx.

55. *14 Penn Plaza LLCV v. Pyett*, No. 07-581 (S. Ct. 2009).

56. Steven Greenhouse, "Wisconsin's Legacy for Unions," *New York Times*, February 22, 2014, http://www.nytimes.com/2014/02/23/business/wisconsins-legacy-for-unions.html?_r=0.

57. SHRM Knowledge Center, "Collective Bargaining: What Subjects Are to Be Considered during Collective Bargaining?" *SHRM Online*, June 1, 2012, http://www.shrm.org/templatestools/hrqa/pages/collectivebargainingsubjects.aspx.

58. BLS.gov, "Work Stoppages Involving 1,000 or More Workers, 1947–2013," http://www.bls.gov/news.release/wkstp.t01.htm.

59. Based on Holman Jenkins, "Why Boeing's Win Matters," *Wall Street Journal*, January 8, 2014; Jon Ostrower, "New Boeing Pact Wins Cost Controls," *Wall Street Journal*, January 6, 2014, p. B3; Jon Ostrower, "Boeing, Union Trade Barbs after Talks Fail," *Wall Street Journal*, December 14, 2013.

60. Dale Kasler, "Unions Fight to Retain Role in Workplace," *Denver Post*, May 6, 2012, p. 4K.

61. Angela H. France, "Plant Closure Plan Halted for Violation of Collective Bargaining Agreement," *HR Magazine*, October 2010, p. 102.

62. Deborah Balser and Anne Winkler, "Worker Behavior on the Job: A Multi-Methods Study of Labor Cooperation with Management," *Journal of Labor Research* 33, no. 3 (September 2012), 388–413.

63. Jonathan Segal, "Affinity Group Danger Zones," *HR Magazine*, September 2013, pp. 75–80.

64. Bernard Walker and Robert T. Hamilton, "Employee-Employer Grievances: A Review," *International Journal of Management Reviews* 13 (2011), 40–58.

65. Alexander Colvin, "Participation versus Procedures in Non-Union Dispute Resolution," *Industrial Relations* 52, supp. 1 (January 2013), 259–283.

66. Yost, Edward, "What Are the Steps Typically Found in a Grievance Procedure?" *HR Magazine* 57, no. 5 (May 2012), 21.

67. SHRM Knowledge Center, "Dispute Resolution: Arbitration. What Are the Steps of the Arbitration Process?" *SHRM online*, June 1, 2012, http://www.shrm.org/templatestools/hrqa/pages/arbitrationprocess.aspx.

68. Syed Zain Al-Mahmood and Shelly Banjo, "In Bangladesh, Labor Activists Say They Were Beaten," *Wall Street Journal*, April 14, 2014, p. B3.

69. Organization for Economic Co-Operation and Development, "Trade Union Density," *OECD .Stat Extracts*, November 30, 2014, http://stats.oecd.org/Index .aspx?DataSetCode=UN_DEN.

70. William Boston and Natalia Drozdiak, "Lufthansa's Pilots Prepare to Strike in Benefits Dispute," *Wall Street Journal*, December 1, 2014, p. B3; David Gauthier-Villars, "Air France Pilots Defend 'Gourmet' Contracts," *Wall Street Journal*, September 26, 2014, p. B1; Caitlan Reeg, "Lufthansa Pilots Walk out to Protest Benefit Changes," *Wall Street Journal*, April 3, 2014, p. B5.

71. Devon Maylie, "South Africa Unionist Sparks Alarm," *Wall Street Journal*, October 28, 2013; Devon Maylie, "South Africa's Troubles Hit Car Makers," *Wall Street Journal*, October 5, 2013.

72. Ana Garcia, "Spanish Court Voids Layoffs at Coca-Cola Bottler," *Wall Street Journal*, June 14, 2014, p. B4; Matt Moffett and Ana Garcia, "Spanish Coke Bottler Clashes with Unions," *Wall Street Journal*, February 24, 2014, p. B3.

73. Holman Jenkins, "Tennessee vs. Germany at VW," *Wall Street Journal*, September 18, 2013.

74. Christina Rogers, "UAW Plans Another Push at Volkswagen," *Wall Street Journal*, September 8, 2014, p. B3; Zan Blue and David Phippen, "UAW Puts Brakes on Objections to Volkswagen Election," *SHRM online*, April 22, 2014, http://www.shrm.org/legalissues/federalresources/pages/uaw-volkswagen-election.aspx; Kerri Reeves, "Will Works Councils Work Here?" *HRE Online*, March 27, 2014, http://www.hreonline.com/HRE/view/story.jhtml?id=534356876; Melanie Trottman, "UAW Wants U.S. to Call for Revote at Volkswagen," *Wall Street Journal*, February 22, 2014, p. B4; Holman Jenkins, "The UAW Never Had a Chance," *Wall Street Journal*, February 19, 2014, p. A11.

PHR® and SPHR® Bodies of Knowledge and Test Specifications[1]

The Professional in Human Resources (PHR®) and Senior Professional in Human Resources (SPHR®) exams are created using the PHR and SPHR Body of Knowledge, which outlines the responsibilities of and knowledge needed by today's HR professional. The PHR and SPHR Body of Knowledge is created by HR subject matter experts through a rigorous practice analysis study and validated by HR professionals working in the field through an extensive survey instrument. It is updated periodically to ensure it is consistent with current practices in the HR field.

Functional Areas:

01: Business Management & Strategy (11%/30%)

Developing, contributing to, and supporting the organization's mission, vision, values, strategic goals and objectives; formulating policies; guiding and leading the change process; and evaluating organizational effectiveness as an organizational leader.

Responsibilities:

01 Interpret and apply information related to the organization's operations from internal sources, including finance, accounting, business development, marketing, sales, operations, and information technology, to contribute to the development of the organization's strategic plan.

02 Interpret information from external sources related to the general business environment, industry practices and developments, technological advances, economic environment, labor force, and the legal and regulatory environment, to contribute to the development of the organization's strategic plan.

03 Participate as a contributing partner in the organization's strategic planning process (e.g., provide and lead workforce planning discussion with management, develop and present long-term forecast of human capital needs at the organizational level). *SPHR only*

04 Establish strategic relationships with key individuals in the organization to influence organizational decision making.

05 Establish relationships/alliances with key individuals and outside organizations to assist in achieving the organization's strategic goals and objectives (e.g., corporate social responsibility and community partnership).

06 Develop and utilize business metrics to measure the achievement of the organization's strategic goals and objectives (e.g., key performance indicators, balanced scorecard). *SPHR only*

07 Develop, influence, and execute strategies for managing organizational change that balance the expectations and needs of the organization, its employees, and other stakeholders.

---

[1] Information taken from PHR® and SPHR® BODIES OF KNOWLEDGE document (HRCI), http://www.hrci.org/docs/default-source/web-files/phr_sphr-body-of-knowledge-pdf.pdf?sfvrsn=14.

08   Develop and align the human resource strategic plan with the organization's strategic plan. *SPHR only*

09   Facilitate the development and communication of the organization's core values, vision, mission, and ethical behaviors.

10   Reinforce the organization's core values and behavioral expectations through modeling, communication, and coaching.

11   Provide data such as human capital projections and costs that support the organization's overall budget.

12   Develop and execute business plans (i.e., annual goals and objectives) that correlate with the organization's strategic plan's performance expectations to include growth targets, new programs/services, and net income expectations. *SPHR only*

13   Perform cost-benefit analyses on proposed projects. *SPHR only*

14   Develop and manage an HR budget that supports the organization's strategic goals, objectives, and values. *SPHR only*

15   Monitor the legislative and regulatory environment for proposed changes and their potential impact to the organization, taking appropriate proactive steps to support, modify, or oppose the proposed change.

16   Develop policies and procedures to support corporate governance initiatives (e.g., whistle-blower protection, code of ethics). *SPHR only*

17   Participate in enterprise risk management by ensuring that policies contribute to protecting the organization from potential risks.

18   Identify and evaluate alternatives and recommend strategies for vendor selection and/or out-sourcing. *SPHR only*

19   Oversee or lead the transition and/or implementation of new systems, service centers, and outsourcing. *SPHR only*

20   Participate in strategic decision-making and due-diligence activities related to organizational structure and design (e.g., corporate restructuring, mergers and acquisitions [M&A], divestitures). *SPHR only*

21   Determine strategic application of integrated technical tools and systems (e.g., new enterprise software, performance management tools, self-service technologies). *SPHR only*

Knowledge of:

01   The organization's mission, vision, values, business goals, objectives, plans, and processes

02   Legislative and regulatory processes

03   Strategic planning process, design, implementation, and evaluation

04   Management functions, including planning, organizing, directing, and controlling

05   Corporate governance procedures and compliance (e.g., Sarbanes-Oxley Act)

06   Due diligence processes (e.g., M&A, divestitures). *SPHR only*

07   Transition techniques for corporate restructuring, M&A, off-shoring, and divestitures. *SPHR only*

08   Elements of a cost-benefit analysis during the life cycle of the business (such as scenarios for growth, including expected, economic stressed, and worst-case conditions) and the impact to net worth/earnings for short-, mid-, and long-term horizons

09   Business concepts (e.g., competitive advantage, organizational branding, business case development, corporate responsibility)

02: Workforce Planning and Employment (24%/17%)

Developing, implementing, and evaluating sourcing, recruitment, hiring, orientation, succession planning, retention, and organizational exit programs necessary to ensure the workforce's ability to achieve the organization's goals and objectives.

Responsibilities:

01   Ensure that workforce planning and employment activities are compliant with applicable federal laws and regulations.

02   Identify workforce requirements to achieve the organization's short- and long-term goals and objectives (e.g., corporate restructuring, workforce expansion or reduction).

03   Conduct job analyses to create and/or update job descriptions and identify job competencies.

04   Identify, review, document, and update essential job functions for positions.

05 Influence and establish criteria for hiring, retaining, and promoting on the basis of job descriptions and required competencies.

06 Analyze labor market for trends that impact the ability to meet workforce requirements (e.g., federal/state data reports).

07 Assess skill sets of internal workforce and external labor market to determine the availability of qualified candidates, utilizing third-party vendors or agencies as appropriate.

08 Identify internal and external recruitment sources (e.g., employee referrals, diversity groups, social media) and implement selected recruitment methods.

09 Establish metrics for workforce planning (e.g., recruitment and turnover statistics, costs).

10 Brand and market the organization to potential qualified applicants.

11 Develop and implement selection procedures (e.g., applicant tracking, interviewing, reference and background checking).

12 Develop and extend employment offers and conduct negotiations as necessary.

13 Administer post-offer employment activities (e.g., execute employment agreements, complete I-9/E-Verify process, coordinate relocations, and immigration).

14 Develop, implement, and evaluate orientation and on-boarding processes for new hires, re-hires, and transfers.

15 Develop, implement, and evaluate employee-retention strategies and practices.

16 Develop, implement, and evaluate the succession planning process. *SPHR only*

17 Develop and implement the organizational exit/off-boarding process for both voluntary and involuntary terminations, including planning for reductions in force (RIF).

18 Develop, implement, and evaluate an affirmative action plan (AAP) as required.

19 Develop and implement a record-retention process for handling documents and employee files (e.g., pre-employment files, medical files, and benefits files).

Knowledge of:

11 Applicable federal laws and regulations related to workforce planning and employment activities (e.g., Title VII, ADA, EEOC Uniform Guidelines on Employee Selection Procedures, Immigration Reform and Control Act)

12 Methods to assess past and future staffing effectiveness (e.g., costs per hire, selection ratios, adverse impact)

13 Recruitment sources (e.g., employee referral, social networking/social media) for targeting passive, semi-active and active candidates

14 Recruitment strategies

15 Staffing alternatives (e.g., outsourcing, job sharing, phased retirement)

16 Planning techniques (e.g., succession planning, forecasting)

17 Reliability and validity of selection tests/tools/methods

18 Use and interpretation of selection tests (e.g., psychological/personality, cognitive, motor/physical assessments, performance, assessment center)

19 Interviewing techniques (e.g., behavioral, situational, panel)

20 Impact of compensation and benefits on recruitment and retention

21 International HR and implications of global workforce for workforce planning and employment; *SPHR only*

22 Voluntary and involuntary terminations, downsizing, restructuring, and outplacement strategies and practices

23 Internal workforce assessment techniques (e.g., skills testing, skills inventory, workforce demographic analysis)

24 Employment policies, practices, and procedures (e.g., orientation, on-boarding, and retention)

25 Employer marketing and branding techniques

26 Negotiation skills and techniques

03: Human Resource Development (18%/19%)

Developing, implementing, and evaluating activities and programs that address employee training and development, performance appraisal, and talent and performance management to ensure that the knowledge, skills, abilities, and performance of the workforce meet current and future organizational and individual needs.

Responsibilities:

01 Ensure that human resources development activities are compliant with all applicable federal laws and regulations.

02 Conduct a needs assessment to identify and establish priorities regarding human resource development activities.

03 Develop/select and implement employee training programs (e.g., leadership skills, harassment prevention, computer skills) to increase individual and organizational effectiveness.

04 Evaluate effectiveness of employee training programs through the use of metrics (e.g., participant surveys, pre- and post-testing). *SPHR only*

05 Develop, implement, and evaluate talent-management programs that include assessing talent, developing career paths, and managing the placement of high-potential employees.

06 Develop, select, and evaluate performance appraisal processes (e.g., instruments, ranking and rating scales) to increase individual and organizational effectiveness.

07 Develop, implement, and evaluate performance management programs and procedures (includes training for evaluators).

08 Develop/select, implement, and evaluate programs (e.g., telecommuting, diversity initiatives, repatriation) to meet the changing needs of employees and the organization. *SPHR only*

09 Provide coaching to managers and executives regarding effectively managing organizational talent.

Knowledge of:

27 Applicable federal laws and regulations related to Human Resources development activities (e.g., Title VII, ADA, Title 17 [Copyright law])

28 Career development and leadership development theories and applications (e.g., succession planning, dual career ladders)

29 Organizational development (OD) theories and applications

30 Training program development techniques to create general and specialized training programs

31 Facilitation techniques, instructional methods, and program delivery mechanisms

32 Task/process analysis

33 Performance appraisal methods (e.g., instruments, ranking and rating scales)

34 Performance management methods (e.g., goal setting, relationship to compensation, job placements/promotions)

35 Applicable global issues (e.g., international law, culture, local management approaches/ practices, societal norms); *SPHR only*

36 Techniques to assess training program effectiveness, including use of applicable metrics (e.g., participant surveys, pre- and post-testing)

37 Mentoring and executive coaching

04: Compensation and Benefits (19%/13%)

Developing/selecting, implementing/administering, and evaluating compensation and benefits programs for all employee groups in order to support the organization's goals, objectives, and values.

Responsibilities:

01 Ensure that compensation and benefits programs are compliant with applicable federal laws and regulations.

02 Develop, implement, and evaluate compensation policies/programs (e.g., pay structures, performance-based pay, internal and external equity).

03 Manage payroll-related information (e.g., new hires, adjustments, terminations).

04 Manage outsourced compensation and benefits components (e.g., payroll vendors, COBRA administration, employee recognition vendors). *PHR only*

05 Conduct compensation and benefits programs needs assessments (e.g., benchmarking, employee surveys, trend analysis).

06 Develop/select, implement/administer, update and evaluate benefit programs (e.g., health and welfare, wellness, retirement, stock purchase).

07 Communicate and train the workforce in the compensation and benefits programs, policies and processes (e.g., self-service technologies).

08 Develop/select, implement/administer, update, and evaluate an ethically sound executive compensation program (e.g., stock options, bonuses, supplemental retirement plans). *SPHR only*

09 Develop, implement/administer and evaluate expatriate and foreign national compensation and benefits programs. *SPHR only*

Knowledge of:

38 Applicable federal laws and regulations related to compensation, benefits, and tax (e.g., FLSA, ERISA, FMLA, USERRA)

39 Compensation and benefits strategies

40 Budgeting and accounting practices related to compensation and benefits

41 Job evaluation methods

42 Job pricing and pay structures

43 External labor markets and/or economic factors

44 Pay programs (e.g., variable, merit)

45 Executive compensation methods; *SPHR only*

46 Noncash compensation methods (e.g., equity programs, noncash rewards)

47 Benefits programs (e.g., health and welfare, retirement, Employee Assistance Programs [EAPs])

48 International compensation laws and practices (e.g., expatriate compensation, entitlements, choice of law codes); *SPHR only*

49 Fiduciary responsibilities related to compensation and benefits

05: Employee and Labor Relations (20%/14%)

Developing, implementing/administering, and evaluating the workplace in order to maintain relationships and working conditions that balance employer/employee needs and rights in support of the organization's goals and objectives.

Responsibilities:

01 Ensure that employee and labor relations activities are compliant with applicable federal laws and regulations.

02 Assess organizational climate by obtaining employee input (e.g., focus groups, employee surveys, staff meetings).

03 Develop and implement employee-relations programs (e.g., recognition, special events, diversity programs) that promote a positive organizational culture.

04 Evaluate effectiveness of employee relations programs through the use of metrics (e.g., exit interviews, employee surveys, turnover rates).

05 Establish, update, and communicate workplace policies and procedures (e.g., employee handbook, reference guides, or standard operating procedures), and monitor their application and enforcement to ensure consistency.

06 Develop and implement a discipline policy on the basis of organizational code of conduct/ethics, ensuring that no disparate impact or other legal issues arise.

07 Create and administer a termination process (e.g., reductions in force [RIF], policy violations, poor performance) ensuring that no disparate impact or other legal issues arise.

08 Develop, administer, and evaluate grievance/dispute-resolution and performance-improvement policies and procedures.

09 Investigate and resolve employee complaints filed with federal agencies involving employment practices or working conditions, utilizing professional resources as necessary (e.g., legal counsel, mediation/arbitration specialists, investigators).

10 Develop and direct proactive employee relations strategies for remaining union-free in nonorganized locations. *SPHR only*

11 Direct and/or participate in collective bargaining activities, including contract negotiation, costing, and administration.

Knowledge of:

50 Applicable federal laws affecting employment in union and nonunion environments, such as laws regarding antidiscrimination policies, sexual harassment, labor relations, and privacy (e.g., WARN Act, Title VII, NLRA)

51 Techniques and tools for facilitating positive employee relations (e.g., employee surveys, dispute/conflict resolution, labor/management cooperative strategies)

52 Employee involvement strategies (e.g., employee management committees, self-directed work teams, staff meetings)

53 Individual employment rights issues and practices (e.g., employment at will, negligent hiring, defamation)

54 Workplace behavior issues/practices (e.g., absenteeism and performance improvement)

55 Unfair labor practices

56 The collective bargaining process, strategies, and concepts (e.g., contract negotiation, costing, and administration)

57 Legal disciplinary procedures

58   Positive employee relations strategies and non-monetary rewards
59   Techniques for conducting unbiased investigations
60   Legal termination procedures

06: Risk Management (8%/7%)

Developing, implementing/administering, and evaluating programs, procedures, and policies in order to provide a safe, secure working environment and to protect the organization from potential liability.

Responsibilities:

01   Ensure that workplace health, safety, security, and privacy activities are compliant with applicable federal laws and regulations.
02   Conduct a needs analysis to identify the organization's safety requirements.
03   Develop/select and implement/administer occupational injury and illness prevention programs (i.e., OSHA, workers' compensation). *PHR only*
04   Establish and administer a return-to-work process after illness or injury to ensure a safe workplace (e.g., modified duty assignment, reasonable accommodations, independent medical exam).
05   Develop/select, implement, and evaluate plans and policies to protect employees and other individuals, and to minimize the organization's loss and liability (e.g., emergency response, workplace violence, substance abuse).
06   Communicate and train the workforce on security plans and policies.
07   Develop, monitor, and test business continuity and disaster recovery plans.
08   Communicate and train the workforce on the business continuity and disaster recovery plans.
09   Develop policies and procedures to direct the appropriate use of electronic media and hardware (e.g., e-mail, social media, and appropriate Web site access).
10   Develop and administer internal and external privacy policies (e.g., identity theft, data protection, workplace monitoring).

Knowledge of:

61   Applicable federal laws and regulations related to workplace health, safety, security, and privacy (e.g., OSHA, Drug-Free Workplace Act, ADA, HIPAA, Sarbanes-Oxley Act)
62   Occupational injury and illness prevention (safety) and compensation programs
63   Investigation procedures of workplace safety, health and security enforcement agencies
64   Return-to-work procedures (e.g., interactive dialog, job modification, accommodations)
65   Workplace safety risks (e.g., trip hazards, bloodborne pathogens)
66   Workplace security risks (e.g., theft, corporate espionage, sabotage)
67   Potential violent behavior and workplace violence conditions
68   General health and safety practices (e.g., evacuation, hazard communication, ergonomic evaluations)
69   Organizational incident and emergency response plans
70   Internal investigation, monitoring, and surveillance techniques
71   Employer/employee rights related to substance abuse
72   Business continuity and disaster recovery plans (e.g., data storage and backup, alternative work locations, procedures)
73   Data integrity techniques and technology (e.g., data sharing, password usage, social engineering)
74   Technology and applications (e.g., social media, monitoring software, biometrics)
75   Financial management practices (e.g., procurement policies, credit card policies and guidelines, expense policies)

Core Knowledge

76   Needs assessment and analysis
77   Third-party or vendor selection, contract negotiation, and management, including development of requests for proposals (RFPs)
78   Communication skills and strategies (e.g., presentation, collaboration, sensitivity)
79   Organizational documentation requirements to meet federal and state guidelines
80   Adult learning processes

81 Motivation concepts and applications
82 Training techniques (e.g., virtual, classroom, on-the-job)
83 Leadership concepts and applications
84 Project management concepts and applications
85 Diversity concepts and applications (e.g., generational, cultural competency, learning styles)
86 Human relations concepts and applications (e.g., emotional intelligence, organizational behavior)
87 Ethical and professional standards
88 Technology to support HR activities (e.g., HR Information Systems, employee self-service, e-learning, applicant tracking systems)
89 Qualitative and quantitative methods and tools for analysis, interpretation, and decision-making purposes (e.g., metrics and measurements, cost/benefit analysis, financial statement analysis)
90 Change management theory, methods, and application
91 Job analysis and job description methods
92 Employee records management (e.g., electronic/paper, retention, disposal)
93 Techniques for forecasting, planning, and predicting the impact of HR activities and programs across functional areas
94 Types of organizational structures (e.g., matrix, hierarchy)
95 Environmental scanning concepts and applications (e.g., Strengths, Weaknesses, Opportunities, and Threats [SWOT], and Political, Economic, Social, and Technological [PEST])
96 Methods for assessing employee attitudes, opinions, and satisfaction (e.g., surveys, focus groups/panels)
97 Budgeting, accounting, and financial concepts
98 Risk-management techniques

The HR Certification Institute, established in 1976, is an internationally recognized certifying organization for the human resource profession. Today, more than 115,000 HR professionals worldwide proudly maintain the HR Certification Institute's credentials as a mark of high professional distinction.

The HR Certification Institute is a global leader in developing rigorous exams to demonstrate mastery and real-world application of forward-thinking HR practices, policies and principles.

To learn more, visit www.hrci.org

The PHR, SPHR, GPHR, PHR-CA and SPHR-CA are trademarks of the HR Certification Institute, registered in the United States and other countries. The PHR, SPHR, GPHR, PHR-CA and SPHR-CA Bodies of Knowledge are copyrighted by the HR Certification Institute. ©2014–2015 HR Certification Institute. All rights reserved.

	Professional in Human Resources (PHR®)	Senior Professional in Human Resources (SPHR®)	Global Professional in Human Resources (GPHR®)
Exam Eligibility Requirements	Minimum of one year of experience with a Master's degree or higher, OR two years of experience with a Bachelor's degree, OR four years of experience with less than a Bachelor's degree.	Minimum of four years of experience with a Master's degree or higher, OR five years of experience with a Bachelor's degree, OR seven years of experience with less than a Bachelor's degree.	Minimum of two years global experience with a Master's degree, OR three years experience with a Bachelor's degree, OR four years experience with a less than a Bachelor's degree.
Profile of a Successful Candidate	Has one to four years of professional (exempt-level) generalist experience.	Has four to seven years of progressive professional (exempt-level) experience.	Responsible for HR activities in more than one country.
	Focuses on program implementation rather than creation.	Designs and plans rather than implementation.	Establishes HR policies and practices to support organizational's global growth and reputation.
	Focuses within the HR function rather than organization-wide.	Makes decisions that have an impact within and outside the organization.	Develops and implements international HR strategies that affect international HR assignments and operations.

Human Resource Management Resources

Students are expected to be familiar with the professional resources and literature in their areas of study. Four groups of resources are listed in this appendix.

A. Research-Oriented Journals

In the field of HR management, academic journals are often a communication link between researchers and practicing managers. These journals contain articles that report on original research studies that expand the discipline. They often contain quantitative verifications of the author's findings or conceptual models and literature reviews of previous research.

Academy of Management Journal
Academy of Management Review
Administrative Science Quarterly
American Behavioral Scientist
American Journal of Health Promotion
American Journal of Psychology
American Journal of Sociology
American Psychologist
American Sociological Review
Annual Review of Psychology
Applied Psychology: An International Review
British Journal of Industrial Relations
British Journal of Management
Business Ethics Quarterly
Career Development Quarterly
Decision Sciences
Dispute Resolution Quarterly
Employee Relations
Employee Responsibilities and Rights Journal
Entrepreneurship Theory and Practice
Ethics and Critical Thinking Journal
Group & Organization Management
Human Organization
Human Relations
Human Resources Development Quarterly
Human Resource Development Review
Human Resource Management
Human Resource Management Journal
Human Resource Management Review

Human Resources Abstracts
Industrial and Labor Relations Review
Industrial Relations
Industrial Relations Journal
Industrial Relations Law Journal
International Journal of Entrepreneurial Behavior
    and Research
International Journal of Human Resource
    Management Education
International Journal of Management Reviews
International Journal of Selection and Assessment
International Journal of Training and Development
Journal of Abnormal Psychology
Journal of Applied Behavioral Science
Journal of Applied Business Research
Journal of Applied Psychology
Journal of Applied Social Psychology
Journal of Business and Industrial Marketing
Journal of Business and Psychology
Journal of Business Communication
Journal of Business Ethics
Journal of Business Research
Journal of Business Strategy
Journal of Collective Negotiations
Journal of Comparative International
    Management
Journal of Compensation and Benefits
Journal of Counseling Psychology
Journal of Employment Counseling

Journal of Experimental Social Psychology
Journal of Human Resources
Journal of Industrial Relations
Journal of International Business Studies
Journal of International Management
Journal of Knowledge Management
Journal of Labor Economics
Journal of Labor Research
Journal of Leadership and Organizational Studies
Journal of Management
Journal of Management Development
Journal of Management Education
Journal of Management Studies
Journal of Managerial Psychology
Journal of Occupational and Organizational
    Psychology
Journal of Organizational Behavior
Journal of Organizational Change Management
Journal of Organizational Excellence
Journal of Personality and Social Psychology
Journal of Personal Selling & Sales Management
Journal of Quality and Participation
Journal of Social Issues
Journal of Social Psychology
Journal of Vocational Behavior
Journal of Workplace Learning
Journal of Workplace Rights
Management Communication Quarterly
New Technology, Work, and Employment
Organization Behavior and Human Decision
    Processes
Personnel Psychology
Personnel Review
Psychological Bulletin
Psychological Review
Public Personnel Management
Quarterly Review of Distance Education
Small Group Research
Social Forces
Social Science Research
Work and Occupations

B. Selected Professional/ Managerial Journals

These journals generally cover a wide range of applied topics. Articles in these publications are often aimed at HR professionals, organizational managers, and other business leaders. Most articles in these publication outlets are written to interpret, summarize, or discuss the implications of research. They also provide operational and administrative ideas.

Academy of Management Perspectives
Australian Journal of Management
Benefits and Compensation Solutions
Berkeley Journal of Employment and Labor Law
Business Horizons
Business Journal
Business Week
California Management Review
Columbia Journal of World Business
Compensation and Benefits Review
Corporate Governance
Directors and Boards
Economist
Employee Benefit Plan Review
Employee Benefits News
Employee Relations
Employment Relations Today
Forbes
Fortune
Global HR
Harvard Business Review
Health Resources and Services Administration
HR Magazine
Human Capital Management
Human Resource Development International
Human Resource Executive
Human Resource Management International
    Digest
IHRIM Link
INC.
Industry Week
International Management
Journal of Network and Systems Management
Labor Law Journal
Long Range Planning
Management Research News
Management Review
Management Today
Managers Magazine
Monthly Labor Review
Nation's Business
Occupational Health and Safety
Occupational Outlook Quarterly
Organizational Dynamics
Pension World
People & Strategy Journal
Personnel Management

Psychology Today
Public Administration Review
Public Manager
Public Opinion Quarterly
SAM Advanced Management Journal
Security Management
Sloan Management Review
TD Magazine
Training
Training and Development
Workforce Management
Working Woman
Workplace Visions
Workspan
WorldatWork Journal

C. Selected Human Resource Associations/Organizations

Academy of Management
www.aom.pace.edu
American Arbitration Association
www.adr.org
American Federation of Labor/Congress
  of Industrial Organizations (AFL-CIO)
www.aflcio.org
American Institute for Managing Diversity
www.aimd.org
American Management Association
www.amanet.org
American Payroll Association
www.americanpayroll.org
American Psychological Association
www.apa.org
American Society for Industrial Security
www.asisonline.org
Association for Talent Development
www.td.org
Australian Human Resource Institute
www.ahri.com.au
Chartered Institute of Personnel
  and Development (UK)
www.cipd.co.uk
CPR International Institute for Conflict
  Prevention and Resolution
www.cpradr.org
Employee Benefit Research Institute
www.ebri.org
Foundation for Enterprise Development
www.fed.org

Hong Kong Institute of Human Resource
  Management
www.hkihrm.org
HR People & Strategy
www.hrps.org
Human Resource Certification Institute
www.hrci.org
International Association for Human Resource
  Information Management
www.ihrim.org
International Association of Industrial Accident
  Boards and Commissions
www.iaiabc.org
International Foundation of Employee
  Benefit Plans (IFEBP)
www.ifebp.org
International Institute of Human Resource
  Management
www.iihrm.org
International Personnel Assessment Council
www.ipacweb.org
International Personnel Management Association
www.ipma-hr.org
Labor and Employment Relations Association
www.lera.uiuc.edu
National Center for Employee Ownership
www.nceo.org
National Health Information Resource Center
www.nhirc.org
Social Media Policies
Society for Industrial and Organizational
  Psychology
www.socialmediagovernance.com
Society for Human Resource Management
www.shrm.org
Union Resource Network
www.unions.org
World at Work
www.worldatwork.org
World Federation of People Management
  Associations
www.wfpma.com

D. Selected Government Agencies Related to HR

Bureau of Labor Statistics
www.bls.gov
Census Bureau
www.census.gov

Department of Labor
www.dol.gov
Employment and Training Administration
www.doleta.gov
Equal Employment Opportunity Commission
www.eeoc.gov
FedStats
www.fedstats.gov
National Institute of Environmental
    Health Sciences
www.niehs.nih.gov
National Institute for Occupational Safety
    and Health (NIOSH)
www.cdc.gov/niosh
National Labor Relations Board
www.nlrb.gov

Occupational Safety and Health Administration
www.osha.gov
Office of Personnel Management
www.opm.gov
Pension and Welfare Benefits Administration
www.dol.gov/ebsa
Pension Benefit Guaranty Corporation
www.pbgc.gov
Small Business Administration
www.sba.gov
Social Security Administration
www.ssa.gov
U.S. House of Representatives
www.house.gov
U.S. Senate
www.senate.gov

APPENDIX C

Major Federal Equal Employment Opportunity Laws and Regulations

Act	Year	Key Provisions	Covered Employers
Broad-Based Discrimination			
Title VII, Civil Rights Act of 1964	1964	Prohibits discrimination in employment on the basis of race, color, religion, sex, or national origin	Employers with 15+ employees
Executive Orders 11246 and 11375	1965 1967	Require federal contractors and subcontractors to eliminate employment discrimination and prior discrimination through affirmative action	Federal contractors with 50+ employees and a government contract of $50,000 or more
Civil Rights Act of 1991	1991	Overturns several past Supreme Court decisions and changes damage claims provisions	Employers with 15+ employees
Congressional Accountability Act	1995	Extends EEO and Civil Rights Act provisions to U.S. congressional staff	U.S. Congress
Military Status			
Vietnam Era Veterans' Readjustment Assistance Act	1974	Prohibits discriminations against Vietnam-era veterans; requires affirmative action and annual reporting of veteran employment	Federal contractors and subcontractors with a contract of $25,000 or more
Uniformed Services Employment and Reemployment Rights Act	1994	Protects members of the uniformed services from discrimination in employment and provides for reinstatement to their job upon return from active duty	All employers
National Origin Discrimination			
Immigration Reform and Control Act	1986 1990 1996	Establishes penalties for employers who knowingly hire illegal aliens/immigrants; prohibits employment discrimination on the basis of national origin or citizenship	Employers with 15+ employees

(Continued)

Act	Year	Key Provisions	Covered Employers
Gender/Sex Discrimination			
Equal Pay Act	1963	Requires equal pay for men and women performing substantially the same work	All employers
Pregnancy Discrimination Act	1978	Prohibits discrimination against women affected by pregnancy, childbirth, or related medical conditions; requires that they be treated as all other employees for employment-related purposes, including benefits	Employers with 15+ employees
Age Discrimination			
Age Discrimination in Employment Act (as amended in 1978 and 1986)	1967	Prohibits discrimination against persons over age 40 and restricts mandatory retirement requirements, except where age is a bona fide occupational qualification	Employers with 20+ employees
Older Workers Benefit Protection Act of 1990	1990	Prohibits age-based discrimination in early retirement and other benefit plans	Employers with 20+ employees
Disability Discrimination			
Vocational Rehabilitation Act and Rehabilitation Act of 1974	1973 1974	Prohibits federal contractors from discriminating against individuals with disabilities	Federal contractors and subcontractors with a contract of $25,000 or more
Americans with Disabilities Act	1990	Requires employer accommodations for individuals with disabilities	Employers with 15+ employees
Genetic Information Nondiscrimination Act	2009	Prohibits employers and health insurers from using genetic information in employment and insurance coverage decisions	Employers with 20+ employees

Uniform Guidelines on Employee Selection

The 1978 Uniform Guidelines on Employee Selection Procedures are used by the U.S. Equal Employment Opportunity Commission (EEOC), the U.S. Department of Labor's Office of Federal Contract Compliance Programs (OFCCP), the U.S. Department of Justice, and the U.S. Office of Personnel Management. These guidelines explain how an employer should deal with hiring, retention, promotion, transfer, demotion, dismissal, and referral. Under the uniform guidelines, if sued, employers can choose one of two routes to prove they are not illegally discriminating against employees: no disparate impact and job-related validity.

No Disparate Impact Approach

In general, the most important issue regarding discrimination in organizations is the *effect* of employment policies and procedures, regardless of the *intent* of the employer. *Disparate impact* occurs when members of a protected class are substantially underrepresented in employment decisions. Under the guidelines, disparate impact is determined with the *4/5ths rule*. If the selection rate for a protected group is less than 80% (4/5) of the selection rate for the majority group or less than 80% of the majority group's representation in the relevant labor market, discrimination exists. Thus, the guidelines have attempted to define discrimination in statistical terms. The use of the statistical means has been researched, and some methodological issues have been identified. However, the guidelines continue to be used because disparate impact is checked by employers both internally and externally.

Internal Metrics for Disparate Impact Internal disparate impact metrics compare the results of employer actions involving by protected-class members with those involving nonprotected-class members within the organization. HR activities that can be checked most frequently for internal disparate impact include the following:

- Selection of candidates for interviews from those recruited
- Pass rates for various selection tests
- Performance appraisal ratings as they affect pay increases
- Promotions, demotions, and terminations
- Identification of individuals for layoffs

The calculation that follows computes the internal disparate impact for men and women who were interviewed for jobs at a firm. In this case, the figure indicates that the selection process does have a disparate impact internally. The practical meaning of these calculations is that statistically, women have less chance of being selected for jobs than men do. Thus, illegal discrimination may exist unless the firm can demonstrate that its selection activities are specifically job related.

Internal Disparate Impact Example

Female applicants: 25% were selected for jobs
Male applicants: 45% were selected for jobs

Disparate Impact Determination (4/5 = 80%)

• Male selection rate of 45% × (80%) = 36%
• Female selection rate = 25%

Disparate impact exists because the female selection rate is less than 4/5 of the male selection rate.

External Metrics for Disparate Impact Employers can check for disparate impact externally by comparing the percentage of protected-class members in their workforces with the percentage of protected-class members in the relevant labor markets. The relevant labor markets consist of the areas where the firm recruits workers, not just where those who are employed live. External comparisons can also consider the percentage of protected-class members who are recruited and who apply for jobs to ensure that the employer has drawn a "representative sample" from the relevant labor markets. Although employers are not required to maintain exact proportionate equality, they must be "close." Courts have applied statistical analyses to determine if any disparities that exist are too high.

The following example illustrates external disparate impact metrics using analyses for a sample metropolitan area, Valleyville. Assume that a firm in that area, Acme Company, has 500 employees, including 50 African Americans and 75 Latinos/Hispanics. To determine if the company's workforce reflects external disparate impact, it is possible to make the following comparisons:

Protected Class	% of Total Employees at Acme Company	4/5 of Group in the Population	Disparate Impact?
African American	10% (50/500)	13.6%	Yes (10% < 13.6%)
Latino/Hispanic	15% (75/500)	14.4%	No (15% > 14.4%)

At Acme, external disparate impact exists for African Americans because the company employs fewer of them than the 4/5 threshold of 13.6%. However, because Acme has more Latino/Hispanic employees than the 4/5 threshold of 14.4%, there is no disparate impact for this group.

Statistical comparisons for determining disparate impact may use more complex methods. HR professionals need to know how to perform such calculations because external disparate impact must be computed and reported in affirmative action plans that government contractors submit to regulatory agencies.

Racial Distribution in Valleyville (Example)

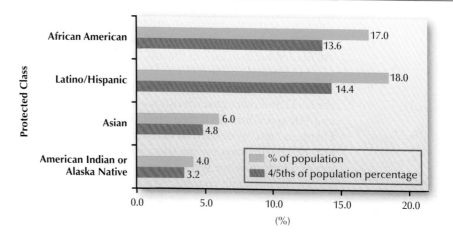

Job-related Validation Approach

Under the job-related validation approach, virtually every factor used to make employment-related decisions is considered an employment "test." Such activities as recruiting, selection, promotion, termination, discipline, and performance appraisal all must be shown to be job related. Hence, two basic concepts, reliability and validity, affect many of the common means used to make HR decisions. Ideally, employment-related tests will be both reliable and valid.

Reliability and Validity *Reliability* refers to the consistency with which a test measures an item. For a test to be reliable, an individual's score should be about the same every time the individual takes the test (allowing for the effects of practice). Unless a test measures a factor consistently (reliably), it is of little value in predicting job performance.

Validity is simply the extent to which a test actually measures what it says it measures. The concept relates to inferences made from tests. For instance, it may be valid to assume that performance on a mechanical knowledge test may predict performance of a machinist in a manufacturing plant. However, it is probably not valid to assume that the same test scores indicate general intelligence or promotability for a manufacturing sales representative. Another example would be a general intelligence test; for it to be valid, it must actually measure intelligence, not just a person's vocabulary. Therefore, an employment test that is valid must measure the person's ability to perform the job for which she or he is being hired.

Validity and Equal Employment If a charge of discrimination is brought against an employer on the basis of disparate impact, a *prima facie* case must be established. The employer then must be able to demonstrate that its employment procedures are valid and job related. A key element in establishing job relatedness is conducting a *job analysis* to identify the *knowledge, skills, and abilities (KSAs)* along with other characteristics needed to perform a job satisfactorily. In one sense, then, current requirements have done management a favor by forcing employers to use job-related employment procedures.

There are two categories of validity in which employment tests attempt to predict how well an individual will perform on the job. In measuring *criterion-related validity*, a test is the *predictor*, and the measures for job performance are the *criterion variables*. Job analysis determines as exactly as possible what KSAs and behaviors are needed for each task in the job. Two types of criterion-related validity are *predictive validity* and *concurrent validity*.

Content validity is validity measured by a logical, nonstatistical method to identify the KSAs and other characteristics necessary to perform a job. Managers, supervisors, and HR specialists must then identify the most important KSAs needed for the job. Finally, a "test" is devised to determine if individuals have the necessary KSAs. The test may be an interview question about previous supervisory experience, an ability test in which someone types a letter using a word-processing software program, or a knowledge test about consumer credit regulations.

A test has content validity if it reflects an actual sample of the work done on the job in question. For example, an arithmetic test for a retail cashier might contain problems about determining amounts for refunds, purchases, and merchandise exchanges. Content validity is especially useful if the workforce is not large enough to allow other, more complex statistical approaches.

Many practitioners and specialists see content validity as a commonsense standard for validating staffing and other employment dimensions and as more realistic than other means. Research and court decisions have shown that content validity is consistent with the Uniform Guidelines. Consequently, content validity approaches are growing in use.

Pre-Employment Inquiries

Many equal employment opportunity (EEO) complaints occur because of inappropriate pre-employment inquiries. Questions asked of applicants may be viewed as discriminatory or biased against applicants of a protected class. This appendix identifies pre-employment inquiries that may or may not be discriminatory. Based on the findings of court cases, the pre-employment inquiries labeled "may be discriminatory" should be avoided in almost all cases. Those labeled "may not be discriminatory" are legal, but only if they reflect a business necessity or are job related. Once an employer tells an applicant he or she is hired (the "point of hire"), inquiries that were prohibited earlier may be made. After hiring, medical examination forms, group insurance cards, and other enrollment cards containing inquiries related directly or indirectly to sex, age, or other bases may be requested.

Guidelines to Lawful and Unlawful Pre-Employment Inquiries

Subject of Inquiry	It May Not Be Discriminatory to Inquire about ...	It May Be Discriminatory to Inquire about ...
1. Name	a. Whether applicant has ever worked under a different name	a. The original name of applicant whose name has been legally changed b. The ethnic association of applicant's name
2. Age	a. If applicant is over the age of 18 b. If applicant is under the age of 18 or 21 if that information is job related (e.g., for selling liquor in a retail store)	a. Date of birth b. Date of high school graduation
3. Residence	a. Applicant's place of residence b. Alternative contact information	a. Previous addresses b. Birthplace of applicant or applicant's parents c. Length lived at current and previous addresses
4. Race or color		a. Applicant's race or color of applicant's skin

(*Continued*)

Subject of Inquiry	It May Not Be Discriminatory to Inquire about ...	It May Be Discriminatory to Inquire about ...
5. National origin and ancestry		a. Applicant's lineage, ancestry, national origin, parentage, or nationality b. Nationality of applicant's parents or spouse
6. Sex and family composition		a. Sex of applicant b. Marital status of applicant c. Dependents of applicant or child care arrangements d. Whom to contact in case of emergency
7. Creed or religion		a. Applicant's religious affiliation b. Applicant's church, parish, mosque, or synagogue c. Holidays observed by applicant
8. Citizenship	a. Whether the applicant is a U.S. citizen or has a current permit/visa to work in the United States	a. Whether applicant is a citizen of a country other than the United States b. Date of citizenship
9. Language	a. Language applicant speaks and/or writes fluently, if job related	a. Applicant's native language b. Language used at home
10. References	a. Names of persons willing to provide professional and/or character references for applicant b. Previous work contacts	a. Name of applicant's religious leader b. Political affiliation and contacts
11. Relatives	a. Names of relatives already employed by the employer	a. Name and/or address of any relative of applicant b. Whom to contact in case of emergency
12. Organizations	a. Applicant's membership in any professional, service, or trade organization	a. All clubs or social organizations to which applicant belongs
13. Arrest record and convictions	a. Convictions, if related to job performance (disclaimer should accompany)	a. Number and kinds of arrests b. Convictions, unless related to job requirements and performance
14. Photographs		a. Photographs with application, with résumé, or before hiring
15. Height and weight		a. Any inquiry into height and weight of applicant, except where a bona fide occupational qualification (BFOQ) exists

(Continued)

Subject of Inquiry	It May Not Be Discriminatory to Inquire about ...	It May Be Discriminatory to Inquire about ...
16. Physical limitations	a. Whether applicant has the ability to perform job-related functions with or without accommodation	a. The nature or severity of an illness or physical condition b. Whether applicant has ever filed a workers' compensation claim c. Any recent or past operations, treatments, or surgeries and dates
17. Education	a. Training applicant has received, if related to the job b. Highest level of education applicant has attained, if validated that having certain educational background (e.g., high school diploma or college degree) is needed to perform the specific job	a. Date of high school graduation
18. Military	a. Branch of the military applicant served in and ranks attained b. Type of education or training received in military	a. Military discharge details b. Military service records
19. Financial status		a. Applicant's debts or assets b. Garnishments

Equal Employment Opportunity Enforcement

Enforcement of equal employment opportunity (EEO) laws and regulations in the United States is often viewed as a work in progress that can be inconsistent and confusing for managers. The court system is left to resolve the disputes and interpret the laws, but the lower courts often issue conflicting rulings and interpretations. The ultimate interpretation rests on decisions by the U.S. Supreme Court, although those rulings have also been interpreted differently.

EEO Enforcement Agencies

Government agencies at several levels can investigate illegal discriminatory practices. At the federal level, the two most prominent agencies are the Equal Employment Opportunity Commission (EEOC) and the Office of Federal Contract Compliance Programs (OFCCP).

Equal Employment Opportunity Commission The EEOC has enforcement authority for charges brought under a number of federal laws. Further, the EEOC issues policy guidelines on many topics that influence EEO. Although the policy statements are not "law," they are "persuasive authority" in most cases.

Office of Federal Contract Compliance Programs While the EEOC is an independent agency, the OFCCP is part of the U.S. Department of Labor and ensures that federal contractors and subcontractors use nondiscriminatory practices. A major goal of the OFCCP efforts is to ensure that covered employers take affirmative action to counter prior discriminatory practices.

State and Local Agencies In addition to federal laws and orders, many states and municipalities have enacted their own laws prohibiting discrimination on a variety of bases, and state and local enforcement bodies have been established. Compared with federal laws, state and local laws sometimes provide greater remedies, require different actions, or prohibit discrimination in more areas.

EEO Compliance

Employers must comply with a variety of EEO regulations and guidelines, and to do so, it is crucial that all employers have a written EEO policy statement. They should widely communicate this policy by posting it on bulletin boards, printing it in employee handbooks, reproducing it in organizational newsletters, and reinforcing it in training programs. The contents of the policy should clearly state the organization's commitment to equal employment and incorporate a list of the appropriate protected classes.

Additionally, employers with 15 or more employees may be required to keep certain records that can be requested by the EEOC, the OFCCP, or numerous other state and local enforcement agencies. Under various laws, employers are also required to post an "officially approved notice" in a prominent place for employees. The notice must state that the employer is an equal opportunity employer and does not discriminate.

EEO Records Retention All employment records must be maintained as required by the EEOC. Such records include application forms and documents concerning hiring, promotion, demotion, transfer, layoff, termination, rates of pay or other terms of compensation, and selection for training and apprenticeship. Even application forms or test papers completed by unsuccessful applicants may be requested. The length of time documents must be kept varied, but generally three years is recommended as a minimum. Complete records are necessary to enable an employer to respond should a charge of discrimination be made.

EEOC Reporting Forms Many private-sector employers must file a basic report annually with the EEOC. Slightly different reports must be filed biennially by state/local governments, local unions, and school districts. The following private-sector employers must file the EEO-1 report annually:

- All employers with 100 or more employees, except state and local governments
- Subsidiaries of other companies if the total number of all combined employees equals 100 or more
- Federal contractors with at least 50 employees and contracts of $50,000 or more
- Financial institutions with at least 50 employees, in which government funds are held or saving bonds are issued

Details on employees must be reported by gender, race/ethnic group, and job levels. Employees may be classified as belonging to two or more races which reflects the diverse nature of a growing proportion of the workforce.

Applicant-Flow Data Under EEO laws and regulations, employers may be required to show that they do not discriminate when recruiting and selecting members of protected classes. Because employers are not allowed to collect such data on application forms and other pre-employment records, the EEOC allows them to do so with a separate applicant-flow form that is not used in the selection process. Applicants voluntarily complete *applicant-flow forms*, and the data must be maintained separately from other selection-related materials. Since many applications are submitted online, employers must collect this data electronically to comply with regulations on who is an applicant. Analyses of the data collected in applicant-flow forms may help to show whether an employer has underutilized a protected class because of an inadequate flow of applicants from that class, in spite of special efforts to recruit them. Also, these data are reported as part of affirmative action plans that are filed with the OFCCP.

EEOC Compliance Investigation Process When a discrimination complaint is received by an employer, it must be processed, whether it is made internally by a disgruntled employee or by an outside agency. The following chart shows the steps required in an employer's response to an EEO complaint.

Notice that the employer should have a formal complaint process in place and should be sure that no retaliatory action occurs. Internal investigations can be conducted

Stages in the Employer's Response to an EEO Complaint

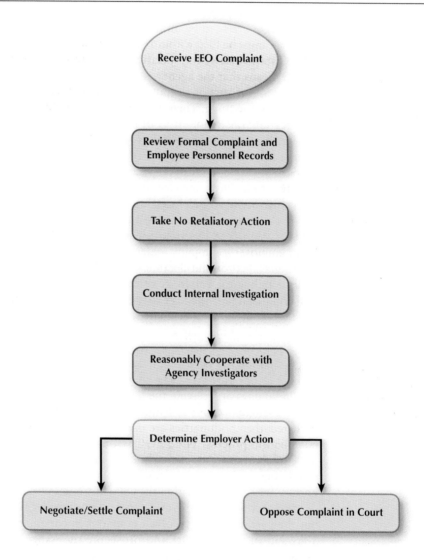

by HR staff, but HR departments often utilize outside legal counsel to provide expert guidance when dealing with agency investigations. Internal investigations should also occur when employees make complaints without filing them with outside agencies. Once the employer has completed the investigation, the decision must be made whether to negotiate and settle the complaint or oppose the complaint.

EEOC Complaint Process To handle the growing number of complaints, the EEOC and other agencies have instituted a system that puts complaints into three categories: *priority*, *needing further investigation*, and *immediate dismissal*. If the EEOC decides to pursue a complaint, the process outlined here is used, and the employer must determine how to respond.

A typical EEO complaint goes through several stages before the compliance process is completed. On average, a complaint takes 182 days to resolve. First, the charges are filed by an individual, a group of individuals, or a representative. A charge must be filed within 180 days of the alleged discriminatory action. Then the EEOC staff reviews the specifics of the charge to determine if it has *jurisdiction*, which means that the agency is authorized to investigate that type of charge. If the EEOC has jurisdiction, it must serve a notice of the charge on the employer within 10 days of the filing. Then the employer is asked to respond. Following the charge notification, the major effort of the EEOC turns to investigating the complaint.

Prior to undertaking its investigation, the EEOC will attempt to resolve the charge through mediation or settlement. This voluntary process must be agreed to by both parties, and it can greatly reduce the documentation burden on the company and save time. However, electing to mediate or settle is a business decision that the company should consider carefully before choosing a course of action.

If the parties elect not to mediate or settle, then the EEOC will begin its investigation. The investigation may involve interviews with the complainants, other employees, company managers, and supervisors. The agency may also request additional records and documents from the employer and ask for a position statement detailing the employer's side of the story. In some cases, EEOC investigators will conduct an on-site visit to gather additional information. After all information has been collected and evaluated, the EEOC investigator will come to a conclusion on the merits of the charge.

The EEOC may determine that there is no reasonable cause to believe that illegal discrimination has occurred. In such a case, the charging party is issued a dismissal and notice of rights letter. The charging party may then file a lawsuit in federal court within 90 days of receiving the letter.

If sufficient cause is found to support charges that alleged discrimination occurred, then both parties are invited to resolve the complaint through a voluntary conciliation process. The EEOC strongly encourages the use of conciliation, and 47% of charges were resolved in this manner in 2014. If the employer agrees that discrimination has occurred and accepts the proposed settlement, then the employer posts a notice of relief within the company and takes the agreed-on actions.

In cases where the EEOC determines that illegal discrimination has occurred but the parties cannot resolve the matter in conciliation, then the agency will file a lawsuit in federal court and prosecute the issue. In the litigation stage, a trial takes place in the appropriate state or federal court. At that point, both sides retain lawyers and rely on the court to render a decision. The Civil Rights Act of 1991 provides for jury trials in most EEO cases. If either party disagrees with the court ruling, an appeal can be filed with a higher court. The U.S. Supreme Court becomes the ultimate adjudication body.

Sample HR-Related Job Descriptions and Job Specifications

Sample Job Description and Job Specification for Human Resource Manager

Identification Section:
Position Title: Human Resource Manager
Department: Human Resources   EEOC Class: O/M
Reports to: President   FLSA Status: Exempt

General Summary: Directs HR activities of the firm to ensure compliance with laws and policies, and assists President with overall HR planning

Essential Job Functions:
1. Manages compensation and benefits programs for all employees, resolves compensation and benefits questions from employees, and negotiates with benefits carriers (20%)
2. Ensures compliance with both internal policies and applicable state and federal regulations and laws, including EEO, OSHA, and FLSA (20%)
3. Identifies HR planning issues and suggests approaches to President and other senior managers (15%)
4. Assists managers and supervisors to create, plan, and conduct training and various development programs for new and existing employees (15%)
5. Recruits candidates for employment over telephone and in person; interviews and selects internal and external candidates for open positions (10%)
6. Reviews and updates job descriptions, assisted by department supervisors, and coordinates performance appraisal process to ensure timely reviews are completed for all employees (10%)
7. Administers various HR policies and procedures and helps managers resolve employee performance and policy issues (10%)
8. Performs other duties as needed and directed by President

Knowledge, Skills, and Abilities:
- Knowledge of HR policies, HR practices, and HR-related laws and regulations
- Knowledge of company products, services, policies, and procedures
- Knowledge of management principles and practices
- Skill in operating equipment such as personal computer, software, and IT systems
- Skill in oral and written communication
- Ability to communicate with employees and various business contacts in a professional and courteous manner
- Ability to organize multiple work assignments and establish priorities
- Ability to negotiate with others and resolve conflicts, particularly in sensitive situations
- Ability to pay close attention to detail and to ensure accuracy of reports and data
- Ability to make sound decisions using available information while maintaining confidentiality
- Ability to create a team environment and sustain employee commitment

Education and Experience: Bachelor's degree in HR management or equivalent, plus 3–5 years' experience

Physical Requirements:	Percentage of Work Time Spent on Activity			
	0%–24%	25%–49%	50%–74%	75%–100%
Seeing: Must be able to read computer screen and various reports				X
Hearing: Must be able to hear well enough to communicate with employees and others				X
Standing/walking	X			
Climbing/stooping/kneeling	X			
Lifting/pulling/pushing	X			
Fingering/grasping/feeling: Must be able to write, type, and use phone system				X

Working Conditions: Good working conditions with the absence of disagreeable conditions

Note: The statements herein are intended to describe the general nature and level of work performed by employees, are not a complete list of responsibilities, duties, and skills required of personnel so classified. Furthermore, they do not establish a contract for employment and are subject to change at the discretion of the employer.

Sample Job Description and Job Specification for Compensation Manager

Job Title: Compensation Manager	**JOB CODE:** _____
Supervisor's Title: Vice President of Human Resources	**GRADE:** _____
Department: Human Resources	**FLSA STATUS:** Exempt
	EEOC CLASS: O/M

General Summary: Responsible for the design and administration of all cash compensation programs, ensures proper consideration of the relationship of compensation to performance of each employee, and provides consultation on compensation administration to managers and supervisors

Essential Duties and Responsibilities:
1. Prepares and maintains job descriptions for all jobs and periodically reviews and updates them; responds to questions from employees and supervisors regarding job descriptions (25%)
2. Ensures that Company compensation rates are in line with pay structures; obtains or conducts pay surveys as necessary and presents recommendations on pay structures on an annual basis (20%)
3. Develops and administers the performance appraisal program and monitors the use of the performance appraisal instruments to ensure the integrity of the system and its proper use (20%)
4. Directs the job evaluation process by coordinating committee activities and resolves disputes over job values; conducts initial evaluation of new jobs prior to hiring and assigns jobs to pay ranges (15%)
5. Researches and provides recommendations on executive compensation issues; assists in the development and oversees the administration of all annual bonus payments for senior managers and executives (15%)
6. Coordinates the development of an integrated HR information system and interfaces with the Management Information Systems Department to achieve departmental goals for information needs (5%)
7. Performs related duties as assigned or as the situation dictates

Required Knowledge, Skills, and Abilities:
1. Knowledge of compensation and HR management practices and approaches
2. Knowledge of effective job analysis methods and survey development and interpretation practices and principles
3. Knowledge of performance management program design and administration
4. Knowledge of federal and state wage and hour regulations
5. Skill in writing job descriptions, memorandums, letters, and proposals
6. Skill in use of word processing, spreadsheet, and database software
7. Ability to make presentations to groups on compensation policies and practices
8. Ability to plan and prioritize work

Education and Experience: Equivalent of a college degree in Business Administration, Psychology, or related field plus 3–5 years' experience in HR management, 2–3 of which should include compensation administration experience. An advanced degree in Industrial Psychology, Business Administration, or HR Management preferred, but not required.

Physical Requirements:	Rarely (0%–12%)	Occasionally (12%–33%)	Frequently (34%–66%)	Regularly (67%–100%)
Seeing: Must be able to read reports and use computers				X
Hearing: Must be able to hear well enough to communicate with coworkers				X
Standing/walking	X			
Climbing/stooping/kneeling	X			
Lifting/pulling/pushing	X			
Fingering/grasping/feeling: Must be able to write, type, and use phone system				X

Working Conditions: Normal office working conditions with the absence of disagreeable elements

Note: The statements herein are intended to describe the general nature and level of work being performed by employees, and are not to be construed as an exhaustive list of responsibilities, duties, and skills required of personnel so classified. Furthermore, they do not establish a contract for employment and are subject to change at the discretion of the employer.

GLOSSARY

A

Absenteeism Any failure by an employee to report for work as scheduled or to stay at work when scheduled.

Acceptance rate Percentage of applicants hired divided by total number of applicants offered jobs.

Active practice Trainees perform job-related tasks and duties during training.

Adult learning (also known as andragogy) Ways in which adults learn differently than do younger people.

Adverse selection Situation in which *only* higher-risk employees select and use certain benefits.

Affinity groups Groups for employees with a common interest or characteristic.

Affirmative action Proactive employment practices to make up for historical discrimination against women, minorities, and individuals with disabilities.

Affirmative action program (AAP) A document that outlines proactive steps the organization will take to attract and hire members of underrepresented groups.

Alternate work arrangements Nontraditional schedules that provide flexibility to employees.

Applicant pool All persons who are actually evaluated for selection.

Applicant population A subset of the labor force population that is available for selection using a particular recruiting approach.

Arbitration Process that uses a neutral third party to make a binding decision.

Assessment centers Collections of test instruments and exercises designed to diagnose an individual's development needs.

Attitude survey A survey that focuses on employees' feelings and beliefs about their jobs and the organization.

Attraction-selection-attrition (ASA) theory Job candidates are attracted to and selected by firms where similar types of individuals are employed, and individuals who are very different quit their jobs to work elsewhere.

Auto-enrollment Process by which employee contributions to a 401(k) plan are started automatically when an employee is eligible to join the plan.

Autonomy Extent of individual freedom and discretion in the work and its scheduling.

B

Balanced scorecard A framework organizations use to report on a diverse set of performance measures.

Bargaining unit Employees eligible to select a single union to represent and bargain collectively for them.

Base pay Basic compensation that an employee receives, often as a an hourly wage or salary.

Behavioral interview Interview in which applicants give specific examples of how they have performed a certain task or handled a problem in the past.

Behavioral modeling Copying someone else's behavior.

Behaviorally anchored rating scale Scale that describes specific examples of job behavior, which are then "anchored" or measured against a scale of performance levels.

Benchmark jobs Jobs that are found in many other organizations that can be used for the purposes of comparison.

Benchmarking The process of comparing an organization's business results to industry standards or best practices.

Benefit Indirect reward given to an employee or group of employees as part of membership in the organization, regardless of performance.

Blended learning Learning approach that combines short, fast-paced, interactive computer-based lessons and teleconferencing with traditional classroom instruction and simulation.

Bona fide occupational qualification (BFOQ) Characteristic providing a legitimate reason an employer can exclude persons on otherwise illegal bases of consideration.

Bonus One-time payment that does not become part of the employee's base pay.

Bring your own device (BYOD) The practice of employees using their own mobile devices such as smartphones and digital tablets in the workplace.

Broadbanding Practice of using fewer pay grades with much broader ranges than in traditional compensation systems.

Bullying Behavior that the target perceives as oppressive, humiliating, threatening, or infringing on the target's human rights and that occurs over an extended period of time.

Burden of proof What individuals who file suit against employers must prove to establish that illegal discrimination has occurred.

Business necessity A practice necessary for safe and efficient organizational operations.

C

Cafeteria benefit plan Employees are given a budget and can purchase the bundle of benefits most important to them from the "menu" of options offered by the employer.

Career Series of work-related position a person occupies throughout life.

Career paths Represent employees' movements through opportunities over time.

Cash balance plan Retirement program in which benefits are determined on the basis of accumulation of annual company contributions plus interest credited each year.

Central tendency error Occurs when a rater gives all employees a score within a narrow range in the middle of the scale.

Churn Hiring new workers while laying off others.

Closed shop Firm that requires individuals to join a union before they can be hired.

Coaching A collaborative process focused on improving individual performance.

Codetermination Practice in which union or worker representatives are given positions on a company's board of directors.

Cognitive ability tests Tests that measure an individual's thinking, memory, reasoning, verbal, and mathematical abilities.

Collective bargaining Process whereby representatives of management and workers negotiate over wages, hours, and other terms and conditions of employment.

Commission Compensation computed as a percentage of sales in units or dollars.

Compa-ratio Pay level divided by the midpoint of the pay range.

Compensable factor Job dimension commonly present throughout a group of jobs within an organization that can be rated for each job.

Competencies Individual capabilities that can be linked to enhanced performance by individuals or teams.

Competency-based pay Rewards individuals for the capabilities they demonstrate and acquire.

Complaint Indication of employee dissatisfaction.

Compressed workweek A workweek in which a full week's work is accomplished in fewer than five days of eight working hours each.

Conciliation Process by which a third party facilitates the dialogue between opposing parties to reach a voluntary settlement.

Concurrent validity Measured when an employer tests current employees and correlates the scores with their performance ratings.

Constructive discharge Process of deliberately making conditions intolerable to get an employee to quit.

Consumer-driven health (CDH) plan Health plan that provides employer financial contributions to employees to help cover their health related expenses.

Contingent worker Someone who is not an employee but is a temporary or part-time worker for a specific period of time and type of work.

Contractual rights Rights based on a specific contract between an employer and an employee.

Contrast error Tendency to rate people relative to others rather than against performance standards.

Copayment The portion of medical expenses paid by the insured individual.

Core competency A unique capability that creates high value for a company.

Core workers Employees that are foundational to the business.

Cost–benefit analysis Comparison of costs and benefits associated with human resource practices.

Cross-training Training people to do more than one job.

Cumulative trauma disorders (CTDs) Musculoskeletal injuries that occur when workers repetitively use the same muscles when performing tasks.

D

Decertification Process whereby a union is removed as the representative of a group of employees.

Deductible Money paid by an insured individual before a health plan pays for medical expenses.

Defined benefit plan Retirement program in which employees are promised a pension amount based on age and service.

Defined contribution plan Retirement program in which the employer or employee makes an annual payment to an employee's pension account.

Development Efforts to improve employees' abilities to handle a variety of assignments and to cultivate their capabilities beyond those required by the current job.

Discipline A process of corrective action used to enforce organizational rules.

Disparate impact Occurs when an employment practice that does not appear to be discriminatory adversely affects individuals with a particular characteristic so that they are substantially underrepresented as a result of employment decisions that work to their disadvantage.

Disparate treatment Occurs when individuals with particular characteristics that are not job related are treated differently from others.

Distributive justice Perceived fairness of how rewards and other outcomes are distributed.

Draw Amount advanced against, and repaid from, future commissions earned by the employee.

Dual-career ladder System that allows a person to advance through either a management or a technical/professional ladder.

Due diligence A comprehensive assessment of all aspects of a business being acquired.

Due process Occurs when an employer is determining if there has been employee wrongdoing and uses a fair process to give an employee a chance to explain and defend his or her actions.

Dues checkoff clause Provides for the automatic deduction of union dues from the payroll checks of union members.

Duty Larger work segment comprised of several tasks that are performed by individuals.

E

Effectiveness The ability to produce a specific desired effect or result that can be measured.

Efficiency The degree to which operations are carried out in an economical manner.

E-learning Use of web-based technology to conduct training online.

Emotional intelligence The ability to recognize and manage our own feelings and the feelings of others.

Employee assistance program (EAP) Program that provides counseling and other help to employees having emotional, physical, or other personal problems.

Employee engagement The extent to which an employee's thoughts an behaviors are focused on his or her work and their employer's success.

Employee handbook A physical or electronic manual that explains a company's essential policies, procedures, and employee benefits.

Employee stock ownership plan (ESOP) Designed to give employees significant stock ownership in their organizations.

Employment at will (EAW) A common-law doctrine states that employers have the right to hire, fire, demote, or promote whomever they choose, unless there is a law or a contract to the contrary, and employees may quit at any time with or without notice.

Employment brand Distinct image of the organization that captures the essence of the company to engage employees and outsiders.

Employment contract Formal agreement that outlines the details of employment.

Entitlement philosophy Assumes that individuals who have worked another year with the company are entitled to pay increases with little regard for performance differences.

Environmental scanning The assessment of external and internal environmental conditions that affect the organization.

Equal employment opportunity Employment that is not affected by illegal discrimination.

Equity The perceived fairness of what the person does compared with what the person receives for doing it.

Equity theory States that individuals judge fairness (equity) in compensation by comparing their inputs and outcomes against the inputs and outcomes of referent others.

Ergonomics Study and design of the work environment to address physical demands placed on individuals.

Essential job functions Fundamental job duties.

Exclusive remedy Workers' compensation benefits are the only benefits injured workers may receive to compensate for a work-related injury.

Exempt employees Employees who hold positions for which they are not paid overtime.

Exit interview An interview in which individuals who are leaving an organization are asked to explain their reasons.

Expatriate A citizen of one country who is working in a second country and employed by an organization headquartered in the first country.

Expectancy theory States that an employee's motivation is based on the probability that his or her efforts will lead to an expected level of performance that is linked to a valued reward.

Extrinsic rewards Rewards that are external to the individual.

F

Feedback Information employees receive about how well or how poorly they have performed.

Flexible benefits plan Program that allows employees to select the benefits they prefer from groups of benefits established by the employer.

Flexible workers Employees that are hired on an "as-needed" basis.

Forced distribution Performance appraisal method in which ratings of employees' performance levels are distributed along a bell-shaped curve.

Forecasting Using information from the past and present to predict future conditions.

401(k) plan Plan in which a percentage of an employee's pay is withheld and invested in a tax-deferred account.

Free rider A member of the group who contributes little.

G

Gainsharing System of sharing with employees greater than expected gains in profits and/or productivity.

Games Exercises that entertain and engage.

Gamification Using game thinking and software to engage people in solving problems.

Garnishment A court order that directs an employer to set aside a portion of an employee's wages to pay a debt owed to a creditor.

Glass ceiling Discriminatory practices that have prevented women and minority status employees from advancing to executive-level jobs.

Graphic rating scale Scale that allows the rater to mark an employee's performance on a continuum indicating low to high levels of a particular characteristic.

Green-circled employee Incumbent who is paid below the range set for a job.

Grievance Complaint formally stated in writing.

Grievance arbitration Means by which a third party settles disputes arising from different interpretations of a labor contract.

Grievance procedures Specific steps used to resolve grievances.

Gross-up To increase the net amount of what the employee receives to include the taxes owed on the amount.

Group interview Several job candidates are interviewed together by a hiring authority.

H

Halo effect Occurs when a rater scores an employee high on all job criteria because of performance in one area of the assigned work responsibilities.

Headhunters Employment agencies that focus their efforts on executive, managerial, and professional positions.

Health General state of physical, mental, and emotional well-being.

Health promotion Supportive approach of facilitating and encouraging healthy actions and lifestyles among employees.

HiPos Individuals who show high promise for advancement in the organization.

Home country–based approach Maintains the standard of living the expatriate had in the home country.

Horns effect Occurs when a low rating on one characteristic leads to an overall low rating.

Host country–based approach Compensates the expatriate at the same level as workers from the host country.

Hostile environment Sexual harassment occur when an individual's work performance or psychological well-being is unreasonably affected by intimidating or offensive working conditions.

HR analytics An evidence-based approach to making HR decisions on the basis of quantitative tools and models.

HR audit A formal research effort to assess the current state of an organization's HR practices.

HR generalist A person who has responsibility for performing a variety of HR activities.

HR metrics Specific measures of HR practices.

HR specialist A person who has in-depth knowledge and expertise in a specific area of HR.

Human capital The collective value of the capabilities, knowledge, skills, life experiences, and motivation of an organization's workforce.

Human capital return on investment (HCROI) Directly shows the amount of operating profit derived from investments in labor.

Human capital value added (HCVA) Calculated by subtracting all expenses *except* labor expenses from revenue and dividing by the total full-time head count.

Human economic value added (HEVA) Wealth created per employee.

Human resource management Designing formal systems in an organization to manage human talent for accomplishing organizational goals.

Human resource planning The process of analyzing and identifying the need for and availability of people so that the organization can meet its strategic objectives.

I

Illegal issues Collective bargaining issues that would require either party to take illegal action.

Immediate confirmation Based on the idea that people learn best if they receive reinforcement and feedback as soon as possible after training.

Implied contract An unwritten agreement created by the actions of the parties involved.

Incentives Tangible rewards that encourage or motivate action.

Incivility Rude behavior that offends other employees.

Individual-centered career planning Career planning that focuses on an individual's responsibility for a career rather than on organizational needs.

Informal training Training that occurs through interactions and feedback among employees.

Instructional systems design (ISD) A step-by-step process to ensure that the right learning materials are provided to the right people at the right time.

Intangible rewards Elements of compensation that cannot be as easily measured or quantified.

Integrated talent management (ITM) A holistic approach to leveraging and building human capital.

Interactional justice The extent to which a person affected by an employment decision feels treated with dignity and respect.

Intrinsic rewards Rewards that are internal to the individual.

J

Job Grouping of tasks, duties, and responsibilities that constitutes the total work assignment for an employee.

Job analysis Systematic way of gathering and analyzing information about the content, context, and human requirements of jobs.

Job description Identifies a job's tasks, duties, and responsibilities.

Job design Organizing tasks, duties, responsibilities, and other elements into a productive unit of work.

Job duties Important elements in a given job.

Job enlargement Broadening the scope of a job by expanding the number of different tasks that are performed.

Job enrichment Increasing the depth of a job by adding responsibility for planning, organizing, controlling, and/or evaluating the job.

Job evaluation Formal, systematic means to determine the relative worth of jobs within an organization.

Job posting System in which the employer provides notices of job openings, and employees respond by applying for specific openings.

Job redesign Changing existing jobs in different ways to improve them.

Job rotation Process of moving a person from job to job.

Job satisfaction The positive feelings and evaluations derived from an individual's employment in a job.

Job sharing Scheduling arrangement that has two employees perform the work of one full-time job.

Job specifications The knowledge, skills, and abilities (KSAs) an individual needs to perform a job satisfactorily.

Job-relatedness A qualification or requirement in selection that is significantly related to successful performance of job duties.

Just cause Reasonable justification for taking employment related action.

K

Key performance indicators (KPIs) Measures that tell managers how well the organization is performing relative to critical success factors.

Knowledge management The way an organization identifies and leverages knowledge to be competitive.

L

Labor force participation rate The percentage of the population that is working or seeking work.

Labor force population All individuals who are available for selection if all possible recruitment strategies are used.

Labor markets The supply pool from which employers attract employees.

Leniency error Occurs when ratings of all employees fall at the high end of the scale.

Line of sight Idea that employees can clearly see how their actions and decisions lead to desired outcomes.

Lockout Shutdown of company operations undertaken by management to prevent union members from working.

Loyalty Being faithful to an institution or employer.

Lump-sum increase (LSI) One-time payment of all or part of a yearly pay increase.

M

Make-or-buy Develop competitive human resources or hire individuals who are already developed from somewhere else.

Managed care Approaches that monitor and reduce medical costs through restrictions and market system alternatives.

Management by objectives (MBO) A specific performance appraisal method that highlights the performance goals that an individual and manager identify together.

Management mentoring A relationship in which experienced managers aid individuals in the earlier stages of their careers.

Management rights Rights reserved so that the employer can manage, direct, and control its business.

Mandatory issues Collective bargaining issues identified specifically by labor laws or court decisions as subject to bargaining.

Marginal job functions Duties that are part of a job but that are incidental or ancillary to the purpose and nature of the job.

Market banding Grouping jobs into pay grades based on similar market survey amounts.

Market line Graph line that shows the relationship between job value as determined by job evaluation points and job value as determined pay survey rates.

Market pricing Use market pay data to identify the relative value of jobs based on what other employers pay for similar jobs.

Mediation Process by which a third party suggests ideas to help the negotiators reach a settlement.

Microunit Bargaining unit that includes only one job category or department within a company.

M-learning Use of mobile technology to conduct training.

Modeling Copying someone else's behavior.

MOOCs Massive open enrollment online courses.

Motivation The desire that exists within a person that causes that individual to act.

Multinational corporation (MNC) An organization that has facilities and other assets in at least one country other than its home country.

N

Negligent hiring Occurs when an employer fails to check an employee's background and the employee injures someone on the job.

Negligent retention Occurs when an employer becomes aware that an employee may be unfit for work but continues to employ the person, and the person injures someone.

Nepotism Practice of allowing relatives to work for the same employer.

Nine-Box Talent Grid A matrix showing past performance and future potential of all employees.

No-fault insurance Injured workers receive benefits even if the accident was their fault.

Noncompete agreements Agreements that prohibit individuals who leave an organization from working with an employer in the same line of business for a specified period of time.

Nondirective interview Interview that uses questions developed from the answers to previous questions.

Nonexempt employees Employees who must be paid overtime.

O

Offshoring A company's relocation of a business process or operation from one country to another.

Ombuds Individual outside the normal chain of command who acts as independent problem solver for both management and employees.

On-the-job training The most common training because it is flexible and relevant.

Open enrollment A time when employees can change their participation level in various benefit plans and switch between benefit options.

Open shop Firm in which workers are not required to join or pay dues to a union.

Open-door policy A policy that allows anyone with a complaint to talk with someone in management.

Organizational citizenship behavior Occurs when an employee acts in a way that improves the psychological well-being and social environment of an organization.

Organizational commitment The degree to which workers believe in and accept organizational objectives and want to remain employed at a company.

Organizational culture The shared values and beliefs that give members of an organization meaning and provide them with rules for behavior.

Organizational justice The fairness of decisions and resource allocations in an organization.

Organizational mission The core reason for the existence of the organization and what makes it unique.

Organization-centered career planning Career planning that focuses on identifying career paths that provide for the logical progression of people between jobs in an organization.

Orientation Planned introduction of new employees to their jobs, coworkers, and the organization.

Outsourcing Transferring the management and performance of a business function to an external service provider.

P

Paid-time-off (PTO) plans Plans that combine all sick leave, vacation time, and holidays into a total number of hours or days that employees can take off with pay.

Panel interview Interview in which several interviewers meet with the candidate at the same time.

Passive job candidates Qualified individuals who aren't actively looking for work but might be interested if the right job comes along.

Pay compression Occurs when the pay differences among individuals with different levels of experience and performance become small.

Pay equity The idea that pay for jobs requiring comparable levels of knowledge, skill, and ability should be similar, even if actual duties differ significantly.

Pay grades Groupings of individual jobs that have approximately the same value to the organization.

Pay survey Collection of data on compensation rates for workers performing similar jobs in other organizations.

Pay-for-performance philosophy Assumes that compensation changes reflect performance differences.

Performance appraisal Process of determining how well employees do their jobs relative to a standard and communicating that information to them.

Performance management Series of activities designed to ensure that the organization gets the performance it needs from its employees.

Performance standards Indicators of what the job accomplishes and how performance is measured in key areas of the job description.

Permissive issues Collective bargaining issues that are not required but might relate to certain jobs or practices.

Perquisites (perks) Special benefits—usually noncash items—for executives.

Person with a disability Someone who has a mental or physical challenge that greatly reduces the ability to perform important life functions, who possesses a record of such a challenge, or who is thought to have such a challenge.

Person/group fit The congruence between individuals and group or work unit dynamics.

Person/job fit Matching the knowledge, skills, abilities, and motivations of individuals with the requirements of the job.

Person/organization fit The congruence between individuals and organizational factors.

Phased retirement Approach that enables employees to gradually reduce their workloads and pay levels.

Physical ability tests Tests that measure an individual's physical abilities such as strength, endurance, and muscular movement.

Piece-rate system Pay system in which wages are determined by multiplying the number of units produced by the piece rate for one unit.

Placement Fitting a person to the right job.

Policies General guidelines that focus organizational actions.

Portability A pension plan feature that allows employees to move their pension benefits from one employer to another.

Predictive validity Measured when applicants' test results are compared with subsequent job performance.

Predictors of selection criteria Measurable or visible indicators of selection criteria.

Prevailing wage An hourly wage determined by a formula that considers the rate paid for a job by a majority of the employers in the appropriate geographic area.

Previous job tenure A measure of how long the applicant has stayed on jobs held in the past.

Primacy effect Occurs when a rater gives greater weight to information received first when appraising an individual's performance.

Procedural justice Perceived fairness of the process and procedures used to make decisions about employees, including their pay.

Procedures Customary methods of handling activities.

Productivity Measure of the quantity and quality of work done, considering the cost of the resources used.

Profit sharing System to distribute a portion of an organization's profits to employees.

Protean career A process whereby an individual makes conscious career plans to achieve self-fulfillment.

Protected characteristics Individual attributes that are protected under EEO laws and regulations.

Protected concerted activities Actions taken by employees working together to try to improve their pay and working conditions, with or without a union.

Psychological contract The unwritten expectations employees and employers have about the nature of their work relationships.

Psychomotor tests Tests that measure dexterity, hand–eye coordination, arm–hand steadiness, and other factors.

Pulse surveys Short questionnaires used to solicit anonymous employee feedback.

Q

Qualifying event An event that causes a plan participant to lose group health benefits.

Quid pro quo Sexual harassment that links employment outcomes to the granting of sexual favors.

R

Ranking Performance appraisal method in which employees are listed from highest to lowest based on their performance levels and relative contributions.

Rater bias Occurs when a rater's values or prejudices distort the rating.

Ratification Process by which union members vote to accept the terms of a negotiated labor agreement.

Realistic job previews Process through which a job applicant receives an accurate picture of a job.

Reasonable accommodation A modification to a job or work environment that gives a qualified disabled individual an equal employment opportunity to perform.

Recency effect Occurs when a rater gives greater weight to recent events when appraising an individual's Performance.

Recruiting Process of generating a pool of qualified applicants for organizational jobs.

Red-circled employee Incumbent who is paid above the range set for a job.

Reinforcement Based on the idea that people tend to repeat responses that give them some type of positive reward and to avoid actions associated with negative consequences.

Reliability The extent to which a test or measure repeatedly produces the same results over time.

Repatriation Process that involves planning and training for the reassignment of global employees back to their home countries.

Rerecruiting Seeking out former employees and recruiting them again to work for an organization.

Responsibilities Obligations that individual have to perform certain tasks and duties within a job.

Restricted stock option Company stock shares paid as a grant of shares to individuals, usually linked to achieving specific performance criteria.

Retaliation Punitive actions taken by employers against individuals who exercise their legal rights.

Retirement plan Retirement program established and funded by the employer and employees.

Return on investment (ROI) Calculation showing the value of investments in human capital.

Right to privacy An individual's freedom from unauthorized and unreasonable intrusion into personal affairs.

Rights Powers, privileges, or interests derived from law, nature, or tradition.

Right-to-work laws State laws that prohibit requiring employees to join unions as a condition of obtaining or continuing employment.

Risk management Involves the responsibility to consider physical, human, and financial factors to protect organizational and individual interests.

Rules Specific guidelines that regulate and restrict individuals' behavior.

S

Sabbatical Time off the job to develop and rejuvenate.

Safety Condition in which people's physical well-being is protected.

Salary Consistent payments made each period regardless of the number of hours worked.

Salary inversion Occurs when the pay given to new hires is higher than the compensation provided to more senior employees.

Salary plus commission Combines the stability of a salary with a commission based on sales generated.

Salting Practice in which unions hire and pay people to apply for jobs at certain companies to begin organizing efforts.

Security Protection of employees and organizational facilities.

Security audit Comprehensive review of organizational security.

Selection The process of choosing individuals with the correct qualifications needed to fill jobs in an organization.

Selection criterion Characteristic that a person must possess to successfully perform job duties.

Selection rate Percentage hired from a given group of candidates.

Self-directed team Organizational team comprised of individuals who are assigned a cluster of tasks, duties, and responsibilities to be accomplished.

Self-efficacy People's belief that they can successfully learn the training program content.

Self-service Technology that allows employees to change their benefit choices, track their benefit balances, and submit questions to HR staff members and external benefit providers.

Seniority Time spent in an organization or working in a particular job.

Separation agreement Agreement in which a terminated employee agrees not to sue the employer in exchange for specified benefits.

Serious health condition An illness or injury that requires inpatient care or continuing treatment by a health care provider for medical problems that exist beyond three days.

Severance benefits Temporary payments made to laid-off employees to ease the financial burden of unemployment.

Sexual harassment Unwelcome verbal, visual, or physical conduct of a sexual nature that is severe and affects working conditions or creates a hostile work environment.

Simulations Reproduce parts of the real world so that they can be experienced and manipulated, and learning can occur.

Situational interview Structured interview that contains questions about how applicants might handle specific job situations.

Situational judgment tests Tests that measure a person's judgment in work settings.

Skill variety Extent to which the work requires several activities for successful completion.

Special-purpose team Organizational team formed to address specific problems, improve work processes, and enhance the overall quality of products and services.

Status-blind Employment decisions are made without regard to individuals' personal characteristics.

Statutory rights Rights based on laws or statutes passed by federal, state, or local governments.

Stock option plan Gives employees the right to purchase a fixed number of shares of company stock at a specified price for a limited period of time.

Strategic HR management The appropriate use of HR management practices to gain or keep a competitive advantage.

Strategic planning The process of defining organizational strategy, or direction, and allocating resources toward its achievement.

Strategic talent management The process of identifying the most important jobs in a company that provide a long-term competitive advantage and then creating appropriate HR policies to develop employees so that they can effectively work in these jobs.

Strategy A plan an organization follows for how to compete successfully, survive, and grow.

Stress The harmful physical or psychological reaction that occurs when people are subject to excessive demands or expectations.

Strictness error Occurs when a manager uses only the lower end of the scale to rate employees.

Strike Work stoppage in which union members refuse to work in order to put pressure on an employer.

Structured interview Interview that uses a set of prepared job-related questions that are asked of all applicants.

Substance abuse Use of illicit substances or misuse of controlled substances, alcohol, or other drugs.

Succession planning The process of identifying a plan for the orderly replacement of key employees.

T

Talent acquisition Process of finding and hiring high-quality talent needed to meet the organization's workforce needs.

Tangible rewards Elements of compensation that can be quantitatively measured and compared between different organizations.

Task Distinct, identifiable work activity comprised of motions that employees perform.

Task identity Extent to which the job includes a recognizable unit of work that is carried out from start to finish and results in a known consequence.

Task significance Impact the job has on other people and the organization as a whole.

Team interview Interview in which applicants are interviewed by the team members with whom they will work.

Telework Employees complete work through electronic interactions, telecommunications, and Internet technology.

Termination When an employee is removed from a job at an organization.

Third-party administrator (TPA) A vendor that provides administrative services to an organization.

Three-legged stool A model showing the three sources of income to fund an employee's retirement.

Total rewards Monetary and nonmonetary rewards provided by companies to attract, motivate, and retain employees.

Training Process whereby people acquire capabilities to perform jobs.

Turnover The process in which employees leave an organization and have to be replaced.

U

Undue hardship Significant difficulty or expense imposed on an employer when making an accommodation for individuals with disabilities.

Unfair labor practices Actions that employers are legally prohibited from taking to prevent employees from unionizing.

Union authorization card Card signed by employees to designate a union as their collective bargaining agent.

Union Formal association of workers that promotes the interests of its members through collective action.

Union security provisions Contract clauses to help the union obtain and retain members and collect union dues.

Unit labor cost Computed by dividing the average cost of workers by their average levels of output.

V

Validity The extent to which a test measures what it claims to measure.

Variable pay Compensation linked directly to individual, team, or organizational performance.

Vesting A benefit that cannot be taken away.

Virtual team Organizational team that includes individuals who are separated geographically but who are linked by communications technology.

W

Wages Payments calculated directly on the basis of time worked by employees.

Wellness programs Programs designed to maintain or improve employee health before problems arise.

Whistle-blowers Individuals who report real or perceived wrongs committed by their employers.

Work Effort directed toward accomplishing results.

Work sample tests Tests that require an applicant to perform a simulated task that is a specified part of the target job.

Workers' compensation Security benefits provided to workers who are injured on the job.

Workflow analysis Study of the way work (inputs, activities, and outputs) moves through an organization.

Work–life balance Employer-sponsored programs designed to help employees balance work and personal responsibilities.

Wrongful discharge Termination of an individual's employment for reasons that are illegal or improper.

Y

Yellow dog contracts Pledges by workers not to join a labor union.

Yield ratio Comparison of the number of applicants at one stage of the recruiting process with the number at the next stage.

AUTHOR INDEX

SUBJECT INDEX

Page numbers followed by "f" indicate figures.

A

Ability tests, 254–255
Absenteeism, 177–179
Acceptance rate, 232
Accidents, 544, 545f, 547, 547f
Accountability, 302
Achievement tests, 254
Across-the-board increases, 437
Active practice, 300
Activities, 131–132
ADA. *See* Americans with Disabilities Act (ADA)
ADA Amendments Act (ADAAA), 102, 104
ADDIE model, 292–293, 293f
Adequate performance, 367
Administrative HR role, 18
Adoption benefits, 517–518
ADR. *See* Alternative Dispute Resolution (ADR)
Adult learning, 298
Adverse selection, 491
Affinity groups, 642
Affirmative action, 92
Affirmative action plan (AAP), 92, 207
Age/age discrimination, 107–109, 126–127
  managing, 108–109
  retirement benefits and, 505–506
  in workforce, 25–26
Age Discrimination in Employment Act (ADEA), 107–108, 505
Agency shops, 626, 636
Alternative Dispute Resolution (ADR), 581–583
  arbitration, 581
  mediation, 582–583
  ombuds, 581
  peer review panels, 581
  setting up, 582
Alternative work arrangements, 65–66
Alumni networks, 223
American Productivity & Quality Center, 313
Americans with Disabilities Act (ADA), 101–102, 153, 510, 533, 583, 593
  amendments to, 102–103
  job requirements related to, 103–106
  jobs analysis related to, 153
  medical examinations/ inquiries and, 267
  medical information related to, 105–106
  restrictions related to, 105–106
Appearance discrimination, 114
Applicant flow, documenting, 211
Applicant job interest, 249
Applicant pool, 211
Applicant population, 210
Applicant tracking system, 211, 232

Application disclaimers, 250–251
Application forms, 251, 252f
Application time limit, 251
Appraisal by results, 389
Appraisal responsibilities, 376
Appraisals feedback, 393–394
  appraisal interview and, 393, 394f
  performance management and, 394
  reactions of employees, 393–394
  reactions of managers, 393–394
Apprenticeships, 307
Apprentice training, 306
Arbitration, 581, 639
Assessment centers, 255, 347–348
Assessments, 292
Assets
  financial, 9
  human, 9
  intellectual property, 9
  physical, 9
  reallocation of strategic, 46
Association for Talent Development (ATD), 35–36, 217, 282, 284, 308, 313
Attitude survey, 173
Attitude training, 295
Attraction-selection-attrition (ASA) theory, 241
Attrition, 63
At-will employment, 250, 602
Auditory learning, 298
Authorization cards, 631
Auto-enrollment, 504
Autonomy, 136
Available workforce, 54

B

Baby boomers, 126, 299
Background investigations, 266–271
  additional selection criteria, 269–270
  Fair Credit Reporting Act and, 267
  job offers, 270–271
  legal constraints on, 266–267
  medical examinations/ inquiries and, 267–268
  personal references for, 269
  previous employment checks, 269
Balanced scorecard, 72–73, 72f
Ban-the-box legislation, 268
Bargaining impasse, 638–639
Bargaining unit, 632
Base pay, 405
Base pay systems, 425–430
  job evaluation methods for, 426–428

market pricing and, 428–429
  pay surveys and, 429–430
Basic and remedial skills training, 290
Behavior
  counterproductive, 587–588
  off-duty, 588
  training, 312
Behavioral assessments, 258
Behavioral competencies, 146
Behavioral dimensions, 383
Behavioral interview, 261
Behaviorally anchored rating scale (BARS), 385
Behavioral modeling, 300
Behavior-based information, 369–370
Behavior-based safety (BBS), 548
Benchmarking/benchmarks, 71–72, 313, 370
Benchmark jobs, 429
Benefits/benefits management, 484. *See also* specific types of benefits
  administration, 492–496, 494f
  adoption, 517–518
  communications and, 492–496
  as competitive advantage, 486–487
  cost control, 494
  defined, 406, 484
  designing of, 490–492
  domestic partner, 492
  family-care, 517–518
  family-oriented, 515–518
  financial, 513–515, 513f
  flexible, 490–491
  global, 487–489
  health care, 506–513
  HR metrics for, 494f
  HR strategies for, 485–490
  HR technology and, 493
  insurance, 513–514
  measurement of, 493–494
  older workers benefit needs, 492
  paid-time-off, 518–521
  part-time employee, 491
  public-sector, 489–490
  retention and, 508–509
  retirement, 500–504
  security, 496–498
  statements of personal, 495
  tax-favored, 487
  types of, 495–496, 496f
  voluntary, 520
  workforce attraction and, 531–533
Bereavement leave, 520
"Best-in-class" organizations, 71
Biases, 265
"Big Five" personality, 256, 256f
Biographical interview, 261
Blended learning, 310

Blogs, 27, 215, 219
Bloodborne pathogens, 540
Bloomberg, 223
Board of directors, 98, 322, 473
Body appearance, 588
Bona fide occupational qualification (BFOQ), 88
Bonuses, 454–456, 468
  annual executive, 473
Boomerangs, 223
Brain drain, 25, 56
"Breaking the glass," 98
Bring your own device (BYOD), 586
  dangers, 557
  policy, 27
Broadbanding, 432–433
Broad-based discrimination laws, 90–93
Bullying, 560
Burden of proof, 88
Bureau of Labor Statistics, 34, 125, 134, 339, 344, 429, 471
Business necessity, 87–88, 91, 248–249

C

Cadillac health benefits, 508
Cafeteria benefit plan, 496
Campaigns for unions, 629–630
CareerBuilder, 216
Career planning, 221, 335–343
  career progression, 340–342
  career transitions, 342–343
  changing nature of careers, 335–336
  employer websites and, 338
  individual-centered, 337f, 338–340
  organizational-centered, 337–338, 337f
Career(s)
  changing nature of, 335
  defined, 335
  development, 181, 189
  development centers, 350
  goals, setting, 339
  issues concerning, 341, 343–345
  paths, 338
  phases, 341f
  plans, 221
  plateaus, 341–342
  progression considerations for, 340–342
  training, 188–189
  transitioning into, 338, 342–343
  views on, 335–336
  websites, 217
Carpal tunnel syndrome, 540–541
Case study interview, 261
Cash balance plan, 504
Category scaling methods, 383
Central tendency errors, 392